HALSBURY'S
LAWS OF ENGLAND

ANNUAL ABRIDGMENT
2013

HALSBURY'S
Laws of England

ANNUAL ABRIDGMENT 2013

 LexisNexis®

Members of the LexisNexis Group worldwide

UNITED KINGDOM	LexisNexis, a Division of Reed Elsevier (UK) Ltd, Lexis House, 30 Farringdon Street, London, EC4A 4HH, and London House, 20–22 East London Street, **Edinburgh**, EH7 4BQ
Australia	LexisNexis Butterworths, Chatswood, **New South Wales**
Austria	LexisNexis Verlag ARD Orac GmbH & Co KG, **Vienna**
Benelux	LexisNexis Benelux, **Amsterdam**
Canada	LexisNexis Canada, Markham, **Ontario**
China	LexisNexis China, **Beijing** and **Shanghai**
France	LexisNexis SA, **Paris**
Germany	LexisNexis GmbH, **Dusseldorf**
Hong Kong	LexisNexis Hong Kong, **Hong Kong**
India	LexisNexis India, **New Delhi**
Italy	Giuffrè Editore, **Milan**
Japan	LexisNexis Japan, **Tokyo**
Malaysia	Malayan Law Journal Sdn Bhd, **Kuala Lumpur**
New Zealand	LexisNexis NZ Ltd, **Wellington**
Poland	Wydawnictwo Prawnicze LexisNexis Sp, **Warsaw**
Singapore	LexisNexis Singapore, **Singapore**
South Africa	LexisNexis Butterworths, **Durban**
USA	LexisNexis, Dayton, **Ohio**

© Reed Elsevier (UK) Ltd 2014
Published by LexisNexis UK
This is a Butterworths title

A CIP Catalogue record for this book is available from the British Library.

ISBN for this volume
ISBN 13: 9781 405 787 765

ISBN 978-1-4057-7986-9

9 781405 779869

Typeset by Letterpart Ltd, Caterham on the Hill, Surrey CR3 5XL
Printed and bound by CPI Group (UK) Ltd, Croydon, CR0 4YY
Visit LexisNexis at www.lexisnexis.co.uk

PUBLISHERS' NOTE

This is the fortieth *Annual Abridgment* and covers the year 2013. The *Abridgment* constitutes year by year a comprehensive survey of English case law, statute law and subordinate legislation. European Union law and decisions of Commonwealth courts are given attention commensurate with their importance. Further noteworthy items are derived from government papers and legal periodicals. The alphabetical arrangement and the comprehensive tables and index make the work an ideal aid to research.

Each *Annual Abridgment* is complete without recourse to any other publication.

When referring to this volume reference should be made to both the year and the relevant paragraph number: eg '2013 Abr para 1980'.

This volume covers the law made in 2013.

LEXISNEXIS BUTTERWORTHS

TABLE OF STATUTORY INSTRUMENTS

PARA

C

D

E

I

L

M

X

Y

Z

Decisions of the European Court of Human Rights are listed below numerically. These decisions are also included in the preceding alphabetical table where appropriate.

INJURY	PSLA	SEX/AGE	CITATION & PARA NUMBER
	£2,255	Male/25	*Bromley v Roberts* (Walsall County Ct), para 873
	£2,250	Female/49	*Parveen v Kovac* (Dudley County Ct), para 874
	£2,200	Male/9	*F (a child) v Flynn* (Basildon County Ct), para 875
	£1,800	Male/43	*Major v Egyeslet* (Dartford County Ct), para 876
	£1,000	Male/40	*Krafft v Bushell* (Canterbury County Ct), para 878
	£1,000	Male/13	*C v Zurich Insurance plc* (Slough County Ct), para 877
Neck and chest	£7,000	Female/10	*F (a child) v Faux* (Birmingham County Ct), para 880
Shoulder	£30,000	Female/76	*Palfrey v Wm Morrisons* (Plymouth County Ct), para 851
	£1,300	Female/27	*Morley v Andrews* (*Sheffield*) (*t/a Stagecoach Yorkshire*) (Sheffield County Ct), para 881
Back	£3,500	Male/30	*Milner v S Barrett Construction* (Kingston-upon-Hull County Ct), para 883
	£3,300	Male/55	*Hibbert v Lownds* (Harrogate County Ct), para 864
	£2,000	Male/37	*Cole v Talbot* (Northampton County Ct), para 866
Chest	£2,300	Male/11	*C (a child) v Smith* (Birmingham County Ct), para 885
Chest and back	£2,900	Male/8	*D (a child) v Ferguson* (Bow County Ct), para 886
Elbow	£5,350	Male/35	*Davis v Wokingham BC* (*Reading County Ct*), para 887
Wrist	£9,000	Female/13	*H (a child) v Peterborough City Council* (Peterborough County Ct), para 888
	£4,500	Male/5	*H (a child) v Reading BC* (Reading County Ct), para 889
Hip	£25,000	Male/36	*Ballinger v Robinson* (Preston County Ct), para 890
Leg	£3,300	Male/55	*Hibbert v Lownds* (Harrogate County Ct), para 864
Ankle	£3,000	Female/27	*Maynard v Wigan MBC* (Liverpool County Ct), para 892

INJURY	PSLA	SEX/AGE	CITATION & PARA NUMBER
Minor injuries	£6,000	Female/14	C (*a child*) *v Ross* (*t/a Rapunzels Hair Dressers*) (Exeter County Ct), 893
	£1,250	Female/2	P (*a child*) *v Banovallum Veterinary Group* (Newport County Ct), para 894
	£850	Male/3	B (*a child*) *v Hewson* (Medway County Ct), para 895

TABLE OF ARTICLES

AIR LAW

European Commission Acts to Clarify Stance on Cancelled and Delayed Flights, Paul Stanley: (2013) 157 Sol Jo (no 12) 23
While interpretation of the rules relating to delayed flights seems to benefit travellers, forthcoming changes could shift the balance to favour airlines.

ANIMALS

An Animals' Ombudswoman, Noël Sweeney: (2013) 177 JPN 667
Whether it is a democracy or dictatorship, animals are always equally unequal and denied the means of dissent.
Dangerous Dog Offences—The Proposed New Sentencing Limits, Neil Parpworth: (2013) 177 JPN 759
Reforming the Dangerous Dogs Act 1991, Neil Parpworth: (2013) 177 JPN 378
What are the main reforms under the draft Dangerous Dogs (Amendment) Bill?

ARBITRATION

Anti-Suit Injunctions and Arbitration: Parasitic or Free Standing? Hakeem Seriki: [2013] JBL 267
Are English courts willing to grant anti-suit injunctions?
Application of the Unidroit Principles of International Commercial Contracts in Arbitration, Maud Piers and Johan Erauw: (2013) 8(3) J Priv Int L 441
An analysis of the Unidroit Principles and their prominence in international arbitration.
Assess Now or Pay Later, James Harrison: 163 NLJ 14
The recent case of *Moondance Maritime Enterprises SA v Carbofer Maritime Trading APS* [2012] EWHC 3618 (Comm), [2012] All ER (D) 238 (Dec) (2012 Abr para 71) has shed light on how the courts will deal with the question of costs where an arbitration award is being challenged.
Because I'm Worth It? Vijay Bange: (2013) 24(1) Cons Law 20
A recent decision by the Court of Appeal ruled that an adjudicator was not entitled to the payment of his fees where there had been a breach of the rules of natural justice.
Commercial Suicide Fears are no Defence, Ann Levin and Estelle Katsimani: (2013) 24(9) Cons Law 23
In *Morris Homes (West Midlands) Ltd v Keay* [2013] EWHC 932 (TCC), [2013] All ER (D) 173 (Apr) specific events which required the works to be completed as soon as possible were considered to be one-off events.
Court Takes Pragmatic Approach, Ann Levin and Jessica Rajwan: (2013) 24(1) Cons Law 14
The case of *Turville Health Inc v Chartis Insurance UK Ltd* [2012] EWHC 3019 (TCC), [2012] All ER (D) 10 (Nov) is a good illustration of the court's wide ranging powers to manage and control the dispute resolution process.
International Arbitration—An Industry Perspective, Rachel Chaplin: (2013) 24(6) Cons Law 32
The survey reveals continuing and wide support across the industry for the use of arbitration to resolve international disputes.
New Arbitration Guidance, Alexander Whyatt: (2013) 24(5) Cons Law 32
What are the circumstances in which an agreement to arbitrate survives a contract becoming invalid or void? On *Hyundai Merchant Marine Ltd v Americas Bulk Transport Ltd, The Pacific Champ* [2013] EWHC 470 (Comm), [2013] 2 All ER (Comm) 649 (REVIEW para 54).
A Novel Implication, Stuart Pemble: Estates Gazette, 9 February 2013, p 103
The decision in *Interserve Industrial Services Ltd v Zre Katowice SA* [2012] EWHC 3205 (TCC), [2012] All ER (D) 09 (Dec), may widen the scope for implying arbitration agreements into contracts.
Route 66: An Easy Journey? Clare Arthurs and Margaret Tofalides: 163 NLJ 315
The Arbitration Act 1996 s 66 (1996 Abr para 157) allows a successful party to arbitration to enforce the award using the mechanisms available to the court in respect of court judgments.

Speaking Up for Others, Guy Fetherstonhaugh: Estates Gazette, 5 February 2013, p 94
  Why is oral advocacy considered unimportant in arbitration?
Stop Scrabbling Around, Tony Bingham: Building, October 2013, p 40
  CG Group Ltd v Breyer Group plc [2013] EWHC 2722 (TCC), [2013] All ER (D) 73
  (Oct) highlights that that court is likely to enforce an adjudicator's decision, even if the
  losing party finds a reason why it should not pay.
Stormy Skies: Uncovering the Problems of s 8 of the Contracts (Rights of Third Parties)
  Act 1999, Hamid Khanbhai: (2013) 7 JIBFL 421
  How is a right or benefit conferred by the parties to a contract on a third party enforced
  by the third party if the contract contains an arbitration clause? On *Fortress Value
  Recovery Fund I LLC v Blue Skye Special Opportunities Fund LP* [2013] EWCA Civ 367,
  [2013] 1 Lloyd's Rep 606, [2013] All ER (D) 115 (Apr) (REVIEW para 540).
A Study of the Use of Sharia Law in Religious Arbitration in the United Kingdom and the
  Concerns That This Raises for Human Rights, Jessie Brechin: (2013) 15 Ecc LJ 293
  To what extent are sharia 'courts' able to operate within the legal systems of the United
  Kingdom through the means of arbitration?
Written Arbitration Agreements—What Written Arbitration Agreements? Hong-Lin Yu:
  (2013) 32 CJQ 68
  While signatories to the New York Convention are obliged to recognise all written
  arbitration agreements, in reality it is acknowledged that formal requirements are not
  always followed in practice.

ARMED CONFLICT AND EMERGENCY

Syria—Justice After Assad, John Cammegh: (2013) 177 JPN 763
  Dissidents want a war crimes tribunal that adheres to international standards.

ARMED FORCES

Armed Forces Divorce: Service Issues, Juliet McDermott: Fam LJ, March 2013, p 15
  Divorces involving members of the armed forces require unique considerations, such as
  the division of a forces pension.
Claims Can Proceed for Soldiers' Deaths in Iraq, Robert Weir: Personal Injury Law Journal,
  July 2013, p 22
  In what circumstances is the Ministry of Defence liable of the deaths of soldiers in
  combat?
In Combat, Robert Weir: 163 NLJ 15
  The Supreme Court has upheld the human rights of British soldiers.
The Judicialisation of War? Richard Scorer: 163 NLJ 14
  The recent decision of the Supreme Court in *Allbutt v Ministry of Defence; Ellis v
  Ministry of Defence; Smith v Ministry of Defence* [2013] UKSC 41, [2013] All ER (D) 167
  (Jun) (REVIEW para 77) has attracted fierce criticism from many commentators who feel
  that the case takes human rights remedies a step too far.

BANKRUPTCY AND INDIVIDUAL INSOLVENCY

At the Crossroads: The European Insolvency Regulation and the UK's Choice to Adhere,
  Paul Omar: (2013) 3 CRI 86
  The United Kingdom has chosen to opt in to the proposals to revise Council Regulation
  (EC) 1346/2000.
Debt Settlement Arrangements: A Step-by-Step Analysis, Patrick O'Sullivan: (2013) 20(3)
  CLP 58
  What are the eligibility criteria for a debt settlement arrangement under the Personal
  Solvency Act 2012, and what role does the personal solvency practitioner play?
Down & Out, Edward Heaton: 163 NLJ 309
  Against the spectre of bankruptcy, *McRoberts v McRoberts* [2012] EWHC 2966 (Ch),
  [2013] BPIR 77, [2012] All ER (D) 12 (Nov) (2012 Abr para 96) provides some
  reassurance in cases involving long-standing obligations such as lump sums payable by
  instalment.
If it Aint Broke, Don't Fix It?—The Potential Impact of Article 3(b)(3), Adrian Cohen:
  (2013) 3 CRI 83
  Will insolvency practitioners become more cautious if foreign creditors are permitted to
  challenge the opening of insolvency proceedings?

available in relation to shares in 'trading' companies, and individuals holding such shares are likely to want to rely on one or other of these reliefs at some point.
Where's it Gone? David Bowes: Taxation, 21 February 2013, p 16
What value attaches to the valuable goodwill that would normally form part of any successful trading business?

CARRIAGE AND CARRIERS

Repudiation, Anticipatory Breach and Conditions in a Contract for Services, Rose O'Donnell: In-House Lawyer, July/August 2013, p 32
Following a recent case, under an amended supplytime or a bespoke charter, owners may be able to claim damages for the unexpired length of the charter following withdrawal arising out of late payment of hire.

CHARITIES

Charitable Simplification, David Oliver: Taxation, 6 June 2013, p 10
What are the gift aid changes that were introduced for the new financial year?
Charitable Trusts and Waqfs: Their Parallels, Registration Process, and Tax Reliefs in the United Kingdom, Zia Akhtar: (2013) 13 Stat LR 281
Questions of Definition, Nicholas Dobson: LS Gaz, 22 July 2013, p 34
Would occupation afford relief from non-domestic rates on the ground that the organisation is a charity in occupation of the relevant hereditament?
A Relief for Charities, Stephanie Howarth: Trusts and Estates Law & Tax Journal, November 2013, p 19
Pollen Estate Trustee Co Ltd v Revenue and Customs Comrs [2013] EWCA Civ 753, [2013] 3 All ER 742 confirms that stamp duty land tax relief applies when a charity acts as a joint purchaser with non-charitable bodies.
Time for a Change, Marion Shanley: (2013) 157 Sol Jo (no 22) 15
What legal structures are available for charities and social enterprises, and in what circumstances can they be changed?
Vanishing Act, James Kilby: (2013) 157 Sol Jo (no 14) 15
What happens when a gift is made to a non-existent charity?
What Makes a Charity? Kenneth Dibble: (2013) 157 Sol Jo (no 18) 15
What makes a charity, and who makes the decision?

CHILDREN AND YOUNG PERSONS

Adoption: Human Rights, Rebecca Bailey-Harris: Fam LJ, June 2013, p 659
Visual impairment, child care and the Human Rights Act 1998 (1998 Abr para 1800).
All Change, Chris McIntosh: Fam LJ, October 2012, p 2
The intention behind the proposed new statutory child maintenance service is said to be to support parents from an early stage to reach maintenance agreements directly.
All Change, Elizabeth Isaacs: Family LJ, May 2013, p 2
The Children and Families Bill 2013 will lead to increased challenges to local authority childcare decisions.
Arbitration in Children Cases, Nasreen Pearce HHJ: Fam LJ, April 2013, p 416
What issues surround the use of arbitration in cases concerning children?
Balancing Rights, Amy Harris: Fam LJ, March 2013, p 5
The courts must already balance various factors in contact cases, so is a change in the law to the presumption of shared parenting really necessary?
A Capital Idea, Kim Beatson: 163 NLJ 11
Arguments over the capitalisation of maintenance are best settled via dispute resolution processes.
Care Proceedings: Appeal, Caroline Bridge: Fam LJ, August 2013, p 946
The decision in B (a child) (care order: proportionality: criteria for review) [2013] UKSC 33, [2013] 3 All ER 929 (REVIEW para 171) provides an examination of the threshold in the Children Act 1989.
Changes to Rules on Instructing Experts, Safda Mahmood: Fam LJ, June 2013, p 709
There has been a tightening of the law with regard to employing experts in cases to do with family law and there is a need to lay down strict guidelines.
Child Abduction, David Ormerod: [2013] Crim LR 54
Does failing to return a child constitute 'taking' them outside the United Kingdom?

CHOSES IN ACTION

CIVIL PROCEDURE

fraud was carried out by its sole shareholder and directors. On *Bilta (UK) Ltd (in liquidation) v Nazir* [2013] EWCA Civ 968, [2014] 1 All ER (Comm) 176 (REVIEW para 357).

Upsetting the Balance, Simon Duncan: 163 NLJ 135
Liquidators can apply the hindsight principle when assessing whether a company is past the point of no return.

A Useful Tool for the Large Retailer, Morgan Bowen, Nishi Gandesha and Emma Lloyd: Property Law Journal, 10 September 2012, p 8
Recent years have seen the use, by large retailers who are in financial difficulty, of the company voluntary arrangement procedure to restructure their rent obligations.

What Lies Beneath, Joe Speakman: (2013) 4 CRI 105
'Centrebinding', the process whereby a liquidator realises a company's assets in the period between appointment and the calling of the first creditors' meeting, was a once popular, and sometimes inappropriately exploited, procedure.

When Creditors' Interests Intrude: The Effect of Doubtful Solvency on Directors' Duties, Simon Passfield: (2013) 6 CRI 176
Directors owe a duty to act in the best interests of the members of a company as a whole.

When is a Company Insolvent? Katie Harding: LS Gaz, 5 August 2013, p 28
The Supreme Court decision in *BNY Corporate Trustee Services Ltd v Eurosail-UK 2007–3BL plc* [2013] UKSC 28, [2013] 3 All ER 271 (REVIEW para 396) concerned the interpretation of what constitutes balance sheet insolvency, and in this context the treatment of contingent and prospective liabilities.

When is a Petition to Wind Up a Company an Abuse of Process? Rory Brown: (2013) 5 CRI 125
In every case the court must consider the petition, or proposed petition, against the backdrop of the particular facts of the case, and the purposes and principles of the insolvency regime.

Who Would be a Creditor? Prest in the Supreme Court and the Effect of Trusts on Insolvency, John Tribe: (2013) 4 CRI 91
Can trusts be used to benefit a creditor?

COMPETITION

Analysing the Information, Muthmainur Rahman and Matt Rees: Competition Law Insight, Vol 12, Issue 3, p 17
Data analytics have a crucial role to play in competition cases.

Benefits and Costs of Co-Operating under the European Commission's Leniency Notice, Niels Christian Ersbøll and Luc Gyselen: In-House Lawyer, April 2013, p 16
Seeks to highlight importance with co-operating with the European Commission in helping to bring down illegal trading cartels.

Cartel Enforcement in the European Union: Determinants of the Duration of Investigations, Kai Hüschelrath, Ulrich Laitenberger and Florian Smuda: [2013] ECLR 33
Assessing cartel enforcement decisions in the last decade.

The Cartel Penumbra: Where Public and Private Enforcement Policies Intersect, Roger Gamble: (2013) 42(1) CLWR 23
The EU and Australia share a strong tradition of the public enforcement of anti-cartel laws with relatively few private actions by victims seeking compensation.

Changes to the Takeover Code, Andrew Pearson, Bernard Wall: (2013) 37 CSR 5, p 38
What are the changes to the scope of the Takeover Code which come into force from the end of September this year?

Competition Law Compliance Across Europe: A Multi-Jurisdictional Challenge, Frédéric Manin and others: [2013] ECLR 6
What are the jurisdictional differences in competition law?

Cornering the Market, Nicholas Wood: Estates Gazette, 16 March 2013, p 75
Two years on, how is the Competition Act 1998 (Land Agreements Exclusion Revocation) Order 2010, SI 2010/1709 (2010 Abr para 485), affecting retail exclusivity agreements?

Counterfactual Analysis in Predation Cases, Kay Winkler: [2013] ECLR 410
Recent contributions on predatory pricing discuss the validity of counterfactual tests.

The Criminal Cartel Offence, Alison Jones and Martin McElwee: Competition Law Insight, June 2013, p 3
Dropping the dishonesty requirement has proved distinctly contentious.

The best way of ensuring that wide-ranging and onerous duties of good faith are not implied on parties is to deal with the issue in the contract expressly. On *Compass Group UK and Ireland Ltd (t/a Medirest) v Mid Essex Hospital Services NHS Trust* [2013] EWCA Civ 200, [2013] BLR 265, [2013] All ER (D) 200 (Mar).

An Implied Term of Good Faith: A Watershed or a Damp Squib? Helen Pugh: (2013) 6 JIBFL 347

The decision in *Yam Seng Pte Ltd v International Trade Corporation Ltd* [2013] EWHC 111 (QB), [2013] 1 All ER (Comm) 1321 has opened the door to an implied duty of good faith in commercial contracts.

Keay v Morris Homes and Section 2 Law of Property (Miscellaneous Provisions) Act 1989, Emma Lees: [2013] Conv 68

Do oral agreements comply with the Law of Property (Miscellaneous Provisions) Act 1989 s 2? On *Keay v Morris Homes (West Midlands) Ltd* [2012] EWCA Civ 900, [2012] 1 WLR 2855, [2012] All ER (D) 106 (Jul) (2012 Abr para 653).

Keeping the Faith, Vijay Bange: (2013) 24(6) Cons Law 26

Good faith clauses seem to be growing in use, but not all parties seem to be fully aware of their significance.

Litigation, Nicholas Peacock and Hannah Ambrose: Corporate Briefing, June 2013, p 8

How has the Court of Appeal grappled with the relationship between an arbitration clause and the rights of third parties?

The Meaning of Good Faith and Material Breach, Ewan McKendrick: Building Law Monthly, April 2013, p 10

The general and the specific.

Once More Unto the Breach, Rachel Barnes: Building, 7 June 2013, p 49

Ampurius Nu Homes Holdings Ltd v Telford Homes (Creekside) Ltd [2013] EWCA Civ 577, [2013] BLR 400, [2013] All ER (D) 305 (May) (REVIEW 535) highlights why care should be taken when treating a breach of contract as repudiatory.

A Principled Approach to Choice of Law in Contract? Andrew Dickinson: (2013) 3 JIBFL 151

The draft Hague Principles on Choice of Law in International Contracts are concerned with the law applicable to international commercial contracts, including banking and financial contracts, and, more specifically, with the possibility of a choice of the legal rules governing such contracts.

The Reform of Insurance Warranties: A Behavioural Economics Perspective, James Davey: [2013] JBL 118

The 'nudge theory' is applied to insurance warranty reform.

Spot the Difference, Michael Twomey: 163 NLJ 263

If warranties were representations, could a buyer sue for misrepresentation and sidestep the limitations?

Stormy Skies: Uncovering the Problems of s 8 of the Contracts (Rights of Third Parties) Act 1999, Hamid Khanbhai: (2013) 7 JIBFL 421

How is a right or benefit conferred by the parties to a contract on a third party enforced by the third party if the contract contains an arbitration clause? On *Fortress Value Recovery Fund I LLC v Blue Skye Special Opportunities Fund LP* [2013] EWCA Civ 367, [2013] 1 Lloyd's Rep 606, [2013] All ER (D) 115 (Apr) (REVIEW para 540).

Talk is Not So Cheap for Employers, Joanne Owers: The Lawyer, 13 May 2013, p 9

The decision of *Commerzbank AG v Keen* [2006] EWCA Civ 1536, [2007] IRLR 132 (2006 Abr para 1209) highlights how the Court of Appeal relies on common law contractual principles.

Warranties and Representations—Why it Matters, Emma Dolphin: Legal Week, 26 April 2013, p 21

Highlighting the distinction between warranties and representations.

When is a Collateral Warranty a Contract? James Ladner: (2013) 24(9) Cons Law 17

CONVEYANCING

Chancel Repair, Jennifer Slade: LS Gaz, 31 March 2014, p 24

Don't Pay the Price, Malcolm Warner and Peter Blair: Estates Gazette, 13 July 2013, p 74

What constitutes bribery and when does an estate agent cross the legal line?

COPYRIGHT

DEEDS AND OTHER INSTRUMENTS

Setting the Record Straight, Hugh Elder: (2013) 157 Sol Jo (no 18) 14

There are various issues to consider when a client seeks rectification of a voluntary settlement, which is only intended to correct a mistake in a document.

DEFAMATION

Can New Act Clean Up Libel Law? David Allen: The Lawyer, 6 May 2013, p 9

The Defamation Act 2013 (REVIEW para 840) will go some way to restoring the reputation of libel law by discouraging bad claims.

Can the Trolls be Put Back Under the Bridge? Sarosh Khan: (2013) 19(1) CTLR 9

How the law should deal with internet trolls.

Costs Protection and Defamation, Katy Manley and Amali de Silva: LS Gaz, 25 November 2013, p 22

Not So Innocent After All, Julian Pike: LS Gaz, 17 June 2013, p 23

2013 is shaping up to be a bad year in the courts for those who misjudge their use of social media. On *McAlpine v Bercow* [2013] EWHC 1342 (QB), [2013] All ER (D) 301 (May) (REVIEW para 844).

DISCRIMINATION

All Marriages are Equal ... Janet Barlow and Rebecca Mason: 163 NLJ 15

While the Marriage (Same Sex Couples) Act 2013 purports to give same-sex couples equality with that of heterosexual couples, on closer examination this does not appear to be the case.

Appealing Options, Chris Bryden, Michael Salter: 163 NLJ 9

Who should be named as respondents when clients allege they have been the victim of discrimination?

Back to Square One, Hannah White: (2013) 142 Em LJ 16

Is post-termination victimisation unlawful?

The Balancing Act, Sarah Johnson: 163 NLJ 306

The decision in Applications 48420/10, 59842/10, 51671/10 and 36516/10 *Eweida v United Kingdom* [2013] All ER (D) 69 (Jan), ECtHR (REVIEW para 2165), makes successful discrimination claims easier to bring.

Business Tenancies and the Equality Act, Simon Butler and William East: (2013) 157 Sol Jo (no 21) 10

How the Equality Act 2010 (2010 Abr para 985) affects a local authority's possession of a property.

Definition of Disability, Darren Newman: Equal Opportunities Review, May 2013, p 28

Symptoms compounded by obesity could amount to disability.

The Development of EU Case-Law on Age Discrimination in Employment: 'Will You Still Need Me? Will You Still Feed Me? When I'm Sixty-Four', Elaine Dewhurst: [2013] 19 ELJ 517

Mandatory retirement policies may no longer be compatible with European Union law and there is a need to move towards more flexible retirement policies.

Dismissal Due to Sickness Continuing after Maternity Leave Was Not Discrimination, Sue Johnstone: Equal Opportunities Review, May 2013, p 31

There was no discrimination where sickness continued after maternity leave.

Education Update, Salima Mawji: (2013) 157 Sol Jo (no 21) 22

Considers the rising trend of discrimination against those who are disabled at university.

Employers Liability for Employee References and Victimisation, Sam Middlemiss: (2013) 34(2) Stat LR 138

The Equality Act 2010 (2010 Abr para 985) represents the most fundamental change in equality since it was first introduced and, although most commentators commend its introduction, there are some who are critical of the breadth of the changes it has introduced.

[Enterprise and Regulatory Reform Act 2013] and Discrimination Law: An [Equal Opportunities Review] Guide, Michael Rubenstein: Equal Opportunities Review, July 2013, p 26

The problems with the Enterprise and Regulatory Reform Act 2013 (REVIEW para 414) in relation to discrimination law.

What are the ways in which being a woman priest in the Church and a potential candidate for the episcopacy is conceived in secular law?

ECCLESIASTICAL LAW

Chancel Repair, Jennifer Slade: LS Gaz, 31 March 2014, p 24

The Devil's Law Cases, Duncan Henderson: (2013) 15 Ecc LJ 28
What is the proper role and authority of the ecclesiastical courts?

Methodist Ministers: Employees or Office-holders? Frank Cranmer: (2013) 15 Ecc LJ 316
The issue of whether a minister of religion is an employee or an office-holder came before the Supreme Court in *President of the Methodist Conference v Preston* [2013] UKSC 29, [2013] 2 AC 163, [2013] 4 All ER 477 (REVIEW para 1003) an action for unfair constructive dismissal against the Methodist Church.

Succession to the Crown Bill: Possible Untoward Effects? Bob Morris: (2013) 15 Ecc LJ 186
The threats to the Church's status come less from the legislature than from larger societal changes.

The Teaching of Church Law: An Ecumenical Exploration Worldwide, Norman Doe: (2013) 15 Ecc LJ 267
Each of the churches across the ecclesiastical traditions employs law or other system of regulatory instruments, from canons to charters, from constitutions to covenants.

Terms of Service, Mark Hill: 163 NLJ 10
The case of *President of the Methodist Conference v Preston* [2013] UKSC 29, [2013] 2 AC 163, [2013] 4 All ER 477 (REVIEW para/13/1282) considers the legal obligations owed by the Methodist Church to its ministers as a matter of secular employment law today.

Women Bishops: Equality, Rights and Disarray, Rob Clucas and Keith Sharpe: (2013) 15 Ecc LJ 158
What are the ways in which being a woman priest in the Church and a potential candidate for the episcopacy is conceived in secular law?

EDUCATION

Decisions, Decisions: Choice of School and the 'Judicial Reasonable Parent', Simon Johnson: Fam LJ, August 2013, p 1103
What is the role of the law in cases where parents are unable to agree on what school their children should attend?

Education Update, Salima Mawji: (2013) 157 Sol Jo (no 21) 22
Considers the rising trend of discrimination against those who are disabled at university.

Education Update, Salima Mawji and Asma Nizami: (2013) 157 Sol Jo (no 8) 23
Is plagiarism a strict liability offence?

Equality Challenge Unit: Kick-Starting Change, David Ruebain: Equal Opportunities Review, October 2013, p 11
The Equality Challenge Unit has developed an equality charter to kick-start change in the higher education sector.

ELECTIONS AND REFERENDUMS

Legal Issues Surrounding the Referendum on Independence for Scotland, Stephen Tierney: [2007] ECLR 359

EMPLOYMENT

The Adviser Q&A: NHS agency: Healthy VAT Saving or Avoidance? Chris Silk: Tax J, Issue 1176, p 7
With the current interest in perceived corporate tax avoidance, it seemed only a matter of time before an NHS scheme designed to avoid value added tax on agency staff came into the media spotlight.

An Alternative Exit Tool, Julian Yew and Anna Henry: 163 NLJ 9
The government recently announced that it plans to introduce protected conversations so that 'a boss and an employee feel able to sit down together and have a frank conversation at either's request'.

Awards for Failure to Engage with Employees, Sarah Ozanne: (2013) 142 Em LJ 11
The penalties for engagement failure.

Ruiz Zambrano as an Illustration of How the Court of Justice of the European Union Constructs Its Legal Arguments, Urška Šadl: (2013) E Con LR 205
The conclusion of the Court of Justice of the European Union in Case C-34/09 *Ruiz Zambrano v Office National de l'Emploi (ONEm)* [2012] QB 265, [2011] All ER (EC) 491, ECJ (2011 Abr para 2484), is based on three mutually reinforcing arguments: (1) an argument from TFEU art 20; (2) a judge-made rule of the intended fundamental status and cases cited in the opinion of the court; and (3) by the argument from practical consequences of the decision.

Same-Sex Couples and the Harmonisation of EU Matrimonial Property Regimes: Unjustifiable Discrimination or Missed Opportunities? Stuart Davis: [2013] CFLQ 19
Despite the different treatment afforded to same-sex couples, the European Commission's proposed harmonisation measures should be tolerated.

Separation Versus Fusion—Or: How to Accommodate National Autonomy and the Charter? Daniel Thym: [2007] ECLR 391
The precise delimitation of the Charter of Fundamental Rights reveals deeper conflicts about how to resolve jurisdictional overlap.

Thank You for Not Smoking: The Commission's Proposal for a New Tobacco Products Directive—Legally Sound but Does It Hit the Spot? Matthew Elsmore and Viktoria Obolevich: (2013) 38 EL Rev 552
The European Commission has proposed a policy shift towards fully standardising the packaging and labeling of tobacco products consumed in the European Union.

Time to Seize the (Red) Bull by the Horns: The European Union's Failure to Protect Children from Alcohol and Unhealthy Food Marketing, Oliver Bartlett and Amandine Garde: (2013) 38 EL Rev 498
Weaknesses within European Parliament and Council Directive (EU) 2010/13 mean the European Union is failing to do all it can to prevent children being targeted by the alcohol and food industries.

TLLC Ltd: VAT Recovery on Fees for Professional Services, Chris Bates and Julia Lloyd: Tax J, Issue 1189, p 18
The First-tier Tribunal case of *TLLC Ltd v HMRC* [2013] UKFTT 467 (TC), (3 September 2013, unreported) looks in some detail at the principles established by the European Court of Justice in relation to the recovery of input VAT.

Variations in Member States' Preliminary References to the Court of Justice—Are Structural Factors (Part of) the Explanation? Morten Broberg and Niels Fenger: [2013] 19 ELJ 488
Many of the variations in the number of preliminary references from member state judiciaries may be attributed to structural factors rather than be seen as a reflection of the willingness of different member state courts to make use of the TFEU art 267 on such references.

Widening the Net: The General Court Extends the Principle of Successor Liability, Adrian Brown and Morris Schonberg: [2013] ECLR 1
The decisions in Case T-349/08 *Uralita v European Commission* [2012] 4 CMLR 193, EGC, and Case T-194/06 *SNIA SpA v European Commission* (16 June 2011, unreported), EGC, complicate rules on successor liability.

EXTRADITION
Warranted Objection, Andrew Smith: LS Gaz, 27 May 2013, p 21
Emerging pilot judgments could be useful for lawyers contesting extradition requests.

FINANCIAL SERVICES AND INSTITUTIONS
[Alternative Investment Fund] Depositaries: All Clear Now? Madeleine Yates: (2013) 4 JIBFL 220
Despite the publication of the Alternative Investment Fund Managers Level 2 Regulation in final form, there are still significant areas of uncertainty regarding the meaning and application of provisions of both Alternative Investment Fund Managers and the Level 2 Regulation.

The Alternative Investment Fund Managers Directive, Fund Management LLPs and Partnership Tax Issues, Peter Trevett: Tax J, Issue 1184, p 10
The European Securities and Markets Authority has now produced its guidelines on sound

Letters of Credit: Existence of a Duty to Return Documents Listed in a Rejection Notice, Ebenezer Adodo: [2012] JIBLR 456
    Do banks have a duty to return documentation under a letter of credit after rejecting it?
The LIBOR Scandal—The UK's Legislative Response, Victoria Callaghan and Zia Ullah: [2013] JIBLR 160
    Can the Prudential Regulation Authority and Financial Conduct Authority restore the reputation of the City following the LIBOR scandal?
The LIBOR Scandal: What If A Bank Faced Prosecution Under The Bribery Act 2010? Richard Lissack and Eleanor Davison: (2013) 4 JIBFL 215
    An analysis of the Bribery Act 2010 s 7 makes for very interesting reading when viewed through the prism of the range of cases preoccupying banks at present, and in particular the London Interbank Offered Rate.
The Mechanics of Refusal in Documentary Letters of Credits: An Analysis of the Procedures Introduced by Article 16 UCP 600, Mohd Hwaidi and Brian Harris: [2013] JIBLR 146
    New procedures for refusal notices introduced by the ICC Uniform Customs and Practice for Documentary Credits (UCP600) art 16 may have considerable impact on the substantive entitlements of bankers under English law.
Negotiating Indemnity Clauses in the Investment Management Context, Carole Cotter: (2013) 10 JIBFL 645
    What are the drafting techniques when negotiating indemnity clauses in investment management agreements?
No Guarantees, Gita Chakravarty: (2013) 157 Sol Jo (no 21) 9
    Is refusing to lend without a personal guarantee legitimate?
No Place for the Hindsight Principle When Valuing Client Trust Monies, Neil Henderson: (2013) 3 JIBFL 157
    In Re MF Global UK Ltd (in special administration) [2013] EWHC 92 (Ch), [2013] All ER (D) 221 (Jan) (REVIEW para 1209), the court considered an application for directions as to the appropriate method for valuing client trust monies held by an insolvent broker dealer.
Out of Proportion, Karen Anderson: LS Gaz, 22 July 2013, p 9
    New government plans to sanction directors of failed banks are deeply flawed.
The Pitfalls of Guarantees, Allyson Colby: Estates Gazette, 13 July 2013, p 83
    Principals should always consult guarantors when varying terms of the underlying contract.
Profile, Jonathan Rayner: LS Gaz, 16 September 2013, p 26
    How did the Financial Services Authority allow the once respected banking profession to sink so low?
Reaching The Parts Other Investigations Cannot Reach, Rick Brown: (2013) 20(3) JFC 259
    Financial investigation was often introduced at the pre-arrest stage in an investigation, although there were still opportunities to introduce financial investigation earlier in the case in some instances.
Recent Developments on the Banking Code of Practice, Tony Beare: Tax J, Issue 1188, p 8
    Reviews draft guidance of the Banking Code of Practice.
The Regulatory Powers and Purview of the Bank of England: Pre- and Post-Crisis, Graham Nicholson and Michael Salib: (2013) 10 JIBFL 636
    What is the Bank of England's pre-crisis role in the United Kingdom's financial regulation framework?
Restrictions on the Transfer of Rights in Loan Contracts, Philip Rawlings: (2013) 9 JIBFL 543
    Large loans, particularly syndicated loans, normally restrict the lender's ability to transfer rights and obligations.
A Review of the Jurisdiction and Procedure of the Financial Services Ombudsman and Recent Trends, Trevor Murphy: (2013) 20(5) CLP 102
    Given the recent spate of litigation against the Financial Services Ombudsman, is it time for the legislature to review its purpose?
Rise and Fall of Regulatory State in Financial Markets, Bruno Nickolic: [2013] JIBLR 1
    How has the regulatory state fared in the financial crisis?
Saltri III and the Shortcomings of Scheme/Intercreditor Release Mechanisms, David Eaton Turner: (2013) 2 CRI 49
    What are the duties owed by a security trustee to mezzanine lenders on enforcement?

Sanctions for Bank Directors and Ring Fencing, Gregory Mitchell: (2013) 5 JIBFL 287
Under existing English civil law, are there sanctions which do or could provide significant deterrents to the directors of banks against wrongful conduct, both for what has already occurred to date and what might occur in the future once a ring fence is introduced?

The United Kingdom's New Financial Services Regulatory Structure—The Shape of Things to Come, Jeremy Hill and Edite Ligere: [2013] JIBLR 156
The Financial Services Act 2012 (2012 Abr para 1243) introduces structural changes to the United Kingdom's financial services regulatory structure.

Upper Tribunal Finds 'Layering' Constitutes Market Abuse, Hannah Laming and Tommy Dutton: (2013) 3 JIBFL 164
In *7722656 Canada Inc (formerly t/a Swift Trade Inc) v Financial Services Authority* [2013] All ER (D) 266 (Feb), the Upper Tribunal was called on to consider whether the practice known as 'layering' was abusive and so contrary to the Financial Services and Markets Act 2000 (2000 Abr para 1558).

When Can A Material Adverse Change Clause Be Relied On? Jo Windsor: (2013) 8 JIBFL 497
While material adverse change clauses are included in a broad range of financial and commercial transactions, it is often observed that nobody ever really relies on them.

FOOD AND DRINK

The Mane Line, Max Weaver: 163 NLJ 223
What remedy, if any, might be available to consumers duped into eating horsemeat?

No Smoke Without Fire, Lindsay Cook: Intellectual Property Magazine, February 2013, p 42
Following the introduction of restrictions on tobacco branding, could junk food be next?

The Protection of Traditional Foods in the EU: Traditional Specialities Guaranteed, Andrea Tosato: [2013] 19 ELJ 545
Since the dawn of the common market, the European Union has enacted abundant legislation regulating the employment of specific food names, a process leading to the introduction of a regulatory framework for wines and spirits, and four quality schemes for food products.

Time to Seize the (Red) Bull by the Horns: The European Union's Failure to Protect Children from Alcohol and Unhealthy Food Marketing, Oliver Bartlett and Amandine Garde: (2013) 38 EL Rev 498
Weaknesses within European Parliament and Council Directive (EU) 2010/13 mean the European Union is failing to do all it can to prevent children being targeted by the alcohol and food industries.

GIFTS

How to Make an Effective Gift, Emma Hunt: Simon's Tax Briefing, 1 June 2013, p 83
If structured correctly, lifetime giving can be a tax efficient way of reducing an individual's taxable estate, but care is needed to ensure the gift does not come back to the estate on death.

In Contemplation of Death, Jennifer Lee: Trusts and Estates Law & Tax Journal, November 2013, p 15
How does the law in relation to donation mortis causa work in practice?

Probate: Double Portions, Lesley King: LS Gaz, 25 March 2013, p 38
Establishing the testator's intention at the time of making a lifetime gift is critical.

Vanishing Act, James Kilby: (2013) 157 Sol Jo (no 14) 15
What happens when a gift is made to a non-existent charity?

HEALTH AND SAFETY AT WORK

Balance of Probability or Material Contribution? Establishing Causation in Occupational Cancer Claims, Robert O'Leary: [2013] JPIL 19
What is the difference between establishing causation on the balance of probabilities using the 'doubles the risk' approach, and using material contribution in occupational cancer cases?

Buyer Beware, Matthew Judson: Tolley's Health and Safety at Work, November 2013, p 36
The consequences of wearing personal protective equipment that does not protect the worker can be fatal, and employers are responsible for ensuring it meets the necessary standard.

The Standard of Proof in Civil Cases: An Insurance Fraud Perspective, Johanna Hjalmarsson: (2013) EvPro 17(1) 47
Insurance law generally operates without presumptions, for which reason the basic rule on the burden of proof will more often than not find application.

Taking No Credit, William Irwin: (2013) 157 Sol Jo (no 28) 14
Road traffic accident victims hiring a replacement car on credit may face unexpected claims as new costs recovery rules could make credit hire companies turn to them to recoup full hire costs.

INTERNATIONAL RELATIONS LAW

Chapter VII½: Is Jus Post Bellum Possible? Antonia Chayes: [2013] 24(1) EJIL 291
What would help to create a more robust obligation, if not a jus post bellum?

Enforced Equations, Dino Kritsiotis: [2013] 24(1) EJIL 139
How does international law view the initiation of force in hostilities conducted between states?

Far Be It from Thee to Slay the Righteous with the Wicked: An Historical and Historiographical Sketch of the Bellicose Debate Concerning the Distinction between Jus ad Bellum and Jus in Bello, J H H Weiler and Abby Deshman: [2013] 24(1) EJIL 25
The question whether jus in bello and jus ad bellum should interact, or remain in hermetically sealed spheres, has generated a voluminous and vociferous body of contemporary literature.

A Formal Approach to Article 38(1)(d) of the [International Court of Justice] Statute from the Perspective of the International Criminal Courts and Tribunals, Aldo Zammit Borda: [2013] 24(2) EJIL 649
What is the meaning of the phrase 'as subsidiary means for the determination of rules of law' in the Statute of the International Court of Justice art 38(1)(d)?

From Right to Intervene to Duty to Protect: Michael Walzer on Humanitarian Intervention, Terry Nardin: [2013] 24(1) EJIL 67
The occasional inconsistencies in Walzer's arguments reflect his political character and his resistance to turn political questions into philosophical ones.

Imagining Warfare, Paul Kahn: [2013] 24(1) EJIL 199
War and law enforcement refer to structures of the political imaginary before they refer to legal norms.

The Inherent Right to Self-Defence and Proportionality in Jus Ad Bellum, David Kretzmer: [2013] 24(1) EJIL 235
While necessity of the force used is indeed the main issue in jus ad bellum, there is still place for assessing narrow proportionality.

Moral Internationalism and the Responsibility to Protect, Anne Orford: [2013] 24(1) EJIL 83
Moralism has emerged as an important feature of the contemporary internationalist landscape.

A Non-Response to Weiler and Deshman, Marko Milanovic: [2013] 24(1) EJIL 63
What Weiler and Deshman's broader narrative shows is that, while the separation principle has always been the mainstream view in legal scholarship, it has also never been without significant challenge.

Pre-empting Proliferation: International Law, Morality, and Nuclear Weapons, Michael Glennon: [2013] 24(1) EJIL 109
Neither international law, practical morality, nor a consequentialist calculus of national interest can eliminate the need for judicious choice and subjective judgment.

The Quest for Peace, Marc Weller: 163 NLJ 12
What are the origins and the compliance issues associated with the prohibition of the use of force in international relations?

Regulating Resort to Force: A Response to Matthew Waxman from a 'Bright-Liner', Olivier Corten: [2013] 24(1) EJIL 191
What are the difficulties raised by Matthew Waxman's article in correctly assessing what he designates as the 'Bright-Liners' view?

Regulating Resort to Force: Form and Substance of the UN Charter Regime, Matthew Waxman: [2013] 24(1) EJIL 151
Much of the international legal debate about regulating force and self-defence takes place on a substantive axis, focusing on the scope of force prohibitions and exceptions.

Syria—Justice After Assad, John Cammegh: (2013) 177 JPN 763
  Dissidents want a war crimes tribunal that adheres to international standards.
What to Make of Jus Post Bellum: A Response to Antonia Chayes, Guglielmo Verdirame:
  [2013] 24(1) EJIL 307
  When the distinction between war and peace and the discreteness of jus in bello are called
  into question, what is the point of inventing a new field of international law defined by the
  ever more elusive notion of war?

JUDICIAL REVIEW

Concurrent Proceedings in Tax Residence Cases, Ryan Hawthorne: Tax J, Issue 1160, p 22
  In *Daniel v Revenue and Customs Comrs* [2012] EWCA Civ 1741, [2013] All ER (D) 189
  (Jan) (2012 Abr para 1471), the Court of Appeal considered the order in which
  concurrent proceedings—a statutory appeal in the First-tier Tribunal and a judicial review
  hearing in the Upper Tribunal—should be heard.
GSTS Pathology LLP: When Do Legitimate Expectations End? Kevin Smith and Richard
  Doran: Tax J, Issue 1177, p 16
  Interim relief to prevent the immediate implementation of a proposed change in tax
  treatment may be available to a taxpayer making an application for judicial review. On
  R (on the application of GSTS Pathology LLP) [2013] EWHC 1823 (Admin), (21 June
  2013, unreported).
Judicial Review Update, Gareth Mitchell: (2013) 157 Sol Jo (no 12) 31
  In *BA v Secretary of State for the Home Department* [2012] EWCA Civ 944, [2012] All
  ER (D) 107 (Jul) (2012 Abr para 378) the Court of Appeal considered whether it is an
  abuse of process to bring a private law claim where the challenge might have been
  included in an earlier judicial review.
Legitimate Expectation in the Tribunal, Angela Savin: Tax J, Issue 1162, p 22
  Since the High Court decision in *Oxfam v Revenue and Customs Comrs* [2009] EWHC
  3078 (Ch), [2010] STC 686 (2010 Abr para 1830), there has existed a state of confusion
  over the question of the First-tier Tribunal's jurisdiction to determine cases on the basis of
  public law arguments.
Make Unmeritorious Litigants Foot Judicial Review Bill, Daniel Levy: Property Week,
  10 May 2013, p 61
  The government's plans to reduce unmeritorious cases seeking judicial review are
  welcome, but unlikely to deter groups determined to stop a development.
Making Urgent Judicial Review Application, Richard Honey: (2013) 157 Sol Jo (no 12) 21
  In recent cases, the Queen's Bench Division has given guidance for solicitors applying for
  urgent consideration in judicial review.
New Costs Regime 'May Lead to Surge in Claims', Jamie Carpenter: Planning, 9 April
  2013, p 4
  New rules to cap claimants' exposure to legal costs in environmental judicial reviews
  could lead to an upsurge in cases.
Reluctant Reformers, Claire Dutch and Victoria du Croz: Legal Week, 19 July 2013, p 16
  The problems with the judicial review planning reforms.
Taking Frivolity Out of Judicial Review, Nigel Hewitson: Estates Gazette, 22 June 2013,
  p 105
  How effective will the government's proposed reforms to the judicial review system
  actually be?
Time's Winged Chariot, Nicholas Dobson: 163 NLJ 14
  Time in judicial review runs from when the substantive determinative decision is made.
  On *R (on the application of Nash) v Barnet LBC* [2013] EWHC 1067 (Admin), [2013] All
  ER (D) 60 (May).
Where Do We Stand? Charles Brasted and Ben Gaston: 163 NLJ 18
  Will proposals for further judicial review reform make any difference?

JURIES

Common Sense and a Sharp Eye, Jeannie Mackie: (2013) 157 Sol Jo (no 10) 7
  As highlighted in *R v Ramin Pouladian-Kari* [2013] EWCA Crim 158, [2013] All ER
  (D) 314 (Feb) (REVIEW para 1649), sometimes a juror will notice a detail missed by the
  legal teams and court.

LANDLORD AND TENANT

Freedom of Information, Practically Speaking—Game, Data Set and Match, Paul Gibbons: (2013) 9(4) FOI 3

The biggest challenge for Freedom of Information Officers will be keeping published datasets up to date.

In Practice, Nicholas Dobson: LS Gaz, 11 March 2013, p 18

What are the latest significant developments in the history of local government lawyers?

Keeping it Local, Alison Murrin: Estates Gazette, 6 April 2013, p 82

Will the community right to bid lead to groups running local assets, or just derail unpopular developments?

LOCAL GOVERNMENT FINANCE

Contracting Out Local Taxation Functions—Completion Notices, Christopher Lewsley: [2013] RVR 65

An examination of the relevant legislation calls into question the notion that the service of completion notices can be a lawfully contracted out function.

Help for Council Tax Payers—Part 1: Appeals About Reductions, Jan Luba and Catherine O'Donnell: LA, July/August 2013, p 17

People of limited means will often have difficulty paying their local council tax bill.

Questions of Definition, Nicholas Dobson: LS Gaz, 22 July 2013, p 34

Would occupation afford relief from non-domestic rates on the ground that the organisation is a charity in occupation of the relevant hereditament?

Take Stock of the Recent Rating Cases, Blake Penfold: Estates Gazette, 15 June 2013, p 98

A flurry of recent decisions has shed light on the issue of liability for business rates.

MATRIMONIAL AND CIVIL PARTNERSHIP LAW

Agreements: Reaching Conclusions, Claire Glaister: Fam LJ, March 2013, p 19

Courts may uphold a financial agreement; even if one party disputes whether an agreement has been reached.

All About The Evidence, Anna Heenan: 163 NLJ 284

The decision in *Davies v Davies* [2012] EWCA Civ 1641, [2013] 1 FCR 459 is likely to be of use to practitioners for its consideration of how to deal with an inherited business to which the wife had made a significant contribution during a short marriage.

All Marriages are Equal ..., Janet Barlow and Rebecca Mason: 163 NLJ 15

While the Marriage (Same Sex Couples) Act 2013 purports to give same sex couples equality with that of heterosexual couples, on closer examination this does not appear to be the case.

All's Fair in Love and ... Jonathan Herring: 163 NLJ 10

The decision in *T v T* [2013] EWCA Civ 774, [2013] All ER (D) 118 (Jul) acknowledges that, especially where the resident parent is working, childcare costs can be a significant expense, even for school age children.

Am I Married? Three Recent Case Studies on the Effect of Non-Compliant Marriage Ceremonies, Ruth Gaffney-Rhys: [2013] IFL 53

Recent cases suggest there is a certain lack of awareness of the formalities required to create a valid marriage under English law; particularly amongst parties from outside the United Kingdom.

Appeal: Test for Permission, Gillian Douglas: Fam LJ, August 2013, p 938

What constitutes a real prospect of success? On *CR v SR (financial remedies: permission to appeal)* [2013] EWHC 1155 (Fam), (22 January 2013, unreported).

Armed Forces Divorce: Service Issues, Juliet McDermott: Fam LJ, March 2013, p 15

Divorces involving members of the armed forces require unique considerations, such as the division of a forces pension.

Brave New World? David Lister: Family LJ, May 2013, p 15

How do legal services orders differ from costs allowance orders?

A Capital Idea, Kim Beatson: 163 NLJ 11

Arguments over the capitalisation of maintenance are best settled via dispute resolution processes.

Changes to Rules on Instructing Experts, Safda Mahmood: Fam LJ, June 2013, p 709

Shows tightening in laws with regard to employing experts in cases to do with family law, and the need to lay down strict guidelines.

Lost in Translation, Tom Bailey: (2013) 157 Sol Jo (no 12) 16
   Two Supreme Court cases on piercing the corporate veil could have implications for the
   application of the Matrimonial Causes Act 1973.
Lump Sum Orders: Providing Clarity, Alex Davies: Fam LJ, March 2013, p 2
   Hamilton v Hamilton [2013] EWCA Civ 13, [2013] All ER (D) 201 (Jan) highlights the
   significance in the difference between a series of lump sums and a lump sum payable by
   instalments.
The Lump Sum Trap, Margaret Hatwood and Rebecca Carter: 163 NLJ 12
   Most people going through a divorce want to achieve future certainty in their financial
   arrangements by what is known as a 'clean break'.
A Matter of Trust ... Geraldine Morris: 163 NLJ 11
   In *Prest v Petrodel Resources Ltd* [2013] UKSC 34, [2013] 2 AC 415, [2013] All ER
   (D) 90 (Jun) (REVIEW para 1819), the wife's argument to pierce the corporate veil failed,
   with the Supreme Court finding in favour of a trust scenario.
New Signposts? Clare Renton: 163 NLJ 13
   What does the future hold for the concept of habitual residence?
Passing the Buck, Frances Bailey and Nikki Saxton: Fam LJ, October 2012, p 5
   To remove the discretion and to say that cohabitation per se will terminate financial
   obligations that have arisen as a result of the marriage and not the cohabitation would
   swing the pendulum too far.
Piercing the Corporate Veil, Nicholas Bennett: LS Gaz, 15 July 2013, p 28
   What are the ramifications of the latest big money divorce judgment? On *Prest v Petrodel
   Resources Ltd* [2013] UKSC 34, [2013] 2 AC 415, [2013] All ER (D) 90 (Jun) (REVIEW
   para 1819).
Prenuptial Agreements: Lady Hale and a Lesson from America, Nick Rees: [2013] IFL 59
   There are crucial distinctions between ante-nuptial and post-nuptial agreements that
   should not be overlooked, despite the ruling in *Radmacher (formerly Granatino) v
   Granatino (pre-nuptial contract)* [2010] UKSC 42, [2011] 1 AC 534, [2011] 1 All ER 373
   (2010 Abr para 2000).
Prenuptial Agreements, Muslim Marriages and UK Law, Zia Akhtar: [2013] IFL 63
   Are talaq agreements enforceable under English law?
Prenuptial Agreements: The Implications of Gender, Somaya Ouazzani: Fam LJ, April 2013,
   p 421
   Operation of prenuptials and protection for female spouse.
Prest: A Very English Solution, Hazel Wright, Tom Bailey and Chris Bryden: (2013) 157 Sol
   Jo (no 21) 12
   In *Prest v Petrodel Resources Ltd* [2013] UKSC 34, [2013] 2 AC 415, [2013] All ER
   (D) 90 (Jun) (REVIEW para 1819), the Supreme Court kept company law principles intact
   and used property and trust law to reach a fair conclusion – but not all agree with
   Lord Sumption.
Prest v Petrodel Resources Ltd and Others [2013] UKSC 34, Rebecca Bailey-Harris: Fam LJ,
   August 2013, p 953
   The decision in *Prest v Petrodel Resources Ltd* [2013] UKSC 34, [2013] 2 AC 415, [2013]
   All ER (D) 90 (Jun) (REVIEW para 1819) may not be a repeatable victory for wives.
Recession Impacts Divorce Decisions, Jan Miller: 63 NLJ 4 (1)
   Divorce rate falling but financial trickery is on the rise.
Revealing Assets, Robert Hines: 163 NLJ 11
   A careful consideration of the ultimate beneficial ownership of assets held behind the
   'corporate veil' may make such assets available for division on divorce.
Same-Sex Couples and the Harmonisation of EU Matrimonial Property Regimes:
   Unjustifiable Discrimination or Missed Opportunities? Stuart Davis: [2013] CFLQ 19
   Despite the different treatment afforded to same-sex couples, the European Commission's
   proposed harmonisation measures should be tolerated.
Scuppering Unscrupulous Spouses, Ed Heaton and Anna Heenan: 163 NLJ 14
   What are the implications of a court setting aside a disposal made by a divorcing spouse to
   a third party?
Spousal Support, Andrew Newbury: LS Gaz, 11 February 2013, p 19
   In the case of *S v M* [2012] All ER (D) 175 (Nov), the court addressed the issue of the
   unrealistic time estimate of 30 minutes given to deal with the maintenance pending suit
   application where there was a significant difference in the evidence of the parties.

Stop, Collaborate and Listen, Bindu Bansal: (2013) 157 Sol Jo (no 37) 17
  The use of collaborative law in divorce cases could become more popular as parties look
  to reduce costs and avoid court.
Striking the Right Note? Andrew Newbury: LS Gaz, 9 September 2013, p 24
  The introduction of the Family Procedure Rules 2010, SI 2010/2955, r 4.4(1) (2010 Abr
  para 266) is a significant development in family proceedings.
What's Mine is Mine ..., Ed Heaton: 163 NLJ 7585, p 9
  What are the rights of cohabitants?

MEDICAL PRODUCTS AND DRUGS

'He Was Like a Zombie': Off-Label Prescription of Antipsychotic Drugs in Dementia, Rosie
  Harding and Elizabeth Peel: (2013) 21 Med Law Rev 243
  Does the practice of off-label prescribing require regulatory intervention in order to
  protect vulnerable patients?
Time for a Litigation Supplement? Sarah Moore: 163 NLJ 9
  It is vital that manufacturers are compelled to either substantiate their products' claims to
  medical efficacy, or remove them.

MEDICAL PROFESSIONS

Brustle v Greenpeace, Embryonic Stem Cell Research and the European Court of Justice's
  New Found Morality, Ciara Staunton: (2013) 21 Med Law Rev 310
  The decision in Case C-34/10 Brustle v Greenpeace [2012] All ER (EC) 809, ECJ,
  concerns a referral from the Federal Court of Justice of Germany to the European Court
  of Justice for an interpretation of three issues under Council Directive (EC) 98/44.
Cutting to the Chase, Giles Eyre: 163 NLJ 20
  Many medical reports prepared for civil litigation, whether obtained through a medical
  reporting agency or direct from a clinician, are not fit for purpose.
Delayed Diagnosis in Cancer Cases and Proof of Causation, Julian Matthews: Personal
  Injury Law Journal, May 2013, p 17
  Recent cases including Oliver v Williams [2013] EWHC 600 (QB), [2013] All ER (D) 193
  (Mar) leave potential litigants in delayed cancer diagnosis cases with little redress.
Disclosure of Confidential Patient Information and the Duty to Consult: The Role of the
  Health and Social Care Information Centre, Jamie Grace and Mark Taylor: (2013) 21
  Med Law Rev 415
  There is currently a responsibility on health professionals to consult with a patient
  wherever practicable before disclosing confidential patient information for purposes not
  directly related to the patient's care and treatment.
Doctrinal Incoherence or Practical Problem? Minor Parents Consenting to their Offspring's
  Medical Treatment and Involvement in Research in England and Wales, Sara Fovargue:
  [2013] CFLQ 1
  Who can give medical consent for a child when both parents are minors themselves?
Inherent Jurisdiction, Caroline Bridge: Fam LJ, August 2013, p 964
  What is the legality of tissue testing a corpse? On CM v The Executor of the Estate of EJ
  (deceased) [2013] EWHC 1680 (Fam), [2013] All ER (D) 148 (Jun).

MENTAL HEALTH AND CAPACITY

Clients Without Capacity—Managing Their Property and Affairs, Araba Taylor: Personal
  Injury Law Journal, May 2013, p 10
  Clients without capacity present complex issues of property management, which includes
  existing property and that acquired following the injury.
Comparison Contrast, David Hewitt: (2013) 157 Sol Jo (no 16) 9
  Should the subjective approach taken to the Deprivation of Liberty Safeguards Code of
  Practice be replaced with an objective one?
Doctrinal Incoherence or Practical Problem? Minor Parents Consenting to their Offspring's
  Medical Treatment and Involvement in Research in England and Wales, Sara Fovargue:
  [2013] CFLQ 1
  Who can give medical consent for a child when both parents are minors themselves?
The Inherent Jurisdiction over Vulnerable Adults, Ruth Hughes: [2013] PCB 132
  Despite the delineation of the Court of Protection's powers in the Mental Capacity
  Act 2005 (2005 Abr para 2174), the inherent jurisdiction of the High Court has survived
  in certain cases involving vulnerable adults.

PERSONAL PROPERTY

Commercial Property, Suzanne Gill: LS Gaz, 2 September 2013, p 24
  When is a chattel annexed to the realty?
Value Judgment, Robin Ellison: Pensions World, January 2013, p 14
  Pension rights do not fit well into conventional definitions of property.

PLANNING

An Addition to the Armoury, Martin Edwards and John Martin: Estates Gazette, 9 February
  2013, p 102
  The government wants to make temporary stop notices available to local authorities in
  cases of unauthorised traveller sites.
An Analysis of s 124 of the Localism Act 2011, Emma Hatfield: [2013] Conv 48
  Hard cases make bad law—the problems with the Localism Act 2011 (2011 Abr
  para 1784).
At the Court's Discretion, Martin Edwards and John Martin: Estates Gazette, 8 June 2013,
  p 69
  Two recent cases suggests planning permission may stand despite non-compliance with the
  Town and Country Planning (Environmental Impact Assessment) Regulations 2011,
  SI 2011/1824 (2011 Abr para 2015).
Beware the Newts, Bill Bidder and Kate Egan-Martin: Building, 10 May 2013, p 48
  Development in areas of special scientific interest.
Both Sides Bungle Greenfield Debate, Tony Fyson: Planning, 14 December 2012, p 15
  The case for new towns and planned mitigation.
[Compulsory Purchase Orders]: Powers, Procedures and Pitfalls, John Bowman and Emily
  Murray: Estates Gazette, 4 May 2013, p 96
  Information gathering and the full referencing exercise are essential to ensure a
  compulsory purchase order does not encounter difficulties.
Concealed Development: Did We Really Need Section 124? Emma Hatfield: [2013] JPL 19
  The government has reacted with unnecessary regulation without considering existing
  options.
The Concepts of 'Harmful by Definition' and 'Very Special Circumstances' in the
  Application of Green Belt Policy: A Case for Reassessment? John Brearley: [2013] JPL 798
  Green Belt policy is an area particularly prone to generate polarised views and conceptual
  rigidities, the concept of something being 'by definition' harmful being perhaps the
  cardinal example.
Determining a 'Neighbourhood Area': Plan-Led Paradigm or Broad Discretion? Ashley
  Bowes: [2013] JPL 926
  The neighbourhood plan process should be firmly framed in the plan-led system and the
  legislation must be construed accordingly.
Distinguishing Between Various Types of Dwelling House or Residential Uses, Michael
  Purdue: [2013] JPL 1
  Clarifying material change of use in planning law.
Enlightening Thoughts, Martin Edwards and John Martin: Estates Gazette, 11 May 2013,
  p 89
  Along with increased power over planning decisions, local authorities have acquired new
  responsibilities.
Ex-Gratia Payments for Maladministration by the Planning Inspectorate, Michael Purdue:
  [2013] JPL 2
  Change of policy on ex gratia payments.
Filling the Void: Minor Glitch or System Failure? Nicholas Dobson: LS Gaz, 4 February
  2013, p 19
  Can a local authority prosecute for failure to have a valid caravan site licence in place,
  when the initial licence the authority had purported to grant was ultra vires?
Growth and Infrastructure Act 2013, Alec Samuels: [2013] JPL 931
  Despite the contemporary move towards localism there remains a significant element of
  centralism in the Growth and Infrastructure Act 2013 (REVIEW para 2022).
How to Live With the Levy, Roy Pinnock and Stephen Ashworth: Estates Gazette, 16 March
  2013, p 76
  Despite recent changes, the community infrastructure levy remains flawed and open to
  abuse.

POLICE AND INVESTIGATORY POWERS

Step in the Right Direction, Leslie Keegan: (2013) 157 Sol Jo (no 21) 22
There is no perfect solution to the issues surrounding the right-to-die debate but the new bill will help.
A Study of the Use of Sharia Law in Religious Arbitration in the United Kingdom and the Concerns That This Raises for Human Rights, Jessie Brechin: (2013) 15 Ecc LJ 293
To what extent are sharia 'courts' able to operate within the legal systems of the United Kingdom through the means of arbitration?
Use of the Human Rights Act in Clinical Negligence Litigation, Richard Lodge and Raoul Lumb: Personal Injury Law Journal, May 2013, p 12
The Human Rights Act 1998 has had a significant impact on clinical negligence cases, but article 8 claims have met with little success.
You Must Be Joking: Protecting 'Free Speech', Steve Foster: (2013) 177 JPN 75
Do we have a right under the European Convention on Human Rights art 10 to make jokes, and is anything we say or write truly speech or expression under that fundamental provision?

ROAD TRAFFIC

Against the Odds, Andrew Ritchie: 163 NLJ 8
Dealing with the Motor Insurers' Bureau under the Untraced Drivers Agreement 2003 has become much clearer after a recent arbitration ruling.
Asleep at the Wheel? Nicholas Bevan: 163 NLJ 10
Can the government wash its hands of the many imperfections in its provision for motor accident victims?
Insurance Obligations, the Road Traffic Act 1988 and Deliberately Caused Damage, Margaret Hemsworth: [2013] JBL 354
What is the insurance obligation when damage is deliberate?
On the Right Road? Nicholas Bevan: 163 NLJ 94, 130, 160
Examines how effectively national law implements EU law on compulsory motor insurance and compensation in respect of uninsured drivers.
Resident Evil? Nicholas Dobson: 163 NLJ 15
The Road Traffic Regulation Act 1984 is not a fiscal measure and does not authorise local authorities to use powers to charge local residents for parking to raise surplus revenue for other transport purposes.
Road Traffic Update, Roger Cooper: (2013) 157 Sol Jo (no 22) 27
The decisions in *Ayres v Odedra* [2013] EWHC 40 (QB), [2013] All ER (D) 114 (Jan) (REVIEW para 1898) and *Rehill v Rider Holdings* [2012] EWCA Civ 628, [2012] All ER (D) 206 (May), highlight how the courts are taking a more nuanced approach to road traffic cases involving pedestrians.

SALE OF GOODS AND SUPPLY OF SERVICES

Retention of Title, Stephen Cogley and Jeremy Richmond: LS Gaz, 11 November 2013, p 24
A recent case has settled the longstanding debate as to whether Sale of Goods Act 1979 s 49 provides the exclusive remedy for the price of goods or simply a statutory alternative.
Tortious Duties of Care Owed in Letters of Credit between Parties to the Autonomous Contracts, Cristin Toman: (2013) 9 JIBFL 568
A third party inspection company engaged by the seller and designated to inspect and certify goods in connection with a letter of credit may owe a duty of care to the buyer as an applicant under the letter of credit.

SENTENCING AND DISPOSITION OF OFFENDERS

An 'Aggravating' Factor in Sentencing, Claire Hargreaves and Daniel Prince: Police Professional, 22 August 2013, p 23
What effect should the use of technology in a crime have on sentencing?
A Behaviour-Based Approach to Sentencing for Sexual Offences, Lyndon Harris and Felicity Gerry: (2013) 177 JPN 239
The only method of assessing the true culpability of an offence is by reference to behaviour, as opposed to an arbitrary list of factors defined by the statutory offence charged.

to consider whether the 'football creditor' rule operated by the Football League was void for offending the pari passu principle and the so-called anti-deprivation principle.

Local Government: Public Order Charges, Nicholas Dobson: LS Gaz, 15 April 2013, p 21
When can the police charge for policing football matches?

Tackling Ticket Touting, Alec Samuels: (2013) 177 JPN 635
Should there be a simple statutory regulation prohibiting touting?

STAMP TAXES

Examining the Scope of FA 2003 s 75A, Sharon McKie: Tax J, Issue 1169, p 15
Revenue and Customs takes the view that the stamp duty land tax anti-avoidance provision in the Finance Act 2003 s 75A (2003 Abr para 2258) applies only where there is avoidance of tax and, on that basis, it will not seek to apply s 75A where it considers transactions have already been taxed appropriately.

Many Happy Returns, Paul Clark: [2013] Conv 7
The legal problems with stamp duty.

Pollen Count, Graham Elliott: Taxation, 18 July 2013, p 17
Her Majesty's Revenue and Customs seem to have had an allergic reaction to granting stamp duty land tax relief.

Pollen Estate: [Stamp Duty Land Tax] and Joint Purchasers, Jonathan Legg: Tax J, Issue 1177, p 10
What are the fundamental principles of how stamp duty land tax applies to joint purchasers of land?

A Relief for Charities, Stephanie Howarth: Trusts and Estates Law & Tax Journal, November 2013, p 19
Pollen Estate Trustee Co Ltd v Revenue and Customs Comrs [2013] EWCA Civ 753, [2013] 3 All ER 742 confirms that stamp duty land tax relief applies when a charity acts as a joint purchaser with non-charitable bodies.

[Stamp Duty Land Tax] and Connected Parties, Annette Morley: Simon's Tax Briefing, 2 January 2013, p 11
There are exceptions to the Finance Act 2003 s 53 (2003 Abr para 2258), but it is important for tax advisers to be aware of the rules relating to stamp duty land tax and connected parties.

[Stamp Duty Land Tax] on Incorporation, Peter Rayney: Tax J, Issue 1152, p 22
Where property is transferred by a partnership to an 'unconnected company', the stamp duty land tax is generally based on the actual consideration given for the property.

[Stamp Duty Land Tax] Transfer of Rights Rules, Marc Selby: Tax J, Issue 1165, p 20
The new rules on the transfer of rights in the Finance Act 2003 Sch 2A (2003 Abr para 2258) provide greater clarity than the existing rules in certain important respects, such as the identity of the vendor.

Taxation of Demergers, Bradley Phillips and Perminder Gainda: Tax J, Issue 1190, p 13

Taxpayer Wins Right to Reclaim Overpaid [Stamp Duty Land Tax], Jessica Ganagasegaran: Property Law Journal, 3 June 2013, p 15
The grant of a lease may now be the 'the transfer of a business as a going concern' for VAT purposes. On *Robinson Family Ltd v Revenue and Customs Comrs* [2013] UKFTT 360 (TC), (29 May 2012, unreported).

Too Hot to Handle, Peter Rayney: Taxation, 17 January 2013, p 8
Is it time to drop the idea of holding United Kingdom property through offshore companies?

Triple Jump, Sean Randall: Taxation, 26 September 2013, p 18
Is responsible stamp duty land tax planning still possible?

STATUTES AND LEGISLATIVE PROCESS

The Day the Supreme Court Was Unable to Interpret Statutes, Catrin Fflur Huws: (2013) 13 Stat LR 221
What are the problems that arise from a dual legislature within a monolingual courts system?

Enacting Legislation—A Civil Servant's Perspective, Paul Regan: (2013) 34 Stat LR 32
A Bill can be brought before Parliament for many reasons, such as to give effect to a manifesto commitment, to take forward a policy long in gestation, to enable the United Kingdom to comply with international obligations and to respond to a crisis.

TELECOMMUNICATIONS

TORT

TRADE AND INDUSTRY

On the Scrapheap, Steven King: 163 NLJ 19
What is the likely effectiveness of the Scrap Metal Dealers Act 2013 (REVIEW para 2387)?

TRADE MARKS AND TRADE NAMES

Confused in the Dotcom, Michael Hart: (2013) 157 Sol Jo (no 28) 12
Using competitors' names as keywords in search engines will be lawful provided advertisers make it clear they have no association with the brand.
Harmonisation of Intellectual Property Law in Europe: The ECJ Trade Mark Case Law 2008–2012, Annette Kur: [2013] CML Rev 773
What is the past, present and future of European trade mark law?
Not in My Name, Jim McDonnell: LS Gaz, 25 February 2013, p 20
The judgment in *Hotel Cipriani SRL v Fred* [2013] EWHC 70 (Ch), [2013] All ER (D) 250 (Jan) provides another useful insight into the 'own name' defence and the enforcement of injunctions.
Not in My Name, Stephen Boyd: 163 NLJ 6
The utility of passing off as a cause of action to be deployed by a celebrity whose image had been exploited without consent was brought to the fore by *Irvine v Talksport Ltd* [2002] EWHC 367 (Ch), [2002] 2 All ER 414 (2002 Abr para 2967).
Rihanna v Topshop: A Long-Awaited Success for the Celebrity Industry, Lisa Broad: Corporate Briefing, October 2013, p 2
In *Fenty v Arcadia Group Brands Ltd* [2013] EWHC 2310 (Ch), [2013] All ER (D) 410 (Jul) (REVIEW para 2398), the High Court held that the use of a celebrity's image on clothing without her permission amounted to passing off.

TRUSTS AND POWERS

Charitable Trusts and Waqfs: Their Parallels, Registration Process, and Tax Reliefs in the United Kingdom, Zia Akhtar: (2013) 13 Stat LR 281
Clarifying Intentions, Sarah Greenan: Family LJ, May 2013, p 19
How should the issue of equitable accounting be approached?
Common Intention Constructive Trusts: A Way Forward, Annika Newnham: Fam LJ, June 2013, p 718
How the law treats separating cohabitants.
The Cost of Occupation, Geraldine Morris: 163 NLJ 157
What are the issues of occupation rent and equitable accounting in cohabitant cases?
Cutting Through the Hedge, Emily Saunderson: (2013) 5 JIBFL 267
What is the essence of the knowledge that lies at the heart of a dishonest assistance claim?
Declarations of Trust in the Family Home, Mark Pawlowski: Trusts and Estates Law & Tax Journal, April 2013, p 4
Are express trusts conclusive? On *Pankhania v Chandegra (by her litigation friend, Ronald Andrew Eagle)* [2012] EWCA Civ 1438, [2013] 1 P & CR 238, [2012] All ER (D) 132 (Nov).
In the Wrong Hands, Christopher Stone and Alison Padfield: (2013) 157 Sol Jo (no 18) 10
Can solicitors escape liability for breach of trust claims in failed conveyancing transactions?
Letting the Cat Out of the Bag: The Law of Trust Disclosure, William East: [2013] PCB 106
The decision in *Schmidt v Rosewood Trust Ltd* [2003] UKPC 26, [2003] 2 AC 709, [2003] 3 All ER 76 (2003 Abr para 2739) has provided a uniform approach for the courts to take on questions of trust disclosure.
A Matter of Discretion, Francesca Kaye and Mary Hodgson: 163 NLJ 8
What constitutes completion and breach of trust?
Monetary Mistakes, Michael Firth: Taxation, 23 May 2013, p 14
It was uncontroversial that the fiduciaries in *Pitt v Holt; Futter v Futter* [2013] UKSC 26, [2013] 2 AC 108, [2013] 3 All ER 429 (REVIEW para 2480) had the power to make the type of disposition that they made, and that they were not exercising it for an improper purpose, so the Supreme Court was considering two cases of inadequate deliberation.
Oh, Grow Up! Jan Miller: Pensions World, February 2013, p 14
There is a need for more involvement of trust law and less regulation.
Prest: A Very English Solution, Hazel Wright, Tom Bailey and Chris Bryden: (2013) 157 Sol Jo (no 21) 12
In *Prest v Petrodel Resources Ltd* [2013] UKSC 34, [2013] 2 AC 415, [2013] All ER

VALUE ADDED TAX

[2013] All ER (D) 273 (Jan), ECJ (REVIEW para 2548), is interesting with regard to the context of wider VAT debates that exist around the questions of single versus multiple supplies and the treatment of recharges.

Budget Analysis—VAT Measures, Marc Welby: Tax J, Issue 1163, p 24
What are the VAT measures announced in this year's budget?

Developments on Single v Multiple Supplies, David Anderson and Nicole Kostic: Tax J, Issue 1171, p 18
What developments have there been in the case law on the analysis to be applied to a single, multiple or a composite supply, to determine the VAT liability of part or all of the supply?

Digital Mayhem, Robin Williamson: Taxation, 24 October 2013, p 10
In *LH Bishop Electric Company Ltd* [2013] UKFTT 522 (TC), (30 September 2013, unreported), the First-tier Tribunal held that Her Majesty's Revenue and Customs acted illegally when it issued a notice requiring three taxpayers to file their VAT returns online.

Esporta: VAT on Recovered Membership Fees, Vinny McCullagh: Tax J, Issue 1169, p 19
In *Revenue and Customs Comrs v Esporta* [2013] UKUTT 0173 (TCC), (26 April 2013, unreported), the Upper Tribunal overturned the First-tier Tribunal's decision that unpaid membership fees recovered through debt collection agencies were outside the scope of VAT.

Eternal Triangles, Mike Thexton: Taxation, 11 April 2013, p 20
Where two businesses are involved in supplying something to one customer, it is essential to determine the lines of supply.

The Financial Services Exemption, Kevin Hall: Tax J, Issue 1170, p 18
Which services qualify for the financial services exemption and which follow the normal rules?

GfBk and Special Investment Funds, Nick Skerrett and Matthew Rees: Tax J, Issue 1164, p 23
While funds may already have structured their operations to benefit from the exemption, in Case C-275/11 *GfBk Gesellschaft fur Borsenkommunikation mbH v Finanzamt Bayreuth* [2013] All ER (D) 118 (Mar) the European Court of Justice has taken a wide view.

Gone Missing, Neil Warren: Taxation, 16 May 2013, p 14
How can a claim for input tax still be made by a business in the absence of a tax invoice?

Legitimate Expectation in the Tribunal, Angela Savin: Tax J, Issue 1162, p 22
Since the High Court decision in *Oxfam v Revenue and Customs Comrs* [2009] EWHC 3078 (Ch), [2010] STC 686 (2010 Abr para 1830), there has existed a state of confusion over the question of the First-tier Tribunal's jurisdiction to determine cases on the basis of public law arguments.

NEC: VAT and Booking Fees, Julie Park: Tax J, Issue 1172, p 18
The First-tier Tribunal recently released its judgment in the case of *National Exhibition Centre Ltd* [2013] UKFTT 289 (TC) (17 May 2013, unreported) and found in favour of the taxpayer.

Ocean Finance: Economic and Commercial Reality, Anbreen Khan and Emma Hughes: Tax J, Issue 1175, p 24
What weight is to be attributed to contracts in determining the VAT supply position? On Case C-653/11 *Newey v Revenue and Customs Comrs* [2013] All ER (D) 254 (Jun), ECJ.

Pactor Vastgoed—A Possible Challenge to the [UK Capital Goods Scheme], Gary Richards and Alan Sinyor: Tax J, Issue 1190, p 18
In C-622/11 *Staatssecretaris van Financen v Pactor Vastgoed BV* [2013] All ER (D) 246 (Oct), ECJ, it was held that any adjustment to a deduction from which a taxable person had benefited must be made on that person.

A Problem Like Maria, Neil Warren: Taxation, 14 February 2013, p 14
It is recommended for a practitioner to consider all non-United Kingdom clients to make sure that they are not classed as a non-established taxable person where VAT registration could now be needed as a result of the zero threshold from 1 December 2012.

Rank: VAT and Gaming Machines, Stephen Hignett and Matthew Wentworth-May: Tax J, Issue 1193, p 18
The decision in *Revenue and Customs Comrs v Rank Group plc* [2013] EWCA Civ 1289, [2013] All ER (D) 337 (Oct) was the result of a new argument as to the VAT treatment of slot machines.

regulations consequential on European Parliament and Council Regulation (EU) 1308/2013, establishing a common organisation of the markets in agricultural products and repealing Council Regulation (EEC) 922/72, Council Regulation (EEC) 234/79, Council Regulation (EC) 1037/2001, and Council Regulation (EC) 1234/2007, by replacing references to Regulation 1234/2007 with references to Regulation 1308/2013.

11   Common agricultural policy—cross compliance

The Agriculture (Cross compliance) (No 2) (Amendment) Regulations 2013, SI 2013/3231 (in force on 1 January 2014), further amend the 2009 Regulations, SI 2009/3365, by adding specified provisions relating to groundwater activities, set out in the Environmental Permitting (England and Wales) Regulations 2010, SI 2010/675, to the list of provisions of which a breach constitutes a failure of cross compliance by a claimant of subsidy under the single payment scheme.

12   Control of pollution—gaseous and particulate pollutants—agricultural and forestry tractors

See para 1127.

13   Control of pollution—water—silage, slurry and agricultural fuel oil—England

See para 1147.

14   Feeding stuffs—hygiene and enforcement—England

The Feed (Hygiene and Enforcement) and the Animal Feed (England) (Amendment) Regulations 2013, SI 2013/3133 (in force on 17 January 2014), further amend (1) the Feed (Hygiene and Enforcement) (England) Regulations 2005, SI 2005/3280, so as to (a) re-state the definition of European Parliament and Council Regulation (EC) 183/2005 laying down requirements for feed hygiene so that, by virtue of the Interpretation Act 1978 s 20A, it includes the amendments made by Commission Regulation (EU) 225/2012; (b) provide that any reference to an Annex to Regulation 183/2005 is to be construed as a reference to that Annex as it may be amended from time to time; (c) designate the competent authorities for the purposes of enforcing certain provisions of Regulation 225/2012; and (d) provide for the fee to be paid for approval of specified establishments; and (2) the Animal Feed (England) Regulations 2010, SI 2010/2503, so as to (a) remove references to an EU instrument which has been repealed; and (b) clarify the drafting of enforcement provisions relating to European Parliament and Council Regulation (EC) 767/2009 on the placing on the market and use of feed.

15   Feeding stuffs—hygiene and enforcement—Wales

The Feed (Hygiene and Enforcement) and the Animal Feed (Wales) (Amendment) Regulations 2013, SI 2013/3207 (in force on 12 January 2014), (1) further amend the Feed (Hygiene and Enforcement) (Wales) Regulations 2005, SI 2005/3368, so as to (a) re-state the definition of European Parliament and Council Regulation (EC) 183/2005 laying down requirements for feed hygiene so that, by virtue of the Interpretation Act 1978 s 20A, it includes the amendments made by Commission Regulation (EU) 225/2012; (b) provide that any reference to an Annex to Regulation 183/2005 is to be construed as a reference to that Annex as it may be amended from time to time; (c) designate the competent authorities for the purposes of enforcing certain provisions of Regulation 225/2012; and (d) provide for the fee to be paid for approval of specified establishments; and (2) amend the Animal Feed (Wales) Regulations 2010, SI 2010/2652, so as to (a) remove references to an EU instrument which has been repealed; and (b) clarify the drafting of enforcement provisions relating to European Parliament and Council Regulation (EC) 767/2009 on the placing on the market and use of feed.

16   Plant health—control of pests—England

The Plant Health (England) (Amendment) Order 2013, SI 2013/23 (in force on 17 January 2013), further amends the 2005 Order, SI 2005/2530, so as to (1) make minor amendments to the matters which are required to be notified under art 19(4); and (2) make provision to prohibit a person from landing in England certain plants which have been grown or are suspected to have been grown in another member state or in Switzerland, unless prior written notification has been given to an authorised inspector.

The Plant Health (England) (Amendment) (No 2) Order 2013, SI 2013/1477 (in force on 15 July 2013), further amends the 2005 Order above by (1) revising the definition of 'protected zone' to take account of Commission Regulation (EC) 690/2008 recognising protected zones exposed to particular plant health risks; and (2) recognising Serbia as being free from *Clavibachter michiganensis* ssp *Sepedonicus*, in implementation of Commission Decision (EU) 2012/219.

The Plant Health (England) (Amendment) (No 3) Order 2013, SI 2013/2687 (in force on 11 November 2013), further amends the 2005 Order above so as to (1) alter the existing control measures to prevent the introduction and spread of *Ceratocystis fimbriata f spp Walter and Cryphonectria parasitica* (Murrill) Barr; (2) implement Commission Implementing Decision (EU) 2013/253 amending Commission Decision (EC) 2006/473 as regards the recognition of certain third countries and certain areas of third countries as being free from *Xanthomonas campestris*, *Cercospora angolensis Carv et Mendes* and *Guignardia citricarpa* Kiely; (3) prohibit a person from landing in England plants of *Pinus* L intended for planting unless prior written notification has been given to an authorised inspector; and (4) provide for reference to Decision 2006/473 to be read as reference to Decision 2006/473 as amended from time to time.

17　Plant health—control of pests—Wales

The Plant Health (Wales) (Amendment) Order 2013, SI 2013/888 (in force on 10 May 2013), further amends the 2006 Order, SI 2006/1643, so as to include emergency measures to prevent the introduction and spread of *Chalara fraxinea* T Kowalski including its teleomorph Hymenoscyphus pseudoalbidus. In particular, the order (1) prohibits the landing in or the spread within Wales of *Chalara fraxinea* T Kowalski; (2) prohibits the landing in or the movement within Wales of plants intended for planting of Fraxinus L which are infected with *Chalara fraxinea* T Kowalski; (3) imposes additional requirements on the landing in or movement within Wales of plants intended for planting of Fraxinus L; (4) imposes additional requirements on the consignment from Wales to other parts of the European Union of plants intended for planting of Fraxinus L; and (5) confers powers on the Welsh Ministers to grant licences for trial or scientific purposes or for work on varietal selections in relation to certain plant pests.

The Plant Health (Wales) (Amendment) (No 2) Order 2013, SI 2013/2939 (in force on 13 December 2013), further amends the 2006 Order above so as to prohibit anyone from landing in Wales certain plants which have been grown, or are suspected to have been grown, in another member state or in Switzerland, unless prior written notification has been given to an authorised inspector.

18　Plant health—export certification—England

The Plant Health (Export Certification) (England) (Amendment) Order 2013, SI 2013/572 (in force on 6 April 2013), further amends the 2004 Order, SI 2004/1404, by increasing the fees for services in respect of applications for certificates and for pre-export services.

19　Plant health—export certification—Wales

The Plant Health (Export Certification) (Wales) (Amendment) Order 2013, SI 2013/1658 (in force on 31 July 2013), amends the 2006 Order, SI 2006/1701, by increasing fees for services in respect of applications for certificates and fees for pre-export services.

20　Plant health—import inspection fees—England

The Plant Health (Fees) (England) Regulations 2013, SI 2013/494 (in force on 6 April 2013), replace the 2012 Regulations, SI 2012/745, so as to specify fees payable to the Secretary of State in the field of plant health. The fees are payable in relation to specified inspections and other operations carried out pursuant to Council Directive (EC) 2000/29 (on protective measures against the introduction into the Community of organisms harmful to plants or plant products and against their spread within the Community).

The Plant Health (Fees) (England) (Amendment) Regulations 2013, SI 2013/3050 (in force on 1 January 2014), amend SI 2013/494 above by specifying revised import inspection fees and inspection rates in respect of certain plants.

21   Plant health—import inspection fees—Wales

The Plant Health (Fees) (Wales) Regulations 2013, SI 2013/1700 (in force on 2 August 2013), replace the 2012 Regulations, SI 2012/1493, and specify fees payable to the Welsh Ministers in the field of plant health in relation to specified inspections and other operations carried out pursuant to Council Directive (EC) 2000/29, on protective measures against the introduction into the Community of organisms harmful to plants or plant products and against their spread within the Community.

22   Seeds—marketing—Wales

The Seed Marketing (Wales) (Amendment) Regulations 2013, SI 2013/889 (in force on 10 May 2013), amend the 2012 Regulations, SI 2012/245, so as to (1) add Council Decision (EC) 2003/17 on the equivalence of field inspections carried out in third countries on seed-producing crops and on the equivalence of seed produced in third countries to the list of European Union instruments in respect of which references in the 2012 Regulations are to be construed as references to those instruments; and (2) allow the Welsh Ministers to license exemptions for temporary experiments organised under Council Directive (EC) 2002/54 (on the marketing of beet seed), Council Directive (EEC) 66/402 (on the marketing of cereal seed), Council Directive (EEC) 66/401 (on the marketing of fodder plant seed), Council Directive (EC) 2002/57 (on the marketing of seed of oil and fibre plants), or Council Directive (EC) 2002/55 (on the marketing of vegetable seed).

23   Uplands farming—transitional payments—England

The Uplands Transitional Payment Regulations 2013, SI 2013/109 (in force on 15 February 2013), (1) define the conditions of eligibility for an uplands transitional payment; and (2) provide that payment is payable only in relation to severely disadvantaged land at the rates specified. SI 2006/225, SI 2006/518, SI 2007/619 and SI 2008/51 are revoked.

AIR LAW

Halsbury's Laws of England (5th edn) vol 2 (2008) paras 1–700

Articles

For articles relating to this title please refer to the Table of Articles at the beginning of the Abridgment.

24   Air navigation—general

The Air Navigation (Amendment) Order 2013, SI 2013/3169 (in force on 27 January 2014), further amends the 2009 Order, SI 2009/3015, so as to (1) provide that a student pilot with a valid medical declaration or with a certificate issued under relevant European legislation can, subject to other conditions, fly solo for the purpose of becoming qualified for the grant or renewal of a pilot licence or for the inclusion or variation of any rating in such a licence; (2) alter what constitutes time in flight for a helicopter for the purpose of recording time in a 'personal flying log'; (3) designate the Civil Aviation Authority as the competent authority for the purposes of Commission Regulation (EU) 965/2012 (laying down technical requirements and administrative procedures related to air operations); and (4) provide that it is an offence to hold anyone out as being one who can offer flights in an aircraft registered in the United Kingdom for the purpose of commercial air transport or public transport unless that person holds, in the case of a public transport flight, a valid national air operator's certificate or a valid EU-OPS air operator certificate, or in the case of a commercial air transport flight, a valid EU-OPS air operator certificate.

25   Air navigation—overseas territories

The Air Navigation (Overseas Territories) Order 2013, SI 2013/2870 (in force on 1 January 2014), replaces the 2007 Order, SI 2007/3468, and sets out the provisions applicable to listed overseas territories to enable the United Kingdom to comply with the Convention on International Civil Aviation. The order contains substantially the same provisions as the 2007 Order, except that (1) certain information has been omitted where adequate provision has been made in corresponding Overseas Territories Aviation Requirements Parts; (2) the requirement for the principal place of business, in addition to the registered office, of an applicant for aircraft registration to be located in a particular territory has been removed; (3) a provision relating to aircraft equipment has been amended by deleting the specific details of the type of instructions to be given regarding the actions to be taken in an emergency; (4) it has been clarified that an operator's minimum equipment list requires approval by the regulatory authority; (5) references to pressurisation, in relation to crewing requirements, and provisions relating to flight navigators and flight engineers have been removed; (6) in relation to restrictions on flying, the term 'issue instructions' has been used in place of the term 'make regulations', thereby enabling the governor of a territory to act without needing to follow the formal process of making and gazetting regulations; (7) provisions relating to increasing unmanned aerial activities have been revised to mirror those applicable in the United Kingdom; (8) certain performance requirements relating to aircraft have been revised in order to align them more closely with International Civil Aviation Organisation Standards; and (9) in relation to aerial works, the order imposes requirements relating to the assessment of risk and the development of standard operating procedures as an alternative to an operations manual. SI 2008/3125 and SI 2011/237 are revoked.

26   Air navigation—single European sky—penalties

The Air Navigation (Single European Sky) (Penalties) (Amendment) Order 2013, SI 2013/2874 (in force on 12 December 2013), amends the 2009 Order, SI 2009/1735, by providing that it is an offence (1) to fail to comply with specified provisions of Commission Regulation (EU) 255/2010, laying down common rules on air traffic flow management which concern obligations on air traffic service units, operators and airport managing bodies, obligations concerning critical events, consistency between flight plans and airport slots and monitoring of compliance to air traffic flow management measures; (2) for a local air traffic management unit, when requested by an airport slot co-ordinator or a managing body of a co-ordinated airport, to fail to provide the accepted flight plan of a flight operating at that airport before that flight takes place; and (3) to fail to comply with an obligation imposed by certain implementing rules. The order also replaces a reference to Commission Regulation (EC) 2096/2005 with a reference to the superseding Commission Implementing Regulation (EU) 1035/2011 and requires the Secretary of State to review the operation and effect of the 2009 Order and to publish a report containing the conclusions of the review.

27   Air passenger duty—exemption—connected flights

See *Ryanair Ltd v Revenue and Customs Comrs*, para 756.

28   Air services—Community air services—operation

The Operation of Air Services in the Community (Pricing etc) Regulations 2013, SI 2013/486 (in force on 6 April 2013), make provision implementing European Parliament and Council Regulation (EC) 1008/2008 on common rules for the operation of air services in the European Community. The 2013 Regulations (1) require the Secretary of State to review the operation and effect of the new requirements and publish a report within five years after they come into force and within every five years after that; (2) specify the Civil Aviation Authority and the Office of Fair Trading as the enforcement authorities ('enforcers'); (3) create an enforcement regime that provides powers for (a) the courts to make an enforcement order on the application of an enforcer; (b) the courts to make an interim enforcement order on the application of an enforcer; (c) an enforcer to accept an undertaking instead of seeking an enforcement order; (d) further proceedings to be taken by an enforcer following breach of an undertaking, enforcement order or an interim enforcement order; (e) enforcers to seek information for the purpose of ascertaining whether there is an infringement of the requirements or whether a person has complied with an order; (f) officers of an enforcer to enter premises with or without a warrant; and (g) officers of an enforcer to observe the business and inspect goods and documents on the premises, to

preliminary investigation committee there is to be at least one lay person and one registered person and within the quorum of five for the disciplinary committee there is to be at least two lay persons and two registered persons; (5) persons registered in the supplementary veterinary register will not be treated in the same way as registered persons for the purpose of any proceedings and also in relation to their entitlement to sit on the committees; (6) a person may not be appointed to a committee more than twice; and (7) the Council may stipulate conditions as to fitness to serve as members of the committees.

47 Veterinary surgeons—professional qualifications—recognition—Switzerland and Croatia

The Veterinary Surgeons' Qualifications (Recognition) (Switzerland and Croatia) Regulations 2013, SI 2013/2985 (in force on 18 December 2013), amend the Veterinary Surgeons Act 1966 so as to (1) extend the definition of 'national' to include all EEA states and Switzerland; (2) provide for the recognition of a specified Swiss veterinary qualification on the same basis as the equivalent veterinary qualifications awarded in specified EEA states; and (3) provide for the recognition of specified Croatian veterinary qualifications.

ARBITRATION

Halsbury's Laws of England (5th edn) vol 2 (2008) paras 1201–1307

Articles

For articles relating to this title please refer to the Table of Articles at the beginning of the Abridgment.

48 Arbitral proceedings—determination of jurisdiction—approach of court

A dispute arose between the claimant (Habas) a company incorporated in Turkey, and the defendant (VSC), a company incorporated in Hong Kong, in respect of an alleged contract for the sale by Habas and purchase by VSC of a quantity of steel (the steel) for shipment from Turkey to Hong Kong (the VSC contract). The steel was not delivered and VSC commenced arbitration proceedings claiming damages pursuant to a London arbitration clause allegedly agreed. Habas denied that any such arbitration agreement had been made. An arbitration tribunal, having concluded that it had substantive jurisdiction, issued an award (the award). The award provided that Habas' agents, Steel Park and Charter Alpha, had had ostensible authority to conclude the VSC contract and the arbitration agreement, and that there was a binding contract made containing a binding London arbitration agreement. The tribunal further held that Habas was in breach of contract for non-supply of the steel and awarded VSC the sum of US$3,142,500 plus interest and costs (to be assessed). Habas appealed against the tribunal's conclusion on jurisdiction and its award pursuant to the Arbitration Act 1996 ss 67, 69. In respect of the appeal under s 67, Habas submitted that the tribunal had erred in finding that there had been a binding arbitration agreement made between the parties because, it contended (1) Steel Park and/or Charter Alpha did not have actual or ostensible authority to conclude the London arbitration agreement on behalf of Habas; and (2) there was no binding consensus on the terms of the London arbitration agreement. The first issue for consideration was whether Habas' contention in the proceedings that the issue of authority to enter into the arbitration agreement was governed by Turkish law and that there was no requisite authority, constituted a new ground of objection to jurisdiction which it was not open to Habas to make or, alternatively, whether Habas' case that there was no valid arbitration agreement because the formal requirements under Turkish law for making such an agreement were not met, was a new ground which was not open to Habas to make. Consideration was given to s 73. The second issue for determination was whether there had been a binding consensus to a London arbitration agreement. Consideration was given to whether it had been contemplated by the parties that there would be a signed contract, and that it would be signed by Steel Park on behalf of Habas. The third issue related to the applicable law. Habas contended that the contract was governed by the law of Turkey. It submitted that if, contrary to that contention, the applicable law to issues of authority was English law, the effect of the Overseas Companies (Execution of Documents) Regulations 2009, SI 2009/1917, was to make issues of actual authority and compliance with formalities subject to Turkish law, as the law of the territory in which Habas was incorporated. The fourth issue was whether, as a matter of English law, Charter Alpha and/or Steel Park had ostensible authority to agree the London arbitration clause. In respect of the application under the 1996 Act s 69, Habas also challenged the tribunal's decision as to the date for assessment of damages. Consideration was given to *Sul America Cia Nacional De Seguros Sa v Enesa Engenharia SA*. Held, (a) it was settled law that the principle of openness and fair dealing between the parties to an arbitration demanded not merely that, if jurisdiction was to be challenged under the 1996 Act s 67, the issue as to jurisdiction had to normally have been raised, at least on some grounds, before the arbitrator but that each ground of challenge to his jurisdiction had to previously have been raised before the arbitrator if it was to be raised in an application under s 67 challenging the award. It was clear from authority that the term 'any objection' in s 73(1) was intended to mean 'any ground of objection'. Adopting a broad approach, in the circumstances of the instant case, Habas' arguments on actual and ostensible authority based on Turkish law fell within the ground of objection based on lack of authority made at the arbitration. However, Habas' objection based on failure to comply with the formal requirements for an arbitration agreement under Turkish law had nothing to do with authority. It was a new ground of objection and as such was not open to Habas on its application by reason of s 73. (2) The fact that parties contemplated that there would be a signed contract did not necessarily mean that there could be no binding agreement until the contract was signed. Each case depended on its facts. On the facts, Habas' case that there was no binding consensus to the London arbitration agreement would be rejected. (3) In respect of determining the applicable law, it was settled that, even if an arbitration agreement formed part of a contract, its proper law might not be the same as that of the contract. The proper law was to be determined by undertaking a three-stage inquiry into (i) express choice; (ii) implied choice; and (iii) the system of law with which the arbitration agreement had the closest and most real connection. Where the contract did not contain an express governing law clause, the significance of the choice of seat of the arbitration was likely to be 'overwhelming'. That was because the system of law of the country seat would usually be that with which the arbitration agreement had its closest and most real connection. Where the contract contained an express choice of law, that was a strong indication or pointer in relation to the parties' intention as to the governing law of the agreement to arbitrate, in the absence of any indication to the contrary. The choice of a different country for the seat of the arbitration was a factor pointing the other way. However, it might not, in itself, be sufficient to displace the indication of choice implicit in the express choice of law to govern the contract. Where there were sufficient factors pointing the other way to negate the implied choice derived from the express choice of law in the contract, the arbitration agreement would be governed by the law with which it had the closest and most real connection. That was likely to be the law of the country of seat, being the place where the arbitration was to be held and which would exercise the supporting and supervisory jurisdiction necessary to ensure that the procedure was effective. Further, the terms of the arbitration clause might themselves connote an implied choice of law. There was clear authority that the 2009 Regulations did not affect the question of ostensible authority. The instant case was one where there was no express choice of law in the contract. In such a case, Sul America was clear authority that the applicable law would be that of the country of seat. Applying settled law to the facts, even if it was the case that there was no actual authority to agree the London arbitration clause, the applicable law to the arbitration agreement would remain English law, even if the applicable law of the contract was Turkish law. It followed that the law governing the question whether Charter Alpha (or, if relevant, Steel Park) had ostensible authority to bind Habas to an arbitration agreement with VSC, was English law. (d) As a matter of English law, it was clear that Charter Alpha and Steel Park had had ostensible authority to agree the London arbitration clause pursuant to the agency letter. On the facts, there had been ostensible authority to conclude the arbitration agreement. It followed that a valid and binding arbitration agreement had been made as between Habas and VSC. There had been a binding consensus to that agreement and there had been ostensible authority to enter into it. In any event, it had not been shown, if relevant, that there was no actual authority to do so. The 1976 Act s 67 application, therefore, had to be dismissed. The application under s 69 was not a question of law which the tribunal had been asked to determine. Accordingly, the application would be dismissed.

Habas Sinai Ve Tibbi Gazlar Istihsal Endustrisi AS v VSC Steel Co Ltd [2013] EWHC 4071 (Comm), [2014] All ER (D) 1 (Jan) (Queen's Bench Division: Hamblen J). *Sul America Cia Nacional De Seguros Sa v Enesa Engenharia SA* [2012] EWCA Civ 638, [2012] All ER (D) 145 (May) (2012 Abr para 61) applied.

49   Arbitral proceedings—existence—hearing before appeal panel of sporting body

The claimant was the governing body of cricket in England and Wales. In the course of appeal proceedings under the claimant's disciplinary regulations, an application was made for a witness summons under the Arbitration Act 1996 s 43. It was accepted that the witness in question was a central witness in the case. It fell to be determined whether the proceedings before the claimant's appeal panel, constituted under the claimant's disciplinary regulations, were arbitration proceedings within the meaning of the 1996 Act. *Held*, the hallmark of the arbitration process was that it was a procedure to determine the legal rights and obligations of the parties judicially, with binding effect, which was enforceable in law, thus reflecting in private proceedings the role of a civil court of law. Applying settled law, the appeal panel was an arbitral body and the proceedings before it were arbitration proceedings. It followed that, as it was accepted that the witness in question was a central witness whose presence was desirable for justice to be done, the witness summons should be issued. Judgment would be given accordingly.

England and Wales Cricket Board Ltd v Kaneria [2013] EWHC 1074 (Comm), [2013] All ER (D) 47 (May) (Queen's Bench Division: Cooke J).

50   Arbitral proceedings—powers of court—interim injunction

The parties, who were shareholders in a Mauritian company, entered into a share purchase agreement with a Mauritian law and jurisdiction clause. The defendant threatened to exercise its rights under the agreement to transfer shares on the basis of a valid debt under a put option agreement. That proposed course would have given the defendant the entire share capital and it would have been likely to sell the business to recoup the debt. The claimant issued arbitral proceedings, submitting that it would be prejudiced if the defendant took that action. The tribunal rejected that application. The claimant applied to the court under the Arbitration Act 1996 s 44 and/or the Senior Courts Act 1981 s 37 for an injunction restraining the defendant from exercising its rights under the share purchase agreement pending arbitration. It contended that there would be no prejudice, as the defendant's takeover would merely be delayed by six months. The claimant contended that the tribunal had ruled that it had no power to grant interim relief. It fell to be determined whether the tribunal had determined that it had no power to grant interim relief, and whether the court should grant relief on the facts. *Held*, it was inconceivable that the 1996 Act intended or should be treated in the absence of express provision as effectively abrogating the protection enjoyed under the 1981 Act s 37 in respect of the negative rights under an arbitration agreement by those who stipulated for an arbitration with an English seat. In the present case, there was ambiguity about what the tribunal had decided, which needed to be decided before the court could determine the matter. The proper course was to go back to the tribunal to determine whether it had decided that it had no power to act. On the facts, the court had jurisdiction to order short-term interim relief, as the tribunal might have ruled that it was unable or at present unable to grant interim relief. The relatively low threshold of a serious issue to be tried had been met. The balance of convenience favoured the grant of relief to preserve the status quo. The claimant's delay was not such a weighty factor as to point against the justice of granting the injunction. Accordingly, the application would be allowed.

Barnwell Enterprises Ltd v SCP Africa FII Investments LLC [2013] All ER (D) 117 (Aug) (Queen's Bench Division: Hamblen J). *American Cyanamid Co v Ethicon Ltd* [1975] 1 All ER 504, CA (1974 Abr para 2459), applied.

51   Arbitration clause—incorporation in external document—general conditions

The claimant and defendant were both engaged in the shipping industry, with the claimant operating a ship repair yard and the defendant managing a number of ships. They agreed a fleet repair contract, but not before eight or twelve individual ship repair contracts had been agreed between numerous ship owners and the claimant for ships managed by the defendant. The defendant had not signed any of these contracts, but was aware of their

general terms and it was common ground that they incorporated the claimant's general
conditions, which included a binding arbitration clause. When the claimant tendered for the
fleet repair contract it made specific reference to these general conditions, but not the
arbitration clause. After this arrangement came to an end, the defendant made a claim under
the fleet contract for a contractually defined rebate, and this dispute led to arbitration
proceedings. By a majority, the tribunal decided that it had jurisdiction to hear the claim
based on the relationship between the fleet agreement and the ship repair contracts, as
reflected by the use of the words 'ship-repair' in the fleet agreement. On the claimant's
appeal, the question was whether the fleet agreement incorporated the arbitration clause in
the claimant's general conditions of contract, notwithstanding the absence of any specific
reference within the fleet contract. *Held*, on the true construction of the documents, the role
of the fleet agreement was to amend, alter or supersede certain of the provisions of the
conditions for the purposes of ship repair contracts that might in the future be entered into,
but that did not cause any of the provisions of the conditions to flow in the other direction
into the agreement. Further, while the arbitrators had been correct to conclude that there
had been a close relationship between the agreement and the ship repair contracts, and the
use of the words 'ship repair' in the title of the agreement reflected that, the closeness of the
relationship did not make it obvious that the arbitration clause in the conditions should be
applicable to the agreement. As for the reference in the agreement to the defendant as the
'owners', it was common ground that the defendant was not (and was known not to be) the
owner of any vessels and the assessment of the facts had to be by reference to what the
parties had known and not by reference to any false appellation. It followed that the arbitral
award should be set aside and a declaration made that the tribunal did not have jurisdiction.
Accordingly, the appeal would be allowed.

Lisnave Estaleiros Navais SA v Chemikalien Seetransport GmbH [2013] EWHC 338
(Comm), [2013] All ER (D) 354 (Feb) (Queen's Bench Division: Colin Edelman QC).
McCutcheon v David MacBrayne Ltd [1964] 1 All ER 430, HL; *Fiona Trust & Holding
Corp v Privalov* [2008] EWHC 1748 (Comm), [2008] All ER (D) 292 (Jul); and *A-G of
Belize v Belize Telecom Ltd* [2009] UKPC 10, [2009] 2 All ER 1127 (2009 Abr para 1126)
considered.

52   Arbitrator—jurisdiction—challenge—foreign court ruling arbitration clause invalid

See *AES Ust-Kamenogorsk Hydropower Plant LLP v Ust-Kamenogorsk Hydropower Plant
JSC*, para 449.

**53   Award—appeal—permission to appeal—question of law of general public
        importance**

The Arbitration Act 1996 s 69(8) provides that the decision of the court on an appeal under
s 69 is to be treated as a judgment of the court for the purposes of a further appeal; but no
such appeal lies without the leave of the court which is not to be given unless the court
considers that the question is one of general importance or is one which for some other
special reason should be considered by the Court of Appeal.

The defendant shipowner contended that a charterparty with the claimant charterer had
been frustrated after the vessel was seriously damaged during the charter. The matter was
referred to arbitration, which ruled in the defendant's favour. The claimant sought to appeal
pursuant to the 1996 Act s 69. The application was determined on paper, and permission
was granted on the basis that the question of law posed had raised a question of general
public importance. On appeal, the Commercial Court rejected the existence of such a
principle and found that an insurance clause in the charterparty created an assumption of
risk and responsibility on the part of the claimant to repair the damage up to the figure for
which the vessel had been insured. The claimant applied pursuant to s 69(8) for permission
to appeal. The judge refused the application on the ground that the case had turned on the
correct construction of particular clauses in a particular charterparty. He was not convinced
that there would be a real prospect of success if permission were granted, the case was not
one of general importance, and the interests of justice favoured finality. The claimant
applied to the Court of Appeal for permission to appeal, or alternatively to set aside the
decision of the judge refusing permission to appeal. The claimant submitted that, once it had
been decided on the papers that the question of law had raised a question of general public
importance, the judge had had no business to say that, in his view, the case had turned on

Arsanovia Ltd v Cruz City 1 Mauritius Holdings [2012] EWHC 3702 (Comm), [2013] 2 All ER (Comm) 1 (Queen's Bench Division: Andrew Smith J).

57   Award—challenge—serious irregularity—duties of arbitral tribunal

The claimants agreed to sell metallurgical coke to the defendant. The defendant made a pre-payment for the coke, but the claimants did not deliver it within the contractual delivery period. The defendant sought repayment of the pre-payment, but the claimants repaid only part of it. The defendant began arbitration proceedings claiming the balance of the payment. The parties reached a settlement under which the claimants agreed to pay a sum to the defendant. The settlement provided that, in the event of the claimants failing to pay, the defendant was entitled to resume the arbitration proceedings and to an immediate consent award, without the need for any pleadings or hearings. The claimants failed to make the agreed payment and the defendant asked the arbitral tribunal to proceed immediately to make an award in its favour. The tribunal responded that the claimants had until the close of business on the following day to respond. Communication continued between the parties and the claimants argued that the award should not be made. A week later, the tribunal directed payment of the sum agreed to the defendant. The claimants failed to make the payment and applied to the court to challenge the award on the grounds that there was obvious and serious irregularity and that the Arbitration Act 1996 s 33 prevented the defendant from circumventing the tribunal's general duty to afford a reasonable opportunity to the claimants to present their case. *Held*, the court had to ask itself if the case was an extreme one justifying its intervention and determine if the tribunal had gone so wrong in its conduct of the arbitration that justice called for it to be corrected. The question of substantial injustice did not arise unless the claimants established the requisite irregularity. If the tribunal was considering a new case in which the claimants sought to put forward their defences to a claim, the procedure adopted would have been irregular and unfair. However, the claimants were not at the beginning of a new case. They were not entitled to put forward and develop, at great further expense and delay, new defences as though they were in the early stages of a legal process, nor was there a breach of s 33. Given what the parties agreed in the settlement, the tribunal gave them a reasonable opportunity of putting their case and adopted a suitable procedure. Accordingly, the application would be dismissed.

Gujarat Nre Coke Ltd v Coeclerici Asia (PTE) Ltd [2013] EWHC 1987 (Comm), [2013] All ER (D) 137 (Jul) (Queen's Bench Division: Judge Mackie QC).

58   Award—enforcement—challenge—arbitration clause—jurisdiction

A vessel carrying a cargo of fuel oil sank after suffering damage in a storm. The resulting oil spill was an ecological disaster, severely polluting parts of the Spanish coastline, with its effects spreading as far as France. Criminal proceedings were instituted in Spain against the Master, Chief Officer, Chief Engineer and the Spanish official and civil claims were also brought under the Convention on Civil Liability and the Spanish penal code against the owners of the vessel and the owners' protection and indemnity insurer, the claimant. France subsequently joined the Spanish proceedings. The claimant acknowledged its liability under the Convention but, in respect of the other claims, contended that the parties were bound by the terms of the contract of insurance to bring those claims in arbitration and by way of an English law clause. The claimant played no part in the Spanish proceedings, but commenced arbitration proceedings in England seeking negative declaratory relief in respect of any non-Convention liability to Spain and France. The tribunal upheld most of the claimant's claims for negative declaratory relief and the claimant sought permission, pursuant to the Arbitration Act 1996 s 66, to enforce two arbitration awards as judgments and/or to have judgments entered in their terms. France and Spain resisted the application as a matter of jurisdiction on the grounds that they had state immunity and as a matter of discretion. They also challenged the substantive jurisdiction of the tribunal pursuant to s 67 and/or s 72 on the basis that they were not bound by the arbitration agreement as their direct action rights were in essence independent rights under Spanish law rather than contractual rights, and also on the grounds of non-arbitrability and, in relation to France only, waiver. *Held,* in the light of the court's findings as to the nature of the direct action under Spanish law, in respect of the proper characterisation of the right as a matter of English law, the direct action right conferred by Spanish law against liability insurers was in substance a right to enforce the contract rather than an independent right of recovery. Moreover, it had not been shown that the dispute referred to represented an attempt to delegate to arbitrators a matter of public interest which could not be determined within the limitations of a private contractual process or that such a reference engaged, still less was prohibited by, English statute or English public policy or was otherwise inarbitrable. It had already been decided that the claims were, in substance, claims to enforce a contract. The claims of Spain and France were all monetary claims for damages, and the claimant's alleged liability was fundamentally civil in nature. Even if France and Spain were fulfilling constitutional or domestic public functions of protecting the environment, or recovering civil damages flowing from criminal offences, the claims pursued were, fundamentally, civil claims which were no different from the claims brought by private parties in respect of the same acts. Arbitrating such claims was not contrary to any identified English statute or English rule of public policy. As to the question of waiver, on the evidence, the only claim made against the claimant in the French proceedings was a Convention claim and, therefore, the issue of waiver of the right to arbitrate non-Convention claims did not arise and the challenge to the jurisdiction of the tribunal on the grounds of waiver failed. In relation to the question of state immunity, applying the State Immunity Act 1978 s 14, Spain and France were prima facie immune from the jurisdiction of the English court. That immunity would only be lost to the extent that they fell within one of the exceptions set out in the 1978 Act. The question was whether a state, which became a party to an arbitration agreement, had agreed in writing to submit a dispute to arbitration within the meeting of s 9(1). The court was satisfied that it had. Authority held that the government could not go behind the arbitrators' decision that they were bound by the arbitration agreement and that was sufficient for the purposes of s 9(1). Applying settled law, there was a clear utility in granting the declarations sought and no good reason had been shown why the court should refuse to allow the claimant to seek to realise the full benefit of the awards it had obtained. It followed that in the exercise of the court's discretion and in the interests of justice the claimant's application under the 1996 Act s 66 would be granted, while the defendants' applications under ss 67, 72 would be refused. Judgment would be given accordingly.

London Steam Ship Owners Mutual Insurance Association Ltd v Kingdom of Spain [2013] EWHC 3188 (Comm), [2013] All ER (D) 299 (Oct) (Queen's Bench Division: Hamblen J). *Through Transport Mutual Insurance Association (Eurasia) Ltd v New India Assurance Co Ltd, The Hari Bhum* [2003] EWHC 3158 (Comm), [2004] 1 Lloyd's Rep 206, [2003] All ER (D) 360 (Dec); *Fulham Football Club (1987) Ltd v Richards* [2011] EWCA Civ 855, [2012] Ch 333, [2012] 1 All ER 414 (2011 Abr para 430); and *West Tankers Inc v Allianz Spa, The Front Comor* [2012] EWCA Civ 27, [2012] 2 All ER (Comm) 113 (2012 Abr para 72) applied.

59   Award—enforcement—challenge—lack of jurisdiction

Considerable oil pollution damage was caused when a vessel broke up off the coast of Spain. The vessel was entered with, and her owners and managers were members of, the claimant whose rules provided protection and indemnity insurance, along with freight, demurrage and defence insurance, in respect of the vessel. The claimant declined to participate in civil claims advanced against it. On the footing that the claims were made by the defendant, the kingdom of Spain, the claimant served on the defendant a notice of arbitration. The defendant denied any obligation to arbitrate. An award was later published and the claimant issued an arbitration form against the defendant, seeking leave to enforce the arbitration award and the entry judgment in terms of the award under the Arbitration Act 1996 s 66, and service out of the jurisdiction and by alternative means. The court granted the order for service out of the jurisdiction, but not for the order under s 66. The defendant sought an extension of time in order to make a jurisdictional challenge to the award under s 67 and/or s 72. The claimant contended that the defendant's inaction following the arbitrator's award, but prior to notice of the application to enforce, had to count against the defendant when seeking extension of time. *Held,* in the exercise of discretion, it would be in the interests of justice to grant such extensions as would be necessary to ensure that the defendant could deploy its full armoury of objections to enforcement of the award and the award itself. The issue with respect to the defendant's participation was concerned with matters which, if established, undermined the legitimacy of the award as giving rise to a binding obligation created in accordance with the will of the parties as expressed in the arbitration agreement. In the circumstances, the claimant's

75 Gurkha soldiers—dependants—leave to remain in United Kingdom

See *R (on the application of Sharmilla) v Secretary of State for the Home Department*, para 1441.

76 Legislation—continuation

The Armed Forces Act (Continuation) Order 2013, SI 2013/2603 (made on 9 October 2013), continues in force, until 2 November 2014, the Armed Forces Act 2006.

77 Member of armed forces—solider on active service overseas—death—application of European Convention on Human Rights

The proceedings arose out of the deaths of three soldiers who lost their lives while serving in the British Army in Iraq and the suffering by two other servicemen of serious injuries. Before the Supreme Court it fell to be determined whether, at the time of their deaths, the soldiers in the first and second matters had been within the jurisdiction of the United Kingdom for the purposes of the European Convention on Human Rights art 1 and if so, whether art 2 imposed positive obligations on states with a view to preventing the deaths of their own soldiers in active operations against the enemy. It was also to be determined whether allegations of negligence in the second and third matters should be struck out because they fell within the scope of combat immunity or because it would not be fair, just or reasonable to impose a duty to take care to protect against such death or injury. *Held*, the jurisdiction of the United Kingdom under art 1 extended to securing the protection of art 2 to members of the armed forces when they were serving outside its territory. Therefore, at the time of their deaths, the soldiers in the first and second matters had been within the jurisdiction of the United Kingdom for the purposes of art 1. Further, a finding that deaths or injuries in combat that resulted from the conduct of operations by the armed forces were outside the scope of art 2 would not be sustainable. It would amount, in effect, to a derogation from the state's substantive obligations under that article. However, the circumstances were such that a decision on liability should be deferred until after trial. The procurement issues might give rise to questions that were essentially political in nature, but it was not possible to decide whether that was the case without hearing evidence. It was far from clear that the claimants would be able to show that the implied positive obligation under art 2(1), to take preventative operative measures, had been breached. The extension of combat immunity to the planning of and preparation for military operations applied to the planning of and preparation for the operations in which injury had been sustained, and not to the planning and preparation, in general, for possible unidentified further operations. In the circumstances, to apply the doctrine of combat immunity to the claims would involve an extension of that doctrine beyond the cases to which it had previously been applied. With respect to the third matter, at the stage when men were being trained, whether pre-deployment or in theatre, or decisions were being made about the fitting of equipment to tanks or other fighting vehicles, there was time to think things through, to plan and to exercise judgment. Those activities were sufficiently far removed from the pressures and risks of active operations against the enemy for it not to be unreasonable to expect a duty of care to be exercised, so long as the standard of care that was imposed had regard to the nature of the activities and to their circumstances. With respect to the negligence claim, it was less obviously directed to things done away from the theatre in which the solider had been engaged at the time of his death. Therefore, the details that were needed to place the claims in context would only emerge if evidence was permitted to be led in support of them and it would be premature for them to be struck out on the ground of combat immunity. Judgment would be given accordingly.

Smith v Ministry of Defence; Ellis v Ministry of Defence; Allbutt v Ministry of Defence [2013] UKSC 41, [2014] AC 52, [2013] All ER (D) 167 (Jun) (Supreme Court: Lord Hope DP, Lord Walker, Lady Hale, Lord Mance, Lord Kerr, Lord Wilson and Lord Carnwath SCJJ). *A v Secretary of State for the Home Department; X v Secretary of State for the Home Department* [2004] UKHL 56, [2005] 2 AC 68, [2005] 3 All ER 169 (2004 Abr para 290) applied. Application 55721/07 *Al-Skeini v United Kingdom* [2011] All ER (D) 70 (Jul), ECtHR (2011 Abr para 1402), adopted. *Mulcahy v Ministry of Defence* [1996] QB 732, [1996] 2 All ER 758, CA (1996 Abr para 2209); and *Re Post Traumatic Stress Disorder Group Litigation; Multiple Claimants v Ministry of Defence* [2003] EWHC 1134 (QB),

[2003] All ER (D) 301 (May) (2003 Abr para 175) approved. Decision of Court of Appeal [2012] EWCA Civ 1365, [2013] 1 All ER 778 (2012 Abr para 2204) reversed.

78 Pensions—disablement and death

The Naval, Military and Air Forces Etc (Disablement and Death) Service Pensions (Amendment) Order 2013, SI 2013/241 (in force on 8 April 2013), further amends the 2006 Order, SI 2006/606, which makes provision for pensions and other awards in respect of disablement or death due to service before 6 April 2005 in the naval, military and air forces, by (1) correcting a minor error in a provision dealing with relationships subsequent to the award of a pension so as to refer to 'person' instead of 'widow'; (2) correcting a typographical error in the formula to determine the degree of disablement; and (3) varying the rates of retired pay, pensions, gratuities and allowances in respect of disablement or death due to service in the armed forces.

79 Service courts—proceedings—interpretation and translation

The Armed Forces (Interpretation, Translation, Alcohol and Drug Tests) Rules 2013, SI 2013/2527 (in force in part on 27 October 2013 and in part on 1 November 2013), amend the Armed Forces (Custody Proceedings) Rules 2009, SI 2009/1098, the Armed Forces (Service Civilian Court) Rules 2009, SI 2009/1209, the Armed Forces (Summary Appeal Court) Rules 2009, SI 2009/1211, and the Armed Forces (Summary Hearing and Activation of Suspended Sentences of Service Detention) Rules 2009, SI 2009/1216, and further amend the Armed Forces (Court Martial) Rules 2009, SI 2009/2041, so as to give effect to European Parliament and Council Directive (EU) 2010/64, on the right to interpretation and translation in criminal proceedings, by requiring the provision of interpretation and translation services for persons accused or convicted of service offences, including persons with hearing or speech impediments, who need such services. The 2013 Rules also allow, except in relation to SI 2009/1098, for the use of breath, blood or urine specimens in proceedings for certain service offences relating to alcohol or drugs.

80 Servicemen—death of detainees—effective investigation

See *R (on the application of Mousa) v Secretary of State for Defence (No 2)*, para 2191.

81 Visiting forces—designation order

The Visiting Forces (Designation Order) 2013, SI 2013/540 (in force on 6 April 2013), designates the countries to which the Visiting Forces Act 1952 s 9A applies.

BANKRUPTCY AND INDIVIDUAL INSOLVENCY

Halsbury's Laws of England (5th edn) vol 5 (2013) paras 1–949

Articles

For articles relating to this title please refer to the Table of Articles at the beginning of the Abridgment.

82 Bankruptcy—annulment—trustee in bankruptcy—costs

Bankruptcy orders were made against the appellants. They had sufficient assets to meet all possible claims against them but refused to pay the first respondent. Despite the discharge of their bankruptcies after one year, the second respondent was appointed as trustee in bankruptcy. He applied for possession of four properties belonging to the appellants. The appellants' applications to have the bankruptcies annulled under the Insolvency Act 1986 s 282(1)(a) were dismissed. On their appeals, the appellants were permitted to adduce fresh evidence regarding the striking off from the Roll of Solicitors of their former solicitor. The appeals were allowed and the bankruptcies were annulled on the basis that the orders should not have been made. The annulment of the bankruptcies was made conditional on payments being made by the appellants of the substantial costs of the second respondent. The appellants appealed. *Held*, the guiding principle was that the proper expenses of the trustee would normally be paid or provided for before the assets were removed from him by an annulment order. It would be unusual for the court to take away that right without providing for the trustee's position to be adequately protected. Usually, when the court made an annulment order on the ground that the bankruptcy order should never have been made, it would go on to order that the petitioning creditor should pay the costs of the trustee. Assuming that the petitioning creditor could pay those costs, that order would have the effect that the burden of the expenses was transferred from the innocent estate to the culpable party. In the circumstances, the appellants could not pay the second respondent's costs, the second respondent had done nothing that would deprive him of any rights to his costs, the costs could, if disputed, be quantified on a separate application to the court before payment, and, if the second respondent had not obtained an order against the appellants and their estates had turned out to be insufficient to pay his expenses, then the burden of non-payment of those expenses would have fallen on the second respondent since those expenses would not have been paid. Consequently, the judge had been entitled to make the order which he had made. Further, there was no general rule that the second respondent's costs could not be ordered to be paid by a party who had successfully applied to annul his bankruptcy when that party was entirely innocent vis à vis the petitioning creditor. When considering whether to make an order that the bankrupt pay the trustee's costs in light of an actual or anticipated annulment under s 282(1)(a), the court needed to be careful to examine the matter not only from the bankrupt's perspective, but also from the trustee's perspective. The court had an unfettered discretion to decide whether, and if so by whom, the trustee's costs would be paid. Normally, a trustee who had acted could expect to have his reasonable remuneration provided for. It was inconceivable that the judge had meant that, however bad the second respondent's conduct, he could never be persuaded not to make an order depriving him altogether of his costs. From his judgment, it was clear that he had concluded that there were at least some costs of the second respondent that the court would be bound to find were reasonably and properly incurred and that should be borne by the appellants. Nevertheless, there had been disputes which the judge could not resolve as to the second respondent's conduct that might have reduced the costs payable to him. The judge could not have resolved those disputes and they had been irrelevant in that they had not required further analysis before him on that occasion. Accordingly, the appeal would be dismissed.

Oraki v Dean & Dean (a firm) [2013] EWCA Civ 1629, [2014] BPIR 266, [2013] All ER (D) 170 (Dec) (Court of Appeal: Arden, Davis and Floyd LJJ).

83 Bankruptcy—divorce—financial provision—concealing assets

See *Young v Young*, para 1818.

84 Bankruptcy—statutory demand—application to set aside—order not specifying date on which bankruptcy petition to be presented

The Insolvency Rules 1986, SI 1986/1925, r 6.5(6) provides that, if the court dismisses an application to set aside a statutory demand, it must make an order authorising the creditor to present a bankruptcy petition either as soon as reasonably practicable, or on or after a date specified in the order.

The respondents served a statutory demand on the appellant, and the appellant's application to set aside the demand was dismissed. It was common ground that the order failed to specify a date on or after which the respondents could present a petition for a bankruptcy order to be made against the appellant. The respondents presented their petition the following day. A district judge adjudged the appellant to be bankrupt on the petition presented by the respondents. The appellant appealed against the bankruptcy order, submitting that (1) there had been an absence of any order by the judge under the 1986 Rules r 6.5(6) in that the order failed to specify a date on or after which the respondents could present a petition, and that, once an application was made to set aside a statutory demand, the creditor could not then present a petition; (2) the district judge had been wrong to proceed to a substantive determination of the petition and she should have adjourned the matter for a substantive hearing at a later date with directions for the filing of evidence in the meantime; and (3) there were cross-claims concerning the alleged sale by the respondents of a property from which they had realised a sum, and in relation to an assigned trust, which ought to be set against the debt. *Held*, once the application to set aside the statutory demand was dismissed, the restriction on filing a petition automatically fell away. In the absence of any request by the debtor for more time, or even if a request was made, if no justification was provided, it was for the court to authorise the presentation of a petition forthwith. It followed that r 6.5(6) should not be interpreted as prohibiting the petitioner from presenting a petition forthwith if no date was specified in the order. However, on the facts, the district judge had not been entitled summarily to dispose of the petition in the way that she had without giving the appellant the chance to substantiate the grounds of opposition that he had set out in his notices of opposition by evidence. There was no reason to doubt that the appellant had a real prospect of success in relation to the cross-claim in respect of the property. In respect of the trust claim, the district judge was not entitled to dismiss it out of hand without giving the appellant the opportunity to file evidence in support of it. The district judge had not really got to grips with the point that, if all three cross-claims were added together and were sufficiently substantiated to the relevant standard, then they would extinguish the petition debt. Accordingly, the appeal would be allowed.

Darbyshire v Turpin [2013] EWHC 954 (Ch), [2013] All ER (D) 161 (May) (Chancery Division: Arnold J).

85   Bankruptcy—transaction at an undervalue—financial provision—wife seeking to set aside transactions

A wife filed a petition for divorce. She applied to set aside a number of earlier money transfers under the Matrimonial Causes Act 1973 s 37 so as to bring the money back within the assets available to the financial remedy proceedings. The wife obtained an ex parte freezing order in respect of the husband's assets. In turn, the husband's son ('I') was joined as a second respondent. Later, the husband became ill and was unable to give instructions, medical opinion was that he lacked capacity to litigate and the Official Solicitor became involved. One of the transfers from the husband to I was set aside by the district judge. She dismissed the applications in respect of the other transfers. I appealed and the High Court set aside the earlier order. The wife applied under the Insolvency Act 1986 s 423 for an order to restore the husband's financial position to that which would have existed had he not made the transfers to I and for an order waiving compliance with any other procedural requirements that might otherwise had existed in respect of that application. Due to the hearing over-running the parties were to submit further submissions by way of written representations. The husband died. It was agreed that the right to pursue an application to judgment did not extend past joint lives and the jurisdiction under the 1973 Act s 37 had ended. Under the husband's will, the wife was to receive nothing. She wished to commence proceedings under the Inheritance (Provision for Family and Dependants) Act 1975. Therefore, the wife queried whether there had been an application for probate. Counsel for the husband confirmed that probate had not been obtained. The wife confirmed that her intention had been that the application under the 1973 Act s 37 be replaced with an application under the 1975 Act s 10 and that the 1986 Act s 423 application be deployed in the context of the 1975 proceedings. *Held*, the 1986 Act s 423 provided an additional remedy which might be of utility to the wife in the circumstances. Such an application could be issued in its own right pending the making of a claim. It did not require formal insolvency, it was the existence of debt which triggered the remedy. The husband or his estate might be characterised as the debtor and the wife as a victim of the transaction. The test under s 423 was wider than the test under the 1975 Act s 10 and the remedy was different. The 1986 Act s 423 applied to the case where the applicant had or might make a claim. As at the date of the hearing, the wife had not been able to make a claim because there had been no grant of probate. As a matter of practical application, in the absence of a freezing order, before the wife was in a position to make a claim, dissipation might take place with impunity. Her application would be made in support of an application under the 1975 Act. Injunctive relief was required to preserve the position before the wife was able to make a claim. Judgment would be given accordingly.

W v H [2013] EWHC 3755 (Fam), [2013] All ER (D) 36 (Dec) (Family Division: Parker J). *Hill v Spread Trustee Co Ltd* [2006] EWCA Civ 542, [2007] 1 All ER 1106 (2006 Abr para 278); *Trowbridge v Trowbridge* [2002] EWHC 3114 (Ch), [2004] 2 FCR 79; and *AC v DC (financial remedy: effect of s 37 avoidance order)* [2012] EWHC 2032 (Fam), 15 ITELR 811 applied.

86   Insolvency—corporate insolvency

See COMPANY AND PARTNERSHIP INSOLVENCY.

changes to the class of wireless telegraphy apparatus whose establishment, installation and use are exempted from the requirement to be licensed under the Wireless Telegraphy Act 2006 s 8(1).

105 Wireless telegraphy—licence—limitation of number

The Wireless Telegraphy (Limitation of Number of Licences) Order 2013, SI 2013/1787 (in force on 29 July 2013), (1) provides that a limited number of licences will be granted by the Office of Communications ('OFCOM') for the use of frequencies in the specified frequency band; (2) sets out the criteria that OFCOM will apply in determining the number of licences to be granted; and (3) sets out the criteria that OFCOM will apply in determining the persons to whom those licences will be granted.

106 Wireless telegraphy—licence—mobile spectrum trading

The Wireless Telegraphy (Mobile Spectrum Trading) (Amendment) Regulations 2013, SI 2013/646 (in force on 5 April 2013), amend the 2011 Regulations, SI 2011/1507, so as to extend their application to licences in the spectrum access licence class for frequencies in specified frequency bands.

107 Wireless telegraphy—licence—register

The Wireless Telegraphy (Register) (Amendment) Regulations 2013, SI 2013/640 (in force on 5 April 2013), amend the 2012 Regulations, SI 2012/2186, by adding the specified frequency bands to the list of frequency bands in relation to which the Office of Communications is required to establish and maintain a public register of relevant information.

BUILDING CONTRACTS

Halsbury's Laws of England (5th edn) vol 6 (2011) paras 201–600

Articles

For articles relating to this title please refer to the Table of Articles at the beginning of the Abridgment.

108 Building contract—adjudication—award—enforcement—jurisdiction

The proceedings arose from a dispute between the parties, concerning the alleged failure of the defendant company to pay sums owed under a building contract to the claimant company. A dispute arose over the sums payable and due. The claimant issued and served a notice of adjudication. The claimant contended that, due to late payment, a breach of contract had occurred, and sought the appointment of an adjudicator. The adjudicator decided in favour of the claimant. The claimant issued proceedings to enforce the adjudicator's decision. The defendant challenged the adjudicator's decision. It fell to be determined whether the adjudicator had had jurisdiction to make the decision. *Held*, the adjudicator had had jurisdiction to decide what he did. The defendant had waived its right to challenge on jurisdictional grounds because it had failed to raise an alternative argument early enough. There had been no breach of natural justice. Consequently, there was no good reason why the decision should not be enforced. Accordingly, the claim would be allowed.

    Brim Construction Ltd v A2M Developments Ltd [2013] EWHC 3262 (TCC), [2013] All ER (D) 317 (Oct) (Queen's Bench Division: Akenhead J). *Cantillon Ltd v Urvasco Ltd* [2008] EWHC 282 (TCC), 117 ConLR 1, [2008] All ER (D) 406 (Feb); OSC *Building Services Ltd v Interior Dimensions Contracts Ltd* [2009] EWHC 248 (TCC), [2009] All ER (D) 129 (Mar); *Durham CC v Kendall* [2011] EWHC 780 (TCC), [2011] All ER (D) 351 (Mar); *Witney Town Council v Beam Construction (Cheltenham) Ltd* [2011] EWHC 2332 (TCC), [2011] All ER (D) 141 (Sep) considered.

109 Building contract—adjudication—award—jurisdiction

The defendant housing association was responsible for a large number of properties. The claimant agreed to provide gas servicing for the defendant's housing stock. The contract was based on the ACA Standard Form of Contract for Term Partnering. The term of the contract was to be an initial period of four years extendable at the defendant's sole option for a further period of one year. The defendant terminated the claimant's appointment under the contract. No specific reason was given for the termination. However, an email suggested that the decision was based on 'current issues, communication, compliancy and risk for the defendant going forward'. The claimant sought adjudication in relation to whether it was entitled to payment on the open book basis for the period up to the termination date. The adjudicator held that the claimant was entitled to a sum plus interest. That sum was paid. Subsequently, the claimant served a notice of adjudication which related to its 'position statement' supporting three financial heads of claim. The defendant contended that the referral notice referred to three distinct disputes when the relevant scheme only permitted a single dispute to be referred to adjudication at any one time. The adjudicator considered that he did have jurisdiction and found that the claimant was entitled to payment of sums associated with the termination of the appointment and ordered the defendant to pay its fees. The claimant brought proceedings to enforce the adjudicator's decision. The court also considered a CPR Pt 8 claim for declarations relating to jurisdictional issues in adjudication, whether more than one dispute could be referred to an adjudicator and the scope and applicability of good faith and reasonableness in a termination for convenience clause in a contract between the parties. *Held*, a dispute could comprise a single issue or any number of issues. However, a dispute between parties did not necessarily comprise everything which was in issue between them at the time that one party initiated adjudication. What a dispute in any given case was about would be a question of fact. The authorities were now sufficiently well established to suggest that only one dispute could be referred to adjudication, albeit that the courts adopted a sensible and commercial approach in determining the relative width of any given dispute. On the facts, there was no doubt that there was only one dispute referred to adjudication, albeit that it comprised three primary strands or issues. The claimant's compensation claim was one claim comprising three primary alleged financial entitlements which had been effectively challenged or at least not admitted prior to the initiation of the adjudication. The adjudicator had jurisdiction to resolve all the issues put before him. The contract entitled either party to terminate for any or even no reason. Having exercised its right to serve notice to terminate the contract the claimant had no entitlement, whether as damages for breach of contract, or as a sum due under the contract, to receive monies and/or compensation in respect of overheads and profit which it would have recovered over the balance of the term of the contract following termination had the contract not been terminated. There was no implied term of good faith in reference to a termination for convenience clause in the contract. It followed that the adjudicator had been wrong to order that the defendant should pay the claimant in relation to overheads and profit. The adjudicator had jurisdiction to decide that which he had, although he had reached the wrong conclusion. The defendant should pay the adjudicator's fee. Judgment would be given accordingly.

TSG Building Services plc v South Anglia Housing Ltd [2013] EWHC 1151 (TCC), [2013] All ER (D) 102 (May) (Queen's Bench Division: Akenhead J).

110   Building contract—contractual term—implied warranty—insurance

The claimant housing association leased six floors in a large building that was being developed by a developer. The developer was a special purpose vehicle which had been created for the purposes of developing the property. It was engaged by the claimant to construct a number of residential units on those floors. The claimant decided to take out insurance with the defendant insurers. Acting as agents for the claimant, the developer arranged that insurance, which included additional cover in respect of the risk of insolvency of the builder during construction. However, the proposal form stated incorrectly that the builder was to be another company in the same group of companies as the developer. The proposal form contained a declaration to the effect that it formed the basis of the contract between the claimant and the defendant. On the basis of the proposal form, the defendant agreed to insure the claimant's development in the building and a policy was issued. It was stated in the policy that it would be voidable in the event of misrepresentation by the policyholder with the intention to defraud. The developer became insolvent and administrators were appointed. The claimant engaged other contractors to complete the development and sought an indemnity in respect of losses suffered as a result of the insolvency of the developer. It was found that the statement in the proposal form that the other company would be the builder had been a warranty incorporated into the insurance contract and the claimant had been in breach of that warranty. Therefore, the claimant was unable to recover under the policy. The claimant appealed. *Held*, where a proposal form contained a 'basis of contract' clause, the proposal form had contractual effect even if the policy contained no reference to the proposal form and all statements in the proposal form constituted warranties on which the insurance contract was based. Those principals could not be displaced merely be omitting the proposal form from the list of contractual documents set out in the policy. If the parties intended to deprive of contractual effect a proposal form which purported to be the basis of their contract, they had to do so by clear and unequivocal language. In the circumstances, the policy contained no such express words. Therefore, the proposal form had been of contractual effect and the statements in it had become warranties forming the basis of the policy. The claimant had warranted, without qualification, that the other company in the group would be the builder. The condition was not expressed as a limiting provision, it did not state that the policy would be voidable only in the circumstances there mentioned. It could only be read as a provision conferring additional express rights on the defendant, regardless of whether those express rights served any useful purpose. It could not be read as cutting down the defendant's general right to avoid for misrepresentation. Therefore, by reason of the misstatement concerning the builder in the proposal form, the policy was or became void. Accordingly, the appeal would be dismissed.

Genesis Housing Association Ltd v Liberty Syndicate Management Ltd [2013] EWCA Civ 1173, [2013] All ER (D) 51 (Oct) (Court of Appeal: Lord Dyson MR, Jackson and Gloster LJJ). Decision of Akenhead J [2012] EWHC 3105 (TCC), [2012] All ER (D) 150 (Nov) (2012 Abr para 138) affirmed.

111   Construction contract—adjudication—award—jurisdiction—property occupied as residence

The Housing Grants, Construction and Regeneration Act 1996 s 106(1)(a) provides that Pt 2 (ss 104–117) does not apply to a construction contract with a residential occupier. A construction contract with a residential occupier means a construction contract which principally relates to operations on a dwelling which one of the parties to the contract occupies, or intends to occupy, as his residence: s 106(2).

The defendant employed the claimant contractor under a construction contract to carry out refurbishment work at a property. A dispute arose between the parties in respect of the defendant's non-payment of a valuation. The matter was referred to adjudication and the adjudicator made an award in the claimant's favour. The claimant applied to enforce the decision. In his defence, the defendant contended that the 1996 Act s 106 excluded the adjudicator's jurisdiction to decide the dispute because the construction contract was in respect of property which he had occupied as a residence and intended to occupy in the future. *Held*, occupation was an ongoing process and could not be tested by reference to a single snapshot in time. The word 'occupies' in s 106 carried some reflection of the future and indicated that the employer occupied and would remain at, or intended to return to the property. The evidence about the position at the date that the contract was made had to be considered in context of all of the evidence of occupation and intention, both before and after the agreement of the contract. On the evidence, at the time the contract was made the defendant had intended to let out the property when the works were completed. It followed that the residential occupier exception did not apply. Accordingly, the challenge to the adjudicator's jurisdiction failed and the claimant was entitled to the sum sought by way of summary judgment.

Westfields Construction Ltd v Lewis [2013] EWHC 376 (TCC), [2013] 1 WLR 3377, [2013] All ER (D) 328 (Feb) (Queen's Bench Division: Coulson J).

112   Construction contract—adjudication—payment in compliance with decision—action for repayment—limitation period

The defendant construction company hired the claimant company to carry out an asbestos survey at a housing estate. The defendant later alleged that the claimant had underestimated the amount of asbestos at the site, which had led to delays in development and a larger bill for asbestos removal than had been expected. Following an adjudication, the claimant paid a sum in damages to the defendant. More than six years after the supposed breach of contract or duty, but less than six years after having made the payment, the claimant began proceedings to recover that sum. The defendant served a defence and counterclaim, claiming the amount claimed in the adjudication. Subsequently, the defendant pleaded that the claim was time-barred. At a trial of various preliminary issues, a judge determined that it had not been an implied term of the parties' contract that an unsuccessful party to an adjudication would be entitled to seek a final determination by litigation and (if successful) recover any payment made, that the limitation period that had applied to the defendant's counterclaim was six years and that the claimant did not have a claim in restitution. Although not formally one of the preliminary issues, the judge also found that a declaration of non-liability was an assertion of a cause of action and was time-barred on the facts of the case because the claim form had been issued more than six years after the alleged breach of contract or duty. The claim was dismissed. On the claimant's appeal against that decision, it fell to be determined whether a claim by the losing party to an adjudication for repayment of sums paid over to the successful party was subject to a time bar accruing at the time of the (supposed) original breach of contract or duty or only from the date of the (supposedly) unnecessary payment made as a result of the adjudication. *Held*, the contract that incorporated the scheme expressly provided that the adjudication was to be binding only until the dispute was finally determined. That contemplated that the final determination might be different from the adjudication and that it was the final determination which was to the determinative of the rights of the parties. If the final determination decided that a particular party had paid too much, repayment had to be made. To the extent that there was no reference to such payment in the scheme was implicit. The accrual of the cause of action for recovery of any overpayment was the date of overpayment since the losing party was 'entitled' to have the overpayment returned to him. It had been an implied term of the parties' contract that an unsuccessful party to an adjudication would be entitled to seek a final determination by litigation and (if successful) recover any payment made. The applicable limitation period for a claim that sought to enforce that implied term was six years, and the limitation period that had applied to the defendant's counterclaim was six years. Accordingly, the appeal would be allowed.

Aspect Contracts (Asbestos) Ltd v Higgins Construction plc [2013] EWCA Civ 1541, [2013] All ER (D) 339 (Nov) (Court of Appeal: Longmore, Rimer and Tomlinson LJJ). Decision of Akenhead J [2013] EWHC 1322 (TCC), [2013] BLR 417, [2013] All ER (D) 296 (May) reversed.

113   Construction products—safety requirements

See para 506.

BUILDING

Halsbury's Laws of England (5th edn) vol 6 (2011) paras 1–200

Articles

For articles relating to this title please refer to the Table of Articles at the beginning of the Abridgment.

114   Building regulations—energy performance—certificates

The Energy Performance of Buildings (England and Wales) etc (Amendment) Regulations 2013, SI 2013/10 (in force on 27 January 2013), further amend the Building Regulations 2010, SI 2010/2214, and amend the 2012 Regulations, SI 2012/3118, in connection with the green deal energy efficiency scheme created by the Energy Act 2011 Pt 1 Ch 1 (ss 1–41). In particular, the regulations (1) add a number of new definitions relating to the green deal scheme; (2) add new provision so that energy performance certificates which relate to a property where there is a green deal plan are required to include certain information about that plan; and (3) add new provisions relating to the validity of energy performance certificates containing green deal information when those certificates are being used to comply with the green deal disclosure obligations contained in the 2011 Act s 12 and the Green Deal Framework (Disclosure, Acknowledgment, Redress etc) Regulations 2012, SI 2012/2079, Pt 7 (regs 41–50). In addition, the regulations amend the 2012 Regulations, SI 2012/3118, so as to (a) ensure that green deal information is added

Revenue imposed a penalty charge on the taxpayer pursuant to the Finance Act 2007 Sch 24 on the grounds that there was an inaccuracy in his tax return which was careless. The taxpayer appealed against the penalty charge on the grounds that he had taken reasonable care to avoid the inaccuracy. *Held,* the effect of Sch 24 para 18 was to remove the liability of a taxpayer to a penalty where a return was completed and lodged by an agent, and inaccuracy in the return was the result of something done or omitted by the agent and the taxpayer took reasonable care to avoid the inaccuracy. What constituted reasonable care would depend on all the circumstances of a particular case. If a taxpayer reasonably relied on a reputable accountant for advice in relation to the content of his tax return then he would not be liable to a penalty under Sch 24. The extent to which a taxpayer could reasonably rely on the advice of his agent would depend on the particular circumstances of each case. A taxpayer could not simply leave everything to his agent and had to satisfy himself that the agent had not made any obvious error. However, in matters that would not be straightforward to a reasonable taxpayer and where advice from an agent was sought which was within the agent's area of competence the taxpayer was entitled to rely on that advice. It was for the Revenue to show the inaccuracy on the taxpayer's tax return was as a result of the carelessness of the taxpayer or the accountants. It was clear that the accountants had acted carelessly. In the circumstances of the case, the taxpayer had discharged the burden of showing that he had taken reasonable care to avoid the inaccuracy. Accordingly, the appeal would be allowed.

JR Hanson v Revenue and Customs Comrs [2012] UKFTT 314 (TC), [2012] WTLR 1769 (First-tier Tribunal: Judge Cannan).

122 Disposal of assets—shares—derivative transactions

The taxpayer company was acquired as part of a scheme to avoid the payment of tax on the sale of a large number of shares. The shares were transferred to the taxpayer, which subsequently sold the shares in the open market, causing a large net chargeable gain to accrue to the taxpayer. Seeking to avoid the payment of corporation tax on the gain, the taxpayer then entered into a series of derivative contracts. After closing out one such contract at a considerable loss, it took out a similar contract which had the effect of locking in the profit that was latent in another contract. It was hoped that that the profit would be sheltered by selling the taxpayer to a company with capital losses. However, in the event no such sale was made. The taxpayer claimed that the closing out of the contract gave rise to an accounting loss, offsetting its gain on the shares. Shortly afterwards, the taxpayer closed out the other derivative contracts, on the basis of which it claimed to have achieved an equivalent chargeable gain. At the same time, three recently acquired subsidiaries of the taxpayer entered into further derivative contracts, as part of an arrangement designed to avoid the tax that would otherwise be payable on the gain. Several months later, the taxpayer sold its shares in one of those subsidiaries to unconnected third parties for a nominal sum. The taxpayer contended that an allowable capital loss arose on the sale and that it was entitled to set that against the almost identical gain that, on its case, had arisen in the same accounting period. The Revenue decided that the transactions did not give rise to any gains, profits or losses so that the taxpayer was liable to tax on the gain realised when it sold the shares. The taxpayer unsuccessfully appealed against that decision and, on its further appeal, *held,* even if the taxpayer could be said to have gained and lost on the derivative transactions, the gains and losses did not have the character of income. The transactions were one-off, stand-alone transactions. Moreover, they were not undertaken in the hope that they would, of themselves, produce any profit. The immediate objective had been to achieve a loss, albeit one balanced by a locked-in gain. There was no question of the taxpayer ultimately achieving a profit, nor any prospect of it being out of pocket. The transactions had not been entered into with a view to producing, in the result, income or revenue for the taxpayer. If the first derivative contracts were looked at together, it was plain that they had not been entered into for ordinary commercial purposes. While the form and content of a transaction were important, the purpose for which the transaction was entered was also relevant. Accordingly, the appeal would be dismissed.

Explainaway Ltd v Revenue and Customs Comrs [2012] UKUT 362 (TCC), [2012] STC 2525 (Upper Tribunal: Newey J presiding).

123   Disposal of assets—value shifting—tax-free benefit—shares

The taxpayer was involved in the business of property investment and management for profit. Prior to the transactions with which the present case was concerned, another company in the taxpayer's group had in issue nine unclassified shares (out of its authorised share capital of 100 shares). In a scheme proposed by a third party, part of the unissued share capital (but not the nine shares) was developed into a different class of share and offered to a subsidiary company of the taxpayer. This was part of a joint venture between the taxpayer and the third party in various financial dealings, partly used as collateral or offered as joint securities. Later, the taxpayer and third party entered into a cash-settled forward agreement, the broad effect of which was that, should the amount payable for the nine shares on exercise of either the put or the call option differ from a specified amount, an adjustment payment would be made between the parties to restore the net position to that amount. Prior to completion of the purchase of the nine shares, the taxpayer repaid the loan balance to its subsidiary. The Revenue decided that the principal purpose of the taxpayer in entering into those transactions had been to establish a capital loss for the purposes of corporation tax on chargeable gains in excess of the loan sum, and the loss relief on the wider scheme should not be allowed. The taxpayer's appeal to the First-tier Tribunal against that decision was dismissed, and on its further appeal consideration was given to the Taxation of Chargeable Gains Act 1992 s 30. *Held*, s 30(9) was not a computational provision or one that involved the application of computational rules. Rather, it was an enabling or 'threshold' provision defining the circumstances in which a particular form of computational adjustment fell to be made. For this reason, the Tribunal's approach of considering the applicability of s 30(9) on notional rather than actual facts meant that decision could not be upheld on its terms. On the proper interpretation of s 30(9) to the indisputable facts, the present case was one in which the disposal of an asset preceded its acquisition. That did not involve any process of 'deeming' or preferring notional facts to actual facts. In the context of the share development scheme, the relevant acquisition in respect of the disposal of the shares had been the acquisition of the same shares within the prescribed period following their disposal which had been at the heart of the scheme. The wording of s 30(9) was not to be applied without regard to the scheme effected or arrangements made of which the disposal of the asset formed part, and clearly the whole of s 30 had to be read together. In the circumstances of the present case, the just and reasonable adjustment to make within the confines of that power to increase any allowable loss or chargeable gain in s 30(5) was to increase the consideration for the disposal of the nine shares to the extent necessary to eliminate the loss claimed. Accordingly, the appeal would be dismissed.

Land Securities plc v Revenue and Customs Comrs [2013] UKUT 0124 (TCC), [2013] All ER (D) 244 (Mar) (Upper Tribunal: Roth J presiding). *Davies (Inspector of Taxes) v Hicks* [2005] EWHC 847 (Ch), [2005] STC 850 (2005 Abr para 380) applied.

124   Disposal of assets—wasting asset—meaning of 'plant'—sale of painting

The Taxation of Chargeable Gains Act 1992 s 44(1)(c) provides that 'wasting asset' means an asset with a predictable life not exceeding 50 years, but plant and machinery is in every case to be regarded as having a predictable life of less than 50 years, and in estimating that life it is to be assumed that its life will end when it is finally put out of use as being unfit for further use, and that it is going to be used in the normal manner and to the normal extent and is going to be so used throughout its life as so estimated.

The deceased had owned a painting that he kept on his estate. He allowed the company that owned the estate to use the painting in exchange for bearing the costs of the insurance, maintenance, restoration and security of the painting. There had been no formal lease, hire or loan in relation to the use of the painting by the company. Following the deceased's death, the executors continued the arrangement for 17 years before selling the painting. The executors' trust and estate tax return for the tax year in which the painting was sold included the gain accruing on the disposal of the painting as a chargeable gain. The executors sought to amend the return on the basis that the gain accruing on the sale of the painting was exempt from capital gains tax by virtue of the 1992 Act s 45, as a gain accruing on the disposal of tangible movable property which was 'plant' and therefore, by virtue of s 44(1)(c), a wasting asset. The Revenue rejected the contention that the painting was plant, and issued a closure notice. The taxpayer's appeal to the First-tier Tribunal against that decision was dismissed and, on its further appeal, *held*, it was established law that 'plant', in its ordinary sense, included whatever apparatus was used by a businessman for carrying on his business. It did not include his stock-in trade, but included all goods and chattels, fixed or moveable, live or dead, which he kept for permanent employment in his business. A permanent structure might be plant. The most useful description, where one was concerned with something done to premises, was to be found in that of 'setting'. To provide a setting for the conduct of a trade or business was not to provide plant. On the findings of fact that had been made by the Tribunal, the painting had satisfied the criteria as to function and permanence in the established test as to the meaning of plant. Further, the meaning of plant in s 44(1)(c) had not permitted a finding that an asset had been plant in the hands of a person using the asset in his business but, at the same time, not plant in the hands of the owner of the asset. It followed that the painting had been plant within the meaning of s 44(1)(c), and, in the absence of any argument that the painting had ceased to be plant a short time before it had been disposed of by the executors, the executors were entitled to the exemption conferred by s 45(1). Accordingly, the appeal would be allowed.

Executors of Lord Howard of Henderskelfe v Revenue and Customs Comrs [2013] UKUT 129 (TCC), [2013] STC 1025 (Upper Tribunal: Morgan J presiding).

This decision has been affirmed on appeal: [2014] EWCA Civ 278, [2014] All ER (D) 176 (Mar).

125   Exchange gains and losses—bringing into account gains or losses—foreign exchange risk—loan relationships and derivative contracts

The Exchange Gains and Losses (Bringing into Account Gains or Losses) (Amendment) Regulations 2013, SI 2013/1843 (in force on 12 August 2013), further amend the 2002 Regulations, SI 2002/1970, so as to make provision in relation to the calculation of the gain or loss arising on a loan relationship or derivative contract used to hedge any foreign exchange risk in relation to the disposal in a foreign currency of a ship, an aircraft or an interest in shares.

126   Exemptions and reliefs—annual exempt amount

The Capital Gains Tax (Annual Exempt Amount) Order 2013, SI 2013/662 (made on 19 March 2013), provides that, for the tax year 2013–14, an individual is exempt from capital gains tax on gains not exceeding £10,900 unless Parliament determines otherwise.

127   Exemptions and reliefs—collective investment schemes—tax transparent funds— exchanges, mergers and schemes of reconstruction

The Collective Investment Schemes (Tax Transparent Funds, Exchanges, Mergers and Schemes of Reconstruction) Regulations 2013, SI 2013/1400 (in force on 8 June 2013), amend the Taxation of Chargeable Gains Act 1992 so as to make provision in relation to the capital gains tax treatment of participants in collective investment schemes. In particular, the regulations (1) make provision in relation to a new type of collective investment scheme, an authorised contractual scheme which is a co-ownership scheme; (2) disregard a participant's interests in property subject to such a scheme for the purposes of the 1992 Act and provide that the participant's holding of units issued under the scheme is treated as an asset for capital gains tax purposes; (3) provide relief for insurance companies which transfer assets into a co-ownership scheme, or certain offshore funds which are directly comparable to co-ownership funds, in exchange for units in the scheme; (4) add an interest in a co-ownership fund to the types of collective investment scheme in relation to which an insurance company is treated as disposing of and reacquiring its interest at the end of each accounting period; (5) provide that, where the relief set out in head (3) has applied in relation to the acquisition of units, if those units are disposed of within three years after the end of the accounting period in which the acquisition took place, any allowable loss or chargeable gain which has been deferred and not already treated as accruing will be brought into account at the end of the period in which the disposal occurs; (6) extend the treatment provided in relation to umbrella funds to other types of collective investment scheme; (7) omit a redundant provision relating to collective investment schemes with property divided into separate parts; (8) apply, with modifications, provisions of the 1992 Act which relate to exchanges, mergers and schemes of reconstruction to specified types of collective investment scheme in a range of specified circumstances; and (9) make anti-avoidance provision. The regulations also make consequential amendments to the Authorised Investment Funds (Tax) Regulations 2006, SI 2006/964, and the Offshore Funds (Tax) Regulations 2009, SI 2009/3001.

128　Exemptions and reliefs—gilt-edged securities

The Taxation of Chargeable Gains (Gilt-edged Securities) Order 2013, SI 2013/13 (made on 10 January 2013), specifies six gilt-edged securities, disposals of which are exempt from tax on chargeable gains in accordance with the Taxation of Chargeable Gains Act 1992 s 115.

The Taxation of Chargeable Gains (Gilt-edged Securities) (No 2) Order 2013, SI 2013/2983 (in force on 25 November 2013), specifies five securities as 'gilt-edged securities'.

129　Exemptions and reliefs—intra-Community transfer of branch—substitute tax

The taxpayer was a capital company with its corporate seat in Italy. It transferred a branch of its business that was also located in Italy to a company established in Luxembourg. Following that transaction, the taxpayer received shares in the Luxembourg company, and the branch that had been transferred became a permanent establishment, in Italy, of the Luxembourg company. The transferred shares were recorded on the taxpayer's balance sheet at a higher value than the value for tax purposes of the branch that had been transferred. Later, the taxpayer elected to pay substitution tax at a rate of 19 per cent in respect of that transaction, as provided for by Italian law, thereby foregoing the regime of fiscal neutrality provided for in earlier Italian law. After the payment of that tax, the capital gains listed in the accounts following the transfer were distributed, since the difference between the value for tax purposes of the branch of activity that had been transferred and the value that had been attributed to the shares received as payment for the transfer had also been recognised for tax purposes. Later, the taxpayer asked the Italian tax authorities to refund the substitution tax that it had paid. It argued that national law was incompatible with Council Directive (EC) 90/434 (on the common system of taxation applicable to mergers, division, transfers of assets and exchanges of shares concerning companies of different member states) in that it made the neutrality of the transfer subject to conditions not contemplated by that directive. It was claimed by the taxpayer that it had mistakenly believed that the conditions set out in national law were lawful and that, because of that mistake, it had opted for the substitution tax rather than for the regime of fiscal neutrality. After the request for reimbursement had been implicitly rejected, the taxpayer brought an action before the national court. That action was rejected on the ground that the taxpayer had freely chosen the regime of substitution tax and that it had obtained the benefit of having the difference in value taxed at a rate that had been highly favourable in comparison with that at which the taxpayer would normally have had to pay tax in the event of realisation of the capital gain. On the taxpayer's appeal, it was found that national law, in so far as it imposed an obligation to carry over in the transferring company's balance sheet a reserve fund for suspension of tax following an intra-Community transfer, on pain of incurring taxation of any capital gain arising from the transfer, was contrary to Directive 90/434 and to the settled case law of the European Court of Justice, which had declared that measures which impeded the free circulation of capital and the freedom of establishment were unlawful. In order to avoid such incompatibility with European Union law, the court took the view that the member states should delay the taxation of capital gains until the point in time at which the capital gains were actually realised, without making the deferral of taxation subject to conditions that excessively limited those fundamental freedoms. In the circumstances, the court decided to stay the proceedings and seek a preliminary ruling. *Held*, arts 2, 4 and 9 had to be interpreted as not precluding the consequence of a transfer of assets being the taxation of the transferring company on the capital gain arising from that transfer, unless the transferring company carried over in its own balance sheet an appropriate reserve fund equivalent to the capital gain arising on that transfer.

Case C-207/11 *3D I Srl v Agenzia delle Entrate – Ufficio di Cremona* [2013] All ER (D) 40 (Feb) (ECJ: First Chamber).

Council Directive (EC) 90/434 replaced: Council Directive (EC) 2009/133.

130　Exemptions and reliefs—unauthorised unit trusts

See para 1524.

to preclude the shipowner from cancelling his nominated agent's authority to act on his behalf in receiving the freight, before such payment was made, and requiring it to be made to himself. In the present case, there was no difficulty in the first claimant countermanding his direction to the second defendant to pay freight to a third party, provided that it did so, as it had done, before the second defendant made payment as initially directed. Accordingly, the appeal would be dismissed.

Dry Bulk Handy Holding Inc v Fayette International Holdings Ltd, The Bulk Chile [2013] EWCA Civ 184, [2013] 2 All ER (Comm) 295 (Court of Appeal: Pill, Toulson and Tomlinson LJJ). Decision of Andrew Smith J [2012] EWHC 2107 (Comm), [2013] 1 All ER (Comm) 177 (2012 Abr para 175) affirmed.

143 Charterparty—construction—overage freight—mistaken payment

The claimant company chartered a vessel from the defendant owners. The vessel was to load a cargo of fuel oil at ports in the Ukraine or Black Sea and discharge in the European Mediterranean and/or in the claimant's option ports in the Singapore/Japan range. The claimant paid the defendant's invoice, which had been calculated on the basis that freight was payable in respect of all of the oil carried. The claimant subsequently contended that no transatlantic overage freight was payable as the parties had agreed that it was to pay no overage freight unless the charterparty so provided and the only overage freight that had been agreed was 50 per cent overage freight in the event of discharge in the European Mediterranean. The judge held that the defendant was not entitled to freight at the charterparty rate based on the entire quantity shipped, but that the claimant had not been entitled to pay nothing in respect of freight for tonnage carried in excess of the minimum. Since the parties had not made any express agreement as to the amount due in that respect, the judge ordered an inquiry into what would be a reasonable figure for the defendant to recover over and above the amount of freight calculated on the minimum quantity. The parties appealed against that decision. The claimant submitted that freight payable for any cargo loaded in excess of the minimum was to be the overage rate stated in the charterparty, with the effect that no freight payable for any cargo loaded in excess of the minimum quantity. The defendant submitted that it could not be supposed that it was carrying any cargo in excess of the minimum rate for nothing. *Held*, in the absence of any agreement to the contrary, the parties had agreed that overage was to be 50 per cent of the freight rate. It followed that, even in the absence of a stated rate, overage would be payable. If the parties had wanted to agree that no overage had been payable, they would have said so in terms. The parties had not expressly stated that there was to be no overage in other circumstances. The judge had therefore been entitled to find that the claimant's construction had not been correct. With regard to the defendant's contention, it could not be accepted that the contract had required, or the parties had intended, any inquiry to have been made as to what a reasonable freight should have been. The freight provisions were, if not extensive, at least apt to cover the relationship between the parties. Once it had been concluded that the claimant's construction had been impossible, the only reliable alternative was that the agreed freight rate had applied to all of the cargo for the relevant voyage. Accordingly, the claimant's appeal would be dismissed and the defendant's appeal would be allowed.

BP Oil International Ltd v Target Shipping Ltd [2013] EWCA Civ 196, [2013] All ER (D) 144 (Mar) (Court of Appeal: Ward, Longmore and Moses LJJ). Decision of Andrew Smith J [2012] EWHC 1590 (Comm), [2012] 2 Lloyd's Rep 245, [2012] All ER (D) 169 (Jun) (2012 Abr para 162) reversed in part.

144 Charterparty—construction—safe port warranty

A vessel had sought to leave a port in Japan during a severe gale. The vessel went aground and was abandoned by the crew. The vessel broke apart and a wreck removal contract was concluded. At the time of the casualty, the vessel was demised to a fourth party. The demise charterparty provided that the vessel was to be employed 'only between good and safe ports'. By a time charterparty, the fourth party chartered the vessel to the defendant or its predecessor in title. The defendant in turn sub-chartered the vessel to the third party. The claimants, the hull underwriters, issued proceedings as assignees of the registered owner and the fourth party. The defendant brought third party proceedings against the third party. The claimants submitted that the casualty had been caused by the unsafe nature of the port to which the defendant had ordered the vessel to discharge cargo. The defendant and the third party contended that the port was not unsafe. They alternatively contended that the cause of the casualty had not been that of lack of safety, but a misapprehension by the vessel's master that the vessel had been ordered to leave the port on the captain's advice and/or the negligent navigation of the master when leaving the port. The defendant and the third party further contended that the parties had not intended that the fourth party would have been liable to the owner for breach of the safe port warranty in respect of losses covered by the hull insurance taken out by the fourth party at its expense in the joint names of both the owner and itself. It fell to be determined whether the port was a safe port, whether the chain of causation had been broken and whether the value of the vessel was recoverable. *Held*, it was settled law that a port would not be safe unless, in the relevant period of time, the particular ship could reach it, use it and return from it without, in the absence of some abnormal occurrence, being exposed to danger which could not be avoided by good navigation and seamanship. When the defendant and third party had ordered the vessel to discharge her cargo at the port, it had prospectively been unsafe for the vessel. There had been a risk that the vessel might have to leave, or be advised to leave, the port on account of long waves or bad weather at a time when the wind and sea conditions in the channel had been such that more than ordinary seamanship and navigation had been required to enable the vessel to leave the port safely. There had been no system to ensure that, when any such departure had been necessary or advised, the vessel could safely leave. There had been no break in the chain of causation running from the captain's advice to leave the port to the actual departure. The effective cause of the casualty had remained the advice to leave given by the captain, which advice, given without considering whether it had been safe to leave, had reflected the unsafe nature of the port. Any negligence of the master had been the product of that lack of safety. The lack of safety of the port had meant that it had been difficult for the vessel to maintain the desired course and that difficulty had been reflected in the navigation of the vessel. On the true construction of the charterparty as a whole, the fourth party, as the demise charterer, was liable to the owner, in damages for breach of the safe port warranty, notwithstanding that the value of the vessel was recoverable and had been recovered by the owner from the claimants. The claimants would be entitled to the sums claimed from the defendant and the defendant would be entitled to the sums claimed from the third party. Accordingly, the claim would be allowed.

Gard Marine & Energy Ltd v China National Chartering Co Ltd [2013] EWHC 2199 (Comm), [2013] 2 All ER (Comm) 1058 (Queen's Bench Division: Teare J).

145   Charterparty—construction—suspension of services—term as to notice of suspension

See *Greatship (India) Ltd v Oceanografia SA de CV, The Greatship Dhriti*, para 549.

146   Charterparty—demurrage—cargo loaded without clearance of terminal authority—force majeure

The defendant chartered an oil tanker owned by the claimant in order to transport crude oil from a port in Nigeria. It was a requirement that an official from the Nigerian Department of Petroleum Resources (the 'NDPR') be present during the loading of vessels in order to verify the actual quantity of oil being loaded. When the vessel was ready to load, a representative of the NDPR was not at the terminal. Believing that the NDPR's head of operations had given verbal authorisation for the loading operation to begin, loading commenced in due course. A representative of the NDPR later arrived who took no steps to prevent the loading from continuing. The NDPR's head office then issued clearance to load, which was transmitted to its representative on board. However, later the same day the clearance was revoked. Consequently the necessary cargo documents were not completed and the vessel could not leave Nigeria. The terminal operator was ordered to pay a fine before the NDPR completed the cargo documents and the vessel was eventually allowed to leave the country several weeks later. The claimant brought proceedings against the defendant for demurrage and other sums. The judge held that the vessel had been on demurrage until the cargo documents had been placed on board and that a change in the underlying reason for the delay in the provision of cargo documents did not affect the application of the force majeure clause in the charterparty concerning delay after the disconnection of hoses. He stated that, on the facts, there was no question of the delay until the minister intervened. The defendant appealed. *Held*, (1) it was settled law that a force majeure clause had to be construed in accordance with its own terms. A force majeure clause was an exceptions clause and any ambiguity had to be resolved against the party seeking to rely on it. In the present case, the delay caused to the vessel had not been beyond the terminal operator's 'reasonable control' if one looked at the terminal operator as one entity. The terminal operator in Nigeria had not asked for official loading clearance from the NDPR in Lagos before the vessel had begun to load. The terminal operator had preferred to deal with the NDPR representative in port. However, in circumstances in which the judge had found that there was an official channel of communication in Nigeria for loading clearance, it had been a choice which had carried a risk. Exercising a choice which carried a risk was doing something which had been within one's control. The intention of the charterparty was that if anything went wrong with the loading operation for any reason that was the charterers' responsibility. It would not have been consistent with the concept of the charterers being responsible for defaults in loading that they should be able to excuse themselves on the basis that the event causing the damage had been outside the control of themselves or their immediate contracting party. The defendant had initiated a chain of contracts which had led to the actual loading of the vessel being done by the terminal operator. (2) The defendant's contract with a further seller of the oil in the chain of contracts excused that seller for delay in the performance of its obligations if performance was delayed by the occurrence of an unforeseen act or event which was beyond the control of either party. That had meant that that seller had been responsible for anything that had gone wrong during the loading operation since acts or events beyond the reasonable control of either party had meant beyond the reasonable control of that party or any other party to whom the contractual performance of that party's obligation had been delegated by that party. The result had been that the contravention of the procedure guides had put that seller in breach of its obligations, and damages for that breach were the sums for which the defendant was itself liable by way of demurrage to the claimant. It would be absurd if that seller had been able to excuse itself from the consequences of that breach by reference to the force majeure clause when it was its own breach of contract that had caused the supposed force majeure in the first place. The same considerations applied to another seller. (3) The Nigerian authority's abuse or arbitrary exercise of power was not a new intervening cause which had displaced the original breaches of contract by the sellers. Therefore, the claimant's claim for demurrage succeeded in full and that claim would be passed by the defendant on to the other oil sellers. Accordingly, the appeal would be allowed.

Great Elephant Corpn v Trafigura Beheer BV [2013] EWCA Civ 905, [2013] All ER (D) 315 (Jul) (Court of Appeal: Longmore, Tomlinson and Underhill LJJ). Decision of Teare J [2012] EWHC 1745 (Comm), [2013] 1 All ER (Comm) 415 (2012 Abr para 164) reversed.

147 Charterparty—demurrage—claim—delay

The claimant was the charterer of a vessel from the defendant owner pursuant to a charterparty. The charterparty provided that 'in the event that whilst at or off the loading place or discharging place the loading and/or discharge of the vessel is prevented or delayed by mechanical breakdown at the mechanical loading plants, time so lost shall not count as laytime'. A week before the vessel arrived at the load port, the parties were advised that a fire at the terminal used by the charterer had destroyed the conveyor belt system linking the terminal to the warehouse. The parties were advised to alter their berthing programme. Delays were caused at the alternative terminal. The claimant contended that, as a result of the fire, loading of the vessel was delayed by the mechanical breakdown of the conveyor belt system within the meaning of the charterparty and the time lost did not count as laytime. Arbitrators determined that the claimant was not able to rely on the charterparty because the inoperability of the conveyor belt was the result of physical damage due to the fire rather than a mechanical breakdown. On the claimant's appeal, the judge upheld the arbitrators' award. On further appeal, the claimant submitted that there was a mechanical breakdown of the conveyor belt system because, as a result of the fire, the machinery no longer functioned as a conveyor belt system. *Held*, on the facts, there was no mechanical breakdown of the conveyor belt system. It was possible that further investigations, not undertaken by the parties before the arbitration, might have revealed that the fire itself was caused by mechanical breakdown. However, the claimant did not advance any evidence before the arbitrators to establish if that was the case. Destruction of machinery by fire did not, without more, amount to a mechanical breakdown for the purposes of the charterparty, and the claimant failed to establish that it was entitled to invoke its protection. Accordingly, the appeal would be dismissed.

ED & F Man Sugar Ltd v Unicargo Transportgesellschaft GmbH [2013] EWCA Civ 1449, [2013] All ER (D) 213 (Nov) (Court of Appeal: Patten, Tomlinson and Christopher Clarke LJJ). Decision of Eder J [2012] EWHC 2879 (Comm), [2012] 2 Lloyd's Rep 660, [2012] All ER (D) 256 (Oct) (2012 Abr para 165) affirmed.

148　　Charterparty—exclusive jurisdiction clause—anti-suit injunction to restrain foreign proceedings

The claimant company was the owner of a vessel and was the contractual carrier of the cargo on the voyage under a bill of lading. The first defendant, a Moroccan company, was the receiver of the cargo and the second to sixth defendants were the insurers of the cargo. By a contract on an amended New York Produce Exchange form, the claimant chartered the vessel to a third party ('U') for the carrying of coal from the Netherlands to Morocco. U concluded the charter in order to perform a shipment which it had agreed to perform under a voyage charter contract with a company ('G'). The voyage charterparty between U and G was in the form of an email fixture. It concluded, otherwise as per proforma a specified pre-existing charter. That charter specified that the charterparty would be governed by English law, and that any dispute arising from it would be submitted to the jurisdiction of England and Wales. Subsequently, a bill of lading was drawn up naming G as the shipper and was consigned to the order of the first defendant. It took effect as a contract between the claimant and G. During the voyage, the temperature of the cargo was found to have increased considerably. Once the vessel was in harbour, it was decided to douse the hold with water to halt the self-heating effect. The cargo was doused. It was claimed by the first defendant that the dousing had damaged the cargo, rendering it unsuitable for their purposes. The claimant issued proceedings, seeking a declaration of non-liability. The first defendant was made aware of the English proceedings, but there were delays in serving the proceedings on the defendants in Morocco. Sometime later, the second to sixth defendants commenced proceedings in the Moroccan courts. They challenged the jurisdiction of the English court. Later, the claimant issued an application for an anti-suit injunction to restrain pursuit of the Moroccan proceedings on the ground that they constituted a breach of an exclusive jurisdiction clause in the charterparty that, they contended, had been incorporated into the bill of lading. *Held*, the express reference to the governing law of the charterparty amounted to an irrefutable case that the parties to the bill of lading had intended their contracts to be governed by the same law as was applicable to the charterparty. Since the form used was commonly used, there was nothing surprising or unusual about the choice of English law. Consequently, the owners had a good arguable case that the bill of lading was a contract governed by English law. Therefore, discretion would be exercised on the basis that the claimant had an extremely strong case that the bill of lading was subject to an express choice of English law. Further, general words of incorporation would not be effective to incorporate an arbitration or jurisdiction clause because such clauses were ancillary to the main contract to which they related. However, specific reference to an arbitration of jurisdiction clause would be effective and, providing that there was such a specific reference demonstrating an intention to arbitrate, it did not matter that the wording of the charterparty arbitration clause might require some degree of verbal manipulation in order to make it applicable to the bill of lading. There was no doubt that the dispute resolution clause did form part of the charterparty between U and G, which was in turn incorporated into the bill of lading. Therefore, the bill of lading contained a term requiring any dispute to be submitted to the exclusive jurisdiction of the English court. Judgment would be given accordingly.

Caresse Navigation Ltd v Office National de L'Electricitie [2013] EWHC 3081 (Comm), [2013] All ER (D) 188 (Oct) (Queen's Bench Division: Males J). *Chartbrook Ltd v Persimmon Homes Ltd* [2009] All ER (D) 12 (Jul) (2008 Abr para 859) applied.

149　　Charterparty—formation of contract—jurisdiction of arbitral tribunal

See *Hyundai Merchant Marine Co Ltd v Americas Bulk Transport Ltd*, para 54.

150   Charterparty—off-hire clause—loss of time due to drifting—obligation to show net loss of time

The claimant was the owner of a vessel which was chartered by a time charterparty to the defendant who sub-chartered to the second defendant on the same terms. Both charters provided that, in the event of the loss of time from default of master, officers or crew or deficiency of men or stores, fire, breakdown or damages to hull, machinery or equipment, grounding, detention by average accidents to ship or cargo, dry docking for the purpose of examination or painting bottom, or by any other cause preventing the full working of the vessel, the payment of hire would cease for the time lost, unless caused by the defendants or their agents, and all extra expenses directly incurred would be for the claimant's account. The sub-charter was for a one time charter trip with redelivery at Syria or the Egyptian Mediterranean at the second defendant's option. On the vessel's arrival at Syria, the authorities forbade the cargo's import. The second defendant instructed the master that discharge was to be in Libya. The second defendant instructed the master to anchor at the roads off the port and await further instructions. The second defendant informed the master that he was not complying with their instructions to proceed to the roads off the port and that they would treat the vessel as off-hire until she departed from the drifting position. The vessel continued to drift in international waters before resuming her voyage. Two arbitrations were issued and heard together. It fell to be determined whether the vessel had been off-hire or, if not, whether the second defendant could nonetheless recover the hire paid as damages for breach of the charterparties, on the footing that the master had both failed to prosecute the ordered voyage with the utmost despatch and/or that the master, who had been under the orders of the second defendant, had failed to comply with its orders. It was found that had the vessel proceeded directly to Libya, she would have berthed no earlier than she had and the breaches of contract by the claimant had caused no loss. The claimant's appeal succeeded. On appeal by the second defendant, *held*, the charters were concerned to identify an actual period of real time during which time was being lost, not an identifiable length of time by which the chartered service could be said to have been delayed. That enabled the parties to know where they stood without having to wait on events subsequent to the period of inefficiency. Use by the judge of the word 'overall' begged the question of what was the beginning and the end points of what was being measured. Without more, 'the charter service overall' seemed to be a reference to the entirety of the service to be performed under the charter. It was apparent that it would lead to precisely those intricate and speculative inquiries which had been deprecated by previous authority. It would also give rise to the distinct possibility that the same triggering event could give rise to different consequence in terms of off-hire in back to back charterparties of differing length. The service immediately required of the vessel while drifting had been to proceed to the roads at the port. It was not to the point in computing the time lost by reason of the master's default that a similar length of time, although not obviously the same precise period of time might have been lost had there been brought forward the moment at which the service immediately required of the vessel had become not the sea passage but rather berthing and discharge. Accordingly, the appeal would be allowed.

Minerva Navigation Inc v Oceana Shipping AG; Oceana Shipping AG v Transatlantica Commodities SA [2013] EWCA Civ 1723, [2014] 1 All ER (Comm) 552 (Court of Appeal: Tomlinson, Lewison and Underhill LJJ). *Hogarth v Miller, Brother & Co* [1891] AC 48, HL; *Vogermann v Zanzibar SS Co* (1902) 7 Com Cas 254, CA; *Tynedale Steam Shipping Co Ltd v Anglo-Soviet Shipping Co Ltd* [1936] 1 All ER 389, CA; and *Bergesen (Sig) DY A/S v Mobil Shipping and Transportation Co, The Berge Sund* [1992] 2 Lloyd's Rep 453, CA, applied. Decision of Walker J [2012] EWHC 3608 (Comm), [2013] 2 All ER (Comm) 28 (2012 Abr para 173) reversed.

151   Charterparty—repudiation—affirmation by shipowners prior to termination

See *White Rosebay Shipping SA v Hong Kong Chain Glory Shipping Ltd*, para 533.

152   Charterparty—repudiation—unpaid hire—worldwide freezing order—grounds for discharge

See *E v M*, para 310.

CHARITIES
Halsbury's Laws of England (5th edn) vol 8 (2010) paras 1–648

Articles
For articles relating to this title please refer to the Table of Articles at the beginning of the Abridgment.

153   Charitable trust—imperfect trust provision—validation

The Charitable Trusts (Validation) Act 1954 s 2(2) provides that the Act does not apply to a disposition if, before 16 December 1952, property comprised in the disposition had been applied for the benefit of the persons entitled by reason of the invalidity of the disposition in question.

A tennis and social club had a current and historic association with a nearby church although now only a minority of its members were members of the church. The club members played on courts on land which was held by the trustees of a deed made in 1938. The trust deed stated that the trustees were to hold the land for the purpose of tennis by persons associated with the church, and that in the event of any sale of the land the net proceeds were to be used for purposes in connection with the church. The church requested the trustees to consider the sale of the land and to make the proceeds available to the church. The club took legal advice as a result of which it challenged the validity of the trust deed. The Charity Commissioners advised the trustees that the trust deed had not created a charitable trust. The question arose whether any invalidity in the trust deed was validated by the provisions of the 1954 Act. *Held*, the purpose of s 2(2) was to prevent the 1954 Act being applied where an imperfect trust provision had already been recognised to be invalid and the invalidity acted on. The phrase 'entitled by reason of the invalidity of the disposition in question' did not describe the class of persons whose entitlement arose from the invalidity of the disposition. Rather it described what had happened: that meant the persons who had received benefit because the disposition was invalid. As the trust deed had been applied for the benefit for the members of the club at all times prior to 16 December 1952, the 1954 Act was not disapplied by s 2(2). However, the trust deed was not validated by the 1954 Act, because the 1954 Act provided for validation where property could be used for exclusively charitable purposes. On its face, the trust deed sought to create a perpetual trust primarily for a non-charitable purpose, to enable the members of the club to play tennis. If the trust deed were to be restricted to exclusively charitable trusts for the benefit of the church, the club would be deprived of the benefit which it had been intended to have and had in fact enjoyed for many years. Accordingly, the trust deed was invalid and was not validated by the 1954 Act.

Re St Andrew's (Cheam) Lawn Tennis Club Trust; Philippe v Cameron [2012] EWHC 1040 (Ch), [2012] 3 All ER 746 (Chancery Division: Arnold J). *Ulrich v Treasury Solicitor* [2005] EWHC 67 (Ch), [2006] 1 WLR 33, (2005) 7 ITELR 552 (2005 Abr para 398) applied.

154   Charities Act 2011—appointed day

The Charities Act 2011 (Commencement No 2) Order 2013, SI 2013/1775, appoints 1 September 2013 as the relevant commencement date for the purposes of specified provisions of the 2011 Act Sch 9 (transitory modifications), except that each provision comes into force on that date in relation to specified exempt charities only. The specified exempt charities are Saint David's Catholic College, further education corporations generally, and charities connected to them. Transitional provisions and savings are also made. For a summary of the Act, see 2011 Abr para 189.

155   Exempt charities—principal regulators

The Charities Act 2011 (Principal Regulators of Exempt Charities) Regulations 2013, SI 2013/1764 (in force on 1 September 2013), prescribe (1) the Secretary of State for Business, Innovation and Skills as the principal regulator of further education corporations in England and their connected charities; and (2) the Welsh Ministers as the principal regulator of further education corporations and connected charities in Wales, and of Saint

David's Catholic College. The regulations also define 'responsible person' in relation to the principal regulators for the purposes of unauthorised disclosure offences.

156   Incorporated Church Building Society—object of charity—administration

The Charities (Incorporated Church Building Society) (England and Wales) Order 2013, SI 2013/641 (in force on 27 March 2013), gives effect to a scheme of the Charity Commission relating to the Incorporated Society for Promoting the Enlargement, Building and Repairing of Churches and Chapels, a charity regulated by the Church Building Society Act 1828. The scheme specifies that the object of the charity is to maintain, build, enlarge and repair consecrated or dedicated churches and chapels and other places of worship of the Church of England by making grants on application. The scheme also makes provision for the administration of the charity and disapplies provisions of the 1828 Act which are inconsistent with, or rendered otiose by, the provisions of the scheme.

157   Small charitable donations—top-up claims, top-up payments and overpayments

See para 1564.

158   Trusts (Capital and Income) Act 2013

See para 2482.

CHILDREN AND YOUNG PERSONS

Halsbury's Laws of England (5th edn) vol 9 (2012) paras 1–704, vol 10 (2012) paras 705–1336

Articles

For articles relating to this title please refer to the Table of Articles at the beginning of the Abridgment.

159   Adoption—adoption agencies

The Adoption Agencies (Miscellaneous Amendments) Regulations 2013, SI 2013/985 (in force on 1 July 2013), further amend the 2005 Regulations, SI 2005/389, so as to (1) require adoption agencies to refer to the adoption register, within the required timescale, details of children who, it has been determined, should be placed for adoption; (2) introduce a two-stage approval process for prospective adopters, comprising a pre-assessment process and an assessment decision; (3) require an adoption agency to prepare a written plan in consultation with a prospective adopter, which must include information about the role of the agency and the prospective adopter in the pre-assessment process; (4) set out the pre-assessment information which an adoption agency must obtain and provide that an agency must decide, in light of that information, whether the prospective adopter may be suitable to adopt a child; (5) require an adoption agency to reach a pre-assessment decision within two months of the date on which the agency has notified a prospective adopter that the pre-assessment process is to proceed, except where the agency delays making such a decision because it is satisfied that there are good reasons for doing so or because the prospective adopter has requested it to do so; (6) require an adoption agency to prepare, after a prospective adopter has successfully completed the pre-assessment process, a written plan in consultation with the prospective adopter, which must include information about the procedure for assessing the prospective adopter's suitability to adopt a child; (7) require an adoption agency to decide whether a prospective adopter is suitable to adopt within four months of being notified that the prospective adopter wishes to proceed with the assessment process, except where the agency delays making such a decision because it considers that there are exceptional circumstances which mean it cannot make the decision within that time or because the prospective adopter has requested it to delay making the decision; (8) modify the new provisions in cases where an adoption agency is satisfied that a prospective adopter is an approved foster parent or has previously adopted a child; (9) require adoption agencies to refer to the adoption register, within the required timescale, details of approved prospective adopters; and (10) provide that, in most cases, an adoption agency must prepare a written plan in consultation with an approved prospective adopter which is to include information about the duties of the agency in relation to placement and reviews. The regulations also make various consequential amendments.

160   Adoption—adoption order—leave to oppose

Two children had been removed from their mother's care and made the subject of care and placement orders, the court dispensing with the mother's consent in accordance with the Adoption and Children Act 2002 s 52(1)(b). The children were placed with prospective adopters and an application was made for their adoption. The mother applied under s 47(5) for leave to oppose the adoption. Although the judge acknowledged that there had been a change in circumstances, she refused the application on the basis that opposition proceedings were not in the children's best interests. The mother appealed. *Held*, there was a real concern about the recurrent inadequacy of the analysis and reasoning put forward in support of the case for adoption, both in the materials put before the court by authorities and guardians and also in too many judgments. When the court was being asked to approve a care plan for adoption and when it was being asked to make a non-consensual placement order or adoption order, two things were essential. First, there had to be proper evidence both from the authority and the guardian which addressed all the options which were realistically possible and contained an analysis of the arguments for and against each option. Second, there was an adequately reasoned judgment. The judge had to evaluate all the options, undertaking a global, holistic and multi-faceted evaluation of the child's welfare which took into account all the pros and cons of each option. It was settled law that an application for leave to defend adoption proceedings under s 47(5) involved a two-stage process. First, the court had to be satisfied that there had been a change in circumstances within s 47(7). Second, if the court was so satisfied, it had to decide whether to exercise its discretion to permit opposition proceedings, with the child's welfare throughout his life being the paramount consideration. In relation to the second stage, the court would need to consider all the circumstances, in particular, the parent's ultimate prospect of success if given leave and the impact on the child if the parent was, or was not, given leave to oppose. In this regard, prospect of success related to the prospect of resisting the making of an adoption order, not the prospect of ultimately having the child restored to the parent's care. If it were concluded that there had been a change of circumstances and that the parent had solid grounds for seeking leave, the judge had to consider very carefully indeed whether the child's welfare really did necessitate the refusal of leave, bearing in mind that adoption was the last resort and that the child's interests included being brought up by the parents or wider family unless the overriding requirements of the child's welfare made that not possible. The mere fact that the child had been placed with prospective adopters or the mere passage of time could not be determinative. In the present case, the judge had conflated the stages applicable for consideration of the mother's application pursuant to s 47(5). However, that error of law had not vitiated the judge's essential reasoning or her conclusion, and it could not be said that her decision refusing leave had been wrong. Accordingly, the appeal would be dismissed.

Re B-S (children) (adoption order: leave to oppose) [2013] EWCA Civ 1146, [2014] 1 WLR 563, [2013] 3 FCR 481 (Court of Appeal: Sir James Munby P, Lord Dyson MR and Black LJ). *Re P (a child) (adoption order: leave to oppose making of adoption order)* [2007] EWCA Civ 616, [2007] 1 WLR 2556, [2007] 2 FCR 407 (2007 Abr para 492) applied. *Re W (a child) (adoption order: set aside and leave to oppose)* [2010] EWCA Civ 1535, [2011] 1 FCR 342 (2010 Abr para 195) considered.

The present judgment concerned two separate appeals which were heard together as they raised similar issues with regard to parents who had been refused leave to oppose adoption orders made in respect of their children. In each case the judgments had been delivered prior to the Court of Appeal's decision in *Re B-S (children) (adoption: application of threshold criteria)*. It fell to be determined how to apply the guidance in *Re B-S* to cases which had been determined before that decision. Held, in the case of judgments given before the decision in *Re B-S*, the Court of Appeal had to have regard to and make appropriate allowance for that fact. The focus had to be on substance rather than form. The judgment had to make clear that the judge had the two-stage process in mind, first, whether there had been a change in circumstances and, if the answer to that question was in the affirmative, then the second question was whether leave to oppose should be given. Where the answer to the first question was in the negative that was the end of the matter. In addressing the

168   Care order—judicial guidelines—validity

The present proceedings were care proceedings commenced by a local authority in respect of a child, who was 21 months old. Prior to the child's birth, the mother had made serious allegations that she had been sexually and physically abused by her older brothers and her parents. Following the child's birth, and in the light of the allegations made by the mother, the authority commenced care proceedings in regard to the child. The issue was the nature and extent of the risk to the child presented by the various members of the family. The mother withdrew her allegations and the truth of them became an issue. The authority's case was that the mother's allegations of abuse were probably true. The mother's case was that she had fabricated the allegations and that there was no risk. The authority made it clear that, if the mother was found to have been lying, it would not seek to argue that the jurisdictional threshold of the Children Act 1989 s 31 was satisfied and would not want an order. The mother was found to have been lying about the allegations. A report was prepared by an independent expert in psychology who was of the view that the mother continued to lie and make allegations against anybody, and had aggressive and violent motives. The judge held that the risk of emotional harm to the welfare of the child was substantial and stemmed from the mother's maladaptive behaviours. There was a significant disagreement between the authority and the mother on the one hand, and the child's guardian and the court on the other, as to whether the authority's proposals, as reflected by a care plan pursuant to s 31A, had met the risk identified by the court. The mother appealed, submitting that the care order was disproportionate, that it was not necessary for the authority to have shared parental responsibility with the mother, and that the judge did not have sufficient evidence about the benefits and detriments of statutory intervention in the lives of the mother and the child to be able to analyse what was proportionate. *Held,* the authority was in complete charge of the decision to make an application, but from that moment on, it became subject to the procedural obligations imposed by the rules and practice directions of the court and the orders of the allocated judge. It was the function of the court to come to a value judgment and it was not open to an authority within proceedings to decline to accept the court's evaluation of risk, no matter how much it might disagree. Furthermore, it was that evaluation which informed the proportionality of the response which the court decided was necessary. Although it was for the authority to decide what services to supply, as a matter of law it had to supply sufficient services to prevent the state's intervention becoming disproportionate. Not all services would be practicable and it was for those reasons that the court needed to know what services were practicable in support of each of the placement options and orders that the court might approve and make. It ought to form no part of an authority's case that the authority declined to consider or ignored the facts and evaluative judgments of the court. While within the process of the court, the State's agencies were bound by its decision and had to act on them. If the authority disagreed with the judge's risk evaluation, it had to, in a case that it was wrong, appeal it. If the welfare evaluation was not appealed, then it stood and the authority had to respect it and work with it while the proceedings were outstanding. To do otherwise risked disproportionate, irrational or otherwise unlawful conduct by the authority. There was no purpose in Parliament having decided to give the decision whether to make an order and the duty to consider the basis on which the order was made to the judge if the authority that made the application could simply ignore what the judge had decided. In the present case, there had been a lack of evidence before the judge about the benefits and detriments of statutory intervention in the lives of the mother and the child for the judge to be able to analyse what was proportionate. That lack of evidence had been a consequence of the authority's stance. The remedy in the court had been to direct the evidence that had been missing to be filed. However, the lack of reasoning had vitiated the exercise of determining the proportionality of the order made. Therefore, in the circumstances, the care order would be set aside and an interim care order substituted in its place. Accordingly, the appeal would be allowed.

Re W (a child) (care proceedings: welfare evaluation) [2013] EWCA Civ 1227, [2014] 1 FCR 260 (Court of Appeal: Sir James Munby P, McCombe and Ryder LJJ).

169   Care order—placement order—threshold criteria—non-accidental injuries—known perpetrator—rights of other parent to retain care

A family were from Bangladesh. The husband had moved to London to study and the mother and their two children subsequently joined him. The landlord of the flat where they lived had an agent who lived in another flat at the property. The mother and the agent formed a relationship which resulted in the birth of a third child. The third child lived with the family; the husband being unaware that the agent was the father. The agent occasionally cared for the children. The third child was taken to hospital and underwent immediate surgery for an acute subdural haematoma, retinal haemorrhage and encephalopathy. The local authority commenced care proceedings. The third child was taken into foster care. The husband learnt that the third child was not his and the mother moved out to live with the agent. One of the older children went with her while the other stayed with the husband. The husband sought a residence order in respect of the two older children. A fact finding hearing took place regarding the third child and the identity of the person responsible for her injuries. The process led to a conclusion that the third child had been assaulted by violent shaking. The judge was clear that the agent had been responsible and findings were made regarding his history of violence towards adults and that he had directed his anger towards the mother's older children. The mother was absolved from knowledge of the abuse although she had known that the agent had an intolerance of small children. Following judgment in the fact finding hearing, the mother continued living with the agent. She had had no alternative as she was an overstayer. She then moved to a refuge. However, the authority remained concerned that the mother remained involved with the agent. The father was granted a final residence order in respect of the two older children. The mother was permitted staying contact on condition that the children did not have contact with the agent. The authority sought care and placement orders for the adoption of the third child. The mother sought her return to her care. The judge found that the mother was in thrall to the agent. The judge made the care order sought and, having dispensed with the mother's consent under the Adoption and Children Act 2002 s 52, made a placement order for the third child's adoption. The mother appealed. *Held*, a court had to demonstrate that it had the relevant factors in mind and that its analysis was compatible with the law. The test for dispensing with a parent's consent under s 52 was the tipping point where the state could interfere with family life. A judge who expressly referred to the test could more readily identify the present proceedings against the tipping point. In all the circumstances, the conclusion that the third child should be adopted had not been a proportionate outcome. In virtually every other aspect of parenting, other than her relationship with the agent, the mother had been found to have much to offer the third child and no criticism had been made of her care of the older children. In such a case, the judge had been unwise not to have grounded her conclusions by reference to the welfare checklist. The question that the judge had focused on was whether the mother could be regarded as a safe parent in the future given her past relationship with the agent. That had been one of a range of factors that had had to be considered. Part of the proportionality assessment was to look at what a local authority could do to help keep a family together. The placement order would be set aside. The care order would be set aside and replaced with an interim care order. The matter would be remitted to the first instance judge to decide whether it was appropriate for her to undertake future planning. Accordingly, the appeal would be allowed.

Re E (*a child*) (*adoption order: proportionality of outcome to circumstances*) [2013] All ER (D) 343 (Oct) (Court of Appeal: Laws, McFarlane and Gloster LJJ).

170   Care order—threshold criteria—balancing exercise

The Nigerian mother of a young child claimed asylum in Ireland and subsequently settled in the United Kingdom. The child, who was autistic, had previously been in the care of Irish social services and an interim care order was made in the United Kingdom. When the child was aged eight, a district judge in the United Kingdom granted a full care order on the basis that the child had suffered and was at risk of suffering significant harm due to the care he had received and would receive if the order was not made. The mother's appeal against that decision was dismissed by a circuit judge. On her further appeal, the mother submitted that the district judge had failed to undertake an adequate balancing exercise or to consider the proportionality of permanent separation between mother and child when set against the adverse findings that had been made. *Held*, the authorities had made it clear that, following the process of finding any relevant facts, the court in a public law children case had to first make an evaluation to determine whether the statutory threshold criteria in the Children Act 1989 s 31 were established with respect to the individual child or children as at the relevant date. If the threshold criteria were established, the final stage of the proceedings involved the court evaluating which set of arrangements for the child's future care were to be endorsed by the court's order, and the evaluation was conducted by affording paramount consideration to the child's welfare. A judge could not properly decide that a care order should be made in such circumstances unless the order was proportionate bearing in mind the requirements of the European Convention on Human Rights art 8. The judicial exercise should not be a linear process. On the facts, the district judge had erred in the manner in which she had conducted the first instance welfare determination. The first appeal should therefore have been allowed on the basis that the district judge had failed to carry out the required balancing exercise. It followed that the circuit judge had erred in dismissing the appeal. The care order would therefore be set aside. Accordingly, the appeal would be allowed.

Re G (a child) (care proceedings: welfare balancing exercise: proportionality) [2013] EWCA Civ 965, [2013] 3 FCR 293 (Court of Appeal: Longmore, McFarlane and Davis LJJ).

171 Care order—threshold criteria—behaviour of parents—future harm to child

A mother suffered from somatisation disorder, which was a chronic psychiatric disorder, the main features of which would drive a sufferer to misuse physical symptoms in order to elicit care from others. Following the birth of her daughter, the local authority commenced care proceedings, removing the daughter from her parents, and sought an interim care order. Expert evidence stated that, beyond abnormal personality traits and in addition to, and more significantly than, her somatisation disorder, the mother suffered a factitious disorder of mild-to-moderate intensity. The judge found that there would be risks if the daughter were placed in the care of her mother in that the mother might present the daughter for medical treatment and that the daughter might receive unnecessary medical treatment and that, in any event, she might grow up to believe that the way in which the mother had presented herself for treatment was appropriate and might model herself on it. The judge's concerns were far wider than this, driving him to the key conclusion that it would not be safe for the daughter to be placed with her parents. The judge granted the care order and found that adoption was the only viable option for the daughter's future care. The parents' appeal was dismissed and they appealed further. *Held*, it was not the case, generally and in the current circumstances, that the threshold set by the Children Act 1989 s 31(2) was not crossed if the deficits related only to the character of the parents rather than to the quality of their parenting. The character of the parents was relevant to each stage of the inquiry whether to make a care order only to the extent that it affected the quality of their parenting. It was misconceived to submit that harm suffered, or likely to be suffered, by a child as a result of parental action or inaction might cross the threshold only if, in so acting or failing to act, the parent or parents deliberately or intentionally caused, or were likely to cause, such harm. There was no requisite mental element to accompany the actions or inactions. The judge had been fully justified in coming to the conclusion that the threshold had been crossed on the facts as he had found them, and in light of his assessment of the witnesses and of the risks facing the daughter. The judge had not been wrong to proceed to make a care order in relation to the daughter with a view to her adoption. There was a sufficient likelihood that the way in which the parents' care for the daughter, however well-intentioned, would be blighted by the parents' well-established difficulties and that the daughter's emotional well-being and development would suffer significantly. Accordingly, the appeal would be dismissed.

Re B (a child) (care order) [2013] UKSC 33, [2013] All ER (D) 103 (Jun) (Supreme Court: Lord Neuberger P, Lady Hale, Lord Kerr, Lord Clarke and Lord Wilson SCJJ). *Biogen Inc v Medeva plc* (1996) 38 BMLR 149, HL(1996 Abr para 2283); and *Re J (children) (care proceedings: threshold criteria)* [2013] UKSC 9, [2013] 1 AC 680, [2013] 3 All ER 1 (para 174) applied.

172 Care proceedings—care order—judicial review—availability of alternative remedy

See *R (on the application of CB) v Sheffield CC*, para 1634.

173 Care proceedings—expert evidence—expert witness—evidence necessary to assist court in resolution of proceedings

A child was born with spondylocostal dysostosis, which was a rare genetic disorder that required continuous medical monitoring by a team of local specialists. The child was found to have sustained bruising to her face and body and the appellant, the child's mother, on the advice of her local GP, took the child to hospital. The local authority subsequently commenced care proceedings in respect of the child and, during the course of those proceedings, the appellant applied for permission to instruct three expert medical witnesses, including a geneticist, a haematologist and a paediatrician. The hearing was listed as an issue resolution hearing and the only medical evidence filed was from the local authority, which consisted of evidence from various clinicians based at the hospital who either had direct contact with the child on the day of her referral to hospital and the immediate days following, or who were more generally part of the clinical team responsible for her case. The judge refused the appellant's application, holding that the factual parameters of the matter did not reach the test of necessity embodied in the Family Procedure Rules 2010, SI 2010/2955, r 25.1. The appellant appealed. *Held*, 'necessary', for the purposes of r 25.1, meant necessary. It was an ordinary English word and was a familiar expression in family law. Under established authority, albeit in a different context, its precise meaning had been held to be lying somewhere between 'indispensable', on the one hand, and 'useful', 'reasonable' or 'desirable' on the other, having the connotation of the imperative, what was demanded rather than what was merely optional or reasonable or desirable. It followed that the court would allow the instruction of a geneticist to answer two or three targeted questions based on matters of principle, without a need to consider the papers. Dependent on his answers, the geneticist's further involvement would be a matter to be dealt with by the judge in the ordinary way. The appeal in respect of the instruction of a haematologist and a paediatrician would be dismissed. Accordingly, the appeal would be allowed in part.

Re H-L (a child) (care proceedings: 'necessary' expert evidence) [2013] EWCA Civ 655, [2013] 2 FLR 1434, [2013] All ER (D) 112 (Jun) (Court of Appeal: Sir James Munby P, McFarlane and Treacy LJJ).

174　　Care proceedings—local authority care plan—evidence from previous care proceedings

A local authority initiated care proceedings in respect of three children living with their mother and her partner, on the sole ground that a judge had found previously that physical injuries sustained prior to the death by asphyxia of the mother's first child, when the mother had been living with a previous partner, had been caused by either the mother or the previous partner or both of them. It was held that the authority had not made out a case of likely harm to the three children for the purposes of the Children Act 1989 s 31(2). The authority's appeal was dismissed and it appealed further. *Held*, the 1989 Act tried to balance the two objectives of protecting the family from unwarranted intrusion while at the same time protecting children from harm. It did so by setting a threshold which had to be crossed before a court could consider what order, if any, should be made to enable the authorities to protect a child. The threshold, defined in s 31(2), was designed to restrict compulsory intervention to cases which genuinely warranted it, while enabling the court to make the order which would best promote the child's welfare once the threshold had been crossed. The three questions to be answered in any care case were: (1) whether there was harm or a likelihood of harm; (2) to what was that harm or likelihood of harm attributable; and (3) what would be best for the child. The court was concerned with the second limb of the first question. It had twice been held in the House of Lords that the mere possibility, however real, that another child might have been harmed in the past by a person who was now looking after a child with whom the court was presently concerned was not sufficient. The court had to be satisfied on the balance of probabilities that the person actually had harmed that other child but, in both those cases, it had not been established that the other child had been harmed at all. The issue in the present case was whether it made a difference that another child had indeed been harmed in the past and there was a possibility that the parent had been responsible for that harm. That remained a correct statement of the law. Only a finding that a child had been harmed by a parent in a way that was not accidental could be sufficient to found a prediction that, because it had happened in the past, the same was likely to happen in the future. A possibility that a parent had harmed some other child in the past did not establish that children now in that parent's care were likely to suffer significant harm for the purpose of s 31(2)(a). It was, of course, a fact that a previous child had been injured or even killed while in the same household as the parent. No-one had ever suggested that that fact should be ignored but such a fact normally came associated with

59(2); and (2) on 31 July 2013, in relation to specified local authority areas, ss 57, 58(1), (3)–(5), (6)(a), (7)–(9), (11)–(14), 59–62, 64, 65.

For a summary of the Measure, see 2010 Abr para 251. See also the commencement table in the title STATUTES AND LEGISLATIVE PROCESS.

197   Children and Young Persons Act 2008—commencement

The Children and Young Persons Act 2008 (Commencement No 5) (England) Order 2013, SI 2013/2606, brings ss 1 (so far as not already in force) and 4 into force in England on 12 November 2013. For a summary of the Act, see 2008 Abr para 512. See also the commencement table in the title STATUTES AND LEGISLATIVE PROCESS.

198   Children, Schools and Families Act 2010—commencement

The Children, Schools and Families Act 2010 (Commencement No 3) Order 2013, SI 2013/668, brings s 8 into force on 15 April 2013.

The Children, Schools and Families Act 2010 (Commencement No 4) Order 2013, SI 2013/1573, brings s 10 into force on 3 July 2013.

For a summary of the Act, see 2010 Abr para 1030. See also the commencement table in the title STATUTES AND LEGISLATIVE PROCESS.

199   Children's homes—England

The Children's Homes and Looked after Children (Miscellaneous Amendments) (England) Regulations 2013, SI 2013/3239 (in force in part on 27 January 2014 and in part on 1 April 2014), further amend (1) the Children's Homes Regulations 2001, SI 2001/3967, so as to (a) define the qualifications required by managers of children's homes and persons working in care roles in children's homes; (b) set out the date by which the qualifications must be attained or held; (c) require the registered person to notify the local authority when a child is admitted to, or discharged from, a children's home and specify the information which the notification must contain; (d) alter the requirements for children's homes to have a policy regarding missing children and provide for consultation with local services before implementing the policy; (e) provide for an annual risk assessment in relation to the location of premises used for the purposes of a children's home; (f) make provision for visits to, and reporting on, a children's home by an independent person and for the appointment of the independent person; and (g) set out the matters to be included in a children's home's statement of purpose and the matters to be monitored and reported on by the registered person; (2) the Care Planning, Placement and Case Review (England) Regulations 2010, SI 2010/959, so as to (a) add a new definition of a placement of a looked after child 'at a distance'; (b) require that the decision to put a child in such a placement is approved by the local authority's director of children's services; (c) prescribe consultation and notification requirements in relation to such placements; (d) require the local authority to hold a review of a child's case whenever a child has been persistently absent from a placement, or where there are concerns that the child may be at risk of harm; (e) provide that, where a chid aged 16 or 17 is looked after other than by virtue of a care order, the decision of the local authority to cease looking after the child must be approved by the authority's director of children's services; and (f) require that, in any case where there are child protection concerns relating to a child, or the child has gone missing from a placement, the child's care plan must record the day-to-day arrangements put in place to keep the child safe; and (3) the Care Standards Act 2000 (Registration) (England) Regulations 2010, SI 2010/2130, and the Fostering Services (England) Regulations 2011, SI 2011/581.

200   Children's services—registration and inspection—holiday schemes for disabled children—England

The Care Standards Act 2000 (Extension of the Application of Part 2 to Holiday Schemes for Disabled Children) (England) Regulations 2013, SI 2013/253 (in force on 4 March 2013), apply with modifications the Care Standards Act 2000 Pt 2 (ss 11–42) to a person who carries on or manages a holiday scheme for disabled children.

201   Contact order—application by father—child conceived by artificial insemination—mother in same-sex relationship

The first and second applicants were a male couple who had been together for 20 years. The first applicant was the biological father of two children, and the second applicant was the biological father of one child. All three children were born as a result of artificial insemination. The children's mothers, who were known to the applicants, were both in civil partnerships. As a result of the Human Fertilisation and Embryology Act 2008, legal parenthood of two of the children was vested in the mothers and the mothers' respective civil partners, to the exclusion of the applicants who therefore had no right to apply for orders in respect of the children without the leave of the court. The applicants sought leave to apply under the Children Act 1989 s 8 for contact orders in respect of those two children. They relied in part on their right to a family life under the European Convention on Human Rights art 8. *Held*, when considering an application by a biological father for leave to apply for an order under the 1989 Act s 8 in respect of a child conceived using his sperm by a woman who, at the time of her artificial insemination, was party to a civil partnership, the reforms implemented in the 2008 Act ss 42, 45 and 48, and the policy underpinning those reforms, namely to put lesbian couples and their children in exactly the same legal position as other types of parent and children, were relevant factors to be taken into account by the court, alongside all other relevant considerations, including the factors identified in the 1989 Act s 10(9). In some cases, the reforms, and the policy underpinning those reforms, would be decisive. Each case, however, was fact specific. The position of a lesbian couple who had been granted the status of legal parents by the 2008 Act was exactly the same as any other legal parent. Having taken those rights into account, however, it was still open to the court, after considering all relevant factors, to grant leave to other persons to apply for orders under the 1989 Act s 8. In that regard, the position of biological fathers who had been deprived of the status of legal parent by the 2008 Act was the same as any other person. Applying those principles, it was appropriate to grant the applicants leave to apply for contact orders. It was plainly arguable that the relationships which the children's mothers allowed the applicants to establish with their children amounted to family or private life. Accordingly, the applications would be allowed.

Re G (a child) (sperm donor: contact order); Re Z (a child) (sperm donor: contact order) [2013] EWHC 134 (Fam), [2013] 1 FLR 1334, [2013] All ER (D) 19 (Feb) (Family Division: Baker J).

202   Contact order—application by father—wishes of child

The first application by a father for contact with his daughter was made shortly after her birth. In the course of lengthy proceedings, the father was heavily criticised for his conduct. The guardian ad litem recorded that, although the father clearly loved the daughter, he was angry and frustrated in not playing a significant part in her life, that he used bullying tactics in order to get his own way, and that his behaviour aroused concern with regard to any future contact arrangement with her. A consultant clinical psychologist reported that the father showed evidence of being obsessed with his daughter, that he could be demanding and aggressive. An order was made which provided that the father should have direct contact with his daughter three times a year, that the father have indirect contact, as defined, that the father be prohibited from contacting her school, and that he be prevented from making further applications for orders under the Children Act 1989 s 8 without leave of the court. Following the expiry of that order, the father sought the mother's agreement to extend contact. When the mother refused, the father issued an application to extend contact to two days per month for two months, to be followed by significant additional contact during school holidays. A report was prepared by a National Youth Advocacy Service caseworker, who reported that there was still a risk of manipulation and controlling behaviour by the father, but that the daughter had expressed her view that, while she did want to extend contact with her father and was content to change contact to see the father six times a year, she opposed staying contact. The father asserted that the views expressed by his daughter had been a reflection of the mother's views. *Held*, in carrying out an assessment under s 1(3), the daughter was at an age when the court was likely to place significant weight on her expressed wishes and feelings. The wishes and feelings of the daughter, which had been consistently expressed, were rational, congruent and genuine. Her emotional welfare required that she be protected against the kind of behaviour previously exhibited by the father which had been so roundly criticised in earlier judgments. It was clear that, if there was any repetition of the father's behaviour, there was a real risk that that would cause the daughter emotional harm. There was a wide gulf between the contact sought by the father and the increased, but limited, contact sought by the daughter. The welfare check list, pursuant to s 1(3), did not support the extensive contact sought by the father. Therefore, an order for contact would be made that was less extensive than that sought by the father, but more extensive than that which had previously been in place. Judgment would be given accordingly.

Re G (a child: intractable contact) [2013] EWHC 2948 (Fam), [2013] All ER (D) 08 (Oct) (Family Division: Judge Clifford Bellamy).

203 Contact order—restrictions on contact—direction hearing—relaxation of restrictions—pre-emption of full hearing

The parents of a child separated and the mother obtained a non-molestation order against the father. A contact order made with regard to the child recorded that the mother did not consent to contact meetings taking place at the father's home. Contact was extended to the father but the mother continued to object, claiming that the child had made allegations to her that the father had physically abused him during contact meetings. The contact order was varied to require contact to take place in a public place. A CAFCASS officer and social worker reported that the child greatly enjoyed spending time with the father and recommended that more contact between them was desirable. The mother suspended contact, alleging that the father regularly breached the order not to take the child to the father's home. A directions hearing took place and the date for a full hearing was fixed to take place nine months later. The father applied to revoke his undertaking not to take his son to his home and for an extension of contact as recommended by the CAFCASS officer. A second directions hearing took place and, having heard the matter on submissions only, the judge extended the duration of contact and lifted the restrictions on the father taking his son to his home. The mother appealed. The court considered whether the judge had failed to comply with PD 12J and had wrongly deviated from a course that had been set by the earlier hearings. The mother submitted that the judge's relaxation of the restrictions on contact had pre-empted the full hearing which, therefore, was redundant. *Held*, PD 12J did not prevent a judge from making an order for contact without making findings of fact in relation to disputed allegations of domestic violence. The issue of domestic violence had to be kept in mind at all times, including the interim stage before findings had been made. In an appropriate case, a conscious decision could be made either not to make findings of fact at all or not to do so in a separate fact finding hearing. PD 12J should be read as imposing an obligation on the court to determine whether findings needed to be made about factual obligations at all and, if so, whether that should be done in a separate fact finding hearing or as part and parcel of a composite fact finding and welfare hearing. If it decided that a separate fact finding hearing was necessary, then it had to give directions for that and it had to be sure to fix the welfare hearing there and then. Having a two-stage process of fact finding and welfare hearings would not be consistent with guidance that sought to limit the proliferation of split hearings. The judge had conformed with PD 12J. Although he had not referred specifically to PD 12J, he had been well aware of the need to consider the likely impact of the domestic violence issue on the conduct and outcome of the proceedings and in particular whether the nature and effect of the violence alleged had been such that, if proved, the decision of the court would be likely to be affected. The judge had been within the bounds of his discretion to make the order which he had supported as it was by the evidence and as explained in his judgment. He was entitled to take the view that the then present arrangements had not been satisfactory and that, as stopgap arrangements, they would be in place for a much longer time than anticipated because of the nine-month delay before the full hearing. Accordingly, the appeal would be dismissed.

Re H (interim contact: domestic violence allegations) [2013] EWCA Civ 72, [2014] 1 FLR 41, [2013] All ER (D) 331 (Feb) (Court of Appeal: Arden, Elias and Black LJJ). *Piglowska v Piglowski* [1999] 3 All ER 632, HL (1999 Abr para 1257), applied. *Re Z (unsupervised contact: allegations of domestic violence)* [2009] EWCA Civ 430, [2009] 3 FCR 80 (2009 Abr para 427); *Re F-H (children) (fact-finding hearing)* [2008] EWCA Civ 1249, [2009] 1 FCR 749 (2008 Abr para 530); *President's Guidance in relation to Split Hearings* [2010] 2 FCR 271 (2010 Abr para 278); *Re C (children) (residence order: application being*

dismissed at fact-finding stage) [2012] EWCA Civ 1489, [2012] All ER (D) 223 (Nov); and
Re TG (a child) (care proceedings: biomechanical engineering evidence) [2013] EWCA Civ
5, [2013] 1 FCR 229 considered.

204   Criminal proceedings—reporting restrictions—child not directly concerned in proceedings—protection of child

The claimant, an elected councilor, pleaded guilty to a charge of being drunk in a public place while having the charge of a child under the age of seven years, contrary to the Licensing Act 1902 s 2(1), and a fine of £100 was imposed on her. Immediately after sentencing, the claimant applied for an order, pursuant to the Children and Young Persons Act 1933 s 39, submitting that she ought not to be identified because of her health. In the summary grounds of defence of the defendant magistrates' court, a legal adviser, who had been present in court during the proceedings against the claimant, stated that no evidence had been provided by her relating to how the daughter would be affected by the claimant's name being released to the press, other than the fact that the daughter ought to be protected from publicity on the matter. The legal adviser had advised the justices that they did not need to consider the impact on the claimant of an order under s 39, but that they only needed to consider the impact on the daughter. The justices stated that, having considered such advice, they would refuse the application for reporting restrictions. In judicial review proceedings, the claimant contended that the justices had erred in law in refusing to make the s 39 order. Questions arose as to whether the daughter was 'concerned' in the proceedings and as to the relevant considerations the justices had to take into account. *Held*, under the 1902 Act s 2(1), it was unnecessary to show that a defendant positively inflicted physical or psychological harm on the young child, or even that a defendant in the particular circumstances was likely to do so. In that strict sense, the child might not be considered a victim as in the case of a violent or sexual assault, or of child cruelty. However, whatever the original intent of s 2(1), the court was prepared to give it an interpretation that would best promote public policy in modern conditions, namely, that it should protect the welfare of small children who could be at risk of physical or psychological harm, because the person responsible for their welfare was intoxicated. Thus, the child who was specifically referred to in any charge under s 2(1) was in a real sense a subject of the criminal proceedings. In the context of civil proceedings, it would ordinarily be straightforward to determine whether a child or young person was bringing the proceedings, or whether the proceedings had been brought against him, or whether the child or young person was in substance the subject of civil proceedings brought by others. In a strictly formal sense, it might be argued that the only two parties to criminal proceedings were the prosecution and the defendant and that criminal proceedings were not taken 'in respect of' any other person'. However, it was plain that the legislature, in enacting the 1933 Act s 39, had sought to capture, in wide language, at least the central participants in proceedings, whether civil or criminal, who would, for that very reason, be likely to be the focus of any report of the proceedings. A narrow interpretation of s 39 would tend to defeat the main objective of protecting, where appropriate, the identity of a child or young person in that position. A broad interpretation of s 39 was also supported by the Convention art 8 and the jurisprudence emphasising the best interests of children as a primary consideration. On any sensible construction of the 1933 Act s 39, the proceedings had been taken 'in respect of' and thus 'concerned' the child. It was clear that the application of s 39 engaged important and competing principles, namely, the private and family life of a child, the best interests of that child and the freedom of the media to publish, and of the public to receive, information or comment and the requirements of open justice. Those principles were enshrined on one side in the European Convention on Human Rights art 8, which guaranteed the right to a private and family life, and in the jurisprudence recognising the best interests of the child as a primary consideration, and on the other, in arts 6 and 10 which guaranteed the rights to a fair hearing and to freedom of expression. In all the circumstances of the case, the justices had had a reasonable basis for concluding that no order under the 1933 Act s 39 had been justified. The balance of the relevant competing principles had come down firmly in favour of the Convention art 10 and open justice, given the immediate, direct and considerable extent of the interference with those rights and taking due account of the much weaker, remote and uncertain impact on the daughter's rights under art 8 and on her best interests. For the avoidance of doubt, if it were necessary, the court would also hold that the decision reached by the justices had been correct. Accordingly, the application would be dismissed.

that the allocated social worker had been aware of the guidance, and its s 37 report had been deficient for absence of thorough investigation, assessment, analysis or any logical or coherent thinking. The failure to follow the relevant guidance had itself been a serious failing. Further, the authority's hard-pressed financial resources could not allow it to be released from its clear statutory responsibility to investigate in accordance with the provisions of s 37 in fulfilment of a specific court direction. The authority's failings carried the case over the exceptionality threshold. Therefore, the father was entitled to his costs of the wasted hearings from the authority. Accordingly, the application would be allowed.

HB v PB [2013] EWHC 1956 (Fam), [2013] All ER (D) 138 (Jul) (Family Division: Cobb J). *Phillips v Symes; Symes v Phillips* [2004] EWHC 2330 (Ch), [2005] 4 All ER 519 (2005 Abr para 866); and *Re X (emergency protection orders)* [2006] EWHC 510 (Fam), [2007] 1 FCR 551 (2006 Abr para 483) applied.

213 Family proceedings—jurisdiction—care proceedings in the United Kingdom—other member state seeking transfer

A Slovakian district court made an order placing the mother, who was a Slovakian citizen, in a children's home. When she was 15 years old, the mother became pregnant. A court ordered that the mother be transferred to a children's home which had a special unit for underage mothers. The mother ran away with the father, who was also a Slovakian citizen. They travelled to the United Kingdom where their child was born. The applicant local authority undertook an assessment immediately after the birth. Although the mother was allowed to take the child to her mother's home in the United Kingdom, that placement broke down and they were moved to a mother and baby unit for assessment. The applicant issued care proceedings and sought a placement order. The mother left the unit. The director of the children's home in Slovakia wrote to the applicant stating 'our interest is that the mother be returned to the children's home, as she is entrusted to our care by the courts'. The authorities in Slovakia sought the return of the child. The Slovakian Central Authority contended that the case was one where a request ought to be made by the present court under Council Regulation (EC) 2201/2003 (concerning jurisdiction and the recognition and enforcement of judgments in matrimonial matters and the matters of parental responsibility) art 15 for a transfer to the Slovakian courts of the proceedings. *Held,* the applicable principles were (1) art 15 applied to public law as well as private law proceedings; (2) as a precondition, the court had to be satisfied within the meaning of art 15(3) that the child had a particular connection with the relevant other member state; (3) the applicant had to satisfy the court that the other court would be better placed to hear the case and, in making that evaluation, the applicant had to show that the other court was clearly the more appropriate forum; (4) in assessing the appropriateness of each forum, the court had to discern the forum with which the case had the more real and substantial connection in terms of convenience, expense and availability of witnesses; (5) if the court were to conclude that the other forum was clearly more appropriate, it should issue the transfer request and grant a stay unless other more potent factors were to drive the opposite result; (6) in the exercise to be conducted at (3)–(5), the best interests of the child was an important, but not the paramount, consideration; (7) in making the best interests analysis at (6) the court would not embark on a profound investigation of the child's situation and upbringing but would dwell in an attenuated inquiry on the sort of considerations which came into play when deciding on the most appropriate forum. In the present case, all the requirements of art 15 when read conformably with established principles were satisfied. The plan outlined by the Slovakian Central Authority best promoted the possibility of preserving the child's Slovakian and Romanian heritage. The promotion of the child's heritage was of great importance and neither the applicant nor the guardian had had sufficient regard to that factor. The analysis of best interests only went to inform the question of forum and ought not to descend into some kind of divisive value judgment about the laws and procedures of other European countries. The present proceedings would be stayed but the child would remain where he was under a sequence of interim care orders made administratively until the Slovakian court made a decision about his interim arrangement. Judgment would be given accordingly.

Re T (a child: article 15 of Brussels II revised) [2013] EWHC 521 (Fam), [2013] Fam 253, [2013] All ER (D) 192 (Mar) (Family Division: Mostyn J).

214   Family proceedings—jurisdiction—child habitually resident in another member state—making inquiries of foreign judge

A five-year-old child and her mother, who were habitually resident in Sweden, visited England. During the course of the visit, the authorities became concerned about the behaviour of the mother, who had significant mental health problems, and the child was taken into care. Care proceedings were subsequently issued in relation to the child by the relevant local authority. The mother applied for a declaration under Council Regulation (EC) 2201/2003 art 17 that the English court lacked jurisdiction. Inquiries were made through the International Hague Network of Judges (the 'judicial network') regarding the jurisdiction of the Swedish courts. The Swedish court's view, promulgated by an unnamed Swedish network judge, was that, at that stage, there were no live proceedings in Sweden so that it had no current jurisdiction in relation to the child. The English judge decided on that basis that any jurisdiction the Swedish courts had had been declined, with the effect that no member state had jurisdiction pursuant to arts 8–18. The judge therefore ruled that jurisdiction ought to be determined in accordance with the law of the present jurisdiction. The mother appealed against that decision, submitting that (1) the judge had incorrectly applied the provisions of arts 8, 14 and 17; and (2) the judge had fallen into error in the manner in which she had dealt with the opinion of the unnamed Swedish network judge because the process of judicial liaison adopted by the judge had denied the mother of her right to a fair trial pursuant to the European Convention on Human Rights art 6. *Held*, it was outside the scope of the judicial network for it to be used to obtain an authoritative determination from the court of the requested network judge on the issues relating to a particular child where either there were no proceedings relating to that child before that court or, if there were proceedings, the determination sought was one that was made outside those proceedings. In the context of liaison between judges in Europe, each was governed by the fair trial requirements of art 6. In the present case, the questions asked of the Swedish network judge had fallen outside what could properly have been requested via the judicial network. The questions had sought the determination of fundamental matters of status in a case where those very issues had been fully contested. It was wholly inappropriate for the English court to have asked such questions both as a matter of substance and also because, had the Swedish court sought to give a binding reply, such a process would have been bound to have breached art 6. The expressions of opinion given by the Swedish network judge could not have formed the basis for a finding that the courts in Sweden had actually declined jurisdiction as the English judge had concluded. Courts in a member state could decline jurisdiction only in the context of a proper judicial process, conducted within ongoing court proceedings in that state where, as Regulation 2201/2003 art 17 made plain, that court was seised of the case relating to the particular child. It followed that both the process and the internal reasoning adopted by the English judge could not stand and had to be set aside. In the circumstances, a declaration would also be made under art 17 that the English courts had no jurisdiction. Accordingly, the appeal would be allowed.

Re B (a child) (care order: jurisdiction) [2013] EWCA Civ 1434, [2013] All ER (D) 142 (Nov) (Court of Appeal: McFarlane, Gloster and Floyd LJJ).

215   Family proceedings—jurisdiction—dispute—child habitually resident in United Kingdom

A child born in the United States of America was a United States national. Her parents were also United States nationals. At the time of the child's birth, the parents lived together but were not married. They separated and the child remained living with the mother in the United States, enjoying contact with the father. The mother married a British national, who became the child's stepfather, and asked the father whether she could take the child to the United Kingdom for a holiday. The father sought sole custody of the child, and applied for an order prohibiting the child's removal from the United States. The mother cross-applied for permission to relocate with the child, for a period of two years, to the jurisdiction of England and Wales. A full custody hearing followed in the United States, and the court ordered that the mother be granted permission to relocate. The parties were awarded shared parental responsibility of the child, with the mother being designated as the primary residential parent and the father as the secondary residential parent. The child and her mother went to England where they remained. The parents agreed to extend the period in which the child could remain living in England. The extension provided for a review after one year, and gave the father the right to call for an early return after one year if there were substantial reasons. The agreement made it clear that the final decision as to whether the child should return needed to be finalised. The father issued proceedings in the United States seeking an order that the child be returned to the jurisdiction. The mother issued proceedings in the United Kingdom seeking a residence order and an order that the father have defined contact. The father contested the jurisdiction of the English court. *Held*, the general rule of jurisdiction was contained in Council Regulation (EC) 2201/2003 (concerning jurisdiction and the recognition and enforcement of judgments in matrimonial matters) art 8 to the effect that the courts of a member state were to have jurisdiction in matters of parental responsibility over a child who was habitually resident in that member state at the time the court was seised. It was established law that the concept of habitual residence had to be interpreted as meaning that such residence corresponded to the place which reflected some degree of integration by the child in a social and family environment. It was a question of fact and not a legal concept such as domicile. In the circumstances, the child had lived in England for nearly half of her life. Her mother and stepfather had full-time employment in England. The child was habitually resident in England and Wales. It followed that the court of England and Wales undoubtedly had jurisdiction to entertain the mother's application for substantive welfare-based orders in respect of the child. Any welfare-based inquiry focusing of the child's best interests going forward would surely be best conducted in the country which had been her home for a significant time, and in which she was habitually resident. Therefore, the residence order would be confirmed and the issue of defined contact adjourned. Judgment would be given accordingly.

Re M (a child) (habitual residence: jurisdiction) [2013] EWHC 2774 (Fam), [2013] All ER (D) 159 (Sep) (Family Division: Cobb J). *Re I (a child) (jurisdiction: habitual residence outside European Union)* [2009] UKSC 10, [2010] 1 AC 319, [2010] 1 All ER 445 (2009 Abr para 429); *Re A (children) (jurisdiction: return of child)* [2013] UKSC 60, [2013] All ER (D) 66 (Sep) (para 179); and *Mercredi v Chaffe* [2011] EWCA Civ 272, [2011] 2 FCR 177 applied.

216   Family proceedings—without notice applications—procedural guidance

The court has, on an appeal by a father against an order refusing him direct contact with his child, given the following guidance as to the proper approach to be adopted in family proceedings when considering a without notice application for a prohibited steps order and the making of a contact order: (1) It was an established principle that due process had to involve scrutiny of the details of that which was alleged and asked for. It had to be clear, where a 'tick box' formula was used to identify the existence of abduction and/or domestic violence, it should be a requirement not a request that relevant particulars were given and that requirement should be made clear on the form. The notice and form would be of much greater use to the judges of the court if they contained in template form a short sequence of narrative paragraphs whose completion was mandatory dealing with the order applied for, the precipitating circumstance, the allegations, the specific proposal relating to the application and the required particulars of exceptional urgency and notice. In that context, the Family Procedure Rules Committee might wish to consider whether the forms were a sufficient reflection of the duty of full and frank disclosure which existed on those who sought to use a without notice procedure. (2) FPR rr 12.16(4), (5) required that an application notice and order made without notice were served within 48 hours of the order being made. In accordance with r 18.10(2), the service of evidence on a respondent in support of a without notice application was mandatory unless the court ordered otherwise. Where in private law children proceedings there would often be no written evidence in support because leave to file the same had not yet been given under r 12.19(2), it was an essential procedural protection that the court ordered the applicant to file and serve a statement setting out the matters relied on orally before the court in the absence of the respondent and/or, where appropriate, to obtain and serve a transcript of the proceedings. Any abrogation or variation of that procedural protection had to be explained, namely, reasoned by the court and the reason should be stated in the order where, as was likely, there would be no formal judgment. The magistrates in the family proceedings court and each of the divisions of the High Court had precedent forms of order that were in regular use for paper and without notice orders that helpfully prompted the court to give reasons for the order on the face of the same. In future, that should be regarded as good practice in all family courts where written reasons or a judgment were not otherwise readily available. (3) The father's right to apply to set aside or vary the order was contained in r 18.11. It was an absolute right which had to be set out in a statement on the order in accordance with r 18.10(3). (4) A prohibited steps order was a statutory restriction on a parent's exercise of their parental responsibility for a child. It could have profound consequences. Once made, the terms of the Children Act 1989 s 8 did not allow parents to relax the prohibition by agreement. It could only be relaxed by the court. There was accordingly a high responsibility not to impose such a restriction without good cause and the reason had to be given. Further, where a prohibition was appropriate, consideration should always be given to the duration of that prohibition. Hence, the finite nature of an order had to be expressed on the face of the order. (5) When a court was concerned with a prohibited steps order it was an established principle that the court should engage itself with the welfare of the child concerned. On a without notice application there would of necessity be no evidence to contradict that which the applicant asserted and the court had to decide whether there was a prima facie case for the order. There had to be a persuasive case supported by evidence of objective fact, rather than expressions of suspicion or anxiety, that the respondent intended to exercise his parental responsibility in a manner which was likely to harm the child or otherwise be adverse to the child's welfare having regard to the factors described in s 1(3). The applicant had to give evidence of the alleged underlying facts and the sources of any information and belief that were relied on. (6) One of the six exclusive reasons for a without notice application, as set out in FPR PD 18A para 5.1, was that there was 'exceptional urgency'. There were ordinarily two bases for exceptional urgency: the imminence of the event to be prohibited, and hence usually of the risk of harm to the child, or the need to make an order about that event without alerting the respondent, namely where notice would arguably defeat the ends of justice. It was in the nature of due process that where exceptional urgency was relied on steps should be taken to notify a respondent informally and/or to give him short notice rather than no notice at all. (7) A more inquisitorial process might help those judges who needed to deal with very difficult cases involving litigants in person where emotions could run very high. At the hearing and given that it would have been clear whether the key issues included the need to make findings of fact, the judge could control the process to ensure that it was fair. Having been sworn, each party could be asked to set out their proposals and to confirm their version of the disputed key facts. They could then be asked by the judge what questions they would like to ask of the other party. Where lawyers were not instructed the judge could then assimilate the issues identified into his or her own questions and ask each party the questions that the judge thought were relevant to the key issues in the case. It might be appropriate to give the parties the opportunity to give a short reply. In that way the issues could be proportionately and fairly considered.

Re C (a child) [2013] EWCA Civ 1412, [2014] 1 FCR 239 (Court of Appeal: Sullivan, Ryder and Macur LJJ). *R (on the application of Casey) v Restormel BC* [2007] EWHC 2554 (Admin), [2007] All ER (D) 96 (Nov) applied. *Re S (a child) (Family Division: without notice orders)* [2001] 1 All ER 362 (2000 Abr para 2594) considered.

217 Fostering—foster carers—financial assistance—reduced payment for related carers—lawfulness of policy

The claimant was the foster mother of her two nephews and one niece. All three children were disabled and difficult to care for. The claimant was paid a certain sum in benefits every year in respect of her position as foster mother for the children. However, she was paid substantially less than the amount which she would have received if she were unrelated to the children. The claimant applied for judicial review of the policy and practice of the defendant local authority to pay family foster carers less money than unrelated foster carers. The judge concluded that the defendant's policy was unlawful to the extent that it discriminated on the grounds of the pre-existing relations with the child between family and unrelated family carers. On the defendant's appeal, *held*, on the facts, there was no doubt that the defendant had not complied with the statutory guidance which, when read as a whole, sought to ensure that allowances and fees paid to family foster carers should not be less than those paid to their unrelated colleagues. On any view, the claimant was being treated unequally, in particular in relation to fees, and the judge had been incontrovertibly right about that. A departure from the statutory guidance might be justified by cogent reasons objectively established as such through litigation, even if they had not been carefully considered at the time of departure. However, it was impossible to say that the judge had reached a wrong conclusion about the absence of cogent reasons. The statutory guidance had at its heart a policy that, in the absence of cogent reasons, there should be no differentials between family and unrelated foster carers. Accordingly, the appeal would be dismissed.

R (on the application of X) v Tower Hamlets LBC [2013] EWCA Civ 904, [2013] All ER (D) 276 (Jul) (Court of Appeal: Maurice Kay VP, Lewison and Gloster LJJ). Decision of Males J [2013] EWHC 480 (Admin), [2013] All ER (D) 102 (Mar) affirmed.

218 Fostering—fostering services—establishments and agencies—registration and inspection—England

See para 199 and para 165.

219 Her Majesty's Chief Inspector of Education, Children's Services and Skills—appointments

The Inspectors of Education, Children's Services and Skills (No 5) Order 2013, SI 2013/1448 (in force on 14 June 2013), appoints the specified persons as Her Majesty's Inspectors of Education, Children's and Skills.

220 Her Majesty's Chief Inspector of Education, Children's Services and Skills—fees and frequency of inspections

The Her Majesty's Chief Inspector of Education, Children's Services and Skills (Fees and Frequency of Inspections) (Children's Homes etc) (Amendment) Regulations 2013, SI 2013/523 (in force on 1 April 2013), further amend the 2007 Regulations, SI 2007/694, so as to (1) specify the annual fees that are paid under the Care Standards Act 2000, the Education and Inspections Act 2006 and the Children Act 1989 to Her Majesty's Chief Inspector of Education, Children's Services and Skills in respect of voluntary adoption agencies, adoption support agencies, children's homes, residential family centres, boarding schools, residential colleges, residential special schools and in respect of local authority fostering and adoption functions; and (2) remove the requirement that the chief inspector inspect premises used by local authorities in their performance of relevant functions at least once in every three year period. The 2013 Regulations also further amend the Children's Act 2004 (Children's Services) Regulations 2005, SI 2005/1972, so as to update the definition of 'children's services' following amendments to the Health and Social Care (Community Health Standards) Act 2003.

221 Local safeguarding children boards—review—England

The Local Safeguarding Children Boards (Review) Regulations 2013, SI 2013/2299 (in force on 9 October 2013), make provision for the review of local safeguarding children boards by Her Majesty's Chief Inspector of Education, Children's Services and Skills. The regulations (1) specify the functions of a board for the purposes of the Children Act 2004 s 15A; (2) provide that the Chief Inspector may conduct a review of any or all of the specified functions and must conduct a review at the request of the Secretary of State; (3) require the Chief Inspector to make a report of the review and to send it to the local authority with responsibility for establishing the board, the chair of the board, the board's partners, the relevant inspectorates for each of the board's partners, any other body represented on the board and the Secretary of State; (4) make provision about publication of the report by the board and the Chief Inspector; and (5) enable the Chief Inspector to request documents, interview specified individuals and attend meetings of the board, for the purposes of a review.

222 Parental responsibility order—termination—parent convicted of sexual offences

The claimant was the mother and the defendant the father and of a young boy. The defendant had parental responsibility for the child pursuant to the Children Act 1989 s 4. The defendant was charged with a series of sexual offences involving two of the claimant's other children, who had been born before the parties had met. The defendant pleaded guilty at trial and was sentenced to four years' imprisonment. The claimant filed an application for an order terminating the defendant's parental responsibility. The defendant then sought a specific issues order requiring the claimant to supply annual reports on the child's progress. In a psychological assessment, the defendant maintained that he was innocent of all the charges and that he had pleaded guilty only to spare the children the ordeal of giving evidence. However, the defendant later accepted that the convictions were justified and did not invite the court to reconsider them. Consideration was given to the defendant's right to a family life under the European Convention on Human Rights art 8. *Held*, because of his parentage, the child's position in the family was difficult, and there was a risk of his suffering further harm and stigma if he continued to be perceived and treated in any way as the son of the man who perpetrated acts of sexual abuse on his older siblings. The child had expressed a wish to have no involvement with his defendant. Although to a considerable extent that wish had been influenced by his claimant and siblings, it was rooted in the reality of his life. Moreover, were the defendant to retain parental responsibility, the claimant would be placed under very great strain, given the probability that the defendant would subsequently apply for contact, and that he would seek to be further involved in the child's life. In certain circumstances the principle that a child should have a relationship with each biological parent had to give way to more important considerations, and in particular the need for emotional security. Equally, while acknowledging that, as an aspect of their respective rights under art 8, both the child and the defendant had a family life together, that aspect was outweighed by the child's overriding need, as part of his art 8 rights, to security within his family. An order would therefore be made terminating the defendant's parental responsibility, and the application for the specific issues order would be denied. Judgment would be given accordingly.

CW v SG [2013] EWHC 854 (Fam), [2013] All ER (D) 117 (Apr) (Family Division: Baker J).

223   Paternity—determination—DNA testing—power of court—international child abduction proceedings

A child lived with her parents in Latvia. After the parents separated, the child resided mainly with her mother, but had frequent contact with the father. A dispute arose as to the contact arrangements and the father issued proceedings in Latvia. The mother took the child to the United Kingdom with the father's consent. The intention was that the father would later travel to the United Kingdom to collect the child and return with her to Latvia. However, the mother failed to contact the father and he issued child abduction proceedings in which the mother asserted, for the first time, that the father was not the child's biological father. An issue therefore arose as to whether the father had rights under Latvian law or the Hague Convention on the Civil Aspects of International Child Abduction 1980. The judge ordered a DNA test to be carried out on the father in order to determine the child's paternity. The father appealed, submitting that the order was premature, that the Latvian court had presupposed that he was the child's father and, unless and until that order was set aside, DNA testing was inappropriate. The mother submitted that the order had been sensible and was in any event a case management decision with which the court should not interfere. *Held*, DNA testing to establish paternity was a serious step for any court to take and should not be ordered unless it was necessary to enable a conclusion to be reached. If DNA testing was to be done at all, it should be done only as a last resort. A determination of paternity was best carried out in a welfare context and by the court of the child's habitual residence. Such a determination should be made only in the context of a Hague Convention application if it was clear that this was necessary for the purpose of a decision which the court had to make. The DNA testing was not a mere case management decision. If the father had a right of custody under Latvian law, or if, despite any conclusion of Latvian law, the father had a right of custody on the true construction of the Hague Convention, any question of DNA testing would have fallen away. However, if the court concluded that the father had no right of custody on which he could rely unless he was actually the child's biological father, then the question of DNA testing would have to be revisited. However, it should only be at that stage that any order should be made. Accordingly, the appeal would be allowed.

Re M (*abduction: paternity: DNA testing*) [2013] EWCA Civ 1131, [2014] 1 FLR 695, [2013] All ER (D) 148 (Sep) (Court of Appeal: Longmore, Underhill and Macur LJJ).

224   Protection of children—child involved in proceedings—identification—victim of cyberbullying

See *AB (by her litigation guardian CD) v Bragg Communications Inc*, para 425.

225   Protection of children—child's welfare—local authority inquiry—parental consent

The claimants were the parents of a child and were both experienced qualified social workers. An unsigned letter sent to the defendant local authority indicated that the writer, a neighbour, had concerns about the way in which the claimants' child was being treated. The defendant's response through its appropriately qualified officer was to purportedly start an inquiry under the Children Act 1989 s 47. It commenced an initial data-gathering exercise seeking information from the child's doctor and from her school. The only indication that such an inquiry had been taken was a letter sent to the claimants stating that the defendant was undertaking the investigation. The claimants sought judicial review of the decision of the defendant to undertake the s 47 inquiry into whether their child was suffering or was likely to suffer significant harm. *Held*, s 47 inquiries involved an in-depth child-centred assessment of a child's development needs, of the harm she was suffering or might suffer, of the capacity of the child's parents or carers to respond to the child's needs and of the family and environmental factors that were playing a role in the harm she was suffering or may suffer. For s 47 inquiries, three distinct phases of assessment were provided for, the screening assessment, the initial assessment and the core assessment. In the circumstances, a s 47 decision had not been taken and the defendant's insistence that one had been taken was erroneous and unlawful. It the defendant had succeeded in making a s 47 decision that decision would have been unlawful and should be set aside. Further, the initial data-gathering exercise was unlawful in that the initial request for data sent to the child's doctor was accompanied by erroneous information and in the absence of parental consent. Nor had the consent of the claimants been obtained before the school was approached. The claimants were entitled to a quashing order quashing the purported s 47 inquiry decision and to declarations that there never was a s 47 inquiry decision, that the initial assessment was terminated because the child was not at risk of significant harm and because it was highly likely that the anonymous referral was malicious. Further argument was needed on both the entitlement and amount of damages. Judgment would be given accordingly.

R (on the application of AB and CD) v Haringey LBC [2013] EWHC 416 (Admin), [2013] All ER (D) 212 (Mar) (Queen's Bench Division: Judge Anthony Thornton).

226   Protection of children—exchange of criminal conviction information

The Working with Children (Exchange of Criminal Conviction Information) (England and Wales and Northern Ireland) Regulations 2013, SI 2013/2945 (in force on 18 December 2013), implement European Parliament and Council Directive (EU) 2011/93 on combating the sexual abuse and sexual exploitation of children and child pornography by, in particular, (1) placing an obligation on a chief officer of a police force to comply with the information-sharing requirements of the directive; (2) requiring the Secretary of State to identify a chief officer of a police force to carry out those obligations; and (3) allowing that officer to request relevant information relating to disqualification from working with children from the Disclosure and Barring Service, which is in turn obliged to provide such information.

227   Protection of children—injunction to prevent identification—contra mundum injunction—child subject of care proceedings—father posting material on internet

A mother and father had four children, all of whom had been the subject of care proceedings. The father had posted material about all four children on the internet, including their names and photographs. The youngest child was made the subject of an emergency protection order on the day of birth. The father announced the birth on a social networking website and described social workers arriving to remove the child. He later posted on the site what the applicant local authority claimed was covert filming of the execution of the emergency protection order. The father and the mother were referred to by name. The father subsequently gave an undertaking to remove all the material posted on the internet and within his control that would identify any of the children as being or having been subject to care proceedings. Footage of the parents at court was later posted. The father was given a suspended prison sentence for breach of the undertaking and material about the youngest child remained on the internet. The applicant sought a contra mundum injunction restricting the publication or broadcasting of information in respect of the youngest child. The draft order prohibited the publishing or broadcasting of the names and addresses of the youngest child, the parents, the applicant and any employee of the applicant, as well as any picture, image, voice or video recording of the same, if such publication was likely to lead the identification of the youngest child as being a child subject to proceedings or who had been removed from the care of its parents. The principal issue was whether there was justification for extending the youngest child's anonymity beyond the point at which the Children Act 1989 s 97 ceased to have effect, namely once proceedings had come to an end. *Held*, the court had power both to relax and add to the 'automatic restraints' on the publication of information relating to proceedings under s 97 and the Administration of Justice Act 1960 s 12. In exercising that jurisdiction, the court had to conduct the balancing exercise described in the authorities. Although the court might, by an appropriate injunction, extend the anonymity of the youngest child beyond the point at which the 1989 Act s 97 ceased to have effect, the authorities expressed doubt as to the likely need for specific orders protecting a child's identity beyond the conclusion of the proceedings. Further, while it might likewise afford anonymity to other participants in the process, it was an established principle that such injunctions would not readily be granted. More generally, there was a compelling need for transparency in the family justice system as a matter of both principle and pragmatism. Furthermore, an injunction which could not otherwise be justified was not to be granted because of the manner or style in which the material was being presented on the internet or to spare the blushes of those being attached, however abusive and unjustified those attacks were. The only justification for an injunction was if restraint was necessary in order to protect the child's rights under the European Convention on Human Rights art 8 and, in particular, his privacy and anonymity. However, there was a crucial difference in this case, which was concerned with a one-day-old baby, although the same point would no doubt apply to somewhat older children, between restraining publication of the child's name and restraining publication of visual images of the child. Firstly, the reality was that, although anyone could identify a baby by its name, it was almost impossible, except for the parent, to distinguish between photographs of children of that age who had the same general appearance. Secondly, the reality, at least with current technology where searches of the internet were by word, in particular a name and not an image, was that unless one had a name, or a mass of other identifying details, it was going to be very difficult to locate anonymous postings about an individual. Thirdly, although there might be a powerful argument for asserting that the baby who featured in a filmed episode should not be named, there were at least as powerful arguments for asserting that the publication on the internet of film, commenting on the operation of the care system and conveying a no doubt powerful and disturbing message, should not be prevented merely because it included images of a baby. Assessing those three factors together, there was a very powerful argument that the balance between the public interest in discussing the workings of the system and the personal privacy and welfare interests of the child was best and most proportionately struck by restraining the naming of the child while not restraining the publication of images of the child. The effect was that (1) the essential vice, the identification of the child, was in large measure prevented; (2) internet searches were most unlikely to provide any meaningful 'link' in the searcher's mind with the particular child; and (3) the public debate was enabled to continue with the public having access to the footage albeit not knowing who the anonymous child was whose image was on view. Further, the naming of the applicant, the social workers, the applicant's legal representative or the children's guardian, or even all of them, in the draft order could not in any realistic way be said to make it likely that the youngest child would be identified, even indirectly. The risk was merely fanciful. If this was so, then inclusion of reference to those persons was likely to mislead. The casual reader might think that the order prohibited the naming of any of them. The more careful reader would realise that this was not so, but might nonetheless assume that the court thought that naming them might lead to the identification of the youngest child and might thus be deterred from doing so for fear of falling foul of the order. Either way, the effect was highly undesirable, tending to confer indirectly the very anonymity which the court had not intended. Accordingly, the application would be allowed and an injunction granted.

Re J (reporting restriction: internet: video) [2013] EWHC 2694 (Fam), [2014] 1 FLR 523, [2013] All ER (D) 45 (Sep) (Family Division: Sir James Munby P). *Re S (a child)* (*identification: restriction on publication*) [2004] UKHL 47, [2005] 1 AC 593, [2004] 4 All ER 683 (2004 Abr para 2258) applied. *R v Secretary of State for the Home Department, ex p Simms* [2000] 2 AC 115, [1999] 3 All ER 400 (1999 Abr para 2785); *Clayton v Clayton* [2006] EWCA Civ 878, [2007] 1 All ER 1197 (2006 Abr para 482); *A v Ward* [2010] EWHC 16 (Fam), [2010] All ER (D) 2 (Oct) (2010 Abr para 617); and *Re B (a child) (disclosure)* [2004] EWHC 411, [2004] 3 FCR 1 (2004 Abr para 418) considered.

228 Protection of children—privacy for children involved in proceedings—publication of information—reporting restriction order

A mother came to the United Kingdom with which she had no, or little, previous connection. She was on a short visit and was pregnant. Following a panic attack, she was detained pursuant to the Mental Health Act 1983 s 3. The relevant NHS trust made an urgent application to the Court of Protection. Having concluded that the mother lacked capacity to decide for herself, the judge authorised the performance of a Caesarean section and, if necessary and appropriate, the use of restraint. The child was born by Caesarean section. The relevant local authority began care proceedings. A judge granted an interim care order and authorised the authority to refuse contact with the mother in accordance with the Children Act 1989 s 34(4). The mother had some contact with the child who was placed in foster care. Prominent accounts of the case were published in two Sunday newspapers. An application was made by the authority seeking a reporting restriction order prohibiting publication of the child's name and date of birth and the names of the child's parents and any member of the mother's family and any pictures of the family if such publication was likely to lead to the identification of the child. It was decided that the circumstances were not such as to justify, having regard to the Human Rights Act 1998 s 12(2), the making of any order unless steps had first been taken by the authority to notify the media of the application. The application was renewed on notice. It fell to be determined whether and to what extent a reporting restriction order should be made. *Held*, the court had to conduct a balancing exercise, focusing on the comparative importance of the specific rights in play in the individual case and treating the child's interests, although not paramount, as a primary consideration. A number of competing interests, protected by the European Convention on Human Rights arts 6, 8, 10, were engaged. Three competing interests, in particular, had to be considered. The public had an interest in knowing and discussing what had been done in the case. Given the circumstances of the case and the extreme gravity of the issues which confronted the courts, it was hard to imagine a case which more obviously and compellingly required that public debate be free and unrestricted. The mother had an equally obvious and compelling claim to be allowed to tell her story to the world. The child also had an equally compelling claim to privacy and anonymity. Accordingly, an appropriate order would be made.

Re P (a child) [2013] EWHC 4048 (Fam), [2013] All ER (D) 188 (Dec) (Family Division: Sir James Munby P).

229 Protection of children—social work services—providers—regulation and registration—England

The Providers of Social Work Services (England) Regulations 2013, SI 2013/2668 (in force on 12 November 2013), make provision in relation to the regulation and registration of providers of social work services entering into arrangements with local authorities under the Children and Young Persons Act 2008 s 1. In particular, the regulations (1) disapply the Care Standards Act (Registration) (England) Regulations 2010, SI 2010/2130, in relation to registered providers of social work services; (2) make provision as to the fitness of registered providers, managers, employees and premises; (3) prescribe the information and documents which must be provided to Her Majesty's Chief Inspector of Education, Children's Services and Skills on an application for registration as a registered provider; (4) provide for the keeping of a register of providers of social work services and for certificates of registration; (5) make provision in relation to conditions and cancellations of registration; and (6) permit the electronic transmission of documents and information.

230 Residence order—best interests of child—habitual residence—jurisdiction of court

Following the break-up of her marriage, the mother removed the child, a United States citizen, and herself to the United Kingdom. She was ordered to return to the United States for the purpose of completing divorce proceedings. Following a welfare-based custody hearing, to which the mother raised no jurisdictional objections, the court decided that the it was in the child's best interests that the father should have the exclusive right to designate his primary residence. Therefore, the child lived with his father in the United States, save for vacations in England. Later, the child and the mother returned to England pursuant to an order under the Hague Convention on the Civil Aspects of International Child Abduction. In turn, the mother obtained a residence order in England on a summary basis. Soon after, the order under the Convention was vacated on appeal and the mother was ordered to return the child to his father in the United States and thereafter to comply with the terms of the original American order. Following breach of that order, the father issued proceedings in England, asserting that the mother's retention of the child was wrongful, as the child was still habitually resident in the United States when the mother's disobedience of the order had become wrongful. He alternatively contended that the English court should exercise its inherent jurisdiction to return the child, even if not required to do so under the terms of the Convention. The judge considered that he could not reasonably conclude that it would be in the child's best interests to leave the mother and England for the father and the United States. The Court of Appeal dismissed the father's appeal. On further appeal by the father, *held*, habitual residence was a question of fact which should not be glossed with legal concepts which would produce a different result from that which the factual inquiry would produce. The concept corresponded to the place which reflected some degree of interpretation by the child in a social and family environment. Further, it was clear that parental intent did play a part in establishing or changing the habitual residence of a child. That would have to be factored in, along with all the other relevant factors in deciding whether a move from one country to another had a sufficient degree of stability to amount to a change of habitual residence. In the circumstances, the child had become integrated in England. Looked at from his point of view, the judge had been entitled to find that the child had become habitually resident in England. Further, it was well established that the High Court had power to exercise its inherent jurisdiction in relation to children by virtue of the child's habitual residence or presence in the United Kingdom. However, the judge had asked himself the wrong question and the Court of Appeal had not addressed that essential point. That being the case, it fell to be determined whether it was in the child's best interests to remain in the United Kingdom so that the dispute between his parents was decided here or to return to the United States so that the dispute could be decided there. The crucial factor was that the child was a United States national who was being denied a proper opportunity to develop a relationship with his father and with his country of birth. While conflicting orders remained in place, he was effectively denied access to his country of origin. The best chance that the child had of developing a proper relationship with both parents was for the United States court to consider where his best interests lay in the long term. Therefore, an order for the return of the child to the United States would be made. Accordingly, the appeal would be allowed.

Re KL (a child) [2013] UKSC 75, [2014] 1 FCR 69, [2013] All ER (D) 24 (Dec) (Supreme Court: Lord Neuberger P, Lady Hale DP, Lord Wilson, Lord Hughes and Lord Hodge SCJJ). Case C-497/10PPU *Mercredi v Chaffe* [2012] Fam 22, ECJ, adopted. *Re J (a child)* (*return to foreign jurisdiction: convention rights*) [2005] UKHL 40, [2006] 1 AC 80, [2005] 3 All ER 291 (2004 Abr para 1454); and *Re A (children) (jurisdiction: return of child)* [2013] UKSC 60, [2013] All ER (D) 66 (Sep) (para 179) applied. Decision of Court of Appeal [2013] EWCA Civ 865, [2013] 3 FCR 69 reversed.

231   Residence order—removal of child from jurisdiction—welfare of child

A family moved to England from Spain when the father was offered a posting there by his employer. The family returned to Spain for a holiday. The parents' relationship subsequently broke down and the father returned to England ahead of the mother and the child. The mother only stayed in England for a few days before returning to Spain, leaving the child in England with the father. The parents each sought a residence order, the father seeking to have the child living with him in England and the mother seeking leave to remove the child from the jurisdiction and take him to live with her in Spain. The judge decided that he was entitled to look at the decision in *Payne v Payne* and thereafter embarked on the discipline approach identified in that decision, concluding that the mother's application had been genuinely concerned for the future of the child's welfare. The judge made a shared residence order in favour of both parents, but ordered that the mother had permission permanently to remove the child from the jurisdiction. The father appealed, contending that the judge did not consider the importance of the child's status quo and erred in applying the decision in *Payne v Payne* because the applicant seeking removal from the jurisdiction, the mother, had not been the primary carer and, by doing so, the judge had approached the case with a presumption in favour of the mother. *Held*, although the present case had not been one where the application was being made by the primary carer, the judge had been entitled to have regard to the discipline approach as set out in *Payne v Payne*. The judge correctly appreciated that the case had to be decided by reference to the child's best interests and he had carefully taken into account the child's current circumstances in England, the quality of his father's care for him and the father's own plans, wishes and feelings. There was nothing which suggested that the judge had started off with any presumption in favour of the mother's claim. The judge had taken into account and given appropriate weight to each of the factors to which the father had drawn attention. He acknowledged that the father was the primary carer and recognised the importance the father was attaching to the argument based on the status quo. He had given appropriate weight to both points, while correctly appreciating that neither could be decisive. There was no sustainable basis for any complaint that the judge had either taken into account irrelevant factors or failed to take into account any relevant factors. Nor was there any sustainable basis for complaint that the judge erred either in the weight he had chosen to attach to the various factors he had to take into account or his evaluative decision as to where the ultimate balance had fallen. Accordingly, the appeal would be dismissed.

Re F (a child) (permission to relocate) [2012] EWCA Civ 1364, [2012] 3 FCR 443 (Court of Appeal: Pill, Toulson and Munby LJJ). *Payne v Payne* [2001] EWCA Civ 166, [2001] Fam 473, [2001] FCR 425 (2001 Abr para 486) considered.

232 Residential family centres—England

The Residential Family Centres (Amendment) Regulations 2013, SI 2013/499 (in force on 1 April 2013), further amend the 2002 Regulations, SI 2002/3213, by (1) changing references to a 'general practitioner'; (2) clarifying that an establishment which provides accommodation and services to families but whose principal purpose is not the assessment or monitoring of parenting capacity is not a residential family centre; (3) prescribing the information which registered persons must include in the centre's resident's guide, and providing that the guide must also be supplied to persons who are not residents but in respect of whom accommodation in the centre is being considered; (4) clarifying that registered persons must ensure that the centre is conducted in a way which promotes and makes provision for the physical, mental and emotional health of the residents; (5) ensuring that the placement plan drawn up by centres includes an assessment of the risks which a resident may present; (6) requiring centres to ensure that assessments or monitoring of parenting capacity are carried out by suitably qualified persons and in accordance with appropriate and generally recognised methods of assessment; (7) providing that conclusions or recommendations must be made as a result of the assessment and they must be objective and accessible to the persons who will need to consider them; (8) setting out the registered person's duties with regards to the premises and accommodation; (9) clarifying that records maintained in the centre, including records made in relation to the centre's complaints procedure, may be kept in electronic form; (10) providing that monitoring devices must be used in the centre only for the purpose of safeguarding the residents' welfare or for the assessment or monitoring of parenting capacity; (11) providing that the use of monitoring devices must be no more intrusive than necessary and residents must be informed in advance of the intention to use them; (12) providing that, if the devices are to be used for the purpose of assessing a resident's parenting capacity, the resident being assessed must consent to their use and it must be provided for in the placement plan; (13) requiring the centre's system for reviewing and improving care to take into account the views of the persons working at the centre about matters relating to the conduct of the centre; (14) removing the requirement for the registered provider to inspect the centre's daily log of events during the provider's visit to the centre; (15) omitting provision making that made it a criminal offence to contravene or fail to comply with the requirements; (16) ensuring that the centre's statement of purpose includes details of the types of assessment or monitoring which will be used in the centre and a description of any electronic or mechanical means of surveillance; (17) requiring information resulting from the assessment or monitoring of parenting capacity to be included in the centre's case records; and (18) removing the requirement that a daily log of events at the centre must be maintained.

233   Secure accommodation—Wales

The Children (Secure Accommodation) (Amendment) (Wales) Regulations 2013, SI 2013/663 (in force on 18 April 2013), which apply in relation to Wales only, further amend the 1991 Regulations, SI 1991/1505, so as to provide that the modified criteria set out in reg 6(2) will continue to apply to children who are aged 12 or over but who are under the age of 17 who have been detained by the police under the Police and Criminal Evidence Act 1984 s 38(6).

234   Youth conditional cautions—code of practice

The Crime and Disorder Act 1998 (Youth Conditional Cautions: Code of Practice) Order 2013, SI 2013/613 (in force on 8 April 2013), brings into force a revised code of practice in relation to youth conditional cautions. SI 2010/127 is revoked.

235   Youth conditional cautions—financial penalties—maximum amount

The Crime and Disorder Act 1998 (Youth Conditional Cautions: Financial Penalties) Order 2013, SI 2013/608 (in force on 8 April 2013), (1) prescribes the descriptions of offences in respect of which, where a youth conditional caution is given, a condition may be attached which requires the offender to pay a financial penalty; (2) sets (a) different maximum amounts of penalty that the offender may be required to pay, depending on the description of offence; and (b) different maximum penalty amounts depending on the age of the offender at the time the youth conditional caution is given. SI 2009/2781 is revoked.

CHOSES IN ACTION

Halsbury's Laws of England (5th edn) vol 13 (2009) paras 1–200

Articles

For articles relating to this title please refer to the Table of Articles at the beginning of the Abridgment.

236   Assignment—right of action—right to appeal against tax assessment—company in liquidation

The claimant was the liquidator of a company. The defendants were the former directors of the company, which had sold its business and assets. The claimant commenced proceedings seeking recovery of a sum paid to the defendants for their shares in the company, in respect of payments which, the claimant maintained, the defendants had not proved were lawfully and properly authorised by them in accordance with their duties owed to the company. The Commissioners for Her Majesty's Revenue and Customs raised assessments of the company's corporation tax liability resulting from the company's sale of its assets. At the request of the defendants, the claimant caused the company to serve a notice of appeal against the assessments, although he made it clear that he did not have the means to finance the appeals and that he had doubts as to their merit. Following a request by the defendants that the claimant assign the appeals to them, the claimant sought directions on whether he had power to do so and, if so, whether it ought to be exercised. *Held*, the classical definition of a chose in action was that it described 'all personal rights of property which could only be claimed or enforced by action and not by taking physical possession'. A bare right to appeal against what would otherwise be a liability did not satisfy that definition. The authorities maintained a distinction between a chose and the remedies available for its enforcement. The right to a remedy was an incident of the ownership of the chose. It was not something that was capable of being sold or assigned separately from the right to which it related. The right of appeal was a right conferred on the company by statute by reason of it having been assessed to tax. The liability to which the bare right to appeal was appurtenant could not on conventional analysis be assigned. All that could be assigned would be the right to appeal. That analysis was entirely consistent with the orthodox approach to whether a bankrupt had locus to appeal. A bare right to appeal was not property for the purposes of the Insolvency Act 1986 s 436. Therefore, it was not open to the claimant to assign the company's right to appeal against the tax assessments to which it had become subject. Judgment would be given accordingly.

Re GP Aviation Group International (in liquidation) Ltd; Williams v Glover [2013] EWHC 1447 (Ch), [2013] BPIR 576, [2013] All ER (D) 41 (Jun) (Chancery Division: Judge Pelling QC). Torkington v Magee [1902] 2 KB 427, DC; and Heath v Tang; Stevens v Peacock [1993] 4 All ER 694, CA (1993 Abr para 186), applied. Ruttle Plant Hire Ltd v Secretary of State for the Environment and Rural Affairs [2007] EWHC 2870 (TCC), [2008] 2 All ER (Comm) 264 (2007 Abr para 642) considered.

CIVIL PROCEDURE

Halsbury's Laws of England (5th edn) vol 11 (2009) paras 1–1108, vol 12 (2009) paras 1109–1836

Articles

For articles relating to this title please refer to the Table of Articles at the beginning of the Abridgment.

237   Abuse of process—striking out—discretion of court—claim with real prospect of success

The defendant had been held liable to the claimant in relation to a fraudulent operation of letters of credit. A receiver was appointed as receiver of the receivership assets which included the assets of two English companies which held shares in a French company. In proceedings against the claimant and the receiver, the defendant claimed that he had suffered loss as a result of the liquidation of the French company in which he had a shareholding via the two English companies in which he owned shares. He contended that, as he was the beneficial owner of the two English companies, he was interested in the French company. Included in the claim was an allegation that he had made a substantial loss in respect of capital and interests in the French company. The claimant and the receiver applied to strike out the defendant's claim. Held, it was settled law that, where a company suffered loss caused by a breach of duty owed to it, only the company might sue in respect of that loss. No action lay at the suit of a shareholder suing only in that capacity to make good a diminution in the value of the shareholder's shareholding where that merely reflected the loss suffered by the company. A claim would not lie by a shareholder to make good a loss which would be made good if the company's assets were replenished through action against the party responsible for the loss, even if the company, acting through its constitutional organs, had declined or failed to make good that loss. The defendant's claims against the claimant would be struck out pursuant to CPR 3.4. It was a matter for the court's discretion whether to grant permission to bring a claim against a receiver. The defendant had failed to demonstrate any genuine claim that the receiver had acted in breach of duty or that the defendant had any real prospect of establishing such a claim. The claim was not a genuine one and had no real prospect of success. Accordingly, the claims against the receiver would be struck out pursuant to CPR 3.4.

Barclays Pharmaceuticals Ltd v Waypharm LP [2013] EWHC 503 (Comm), [2013] All ER (D) 131 (Mar) (Queen's Bench Division: Gloster J). Medforth v Blake [2000] Ch 86, [1999] 3 All ER 97, CA (1999 Abr para 2377); and Silven Properties Ltd v Royal Bank of Scotland plc [2003] EWCA Civ 1409, [2004] 4 All ER 484 (2004 Abr para 2007) applied. Johnson v Gore Wood & Co (a firm) [2002] 2 AC 1, [2001] 1 All ER 481, HL (2000 Abr para 2543); Burgess v Auger; Burgess v Vanstock Ltd [1998] 2 BCLC 478; and McGowan v Chadwick [2001] All ER (D) 109 (Dec) considered.

238   Adjournment—application—refusal—decision of First-tier Tribunal

The taxpayer had applied to the First-tier Tribunal ('FTT') for an adjournment of an appeal hearing. A medical certificate was sent to the FTT by a chartered accountant who had represented the taxpayer at various times. Soon after, the FTT made an unless direction that unless a signed medical certificate with details of the taxpayer's incapacity and explaining when he would be fit to attend a tribunal hearing was received, the hearing would go ahead.

In turn, the FTT received a signed version of the previously unsigned certificate. The judge decided not to adjourn the hearing. That same day, the chartered accountant emailed the FTT giving details of the state of the taxpayer's health. Another email stated that the taxpayer had visited his doctor's surgery and that the surgery had confirmed that an email and a letter had been sent and that the taxpayer's doctor had been ill and unable to sign the original medical certificate. Later, the FTT decided to proceed despite the absence of the taxpayer or any representative on his behalf, and despite the earlier application for an adjournment. At the hearing, the FTT reserved its decision on the question of whether to adjourn and went on to hear and consider the evidence. Subsequently, the FTT released a decision which announced its conclusion that the right course to have adopted had been to proceed with the hearing, and also set out its decision on the substantive appeal. Normally the FTT would grant an adjournment on health grounds, however, it had concluded that it should not follow its normal practice. The taxpayer had failed to provide any medical opinion as to when he might be fit to attend a hearing of the appeal, and that raised a real prospect of indefinite adjournments and an infinitely postponed disposition of the appeal. On appeal by the taxpayer, *held*, the evidence before the FTT had not permitted it to conclude that the taxpayer and the chartered accountant had known that the unless direction had not been complied with. However, neither had the evidence compelled the FTT to conclude that the taxpayer or the chartered accountant had thought that the unless direction had been complied with. The FTT's comment that the taxpayer had 'failed to provide any medical opinion as to when he might be fit to attend' was accurate although the FTT had given no consideration to the ability of the taxpayer to understand or ensure compliance with the unless direction. If the FTT had restricted itself to balancing the undoubted prejudice the taxpayer would suffer if the appeal went ahead against the possibility of uncertain delay if it postponed the appeal, the decision it reached could not have been regarded as unreasonable. The FTT had been entitled to reach a balance which favoured proceedings. However, whether the taxpayer would be pleased by an adjournment was not relevant in assessing the balance of prejudice it might cause. Those considerations had been either irrelevant or could not have led to a reasonable doubt over the state of the taxpayer's health as expressed in the medical certificate. Those doubts had been an irrelevant consideration. Therefore, the FTT had taken into consideration a materially irrelevant factor. The decision would be set aside. Accordingly, the appeal would be allowed.

Wright v Revenue and Customs Comrs [2013] UKUT 0481 (TCC), [2013] All ER (D) 73 (Dec) (Upper Tribunal: Judge Charles Hellier and Judge Jill Gort).

239 Admission of liability—withdrawal of admission—arguable defence to claim

The claimant was employed by the defendant football club as club manager. The terms of his contract of employment were contained in a service agreement signed on behalf of the defendant by its managing director. The agreement provided that it would continue for a fixed term. However, the defendant terminated the claimant's employment shortly after the agreement was signed. The claimant sought a sum due to him under the agreement which provided for compensation in the event of early termination. The defendant admitted liability to pay the sum claimed, but later applied to withdraw its admission pursuant to CPR 14.1(5). It fell to be determined whether it was at least realistically arguable that the compensation clause was a penalty and as such unenforceable beyond the sum that represented the claimant's actual loss; and that the managing director did not have authority to enter into the agreement on the defendant's behalf. *Held*, the correct way of approaching such an application was to begin by asking whether the defendant demonstrated that, if permitted to withdraw its admission, it would have a realistically arguable defence. If it did not, it was not necessary to consider other factors because a summary judgment application was bound to succeed if permission to withdraw the admission was granted and no useful purpose would be served by giving permission. The contention that the compensation clause was a penalty was not realistically arguable. Under the agreement, the termination of the claimant's employment prior to the expiry of the fixed term did not constitute a breach of contract on which a sum of money became payable by the defendant to the claimant. Payment became due on the occurrence of an event other than a breach of contract. In such circumstances, the law relating to penalty clauses was not engaged and the defendant's contention to the contrary was not arguable. Further, the defendant's case that the managing director did not have authority to sign the agreement was also unarguable. Accordingly, the application would be dismissed.

Berg v Blackburn Rovers Football Club & Athletic plc [2013] EWHC 1070 (Ch), [2013] IRLR 537 (Chancery Division: Judge Pelling QC).

240 Appeal—grounds of appeal—findings of fact—erroneous finding—serious irregularity

An action by an employer alleging the wrongful extraction, retention and use of confidential customer information by an employee was dismissed. The judge handed down her written judgment without the prior confidential circulation of a draft judgment to counsel for consideration of typing corrections and obvious errors in writing. The judge subsequently declined to make an amendment to the judgment to correct a finding that the key documents relied on by the employer had not contained the confidential information in question. The judge refused permission to appeal on the ground that the judgment was fact-based but stated that her refusal of permission was 'despite a finding which was plainly wrong at the start of the judgment'. She did not accept that the finding was the result of a typographical error capable of correction by her and explained that 'the inferences which the claimant asked the court to draw could not be drawn from the facts found'. The employer was subsequently granted permission to appeal. It fell to be determined whether the appeal ought to be allowed pursuant to CPR 52.11(3) on the basis that the judge's decision in dismissing the action had been unjust because of a serious procedural error or other irregularity in the proceedings in the lower court. *Held*, the uncorrected sentence in the judgment indicated that the judge might have proceeded on a mistaken view of the contents of the employer's confidential customer documents. That mistake was material because it was not possible to say, with sufficient confidence to uphold the judgment, that the judge's findings and conclusions on other issues in the case would probably have been the same, even if she had not made that mistake. The retention of the erroneous finding could properly be described as an 'irregularity in the proceedings' which made the decision an unjust one. The matter would be remitted to the High Court to be retried by a different judge. Accordingly, the appeal would be allowed.

Space Airconditioning plc v Guy [2012] EWCA Civ 1664, [2013] 1 WLR 1293, [2012] All ER (D) 149 (Dec) (Court of Appeal: Mummery, Rimer and Sullivan LJJ). Decision of Proudman J [2011] EWHC 2107 (Ch), [2011] All ER (D) 04 (Aug) reversed.

241 Case management—allocation to particular track—likely level of damages—copyright infringement

See *Sheldon v Daybrook House Promotions Ltd*, para 579.

242 Case management—disclosure—ability of party to conduct litigation

A large number of claimants brought proceedings against the defendant and other companies alleging that they had been supplied with faulty breast implants. Evidence indicated that the defendant's parent company was technically insolvent. The defendant had guaranteed the liability of its parent by a loan. Questions were raised as to the liquidity of the defendant. There were concerns that, if the claimants obtained judgment against it, the defendant would not be able to pay the sums owed. The claimants therefore applied for a direction as to whether the defendant had sufficient insurance (1) to fund its participation in the litigation to the end of the trial; (2) to meet any order for damages; and (3) to meet any order for costs. An issue arose as to whether the court could order the defendant to give answers to those questions pursuant to CPR 3.1(2)(m). *Held*, CPR 3.1(2)(m) was a case management rule. Whether the claimants would be able to enforce judgment was not a matter that would affect case management. Therefore, it would not be appropriate to make any order requiring the defendant to provide the answers to the questions under heads (1) and (2). However, CPR 3.1(2) gave the court the power to order the defendant to provide a witness statement setting out whether it had adequate insurance to fund its participation in the litigation to the completion of the trial and the conclusion of any appeal. That knowledge would allow the litigation to be managed on the basis of adequate information. That would be in accordance with the overriding objective, would give no unfair advantage to the claimants, and no prejudice to the defendant. Judgment would be given accordingly.

X Y Z v Various [2013] EWHC 3643 (QB), [2013] All ER (D) 278 (Nov) (Queen's Bench Division: Thirlwall J).

243   Case management—relief from sanctions—failure to comply with unless order—failure to disclose assets

CPR 3.9 provides that on an application for relief from any sanction imposed for a failure to comply with any rule, practice direction or court order the court will consider all the circumstances of the case so as to enable it to deal justly with the application, including the need for litigation to be conducted efficiently and at proportionate cost, and to enforce compliance with rules, practice directions and orders.

A dispute arose between the claimant and defendants relating to a number of commercial property transactions. The claimant obtained an unless order requiring the defendants to disclose their assets and liabilities by a specified date. Following the defendants' failure to comply with their disclosure obligations by the specified date the court acceded to an application by the claimant for an order striking out the defendants' defence and counterclaim. The defendants made an application under CPR 3.9 for relief from the sanctions imposed on the basis that the disclosure requirements had now been complied with, the delay was in part due to the wide-ranging nature of the disclosure sought and their failure to comply with the unless order was in part due to their reliance on their former solicitors. *Held*, while the new CPR 3.9 did not require the judge to go through the items listed in the old CPR 3.9, the matters contained in those items remained of relevance to an application for relief from sanction. In exercising its discretion to decide the consequence of non-compliance with an unless order, the court was not fettered by any binding principle that the default, whether an act or omission, of a litigant's solicitor should be visited on the litigant himself. What was required for relief from sanction under the new CPR 3.9 was either some material change in circumstances between the date of the making of the unless order and the hearing of the application for relief or some good reason to excuse continued non-compliance. What constituted disclosure to the best of one's ability had to be determined by assessing the particular position and difficulties in which the defendant was placed at the time when he was required to comply with the order. In the circumstances in which the court had imposed wide-ranging disclosure obligations the defendants had been justified in relying on their solicitors to ensure that they had complied with those orders. On the facts, the extent of the non-disclosure was de minimis and a finding that the defendants had failed to comply with their disclosure obligations was not justified. The interests of justice in the present case dictated that the defendants should be granted relief from sanction. Accordingly, the application would be allowed.

Thevarajah v Riordan [2013] EWHC 3179 (Ch), [2013] All ER (D) 239 (Oct) (Chancery Division: Andrew Sutcliffe QC).

244   Case management—relief from sanctions—failure to comply with unless order—failure to submit costs schedule

During the course of personal injury proceedings issued by the claimant against the defendant company, the parties were required pursuant to CPR 26.3(6) to file and serve an allocation questionnaire. The claimant's solicitor missed that deadline, and subsequently submitted an incomplete questionnaire. The defendant complained to the court, which ordered the claimant's solicitor to file and serve the missing costs schedule by a specified date. It was not served by that time and, six weeks later, the court, of its own motion and without giving the claimant an opportunity to make representations, made an order that, unless the costs schedule was filed and served within the next two weeks, the claim would be struck out. The solicitor again failed to submit the schedule in time, and in due course the claim was struck out. Pursuant to CPR 3.9, the claimant applied for relief from that sanction, including the costs schedule and a supporting witness statement in the application. The deputy district judge refused relief, finding that, although the default had not been intentional, the delay had been entirely attributable to the claimant. On the claimant's appeal against that decision, the judge ruled that the deputy district judge had erred in his assessment of the CPR 3.9 factors, and in particular had failed to give due regard to the value of the claim, the fact that the claimant had not breached the court order deliberately, and the fact that the breach of the order had not in itself caused substantial delay. The judge allowed the appeal and the defendant appealed against that decision. *Held*, the judge had been entitled to rule that the deputy district judge had fallen into error and therefore that he had had to exercise his discretion afresh. The decision of the court to make an unless order of its own motion without giving the claimant the opportunity to be heard or even to make written representations created a powerful argument for the grant of relief. On a consideration of CPR 3.9, there had been sound reasons why relief should have been granted and no very strong reason why it should have been refused. Although there were several points of criticism of the claimant's conduct of the claim, those criticisms, even when considered collectively, had not amounted to the kind of conduct which justified striking out an action when its overall effects on the action were considered together with the severe prejudicial effect on the claimant of the refusal of relief. Accordingly, the appeal would be dismissed.

Beever v Ryder plc [2012] EWCA Civ 1737, [2013] 2 Costs LO 364, [2012] All ER (D) 249 (Dec) (Court of Appeal: Etherton and Janet Smith LJJ).

245   Case management—relief from sanctions—failure to comply with unless order—failure to submit witness statements

CPR 3.9(1) provides that on an application for relief from any sanction imposed for a failure to comply with any rule, practice direction or court order, the court will consider all the circumstances of the case, so as to enable it to deal justly with the application, including the need for litigation to be conducted efficiently and at proportionate cost, and to enforce compliance with rules, practice directions and orders. An application for relief must be supported by evidence: CPR 3.9(2).

The first defendant had acted as the claimant's solicitor for a number of years. The claimant sold his business. The proceeds of sale were retained by the first defendant who alleged that he was a partner in the business and entitled to 50 per cent of those proceeds. The claimant brought a claim against the defendant seeking to set aside two deeds of trust on the grounds of fraudulent misrepresentation and an order for payment of the proceeds of sale. The claimant's then solicitor allegedly held back witness statements that could have been served as 'some form of tactic' until seven days before the anticipated start of the trial. An order was made striking out the claim for failure to comply with an unless order to serve witness statements and to give disclosure. The claimant instructed new solicitors and applied for relief from sanctions. *Held*, in a case of non-compliance with an unless order a party was required to show a material change of circumstances in order to obtain relief from sanctions under CPR 3.9 as amended. Although the checklist of relevant considerations in the unamended CPR 3.9 had been removed, they nonetheless represented matters which continued to be relevant as considerations for the court in making the overall assessment required by the terms of the amended rule. It was settled law that the court should be less ready to grant relief under the amended rule and that in order to do so the court had to be fully satisfied that relief from sanctions was appropriate and just in the particular case, and that the court would be slow to draw such a conclusion. In the present case, CPR 3.9 applied. It was highly relevant that the claimant was not yet in a position to correct the default that led to the striking out order. As far as witness statements were concerned, there was nothing in the evidence itself to say that the claimant was ready to serve the witness statements. Focusing on the overall justice of the application, the case was one in which the conduct of the case by the claimant's then solicitor was very seriously inefficient. He had failed to comply with the district judge's order, failed to seek an extension of time, got himself in a position, both at the pre-trial review and subsequently, that the trial listed either could not proceed at all or would be ineffective so far as the claimant's case was concerned because he was unable to lead any witness evidence and had not made proper disclosure of documents such as would allow the trial to be conducted fairly. In all the circumstances, the right order was to refuse the claimant relief from sanctions and that, if he were to maintain the position that he sought to advance in the claim, he should start again having paid the costs of the action and the costs of the application with fresh proceedings based on the form of relief that he sought to pursue to trial and in circumstances where he would be freshly advised and able to focus on that litigation with a clean start. Accordingly, the application would be dismissed.

Michael v Middleton [2013] All ER (D) 124 (Oct) (Chancery Division: Judge David Cooke). *Fred Perry (Holdings) Ltd v Brands Plaza Trading Ltd* [2012] EWCA Civ 224, [2012] All ER (D) 77 (Jun); and *Tarn Insurance Services Ltd (in administration) v Kirby* [2009] EWCA Civ 19, [2009] All ER (D) 211 (Jan) (2009 Abr para 572) considered.

246   Case management—relief from sanctions—failure to file costs budget—guidance

CPR 3.9(1) provides that on an application for relief from any sanction imposed for a failure to comply with any rule, practice direction or court order, the court will consider all the circumstances of the case, so as to enable it to deal with the application, including the need for litigation to be conducted efficiently and at proportionate cost and to enforce compliance with the rules, practice directions and orders.

The claimant issued proceedings against the defendant alleging defamation. The proceedings were subject to *Practice Direction-Defamation Proceedings Cost Management Scheme* PD 51D, which provided that the parties had to exchange and lodge their costs budget not less than seven days before the date of the hearing for which the costs budget was required. It was not until the day before the case management and costs budget hearing that the claimant filed his costs budget. As a result, at the hearing, the master stated that there was insufficient time to consider the claimant's budget. Solicitors acting for the claimant informed the master that the reason why the budget had not been filed until the previous day was due to pressure of litigation elsewhere in the firm. The master found that there was a mandatory sanction that, where a party failed to file a costs budget within seven days prior to the date of the first hearing, the party was deemed to have filed a budget that was limited to court fees. In turn, the claimant applied for relief under CPR 3.9, submitting that the defendant had suffered no prejudice as a result of the claimant's defaults and that, if relief was refused, the defendant would receive a windfall in the form of costs protection. It was found that the new overriding objective and wording in CPR 3.9 highlighted the emphasis to be placed on rule compliance. Therefore, the master found that, applying the stricter approach to CPR 3.9, the application for relief from the sanction imposed in her earlier decision would be dismissed. The claimant appealed. *Held*, the obligations in CPR 3.9 had to be regarded as of paramount importance and given great weight. In practice, it would usually be appropriate to start by considering the nature of the non-compliance with the relevant rule, practice direction or court order. If that could properly be regarded as trivial, the court would usually grant relief provided that an application was made promptly. If the non-compliance could not be characterised as trivial, then the burden was on the defaulting party to persuade the court to grant relief. The court would want to consider why the default occurred. If there was a good reason for it, the court would be likely to decide that relief should be granted. The need to comply with rules, practice directions and court orders was essential if litigation was to be conducted in an efficient manner. If departures were tolerated, then the relaxed approach to civil litigation would continue. In the circumstances, the master had not misdirected herself in any material respect, nor did she reach a conclusion that had not been open to her. The decision had been robust. The defaults by the claimant had not been minor or trivial and there was no good excuse for them. They had resulted in an abortive costs budgeting hearing and an adjournment which had serious consequences for other litigants. Accordingly, the appeal would be dismissed.

Mitchell v News Group Newspapers Ltd [2013] EWCA Civ 1537, [2014] 1 WLR 795, [2013] All ER (D) 314 (Nov) (Court of Appeal: Lord Dyson MR, Richards and Elias LJJ).

247   Case management—relief from sanctions—failure to file witness statements

The claimant brought civil proceedings against the defendant constabulary after being acquitted of a public order offence. Following a number of hearings, a judge gave directions for the exchange of witness statements by a specified date. The defendant failed to comply with the direction, and the claimant did not agree to an extension. The judge then made an order requiring the defendant to serve any witness statements by a given date, which was the only evidence on which it would be entitled to rely at the hearing. The defendant's solicitor sent to the claimant the statements of two police officers shortly after that deadline. Two months later, the solicitor applied to the court for relief from sanction to allow the defendant to rely on witness evidence in the claim. The following month, the defendant made a further application for relief from sanction so as to allow two more officers to be called as witnesses. In determining the two applications for relief from sanctions, the trial judge ruled that, despite the requirement under CPR 3.9 to enforce compliance with rules, practice directions and orders, there was a public interest in the court scrutinising the actions of police officers when it had heard all of the evidence from both sides. It was that factor in particular which persuaded the judge to grant relief from sanctions sought and permitted the defendant's witnesses to give evidence in the case. The judge also allowed the defendant's subsequent application for an adjournment, to a date to be fixed. The claimant appealed, submitting that the recent decision in *Mitchell v News Group Newspapers Ltd* indicated that a stricter line was to be taken by the court in enforcing case management decisions of the court. *Held*, it was vital that decisions under CPR 3.9 that failed to follow the robust approach laid down in *Mitchell* should not be allowed to stand. Failure to follow that approach constituted an error of principle entitling an appeal court to interfere with the discretionary decision of the first instance judge. It was likely also to lead to a decision that was plainly wrong, justifying intervention on that basis too. There was no doubt that the judge in the present case had erred in principle and reached a decision that was plainly wrong. Firstly, the judge had not had sufficiently in mind that the sanction imposed by the first order had been itself a proportionate sanction which complied with the overriding objective. Secondly, although the judge had purported to proceed on the basis that a much stronger and less tolerant approach was required under the new CPR 3.9 towards failures to comply with time limits, it was evidence that he had not approached the exercise with the focus or degree of toughness called for by the guidance in *Mitchell*. In the result, he had granted relief from sanction in circumstances which could not be justified on any proper application of CPR 3.9. It followed that relief from sanction should be refused in respect of the witness statements. Accordingly, the appeal would be allowed.

Durrant v Chief Constable of Avon and Somerset Constabulary [2013] EWCA Civ 1624, [2013] All ER (D) 186 (Dec) (Court of Appeal: Richards, Lewison and Coleridge LJJ). *Mitchell v News Group Newspapers Ltd* [2013] EWCA Civ 1537, [2013] All ER (D) 314 (Nov) (para 246) applied.

248   Case management—relief from sanctions—failure to provide security for costs

The defendants were alleged to have combined to make a false denunciation to the Romanian authorities with the intention of inflicting harm on the business of the claimant. A judge dismissed an application by the defendants for summary judgment and gave directions on disclosure. The claimant was ordered to provide security up to and including the exchange of disclosure lists. Security was to be provided within 28 days. However, security was not provided within that period and no application was made by the claimant for further time before the period ordered expired. Soon after, the first and second defendants applied for an order striking out the claim against them because security had not been provided. The judge declined to strike out the claim but ordered that, in the event of the claimant failing to comply with the order for security within an extended period allowed, the claim would be automatically struck out without the need for further order. Security was not provided within the extended period allowed. On the day of the expiry of that period, the claimant applied for an extension of time in which to provide security, under CPR 3.1(2), and for relief from sanctions, under CPR 3.9(1). At the time of the application the security ordered had still not been provided. *Held*, if security was ordered and not given, the Admiralty and Commercial Court Guide made it clear that in the Commercial Court the practice was ultimately to dismiss the case. It was settled that the starting point was to consider the nature of the non-compliance with the relevant rule, practice direction or court order. If the non-compliance could not be characterised as trivial, then the burden was on the defaulting party to persuade the court to grant relief. The court would want to consider why the default occurred. If there was a good reason for it, the court would be likely to decide that relief should be granted. Later developments in the course of the litigation process were likely to be a good reason if they showed that the period for compliance originally imposed was unreasonable. Good reasons were likely to arise from circumstances outside the control of the party in default. On an application for relief from a sanction, a submission that the sanction should not have been imposed in the first place would be misguided. The starting point should be that the sanction had been properly imposed and complied with the overriding objective. An application for relief from a sanction presupposed that the sanction had, in principle, been properly imposed. If a party wished to contend that it was not appropriate to make the order that should be by way of appeal, or exceptionally, by asking the court which imposed the order to vary or revoke it under CPR 3.1(7). In the circumstances, the extension of time sought and the relief from the sanction ordered by the judge would be refused. Overall, taking account of all the circumstances of the case, so as to deal justly with the application, and including the need for litigation to be conducted efficiently and to enforce compliance with orders, it was not an appropriate case in which to extend time further or grant relief from the sanction. Accordingly, the application would be dismissed.

SC DG Petrol SRL v Vitol Broking Ltd [2013] EWHC 3920 (Comm), [2013] All ER (D) 117 (Dec) (Queen's Bench Division: Robin Knowles QC). Mitchell v News Group Newspapers Ltd [2013] EWCA Civ 1537, [2013] All ER (D) 314 (Nov) (para 246) applied.

249   Cause of action estoppel—res judicata—patent infringement—ruling of European Patent Office

See Virgin Atlantic Airways Ltd v Zodiac Seats UK Ltd (formerly Contour Aerospace Ltd), para 1931.

250   Charging order—orders for sale—financial thresholds

The Charging Orders (Orders for Sale: Financial Thresholds) Regulations 2013, SI 2013/491 (in force on 6 April 2013), set a financial threshold of £1,000 for orders for sale to enforce a charge imposed by a charging order in cases where the charging order was made to secure the payment of money due under a judgment made for the purpose of enforcing payment of money owed under an agreement which is a regulated agreement under the Consumer Credit Act 1974, so that if the amount of the judgment debt which remains unpaid at the date of the making of the application to enforce is less than £1,000, no order for sale may be made.

251   Civil Procedure Rules 1998

The Civil Procedure (Amendment) Rules 2013, SI 2013/262 (in force on 1 April 2013), further amend the CPR so as to (1) make amendments in relation to costs management, including (a) changing the overriding objective to include the objective to deal with cases at proportionate cost; (b) dividing Pt 3 into Sections, the first containing current rules on case management, the second containing new rules on costs management, and the third containing rules on costs capping; and (c) adding to the Glossary the definition of 'budget'; (2) add a new rule relating to monitoring parties' compliance with directions; (3) replace allocation questionnaires with directions questionnaires; (4) make amendments in relation to standard directions in the multi-track, to add a provision that the parties and the court should take standard and model directions as a starting point for directions; (5) make amendments in relation to timetabling and the steps following allocation to the multi-track; (6) make amendments in relation to disclosure in multi-track cases; (7) make amendments in relation to court directions about factual witness statements; (8) amend the rules relating to the costs of expert evidence by providing that, when a party applies for permission to call an expert, the party must provide an estimate of the costs of the proposed expert evidence and identify the issues which the expert evidence will address; (9) provide that where judgment against a defendant is at least as advantageous to the claimant as the proposals contained in a claimant's Pt 36 offer, the court may order that the claimant is entitled to an additional amount, not exceeding £75,000, calculated by applying the prescribed percentage; (10) revoke Pt 43 and replace Pts 44–48 with new Pt 44 (General rules about costs); Pt 45 (Fixed costs); Pt 46 (Costs: special cases); Pt 47 (Procedure for detailed assessment of costs and default provisions); and Pt 48 (Legal Aid, Sentencing and Punishment of Offenders Act 2012 Pt 2 (ss 44–62) relating to civil litigation funding and costs: transitional provision in relation to pre-commencement funding arrangements); (11) make various consequential amendments resulting from the introduction of new CPR Pts 44–48; (12) make new provision in relation to appeal costs by providing that, in any proceedings in which costs recovery is normally limited or excluded at first instance, an appeal court may make an order that the recoverable costs of an appeal will be limited to the extent which the court specifies; (13) add the definition of 'damages-based agreement' to the Glossary; (14) increase, from £5,000 to £10,000, the small claims track limit; (15) make an amendment in relation to Aarhus Convention claims; and (16) omit CCR Ord 27 r 7A(3) as a consequence of the introduction of CPR Pt 81 (applications and proceedings in relation to contempt of court).

The Civil Procedure (Amendment No 2) Rules 2013, SI 2013/515 (in force on 1 April 2013), further amend the CPR so as to (1) provide that in addition to not applying to multi-track cases commenced on or after 1 April 2013 in the Admiralty and Commercial

Henry v News Group Newspapers Ltd [2013] EWCA Civ 19, [2013] 2 All ER 840 (Court of Appeal: Moore-Bick, Aikens and Black LJJ).

264 Costs—assessment of costs—personal injury claim—choice of solicitor—reasonable costs

The respondent, who was employed as a senior radiographer at the appellant trust, was medically retired after developing repetitive strain injury. She was a member of a society that assisted members who incurred personal injury through their work and, due to the complexity of the claims it supported, the society usually referred all of its personal injury work to a particular solicitors' firm in central London. However, in the respondent's case it advised her to consult a local firm, which advised that it did not consider there to be any reasonable prospect of establishing legal liability. The society agreed to fund a second opinion, but insisted that the respondent consult the London firm. Proceedings were issued and the appellant denied liability. The respondent accepted a settlement and there was a dispute between the parties as to costs and, in particular, the choice of solicitor. The appellant objected to the use of the London firm and submitted that it would have been reasonable to have instructed local solicitors who had reasonable expertise in claims for repetitive strain injury. A costs judge held that the costs, although large, had not been disproportionate in the circumstances of the case, that the appropriate grade of fee earner had been grade A and, although the case had been a six figure claim and merited a grade A fee earner, on balance, it had not warranted a grade A fee earner in central London. Firms outside London could have conducted it and, to the extent that it had been out of the ordinary, it could have been addressed by uprating the hourly rate, rather than by altering the locality. The appellant appealed, contending that the judge erred in allowing a specified hourly rate, and the respondent cross-appealed, contending that, in allowing the specified hourly rate, there had been a failure to accept that the local firm turned down the claim and to consider whether, in light of the local firm's repudiation, it had been reasonable for the respondent to instruct the London firm. *Held*, it had been reasonable for the respondent to instruct the London firm and there had been an error with regard to the failure to consider the reasonableness of the decision to instruct the firm in light of the local firm declining to act on the merits. The assessment of whether it had been reasonable to instruct the London firm was to be made in light of the circumstances at the time the decision had been made. All that the respondent and the society had at the time that the decision was made was a letter, which made clear that the local firm believed that the claim would not succeed on the merits. It had been in the light of that assessment that the society supported the respondent obtaining a second opinion. On the facts, there had been no error in the judge's reference to local rates. As to the uplift, that had been a matter within the judge's discretion. He had heard the evidence about the nature of the claim and had been in a good position to assess its complexity. Accordingly, the appeal would be dismissed and the cross-appeal would be allowed.

Royal Devon and Exeter NHS Foundation Trust v Acres [2013] EWHC 652 (QB), [2013] All ER (D) 238 (Mar) (Queen's Bench Division: Cranston J). *Ladd v Marshall* [1954] 3 All ER 745, CA; *G v G* [1985] 2 All ER 225, HL (1985 Abr para 1744); *Truscott v Truscott; Wraith v Sheffield Forgemasters Ltd* [1998] 1 All ER 82, CA (1998 Abr para 2632); *Griffiths v Solutia UK Ltd (formerly Monsanto Chemicals Ltd)* [2001] EWCA Civ 736, [2001] All ER (D) 196 (Apr); and *Gazley v Wade* [2004] EWHC 2675 (QB), [2004] All ER (D) 291 (Nov) applied.

265 Costs—assessment of costs—summary assessment—challenge to sums claimed

The court had made an order for the intervener to pay the claimants' costs in patent proceedings. The present proceedings concerned a summary assessment of those costs. The intervener challenged the claimants' costs on the grounds that the court should take into account and effectively split the preparation time equally between three documents in relation to which the intervener had failed and three documents in relation to which it had succeeded. Furthermore, the intervener contended that the rates that the claimants' solicitors charged had been higher than the normal guideline rates, given that the matter was a procedural application, and that the 15 hours other than partner time that the claimants' solicitors had taken in preparing the matter had been excessive. *Held*, the intervener's analysis of the split of preparation time on the documents was not fair. Even if it had otherwise been legitimate to take that matter into account, there was no good reason for making a deduction for those. Further, the application had related to documents which had played a part at trial, and it had been proportionate and entirely reasonable for the claimants to have employed the same firm at the same rates as it had dealt with at trial. If a different charging rate had been imposed on the basis that the present application had been a procedural application, that would create an incentive on a party in a patent case to try and instruct a new solicitors, who had not been experts in the case, at a lower rate which would no doubt increase the costs very substantially. It had been plainly right for the solicitors who had handled the case to deal with it. However, the time taken had been more than had been really reasonable or necessary to deal with the application. The matter could have been done in about ten hours of the time of the relevant senior associate, junior associate and paralegal. The costs of the junior associate in the case would therefore be deducted. Judgment would be given accordingly.

Nestec SA v Dualit Ltd [2013] EWHC 2738 (Pat), [2013] All ER (D) 100 (Oct) (Chancery Division: Birss J).

266   Costs—divorce proceedings

See MATRIMONIAL AND CIVIL PARTNERSHIP LAW.

267   Costs—family proceedings

See CHILDREN AND YOUNG PERSONS.

268   Costs—interest on costs—credit agreement—pre-judgment disbursements

In the course of group litigation, the claimants entered into a credit agreement with their solicitors, whereby the solicitors undertook to provide credit in such sums as were required from time to time to pay disbursements relating to the claimants' claim up to a maximum amount, in return for payment of a credit charge at four per cent above base rate. It further provided that, if the claim was successful, the credit charge would be paid by the claimants out of their damages. Following judgment of the group litigation the court handed down judgment on costs, providing that the defendants should pay 80 per cent of the claimants' costs of the action as agreed or assessed. The claimants sought an order that the defendants should also pay interest on the disbursements that had been paid, from the date of payment of the relevant sums to the date of judgment. It was conceded by the defendants that the claimants were entitled to pre-judgment interest on disbursements, but disputed the rate of that interest. *Held*, it was likely that the interest demanded by a third party for an unsecured loan in order to fund disbursements would have been significantly in excess of the four per cent above base rate which had been agreed with the solicitors. Furthermore, such loans would not have been contingent, as the agreement had been. The position was no different from that which would have existed if the claimants had taken out loans from a bank to fund their disbursements and had agreed to pay interest to the bank. In that event, they would clearly have been entitled to claim from the defendant the monies paid by way of interest. However, the fact that, under the agreement, the claimants' liability to pay the credit charges had been contingent on the success of their claims had not altered the nature of the agreement. The fact was that the agreement had provided that, since the claims had succeeded, the claimants were liable to pay the credit charges. That being the case, and absent any suggestion that the agreed rate of interest had been excessive or unreasonable, the appropriate rate of interest on pre-judgment disbursements was four per cent above base rate. Accordingly, the application would be allowed.

Jones v Secretary of State for Energy and Climate Change [2013] EWHC 1023 (QB), [2013] 3 All ER 1014 (Queen's Bench Division: Swift J). For related proceedings see [2012] EWHC 3647 (QB), [2013] All ER (D) 81 (Feb).

This decision has been affirmed on appeal: [2014] EWCA Civ 363, [2014] All ER (D) 255 (Mar).

269   Costs—matrimonial proceedings

See MATRIMONIAL AND CIVIL PARTNERSHIP LAW.

270 Costs—order for costs—after the event insurance premium—recoverability

The claimant brought proceedings for the rectification of a contract it had made with the defendants. The claim was allowed with costs and the defendant appealed. One day before the appeal was due to be heard, the claimant obtained after the event insurance cover, protecting it against having to pay the costs of the action and its costs of the appeal if the appeal was allowed. The appeal was dismissed and the defendant was ordered to pay the claimant's costs of the appeal, including, pursuant to the Access to Justice Act 1999 s 29, costs in relation to the insurance premium. The defendant challenged the recoverability of the premium in so far as it related to the costs of the claim up to and including the trial, submitting that, on a proper construction, s 29 would not allow recovery of the premium relating to the costs of the trial because the cover had to be limited to the risk of incurring a liability in the proceedings in which the costs order was made, which in the present case was the appeal not the first instance trial. *Held,* the word 'proceedings' in s 29 should be given its traditional meaning which distinguished between proceedings at trial and on appeal. The risk that the incidence of costs at trial might be changed by the costs order of the appeal court might be a new risk of the appeal, but the costs liability and costs order in question remained those of the trial. It followed that the costs liability in respect of which the premium had been taken out remained a costs liability in the trial proceedings, not the appeal proceedings. The result was that the costs concerned, which could only be costs in the appeal, under the 1999 Act were justifiable as neither costs of the appeal nor as costs of a trial which had already terminated. If it were otherwise, costs of trial could in effect be increased retrospectively, to the prejudice of the opposing party. Accordingly, the appeal would be allowed.

Hawksford Trustees Jersey Ltd v Stella Global UK Ltd (No 2) [2012] EWCA Civ 987, [2012] 1 WLR 3581, [2012] All ER (D) 337 (Jul) (Court of Appeal: Rix, Etherton and Patten LJJ). *Masson Templier & Co v De Fries* [1909] 2 KB 831, CA; *Wright v Bennett* [1948] 1 KB 601, [1948] 1 All ER 410; *Aiden Shipping Co Ltd v Interbulk Ltd, The Vimeira (No 2)* [1986] AC 965, [1986] 2 All ER 409, HL (1986 Abr para 1964); and *Callery v Gray* [2001] EWCA Civ 1246, [2001] 4 All ER 1 (2001 Abr para 709) considered.

271 Costs—order for costs—apportionment between parties—apportionment according
       to timing of settlement offers

The claimant sought contractual payment of a sum from the defendant. The defendant's offers of pro rata payment were refused and the claimant issued proceedings. The defendant made a *Calderbank* offer which remained open for 21 days and also offered to pay the claimant's costs on the standard basis. The offer was rejected, as was a subsequent higher offer. The claimant made an offer under CPR Pt 36. On the same day, the defendant requested confirmation of the claimant's costs in order to consider the offer. The claimant did not respond. The matter proceeded to a hearing and the claimant was awarded a sum equivalent to one third of its original claim. In relation to costs, the judge ordered that (1) the defendant pay the claimant its costs relating to the claim for the period from the issue of proceedings to the date on which the *Calderbank* offer expired; and (2) the claimant pay the defendant's costs relating to the period after the expiry date of the *Calderbank* offer. On appeal by both parties on the basis that the judge was wrong in the exercise of his discretion as to costs, *held,* (1) the CPR Pt 36 offer made by the claimant was at least as advantageous as the judgment. A relevant consideration pursuant to CPR 36.14(4)(c), (d) was the lack of clarification of costs which led to the defendant's unanswered request of the same day for confirmation of those costs. It was inevitable that that the judge should have had regard to the whole litigation history in considering CPR 36.14(4) and to have placed the offer in the context of those previously made. He was not obliged to isolate his consideration to events from the time of the making of the offer. (2) The judge's award of costs to the defendant for the period after the expiry of the *Calderbank* offer underlined the positive evaluation he made of the balance he had to draw and was unassailable. In the circumstances, it was entirely unrealistic for the claimant to have expected the court to adopt a blunt approach of 'winner takes all' with regard to costs. The judge identified the *Calderbank* offer as a significant event and, consequently, a relevant date in the proceedings. He was entitled to give considerable weight to the fact of an entirely realistic offer in monetary terms. The judge did not fail to take into account all factors relevant to his discretion and accorded sufficient weight to those in favour of the claimant. Accordingly, the appeals would be dismissed.

Thinc Group Ltd v Kingdom [2013] EWCA Civ 1306, [2013] All ER (D) 331 (Oct) (Court of Appeal: Arden, Ryder and Macur LJJ).

272   Costs—order for costs—claimant's offer to settle—offer not accepted—both parties claiming to be successful party

The parties to court proceedings sought costs orders. The claimant contended that it was the successful party as its liability to pay a much lesser sum than its potential liability should not be regarded as a failure and it had obtained two of the three declarations it had sought. It further relied on the defendants' rejection of its previous offer exceeding the capitalised value of liability to establish what the parties considered to be the true measure of success. The claimant further drew attention to the fact that only the defendants had made any application for permission to appeal. The defendants invoked the mechanical test of identifying which of the parties was compelled to pay money to the other and contended that the claimant's offer did not comply with the mandatory requirements of CPR 36.2(c). They further contended that it would be unjust to visit on them the consequences of CPR 36.14 because the offer was, in substance, a defendant's offer and failure to accept or beat a defendant's offer did not occasion any of the consequences of CPR 36.14(3). *Held*, (1) it was settled law that a judge had to look closely at the facts of the particular case before him and ask who, as a matter of substance and reality, had won. The fact that at the end of the day the claims were about money and one of the parties had been required to pay the other did not necessarily signify that the party paying had lost. In the present case, as a matter of substance and reality, the claimant was, overall, the successful party. That was so even though it had to write a cheque and notwithstanding that it had not succeeded on every point. Further, it was relevant that the defendants were seeking permission to appeal. They self-evidently wished to appeal because they had not secured the prize they wanted and they were not sufficiently satisfied with what they had achieved to allow the matter to rest there. (2) On its proper construction, the use of the defined terms 'offeror' and 'offeree' in CPR Pt 36 denoted that the offeror might be either the claimant or the defendant. Thus, CPR 36.6(1), CPR 36.7, CPR 36.8 and CPR 36.9 all used those terms because all those rules applied to both claimant's offers and defendant's offers. Further, the term 'claimant' was used precisely and carefully where it appeared in CPR Pt 36 to denote just that: it was not to be read as if it had been intended to mean 'claimant or defendant', which would be the effect of substituting the term 'offeree'. Further, different consequences were provided according to whether the offer was made by a defendant and not accepted by a claimant or vice versa. On the facts, the objective of CPR Pt 36 would be advanced by reading CPR 36.2(2)(c) as requiring a claimant who sought their costs to specify a period of not less than 21 days within which the defendant would be liable to pay them. The offer would be treated as compliant with CPR Pt 36. (3) It was neither required nor permissible to go behind the formal status of the parties for the purposes of determining compliance with CPR Pt 36 and the prima facie effect of a compliant offer. For those purposes, the description in the record was conclusive. However, the substance of the claim and which of the parties was seeking to establish liability and which to oppose it, was one of the circumstances to be considered by the court in determining whether it would be unjust to make orders for indemnity costs for the purposes of CPR 36.14(3). Further, properly understood, the making of an indemnity costs order in a case to which CPR 36.14 applied indicated only that the court had not considered it unjust to make the order for indemnity costs. In the present case, there was force in the argument that, in substance, the claimant had really been in the position of a defendant, and that, further or alternatively, the rationale in CPR Pt 36 for giving a special incentive to claimants to put forward offers to settle was not easily applicable. It would not be just to make an order under CPR 36.14(3), but the just order would be for the defendants to bear all of the claimant's post-offer costs on the standard basis. Judgment would be given accordingly.

Procter & Gamble Co v Svenska Cellulosa Aktiebolaget SCA [2012] EWHC 2839 (Ch), [2013] 1 WLR 1464, [2012] All ER (D) 282 (Oct) (Chancery Division: Hildyard J). For earlier related proceedings see [2012] EWHC 1257 (Ch), [2012] IRLR 733.

273   Costs—order for costs—conditional fee agreement—cost capping order

The court had previously given judgment in patent proceedings in the defendant's favour. The present proceedings concerned the appropriate costs orders. The claimant contended that, although the defendant had clearly won the action, there should be a general discount to reflect the fact that it had lost so many points on non-infringement. It raised further issues with respect to various issues in the defendant's schedule. The defendant had entered into a conditional fee agreement with its solicitors at an early stage in the proceedings, with an uplift of 100 per cent. The claimant objected to the court taking that into account, as there should have been a more optimistic view and the risk assessment should have changed. It fell to be determined: (1) whether there should be a general discount to reflect the points the defendant lost; (2) whether there should be a reduction from the defendant's schedule; and (3) whether the conditional fee agreement should be considered. *Held,* (1) dealing with the defendant's points was part of the process of educating the court about the overall meaning of the claim. The defendant, which had had no choice but to defend itself, should not be penalised in costs over points of such nature, as the lost points had not been improperly taken and had not led to very significant additional expenditure. (2) There was no pressing reason to depart from the relevant guidelines in the present case. The total of the various sums would be an appropriate sum, well under the applicable £50,000 cap. (3) At the early stage in the proceedings, when the conditional fee agreement had been entered, it had been entirely reasonable for the defendant's solicitors to advise that the matter had been extremely uncertain. Further, there was no justification for saying that the parties to a conditional fee agreement should be continually adjusting the relevant uplift according to their instantaneous perception of the chances of success. Accordingly, absent any other reason not to give full effect to the conditional fee agreement, it was necessary to double the figures payable by the claimant to the defendant, taking into account both the overall cap of £50,000 and the appropriate cap for each individual stage. Judgment would be given accordingly.

Scopema Sarl v Scot Seat Direct Ltd [2013] EWPCC 37, [2013] All ER (D) 153 (Sep) (Patents County Court: Alastair Wilson QC). For related proceedings see [2013] EWPCC 32, [2013] All ER (D) 152 (Sep) (para 1925).

274   Costs—order for costs—indemnity basis—variation of costs management order

The claimant unsuccessfully brought a claim against the defendant for breach of contract. At a case management conference, the judge ordered that the defendant file and serve its costs budget in accordance with *Practice Direction–Costs Management in Mercantile Courts and Technology and Construction Courts* PD 51G pilot scheme. At the pre-trial review hearing the costs management orders were increased to cover the costs of daily transcripts at the forthcoming trial, which had the effect of enlarging the defendant's approved costs budget. At no time before or at the trial did either side apply to increase or revise the costs budgets which were the subject of the costs management order. A month before the trial, the defendant sent the claimant and the court a revised costs budget which doubled the previous estimate. The claimant objected to the revised budget and informed the defendant of a small increase in its own budget figure. The claimant accepted that it was liable to pay the defendant's costs. However, disputes arose as to the basis of assessment of those costs and the interaction between the existing costs management order, which approved the defendant's budget costs, and the total costs sought. It fell to be determined (1) whether the defendant was entitled to its costs on an indemnity basis; (2) if so, what was the relevance, if any, of the existing costs management order; and (3) if the costs were assessed on the standard basis, whether the defendant could recover more than its initial budget either by seeking to amend the costs budget after judgment, or by asserting good reasons to depart from the existing costs budget. *Held,* the present case was not one where indemnity costs were appropriate. That was principally because, although the claimant had lost, the various matters raised were plainly arguable. The particular circumstances required for the indemnity basis of costs assessment had not been made out. Also, the costs management order was expressed to be relevant only to an assessment of costs on a standard basis. However, as a matter of logical analysis, the costs management order should also be the starting point of an assessment of costs on an indemnity basis, even if the good reasons to depart from it were likely to be more numerous and extensive if the indemnity basis was applied. In any given case, an award of indemnity costs, which did not require any assessment of proportionality, might be a good reason to depart from the costs budget approved by the court pursuant to PD 51G. In the circumstances, the defendant could not seek, retrospectively, to revise the budget under PD 51G para 6 so as to all but double the original costs budget approved in the costs management order. If a defendant wanted the court to approve significant changes to its costs budget, it had to seek such approval formally. It was not enough simply to file the material at court. An application to revise or amend a costs management order ought to be made immediately after it became apparent that the original budget for costs had been exceeded by a more than minimal amount. Judgment would be given accordingly.

Elvanite Full Circle Ltd v AMEC Earth & Environmental (UK) Ltd [2013] EWHC 1643 (TCC), [2013] 4 All ER 765 (Queen's Bench Division: Coulson J).

275   Costs—order for costs—intellectual property rights—infringement—discretion of court

The claimant alleged that the defendants, who included two companies and certain of their directors and shareholders, had used confidential customer data taken from the claimant's customer databases for the purposes of marketing extended warranty service plans for the claimant's satellite equipment and had infringed the claimant's marks so as to be guilty of passing off through the use of deceptive marketing activities. A court granted declarations that the defendants were liable for breaches of confidence, database right, trade mark infringement and passing off. The judge declined to grant any relief against the two companies themselves because of a statutory stay imposed by the Insolvency Act 1986 s 130(2) since they were in compulsory winding-up. The claimant sought to recover all of its costs. *Held*, the court was not willing to grant judgment against the two companies. It followed that it would not be open to the claimant to pursue, against the two companies, the inquiry as to damages. There was no reason why the claimant should not be free to pursue one or other remedy against the other defendants. It was premature to deal with the claimant's costs so far as they had been incurred in its pursuit of the two companies up to the time of the stay. The court was not persuaded that it should make any order for costs in respect of the two companies. The general rule was that costs should follow the event, namely that the unsuccessful party would be ordered to pay the costs of the successful party. There was no general rule that a finding of dishonest conduct by the successful party would replace the usual starting point. Where a defendant's liability for costs was shared with another that liability would be shared equally with that other but would be joint as regards the payee. Where the case against one defendant had failed only because he had lied, it was just for the claimant to recover its costs. Where the claimant had acted reasonably in pursuing a second defendant to trial, it would be wrong to order the claimant to pay his costs. As to each of the remaining defendants, there was no reason why they should not be ordered to pay costs. Accordingly, orders for costs would be granted.

British Sky Broadcasting Group plc v Digital Satellite Warranty Cover Ltd (in liquidation) [2012] EWHC 3679 (Ch), [2012] All ER (D) 193 (Dec) (Chancery Division: Sir William Blackburne).

276   Costs—order for costs—order against joint defendant—judgment against defendant company but not co-defendant sole director and shareholder

The claimant brought an action against the first defendant company for breach of his employment contract and claimed an entitlement to a 20 per cent share of its equity. The second defendant, the first defendant's sole director and shareholder, was joined to the action because any order for specific performance would require him to transfer or cause the allotment of shares. It was held that the claimant had been entitled to the claimed share in the first defendant's equity or, at his option, payment in lieu. The first defendant accepted that it should pay the claimant's costs. However, the judge refused the claimant's application for an order that the second defendant should be jointly and severally liable for costs on the basis that he would been made the subject of a non-party costs order if he had not been joined as a party to the action. The first defendant subsequently went into insolvent liquidation and the claimant appealed against the costs order. *Held*, if a non-party costs order was made against a company director, it was quite wrong to characterise it as piercing or lifting the corporate veil. The purpose of the concept of corporation personality was to deal with legal rights and obligations, whereas the exercise of discretion to make a non-party costs order left rights and obligations where they were. The very fact that the making of such an order was discretionary demonstrated that the question was not one of rights and obligations of a non-party, for no obligations existed unless and until the court exercised its discretion. Moreover the fact that the discretion, if exercised, was exercised against a non-party underlined the proposition that the non-party had no substantive liability in respect of the cause of action in question. The judge's reasons for refusing to make an order against the second defendant had all related to a question of substantive liability. However, although it had been common ground that the application should have been considered by analogy with a claim for costs against a non-party, the judge had given no consideration to the principles on which such orders were made. This omission had vitiated the judge's exercise of her discretion, and so it was open to the court to exercise that discretion afresh. It was not enough to say that the second defendant had been a director of the company, but in deciding whether to make such an order, the court was not fettered by the legal realities. It was entitled to look to the economic realities. In the circumstances, it was just to order the second defendant to pay the claimant's costs. Accordingly, the appeal would be allowed.

Threlfall v ECD Insight Ltd [2013] EWCA Civ 1444, [2013] All ER (D) 195 (Nov) (Court of Appeal: Richards, Tomlinson and Lewison LJJ). *Goodwood Recoveries Ltd v Breen* [2005] EWCA Civ 414, [2006] 2 All ER 533 (2006 Abr para 699) applied; *Systemcare (UK) Ltd v Services Design Technology Ltd* [2011] EWCA Civ 546, [2012] 1 BCLC 14 (2012 Abr para 363) considered. Decision of Lang J [2012] EWHC 3543 (QB), [2013] IRLR 185 reversed in part.

277 Costs—order for costs—payment on account

In earlier proceedings, it had been found that the sale in a shop of t-shirts bearing an image of a pop star without her approval was an act of passing off. Questions arose as to the appropriate costs and to any further orders to be applied in light of the judgment in the earlier proceedings. *Held*, the claimants were entitled to costs. The correct course was to order the defendants to pay the claimants' costs subject to a detailed assessment. It followed that general costs would be ordered to go the general way. The court was satisfied that the order proposed by the defendants, that the claimants' costs for obtaining, preparing and filing of the three witness statements should be disallowed, was appropriate and fair in the circumstances. The claimants had incurred costs and it was appropriate to order interim payment on account of costs. However, the court was not satisfied that it could safely use the figure proposed because it was so much higher than the estimate given earlier in the proceedings. The increase in the estimate of costs, without explanation, was startling. The only safe basis that the court was able to make an order for payment on account of costs was to use the earlier estimate provided in the course of the proceedings. Further, it was right and fair that an injunction be granted to prevent any future similar wrong use of the pop star's image by the defendants. The claimants would be awarded their costs subject to the reduction indicated in respect of the pre-trial applications. Judgment would be given accordingly.

Fenty v Arcadia Group [2013] All ER (D) 225 (Sep) (Chancery Division: Birss J). For earlier proceedings, see [2013] EWHC 2310 (Ch), [2013] All ER (D) 410 (Jul) (para 2398).

278 Costs—order for costs—third party order—personal injury action—alleged failure by claimant's solicitors to obtain after the event insurance

In personal injury proceedings against his employer, the claimant instructed a firm of solicitors under a conditional fee arrangement. The employer's costs in defending the action were funded by its insurers. A notice of funding served on the insurers made it clear that there was no after-the-event insurance in place. The solicitors had drafted a proposal for after-the-event insurance but neither submitted nor sought instructions from the claimant as to whether it should be submitted. A number of offers and counter-offers were made between the parties, the level of offers varying in light of differing medical opinions being received. In the course of one offer, the insurers asserted that they were aware that the claimant was placing himself at significant financial risk given that he had no after-the-event insurance. At one stage, the claimant paid an invoice for disbursements which, at least in part, had been advanced by the solicitors without being in funds. At trial, the claimant was awarded an amount by way of general damages that was less than the offers made by the insurers to compromise the claim. The result was that the claimant was ordered to pay the employer's costs from the date of the first offer made by the insurers. The insurers then applied under CPR 48.2 to join the solicitors for the purposes of costs, and made an application under the Senior Courts Act 1981 s 51 for a non-party costs order against the solicitors. The insurers submitted that the solicitors' failure to obtain after-the-event insurance for the claimant meant that there was an undeclared conflict of interest between them and their client that had motivated the solicitors to continue with the case in an effort to obtain a conclusion by which the claimant was not liable for the employer's costs. The judge rejected that contention on the ground that there was no evidence that the solicitors had appreciated the supposed conflict of interest. The solicitors had had substantial control over the way the case had developed, but, except for the after-the-event insurance, nothing untoward in the conduct of the case. The judge concluded that the case was not outside the ordinary run of cases and dismissed the application. The insurers appealed. *Held*, a non-party costs order could exceptionally be made against legal representatives. However, where a non-party not merely funded the proceedings, but substantially also controlled or at any rate was to benefit from them, justice would ordinarily require that, if the proceedings failed, he would pay the successful party's costs. The non-party in those cases was not so much facilitating access to justice by the party funded, as himself gaining access to justice for his own purposes, and he himself was 'the real party' to the litigation. A solicitor was entitled to act on a conditional fee agreement for the impecunious client whom he knew or suspected would not be able to pay its own, or the other side's, costs. As far as the other side was concerned, whether the solicitor had negligently failed to obtain after-the-event insurance to protect his client did not impact on the costs he would incur unless it was demonstrably proved that the costs would not have been incurred. The insurers' application had to be put on the basis that the failure of the solicitors to have obtained after-the-event insurance, and the subsequent failure to admit that fact to the claimant, had itself been sufficient not only to give rise to a breach of duty to him but, in addition, to demonstrate that the solicitors had become a 'real party' to the litigation, the person with the principle interest in its outcome, or who had been acting primarily for his own sake. If that was so, every act of negligence by a solicitor in the conduct of litigation, thereby giving rise to a conflict, which meant that an opposing party had incurred costs which might not otherwise have been incurred, would be sufficient. However, the law had not gone that far. Accordingly, the appeal would be dismissed.

Heron v TNT (UK) Ltd [2013] EWCA Civ 469, [2013] All ER (D) 28 (May) (Court of Appeal: Leveson, Beatson and Gloster LJJ).

279 Costs—order for costs—third party order—personal injury action—payment by solicitor of disbursements

The claimants in two conjoined appeals had instructed the same firm of solicitors to represent them in personal injury claims that were ultimately unsuccessful. The claimants' solicitors had been instructed under conditional fee agreements but without after-the-event insurance cover. In each case the defendant's solicitors had sought orders requiring the claimant's solicitors to disclose information of the source of funding. On appeal, the solicitors were ordered to provide that information, the judge holding that, even though the claimant in each case might have recovered compensation for himself if successful, the solicitors could still be regarded as having benefited, or potentially benefited from the case to the extent that a third party costs order could be made against them on the basis that, by funding disbursements, it was possible that the solicitors had stepped outside the normal role of a solicitor. The claimants' solicitors appealed against those decisions, and it fell to be determined whether a third party costs order could or should be made against them on the grounds that they had funded disbursements, and, if so, whether it was appropriate to order disclosure and information regarding the funding of each case. *Held*, once it had been conceded that a solicitor did not have to be in funds before incurring costs, those costs had been borne by the solicitor and became an expense of providing advocacy or litigation services. The costs might have to be the subject of an account to the client as a disbursement, but the credit afforded to the client in respect of the costs was part of the service provided by the solicitor to the client. The Courts and Legal Services Act 1990 visualised the possibility that a solicitor might fund disbursements and, in that event, it would not be right to conclude that such a solicitor was a real party to the litigation. Whether a litigant could afford an expert report or the court fee said nothing about his ability to fund the costs incurred by opponents in an unsuccessful claim, and a solicitor could advance disbursements with a technical, albeit improbable, obligation for repayment.

SI 2009/2725, under Pt 5 of the 2008 Act; the order directed all persons operating in the financial sector not to enter into or continue to participate in any transaction or business relationship with two companies, one of which was an Iranian bank operating in the United Kingdom. The bank issued proceedings under Pt 6 to set the order aside. The government considered that some of the evidence relied on by the Treasury was of such sensitivity that it could not be shown to the bank or its representatives. The High Court judge accepted the government's case that that evidence should be put before the court and that a 'closed material procedure' should be adopted under which the court would consider the material and hear submissions about it without the bank seeing the material or being present. An open hearing and a closed hearing were held; the closed hearing was conducted in private, without the presence of the bank, its lawyers or the public. The bank was provided with a document giving the gist of the closed material and 'special advocates', who had been cleared to see the closed material, made submissions on behalf of the bank at the closed hearing. The judge handed down an open judgment dismissing the bank's application, and a closed judgment, which was seen by the Treasury but not by the bank and was not available to the public. The bank appealed. The Court of Appeal held an open hearing and a short closed hearing at which they considered the closed judgment. They dismissed the bank's appeal in an open judgment. The bank appealed to the Supreme Court. Under s 40(2)b of the Constitutional Reform Act 2005 an appeal lay to the Supreme Court from any order or judgment of the Court of Appeal in England and Wales in civil proceedings; under s 40(5) of the 2005 Act the Supreme Court had power to determine any question necessary to be determined for the purposes of doing justice in an appeal to it under any enactment. In the bank's appeal the Treasury asked the Supreme Court to adopt a closed material procedure in order to consider the closed judgment of the High Court judge. The Supreme Court considered whether it could conduct a closed hearing. *Held*, (1) (Lord Hope, Lord Kerr and Lord Reed dissenting), the Supreme Court had power to entertain a closed material procedure on appeals against decisions of the courts of England and Wales on applications brought under s 63(2) of the 2008 Act. Under s 40(2) of the 2005 Act an appeal lay against 'any' judgment of the Court of Appeal; that must extend to a judgment which was wholly or partially closed; in order for an appeal against such a judgment to be effective, the hearing would have to involve a closed material procedure. That conclusion was reinforced by the power accorded to the Supreme Court by s 40(5) of the 2005 Act to determine any question necessary for the purposes of doing justice, as justice would not be able to be done in certain cases if the Supreme Court could not consider closed material. Where the Supreme Court was satisfied that it might be necessary to conduct a closed material procedure in order to dispose of an appeal, the court could do so. (2) (Lord Hope, Lord Kerr, Lord Dyson and Lord Reed dissenting), in the instant case, the court would adopt a closed material procedure. Judgment would be given accordingly.

Bank Mellat v HM Treasury [2013] UKSC 38, [2013] 4 All ER 495 (Supreme Court: Lord Neuberger P, Lord Hope DP, Lady Hale, Lord Kerr, Lord Clarke, Lord Dyson, Lord Sumption, Lord Reed and Lord Carnwath SCJJ).

289 Disclosure—documents—exceptions to disclosure obligation—public interest immunity—adoption of 'confidentiality ring'

The claimant was in prison in Afghanistan and began judicial review proceedings against the defendant with respect to his detention. There was before the court information in respect of which public interest immunity had been claimed. The claimant's legal team applied to make available some of that information on a lawyer-only basis. The mechanism was described as a 'confidentiality ring'. The respondent opposed the application. The respondent submitted that the practice of providing documents on a lawyer-only basis had been ruled impermissible by *Al Rawi*. Further the respondent expressed a fear that the ring would fail to maintain the confidentiality necessary to protect the public interest. *Held*, there was no principle which prohibited a court considering whether to uphold a claim for public interest immunity from ordering that, while the claim should not be upheld, nonetheless the documents or material should only be disclosed to those identified within a confidentiality ring on the terms specified in the parties' undertaking. The free and unencumbered ability to give and receive instructions was an important facet of open and fair trials. The ability was hampered if in some respects the lawyer was unable to disclose all the relevant evidence and material and, in that respect, the client was deprived of the opportunity to give informed instructions. The degree to which that was of importance varied from case to case. No lawyer should consent to such a ring unless they were satisfied they could do so without harming their client's case. However, provided the legal advisors were satisfied they could safely continue to act under a restriction, the inability to communicate fully with the client would not in such circumstances undermine the fundamental principles on which a fair application for judicial review depended. There was no principle which precluded a confidentiality ring once the judge had an opportunity to consider whether the public interest immunity claim should be upheld. Further, the respondent's objections related not to matters of principle but to the circumstances of any particular case, in the context of the documents or information in respect of which the claim was made. There was no reason why the nature and description of that which had to be confined to the ring should not be carefully prescribed. If it could not be, then that would be a powerful argument against the use of the ring. In the present case, some information in respect of which public interest immunity had been claimed could, as a matter of principle, be provided to the claimant's lawyers only and considered in camera. Accordingly, the application would be allowed.

R (on the application of Mohammed) v Secretary of State for Defence [2012] EWHC 3454 (Admin), [2013] 2 All ER 897 (Queen's Bench Division: Moses LJ). Al Rawi v Security Service [2011] UKSC 34, [2012] 1 All ER 1 (2011 Abr para 327) considered.

290 Disclosure—documents—order against party in other regulation state—compliance with order prohibited under national law

Two separate sets of proceedings were brought concerning allegations breach of competition law and/or abuse of a dominant position in breach of European Union law against a number of defendants, some of which were French. In the first action, an order was made pursuant to CPR Pt 18 requiring the French defendants to serve a response to the claimants' request for further information. In the second action, the French defendants were required to give disclosure under specified heads pursuant to CPR Pt 31. In both cases, the French defendants contended that they should not have the respective orders made against them because compliance would put them in breach of a French statute. That statute prohibited an individual from disclosing documents or information of an economic, commercial, industrial, financial or technical nature with a view to establishing evidence in foreign judicial or administrative proceedings. In each action, the judge held that the risk of prosecution to which the relevant parties might have been exposed by the orders had been theoretical and that the mandatory procedure set out in Council Regulation (EC) 1206/2001 (on cooperation between the courts of the member states in the taking of evidence in civil or commercial matters) only applied where the taking or obtaining of the relevant evidence had involved collaboration between public authorities of each member state involved. In both cases, the French defendants appealed. Held, orders for the provision of further information and disclosure were of a procedural nature and their making had been, therefore, governed by the lex fori, the law of England and Wales. It was no defence to the making of such orders that compliance with them might expose the parties subject to them to the risk of prosecution under a foreign law. However, the English court had discretion as to whether to exercise its jurisdiction to make them. While the Regulation enabled a domestic court to obtain evidence with the assistance of that member state's judicial or other public authorities, it did not limit or reduce the options available to a domestic court in the way it obtained evidence or disclosure from the parties to the litigation before it. Accordingly, the appeals would be dismissed.

Secretary of State for Health v Servier Laboratories Ltd; National Grid Electricity Transmission plc v ABB Ltd [2013] EWCA Civ 1234, [2013] All ER (D) 238 (Oct) (Court of Appeal: Laws, Rimer and Beatson LJJ). C-332/11 ProRail BV v Xpedys NV [2013] All ER (D) 298 (Feb), ECJ, explained. Decisions of Henderson J [2012] EWHC 2761 (Ch), [2012] EWHC 3663 (Ch) and decision of Roth J [2013] EWHC 822 (Ch), [2013] All ER (D) 51 (Apr) affirmed.

291 Disclosure—documents—possession of documents

The claimant brought proceedings contending that the first and third defendants paid a substantial bribe to the chief risk officer of a German bank in order to induce the bank to sell its stake in a particular group at an undervalue. The transaction took place through the fourth defendant company. The defendants contended that the stake was sold at its market value. The claimant made applications for (1) further disclosure against the first defendant under CPR 31.12; and (2) non-party disclosure against the fourth to ninth defendants under CPR 31.17. It fell to be determined whether the first defendant had physical possession of the documents of the group such that he ought to be ordered to disclose them. In respect of disclosure against the other defendants, consideration was given to (a) whether it had been shown that each of the documents in the category or the class of documents might help the claimant's case or damage the defendant's case; (b) whether disclosure of the documents was necessary to dispose fairly of the claim or to save costs; (c) whether the definition of the documents was sufficiently clear and specific so that no judgments about the issues in the case were required by the defendants; and (d) whether, as a matter of overall discretion, disclosure of that class of documents should be ordered. *Held*, on the evidence, the first defendant had not been shown to be in physical possession of the documents of which disclosure was sought. It was clear from the fact the defendants had opposed the application that those companies had not regarded it as in their interests to disclose the documents sought in the application. In the circumstances, the court had to be bound by the decision of a company's own board of directors as to what was in its best interests. In respect of the disclosure sought against the fourth to ninth defendants, although it had been asked for late and should have been requested some time earlier than it had been, the disclosure was necessary for the fair disposal of the claim. The mere fact that the claimant had not moved as quickly as it should have to make the application did not justify refusing the disclosure sought. Judgment would be given accordingly.

Constantin Medien AG v Ecclestone [2013] EWHC 2674 (Ch), [2013] All ER (D) 30 (Sep) (Chancery Division: Vos J).

292 Disclosure—documents—public interest immunity—closed material application

The claimants were British citizens of Somali descent. They were both detained by the Somali authorities pending removal to the United Kingdom. Each claimed that they were unlawfully detained, tortured and mistreated during the period of detention in Somalia. Pursuant to case management orders, the defendant had signed a public interest immunity ('PII') certificate in relation to material referred to in a sensitive schedule to that certificate. The court directed the trial of (1) the PII application, in so far as it related to material the disclosure of which was not claimed by the defendant to be damaging to the interests of national security; and (2) whether the court would make a declaration that a closed material application might be made to the court, provided that the Justice and Security Act 2013 by a specified date and rules under the 2013 Act were in force, having been laid before Parliament and not having ceased to have effect. The claimants contended that the PII process was necessarily fairer than the process which would follow a declaration under the 2013 Act s 6 and a PII process should always be concluded before a declaration was made under the 2013 Act. They further argued in favour of alternative mechanisms to PII and, by extension, an order permitting a closed material procedure, including a confidentiality ring. The defendant responded that Parliament had declined to make it a pre-condition of a declaration that PII proceedings should be conducted in every case and had expressly provided that an application need not be based on all of the material that might meet the conditions under s 6(6). *Held*, the 2013 Act permitted the state to establish a regime, if the relevant criteria were established, allowing evidence to be adduced in private, under strict conditions which did not threaten national security. That could avoid the need for a concession which threatened or carried injustice for the state. It imported a corresponding risk of injustice to the claimant acting against the state, whose case would be met by evidence he would never hear and could not answer. The question of whether it was in the interests of the fair and effective administration of justice in the proceedings to make a declaration, had to turn on the specific circumstances of the case at hand and could not properly turn on objections which would arise in every case and which would, therefore, if successful, subvert the intention of Parliament. It would be declared, pursuant to s 6(1), that a closed material application ('CMP') could be made to the court. The defendants were correct that the court might make a declaration and adopt a CMP, before disclosure had been given and without a PII claim having been made or determined. Applying established principles, the application for PII would succeed in respect of a number of specific applications for PII on the ground of potential damage to the international relations of the United Kingdom. The reasons for excluding the material on the ground of likely damage to international relations did not touch on the core of the case between the claimants and defendant. The decisions turned on broader considerations, most notably the pressing requirement to preserve confidence and the capacity for frank communication between the various parties involved.

CF v Security Service; Mohamed v Foreign and Commonwealth Office [2013] EWHC 3402 (QB), [2013] All ER (D) 349 (Nov) (Queen's Bench Division: Irwin J).

293   Disclosure—documents—subsequent use of disclosed documents—patent proceedings

The claimant company brought a claim for the revocation of the defendant's European patent. The defendant counterclaimed for infringement against the claimant's subsidiary. The claimant applied for specific disclosure of documents from the defendant. In the course of giving disclosure pursuant to a court order, the defendant disclosed a memorandum giving certain experimental results. Prior to the action coming to trial, the patent was revoked in proceedings before the European Patent Office. At a hearing of an application for an adjournment of the present proceedings, the claimant successfully applied for permission to use the defendant's documents in foreign proceedings other than those before the European Patent Office. The claimant then applied for a declaration that it was entitled to use the documents in all proceedings relating to the patent and divisional applications in, among others, national courts and tribunals, intellectual property offices and the European Patent Office. The defendant contended that the permission in the order was not wide enough to cover proceedings which were not pending at the date of the order. *Held*, there was no reason why the judge would have wished to prevent the use of the documents in relation to a divisional patent, which had the same disclosure as the patent but different claims. Likewise, there was no reason why related rights properly described as members of the same patent family, such as utility models, would have been excluded. It followed that the documents might be used by the claimant and its subsidiary in inter partes proceedings in Europe, whether those inter partes proceedings were in courts or patent offices, and were in relation to the validity and/or infringement of, but not ownership of, patent and related rights in the same family as the patent in suit, whether or not those proceedings were pending. A declaration would therefore be granted in those terms. Judgment would be given accordingly.

Dupont Nutrition Biosciences ApS v Novozymes A/S [2013] EWHC 155 (Pat), [2013] All ER (D) 70 (Feb) (Chancery Division: Floyd J).

294   Disclosure—legal professional privilege—disclosure by third party

The claimants brought a claim against the defendant regulatory body relating to an investigation carried out by the defendant. The present proceedings concerned an application by the claimants under CPR 31.17 for third party disclosure from the joint liquidators of a particular company. In particular, disclosure was sought of five reports, four of which did not state the date they had been commissioned, which had been prepared by a firm of accountants on the instructions of the joint liquidators. The reports had been shown to the defendant by the accountants, but not permitted to be copied by the defendant. The claimants contended that the reports played a key role in the information placed before the judge by the defendant in support of the orders then sought by the defendant and the obtaining of warrants. The joint liquidators claimed that the reports should not be disclosed on the grounds, firstly, that they were protected by litigation privilege, and, secondly, that the test of necessity and relevance under CPR 31.17(3) was not satisfied. With respect to litigation privilege, the joint liquidators relied on a solicitor's statement relating to the purpose for which the reports were prepared. *Held*, on the facts, and subject to the question of litigation privilege, the requirements of CPR 31.17 were satisfied and the case was an appropriate one for the exercise of the court's discretion. It followed that it was, in principle, necessary and appropriate to make an order against the joint liquidators for disclosure of the reports, subject to litigation privilege and any special order with regard to confidentiality and use of the reports. Litigation privilege would attach to a document where the document had been produced for the dominant purpose of obtaining information or advice in connection with pending or contemplated litigation, or of conducting or aiding in the conduct of such litigation. The mere fact that a document was produced for the purpose of obtaining information or advice in connection with pending or contemplated litigation, or of conducting or aiding in the conduct of such litigation was not sufficient to founder a claim for litigation privilege. In the present case, the dominant purpose test had not been satisfied in respect of the reports. Accordingly, the application would be allowed.

Tchenguiz v Director of the Serious Fraud Office [2013] EWHC 2297 (QB), [2013] All ER (D) 357 (Jul) (Queen's Bench Division: Eder J).

295 Disclosure—legal professional privilege—litigation privilege—dominant purpose of instruction

The parties entered into a contract pursuant to which the defendant was entitled to deferred consideration following its sale of a European brewing business. The claimant brought proceedings applying for disclosure of documents that related to advice received from a bank concerning the structuring of the consideration for sale dealings with an auditor relating to work done for an agreement. The defendant submitted that the documents were covered by litigation privilege. The claimant sought an order pursuant to CPR 31.19(5) challenging the claim of the defendant to withhold inspection of the documents on the ground of litigation privilege. It fell to be determined whether the documents had been prepared for the dominant purpose of litigation. *Held*, it was established law that the burden of proof was on the party claiming litigation privilege to establish it. It was necessary for the judge to subject the evidence to anxious scrutiny. In relation to the bank documents, it had not been established that the dominant purpose of instructing the bank to provide advice was in connection with anticipated litigation. The bank's role had been investigatory. The claim for litigation privilege relating to that advice had accordingly not been made out. In relation to the auditor's documents, the defendant had not sought to address, and still less explain, the evidence that contradicted the assertion of privilege. There was inherent implausibility in the claim of privilege. Litigation had not been the dominant purpose of instructing the auditor. It followed that the documents should be disclosed. Accordingly, the application would be allowed.

Starbev GP Ltd v Interbrew Central European Holding BV [2013] EWHC 4038 (Comm), [2014] All ER (D) 116 (Jan) (Queen's Bench Division: Hamblen J).

296 Disclosure—legal professional privilege—scope—legal advice given by accountant

The claimant companies instructed an international firm of chartered accountants to advise them in connection with overseas holdings. The claimants implemented a scheme suggested to it by the accountants and the inspector of taxes, considering it necessary to look into the details of the transactions, served notice on the claimants pursuant to the Taxes Management Act 1970 s 20, requiring that they make available specified classes of documents. The claimants refused disclosure of the documents and applied for judicial review of the decision requiring them to do so, challenging the validity of the notices on the ground that they sought disclosure of documents which related to the seeking and giving of legal advice in connection with the transactions, which were excluded from the requirements of s 20 by virtue of legal advice privilege. The application was rejected on the basis that, although the disputed documents would have attracted legal advice privilege if the advice in question had been sought from, and provided by, a member of the legal profession, no such privilege extended to advice, even if identical in nature, provided by a professional person who was not a qualified lawyer. The claimants appealed. *Held,* it was universally believed that legal advice privilege only applied to communications in connection with advice given by members of the legal profession. It ought not to be extended to communications in connection with advice given by professional people other than lawyers, even where that advice was legal advice which that professional person was qualified to give. There was a strong case in terms of logic for allowing the appeal. However, where a common law rule was valid in the modern world, but it had an aspect or limitation which appeared outmoded, it was by no means always right for the courts to modify the aspect or remove the limitation. In any such case, the court had to consider whether the implications of the proposed modification or removal were such that it would be more appropriate to leave the matter to Parliament. If the appeal were allowed, the court would be extending the legal advice privilege beyond what had, for a long time, been understood to have been its limits. Moreover, it would be extending it considerably, as the issue could not simply be treated as limited to the question as to whether tax advice given by expert accountants was covered by legal advice privilege. To have concentrated on tax advice given by accountants would have been wrong, because it would have ineluctably have followed from accepting the claimants' argument that legal advice given by some other professional people would also have been covered. Accordingly, the appeal would be dismissed.

R (on the application of Prudential plc) v Special Comr of Income Tax [2013] UKSC 1, [2013] 2 AC 185, [2013] 2 All ER 247 (Supreme Court: Lord Neuberger P, Lord Hope DP, Lord Walker, Lord Mance, Lord Clarke, Lord Sumption and Lord Reed SCJJ). *R (on the application of Morgan Grenfell & Co Ltd) v Special Comr of Income Tax* [2002] UKHL 21, [2003] 1 AC 563, [2002] 3 All ER 1 (2002 Abr para 1792); and *Three Rivers DC v Governor and Company of the Bank of England* [2004] UKHL 48, [2005] 1 AC 610, [2005] 4 All ER 948 (2004 Abr para 2212) considered. Decision of Court of Appeal [2010] EWCA Civ 1094, [2011] QB 669, [2011] 1 All ER 316 (2010 Abr para 343) affirmed.

297   Enforcement—taking control of goods

The Taking Control of Goods Regulations 2013, SI 2013/1894 (in force on 6 April 2014), make provision relating to the procedure for taking control of goods under the Tribunals, Courts and Enforcement Act 2007 Sch 12 and the procedure for commercial rent arrears recovery under s 72. In particular, the 2013 Regulations (1) make provision as to the notice that must be given to a debtor prior to the taking of control of goods; (2) deal with the actual taking of control, both regarding goods on premises and goods on a highway; (3) prescribe particular protection for children and vulnerable persons so that an enforcement agent may not take control of goods where either the debtor is a child, or a child or vulnerable person is or are alone on the premises; (4) deal with the time limit for taking control, the circumstances in which control should not be taken, and the days and hours when control of goods may be taken; (5) provide for controlled goods agreements, under which the debtor is permitted to retain custody of the goods but must not remove, dispose of or permit another person to deal with them pending a payment of the debt; (6) deal with securing the goods of the debtor; (7) make provision relating to entry to premises, including the method of entry, when entry or re-entry may occur, restrictions on entry, re-entry and remaining on premises, and the necessary notice of entry where so required; (8) set out the circumstances in which a court can issue a warrant permitting the use of reasonable force by the enforcement agent to enter premises or to take control of goods on the highway; (9) prescribe the procedure following entry and taking control of goods; (10) provide for the sale of the controlled goods; (11) make provision for notice to the debtor and any co-owner of a sale, and for the conduct of the sale; (12) provide for the holding, protection and disposal of securities of the debtor by the enforcement agent, and also the notice procedure where the creditor exercises the right to take proceedings; (13) provide that, where the debtor fails to collect the goods within 28 days, the court can make orders concerning the disposal of the goods; (14) deal with underpayments where a person who claims that the goods of which control has been taken belong to him, and not the debtor, makes an application to the court; (15) make provision relating to authorisation by a landlord to another person to exercise the commercial rent arrears recovery procedure on his behalf, and define the minimum amount of net unpaid rent; and (16) deal with the notice requirements for the landlord's right to recover rent from the sub-landlord, including the withdrawal of such a notice.

298   Evidence—expert evidence—admissibility—late stage of proceedings

In the course of trade mark proceedings, at a case management conference, the need for expert evidence was discussed. The court made an order that each party had permission to apply for leave to adduce oral expert evidence. No application was forthcoming from the claimant companies. Later, when witness statements were exchanged, the claimants gave notice that it intended to rely on documents. Those documents included reports and academic articles. The defendant objected to some of the documents being adduced. Its primary objection was that the statements constituted expert evidence and hence were admissible in accordance with CPR 35 and not otherwise. In the alternative, it contended that the court ought to exercise its case management powers under CPR 1.4(1), 1.4(2)(h) and 32.1(2) to exclude the evidence, even if it was technically admissible. It contended that if an application had been made to adduce the evidence by way of an expert's report, such an application would have had to have been made in due time before trial. Therefore, due notice would have had to have been given to the defendant of the nature of the material that was being relied on and for what purpose, which would have given the defendant a proper opportunity to deal with the material. *Held*, references to experts and to the evidence and reports of experts in CPR 35 had to be read as references to experts as defined in CPR 35.2(1). That was to say, persons who had been instructed to give or prepare expert evidence for the purpose of proceedings. Thus, CPR 35 controlled the giving of evidence by experts as so defined. It did not control the admission of other types of evidence that could be described as expert evidence. The defendant's objection was not well founded in that it was based on the proposition that such material would only have been admissible in the form of an expert's report, or possibly an exhibit to an expert's report, properly tendered in accordance with CPR 35. Further, the mere fact that the material came into the case at a rather late stage was not sufficient reason in itself to regard the claimants' reliance on it as unfair or prejudicial to the defendant. Ultimately, it was not sufficiently unfair that the evidence should be excluded. If the defendant had not undertaken the kind of search of official reports and academic literature that the claimants had taken, then it only had itself to blame. Therefore, the court would decline to exclude any of the evidence. Judgment would be given accordingly.

Interflora Inc v Marks and Spencer plc [2013] EWHC 936 (Ch), [2013] All ER (D) 314 (May) (Chancery Division: Arnold J).

299 Evidence—expert evidence—admissibility—relevance of evidence

The proceedings concerned an accident which occurred when an aircraft piloted by the defendant crashed, killing its passenger. The claimants were the executors of the estate and the dependants of the deceased. They commenced proceedings seeking compensation for his death. They alleged that the accident had been caused by the defendant's negligence, in that he had attempted to perform aerobatics, for which he had no training, at a dangerously low altitude. The defendant claimed that the rudder pedals of the aeroplane had jammed, and he had been unable to prevent it from stalling and entering a spin from which it had been impossible to recover. The Air Accident Investigation Board of the Department for Transport carried out an investigation, and produced a report, which contained both statements of fact and opinion, including the opinions of experts. The claimants sought to rely on findings in the report as evidence. The defendant sought an order that the parts of the claimants' statements relying on the report be struck out and a declaration that the report was inadmissible in the proceedings. The defendant contended that the report consisted of inadmissible opinion evidence. Alternatively, he contended that it would be unsafe and undesirable to allow the report to be admitted in evidence. He submitted that, in any event, the court should use its discretion to exclude the report on the basis that the report was an anonymised document whose authors could not be identified, and, as such, it would be unsafe for any court to give any weight at all to anything in the report. Secondly, he submitted that, as a matter of policy, if information contained in the report were allowed to be used as evidence in litigation that would deter people able to assist in the investigation of air accidents from doing so in future, which would impede the Board's effectiveness and jeopardise aviation security. Consideration was given to the rule in *Hollington v Hewthorn* which stated that all evidence that was relevant to an issue was admissible, while all that was irrelevant should be excluded. *Held*, the responsibility of a judge to make his own independent assessment of the evidence entailed that weight should not be attached to conclusions reached by another judge. The rule in *Hollington v Hewthorn* as usually stated applied only to previous judicial findings. The line between judicial findings and expert opinions was not a bright one. Where there were statements of opinion based on an evaluation of factual evidence of a kind that did not deploy any expert knowledge and which the court was as well placed to make as the author of the report, it was preferable to treat that as a question of weight rather than of admissibility, particularly since there was no clear point at which an expert's specialised knowledge and experience ceased to inform and give some added value to the expert's opinions. The whole of the report would be admissible with it being a matter for the judge to make such use of the report as he thought fit. Even if the report had contained some inadmissible material, it would not have been sensible to engage in an exercise of editing out parts of it. With regard to anonymity, while it had to be taken into account by the judge when assessing what weight should be given to statements made in the report it was not sufficient to exclude the report from the evidence. Accordingly, the application would be dismissed.

Rogers v Hoyle [2013] EWHC 1409 (QB), [2013] All ER (D) 21 (Sep) (Queen's Bench Division: Leggatt J). *Hollington v F Hewthorn and Co Ltd* [1943] KB 587, [1943] 2 All ER 35, CA, considered.

300 Evidence—expert witness—professional negligence—rejection of evidence—need for careful scrutiny of reasoning

Jamaica

The claimant company intended to acquire a majority shareholding of another company ('the company'). Before going ahead with the acquisition, the claimant instructed the defendant firm of accountants to carry out a valuation of the company. In reaching a valuation, the defendant took the view that the surplus of the company's pension fund was an asset. At the date of the defendant's valuation, the company had borrowed sums from the pension fund, but this had not been recorded in a report provided by a firm of consulting actuaries. The claimant brought an action in negligence and breach of contract against the defendant, asserting that it had been negligent in considering that the pension fund surplus was an asset when in fact it had been materially depleted by the company borrowing from it. The parties each relied on expert evidence. The defendant's expert witness stated that it had been commonplace for pension plan surpluses to be used to reduce the company's contribution rate to the pension plan and, in that event, the surplus could be seen as an asset. The trial judge rejected this evidence, holding that the defendant ought to have realised the importance of the status and value of the surplus to the whole valuation exercise and the valuation had required 'the application of common sense' which did not 'require any expertise in share valuation'. The defendant appealed. The appellate court held that had the trial judge given due value and weight to the evidence of the defendant's expert witness he would not have found that the defendant was negligent. The claimant appealed. *Held*, the trial judge's finding that the defendant's case that the pension fund surplus could have been brought back into the company as an asset was unsound had been based on a view of the judge that had not been put to the defendant's expert witness. The effect of the pension fund surplus was properly a matter for a professional opinion, based on accounting standards and practices at the relevant time. Further, the trial judge had been wrong to regard as a matter of obvious common sense that the defendant had been negligent, not requiring any expertise in share valuation. While in principle a court could reject an expert witness's opinion, it was essential that the reasons given by the expert for reaching his opinion were carefully scrutinised. The defendant's expert had advanced reasoned grounds in support of his conclusion. Had the trial judge given due weight to that evidence he would not have concluded that the defendant had been negligent. Accordingly, the appeal would be dismissed.

Caribbean Steel Co Ltd v Price Waterhouse [2013] UKPC 18, [2013] All ER (D) 74 (Aug) (Privy Council: Lord Hope, Lord Wilson, Lord Sumption, Lord Carnwath and Lord Toulson). *Sanson v Metcalfe Hambleton & Co* (1997) 57 ConLR 87, CA (1997 Abr para 856), applied.

301 Evidence—fresh evidence—admissibility—evidence demonstrating earlier evidence to be fraudulent

Four appeals were heard together which raised common issues regarding charges incurred in hiring a replacement car on credit terms following a road traffic accident in which the claimant was not to blame. In each case a specialist car hire and claims management company (the 'hire company') had provided a replacement car on credit hire terms to the claimant. Another company (the 'forensics company') had in each case provided a forensic report concerning the daily rate of hire that could be recovered by the hire company. The hire company brought proceedings against the forensics company, alleging that it had falsified evidence concerning the hire rates applicable, which had caused the hire company financial loss. An analysis, which was not disputed, of the forensics company's business records demonstrated that (1) historic basic hire rate data had been fabricated by its rate surveying staff; (2) those fabrications had affected its database of hire rate information as well as the reports that it had generated; and (3) witness evidence had been routinely altered by its employees. In the four present appeals, each claimant had claimed damages for the loss of use of the car that had been damaged as a result of the negligence of the defendant. In each case, the judge had accepted, to a greater or lesser extent, the forensics company's matter went to arbitration in Malaysia. An award was issued in favour of the claimants as contractual compensation for the defendant's termination of the agreement. The claimants took steps in a number of different jurisdictions to enforce the award. The agreement contained an express waiver of immunity from execution by the defendant which commenced proceedings in Malaysia to set aside the award. The claimants applied for judgment of the award together with an application from the defendant for an adjournment of the hearing pending the forthcoming hearing of its application to set aside the award. The defendant was ordered to pay the full amount into court as a condition of adjourning the application. It failed to pay and judgment was entered against it. The Malaysian court set aside the award. The claimants obtained a freezing order in standard form except that it was stated that the prohibition included any assets held in an account in which the defendant had a beneficial interest, whether maintained in its own name or the name of the central bank. Special instructions to banks and other financial institutions were also made. The effect of the freezing order was that the central bank's accounts remained frozen for over three working days and seriously impacted on its ordinary business operations. An application was made by the central bank to discharge a domestic freezing order made against the defendant. On the return date, the central bank as a non-party, sought to set aside the entirety of the freezing order, alternatively the two provisions, together with directions for an inquiry under the cross-undertaking into the damages which it claimed to have suffered as a result of the order and further fortification of that cross-undertaking. *Held*, there had not been a fair presentation to the judge of the nature and consequence of the relief sought in the two provisions, how they could be justified and what the countervailing arguments might be. There had been serous failures to explain and justify the relief sought against bank accounts in the central bank's name. Although the breaches of duty were serious, it would not be just to deprive the claimants of the continuation of the freezing order against the defendant as a result of them. The breaches related solely to the two provisions and had no logical relevance to the continuation of the freezing order and in all its other respects against the defendant. As the breaches were not deliberate, the court would not require the claimant to give an undertaking. There would be an inquiry into damages as, once it had been decided that the central bank should be compensated for losses caused, all that was required was credible evidence sufficient to show that an inquiry was not clearly futile or disproportionate. The evidence adduced on behalf of the central bank had been sufficient to meet that test. Fortification would not be ordered with the cross-undertaking. The freezing order would be continued in a form varied by deletion of the two provisions, and directions would be given for an inquiry into damages under the undertaking. There would be no fortification of the cross-undertaking for the purposes of such inquiry. Judgment would be given accordingly.

Thai-Lao Lignite (Thailand) Co Ltd v Government of Lao People's Democratic Republic [2013] EWHC 2466 (Comm), [2013] 2 All ER (Comm) 883 (Queen's Bench Division: Popplewell J). *Miller Brewing Co v Mersey Docks and Harbour Co* [2003] EWHC 1606 (Ch), [2004] IP & T 542 (2003 Abr para 2689) applied.

309   Freezing order—discharge—misappropriation and misuse of funds

The claimant, who was a Russian banker, acquired a percentage of the defendant bank, which was incorporated in Lithuania. The defendant became insolvent and brought proceedings against the claimant in England, claiming that he seriously abused his position as chairman and appropriated assets. The Lithuanian government, by compensating depositors with the defendant, became the largest creditor in the defendant's bankruptcy. The Lithuanian prosecuting authorities sought the extradition of the claimant in connection with criminal charges and the court granted a world-wide freezing order against him. The claimant applied to the court to discharge the order on the basis that there had been material non-disclosure by the defendant in relation to various matters, misrepresentations by the defendant that were highly relevant to the need for relief and the scope of any order, the risk of dissipation and the issue of delay, no significant risk of asset dissipation to justify making the order, and considerable delay since the date on which the defendant contemplated bringing civil proceedings against the claimant and the date on which the application for the order had been made. Moreover, the claimant contended that the order should be varied so that he did not have to provide disclosure of his current assets, submitting that information provided by him would, in breach of his rights under the

European Convention on Human Rights, be passed to the Lithuanian prosecuting authorities and would be used against him in the criminal investigation. *Held*, in relation to the discharge of the freezing order, although there had arguably been non-disclosure in relation to some matters, there was nothing sufficiently material to be taken into account in deciding whether to grant relief without notice. In particular, none of the alleged non-disclosures, misrepresentations or inadequate descriptions of events in any way impacted on the merits of the defendant's claims. Taking into account all the circumstances, it would be wholly inappropriate and disproportionate to discharge the order, or to discharge it and re-grant it at a later date. Further, there was clearly a risk of dissipation and the fact that the defendant had not made the application for the order until a later date was no reason for not continuing the injunctions. Moreover, the claimant would be ordered to comply with the terms of disclosure in the order and no variation would be made. Given the nature and amount of the claim, and the evidence relating to the claimant's alleged misappropriations, a disclosure order was necessary to make the freezing order effective. The defendant would be under the standard undertaking not to use any information given by the claimant for any purposes except that of the present proceedings. While it was possible that information could fall into the hands of the Lithuanian prosecuting authorities that did not outweigh the need and obligation for the claimant to provide disclosure. Accordingly, the applications would be dismissed.

Akciné Bendrové Bankas Snoras (in bankruptcy) v Antonov [2013] EWHC 131 (Comm), [2013] All ER (D) 49 (Feb) (Queen's Bench Division: Gloster J). *Brink's Mat Ltd v Elcombe* [1988] 3 All ER 188, CA (1988 Abr para 1379); *Dubai Bank Ltd v Galadari* [1990] Ch 98, [1989] 3 All ER 769 (1989 Abr para 691); and *Re Stanford International Bank Ltd* [2010] EWCA Civ 137, [2011] Ch 33, [2010] All ER (D) 219 (Apr) (2010 Abr para 557) applied.

310   Freezing order—discharge—worldwide order—grounds for discharge

The claimant let a vessel to the defendant under a charterparty. The defendant did not pay hire and the claimant obtained two interim partial awards for unpaid hire in arbitration proceedings. The claimant subsequently terminated the charterparty prematurely, contending that the defendant was in repudiatory breach of the charterparty. The claimant sought damages for the breach and obtained a worldwide freezing order over the defendant's assets. The defendant applied to discharge the order on the basis that the claimant's arrest of the vessel in another jurisdiction breached an undertaking to the court not to seek to enforce the order outside the jurisdiction without the court's permission. *Held*, the principle applying to the grant of permission to enforce a worldwide freezing order abroad was that the grant of the permission had to be just and convenient for the purpose of ensuring the effectiveness of the order and, in addition, that it was not oppressive to the parties to the English proceedings or to third parties who might be joined to the foreign proceedings. Obtaining a specific form of security order abroad such as an arrest had nothing to do with ensuring the effectiveness of the order. The arrest of the vessel did not involve a breach of the undertaking because it did not involve seeking an order of a similar nature to the worldwide freezing order. Accordingly, the application would be refused.

E v M [2013] EWHC 895 (Comm), [2013] All ER (D) 277 (May) (Queen's Bench Division: Hamblen J). *Dadourian Group International Inc v Simms* [2006] EWCA Civ 399, [2006] 3 All ER 48 (2006 Abr para 1705) applied.

311   Freezing order—interim order—continuation—jurisdiction

The Civil Jurisdiction and Judgments Act 1982 s 25(1) provides that the High Court has power to grant interim relief where (a) proceedings have been or are to be commenced in a Brussels or Lugano contracting state, a state bound by the Lugano Convention or a Brussels I Regulation state or a European Maintenance Regulation state other than the United Kingdom; and (b) they are or will be proceedings whose subject matter is either within the scope of the Brussels Regulation or the Maintenance Regulation or within the scope of the Convention, whether or not the Brussels Regulation, the Maintenance Regulation or the Convention has effect in relation to the proceedings. On an application for interim relief under the 1982 Act s 25(1), the court may refuse to grant relief if, in its opinion, the fact that the court has no jurisdiction apart from s 25 in relation to the subject matter of the proceedings makes it inexpedient for the court to grant it: s 25(2).

The claimant was a Russian bank that made substantial loans to a number of companies in a Russian group under loan agreements. Each of the loan agreements was guaranteed by the first defendant, who was resident in Russia. The second and third defendants were limited liability partnerships in England owned by trusts of which the first defendant was the discretionary beneficiary. In support of Russian proceedings arising out of the loans, interim freezing orders under the 1982 Act s 25 were made in respect of all the defendants. On a hearing to decide whether to continue the orders, an issue arose as to whether the court had jurisdiction to make the orders against the second and third defendants. *Held*, the connection or lack of it with the United Kingdom was to be considered under s 25(2) under the heading of 'inexpediency'. The court had to consider first whether the facts warranted the relief sought if the substantive proceedings were brought in England. If the answer to that question was in the affirmative, the court then had to consider whether in the terms of s 25(2) the fact that it had no jurisdiction made it inexpedient to grant the interim relief sought. The statutory test expressly provided for how the approach was to be taken, namely that the court could grant the order but might refuse it within s 25(2). Although s 25 was an exorbitant jurisdiction, it was intended to assist foreign proceedings and foreign courts. However, the court would, obviously, proceed with caution. In the circumstances, the court was satisfied that it had jurisdiction in accordance with s 25 and the relief sought by the claimant would be continued.

Joint Stock Co VTB Bank v Skurikhin [2012] EWHC 3916 (Comm), [2013] 2 All ER (Comm) 418 (Queen's Bench Division: Burton J).

312   Freezing order—scope—general freezing of assets—lawfulness

The claimant was the partner of the defendant, with whom she had two children. She brought a claim against the defendant contending that he had promised her a share of the proceeds of sale of the house in which they had lived and to buy her a new home. She also contended that she was the ultimate beneficial owner of two properties in France, which were held through companies and trusts. A sale of the relevant properties was being planned, and the claimant was fearful that she would not receive the proceeds. She therefore applied without notice for an interim freezing order against the defendant in respect of the proceeds of the sale of the house, the relevant part of the litigation settlement proceeds, and the French properties. The order was granted and the defendant's assets were frozen generally to the extent of £200m. The defendant applied to discharge the freezing order, submitting that there was insufficient evidence of a relevant risk of dissipation to found an application for a freezing order, and that the evidence was also insufficient to justify a without notice application. *Held*, the evidence did not go so far as to establish that there was a risk that the claimant would dissipate his assets generally in order to keep them away from being able to satisfy the claimant's claims should she establish them. Further, while there had been justification for making an application without notice, the full scope of the relief obtained could not be justified. The evidence demonstrated a sufficient degree of likelihood that the defendant would take steps in relation to the particular assets to frustrate the claimant's claim to those assets. But the defendant was not found to have demonstrated a tendency to take steps in relation to his assets generally to frustrate any consequential contractual claims the claimant might have. In those circumstances, it would be wrong to freeze his assets generally. The assets which should be frozen should be those which were at risk, namely the three assets in which the claimant had been promised or in which she had been assured an interest. Accordingly, the appeal would be allowed in part.

Gorbunova v Berezovsky [2013] EWHC 76 (Ch), [2013] All ER (D) 179 (Jan) (Chancery Division: Mann J).

313   Funding—funding agreement—damages-based agreement

The Damages-Based Agreements Regulations 2013, SI 2013/609 (in force on 1 April 2013), prescribe the requirements with which a damages-based agreement ('DBA') must comply in order to be enforceable under the Courts and Legal Services Act 1990 s 58AA following the amendment of that provision to permit and regulate the use of DBAs in all civil litigation. The 2010 Regulations, SI 2010/1206, which applied only to employment matters, are revoked. In particular, the regulations (1) provide that the payment from a client's damages must be the sum agreed to be paid (which, where relevant, will include any disbursements incurred by the representative in respect of counsel's fees) net of any costs (including fixed costs) and any sum in respect of counsel's fees, payable to the representative by another party to the proceedings; (2) provide that in a claim for personal injuries, the amount to be paid by a client, including VAT, must not be greater than 25 per cent of the combined total of the damages recovered by the client in the proceedings for pain, suffering and loss of amenity and pecuniary loss (other than future pecuniary loss), net of any sums recoverable by the Compensation Recovery Unit; the 25 per cent cap will only apply to claims or proceedings at first instance; (3) provide that in any other claim or proceedings to which the regulations apply, the amount of the payment, including VAT, must not be greater than 50 per cent of the sums ultimately recovered by the client; the 50 per cent cap will only apply to claims or proceedings at first instance; and (4) in relation to employment matters only (a) specify the information that a representative must provide before a DBA is made; (b) specify that additional causes of action can be added to the agreement by written and signed amendment; (c) provide for the maximum amount that is payable to the representative from a client's damages under a DBA in respect of an employment matter, so that the amount of the payment, including VAT, must not be greater than 35 per cent of the sums ultimately recovered by the client in the claim or proceedings; and (d) state that the terms and conditions of an agreement that provide for the termination of the DBA in an employment matter must comply with the following requirements: if the agreement is ended then the representative cannot charge more than his or her costs and expenses for the work done in respect of the client's claim or proceedings; the client may not end the agreement at particular stages; the representative may not end the agreement unless the client has been or is being unreasonable; and nothing in the regulations prevents a party from exercising a right under the general law of contract to terminate the agreement, for example for misrepresentation or fundamental breach.

314   Hearing—private hearing—disciplinary proceedings brought by Financial Services Authority—protection of claimant's identity

The claimant was the group finance director of a bank. The defendant, which was the former statutory regulator of the financial services industry, issued a decision notice to the claimant and imposed a penalty for failing to comply with principles laid down by the Financial Services and Markets Act 2000. In judicial review proceedings, the claimant alleged that, contrary to s 388, the defendant had failed to give adequate reasons for issuing the notice. The hearing was conducted in private, and the judgment was published in a redacted and anonymised form in order to protect the claimant's identity. The defendant appealed against the substantive decision reached by the judge in the judicial review proceedings. At the beginning of the appeal, the claimant applied for the hearing to be held in private. *Held*, in civil cases between adult parties, the public interest in open justice would usually outweigh other considerations, except where publication would significantly undermine the effectiveness of any relief the court might grant. No doubt the proceedings would have been embarrassing to the claimant if his identity had been made public, and it might have been that they would have caused some damage to his professional reputation, but he would not have been entitled to have his identity protected on those grounds if, for example, he had for some reason been facing criminal charges. Further, there was no positive evidence that he would suffer significant harm if the existence of the proceedings was disclosed at the present stage. Although the defendant's disciplinary proceedings had been in private, once the claimant had stepped outside of those proceedings, whether by referring the matter to the Upper Tribunal or by making a claim for judicial review, he had brought the matter into the public forum where the principle of open justice applied. The primary object of the proceedings had not been to protect the claimant, but to ensure that the procedure adopted by the defendant had complied with the statutory requirements and to quash the existing decision notice to enable the defendant to reconsider the matter. In those circumstances, it had not been strictly necessary in the interests of justice to publish the judgment in a form that would prevent the claimant's identification. Accordingly, the application would be dismissed.

R (on the application of Willford) v Financial Services Authority [2013] EWCA Civ 674, [2013] All ER (D) 115 (Jun) (Court of Appeal: Moore-Bick and Black LJJ and Sir Malcolm Pill).

management, had fraudulently misappropriated large sums through a number of offshore companies controlled and managed on his behalf. The offshore companies included five incorporated in the British Virgin Islands ('the BVI companies'). The defendant had failed to attend the handing down of a judgment by the High Court in committal proceedings and he subsequently absconded from the jurisdiction. In those proceedings the judge found that the defendant was the beneficial owner of at least one of the BVI companies ('the first BVI company'). Default judgments were entered against him but none of those judgments had been satisfied. The claimant applied for summary judgment against the defendant. *Held*, it was settled law that summary judgment would be granted where a defendant had no real prospect of a defending the claim. The simpler the case, the easier it was likely to be to take the view and resort to summary judgment. More complex cases were unlikely to be capable of being resolved without conducting a mini-trial on the documents, without discovery and without oral evidence. Where the application in such complex cases relied on inferences of fact, the overriding objective might well require the claim to go to trial in the interest of a fair trial. However, it did not follow that summary judgment could never be appropriate in a complex case where fraud was alleged. On the facts, the defendant was the ultimate beneficial owner of all five of the BVI companies and there was no reasonable prospect of the court reaching a contrary conclusion if the case were to go to trial. Applying settled law, the committal judgment was a judgment of the High Court and was final and conclusive. It followed that the court could safely proceed on the assumption that, if the case were to go to trial, the defendant would be estopped from denying his beneficial ownership of the first BVI company. It was not credible to suppose that the transactions relating to the fraudulent activities could have taken place without the defendant's authority, knowledge and involvement. In addition to his beneficial ownership of the BVI companies, and the circumstantial evidence linking him to the alleged fraud, there was evidence directly implicating him in the transactions. Accordingly, the application would be allowed.

JSC BTA Bank v Ablyazov [2013] EWHC 3691 (Ch), [2013] All ER (D) 293 (Nov) (Chancery Division: Henderson J). *Mentmore International Ltd v Abbey Healthcare (Festival) Ltd* [2010] EWCA Civ 761, [2010] All ER (D) 62 (Jul) applied.

326   Judgment—summary judgment—real prospect of successful defence—gift of property

For six months the defendant lived in a property which the director and shareholder of the claimant company (the 'director') provided for her, but which was held in the defendant's name. It was common ground that the claimant provided bridging finance for the purchase of a flat, as the flat was to be purchased before completion of the sale of the property. The defendant was the registered owner of the flat. The claimant contended that it provided the funds for the purchase of the flat by way of bridging finance on terms contained in a letter handed to the defendant by the director, providing that the legal title would be held by the defendant as a bare trustee, but that the claimant was beneficially entitled to the flat and had a right to possession. The claimant also claimed to have an equitable title in the flat on the basis that (1) it was fanciful that the director would gift the property to the defendant, given their casual sexual relationship; (2) the director was unable to effect such a gift because the property did not belong to the director, but to the claimant; and (3) the formalities required by the Law of Property Act 1925 s 53 for the disposition of an equitable interest had not been complied with. In the resulting proceedings, the claimant sought summary judgment. *Held*, if the defendant's denial of receiving and agreeing to the terms of the letter could be substantiated, that would appear to dispose of the claimant's case in relation to the flat. Although there were contemporary documents which referred to the provision of bridging finance, there had been no document which had provided that the director had handed the letter to her as he had said he had. It followed that that was a factual issue which was not suitable for summary judgment. Assuming that the terms of the letter had been agreed by the defendant so as to constitute a binding contract, that had not provided the claimant with an unanswerable case. Moreover, there was at least some apparently compelling evidence that the defendant had more than a casual relationship with the director. There was also at least an arguable case with a real prospect of success that the property had been beneficially as well as legally owned by the defendant and that, fanciful or not, there was a real prospect of showing that the director had made such a gift. The claimant's argument based on s 53 failed to take account of the impact of repayment of the bridging loan. As there were reasonable arguments that the effect of the letter had been that the claimant's equitable interest had only been intended to subsist until repayment of the loan out of the property proceeds of sale, after which the defendant had been intended to have both the legal and beneficial interest in the flat, and that the bridging loan had been repaid in its entirety, effect had to be given to the parties' contractual agreement to that effect. Accordingly, the application would be dismissed.

Sargespace Ltd v Eustace [2013] EWHC 2944 (QB), [2013] All ER (D) 26 (Oct) (Queen's Bench Division: Males J).

327   Judgment—summary judgment—reasonable prospect of success—lack of evidence—phone hacking

Four claimants brought proceedings contending that journalists employed by the defendant newspaper proprietor had hacked their mobile phones and listened to messages in their voicemail boxes without their consent. The claimants argued that the newspapers published by the defendant had therefore been able to publish stories about their private lives. It was contended that that activity infringed the claimants' privacy rights. However, none of the claimants pleaded direct evidence of hacking in their particular cases in the sense of direct first-hand evidence or records of particular hacking events. Instead, the particulars of claims were based on inferences from various generic facts. The defendant applied for summary judgment in two of the actions, and for the particulars of claim to be struck out in all four cases. It fell to be determined whether there was a realistic prospect of the claims succeeding for the purposes of CPR Pt 24. The defendant submitted that a case should not be allowed to go for trial simply because it was asserted that some further evidence might turn up. *Held*, summary judgment might be given against a claimant if it was clear beyond question that the statement of facts was contradicted by all the documents or other material on which it was based. The simpler the case, the easier it would be to take that view. However, more complex cases were unlikely to be capable of being resolved in that way without conducting a mini-trial on the documents, without discovery and without oral evidence. CPR Pt 24 was designed to deal with cases that were not fit for trial at all. The present cases were capable of falling into the category of cases which required full investigation. Provided that there was enough to prevent them falling into the category of the purely speculative, the nature of the wrong or alleged wrong was such that the claimants would or might have little knowledge and evidence of their own at the present stage and would need the benefits of pre-trial procedures in order to add to their case. The alleged activities in the present case had been covert and, of their very nature, would be activities of which the victims would know little or nothing. Better evidence of what happened would lie with the defendant. There was nothing wrong with pleading a starting point, on an appropriate basis, and then expecting the case to become clearer after pleading and disclosure. The present case was not one in which the cause of action was couched in dishonesty, or which involved a particular state of mind. It was based on acts which were said to be a civil wrong, and which also happened to be a criminal offence. Accordingly, the applications would be dismissed.

Gulati v MGN Ltd [2013] EWHC 3392 (Ch), [2013] All ER (D) 66 (Nov) (Chancery Division: Mann J).

328   Judgment—summary judgment—striking-out—malicious falsehood

See *Niche Products Ltd v Macdermid Offshore Solutions LLC*, para 848.

329   Justice and Security Act 2013

See para 475.

330   Litigation funding—personal injury cases—referral fees—prohibition

See *R (on the application of Association of Personal Injury Lawyers) v Secretary of State for Justice*, para 1642.

331   Parties—right to anonymity—child victim of cyberbullying

See *AB (by her litigation guardian CD) v Bragg Communications Inc*, para 425.

332   Parties—substitution—patent proceedings—assignment of patent

The first defendant was an American company which owned various pharmaceutical patents. The claimant companies brought claims against the first defendant for revocation of one of the patents and for a declaration that any supplementary protection certificate based on the patent would not be valid. The claimants also brought a claim against the first defendant and the second defendant, which was a wholly owned subsidiary of the first defendant, for a declaration that dealing in a specified product would not amount to infringement of the patent. At the dates on which the claims were brought, the first defendant was the registered proprietor of the patent, although it had assigned the patent to the second defendant. It was common ground that the claimants were unaware of that assignment. Pursuant to CPR 19.2, the defendants applied for orders that the second defendant be substituted for the first defendant in the proceedings and that the first defendant cease to be a party to the claims. *Held*, it was settled law that CPR 19.2 conferred a very wide power to enable parties who might be affected by a finding in any proceedings to be joined. That power might be exercised to add (and therefore to retain) a party even if no existing party was in a position to assert a claim against the party sought to be joined. The Patents Act 1977 s 32(9), the Patents Rules 2007, SI 2007/3291, r 103, and CPR 63.14(2)(a) made it clear that a person was entitled to consult the register of patents and commence revocation proceedings by serving those proceedings on the proprietor at the address that he found in the register. Even when a claimant knew that the patent in suit had been assigned to another party, the registered proprietor remained a proper party, in order to ensure that any order obtained was fully effective. The power of the court to grant declaratory relief was discretionary. There had, in general, to be a real and present dispute between the parties before the court as to the existence or extent of a legal right between them. In the present case, in considering whether to grant declaratory relief, it was sufficient for the court to decide whether the claimants had a real prospect of successfully claiming declaratory relief against the first defendant. Applying settled law, there was such a prospect. The fact that the first defendant did not own the legal right in question was not determinative. The key question was whether that party would be affected by the court's determination of the issues concerning that right so that, where one party sought to be made a defendant, the opposing party had a legitimate interest in ensuring that the other party was bound by that determination. It was arguable that the first defendant would be affected by the court's determination of the issues concerning the patent in a number of ways. On the evidence, there appeared to be nothing to prevent the first defendant from procuring that the second defendant assign the patent back to it at any time. Further, the first defendant remained the owner of the other patents in the family. Accordingly, the application would be dismissed.

Teva Pharma BV v Amgen Inc [2013] EWHC 3711 (Pat), [2013] All ER (D) 317 (Nov) (Chancery Division: Arnold J).

333   Settlement of proceedings—offers to settle

The Offers to Settle in Civil Proceedings Order 2013, SI 2013/93 (in force on 12 February 2013), prescribes the percentage of the amount awarded to the claimant that a defendant may be ordered to pay as an additional amount under the Legal Aid, Sentencing and Punishment of Offenders Act 2012 s 55, where the defendant does not accept the claimant's offer to settle, and the court subsequently gives judgment for the claimant which is at least as advantageous to the claimant as the claimant's offer. The order also provides (1) that in those proceedings which include both a claim for money and a non-money claim, the amount to be paid by the defendant to the claimant will be calculated as a percentage of the amount awarded to the claimant by the court in respect of the claim for money; (2) that in a non-money claim only, the amount to be paid will be calculated as a percentage of the costs that the defendant is ordered to pay the claimant; in these instances the maximum amount that a defendant may be ordered to pay is £75,000; and (3) that rules of court may include provision as to the assessment of whether a judgment is at least as advantageous as an offer to settle and may further make provision as to how the value of a non-monetary benefit awarded to a claimant may be calculated.

334   Settlement of proceedings—Part 36 offer—expiry of offer—judgment—costs

The claimant issued proceedings in which it was alleged that the defendants, who had been engaged to act for the claimant in a property transaction, purchased the property themselves, making use of the legal advice and valuation report that had been prepared for the claimant. The claimant sought an account of profits for breach of fiduciary duty arising from misuse of his confidential information. The defendants made an offer under CPR Pt 36, but the claimant did not accept the offer within the required time. The claimant subsequently failed to obtain a judgment more advantageous than the defendant's offer, the judge having rejected the claimant's claim for an account of profits, but awarding him nominal damages for the defendants' use of the information. The judge gave a separate decision in relation to costs, ordering the claimant to pay 90 per cent of the defendants' costs down to and including the date on which the offer under Pt 36 expired and all of their costs thereafter. The judge found that the principal issue in the case was the claim by the claimant to be entitled to an account of the profits made by the defendant from the acquisition of the property and that, while the claimant recovered money as a result of the judgment and was entitled to recover his costs of the issue on which he had been successful, by the same token the defendants were entitled to recover their costs attributable to resisting the remaining issues and the costs common to both. The claimant appealed, submitting that the judge should have had specific regard to the fact that most of the costs incurred by the defendants during the period prior to the date on which the Pt 36 offer expired were attributable to their unsuccessful defence. *Held*, the consequence of the claimant's rejection of the Pt 36 offer had been that the only costs in issue had been those for the period down to the day the Pt 36 offer expired. For the reasons that he had given, the judge's first assessment had been that the case had all been about the claimant's claim for an account of profits, and had hardly at all been about his alternative claim for damages, although the defendants resisted the latter claim on two grounds that failed, whereas they could have conceded it. As the defendants had won on the account of profits issue, the judge concluded that they had been the substantially successful parties, although their success should have been regarded as reduced by their unsuccessful resistance of the damages claim. That had meant that they had not been the successful party on all issues, just as the claimant had not been the unsuccessful party on all issues. In all the circumstances, the judge's order that the claimant was to pay 90 per cent of the defendants' costs of the claim had been unexceptionable. Accordingly, the appeal would be dismissed.

Walsh v Shanahan [2013] EWCA Civ 675, [2013] All ER (D) 180 (Jun) (Court of Appeal: Laws, Hallett and Rimer LJJ).

335   Settlement of proceedings—Part 36 offer—rejection of offer—subsequent acceptance—costs

The claimant company issued proceedings against the defendant company in relation to the refurbishment of a commercial property. The defendant denied liability. Shortly before the commencement of proceedings, the claimant made an offer to settle pursuant to CPR Pt 36. Standard directions for disclosure and expert evidence were ordered. A further CPR Pt 36 offer was subsequently refused by the defendant, which also failed to respond to the claimant's offer to take part in an early mediation. The defendant's own offer to settle was rejected by the claimant. Three months later, the claimant sent a further invitation to the defendant to mediate, but again the defendant did not respond. The day before the commencement of the trial, the defendant changed its defence, with the result that the claimant decided to accept the defendant's settlement offer. The ordinary consequences of that acceptance would have been that the claimant would have been obliged to pay the defendant's costs. However, the claimant decided to challenge the award of costs to the defendant, submitting that the defendant's refusal to participate in alternative dispute resolution ('ADR') had been unreasonable. The defendant denied that its silence had amounted to refusal and that any deemed refusal was unreasonable, and asserted that the expenditure during the relevant period had been attributable to the claimant's failure to accept a reasonable CPR Pt 36 offer until the day before the trial. The judge ruled that the defendant's silence had amounted to a refusal and that the refusal had been unreasonable. In those circumstances, although the judge refused to accede to the claimant's submission that it should have its costs for the relevant period, he made an order depriving the defendant of its costs which it would otherwise have been entitled. The defendant appealed against that decision. *Held*, silence in the face of an invitation to participate in ADR was, as a general rule, of itself unreasonable, regardless of whether an outright refusal, or a refusal to engage in the type of ADR requested, or to do so at the time requested, might have been justified by the identification of reasonable grounds. There might be rare cases where ADR was so obviously inappropriate that to characterise silence as unreasonable would be pure formalism. There might also be cases where the failure to respond at all was a result of some mistake, leading to a failure to appreciate that the invitation had been made. However, in such cases, the onus lay squarely on the recipient of the invitation to make that explanation good. On the face of the correspondence between the parties, the defendant's silence in the face of two requests to mediate had itself been unreasonable conduct of litigation sufficient to warrant a costs sanction. However, the sanction imposed by the judge had followed his determination that there had indeed been a refusal, and that it had been unreasonable. In that regard, the judge's exercise of the discretion to depart from the otherwise automatic consequences of CPR Pt 36 had been entirely correct. Accordingly, the appeal would be dismissed.

PGF II SA v OMFS Co 1 Ltd [2013] EWCA Civ 1288, [2013] All ER (D) 264 (Oct) (Court of Appeal: Maurice Kay, McFarlane and Briggs LJJ). *Halsey v Milton Keynes General NHS Trust; Steel v Joy* [2004] EWCA Civ 576, [2004] 4 All ER 920 (2004 Abr para 645) applied.

336 Settlement of proceedings—reservation of right to sue—joint tortfeasors

See *Gladman Commercial Properties v Fisher Hargreaves Proctor*, para 2371.

337 Stay of proceedings—parallel proceedings—enforcement of competition law—same issues arising in Scottish and English proceedings

See *Scottish Ministers v Servier Laboratories Ltd*, para 463.

CLUBS

Halsbury's Laws of England (5th edn) vol 13 (2009) paras 201–300

Articles

For articles relating to this title please refer to the Table of Articles at the beginning of the Abridgment.

COMMONHOLD

Halsbury's Laws of England (5th edn) vol 13 (2009) paras 301–400

Articles

For articles relating to this title please refer to the Table of Articles at the beginning of the Abridgment.

COMMONS

Halsbury's Laws of England (5th edn) vol 13 (2009) paras 401–700

Articles

For articles relating to this title please refer to the Table of Articles at the beginning of the Abridgment.

338 Growth and Infrastructure Act 2013

See para 2022.

339 Registration—town or village green—beach—conflict with use of land as port

The claimant owned and operated a port which included an area of beach. The interested party town council applied to the defendant local authority for the registration of the beach as a town or village green under the Commons Act 2006. The application was supported by significant evidence that the beach had been used by local inhabitants as of right for lawful sports and pastimes for at least 20 years before the claimant fenced off public access. The claimant sought judicial review of the defendant's decision to register the beach as a town or village green. The application was refused on the basis that registration was incompatible with the statutory purpose for which the claimant held the land, which was the maintenance and operation of the port. The defendant and town council appealed. *Held*, Lewison LJ dissenting, if Parliament had wished to preclude registration of land as a town or village green on grounds of incompatibility with the landowner's statutory functions, it would have included express provision to that effect. While the court did not underestimate the consequences that registration of the beach as a town or village green might have on the future discharge of the claimant's statutory functions, those consequences did not provide a proper ground for holding that the land was not registrable. Unlike the law relating to public highways and private rights of way, registration as a town or village green did not depend on actual or presumed grant or on actual or implied dedication. It depended instead on use of a specified character over a specified period, in accordance with the statutory conditions. Neither the absence of any general common law right in respect of use of the foreshore for recreational purposes nor the history of tolerance of such use precluded a finding that recreational use of a particular beach was use as of right, if such a finding was otherwise justified by the evidence. Accordingly, the appeal would be allowed.

R (on the application of Newhaven Port and Properties Ltd) v East Sussex CC [2013] EWCA Civ 276, [2014] QB 186, [2013] 3 All ER 677 (Court of Appeal: Richards, McFarlane and Lewison LJJ). *R (on the application of Beresford) v Sunderland City Council* [2003] UKHL 60, [2004] 1 AC 889, [2004] 1 All ER 160 (2003 Abr para 435) considered. Decision of Ouseley J [2012] EWHC 647 (Admin), [2012] 3 All ER 1361 (2012 Abr para 389) reversed.

340   Registration—town or village green—landowner statements and declarations

The Commons (Registration of Town or Village Greens) and Dedicated Highways (Landowner Statements and Declarations) (England) Regulations 2013, SI 2013/1774 (in force on 1 October 2013), apply to applications in England to deposit a statement and map, or lodge a declaration under the Highways Act 1980 s 31(6) or deposit a statement and map under the Commons Act 2006 s 15A. Specifically, the regulations (1) prescribe requirements as to the form such applications must take, including a prescribed application form, the scale requirements for an accompanying map, and fees required in respect of such applications; (2) make provision relating to when a statement made under s 15A(1) is treated as having been deposited with a commons registration authority; (3) prescribe that where an application to make such a deposit is combined with an application to deposit a statement and map or lodge a declaration under the 1980 Act s 31(6), the combined application will be treated as having been given to an appropriate authority at the same time as an application to deposit a statement and map or lodge a declaration under s 31(6) would be so treated under s 322(2), (3); (4) set out the steps which the authority receiving such an application must take on receipt of a validly made application; (5) require an authority to create a new part of the register under the 2006 Act s 15B(3); (6) prescribe the information which the register must include and the manner in which the register must be kept; and (7) specify circumstances in which information can be removed from the register. In addition, the regulations further amend the Dedicated Highways (Registers under Section 31A of the Highways Act 1980) (England) Regulations 2007, SI 2007/2334, so as to provide for paper registers kept under the 1980 Act s 31A to be held and inspected at a specified office or the principal office of the appropriate council. References to statutory declarations are removed and the period in which declarations under s 31(6) can be made following the deposit of an initial statement and map or the deposit of a previous declaration is extended.

341   Registration—town or village green—user as of right—compatibility with landowner's property rights

A town council applied under the Commons Act 2006 s 15(4) to a county council to register a beach owned by the claimant port as a town or village green. The claimant had recently fenced off an area of the beach that had been used by members of the public for recreational activities. According to the application, the claimed use of the land as of right had ended some months earlier. An inspector recommended that the application should be accepted and that recommendation was accepted by the county council, which duly registered the land as a town or village green. The claimant applied for judicial review of that decision. The judge allowed the application and quashed the registration. However, registration was restored on appeal by the defendant Secretary of State. Subsequently, the claimant appealed on one of the grounds of challenge which the judge had rejected, that s 15(4) was incompatible with the claimant's rights under the European Convention on Human Rights First Protocol art 1. *Held*, it was plain that a policy which recognised and regularised a long-standing state of affairs, the use of land 'as of right' for 20 years for lawful sports and pastimes. That was a legitimate aim. It was the basis of the law of adverse possession and the acquisition of easements by prescription. The aim was the more legitimate where the long-standing state of affairs was itself dependent on the acquiescence of the landowner and the rights created by the regularisation of that state of affairs were, effectively, public rights. In the present case, the aim of the 2006 Act s 15(4) was to give local inhabitants a longer period of grace in order to take account of the fact that the threat to their continued use had not been as obvious as in cases of cessation after the 2006 Act. That was a legitimate aim, and it was consistent with the overall policy that once 20 years use as of right had been established it should be possible to get the land registered as a town or village green. Since the decision in *R v Oxfordshire CC, ex p Sunningwell Parish Council*, all landowners had effectively been put on notice that those using their land for recreational purposes might well have been asserting a public right to do so if their use of the land was more than trivial or sporadic. The fact that the claimant's predicament had come about because of its own acquiescence in a long-standing state of affairs meant that the case for compensation was a particularly weak one. Further, s 15(5) gave a substantial measure of protection to landowners, which was not available under s 15(3). The fact that s 15(5) existed at all showed that Parliament had balanced the interests of local inhabitants and landowners. The Secretary of State had demonstrated that s 15(4) pursued a legitimate aim and that the means by which it pursued that aim were not manifestly without reasonable foundation. Accordingly, the appeal would be dismissed.

R (on the application of Newhaven Port and Properties Ltd) v East Sussex CC (No 2) [2013] EWCA Civ 673, [2013] 3 All ER 719 (Court of Appeal: Lloyd, Lewison and Gloster LJJ). *R v Oxfordshire CC, ex p Sunningwell Parish Council* [1999] 3 All ER 385, HL (1999 Abr para 463), considered. For earlier related proceedings see *R (on the application of Newhaven Port and Properties Ltd) v East Sussex CC* [2013] EWCA Civ 276, [2013] LGR 570 (para 339).

COMMONWEALTH

Halsbury's Laws of England (5th edn) vol 13 (2009) paras 701–871

342   Overseas territories—legislation—validity—review powers of English courts

See *R (on the application of Barclay) v Lord Chancellor (No 2)*, para 343.

343   Sark—constitution—plurality of offices—human rights

The Reform (Sark) Law 2008 provided for the dual role of the Seneschal as Chief Judge and President of the legislature of the Island of Sark. The claimants successfully challenged the legality of that enactment as being incompatible with the requirement under the European Convention on Human Rights art 6 for courts to be independent and impartial. As a result, the Reform (Sark) (Amendment) (No 2) Law 2010 was enacted. The Secretary of State had given advice to the Committee for the Affairs of Jersey and Guernsey in relation to the compatibility of the 2010 Law with the Convention. The present proceedings were instituted by the claimants in the belief that the advice given by the Secretary of State was unlawful as the 2010 Law also did not meet the requirements of the Convention art 6. It fell to be determined (1) whether the courts of England and Wales had jurisdiction to review the lawfulness of any advice given by the Secretary of State in relation to the approval of a projet de loi and of the recommendation of the Committee; (2) whether the lawfulness of the advice given by the Secretary of State in relation to the compatibility of the 2010 Law with the Convention as a treaty made by the United Kingdom was justiciable in England and Wales; and (3) whether the 2010 Law complied with the Convention art 6. *Held*, it was settled law that there was no reason why prerogative legislation should not be subject to review on ordinary principles of legality, rationality and procedural impropriety in the same way as any other executive action. On the facts, it would not be right for the court to decline jurisdiction on the basis that the proper court for the determination of the compatibility of the 2010 Law with the Convention was a court of the Bailiwick of Guernsey and to hold that proceedings should be brought in the courts of the Bailiwick. It was also an established principle that the law permitted the review of a decision based on the interpretation of the Convention where a decision was impugned on the basis that the decision-maker had erred in law in the interpretation of the Convention. In the present case, the issue was justiciable. Although the correctness of the advice of the Secretary of State formed the basis of the challenge, the challenge was to the decision of the Committee on the ground that it had misdirected itself in following the incorrect advice of the Secretary of State as to the interpretation of art 6. The correctness of that advice could be determined by reference to the considerable body of authority. Further, in the circumstances, the provisions of the 2010 Law with respect to the Seneschal's appointment, removal and renewal after the age of 65 had complied with the Convention art 6. However, the provision containing the unqualified power to make a reduction in the remuneration was open to arbitrary use. That provision on its own was sufficient to constitute a violation of art 6. Accordingly, the application would be allowed in part.

R (*on the application of Barclay*) *v Lord Chancellor* (*No 2*) [2013] EWHC 1183 (Admin), [2014] 1 WLR 415, [2013] All ER (D) 123 (May) (Queen's Bench Division: Sir John Thomas P and Burnett J). For earlier related proceedings see R (*on the application of Barclay*) *v Secretary of State for Justice* [2009] UKSC 9, [2010] 1 AC 464, [2010] 3 LRC 702 (2009 Abr para 587).

COMPANIES

Halsbury's Laws of England (5th edn) vol 14 (2009) paras 1–692, vol 15 (2009) paras 693–1841

Articles

For articles relating to this title please refer to the Table of Articles at the beginning of the Abridgment.

344   Accounts and audit—auditors—statutory and third country auditors

The Statutory Auditors and Third Country Auditors Regulations 2013, SI 2013/1672 (in force in part on 31 July 2013 and in part on 1 October 2013), make provision in relation to third country auditors and, specifically, (1) require the Financial Reporting Council Limited ('the Council') to keep the statutory register of third country auditors; (2) prescribe the information which the register must contain; (3) require the register to be kept in electronic form and to be available for inspection; (4) set out matters with which a third country auditor must comply in order to become registered; (5) set out the circumstances in which the Council may or may not register an applicant; (6) require the Council to allocate a registered number to a successful applicant on registration; (7) impose a duty on registered third country auditors to provide the Council with updated information so as to ensure that the information on the register remains correct; (8) make provision in relation to the removal of third country auditors from the register; (9) delay the coming into force of certain amendments to the Companies Act 2006 so that member states may continue, until 31 July 2016, to allow the transfer of audit working papers to specified American bodies; and (10) amend the 2006 Act so as to (a) allow an entity carrying out inspections of third country audit functions performed by statutory auditors to determine sanctions against such auditors where its inspections reveal breaches of the relevant rules of the auditor's professional body; (b) oblige a professional body to treat such sanctions as if they were sanctions imposed by itself; and (c) allow hearings in connection with disciplinary proceedings involving registered third country auditors to be waived. SI 2008/499, SI 2008/2639 and SI 2009/2798 are revoked. SI 2007/3494, SI 2010/2537 and SI 2011/1856 are amended.

345   Accounts and audit—partnerships and unlimited companies

The Companies and Partnerships (Accounts and Audit) Regulations 2013, SI 2013/2005 (in force on 1 September 2013), amend certain accounting and auditing provisions in the

375   Shareholder—minority shareholder—multiple derivative action—status of action at common law

The proceedings concerned an application by a company for permission to continue a derivative action concerning a claim for breach of fiduciary duty against the defendants in respect of a joint venture to develop a former coastal battery. The application raised related legal questions because the action was a 'double derivative action'. The applicant was not a shareholder in the company in which the cause of action was alleged to be vested but was a member of a limited liability partnership, which owned all the shares in that company. The issues for consideration were (1) whether a multiple derivative action was known to English common law before the coming into force of the Companies Act 2006 and, if so, whether the multiple derivative action had survived the coming into force of the 2006 Act; and (2) whether permission to continue the derivative action ought to be given. It was conceded that the particulars of claim and the evidence in support of them disclosed a sufficient prima facie case of a wrong done to the company. However, it was submitted on behalf of the defendants that the present case was not the type of case where the necessity of a derivative claim was sufficiently demonstrated since there were obvious alternative remedies such as a claim under the joint venture agreement or an unfair prejudice claim. *Held,* the 2006 Act had not done away with the multiple derivative action. Parliament had identified the main version of the procedural device, where locus standi was accorded to the wronged company's members, labelled it a 'derivative claim' and enacted a comprehensive statutory code in relation to it. As a matter of language, s 260 applied Pt 11 (ss 260–264) only to that part of the old common law device thus labelled, leaving other instances of its application unaffected. There had been a common law procedural device called the derivative action by which the court could permit a person with the closest sufficient interest to litigate on behalf of a company by seeking for the company relief in respect of a cause of action vested in it. Those persons would usually be a minority of the company's members, but might, if the company was wholly owned by another company, be a minority of the holding company's members. Applying the well-established relevant principle of construction, Parliament had not expressly abolished the whole of the common law derivative action in relation to companies. The court had a discretion whether to permit any common law claim to continue which was not limited to a cold analysis of whether the common law requirements set out in authority were met. It was settled law that in cases where neither side sought a buy-out, so that the only remedy for unfairly prejudicial conduct would be for the court to authorise a derivative claim, the consequential multiplicity of proceedings was itself a good reason for giving permission for a derivative claim in the first place. On the facts, the alternative remedies were not of sufficient substance to displace a multiple derivative action. A refusal of permission to continue the multiple derivative action would be less likely to focus the parties on the negotiation of a just solution to their dispute than would permission to continue, coupled with an order for a relatively short stay for mediation. Permission for the claim to continue would be granted. Judgment would be given accordingly.

Universal Project Management Services Ltd v Fort Gilkicker Ltd [2013] EWHC 348 (Ch), [2013] Ch 551, [2013] 3 All ER 546 (Chancery Division: Briggs J). *Stainer v Lee* [2011] 1 BCLC 537 considered.

376   Shareholder—minority shareholder—public company—application to re-register as private limited company

The second defendant company was incorporated in England as a public company but operated from Germany and its shares were only listed for trading on German exchanges. There were two registered shareholders: the first holding one share and the second holding the balance. The second defendant sold one of its subsidiaries and announced its intention to make a dividend distribution to its shareholders. The proposed dividend distribution was rejected by a majority of the shareholders, which included the first defendant company. Subsequently, a new board announced its intention to propose, at an annual general meeting, the cancellation of the listing of the second defendant's shares on the German exchanges and to re-register the second defendant as a private limited company. That announcement had an impact on the marketability of the second defendant's shares. The claimants claimed to be minority shareholders of the second defendant but were not registered shareholders. They commenced CPR Pt 8 proceedings alleging that their aggregate holding of the second defendant's shares gave them standing to apply under the

Companies Act 2006 s 98 for the cancellation of the resolution for the re-registration of the company as a private company. They sought an order for cancellation of the resolution unless the first defendant offered to purchase their shares at a fair price or, alternatively, an order that the second defendant should purchase their shares at a fair price and for its share capital to be reduced accordingly. The defendants applied to strike out the claim form pursuant to CPR 3.4(2)(a) as disclosing no reasonable grounds for bringing the claim, or alternatively for summary judgment. *Held*, on its true construction, the 2006 Act s 98 did not apply to the holders of an economic interest in shares and did not enable the holder of the ultimate economic interest to exercise rights otherwise vested in a member to protect the economic value of the shares. Membership, not ownership of an economic interest, defined the class from whom interest might be acquired of dissentient members. It was settled law that registration conferred title. Without registration, an applicant was not the holder of a share or a member of the company: the share had not been issued to him. Section 145 did not confer rights enforceable against a company by anyone other than the registered shareholders. The architecture of company law employed the concept of 'member' or 'shareholder' as a key element. Applying that interpretation of ss 98, 145, the claimants were not 'holders' of shares of the relevant value so as to entitle them to bring the claim. The proceedings commenced by the claim form had no real prospect of success. Summary judgment would be granted in favour of the defendants. Judgment would be given accordingly.

Eckerle v Wickeder Westfalenstahl GmbH [2013] EWHC 68 (Ch), [2013] All ER (D) 150 (Jan) (Chancery Division: Norris J). *National Westminster Bank plc v IRC* [1994] 3 All ER 1, HL (1994 Abr para 527), applied. *Farstad Supply A/S v Enviroco Ltd* [2011] UKSC 16, [2011] 3 All ER 451 (2011 Abr para 418) considered.

377   Shares—acquisition of company's own shares—instalments

The Companies Act 2006 (Amendment of Part 18) Regulations 2013, SI 2013/999 (in force on 30 April 2013), amend the Companies Act 2006 Pt 18 (ss 658–737) so as to (1) remove the requirement for private limited companies to pay on purchase the price of shares in full in cases where the buyback is for an employees' share scheme, thus allowing a private company to pay for its shares by instalments; (2) permit private companies to use cash without having to identify it as distributable reserves to finance the buyback of its own shares, up to the value of £15,000 or 5 per cent of the share capital of the company in each financial year; (3) change the requirements for shareholder authorisations concerning contracts for share buyback to be passed; instead of the authorisation being given by special resolution, it may be given by ordinary resolution; (4) allow a company to make off-market purchases of its own shares without having each buyback contract approved by shareholder resolution, as long as the company has a resolution from the shareholders authorising this; (5) amend the requirements that a company must fulfil when buying back its own shares using capital in cases where the buyback is for the purposes of or pursuant to an employees' share scheme so as to reduce the requirement to a statement by the directors that the company is solvent and a special resolution by the shareholders; and (6) allow a company limited by shares to hold its own shares in treasury, to deal with such shares as treasury shares, and allow shares bought back with cash to be held as treasury shares.

378   Unfair prejudice to members—petition—means used to obtain control of company

The petitioner held 36·2 per cent of the issued share capital in a private company. A second shareholder had executed two charges against his shares in favour of a bank. Under a shareholders' agreement and the company's articles of association, the petitioner had pre-emption rights in respect of the shares of other shareholders in particular circumstances. The petitioner alleged that the appropriate offer had not been made to him when it should have been so that the second shareholder's 35·4 per cent shareholding came under the control of a family settlement without having gone through the pre-emption provisions. A petition was issued under the Companies Act 2006 s 994 for relief against unfairly prejudicial conduct. The relief sought was an order entitling the petitioner to purchase the second shareholder's shareholding or exercise his pre-emption rights. The petition was dismissed on the basis that the companies controlled by the family settlement had achieved practical control over the second shareholder's shareholding. However, the judge found that there had not been a breach of the agreement, as it had fallen deliberately short of the transfer of an interest in the shares because the parties had wanted to avoid triggering the pre-emption rights, and that neither of the charges had become enforceable for the purposes of the agreement. On appeal by the petitioner, *held*, the arrangements by which control in the second shareholder's shares had passed to the family settlement had not amounted to the transfer either of the shares or of any interest in them, in circumstances where the court and the parties were bound by an earlier decision that 'interest' in a share for the purpose of the prohibition of the transfer of interest in shares in the agreement meant a direct proprietary interest. In the circumstances, the arrangements had not involved the transfer of a proprietary interest in the second shareholder's shares contrary to the agreement. Further, the arrangements whereby control of the second shareholder's shares had ended up in the hands of the family settlement had not involved any breach of the good faith clause in the agreement. There was no question of any act or omission which had been unfairly prejudicial to the petitioner within the meaning of s 994(1). Although the first charge had become enforceable, the second shareholder had been unaware of that fact at the relevant time and, therefore, had been unable to consider whether to exercise his right under the agreement so as to treat the second shareholder as having given a transfer notice while he still had the power to do so. However, its failure had not involved any breach of the petitioner's rights and could not be regarded as having caused him unfair prejudice. Furthermore, the later charge had become enforceable. There had been no need for an enforcement declaration. The company had not known that the later charge had become enforceable before the expiry of the time limit set out in the agreement. There was no implied term that had the effect of extending the one-month period. Accordingly, the appeal would be dismissed.

McKillen v Misland (Cyprus) Investments Ltd [2013] EWCA Civ 781, [2013] All ER (D) 52 (Jul) (Court of Appeal: Arden, Moore-Bick and Rimer LJJ). *Re Coroin Ltd; McKillen v Misland (Cyprus) Investments Ltd* [2012] EWCA Civ 179, [2012] 2 BCLC 611 (2012 Abr para 437) applied. *Tett v Phoenix Property and Investment Co Ltd* [1986] BCLC 149, CA (1985 Abr para 336), distinguished. Decision of David Richards J [2012] EWHC 2343 (Ch), [2012] All ER (D) 71 (Aug) (2012 Abr para 438) affirmed.

379   Unfair prejudice to members—petition—minority shareholder—valuation of shares

In proceedings in which a petitioner under the Companies Act 2006 s 994 established that she had been unfairly prejudiced as a minority shareholder of a company and an order was made that she be bought out by the majority shareholders, it has been held that the judge, in determining the price to be paid to the petitioner for her shares, erred in drawing a distinction between a bank debt and other debts.

Kohli v Lit [2013] EWCA Civ 667, [2013] All ER (D) 143 (Jun) (Court of Appeal: Laws and Black LJJ and Mann J).

380   Unfair prejudice to members—petition—pre-emption provisions

See *McKillen v Misland (Cyprus) Investments Ltd*, para 378.

381   Unfair prejudice to members—petition—service out of jurisdiction

The petitioner company was incorporated in the Seychelles and was owned and controlled by a Jordanian businessman. The third and fourth respondents were the directors of the second respondent company, a company incorporated in the British Virgin Islands. Both the petitioner company and the second respondent held shares in the first respondent, a company incorporated in England. A petition was presented by the petitioner company against the respondents under the Companies Act 2006 s 994 seeking an order that the second to fifth defendants should be ordered to purchase the petitioner company's shares in the first respondent at a fair and proper valuation pursuant to the Companies Act 2006 s 996. In its petition the petitioner company relied on unfairly prejudicial conduct. It was claimed that the third respondent had retained the post of chairman of the first respondent while refusing to become a de jure director of it. Further, the third and fourth respondents had caused, and the second respondent had knowingly permitted, the first respondent to become involved in unlawful activities relating to money laundering, for the actual or intended benefit of the third and fifth respondents and that the second to fifth respondents had pursued a campaign of threats and other unlawful conduct against the petitioner company and the Jordanian businessman. It was also claimed that for a period of time the third and fourth respondents had been hostile to the Jordanian businessman and had refused to co-operate with him in the running of the first respondent. The petitioner company issued an application notice seeking the court's permission to serve its petition on each of the second to fifth respondents outside the jurisdiction on the grounds that the shareholders' agreement and an alleged share sale agreement were governed by English law and jurisdiction and/or that it was brought under an enactment, namely s 994, which allowed it to be brought. Permission was duly granted by the registrar of companies. The third to fifth respondents applied to set aside the permission. *Held*, it was clear that if the facts alleged were established, relief under s 996 should be granted against one or more of the third, fourth and fifth respondents. It was clear that each of the third to fifth respondents was alleged to have been responsible for the conduct that had destroyed the petitioner company's confidence in the second respondent. Further, there was a serious case to be tried as to whether the first respondent's affairs were being or had been conducted in a manner that was unfairly prejudicial to the interests of the petitioner company within s 994. The court could not accept that the claims were far-fetched, incredible and fanciful. They might be found at trial to be one or more of those things, either in whole or in part, but at the present stage, the allegations raised a serious case to be tried and were supported by documents and materials that, if believed, evidenced them. In the circumstances, the requirements of the necessary or proper party gateway were satisfied in respect of each of the third to fifth respondents. The Jordanian businessman wished to serve the claim form on each of the third to fifth respondents and each of those respondents was both a necessary and a proper party to the claim. The registrar of companies had been right to permit the petition to be served out of the jurisdiction. Judgment would be given accordingly.

Apex Global Management Ltd v Fi Call Ltd [2013] EWHC 1652 (Ch), [2013] All ER (D) 194 (Jun) (Chancery Division: Vos J).

382   Unregistered companies—application of provisions of Companies Act 2006

The Unregistered Companies (Amendment) Regulations 2013, SI 2013/1972 (in force on 1 October 2013), further amend the 2009 Regulations, SI 2009/2436, so as to make changes in consequence of amendments made to the Companies Act 2006 by the Companies Act 2006 (Strategic Report and Directors' Report) Regulations 2013, SI 2013/1970 (see para 347), and the Enterprise and Regulatory Reform Act 2013 (see para 414), with the effect that the 2006 Act ss 414A–414D, 426–429, 420–422A and 439–440 are disapplied in relation to unregistered companies.

COMPANY AND PARTNERSHIP INSOLVENCY

Halsbury's Laws of England (5th edn) vol 16 (2011) paras 1–629, vol 17 (2011) paras 630–1370

Articles

For articles relating to this title please refer to the Table of Articles at the beginning of the Abridgment.

383   Company insolvency—administration—application for order—application by sole director—opposition by shareholders

The claimant was the sole director of a company engaged in the development of software. The company became insolvent, and the claimant applied under the Insolvency Act 1986 Sch B1 para 12 for the appointment of administrators on the ground that the company was unable to pay its debts. After that application had been made, two shareholders ('the shareholders') in the company's parent company appointed themselves as directors of the company pursuant to a shareholders' agreement. The shareholders opposed the claimant's application on the basis that there was the prospect of sufficient business for the company to enable it to continue in business and pay its liabilities in the ordinary course. An issue arose as to whether the shareholders were entitled to exercise rights to appoint or remove directors, including to appoint themselves as directors, under the shareholders' agreement, and whether the court had jurisdiction to make the order where the application for an administration order had been made by the one director who was on the board at the time the application was issued, but was opposed by two out of the three persons who were

652, CA; and *Glenister v Rowe* [2000] Ch 76, [1999] 3 All ER 452, CA, disapproved. Decision of Court of Appeal [2011] EWCA Civ 1124, [2012] 1 All ER 1455 (2011 Abr para 441) reversed.

392   Company insolvency—company voluntary arrangement—pre-arrangement debt—adjudicator's award

The defendants employed the claimant company to carry out sub-structure work for a house under a contract which provided for adjudication of disputes arising under it. Completion of the works was delayed and the claimant referred a claim in relation to the delay to adjudication. The claimant then entered into a company voluntary arrangement ('CVA'). During the adjudication proceedings, the defendants claimed that they had a valid and substantial counterclaim for negligence. The adjudicator subsequently determined that the defendants were liable to the claimant. The defendants wrote to the CVA supervisor to put the supervisor on notice that they intended to launch a claim against the claimant in respect of the cost of remedying defective work, and informed the supervisor that the claim for defects had not been considered in the adjudication proceedings. The claimant issued proceedings seeking summary judgment to enforce the adjudicator's decision. *Held*, as a matter of jurisdiction, the existence of a CVA did not act as a bar on adjudication which prevented a company from pursuing adjudication for a pre-CVA debt. The adjudicator had been right to disregard the existence of the CVA as a valid challenge. No set-off or cross-claim had been raised by the defendants before the adjudication, and neither the claimant nor the supervisors could be criticised for not actually then knowing that the defendant had or might have a viable cross-claim. In accordance with the Insolvency Act 1986 s 5, the conditions of the CVA were to be construed as contractually binding as between the parties. This had to be done in the context of the defendants having submitted a credible challenge to the substance of the adjudicator's decision, as well as raising an arguable counterclaim. On the facts, the court could not say that the claims were so lacking in support as not to be bona fide. Accordingly, the application for summary judgment would be dismissed.

Westshield Ltd v Whitehouse [2013] EWHC 3576 (TCC), [2014] BPIR 317, [2013] All ER (D) 292 (Nov) (Queen's Bench Division: Akenhead J). *Bouygues (UK) Ltd v Dahl-Jensen (UK) Ltd* [2001] 1 All ER (Comm) 1041, CA (2000 Abr para 390), applied. *Mead General Building Ltd v Dartmoor Properties Ltd* [2009] EWHC 200 (TCC), [2009] BLR 225, [2009] All ER (D) 224 (Mar) (2009 Abr para 319) considered.

393   Company insolvency—compulsory sale—event chargeable to value added tax

See Case C-125/12 *Promociones y Construcciones BJ 200 SL*, para 2563.

394   Company insolvency—cross-border insolvency—conflict of laws—jurisdiction

See *Joint Administrators of Heritable Bank plc v Winding up Board of Landsbanki Islands hf*, para 454.

395   Company insolvency—cross-border insolvency—co-operation between courts—request for assistance

The Insolvency Act 1986 s 426(4) provides that courts having jurisdiction in relation to insolvency law in any part of the United Kingdom are to assist the courts having the corresponding jurisdiction in any other part of the United Kingdom or any relevant country or territory.

The claimant company was registered in Jersey, but its main business activity was in England. The claimant had borrowed a large sum from the defendant bank in order to purchase and develop property in England. That venture had been a substantial failure, and the defendant had become the claimant's main creditor. The director of the claimant and the bank had arranged for sale of the property to occur, but considered it appropriate that a form of insolvency procedure occur before sale. It was not considered that Jersey insolvency proceedings would be appropriate, as the only available Jersey procedure would conclude certain contracts that needed to remain. An English administration was felt desirable by both parties, and they therefore made a request under the 1986 Act s 426 and invited the court to appoint administrators. An issue arose as to the meaning and effect of the word 'assist' in s 426(4). The court refused the claim, ruling that s 426 had no application where the foreign court was not actually doing anything, or apparently intending to do anything, in its insolvency jurisdiction. The defendant appealed against that decision, submitting that the judge's interpretation of s 426 was erroneous. *Held*, s 426(4) was not, by its actual working, applicable to courts exercising jurisdiction in relation to insolvency law; it was applicable to courts having jurisdiction, or the corresponding jurisdiction, in insolvency law. Under established authorities, s 426(4) and (5) were to be given a broad interpretation. The words of s 426(4), broadly read, were amply sufficient to enable the English court to 'assist' the Jersey court in the way requested. The approach of the judge had seemed to require the maintenance of separate formal insolvency processes in the requesting state, even where such process was not desired, would serve no purpose and would run up needless costs. Further, it was demonstrable that the Jersey court had been engaged in an endeavour. That endeavour had been to further the interests of the claimant and its creditors and to facilitate the most efficient collection and administration of the claimant's assets. In all the circumstances, there had been no good reason to have refused to acknowledge it as an exercise of insolvency jurisdiction simply because formal proceedings for an unwanted order had not been issued or contemplated. Accordingly, the appeal would be allowed.

HSBC Bank plc v Tambrook Jersey Ltd [2013] EWCA Civ 576, [2013] All ER (D) 247 (May) (Court of Appeal: Longmore, McFarlane and Davis LJJ). Decision of Mann J [2013] EWHC 866 (Ch), [2013] All ER (D) 116 (Apr) reversed.

396   Company insolvency—determination of insolvency—inability to pay debts—balance sheet test

The Insolvency Act 1986 s 123(2) provides that a company is deemed unable to pay its debts if it is proved to the satisfaction of the court that the value of the company's assets is less than the amount of its liabilities, taking into account its contingent and prospective liabilities.

An issuer of interest-bearing notes in a securitisation transaction agreed that an enforcement notice could be served on its associated company on behalf of the holders of the notes if a specified event of default occurred. The issuer hedged its risk in relation to the notes with companies which failed to meet their obligations and entered into liquidation. In the course of proceedings arising out of the transaction, it was found that the issuer could not be deemed unable to pay its debts within the meaning of the 1986 Act s 123(2). That decision was affirmed on appeal. On appeal by a section of the noteholders, *held*, the provisions of s 123(1), (2) had to be seen as making little significant change in the law that had existed before the 1986 Act. The changes in form served to underline that the 'cash flow' test was concerned with debts falling due from time to time in the reasonably near future, as well as to debts currently due. What was the reasonably near future would depend from case to case on all the circumstances, but especially on the nature of the company's business. Whether the test of balance-sheet insolvency was satisfied would depend on the available evidence as to the circumstances of the particular case. Once the court had to move beyond the reasonably near future, any attempt to apply a cash-flow test would become completely speculative, and a comparison of present assets with present and future liabilities would become the only sensible test. However, that was still very far from an exact test, and the burden of proof had to be on the party which asserted balance-sheet insolvency. Whether the test of balance-sheet insolvency was satisfied had to depend on the evidence in the individual case. The issuer's ability or inability to pay all its debts, present or future, might not be fully determined until much closer to the final repayment date. The complex documentation under which the loan notes were issued contained several mechanisms for ensuring that liabilities in respect of principal were, if necessary, deferred until the final redemption date, unless the post-enforcement regime came into operation. The movement of currencies and interest rates in the meantime, if not entirely speculative, were incapable of prediction with any confidence. It could not with any satisfaction be said that there would eventually be a deficiency. The court of first instance and the Court of Appeal had been correct on the issues. Accordingly, the appeal would be dismissed.

BNY Corporate Trustee Services Ltd v Eurosail-UK 2007–3BL plc [2013] UKSC 28, [2013] 3 All ER 271 (Supreme Court: Lord Hope DP, Lord Walker, Lord Mance, Lord Sumption and Lord Carnwath SCJJ). *Byblos Bank SAL v Al-Khudhairy* [1987] BCLC 232, CA (1986 Abr para 324); and *Re Cheyne Finance plc* [2007] EWHC 2402 (Ch), [2008] 2 All ER 987 (2007 Abr para 640) applied. Decision of Court of Appeal [2011] EWCA Civ 227, [2011] 3 All ER 470 (2011 Abr para 449) affirmed.

The appellant, the liquidator of a company, issued proceedings to recover from the respondent payments, consisting of remuneration and pension contributions in respect of services which the respondent claimed to have provided to the company, made under the Insolvency Act 1986 s 238 as payments at an undervalue. The judge decided that the payments constituted transactions at an undervalue but that they were not recoverable because the time of each payment was not a relevant time by virtue of s 240(2) as the company was not unable to pay its debts within the meaning of s 123 and did not become unable to do so as a result of the payments. Two experts agreed that the company was marginally insolvent on a balance-sheet basis as from a date specified and held that the company's directors' loan accounts might be current liabilities, but that the company had not reached the point of no return if they had no immediate intention of calling the loans in. The appellant appealed, contending that the company was unable to pay its debts within the meaning of s 123 and that the experts agreed that the company was balance-sheet insolvent at all material times, if a loan, which had been valued as an asset, was valued at nil. *Held*, since the point of no return did not provide the right test, it became irrelevant whether the judge had been right or wrong. The question was whether, applying the correct test, the court was in a position to be able to decide whether the company had been unable to pay its debts, giving due weight to the relevant factors. Reading ss 123 and 240(2) together, it was necessary for the respondent to prove to the satisfaction of the court both that the company had been, at material times, not unable to pay its debts as they had fallen due and the value of the company's assets equalled or exceeded the amount of its liabilities, taking into account its contingent and prospective liabilities. Further, if all of a company's liabilities were immediate or would be so within the reasonably near future, s 123(2) did not come into play. Therefore, when applying the cash-flow test under s 123(1)(e), all of the company's liabilities were taken into account and there was no need to look further to s 123(2). The respondent was unable to rebut the presumption which arose under s 240(2) in respect of balance-sheet insolvency. The company was, at all material times, in a position of having net liabilities as disclosed by the balance sheets prepared by both experts if the loan was valued at nil. It could not be suggested that, had the company stopped trading on any particular date after the date on which it became marginally balance-sheet insolvent, it would have been able to meet all of its liabilities. Its balance sheet showed an excess of liabilities over assets. It could not be said that the company had been able to pay its debts as they had fallen due. Accordingly, the appeal would be allowed.

Carman v Bucci [2013] EWHC 2371 (Ch), [2013] All ER (D) 03 (Aug) (Chancery Division: Warren J). *BNY Corporate Trustee Services Ltd v Eurosail-UK 2007–3BL plc* [2013] UKSC 28, [2013] 3 All ER 271 above applied.

397 Company insolvency—determination of insolvency—inability to pay debts—duty of director

The claimants were the joint liquidators of a company of which the defendant was the principal director. The company was a holding company for a Portuguese entity, and there were also a number of associated companies and/or subsidiaries in the United Kingdom. Much of the company's business was conducted through four direct subsidiaries. The company's net current liabilities, retained losses and shareholders' deficit increased steadily over the course of several years. The company also had contingent liabilities. The claimants brought proceedings seeking financial relief against the defendant in respect of a number of payments which he caused the company to make. They alleged that the defendant breached his duties owed to the company as a director under the common law and the Companies Act 2006. Consideration was given to the Insolvency Act 1986 s 123, which made provision for determining when a company was deemed to be unable to pay its debts. *Held*, the court's function under s 123(2) was not simply to aggregate all contingent and present liabilities at their face value with debt presently due, but rather to judge whether it had been established that, looking at the company's assets and making proper allowance for its prospective and contingent liabilities, it could not reasonably be expected to be able to meet those liabilities. In the present case, the company's accounts themselves had provided strong prima facie evidence of insolvency under both s 123(1)(e) and 123(2), which was reinforced by a number of further, practical indicators, apparent from the evidence, of the company's inability to pay its debts as they had fallen due over a number of years. On the evidence, the company had been unable to pay its debts as they had fallen due for the purposes of s 123(1)(e), and, for the purposes of s 123(2), the value of its assets was less than the amount of its liabilities, taking into account its contingent and prospective liabilities throughout the period during which the payments complained of were made. The decision to make the payments was made by the defendant without any consideration to the best interests of the company's creditors as a whole, nor those of its contingent creditor, despite the company having substantial creditors, substantial net liabilities and overall net liabilities, no live projects or revenue stream, and no realistic prospect of gaining any. The defendant had, in effect, been choosing which creditors to pay, and which to leave exposed to a real risk of being left unpaid. An intelligent and honest man in the defendant's position could not, in the circumstances, have reasonably believed that making the payments had been for the benefit of the company, nor of its creditors as a whole. It followed that breach of duty had been made out in regard to the payments. Accordingly, the application would be allowed.

Hellard v Carvalho [2013] EWHC 2876 (Ch), [2013] All ER (D) 240 (Sep) (Chancery Division: John Randall QC).

398   Company insolvency—fraudulent trading—meaning of victim

The second and third defendants were the managers of an investment structure in which the claimants were investors. The investment structure, as originally set up, was based around the first defendant, an English limited partnership which held indirectly the whole interest in the underlying assets of the structure. The principal limited partner in the first defendant was the fourth defendant, which acquired its interest in the first defendant through a loan from the second claimant. Pursuant to that loan, the fourth defendant assigned to the first claimant all of its rights and interest in the first defendant. The claimants instituted proceedings alleging that the defendants had designed and implemented a dishonest scheme to reorganise the first defendant and its assets, in such a way as to diminish or eliminate the claimants' rights and interests in the investment property and underlying assets, and to take the control and benefit of the assets for themselves. The first and second claimants claimed against the fourth defendant for breach of a loan agreement and of the security assignment respectively. Further, the first and second claimant's claimed in tort against all the defendants, except the fourth defendant, for unlawful means conspiracy and unlawful interference. The second claimant claimed against all the defendants, except the fourth defendant, in tort for procuring breach by the fourth defendant of various agreements. All the claimants sought orders under the Insolvency Act 1986 ss 423–425, unwinding the reorganisation of the structure and restoring the economic substance to what it was prior to the scheme. The fourth defendant had been declared bankrupt by a court in Luxembourg and an official receiver was appointed. It was concluded that there had been a fraudulent scheme of which the fourth defendant had also been a victim. The official receiver instructed solicitors to issue a CPR Pt 20 claim. Subsequently, the second, third, fifth to twelfth, fifteenth, seventeenth and twenty-first defendants ('R') issued proceedings in Luxembourg to set aside the CPR Pt 20 proceedings. The claimants sought to amend the particulars of claim to allege that the second claimant had suffered loss in that the value of its security for the loan had been lost or diminished. R applied to strike out the amended proceedings of claim or, alternatively, for summary judgment against the claimants on the grounds of the applicable law of the claims. *Held*, it was not appropriate to decide the issue of applicable law on a summary basis. In the circumstances, the claimants had a real prospect of establishing at trial that the applicable law of the tortious acts and conduct as alleged was English law and the defendants' application to have the issue determined in their favour summarily had to be dismissed. The second claimant was a secured creditor. It was clearly arguable that the rule against reflective loss did not apply to a secured creditor. Furthermore, the claim for the loss of the second claimant was not a claim for reflective loss but for diminution in the value of the security for the loan. Further, it was settled law that the word 'victim' in the Insolvency Act 1986 s 423(5) was not limited to creditors. Applying settled law, s 423(3) was not restricted in the way suggested by the defendants and included prejudicing a claim that would be made by indirect means. If the claimants' allegations were made out, they were arguably entitled to bring a claim under s 423 on the basis that the scheme was a transaction which had the purpose of defeating a claim by the fourth defendant or the first defendant and that the plea was a sustainable one. Therefore, the applications to strike out and for summary judgment would be dismissed, save with respect to an award of costs and a pending claim. Judgment would be given accordingly.

Fortress Value Recovery Fund I LLC v Blue Skye Special Opportunities Fund LP (*a firm*) [2013] EWHC 14 (Comm), [2013] 1 All ER (Comm) 973 (Queen's Bench Division: Flaux J). Case C-364/93 *Marinari v Lloyds Bank plc* [1996] QB 217, [1996] All ER (EC) 84, ECJ (1995 Abr para 3105); *Hill v Spread Trustee Co Ltd* [2006] EWCA Civ 542, [2007] 1 All ER 1106 (2006 Abr para 278); *London Helicopters Ltd v Heliportugal LDA-INAC* [2006] EWHC 108 (QB), [2006] 1 All ER (Comm) 595 (2006 Abr para 609); and *Hillside* (*New Media*) *Ltd v Bjarte Baasland* [2010] EWHC 3336 (Comm), [2010] All ER (D) 262 (Dec) applied.

399   **Company insolvency—liquidation—company property—assignment—right of action—right to appeal against tax assessment**

See *Re GP Aviation Group International* (*in liquidation*) *Ltd; Williams v Glover*, para 236.

400   **Company insolvency—transaction at undervalue—connected companies—sums received for dividends of company**

The Insolvency Act 1986 s 238 provides that where a company which goes into liquidation has at a relevant time entered into a transaction with any person at an undervalue, the liquidator may apply to the court for such order as it thinks fit for restoring the position to what it would have been if the company had not entered into that transaction.

The defendant was appointed joint liquidator of two connected companies which were indebted to a third company which was entitled to a substantial dividend from the liquidation of the connected companies. The third company entered into a fee agreement with its accountant in order to reward the accountant for the work which he had carried out for it in formulating its claim in the liquidation of the connected companies. The fee agreement authorised the accountant to receive any distributions from the liquidation of the connected companies, to hold those distributions in an account to the order of the third company, and to transfer to his own account agreed fees. The third company authorised the defendant, as liquidator of the connected companies, to pay the dividends due to the third company into a client account maintained by the accountant. The fee agreement was varied to amend the fees which the accountant was able to retain out of the dividends of the connected companies. Distributions were made from the connected companies in favour of the third company and paid by the accountant into the client account out of which the accountant made a series of payments, a proportion of which were made to the defendant. The defendant and one of his partners were appointed joint administrators of the third company and it was subsequently placed in creditors' voluntary liquidation. The claimant was appointed liquidator of the third company. He issued proceedings pursuant to the 1986 Act ss 238 and 241 and alleged that the payments received by the defendant had been payments at an undervalue. The claimant submitted that the payments to the defendant had either been transactions between the third company and the defendant, or, alternatively, had been transactions between the third company and the accountant and the court had power to make an order against the defendant as a third party who had received benefits from those transactions. The judge found that the claimant's case under each limb was unarguable. He found that the payments made to the defendant had not been transactions which, for the purposes of s 238, the third company had entered into, as they were either payments which the accountant had been authorised to make or they were not payments which he had been authorised to make. In the former case, they could not have been attacked unless the agreements were themselves challenged, which the claimant had not done, and in the latter case, the payments had constituted a breach of trust and so could not have been attributed in any way to the company. On that basis he struck out the claim against the defendant. The claimant appealed. *Held*, a claim under s 241 could only succeed if a claim under s 238 was first established. The requirement that the third company had itself entered into a transaction was an essential part of any claim under s 238 and comprised two interrelated elements (1) that there was a transaction; and (2) that the transaction was something which the company had itself entered into. The expression 'entered into' connoted the taking of some step or act or participation by the company. Thus, the composite requirement required the third company to have made the gift or to have made the arrangement or in some other way have been party to or involved in the transaction in issue so that it could properly be said to have entered into it, and to have done so within the period prescribed by s 240. The improper withdrawal by the accountant of the funds which he had held on trust, if that was what he had done, had not constituted a dealing between him and the third company nor could it be said that the accountant had been acting as agent for the third company in making the impugned payments. The accountant had been a trustee of the funds, but a trustee in English law was not an agent for his beneficiary. He had contracted in his own name with a right of indemnity against the beneficiary for the liabilities which he had incurred. When the accountant had taken the funds from the client account and paid them over to the defendant, it had required no further act or step by the third company beyond the fee agreement and the variation, and neither of those was said to have constituted or formed part of a relevant transaction. The payments themselves had not been a gift by the third company to the accountant nor had it entered into a further transaction of any kind with him. If had followed that the actions of the accountant in withdrawing the funds from the client account and paying them over to the defendant had not been transactions entered into by the third company. The claim against the defendant under ss 238 and 241 failed and the judge had been right to strike it out. Accordingly, the appeal would be dismissed.

Re Ovenden Colbert Printers Ltd, Hunt v Hosking [2013] EWCA Civ 1408, [2013] All ER (D) 188 (Nov) (Court of Appeal: Elias, Kitchin and McCombe LJJ). Stone & Rolls Ltd (in liq) v Moore Stephens (a firm) [2009] UKHL 39, [2009] AC 1391, [2009] 4 All ER 431 (2009 Abr para 1448); Smith (Administrator of Cosslett (Contractors) Ltd) v Bridgend CBC [2001] UKHL 58, [2002] 1 AC 336, [2002] 1 All ER 292 (2001 Abr para 543); Manson v Smith (liquidator of Thomas Christy Ltd) [1997] 2 BCLC 161, CA; and Re Brabon, Treharne v Brabon [2001] 1 BCLC 11 applied. Decision of Peter Smith J [2013] EWHC 311 (Ch), [2013] 2 BCLC 388 affirmed.

401   Company insolvency—winding up—compulsory winding up—actions of director

The accounts of a company showed that it was solvent but had substantial debts owed to it by two of its directors. The company experienced severe financial difficulties and attempted to use a winding-up petition to recover an alleged debt from a client company. The petition was dismissed and costs were awarded against the company. One of the company's directors asserted that the company had not been paid a 'success fee' due from another client. The client company presented a winding-up petition in respect of the costs award, which had not been paid. When the petition was first heard, the company obtained an adjournment for the purpose of paying the petition debt. No proposals were forthcoming for payment and, instead, the first director applied for an administration order in respect of the company pursuant to the Insolvency Act 1986 Sch B1 para 12(1)(b). The client company opposed the administration order application. Both the petition and the administration order application were heard together. By the time of the hearing, the first director's evidence was that the company was insolvent and that the debts owed to it by the two directors had been repaid by set-off against expenses and salaries due to them and other payments made by the first director on behalf of the company. Held, it was plain that the company had no assets with which to discharge any of the debts which were due and owing, including the petition debt. However, an administration order was not reasonably likely to achieve the purpose of the proposed administration. The merits of the claim would have been the same in an administration or a liquidation and it was not the case that funding would have been available to pursue the claim in an administration. Further, it was not the case that such funding as might have been available in an administration would not have been available in a liquidation. Even if funding could have been obtained, the pursuit of the claim would not have been for the benefit of the creditors of the company as a whole, nor would it have enabled the company to be rescued. Furthermore, there were real grounds for believing that the company might have had claims against the directors which would not have been available to it in an administration but might have been available in a liquidation. That was a significant factor in favour of making a winding-up order. The administration order application had been a tactical ploy by the first director to avoid or at least postpone the liquidation of the company and the independent investigation of his conduct of its affairs. The application for an administration order would be dismissed and a compulsory winding-up order would be made. Judgment would be given accordingly.

Re Integeral Ltd [2013] EWHC 164 (Ch), [2013] All ER (D) 63 (Feb) (Chancery Division: Richard Snowden QC).

402   Company insolvency—winding up—costs—winding-up petition followed by administration—treatment of solicitor's fees relating to winding-up petition as expense of administration

See *Re Portsmouth City Football Club Ltd; Neumans LLP v Andronikou*, para 385.

403   Company insolvency—winding up—liquidator—data protection—data controller— right to dispose of personal data

See *Re Southern Pacific Personal Loans Ltd*, para 426.

404   Company insolvency—winding up—proof of debts—valuation of claims

The applicants were creditors of a company pursuant to a sale and purchase agreement. Under the agreement, the applicants acquired the issued share capital in a number of entities and the company agreed to indemnify the applicants in respect of the pre-completion tax liabilities of the entities that it had acquired. The company entered into a members' voluntary liquidation. At the commencement of the liquidation, the applicants had crystallised and contingent claims under the indemnities in the agreement. The contingent claims consisted of potential tax liabilities for the relevant acquired entities, the quantification of which had yet to be determined. The respondent liquidators of the company gave notice to the creditors pursuant to the Insolvency Rules 1986, SI 1986/1925, r 4.182A informing them that they proposed to make a final distribution to creditors and requiring them to prove their debts. The applicants set out the details of the tax liabilities and provided an estimate of the maximum value of the contingent claims. The applicants requested that the respondents deferred taking any further steps until all of the applicants' claims could be quantified, and that the liquidators should ring fence a sufficiently large reserve prior to any distribution to other creditors and members out of which the contingent claims under the indemnities, once crystallised, could be paid. The respondents took the view that they had been obliged to value any contingent claims under r 4.86, and that the claims could be valued with a good degree of accuracy or, failing that, a realistic estimate made of the worst case outcome so as to enable an appropriate reserve to be set aside to meet the claims. The applicants issued an application seeking directions under the Insolvency Act 1986 s 112 that the respondents should be required to make a retention of the maximum value of the contingent claims, and that sum should not become available for distribution to members until either the contingent claims had crystallised or until the date on which the indemnity period under the agreement ended, which was one year away. The judge dismissed the application. The applicants appealed. *Held*, a liquidator was not obliged to set aside a reserve fund to meet contingent claims in full. Contingent claims of creditors fell to be satisfied through the valuation of their claims under the 1986 Rules r 4.86. While there might be cases where a contingent debt was so imminent that the liquidator could sensibly wait for the event to occur rather than spending time in a valuation of the chances of the claim ultimately materialising, and even where such a degree of imminency did not exist and the valuation of contingent claims remained open to variation in the light of subsequent events under r 4.84 right up to the completion of the liquidation in accordance with the 1986 Act s 107, there was no legal duty on a liquidator who had already valued the contingent claims and had so admitted them to proof in the amount of the valuation to provide for the contingency in full by making a reserve against any distribution to members. In the present case, where the contingency had remained a year away, there was no basis on which the respondents had fallen under a legal duty to make the retention sought. The respondents were entitled to proceed to a distribution to members on the basis of the debts admitted to proof. There was nothing in the 1986 Rules r 4.86 which required the liquidator of a company to guarantee a 100 per cent return on a contingent debt by assuming a worst-case scenario in favour of the creditor. To do so would produce a valuation, which was unfair to the company and its other creditors. Any valuation of a contingent liability had to be based on a genuine and fair assessment of the chances of the liability occurring. The respondents had had to use their own expertise and that of any relevant advisors to make a realistic estimate of the likelihood of the acquired entities sustaining the tax liabilities. Therefore, there had been no error by the respondents. Accordingly, the appeal would be dismissed.

Ricoh Europe Holdings BV v Spratt; Re Danka Business Systems plc (in members' voluntary liquidation) [2013] EWCA Civ 92, [2013] All ER (D) 217 (Feb) (Court of Appeal:

Mummery, Patten and Treacy J). *Re R-R Realisations Ltd (formerly Rolls-Royce Ltd)* [1980] 1 All ER 1019 (1980 Abr para 398); *Tombs v Moulinex SA* [2004] EWHC 454 (Ch), [2004] All ER (D) 208 (Mar) distinguished. Decision of Judge Pelling QC [2012] All ER (D) 146 (Mar) affirmed.

COMPETITION

Halsbury's Laws of England (5th edn) vol 18 (2009) paras 1–500

Articles

For articles relating to this title please refer to the Table of Articles at the beginning of the Abridgment.

405   Abuse of dominant position—decision of European Commission—decision pending investigation—proceedings in national court—stay of disclosure

The claimant, which was a start-up internet company that operated as a vertical search engine allowing users to compare products or services from information on third party websites, brought a claim for damages against the defendant, an operator of a well-known search engine, for an alleged breach of European Union and United Kingdom competition law, contending that the defendant was in a dominant position in the market and abused that position contrary to the TFEU art 102 and the Competition Act 1998 s 18. The defendant denied the contention and the claimant lodged a complaint with the European Commission. The defendant disclosed numerous documents to the Commission as part of its investigation. The Commission reached the preliminary conclusion that one of the defendant's business practices that might be considered to be an abuse of dominance was that it might give preferential treatment to its own vertical search services compared with competing vertical search services. The defendant offered certain commitments to the Commission in relation to its concerns and the Commission sought feedback on those commitments. Discussions continued and there was a possibility of reaching an agreement at the point when the matter was heard in the English court. The defendant sought a stay of proceedings pending further progress of an investigation by the Commission, whereas the claimant sought an order for standard disclosure. The parties agreed to the case proceeding to trial on the assumption that the defendant was dominant and it fell to be determined what the position was under European law where there was the possibility of a Commission decision being issued in the future and whether a stay of disclosure by the defendant ought to be granted in all the circumstances. *Held*, the case concerned a stand-alone action, not a follow-on action that proceeded on the basis of a decision by the Commission finding an infringement. However, there was clearly the possibility of a Commission decision being issued in the future and in that regard Council Regulation (EC) 1/2003 (on the implementation of the rules on competition laid down in articles 81 and 82 of the EC Treaty) art 16(1) applied. There was no objection, as a matter of European Union law, to the national proceedings continuing to a point short of an actual decision or judgment. It was in the courts discretion to determine what steps short of trial should be taken in the proceedings. That discretion was to be exercised having regard to the overriding objective and the requirement to avoid a decision that was counter to that of the Commission or the European Union courts. The parties were invited to agree that the case should proceed to trial on the assumption that the defendant was dominant as alleged. If the court then found for the defendant on the allegations of abuse, that would be the end of the case. If the court found against the defendant, the defendant would proceed to fight the case on dominance at a further trial. It followed that there need be no disclosure regarding the potentially wide-ranging issues that went to dominance and the definition of the relevant upstream markets. On the question of abuse, it was not appropriate to order blanket, standard disclosure. The position could be reviewed once the Commission clarified its position. All the allegations made in the proceedings were apparently contained in the claimant's complaint to the Commission and, therefore, it would be directed that disclosure by the defendant should be limited, save for some narrow specified categories, to the material documents within the disclosure already made to the Commission. Judgment would be given accordingly.

Infederation Ltd v Google Inc [2013] EWHC 2295 (Ch), [2014] 1 All ER 325 (Chancery Division: Roth J). *Purple Parking Ltd v Heathrow Airport Ltd* [2011] EWHC 987 (Ch), [2011] All ER (D) 169 (Apr); and *WM Morrison Supermarkets plc v MasterCard Incorporated* [2013] EWHC 1071 (Comm), [2013] All ER (D) 54 (May) applied.

406 Agreements preventing, restricting or distorting competition—agreement to terminate business with unlicensed competitor—prohibition—exception

The Slovakian competition authority found that three Slovakian banks infringed TFEU art 101 prohibiting, subject to an exception, as incompatible with the internal market all agreements between undertakings, decisions by associations of undertakings and concerted practices which might affect trade between member states and which had as their object or effect the prevention, restriction or distortion of competition within the internal market by entering into an agreement not to do business with a competitor Czech finance company. The Czech company did not have the requisite licence from the Slovakian authorities to carry out its activities. One of the banks successfully challenged the decision in the Slovakian court. The competition authority appealed. On a reference for a preliminary ruling, issues arose as to the interpretation of art 101. *Held*, art 101 had to be interpreted as meaning that the fact that an undertaking that was adversely affected by an agreement whose object was the restriction of competition was allegedly operating illegally on the relevant market at the time when the agreement was concluded was of no relevance to the question whether the agreement constituted an infringement of that provision. In order to find that an agreement was restrictive of competition under art 101(1), it was not necessary to demonstrate personal conduct on the part of a representative authorised under the constitution of the undertaking concerned or the personal assent, in the form of a mandate, of that representative to the conduct of an employee of the undertaking who participated in an anti-competitive meeting. The exceptions in art 101(3) could apply to an agreement prohibited under art 101(1) only when the undertaking that was relying on the exception proved that the four cumulative conditions laid down in art 101(3) were met.

Case C-68/12 *Protimonopolny urad Slovenskej republiky v Slovenska sporitelna as* [2013] Bus LR 1011, [2013] All ER (D) 149 (Aug) (ECJ: First Chamber).

407 Agreements preventing, restricting or distorting competition—calculation of fine—duration of infringement

The European Commission decided that the appellant companies had participated in various anti-competitive agreements and concerted practices in the methacrylates industry. Concerning the duration of the activities, the Commission found that, as the appellants had been involved in the infringement for a period of two years and three months, the starting amount of the fine should be increased by 20 per cent, or 10 per cent for each full year of participation. However, the Commission accepted the appellants' argument that they had had only a passive and minor role in the infringement, and on that basis granted them a 50 per cent reduction in the fine which would otherwise have been imposed. The appellants' appeal against that decision to the General Court of the European Union was dismissed, and, on their further appeal, they submitted that, in reviewing the Commission's assessment of the duration of the infringement, the General Court had failed to observe the general principles of European Union law relating to the presumption of innocence, the protection of legitimate expectations and the recognition of equal treatment. *Held*, the system of competition established by TFEU arts 101 and 102 was concerned with the economic consequences of agreements, or of any comparable form of concertation or co-ordination, rather than with their legal form. Consequently, in the case of agreements which had ceased to be in force, it was sufficient in order for art 101 to apply that they produced their effects beyond the date on which the unlawful contacts formally came to an end. It followed that the duration of an infringement might be assessed by reference to the period during which the undertakings concerned had engaged in conduct prohibited by that article. In the present case, the General Court had adopted an approach which was favourable to the appellants and had not made an error of law so far as the assessment of the duration of the infringement was concerned. Further, the appellants' argument relating to the alleged infringement of the principle of equal treatment did not satisfy the requirements which should be met by an appeal. Also, although the Commission had to observe the principle of the protection of legitimate expectations when it applied its self-imposed guidelines, that principle could not bind the European courts in the same way, in so far as they did not propose to apply a specific method of setting fines in the exercise of their unlimited jurisdiction, but considered the situations before them on a case-by-case basis, taking account of all the matters of fact and of law relating to those situations. Accordingly, the appeal would be dismissed.

Case C-70/12P *Quinn Barlo Ltd v European Commission* [2013] 5 CMLR 637, [2013] All ER (D) 181 (Sep) (ECJ: Seventh Chamber).

408   Agreements preventing, restricting or distorting competition—cartel offence—claim in conspiracy—intent to injure

The defendant group of companies was a supplier of copper plumbing tubes. The claimant group of companies purchased copper plumbing supplies from the defendant. The European Commission found that the defendant had been party to an international cartel contrary to TFEU art 101. A fine was imposed. The claimant wished to recover losses and issued proceedings under the Competition Act 1998 s 47A alleging conspiracy and breach of statutory duty imposed by TFEU art 101. The judge held that the 1998 Act s 47A could apply to claims in conspiracy, provided that the cause of action was based on findings of infringement in the Commission's decision. He also held that the element of the tort of conspiracy that the conspirators had to have intended to harm the claimant had been established on the basis of the findings in the Commission's decision. The defendant appealed. *Held*, on its true interpretation, s 47A permitted a claimant to bring a conspiracy claim provided that all the ingredients of the cause of action could be established by infringement findings in the Commission's decision. The Commission's findings had not satisfied the requirement of an intent to injure for the claimant's conspiracy claim. The inference that the judge had drawn that intent to injure had flowed from the fact that the cartelists had intended to benefit their own businesses had not necessarily followed. The defendant might have had absolutely no intent as regards the claimant. It had not followed that the claimant would inevitably have suffered loss. The claimant might have passed the price increases on or might have made a profit if it had been able to raise its prices in advance of becoming liable to pay price increases to the defendant. Although the Commission had found that the defendant had been involved in making arrangements, for example, as to the allocation of market shares, the crucial point was that no intent to injure had been found. Consequently, the claimant had succeeded on the interpretation of s 47A, namely that a conspiracy claim might be brought under s 47A if the Commission's infringement findings supported it. However, the infringement findings had not supported the intent to injure required for that claim. Accordingly, the appeal would be allowed in part.

WH Newson Holding Ltd v IMI plc [2013] EWCA Civ 1377, [2014] Bus LR 156, [2013] All ER (D) 124 (Nov) (Court of Appeal: Arden, Patten and Beatson LJJ). *OBG Ltd v Allan; Douglas v Hello! Ltd (No 3); Mainstream Properties Ltd v Young* [2007] UKHL 21, [2008] 1 AC 1, [2007] 4 All ER 545 (2007 Abr para 673) considered. Decision of Roth J [2012] EWHC 3680 (Ch), [2012] All ER (D) 210 (Dec) reversed in part.

409   Agreements preventing, restricting or distorting competition—cartel offence—price fixing

See *Ryanair Ltd v Esso Italiana Srl*, para 456.

410   Competition Act 1998—commencement

The Competition Act 1998 (Commencement No 6) Order 2013, SI 2013/284, brings into force, on 10 March 2013, so far as not already in force, s 1 and various repeals in Sch 14 Pt 1. For a summary of the Act, see 1998 Abr para 3140. See also the commencement table in the title STATUTES AND LEGISLATIVE PROCESS.

411   Competition and Markets Authority—establishment—disqualification of members from election to National Assembly for Wales

The Enterprise and Regulatory Reform Act 2013 (Competition and Markets Authority) (Consequential Amendments) Order 2013, SI 2013/2268 (in force on 1 October 2013), further amends the National Assembly for Wales (Disqualification) Order 2010, SI 2010/2969, so as to disqualify members of the Competition and Markets Authority from election to the National Assembly for Wales.

412 Competition Commission—investigation of price control—referral by Office of Communications—customer response evidence

See *British Telecommunications plc v Competition Commission*, para 2362.

413 Disclosure of information—facilitation of exercise of statutory functions

The Enterprise Act 2002 (Part 9 Restrictions on Disclosure of Information) (Specification) Order 2013, SI 2013/1808 (in force on 16 August 2013), enables a public authority, pursuant to the Enterprise Act 2002 s 241(3), to disclose restricted specified information which it holds for the purposes of facilitating the exercise of functions under the Green Deal Framework (Disclosure, Acknowledgment, Redress etc) Regulations 2012, SI 2012/2079.

414 Enterprise and Regulatory Reform Act 2013

The Enterprise and Regulatory Reform Act 2013 makes provision about the UK Green Investment Bank and employment law, establishes and makes provision about the Competition and Markets Authority, abolishes the Competition Commission and the Office of Fair Trading and amends the Competition Act 1998 and the Enterprise Act 2002. The 2013 Act makes provision for the reduction of legislative burdens, makes provision about copyright and rights in performances, about payments to company directors and redress schemes relating to lettings agency work and property management work. The Act also makes provision about the supply of customer data, makes provision for the protection of essential supplies in cases of insolvency, makes provision about certain bodies established by royal charter and amends the Equality Act 2010 s 9(5). The 2013 Act received the royal assent on 25 April 2013 and certain provisions came into force on that day. Further provisions came into force on and between 25 June 2013 and 31 March 2014: SI 2013/1455 (amended by SI 2013/2271), SI 2013/1648, SI 2013/2227, SI 2013/2271, SI 2013/2979. The remaining provisions come into force on a day or days to be appointed. For details of commencement, see the commencement table in the title STATUTES AND LEGISLATIVE PROCESS.

Part 1 (ss 1–6) UK Green Investment Bank
Section 1 defines the green purposes, for the purposes of the Act, as the reduction of greenhouse gas emissions, the advancement of efficiency in the use of natural resources, the protection or enhancement of the natural environment, the protection or enhancement of biodiversity and the promotion of environmental sustainability. The Secretary of State may by order under s 2, subject to certain conditions, designate the UK Green Investment Bank for the purposes of ss 3–6, by virtue of which the bank may, on certain conditions, alter the objects in its articles of association (s 3), provision may be made for appropriate financial assistance to be given to the bank, with Treasury consent, at any time when the Crown owns more than half of the bank's issued share capital (s 4), the bank may be subject to certain enhanced obligations under the Companies Act 2006 and must report each year on the contribution of its investment activities to a reduction of global greenhouse gas emissions (2013 Act s 5) and the Secretary of State is required to lay a copy of the bank's annual accounts and reports before Parliament, if, at the date of the bank's general meeting, the Crown owns at least one share in the bank (s 6).

Part 2 (ss 7–24) Employment
By virtue of s 7, Sch 1, a prospective claimant must provide, except in certain circumstances, prescribed information to ACAS before lodging his claim at an employment tribunal so that a conciliation officer may endeavour to promote a settlement between the prospective parties to the proceedings; and ACAS has other duties to promote conciliation between prospective parties to proceedings where the services of a conciliation officer are requested by a person where it is likely that a matter (if not settled) is likely to give rise to proceedings by or against that person. Section 8, Sch 2 provide for the extension of limitation periods to allow for conciliation. The power of the Secretary of State and Lord Chancellor to amend the list of relevant proceedings for conciliation purposes is extended by s 9. ACAS, or a person appointed by ACAS, is prohibited by s 10, except in specified circumstances, from

releasing information relating to a worker, employer of a worker, or a trade union, held by ACAS in connection with the provision of a service by it; and the contravention of the prohibition is a criminal offence punishable by a fine. Legal officers are enabled by s 11 to make determinations of certain employment tribunal proceedings of a specified description where all the parties to the proceedings consent in writing. Section 12 provides for proceedings before the Employment Appeal Tribunal to be heard by a judge alone but a judge may direct that proceedings are to be heard by a judge and either two or four appointed members or, with the consent of the parties, by a judge and either one or three appointed members. The two-year qualification period for bringing unfair dismissal proceedings does not apply if the reason or principal reason for the dismissal is, or relates to, the employee's political opinions or affiliation: s 13. By virtue of s 14, evidence of pre-termination negotiations is inadmissible except in cases where the employee claims to have been dismissed for an automatically unfair reason. The Secretary of State has power under s 15 to increase or decrease, within certain limits, the amount of the compensatory award for unfair dismissal. An employment tribunal determining a claim involving an employer and a worker has a discretion to impose a financial penalty on the employer, having regard to the employer's ability to pay, where there has been a breach of the worker's employment rights and the tribunal considers that the employer's behaviour in committing the breach had one or more aggravating features: s 16, Sch 3. Under s 17, a disclosure is not protected unless reasonably believed by the worker making the disclosure to be made in the public interest. Compensation may be reduced by virtue of s 18 by no more than 25 per cent where it appears that a disclosure has not been made in good faith. Where a worker is subjected to detriment by another worker by anything done by such other worker, in the course of his employment with the employer, on the ground that the worker made a protected disclosure, such detriment is a legal wrong and is actionable against both the employer and the other worker: s 19. Section 20 extends the meaning of 'worker'. Existing powers to make employment tribunal procedure regulations are amended by s 21. The time at which orders made in relation to the indexation of specified amounts are to come into force and the calculation which is to be used to increase or decrease the relevant limits are amended by s 22. The terms 'compromise agreement' and 'compromise contract' in specified legislation relating to employment matters are renamed by s 23 as 'settlement agreement'; and the term 'compromise' is renamed as 'settlement'. Section 24 makes transitional provision.

Part 3 (ss 25–28) The Competition and Markets Authority
Section 25, Sch 4 establish, and make provision for, the Competition and Markets Authority ('CMA') and its functions; s 26 and Schs 5, 6 abolish, and make provision for the abolition of, the Competition Commission and the Office of Fair Trading ('OFT'); and s 27 confers power on the Secretary of State to make transfer schemes in connection with the establishment of the CMA and the abolition of the Commission and the OFT. Transitional provision is made by s 28 for consultation by the CMA and the Commission and the OFT.

Part 4 (ss 29–58) Competition Reform

Chapter 1 (ss 29–32) Mergers
Investigation powers in relation to mergers are extended by s 29 to assist the CMA in carrying out its functions. The interim measures powers available to the CMA are amended by s 30, Sch 7, to make it easier for it to suspend the integration of companies involved in a merger during a Phase 1 investigation. The CMA may impose a financial penalty on a person who, without a reasonable excuse, fails to comply with interim measure at either Phase 1 or Phase 2 of an investigation: s 31. Provision is made by s 32, Sch 8 about time limits in relation to the mergers reference regime under the Enterprise Act 2002 Pt 3 (ss 22–130).

Chapter 2 (ss 33–38) Markets
Under its power to make market investigation references, the CMA has power, by virtue of the 2013 Act s 33, to carry out an investigation into practices across more than one market (ie a cross-market reference); the corresponding ministerial power is similarly extended by s 34, Sch 9. The Secretary of State has power by s 35, Sch 10 to request the CMA to investigate public interest issues alongside competition issues as part of a market investigation and to propose remedies which address any adverse effect on competition and

Sections 21, 22 contain consequential amendments, transitional provisions and definitions. Sections 23–26 deal with the making of orders, extent, commencement and short title.

Amendments and repeals
Specific provisions of the following Acts are amended: Parliamentary Commissioner Act 1967 Sch 2; House of Commons Disqualification Act 1975 Sch 1 Pt III; Freedom of Information Act 2000 Sch 1 Pt VI; Enterprise Act 2002 Schs 14, 15.

416 Office of Fair Trading—transfer of consumer advice functions—modification of enforcement functions

The Public Bodies (The Office of Fair Trading Transfer of Consumer Advice Scheme Function and Modification of Enforcement Functions) Order 2013, SI 2013/783 (in force on 28 March 2013), (1) transfers the power of the Office of Fair Trading ('the OFT') to support a consumer advice scheme to the National Association of Citizens Advice Bureaux, modifies the OFT's consumer enforcement functions and makes consequential amendments to primary legislation; (2) replaces the requirement for enforcers, within the meaning of the Enterprise Act 2002 s 213 (other than the OFT), to consult with the OFT before making an application for an enforcement order with a requirement to notify the OFT that they are making an application; and (3) amends the Unfair Terms in Consumer Contracts Regulations 1999, SI 1999/2083, the Consumer Protection (Distance Selling) Regulations 2000, SI 2000/2334, the Business Protection from Misleading Marketing Regulations 2008, SI 2008/1276, and the Consumer Protection from Unfair Trading Regulations 2008, SI 2008/1277, so as to provide that the OFT has a power rather than a duty to enforce those regulations.

417 Restrictive Practices Court—abolition

See para 621.

COMPULSORY ACQUISITION OF LAND
Halsbury's Laws of England (5th edn) vol 18 (2009) paras 501–910

Articles

For articles relating to this title please refer to the Table of Articles at the beginning of the Abridgment.

418 Compulsory purchase order—approval—decision of planning inspector—validity

The claimant was the owner of an amusement park and associated tourist site. It was universally recognised that the area was in urgent need of regeneration. Initially, the second defendant local authority was in discussion with the claimant about redeveloping the land, under which the claimant would have provided part of the funding. However, negotiations broke down, principally over the nature, size and character of the proposed residential development in two areas of the land. In the event, the second defendant resolved to adopt a different funding package that did not rely on any funding from the claimant but did involve the compulsory purchase of the land if negotiations ultimately failed (the 'adopted scheme'). An expert consultant subsequently produced a business plan (the 'first plan') which concluded that the adopted scheme had operational viability. A separate business plan (the 'second plan') was prepared by another consultant, which envisaged the regeneration being achieved together with some residential development of two parts of the land and did not include the requirement of a compulsory purchase order. A planning inspector appointed by the first defendant Secretary of State considered the alternative business plans, and concluded that the residential development of part of the area would have restricted the regenerative effect of the development. The inspector therefore recommended proceeding with the adopted scheme. The claimant brought proceedings challenging that decision, submitting that the first plan was flawed and the Secretary of State had been misled as to the nature of an offer from the claimant to sell the land which, if accepted, would have removed the need for any compulsory purchase order. *Held*, it would have been surprising that public bodies or charities would have been willing to give grants, in some cases amounting to millions of pounds, without a careful evaluation of the viability of the scheme under consideration. Given, in particular, the strong commitment which the second defendant had shown to implementing the adopted scheme, the inspector's assessment that the first plan was prudent and cautious, and the willingness of third parties to support the adopted scheme by giving substantial sums of money, the inspector's conclusion that the adopted scheme was operationally viable was plainly sustainable. Further, even if there had been a material misstatement of the claimant's position, the first defendant would inevitably have approved the scheme even if he had been accurately informed of the position. The need for regeneration for the economic and social benefit of the area was overwhelming. There had been two schemes in play, only one of which was, in the inspector's view, satisfactory. The proposed development had required the whole land, and the compulsory purchase order had been necessary to secure the relevant land because the claimant had not been willing to transfer it voluntarily. The offer to sell only part of the land had been insufficient to achieve the second defendant's objective. Accordingly, the appeal would be dismissed.

Margate Town Centre Regeneration Co Ltd v Secretary of State for Communities and Local Government [2013] EWCA Civ 1178, [2013] All ER (D) 74 (Oct) (Court of Appeal: Goldring and Elias LJJ and Sir David Keene).

419   Growth and Infrastructure Act 2013

See para 2022.

CONFIDENCE AND INFORMATIONAL PRIVACY

Halsbury's Laws of England (5th edn) vol 19 (2011) paras 1–300

Articles

For articles relating to this title please refer to the Table of Articles at the beginning of the Abridgment.

420   Confidential information—disclosure—emails—proprietary right to content

The defendant was the chief executive officer of, but not an employee of, the claimant company. In the course of providing his services to the claimant, the defendant received emails which were forwarded to his private email address. Those emails were automatically deleted from the claimant's server without retaining copies. After the claimant terminated the defendant's contract, the defendant refused to allow the claimant to have access to emails sent to and contained on the defendant's personal computer that related to the claimant's business. The claimant brought proceedings seeking an order requiring the defendant to grant such access, contending that it had an enforceable proprietary right to the content of the emails. The judge refused the claim, ruling that the content of the emails was information, and there was no property in information. He considered that the law provided protection against misuse of information contained in emails by way of the laws of confidence and copyright. The claimant appealed against that decision, submitting that the relationship between the parties was one of agency, and a principal was entitled to inspect and copy correspondence held by its agent whether in hard copy or electronically. *Held*, the reference in the earlier proceedings to a proprietary right had been a distraction from the centrality of the agency relationship and its legal incidents. The assertion of a right to inspect and copy the content of the emails on the defendant's computer relating to the claimant's business affairs had arisen from the legal incidents of an agency relationship that had survived its termination. It had been unnecessary to explore the question of whether information in the content of the emails was property owned by the claimant. The absence of a proprietary right had not affected the legal right of the claimant as principal to an inspection and copying remedy against a former agent in respect of the emails. As a general rule, it was a legal incident of an agency relationship that a principal was entitled to require production by the agent of documents relating to the affairs of the principal, and that materials held and stored on a computer, which might be displayed in readable form on a screen or printed out on paper were, in principle, covered by the same incidents of agency as applied to paper documents. Accordingly, the appeal would be allowed.

Fairstar Heavy Transport NV v Adkins [2013] EWCA Civ 886, [2013] All ER (D) 239 (Jul) (Court of Appeal: Mummery, Patten and Black LJJ). Decision of Edwards-Stuart J [2012] EWHC 3294 (TCC), [2012] All ER (D) 274 (Nov) (2012 Abr para 492) reversed.

421   Confidential information—disclosure—employee—trade secrets—breach of confidence

The claimants were involved in the development, manufacture and marketing of insecticidal bednets. The defendant was a former employee of the claimants who had set up a company selling products in direct competition with them. The defendant's contract of employment contained a confidentiality clause that restricted her from disclosing information obtained during the course of her employment. The clause stated that the duty of confidentiality also applied after the contract came to an end. The claimants brought proceedings against the defendant seeking damages and other relief for misuse of their confidential information. The claim was allowed, but the decision was reversed on appeal. The claimants appealed, contending that the defendant was liable for breach of confidence on the basis of (1) the terms of her contract of employment; (2) a common design to develop a rival product that used the claimants' trade secrets; and (3) her conduct in forming and working for a company that was responsible for the design, manufacture and marketing of a rival product, and in hiring a consultant who had also performed work for the claimants. *Held*, each of the claimants' arguments had to fail because of the combination of two crucial facts. First, the defendant did not herself ever acquire the confidential information in question, whether during the time of her employment with the claimants or afterwards. Secondly, until some point during the currency of the proceedings, the defendant was unaware that her own company's product had been developed using the claimants' trade secrets. In those circumstances, unless the defendant's employment contract with the claimants imposed such a liability, the defendant could not be primarily liable for misuse of confidential information, because she had received no confidential information, or at least no relevant confidential information. Further, subject to the same qualification, she could not be secondarily liable for such misuse, as she had not known that the consultant was using, or had used, the claimants' confidential information in order to develop the competing product. The confidentiality clause in the employment contract was of no use to the claimants as the confidential information wrongly used was not obtained by the defendant herself. It was also not seriously arguable that a term could properly be implied into the contract to the effect that the defendant would not assist another person to abuse trade secrets owned by the claimants, in circumstances where she did not know the trade secrets and was unaware that they were being misused. Moreover, in order for a person to be party to a common design, he had to share with the other party, or parties, to the design, each of the features of the design which made it wrongful. If, and only if, all those features were shared, the fact that some parties to the common design did only some of the relevant acts, while others did only some other relevant acts, would not stop them all from being jointly liable. The contention that the defendant had 'blind-eye' knowledge of the fact that the consultant was using the claimants' trade secrets could not succeed without a finding of dishonesty against the defendant, which had not been made. Accordingly, the appeal would be dismissed.

Vestergaard Frandsen A/S v Bestnet Europe Ltd [2013] UKSC 31, [2013] All ER (D) 252 (May) (Supreme Court: Lord Neuberger P, Lord Clarke, Lord Sumption, Lord Reed and Lord Carnwath SCJJ).

422   Confidential information—disclosure—employee—trade secrets—employee establishing competing business

The claimant company printed magazines. Following the resignation of the first three defendants from their employment with the claimant, it was discovered that they had set up the fourth defendant, another company. It was contended that the fourth defendant was, and had been prior to the termination of first three defendants' employment, in competition with the claimant. The claimant commenced proceedings, seeking damages for breach of fiduciary duty and/or infringement of its database rights under the Copyright and Rights in Database Regulations 1997, SI 1997/3032, and for a permanent injunction restraining the defendants from using and disclosing the claimant's confidential information obtained during the defendants' employment. *Held*, there was a strong case that the defendants had been taking steps for over a year to compete against the claimant. Those steps had been more than merely preparatory and were taken with more than just the intention to set up another company. They had been active steps to compete. Further, the defendants had been competing with the claimant while still employed by it. They had clearly sought to act in secrecy. Furthermore, there was a strong case that the circulation database and the customer database had been the claimant's confidential information. Therefore, there was also a strong case that the business cards had provided the defendants with a competitive advantage, so that springboard relief should be granted. The claimant had a very good chance of succeeding at trial. Interim relief would be granted. Accordingly, the application would be allowed.

Whitmar Publications Ltd v Gamage [2013] EWHC 1881 (Ch), [2013] All ER (D) 57 (Jul) (Chancery Division: Peter Leaver QC). *Customer Systems plc v Ranson* [2012] EWCA Civ 841, [2012] IRLR 769 (2012 Abr para 1046) applied.

423   Confidential information—disclosure—exceptions—European Commission— protection of decision-making process

The applicant was a company limited by guarantee under English law. It pursued objectives relating to the protection of the environment. Documents were received by the European Commission concerning the transposition of directives on the environment and the applicant applied to the Commission for access to the documents under European Parliament and Council Regulation (EC) 1049/2001 (regarding public access to European Parliament, Council and Commission documents) and European Parliament and Council Regulation (EC) 1367/2006 (on the application of the provisions of the Aarhus Convention on access to information, public participation in decision-making and access to justice in environmental matters to Community institutions and bodies). The Commission rejected the application in part, sending to the applicant one of the documents requested, but stating that the others were covered by the exceptions provided for in Regulation 1049/2001 art 4(2) and (3), relating to the protection of the purpose of inspections, investigations and audits and the protection of the decision-making process of the institutions. The applicant submitted, pursuant to art 7(2), a confirmatory application asking the Commission to reconsider its position and the Commission adopted an express decision of the confirmatory application. The applicant submitted that there had been an infringement of art 4(2) in that the Commission had disregarded the limits attaching to the exception laid down by art 4(2) and that there had been an infringement of the Aarhus Convention art 4(1), (2) and (4), in that no exception was allowed to the right of access to documents intended to protect the purpose of investigations other than those of a criminal or disciplinary nature. The applicant further submitted that, when an institution was asked to disclose a document, it had to assess, in each individual case, whether that document was covered by the exceptions to the right of access and that the Commission's examination of the studies in issue had been general and abstract. *Held,* it was settled law that the Commission could legitimately rely on the exception in Regulation 1049/2002 art 4(2) in order to refuse access to documents relating to investigations of a possible contravention of European Union law that might lead to the initiation of infringement proceedings or which had led to the initiation of such proceedings. In those circumstances, refusal of access was considered to be justified because the member states concerned were entitled to expect the Commission to observe confidentiality as regards investigations, even where a period of time had elapsed since the closure of those investigations. It could not be said that there had been an infringement of art 4(2). Further, the applicant's argument that art 4(2), as applied by the Commission in the express decision, was incompatible with the Aarhus Convention art 4(4), in that art 4(4) had not allowed any exception to the right of access to documents intended to protect the purpose of investigations other than those of a criminal or disciplinary nature, could not be upheld. The applicant had failed to demonstrate that the Commission had committed an error in refusing to disclose the studies at issue in order to protect the purpose of its investigations. The applicant had not presented any argument capable of demonstrating that, in relation to the studies at issue, there was any pressing public concern. The applicant had done no more than refer to non-specific considerations unrelated to the particular circumstances of the case. Non-specific considerations could not provide an appropriate basis for establishing that the principle of transparency represented in a specific case an issue of particularly pressing concern that prevailed over the reasons justifying the refusal to disclose the documents requested. Accordingly, the application would be dismissed.

done by men. The appellant refused the request, contending that such information was personal data and disclosure would contravene the Data Protection Act 1998. The third party complained to the respondent commissioner. The respondent drew the third party's attention to Sch 2 para 6 as the only condition which might apply to the circumstances and requested the third party's submissions and further information in support of his position. The respondent also received letters from two members of the Scottish Parliament in support of the third party's request, but neither the respondent's request for further information nor the letters were revealed to the appellant. The respondent determined that the data requested was not personal data, that the third party had a legitimate interest in obtaining the information, that the matter was not an intrusion of any significance on the privacy of the individuals concerned and, on balance, Sch 2 para 6 had been met. The appellant's appeal to the Inner House was dismissed. The appellant appealed and it fell to be determined what the proper interpretation of Sch 2 para 6 was and whether the respondent acted in breach of natural justice by failing to disclose to the appellant the communications between the respondent, the third party and the members of the Scottish Parliament during the course of the investigation. *Held,* under Sch 2 para 6 three questions had to be answered, namely whether the data controller or the third party to whom the data were disclosed were pursuing a legitimate interest, whether the processing involved was necessary for the purposes of those interests, and whether the processing was unwarranted in the case by reason of prejudice to the rights and freedoms or legitimate interests of the data subject. As the processing requested would not enable the discovery of the identity of the data subjects, it was difficult to see why there was any interference with their right to respect for their private lives. The respondent adopted a test which was probably more favourable to the appellant than required and certainly no less favourable and, in any event, it was clear that he was entitled to reach the conclusion that he had. Moreover, although the respondent had to provide notice of any new material which his inquiries elicited and which was adverse to the appellant's interests, it did not follow that every communication had to be copied to the appellant and, in the circumstances, it had not been a breach of the rules of natural justice for the respondent to refrain from copying the correspondences to the appellant. Accordingly, the appeal would be dismissed.

South Lanarkshire Council v Scottish Information Comr [2013] UKSC 55, [2013] IRLR 899 (Supreme Court: Lady Hale DP, Lord Kerr, Lord Wilson, Lord Reed and Lord Carnwath SCJJ). *Corporate Officer of the House of Commons v Information Comr* [2008] EWHC 1084 (Admin), [2009] 3 All ER 403 (2008 Abr para 782) applied.

430   Freedom of information

See CONSTITUTIONAL AND ADMINISTRATIVE LAW.

CONFLICT OF LAWS

Halsbury's Laws of England (5th edn) vol 19 (2011) paras 301–783

Articles

For articles relating to this title please refer to the Table of Articles at the beginning of the Abridgment.

431   Applicable law—tort—assessment of damages—expert evidence—law of forum or applicable law

The claimant sustained severe personal injuries when his motorcycle collided with a motor vehicle while he was on holiday in France. The collision occurred as a result of the motorist's negligence. The claimant issued a claim form in England naming the motorist's insurers as defendant. Judgment was entered for the claimant for damages to be assessed. CPR 35 applied to the case as the rules as to expert evidence which it contained were plainly a matter of procedure. The claimant requested permission to call a number of experts. The defendant submitted that permission ought to be given for the calling of a single expert witness of a kind who was appointed in French personal injury litigation in accordance with French law. It further submitted that 'law' within the meaning of European Parliament and Council Regulation (EC) 864/2007 art 15(c) included the practices, conventions and guidelines regularly used by judges in assessing damages in the courts of the state whose law was the applicable law. The only way in which the legislative purposes of Regulation 864/2007 would be achieved was by rejecting the English 'panoply of experts' and permitting only a single expert of the kind customarily appointed by French courts, so as to arrive at a figure that would actually be awarded in France. Any other interpretation would give an undue weight to the law of the claimant's domicile. The claimant contended that whether to give permission to the parties to adduce expert evidence, whether to order a single joint expert or to refuse permission for any expert evidence were questions of case management. *Held*, on the facts, the question of what expert evidence the court should order and, in particular, whether there ought to be one single joint expert pursuant to CPR 35 were matters of procedure within Regulation 864/2007 art 1(3). The court was not required to put itself in the position of a court in France and was not required to adopt new procedures. Judgment would be given accordingly.

Wall v Mutuelle de Poitiers Assurances [2013] EWHC 53 (QB), [2013] 2 All ER 709 (Queen's Bench Division: Tugendhat J).

432   Family law—child care proceedings—transfer—best interests of child

See *Re LM* (*a child*) (*transfer of Irish proceedings*), para 177.

433   Family law—orders relating to children—habitual residence

See *Re KL* (*a child*), para 230.

434   Family law—parental responsibility—habitual residence

See *Re M* (*a child*) (*habitual residence: jurisdiction*), para 215.

435   Jurisdiction—anti-suit injunction to restrain foreign proceedings—application for summary judgment—delay pending jurisdiction hearing

The claimant company time-chartered a ship. The defendant, a Jordanian company, alleged that the cargo was of deficient quality on arrival and commenced proceedings in Jordan. The claimant commenced proceedings in England, seeking an anti-suit injunction restraining the defendant from further prosecuting the Jordanian proceedings, as well as declarations of non-liability in relation to the substantive claim that formed the subject matter of the Jordanian proceedings. The defendant challenged the jurisdiction of the English court. The claimant applied for summary judgment and for an order that the two applications should be listed together. *Held*, the CPR contemplated that a foreign defendant who had entered an acknowledgment of service indicating a challenge to jurisdiction should have a further opportunity, once that jurisdiction challenge had failed, to consider whether to contest the claim on the merits and therefore participate, or to take no part in the English proceedings, with the potential effect that this could have in relation to the enforcement of the judgment. It was wrong in principle for a foreign defendant, who was challenging the jurisdiction of the English court to determine the claim on the merits, to have to prepare for a hearing on the merits by preparing for a summary judgment application, before his jurisdiction challenge was heard. There would be no undue delay or unfairness if the summary judgment application had to await the outcome of the jurisdiction challenge and be listed for a further subsequent hearing if the jurisdiction challenge failed nor would the summary judgment application have had any immediate practical effect on the Jordanian proceedings. The two applications would not be listed together. The jurisdiction challenge would be listed while the summary judgment application would depend on the outcome of the jurisdiction challenge. Accordingly, the application would be dismissed.

Navig8 PTE Ltd v Al-Riyadh Co [2012] EWHC 3925 (Comm), [2013] All ER (D) 174 (Feb) (Queen's Bench Division: Popplewell J).

436   Jurisdiction—anti-suit injunction to restrain foreign proceedings—appropriate forum

The claimant buyer entered into contracts for the purchase of two cargoes of oil from the first defendant which provided warranties, expressly governed by English law, that it had good title to the oil. The second and third defendants, two companies incorporated in the United Arab Emirates ('UAE'), claimed that the oil had been dishonestly misappropriated from them by the first defendant, a company operated by a former employee of the second and third defendants, so that the first defendant did not have good title and, therefore, could not pass a good title to the claimant. Proceedings were commenced by the second and third defendants in the UAE. In English proceedings, the claimant sought a declaration that the first defendant had good title to the cargoes so that it had transferred good title to the claimant. Jurisdiction was established by reason of the exclusive English jurisdiction clause in the warranties of title and, as between the claimant and the first defendant, England was the agreed venue for determination of any issue about the first defendant's title. The claimant was granted an anti-suit injunction to prevent the second and third defendants from pursuing any application to join the claimant to proceedings commenced in the UAE and from making any claim against it in connection with the title to other cargoes of oil. The claimant sought an order to continue the anti-suit injunction. *Held*, it was settled law that an anti-suit injunction would be granted where there was either an agreement for exclusive jurisdiction or its equivalent, an agreement for arbitration in England, in which case the court would ordinarily enforce the parties' agreement by granting an anti-suit injunction in the absence of a strong reason not to do so, or where England was the natural forum for the resolution of the dispute and the conduct of the party to be injuncted was unconscionable. The English court would not grant an anti-suit injunction merely because pursuit of foreign proceedings was vexatious, but would only do so if it had some interest of its own to protect. In the circumstances, the question of title should be determined in the UAE. The real parties between whom that question arose were the second and third defendants and the first defendant, none of whom had any connection with the United Kingdom and between whom there was no contract of any kind. Most of the relevant evidence and witnesses were in the UAE. None of them were in the United Kingdom. The only connection with England was the warranties of title given by the first defendant. They were subject to English law and exclusive jurisdiction, but as between the claimant and the first defendant there was no dispute. As between the claimant and the first defendant, there was nothing to litigate unless and until the second and third defendants made good their claim. The anti-suit injunction would not be ordered to continue and judgment would be given accordingly.

Vitol Bahrain EC v Nasdec General Trading LLC [2013] EWHC 3359 (Comm), [2013] All ER (D) 14 (Nov) (Queen's Bench Division: Males J). *Airbus Industrie GIE v Patel* [1999] 1 AC 119, [1998] 2 All ER 257, HL (1998 Abr para 583); and *Star Reefers Pool Inc v JFC Group Co Ltd* [2012] EWCA Civ14, [2012] 2 All ER (Comm) 225 (2012 Abr para 527) applied.

The claimant brought an action in England against the defendant for indemnity pursuant to contracts of reinsurance. The defendant brought certain counterclaims. Following negotiations between the parties, the claimant launched a claim in New York, allegedly without informing the defendant. The defendant applied for an anti-suit injunction in respect of the claim in New York and the claimant applied for a stay of the English proceedings pending the New York court's determination of the defendant's motions for a stay. *Held*, it was settled law that the English court should favour its own conflict of law rules and, under those rules, it was overwhelmingly likely that English law governed the formation and meaning and effect of the reinsurance contracts. Where a claimant had brought a claim against the same defendants for essentially the same relief arising out of the same facts in two jurisdictions, in the absence of special circumstances, it would be wrong for the court to grant a stay of one set of proceedings at the instigation of the claimant. In the present case, the applicability of English law to the claims meant that the English court was the appropriate forum. On the facts, wasted costs were not a foundation for an anti-suit injunction. In all the circumstances, unsatisfactory as the claimant's manner of proceeding had been, it ought not to be restrained from continuing with the New York proceedings. It would be in the interests of justice that the English action, including the defendant's counterclaim, to be continued with the claimant having the burden of seeking an order of discontinuance or dismissal of its claim should the New York court dismiss the defendant's stay motions. By reason of the manner in which it had negotiated with the defendant by reference to contemplated English proceedings without informing the defendant it would sue in New York if the negotiations failed, the claimant had failed to show that the present case was one of those exceptional cases where a claimant, having brought an action against a defendant, should be granted a stay even of a temporary nature pending the outcome of interlocutory proceedings started in another court. Judgment would be given accordingly.

Insurance Co of the State of Pennsylvania v Equitas Insurance Ltd [2013] EWHC 3713 (Comm), [2014] Lloyd's Rep IR 195, [2013] All ER (D) 18 (Dec) (Queen's Bench Division: Field J).

437   Jurisdiction—anti-suit injunction to restrain foreign proceedings—exclusive jurisdiction clause

See *Caresse Navigation Ltd v Office National de L'Electricitie*, para 148.

438   Jurisdiction—arbitration—exclusive jurisdiction clause—proper law of arbitration

See *Arsanovia Ltd v Cruz City 1 Mauritius Holdings*, para 56.

439   Jurisdiction—Brussels Regulation—assignment of jurisdiction—jurisdiction derived from choice of court agreement

A property developer had renovation work carried out in France. It was insured by the respondent whose registered office was in France. In the course of the work, air-conditioning units were installed. The units were equipped with compressors which were manufactured by the applicant, whose registered office was in Italy, purchased from that company and fitted by a second company whose registered office was also in Italy, then sold to the property developer by a third company to whose rights a fourth company was subsequently subrogated. The fourth company, whose registered office was in France, was insured by another insurance company, in the same group as the respondent, which was also established in France. Irregularities occurred in the air-conditioning system and an expert's report established that the failures had been caused by a defect in the manufacturing of the compressors. Subrogated to the rights of the property developer, to which it paid compensation, the respondent, in French proceedings, sued the manufacturer, the applicant, the fitter, the second company, and the seller, the fourth company, seeking an order that they pay compensation for the damage suffered. A question arose as to the jurisdiction of the French court. *Held*, Council Regulation (EC) 44/2001 art 23(1) clearly indicated that its scope was limited to cases in which the parties had 'agreed' on a court. It was that consensus between the parties which justified the primacy granted, in the name of the principle of the freedom of choice, to the choice of a court other than that which might have had jurisdiction under Regulation 44/2001. The French court had held, with regard to art 17, that, by making the validity of a jurisdiction clause subject to the existence of an 'agreement' between the parties, that provision imposed on the court the duty of examining, first, whether the clause conferring jurisdiction on it had in fact been the subject of consensus between the parties. Article 23(1) should be interpreted as meaning that, like the aim pursued by art 17, ensuring the real consent of the parties was one of the aims of that provision. It followed that the jurisdiction clause incorporated in a contract might produce, in principle, effects only in the relations between the parties who had given their agreement to the conclusion of that contract. In order for a third party to rely on the clause, it was necessary, in principle, that the third party had given his consent to that effect. In a chain of contracts transferring ownership, the relationship of succession between the initial buyer and the sub-buyer was not regarded as the transfer of a single contract or the transfer of all the rights and obligations for which it provided. In such a case, the contractual obligations of the parties might vary from contract to contract, so that the contractual rights which the sub-buyer could enforce against his immediate seller would not necessarily be the same as those which the manufacturer would have accepted in his relationship with the first buyer. Further, the agreement of the national legal systems with respect to the effects of the transfer of the bill of lading to a third party was not found in relation to contracts transferring ownership, with regard to which it appeared that the relationships between manufacturer and sub-buyer were perceived differently in the member states. In such circumstances, to refer the assessment as to whether the sub-buyer might rely on a jurisdiction clause incorporated in the initial contract between the manufacturer and the first buyer to national law, as the applicant had suggested, would give rise to different outcomes among the member states liable to compromise the aim of unifying the rules of jurisdiction. Such a reference to national law would also be an element of uncertainty incompatible with the concern to ensure the predictability of jurisdiction which was one of its objectives. In the light of all of the foregoing considerations, art 23 should be interpreted as meaning that a jurisdiction clause agreed in the contract concluded between the manufacturer of goods and the buyer could not be relied on against a sub-buyer who, in the course of a succession of contracts transferring ownership concluded between parties established in different member states, purchased the goods and wished to bring an action for damages against the manufacturer, unless it was established that that third party had actually consented to that clause under the conditions laid down in art 23.

Case C-543/10 *Refcomp SpA v Axa Corporate Solutions Assurance SA* [2013] All ER (D) 224 (Feb) (ECJ: First Chamber).

440   Jurisdiction—Brussels Regulation—attachment order—conspiracy to commit value added tax fraud

Following an alleged value added tax 'carousel' type fraud which had permitted evasion of output VAT, to the detriment of the United Kingdom Treasury, the Commissioners for Her Majesty's Revenue and Customs brought court proceedings in the United Kingdom and Denmark. In the United Kingdom, the proceedings had been brought against a number of natural and legal persons established in Denmark, including the respondent company. The question was whether the Revenue could claim, from non-residents, damages corresponding to the amount of VAT not paid by a person subject to VAT in the United Kingdom, on the ground that those non-residents had taken part in a tortious conspiracy to defraud within the meaning of English law. The Revenue maintained that those non-residents had been guilty in the United Kingdom of a VAT 'carousel' type fraud. The Revenue further submitted that those non-residents, who were not subject to VAT in the United Kingdom, had been the real beneficiaries of the sums obtained by that tax evasion mechanism. The person subject to VAT in the United Kingdom who was not in that VAT carousel was not a party to the proceedings before the United Kingdom court. The Revenue issued proceedings in Denmark, which had made attachment orders in respect of assets belonging to the respondent situated on Danish territory. The respondent's appeal against the orders was dismissed. By a separate application lodged in Denmark, the Revenue, acting on the basis of Danish law, asked the court to confirm the orders and also claimed payment of the VAT evaded. The Danish court decided to deal separately with the question of whether it should stay the proceedings until the United Kingdom proceedings had been completed. It was uncertain as to whether an action such as that lodged, before the United Kingdom courts fell within the scope of Council Regulation (EC) 44/2001 (on the jurisdiction and the recognition and enforcement of judgments in civil and commercial matters), so that a judgment delivered by those courts might be recognised and enforced in Denmark. It fell to be determined whether the concept of 'civil and commercial matters' within the meaning of art 1(1) was to be interpreted as meaning that it included an action whereby a public authority of one member state claimed, from natural and legal persons resident in another member state, damages in respect of loss caused by a conspiracy to commit VAT fraud in the first member state. *Held*, the concept of 'civil and commercial matters' within the meaning of art 1(1) should be interpreted as meaning that it covered an action whereby a public authority of one member state claimed, as against natural and legal persons resident in another member state, damages for loss caused by a tortious conspiracy to commit VAT fraud in the first member state.

Case C-49/12 *Revenue and Customs Comrs v Sunico ApS* [2013] 2 All ER (Comm) 1117 (ECJ: Third Chamber).

441   Jurisdiction—Brussels Regulation—exclusive jurisdiction agreement—breach—effect of acknowledgment of service

The claimant company brought proceedings against the defendant insurers in respect of the loss of a vessel. An exclusive jurisdiction clause in the insurance policies provided for English law and for the jurisdiction of the courts of England and Wales. Settlement agreements between the parties were made in full and final settlement of all and any claims the claimant might have in relation to the loss of the vessel. The agreements were stated to be subject to English law and required the claimant to obtain a stay by way of a Tomlin order. The claimant subsequently issued a number of sets of proceedings in Greece alleging that it had suffered considerable loss as a result of the alleged dissemination of false information to third parties and fabrication of false evidence with the purpose of avoiding payment of the insurance indemnity. The defendants then brought proceedings in England to enforce the settlement agreements and seeking relief for breach of the exclusive jurisdiction clause in the insurance policies by virtue of the issue of the Greek proceedings. It second company in the same group, which also had its registered office in Switzerland, held several patents protecting special forms for sending a letter together with a membership card, and the base material for those card forms. A company established in Italy produced various kinds of laminates and multilayer film. The Italian company claimed that the first Swiss company's distribution policy and its refusal to grant patent licences had been contrary to competition law. The Swiss companies brought an action before the Swiss court for a negative declaration stating that (1) the first Swiss company was not obliged to desist from its sales practice in relation to the granting of discounts and the terms of its distribution contracts; and (2) the Italian company had no right either to have that sales practice terminated or to obtain compensation. The Swiss companies further sought a declaration that the second Swiss company was under no obligation to grant a licence for its patents, which protected the manufacture of forms and the base materials for their manufacture. The Italian company and a subsidiary established in Switzerland brought an action for performance before the Italian court, arguing that the conduct of the Swiss companies was anti-competitive and seeking an award of damages as well as an order requiring the second Swiss company to grant licences for the patents in question. The action for a negative declaration was dismissed as inadmissible. That decision was confirmed on appeal on the ground that the jurisdiction in matters relating to tort or delict provided for in Council Regulation (EC) 44/2001 art 5(3) could not be applied in the case of an action for a negative declaration, since the very purpose of such an action was to establish that no tort or delict had been committed. The German court, before which the Swiss companies had brought an appeal on a point of law, raised the question whether the jurisdiction provided for was also established where the potential injuring party brought an action for a negative declaration seeking a declaration that the potential injured party had no claim based on a tort or delict. On a reference for a preliminary ruling, *held*, in light of established authority, the rule establishing special jurisdiction laid down, by way of derogation from the principle that jurisdiction lay with the courts of the defendant's place of domicile, in art 5(3) was based on the existence of a particularly close connecting factor between the dispute and the courts of the place where the harmful event had occurred or might occur, which justified the attribution of jurisdiction to those courts for reasons relating to the sound administration of justice and the efficacious conduct of proceedings. In matters of tort or delict, the courts of the place where the harmful event had occurred or might occur were usually the most appropriate for deciding the case, in particular on grounds of proximity and ease of taking evidence. Further, the expression 'place where the harmful event occurred or might occur' was intended to cover both the place where the damage occurred and the place of the event giving rise to that damage and, in consequence, the defendant might be sued, at the option of the applicant, in the courts of either of those places. Article 5(3) had to be interpreted as meaning that an action for a negative declaration seeking to establish the absence of liability in tort, delict, or quasi-delict fell within its scope.

Case C-133/11 *Folien Fischer AG v Ritrama SpA* [2013] QB 523, [2014] 1 All ER (Comm) 568 (ECJ: First Chamber). Case C-189/08 *Zuid-Chemie BV v Philippo's Mineralenfabriek NV/SA* [2009] All ER (D) 15 (Sep), ECJ, considered.

445   Jurisdiction—Brussels Regulation—matters relating to tort—defendant domiciled in another state—claim against director of limited liability company

Council Regulation (EC) 44/2001 art 5(3) provides that a person domiciled in a member state may, in another member state, be sued, in matters relating to tort, delict or quasi-delict, in the courts for the place where the harmful event occurred or may occur.

The first defendant, who resided in the Netherlands, was a director of a Swedish company. The second defendant was an investment company, also based in the Netherlands, which held the majority of the shares in the Swedish company. The Swedish company hired two construction companies to work on a hotel which it was building. The Swedish company subsequently ran into financial difficulties and suspended payment. A Swedish court made a company reconstruction order under which the construction companies were paid only part of their claims. The outstanding balance was acquired by the claimant, which brought two actions against the defendants, submitting that they were liable to compensate the claimant under the principles of Swedish limited liability law. As regards the jurisdiction of the Swedish court to hear the dispute at issue, the claimant argued that the harmful event had occurred in Sweden so that the damage had also been sustained there. It fell to be determined whether, as both defendants were domiciled in the Netherlands, the Swedish court did not have jurisdiction to hear the disputes. *Held*, the concept of 'matters relating to tort, delict or quasi delict' in Regulation 44/2001 art 5(3) covered actions brought by a creditor of a limited company seeking to hold liable a member of the board of directors of that company and one of its shareholders for the debts of the company, because they had allowed the company to continue to carry on business even though it had been undercapitalised and had been forced to go into liquidation. Also, the concept of 'the place where the harmful event occurred or may occur' had to be interpreted as meaning that, as regards actions seeking to hold liable a member of the board of directors and a shareholder of a limited company for the debts of that company, that place was situated in the place to which the activities carried out by that company and the financial situation related to those activities were connected. Moreover, the fact that the claim at issue had been transferred by the initial creditor to another had no impact on the determination of the court having jurisdiction under art 5(3).

Case C-147/12 *OFAB, Ostergotlands Fastigheter AB v Koot* [2013] All ER (D) 10 (Aug) (ECJ: Fifth Chamber).

446   Jurisdiction—Brussels Regulation—matters relating to tort—tortfeasors domiciled in different member states

Article 5 of Council Regulation 44/2001 (on jurisdiction and the recognition and enforcement of judgments in civil and commercial matters) provides, so far as material: '(1) A person domiciled in a member state may, in another member state, be sued: ... 3. in matters relating to tort, delict or quasi-delict, in the courts for the place where the harmful event occurred or may occur.'

The applicant was solicited as a client by telephone for the purpose of trading in futures on stock exchanges. His file was managed by WHH, established in Dusseldorf, Germany. That company opened an account for him with MF Global (MFG), a brokerage company established in the United Kingdom. MFG traded in futures for the applicant in return for remuneration. In the period from 2002 to 2003, the applicant paid a total of €172,000 into a specific account. From that amount MFG repaid him €924.88 on 9 July 2003. The applicant claimed the difference as damages. MFG invoiced the applicant for USD$ 120 by way of commission. It retained USD$ 25 and transferred the difference, namely USD$ 95, back to WWH. The applicant commenced proceedings against MFG, alleging that he had not been sufficiently informed about the risks of trading futures on stock exchanges either by WWH or MFG. He further alleged that he had not been effectively informed about the 'kick-back' agreement entered into between MFG and WWH and the conflict of interest which resulted from it. He claimed that MFG was liable in damages for deliberately and unlawfully assisting WWH to cause unfair harm. The Landgericht Dusseldorf (the referring court) considered that the German courts had jurisdiction pursuant to art 5(3) of Council Regulation 44/2001 (on jurisdiction and the recognition and enforcement of judgments in civil and commercial matters) (the Regulation). Since the loss had been sustained in Berlin and not Dusseldorf, the place where the harmful event occurred was therefore decisive. Since MFG only traded in London, the jurisdiction of the courts in Dusseldorf might be based only on the activities of WWH. Nonetheless, the referring court was unsure about its jurisdiction under art 5(3) of the Regulation. Since the loss had been sustained in Berlin and not Düsseldorf, the place where the harmful event had occurred was therefore decisive. Since MFG only traded in London, the jurisdiction of the courts in Düsseldorf might be based only on the activities of WWH. According to the referring court, such a connecting factor as an alternative to the place where the harmful event, which had been committed by joint perpetrators or accomplices, had occurred, was admissible under German civil procedure and was, in the light of the applicant's allegations, conceivable in the instant case. In those circumstances, the referring court decided to stay the proceedings and to refer a question to the Court of Justice of the European Union (the Court) for a preliminary ruling. By its question, the referring court asked essentially whether art 5(3) of the Regulation should be interpreted as meaning that jurisdiction might be established on the ground of a harmful event, imputed to one of the presumed perpetrators of damage who was not a party to the dispute, over another presumed perpetrator of that damage who had not acted within the jurisdiction of the court seised. *Held*, the expression 'place where the harmful event occurred or may occur' in art 5(3) of the Regulation was intended to cover both the place where the damage had occurred and the place of the event giving rise to it, so that the defendant might be sued, at the option of the applicant, in the courts for either of those places. In that connection, according to settled case-law, the rule of special jurisdiction laid down in art 5(3) of the Regulation was based on the existence of a particularly close connecting factor between the dispute and the courts of the place where the harmful event occurred or may occur, which justified the attribution of jurisdiction to those courts for reasons relating to the sound administration of justice and the efficacious conduct of proceedings. In matters relating to tort, delict and quasi-delict, the courts for the place where the harmful event had occurred were usually the most appropriate for deciding the case, in particular on the grounds of proximity and ease of taking evidence. Since the identification of one of the connecting factors recognised by the case law thus enabled the court objectively best placed to determine whether the elements establishing the liability of the person sued were present to take jurisdiction, the relevant connecting factor should be situated within the jurisdiction of the court seised. Article 5(3) of the Regulation should be interpreted as meaning that it did not allow jurisdiction to be established on the ground of a harmful event imputed to one of the presumed perpetrators of damage, who was not a party to the dispute, over another presumed perpetrator of that damage who had not acted within the jurisdiction of the court seised. Judgment would be given accordingly.

C-228/11 *Melzer v MF Global UK Ltd* [2013] QB 1112, [2013] All ER (D) 262 (May) (ECJ: First Chamber).

447　Jurisdiction—Brussels Regulation—meaning of 'judgment'

It has been held, on a reference for a preliminary ruling on the scope of the term 'judgment' in Council Regulation (EC) 44/2001 arts 32, 33 in proceedings involving German companies where a Belgian court claimed to lack jurisdiction due to an Icelandic jurisdiction clause, that (1) a judgment by which a court of a member state rules on its international jurisdiction, whether it accepts or declines jurisdiction, falls within the concept of 'judgment' within the meaning of Regulation 44/2001, regardless of the fact that the judgment is classified as a procedural judgment by the law of the member state addressed; and (2) where the court of the member state of origin has declined jurisdiction after first ruling, in the grounds of its decision, on the validity and scope of an agreement on jurisdiction, the court of the member state addressed is bound by that finding, regardless of whether it is regarded as res judicata by the law of the member state of origin or the member state addressed, except in the cases in which Regulation 44/2001 art 35(3) authorises that court to review the jurisdiction of the court of the member state of origin.

C-456/11 *Gothaer Allgemeine Versicherung AG v Samskip GmbH* [2013] QB 548, [2012] All ER (D) 316 (Nov) (ECJ: Third Chamber).

448　Jurisdiction—Brussels Regulation—stay of proceedings—discretionary stay—related foreign proceedings

The claimant was the German subsidiary of a large international financial services firm. The defendant was a French-registered company engaged in the business of shipping and international trade. The claimant, which was in liquidation, issued a claim in England against the defendant seeking damages for breach of contract. The contract in question was governed by English law. At the time the English proceedings had begun, a French court had already been seised of proceedings concerning disputes between the parties. The relevant rules of law in the French proceedings were those concerned with protection for businesses which were in difficulties. The defendant applied for an order that the English court, being second seised, decline jurisdiction and/or stay the English proceedings pending the final outcome of pending proceedings in France. Consideration was given to Council Regulation (EC) 44/2001 art 28, under which, where related actions were pending in the courts of different member states, any court other than the court first seised could stay its proceedings. *Held*, art 28 should not be applied mechanically. What was required was an assessment of the degree of connection, and then a value judgment as to the expediency of hearing the two actions together (assuming they could be so heard) in order to avoid the risk of inconsistent judgments. That did not say that any possibility of inconsistent judgments meant that they were inevitably related. It was open to the court to acknowledge a connection, or a risk of inconsistent judgments, but to say that the connection was not sufficiently close, or the risk was not sufficiently great, to make the actions related. In all the circumstances, the substantive consideration of the present English proceedings would be more advantageously dealt with after the French courts had determined whether they would decide the French law proposition, and if so what the answer was and why. It was highly relevant that the English proceedings could not be substantively determined in favour of the claimant unless either the French law proposition was wrong or the French law proposition was right but, as a matter of English private international law, it did not assist the defendant. In that regard, there was a substantial degree of connection. Pushing on with the English proceedings would run a substantial risk of trespassing on the French proceedings with the consequent danger of irreconcilable judgments. It followed that the English proceedings should be stayed. Accordingly, the application would be allowed.

Lehman Bros Bankhaus AG I. Ins v CMA CGM [2013] EWHC 171 (Comm), [2013] All ER (D) 68 (Feb) (Queen's Bench Division: Walker J).

449   Jurisdiction—challenge to jurisdiction—arbitration clause—foreign court ruling
        clause invalid

The respondent company was the current grantee and lessee of a concession agreement entitling it to operate an energy-producing hydroelectric plant in Kazakhstan. For a number of years, the concession had been held by its parent or affiliate company. The appellant company was the current owner and grantor of the concession, having succeeded to the concession's original owner and grantor, the Republic of Kazakhstan. The concession agreement was governed by Kazakh law, but contained a London arbitration clause. It was decided by the Kazakhstan court that the arbitration clause was invalid. The appellant brought a claim against the respondent, seeking information about the value of the concession's assets. The respondent's application to dismiss the claim on the ground that it was subject to resolution in an arbitration court, was dismissed by the Kazakhstan court on the basis of the earlier ruling. The respondent obtained a without notice anti-suit injunction to prevent the appellant from commencing or pursuing legal proceedings in Kazakhstan, as well as permission to serve an arbitration claim form out of the jurisdiction on the appellant. The appellant's application for an order that the English court had no jurisdiction to try the respondent's claim or should not exercise any jurisdiction it might have was dismissed. The appellant's appeal against the decision was dismissed and it appealed further. *Held*, unless the Arbitration Act 1996 required a different conclusion, the negative aspect of a London arbitration agreement was a right enforceable independently of the existence or imminence of any arbitral proceedings. Where an injunction was sought to restrain foreign proceedings in breach of an arbitration agreement, whether on an interim or a final basis and whether at a time when arbitral proceedings were or were not on foot or proposed, the source of the power to grant such an injunction was to be found not in s 44, but in the Senior Courts Act 1981 s 37. The general power provided by s 37 had to be exercised sensitively and, in particular, with due regard for the scheme and terms of the 1996 Act when any arbitration was on foot or proposed. It was also open to a court, under the 1981 Act s 37, if it thought fit, to grant any injunction on an interim basis, pending the outcome of current or proposed arbitration proceedings, rather than a final basis. However, it was inconceivable that the 1996 Act had intended or should be treated sub silentio as effectively abrogating the protection enjoyed under the 1981 Act s 37 in respect of their negative rights under an arbitration agreement by those who stipulated for arbitration with an English seat. In some cases where foreign proceedings were brought in breach of an arbitration clause or exclusive choice of court agreement, the appropriate course would be to leave it to the foreign court to recognise and enforce the parties' agreement on forum. The foreign court had refused to do so, and had done so on a basis which the English courts were not bound to recognise and on grounds which were unsustainable under English law which was accepted to govern the arbitration agreement. There had been every reason for the English courts to intervene. It followed that the court had had jurisdiction under s 37 to make the order which it had made and, accordingly, the appeal would be dismissed.

AES Ust-Kamenogorsk Hydropower Plant LLP v Ust-Kamenogorsk Hydropower Plant JSC [2013] UKSC 35, [2014] 1 All ER 335 (Supreme Court: Lord Neuberger P, Lord Mance, Lord Clarke, Lord Sumption and Lord Toulson SCJJ). Decision of Court of Appeal [2011] EWCA Civ 647, [2012] All ER (Comm) 845 (2011 Abr para 500) affirmed.

450   Jurisdiction—challenge to jurisdiction—contract—appropriate forum—domicile of
       defendants

The claimant company designed, supplied and installed wood framed glazed structures. It
maintained three websites. Those websites, among other things, stated a willingness to
solicit business from the United Kingdom, and that the claimant was willing to consider job
applications from the United Kingdom, Europe and the United States of America. They also
stated willingness to look into issues of planning permission across the United Kingdom.
The defendants lived and were domiciled in Scotland. The claimant alleged that the
defendants had unlawfully repudiated contracts that had been concluded for the design,
manufacture and installation of a greenhouse, a garden room and a pool house at their
house. In turn, the defendants applied for an order stating that the English court had no
jurisdiction to try the claim or, alternatively, that it should not exercise any jurisdiction that
it had. They submitted that the claim should be struck out, as exclusive jurisdiction was
vested in Scotland. *Held*, the trader had to have manifested its intention to establish
commercial relations with consumers from one or more other member states including that
of the consumer's domicile. Specifically, in the case of a contract between a trader and a
given consumer, it had to be determined, by reference to the trader's websites and overall
activity, whether before any contract with that consumer was concluded, there had been
evidence demonstrating that the trader had envisaged doing business with consumers in
other member states, including the member state of that consumer's domicile, in the sense
that it was minded to conclude a contract with those consumers. Further, while the
dissemination of traditional forms of advertising in other member states, such as by the
press, radio, television or other medium, might of itself demonstrate an intention of the
trader to direct its activities towards those states, the mere establishment of a website which
was accessible in other member states would not of itself do so since use of the internet
might automatically give worldwide reach without any intention on the part of the trader to
target consumers outside of the state in which it was established. When considering
advertising, whether by the use of the internet or by other media which could reach across
borders without any necessary intention to target consumers in other member states, the
court had to look for clear expressions of the intention to solicit the custom in that state.
Such clear expressions could include mention that it was offering its services or its goods in
one or more member states designated by name, or mention of an international clientele
composed of customers domiciled in various states. However, a finding that an activity was
directed to other member states did not depend solely on the existence of such patent
evidence. In the circumstances, the claimant had a willingness and ability to work in
Scotland. It was willing to solicit the custom of consumers in all parts of the United
Kingdom, including Scotland. Thus, while the primary focus of the claimant's business
might be in England and most of the business it had formerly obtained had been in England,
it was clear that it envisaged doing business with consumers domiciled in Scotland.
Therefore, the proceedings could only be brought against the defendants in Scotland.
Judgment would be given accordingly.
    Oak Leaf Conservatories Ltd v Weir [2013] EWHC 3197 (TCC), [2013] All ER (D) 281
(Oct) (Queen's Bench Division: Stuart-Smith J). Joined Cases C-585/08 and C-144/09
Pammer v Reederei Karl Schluter GmbH & Co KG [2010] All ER (D) 84 (Dec), ECJ (2010
Abr para 539), considered.

451   Jurisdiction—challenge to jurisdiction—contract—appropriate forum—group
       companies

The claimant was the majority state-owned Russian airline. The first and second defendants
were Russians domiciled in the United Kingdom. The claimant alleged that a fraud had been
perpetrated by the first and second defendants through the third to seventh defendant
companies, which were controlled by the first and second defendants. The third defendant
was based in Luxembourg and the seventh defendant was based in the British Virgin Islands.
The claimant alleged that the first defendant had used his influence to insert the second
defendant into the claimant. The second defendant obtained the appointment of the fifth
defendant to act for the claimant pursuant to an advisory mandate. The mandate contract
was governed by Swiss law and contained a Lausanne jurisdiction clause. The fifth
defendant entered into two credit agreements. The amended first credit agreement contained
a Swiss ICC arbitration clause and the amended second credit agreement contained a Zurich

460   Jurisdiction—insolvency—cross-border insolvency—co-operation between courts—request for assistance

See *HSBC Bank plc v Tambrook Jersey Ltd*, para 395.

461   Jurisdiction—international carriage by road—primary carrier and sub-contractor—liability for loss of cargo

See *British American Tobacco Switzerland SA v Exel Europe Ltd*, para 136.

462   Jurisdiction—matters relating to tort—fraudulent misrepresentation

The parties, who were both of Russian nationality, signed a written agreement (the 'principal agreement'), which was in Russian and concerned a joint venture. The principal agreement provided that that agreement and also a shareholders' agreement were to be governed by English law. The claimant, who resided in England, brought proceedings contending that the defendant had made fraudulent representations which had led to her signing the principal agreement and to her participation in the joint venture, including causing a lender to make initial loans. She applied for rescission of the principal agreement or damages in lieu of rescission, together with damages for deceit. The defendant sought a stay of the proceedings. He contended that Russia was the natural forum for the dispute because (1) it was the country with which the claim had its most real and substantial connection; (2) the Russian court was competent to hear the dispute, and was the forum where the dispute could most suitably be tried in the interests of the parties and for the ends of justice; and (3) justice did not require the claim to be heard in England. The defendant further contended that the negotiations in relation to the projects had taken place in Moscow, and that almost all of the contractual agreements in respect of them had been governed by Russian law and provided for Russian court jurisdiction. Consideration was given to the Private International Law (Miscellaneous Provisions) Act 1995 ss 11 and 12. *Held*, there was no doubt that the court should proceed on the footing that the 1995 Act had the result that the tort claims were governed by Russian law. The defendant had rightly pointed out that the negotiations in relation to the projects had taken place in Moscow. In so far as the claimant had been induced by the representations to make the principal agreement and had caused the lender to make the initial loans, it seemed clear that she had done both of those things in Russia. The principal agreement could have been drafted in a way which applied English law to the tortious claims connected with the principal agreement. However, it had not been nor could it be suggested that the transaction had been organised by reference to English law. On the contrary, it had involved numerous contractual agreements, almost all of which had been governed by Russian law and provided for Russian court jurisdiction. On the facts, the links with Russia were overwhelming and the defendant had demonstrated that Russia was an available forum which was clearly and distinctly more appropriate than England. There were no special circumstances such that the interest of justice required that the claim be litigated in the United Kingdom. Accordingly, the application would be allowed.

Baturina v Chistyakov [2013] EWHC 3537 (Comm), [2013] All ER (D) 184 (Nov) (Queen's Bench Division: Walker J).

463   Jurisdiction—stay of proceedings—parallel proceedings—same issues arising in competition law actions in England and Scotland

The United Kingdom health authority commenced proceedings in England against the first defendant alleging anti-competition activity in respect of a patent for a drug. Parallel proceedings were brought against the defendants in Scotland based on similar facts, save that the English proceedings included a claim in tort. The defendants applied for a stay of the Scottish proceedings so as to allow the parallel English proceedings to be heard first to avoid duplication of effort and increased and unnecessary costs. They favoured a stay of the Scottish proceedings because the English proceedings were more advanced, more valuable, and raised a core issue not raised in the Scottish claim. *Held*, while it was accepted that all of the major issues on liability in both sets of proceedings were common, the present matter should be dealt with as a case management decision. Duplication of effort should be controlled by case management techniques. The Scottish Ministers had the right to have their own case advanced by their own representatives and a fair opportunity to influence events in the case. A stay would deprive the Scottish Ministers of all discovery and all opportunity to consider the matter further. It would be unfair to treat the English proceedings as a test trial. The risk of duplication was not sufficient to require the court to take such drastic action. Accordingly, the application would be dismissed.

Scottish Ministers v Servier Laboratories Ltd [2013] All ER (D) 20 (Oct) (Chancery Division: Mann J).

CONSTITUTIONAL AND ADMINISTRATIVE LAW
Halsbury's Laws of England (5th edn) vol 20 (2014) paras 1–663

Articles
For articles relating to this title please refer to the Table of Articles at the beginning of the Abridgment.

464   Central government bodies—estimates and accounts
The Government Resources and Accounts Act 2000 (Estimates and Accounts) Order 2013, SI 2013/488 (in force on 1 April 2013), designates specified central government bodies in relation to named government departments for the purpose of those departments' supply estimates and resource accounts; the designations have effect for the financial year that ends on 31 March 2014.

The Government Resources and Accounts Act 2000 (Estimates and Accounts) (Amendment) Order 2013, SI 2013/3187 (in force on 31 January 2014), amends SI 2013/488 above by designating additional central government bodies, changing the names of certain bodies and providing that certain other bodies are no longer designated.

465   Comptroller and auditor general—resource accounts—alteration of timetables
The Government Resources and Accounts Act 2000 (Alteration of Timetables for Accounts) Order 2013, SI 2013/148 (in force on 30 January 2013), provides that, in relation to the resource accounts prepared by the Department for Culture, Media and Sport for the financial year ending on 31 March 2012, the Treasury is required to lay the certified accounts and the related report before the House of Commons not later than 25 February 2013.

466   Constitutional Reform and Governance Act 2010—commencement
The Constitutional Reform and Governance Act 2010 (Commencement No 8 and Saving Provision) Order 2013, SI 2013/2826, brings into force on 1 November 2013 Sch 6 paras 35(3), 38–41, 47(2) (so far as not already in force). The 2013 Order also provides that the European Parliamentary (United Kingdom Representatives) Pensions (Consolidation and Amendment) Order 1994, SI 1994/1662, and the European Parliamentary (United Kingdom Representatives) Pensions (Additional Voluntary Contributions Scheme) (No 2) Order 1995, SI 1995/739, have effect as if they were schemes made by the Independent Parliamentary Standards Authority under the European Parliament (Pay and Pensions) Act 1979 s 4. For a summary of the 2010 Act, see 2010 Abr para 562. See also the commencement table in the title STATUTES AND LEGISLATIVE PROCESS.

467   Crown Office—fees
The Crown Office Fees Order 2013, SI 2013/986 (in force on 20 May 2013), replaces the 2008 Order, SI 2008/1977, and increases various fees taken in the office of the Clerk of the Crown in Chancery.

468   Designation—European Communities—European Parliament
The European Communities (Designation) Order 2013, SI 2013/1445 (in force on 12 July 2013), (1) designates the Secretary of State, the Lord President of the Council and the Lord Privy Seal in relation to the European Parliament; (2) designates the Secretary of State and the Lord President of the Council in relation to local elections; (3) provides that a new designation does not restrict the scope of designations in other orders and allows ministers and departments designated in relation to the same matters to legislate jointly as well as individually; and (4) revokes two existing designations which are superseded.

469   European Union (Croatian Accession and Irish Protocol) Act 2013

The European Union (Croatian Accession and Irish Protocol) Act 2013 makes provision consequential on the Treaty concerning the accession of the Republic of Croatia to the European Union (Brussels, 9 December 2011) ('the Accession Treaty') and the Protocol on the concerns of the Irish People on the Treaty of Lisbon (Brussels, 16 May 2012) ('the Irish Protocol'); and makes provision about the entitlement of Croatian nationals to enter or reside in the United Kingdom as workers. The Act received the royal assent on 31 January 2013 and came into force on that day.

Sections 1, 2 approve the Accession Treaty and the Irish Protocol for the purposes of the European Union Act 2011 s 2, under which primary legislation is required before a treaty amending the Treaty on European Union or the Treaty on the Functioning of the European Union can be ratified in the United Kingdom. By virtue of the 2013 Act s 3, the Accession Treaty and the Irish Protocol are added to the list of treaties given effect in United Kingdom law by the European Communities Act 1972. The Secretary of State may make regulations under the 2013 Act s 4 providing for the entitlement of Croatian nationals to enter or reside in the United Kingdom as workers, and such regulations may provide that an enactment relating to the rights of nationals of the European Economic Area to enter or reside in the United Kingdom in order to work applies to Croatian nationals. Under s 5, a draft of the first set of regulations made under s 4 must be approved by both Houses of Parliament before they are made. Section 6 provides for extent, commencement and short title.

470   Freedom of information—exempt information—environmental information

The claimant journalist sought disclosure of communications passing between the Prince of Wales and various government departments. The request was declined by the relevant departments. The interested party, the Information Commissioner, ruled that such withholding of the requested information was not in breach of the Freedom of Information Act 2000 or the Environmental Information Regulations 2004, SI 2004/3391. The claimant's appeal succeeded to the extent that it was found that 'advocacy correspondence' could not be lawfully withheld. Neither the interested party nor the departments sought to appeal against the decision but the defendant, the Attorney General, issued a certificate under the 2000 Act s 53, stating that he had formed the opinion, on reasonable grounds, that there was no failure to comply with the relevant provisions of the 2000 Act or the 2004 Regulations, so that the departments were not obliged to disclose the advocacy correspondence. In judicial review proceedings, the claimant questioned the lawfulness of the certificate and sought an order quashing it. *Held*, properly construed, under the 2000 Act s 53, reasonable grounds for the certificate had to exist and, if reasonable grounds did not exist, the certificate was invalid and of no effect. The burden of argument, in practice, was on the accountable person to show that the grounds for certifying were reasonable. In the circumstances, the judgment called for was a value judgment as to where the balance of the public interest lay. The statement of reasons appended to the certificate, once carefully read and analysed, had demonstrated reasonable grounds. The views and reasons expressed as to where the balance of public interest lay were proper and rational. They made sense. In fact, there was no difficulty in holding them to be cogent. The nature of the reasons given showed that individual consideration to each individual piece of correspondence separately had not been called for and the defendant had been entitled to consider the correspondence as a whole. The scheme and language of s 53 was not such as to require the accountable person, before he might properly certify, to form the view on reasonable grounds that the decision proposed to be overridden had itself been unreasonable or otherwise flawed in a public law sense. The statement of reasons had made abundantly clear the essential reasons for the opinion expressed in the certificate and for the exercise of the executive override. Further, Council Directive (EC) 2003/4 (on public access to environmental information) art 6(2) imposed an additional requirement on member states following a review procedure consistent with art 6(1). However, how that requirement was met was left to national law. Article 6(2) was capable of being satisfied in a case under the 2000 Act s 53 by the courts having the power to review the reasonableness of the grounds given by the accountable person in issuing a certificate. Inevitably, therefore, the reasons for the certificate would have to engage with the substance of the original decision of the public authority to withhold. The court would review that even where it was not required to replicate the entire exercise undertaken by the decision-maker. In the circumstances, close scrutiny by the court was called for and such close scrutiny of the reasons given for the accountable person's opinion had to require a close scrutiny by the court of the initial decision to withhold. Section 53 was not incompatible with Directive 2003/4. Since the defendant had had reasonable grounds for certifying as he had, the challenge in so far as it related to requests for disclosure of environmental information failed. Accordingly, the application would be dismissed.

R (on the application of Evans) v A-G [2013] EWHC 1960 (Admin), [2014] 1 All ER 23 (Queen's Bench Division: Lord Judge CJ, Davis LJ and Globe J).

This decision has been reversed on appeal: [2014] EWCA Civ 254, [2014] All ER (D) 100 (Mar).

471   Freedom of information—release of datasets for re-use—fees

The Freedom of Information (Release of Datasets for Re-use) (Fees) Regulations 2013, SI 2013/1977 (in force on 1 September 2013), make provision about the charging of a fee by a public authority in connection with making certain datasets which are relevant copyright works available for re-use in accordance with the Freedom of Information Act 2000 s 11A(2) or a requirement imposed by virtue of s 19(2A)(c). The regulations (1) confer a power on a public authority to charge a fee for such re-use except where the public authority has another statutory power to charge a fee for that re-use; (2) prescribe how any fee that may be charged is to be determined, including how the maximum fee is to be determined; and (3) make provision relating to the establishment of standard fees, including a requirement for a public authority to specify the basis for calculating any fee or standard fee.

472   Global Green Growth Institute—legal capacities

The Global Green Growth Institute (Legal Capacities) Order 2013, SI 2013/785 (in force on a date to be notified in the London Gazette), confers the legal capacities of a body corporate on the Global Green Growth Institute, an international organisation established with the aim of promoting sustainable development of developing and emerging countries.

473   Government accounts—whole of government accounts—designation of bodies

The Whole of Government Accounts (Designation of Bodies) Order 2013, SI 2013/1796 (in force on 9 August 2013), designates specified bodies, in relation to the financial year ending on 31 March 2013, for the purposes of the Government Resources and Accounts Act 2000 so that those bodies are required to prepare and present to the Treasury such financial information in relation to that financial year as the Treasury requires to enable it to prepare whole of government accounts.

474   Interception of communications

See POLICE AND INVESTIGATORY POWERS.

475   Justice and Security Act 2013

The Justice and Security Act 2013 provides for oversight of the Security Service, the Secret Intelligence Service, the Government Communications Headquarters and other activities relating to intelligence or security matters, makes provision about the closed material procedure in relation to certain civil proceedings, and prevents the making of certain court orders for the disclosure of sensitive information. The Act received the royal assent on 25 April 2013 and came into force in part on that day. The remaining provisions came into force on 25 June 2013: SI 2013/1482. For details of commencement, see the commencement table in the title STATUTES AND LEGISLATIVE PROCESS.

Part 1 (ss 1–5) Oversight of intelligence and security activities
Section 1 replaces the Intelligence and Security Committee with a new body called the Intelligence and Security Committee of Parliament ('ISC'), which is to consist of nine members drawn from both Houses of Parliament; and Sch 1 makes provision about the membership and procedure of the ISC. The main functions of the ISC, which are essentially to examine or otherwise oversee the expenditure, administration, policy and operations of the Security Service, the Secret Intelligence Service, and the Government Communications Headquarters, are outlined in s 2. The ISC is required to make an annual report to

Parliament on the discharge of its functions, and is authorised to make such other reports as it considers appropriate concerning any aspect of its functions: s 3. Section 4 defines various terms used in ss 1–3 and Sch 1. Section 5 empowers the Prime Minister to require the Intelligence Services Commissioner to keep under review the carrying out of any aspect of the functions of an intelligence service, a head of an intelligence service, or any part of Her Majesty's forces, or of the Ministry of Defence, so far as engaging in intelligence activities.

Part 2 (ss 6–18) Disclosure of sensitive material
Under s 6, certain courts hearing civil proceedings are permitted to make a declaration that the case is one in which a closed material application may be made in relation to specific pieces of material. Section 7 makes explicit the power of judges to review, and in appropriate cases revoke, a declaration under s 6, and obliges the court to review its decision to grant a declaration after the pre-trial disclosure exercise. By virtue of s 8, rules of court may make provision relating to the process to be followed after a declaration is granted under s 6. A special advocate may be appointed by the Attorney General to represent the interests of an excluded party in closed material proceedings: s 9. Section 10 provides that, subject to ss 8, 9 and 11, rules of court must ensure that the normal rules of disclosure continue to apply to s 6 proceedings. The general provisions to be included in the rules of court relating to s 6 proceedings are set out in s 11. The Secretary of State is required by s 12 to lay a report before Parliament on an annual basis on the operation of the closed material procedure provisions. Section 13 requires a review to be carried out on the operation of the closed material procedure provisions, and sets out the framework for the appointment of the reviewer and the production and timing of his report to be laid before Parliament. Various terms used in ss 6–13 are defined in s 14. Section 15 provides for a right of review on judicial review principles by the Special Immigration Appeals Commission in respect of certain prescribed categories of executive action by the Secretary of State; and s 16 permits the use of intercept evidence in closed material proceedings before an employment tribunal. Section 17 prevents the court in certain circumstances from exercising its residual disclosure jurisdiction so as to order the disclosure of specified types of sensitive government-held information. By virtue of s 18, a party to proceedings in which the Secretary of State has issued a certificate in relation to sensitive material other than intelligence service information may apply to the court for the certificate to be set aside.

Part 3 (ss 19, 20) General
Section 19 gives effect to Sch 2, which makes consequential amendments, and Sch 3, which makes transitional provision. Section 20 deals with commencement and extent, and specifies the short title.

Amendments, repeals and revocations
The list below, which is not exhaustive, mentions repeals and amendments which are or will be effective when the Act is fully in force.
  Specific provisions of a number of Acts are amended or repealed. These include: Intelligence Services Act 1994 ss 10, 11, Sch 3; Regulation of Investigatory Powers Act 2000 s 18.

476 Ministers—transfer of functions—Chequers and Dorneywood Estates

The Transfer of Functions (Chequers and Dorneywood Estates) Order 2013, SI 2013/537 (in force on 17 April 2013), transfers (1) from the Lord Privy Seal to the Chancellor of the Duchy of Lancaster, the statutory functions relating to the Chequers Estate; and (2) to the Chancellor of Duchy of Lancaster, functions relating to the Dorneywood Estate that were originally conferred on the Minister of Works.

477 Ministers—transfer of functions—elections and referendums

The Transfer of Functions (Elections and Referendums) Order 2013, SI 2013/2597 (in force on 6 November 2013), makes provision for various functions of the Secretary of State in relation to elections and referendums, which are exercised under or by virtue of the Town and Country Planning Act 1990, the Local Government Finance Act 1992 and the Local Government Act 2000, to be exercised concurrently with the Lord President of the Council. The order also makes supplementary provision for continuity in relation to the exercise of the functions and makes consequential amendments to those Acts.

478   Overseas territories—legislation—lawfulness—review powers of English courts

See *R (on the application of Barclay) v Lord Chancellor (No 2)*, para 343.

479   Parliamentary Commissioner—bodies subject to investigation

The Parliamentary Commissioner Order 2013, SI 2013/238 (in force on 1 April 2013), further amends the Parliamentary Commissioner Act 1967 by making changes to the list of departments subject to investigation by the Parliamentary Commissioner for Administration.

480   Public Audit (Wales) Act 2013

See para 1802.

481   Public bodies—abolition—Administrative Justice and Tribunals Council

The Public Bodies (Abolition of Administrative Justice and Tribunals Council) Order 2013, SI 2013/2042 (in force on 18 August 2013), abolishes the Administrative Justice and Tribunals Council, which was set up by the Tribunals, Courts and Enforcement Act 2007 s 44.

482   Public bodies—abolition—Disability Living Allowance Advisory Board

The Public Bodies (Abolition of the Disability Living Allowance Advisory Board) Order 2013, SI 2013/252 (in force in part on 7 February 2013 and in part on 8 February 2013), abolishes the Disability Living Allowance Advisory Board. SI 1991/1746 is revoked.

483   Public bodies—abolition—Registrar of Public Lending Right

The Public Bodies (Abolition of the Registrar of Public Lending Right) Order 2013, SI 2013/2352 (in force in part on 1 October 2013 and in part on 2 October 2013), (1) abolishes the Registrar of Public Lending Right; (2) transfers the functions, property, rights and liabilities of the Registrar to the British Library Board; (3) imposes final reporting and accounting obligations on the Board in relation to the period preceding the Registrar's abolition; (4) makes consequential amendments to primary and secondary legislation; and (5) makes provision for various supplementary matters, including the continuing validity and effect of anything done by or in relation to the Registrar after its abolition and the transfer of its functions, property, rights and liabilities to the Board.

484   Public bodies—abolition—Victims' Advisory Panel

The Public Bodies (Abolition of Victims' Advisory Panel) Order 2013, SI 2013/2853 (in force on 5 November 2013), abolishes the Victims' Advisory Panel. Specifically, the order (1) repeals and amends provisions in consequence of the abolition of the Victims' Advisory Panel; and (2) repeals the entry for the Victims' Advisory Panel in the Public Bodies Act 2011 Sch 1.

485   Public procurement—award of contracts—contracts between public bodies—need for tender

A local health authority in Italy hired a public university to carry out a study of the seismic vulnerability of hospital structures in the local area. The study was to include a technical description of any remedial work required to each building. Pursuant to the consultancy contract, the university was authorised to use qualified external collaborators where necessary to carry out parts of the work. Provision was also made for the university to be paid for its costs and services. Various professional associations and undertakings brought proceedings complaining about the award of the contract, contending that it was in contravention of national procurement legislation and European Parliament and Council Directive (EC) 2004/18 on the award of public contracts. An Italian court ruled that the study project constituted a contract for the provision of engineering services and was therefore subject to the requirements of national procurement law. The parties challenged the decision, arguing that the university's remuneration was limited to costs incurred, that the contract fell within its institutional activities, and that the project related to research conducted by means of experiments and analyses. It fell to be determined whether Directive

2004/18 precluded national legislation, which permitted the conclusion, without an invitation to tender, of a consultancy contract between two public entities involving structural evaluations. *Held*, in accordance with art 1(2), a contract for pecuniary interest concluded in writing between an economic operator and a contracting authority, and having as its object the provision of relevant services, was a public contract. It was immaterial whether that operator was itself a contracting authority, or whether it was primarily profit-making, structured as an undertaking or had a continuous presence on the market. In principle, therefore, public universities were entitled to take part in a tendering procedure for the award of a public service contract, subject to regulation by the member states as to the activities in which they were permitted to engage. Activities such as those forming the subject matter of the consultancy contract fell within the framework either of research and development services or of engineering services and related scientific and technical consulting services. A contract was not a public contract merely because the remuneration remained limited to reimbursement of the expenditure incurred to provide the agreed service. However, a contract established co-operation between public entities with the aim of ensuring the performance of a task in the public interest which all the parties had to perform did not fall within the scope of EU public procurement law in so far as it was concluded exclusively by public entities, without the participation of a private party, provided that no private service provider was placed in a position of competitive advantage and implementation of the co-operation was governed solely by considerations relating to the pursuit of public interest objectives. The consultancy contract was largely for activities which corresponded to those usually carried out by engineers and architects and which, even though they had an academic foundation, did not constitute academic research. Consequently, the public task which formed the subject matter of the co-operation between the university and the health authority did not appear to ensure the implementation of a public task which both parties had to perform. Moreover, the contract was capable of bringing about an advantage for private undertakings if the external collaborators to whom the university was permitted to have recourse included private service providers.

Case C-159/11 *Azienda Sanitaria Locale di Lecce and Università del Salento v Ordine degli Ingegneri della Provincia di Lecce* [2013] PTSR 1043 (ECJ: Grand Chamber).

486 Public procurement—award of contracts—technical specifications—specifications referable to specific eco-labels

A Dutch province published a contract notice for the supply and management of automatic tea and coffee machines. The notice emphasised that the province wished to increase the use of organic and fair trade products. The notice referred to specifications, which included statements regarding the importance attached by the province to 'sustainable purchasing' and 'socially responsible business'. An annex to the specifications provided that the province used the 'Max Havelaar' and 'EKO' labels for tea and coffee, and that if possible the other ingredients used for the preparation of drinks other than tea and coffee, such as milk, sugar and cocoa, should comply with those labels. The EKO label was granted to organic products and the Max Havelaar label was intended to promote the marketing of fair trade products. The province subsequently published an information notice to clarify that other labels would also be accepted, in so far as the criteria were equivalent or identical. The European Commission brought an action against the Netherlands for failure to fulfil its obligations on the basis that the specifications infringed European Parliament and Council Directive (EC) 2004/18 (on the co-ordination of procedure for the award of public works contracts, public supply contracts and public service contracts) by imposing the Max Havelaar and EKO labels or labels based on comparable or identical criteria. *Held*, the requirement that certain products to be supplied were to bear a specific eco-label, rather than using the detailed specifications defined by that eco-label, was incompatible with art 23(6). That provision conferred on contracting authorities the option to use the detailed specifications of an eco-label but not the eco-label as such. The obligation of the contracting authority to mention expressly the detailed environmental characteristics it intended to impose, even where it referred to the characteristics defined by an eco-label, was indispensable in order to allow potential tenderers to refer to a single official document, coming from the contracting authority itself and thus without being subject to the uncertainties of searching for information and the possible temporal variations in the criteria applicable to a particular eco-label. The subsequent clarification in the information notice could not compensate for the failure to identify the detailed technical specifications corresponding to the label concerned. The reference in the specifications to specific labels in the award criteria without listing the criteria underlying those labels and without allowing proof that a product satisfied those underlying criteria by all appropriate means was incompatible with art 53(1)(a). Further, the requirements that tenderers comply with the 'criteria of sustainability of purchases and socially responsible business' and 'contribute to improving the sustainability of the coffee market and to environmentally, socially and economically responsible coffee production' were not so clear, precise and unequivocal as to enable all reasonably informed tenderers exercising ordinary care to be completely sure what the criteria governing those requirements were. Those requirements therefore did not comply with the obligation of transparency provided for in art 2.

Case C-368/10 *EU Commission v Netherlands* [2012] 3 CMLR 2342, [2013] All ER (EC) 804 (ECJ: Third Chamber).

487　Public procurement—professional and trade registers—Croatia

The Public Contracts and Defence and Security Public Contracts (Croatia Accession Amendments) Regulations 2013, SI 2013/1431 (in force on 1 July 2013), further amend the Public Contract Regulations 2006, SI 2006/5, and the Defence and Security Public Contract Regulations 2011, SI 2011/2473, by adding to the list of professional and trade registers those professional and trade registers for the Republic of Croatia consequent to its accession to the European Union.

488　Public records—Public Record Office—fees

The Public Record Office (Fees) Regulations 2013, SI 2013/3267 (in force on 1 April 2014), replace the 2012 Regulations, SI 2012/1665, and prescribe a new range of fees to be charged for the provision by the Public Record Office of authenticated copies or extracts from records and of other services.

489　Rights and freedoms

See RIGHTS AND FREEDOMS.

490　Scotland—competence of Scottish Parliament—agricultural holding—security of tenure

Scotland

The Agricultural Holdings (Scotland) Act 2003 s 72(3)–(10) applied to the purported termination of a tenancy as a consequence of the dissolution of a partnership by notice served by a limited partner on or after 16 September 2002. Section 72(10) enabled a landlord, in cases where the tenancy continued to have effect by virtue of s 72(6), notwithstanding the purported termination of the tenancy, to obtain the benefit of s 73, which allowed the landlord to terminate the tenancy by the service of a notice to quit at a time of his own choosing. However, s 72(10)(b)(i) and (ii) added a further qualification which had to be satisfied if s 73 was to apply. The notice of dissolution or 'thing mentioned' in s 72(3) had to have been served or occurred after 1 July 2003. Following the publication of the Agricultural Holdings (Scotland) Bill, the precursor to the 2003 Act, amendments were made to the provisions that were to become s 72 stating that the start date would be moved from 4 February 2003 to 16 September 2002. The amendment was retrospective and was designed to deal with the situation where a large number of dissolution notices had been served due to the desire of landlords to avoid being adversely affected by the proposed changes. A question arose as to whether the right of a landlord, under the European Convention on Human Rights First Protocol art 1, who had served his notice of dissolution on 3 February 2003, had been violated by the 2003 Act s 72. *Held*, the effect of the qualification in s 72(10)(b)(i) and (ii) was to deny the benefit of s 73 to all cases where the tenancy was purportedly terminated between 16 September 2002 and 30 June 2003 but which continued to have effect by virtue of s 72(6). Landlords who served dissolution notices on 3 February 2003 were therefore denied that benefit. They were in a worse position than those who served notices on or after 1 July 2003. So too were landlords who served them at any time after the date when the Bill was introduced. The provision was therefore discriminatory in that it affected a landlord's right to the enjoyment of the

and (4) requiring the Secretary of State to review the 2008 Regulations and to publish a report containing the conclusions of the review. SI 1985/2042 and SI 1987/1979 are revoked.

505   Complaints—Financial Conduct Authority—designated consumer bodies
See para 1217.

506   Construction products

The Construction Products Regulations 2013, SI 2013/1387 (in force on 1 July 2013), make provision necessary for the operation in the United Kingdom of European Parliament and Council Regulation (EU) 305/2011 (laying down harmonised conditions for the marketing of construction products). Specifically, the regulations (1) establish offence provisions in respect of breaches of the principal safety-related provisions of Regulation 305/2011; (2) set out the competent authority in the United Kingdom for the purposes of Regulation 305/2011, and in so far as it applies to construction products, to European Parliament and Council (EC) Regulation 765/2008 (setting out the requirements for accreditation and market surveillance relating to the marketing of products); (3) prescribe an offence were construction products are supplied without accompanying product identification, contact information for manufacturers, importers or distributors, or instructions and safety information; (4) make provision for the service of notices by an enforcement authority suspending the supply of construction products on grounds of the commission of an specified offence; (5) provide for appeal against suspension notices; (6) make provision for forfeiture of construction products on grounds similar to those for the service of suspension notices; (7) provide that enforcement authorities must notify the Secretary of State of any action that they take under heads (4) or (6); (8) make provision for the service of notices by the Secretary of State prohibiting the supply of construction products; (9) require the issue of warnings in relation to construction products, on grounds of the commission of an offence; (10) provide for the service of notices requiring information to assist the Secretary of State in deciding whether to serve prohibition notices and notices to warn, with an offence for non-compliance or provision of false information; (11) specify requirements for the content of prohibition notices and notices to warn; (12) establish a procedure by which representations can be made against the grounds for service of a prohibition notice; (13) provide for notices to be given in advance of service of a notice to warn, and for a procedure for representations to be made against the service of the notice; (14) establish the duty for local weights and measures authorities in England and Wales and in Scotland, and district councils in Northern Ireland, to carry out market surveillance under Regulation 765/2008, as it applies to construction products, and Regulation 305/2011; (15) empower local weights and measures authorities in England and Wales to investigate and prosecute in relation to offences anywhere in England and Wales, and district councils to do the same anywhere in Northern Ireland; (16) govern powers of entry, search and seizure in connection with failures to comply with the requirements of Regulation 305/2011 and other specified offences; (17) establish offences for obstructing or giving false information to an officer of an enforcement authority; and (18) set out an offence provision for disclosure of information obtained in the course of procedures under the regulations or under Regulation 765/2008 art 27(2). SI 1991/6120 is revoked.

507   Consumer contract—contract made in consumer's home or place of work—cancellation

The Cancellation of Contracts made in a Consumer's Home or Place of Work etc Regulations 2008, SI 2008/1816, reg 5 provides that the 2008 Regulations apply to a contract between a consumer and a trader which is for the supply of goods or services to the consumer by a trader and which is made (1) during a visit by the trader to the consumer's home or place of work, or to the home of another individual; (2) during an excursion organised by the trader away from his business premises; or (3) after an offer made by the consumer during such a visit or excursion.

The appellant telephoned the respondent, who was the proprietor of a removal firm, asking for a quotation. The following day, the parties met at the appellant's home and agreed a price for the move. The respondent returned to his office and emailed an acceptance document. Later the same day, the respondent visited the appellant again and was given the completed acceptance document. The appellant subsequently paid a deposit. The respondent's standard conditions provided that, if the agreement were to be cancelled by the appellant, the appellant would be charged a fee according to how much notice he gave. The appellant subsequently obtained a substantially lower quotation from another removals firm. He therefore contacted the respondent to cancel their agreement, agreeing to pay a 50 per cent cancellation charge. However, the appellant subsequently refused to pay the charge, believing that, since he was still within the seven-day cancellation period specified in the 2008 Regulations, the contract was unenforceable because it had been concluded at his home within the meaning of reg 5. The respondent sued the appellant for the amount of the cancellation charge. The judge ruled that the 2008 Regulations did not apply to the present agreement as reg 5 required the contract to have been made over the course of only one visit to the consumer's home rather than multiple visits. He therefore allowed the respondent's claim. The appellant's appeal against that decision was dismissed and, on his further appeal, *held*, the 2008 Regulations applied if the consumer's home was the place where the contract was concluded, irrespective of whether there had been earlier negotiations between the parties there. The target of reg 5 was contract-making in the consumer's home, a place where the consumer was believed to be vulnerable. The respondent had therefore been obliged under reg 7(2) to give the appellant written notice of his right to cancel. As the respondent did not do so, the agreement was unenforceable against the appellant. If such notice had been given, the appellant would have been entitled to cancel the agreement during the cancellation period. Accordingly, the appeal would be allowed.

Robertson v Swift [2012] EWCA Civ 1794, (2013) 177 JP 169 (Court of Appeal: Mummery, Jackson and Lewison LJJ).

508   Consumer contracts—information, cancellation and additional charges

The Consumer Contracts (Information, Cancellation and Additional Charges) Regulations 2013, SI 2013/3134 (in force on 13 June 2014), which supersede the Consumer Protection (Distance Selling) Regulations 2000, SI 2000/2334, and the Cancellation of Contracts made in a Consumer's Home or Place of Work etc Regulations 2008, SI 2008/1816, implement European Parliament and Council Directive (EU) 2011/83 on consumer rights. In particular, the regulations (1) make provision for their periodic review by the Secretary of State; (2) apply to contracts, except for specified excluded contracts, between traders and consumers which are entered into on or after the commencement date; (3) specify the information which a trader must provide to a consumer before entering into an on-premises contract, an off-premises contract or a distance contract; (4) require a trader to provide a consumer with a copy of a signed contract, or confirmation of a contract, within a reasonable time after its conclusion; (5) provide that a term is implied into a contract between a trader and a consumer that the trader has complied with the information requirements; (6) provide that it is a criminal offence for a trader to enter into an off-premises contract without having provided the required information on cancellation rights; (7) give a consumer the right to cancel a distance or off-premises contract, without giving any reason or incurring any costs, within 14 days of the conclusion of the contract or the date of delivery, depending on the type of contract; (8) extend the cancellation period by up to 12 months where a trader fails to provide a consumer with information on cancellation rights; (9) make provision for refunds and return of goods in the event of cancellation; (10) provide that a consumer loses the right to cancel where a service or digital content is supplied during the cancellation period, if the consumer has acknowledged that the right would be lost in those circumstances; (11) specify that an ancillary contract is automatically terminated on cancellation of the main contract; (12) amend the Consumer Protection from Unfair Trading Regulations 2008,SI 2008/1277, so as to provide that a consumer is not required to pay for the unsolicited supply of products; (13) provide that a consumer is not required to make payments in addition to those agreed for a trader's main obligation, unless the consumer has given express consent before the conclusion of the contract; (14) provide that, where a trader operates a telephone line so that consumers can make contact about a contract entered into with the trader, the consumer must not be required to pay above the basic rate for telephone calls; (15) require goods to be delivered to a consumer without undue delay and, in any event, not more than 30 days after the contract has been entered into, unless the trader and consumer have agreed otherwise; (16) make provision in relation to the passing of risk in relation to sales contracts; (17) empower local weights and measures authorities to consider complaints about surcharges and to apply to a court for an injunction against a trader acting in breach of the regulations; and (18) make consequential amendments to primary and secondary legislation. SI 2013/761 is revoked.

The Enterprise Act 2002 (Part 8 EU Infringements) Order 2013, SI 2013/3168 (in force on 13 June 2014), specifies, for the purposes of the Enterprise Act 2002 s 212, the 2013 Regulations above and certain provisions of the Consumer Rights (Payment Surcharges) Regulations 2012, SI 2012/3110, as the United Kingdom law which gives effect to Directive 2011/83 above. The effect of the order is that the enforcement procedures set out in the 2002 Act Pt 8 (ss 210–236) apply in relation to breaches of the 2013 Regulations and of the relevant provisions of the 2012 Regulations.

509   Consumer contracts—unfair terms—tenancy agreements—penalty clause

The defendant company let residential premises to the applicants for non-commercial use. The tenancy agreement was concluded on the basis of standard terms, one of which was a penalty clause pursuant to which the applicants were obliged to pay a stated percentage of interest on unpaid rent. In the event, the applicants failed to make a rental payment, and the defendant successfully brought proceedings seeking termination of the tenancy agreement and an order requiring the applicants to pay a sum representing the unpaid rent and a penalty amount. The applicants appealed, requesting that the amounts granted by way of penalties be reduced, having regard to the discrepancy between, on the one hand, those sums, and, on the other, the detriment suffered by the defendant. The national court decided to stay the proceedings and refer to the European Court of Justice for a preliminary ruling various questions relating to the applicability of Council Directive (EC) 93/13, which prohibited unfair terms in consumer contracts, to tenancy agreements of the present kind. *Held*, Directive 93/13 should be interpreted as meaning that, subject to contractual terms which reflected mandatory statutory or regulatory provisions set out by national law, which was a matter for the national court to ascertain, it applied to a residential tenancy agreement concluded between a landlord acting for purposes relating to his trade, business or profession and a tenant acting for purposes which did not relate to his trade, business or profession. Directive 93/13 should also be interpreted as meaning that, where a national court, before which an action had been brought by a seller or supplier against a consumer concerning the performance of a contract, had the power, under internal procedural rules, to examine of its own motion whether the term on which the claim was based was contrary to national rules of public policy, it should, in the same way, where it had established that that term fell within the scope of Directive 93/13, assess of its own motion whether that term was unfair in the light of the criteria laid down. Where the national court had the power, under internal procedural rules, to annul of its own motion a term which was contrary to public policy or to a mandatory statutory provision the scope of which warranted such a sanction, it should, as a rule, after having invited each of the parties to set out its views on that matter, with the opportunity to challenge the views of the other party, annul of its own motion a contractual term which it had found to be unfair in the light of the criteria laid down by Directive 93/13. Article 6(1) could not be interpreted as allowing the national court, in the case where it established that a penalty clause in a contract concluded between a seller or supplier and a consumer was unfair, to reduce the amount of the penalty imposed on the consumer instead of excluding the application of that clause in its entirety with regard to that consumer. Article 6(1) should also be interpreted as meaning that it did not allow the national court, in the case where it had established that a penalty clause in a contract concluded between a seller or supplier and a consumer was unfair, merely, as it was authorised by national law, to reduce the amount of the penalty imposed on the consumer by that clause, but required it to exclude the application of that clause in its entirety with regard to the consumer.

Case C-488/11 *Brusse v Jahani BV* [2013] 3 CMLR 1217, [2013] All ER (D) 154 (Jun) (ECJ: First Chamber).

510   Consumer safety—cosmetic products

The Cosmetic Products Enforcement Regulations 2013, SI 2013/1478 (in force on 11 July 2013), provide for the enforcement of European Parliament and Council (EC) Regulation 1223/2009 (on cosmetic products). Specifically, the regulations (1) identify the Secretary of State and the specified enforcement authority as the competent authorities for the purpose of Regulation 1223/2009; (2) specify additional requirements for labelling goods that are required to be created under art 19; (3) set out offences, penalties and enforcement; (4) impose duties on the enforcement authorities to enforce the regulations and give them the necessary powers; (5) prescribe how notices of requirements and requests should be given; (6) require enforcement authorities to get authorisation from the Secretary of State before taking provisional measures under art 27; (7) provide that enforcement authorities must notify the Secretary of State of information which is required to be notified to the European Commission or to other member states; (8) set out what information must be provided to the Secretary of State when requesting authorisation of provisional measures for providing notification under heads (6) and (7); (9) set out offences under the regulations; (10) specify penalties; (11) enable the court to order someone to remedy a matter or reimburse the enforcement authority for expenses of enforcement; (12) enable orders for the forfeiture of goods to be made; (13) set out time limits for prosecution, defences and liability of persons other than the principal officer; (14) require the Secretary of State to review the operation and effect of the regulations and publish a report within five years after 11 July 2013 and within every five years thereafter; (15) make provision relating to testing cosmetic products, powers to enter premises, powers to inspect, seize and detain cosmetic products etc, and warrants; (16) re-enact the Cosmetic Products (Safety) Regulations 2008, SI 2008/1284 Sch 10; and (17) specify which provision of Regulation 1223/2009 will result in a criminal offence if breached. SI 2008/1284 is revoked with saving provisions.

511   Designated enforcer—Financial Conduct Authority

The Enterprise Act 2002 (Part 8) (Designation of the Financial Conduct Authority as a Designated Enforcer) Order 2013, SI 2013/478 (in force on 1 April 2013), revokes the Enterprise Act 2002 (Part 8) (Designation of the Financial Services Authority as a Designated Enforcer) Order 2004, SI 2004/935, and designates the Financial Conduct Authority as a designated enforcer under the 2002 Act Pt 8 (ss 210–236) in respect of the enforcement of certain consumer legislation.

512   Misleading and comparative advertising—meaning of 'advertising'—website domain name and metatags

European Parliament and Council Directive (EC) 2006/114 art 2(a) defines 'advertising' as the making of a representation in any form in connection with a trade, business, craft or profession in order to promote the supply of goods or services, including immovable property, rights and obligations.

The parties were companies which produced, manufactured and distributed sorting machines and sorting systems incorporating laser technology in the Belgian market. The name of the claimant was commonly abbreviated to 'BEST'. The defendant, which had the name 'Visys', registered the domain name 'www.bestlasersorter.com'. The content of the website hosted under that domain name was identical to that of the defendant's other main websites, but contained several metatags which contained the word 'best'. The claimant subsequently applied for registration of the Benelux figurative trade mark 'BEST'. The claimant brought proceedings against the defendant, contending that the defendant's conduct infringed the claimant's trade mark and contravened the law concerning misleading and comparative advertising. A regional court in Belgium allowed the claim only to the extent of finding the use of metatags by the defendant contrary to the law on comparative and misleading advertising. The regional court of appeal dismissed the claimant's appeal, and, on its further appeal, the national court referred for a preliminary ruling the question of whether the term 'advertising', as defined by Directive 2006/114 art 2(a), covered (1) the registration of a domain name; (2) the use of such a name; and (3) the use of metatags in a website's metadata. Held, the purpose of Directive 2006/114 in laying down the conditions under which comparative advertising was permitted was to achieve a balance between the different interests which might be affected by allowing comparative advertising, by allowing competitors to highlight objectively the merits of the various comparable products in order to stimulate competition to the consumer's advantage while, at the same time, prohibiting practices which might distort competition, be detrimental to competitors and have an adverse effect on consumer choice. The intention was to establish a complete framework for every form of advertising event, irrespective of whether it induced a contract, to avoid such advertising harming both consumers and traders and leading to distortion of competition within the internal market. It followed that the term 'advertising' could not be interpreted and applied in such a way that steps taken by a trader to promote the sale of his products or services that were capable of influencing the economic behaviour of consumers and, therefore, of affecting the competitors of that trader, were not subject to the rules of fair competition imposed by the law. 'Advertising' should therefore be interpreted as covering the use of a domain name and that of metatags in a website's metadata. However, the registration of a domain name, as such, was not encompassed by that term.

Case C-657/11 *Belgian Electronic Sorting Technology NV v Peelaers* [2013] All ER (D) 191 (Jul) (ECJ: Third Chamber).

513   Packaging—essential requirements

The Packaging (Essential Requirements) (Amendment) Regulations 2013, SI 2013/2212 (in force on 30 September 2013), further amend the 2003 Regulations, SI 2003/1941, so as to substitute the definition of 'packaging' and the list of illustrative examples of packaging referred to in the definition.

514   Property Misdescriptions Act 1991—repeal

The Property Misdescriptions Act 1991 (Repeal) Order 2013, SI 2013/1575 (in force on 1 October 2013), repeals the Property Misdescriptions Act 1991 and makes consequential amendments to other enactments.

515   Unfair commercial practices—sale of security products to vulnerable person—evidence—no case to answer

The defendant sold domestic security systems by cold calling either by telephone or doorstep visits. The defendant sold security products to a 76-year-old customer, who by reason of age and infirmity was vulnerable. A member of the customer's family found that a sum of money had been taken from his bank account which related to a CCTV system which was unplugged and of which the customer appeared to be unaware. Following a complaint, an investigation was commenced and the defendant was charged with engaging in an unfair commercial practice in contravention of the Consumer Protection from Unfair Trading Regulations 2008, SI 2008/1277. The judge acceded to a submission that there was no case to answer. The prosecution appealed. *Held*, it was established law that the definition of 'commercial practices' was wide and included any act, omission, course of conduct or representation, commercial communication including advertising and marketing, by a trader, directly connected with the promotion, sale or supply of a product to consumers. A commercial practice could be derived from a single incident and the concept of commercial practice was concerned with systems rather than individual transactions. There was, on the evidence, a case to answer. Accordingly, the appeal would be allowed.

R v X Ltd [2013] EWCA Crim 818, [2014] 1 WLR 591, [2013] All ER (D) 330 (May) (Court of Appeal: Leveson LJ, Foskett J and Sir Geoffrey Grigson). Case C-304/08 *Zentrale zur Bekampfung unlauteren Wettbewerbs eV v Plus Warenhandelsgesellschaft mbH* [2011] 1 All ER (Comm) 658 (2010 Abr para 615); *Airtours plc v Shipley* (1994) 158 JP 835 (1994 Abr para 2785); *R v Jabber* [2007] All ER (D) 196 (Feb), CA; and *R v Goring* [2011] EWCA Crim 2, [2011] All ER (D) 54 (Jan) considered.

CONTEMPT OF COURT

Halsbury's Laws of England (5th edn) vol 22 (2012) paras 1–200

Articles

For articles relating to this title please refer to the Table of Articles at the beginning of the Abridgment.

516   Breach of court order—application for legal aid—entitlement

See *King's Lynn and West Norfolk Council v Bunning*, para 1692.

517   Breach of court order—committal for contempt—family proceedings—husband's
       financial circumstances

A wife sought financial support from her husband following their separation. It was the
wife's case that the husband was a very wealthy man. She contended that he had hidden his
entire resources to avoid his legitimate obligations towards her and their children. The
husband claimed that he was penniless and bankrupt. A judge ordered the husband to
respond to the wife's questionnaire and attached a penal notice. The husband was ordered
to provide the documentation sought in the questionnaire. He was committed to prison for
six months for contempt of both orders. The term of imprisonment was suspended for 92
days on terms that the husband provide the answers and documents sought. A judge heard
an application for maintenance pending suit and ordered the husband to pay the wife's rent,
the children's school fees and a set sum per month. The husband was subsequently ordered
to produce certain information contained in that order. The wife made two applications.
The first was to commit the husband to prison for contempt of court in relation to the latest
order and the second was to activate the earlier committal order. The court decided that the
correct approach was to deal solely with the first application, although the earlier breach
would remain relevant to sentence. *Held*, the court was satisfied beyond reasonable doubt
that, in certain very important respects, the husband had not complied with the latest order.
In the circumstances, both contempts were so serious that a fine could not be justified. A
suspended sentence of committal could not be justified either. The court rejected the
husband's ill health as a reason for not passing an immediate custodial sentence. Any
harassment alleged to have been committed against the husband by private investigators
instructed by the wife was not a legitimate defence to failure to comply with a court order.
The court would pass the shortest sentence of imprisonment which matched the seriousness
of the husband's contempt, while taking into account the mitigating factors raised by the
husband. As the court was sentencing the husband for the same contempt, the sentence
ought to be the same as that imposed by the earlier committal order. There would not,
however, be double jeopardy and the court would not activate the suspended committal.
Judgment would be given accordingly.

Young v Young [2013] EWHC 34 (Fam), [2014] 1 FLR 269, [2013] All ER (D) 91 (Jan)
(Family Division: Moor J).

518   Breach of court order—undertaking not to publish defamatory allegations—
       requisite knowledge

The claimants were the parents of a child who disappeared at the age of three when she was
on holiday with her family in Portugal. The defendant was a former social worker and
solicitor who had written at very great length about that affair. The claimants believed that
the defendant's writings were libellous and amounted to harassment. Despite offering
undertakings and assurances to the claimants, the defendant continued to direct people to
websites which continued to publish a leaflet of which the claimants had complained. The
claimants issued a claim form for damages for libel and an injunction restraining the
defendant from further publishing the words complained of or similar words defamatory of
them. An order was made setting out the undertakings made by the defendant, which were
(1) to deliver up all hard copies and to destroy any electronic version of a booklet and the
leaflet; (2) to use his best endeavours to delete or otherwise prevent access to any and all
defamatory allegations about the claimants published on websites; and (3) not to repeat the
same or similar allegations about the claimants. The claimants subsequently alleged that the
defendant had breached the undertakings and was therefore in contempt of court. They
relied on 13 publications which they contended bore the meaning that the claimants had, or
it was suspected that they had, murdered their daughter, disposed of her body, and lied to
the police about so doing. The defendant submitted that he did not intend the meanings
alleged, that his statements were honest comment and so were protected by his right, under
the European Convention on Human Rights art 10, to freedom of expression and that he
had complied with requests to take down or cease distribution of the material. *Held*, on the
facts, breach of the undertakings had been proved with respect to the 13 publications which
had borne the meanings alleged by the claimants. The issue was then whether the defendant
had made the publication in the belief that what he had done had been a breach of the order.
In the circumstances, there could be no doubt that the defendant had had the required
knowledge. He had intended to allege that the claimants were to be suspected of causing the

death of their daughter and had, in fact, disposed of her body, lied about what had happened and covered up what they had done. The words were too clear and the repetitions too numerous for any other interpretation to be put on what the defendant had done. Further, the point that the defendant had complied with the undertakings some of the time might be relevant to penalty, but it could not be relevant to the breaches which had been proved. The right to freedom of expression, whether at common law or under art 10, was not an absolute right that prevailed over all others. It was subject to the claimants' rights under the judgment that they obtained incorporating the undertakings, and to the need to uphold the authority of the court which had made that order. Accordingly, the application would be allowed.

McCann v Bennett [2013] EWHC 283 (QB), [2013] All ER (D) 269 (Feb) (Queen's Bench Division: Tugendhat J).

519 Civil contempt—breach of court order—forced marriage protection order—power of police to issue application

A 16-year-old girl contacted the applicant police force and told them that the first respondent, her mother, had assaulted her and that she was afraid her mother would take her to Pakistan and force her into marriage there. The girl was directed to a local firm of solicitors which made a without notice application on her behalf for a forced marriage protection order, which was granted. It was clear that the girl was in the role of applicant and there was no suggestion that she lacked sufficient capacity to instruct her own solicitor and make her own application. The Family Law Act 1996 s 63C provided that, while local authorities could apply for a forced marriage protection order as a matter of right, police forces could only do so if they first obtained the leave of the court. On the return date, the judge made a further order in the prescribed form. The girl and the first respondent both attended in person before the judge and asked him to discharge the order so that the girl could travel to Pakistan. They gave oral evidence that the first respondent's grandmother was seriously ill. The judge declined to discharge the order. He stated his belief that the girl had brought the application under considerable parental oppression. A Muslim ceremony of marriage took place between the girl and a man whom she knew only by sight. The girl alleged that the man had raped her and informed the local authority and the applicant of the events and the allegations in relation to the man. The first respondent was arrested in the exercise of the power of arrest that had been attached to the order. The second respondent, the girl's aunt, was also arrested on the basis that she had been aware of the existence and terms of the order and had been involved in some of the organisation of the wedding. Both respondents were remanded in custody. The girl was made the subject of an interim care order. The applicant issued a formal application for committal of the respondents to prison for contempt of court. The girl claimed that she had not been forced into the marriage but had married voluntarily and that she did not understand that the order prevented a marriage which was a willing one and not a forced one. It fell to be determined whether the police could pursue its application at a substantive hearing. *Held*, in civil contempt proceedings, the hierarchy of recognised applicants was the party who had obtained the order, if he decided not to, the Attorney General, if the public interest required him to intervene in order to enforce the order, and the court would act of its own volition in exceptional cases of clear contempt in which it was urgent and imperative to act immediately. It would not be an incremental step to add in the police as a category of applicants. Unless and until Parliament decided to provide a proper statutory basis for them to do so, the police simply had no standing, and could not act as applicants, to apply for and press for committal in such circumstances. It was the role and duty of the police to prevent crimes and, in conjunction with the Crown Prosecution Service, to prosecute when crimes had been committed. It had not been the role of the police to join in private civil proceedings to apply to enforce the orders of the civil courts. In the circumstances, the applicant could not properly make or pursue the application. In any event, it would be unconscionable to consider committing a person to prison in a situation in which the applicant had no standing. Accordingly, the application would be dismissed.

Bedfordshire Police Constabulary v RU [2013] EWHC 2350 (Fam), [2013] All ER (D) 22 (Aug) (Family Division: Holman J). *Clarke v Chadburn* [1985] 1 All ER 211 (1984 Abr para 2790) applied.

520   Committal for contempt—breach of court order—order in divorce proceedings—satisfaction of debt

See *Constantinides v Constantinides*, para 1820.

521   Committal for contempt—breach of injunction—publication of photographs on internet

Two eleven-year-old boys ('the offenders') were convicted of murdering a two-year-old child and were sentenced to life imprisonment. Prior to their release, the court granted an injunction, binding on the whole world, preventing publication of any depiction, image or voice recording which purported to be of the new identities of the offenders. Both defendants in the present case had used popular social networking platforms on the internet to publish images that were supposedly of the offenders in their new identities. In each case the images had been obtained from elsewhere on the internet. On being informed by the Treasury Solicitor that publication of the images was illegal, the first defendant immediately removed the photographs and deactivated his account. He also apologised, stating that he did not believe he was under restraint as the image had been readily available and he understood that the injunction had only applied to the media. Unlike the first defendant, the second defendant initially refused to co-operate with the Treasury Solicitor and stated that he was aware of the prohibition of the publication of the images. However, the second defendant also subsequently apologised and admitted breaching the injunction. The Attorney-General applied for the defendants to be committed for contempt of court. *Held*, there was no precedent guiding the court on the facts of the present case. The sentence had to make clear the court's determination to protect people and the importance of upholding the rule of law, particularly the injunction and the fact that no one should contemplate taking the law into their own hands by encouraging the punishment of others. On the facts, a fine would be wholly inappropriate to the seriousness of the contempt and the imposition of a custodial sentence was required to punish the defendants and to deter others. There were very serious aggravating factors, including the potential serious consequences to the offenders, and others potentially mistaken for them, and the fact that the defendants knew of the prohibition. It was in no way exculpatory that others had also been publishing the photographs. However, there were mitigating features, including that the defendants had removed the offending photographs very quickly and had made full apologies and prompt admissions. In the circumstances, a sentence of nine months' imprisonment, suspended for fifteen months in view of the strong personal mitigating factors, was appropriate in each case. Judgment would be given accordingly.

A-G v Harkins; A-G v Liddle [2013] All ER (D) 215 (Apr) (Queen's Bench Division: Sir John Thomas P and Tugendhat J). For earlier related proceedings see *Venables v News Group Newspapers Ltd; Thompson v News Group Newspapers Ltd* [2001] Fam 430, [2001] 1 All ER 908 (2000 Abr para 1733).

522   Committal for contempt—interference with administration of justice—hearing in public

The President of the Family Division and of the Court of Protection has issued *Practice Guidance* (2013) Times, 13 May, on 3 May 2013 concerning committal for contempt of court.

The principle that applications for committal for contempt of court be heard in open court applied as much to the Court of Protection and the Family Division as it did to other divisions of the High Court and the discretion to hear a committal application in private should be exercised only in exceptional cases.

1. It is a fundamental principle of the administration of justice in England and Wales that applications for committal for contempt should be heard and decided in public, that is, in open court.

2. This principle applies as much to committal applications in the Court of Protection (the Court of Protection Rules 2007, SI 2007/1744, r 188(2)) and in the Family Division (the Family Procedure Rules 2010, SI 2010/2955, r 33.5(1)) as to committal applications in any other division of the High Court.

problem, but that delay, even with its attendant uncertainties, would only have become a repudiatory breach if and when the delay had been so prolonged as to frustrate the contract. In the context of the agreement to grant a series of 999 year leases, the circumstances had been a long way from that. Accordingly, the appeal would be allowed.

Ampurius Nu Homes Holdings Ltd v Telford Homes (Creekside) Ltd [2013] EWCA Civ 577, [2013] BLR 400, [2013] All ER (D) 305 (May) (Court of Appeal: Longmore, Tomlinson and Lewison LJJ).

536 Breach of contract—rescission—purchase price—part payment—retention by seller—recovery of balance of purchase price

Under a sale agreement, the defendant agreed to purchase two gas plants from the claimant, the purchase price to be paid in instalments. The defendant paid only part of the purchase price. The claimant rescinded the agreement and sought payment of the outstanding instalments. *Held*, the claimant was entitled to retain the sum paid and to recover the payments outstanding at the date of rescission. As a matter of construction, the wording of the sale agreement made plain that the claimant's accrued rights were to be unaffected by the exercise of the right of termination and that such accrued rights had necessarily to include the right to recover the outstanding payments and, given the parties' agreement, also to retain amounts already paid. That conclusion was supported by commercial considerations. Such right might nevertheless be overridden by the grant of relief from forfeiture on equitable grounds. Judgment would be given accordingly.

Cadogan Petroleum Holdings Ltd v Global Process Systems LLC [2013] EWHC 214 (Comm), [2013] All ER (D) 179 (Feb) (Queen's Bench Division: Eder J). *Stockloser v Johnson* [1954] 1 QB 476, [1954] 1 All ER 630, CA, applied. *Export Credits Guarantee Department v Universal Oil Products Co* [1983] 2 All ER 205, HL (1983 Abr para 563); *Murray v Leisureplay plc* [2005] EWCA Civ 963, [2005] IRLR 946; *Dies v British and International Mining and Finance Corpn Ltd* [1939] 1 KB 724 considered.

537 Breach of contract—wrongful repudiation—damages

See *Seagrain LLC v Glencore Grain BV*, para 534.

538 Building contracts

See BUILDING CONTRACTS.

539 Consumer contracts—information, cancellation and additional charges

See para 508.

540 Contractual term—arbitration clause in deed—rights of third parties—stay of actions sought when defendant not party to deed

The two defendants were the managers of an investment structure, the underlying assets of which were businesses in Italy. The investment structure was based around an English limited partnership regulated by a deed of limited partnership. Although not parties to the deed, its terms purported to confer substantial rights on the defendants and expressly provided for their involvement in the operation of the partnership. In particular, the deed extended, or purported to extend to a named class of person substantial exclusions from and indemnities in respect of liability to the partnership or its partners. One of the partners ('S') in the partnership assigned its interest in the partnership together with certain related rights to the claimant as security for a loan. The claimant alleged that the defendants, as managers of the partnership, acting in concert with others, designed and implemented a dishonest scheme to reorganise the fund and its assets, the purpose or effect of which was to diminish or to eliminate the rights and interests of S and others in relation to those assets, to take the control and benefit of the assets themselves, and to enable them and their associated entities to extract fees and other value from the assets without reference to or oversight from S and the claimant. The claimant issued proceedings against the defendant including claims in conspiracy, unlawful interference, procuring a breach of the deed and dishonest assistance. The deed contained an arbitration clause. Pursuant to the Arbitration Act 1996 s 9 the defendants applied for a stay of the claims in reliance on that arbitration clause. It was contended by the defendants that the deed, on its true construction, provided them with an entitlement to rely on the arbitration clause, notwithstanding that they were not parties to the deed, and that the Contracts (Rights of Third Parties) Act 1999 rendered such provision effective. The deed made express reference to the 1999 Act. It was found that the defendants were not entitled to a stay. The defendants appealed that decision. *Held*, there was no express language in the deed to the effect that either the indemnity or the exclusion was subject to the arbitration clause. That result could only be achieved by way of inference. It was, however, to impute to the parties a far reaching intention if it was to be inferred that they had positively intended to bring about the result that third parties would be bound by the outcome of arbitration proceedings which they had not themselves initiated in order to secure a benefit apparently conferred on them by the deed. That was the inevitable consequence of treating third parties as party to the arbitration agreement in the manner prescribed by the 1999 Act s 8(1), in contrast to the consequences of treating them as a party in the manner prescribed by s 8(2). Very clear language would be required to bring about the result that the right of a third party to avail himself of an exclusion clause in an agreement to which he was not party was in turn subject to an arbitration clause in the same agreement. There was no such clear language in the deed. Accordingly, the appeal would be dismissed.

Fortress Value Recovery Fund I LLC v Blue Skye Special Opportunities Fund LP [2013] EWCA Civ 367, [2013] 2 All ER (Comm) 315 (Court of Appeal: Pill, Toulson and Tomlinson LJJ). Decision of Blair J [2012] EWHC 1486 (Comm), [2012] All ER (D) 32 (Jun) (2012 Abr para 648) affirmed.

541   Contractual term—construction—agreement between group companies—effect of side letter

The claimants were the administrators of the appellant, which entered into back to back transactions with the defendant, another company in its group, under a master agreement. The agreement provided for early termination following an event of default. The parties also executed a side letter that provided for automatic termination of an inter-company transaction if the related client transaction terminated, and for the appellant to pay to the defendant only the amount recovered from the client under the related client transaction. The defendant's parent company became insolvent, as a result of which the inter-company transactions terminated before the client transactions. Soon after, the appellant itself went into default under the client transactions. The consequence of that default was that, under the agreement, there was a determination of compensation by closing-out the inter-company transactions in accordance with the agreement, which involved determining gains or losses at the date of the closing-out. Disputes arose between the parties as to the calculation of those close-out amounts. In the resulting proceedings, the judge ruled that the terms of the side letter were not material terms for the purposes of the definition of 'close-out amount' in the agreement and the side letter was excluded from the process of valuation. On appeal, *held*, the terms of the side letter constituted material terms for the purpose of the definition of 'close-out amount'. The use of the words 'including the payments and deliveries by the parties' made it clear that the category of material terms was meant to be larger than the category of payments and deliveries. Effect had to be given to the words in the terms of the agreement, and the side letter was part of those terms. The side letter set out that the determination of the appellant-client transaction, for whatever reason, would trigger the early determination of the related inter-company transactions. Accordingly, the appeal would be allowed.

Joint Administrators of Lehman Bros International (Europe) v Lehman Bros Finance SA; In the matter of Lehman Bros International (Europe) (in administration) [2013] EWCA Civ 188, [2013] All ER (D) 132 (Mar) (Court of Appeal: Sir James Munby P, Arden and Aikens LJJ). Decision of Briggs J [2012] EWHC 1072 (Ch), [2012] All ER (D) 159 (Apr) (2012 Abr para 628) reversed.

542   Contractual term—construction—amendment—inconsistency with existing term

The claimants agreed to purchase an aircraft from the defendants. Prior to the signature of the purchase agreement, the buy-back guarantee clause in the typed agreement was amended by the addition of a hand-written clause. The hand-written clause was introduced by the words 'Buy back cont ...' and changed the starting price and the period of exercise of the typed clause. The claimants subsequently sought a refund and requested that the defendants take the aircraft back pursuant to the buy-back clause. The defendants refused to do so and the claimants resold the aircraft. The claimants sought damages for breach of the buy-back clause on the basis that the hand-written clause was a distinct and free-standing provision that provided an unconditional buy-back guarantee. The defendants submitted that the typed and hand-written clauses had to be read together and the hand-written clause construed as amending the starting price and the period of time within which the buy-back option could be exercised, but otherwise subject to the typed clause conditions. *Held*, the defendants' construction was preferred because it accorded with the general principle of construction that the court was reluctant to hold that clauses of a contract were inconsistent with each other, and would give effect to any reasonable construction which harmonised such clauses. If the inconsistency between the typed and hand-written clauses was limited to the starting price and the period of exercise, they could otherwise be read together and in harmony. On the claimants' construction, the inconsistency, in effect, spread to the whole of the typed clause, since it was rendered entirely redundant. The buy-back guarantee was therefore subject to the conditions in the typed clause. Accordingly, the claim would be dismissed.

Foster v Action Aviation Ltd [2013] EWHC 2439 (Comm), [2013] All ER (D) 65 (Aug) (Queen's Bench Division: Hamblen J).

543   Contractual term—construction—background facts

The claimant had completed his purchase of a large portion of an industrial estate, which included the transfer from a company of a road. The transfer provided that the company covenanted that it and its successors in title would pay such sums as being fair and reasonable proportions of the expenses incurred in the maintenance of the road. The defendant completed his purchase of a unit in the industrial estate by taking a transfer of the freehold from the company. The second transfer provided that the defendant and his successors in title would pay the company for the fair and reasonable proportion of the expenses incurred by the company and its successors in the maintenance of the road. The company assigned to the claimant the benefit of the purchaser's covenant and gave notice of the assignment to the defendant. The claimant issued proceedings for arrears of the contributions to maintenance which he alleged the defendant was liable to pay. The defendant contended that he had no liability to pay either under the terms of the transfers under which he acquired title to the units or more generally under the equitable principle of benefit and burden. The judge determined a series of preliminary issues which related to the defendant's liability to contribute to the cost of maintaining the road. The judge found for the claimant and the defendant appealed. *Held*, it was settled law that, although a reference to successors in title would usually refer to subsequent owners of the relevant property, the meaning to be given to words in any contractual document depended on a consideration of the language against the admissible matrix of background fact. The test was what meaning the relevant words would convey to a reasonable person having all the background knowledge which would reasonably have been available to the parties at the time of executing the document. In the present case, the reasonable person would know that the purpose of the covenant in the second transfer had been to require the owner of the units to contribute to the costs of maintenance to the road carried out by the company or its successors. It was most unlikely that the objective bystander would conclude that what the parties had intended by the words used had been to exclude the very person who would be the owner and repairer of the road for the foreseeable future. That would serve to destroy the commercial purpose of the bargain. The defendant was contractually liable under the covenant in the second transfer to contribute towards the costs of the maintenance works which otherwise fell within the terms of the covenant. Three conditions needed to be satisfied in order for the burden of a positive covenant to be enforceable against the covenantor's successors in title: (1) the benefit and burden had to be conferred in or by the same transaction; (2) the receipt or enjoyment of the benefit had to be relevant to the imposition of the burden in the sense that the former had to be conditional on or reciprocal to the latter; and (3) the person on whom the burden was alleged to have been imposed had to have had the opportunity of rejecting or disclaiming the benefit, not merely the right to receive the benefit. On the facts, there was nothing to support the idea that the company had given only a personal covenant as opposed to accepting the inevitable personal liability attaching to an original covenantor. The second of the three requirements had been satisfied, as there was a clear and obvious link between the rights of way reserved over the road and the obligation to contribute to the cost of repairs. There was no difficulty in principle about equity treating the defendant, as new owner, as liable to contribute a fair and reasonable proportion of the expenses incurred in the maintenance of the portion of the road on which the unit abutted. The judge had been right to reject the defendant's arguments with respect to occupiers and registration. Since the burden in equity of a positive covenant did not have the effect of creating an estate or interest in the registered land, it did not require to be registered in order to bind successors in title of the original covenantor. Accordingly, the appeal would be dismissed.

Elwood v Goodman [2013] EWCA Civ 1103, [2014] 1 P & CR 105, [2013] All ER (D) 35 (Sep) (Court of Appeal: Arden, Patten and Beatson LJJ).

544　Contractual term—construction—commercial sense

An oil production platform was to be made available by the claimant to the defendant. The hire payments under the charter were designed to compensate the claimant for the platform and its rebuilding. The general technical specification was submitted by the defendant to the claimant. However, changes to the specification were being developed as matters progressed and recorded in an annex. At about the same time, the defendant was considering whether to deploy the platform to an alternative oil field. The defendant informed the claimant that it intended to employ the platform at the alternative site. The change necessitated a new design for the upgrade work to the platform. Work began on developing a new specification. There was an unwritten understanding that the parties would go ahead on the basis of the previous agreement which had been reached, with extra compensation to be paid to the claimant for the additional cost of the upgrade. The parties entered into an agreement that recorded their previously unwritten understanding. It provided that the defendant would pay the claimant an amount equal to the reasonable extra cost to the claimant in respect of upgrading the platform in accordance with the amended specification. In proceedings arising from a number of disputes between the parties, the court considered as preliminary issues what would have been involved in upgrading the platform in accordance with the original specification in respect of the compressors and the risers. The general specification provided what the compression capacity would be. The defendant settled on three compressors and that was confirmed between the parties. The judge found that the effect of the compression deviation, when construed against the relevant background, was that, apart from the claimant having to supply the existing compressor and one new compressor, the whole of the cost of installing such further compression systems as might be specified was for the defendant's account. A further deviation had been recorded in the annex to the general specification. The judge held that of the 98 risers required, only 52 could have been accommodated on the central caisson while the others would have had to have been attached to the pontoons. He held that the defendant had been bound to accept a central caisson solution, because it had agreed to it in the riser deviation. The defendant appealed. *Held*, on the true construction of the compression deviation, the defendant's interpretation was to be preferred. The judge's interpretation had resulted in the putting back on to the defendant the essential functions of a contractor in achieving the designed upgrade so far as compression was concerned. There was no such shift in the wording of the annex to the general specification, particularly in the light of the firm language of the opening sentence of the compression deviation. On the evidence, the final form of the riser derivation had remained no more than an agreement in principle. There had been no contractual commitment to the use of the central caisson for riser attachment and, as a result, the defendant could not have been required, on the basis of such a commitment, to have agreed to the wet attachment of the 46 risers. Consequently, since there had been no commitment in terms of that deviation or concept, the claimant's obligation had remained that of accommodating dry attachment of risers on the pontoons. It was common ground that the probable outcome would have been the solution of building a spider deck. Accordingly, the appeal would be allowed.

Petromec Inc v Petroleo Brasileiro SA [2013] EWCA Civ 150, [2013] All ER (D) 30 (Mar) (Court of Appeal: Rix, Moore-Bick and Lewison LJJ). Decision of Field J [2011] EWHC 2997 (Comm), [2011] All ER (D) 175 (Nov) (2011 Abr para 585) reversed.

an offer in relation to which it would have been entitled to commission under the terms of the exclusivity agreement. Despite the various express clauses of that agreement, an agreement was to be implied from the subsequent conduct of the parties that the claimant would be paid a reasonable fee for its services in the event of the disposal of the relevant assets, if it otherwise would have been entitled to a fee under the terms of the exclusivity agreement. Judgment would be given accordingly.

Energy Venture Partners Ltd v Malabu Oil and Gas Ltd [2013] EWHC 2118 (Comm), [2013] All ER (D) 347 (Jul) (Queen's Bench Division: Gloster LJ).

552   Contractual term—unfair term—electronic payment service—termination of service

The claimant, a professional photographer, offered his house as the prize in a competition and charged each contestant an entry fee. He set up an account with the defendant's electronic payment service through which entries to the competition could be received. In setting up the account, he stated that the nature of his business was photography, and provided email addresses relating to both the competition and his business. The defendant suspended and ultimately terminated its service to the claimant because it was concerned that he provided misleading information about the nature of his business, and that there was unusual activity on his account. The claimant brought proceedings, claiming that the suspension and termination were a breach of contract in consequence of which he suffered loss. The defendant contended that it was entitled to suspend or terminate the service as a result of the express provisions of the agreement between itself and the claimant. The court gave summary judgment in favour of the defendant and directed a trial of issues as to the effect of the Unfair Contract Terms Act 1977 and the Unfair Terms in Consumer Contracts Regulations 1999, SI 1999/2083, on the enforceability of the terms relied on by the defendant. *Held*, it was not possible to solve the issue concerning the 1999 Regulations by categorising the claimant's normal business activities and then asking whether the venture in question fell within the scope of such activities. On the evidence, it could not be said that the competition to win the house was an adventure in the nature of trade. It was, in principle, little different from a disposal of the same asset by public auction, which itself differed from a private sale through an estate agent only in the means chosen to achieve the sale. Further, in opening the account, the claimant intended to facilitate the receipt of payments for goods and services that he provided in connection with his photography business. To that extent, when he entered into the contract with the defendant, he was not acting for purposes that were outside his trade, business or profession. The business purpose could not reasonably be regarded as one which was insignificant or negligible. The claimant was not, therefore, entitled to the protection of the 1999 Regulations. On the true construction of the 1977 Act, the defendant was entitled to rely on the exclusion of liability for loss of profits, goodwill, business, contracts, revenue or anticipated savings under the user agreement and on the exclusion of liability for any indirect or consequential loss. However, it was not entitled to rely on the limitation of the amount of any damages in respect of any liability that was not wholly excluded. Further, the defendant's power of summary termination without cause and without notice did not come within the relevant provisions of the 1977 Act. Judgment would be given accordingly.

Overy v Paypal (Europe) Ltd [2012] EWHC 2659 (QB), [2013] All ER (D) 133 (Mar) (Queen's Bench Division: Judge Hegarty QC).

553   Formation—charterparty—jurisdiction of arbitral tribunal dependent on valid formation of contract

See *Hyundai Merchant Marine Co Ltd v Americas Bulk Transport Ltd*, para 54.

554   Formation—existence of contract—repudiation—damages

The claimant was a company incorporated in Switzerland engaged in the business of international trading of oil and gasoline related products. The defendant was a petroleum refining company incorporated in Lithuania. By email, the claimant made what was described as a firm offer to sell to the defendant an option of crude oil mix. Correspondence continued between the parties, culminating in an email from the defendant stating 'Confirmed'. The claimant sent to the defendant a draft detailed written contract. There were further email exchanges and a revised draft was sent by the claimant to the defendant. At that point there was at least one issue in which the parties had not agreed, namely, the documents the claimant would be required to present for payment under a proposed documentary letter of credit. The defendant subsequently wrote informing the claimant that it was withdrawing from the negotiations. A dispute arose about whether dealings between them gave rise to a contract, if so, what were the terms of the contract, and if broken, what, if any damages should be paid. The claimant notified the defendant that it was taking the defendant's failures to open a letter of credit or to take delivery of the cargo as a repudiatory breach of contract, thereby bringing the sale contract to an end. The claimant brought a claim for breach of contract and sought damages. *Held*, terms were not implied because it would be reasonable or useful to do so; necessity was still required. In the circumstances, there was a contract between the parties which the defendant had repudiated. A contract had come into existence following the initial email exchange. It was a classic spot deal where the speed of the market required that the parties agreed the main terms, and left the details to be discussed and agreed later. There was no necessity for an implied term as alleged by the defendant. It followed that the claim to an implied term failed. The defendant would pay the claimant damages. Judgment would be given accordingly.

Proton Energy Group SA v Orlen Lietuva [2013] EWHC 2872 (Comm), [2013] All ER (D) 206 (Sep) (Queen's Bench Division: Judge Mackie). *The Reborn, Mediterranean Salvage and Towage Ltd v Seamar Trading and Commerce Inc* [2009] EWCA Civ 531, [2010] 1 All ER (Comm) 1 (2009 Abr para 356) applied.

555   Formation—offer and acceptance—carriage of goods—email correspondence—acceptance of vessel

The claimant company was engaged in the international trading of oil- and gasoline-related products. The defendant company was a petroleum refining company incorporated in Lithuania. The claimant made an offer via email to sell crude oil mix to the defendant. Email correspondence continued, ending with an email from the defendant stating simply 'confirmed'. In the course of the following week, the defendant accepted that a specified vessel would be appropriate to carry and deliver the crude oil. The defendant subsequently wrote to the claimant, stating that it was withdrawing from the negotiations. The claimant replied that it was taking the defendant's failures to open a letter of credit or to take delivery of the cargo to be repudiatory breaches of contract and was thereby bringing the contract to an end. The claimant applied for summary judgment on the issue of whether there was a binding contract between the parties. The claimant submitted that a contract had been concluded (1) by way of the defendant's email; (2) when the vessel was agreed; or (3) when, a few days after the specification of the vessel, all terms of any substance had been agreed save for the exact wording of the letter of credit. *Held*, there was a real issue that needed to be tried as to whether a legally binding contract had been concluded between the parties in the course of their email exchanges. On the evidence, the defendant's case was by no means implausible or devoid of reality: it had a real as opposed to fanciful prospect of success at trial. It was also not fanciful to suppose that the defendant's acceptance of the vessel had not created a legally binding contract. That acceptance would not, at least on its face, have negated the necessity for the parties to agree the remainder of the contractual terms. The claimant had not satisfactorily explained or elaborated on how the acceptance of the vessel had not been plausibly consistent with a legally binding contract existing only in contemplation and expectation, or had only been realistically consistent with a legally binding contract already having been made. Finally, if no legally binding contract had been concluded via email, because whatever had been agreed was subject to contract or the equivalent, there was a real prospect that the defendant's argument that no contract had ever been entered into would succeed at trial because, despite the claimant's insistence that the contract ought to incorporate a term requiring payment under the proposed letter of credit to be made against the claimant's presentation of a letter of indemnity in the absence of original bills of lading, the defendant had never agreed. Accordingly, the application would be dismissed.

Proton Energy Group SA v Public Co Orlen Lietuva [2013] EWHC 334 (Comm), [2013] All ER (D) 309 (Feb) (Queen's Bench Division: Gavin Kealey QC).

556   Formation—offer and acceptance—unilateral contract—offer to issue parking permit

See *Vehicle Control Services Ltd v Revenue and Customs Comrs*, para 2544.

557   **Frustration—facility agreement with bank—freezing of assets**

A discount facility agreement was agreed between the claimant bank and the defendant company. The agreement was designed to enable the defendant to obtain payment prior to the maturity date of letters of credit and other financial instruments of which it was the beneficiary. The various fees charged by the claimant included commitment fees linked to the number of days for which a facility to purchase was made available. A pricing letter subsequently agreed between the parties provided for the payment of commitment fees if the facility was unutilised on its expiry date. The claimant, which had links to Iran, was then designated under Council Decision (EC) 2008/475, which had the effect of subjecting the claimant to an asset freeze implemented by the Iran (European Community Financial Sanctions) Regulations 2007, SI 2007/1374. In the event, the facility was unutilised. The claimant sought summary judgment for sums it claimed were due and owing from the defendant by way of commitment fees under the terms of the agreement and the pricing letter. The defendant submitted that it had been discharged from all obligations under the agreement and the pricing letter, including the obligation to pay commitment fees, because the agreement between the parties could no longer be performed by the claimant. The defendant contended that the agreement had either been frustrated or had been terminated by the defendant's agreement to a repudiatory breach by the claimant. An issue arose as to whether repudiation of the defendant's breach could be inferred from the defendant's silence or from its failure to take any steps to utilise the facility in the days between the date of designation and the scheduled expiry of the commitment. *Held*, designation of the claimant had not rendered obligations under the agreement and the pricing letter incapable of performance where a licence could be sought and, on the evidence, could be expected to be forthcoming. On its true construction, the agreement expressly contemplated that it was for the defendant to do what had been necessary or take what action had been required. After designation, seeking a licence would readily fall within those provisions the moment that the defendant indicated to the claimant that it had intended to utilise the facility. Further, in a regulated environment such as banking, but in a context other than that of sanctions, it was possible to imagine a great many situations in which, during the period of availability of a facility, additional requirements were introduced before a bank might provide, or the customer might receive, funds under a facility. It followed that the contention that the doctrine of frustration had been engaged was plainly not well founded. Also, acceptance of any repudiation could not be inferred from the defendant's silence or from its failure to take any steps to utilise the facility in the days between the date of designation and the scheduled expiry of the commitment. Those matters provided neither clear nor unequivocal evidence of such an intention. The present case was a plain one for summary judgment in favour of the claimant for the full amount of the commitment fees. Accordingly, the application would be allowed.

Melli Bank plc v Holbug Ltd [2013] EWHC 1506 (Comm), [2013] All ER (D) 165 (May) (Queen's Bench Division: Robin Knowles QC).

558   **Misrepresentation**

See MISREPRESENTATION.

559   **Restitution**

See RESTITUTION.

560   **Sale of goods**

See CONSUMER PROTECTION; SALE OF GOODS AND SUPPLY OF SERVICES.

561   **Sale of land**

See CONVEYANCING.

CONVEYANCING

Halsbury's Laws of England (5th edn) vol 23 (2013) paras 1–600

Articles

For articles relating to this title please refer to the Table of Articles at the beginning of the Abridgment.

562   Contract of sale—completion—notice to complete—failure to comply with notice— alleged repudiatory breach

The claimant company was a property developer. It entered into a contract with the defendants for the grant of a 125 year lease for an apartment in the claimant's development. The defendants had paid a reservation fee and the contract required them to pay additional sums by way of deposit to a total of 10 per cent of the purchase price. The contract did not specify a fixed completion date. Instead, the special conditions of sale which formed part of the contract provided that when the building of the apartment was complete, the claimant's solicitors would send a written notice to the defendants' solicitors and completion would then occur on or before ten days of the date on that notice. Special condition 2.5 provided that, if the claimant was prevented from completing the building works within a reasonable time because of a list of specified occurrences, then the defendant would have no claim against the claimant. Further, that clause provided that the contract could not be cancelled and nor were the defendants entitled to compensation or damages resulting from delay. The defendants were informed by their solicitor that completion would take place in December 2008. The source of that information was said to be 'the developer'. Due to delays in the building works, the anticipated completion date was actually February 2009, but that was not communicated to the defendants until October 2008. Little work took place between then and January 2009, but that information was not passed to the defendants. In January, the defendants were told that the development might be finished in April or May. In March, the defendants' solicitors wrote to the claimant terminating the contract due to unreasonable delay, contending that it had been an implied term that completion would take place within a reasonable time. The defendants had had a mortgage offer based on an anticipated completion date of December 2008, subject to satisfactory assessment, but the claimant had refused to permit access for a valuation and completion had not taken place in December. The defendants sought repayment of their deposit. In July, the development was completed. In August, the claimant's solicitors served on the defendants the ten-day notice under the special conditions. In September, it served a notice to complete. The defendants did not complete and the claimant issued proceedings seeking specific performance of the contract and/or damages for late completion. The defendants served a joint defence and counterclaim alleging that the claimant had repudiated the contract. At trial, the claimant made clear that it sought an award of damages and not specific performance. The judge found that, in the circumstances, the overall delay had been such as to have amounted to a repudiation of the contract which had entitled the defendants to refuse to complete. Accordingly, the claim was dismissed and the claimant was ordered to return the reservation fee and deposit. The claimant appealed. It submitted that the judge had erred in finding that there had been a repudiatory breach of the contract. *Held*, the defendants had not been entitled to terminate the contract on the date that they had purported to do so by their solicitors' letter. Applying established principles to the instant case, in the absence of any express stipulated date, it had been an implied term of the contract that completion of the apartment and the consequential completion of the contract had to be within a reasonable time and, pursuant to the special conditions of the contract, contractual completion had been due to take place at the latest ten days after then. On the facts, the claimant had not been in repudiatory breach by the time when the defendants' solicitor had written to terminate the contract. The burden had been on the defendants to prove that there had been a repudiatory breach by the claimant by that time. It was impossible to conclude that any breach had gone to the root of the contract by that time, which would have entitled the defendants to terminate the contract. The delay of approximately one month between the earliest possible date for contractual completion and the defendants' purported termination of the contract could not be said to have deprived the defendants of a substantial part of the benefit of the contract, let alone substantially the whole of the benefit. The loss of the defendants' opportunity to secure the mortgage had occurred before the contractual completion date. There was no evidence of any other prejudice to them. Such prejudice as there had been in the delay of a month or so could easily have been satisfied by damages, for example, in so far as the defendants' enjoyment of the term of years to be granted by the claimant under the lease had been adversely affected by the delay. Nor was there any question of the claimant having been in anticipatory breach. Consequently, the defendants had been in breach of the contract by having failed to complete in response to the notice to complete. The claimant was therefore entitled to damages for breach of contract and, accordingly, the appeal would be allowed.

even limited to the infringer's profits but the entire proceeds of sale were held on trust for the copyright owner. That might be both unfair and stultify enterprise. The proceeds of an infringement might be out of all proportion to the profits generated. A person might be deterred from pursuing an activity if he perceived there to be even a small risk that the activity would involve a breach of copyright or other intellectual property rights. Having regard to existing authorities, it was clear that a copyright owner did not have a proprietary claim to the fruits of an infringement of copyright. Accordingly, the application would be dismissed.

Twentieth Century Fox Film Corpn v Harris [2013] EWHC 159 (Ch), [2014] Ch 41, [2013] All ER (D) 28 (Feb) (Chancery Division: Newey J). *Lister & Co v Stubbs* (1890) 45 Ch D 1, CA, applied. *A-G v Observer Ltd; A-G v Times Newspapers Ltd* [1990] 1 AC 109, [1988] 3 All ER 545, HL (1988 Abr para 1934); *Westdeutsche Landesbank Girozentrale v Islington LBC* [1996] AC 669, [1996] 2 All ER 961, HL (1996 Abr para 710); *Sinclair Investments (UK) Ltd v Versailles Trade Finance Ltd (in administration)* [2011] EWCA Civ 347, [2012] Ch 453, [2011] 4 All ER 335 (2011 Abr para 2401); and *FHR European Ventures LLP v Mankarious* [2013] EWCA Civ 17, [2013] All ER (D) 219 (Jan) (para 2476) considered. For earlier related proceedings, see *Twentieth Century Fox Film Corpn v Newzbin Ltd* [2010] EWHC 608 (Ch), [2010] IP & T 1122 (2010 Abr para 659).

581 Intellectual property—infringement—injunction

See *Fenty v Arcadia Group*, para 277.

582 Ownership—contract of service—unsigned contract

The claimant company made software, and effectively was the business entity of a developer. The defendant embarked on the development of software for a bank. The claimant was invited to provide input into the project, in particular to provide assistance in the conversion of computer code. The claimant was sent a copy of the consultancy agreement made between the parties. In order to become binding, the agreement required a signature by both parties. Although it was signed by a representative of the defendant, it was not signed by a representative of the claimant. The claimant worked as part of a team with the defendant to develop a product, which supported the management of investments in hedge funds and other managed assets. He invoiced for work and collected payment. When the completed functioning product was ready, a dispute arose as to the claimant's copyright in the product. It was submitted by the defendant that the copyright in the software belonged to it and not to the individual company members who had made it, and that there was an express contractual provision in the developer's consultancy agreement that bound him. *Held,* although the developer had not signed the agreement on behalf of the claimant, he could waive that provision if he chose to do so. He could perform some other act that objectively recognised that the terms of the agreement were binding. What he had chosen to do was continue to undertake work on the project, invoice for the work and accept payment. When he invoiced for work and accepted payment, that was an unequivocal demonstration that he accepted, and asserted, that the terms of the agreement were binding. It was an entirely orthodox alternative to claim that he was estopped from denying that he was bound by the contract. The claimant was bound by the agreement and that conclusion was sufficient to allow the court to find that the action should be dismissed. Judgment would be given accordingly.

Destra Software Ltd v Comada (UK) LLP [2013] EWHC 1575 (Pat), [2013] All ER (D) 80 (Jun) (Chancery Division: Norris J).

583 Infringement—website—injunction to restrain internet service provider from allowing access to website

The claimant was the governing body of the highest level football league in England. It owned the copyright in recordings of television footage of all league matches, and in artistic works which appeared within that footage. The defendants were the six main retail internet service providers in the United Kingdom, which collectively had a fixed line market share of 94 per cent of internet users. Pursuant to the Copyright, Designs and Patents Act 1988 s 97A, the claimant brought proceedings against the defendants seeking an injunction requiring them to take measures to block or at least impede access by their customers to a website that provided links to unauthorised and illegal streams of matches. It fell to be determined whether the court had jurisdiction to make the orders requested. *Held*, s 97A empowered the court to grant an injunction against a service provider where that service provider had actual knowledge of another person using its service to infringe copyright. It was settled law that, where a television broadcast was retransmitted via the internet, there was no need to show that the public to which the retransmission was communicated was any different from the public to which the original transmission was addressed. The fact that it was a separate communication to the public by a different technical means sufficed. In order for the court to have jurisdiction to make the orders sought, four matters had to be established. Firstly, the defendants had to be service providers. Secondly, the users and/or operators of the website had to have infringed the claimant's copyrights. Thirdly, those users and/or operators had to have used the defendants' services to do that. Fourthly, the defendants had to have actual knowledge of that. Applying settled law, the defendants were service providers within the meaning of s 97A. Further, the relevant website had communicated the claimant's copyright works to the public in the United Kingdom and thereby infringed its copyrights in those works. Having considered the proportionality of the orders sought, the court was satisfied that they were proportionate. Accordingly, the application would be allowed.

Football Association Premier League Ltd v British Sky Broadcasting Ltd [2013] EWHC 2058 (Ch), [2013] All ER (D) 189 (Jul) (Chancery Division: Arnold J).

584　Performer's rights—copying recording of performance

The Copyright, Designs and Patents Act 1988 s 182A(1) provides that a performer's rights are infringed by a person who, without his consent, makes a copy of a recording of the whole or any substantial part of a qualifying performance.

The claimant was a singer, songwriter and musician. When aged about 14, she composed the lyrics for a song. She issued a claim against the defendant, a recording company, alleging the infringement of performer's rights in the song. The claimant contended that the defendant had infringed her performer's rights by copying a recording of her performance and issuing copies of the recording to the public. The defendant contended that it had acted pursuant to the contract with another company and that it had acquired the rights to do what it had as a result of that contract. The defendant further contended that the claimant knew about that, and that it released the song with her acquiescence, approval, encouragement and support. It relied on its dealings with the claimant, including her participation in a video, her permission to use her image and her performances of the song in support of the release amongst other things. *Held*, a performer had economic rights and moral rights relating to their performance. The economic rights gave the performer the right to require her consent to the exploitation of her performances. A performer's consent was required to make a recording of her live performance, assuming other criteria were satisfied. That right was one of a performer's so called 'non-property' rights, because it was not really assignable or transmissible at all, only on death. A performer also had other economic rights relating to a recording of her live performance, including a reproduction right, a distribution right, a rental and lending right and a right to make copies available to the public. Those were defined as a performer's property rights. In the circumstances, the release of the song by the defendant was an infringement of the claimant performer's rights. Accordingly, the claim would be allowed.

Henderson v All Around the World Recordings Ltd [2013] EWPCC 7, [2013] All ER (D) 299 (Mar) (Patents County Court: Judge Birss QC).

585　Recording of broadcasts—educational recording agency—certification of licensing scheme

The Copyright (Certification of Licensing Scheme for Educational Recording of Broadcasts) (Educational Recording Agency Ltd) (Amendment) Order 2013, SI 2013/158 (in force on 1 April 2013), further amends the 2007 Order, SI 2007/266, so as to correspond with the variation to the licensing scheme which the Educational Recording Agency Ltd wishes to make.

The Copyright (Certification of Licensing Scheme for Educational Recording of Broadcasts) (Educational Recording Agency Ltd) (Amendment No 2) Order 2013, SI 2013/1924 (in force on 1 October 2013), further amends the 2007 Order above so as to amend the certified licensing scheme to include Open University Worldwide Ltd as a new licensor member.

CORONERS

Halsbury's Laws of England (5th edn) vol 24 (2010) paras 1–300

586   Coroner—areas and assistants

The Coroners and Justice Act 2009 (Coroner Areas and Assistant Coroners) Transitional Order 2013, SI 2013/1625 (in force on 25 July 2013), renames coroners' districts constituted under the Coroners Act 1988 as coroner areas, pursuant to the Coroners and Justice Act 2009, and requires at least one assistant coroner to be appointed for each coroner area.

The Coroners and Justice Act 2009 (Alteration of Coroner Areas) Order 2013, SI 2013/1626 (in force on 26 July 2013), amalgamates 19 of the coroner areas specified in the principal 2013 Order above into 9 new coroner areas.

587   Coroner—consequential provisions

The Coroners and Justice Act 2009 (Consequential Provisions) Order 2013, SI 2013/1874 (in force on 25 July 2013), amends the Coroners Act 1988 so as to (1) replace references to a coroner of a coroner's district in Wales with references to a senior coroner of a coroner area in Wales; (2) substitute certain references to inquests with references to investigations; and (3) allow the High Court to order a senior coroner, area coroner or assistant coroner to investigate a death where another coroner refused or neglected to hold an inquest or investigation which ought to be held, or where a previous inquest or investigation was held, but for one of the certain specified reasons it is necessary in the interests of justice to hold an investigation (or as the case may be, another investigation).

588   Coroners and Justice Act 2009—commencement

The Coroners and Justice Act 2009 (Commencement No 11) Order 2013, SI 2013/250, brings into force, on 12 February 2013, a repeal in Sch 23 Pt 1.

The Coroners and Justice Act 2009 (Commencement No 12) Order 2013, SI 2013/705, brings s 117(4)–(8) into force on 22 April 2013.

The Coroners and Justice Act 2009 (Commencement No 13) Order 2013, SI 2013/1104, brings Sch 17 paras 4, 5 into force on 28 May 2013.

The Coroners and Justice Act 2009 (Commencement No 14) Order 2013, SI 2013/1628, brings ss 43 and 45 into force on 3 July 2013.

The Coroners and Justice Act 2009 (Commencement No 15, Consequential and Transitory Provisions) Order 2013, SI 2013/1869, brings into force on 25 July 2013, ss 1–10, 13–17, 24, 36 (in part), 37, 42, 46, Schs 1–3, Sch 5 paras 1, 2, 6, 7, Schs 6, 7, Sch 10 paras 1, 3, 5, Sch 21 Pt 1 (in part) and Sch 23 Pt 1 (for certain purposes). Transitory modification provision is also made.

The Coroners and Justice Act 2009 (Commencement No 16) Order 2013, SI 2013/2908, brings s 148 into force on 18 November 2013.

For a summary of the Act, see 2009 Abr para 853. See also the commencement table in the title STATUTES AND LEGISLATIVE PROCESS.

589   Inquest—allowances, fees and expenses

The Coroners Allowances, Fees and Expenses Regulations 2013, SI 2013/1615 (in force on 25 July 2013), make provision for (1) the allowances and expenses payable to jurors and witnesses as a result of their attendance at inquest hearings; (2) fees for the disclosure by the coroner of paper copies of documents and for the transcription of inquest hearings; and (3) fees payable to suitable practitioners for carrying out post-mortem examinations.

590   Inquest—evidence—public interest immunity certificate—rejection

The deceased died having ingested a radioactive isotope. At the request of the defendant, the solicitor to the inquest into the deceased's death requested disclosure from all government departments and agencies of documents held by them relating to the circumstances of the death. Prior to the defendant's consideration of the scope of the inquest, counsel to the inquest prepared an open note, stating that material established a prima facie case as to the culpability of the Russian state in the death, but did not establish a prima facie case with respect to the culpability of the British state. Later, the claimant claimed public interest immunity in respect of a number of documents. The claim was, in part, upheld in respect of preventability and Russian state responsibility and, in part, rejected, requiring the gist of certain documents to be provided. It was contended by the claimant that the defendant had failed to accord adequate respect to the assessment of the claimant as to how the balance of the competing public interests should be struck. Further, he had failed to undertake the balancing exercise of the competing public interests by treating his desire to conduct what he considered to be a full and proper inquest as a trump card which overrode all other considerations and had reached a decision on the merits of the claim which no reasonable coroner properly applying the correct legal principles to a decision of that nature could have reached. *Held*, the claimant had carefully and cogently explained why disclosure had involved a real and significant risk to national security. On any view, the nature of the risk of the damage had required that very considerable weight be placed on what he had said. Given the risk described, it would rarely be the case that, in such circumstances, disclosure could reasonably be ordered. The weight the defendant had given the views of the claimant had been insufficient and had amounted to an error of law. Further, the issues for resolution had only concerned national security. The context of the balancing exercise had been that of national security as against the proper administration of justice. There had unarguably been evidence to support the asserted real risk of damaging national security and the defendant had not suggested otherwise. The balancing exercise had to be carried out, as the claimed damage to national security was not plain and substantial enough to render it inappropriate to carry it out. There had been no reasons, let alone cogent or solid ones, to reject the claimant's view regarding the nature and extent of damage to national security which would flow from disclosure. The claimant had known more about national security than the defendant while the defendant had known more about the proper administration of justice than the claimant. In rejecting the certificate, the defendant had to have taken to have concluded that the damage to national security had been outweighed by the damage to the administration of justice by upholding the certificate. It had been incumbent on the defendant to explain how he had arrived at his decision. Had the defendant approached the balancing exercise in the way stated by the court, he would have been bound to have found that prejudice by non-disclosure did not outweigh the real risk of significant damage to national security. Accordingly, the appeal would be allowed.

Secretary of State for Foreign and Commonwealth Affairs v Assistant Deputy Coroner for Inner North London [2013] EWHC 3724 (Admin), [2013] All ER (D) 312 (Nov) (Queen's Bench Division: Goldring and Treacy LJJ and Mitting J). *Conway v Rimmer* [1968] AC 910, [1968] 1 All ER 87, HL; and *Council of Civil Service Unions v Minister for the Civil Service* [1985] AC 374, [1984] 3 All ER 935, HL (1984 Abr para 2789), applied.

591   Inquest—procedure

The Coroners (Inquests) Rules 2013, SI 2013/1616 (in force on 25 July 2013), regulate the practice and procedure relating to inquests conducted as part of an investigation into a death under the Coroners and Justice Act 2009 and make provision, in particular, in relation to (1) the opening, timing and notification of inquest hearings; (2) disclosure of documents, including restrictions on disclosure; (3) the management of inquest hearings; (4) the giving of evidence; (5) jury inquests; and (6) the recording of determinations and findings.

592   Inquest—properly interested person—right to participate in judicial review proceedings

See *Secretary of State for Foreign and Commonwealth Affairs v Assistant Deputy Coroner for Inner North London*, para 1636.

nominated lay representative had been advancing allegations of that nature, with the financial and other risks that such allegations attracted, caution had be attached to allowing that lay representative to act and make those allegations on behalf of the defendant. Therefore, the defendant's application that the lay representative be granted rights of audience to act for her would be dismissed. With regard to costs, they were unlikely to be in the region put forward by the second claimant so that the injunction would be amended but only for a smaller value. It had become apparent since the freezing orders had been made that the legal rights of the first claimant had been assigned to the second claimant and that the defendant had notice of the assignment so that the first claimant's chose in action had become legally owned by the second claimant, with the effect that it had been appropriate to make an order that the second claimant be substituted as the claimant in the first action. Judgment would be given accordingly.

Durkan v Madden; Goff v Madden [2013] All ER (D) 142 (Sep) (Chancery Division: Norris J).

623   Supreme Court—appeal—Scottish proceedings—requirement for permission of Inner House

Scotland

A director of the appellant company sought permission to appeal to the Supreme Court against two orders that were pronounced in a case that was stated for the opinion of the Court of Session under the Administration of Justice (Scotland) Act 1972 s 3. The arbitration proceedings, to which the stated case related, arose out of a contractual dispute between the appellant and the respondent company. The director was refused leave to appeal to the Supreme Court by the Inner House against an order refusing his application to represent his company, and an Extra Division of the Inner House subsequently pronounced a further order in which it dismissed the stated case. The appellant sought to appeal to the Supreme Court. It fell to be determined whether the appellant could competently appeal against the orders to the Supreme Court without the leave of the Inner House. Consideration was given to the Court of Session Act 1988 s 40, which set out the circumstances in which it was competent to appeal to the Supreme Court against a judgment of the Court of Session. *Held*, the basic common law rule that a party was entitled to a fair hearing applied not only to those whom the court found it easy to deal with, but to everyone. The question of competency depended on whether that part of the order which dismissed a stated case was a judgment within the meaning of s 40(1)(a) against which there was a right of appeal to the Supreme Court without the leave of the Inner House. If it was, there being no provision in any other statute of the kind referred to in the preamble to s 40(1), it had to be concluded that the appellant had a right of appeal to which effect had to be given, so long as the appeal raised a question which could responsibly be certified by counsel as reasonable. The only question which the present court could consider was whether the Extra Division's decision to dismiss the stated case was one which was open to it to take under the jurisdiction given to it by the statute. Unless something had gone seriously wrong, however, that was an exercise of judgment on a matter of procedure with which the court would not normally wish to interfere. The decision to dismiss the stated case could not be regarded as an interlocutory judgment of the kind referred to in s 40(1)(b) which was appealable only with leave. In all the circumstances, the appellant could competently appeal to the present court against that part of the second order which dismissed the stated case without the leave of the Inner House. The order was in substance a final order because the proceedings were brought to an end by it. They could not continue and the Court of Session was not in a position to retrieve them. For the same reason, the decision taken by the Extra Division could not be treated as a procedural decision only. Judgment would be given accordingly.

Apollo Engineering Ltd v James Scott Ltd (Scotland) [2013] UKSC 37, [2013] All ER (D) 116 (Jun) (Supreme Court: Lord Hope DP, Lord Clarke and Lord Carnwath SCJJ).

624   Supreme Court—judicial appointments—selection process

The Supreme Court (Judicial Appointments) Regulations 2013, SI 2013/2193 (in force on 1 October 2013), make provision in relation to the selection process applicable to the appointment of persons as judges of the Supreme Court of the United Kingdom and, in particular, (1) make provision in relation to the composition of selection commissions convened to select persons for appointment as President, Deputy President or ordinary judge of the Supreme Court; (2) specify circumstances in which persons are disqualified from membership of a selection commission and make provision for the replacement of members of a selection commission, where necessary, after it has been convened; and (3) set out the selection process.

625   Supreme Court—proceedings—retention of knives

The Retention of Knives (Supreme Court) Regulations 2013, SI 2013/2532 (in force on 1 November 2013), (1) set out the procedure to be followed when a knife is surrendered to or seized by a Supreme Court security officer and is retained by that officer; (2) prescribe the information which a Supreme Court security officer must provide to a person who surrenders a knife or from whom a knife has been seized; (3) require the chief executive of the Supreme Court to keep a written record of any knives retained by Supreme Court security officers; (4) set out the procedure for requesting the return of a retained knife; and (5) provide for the procedure which must be followed when dealing with a request for the return of a retained knife.

626   Tribunals—rent assessment committees

The Amendments to Schedule 6 to the Tribunals, Courts and Enforcement Act 2007 Order 2013, SI 2013/1034 (in force on 29 April 2013), provides for rent assessment committees to be added to the Tribunals, Courts and Enforcement Act 2007 Sch 6. Specifically, Agricultural Land Tribunals for areas in England are added to Pt 1 and the Agricultural Land Tribunal for Wales is added to Pt 7. The order also removes the entry relating to Agricultural Land Tribunal in Pt 4.

627   Tribunals, Courts and Enforcement Act 2007—commencement

The Tribunals, Courts and Enforcement Act 2007 (Commencement No 9) Order 2013, SI 2013/1739, brings into force, on 15 July 2013 (1) s 90; and (2) for the purpose only of exercising any power to make regulations, ss 62(1), 64(2)–(4), 73(8), 77(4), (6), 78(2), 81(5), (6), Sch 12 paras 3(1), 7(2), (4), 8, 11(2), 12(1), 13(3), 14(3), 15(3), 22(1), 24(1), 25(1), (2), 28(2), (3), 31(2), (4), 32(1), (2), 33(2), 34(4), 35(2), 36, 39(2), 40(2), (3), 41(3), (5), 42, 43(1)–(3), 48, 49(3), (4), 50(3), (4), (7), 53(3), 54(2), 56(3), 60(4), (5), 62.

The Tribunals, Courts and Enforcement Act 2007 (Commencement No 10) Order 2013, SI 2013/2043, brings ss 48(1) (in part), 146 (in part), Sch 8 paras 24, 27 and certain repeals in Sch 23 Pt 1 into force on 19 August 2013.

For a summary of the Act, see 2007 Abr para 863. See also the commencement table in the title STATUTES AND LEGISLATIVE PROCEDURE.

628   Upper Tribunal—fees—Lands Chamber

The Upper Tribunal (Lands Chamber) Fees (Amendment) Order 2013, SI 2013/1199 (in force on 1 July 2013), further amends the 2009 Order, SI 2009/1114, so that (1) where a case is transferred from the Property Chamber of the First-tier Tribunal to the Lands Chamber of the Upper Tribunal, the fees payable under the First-tier Tribunal (Property Chamber) Fees Order 2013, SI 2013/1169, continue to apply instead of the fees payable under the 2009 Order; and (2) there is no longer a requirement for any fee due to the Upper Tribunal (Lands Chamber) to be paid by cheque or postal order.

629   Upper Tribunal—Immigration and Asylum Chamber—judicial review

The Upper Tribunal (Immigration and Asylum Chamber) (Judicial Review) (England and Wales) Fees (Amendment) Order 2013, SI 2013/2069 (in force on 1 November 2013), amend the 2011 Order, SI 2011/2344, so as to extend the prescribed fees to applications for certain immigration and asylum judicial reviews from the High Court.

CREMATION AND BURIAL
Halsbury's Laws of England (5th edn) vol 24 (2010) paras 1101–1356

Articles

For articles relating to this title please refer to the Table of Articles at the beginning of the Abridgment.

630   Burial—faculty for exhumation of human remains—reinterment—presumption of permanence of burial—exceptions

The petitioner sought a faculty for the exhumation of the cremated remains of his father so that they would be reinterred in the family plot. The father's remains had been interred in the churchyard in the parish where the petitioner's brother was a vicar. The brother had instigated the petition but had died before it was entered. The petitioner stated that it had always been the wish of the father and his wife that they be buried together in the family plot. *Held*, the exhumation and reinterment in a grave or graves containing more than one existing family member was capable of constituting an exceptional or special reason outweighing the presumption in favour of permanence of burial. Such a reason depended on the strength of the justification that was put forward and on the credibility of the reasons for any delay in seeking exhumation. The evidence presented by the petitioner was sufficient to outweigh the presumption and, accordingly, the petition would be allowed.

   Re Camp's Petition [2013] PTSR 953 (Worcester Consistory Court). *Re Blagdon Cemetery* [2002] Fam 299, [2002] 4 All ER 482 (2002 Abr para 749) applied. *Re Peter's Petition* [2013] PTSR 420 considered.

CRIMINAL LAW
Halsbury's Laws of England (5th edn) vol 25 (2010) paras 1–426, vol 26 (2010) paras 427–792

Articles

For articles relating to this title please refer to the Table of Articles at the beginning of the Abridgment.

631   Administration of justice—witness intimidation—proof—attempt to intimidate

The Criminal Justice and Public Order Act 1994 s 51(1) provides that a person commits an offence if he does an act which intimidates, and is intended to intimidate, another person ('the victim'), he does the act knowing or believing that the victim is a witness or potential witness in proceedings for an offence, and he does it intending thereby to cause the investigation or the course of justice to be obstructed, perverted or interfered with.

   The complainant alleged that two of the defendant's friends persuaded her to go to a flat, where she was assaulted and prevented from leaving and her mobile phone was taken. The friends were charged with assault, false imprisonment and theft. The defendant then sent two messages to the complainant via a social media website. He was charged with witness intimidation under the 1994 Act s 51(1) on the basis of the messages. At trial, the complainant gave evidence that the defendant's messages had been read out to her but she had been very sleepy and could not recall how she felt. The trial judge directed the jury, in accordance with existing authority, that, if the defendant had done an act which had sought to deter the complainant from assisting the investigation, it was not necessary for the prosecution to prove that the complainant had in fact been put in fear. The defendant was convicted of witness intimidation and sentenced to a 12-month youth rehabilitation order with requirements for intensive supervision and curfew. He appealed against conviction. *Held*, the ordinary and natural meaning of s 51(1) required that the prosecution prove that the other person whom the defendant intended to intimidate was in fact intimidated. Section 51 made it clear that the act of intimidation was part of the actus reus of the offence, and as such it had to be proved. It was clear from the verdict of the jury that they had been sure that the defendant had done an act intending to intimidate with the necessary belief and further intention. In the circumstances, although the defendant might not in fact have intimidated the complainant, the jury had to have been satisfied of the alternative offence of an attempt to intimidate. Therefore, the conviction for witness intimidation would be quashed and substituted with a conviction for attempted witness intimidation but the sentence would remain the same. Accordingly, to that extent, the appeal would be allowed.

R v N(Z) [2013] EWCA Crim 989, [2013] 2 Cr App Rep 275, [2013] All ER (D) 159 (Jun) (Court of Appeal: Sir John Thomas P, Leveson and Rafferty LJJ, Foskett and Hickinbottom JJ). R v Patrascu [2004] EWCA Crim 2417, [2004] 4 All ER 1066 (2004 Abr para 811) disapproved.

632 Aggravated trespass—additional act—presence as part of demonstration

The ten appellants took place in a demonstration. As part of the demonstration they marched towards a shop. At one point, a substantial number of protestors rushed through the doors of the shop, forcing their way past security staff. Inside the shop, protestors were shouting, screaming and chanting. Some protestors were masked and many carried placards and handed out flyers. Some customers and staff were recorded as being terrified, frightened, confused, angry, intimidated and tearful, others unable to leave the store. The appellants were charged with aggravated trespass, contrary to the Criminal Justice and Public Order Act 1994 s 68(1)–(3). Only the behaviour of six of the appellants was particularised, and it was argued that the appellants, or at least four of them who had not been named as doing any specific act within the store, had done no more than trespass. The judge found that the appellants had trespassed on the land, and there had been an intention to intimidate. Further, the actual demonstration was a separate and distinct act from their trespass. Therefore, he found that the demonstration was an additional act, over and above the act of trespassing to make up the offence of aggravated trespass. The judge further found that all ten appellants were guilty as principals, even though there was no evidence to identify four of them as committing particular acts. However, the appellants contended that their presence as part of a demonstration was not an additional act for the purposes of s 68(1), it was no more than the act of trespass. Held, to prove an aggravated trespass, the trespass not only had to be proved, but also a further act, accompanied by one or more of the intentions, identified. Whether 'mere occupation of land' could amount to a further act distinct from the act of trespass depended upon the circumstances in which the occupation had taken place. In the circumstances, there was a clear allegation of an act over and above the act of trespass, namely, demonstration. The judge had been entitled to find that the demonstration had been a second act distinct from trespass. It would only have been necessary to consider whether any particular appellant had been an accessory if he had not been guilty as a principal offender but had encouraged the principals to commit the offence. However, if the principal offence had been the demonstration in force within the confines of the shop, it made no sense to distinguish those taking part in that demonstration from those identified as doing some particular activity. There was no basis for saying that any of those participating in the demonstration within the shop had not been guilty of the conduct element of aggravated trespass. The judge had erred by distinguishing between the named appellants and the other four as perpetrators and accessories. Once he had been satisfied that the presence of all the appellants had amounted to an act distinct from trespass, there had been no need and it had been wrong to go on to consider whether the appellants had taken part by encouraging others with their presence. While the judge ought not to have considered whether the appellants' actions had encouraged others, the appellants were guilty of the offence of which they had been charged. Accordingly, the appeal would be dismissed

Bauer v DPP [2013] EWHC 634 (Admin), [2013] 1 WLR 3617, (2013) 177 JP 297 (Queen's Bench Division: Moses LJ and Kenneth Parker J). R v Coney (1882) 8 QBD 534 considered.

633 Conditional cautions—code of practice

The Criminal Justice Act 2003 (Conditional Cautions: Code of Practice) Order 2013, SI 2013/801 (in force on 7 April 2013), brings into force the revised code of practice in relation to criminal cautions made under the Criminal Justice Act 2003 s 25(6).

634 Conspiracy—corrupt payments—agent—consent

The defendants were indicted for conspiracy to bribe agents of the tax authorities, contrary to the Prevention of Corruption Act 1906 s 1. In the course of the trial, the judge ruled that, purportedly signed by famous figures. On the defendant's arrest, his home was searched and an amount of material, including forged signatures, a calligraphy pen and ink, was found. The prosecution proposed to conduct its case on the footing that the signatures purporting to be of Winston Churchill, amongst others, had been forged and that the defendant had known that to be the case. However, latterly, the focus of the prosecution case was that it was the defendant who had forged the signatures and that it followed that he had had to have known that they were forgeries. The defence case was to put the prosecution to prove that the signatures were not genuine, the defendant believed that the signatures on the books were genuine, he had not acted dishonestly, and denied forging the signatures. In his summing up, the judge instructed the jury that they had to consider each count separately. The defendant was convicted of eight counts of fraud by dishonest representation and two counts of possession of articles for use in fraud. He was acquitted of two counts of fraud by dishonest representation, counts seven and eleven, and three counts of the same offence were ordered to be left on the file following the giving of a majority direction, counts one to three. The defendant appealed against conviction. *Held*, there was no logical inconsistency in the overall result and the convictions were safe. The jury had not been logically required to achieve an outcome on all of counts one to six. It was to be noted that the verdicts on counts four to six had not been returned after the majority direction had been given, but had been reached at an earlier stage after several hours of deliberation. It had only been after the majority direction had been given that the jury had indicated that it was unable to agree verdicts on counts one to three. That negated any concern relating to hasty compromise by reason of seen time pressures. It was clear that the verdicts on counts four to six were not simply to be assumed to be unsafe by virtue of the fact that the jury had failed to reach verdicts on counts one to three after many further hours of deliberation. The judge had given clear and separate treatment directions in his summing up. Expert evidence had focused on items comprising separate counts, the jury had not had to make an identical evaluation of the expert evidence on each count. While it was not permissible to speculate as to how the jury reached its verdict, the prosecution contention illustrated that there were logical ways for the jury to have ended up with the result. There was no logical inconsistency in relation to the verdicts on counts seven and eight either. Accordingly, the appeal would be dismissed.

R v Formhals [2013] All ER (D) 297 (Nov) (Court of Appeal: Davis LJ, Nicol J and Judge Edwards DL).

644 Fraud—possession of article—use of article—intention—direction to jury

The Fraud Act 2006 s 6(1) provides that a person is guilty of an offence if he has in his possession or under his control any article for use in the course of or in connection with any fraud.

The defendant was convicted of two offences of fraud by false representation ('counts 1 and 2') and one count of possessing an article for use in a fraud ('count 3'), contrary to the Fraud Act 2006 s 6(1). Counts 1 and 2 concerned the opening of two current accounts by the use of false identity documents containing the defendant's photograph. Each account was afforded an overdraft facility and a debit card, which were used to obtain fuel from filling stations. The defendant used a cannister, which he kept in the boot of his car. On his arrest, the police found the cannister. At the defendant's trial, it was submitted on his behalf that the jury ought to be directed that he could only be convicted of count 3 if it was sure that he had been intending to use the cannister for the purposes of fraud on or after the date of his arrest. The prosecution disagreed and contended that the defendant could be convicted whenever the fraud took place. The judge directed the jury that it just needed to be sure that the cannister had been used for past transactions. He did not direct that it had to be sure that the defendant was in possession of it with the intention of obtaining fuel by fraud on the day he had been arrested or afterwards. The defendant appealed against his conviction on count 3. *Held*, the offence under s 6(1) did not apply to possession of an article which had been used in the course of or in connection with any past fraud. The observations in *R v Ellames* as to the Theft Act 1968 s 25(1) applied with equal force to offences under the 2006 Act s 6(1). If that were not so, it was easy to see how innocent persons who knowingly had in their possession an article used by someone else in connection with a fraud would commit an offence under s 6(1). That could not be the intention of Parliament. On the facts, as the direction to the jury had made clear, or had left it open to it to conclude, that, if the cannister in the defendant's possession had been used for the previous frauds, the defendant had to be guilty, that was a misdirection. The conviction was unsafe and would be quashed. Accordingly, the appeal would be allowed.

R v Sakalauskas [2013] EWCA Crim 2278, [2014] 1 All ER 1231 (Court of Appeal: Goldring LJ, Mitting and Phillips JJ). *R v Ellames* [1974] 3 All ER 130, CA (1974 Abr para 654), applied.

645   Grievous bodily harm—defence—self-defence—insanely-held delusion

The defendant was found in the staff room of a coffee shop. He was not an employee there. When the police arrived, the defendant tried to hide in a void in the ceiling, before throwing some crockery at them. Eventually, the defendant came down, aiming a fire extinguisher at one of the police officers. He was arrested and taken to the police station. A medical examination indicated a negative result for the presence of any drugs or alcohol, although a history of cannabis use was recorded. Observation by CCTV in the cell demonstrated the defendant drinking from the lavatory cistern. During the course of his interview he said that he did 'not feel okay'. The defendant was later seen in his cell by a specialist drugs worker. As he did not feel comfortable alone in the cell with the defendant, the drugs worker asked the defendant to sit on a bench outside the custody suite. The defendant sought to move towards the exit of the custody suite. A police officer calmly approached him and the defendant punched him in the face, knocking him to the ground. He also punched a female police officer hard in the face, displacing her teeth and fracturing her jaw. A further police officer was punched twice and another officer was scratched and gouged. The defendant was sectioned and committed to hospital. His defence statement, which did not entirely reflect his evidence at trial, pleaded insanity; he had woken up on the morning in question feeling paranoid and had felt that he was being watched and pursued by evil spirits. Good spirits had guided him to the coffee shop, where he had believed that the police were agents of the evil spirits and had thought that they would harm him if he came down. At the police station, he had thought that the police who had come towards him were evil and had started defending himself. There was no mention in the defence statement of self-defence. However, he was permitted to introduce that as an issue at trial. The expert psychiatric evidence was to the effect that the defendant had been insane at the time of the offences. It was conceded by the prosecution that the defendant had genuinely believed that he was being confronted by evil spirits intent on harming him, and further, that the first limb of the conventional self-defence direction was satisfied. The only case advanced by the prosecution was that the force used by the defendant had been unreasonable. The defendant was convicted of two counts of affray and one count of inflicting grievous bodily harm and sentenced to a total of 18 months' imprisonment. He appealed against his conviction. *Held*, as was plain from the Criminal Justice and Immigration Act 2008 s 76, the position remained that the second limb of the defence of self-defence included an objective element by reference to reasonableness, even if there might also be a subjective element. An insane person could not set the standards of reasonableness as to the degree of force used by reference to his own insanity. The position still required objective assessment by reference to the circumstances as a defendant believed them to be. It was the case, prior to the 2008 Act, that in self-defence cases the psychiatric characteristics of an accused could not be brought into account on the issue of whether the degree of force used was reasonable. Whatever the purist force in the defendant's argument, there were strong policy objections to the approach. If right, it could mean that the public was exposed to further violence from an individual with a propensity for suffering insane delusions without any intervening preventative remedies being available to the courts in the form of hospital or supervision orders. With regard to the direction submission, having regard to the course of the trial and taking the summing-up as a whole, that point would not of itself render the convictions unsafe. However, while it could be said that the question of insanity had been a jury matter, the court had the greatest unease at the verdicts reached. The judge, within the proper confines of judicial discretion, had himself given the jury repeated steers on the unchallenged psychiatric evidence as to insanity. Further, the prosecution had itself conducted the trial accepting that the defendant had been suffering from insane delusions. Given all that, there was no safe or rational basis for departing from the unchallenged psychiatric evidence or the prosecution's acceptance of it. The court had power to substitute special verdicts pursuant to the Criminal Appeal Act 1968 s 6. The proper verdicts on each of the three counts would have been not guilty by reason of insanity. Such verdicts would be substituted and the court would order a conditional discharge. Judgment would be given accordingly.

R v Oye [2013] EWCA Crim 1725, [2014] 1 Cr App Rep 151, [2013] All ER (D) 143 (Oct) (Court of Appeal: Davis LJ, Keith and Lewis JJ). *R v Keane*; *R v McGrath* [2010] EWCA Crim 2514, [2010] All ER (D) 185 (Oct) applied.

646   Inchoate crimes—encouraging or assisting an offence—belief that act will encourage or assist offence—act done without knowledge of offence to be committed

The Serious Crime Act 2007 s 46(1) provides that a person commits an offence if (a) he does an act capable of encouraging or assisting the commission of one or more of a number of offences; and (b) he believes that one or more of those offences will be committed (but has no belief as to which), and that his act will encourage or assist the commission of one or more of them.

The defendant was accused of supplying cutting agents to drug dealers and to distributors of cutting agents. His defence was that he ran a legitimate business dealing in chemicals and that he had had no idea that they had been sold or supplied for misuse as cutting agents in the drugs trade. He was charged with intentionally assisting in the supply of controlled drugs, contrary to the 2007 Act s 46. The indictment stated that the defendant had supplied various chemicals as cutting agents, that this act was capable of assisting one or more offences of supplying or being concerned in the supply of controlled drugs, that the defendant believed that one or more of those offences would be committed and that the act would assist in the commission of one or more of those offences. On the defendant's appeal against conviction, *held*, s 46 created the offence of encouraging or assisting the commission of one or more offences. Its specific ingredients and the subsequent legislative provisions underlined that an indictment charging an offence under s 46 of encouraging one or more offences was permissible. A defendant might very well believe that his conduct would assist in the commission of one or more of a variety of different offences by another individual without knowing or being able to identify the precise offence or offences which the person to whom he offered encouragement or assistance intended to commit, or would actually commit. The purpose of the s 46 offence was to provide for the relatively common case where a defendant contemplated that one of a variety of offences might be committed as a result of his encouragement. Contrary to the defendant's submissions, the charge fell within the proper ambit of the s 46 offence and it was neither bad for duplicity nor defective for uncertainty. Accordingly, the appeal would be dismissed.

R v Sadique (No 2) [2013] EWCA Crim 1150, [2013] 2 Cr App Rep 352, [2013] All ER (D) 93 (Jul) (Court of Appeal: Lord Judge CJ, Openshaw and Griffith Williams JJ). *DPP for Northern Ireland v Maxwell* [1978] 3 All ER 1140, HL (1978 Abr para 578), considered.

647   Interception of communications

See POLICE AND INVESTIGATORY POWERS.

648   International co-operation—exercise of functions

The Crime (International Co-operation) Act 2003 (Exercise of Functions) Order 2013, SI 2013/2733 (in force on 21 November 2013), enables the Commissioners for Her Majesty's Revenue and Customs and officers of HMRC to exercise certain functions under the Crime (International Co-operation) Act 2003. In particular, the order will enable HMRC to act as a Central Authority in relation to any relevant offence and allow officers of HMRC to exercise certain functions under the 2003 Act. SI 2005/425 is revoked.

649   Iran—European Union financial sanctions

The Iran (European Union Financial Sanctions) (Amendment) Regulations 2013, SI 2013/163 (in force on 31 January 2013), amend the 2012 Regulations, SI 2012/925, so that a breach of the new prohibition on transfers of funds between EU credit and financial institutions and Iranian credit and financial institutions is an offence, subject to a criminal penalty.

650   Manslaughter—killing by unlawful act—foreseeability of harm causing death

The defendants were involved in a violent incident at a nightclub with a number of doormen during which one of the doormen died. The victim believed himself to be in good health, but unknown to anyone he was suffering from a renal artery aneurysm. The cause of death was blood loss resulting from the rupture of the aneurysm. The defendants were charged with manslaughter on the basis that they committed an unlawful act, namely affray, that caused or significantly contributed to the victim's death. The judge ruled that the jury could not reasonably conclude that they were sure that any reasonable and sober person, having the knowledge that the defendants had during the incident, would inevitably have realised that there was a risk that the victim would suffer an increase in blood pressure leading to the fracture of an aneurysm as a result of anything that occurred during the incident. On appeal by the prosecution against the ruling, *held*, since *R v Church* there was no requirement in the offence of unlawful act manslaughter that a defendant personally had to foresee any specific harm, or that the reasonable bystander had to recognise the precise form of harm that ensued. What mattered was whether reasonable and sober people would recognise that the unlawful activities of the defendant inevitably subjected the deceased to the risk of some harm resulting from them. In the present case, there was evidence from which a jury properly directed could conclude that sober and reasonable people observing events would readily have recognised that all the doormen involved in controlling the defendants were at the risk of some harm. Accordingly, the appeal would be allowed.

   R v M [2012] EWCA Crim 2293, [2013] 1 WLR 1083 (Court of Appeal: Lord Judge CJ, Roderick Evans and Thirlwall JJ). *R v Church* [1966] 1 QB 59, [1965] 2 All ER 72, CCA, applied.

651   Misconduct in public office—prison nurse—prison/health officer—requirements of
       public office

The defendants were serving prison officers or nurses at a prison. As part of their job working in a high security prison, the defendants came into contact with dangerous offenders. One prisoner had his cell searched. A mobile phone charger, mobile phone top up receipts, four mobile phones, a home-made weapon and a love letter from the first defendant were found. A further search linked mobile phones, sim cards and top up vouchers to each defendant. They were charged with committing offences of misconduct in public office. There was further evidence from prison staff and other prisoners which stated that the prisoner and the first defendant had been caught engaged in sexual activity at least three times. It was admitted by the second and third defendants that they had stood outside the prisoner's cell while the first defendant and the prisoner were having intercourse inside. Furthermore, the first defendant admitted sending the prisoner love letters and text messages. The primary defence of each of the defendants was that none of them held a public office, each acting solely as a nurse albeit in a prison environment with a different title. The first and second defendants distinguished themselves from the third defendant on the basis that she was a prison/health officer with the powers of arrest of a prison officer whereas they had been employed as registered nurses. It fell to be determined whether any of the defendants held a public office, whether each defendant in turn was guilty of wilful misconduct in the performance of her public duties, and whether the conduct of each in turn had been such as to be deserving of criminal condemnation and sanction. The first and third defendants were each convicted of three counts of misconduct in public office and the second defendant was convicted of two similar counts. The defendants appealed against their convictions. *Held*, the responsibilities of a nurse in a general hospital were to the patients for whose care they were responsible. The responsibilities of a nurse in a prison setting were not only for the welfare of the prisoners; they were also responsible to the public, so far as it was within their power, for the proper, safe and secure running of the prison in which they worked. Therefore, the duties of the defendants more than amply fulfilled the requirements of a public office. That decision had been a decision of law. If there had been an issue as to the facts, the decision as to the facts would have been for the jury; the existence or otherwise of a public office had been for the judge. Accordingly, the appeals would be dismissed.

   R v Cosford [2013] EWCA Crim 466, [2014] QB 81, [2013] 3 All ER 649 (Court of Appeal: Leveson LJ, Mitting and Males JJ).

664   Sexual offence—sexual activity with girl under fourteen—reasonable belief as to age

The appellant, aged 17, had sexual intercourse with the complainant, a girl aged 13. He was arrested and charged with having had unlawful carnal knowledge of a girl under the age of 14 contrary to the Criminal Law Amendment Acts (Northern Ireland) 1885–1923 s 4. The appellant pleaded guilty to the charge on the basis that the offence created by s 4 was one in which reasonable belief that the complainant was over the age of 14 was not available to him as a defence. Subsequently, having received different legal advice, the appellant appealed to the Court of Appeal in Northern Ireland. He submitted that the approach of s 4 had to be informed by a fundamental common law principle which was that there ought to be a mental element for criminal liability unless a clear intention was evinced by the words of a statute that a particular criminal offence ought to be one of strict liability. The presumption that mens rea was required could only be displaced, the appellant submitted, where it could be shown that that was the unmistakable intention of Parliament. Since s 4 was silent on the question of whether proof of mens rea was required, the appellant submitted that the offence could only be regarded as not requiring such proof if that had to be unavoidably and necessarily implied. It was further submitted that, if an implication of strict liability was to be considered as compellingly clear, it had to arise from coherent and consistent legislative scheme and the Acts did not fit that description. The Court of Appeal rejected the appellant's arguments. On further appeal, *held*, s 4 had to be interpreted as not requiring proof that the appellant had not known or reasonably believed that the complainant had been aged 14 or over. There could really be no doubt that s 4 in its original form had been intended to impose criminal liability for carnal knowledge of a female under the age of 13 without proof that the perpetrator knew or had reason to believe that she was below that age. Previously it had been confirmed that proof of knowledge or lack of reasonable belief in the age of the complainant was not required. It was inconceivable that, had it been intended that such proof was required, s 4 would have remained silent on the issue. Further, the juxtaposition of ss 5, 6 made it impossible to conclude that the absence of such a proviso in s 4 signified anything other than a clear intention that a defence of reasonable belief in the complainant's age was not to be available. It seemed unquestionable that the decision not to extend the defence to offences under s 4 had been deliberate and that it clearly signified that the legislature had intended that no such defence would be available in relation to offences under s 4. Finally, there was nothing in the contemporary social context which militated against the denial of the defence of reasonable belief as to age for offences under s 4. Young girls had to be protected and, as part of that protection, it ought not to be a defence that the person accused had believed the girl to be above the prescribed age. Accordingly, the appeal would be dismissed.

R v Brown (Northern Ireland) [2013] UKSC 43, [2013] All ER (D) 251 (Jun) (Supreme Court: Lord Neuberger P, Lady Hale, Lord Kerr, Lord Wilson and Lord Reed SCJJ). *R v G* [2008] UKHL 37, [2009] AC 92, [2008] 3 All ER 1071 (2008 Abr para 1066); and *R v Prince* (1875) LR 2 CCR 154 applied.

665   Sexual offence—trafficking people for exploitation—protection of complainants

The Trafficking People for Exploitation Regulations 2013, SI 2013/554 (in force on 6 April 2013), are made as part of the implementation in England and Wales of European Parliament and Council Directive (EU) 2011/36 on preventing and combating trafficking in human beings and protecting its victims. The regulations, which apply where there is a police investigation into a human trafficking offence, set out measures aimed at the protection of complainants. In particular, the regulations (1) amend the Youth Justice and Criminal Evidence Act 1999 to ensure that the complainant in respect of every human trafficking offence is eligible for 'special measures' under that Act; such 'special measures' are intended to assist and protect certain categories of witnesses in the giving of evidence in criminal proceedings; and (2) require the Secretary of State to review the operation and effect of the regulations and publish a report within five years after they come into force and within every five years after that.

666   Suicide—complicity in another person's suicide—health care professional— defence—necessity

The Suicide Act 1961 s 2(1) provides that a person ('D') commits an offence if D does an act capable of encouraging or assisting the suicide or attempted suicide of another person, and

D's act was intended to encourage or assist suicide or an attempt at suicide. No proceedings may be instituted for an offence under s 2 except by or with the consent of the Director of Public Prosecutions: s 2(4).

The claimants all suffered from permanent and catastrophic physical disabilities, were of sound mind and wished to die at the time of their choosing. However, none of the claimants was physically capable of ending his own life unaided and wished a health care professional to assist the claimant in ending his life. The claimants sought declarations that, on the particular facts of their cases, the defence of necessity should be available to a health care professional who assisted in their deaths, to either complicity in another's suicide under the 1961 Act s 2(1) or murder. In the alternative, the first claimant sought to establish that, even if the person who assisted him to commit suicide might be subject to criminal prosecution, it was incumbent on the Director of Public Prosecutions to clarify his published policy on the circumstances in which he would allow a prosecution for complicity in another person's suicide, so that a person considering providing assistance to a suicide would be able to assess with some confidence the risk of their being prosecuted. The applications were dismissed. The third claimant died prior to the appeal and his widow was added as a party to the appeal as administratrix and in her own right. The issues on appeal were whether the defence of necessity should be available, whether the blanket prohibition on assisting suicide in s 2(1) was compatible with the European Convention on Human Rights art 8 and whether the Director of Public Prosecutions' policy on consent to prosecution under the 1961 Act s 2(4) enabled a health care professional who assisted a person to commit suicide to predict with any confidence whether he would be prosecuted. *Held*, Lord Judge dissenting in part, the common law would not recognise a defence of necessity to a charge of murder where it took the form of euthanasia, or to a charge of assisted suicide for a number of reasons. Firstly, the sanctity of life was, if anything, an even more fundamental principle of the common law reflected in the unqualified right to life in the Convention art 2. There was no self-evident reason why it should give way to the values of autonomy or dignity and there were cogent reasons why sensible people might properly think that it should not. Secondly, there was no right to commit suicide, so there could be no right that required the state to allow others to assist one to die or to kill oneself. Thirdly, it was not appropriate for the court to fashion a defence of necessity; that was a matter for Parliament. Fourthly, any defence provided to those who assisted someone to die would not merely apply to euthanasia but also to assisted suicide. That raised the question of how the court could develop a defence to assisted suicide when Parliament had stated in unequivocal terms that it was a serious criminal offence punishable by imprisonment. It would be inappropriate for the courts to fashion domestic art 8(1) rights that exceeded the protection afforded by the requirements of Strasbourg in direct opposition to the will of Parliament as reflected in the 1961 Act s 2. The courts had to concede a very wide margin of judgment to Parliament in a controversial area that raised difficult moral and ethical issues such as assisted suicide and the current law could not conceivably be said to stray beyond it. While courts could not refuse to carry out the proportionality exercise even where the case fell within the margin of appreciation, they had to adopt a very light touch particularly when dealing with primary legislation. It was not sufficient for the Director of Public Prosecutions' policy on consent to prosecution under s 2(4) merely to list the factors which the Director of Public Prosecutions would take into account in deciding whether to consent to a prosecution under s 2(1). A list of factors which contained no clue as to how the discretion to grant or withhold consent would be exercised was not sufficient to meet the requirements of the Convention art 8(2). The Director of Public Prosecutions was required to maintain a policy on consent to prosecution which identified the facts and circumstances which he would take into account in such a way that a person who was considering providing assistance to a victim to commit suicide was able to foresee, to a degree that was reasonable and adequate in the circumstances, the consequences of providing such assistance. In particular, the Director of Public Prosecutions had failed to provide sufficient clarity as to his prosecution policy with respect to assisted suicide where the suspect had no close or emotional connection with the victim, but who would act out of a sense of compassion and understanding for the victim's position. Accordingly, the appeal would be allowed in part.

R (on the application of Nicklinson) v Ministry of Justice; R (on the application of AM) v DPP [2013] EWCA Civ 961, [2014] 2 All ER 32 (Court of Appeal: Lord Judge CJ, Lord Dyson MR and Elias LJ). *Airedale NHS Trust v Bland* [1993] AC 789, [1993] 1 All ER 821, HL (1992 Abr para 1770); and Application 497/09 *Koch v Germany* [2013]

1 FCR 595, ECtHR, considered. *R (on the application of Pretty) v DPP* [2001] UKHL 61, [2002] 1 AC 800, [2002] 1 All ER 1 (2001 Abr para 1813) applied. *R (on the application of Purdy) v DPP* [2009] UKHL 45, [2009] 4 All ER 1147 (2009 Abr para 942) followed. Decision of Queen's Bench Divisional Court [2012] EWHC 2381 (Admin), [2012] 3 FCR 233 (2012 Abr para 751) reversed in part.

667 Terrorism—dissemination of terrorist publications—videos uploaded onto internet—depiction and praise of attacks on state military forces

The appellant was born in Libya but was a British citizen and had lived much of his life in the United Kingdom. Police officers executing a search warrant at the appellant's house found videos on his computer showing terrorist attacks on military targets, civilians and the police and accompanied by commentaries praising the bravery and martyrdom of the attackers. The videos had been uploaded onto various websites. The appellant was convicted of dissemination of terrorist publications contrary to the Terrorism Act 2006 s 2. His appeal against conviction was dismissed on the basis that the definition of 'terrorism' in the Terrorism Act 2000 s 1 included any or all military attacks by a non-state armed group against any or all state or inter-governmental organisation armed forces in the context of a non-international armed conflict. The appellant appealed further, arguing that (1) the 2000 Act, like the 2006 Act, was intended to give effect to the United Kingdom's international treaty obligations, and the concept of terrorism in international law did not extend to military attacks by a non-state armed group against state or inter-governmental organisation armed forces in the context of a non-international armed conflict and that such a limitation should be implied into the definition of 'terrorism' in the 2000 Act s 1; (2) it would be wrong to read either Act as criminalising in the United Kingdom an act carried out abroad, unless that act would be regarded as criminal by international law norms; and (3) as a matter of domestic law, some qualifications had to be read into the very wide words of the 2000 Act s 1. The prosecution contended that the definition of terrorism in s 1 was very wide and that it would be wrong to interpret it more narrowly. It relied on s 117 which precluded any prosecution without the consent of the Director of Public Prosecutions or, if the activities under consideration occurred abroad, the Attorney General, as recognising the risks of criminalising activities which should not be prosecuted. It fell to be determined whether both domestic law and international law required some qualifications to be read into s 1. The European Convention on Human Rights, and the International Convention for the Suppression of Terrorist Bombings 1997 and the International Convention for the Suppression of the Financing of Terrorism 1999 were considered. *Held*, the definition of terrorism in the 2000 Act s 1 operated so as to include within its scope any or all military attacks by a non-state armed group against any or all state or inter-governmental organisation armed forces in the context of a non-international armed conflict. Properly construed, the wide interpretation favoured by the prosecution accorded with the natural meaning of the words used in s 1(1)(b) and, while it gave the words a wide meaning, there were good reasons for it. The definition of 'terrorism' had been intended to be very wide. Unless it was established, although this was not suggested, that the natural meaning of the legislation conflicted with the European Convention on Human Rights or that such meaning conflicted with any other international obligation of the United Kingdom, the court's function was to interpret the meaning of the definition in its statutory, legal and practical context. In reaching that conclusion, no weight was attached to the provisions of the 2000 Act s 117 as an aid to construction. It might be that any concern which Parliament had about the width of the definition of terrorism in s 1(1) had been mitigated by the existence of the statutory prosecutorial discretion but it was not regarded as an appropriate reason for giving 'terrorism' a wide meaning. The appellant's two arguments with respect to international law faced insuperable obstacles, the common obstacle being that there was no accepted norm in international law as to what constituted terrorism. The definition of 'terrorism' was as wide as it appeared to be and, accordingly, the appeal would be dismissed.

R v Gul [2013] UKSC 64, [2014] 1 All ER 463 (Supreme Court: Lord Neuberger P, Lady Hale DP, Lord Hope, Lord Mance, Lord Judge, Lord Kerr and Lord Reed SCJJ). *Al-Sirri (FC) v Secretary of State for the Home Department; DD (Afghanistan) (FC) v Secretary of State for the Home Department* [2012] UKSC 54, [2013] 1 AC 745, [2013] 1 All ER 1267 (2012 Abr para 1461) applied. Decision of Court of Appeal [2012] EWCA Crim 280, [2012] 3 All ER 83 (2012 Abr para 752) affirmed.

668   Terrorism—offence—dissemination of terrorist publications—admissibility of evidence

The defendant, who was the manager of an Islamic bookshop, was charged with dissemination of terrorist publications by distribution, possession of information likely to be useful to a person committing or preparing an act of terrorism, and dissemination of terrorist publications by possession with a view to distribution. The dissemination counts were founded on terrorist publications in the form of books and DVDs sold in the bookshop and offered for sale on its website. The judge permitted the prosecution to adduce in evidence the possession of material similar or identical to that allegedly disseminated by the defendant by those convicted of terrorism offences to establish whether the items were terrorist publications within the meaning of the Terrorism Act 2006 s 2(3), (4). The judge directed the jury that it was irrelevant whether any person had in fact been encouraged by the publication in question to commit, prepare or instigate a terrorist offence in accordance with s 2(8). The defendant was convicted of dissemination of a terrorist publication by distribution and possession of information likely to be useful to a person committing or preparing an act of terrorism and was sentenced to three years' imprisonment. The defendant appealed on the basis that the evidence of similar publications found in the possession of convicted terrorists should not have been admitted. *Held,* the evidence was admissible, if at all, for the extremely limited purpose of demonstrating that, among the readership of the publications, there had been people who had been prepared to commit terrorist acts. The danger inherent in admitting the evidence, even for that extremely limited purpose, was manifest. The danger was that the jury would condemn the publication purely by reason of its association with known terrorists. Further, the judge's reference to s 2(8) had not been enough to avoid the risk either of the improper use of the evidence to establish encouragement or to remove the risk of prejudice merely by association. Whether it had been treated as relevant evidence at common law, important explanatory evidence, or as substantially probative on an important issue, it had been essential that the limitations and pitfalls of the evidence should be explained to the jury. There had been no direction warning the jury against making improper use of the evidence and it followed that the defendant's convictions for dissemination of a terrorist publication by distribution had been unsafe. Accordingly, the appeal would be allowed.

   R v Faraz [2012] EWCA Crim 2820, [2013] 1 WLR 2615, [2013] All ER (D) 11 (Jan) (Court of Appeal: Pitchford LJ, Kenneth Parker J and Judge Gilbert QC).

669   Terrorism—prevention—financial restrictions—Iran

See *Bank Mellat v HM Treasury*, para 1237.

670   Terrorism—prevention—financial restrictions—Iran—revocation

The Financial Restrictions (Iran) (Revocation) Order 2013, SI 2013/162 (in force on 31 January 2013), revokes the 2012 Order, SI 2012/2904, which contained a direction given by the Treasury prohibiting all persons operating in the United Kingdom financial sector from entering into new transactions or business relationships with Iranian banks, their branches and subsidiaries, and the Central Bank of Iran, or continuing to participate in transactions or business relationships with them.

671   Terrorism—proscribed organisations—listed organisation

The Terrorism Act 2000 (Proscribed Organisations) (Amendment) Order 2013, SI 2013/1746 (in force on 12 July 2013), further amends the Terrorism Act 2000 Sch 2 by adding 'Jama'atu Ahli Sunna Lidda Awati Wal Jihad (Boko Haram)' and 'Minbar Ansar Deen (Ansar Al Sharia UK)' to the list of proscribed organisations.

The Terrorism Act 2000 (Proscribed Organisations) (Amendment) (No 2) Order 2013, SI 2013/3172 (in force on 13 December 2013), further amends the Terrorism Act 2000 Sch 2 by adding 'Imarat Kavkaz (Caucasus Emirate)' to the list of proscribed organisations.

672   Terrorism—proscribed organisations—name changes

The Proscribed Organisations (Name Changes) Order 2013, SI 2013/1795 (in force on 19 July 2013), exercises the power under the Terrorism Act 2000 s 3(6) to specify other the victims, and was sentenced to a total of eleven years' imprisonment. He appealed against conviction on the basis that prejudice had been caused by the absence of witnesses and documents because of the delay between the alleged offences and the trial. *Held*, some of the submissions made by the defendant had been overstated. Also, there appeared to be an assumption from the defendant that the missing evidence complained of would have supported his case. That could not be accepted by the court. The missing evidence complained of by the defendant did not advance the case much more and was often speculative. The court was satisfied that the defendant received a fair trial and had not been disadvantaged by the missing evidence and witnesses. The missing evidence and witnesses had not resulted in serious prejudice to the defendant to an extent that it could not be dealt with by the trial process and proper directions and summing up by the judge, which had taken place. Accordingly, the appeal would be dismissed.

R v Davies [2013] All ER (D) 76 (Sep) (Court of Appeal: Treacy LJ, Hickinbottom and Nicol JJ). *R v Pope* [2012] EWCA Crim 2241, [2012] All ER (D) 72 (Nov) considered.

682   Bail—refusal of bail—provision of surety

The Bail Act 1976 s 3(4) provides that a person granted bail in criminal proceedings may be required, before release on bail, to provide a surety or sureties to secure his surrender to custody.

During the claimant's trial for fraud, he was also charged with fraudulent trading, likely to be joined with the fraud charges. The judge decided to refuse to grant the claimant bail on the ground that he was not certain that a surety taken to ensure compliance with a condition designed to prevent further offending, namely, a condition not to engage in fraudulent activity, would be liable to be forfeited if the condition was breached. The claimant challenged the refusal of bail, contending that, on the proper interpretation of the 1976 Act, there was no impediment to the judge ordering bail, as a condition against commercial activity or fraudulent activity of a commercial nature could be supported adequately by a surety. The claimant further submitted that the statutory language of s 3(4) gave an example of the most common purpose of a surety, namely to secure surrender to custody, but it did not preclude other purposes. He alternatively contended that the judge had retained a general jurisdiction to achieve what he thought to be a just conclusion by other means. It fell to be determined whether bail should be ordered on the basis of the condition. *Held*, Parliament had plainly intended that the obligation of a surety was a personal obligation that could not be delegated to another party. Parliament had intended that a surety should be provided only to secure surrender to custody and not to secure performance of any other condition. The legislation, read as a whole, showed that the provision of surety should be limited to that expressly identified in s 3 and for no other purpose. Further, it was clear that Parliament had intended the 1976 Act to provide a comprehensive code wherever the issue of bail arose. Accordingly, the application would be dismissed.

R (on the application of S) v Crown Court at Winchester [2013] EWHC 1050 (Admin), [2013] All ER (D) 166 (May) (Queen's Bench Division: Pitchford LJ and Kenneth Parker J).

683   Costs—award—dealing with criminal legal aid and recovery of defence costs orders

Lord Judge CJ has issued, on 3 October 2013, the following: *Practice Direction (costs in criminal proceedings)* [2013] All ER (D) 53 (Oct), the full text of which is set out at [2013] EWCA Crim 1632.

The *Practice Direction* will have effect in the Magistrates' Courts, the Crown Court, the High Court and the Court of Appeal, Criminal Division, where the court, in the exercise of its discretion, considers an award of costs in criminal proceedings or deals with criminal legal aid and recovery of defence costs orders. The provisions in this *Practice Direction* come into force on 7 October 2013.

684   Costs—general

The Costs in Criminal Cases (General) (Amendment) Regulations 2013, SI 2013/2526 (in force on 27 October 2013), further amend the 1986 Regulations, SI 1986/1335, so as to (1) reflect the fact that cases are no longer committed by magistrates' courts to the Crown Court for trial; and (2) ensure that intermediaries who are required to assist a defendant in court are able to receive payment out of central funds.

The Costs in Criminal Cases (General) (Amendment) (No 2) Regulations 2013, SI 2013/2830 (in force on 27 January 2014), further amend the 1986 Regulations above so as to provide that, where legal costs are recoverable, in particular where an individual who is ineligible for legal aid in certain Crown Court proceedings to receive a payment out of central funds in respect of his legal costs if he is acquitted, the amounts payable out of central funds in respect of such costs will be calculated in accordance with the rates or scales or other provision made by the Lord Chancellor.

685　Costs—prosecution costs—capacity to pay

See *R v McKenzie*, para 2291.

686　Costs—prosecution costs—costs disproportionate to fine

See *R (on the application of Gray) v Crown Court at Aylesbury*, para 44.

687　Costs—prosecution costs—third party costs order—serious misconduct

The defendant company had an agreement with the Ministry of Justice in relation to the provision of interpreters. The defendant received a request for a Slovak interpreter to attend a Crown Court sentencing hearing and, on the same day, contracted an interpreter to attend. It was subsequently requested that the interpreter attend earlier than originally booked, but the interpreter was not told of the re-scheduled time. At the hearing, the interpreter did not attend at the re-scheduled time and the hearing was adjourned. The judge directed that he would consider making an order under the Prosecution of Offences Act 1985 s 19B, requiring the defendant to pay the prosecution's fee for the hearing. After hearing oral argument, the judge concluded that the defendant won a contract under which it accepted responsibility as a go-between between the courts and interpreters, and found that the defendant had not done its job properly as a result of negligence on its part and that the negligence of the kind shown in the case constituted a serious misconduct. The judge ordered that the defendant pay part of the prosecution's fee for the adjourned hearing after applying the discretion he had under the Costs in Criminal Cases (General) Regulations 1986, SI 1986/1335. The defendant appealed. *Held*, it was clear that a single failure on its own and of the kind that occurred could not, viewed in isolation, have amounted to serious misconduct. A case of serious misconduct might have arisen if there had been before the court evidence that the non-attendance occurred in circumstances where there had been a failure to remedy a defective administrative system which had caused non-attendance in the past. Equally, the failure of a particular interpreter to attend where there had been evidence that there had been similar failures in the past might have constituted serious misconduct for which the defendant had been responsible. It would always be open to a court to ask the defendant to attend, to provide an explanation and, if appropriate, to provide the necessary disclosure. There had been no evidence that the failure had been anything other than an isolated failure and there had been no serious misconduct on the evidence before the judge. Accordingly, the appeal would be allowed.

Re Applied Language Solutions Ltd [2013] EWCA Crim 326, [2013] 2 Cr App Rep 169, [2013] All ER (D) 239 (Mar) (Court of Appeal: Sir John Thomas P, Swift and Cranston JJ). *R v Ahmati* [2006] EWCA Crim 1826, [2006] All ER (D) 131 (Oct) applied.

688　Costs—wasted costs—defence statement—alibi notice—failure to give particulars of witness

See *Re Joseph Hill & Co (wasted costs order)*, para 707.

689　Crime and Courts Act 2013

See para 2052.

690　Criminal injuries—compensation—entitlement—crime of violence—mens rea

The respondent was seriously injured in a motor accident and required full-time residential care as a consequence. The deceased had run into the path of a truck which, in braking, had hit the respondent's road gritter. An open verdict was recorded at the deceased's inquest. Later, the respondent's mother applied on his behalf to the appellant Criminal Injuries Compensation Authority for an award of compensation under the Criminal Injuries

Compensation Scheme 2001. The respondent was informed that an award could not be made under the scheme because it provided that compensation was payable only if the claimant was the victim of a criminal injury. The respondent appealed to the First-tier Tribunal ('FTT'). It was found that it was not open to the FTT to make an award. It was not satisfied that an offence under the Road Traffic Act 1988 s 22A had been committed and neither was it satisfied that any such offence would amount to a crime of violence within the scheme. The FTT further rejected the claim based on the Offences Against the Person Act 1861 s 20 as it was not satisfied that the deceased had intended to cause harm, or had been reckless as to whether harm might be caused by his actions. In its view, the deceased's act had not been a hostile act directed towards a person who had suffered injury as a result and therefore, it had not been proved that an offence of the kind described by s 20 had been committed by him. The respondent's application for judicial review of that decision was dismissed. On further appeal, the Court of Appeal granted judicial review of the FTT's decision. Its view was that it was highly improbable that anyone who ran into the path of traffic would not at the very least foresee the possibility of an accident and, as a consequence, harm being caused to other road users. It remitted the matter to a differently constituted FTT to reconsider the issue of recklessness. The appellant appealed that decision. *Held*, the Court of Appeal had not been able to demonstrate that it had been entitled to interfere with the FTT's decision. There were signs that it had allowed itself to be unduly influenced by its own view that it was highly improbable that anyone who ran into the path of traffic on a busy motorway would not at the least foresee the possibility of an accident and of consequential harm being caused to other road users. The question whether the deceased had actually foreseen that possibility had been for the FTT to answer, not the Court of Appeal. Taking its judgment overall, the Court of Appeal had failed to identify a flaw in the reasoning of the FTT which could be said to amount to an error of law. The FTT had appreciated that the question it had to consider first had been whether an offence under s 20 had been committed. It had correctly identified the tests that had to be applied and had reached the conclusion that it was not satisfied that the deceased had committed that offence. Therefore, the decision of the FTT would be restored, the terms of the scheme did not permit an award of compensation to be made in the circumstances. Accordingly, the appeal would be allowed.

R (on the application of Jones) v First-tier Tribunal [2013] UKSC 19, [2013] 2 AC 48, [2013] 2 All ER 625 (Supreme Court: Lord Hope DP, Lord Walker, Lady Hale, Lord Sumption and Lord Carnwath SCJJ). *R v Criminal Injuries Compensation Board, ex p Webb* [1987] QB 74, [1986] 2 All ER 478 (1986 Abr para 511) applied. Decision of Court of Appeal [2011] EWCA Civ 400, [2011] All ER (D) 101 (Apr) (2011 Abr para 719) reversed.

691 Criminal injuries—compensation—time limit—discretionary extension—particular circumstances of case

The claimant's father was fatally stabbed when the claimant was only a few months old. Since reaching adulthood, the claimant had tried to find out details of the circumstances of his father's death. He had no success until 41 years after the stabbing, when he discovered that his father's attacker had been found guilty of manslaughter and sentenced to 18 months' imprisonment. The year after making the discovery, the claimant made a claim to the Criminal Injuries Compensation Authority on behalf of himself and his family. The Criminal Injuries Compensation Scheme (2008) para 18 prescribed a two-year time limit for claims, which could be extended at the discretion of a claims officer if, by reason of the particular circumstances of the case, it was reasonable and in the interests of justice to do so. The claims officer refused to waive the two-year time limit in the claimant's case on the basis that the Authority had been unable to verify the claimant's account with police records, which had been destroyed. The claimant's application to the Authority for a review of that decision was also refused, on the ground that it was not reasonable to bring a claim 42 years after the event. The First-tier Tribunal dismissed the claimant's appeal against that decision, ruling that it had not been reasonable or in the interests of justice to extend the time limit. The claimant applied for permission to apply for judicial review of the Tribunal's decision, submitting that it had erred in its interpretation of para 18. *Held*, on the proper construction of para 18, the words 'particular circumstances' meant the actual or distinct circumstances of the individual case. They did not mean special circumstances in the sense of being unusual or extraordinary circumstances. The task of the claims officer or reviewing officer was therefore to establish the actual circumstances of the particular case. Having done so, he then had to ask, given the circumstances of the particular case, whether it was reasonable and in the interests of justice to waive the time limit. In performing that exercise, the wording required that the claims officer consider all relevant factors. Those might include the length of the delay in making the claim, the reasons for the delay and the nature of the claim itself. The claims officer had to make an overall decision bearing all those circumstances in mind. In doing so he would have to take account of the fact that the general rule was that claims ought to be brought as soon as possible and, in any event, within two years of the incident giving rise to the claim. It followed that the Tribunal had erred in its construction of para 18 and, accordingly, the appeal would be allowed.

Hutton v First-tier Tribunal [2012] EWCA Civ 806, [2013] 1 WLR 124, [2012] All ER (D) 71 (Jun) (Court of Appeal: Arden, Aikens and McFarlane LJJ).

692   Criminal Justice Act 2003—commencement

The Criminal Justice Act 2003 (Commencement No 31 and Saving Provisions) Order 2013, SI 2013/1103, brings into force on 28 May 2013, in relation to relevant local justice areas, Sch 3 paras 2–12, 16–18, 20(3)–(14), 21, 23–36, 39, 41–52, 54–56, 57(1), (3)–(7), 58–64, 66(1)–(3), (4) (in part), (5)–(8), 67–69, 71(a)–(c), 72–75, and Sch 37 Pt 4 (in part). Saving provision is also made. For a summary of the Act, see 2003 Abr para 642. See also the commencement table in the title STATUTES AND LEGISLATIVE PROCESS.

693   Criminal Justice and Immigration Act 2008—commencement

The Criminal Justice and Immigration Act 2008 (Commencement No 15) Order 2013, SI 2013/616, brings into force on 8 April 2013, so far as they are not already in force, s 148(1) (in part), Sch 9 para 3, Sch 26 paras 59 (in part), 60, 62; and certain repeals in Sch 28. For a summary of the Act, see 2008 Abr para 940. See also the commencement table in the title STATUTES AND LEGISLATIVE PROCESS.

694   Criminal law

See CRIMINAL LAW.

695   Criminal practice directions—amendment

Lord Judge CJ has issued, on 3 October 2013, the following *Criminal Practice Directions* [2013] All ER (D) 52 (Oct), the full text of which is set out at [2013] EWCA Crim 1631.

The *Practice Directions* replace the *Consolidated Criminal Practice Direction* of 8 July 2002 [2002] 3 All ER 904, [2002] 1 WLR 2870, [2002] 2 Cr App Rep 35 (2002 Abr para 830), which is revoked, with the exception of sections III.21, IV.31, IV.32, IV. 33, IV.38 and IV.41.9. The *Practice Directions*, *Practice Notes* and *Practice Statements* listed in Annex A and Annex B of the 2002 consolidation are also revoked. Annexes D, E and F remain in force. The *Practice Directions*, which are to be known as the *Criminal Practice Directions*, take effect from 7 October 2013. They apply to all cases in all the criminal courts of England and Wales from that date.

696   Criminal Procedure Rules

The Criminal Procedure Rules 2013, SI 2013/1554 (in force on 7 October 2013), replace, with amendments, the 2012 Rules, SI 2012/1726. The principal changes include (1) a requirement for the defendant to give notice of the identity of the intended defence trial advocate; (2) a requirement that, where a document may be served by electronic means, the person serving it must normally use that method; (3) provision of a procedure for dealing with applications for access to the material on the basis of which a search warrant has been issued against a person in his absence; (4) an extension of the scope of Pt 6 (investigation orders and warrants) to an application to a justice of the peace for a search warrant, and to an application or appeal concerning the retention of fingerprints, samples and DNA profiles by the police; (5) the omission of the rules about committal for trial and the transfer for trial of serious fraud cases or cases involving children; (6) the replacement of the procedure on an application to dismiss a charge sent to the Crown Court for trial; (7) the replacement of the rules relating to extradition; (8) the inclusion, in the list of information which the magistrates' court officer must give the defendant where bail is withheld, a statutory certificate that the court has heard full argument and a requirement for the defendant, on making an application for bail, to pass the certificate to the Crown Court officer; (9) the removal of the requirement for the Crown Court officer to send information to the High Court on a prosecutor's appeal against a grant of bail from the Crown Court to the High Court; and (10) a requirement for a draft of any proposed sexual offences prevention order to be served not less than two business days before the hearing at which the order may be made.

The Criminal Procedure (Amendment) Rules 2013, SI 2013/2525 (in force on 27 October 2013), further amend the Criminal Procedure Rules 2013 above so as to (1) require the provision of interpretation and translation services for defendants, including those with hearing or speech impediments, where such provision is necessary in order to facilitate the participation of the defendant; and (2) require court officers to record the identity of any interpreter or intermediary and to record any waiver by a defendant of the right to attend a hearing or have a document translated.

The Criminal Procedure (Amendment No 2) Rules 2013, SI 2013/3183 (in force in part on 24 February 2014 and in part on 7 April 2014), further amend the Criminal Procedure Rules 2013 so as to (1) replace the title of the Lord Chief Justice's Practice Directions; (2) require the publication of specified details of cases which are due to be heard; (3) set out the procedure which must be followed by a magistrates' court where two or more defendants being dealt with on the same occasion are jointly charged with an offence which may be tried either in the Crown Court or in a magistrates' court; (4) add new rules on proceedings relating to deferred prosecution agreements; and (5) provide for costs orders to be made in connection with deferred prosecution agreements.

697   Crown Prosecution Service—decision to prosecute—judicial review
The applicant was one of three co-defendants who were convicted of murder and sentenced to life imprisonment. The convictions were subsequently overturned after fresh evidence emerged relating to the reliability of a confession made by one of the other co-defendants. After his release, the applicant brought proceedings against the relevant police authority for malicious prosecution and misfeasance in public office. He submitted that a former detective inspector had fabricated the evidence of a conversation between the applicant and one of the other co-defendants, and had perjured himself when giving evidence about it to the jury. The claim was eventually settled. Following the settlement, the applicant sought to have the detective inspector prosecuted for perverting the course of justice, perjury and/or misfeasance in public office. A fresh police investigation took place and the results were submitted to the Crown Prosecution Service ('CPS'). A prosecutor for the CPS considered that any trial of the detective inspector would be converted into a repeated murder trial. The CPS therefore concluded that there was insufficient evidence to provide a realistic prospect of conviction against the detective inspector for any offence. The applicant sought judicial review of the decision not to prosecute, contending that it had been unreasonable or perverse. *Held*, it was settled law that, for constitutional reasons, the courts were very slow to interfere with a prosecutorial decision. Prosecutorial independence was of great importance. The court could be persuaded to act only if it was demonstrated that the Director of Public Prosecutions, acting through the CPS, had arrived at the decision not to prosecute because (1) of some unlawful policy; (2) he had failed to act in accordance with his own settled policy; or (3) the decision had been perverse in the sense that it had been one at which no reasonable prosecutor could have arrived. In assessing the case, apart from the expert evidence, the prosecutor had importantly overstated one aspect of the case. The anticipation that any trial of the detective inspector would be converted into a repeated murder trial had been a clear error. That issue aside, the judgments of the prosecutor about the non-expert part of the potential case against the detective inspector had been perfectly reasonable. The decision of the prosecutor had not only been reasonable, but correct. Accordingly, the application would be dismissed.
   R (*on the application of O'Brien*) *v DPP* [2013] EWHC 3741 (Admin), [2013] All ER (D) 323 (Nov) (Queen's Bench Division: Lord Thomas CJ and Irwin J).

698   Evidence—admissibility—discretion to exclude—covert recordings in police vehicle
Three men dressed as policemen forced their way into a property and tied up each of the family members with handcuffs and cable ties. The husband was threatened and ordered to

open his safes. The barrel of a gun was pushed against his head. The men produced a syringe containing red liquid and told the husband that it was HIV infected blood. The victims were threatened with torture and killing if they reported the crime. The men made off with valuable items including a watch and a large quantity of cash. Prior to the victims' complaint, the police had received intelligence and conducted a search of the defendants' home and a garage rented by the first defendant. A number of items were found including the watch, police equipment and clothing, tracker devices, shotguns and a syringe containing red liquid. The first defendant's DNA was found on a shirt and glove. One of the tracker devices had been used to track a friend of the husband and the tracker history was consistent with a visit to the area where the victims lived at the time of the burglary. Two mobile phones which were recovered were found to have been used in the area of the victims' home on the night of the attack. The defendants were arrested and taken to a police station for interview in a police vehicle on three separate occasions. Both of the defendants made a numbers of compromising admissions and statements while they were in the police vehicle which were covertly recorded. At the interview, the defendants were told of the three covert recordings. Thereafter, the laptop was analysed and it showed that internet searches had been made for police issue equipment and the home address of the victims. The judge admitted the evidence from the covert recordings at trial and the defendants were convicted of aggravated burglary, false imprisonment and possession of a firearm. They appealed against conviction. *Held*, the defendants' contention that the surveillance had been 'intrusive surveillance' as defined by the Regulation of Investigatory Powers Act 2000, requiring authorisation by the relevant chief constable, was based on the premise that the police vehicle was a private vehicle. However, the police vehicle was not a private vehicle: it was owned by a state entity and had not been used for private purposes but for the purposes of the state. The judge had been fully entitled to find that the Detective Superintendent who had authorised the surveillance had believed that the surveillance was necessary and proportionate. Furthermore, the evidence had been properly admitted and there was no ground to exclude it under the Police and Criminal Evidence Act 1984 s 78. Finally, the evidence from the analysis of the laptop, the searches and the analysis of the mobile phones would have provided a sufficiently strong case to be satisfied that there could be no reasonable doubt about the safety of the convictions. Accordingly, the appeal would be dismissed.

R v Plunkett [2013] EWCA Crim 261, [2013] 1 WLR 3121, [2013] All ER (D) 107 (Mar) (Court of Appeal: Sir John Thomas P, Swift and MacDuff JJ).

699　　Evidence—admissibility—expert evidence—DNA—statistical evaluation

Three criminal appeals that raised a common issue regarding the use of DNA evidence were heard together. The defendant in the first case was convicted of burglary, robbery and manslaughter. The only forensic evidence found during the investigation of the offences was a very small quantity of DNA on two of three chisels at the scene of the crimes. At least three people had contributed to one of the samples and at least two to the other. The experts stated that it was impossible to calculate a robust statistic indicating the strength of the link between the defendant and the DNA in the two samples and the number of experiments done on the samples was not enough to support a statistical evaluation. The defendant in the second case was convicted of sexual assault. The victim's body and clothing contained DNA from several persons, including the defendant. An expert for the prosecution stated that the results were more likely to be consistent with the victim's account of the offence than the defendant's account, but he could not express a view on the strength of the support as no statistical evaluation could be carried out. The defendant in the third case was convicted of various offences including murder, all committed during the course of a robbery. Forensic analysis of the doorbell of the premises concerned and a knife found nearby showed complex mixed profiles with the defendant's DNA present in them all. The prosecution expert stated that the defendant had been a contributor to the samples but, without a statistical evaluation, it was not possible to evaluate the weight to be attached to any of the contributors. In all three cases the defendants were convicted after the trial judge ruled the DNA evidence admissible. In their appeals, issues arose concerning the courts' treatment of such evidence. *Held*, the fact that there was no reliable statistical basis did not mean that a court could not admit an evaluative opinion, provided there was some other sufficiently reliable basis for its admission. Provided the very limited basis on which an evaluation could be made without a statistical database was made clear to the jury, it could be assisted in its consideration of the evidence by an expression of an evaluative opinion by experts. If the judge was satisfied and the evidence was admissible, it had to be made very clear to the jury that the evaluation had no statistical basis and that the opinion expressed was quite different to the usual DNA evidence based on statistical match probability. In all three cases the expert evidence on DNA had been relevant, properly admitted and correctly summed up to the jury. Accordingly, the appeals in the first and second case would be dismissed. The appeal in the third case would be allowed on different grounds.

  R v Dlugosz; R v Pickering; R v MDS [2013] EWCA Crim 2, [2013] All ER (D) 01 (Feb) (Court of Appeal: Kitchin LJ and Cox J).

700   Evidence—admissibility—medical expert evidence—relevance

The defendants were the parents of the two-year-old victim. On a visit by a social worker it was noticed that the victim had breathing difficulties. The victim was found to be suffering from bronchiolitis. A few days later he was given a full skeletal survey and metaphyseal fractures were discovered in both his legs and right arm. The defendants were subsequently charged with cruelty to a person under 16. At trial, the jury heard medical expert evidence. It was stated that metaphyseal fractures were notoriously difficult to date but that they had been inflicted between one and six weeks prior to the skeletal survey. Further, it would have been obvious to a person present at the time that the injuries were sustained that the child had been harmed. The expert stated that direct pressure over the injured area would have caused discomfort for about five to ten days after the injuries but that would probably not have been apparent during day to day handling. There had also been evidence from other witnesses that when they had tried to change the victim's nappies he showed distress. However, there had not been any evidence that either of the defendants had been present at the time of those nappy changes. The judge admitted the evidence and ruled that the evidence was relevant to the issue of neglect. In turn, the defendants were both convicted of the offence and sentenced to a term of imprisonment suspended for 12 months with a supervision requirement. The defendants appealed against conviction. *Held*, the evidence of the metaphyseal fractures had to have been striking to the jury. However, the medical evidence on the fractures had not warranted any relevance to the case. That evidence had not been properly probative of the prosecution's case and it should not have been admitted into evidence. Further, the submission that the conviction was safe in any event could not be accepted as it could not be said that a reasonable jury would have convicted the defendants in the absence of the medical evidence of the fractures. Therefore, the convictions would be quashed and there would be no order for re-trial. Accordingly, the appeal would be allowed.

  R v Courage [2013] All ER (D) 79 (Mar) (Court of Appeal: Laws LJ, Keith J and Judge Wide QC).

701   Evidence—admissibility—terrorist offence—dissemination of terrorist publications

See *R v Faraz*, para 668.

702   Evidence—biometric data—destruction, retention and use

The Protection of Freedoms Act 2012 (Destruction, Retention and Use of Biometric Data) (Transitional, Transitory and Saving Provisions) Order 2013, SI 2013/1813 (in force in part on 31 October 2013 and in part on 31 January 2014), makes transitional, transitory and saving provision in connection with the coming into force of the Protection of Freedoms Act 2012 Pt 1 Ch 1 (ss 1–25), on the destruction, retention and use of biometric data. The effects of the order are that (1) subject to certain exceptions and transitional arrangements, biometric material taken before the 2012 Act Pt 1 Ch 1 comes into force (referred to as 'legacy material') is subject to the same regime for destruction, retention and use as material taken after that date; (2) legacy material taken from people who have not been charged with an offence must be destroyed, without the possibility of any application for its retention being made to the Commissioner for the Retention and Use of Biometric Material; (3) applications to court to extend, from three years to five years, the retention period for fingerprints and DNA profiles will be available in relation to legacy material only where the retention period ends at least three months after the order comes into force; (4) legacy material need not be destroyed if it is, or may become, disclosable under the Criminal Procedure and Investigations Act 1996 or its code of practice; (5) legacy material need not be destroyed where it has been taken consensually and is required in connection with the identification of a missing person; (6) legacy material which has been identified as requiring consideration as to whether it should be retained by virtue of a national security determination is not subject to destruction for a period of two years; and (7) for a limited period, fingerprints and DNA profiles may be retained on their respective databases for up to 63 days before their destruction, so as to allow for checks to be carried out against material on those databases.

The Protection of Freedoms Act 2012 (Destruction, Retention and Use of Biometric Data) (Transitional, Transitory and Saving Provisions) (Amendment) Order 2013, SI 2013/2580 (in force on 31 October 2013), amends the principal 2013 Order above so as to (1) provide that fingerprints and DNA samples taken on the basis of purported consent, before the coming into force of the 2012 Act above Pt 1 Ch 1 (ss 1–25), from a person who was convicted of an offence can be retained even if the taking of the fingerprint or DNA sample from which the DNA profile was derived was unlawful; and (2) in certain circumstances, enable a further sample to be taken where a previous sample proves insufficient, including where the previous sample has been destroyed pursuant to a statutory requirement.

The Protection of Freedoms Act 2012 (Destruction, Retention and Use of Biometric Data) (Transitional, Transitory and Saving Provisions) (Amendment) (No 2) Order 2013, SI 2013/2770 (in force on 31 October 2013), amends the principal 2013 Order so that, where a person's DNA profile or fingerprints are taken before 30 September 2014, if the person is arrested for or charged with a subsequent offence, or is convicted or given a penalty notice for a subsequent offence, then that person's profile or fingerprints can be retained by the rules applicable to that subsequent offence.

703   **Evidence—character of accused—bad character—admissibility—risk of prejudice to trial**

The appellant was one of five men accused of stabbing a person to death. At the appellant's trial, the prosecution adduced forensic evidence in the form of seven fibres matching the victim's clothes and two hairs matching the victim's DNA found on a sweatshirt and jeans recovered from the appellant's bedroom. A forensic expert gave evidence that the risk of cross-contamination was minimal. The appellant's brother testified that the clothes found on the appellant's floor might have belonged to him and not the appellant. In closing, the prosecution submitted that secondary transfer could have occurred in relation to contamination of the clothing found on the appellant's floor. The jury was also shown a DVD that contained footage of the appellant displaying racist and violent behaviour in conversation with his friends. Pursuant to the Criminal Justice Act 2003 s 101(1)(d), the judge admitted the DVD evidence on the basis that it could not be used by the jury in considering the issue of whether contamination of the evidence had occurred, and could be used only as evidence of reprehensible behaviour which showed that the appellant had a violent and racist character. The appellant was convicted and applied for leave to appeal against conviction, submitting that (1) the DVD evidence should not have been admitted, as the risk of it causing substantial prejudice outweighed any probative value it had, and it was not proximate in time to the killing so that it could only invite a negative assessment of his views; and (2) the failure of his counsel to request an adjournment to deal with the prosecution's change of approach in respect of the allegations of secondary transfer had been unfair. *Held*, the DVD evidence undeniably constituted evidence of reprehensible behaviour, and although it post-dated the offence by almost two years, it was relevant to important matters in issue such as whether the appellant had the foresight necessary to render him guilty of murder. The judge had been entitled to conclude that the probative value of the evidence exceeded its potentially prejudicial effect. Moreover, the approach of the prosecution to the possibility of secondary transfer in the context of contamination was not unfair or misleading. The jury had to decide whether the hair and fibres came from the victim and that contamination could be excluded, which involved a consideration of secondary transfer in the context of contamination. No aspect of that possibility had been left unexplored in detail in the judge's summing up. The jury then had to consider the issue of participation in the attack, and central to that issue was how the hair and fibres came to be on garments found in the appellant's bedroom. It was nobody's case that the appellant's brother was involved. Only the defence knew what the appellant's brother's evidence would be, and they could have asked for time to consult experts. Accordingly, the application would be dismissed.

R v Norris [2013] EWCA Crim 712, [2013] All ER (D) 178 (May) (Court of Appeal: Leveson LJ, Foskett and Hickinbottom JJ).

704 Evidence—character of person other than defendant—witness—admissibility

The Criminal Justice Act 2003 s 100(1)(b) provides that in criminal proceedings evidence of the bad character of a person other than the defendant is admissible if and only if it has substantial probative value in relation to a matter which is a matter in issue in the proceedings and is of substantial importance in the context of the case as a whole.

The defendant, a commander in the police force, was convicted at a retrial of misconduct in a public office and perverting the course of justice. The case against him was that he had abused the power and authority of his office to arrest and detain and then make false complaints of threat and assault by an individual. That individual, a dishonest man of bad character, was engaged by the defendant to create a web-site. The incident occurred following a dispute which developed between them over the work done and the absence of payment for it. A successful appeal following the first trial was based on emerging evidence that, contrary to the way in which the case had been presented to the jury, the individual was not a man of good character and in particular, that he was not the honest business man portrayed by the prosecution. At the retrial, there was a significant body of evidence independent of both the defendant and the individual. CCTV footage was revealing about the demeanour and attitude to the respective protagonists and there was also evidence of calls to the emergency services. The judge allowed bad character evidence in respect of the individual to be put before the jury in part. However, the judge found that three additional areas of material relating to his character were, in accordance with the 2003 Act s 100(1), inadmissible as they lacked substantial probative value. The defendant appealed against his conviction. *Held*, in the absence of any statutory equivalent to s 101(3), the question was whether in the context of the bad character of a non-defendant there was an exclusionary discretion to avoid satellite litigation. Provided the judge was satisfied that the pre-conditions to admissibility were satisfied, there was none. When it was assessing the probative value of the evidence in accordance with s 100(1)(b), (3), and consistently with s 100(2), among the factors relevant to the admissibility judgment, the court should reflect whether the admission of the evidence relating to the bad character of the witness might make it more difficult for the jury to understand the remainder of the evidence, and whether its understanding of the case as a whole might be diminished. In such cases, the conclusion might be that the evidence was not of substantial probative value in establishing the lack of creditworthiness of the witness, or that the evidence was not of substantial importance in the context of the case as a whole. If so, the preconditions to admissibility would not be established. A fact-specific judgment directed to the conditions in s 100(1)(b), (3) had to be made whether to admit evidence of bad character. Where it applied, the assumption in s 109 was not determinative of the admissibility question. In the circumstances, the evidence excluded by the judge did not begin to undermine the powerful body of evidence independent of the individual which served to prove that, notwithstanding all the criticisms which could be made of him, the guilty verdict was fully justified. Notwithstanding the omission of the evidence, in accordance with the judge's ruling, the conviction was and remained safe. Accordingly, the appeal would be dismissed.

R v Dizaei [2013] EWCA Crim 88, [2013] All ER (D) 160 (Feb) (Court of Appeal: Lord Judge CJ, Wyn Williams and Globe JJ).

705 Evidence—codes of practice—revised codes

The Police and Criminal Evidence Act 1984 (Codes of Practice) (Revisions to Codes A, B, C, E, F and H) Order 2013, SI 2013/2685 (in force on 27 October 2013), brings into force revised codes of practice under the Police and Criminal Evidence Act 1984 s 66(1), which will supersede the corresponding existing codes of practice.

706 Evidence—conviction for offence of causing grievous bodily harm with intent— subsequent death of victim—murder trial—exclusion of evidence of conviction

The Police and Criminal Evidence Act 1984 s 74(3)(a) provides that, in any proceedings where evidence is admissible of the fact that the accused has committed an offence, if the accused is proved to have been convicted of the offence by or before any court in the United Kingdom, he is taken to have committed that offence unless the contrary is proved. In any proceedings, the court may refuse to allow evidence on which the prosecution proposes to rely to be given if it appears that, having regard to all the circumstances, including the circumstances in which the evidence was obtained, the admission of the evidence would have such an adverse effect on the fairness of the proceedings that the court ought not to admit it: s 78.

In separate cases, the defendants had been convicted of offences contrary to the Offences against the Person Act 1861 s 18 of wounding or of causing grievous bodily harm with intent to cause grievous bodily harm. In both cases, the victim of the original offence subsequently died. In one case, the post-mortem of the victim concluded that the original attack and the death some years later were connected. In the other case, the victim died as a result of complications arising from the head injury he had sustained two years earlier. In each case, at trial, evidence was adduced of the defendant's conviction of the offence under the 1861 Act. The defendants appealed on the basis that the earlier convictions based on the opinion of the juries as expressed in their verdicts were irrelevant and inadmissible at the subsequent trials. *Held*, the enactment of the 1984 Act s 74 had, in effect, extended the provisions of the Civil Evidence Act 1968 to the criminal justice process. It had not revived the doctrine of issue estoppel but, in circumstances like those of the present cases, the earlier conviction of the 1861 Act offence constituted admissible evidence to prove, following the death of the victim, that the defendant was guilty not merely of wounding or causing grievous bodily harm with intent, but of murder. The prosecution was not required to prove all the matters already proved to the criminal standard, and the defendant was not prevented or excluded from denying them. In relation to matters already proved against the defendant, the burden of proof shifted to him. The defendant was fully entitled to advance his defence, and if he did, it remained open to the jury to acquit him. The separate safeguard under the 1984 Act s 78, which permitted the judge to exclude the evidence, could not be used to exclude the evidence of earlier convictions on the basis of a nebulous sense of unfairness. There had been no specific features of the cases, the evidence or the circumstances to lead either judge to exercise the s 78 jurisdiction. Accordingly, the appeals would be dismissed.

R v Clift; R v Harrison [2012] EWCA Crim 2750, [2013] 2 All ER 776 (Court of Appeal: Lord Judge CJ, Fulford and Bean JJ). *DPP v Humphrys* [1977] AC 1, [1976] 2 All ER 497, HL (1976 Abr para 626), considered.

707 Evidence—defence statement—alibi notice—failure to give particulars of witness

The defendant had been charged with violent disorder. In his instructions to the appellant firm of solicitors, the defendant identified three potential alibi witnesses, each of whom was a relative although the defendant was unable or unwilling to say which of them, if any, would be able to come to court to give evidence. Counsel specifically advised that the name and addresses of a potential alibi witness should not be disclosed unless and until that witness had provided the appellant with a signed witness statement and further advised that the existence of potential witnesses should not be disclosed. The appellant accepted the advice. A number of appointments were made for the potential alibi witnesses to attend the appellant's offices but the appointments were not kept. On the day before the trial, the defendant attended the firm's offices with his father, who gave proof of evidence that the defendant had been at home at the relevant time. As part of his evidence, he had said that he had returned home from work at a certain time but his employer's records showed that he had left work much later. There was a delay in the trial while a witness from the employer came to court with the records. The father was recalled to give evidence but was unable to do so until the following morning. Subsequently, the jury returned a not guilty verdict. At the conclusion of the trial, the judge required the appellant to attend court to show cause why a wasted costs order should not be awarded having regard to the fact that a day of court had been wasted because the appellant had failed to comply with the rules as to alibi notices. A wasted costs order was made against the appellant on the basis that there had been a deliberate and ill-advised breach of the requirement in the Criminal Procedure and Investigations Act 1996 s 6A(2)(a) to give notice of the particulars of alibi, conduct which had been improper and unreasonable and had caused wasted costs. On the appellant's appeal against the order, *held*, the first question was whether there had been a breach of the requirement for a defence statement to give particulars of any alibi witness in s 6A(2)(a). That requirement was triggered by the defendant's belief that the witness was able to give evidence in support of the alibi. It was not necessary that the alibi witness could give such evidence, let alone that he or she was also willing to do so, nor was the defendant's belief in the witness's ability to give evidence dependent on the witness giving a proof of evidence. The defendant must have known that his father was able to give evidence in support of his alibi that he was at home. In those circumstances, the judge had been right when he held that there had been a breach of the requirements of s 6A(2)(a). However, although the appellant might have fallen into error, in view of its reliance on counsel's advice in good faith, and evidence that the view taken by counsel and the appellant was quite widely held, it could not be said that the appellant had been acting in a way in which no reasonably competent solicitor could have acted in the circumstances. The appellant's conduct was neither improper nor unreasonable, and the wasted costs order would be quashed. Accordingly, the appeal would be allowed.

Re Joseph Hill & Co [2013] EWCA Crim 775, [2014] 1 WLR 786, [2013] All ER (D) 331 (May) (Court of Appeal: Leveson LJ, Wilkie and Openshaw JJ).

708   Evidence—fingerprints and DNA samples—requirement to provide non-intimate sample—refusal

See *R (on the application of R) v A Chief Constable*, para 2075.

709   Evidence—foreign tribunal—evidence of rendition of terrorist suspects—jurisdiction for obtaining evidence

The claimants were charged in Ugandan criminal proceedings with murder and other offences in connection with bombings. They petitioned the Ugandan Constitutional Court claiming that the prosecution was an abuse of process, unconstitutional and that they were the subject of unlawful rendition from Kenya to Uganda. They submitted that they had been subjected to torture and other cruel and inhumane treatment. Their allegations were denied by the relevant authorities in Uganda. In the present jurisdiction, the claimants commenced proceedings seeking relief under principles established in *Norwich Pharmacal Co v Customs and Excise Comrs* claiming that the defendant Secretary of State for Foreign and Commonwealth Affairs had material in the form of information or evidence which, if provided, would assist or enable the claimants to establish their case in the Ugandan Constitutional Court. Because it was anticipated that there would be relevant material which the Secretary of State would not wish to disclose, special advocates were appointed to represent the claimants. A Queen's Bench Divisional Court gave an order which stated that 'if the court's open judgment does not include the full reasons for its decisions, the court shall serve on the [Secretary of State] and the special advocate a separate closed judgment including those reasons'. The substantive proceedings were conducted pursuant to those directions. The court refused the application. Following judgment, a further order was made which ordered the Secretary of State to file and serve a public interest immunity certificate in relation to the withholding from publication of a summary of closed annexes to the court's judgment. The court rejected the Secretary of State's submission to the effect that the earlier order already provided for closed judgments to be withheld without the need for a public interest immunity process. Subsequently, the Secretary of State produced a public interest immunity certificate. The claimants appealed and the Secretary of State cross-appealed. *Held*, where the scheme of the Crime (International Co-operation) Act 2003 was in play, *Norwich Pharmacal* did not run. Three features of the 2003 Act were the discretion of the Secretary of State, the confinement of requests to foreign courts and prosecuting authorities, and the national security and Crown servant exceptions. None of those features was built into the *Norwich Pharmacal* jurisprudence as a mandatory requirement. Those were substantial differences such that Parliament could not have intended the common law remedy to survive the statutory scheme in that area. The statutory scheme enabled the Secretary of State to retain a degree of control over sensitive information or evidence which the *Norwich Pharmacal* remedy would loosen or might deny. To relegate national security to the status of a material consideration to be weighed on a case-by-case basis at the stage of necessity or discretion in a *Norwich Pharmacal* application would be to subvert the carefully calibrated statutory scheme. The Divisional Court had been correct to conclude that it had had no jurisdiction to entertain a *Norwich Pharmacal* application in the present case. Under settled principles, 'necessity' was a test which had to be satisfied if *Norwich Pharmacal* relief was to follow. In the present context, there was no practical or substantial difference between a requirement of necessity in the interests of justice and a test of what was just and convenient in the interests of justice. It was plain that the decision not to make an application for disclosure against the Ugandan government had been a deliberate and a rational one. In dealing with the issue of necessity, the approach of the Divisional Court had been based on a correct understanding of the law. *Norwich Pharmacal* applications were not the subject of a statutory regime in the way that proceedings in the Special Immigration Appeals Commission were. The starting point was that such issues would be dealt with pursuant to CPR 31.10. In the present case, it could not be said that the insistence on a public interest immunity certificate had been wrong. Neither as a matter of principle nor on a construction of the closed material procedure order had the Divisional Court been constrained to deal with all subsequent issues exclusively pursuant to that order. If the court had rationally considered that, at the stage of judgment, the interests of open justice demanded a more exacting regime, there had been no reason why it should not have imposed the additional requirement of a public interest immunity certificate. Accordingly, the appeal and cross-appeal would be dismissed.

R (on the application of Omar) v Secretary of State for Foreign and Commonwealth Affairs) [2013] EWCA Civ 118, [2014] QB 112, [2013] 3 All ER 95 (Court of Appeal: Lord Judge CJ, Maurice Kay VP and Richards LJ). *Norwich Pharmacal Co v Customs and Excise Comrs* [1974] AC 133, [1973] 2 All ER 943, HL (1974 Abr para 2453), considered. Decision of Queen's Bench Divisional Court [2012] EWHC 1737 (Admin), [2013] 1 All ER 161 (2012 Abr para 781) affirmed.

710   Evidence—fresh evidence—expert evidence—admissibility

New Zealand
The dead bodies of the appellant's wife and seven-year-old daughter were found in the family home. The appellant was charged with their murder, even though at the time he had been away on a business trip approximately 140 km away. The prosecution alleged that the appellant had driven home and carried out the murders. The evidence adduced by the prosecution included: (1) an analysis of the contents of the victims' stomachs, supposedly indicative of their time of death; (2) central nervous system tissue from the wife found on a polo shirt belonging to him; and (3) the statement of a computer expert that the computer in the family home had been manipulated to give the appearance of it having been shut down at a different time from when it had actually had. The appellant was convicted of the two murders and was sentenced to life imprisonment. His appeal against conviction was dismissed. On his further appeal, he submitted that there was fresh evidence available which raised questions about the validity of the three forms of evidence used by the prosecution. *Held*, the proper basis on which admission of fresh evidence ought to be decided was by the application of a sequential series of tests. If the evidence was not credible, it ought not to be admitted. If it was credible, the question then arose whether it was fresh in the sense that it was evidence which could not have been obtained for the trial with reasonable diligence. If the evidence was both credible and fresh, it should generally be admitted unless the court was satisfied at that stage that, if admitted, it would have no effect on the safety of the conviction. If the evidence was credible but not fresh, the court ought to assess its strength and its potential impact on the safety of the conviction. If it considered that there was a risk of a miscarriage of justice if the evidence was excluded, it ought to be admitted, notwithstanding that the evidence was not fresh. The requirement that evidence be fresh could be of less critical importance in cases involving scientific evidence. Where a case against an accused rested exclusively or principally on scientific evidence, when, on an appeal, application was made to have admitted new scientific material which presented a significant challenge to that evidence, the court should not be astute to exclude the new material solely because it might have been obtained before the trial. The proper test to be applied by an appellate court in deciding whether a verdict was unsafe or a miscarriage of justice had occurred, where new evidence had been presented, was whether that evidence might reasonably have led to an acquittal. In the circumstances, although all of the proffered new evidence could have been obtained before trial, the interests of justice demanded that it be admitted. The new evidence on the computer issue, if accepted, directly challenged the plausibility of the central prosecution case against the appellant. Substantial questions about the validity of the central nervous system tissue evidence had been raised by the fresh

material. The new evidence on the time of death issue, if accepted, eradicated scientific support for the claim that that was the time of the death of the victims. Accordingly, the appeal would be allowed.

R v Lundy [2013] UKPC 28, [2013] All ER (D) 135 (Oct) (Privy Council: Lord Hope, Dame Sian Ellis, Lord Kerr, Lord Reed and Lord Hughes).

711   Evidence—fresh evidence on appeal—discredited evidence of police officers

The licensee of a public house was robbed in his flat above the premises. During the course of a police interview, one of the defendant's co-accused stated that someone sharing the same first name as the defendant had been involved in the robbery and had gained access to the public house by removing wooden beading around a window using an iron bar. He also told the interviewing officers that he had arranged to meet the defendant prior to a planned robbery at a post office. Acting on this intelligence, the police met the defendant at the agreed meeting point and recovered from his vehicle a knife, two screwdrivers, two crowbars and a crash helmet. The defendant was arrested and interviewed by two police officers. The police asserted that the defendant acknowledged his participation in the robbery in the police interview, although this was denied by the defendant. The defendant was convicted of robbery and conspiracy to rob. He sought to appeal against both convictions. His case was investigated by the Criminal Cases Review Commission, which concluded that there was fresh evidence concerning the two officers who had interviewed the defendant that gave rise to a real possibility that the convictions were unsafe. The first officer had been part of a serious crime squad which had been found to be involved in numerous instances of corruption and misconduct. In particular, he had been involved in two cases where convictions had been quashed as a result of unreliable police evidence. The second officer had failed to disclose a forensic report which concluded that the tools found in the defendant's vehicle could not have been used to gain entry to the public house, and an entry in his notebook recording a description of the defendant by his co-accused had been altered. *Held*, the conviction for the robbery depended critically on the reliability of the police evidence as to the defendant's interview. Such reliability could have been undermined at the trial if the first officer had been cross examined on his involvement in other cases which had involved fabricated or allegedly fabricated confessions, sometimes in circumstances with similarities to the present case, against the background of his membership of the discredited serious crime squad. The evidence concerning the second officer made it difficult to contend that he had been an entirely untainted witness whose evidence provided independent support for the evidence of the first officer. As the reliability of the police evidence had been called into serious question, the conviction for robbery could not be regarded as safe. In relation to the conspiracy to rob, although no explanation had ever been offered for the defendant's appearance at the time and place predicted by his co-accused, it could not be disputed that on their own neither the evidence of the co-accused nor the circumstances of the defendant's arrest would have been a safe basis for a conviction. Accordingly, the appeals would be allowed.

R v Foran [2013] EWCA Crim 437, [2013] All ER (D) 232 (Apr) (Court of Appeal: Leveson LJ, Mitting and Males JJ).

712   Evidence—identification—inconsistent evidence—admission at trial

The defendant was arrested on suspicion of being involved in a violent altercation between rival drug dealers in which one man was killed and another wounded. One of the witnesses to the attack (the 'relevant witness') telephoned the police on the day after the incident and described the attacker as slim with very short blonde hair, with a very clean appearance, wearing a horizontally striped upper garment. She also stated that she had deliberately taken a good look of the assailant's face and would definitely recognise him again. Those details were recorded in a note, but the relevant witness neither read through nor signed that document. In her later witness statement, the relevant witness described the assailant as having a stocky, quite muscular build with very light brown or mousy, but definitely not blonde, hair. The defendant was subsequently identified by the relevant witness in an identification parade. At the defendant's trial for murder, the judge directed the jury to pay particular attention to the question of whether there had been any material discrepancies or differences between the description of the man given by the relevant witness to the police and in her evidence, as against the actual appearance of the defendant. The defendant was convicted. He appealed against conviction, contending that it was unsafe on the grounds that the note of the relevant witness's statement to the police should have been admitted at trial and that there had no corroboration of the relevant witness's identification of the defendant. *Held*, in view of the way in which the cross-examination had proceeded, there had been sound tactical reasons for leaving the note to one side. However, in any event, making the decision years later, on paper, could not possibly replicate the difficulties involved in the strategic decision about the conduct of a case in which so much turned on the cross-examination of the witness. The decision at the trial had not been unreasonable. There was a sufficient explanation for the decision not to deploy the contents of the note in cross-examination: in essence, the overall effect might have been to diminish the progress which was thought to have been made. Despite that, the interests of justice did require the court to admit the note into evidence. On reflecting and examining the relevant witness's identification of the defendant, if the contents of the note had been used some further inconsistencies in her description would have emerged. However, there would have been a correspondingly increased concentration on what she, at the time, had actually been focusing her attention. The reality was that the correctness of her identification of the defendant had been given very powerful support by the remaining evidence. Without the benefit of the contents of the note, the jury had not entertained any reservations about it, and having examined the contents of the note, it could not be said that the conviction was unsafe. Accordingly, the appeal would be dismissed.

R v Cole [2013] EWCA Crim 1149, [2013] All ER (D) 80 (Jul) (Court of Appeal: Lord Judge LCJ, MacKay and Griffith Williams JJ).

713   Evidence—overseas witnesses—evidence through television link

The Evidence Through Television Links (England and Wales) Order 2013, SI 2013/1598 (in force on 22 July 2013), permits evidence in extradition proceedings in England and Wales to be given by witnesses who are outside the United Kingdom through a television link.

714   Evidence—personal and family impact statements—use and relevance to sentence— guidance

The Court of Appeal has given the following guidance in three cases heard together in which a number of different questions about victim personal statements and, in cases of homicide, family impact statements, arose. With respect to victim personal statements and family impact statements, it is important to emphasise that (1) the decision whether to make a statement has to be made by the victims personally and they have to be provided with information which makes it clear that they are entitled to make a statement but no pressure, either way, should be brought to bear on their decision; (2) when the decision whether to make a statement is being made, it has to be clearly understood that the victim's opinion about the type and level of sentence ought not to be included; (3) the statement constitutes evidence, is admitted on that basis, has to be treated as evidence and has to be served on the defendant's legal advisors in time for the defendant's instructions to be taken, and for any objection to the use of the statement to be prepared; (4) just because the statement is intended to inform the sentencing court of specific features of the consequences of the offence on the victim, responsibility for presenting admissible evidence remains with the prosecution; (5) the statement may be challenged, in cross-examination, and it may give rise to disclosure obligations; and (6) it will seldom be appropriate for a statement to be introduced at a sentencing appeal if it has not been before the sentencing court. The Power of Criminal Courts (Sentencing) Act 2000 s 155 provides a valuable safety net in the sentencing process, enabling the judge to reflect on the sentencing decision and, if so minded within a statutory period, to amend it. However, it is no more and no less than a further hearing in the original case and, as such, ought to be listed so that all the interested parties, not only the defendant, but the victims, and the public and the media may be present if they wish. Further, unless there has been some breakdown in communication, late service of victim impact statements is wholly inappropriate, wrong in principle and must stop.

R v Perkins [2013] EWCA Crim 323, [2013] All ER (D) 313 (Mar) (Court of Appeal: Lord Judge CJ, Simon and Irwin JJ). *R v Nunn* [1996] 2 Cr App Rep (S) 136, CA (1996 Abr para 2716), applied.

715   Evidence—privilege—legal professional privilege—covert surveillance—privileged material recorded but not admitted in evidence

The defendant and the deceased had been in a short but turbulent relationship. The deceased was found dead in the defendant's home. A post mortem was carried out and a pathologist concluded that she had possibly died as a result of asphyxiation involving neck compression but did not conclusively exclude the possibility of death from natural causes. The defendant was arrested and made no comment during interview. Authorisation was given and approved for the use of intrusive surveillance in the defendant's home. While under surveillance the defendant made significant admissions of his responsibility for the death of the deceased. He also talked about discussions he had had with his lawyers, which were subject to legal privilege. The surveillance also revealed strong evidence that the defendant and his parents had been conspiring together to pervert the course of justice. At the trial, the covert surveillance evidence was admitted and the defendant convicted of the murder of the deceased. He appealed against conviction on the grounds that the indictment should have been stayed as an abuse of process arising from the use of intrusive covert surveillance or, alternatively, the evidence derived from that surveillance had been unfairly admitted in evidence when it should have been excluded under the Police and Criminal Evidence Act 1984 s 78. *Held*, if covert surveillance was likely to result in the acquisition of knowledge and matters subject to legal privilege, approval could not be made unless there were exceptional and compelling circumstances justifying it. An application for covert surveillance should explain the steps which would be taken to ensure that any information subject to legal privilege would not be used, either for the purposes of further investigations or during the course of any subsequent criminal trials. Arrangements for covert surveillance had to focus meticulous attention on a need to preserve legal privilege, and where, for one reason or another, the relevant precautions had failed, to ensure that the interests of the potential defendant during the course of the investigation itself, or at any other subsequent trial, were not prejudiced in consequence. In the present case, the covert surveillance had been lawful and the defendant's legal privilege had not been interfered with in any way which undermined the integrity of the administration of justice. Therefore, there had been no ground to justify a stay. None of the evidence of the conversation between the defendant and his family adduced in evidence had been tainted by unfairness falling within s 78. The covert surveillance had secured damaging admissions because the defendant had not realised that he was being recorded. However, the object of the use of covert surveillance had been to discover the truth and, while the evidence of what the defendant had said about the death of the deceased had been before the jury, anything containing even a whisper of conversations protected by legal privilege had been excluded. That had not been unfair. Accordingly, the appeal would be dismissed.

R v Turner [2013] EWCA Crim 642, [2013] All ER (D) 97 (May) (Court of Appeal: Lord Judge CJ, Royce and Globe JJ).

716   Evidence—retraction of evidence

It has been held that in applications or appeals based on evidence of alleged retractions or inconsistent statements made by a prosecution witness there is nothing which requires the witness concerned to be called and cross-examined about the making of the alleged statements. The best and fairest procedure to adopt depends on the particular circumstances of the case.

R v V (S) [2013] EWCA Crim 159, [2013] 1 Cr App Rep 467 (Court of Appeal: Davis LJ, Bean and Griffith Williams JJ).

717   Evidence—witness—credibility—fraud

The respondents were a husband and wife who owned and controlled an insurance broker which had established an insurance product. For a number of years they participated in a packaged scheme devised and managed by a group of companies of which the ultimate holding company had been the appellant. Under the scheme, policies were issued to the clients of the broker, which were underwritten by the American insurer of the appellant. The policies were issued on the American insurer's behalf by the broker under an agency agreement. The American insurer would be reinsured in respect of its liability under the policies under a programme of reinsurances and indemnities, the object of which was to ensure that the profits or losses of the business were indirectly passed back, initially to the broker and then to the respondents personally. The case concerned negotiations for the renewal of the programme for an extra year. Two former employees of the appellant approached the respondents and alleged that the extra year renewal had been procured by fraud, and offered to give evidence in support of those allegations. At trial, the judge reviewed the evidence and rejected the allegations against the appellant. The main reason was that he had not regarded the former employees as reliable witnesses and had not believed the critical parts of their evidence. On appeal by the respondents, it was found that the trial judge should have accepted the evidence of the former employees. It was also found that the former employees' allegations could be supported. On appeal by the appellants, held, the material that the appellate court had relied on for its finding of fraud had been wholly inadequate. The judge at the trial had found that one of the former employees had been inconsistent, evasive and untruthful and that his evidence had been bought for a substantial sum, a fact which he had not disclosed. It was also found that the other former employee had tailored his evidence to suit that of his former colleague. Those considerations appeared to be compelling reasons for treating their evidence with great reserve. Further, it had been common ground that emails had been false and a letter did not bear the weight which the appellate court had placed on it. Accordingly, the appeal would be allowed.

Mutual Holdings (Bermuda) Ltd v Hendricks [2013] UKPC 13, [2013] All ER (D) 73 (Jun) (Privy Council: Lord Neuberger, Lady Hale, Lord Mance, Lord Wilson and Lord Sumption).

718   Evidence—witness—protection of witness—reporting direction

A witness gave evidence at the criminal trial of the first and second accused. The witness was the former partner of the first accused and had four children with him. They had previously appeared a number of times on television and had been the subject of extensive media coverage and public interest. A dispute concerning the children broke out between the witness and the first accused, which led to the first accused starting a fire at his home with the intention that the witness would be held to blame. The fire killed six children. The witness had been concerned that, in giving live oral evidence, her identity and that of her children would be revealed. The witness applied for special measures to be implemented, pursuant to the Youth Justice and Criminal Evidence Act 1999 s 23(1), in order for her evidence to be given behind a screen in court. The judge allowed the special measures to be implemented and also made an order under s 46 prohibiting the publication of photographs of the witness or any of her children until after the trial. An application was made by the appellant media organisations for revocation of the order, but the application was dismissed. The judge was of the view that no-one listening to the case would have found it easy to understand the purpose of the publication of photographs or films of the witness and her children. The appellants' appealed, submitting that the witness had already been identified by previous publications, television programmes and the internet, and that her name and her identification as the mother of the children of whom the first accused was the father was effectively common knowledge. Held, in the overwhelming majority of cases, the identity of every witness was known. If the jurisdiction to make an order under s 46 was restricted in the way suggested by the appellants, the eligibility test would be virtually confined to the rare case of the anonymous witness. Section 46(7) extended beyond the bare naming of the witness. Thus, a still or moving picture of the witness might be prohibited if the eligibility test was satisfied, whether the name and identity of the witness was otherwise known. That approach was reinforced by analysis of the wide ranging excepting direction in s 46(9), which anticipated that the ambit of the reporting restriction might be much wider than the mere naming of the witness. It anticipated that the reporting restriction might impose substantial restrictions on reporting which, in the context of the public interest, were unreasonable. If the appellants were right, neither the provisions in s 46(7) or those in s 46(9) would be necessary. As it was, they demonstrated that the ambit of the reporting direction was much wider than suggested, but s 46(9) also underlined that even when a reporting restriction was appropriate, it should be no wider than necessary to avoid any diminution in the quality of the evidence to be given by the witness. Accordingly, the appeal would be dismissed.

ITN News v R [2013] EWCA Crim 773, [2014] 1 WLR 199, [2013] All ER (D) 258 (May) (Court of Appeal: Lord Judge CJ, Royce and Globe JJ).

719   Evidence—witness—special measures for child witness—sexual offences

The Special Measures for Child Witnesses (Sexual Offences) Regulations 2013, SI 2013/2971 (in force on 18 December 2013), further amends the Youth Justice and Criminal Evidence Act 1999 s 33 so as to extend the presumption that a complainant of a relevant offence whose age is uncertain is under 18 years of age if there are reasons to believe that person is under the age of 18, to victims of sexual offences under the Youth Justice and Criminal Evidence Act 1999 s 62 and victims of indecent image offences under the Protection of Freedom Act 1978 s 1 and the Criminal Justice Act 1988 s 160, thereby making such witnesses eligible for special measures for the protection and assistance of witnesses.

720   Harassment—defence—preventing or detecting crime—test of rationality

See *Hayes v Willoughby*, para 2367.

721   Indictment—amendment—application by prosecution—amendment after guilty plea

The defendants pleaded guilty to burglary contrary to the Theft Act 1968 s 9(1)(a). Prior to sentencing, it was realised that different sentencing provisions came into operation if the indictment referred specifically to a dwelling rather than to a building. The trial judge allowed an application by the prosecution for the indictment to be amended to refer to a dwelling. The defendants were then re-arraigned and again pleaded guilty. On their appeal against conviction, the defendants submitted that the first guilty plea had not been properly vacated. *Held*, an indictment may, on application by the prosecution, be amended even after a guilty plea has been entered and an order may be made for the guilty plea to be vacated. *R v JW* established that the trial judge had power to amend the indictment. Contrary to the defendants' submission, the first guilty plea had been properly vacated. There was no material irregularity, no prejudice to the defendants other than to prevent them from taking advantage of an error, and no unfairness. Accordingly, the appeal would be dismissed.

R v Love; R v Hyde [2013] EWCA Crim 257, [2013] 2 Cr App Rep 43 (Court of Appeal: Richards LJ, Globe J and Judge Kramer QC). *R v JW* (21 April 1999, unreported), CA, considered.

722   Indictment—defect—statement of offence—error—mislabelling—safety of conviction

See *R v Wilson*, para 1256.

723   International co-operation—evidence—power to make production order

The Crime (International Co-operation) Act 2003 s 13(1)(b) provides that where a request for assistance in obtaining evidence in a part of the United Kingdom is received by the territorial authority for that part, the authority may direct that a search warrant be applied for under or by virtue of s 16 or s 17, or in relation to Scotland, s 18.

The Home Office received a request from the United States of America central authority for evidence for use in a criminal investigation. There was no dispute that the evidence was held or that it was received in confidence and constituted special procedure material under the Police and Criminal Evidence Act 1984 s 14. In turn the Court refused to release the documents without a court order. Later, a detective constable applied for a production order under the 2003 Act. The judge of the defendant Crown Court found that he could not make the order because there was no statutory authority permitting the claimant to direct that an application for a production order be made, as she could only direct the application for a warrant. The applicant sought judicial review of that decision. It was contended that the omission of a reference to a production order in s 13(1)(b) had been a mistake, given the provisions of s 16. The applicant relied on the facts that a direction for an application for a production order could be made under the Criminal Justice (International Co-operation) Act 1990 s 7 and that the long title of the 2003 Act had expressly provided that its purpose was 'to make provision for furthering co-operation with other countries in respect of criminal proceedings and investigations'. *Held*, s 13(1)(b) had to be read as 'direct that a search warrant or order be applied for under or by virtue of s 16 or s 17 or, in relation to evidence in Scotland, s 18'. It was settled law that it was the task of the court to make sense of the text of the statutory provision read in its appropriate context and within the limits of the judicial role. The courts had to abstain from any course which might have the appearance of judicial legislation. Therefore, the courts exercised considerable caution before adding or omitting or substituting words. Before interpreting a statute in that way, the court had to be abundantly sure of three matters: (1) the intended purpose of the statute or provision in question; (2) that, by inadvertence, the draftsman and Parliament had failed to give effect to that purpose in the provision in question; and (3) the substance of the provision Parliament would have made, although not necessarily the precise words Parliament would have used, had the error in the Bill been noticed. Sometimes, however, even when those conditions were met, the court might find itself inhibited from interpreting the statutory provision in accordance with what it was satisfied had been the underlying intention of Parliament. The alteration in language might be too far-reaching or the subject matter might call for a strict interpretation of the statutory language, as in penal legislation. Further, law had to be accessible and foreseeable. The restriction on the ability to co-operate, by virtue of the omission in s 13(1)(b) of the power to direct an application for a production order, was a manifest contraction of the clear purpose of the 2003 Act. The clear purpose of s 16 was to include within the extended statutory search power the method of assistance, namely, the obtaining of a production order. Section 16 could only sensibly be deployed if s 13(1)(b) was read to include the power to direct an application for a production order. The omission of such power had been inadvertent. Accordingly, the application would be allowed.

R (on the application of Secretary of the State for Home Department) v Southwark Crown Court [2013] All ER (D) 197 (Dec) (Queen's Bench Division: Moses LJ and Griffith Williams J). *Inco Europe Ltd v First Choice Distribution (a firm)* [2000] 2 All ER 109, HL (2000 Abr para 209); and *R (on the application of Purdy) v DPP* [2009] UKHL 45, [2010] 1 AC 345, [2009] 4 All ER 1147 (2009 Abr para 942) applied.

724 International co-operation—participating countries—designation

The Crime (International Co-operation) Act 2003 (Designation of Participating Countries) (England, Wales and Northern Ireland) Order 2013, SI 2013/296 (in force on 15 February 2013), designates the Republic of Armenia, the Republic of Chile and Ukraine as participating countries for the purposes of the Crime (International Co-operation) Act 2003 ss 31, 47, 48, Sch 2 para 15 so that the United Kingdom may comply with, and benefit fully from, the provisions of an agreement between the European Union and those countries on mutual legal assistance in criminal matters.

725 Legal aid

See LEGAL AID.

726 Miscarriage of justice—compensation—new or newly discovered fact

In several conjoined cases in which the claimants' convictions for criminal offences had been reversed by the Court of Appeal, the court gave the following guidance as to when compensation for a miscarriage of justice was to be awarded under the Criminal Justice Act 1988 s 133 in cases where a new or newly discovered fact so undermined the evidence against the defendant that no conviction could possibly be based on it. The guidance was given in the light of the decision of the Supreme Court in *R (on the application of Adams) v Secretary of State for Justice*, in which the principle that compensation was available in such cases had been established. (1) It was not straightforward to formulate the additional category or categories of case which the Supreme Court had held would qualify as a miscarriage of justice under s 133. However, the useful formulation would be whether the claimant had established, beyond reasonable doubt that no reasonable jury or magistrates, properly directed as to the law, could convict on the evidence to be considered. (2) Circumstances where it would be proper for the Secretary of State to take a different view of a case from that taken by the Court of Appeal could not be conceived of, save where the evidence had evolved after the hearing of the appeal. A statement from the court that, given the state of the evidence, the case should have been withdrawn from the jury at the close of the prosecution case, might well be of particular significance. Broadly, any conclusion and order of the Court of Appeal would carry the greatest weight, but it had to be borne in mind at all times that the court was focused on a different question: was the conviction unsafe. (3) Save in the most exceptional circumstances, after a retrial at which there had been a proper case to go to the jury, a claimant would not be able to establish a valid claim for compensation for miscarriage of justice pursuant to *Adams*. It might occasionally happen that fresh evidence would become available after the second trial which was capable of demonstrating the innocence of a convicted person. However, such a development was no basis for finding that a claimant was not properly convicted at the retrial. All that could be said was that the particular circumstances of each case had to be looked at, and it was not a sufficient exercise of reasoning on the part of the Secretary of State when dismissing a claim simply to recite the fact that the Court of Appeal had granted permission to the prosecution to have a second trial. (4) Under the general principles of public law, a decision which was not successfully challenged was presumed to be valid. (5) Nothing justified the Secretary of State dismissing the law of evidence, or the rulings of judges in given cases. In the absence of a change in the evidence coming later than a given judicial ruling, it would be proper for the Secretary of State to differ from such a ruling only in the rarest of circumstances and only on a fully reasoned basis. The decisions of the Secretary of State were susceptible to judicial review. It was not acceptable for the Secretary of State in effect simply to advance the proposition 'another judge might have decided differently'. If the Secretary of State did intend to take a different conclusion from that reached by a judge, a claimant was entitled to know why. (6) With respect to common law principles, the majority of the Supreme Court in *Adams* had not adopted the substitutionary approach. It was clear from s 133 that Parliament had given the Secretary of State the function of determining whether a new or newly discovered fact showed beyond reasonable doubt that there has been a miscarriage of justice, subject to the control of the courts on the principles of ordinary judicial review. Further, the process of a claim for judicial review satisfied the requirement of the European Convention on Human Rights art 6 that the determination overall be by an independent and impartial tribunal. (7) It was settled law that, if the law was changed or suddenly discovered, it was right that it should be applied in its new form thereafter, but if it was to be applied retrospectively, that had to be subject to some limitation. Judgment would be given accordingly.

R (on the application of Ali) v Secretary of State for Justice [2013] EWHC 72 (Admin), [2013] 2 All ER 1055 (Queen's Bench Division: Beatson LJ and Irwin J). *R (on the application of Adams) v Secretary of State for Justice; Re MacDermott* [2011] UKSC 18, [2012] 1 AC 48, [2011] 3 All ER 261 (2011 Abr para 750) explained.

This decision has been affirmed in part on appeal: [2014] EWCA Civ 194, [2014] All ER (D) 254 (Feb).

727 Perversion of course of justice—scope of offence—breach of restraint order

The defendant was the director of a company that provided finance to other possibly insolvent businesses. A director ('the borrower') of a company that had operated a large-scale tax fraud ('the borrowing company') was the subject of a restraint order pursuant to the Proceeds of Crime Act 2002 that prohibited him from disposing of his own or the borrowing company's assets. The restraint order made no allowance for using the restrained funds to pay legal fees. However, it was permissible for a third party to use its own money to meet a legal bill if it was a genuine gift and not a loan dressed up as a gift. The borrower obtained a 12-month loan from the defendant to pay his legal fees. The borrower subsequently informed the defendant that he was subject to a restraint order and that his solicitors would accept money only if it was a gift and not a loan. The defendant agreed to tell the solicitors that the funds to be transferred to them were a gift. Repayments on the loan were effectively made using the borrowing company's restrained funds. The defendant was charged with conspiracy to pervert the course of justice by dishonestly removing or attempting to remove from the court's control assets which should have remained restrained and available for confiscation. The defence submitted that there was no case to answer on the basis that a breach of a restraint order made under the 2002 Act, involving no illegality beyond the breach of the order itself, should be punished by way of contempt proceedings alone rather than by a prosecution for perverting the course of justice. The defendant was convicted and, on his appeal, *held*, there was no closed list of acts which might give rise to the offence of perverting the course of justice. That said, any expansion of the offence should take place only incrementally and with caution, reflecting both common law reasoning and the requirements of the European Convention on Human Rights. So far as concerned the offence generally, neither authority nor principle supported confining the requisite acts to those giving rise to some other independent criminal wrongdoing. If there was no such limitation generally, then there was no basis for importing such a restriction, as a matter of law, into the elements of the offence where it arose in the context of a breach of a restraint order. It followed that a breach of a restraint order made under the 2002 Act involving no illegality beyond the breach of the order itself was capable, without more, of constituting the offence of perverting the course of justice. In the present case, so far as factual or discretionary considerations were at all relevant, it had not been inappropriate for perverting the course of justice to have been charged. The defendant's actions had formed part of a carefully orchestrated and planned series of measures designed to frustrate the intended effect of the restraint order. Accordingly, the appeal would be dismissed.

R v Kenny [2013] EWCA Crim 1, [2013] 1 Cr App Rep 291, [2013] All ER (D) 09 (Feb) (Court of Appeal: Gross LJ, Burnett J and the Recorder of Bristol). *R v Ludlam* [2011] EWCA Crim 1340 (unreported) distinguished.

728   Plea of guilty—factual basis of plea—sentence—guidance

In four conjoined appeals, the Court of Appeal gave the following guidance as to the approach to be taken when sentencing a defendant who has pleaded guilty on a specified factual basis. (1) A basis of plea should not be agreed on a misleading or untrue set of facts and must take proper account of the victim's interests. In cases involving multiple defendants, the bases of plea for each defendant must be factually consistent with each other. (2) The written basis of plea must be scrutinised by the prosecution with great care such that if a defendant seeks to mitigate on the basis of assertions of fact outside the prosecutor's knowledge, the judge ought to be invited not to accept that version unless given on oath and tested in cross-examination. If evidence is not given in that way, the judge might draw such inference as he thinks fit from that fact. (3) The prosecution advocate must ensure that the defence advocate is aware of the basis on which the plea is accepted and the way in which the case will be opened. Where a basis of plea is agreed, it ought to be submitted to the judge prior to the opening. It should not contain matters that are in dispute. If it is not agreed, the basis of plea ought to be set out in writing identifying what is in issue, and, if the court decides that the dispute is material to sentence, it can direct further representations or evidence in accordance with the principles set out in *R v Newton*. (4) Both sides must ensure that the judge is aware of any discrepancy between the basis of plea and the prosecution case that could potentially have a significant effect on sentence so that consideration could be given to holding a Newton hearing. Even where the basis of plea is agreed between the prosecution and the defence, the judge is not bound by such agreement. However, if the judge is minded not to accept the basis of plea in a case where that might affect sentence, he must say so. (5) There is no obligation to hold a Newton hearing (a) if the difference between the two versions of fact is immaterial to sentence; (b) where the defence version can be described as manifestly false or wholly implausible; or (c) where the matters put forward by the defendant do not contradict the prosecution case but constitute extraneous mitigation where the court is not bound to accept the truth of the matters put forward, irrespective of whether they were challenged by the prosecution. (6) At the conclusion of a Newton hearing, the judge must provide a reasoned decision as to his findings of fact and, following mitigation, proceed to sentence. (7) After conviction following a trial, a judge is bound to honour the verdicts of the jury, but, provided he does so, he is entitled to form his own view of the facts in the light of the evidence. However, it is not correct to say that a Newton hearing is never appropriate after a trial. If an issue not relevant to guilt but relevant to sentence has not been canvassed in the trial, a further hearing may be necessary.

R v Cairns; R v Morris; R v Rafiq; R v Firfire [2013] EWCA Crim 467, [2013] All ER (D) 12 (May) (Court of Appeal: Leveson LJ, Mitting and Males JJ). *R v Newton* (1982) 77 Cr App Rep 13, CA (1983 Abr para 2994), applied.

729   Plea of guilty—indication of sentence by judge in advance of plea—safety of conviction

While the defendant was serving abroad the rented accommodation that he shared was searched and a firearm and ammunition were found. The defendant was charged with possession of a prohibited firearm and possession of ammunition, contrary to the Firearms Act 1968 s 5(1)(aba), (1)(c). On the morning of the trial the defendant's counsel applied for the intermediary was appointed as the defendant's intermediary in the trial. In summing up, the judge directed the jury that no adverse inference should be drawn from the fact that the defendant had not answered questions in interview. However, he did direct the jury that it was open to them to draw an inference from his failure to give evidence. Subsequently, the defendant and co-accused were convicted of murder. The defendant was sentenced to detention, the minimum term specified being 14 years while the co-accused were sentenced to life imprisonment and each received a minimum term of 16 years. It had been agreed between the prosecution and the defence that the appropriate starting point in the defendant's case was 12 years. In relation to the co-accused, the starting point was 15 years. The difference arose because the defendant was 17 at the time of the offence, whereas the co-accused were over 18. The defendant appealed. *Held*, the judge's ruling had been based on wide considerations which appeared to be appropriate. He had been entitled to look beyond the expert material put before him including the defendant's behaviour after the event, the fact that an intermediary had been in place, the anticipated approach of a fair-minded jury, and the nature of the account to be given by the defendant. The judge's approach and assessment of the situation resulted in a decision to which he had been entitled to come. That decision was not incorrect. Further, there was some justification in the defendant's submission that there was a failure to take all possible steps to assist him to understand and participate in the proceedings. However, the defendant had nonetheless been able to participate meaningfully in the trial. He had a grasp of the essential issues. The evidence had not been complicated. The defendant had been able to convey his defence to his legal team. He had understood sufficiently that his potential involvement went beyond his own actions. While, in the defendant's case, a small increase in the minimum term had been justified, it had not justified the extent of the increase given by the judge. The offence had truly been a joint enterprise and the defendant should not have been singled out by a greater increase in the minimum term than his co-defendants. The minimum term that the defendant had to serve before he was eligible for parole would be reduced to 13 years. To that extent the appeal against sentence would be allowed. Judgment would be given accordingly.

R v Dixon [2013] EWCA Crim 465, [2013] 3 All ER 242 (Court of Appeal: Treacy LJ, Saunders J and Judge Milford QC). *R v Tabbakh* [2009] EWCA Crim 464, [2009] All ER (D) 29 (Mar) (2009 Abr para 954) applied.

745   Trial—fitness to plead—person with learning disability—appeal proceedings

Trinidad and Tobago

The appellant was found guilty of murder and received a mandatory death sentence. His appeal against conviction was dismissed and he then instructed a clinical psychologist to assess his mental state. The psychologist concluded that the appellant had a significant learning disability, and expressed doubts that the appellant would have understood the legal process sufficiently well to have offered a competent defence. The appellant sought permission to appeal and to adduce fresh evidence as to his fitness to plead. It fell to be determined whether the appellant had in fact been unfit to plead or stand trial. *Held*, it would be only in an exceptional case that the Privy Council would entertain the argument that an appellant had not been fit to stand trial because he was of low intelligence due to a learning disability when the point was not taken on his behalf by counsel at trial. It was the responsibility of counsel to assess whether his client was fit to stand trial. He was in the best position to judge whether the client was able to understand the charge that had been brought against him and to give instructions for his defence. The Board would not permit the introduction of that issue for the first time at the final stage unless the evidence pointed very clearly to the fact that there had been a miscarriage of justice. The evidence indicated that it was unlikely that the trial court would have held that the appellant was not fit to plead. Accordingly, the appeal would be dismissed.

Taitt v Trindad and Tobago [2012] UKPC 38, [2012] 1 WLR 3730, [2012] All ER (D) 95 (Dec) (Privy Council: Lord Hope, Lord Wilson and Lord Carnwath).

746   Trial—indictment—amendment—unfair prejudice to defendant

The defendant was accused of committing sexual offences against the complainant, a child aged 14. The defendant was charged with a number of counts of sexual activity with a child and one count of rape. At trial, the judge acceded to the prosecution's application to amend the indictment to add a further count charging the defendant with sexual activity with a child as an alternative to the count of rape. He stated that, while the prosecution case remained that the complainant was raped, there were indications in the evidence that, despite her denials, she might have been a willing participant. The judge further observed that it was open to the jury to decide that it was sure that sexual intercourse occurred between the complainant and defendant on the occasion described, but that it was not sure that it was without consent. The defendant's case throughout was that nothing sexual had occurred. The jury acquitted the defendant of rape, but found him guilty on the alternative count. On appeal against conviction, the defendant submitted that the judge's decision to allow the prosecution to amend the indictment was unfairly prejudicial. He argued that had defence counsel known when cross-examining the complainant that the judge would later permit the amendment, he would not, following an interruption by the judge, so easily have stopped his cross-examination of her as to the physical details of her allegation of rape. *Held*, provided that the jury was sure that the act of intercourse occurred between the complainant and defendant, it was open to it to convict on the alternative count solely on the factual basis that it could not be sure that the complainant had protested as she had claimed. The only arguable claim to prejudice arose from the submission that the cross-examination of the complainant on the detail of the alleged intercourse was foreclosed by the intervention of the judge. However, there was no doubt that, had defence counsel elected to continue cross-examining the complainant on the act she described, it could only have redounded to the disadvantage of the defendant. The nature of the defendant's case never changed. At no time did he assert that he had consensual sex with the complainant, rather he always asserted that sexual intercourse never took place. It was, at all times, in the interests of the defendant if defence counsel could establish his point. However, he could not have done so to any extent which could have been to the defendant's benefit. Accordingly, the appeal would be dismissed.

R v B [2013] EWCA Crim 2301, [2013] All ER (D) 223 (Nov) (Court of Appeal: Pitchford LJ, Nicola Davies J and Judge Collier QC).

747   Trial—stay of proceedings—mental state of defendant—discretionary jurisdiction

Prior to a proposed second retrial on counts of sexual exploitation of children or very young adults, the respondent was seen by a general practitioner and diagnosed as suffering from anxiety and depression. Soon after, the respondent was described as not fit to stand trial. His legal representatives applied for a stay of the remaining counts on the indictment. The stay was granted after the judge found that a further trial could justifiably be said to be oppressive and unjust. The Crown applied for leave to appeal pursuant to the Criminal Justice Act 2003 s 58. *Held*, when a judge had exercised his discretion or made his judgment for the purposes of and in the course of a criminal trial, the very fact that he had carefully had to balance conflicting considerations would almost inevitably mean that he might reasonably have reached a different, or the opposite, conclusion to the one he had reached. Leave to appeal under s 67 would not be given unless it was seriously arguable, not that the discretionary jurisdiction might have been exercised differently, but that it had been unreasonable for it to have been exercised in the way that it had. The mere fact that the judge could reasonably have reached the opposite conclusion to the one reached, and that he acknowledged that there had been valid arguments which might have caused him to do so, did not begin to provide a basis for a successful appeal. The core question in the case related to the issue of whether a trial would be oppressive. In that context clearly the medical evidence had been of importance. The judge had been entitled to rely on that evidence and to decline the prosecution's application for a further investigation in the exercise of his discretion. It could not be characterised as an unreasonable decision. Therefore, leave to appeal would be refused and the judge's ruling confirmed. Judgment would be given accordingly.

R v Hussain [2013] EWCA Crim 707, [2013] All ER (D) 125 (May) (Court of Appeal: Treacy LJ, Burnett and Edwards-Stuart JJ). *Prosecution Appeal; R v Bell* [2010] EWCA Crim 3, [2010] All ER (D) 109 (Jan) (2010 Abr para 836) applied.

748   Trial—summing up—direction to jury—adverse inference—no comment interview and prepared statement

The victim was at home when a group attempted to rob him. In an emergency call and in two subsequent witness statements, he said that he had been able to identify two of the individuals who had attempted to rob him as the defendant and the co-accused. The defendant, who was aged 16 at the time, was arrested. In interview, he was represented by a solicitor and an appropriate adult. In his first interview, the defendant provided a no comment response and his solicitor provided a prepared statement which said that he denied any wrongdoing and had not been present at the relevant time. In his second interview, he was asked further questions and provided no comment at all. At the plea and case management hearing the defendant pleaded not guilty and in his defence statement indicated alibi as his defence with three witnesses to be called. At trial, the defendant explained that he had been at home with two witnesses before later going to a shop with a third. Those witnesses did not give evidence at the trial. Following re-examination of the defendant, the judge intervened asking the defendant why in his prepared statement he had not mentioned where and with whom he was with on the relevant day but had mentioned it at trial. The defendant stated that the police always twisted his words and that it had been the advice of his solicitor to give the prepared statement. It was not part of the prosecution case to ask the defendant why he had not mentioned his alibi in his prepared statement and to subsequently seek to draw an adverse inference due to the difference between the prepared statement and the evidence given at trial. Prior to the judge's summing up, defence counsel sought confirmation that the judge would not make an adverse inference direction to the jury in accordance with the Criminal Justice and Public Order Act 1994 s 34. The judge refused and found that that was a jury point which did not go to whether the jury had been entitled to draw the adverse inference but rather whether they would draw such an inference. Subsequently, the judge gave an adverse inference direction to the jury and stated that the jury could only draw the adverse inference if it had concluded that it was reasonable for the defendant to 'come up with' the account he had given at the trial as to why the prepared statement did not have the same details as those provided at trial. The defendant was convicted of attempted robbery. He appealed against conviction. *Held*, the judge's intervention had clearly been based on the ground that he would have to give an adverse inference direction and that it would only be right for the defendant to have his say. Therefore, the judge was perceiving himself to be asking a question that the prosecution should have put to the defendant but had not. However, the judge had put the question to the defendant without prior intimation to either counsel. Difficulties were reinforced in the way the matter was summed up. The use of the phrase 'come up with' might have depreciated the defence case to the jury. Further, the jury did not have the evidence of the detailed questions that the police had put to the defendant in interview. They had only the prepared statement. Furthermore, it was of note that the prosecution counsel had not sought to draw an adverse inference after the defendant's evidence. Taken together, although the judge had been trying to avoid unfairness, unfairness had been created by the judge. Taking the other evidence of the case into consideration, the court was not satisfied that the conviction was safe. Therefore, the conviction would be quashed. Accordingly, the appeal would be allowed.

R v T [2013] All ER (D) 331 (Jul) (Court of Appeal: Davis LJ, Swift and Spencer JJ).

749   Trial—summing up—direction to jury—inference to be drawn from accused's silence

A police officer stopped a vehicle with three occupants. The driver, who gave his name as G, did not have insurance and was given a fixed penalty notice. At the subsequent hearing, the officer realised that G was not the person he had stopped. G showed the officer a photograph of the defendant, whom the officer confirmed was the person he had stopped. The defendant was asked to attend a police station and contacted his friend, who had the necessary accreditation to represent individuals at police station interviews. The friend told the defendant that, if he could not attend the station, he should give a 'no comment' interview. The defendant attended the station and was arrested. When the defendant was asked about legal representation, he explained that he wished to speak to his friend, whom he called his 'private solicitor'. An interview under caution was conducted in which the defendant gave 'no comment' responses. When asked why he was giving such responses, the defendant said that he wanted to talk to his private solicitor. The defendant was charged with perverting the course of justice. At trial, the defendant submitted that he had wanted to speak with his friend before the interview but had been unable to do so as the friend was abroad. In terms of the offence, he said that someone else had been driving the vehicle. In directing the jury, the judge stated that the legal advice the defendant received was an important consideration. The jury was asked to consider whether the defendant had reasonably relied on the advice from his friend or whether that was an excuse to conceal the defendant's potential culpability. The jury was also asked to consider the reasonableness of the defendant not informing the police of his defence at the time of the interview. The defendant was convicted. On his appeal, he argued that the conviction was unsafe because the judge had failed to direct the jury that, if they accepted his reasons for not answering questions, they could not draw an adverse inference. *Held*, the conviction was not unsafe. The guidance for the interview in Code C: Code of Practice for the Detention, Treatment and Questioning of Persons by Police Officers was followed in all significant respects. The judge was not at fault in the directions he gave nor in his failure to say anything specifically in relation to the defendant wanting to have his own solicitor present at the time of the interview. It was up to the jury to assess the situation and to decide, notwithstanding the advice to give 'no comment' responses in the interview, whether it was reasonable for the defendant not to put forward the defence he subsequently put forward at trial. Accordingly, the appeal would be dismissed.

R v Karapetyan [2013] All ER (D) 138 (Jan) (Court of Appeal: Treacy LJ, Edwards-Stuart J and Sir Geoffrey Grigson).

750   Trial—summing up—direction to jury—specimen counts

The defendant had been charged with seven counts of indecent assault on two child complainants. The defendant did not give evidence at trial and all counts were specimen counts due to the complainants each alleging repeated conduct over many years. However, when giving evidence, both spoke with some particularity about specific occasions relating to count one. In summing up, the judge directed the jury with words suggesting that, in specimen counts, it needed to be satisfied only that the offence had happened on at least one occasion. The defendant was convicted of two of the specimen counts. On his appeal, he contended that the conviction was unsafe because (1) the summing up with respect to the failure to give evidence had been confusing, unhelpful and potentially misleading; and (2) the judge's direction with respect to the specimen counts had left open the real possibility that not every juror was sure that the offence had been committed on the same occasion. *Held*, the matters which a judge had to identify in summing up when dealing with the case of a defendant who had chosen to exercise his right to silence were well established. In particular, the judge had to state that the defendant was entitled to remain silent, and for that reason the appropriate question was always whether the prosecution had demonstrated its case beyond reasonable doubt. The judge had covered this in sufficient detail to the extent that the jury would not have been confused. On the second ground, however, a defendant should be allowed to know with such particularity as the circumstances admitted what case he had to meet. Further, it was incumbent on the judge to relate the evidence to the particular counts. In most cases where a specimen count was relied on, it was enough for the judge to tell the jury that it might convict if it was sure that the offence had been committed at least once. If those specific occasions were not particularised in the indictment, it would be incumbent on the judge to tell the jury that it could convict only if it was sure that the offence had been committed on the same occasion, either on an occasion in the course of the unspecified pattern of offending, or on one of the particular occasions identified in the evidence. In the absence of such a direction, it would not be possible to say that the jury had been unanimous with respect to the same occasion. The nature of the incidents in the present case had been such that the members of the jury could on the evidence have been satisfied about the course of conduct but not the specific occasion, or vice versa. In those circumstances, it could not be said that the verdicts were safe and, accordingly, the convictions would be quashed.

R v Hobson [2013] EWCA Crim 819, [2013] All ER (D) 282 (May) (Court of Appeal: Elias LJ, Wilkie J and HHJ Pert QC). *R v Cowan* [1996] QB 373, [1995] 4 All ER 939, CA, applied. *R v Brown* [1984] 3 All ER 1013, CA (1984 Abr para 539); and *R v Rackham* [1997] 2 Cr App Rep 222, CA, considered.

751   Trial—summing up—direction to jury—supplementary written directions

The defendant admitted assaulting the deceased victim, but denied that the injuries he inflicted caused the victim's death. The defendant was charged with murder. At trial, the judge directed the jury that to convict the defendant of murder, they had to be sure that the deceased died from multiple injuries. He further directed that there was no evidence to contradict that proposition, and therefore if the jury were sure that was how the deceased died, then the defendant was responsible for the death if he caused any serious injury as part of those multiple injuries. The judge also produced a 'questions the jury need to answer' document for the jury in relation to the charge of murder, which asked whether the prosecution had made the jury sure that the defendant caused serious injury to the deceased. The defendant was convicted of murder. On appeal against conviction, an issue arose as to whether the judge misdirected the jury as to the elements of the law of murder because he failed to direct them that they had to be sure that any unlawful assault by the defendant led to the death of the deceased. *Held*, the judge posed the right causation question in his direction. Although the jury retired with the document, it had a proper causation direction orally from the judge. Moreover, the evidence on causation was all one way. Therefore, even if the judge had rephrased the document to include a question on causation and emphasised even more than he did orally that the causation issue was a live one for the jury to decide, it was obvious that the jury would have come to the same result. Accordingly, the appeal would be dismissed.

  R v Clarke [2013] EWCA Crim 162, [2013] All ER (D) 18 (Mar) (Court of Appeal: Aikens LJ, Globe J and Judge Kramer QC).

752 Victims—provision of services to victims—code of practice

The Domestic Violence, Crime and Victims Act 2004 (Victims' Code of Practice) Order 2013, SI 2013/2907 (in force on 10 December 2013), brings into operation, on 10 December 2013, the revised code of practice entitled 'The Code of Practice for Victims of Crime', which is made pursuant to the Domestic Violence, Crime and Victims Act 2004 s 33 and replaces the code of practice which was brought into operation on 3 April 2006.

753 Victims' Advisory Panel—abolition

See para 484.

754 Youth Justice and Criminal Evidence Act 1999—commencement

The Youth Justice and Criminal Evidence Act 1999 (Commencement No 13) Order 2013, SI 2013/862, brings s 28 into force in relation to certain proceedings on 30 December 2013. For a summary of the Act, see 1999 Abr para 925. See also the commencement table in the title STATUTES AND LEGISLATIVE PROCESS.

CROWN AND ROYAL FAMILY

Halsbury's Laws of England (4th edn) vol 12(1) (Reissue) paras 1–100

755 Succession to the Crown Act 2013

The Succession to the Crown Act 2013 makes succession of the Crown not depend on gender, and makes provision about royal marriages. The Act received royal assent on 25 April 2013 and came into force on that day.

  Section 1 provides that the gender of a person who was born after 28 October 2011 will have no relevance when determining succession to the throne. A person will not be disqualified from succeeding to the Crown or from being the sovereign due to his marriage to a Roman Catholic, and has retrospective effect: s 2. A person who is one of the six persons next in the line of succession to the Crown must obtain the consent of Her Majesty before marrying: s 3. Section 4 and the Schedule make consequential amendments and s 5 deals with commencement and the short title.

Amendments and repeals
The following provisions are amended: Bill of Rights s 1; Act of Settlement s 2; Treason Act 1351; Royal Marriages Act 1772; Regency Act 1937 s 3.

CROWN PROPERTY

Halsbury's Laws of England (4th edn) vol 12(1) (Reissue) paras 201–377

Articles

For articles relating to this title please refer to the Table of Articles at the beginning of the Abridgment.

CUSTOMS AND EXCISE

Halsbury's Laws of England (5th edn) vol 30 (2012) paras 1–606, vol 31 (2012) paras 607–1256

Articles

For articles relating to this title please refer to the Table of Articles at the beginning of the Abridgment.

756   Air passenger duty—exemption—connected flights

Air passenger duty was payable by a commercial aircraft operator in respect of each passenger travelling on a flight departing from a United Kingdom airport, save for certain flights which were exempt pursuant to the Finance Act 1994 s 30. If flights were connected within the meaning of the 1994 Act and the Air Passenger Duty (Connected Flights) Order 1994, SI 1994/1821, they did not attract the duty. In order to qualify as connected flights, two conditions had to be satisfied. The first was that the interval between connected flights could not exceed a certain number of hours ('the temporal condition') so as to draw a line between true transfers, which qualified for the exemption, and stopovers, which did not. Secondly, the tickets issued in respect of the connecting flights had to be 'conjunction tickets' ('the ticketing condition'). The ticketing condition was legislated at a time when all flight tickets were issued on paper, and required the holder to have the ticket coupons covering his entire journey. With the advent of electronic bookings, flight details were recorded electronically and accessed in the airline's computer system by means of a reference code known as a passenger name reference ('PNR'). Each booking generated a unique PNR. Some airlines made it possible for a customer to purchase, in a single booking, a sequence of flights making up a journey and generating a single PNR. The taxpayer airline formerly issued paper tickets but following its abandonment of paper tickets each flight, or return flight if both legs were booked together, had to be the subject of a separate booking, and each such booking had its own PNR. During the relevant period, the taxpayer had believed that it was not possible for it to claim the benefit of the exemption, and it accounted for the duty in respect of every passenger departing from a United Kingdom airport. It then changed its mind, considering that many of its flights during that period had qualified for the exemption as connected flights. It therefore claimed from the Revenue a refund of the excess duty for which it said it should not have accounted during the relevant period. The Revenue refused the refund on the basis that the taxpayer had failed to satisfy the ticketing condition, as its electronic ticketing system failed to show all the details of connected flights as if they formed a single journey. The taxpayer appealed against the Revenue's refusal and applied for judicial review of the Revenue's decision. *Held*, once it was accepted that conjunction tickets performed a function which was more than that of merely demonstrating satisfaction of the temporal condition, it became obvious that the taxpayer had not been entitled, during the relevant period, to claim an exemption from air passenger duty in respect of those of its flights which had met the relevant temporal condition as the electronic substitutes for tickets which it had provided to its passengers had not satisfied the ticketing condition. The court could only intervene in cases where it was satisfied that the Revenue believed that there was no material difference between one company or taxpayer and another company, and yet treated that other company differently, and that its conduct was outrageously unfair. The taxpayer had not established, as a matter of fact, that any other airline had been permitted to benefit from the exemption despite its using a booking system which had effectively ignored the ticketing condition. The difficulty facing the taxpayer had been that during the relevant period its systems had not made any of those things possible: flights could only have been booked separately, two flights had never had

768 Excise duty—tobacco products—herbal smoking products

The Tobacco Products (Descriptions of Products) (Amendment) Order 2013, SI 2013/2721 (in force on 1 January 2014), amends the 2003 Order, SI 2013/1471, so as to implement changes required by Council Directive (EU) 2011/64 in respect of herbal smoking products. In particular, the order has the effect of including herbal smoking products, that consist in whole or in part of substances other than tobacco, in the definition of a cigarette or other smoking tobacco.

769 Excise duty—warehousing—fraud—liability of warehouse keeper as consignor

The taxpayer company operated a 'tax warehouse', in which it stored goods without excise duty becoming payable. Duty became chargeable when the goods were released for consumption, which included an irregular departure from the duty suspension arrangement, such as fraud or theft. The present proceedings arose after consignments of whisky and vodka, dispatched by the taxpayer from its warehouse at the owner's request to warehouses in Spain and Estonia, were found not to have reached their intended destinations. The taxpayer was unaware of and had not participated in the irregularity in any way. In the case of each consignment, the fraud had resulted in an irregular departure from the suspension arrangement, as a result of which excise duty had become chargeable. In those circumstances, the excise duty point was the date when the goods had been removed from the taxpayer's tax warehouse, and the person liable to pay the duty was the person named as consignor in the accompanying administrative document ('AAD'). The consignor shown on each of the AADs had been the taxpayer. The Revenue made assessments to excise duty against the taxpayer. The taxpayer's appeal to the First-tier Tribunal was dismissed. On the taxpayer's appeal against that decision, it submitted that, by making an innocent third party liable for duty in such circumstances, the law infringed the principles of proportionality and legal certainty and went further than was required by Council Directive (EC) 92/12. *Held*, the relevant regulations made it clear that the warehouse keeper was the consignor for the purposes of the AAD. The warehouse keeper, as consignor, was the person liable to pay the excise duty in circumstances where the goods were lost or stolen in transit, unless he had procured that someone else agreed to arrange the guarantee. It was not possible to read the law in such a way as to introduce a test of culpability (of any kind) before a warehouse keeper could be held liable to pay the duty. The position was the same under Directive 92/12. The default liability for payment of excise duty on goods which went missing from a duty suspension arrangement fell on the warehouse keeper, but he might be relieved of that liability if he could negotiate that the guarantee was put up not by him but by the transporter or owner of the goods. It was clear that Directive 92/12 was intended to place strict liability to pay the unpaid excise duty on the person providing the guarantee, usually the warehouse keeper, in circumstances of an irregularity occurring during the intra-Community movement under duty suspension arrangements. It was objectively justifiable that a default responsibility should be placed on someone for the payment of duty if the goods were stolen and duty was not paid by the person primarily liable. That someone might have been identified as being the consignee of the goods or the transporter. Had it been either of them, the same argument about proportionality might have been raised by them. It was the keeper of a tax warehouse who reaped the benefit of the system of intra-Community transit of goods under duty suspension arrangements. It was the warehouse keeper who accepted instructions to receive and warehouse the goods and, in the case where intra-Community transit was proposed, accepted and carried out the instructions to arrange and effect shipment, by land, sea or air. Further, the warehouse keeper was in a position to protect himself against liability. Accordingly, the appeal would be dismissed.

Butlers Ship Stores Ltd v Revenue and Customs Comrs [2013] UKUT 564 (TCC), [2013] All ER (D) 331 (Nov) (Upper Tribunal: Lord Glennie presiding).

770 Finance Act 2013

See para 2149.

771 Forfeiture—seizure of goods—lawful reason for seizure

The claimant owned goods that were stored in a bonded warehouse in France. The claimant also had an account with a bonded warehouse in the United Kingdom. Goods on which duty had not been paid could be moved between bonded warehouses under prescribed duty suspension arrangements. A consignment of the claimant's goods that was being transported from the French bond to the United Kingdom bond was seized by the United Kingdom Border Agency, under the Customs and Excise Management Act 1979 s 139, on the basis of concerns about paperwork. The driver was given a document called a 'seizure information notice' and a warning letter. The claimant complained that no reason had been provided for the seizure. The defendant informed the claimant that he would receive an official notice of seizure by post stating the reason for the seizure and how it could request restoration and appeal against the seizure once a tally of the goods had been completed. The claimant sought judicial review, arguing that the defendant had not given a lawful reason for the seizure. *Held*, it was not a pre-condition of a lawful seizure that the reasons for it had to be given at the time. There was nevertheless an obligation to serve a notice on an owner who was not present, either by himself or his agent, at the time when the goods had been seized, once his identity became known to the United Kingdom Border Agency. The seizing officer's state of mind was relevant. Arbitrary seizure of goods by agents of the state could not be justified and it would plainly be a breach of the rights conferred by the European Convention on Human Rights First Protocol art 1. When an organisation treated different cases in the same way, or similar cases in a different way, it could be said that its approach was arbitrary. However, that was not an approach that could be applied to a single case. The first requirement of any treatment if it was not to be regarded as arbitrary was that it was done in good faith. A second requirement was that it was not irrational or perverse. A decision might be irrational or perverse if there was no coherent basis for believing it to be justified. Another aspect of the problem was that, in order to satisfy the Convention, seizure of the goods had to be a proportionate step to take in the circumstances. When the officers of the United Kingdom Border Agency had seized the claimant's load, they had done so in good faith and honestly suspecting that the goods were being imported as part of a plan to evade payment of duty. Although there had been no reasonable grounds for suspicion, the court was not able to say that that had been an irrational suspicion. Given the background to the seizure there had been grounds for regarding with suspicion the claimant's operations in general thereby raising a legitimate source of concern. In light of those considerations the decision to seize the load was neither irrational nor perverse. Whether it was ultimately justified under the provisions of the 1979 Act s 139 was an issue that had to be determined in the condemnation proceedings. Accordingly, the application would be dismissed.

R (on the application of Blackside Ltd) v Secretary of State for the Home Department [2013] EWHC 2087 (Admin), [2013] All ER (D) 336 (Jul) (Queen's Bench Division: Edwards-Stuart J).

772 Forfeiture—seizure of vehicle and goods—notice—validity

Her Majesty's Revenue and Customs detained and removed large quantities of alcohol from the warehouse and other premises of the taxpayer. Pursuant to the Customs and Excise Management Act 1979 s 139(6) and Sch 3 para 1, a series of seizure notices were then issued in relation to the detained goods. The taxpayer brought judicial review proceedings challenging the lawfulness of the notices, submitting that they were invalid by virtue of (1) failing to give a legally sufficient reason for detention at the time of detention; or (2) failing to state that duty had not been paid on the alcohol. The judge ruled that there was no power to detain goods pending evidence of duty status, so that the challenge under head (1) succeeded. However, the judge also held that, although it had not been stated directly on the notice, there could be no doubt that Revenue and Customs had been stating that it believed the duty had been owed on the goods in question. The challenge under head (2) therefore failed. Revenue and Customs appealed against the first of those decisions, and the taxpayer appealed against the second decision. *Held*, it was settled law that goods could be liable to forfeiture on grounds that had not been advanced or even known at the point of seizure or detention. Further, there was no requirement that, when detaining goods, the reason for their detention had to be given. There was no requirement in the 1979 Act for any formal written notice of detention, and it was not necessary for the notice required by Sch 3 para 1(1) to be given at the time of seizure. Even in the case of seizure, notice was not required where goods were seized in the presence of the owner or the owner's agent. It followed that the judge had erred in making the first decision. With regard to the taxpayer's appeal, the express reference in the notices to s 100(1)(e) had made it clear that Revenue and Customs' position had been that the alcohol was liable to forfeiture because duty had not been paid on it. Further, in any event, a notice under Sch 3 para 1 was not a requirement for the exercise of the power to seize. Even where a notice had been required, there was no requirement that the notice be given at the time of seizure or decision to seize the goods. It followed that the judge had not erred in making the second decision. Accordingly, Revenue and Customs' appeal would be allowed and the taxpayer's appeal would be dismissed.

R (on the application of First Stop Wholesale Ltd) v Revenue and Customs Comrs [2013] EWCA Civ 183, [2013] All ER (D) 105 (Mar) (Court of Appeal: Jackson, Lewison and Beatson LJJ).

773　Free movement of goods—quantitative restrictions and equivalent measures—alcohol—minimum pricing—protection of health—proportionality

See *Scotch Whisky Association v Lord Advocate*, para 492.

774　Free movement of goods—quantitative restrictions and equivalent measures—certification of products by private body

The claimant, an Italian manufacturer of copper fittings used in gas and water pipes, decided to sell its products in Germany. German law laid down non-mandatory general sales conditions for water supply undertakings and their customers, one of which was that only products that complied with prescribed technological standards were to be used. Such compliance was assumed if the product was certified by the defendant body, a private undertaking whose purpose was to promote the water sector. Although the defendant initially granted the claimant a certificate in respect of its products, it subsequently cancelled the certificate on the ground that the claimant had used a non-approved testing laboratory in Italy. The claimant brought proceedings challenging that decision, submitting that it had restricted its access to the German market in breach of the provisions on free movement of goods contained in TFEU art 34 (ex EC Treaty art 28). The proceedings were dismissed by the German court, which ruled that the defendant, as a private law body, was not bound by TFEU art 34. On the claimant's appeal against that decision, the court decided to stay the proceedings and refer to the European Court of Justice for a preliminary ruling the question of whether private law bodies set up for the purpose of drawing up technical standards in a particular field and certifying products on the basis of those standards were bound by art 34 if national legislation expressly regarded the products in respect of which certificates had been issued as lawful, thus making it more difficult to distribute products not so certified. *Held*, in order to determine whether a private law body which carried out the standardisation and certification of products was subject to the provisions on free movement of goods, it was necessary to determine whether, in the light of the legislative and regulatory context in which the private law body operated, its activities had the effect of giving rise to restrictions on the free movement of goods in the same manner as measures imposed by the state. Where national legislation considered the products certified by such a private law body to be compliant with national law and that had the effect of restricting the marketing of products which had not been certified by that body, art 34 would apply to the standardisation and certification activities of that body. The defendant, by virtue of its authority to certify products such as the claimant's copper fittings, in reality held the power to regulate the entry into the German market of such products and was therefore subject to art 34.

Case C-171/11 *Fra.bo SpA v Deutsche Vereinigung des Gas- und Wasserfaches eV (DVGW) – Technisch-Wissenschaftlicher Verein* [2013] QB 187 (ECJ: Fourth Chamber).

775　Her Majesty's Revenue and Customs—data-gathering powers—relevant data

See para 2053.

776　Her Majesty's Revenue and Customs—officer—detention and investigation—powers

The Police and Criminal Evidence Act 1984 (Application to immigration officers and designated customs officials in England and Wales) Order 2013, SI 2013/1542 (in force on 25 June 2013), applies, subject to modifications, specified provisions of the Police and Criminal Evidence Act 1984 to investigations undertaken by immigration officers and designated customs officials, and to persons detained by designated customs officials. In particular, the order (1) specifies the provisions in the 1984 Act in relation to which, when a person is detained by police in connection with an investigation conducted by an immigration officer or designated customs official, references to a police officer, constable or officer should include references to an immigration officer or designated customs official, as the case may be; (2) provides that immigration officers do not have powers to charge a person, release them on bail or detain them after charge; (3) provides that powers and functions applied to immigration officers under the order may only be exercised with the authority of the Secretary of State; (4) sets out the circumstances in which an immigration officer or designated customs official may use reasonable force in the exercise of a power under the Act; (5) clarifies that the application of the power of arrest under s 24(2) does not affect powers contained in other legislation of immigration officers or designated customs officials to arrest or detain people; (6) confirms when an immigration officer or designated customs official searching premises under the authority of a warrant may also search persons found on the premises; (7) sets out the circumstances in which immigration officers and designated customs officials may seize and retain things found during a lawful search; (8) ensures that an entry is made in a person's custody record specifying the grounds for, and nature of evidence sought during, a search of a detained person's premises; (9) provides that powers of retention do not affect the power immigration officers have to dispose of property, pursuant to the UK Borders Act 2007 s 26; (10) provides that designated customs officials do not have powers to charge a person or release them on bail; (11) makes provision in relation to the transfer of detained persons between different types of detention and to the aggregation of time spent in different types of detention; (12) provides that the Summary Jurisdiction (Process) Act 1881 applies to a warrant issued, on the application of a designated customs official, under s 8; (13) empowers the Secretary of State to designate customs offices for the detention of arrested persons; (14) specifies who may appoint a custody officer for a designated customs office; (15) makes provision as to the calculation of a person's period of detention where that person is arrested outside England and Wales in relation to an investigation conducted by designated customs officials; (16) requires a court to consider the distance and time involved in a transfer, where an application for such a transfer is made in the course of an application for a warrant of further detention in a customs investigation; (17) makes provision for the keeping of records and the publication of an annual report about customs detention; (18) empowers designated customs officials to carry out a protective search of persons in customs detention; (19) requires the Secretary of State to publish, annually, information about searches carried out by designated customs officials under the 1984 Act s 55; and (20) disapplies the provisions of the Borders, Citizenship and Immigration Act 2009 which relate to the transfer of persons between different types of detention.

The Protection of Freedoms Act 2012 (Consequential Amendments) No 3 Order 2013, SI 2013/2343 (in force on 31 October 2013), makes consequential amendments to the principal 2013 Order above as a result of the replacement, by the Protection of Freedoms Act 2012, of the Police and Criminal Evidence Act 1984 s 64.

777   Her Majesty's Revenue and Customs—officer—disclosure of information

The HGV Road User Levy (HMRC Information Gateway) Regulations 2013, SI 2013/3186 (in force on 13 January 2014), make provision enabling officials of Her Majesty's Revenue and Customs to disclose to the Secretary of State for Transport information required for the purposes of, or in connection with, the discharge of the Secretary of State's functions under the HGV Road User Levy Act 2013. The regulations also prohibit, subject to exceptions, the further disclosure of information.

778   Statistics of trade—intra-European Union trade—threshold

The Statistics of Trade (Customs and Excise) (Amendment) Regulations 2013, SI 2013/3043 (in force on 1 January 2014), further amend the 1992 Regulations, SI 1992/2790, so as to increase the threshold, expressed in terms of annual value of intra-European Union trade, at or below which a business is exempt from providing any Intrastat information. In particular, the regulations (1) increase the arrivals exemption threshold; and (2) increase the threshold, also expressed in terms of annual value of intra-European Union trade, above which an additional piece of information known as 'delivery terms' must be provided.

system and the third insurer, exercising its rights of subrogation, brought a claim against the defendants, claiming the total cost of the repairs paid out by it. It fell to be determined whether (1) where a vehicle was damaged as a result of negligence and was reasonably repaired, the measure of the claimant's loss would be taken as the reasonable cost of repair; (2) if a claimant's insurer arranged repair, the reasonableness of the repair charge was to be judged by reference to what a person in the position of the claimant could obtain on the open market or what his insurer could obtain on the open market; and (3) where a vehicle was not a write-off and an insurer indemnified the insured by having repairs performed and paying charges for those repairs, and where the amount claimed was no more than the reasonable cost of repair, that amount was recoverable. The judge decided that, where a vehicle was damaged as a result of negligence and was reasonably repaired, the measure of the claimant's loss would be taken as the reasonable cost of repair and, if a claimant's insurer had arranged repair, the reasonableness of the repair charge would be judged by reference to what a person in the position of the claimant could obtain on the open market. The judge subsequently made orders striking out parts of the defendants' pleaded case that raised points contrary to the judge's conclusions on the preliminary issues. The defendants appealed. *Held*, the argument that the claimants could not recover the full cost of repair to the third insurer because they had to mitigate their loss by having the repairs done at a lower cost was wrong because mitigation was not relevant in respect of that direct loss. That could not be mitigated by having the chattel repaired free or for a lower cost because it was not the cost of the repairs that constituted the loss. The loss was the diminution in value of the chattel. Therefore, the first preliminary issue asked the wrong question because the measure of the claimant's loss that resulted from the damage was the diminution in value of the vehicle. With that important qualification, the answer to the first preliminary issue was in the affirmative because the reasonable cost of repair was taken as representing the diminution in value of the chattel that had been suffered as a result of the damage caused by the negligence of the defendant. The answer to the second preliminary issue was the same as that of the judge in that if the claimant's insurer arranged the repair, the reasonableness of the repair charge was to be judged by reference to what a person in the position of the claimant could obtain on the open market. If, as was assumed by the form of the question in the third preliminary issue, it was the insurer who arranged and paid for the repairs to the claimant's vehicle and the claimant then sued for the cost incurred by the insurer as the sum representing the diminution in value of the vehicle resulting from the negligence of the defendant, the court had only one question to consider. It was whether the actual sum claimed was equal to or less than the notional sum that the claimant would have paid, by way of a reasonable cost of repair, if he had gone into the open market to have those repairs done. The position of the cost of a courtesy car was different, because that cost could not be a part of the repair costs. If a claimant was deprived of his chattel for a time, he could recover a sum by way of general damages for that deprivation. The defendants' attack on the specific charges which had been included in the invoice all missed the point. The question was not whether each of the items actually charged was reasonable, but whether the overall cost charged was reasonable. If the total repair cost paid by the third insurer was more than the reasonable repair cost that the claimant would have paid if he arranged the repairs on the open market, then the sum claimed would simply be reduced to the notional reasonable repair cost. The answer to the third preliminary issue was also in the affirmative. The issue of the courtesy car was different, because it could not be a part of the cost of repairs. However, the reasonable cost of a courtesy car was recoverable by the claimant and he would hold it for the benefit of the third insurer. Accordingly, the appeal would be dismissed.

Coles v Hetherton [2013] EWCA Civ 1704, [2013] All ER (D) 226 (Dec) (Court of Appeal: Moore-Bick, Aikens and Vos LJJ). *Dimond v Lovell* [2002] 1 AC 384, [2000] 2 All ER 897, HL (2000 Abr para 698); and *Bee v Jenson* [2007] EWCA Civ 923, [2007] 4 All ER 791 (2007 Abr para 1455) applied.

792   Negligence—causation—advice of third party

A schoolgirl, aged 14, died while on a school training exercise. She had been on a school trip with ten other children from the second defendant school. The first defendant was employed as a teacher at the school and was responsible for leading the exercise. During the exercise, the children were permitted to proceed on a route unsupervised, with teachers meeting them at various check points. The children were supposed to be met by the first defendant at a specified check point. However, she became lost on her way to the check point and was not present when the children arrived. The children telephoned the first defendant and they were instructed to continue. They came to a fast flowing stream and found that they could not cross. They telephoned the first defendant again and were instructed not to cross the stream but to walk around it. Another adult on the moor informed the children that they could cross the stream at a different location to which he guided them. While crossing at that location, the schoolgirl fell into the stream and was swept away to her death. The claimant, the schoolgirl's mother, brought a claim for damages for personal injury, in the form of a chronic grief reaction and severe post-traumatic stress disorder resulting from the death and, as administratrix of the estate, damages for loss to the estate. She alleged negligence on the part of the first and/or second defendants. The judge found that the defendants had not been negligent and that, in any event, the intervention of the adult broke the chain of causation. The claimant appealed. *Held*, in the circumstances, given the high standard reasonably to have been expected of the first defendant, and the seriousness of the elementary errors made, there had to be a finding of negligence against her. However, it was very speculative as to what course events would have taken had the first defendant been present at the check point. It could not have been concluded, on the evidence, that the first defendant would probably have accompanied the children on the next leg of the route. It was not possible, on the evidence, to conclude that the first defendant's presence at the check point when the children had first arrived would have led to a different outcome or had been causative of the second attempt to cross the stream. Even if the first defendant had stayed, the intervention of the adult, anxious to help and apparently authoritative, would have broken the chain of causation. It could not have been foreseen that the children would have disobeyed instructions from the first defendant. Subsequent events could not have fairly been attributed to the absence of the first defendant from the check point. A finding that her presence there when the children had first arrived would have prevented the second attempt to cross the stream, with its tragic consequences, involved too much speculation to be tenable. Accordingly, the appeal would be dismissed.

Wilkin-Shaw v Fuller [2013] EWCA Civ 410, [2013] All ER (D) 123 (Apr) (Court of Appeal: Pill, Moore-Bick and Black LJJ). Decision of Owen J [2012] EWHC 1777, [2012] All ER (D) 03 (Jul) (2012 Abr para 839) affirmed.

793　Negligence—nervous shock—secondary victim—post-traumatic stress—relevant incident

See *Taylor v A Novo (UK) Ltd*, para 1911.

794　Patent—infringement—copy of design—moral prejudice

See *Xena Systems Ltd v Cantideck*, para 1926.

795　Personal injury—assessment of damages—periodical payments—medical evidence—evidence to be provided annually in advance of payment

The claimant had judgment entered in his favour as a result of serious injuries sustained in a road traffic accident involving the defendant. The claimant and the defendant's insurer reached a compromise with regard to the payment of a lump sum and periodical payments thereafter but certain aspects of the compromise were not agreed and a determination was sought as to the appropriate wording of an order to be enshrined in the settlement. The insurer submitted that, in addition to requiring the claimant to arrange for a medical examination at infrequent intervals, the claimant should also be required to obtain an up-to-date life expectancy figure for the purpose of the insurer being in a position to calculate reserves so as to be able to set aside capital to cover future periodical payments. The claimant opposed this requirement on the grounds that, rather than facilitating the settlement, the requirement facilitated the preferred method of the insurer running its own commercial business. The insurer also sought a requirement that the claimant obtain and provide to the insurer, at least 14 days before the start of each payment year, written confirmation from his doctor that the claimant was still alive, and that if that confirmation were not provided, the insurer would be entitled to suspend payments. The claimant argued that the insurer should only be entitled to suspend payment if it obtained an order from the court. On the examination issue, the judge held that a medical report was necessary, reasonable and proportionate for the insurer to seek to purchase an annuity but that the additional requirement sought had simply been for the purpose of enabling the insurer to review its provisioning. The judge refused to sanction that requirement or the confirmation requirement on the basis that it would be disproportionate for the insurer to withhold payment without a court order. The insurer appealed. *Held*, the judge had adopted a limited approach to the examination issue. An insurer was obliged or expected to maintain a reasonably accurate reserve, and was at a disadvantage in not having accurate information regarding the medical condition of the injured person in a case where the life expectancy was presently assessed at different terms in excess of 45 years. The insurer was entitled to be reassured that the person to whom periodic payments were being made was still alive at the date on which the payment was to be made. There was no reason why that confirmation should not be made available on an annual basis in advance of the payment which followed reassessment of the payment in the light of up-to-date statistical indices dealing with the cost of living. The insurer would be required to provide a reminder of the obligation but, if there was no confirmation, there was no virtue in requiring the insurer to return to court. Accordingly, the appeal would be allowed.

Follett v Wallace [2013] EWCA Civ 146, [2013] All ER (D) 57 (Mar) (Court of Appeal: Mummery, Richards and Leveson LJJ).

796 Personal injury—limitation periods

See LIMITATION PERIODS.

Personal injury—quantum of damages

Examples of awards of damages in personal injury or fatal accident cases are arranged in the following order. Cases involving more than one injury are classified according to the major injury suffered.

Multiple injuries	Neck and back	Thigh
Psychological damage	Chest	Knee
Scarring	Back	Minor injuries
Head	Arm	Neck
Neck	Hand	

797 Multiple injuries

PSLA: £1,700
Total damages: £1,700
Sex: Male
Age at accident/trial: 8/11
Date of accident/trial: 27 October 2009/22 January 2013
Judge/Court: DJ Taylor/Croydon County Court

The claimant sustained multiple injuries in a road traffic accident when the car in which he was travelling was **struck by another car from the passenger's side.** The car was written off. The claimant was **thrown sideways.** He **attended casualty** for treatment to his injuries shortly after the accident and received advice. He consulted his doctor twice and received a prescription for **painkillers.** The claimant was **unable to attend judo lessons or rugby.** The **neck pain resolved within five months, abdominal pain resolved after three weeks,** recurrent **headaches resolved after two weeks, anxiety as a passenger lasted for eight months** and **severe shock and vomiting lasted for a day.**

TW (a child) v Robinson (unreported, 22 January 2013) (Matthew Mason, instructed by MTA Solicitors LLP, Solicitors, for the claimant) (Kindly submitted for publication by Matthew Mason).

798 Psychological damage

PSLA: £5,000
Total damages: £5,000
Sex: Female
Age at accident/trial: 14/17
Date of accident/trial: 29 November 2008/3 July 2012
Judge/Court: DDJ McCulloch/High Wycombe County Court

The claimant was a **front seat passenger** in her father's car. He lost control of the car when he was drunk. The claimant **suffered a whiplash injury to her head, neck and back and the left side of her forehead and right thumb** impacted with the dashboard. She suffered from a **friction burn to her abdomen and bruising to her forehead** that resolved within two weeks and a strain of her thumb that resolved in one week. She was also **shocked for two days and the day after the accident she began to suffer from severe pain and stiffness in her neck and lower back.** She became **very nervous as a passenger** in a car, with a heightened sense of awareness. At medical examinations four months and one year and five months after the accident, the claimant's **physical symptoms were ongoing** although improved and she had undergone **12 sessions of physiotherapy** by the later date but these had only provided temporary relief. At the second medical examination, she had **not taken part in any physical education lessons** since the accident, her **sleep was still disturbed** and she was taking 6–8 paracetamol a day. She initially had missed one week of school and had subsequently been sent home, on approximately seven occasions, due to pain. She would **cry when in the car at night** and **could not be on her own in the rear of a car.** At two years and three months post-accident, the claimant was seen by a clinical psychologist and she was **diagnosed with a specific phobia of travel.** It was recorded that this was **resulting in mood disturbance, general anxiety, sleep disturbance, travel anxiety and passenger avoidance.** The claimant's physical symptoms **resolved after two years** and her psychological symptoms resolved by **two years eight months post-accident,** assisted by the claimant starting driving lessons.

J (*a child*) v Aston (unreported, 3 July 2012) (Joseph England, Counsel, instructed by Gorman Hamilton, Solicitors, for the claimant) (Kindly submitted for publication by Joseph England).

799   Psychological damage

PSLA: £4,000
Total damages: £4,000
Sex: Female
Age at accident/trial: 9/15
Date of accident/trial: 10 December 2006/16 January 2013
Judge/Court: DJ Farquhar/Peterborough County Court

The claimant, a schoolgirl, suffered **travel anxiety and disturbed sleep as well as neck pain from a whiplash injury** as a result of a road traffic accident. She was wearing a seatbelt and travelling in a vehicle that drove into the rear of another. The **vehicle's airbag did deploy.** The claimant **suffered from red marks across her neck and chest that resolved after four days** and **suffered nightmares and nocturnal enuresis every night following the accident.** She was examined approximately four months after the accident and it was noted that her **neck pain had resolved after two months.** She would **initially not get into a car** but by the time of the medical report she would enter a car cautiously and alerted the driver to perceived hazards. A second report obtained from a **child psychologist one year after the accident** confirmed that there was no diagnosis of PTSD or a specific phobia but there had been **mild traumatisation that had been severe for 3–6 months** and that the travel anxiety had resolved by the time of the report. However, the **nightmares and enuresis were reduced but on-going at the time of the second report** and when this later resolved two years and ten months after the accident, the psychologist confirmed that the entire period was attributable to the accident.

L (*a child*) v Reeve (unreported, 16 January 2013) (Joseph England, instructed by Gorman Hamilton, Solicitors, for the claimant) (Kindly submitted for publication by Joseph England).

800   Psychological damage

PSLA: £2,100
Total damages: £2,100
Sex: Female
Age at accident/trial: 332
Date of accident/trial: 20 February 2012/21 January 2013
Judge/Court: DJ Green/Medway County Court

The claimant, a schoolgirl, suffered **back pain from a whiplash injury** and **travel anxiety** as a result of a road traffic accident. She was wearing a seatbelt and travelling as a rear passenger in a vehicle that was moving when it was hit from the side. The vehicle's airbag did not deploy. The claimant was taken by ambulance to hospital after the accident. She later consulted her GP once but was not given a prescription. She was examined approximately two months after the accident and a soft tissue injury was diagnosed. At the time of the examination, her back pain had resolved by approximately 70–80% but her travel anxiety was on-going. She did not refrain completely from travelling in cars but was extra cautious in cars and apprehensive when presented with situations similar to the accident. The claimant's leisure activities were disrupted as a result of the accident. Her back pain resolved seven months after the accident and her travel anxiety resolved after 12 months.

Q (a child) v Kayd (unreported, 21 January 2013) (Joseph England, instructed by Co-operative legal, Solicitors, for the claimant) (Kindly submitted for publication by Joseph England).

801   Psychological damage

PSLA: £1,550
Total damages: £2,005
Sex: Male
Age at accident/trial: 9/12
Date of accident/trial: 4 July 2010/29 January 2013
Judge/Court: DJ Sofaer/Uxbridge County Court

The claimant was a belted rear seated passenger in a motorcar which sustained a frontal impact with another vehicle at moderate speed. The claimant was looking forward at the time of the impact and did not come into contact with anything in the vehicle when thrown forward. He was taken to A&E following the accident and then one follow up visit to his GP. The claimant's neck pain resolved itself after about one week. The claimant's psychological symptoms resolved after about three weeks. As at the time of his medical examination some months after the accident, he was still suffering from intermittent headaches, which eventually resolved within six months of the accident, following a short course of physiotherapy.

PM (a minor) v EM (unreported, 29 January 2013) (representative for the claimant, instructed by Ascot Solicitors, Solicitors; Thomas Crockett, instructed by DAC Beachcroft, Solicitors, for the defendant) (Kindly submitted for publication by Thomas Crockett).

802   Psychological damage

PSLA: £1,500
Total damages: £1,500
Sex: Female
Age at accident/trial: 3/5
Date of accident/trial: 14 October 2010/18 January 2013
Judge/Court: DJ Grey/North Shields County Court

The claimant was a rear seat passenger in a vehicle when the defendant, who was riding a motorbike, collided into the front of the vehicle. The claimant, who was wearing a seatbelt, was thrown forwards and backwards on impact. She was treated by a paramedic at the scene and then attended a walk in centre where she was referred to a hospital where she was examined. Travel anxiety lasted seven to nine months. Sleep disturbance recovered within eight weeks. Neck pain recovered within a day.

KC (a child) v Stewart (unreported, 18 January 2013) (Jim Hester, instructed by MTA Solicitors LLP, Solicitors, for the claimant) (Kindly submitted for publication by Joanne Bloyce).

803   Psychological damage

PSLA: £1,000
Total damages: £1,000
Sex: Female
Age at accident/trial: 2/3
Date of accident/trial: 29 August 2011/2 January 2013
Judge/Court: DJ Robertson/Hartlepool County Court

The claimant was a rear seat passenger in a car, seated in a child seat behind the driver with her seatbelt fastened. While this was stationary at a roundabout, **another vehicle collided with it from the rear** and, as a direct result of this impact, the **claimant was moderately shaken.** Immediately following the accident the claimant was initially quiet but then **started to cry uncontrollably before being eventually consoled.** By the following day it was clear that her **sleep pattern was disturbed** and she was also **anxious about getting into a car.** She was taken to a local walk-in centre where she was assessed and her guardian was advised to keep an eye on her but there was **no evidence of any physical injuries.** During the initial weeks following the accident, the claimant continued to experience disturbed sleep and remained somewhat anxious about getting into a car. There was a **three to four week period of severe psychological upset in the form of disturbed sleep as well as travel related anxiety after which this improved and resolved by four months following the accident.**

F (a child) v Kerr (unreported, 2 January 2013) (Paul Dunn, instructed by Irwin Mitchell LLP, Solicitors, for the claimant) (Kindly submitted for publication by Paul Dunn).

804   Psychological damage

PSLA: £850
Total damages: £850
Sex: Female
Age at accident/trial: 3/4
Date of accident/trial: 6 July 2011/6 July 2012
Judge/Court: DJ Kumrai/Willesden County Court

The claimant, a child, suffered **psychological injury in the form of travel anxiety, loss of confidence and a change of personality,** as well as a **mild soft tissue injury to her abdomen** caused by her seatbelt. The claimant began to **cry and tremble immediately after** the collision and was taken to hospital by her parents. She was given **painkillers** and discharged the same day. She complained of **abdominal pain for 48 hours** after the accident and lost her appetite for a few days. The claimant **recovered from the seatbelt injury within 48 hours** of the collision. She was **reluctant to travel by car and suffered from sleep disturbance for four days.** She exhibited **attention-seeking behaviour and was less interested in playing with her friends. One year after** the accident, the claimant's father confirmed that she had **recovered from the psychological symptoms** in line with the prognosis period of between 4–6 months.

S (a child) v Walsh (unreported, 6 July 2012) (John Reay, Counsel, instructed by Waring & Co, Solicitors, for the claimant) (Kindly submitted for publication by John Reay).

805   Psychological damage

See para 809.

806   Psychological damage

See para 822.

807   Scarring

PSLA: £15,000
Total damages: £19,150
Sex: Female
Age at accident/trial: 4/11
Date of accident/trial: 11 March 2005/26 July 2012
Judge/Court: Recorder Macdonald/Manchester County Court

The claimant suffered **first degree burns to the inside aspect of her right thigh and calf** when it became **trapped behind a radiator** at infant school. The leg was **trapped for 10–15 minutes.** The claimant's **wound became infected** and she was **admitted to hospital for six weeks** where she had **three operations** under general anaesthetic. The claimant was described as poorly during her time as an inpatient. On discharge she was provided with a splint and advised to rest as much as possible. A **scar reduction gel was massaged** into the area by her mother **for several months.** On first medical examination at one year eight months post accident an **18cm red and roughened scar was noted** with a prognosis for the redness to fade. On review at five years eight months the **scar was measured at 20cm** in total and had been **slow to fade** and was noted to **turn purple in cold weather. Revision surgery** was not likely to improve the appearance but some further fading was anticipated. During the initial period of recovery and post operatively the claimant was **unable to go swimming and her physical activities were restricted.** She was due to start senior school in September and was apprehensive about being **teased.** It was likely that in future she would be **self-conscious about the scar** and her **choice of clothing** especially skirts and swimwear **would be affected.** The judge found the fact of the burn, the number of operations, the length of time for which the leg was trapped and the length of stay in hospital of particular relevance.

L (a child) v Manchester City Council (unreported, 26 July 2012) (Katharine Titchmarsh, instructed by Freeclaim (Tranters), Solicitors, for the claimant; R Goddard, instructed by City Council, Solicitors, for the defendant) (Kindly submitted for publication by Katharine Titchmarsh).

808   Scarring

PSLA: £4,750
Total damages: £4,750
Sex: Male
Age at accident/trial: 18/19
Date of accident/trial: 31 May 2011/10 April 2013
Judge/Court: DJ Flanagan/Leeds County Court

The claimant was using a hole saw fitted to a drill when the **saw blade sprang off and struck him on the left cheek.** As a result he suffered an **abrasion/laceration** to the cheek, about **4cm long.** He attended hospital where the **wound was cleaned and closed with steristrips** which he **wore for about ten days.** He returned to work the day after the accident. When examined for the purposes of the claim at **11 months following the accident he had a residual scar on his cheek** which was about **3.5cm long** and **slightly redder** than the surrounding skin. Anterior to the main scar there was a paler 1.5 cm scar, which was only really visible under magnification. There was some **cold-related discomfort around the scars and episodic tingling and stinging.** The claimant was **conscious of the appearance of the main scar** and grew his facial hair longer than it had been before the accident in order partially to conceal the scar. The prognosis was that the **main scar** would become **paler and less visible** and the **residual symptoms of cold related discomfort, tingling and stinging** would resolve by about **two years post-accident.**

Moss v Arcade Warehouse Ltd (unreported, 10 April 2013) (Tom Nossiter, instructed by Slater & Gordon, Solicitors, for the claimant) (Kindly submitted for publication by Tom Nossiter).

809   Scarring

PSLA: £3,500
Total damages: £3,500
Sex: Male
Age at accident/trial: 33/35
Date of accident/trial: 8 January 2011/18 June 2013
Judge/Court: DDJ Hill/Teesside County Court

The claimant was **bitten on the face** by the defendant's **dog.** The **dog's upper teeth went into the claimant's right cheek,** causing a puncture wound, and the **lower teeth** went into the skin broadly midway between the chin and the bottom lip on the left side of the face, causing a 3 cm deep laceration. The claimant **attended a walk in centre and then hospital.** The wounds were cleaned, closed with glue and steristrips. The wounds scabbed over within about two weeks. The scabs dropped off after 4–6 weeks. The puncture wound on the **right cheek healed leaving no scar.** The **laceration** below on the **lower lip left an oblique thin pale scar,** approximately **2 cm long.** It was not tender and was not adhered to the underlying tissues. There was **altered sensation (numbness) within the scar area,** but sensation in the surrounding skin was normal. The claimant was **conscious of the appearance** of the scar. His **job involved selling to members of the public** and he felt that people would consider him thuggish due to the scar. As a result he grew a short beard, which concealed the scar. He still had the scar at the date of trial. The claimant suffered from **permanent numbness within the scar.** Psychological symptoms of anxiety and sleep disturbance lasted 3–4 months. Anxiety about being in the **presence of large dogs lasted one year**. Anxiety about **passing the defendant's home lasted two years**. There was a full psychological recovery thereafter.

Watson v Hall (unreported, 18 June 2013) (Tom Nossiter, instructed by Williamsons, Hull, Solicitors, for the claimant) (Kindly submitted for publication by Tom Nossiter).

810   Head

PSLA: £2,700
Total damages: £2,773
Sex: Female
Age at accident/trial: 22/27
Date of accident/trial: 3 May 2008/8 August 2012
Judge/Court: DJ Ryan/West London County Court

The claimant was walking along the pavement close to the kerb when she was **hit over the back of the head** by the **wing mirror of a passing bus** operated by the defendant. This caused her to fall onto the pavement on the right side of her body and to **black out**. The **right side of the claimant's face became badly bruised and swollen** and a **fracture of the right cheekbone** was suspected, but never confirmed. The claimant **did not require surgery**. She experienced **severe pain and swelling** which was at its **worst for three months post-accident**. Thereafter, the symptoms decreased. At trial, some **four years later**, the claimant still experienced **tenderness** which she described as being 3 to 4 out of 10. She could still feel a **small lump of skin below her right eye** which had not been there prior to the accident.

Ahmed v Abellio London (unreported, 8 August 2012) (Philippa Seal, instructed by Lancasters, Solicitors, for the claimant) (Kindly submitted for publication by Philippa Seal).

811   Head

PSLA: £1,000
Total damages: £1,010
Sex: Male
Age at accident/trial: 1/3
Date of accident/trial: 23 November 2011/29 January 2013
Judge/Court: DDJ Drayson/Luton County Court

The claimant suffered **pain in his head** for **three weeks** as a result of a **road traffic accident**. He was seated in a child seat and travelling in a vehicle that was stationary when it was hit from behind. The claimant took **painkillers for three weeks**. No other injuries were sustained.

W (a child) v Martin (unreported, 29 January 2013) (Joseph England, instructed by Minster Law, Solicitors, for the claimant) (Kindly submitted for publication by Joseph England).

812   Neck

PSLA: £2,500
Total damages: £2,500
Sex: Male
Age at accident/trial: 15/17
Date of accident/trial: 12 August 2010/ 4 March 2013
Judge/Court: DJ Thomas/Bromley County Court

The claimant, a schoolboy, was a front seat passenger wearing a seatbelt. The car was stationary waiting to turn into a main road when the **car was struck by another vehicle from the front offside corner**. At the time of the impact the claimant was leaning slightly towards the window and was **jolted backwards and hit his head on the side window**. The claimant attended A&E and was advised to rest and **take anti-inflammatories together with ice**. The claimant received **massage therapy** and purchased a new **support pillow to ease the pain in his neck**. He was **unable to participate in football and rugby**, and also suffered discomfort while doing **school work** for four weeks. The claimant's neck pain **resolved after eight months** following the accident. His **sleep disruption and heightened traffic awareness** resolved after one month.

F (a child) v Davidson (unreported, 4 March 2013) (Joshua Hedgman, instructed by MTA Solicitors LLP, Solicitors, for the claimant) (Kindly submitted for publication by Joanne Bloyce).

813   Neck

PSLA: £2,000
Total damages: £2,000
Sex: Female
Age at accident/trial: 15/16
Date of accident/trial: 31 October 2011/15 March 2013
Judge/Court: DJ McCormack/Edmonton County Court

The claimant, a schoolgirl, suffered **neck pain from a whiplash injury and travel anxiety** as a result of a **road traffic accident**. She was wearing a seatbelt and travelling as a front passenger in a vehicle that was **stationary when it was hit from behind**. For **one month** following the accident, the claimant **suffered from severe pain and stiffness in her neck**, radiating across her shoulders and with **associated headaches**. Her symptoms reduced to moderate severity after this period and **resolved after four sessions of physiotherapy** by **seven months post-accident**. Her **sleep had been reduced by up to 70%** during the recovery period and she **missed three weeks of physical education**. In addition, the claimant suffered from **travel anxiety** for approximately **eight months** after the accident.

B (a child) v Fountain Holdings (unreported, 15 March 2013) (Joseph England, instructed by Gorman Hamilton, Solicitors, for the claimant) (Kindly submitted for publication by Joseph England).

814   Neck

PSLA: £1,600
Total damages: £1,649.99
Sex: Female
Age at accident/trial: 13/15
Date of accident/trial: 21 July 2011/18 January 2013
Judge/Court: DJ Shanks/Chelmsford County Court

The claimant, a schoolgirl, **suffered neck pain and stiffness from a whiplash injury** in her neck as a result of a **road traffic accident**. She was wearing a seatbelt and travelling as a **front passenger in a vehicle** that was hit on the passenger side. The claimant **attended her doctor once** and received advice. She was examined approximately **three months after the accident** and it was noted that the **neck pain at that time was mild**. She missed one day of school and her **neck pain resolved approximately five months after the accident**.

K (a child) v Ryan (unreported, 18 January 2013) (Joseph England, instructed by Minster Law, Solicitors, for the claimant) (Kindly submitted for publication by Joseph England).

815   Neck

PSLA: £1,600
Total damages: £1,600
Sex: Male
Age at accident/trial: 9/10
Date of accident/trial: 7 October 2011/4 January 2013
Judge/Court: DDJ Jones/Wandsworth County Court

The claimant, a schoolboy, suffered **soft tissue whiplash injury and travel anxiety** following a road traffic collision. The claimant developed **pain in his neck** a day after the incident. He did not seek medical attention but did take **painkillers**. The claimant's **physical symptoms adversely affected his ability to carry out PE** at school for a **period of three months**. The claimant also **experienced travel anxiety** following the incident. The medical expert considered that the claimant had suffered a soft tissue whiplash injury to his neck which **resolved within between four and five months of the collision. Full recovery from travel anxiety occurred within three months**. At the infant approval hearing around 15 months after the collision, it was confirmed that the claimant had recovered in line with the medical opinion.

A (a child) v Long (unreported, 4 January 2013) (John Reay, instructed by Ronald Fletcher & Co, Solicitors, for the claimant) (Kindly submitted for publication by John Reay).

816   Neck

PSLA: £1,350
Total damages: £1,500
Sex: Female
Age at accident/trial: 11/12
Date of accident/trial: 3 December 2011/5 February 2013
Judge/Court: DJ Lewis/Romford County Court

The claimant, a schoolgirl, suffered **neck pain from a whiplash injury in her neck** as a result of a **road traffic accident**. She was wearing a seatbelt and travelling as a front passenger in a vehicle that was struck from the rear. The claimant was able to alight unaided from the vehicle. She took **paracetamol for two weeks** following the accident. She was examined approximately **one month after the accident** and her **neck pain** was described as **mild and constant with full movement**. After a course of approximately **four physiotherapy sessions**, the claimant's **neck pain resolved by four months after the accident.**

D (a child) v Whayling (unreported, 5 February 2013) (Joseph England, instructed by Minster Law, Solicitors, for the claimant) (Kindly submitted for publication by Joseph England).

817   Neck and back

PSLA: £2,600
Total damages: £2,600
Sex: Female
Age at accident/trial: 9/12
Date of accident/trial: 12 April 2010/11 February 2013
Judge/Court: DJ Greenfield/Dartford County Court

The claimant occupied the rear passenger's seat of a car that was stationary at traffic lights when it was **struck by another car from the rear**. She was **thrown forwards**. The claimant consulted her GP about **neck and back pain a week after the accident** and received advice to use **painkillers**. She was **still taking painkillers** at the time of the medico-legal examination at three month's post-accident. Personal care was restricted for a day. Sleep was restricted for six weeks. Dancing and running were still restricted at three month's post-accident. **Neck, upper and low back pain continued for ten months** and **travel anxiety for seventeen months.**

TW (a child) v Zaman (unreported, 11 February 2013) (Matthew Mason, instructed by MTA Solicitors LLP, Solicitors, for the claimant) (Kindly submitted for publication by Matthew Mason).

818   Neck and back

PSLA: £2,010
Total damages: £2,010
Sex: Male
Age at accident/trial: 16/17
Date of accident/trial: 1 March 2012/14 February 2013
Judge/Court: DDJ McGovern/Uxbridge County Court

The claimant, a schoolboy, suffered **a soft tissue whiplash injury to his neck and back** following a road traffic collision while riding his motorcycle. This collision resulted in an **exacerbation of the injuries** suffered in a previous collision **by between 6 and 12 months**. The medical expert considered that **60% of the claimant's symptoms** were **related to the present collision. Full recovery** was expected within **16–22 months** of the present incident. The claimant occasionally **played football** and **was prevented from doing so** following the accident. His daily life was not affected in any other significant manner. He **did not consult his GP** or receive any form of treatment other than occasionally **taking painkillers**.

Smith v Mburu (unreported, 14 February 2013) (John Reay, instructed by Quality Solicitors RJ Gill, Solicitors, for the claimant) (Kindly submitted for publication by John Reay).

819   Neck and back

PSLA: £1,850
Total damages: £1,850
Sex: Male
Age at accident/trial: 5/7
Date of accident/trial: 31 August 2011/20 February 2013
Judge/Court: DJ Chesterfield/Watford County Court

The claimant, a schoolboy, suffered **back and neck pain** as a result of a road traffic accident. He was wearing a seatbelt and travelling as a middle passenger in a people carrier that was stationary when it was hit from behind. He **attended casualty immediately** after the accident and he was advised to **take painkillers**. The neck pain was recorded as 'never severe' and reported by the claimant to have resolved within one month, although a medical examination after **one and half months showed a restriction in movement at the extremes of turning**. His **back pain** was **more severe**, feeling constantly stiff and with pain at the extremes of movement. **Six sessions of physiotherapy** were recommended although only three were completed before the physiotherapy discharge report was completed after two months post-accident. The **resolution of the neck had occurred by approximately two months post-accident** and the **back pain had resolved after approximately five months**.

   M (a child) v Metropolitan Police (unreported, 20 February 2013) (Joseph England, instructed by Minster Law, Solicitors, for the claimant (Kindly submitted for publication by Joseph England).

820   Neck and back

PSLA: £1,650
Total damages: £1,650
Sex: Male
Age at accident/trial: 280
Date of accident/trial: 6 July 2011/4 March 2013
Judge/Court: DJ Kirby/Bury St Edmund's County Court

The claimant, a schoolboy, **suffered neck and back pain from soft tissue injuries and travel anxiety** as a result of a **road traffic accident**. The claimant was wearing a seatbelt and travelling as a rear passenger in a vehicle that was stationary when it was **hit from behind**. He was in **immediate pain and distress** and **had to be cut from the car** by the fire service. He was placed on a spinal board and **taken to hospital**, from which he was **discharged on the same day**. The claimant **took two days off school**, his **sleep was disturbed for three weeks** and his ability to **play regular sports was severely affected for two months**. He suffered from soft tissue injuries in his neck and lumbar spine and these resolved **within three months of the accident**. He also suffered from travel anxiety, resulting in one **emotional flashback** and particularly in circumstances **similar to the accident** and this also **resolved within three months**.

   J (a child) v Atkinson (unreported, 4 March 2013) (Joseph England, instructed by Co-operative Legal, Solicitors, for the claimant) (Kindly submitted for publication by Joseph England).

821   Neck and back

See para 798.

822   Chest

PSLA: £4,500
Total damages: £4,500
Sex: Female
Age at accident/trial: 55/57
Date of accident/trial: 28 July 2011/9 May 2013
Judge/Court: DJ Bishop/Croydon County Court

The claimant, a support worker, sustained a **soft tissue injury** to the right side of the **chest wall**, a soft tissue injury to the **right knee** and consequential **psychological symptoms**, including a fear of crossing the road. She was **crossing a road as a pedestrian when she was struck on her right side by a vehicle**. The claimant was **knocked to the ground**. Immediately after the accident she was in **pain over the right chest** region. She also developed discomfort over the right knee laterally and was taken to hospital by ambulance. Soft tissue injuries to the right side of the chest and the right knee were diagnosed. She was **discharged with two crutches** to aid mobility and advised to take **painkillers** for relief. The claimant used both **crutches for six weeks**. She then mobilised with one crutch intermittently for a few weeks more. After the accident the claimant experienced **daily pain in the right chest** region. The area was particularly **painful on pressure**. In relation to the **right knee, bruising** developed which lasted for around **one month**. Moving the knee was painful and the joint hurt on kneeling. The **acute symptoms** in her **chest and knee lasted for a period of eight weeks**. Thereafter, the symptoms began to improve. The claimant's physical injuries meant that she needed **help** from her partner **with domestic tasks** and **looking after her children**. She required such assistance **for a month** post-accident. In addition, she suffered **symptoms of anxiety** after the accident. On examination **four months after** the accident, she reported that she **still experienced residual right sided chest** problems, especially when pressure was applied to the chest wall. The expert noted that the claimant also had a pre-existing problem with pain below her right breast. The index chest injury was caused against this background of some level of pre-existing pain. The knee was painful on kneeling, which she tried to avoid doing. The expert's prognosis was for the **residual chest, right knee and psychological symptoms to settle within 12–18 months post-accident**.

Fender-Reid v Huie (unreported, 9 May 2013) (Stephen Garner, instructed by Thompsons, Solicitors, for the claimant; Angela Frost, instructed by Lyons Davidson, Solicitors, for the defendant) (Kindly submitted for publication by Stephen Garner).

823   Chest

PSLA: £1,000
Total damages: £1,000
Sex: Female
Age at accident/trial: 6/8
Date of accident/trial: 6 July 2010/25 January 2013
Judge/Court: DJ Silverwood-Cope/Chelmsford County Court

The claimant was a rear seat passenger in a vehicle which was hit at the driver's side front panel by a transit van. The claimant was sitting behind the passenger seat on a booster seat and was wearing a seatbelt. The claimant **developed a bruise and pain at the chest** along the seat belt area on the left side. She was **administered analgesics** by her mother and made a **full recovery within three weeks**.

AY (a child) v Draper (unreported, 25 January 2013) (Matthew Mason, instructed by MTA Solicitors LLP, Solicitors, for the claimant) (Kindly submitted for publication by Matthew Mason).

824   Back

PSLA: £17,000
Total damages: £17,000
Sex: Male
Age at accident/trial: 40/46
Date of accident/trial: 26 November 2007/20 June 2013
Judge/Court: DJ Wright/Brighton County Court

The unemployed claimant sustained an acceleration **injury to the low back**. A wheelbarrow began to twist over and he instinctively reached over to catch the handle. As he did so he felt a sudden **bolt of pain** in his lower back area. Intense pain followed immediately. It **radiated down his left leg into the left foot**. The left leg symptoms were sciatica-like in nature. The pain did not settle down so he **visited his GP** three days later. Mechanical low back pain was diagnosed. He was **prescribed diclofenac and diazepam** for relief. He underwent a course of **nine physiotherapy sessions**. He reported only **temporary relief** from his low back symptoms after each session of physiotherapy treatment. His lumbar muscle spasm was objectively reduced for a short while, but he remained **tender in the left lumbar spine** with **neurological symptoms radiating down the left leg and into the left foot**. The claimant **was unable to bend, stoop or lift properly**. He could **only sit for half an hour** maximally and was **unable to garden**. He **required care and assistance** from his son **around the home**, especially with **shopping and hoovering**. His **intimate life was radically affected**. As a result of his on-going low back symptoms he **never returned to his pre-accident occupation**. An **MRI scan** revealed that he had a **shallow broad-based disc protrusion** and a **disc bulge with loss of disc height**. The medico-legal expert concluded that the claimant had an **underlying history of degenerative back disease**. The present accident caused an **acceleration injury** to his low back for a period of ten years. The **on-going low back symptoms were permanent**, albeit the court **assessed** general damages based on **a ten year acceleration period**, and he would **never be able to return to manual work**.

Morrison v Hanson Aggregates Ltd (unreported, 20 June 2013) (Jonathan Butters, instructed by Dawson Hart, Solicitors, for the claimant; Stephen Garner, instructed by Beachcroft LLP, Solicitors, for the defendant) (Kindly submitted for publication by Stephen Garner).

825   Back

PSLA: £2,750
Total damages: £2,750
Sex: Male
Age at accident/trial: 57/60
Date of accident/trial: 1 October 2010/23 May 2013
Judge/Court: DJ Cope/Bristol County Court

The claimant, a company director, sustained a **soft tissue injury to the low back** with **associated paraesthesia into the left leg**. The claimant suffered **no immediate symptoms** after the accident. However, **two days later** he developed severe low back pain, stiffness and discomfort. He also developed **accompanying paraesthesia** into the **left leg** and **symptoms of travel anxiety**. He **attended hospital** and was advised that he had suffered soft tissue whiplash injuries. The claimant was **absent from work for three days**. For the first month post-accident the claimant medicated with **strong analgesia**. He was referred for **physiotherapy** treatment by his GP. He underwent a course of **six sessions** of treatment. The treatment was beneficial and his symptoms improved. The claimant was **unable to play golf** or **go to the gym** in the short-term because of his on-going symptoms. On examination **four months post-accident** his low back and left leg **symptoms had improved**. At that time, they were **moderate in intensity**. The prognosis was for **all of the physical symptoms to settle by ten months** post-accident. The symptoms of **travel anxiety settled two months after the** accident.

Bundy v Coe (unreported, 23 May 2013) (Jay Jagasia, instructed by Minster Law, Solicitors, for the claimant; Stephen Garner, Counsel, instructed by Cordner Lewis, Solicitors, for the defendant) (Kindly submitted for publication by Stephen Garner).

826   Back

See para 800.

827   Arm

PSLA: £5,500
Total damages: £5,500
Sex: Male
Age at accident/trial: 6/11
Date of accident/trial: 21 July 2008/21 June 2013
Judge/Court: DDJ Thomas/Lambeth County Court

The claimant **tripped on a protruding brick on a path** under the **control of the defendant**. He was immediately aware of **bleeding and extreme pain in his left arm**. The claimant attended his local A&E department, where x-rays revealed a **fracture of the distal fourth of his left radius and ulna in an unacceptable degree of volar angulation**. His left arm was splinted in a backslab, his wounds were treated and dressed and the claimant returned the next day for a closed manipulation and the application of an **above elbow cast**. This was **replaced with a below elbow plaster cast** about one month later. Later x-rays revealed some evidence of **bridging callus**. When the cast was removed, the claimant continued with his **own active mobilisation exercises**. **Left forearm was immobilised in casts for some seven weeks**, which fully resolved after about 14 weeks.

KD (a child) v Gallions Housing Association Ltd (unreported, 21 June 2013) (Thomas Crockett, instructed by Blake Lapthorn, Solicitors, for the claimant) (Kindly submitted for publication by Thomas Crockett).

828   Hand

PSLA: £5,000
Total damages: £5,060
Sex: Female
Age at accident/trial: 45/46
Date of accident/trial: 28 February 2011/9 July 2012
Judge/Court: DDJ Ellis/Brighton County Court

The claimant attended the defendant's tattoo parlour for a tattoo to be applied to the dorsum aspect of her left hand. During the course of her treatment, the claimant complained of excruciating pain. The left hand pain was acute for a week and the associated tenderness and swelling took approximately two weeks to resolve. Shortly after her treatment, the claimant noted a deepening blue discoloration extending from the mid-dorsum of her left hand to the palmar aspect of her left hand. The claimant suffered a very high degree of embarrassment due to the bruised appearance of her hand. On examination, the medical expert diagnosed the claimant as having sustained an injury when tattoo dye was inserted into the subcutaneous space of the left hand. The ink had slowly begun to diffuse through the subcutaneous tissues and the dermal tissues causing discolouration. The leeching extended from the dorsum of the left hand across the radial aspect corresponding to a line between the web space of the ring and middle fingers and the wrist joint itself. It further extended to approximately a centimetre from the bottom edge of the tattoo onto the palmar aspect of the left hand. The prognosis was for the discoloration to be permanent and likely to continue to cause the claimant some embarrassment. As the staining seemed to arise from the actual tattoo, only a local excision of the tattoo and skin grafting or laser treatment could prevent further leeching. However, the cosmetic effects of the excision/grafting were likely to be as embarrassing as the actual discolouration to the claimant's left hand.

Bartlett v Weston (t/a The Wizard of Ink) (unreported, 9 July 2012) (Elizabeth Dwomoh, Counsel, instructed by Mason & Co, Solicitors, for the claimant) (Kindly submitted for publication by Elizabeth Dwomoh).

829   Thigh

See para 807.

830   Knee

PSLA: £4,250
Total damages: £4,250
Sex: Female
Age at accident/trial: 5/9
Date of accident/trial: 14 February 2009/21 August 2012
Judge/Court: Bell DJ/Reigate County Court

The claimant slipped on some spilt water and fell in the defendant's supermarket. Immediately afterwards she was able to weight bear but not without pain in her left knee. She saw her GP three days afterwards who diagnosed a probable medial collateral ligament sprain. Most symptoms resolved after six weeks, after which the claimant resumed normal activities. However she continued to suffer mild and very occasional pain when playing games, particularly whilst running. Following a second medical report this was expressed to be at a nuisance level and possibly permanent.

PD (a child by her litigation friend ND) v Asda Stores (unreported, 21 August 2012) (Thomas Crockett, instructed by Attwaters Jameson Hill, Solicitors, for the claimant) (Kindly submitted for publication by Thomas Crockett).

831   Knee

PSLA: £1,450
Total damages: £1,450
Sex: Female

Age at accident/trial: 5/7
Date of accident/trial: 18 December 2010/7 January 2013
Judge/Court: DJ Bell/Reigate County Court

The claimant was travelling as a rear seat passenger in a **car that was stationary** when it was **hit from behind** by a vehicle being driven by the defendant. The defendant admitted liability for the collision. The claimant was **examined by a medico-legal expert three months post-accident** who opined that as a result of the accident the claimant sustained **moderate right knee pain and swelling (with limping) twenty minutes after the collision.** The swelling settled over one week. As a result the **claimant did not want to walk anywhere for two weeks.** A prognosis of **six months post-accident** was given in respect of the on-going symptoms. At the settlement hearing it was confirmed that the **claimant recovered in accordance with the prognosis.**

AR (*a child*) v *Bynoe* (unreported, 7 January 2013) (Matthew Mason, instructed by MTA Solicitors LLP, Solicitors, for the claimant) (Kindly submitted for publication by Matthew Mason).

832   Minor injuries

PSLA: £1,800
Total damages: £1,800
Sex: Female
Age at accident/trial: 15/17
Date of accident/trial: 19 July 2011/21 February 2013
Judge/Court: DJ Skerrett/Birmingham County Court

The claimant, a schoolgirl, was a rear passenger when the stationary vehicle in which she was in was struck in the rear by the defendant's vehicle at about 30mph. The claimant was **thrown forwards and backwards.** She was able to get out of the vehicle unaided. She experienced **moderate shock immediately** which **resolved after two days.** The claimant did not receive any treatment at the scene of the accident. The claimant later attended **casualty for treatment to her neck and right arm a day after** the accident and received advice to use painkillers and to stay active. The claimant also consulted her GP about her neck and right arm two days after the accident and received further advice to use **painkillers** and to stay active. She sustained **mild bruising** to the right arm, which **resolved after two weeks** and she also suffered moderate right arm pain. A day after the accident the claimant **developed moderated neck and shoulder pain,** three **sessions of physiotherapy** was required and this **resolved within four months.** A week after the accident the claimant developed moderately severe persistent headaches; this was a secondary injury to the neck pain and **resolved within four months.** The claimant **suffered with travel anxiety** which **resolved four months** after the accident. With regards to the claimant's home life she was **unable to walk the dog** and her **sleep was restricted.**

RW (*a child*) v *Pavlou* (unreported, 21 February 2013) (Thea Osmund-Smith, instructed by MTA Solicitors, Solicitors, for the claimant) (Kindly submitted for publication by Natasha Thynne).

833   Minor injuries

PSLA: £1,650
Total damages: £1,650
Sex: Female
Age at accident/trial: 13/14
Date of accident/trial: 5 October 2011/11 January 2013
Judge/Court: DJ England/Walsall County Court

The claimant, a schoolgirl, was a rear seat passenger wearing a seatbelt in a stationary car into the rear of which the defendant's vehicle had collided. The claimant was **thrown forwards** on impact. She **attended her doctor** following the accident where she was examined and received advice. **Pain in her neck and middle back resolved after four months.** Travel anxiety resolved after four months. Disturbed sleep resolved after two weeks.

JB (*a child*) v *Bailey* (unreported, 11 January 2013) (Gemma Roberts, instructed by MTA Solicitors LLP, Solicitors, for the claimant) (Kindly submitted for publication by Joanne Bloyce).

834   Minor injuries

PSLA: £1,150
Total damages: £1,150
Sex: Male
Age at accident/trial: 11/12
Date of accident/trial: 25 April 2011/29 January 2013
Judge/Court: DJ Brown/Telford County Court

The claimant was a front passenger in a stationary vehicle when the defendant collided with the rear of the vehicle. The claimant was thrown forwards then backwards and needed help getting out of the vehicle. He attended a walk-in centre for treatment to his back a day after the accident and received advice to take anti-inflammatories, which he took for two weeks. He developed severe upper back pain and stiffness four hours after the accident which resolved after two weeks. He also developed moderate pain in the shoulders which resolved after 10 days and developed moderate bruising and discomfort of the ribs four hours after the accident and this resolved after 10 days. The claimant was unable to do martial arts or play golf for two weeks and he had to miss a golf competition.

JH (a child) v Finch (unreported, 29 January 2013) (Carol Knotts, instructed by MTA Solicitors LLP, Solicitors, for the claimant) (Kindly submitted for publication by Natasha Thynne).

835   Minor injuries

PSLA: £1,000
Total damages: £1,000
Sex: Male
Age at accident/trial: 9/11
Date of accident/trial: 4 June 2011/21 January 2013
Judge/Court: DJ Silverwood-Cope/Chelmsford County Court

The claimant sustained minor injuries in a road traffic accident when he was the rear-seat passenger when the car collided with another car at about 30mph. The claimant was thrown in all directions. He was treated by a paramedic before given a lift home. He sustained friction burn to his left shoulder and suffered insomnia and moderate travel anxiety. He began taking over-the-counter painkillers shortly after the accident and finished taking them a week later. The claimant's sleep was restricted for a week.

WM (a child) v Denli (unreported, 21 January 2013) (Matthew Mason, instructed by MTA Solicitors LLP, Solicitors, for the claimant) (Kindly submitted for publication by Matthew Mason).

836   Neck

See para 799.

DEEDS AND OTHER INSTRUMENTS

Halsbury's Laws of England (5th edn) vol 32 (2012) paras 201–500

Articles

For articles relating to this title please refer to the Table of Articles at the beginning of the Abridgment.

837   Construction—purpose of deed—change of law—ascertaining profit and loss

See Lloyds TSB Foundation for Scotland v Lloyds Banking Group plc (Scotland), para 547.

DEFAMATION

Halsbury's Laws of England (5th edn) vol 32 (2012) paras 501–787

Articles

For articles relating to this title please refer to the Table of Articles at the beginning of the Abridgment.

838   Defamation—operators of websites—defence

The Defamation (Operators of Websites) Regulations 2013, SI 2013/3028 (in force on 1 January 2014), make provision about the calculation of the time limits which apply to actions which must be taken by a website operator with regard to the Defamation Act 2013 s 5. The 2013 Regulations, in particular, (1) exclude from the calculation of the 48-hour period, where action is to be taken by the operator within 48 hours of any point in time, any time which occurs on a weekend or bank holiday; (2) set out the information which must be contained in a notice of complaint in order for it to be valid; (3) specify the steps which a website operator must take on receiving a valid notice of complaint in order to benefit from the statutory defence; (4) provide that, where a website operator receives a notice alleging that a statement on its website is defamatory but the notice does not comply with the statutory requirements, the website operator must notify the person making the complaint of those requirements; and (5) empower the court to use discretion to treat any action which was taken outside the time required to be treated as though it was taken within that time limit.

839   Defamation—proceedings—trial by judge alone

See para 251.

840   Defamation Act 2013

The Defamation Act 2013 amends the law of defamation. The Act received the royal assent on 25 April 2013 and came into force in part on that day. The remaining provisions came into force on 1 January 2014: SI 2013/3027. For details of commencement, see the commencement table in the title STATUTES AND LEGISLATIVE PROCESS.

Section 1 provides that a statement is not defamatory unless its publication has caused or is likely to cause serious harm to the reputation of the claimant, and that for these purposes harm to the reputation of a body that trades for profit is not serious harm unless it has caused or is likely to cause the body serious financial loss. By virtue of s 2, the common law defence of justification is replaced by a new statutory defence which applies if a defendant shows that the imputation conveyed by the statement complained of is substantially true. Where the statement complained of contains two or more distinct imputations, the defence does not fail if, having regard to the imputations which are shown to be substantially true, those which are not shown to be substantially true do not seriously harm the claimant's reputation: s 2. Pursuant to s 3, the common law defence of fair comment is replaced by a new defence of honest opinion, which applies where a defendant shows that (1) the statement complained of was a statement of opinion; (2) the statement indicated, whether in general or specific terms, the basis of the opinion; and (3) an honest person could have held the opinion on the basis of any fact which existed at the time the statement was published or anything asserted to be a fact in a privileged statement published before the statement. The defence is defeated if the claimant shows that the defendant did not hold the opinion: s 3.

Section 4 replaces the common law defence of publication on a matter of public interest with a new statutory defence on the same basis available where a defendant shows that the statement complained of was, or formed part of, a statement on a matter of public interest and that he reasonably believed that publishing the statement was in the public interest. If the statement complained of was an accurate and impartial account of a dispute to which the claimant was a party, the court must in determining whether it was reasonable for the defendant to believe that publishing the statement was in the public interest disregard any omission of the defendant to take steps to verify the truth of the imputation conveyed by it: s 4. Where an action for defamation is brought against the operator of a website in respect of a statement posted on the website, s 5 creates a new defence for the operator to show that it did not post the statement on the website. The defence is defeated if the claimant shows that (a) it was not possible for him to identify the person who posted the statement; (b) he gave the operator a notice of complaint in relation to the statement; and (c) the operator failed to respond to the notice in accordance with provisions contained in regulations made by the Secretary of State: s 5.

Section 6 creates a new defence of qualified privilege relating to peer-reviewed statements in scientific or academic journals, which applies where the statement relates to a scientific or academic matter and, before the statement was published in the journal, an independent review of the statement's scientific or academic merit was carried out by the editor of the journal and one or more persons with expertise in the matter concerned. Under s 7, the circumstances in which the existing statutory defences of absolute and qualified privilege may be used are extended. Section 8 replaces the principle that each publication of defamatory material gives rise to a separate cause of action which is subject to its own limitation period (the 'multiple publication rule') with a single publication rule to prevent an action being brought in relation to publication of the same material by the same publisher after a one year limitation period from the date of the first publication of that material to the public or a section of the public.

By virtue of s 9, a court does not have jurisdiction to hear and determine an action brought against a person who is not domiciled in the United Kingdom, another EU member state or a state which is a party to the Convention on Jurisdiction and the Recognition and Enforcement of Judgments in Civil and Commercial Matters (Lugano, 30 October 2007) unless it is satisfied that, of all the places in which the statement complained of has been published, England and Wales is clearly the most appropriate place in which to bring an action in respect of the statement. A court does not have jurisdiction to hear and determine an action for defamation brought against a person who was not the author, editor or publisher of the statement complained of unless it is satisfied that it is not reasonably practicable for an action to be brought against the author, editor or publisher: s 10. Section 11 removes the presumption in favour of jury trials in defamation cases. Where a court gives judgment for the claimant in an action for defamation, it may order the defendant to publish a summary of the judgment (s 12), and order the operator of a website on which a defamatory statement is posted to remove the statement or require any person who was not the author, editor or publisher of the statement but is distributing, selling or exhibiting the material to cease disseminating it (s 13). Section 14 provides that the publication of a statement that conveys the imputation that a person has a contagious or infectious disease does not give rise to a cause of action for slander unless the publication causes the person special damage. Sections 15, 16 contain definitions, consequential amendments and savings, and s 17 deals with short title, extent and commencement.

Amendments, repeals and revocations
The list below, which is not exhaustive, mentions repeals and amendments that are effective when the Act is fully in force.

Specific provisions of the following Acts are amended or repealed: Slander of Women Act 1891; Defamation Act 1952 ss 5, 6; Rehabilitation of Offenders Act 1974 s 8; Senior Courts Act 1981 s 69; County Courts Act 1984 s 66; Defamation Act 1996 ss 14, 15, Sch 1.

841   Defamatory statement—meaning—inferences drawn by reasonable person

The claimants manufactured electric cars. The first vehicle they produced was made available for review in a television programme broadcast by the defendant. The review, which lasted about 10 minutes, was included in an edition of the programme and was subsequently shown by the defendant and other television channels on several occasions and remained available to view on the defendant's website. The claimants alleged that a statement in the programme that 'although [the claimants] say it will do 200 miles, we worked out that on our track it would run out after just 55 miles' was defamatory because it meant that they intentionally or recklessly grossly misled potential purchasers of the car. The claimants sought damages for libel and malicious falsehood. The judge found that the words complained of were wholly incapable of conveying the meaning alleged by the claimants and struck out the claim for libel. The judge also ordered that the claim for malicious falsehood be struck out unless the claimants applied for permission to amend it. On appeal against the refusal of permission to amend, an issue arose as to whether the judge was wrong to hold that the words, sounds and images which made up the programme were incapable of bearing the meaning pleaded in the claim. *Held*, it was clear from what the

had acted as he had so that the politician would engage in improper discussion with the representatives of the companies regarding EU tariffs on imports into the EU (the first meaning); and (2) the incident was an example of how the claimant had sought to impress and keep the first third party close to him (the second meaning). In establishing meaning, the judge accepted that the words complained of had included a general allegation that the claimant's alleged conduct in relation to the dinner in Moscow was an example of how the claimant had acted to impress the first third party. The judge decided that the defence of justification had been met as the defendant had established that the words complained of had been substantially true in the meaning which he had found them to bear. The claimant appealed. *Held,* on the facts, the judge had correctly pitched the sting of the Moscow dinner. The language of the article was the language of suspicion, albeit very strong suspicion, but no more. The judge had been entitled to conclude as he had at head (1)(b) of the first meaning. Although the greater part of the article was taken up by the Moscow dinner, it had not been confined to one event. The judge had been right to conclude that it had contained the wider themes to which he had referred. The dinner had been an example of the cross-currents of the relationship between the claimant and the politician. That was what had been conveyed by the judge in his second meaning. On the face of it, out of context, there was nothing disreputable about seeking to impress and keep the first third party close. However, that ignored the judge's finding that the dinner had been an example of the claimant's facilitating role. The sting of the second meaning was the implicit accusation that the claimant had been prepared to use his long-standing friendship with the politician as a means by which to impress and keep the first third party close to him and, in doing so, he should have foreseen that he would bring the politician's public offices and personal integrity into disrepute. Inherent in those findings was the conclusion, critical to the justification defence, that, in acting as he had, the claimant had known or should have foreseen that he would expose the politician to suspicion or accusations of conflict of interest and improper discussions, suspicions or accusations which in fact eventuated. The judge's plain finding that the claimant had known or should have known that that would happen was no more fragile than any of his other conclusions. That was the sting of the Siberia trip; the sting of the proved instance of the general charge. However, it was also, in essence, the sting of the published, unproved instance, the Moscow dinner. Once the proved instance of the general charge, the Siberia trip, was understood against the whole background of the evidence, the claimant had had no more reputation to lose by the false tale of the Moscow dinner. Accordingly, the appeal would be dismissed.

Rothschild v Associated Newspapers Ltd [2013] EWCA Civ 197, [2013] All ER (D) 191 (Mar) (Court of Appeal: Laws and McCombe LJJ and Eady J). *Berezovsky v Forbes Inc* [2001] EWCA Civ 1251, [2001] EMLR 1030, [2001] All ER (D) 452 (Jul) applied. *Turcu v News Group Newspapers Ltd* [2005] EWHC 799 (QB), [2005] All ER (D) 34 (May) considered. Decision of Tugendhat J [2011] EWHC 3462 (QB), [2011] All ER (D) 188 (Dec) (2011 Abr para 1743) affirmed in part.

846   Defence—privilege—qualified privilege—summary judgment—prospects of claimant defeating defence

The claimants were police constables serving in the Metropolitan Police Service. In November 2011, the defendants published or caused to be published a news item concerning a violent arrest of a man, B, which had remained available for viewing on a website since that date, but which had not named or identified the claimants. In November 2012, the claimants issued a claim form seeking damages for libel and an injunction. They contended that the words complained of bore the natural and ordinary meaning that each claimant had dishonestly conspired with the other claimants in order to mislead a police disciplinary tribunal. Further that, each claimant had done so by cynically giving false evidence to the tribunal, dishonestly and in breach of his duties as a police officer, and that, prior to the arrest of B, each claimant had had reason to believe that he carried weapons and had threatened the police before. In November 2013, the defendants gave notice that they were seeking orders that the claim be struck out as an abuse of process under CPR 3.4(2) and, alternatively, summary judgment in their favour under CPR 24.2. They intimated they would rely on defences, including under *Reynolds* that it was a report of a matter of public interest published responsibly and that there was no real prospect of the claimants recovering anything other than minimal damages. To that end, the third defendant gave evidence that, at a briefing, the Metropolitan Police Service had mentioned the explanation attributed to the claimants in the newspaper, namely, that B had a history of carrying weapons and of using violence towards police officers. The claimants contended that the Metropolitan Police Service could not be understood as having stated that the evidence that the claimants gave at the disciplinary hearing was the same as the explanation attributed to them in a newspaper. It fell to be determined whether the claimants had a reasonable prospect of defeating the *Reynolds* defence. *Held*, in essence, the elements of the *Reynolds* defence were that (1) the publication concerned was a matter of public interest; and (2) the steps taken to gather, verify and publish the information had been responsible and fair. Further, on an application for summary judgment under CPR 24.2, the defendants had to establish that the claimants had no real prospect of success and that there was no other compelling reason why the claim should be disposed of at trial. The word 'real' directed the court to the need to consider whether there was a realistic, as opposed to fanciful, prospect of success. The claimants had to have a case which was better than merely arguable. In the context of libel actions and the right to a jury trial, judgment should not be given at any stage which had the effect of depriving the parties of a jury decision in any case where the defence or claim might depend on a finding of fact which would be properly open to a tribunal. On the facts, the claimants had no real prospect of persuading the court to reject the third defendant's evidence in so far as he stated that, at the briefing the Metropolitan Police Service had mentioned the explanation attributed to the claimants in the newspaper. On that finding, there was no real prospect of the claimants defeating the *Reynolds* defence that the defendants had intimated that they would advance if the claims were to go forward. Further, there was no real prospect of the claimants denying or of being believed if they did deny, that at some stage material to the investigation of the events, they had advanced, as a justification for the force they had used, that there had been intelligence that B had had a history of carrying weapons and of using violence towards police officers. Furthermore, any damage to the claimants' reputations would have to be assessed after taking into consideration the damage their reputations had suffered by reason of the finding of discreditable conduct. With respect to continuing publication, in the absence of any clear and convincing denial by the claimants that that had been their case at some point in the investigation, they had no real prospect of defeating the *Reynolds* defence in respect of continuing publication. Accordingly, the application for summary judgment would be allowed.

Kneafsey v Independent Television News Ltd [2013] EWHC 4046 (QB), [2013] All ER (D) 222 (Dec) (Queen's Bench Division: Tugendhat J). *Reynolds v Times Newspapers Ltd* [2001] 2 AC 127, [1999] 4 All ER 609, HL (1999 Abr para 2135), applied.

847   Libel—publication—internet posting—lack of control over content—duty to remove content

The Defamation Act 1996 s 1(1) provides that, in defamation proceedings, a person has a defence if he shows that (1) he was not the author, editor or publisher of the statement complained of; (2) he took reasonable care in relation to its publication; and (3) he did not know, and had no reason to believe, that what he did caused or contributed to the publication of a defamatory statement.

The defendant, an American company, operated a free service that enabled internet users to create an online blog hosted on the defendant's servers. The claimant complained to the defendant about the contents of one such blog that contained statements that he believed were defamatory of him. After approximately four months of communications between the parties involved, the blog and all of the comments were removed. The claimant decided to bring a libel action against the defendant. The judge decided that three of the comments had been arguably defamatory, but that on common law principles the defendant was not a publisher of the words complained of. The judge also stated that, if the defendant was to be regarded as a publisher at common law, it would have a defence under the 1996 Act s 1. The judge accepted that the period between notification and removal of the offending comments had been so short as to give rise to potential liability on the part of the defendant only for a very limited period, such that the court should regard its potential liability as so trivial as not to justify the maintenance of the proceedings. On the claimant's appeal, it fell to be determined whether (a) there was an arguable case that the defendant was a publisher of the comments; (b) if it was a publisher, it would have an unassailable defence under s 1; and

(c) any potential liability had been so trivial as not to justify the maintenance of the proceedings. *Held*, in the period prior to notification of the complaint, it could not be said that the defendant's role had been that of a secondary publisher. However, in relation to the position after notification, additional considerations arose. If the defendant allowed defamatory material to remain on a blog after it had been notified of the presence of that material, it might have been inferred to have associated itself with, or to have made itself responsible for, the continued presence of that material on the blog and thereby to have become a publisher of the material. On the facts, the period during which the defendant might have fallen to be treated as a publisher of the defamatory comments would be a very short one, but it meant that the claim could not be dismissed on the ground that the defendant had not been a publisher at all. The judge had also erred in his interpretation of s 1. Following notification, the defendant had known or had had reason to believe that what it had done had caused or contributed to the continued publication of the comments within the meaning of s 1(1)(c). It followed that, if the defendant were found to be a publisher of the defamatory comments, s 1 would not provide it with an unassailable defence. However, in the circumstances, any damage to the claimant's reputation arising out of the continued publication of the comments during the period between publication on and removal from the blog would have been trivial. Accordingly, the appeal would be dismissed.

Tamiz v Google [2013] EWCA Civ 68, [2013] All ER (D) 163 (Feb) (Court of Appeal: Lord Dyson MR, Richards and Sullivan LJJ). Decision of Eady J [2012] EWHC 449 (QB), [2012] All ER (D) 14 (Mar) (2012 Abr para 906) affirmed.

848   Malicious falsehood—defamatory words—false assertion

The claimant and defendant companies were rivals in the oil business. The claimant brought a claim for malicious falsehood against the defendant in which it contended that the defendant had, in a letter, falsely asserted that a report issued by the claimant, purporting to tell customers that it was appropriate to consider that the claimant's product had the same characteristics as the defendant's product, was misleading and erroneous. In earlier proceedings, the court refused the defendant's application to stay the proceedings in favour of parallel proceedings in the United States of America. The defendant applied to strike out the claim. *Held*, the essential constituents of the tort of malicious falsehood were set out in authority. The defendant had to publish, about the claimant, words which were false and that had been published maliciously, and special damage had to have followed as the direct and natural result of their publication. As to the special damage, it was sufficient if the words published in writing were calculated to cause pecuniary damage to the claimant. Malice would be inferred if it was proved that the words were calculated to produce damage and that the defendant had known when he had published the words that they had been false or that he had been reckless as to whether they were false. In the circumstances, the court rejected the application to strike out the entire claim. The real technical dispute in the case was about the qualities of the defendant's own products. If the defendant's letter had simply asserted that the two products were, in all material respects, the same and if the claimant was basing its claim for malicious falsehood on that assertion alone, then the court would accept the defendant's submissions and strike the claim out. However, that was not the way the claim was constituted. The claim was based on the allegedly false assertion by the defendant that a report issued by the claimant was misleading and erroneous. That was a distinction from the principles articulated in authority. The question was whether the distinction was a sufficient one to render the claim properly arguable. It was. Therefore, the application to strike out the malicious falsehood claim or for summary judgment in the defendant's favour would be dismissed, albeit that some aspects of the claimant's pleadings would need to be addressed. Accordingly, the application would be dismissed.

Niche Products Ltd v Macdermid Offshore Solutions LLC [2013] EWHC 3540 (IPEC), [2013] All ER (D) 169 (Nov) (Chancery Division: Birss J). *Kaye v Robertson* (1990) Times, 21 March, CA (1990 Abr para 1495), applied. For related proceedings see [2013] EWPCC 11, [2013] All ER (D) 129 (Apr).

849   Malicious falsehood—defamatory words—reasonably available meaning—
       imputation of criminal conduct

See *Cruddas v Calvert*, para 843.

850 Proceedings—costs—assessment—costs exceeding approved budget

See *Henry v News Group Newspapers Ltd*, para 263.

851 Proceedings—costs—failure to file costs budget—sanctions

See *Mitchell v News Group Newspapers Ltd*, para 246.

DISCRIMINATION

Halsbury's Laws of England (5th edn) vol 33 (2013) paras 1–352

Articles

For articles relating to this title please refer to the Table of Articles at the beginning of the Abridgment.

852 Age discrimination—employment—redundancy—quantum of payments— proportionate means of achieving a legitimate aim

An employee was 26 years old with almost eight years' service when she applied for voluntary redundancy under the employer's voluntary redundancy scheme. She was entitled to a significantly lower redundancy payment than a person with the same length of service over the age of 35 would have been entitled to. She brought an age discrimination claim before an employment tribunal. The employment tribunal found that statistical evidence showed that there were material differences between the age groups, in particular between those below the age of 30 and those above the age of 35. Individuals in younger age categories could generally be expected to react more easily to the loss of their jobs and with greater flexibility. The employment tribunal concluded that the employee had not been treated less favourably than any comparator over the age of 35 because her circumstances were materially different from his. It further held that, in any event, the aim of the employer's voluntary redundancy scheme was to produce a proportionate financial cushion until alternative employment had been found, or as a bridge to retirement and the receipt of a pension. In view of the statistical evidence, it could not be said that the age bands chosen were inappropriate or disproportionate. The decision was affirmed on appeal and the employee appealed further. *Held*, the employee's age of 26 had not made her case materially different from that of an appropriate comparator, an employee aged 36 or older whose employment situation was otherwise the same. It followed that the employee had suffered age discrimination. In determining the question of objective justification, the employment tribunal's task had been to carefully assess the evidence before it in the course of deciding whether the employer had discharged the burden of showing the disparate treatment of employees in different age groups had been a proportionate means of achieving the aim underlying the employer's voluntary redundancy scheme. The employment tribunal had carried out that exercise and had given careful consideration to the evidence before holding that the employer's scheme was objectively justified. Accordingly, the appeal would be dismissed.

Lockwood v Department for Work and Pensions [2013] EWCA Civ 1195, [2014] 1 All ER 250 (Court of Appeal: Rimer, Lewison and Treacy LJJ). *Shamoon v Chief Constable of the Royal Ulster Constabulary* [2003] UKHL 11, [2003] 2 All ER 26 (2003 Abr para 959) applied.

853 Disability discrimination—duty to make reasonable adjustments—mental health patient—claim for benefits

The claimants suffered from mental health problems. They were required to undertake a work capability assessment ('WCA') for determination of eligibility for employment and support allowance. The WCA was designed to assess an individual's functional ability, focusing on what he could do rather than what he could not do. In judicial review proceedings, the claimants contended that because of their particular difficulties, as mental health patients ('MHPs'), the decision-maker would not necessarily obtain a properly informed appreciation of either their disabilities or their ability to work and might therefore reject claims on a false basis. This was because it was not possible for them to complete accurately the WCA due to their fluctuating mental health condition, lack of insight of their condition, or being unable to accurately describe how the condition affects them. Further, it was submitted that the process of completing the questionnaire and undergoing the interviews caused some MHPs disproportionate stress when compared with applicants suffering from other disabilities. The claimants further submitted that those adverse consequences could be minimised, and even in some cases eliminated, if the Secretary of State amended the procedures in accordance with a duty to make reasonable adjustments under the Equality Act 2010 so as to require the decision-maker in every case to obtain further medical evidence before a decision was reached, save where that information had already been voluntarily provided. The Upper Tribunal was satisfied that the difficulties faced by MHPs placed them at a substantial disadvantage when compared with other disabled persons who did not experience mental health problems. The Tribunal then directed the Secretary of State to carry out an investigation into the reasonableness of the evidence-seeking adjustment and to file further evidence on that matter. The Secretary of State appealed. *Held*, the Tribunal was in principle able to find that prima facie discrimination had been committed against the claimants, and had therefore been entitled to declare, as a step relevant to the establishment of a breach of duty, that the current policy created a substantial disadvantage to MHPs in general. There had been nothing inconsistent in the Tribunal's approach in recognising the force in the proposition that the extent of substantial disadvantage was limited but then nevertheless holding that, looking at the matter more broadly, the adoption of the evidence-seeking adjustment would have made a difference both to outcomes and adverse experiences of the process. The Tribunal had been right when it rejected the submission on the grounds that the premise that the exercise of a function had to necessarily lead either to a benefit or a detriment. It might be both, depending on the circumstances. It had been inappropriate for the Tribunal to issue directions of the nature it had given. The Tribunal had been acting under the misapprehension that it was its task to determine what a reasonable adjustment would be and it was therefore seeking the appropriate evidence to fulfil that function. That was not a proper approach. The Tribunal's task was to determine whether any of the adjustments proposed by the claimants would be reasonable. Further, it was accepted that the Tribunal could properly indicate that it was not satisfied that the material it had seen demonstrated that the proposed adjustment would be unreasonable, and it had been helpful for it to indicate the kind of material it thought might assist it to reach a conclusion on the question. However, it was ultimately for the Secretary of State to adduce such evidence and advance such arguments as he thought appropriate in order to discharge the burden now placed on him. The Tribunal's directions would be quashed and the Secretary of State's submission that the Tribunal had misunderstood the scope of its powers and ought not to have issued the directions it had would be upheld. Accordingly, the appeal would be allowed in part.

R (on the application of MM) v Secretary of State for Work and Pensions [2013] EWCA Civ 1565, [2013] All ER (D) 67 (Dec) (Court of Appeal: Maurice Kay VP, Elias and Vos LJJ). *Eba v Advocate General for Scotland* [2011] UKSC 29, [2012] AC 710, [2011] STC 1705 (2011 Abr para 1649); and *Cooke v Secretary of State for Social Security* [2001] EWCA Civ 734, [2002] 3 All ER 279 applied.

854   Disability discrimination—employment—claim—costs

An employee brought claims of unfair dismissal and disability discrimination against her employer. An employment tribunal dismissed the claims except in relation to the employer's failure to make reasonable adjustments concerning the employee's disability. The tribunal rejected the employee's other discrimination claims on the basis that she was not disabled by reason of her mental impairment. The tribunal subsequently ordered the employee to pay 50 per cent of the employer's costs of the proceedings, partly because the employee had made a series of unspecified and unsupported allegations against her employer during the course of the action. On her appeal, the employee contended that the tribunal had erred in failing to take account of the deduced effect of her illness under the Disability Discrimination Act 1995 Sch 6 para 1, and that the costs order should be set aside. The appeal was dismissed on the ground that, although there had been an error of law on the part of the tribunal as regards the deduced effect of the employee's illness, none of her claims for discrimination arising out of such a disability would have succeeded had the error not been made. On the employee's further appeal, *held*, in the circumstances, an additional finding that the employee was disabled by reason of mental impairment would not have affected the outcome of the case. Applying the relevant test, the conclusion of the tribunal was plainly and unarguably right, irrespective of its failure to address the deduced effect of the employee's treatment. Also, the tribunal's decision as to costs had not been reached contrary to, or in disregard of, any relevant principle, and it had not been plainly wrong. Notwithstanding the exceptional nature of the award and its implications for the employee, the tribunal's decision had come well within the proper exercise of its discretion. The reasons for, and the basis of, the order had been clearly specified, without the tribunal attempting to identify a precise causal link between the unreasonable conduct and the specific costs that were awarded. The tribunal had been exercising its broad discretion, sufficiently identifying the relevant unreasonable conduct and its effect without seeking to go beyond an appropriate broad brush first instance assessment. Accordingly, the appeal would be dismissed.

Sud v Ealing LBC [2013] EWCA Civ 949, [2013] All ER (D) 386 (Jul) (Court of Appeal: Maurice Kay VP, Patten and Fulford LJJ). *Dobie v Burns International Security Services (UK) Ltd* [1984] 3 All ER 333, CA (1984 Abr para 2850), applied.

Disability Discrimination Act 1995 replaced by Equality Act 2010.

855   Disability discrimination—employment—'disabled person'—opinion of
       occupational health advisers

An employee informed his employer that he was suffering from stress, identified a number of symptoms, and the employer referred him to its external occupational health advisers for an assessment for stress counselling. The employee was signed off work due to sickness on a number of occasions and the employer liaised with the advisers with regard to the employee's condition. Medical advisers on behalf of the occupational health advisers wrote to the employer advising it that the employee was likely to remain unfit for the foreseeable future and that he was not covered under the Disability Discrimination Act 1995. The employee subsequently returned to work, but was suspended following allegations of historic bullying. He was then dismissed and commenced proceedings for disability discrimination. He claimed that he was a disabled person for the purposes of the 1995 Act and asserted direct discrimination and a failure by the employer to make reasonable adjustments. At a preliminary stage, an employment tribunal found that the employee had been a disabled person for the purposes of s 1. At a substantive hearing, the tribunal found that, unless the employer had good reason for forming its own different view, it was entitled to rely on the opinion of its medical advisers as to whether the employee was a disabled person. If such advisers had advised the employer of their view that the employee was not a disabled person, then, even if the fact was that he was a disabled person, the employer did not have the knowledge requisite for the engagement of his obligations towards the employee not to discriminate against him directly on the ground of his disability. The tribunal dismissed the disability discrimination claims. Its decision was affirmed on appeal. On further appeal by the employee, *held*, the responsible employer had to make its own judgment as to whether an employee was disabled. In making that judgment, the employer would rightly want assistance and guidance from occupational health or other medical advisers. That assistance and guidance might be to the effect that the employee was a disabled person and, unless the employer had good reason to disagree with the basis of such advice, he would ordinarily respect it in his dealings with the employee. In other cases, the guidance might be that the opinion of the adviser was that the employee was not a disabled person. The employer should not forget that it was still the employer which had to make the factual judgment as to whether the employee was disabled. The employer could not simply rubber stamp the adviser's opinion that he was not. There was a need for the employer, when seeking outside advice from clinicians, not simply to ask in general terms whether the employee was a disabled person within the meaning of the legislation, but to pose specific practical questions directed to the particular circumstances of the putative disability. The answers would then provide real assistance to the employer in forming its judgment as to whether the criteria for disability were satisfied. In the circumstances, the opinions of the occupational health advisers had amounted to no more that assertions of their view of the 1995 Act. No supporting reasoning had been provided. Their opinion was worthless; the employer had to form its own judgment on whether the employee was a disabled person and the occupational health advisers' views on that topic had been of no assistance. Accordingly, the appeal would be allowed.

Gallop v Newport City Council [2013] EWCA Civ 1583, [2014] IRLR 211 (Dec) (Court of Appeal: Longmore and Rimer LJJ and Sir John Mummery).

856   Disability discrimination—employment—discrimination arising from disability—knowledge of disability

An employee was a journalist employed full time by her employer, a magazine publisher, initially as assistant editor and then as features editor. She developed osteoarthritis of the knees and negotiated an arrangement under which she became a part-time copy editor who did additional work for the magazine on a freelance basis. She underwent four operations and was off work for three or four weeks for each and was due to have a further operation, which was known to the employer. The employer merged the teams working on the employee's magazine and another magazine and the publishing director informed the employee that her copy editor post was going to be redundant. Following her dismissal, the employee brought proceedings before an employment tribunal for disability discrimination under the Equality Act 2010 ss 13 and 15. The tribunal held that the absence of any persuasive evidence explaining the employer's failure to ensure that the employee had the opportunity to apply for two posts which had become available, coupled with her record of absences, which were a consequence of her osteoarthritis, constituted facts from which it could conclude that the former had occurred because of the latter. It considered that the combination of those factors shifted the burden of proof under s 136 to the employer to prove that it had not been influenced by the employee's absences. Though the tribunal rejected the employee's claim for direct disability discrimination under s 13, it upheld her claim for discrimination arising from her disability under s 15 on the basis that the employer had failed to consider her for the two vacancies because of her past and anticipated future absences. The employer appealed. *Held*, in terms of s 15(1)(a), an act or omission could occur 'because of' something which arose in consequence of an employee's disability where it operated on the mind of the putative discriminator to a significant extent. The starting point in a case which depended on the thought processes of the putative discriminator was to identify the individual responsible for the act or omission in question. In the present case, the omission was the failure to give the employee the opportunity of applying for the two vacancies. The individual responsible for that failure was the publishing director. The tribunal had not made an explicit finding about whether the publishing director knew about the employee's absences and the facts did not justify a finding that she did. Therefore, there was no basis for the tribunal's finding of discrimination under s 15. Accordingly, the appeal would be allowed.

IPC Media Ltd v Millar [2013] IRLR 707 (Employment Appeal Tribunal: Underhill J presiding). *Nagarajan v London Regional Transport* [2000] 1 AC 501, [1999] 4 All ER 65, HL (1999 Abr para 1215), applied.

857   Disability discrimination—employment—dismissal—employee absent on sick leave

The employee in the first case was employed by a housing authority in Denmark. She was absent from work on several occasions during a six-month period due to constant and untreatable lumbar pain. No prognosis could be made concerning the prospect of her returning to full-time employment, and the defendant employer decided to dismiss her. The employee subsequently started part-time work at another organisation. The employee in the second case was employed as an office assistant by a Danish company. Following a road accident, she was absent on sick leave for three weeks. By agreement, she subsequently went on part-time sick leave for four weeks, and eventually she went on full-time sick leave. Her doctor reported that he could not give an opinion on the duration of her unfitness for work. Her employer decided to dismiss her. In both cases the employees were dismissed in accordance with a provision of Danish law that permitted employers to give a shortened period of notice on account of periods of absence due to sickness. The purpose of the law was to encourage employers to recruit and maintain in their employment workers who were particularly likely to have repeated absences because of illness, by allowing them subsequently to dismiss them with a shortened period of notice, if the absences tended to have been for very long periods. As a counterpart, those workers could retain their employment during the period of illness. The claimant trade union brought anti-discrimination proceedings on behalf of the employees, submitting that they were disabled within the meaning of Council Directive (EC) 2000/78 and that the employers had been obliged to offer them reduced working hours pursuant to their duty under art 5 to accommodate employees with a disability. A preliminary ruling was sought as to whether such legislation was compatible with Directive 2000/78. *Held*, Directive 2000/78 had to be interpreted as precluding national legislation under which an employer could terminate an employment contract with a reduced period of notice if the disabled worker concerned had been absent because of illness, with his salary being paid, for 120 days during the previous 12 months, where those absences were the consequence of the employer's failure to take the appropriate measures in accordance with the obligation to provide reasonable accommodation laid down in art 5. Further, Directive 2000/78 had to be interpreted as precluding national legislation under which an employer could terminate the employment contract with a reduced period of notice if the disabled worker concerned had been absent because of illness, with his salary being paid, for 120 days during the previous 12 months, where those absences were the consequence of his disability, unless that legislation, as well as pursuing a legitimate aim, did not go beyond what was necessary to achieve that aim, that being for the referring court to assess.

Cases C-335/11 and C-337/11 *HK Danmark v Dansk Almennyttigt Boligselskab; HK Danmark v Dansk Arbejdsgiverforening* [2013] IRLR 571 (ECJ: Second Chamber).

858   Disability discrimination—housing benefit—additional requirements of disabled person

The Benefit Cap (Housing Benefit) Regulations 2012, SI 2012/2994, introduced changes to the Housing Benefits Regulations 2006, SI 2006/213. The relevant changes altered the basis on which maximum housing benefit was calculated in relation to rents in the public sector. They reduced the eligible rent for the purpose of the calculation in cases where the number of bedrooms in the property let exceeded the number permitted by reference to criteria set out in the 2006 Regulations reg B13. Regulation A13(1) required the relevant housing authority to determine a maximum rent for accommodation in the public rented sector in accordance with reg B13. The Discretionary Financial Assistance Regulations 2001, SI 2001/1167, made under the Child Support, Pensions and Social Security Act 2000 s 69, empowered the grant of discretionary housing payments by authorities and, while being a broad discretion, was targeted to housing benefit recipients. The issue of whether discretionary housing payments provided a targeted means of mitigating the impact of the changes introduced by the 2012 Regulations was investigated during the evolution of the proposed policy introduced by the 2012 Regulations. The defendant Secretary of State stated that money had been allocated to authorities in regard to discretionary housing payment, that discretionary housing payments guidance would be issued and that he would closely monitor and adjust the implementation of the policy to ensure that the needs of the relevant groups were effectively addressed. The present judicial review proceedings were brought by a number of claimants, each of whom was entitled to housing benefit and each of whom was either disabled and/or shared their accommodation with a disabled person, including, in some instances, a child or children with disabilities. The challenge was mounted on the grounds that the measures introduced by the 2012 Regulations were unlawfully discriminatory because they failed to provide for the needs of people in the claimants' position; the claimants being said to represent a range of individuals who were typical of those who were adversely affected by the changes for reasons relating to disability in a way that violated their rights under the European Convention on Human Rights art 14. They further contended that the new measures constituted or involved a violation by the defendant of the public sector equality duty imposed by the Equality Act 2010 s 149. *Held*, (1) where discrimination was direct it was the rule itself that had to be justified. Where the discrimination was indirect (where a single rule had disparate impact on one group as opposed to another) it was the disparate impact that had to be justified. With discrimination such as in the case of *Thlimmenos v Greece*, what had to be justified was the failure to make a different rule for those adversely affected. Indirect and *Thlimmenos* discrimination were closely allied applications of the principle that like cases should be treated alike and that different cases should be treated differently. The present case could best be regarded as asserting an instance of *Thlimmenos* discrimination. The contention was that the claimants should be treated differently, more favourably, than others who were covered by the rule complained of. (2) It was plain that the public sector equality duty set an important standard for public decision-making. Where the protected characteristics specified in the

868   Sex discrimination—compensation—joint and several liability

See *Sivanandan v Hackney LBC*, para 789.

869   Sex discrimination—difference in treatment—male prisoners subjected to rub-down search conducted by female prison officer

The claimant was convicted of murder and sentenced to life imprisonment. He was granted permission to apply for judicial review of the defendant Secretary of State's policy on 'rub-down' searches which provided that male prisoners could not normally object to such searches being conducted by a female prison officer other than when his case fell within exceptions based on religious or cultural grounds. The cultural exception covered sincere and deeply held beliefs, but did not extend to an objection that cross-gender searching caused discomfort. As a result of the policy, the claimant had been subjected to rub-down searches conducted by female officers on many occasions. At the time of the present hearing, he was a Category D prisoner. The principal issues that fell to be determined were whether the policy: (1) amounted to discrimination on the ground of sex; (2) amounted to discrimination on the ground of lack of religion; (3) infringed the claimant's rights under the European Convention on Human Rights art 8; (4) infringed the claimant's rights under art 14; and (5) constituted a breach of public law principles. The claimant submitted that the existing exceptions based on religious or cultural grounds were too limited. *Held,* (1) the claimant's concession that he did not contend that male prisoners should only ever be searched by male staff showed that it was accepted by him that the fact that male prisoners were treated differently from their female counterparts did not in itself automatically constitute discrimination on the grounds of sex. The lack of other similar complaints after 20 years of the policy's life showed that the exceptions to the policy were fair, proportionate and reasonable. (2) In order to succeed on the claim that the policy amounted to discrimination on the grounds of lack of religion, the claimant had to establish that he had been less favourably treated, that that less favourable treatment had been because of his lack of religious belief when compared with the way in which someone with a religious belief had been or would have been treated and that in the circumstances, their positions were materially the same. In the present case, the reason why the claimant could not object to cross-gender searching was because his claim of distress did not qualify for an exemption under the cultural grounds exception and not because he lacked a religious belief. (3) The searches achieved the aims of preventing escapes, reducing self-harming by prisoners and detecting threats to security by reducing the number of illicit items that were within the prison estate. The exceptions to the policy were a proportionate way of dealing with genuine objections by male prisoners to being searched by female officers. Accordingly, the challenges under both art 8 and art 14 failed as the policy was justified. (4) The width of the exceptions to the policy did not lead to an unacceptable risk of unlawful decision making. The cultural exception was sufficiently wide to cover the case of an objection that arose from a sincerely and deeply held belief. Further, that the cultural exception was to be decided on a case by case basis showed that rational consideration was required by the prison officer. Accordingly, the claim would be dismissed.

R (on the application of Dowsett) v Secretary of State for Justice [2013] EWHC 687 (Admin), [2013] All ER (D) 270 (Mar) (Queen's Bench Division: Silber J).

870   Sex discrimination—employment—entitlement to paternity leave—refusal on ground of mother's self-employed status

See Case C-5/12 *Montull v Instituto Nacional de la Seguridad Social*, para 1046.

871   Sex discrimination—employment—equal pay and treatment—indirect discrimination—justification

Nine female employees brought a claim before an employment tribunal for equal pay on the basis that they had been paid less than two male comparators, who they claimed were employed on 'like work' within the meaning of the Equal Pay Act 1970 s 1(2)(a). It was common ground that there was a genuine and material explanation for the difference in pay, namely the amalgamation of two roles at different seniority levels into a single post and the application of the employer's practice of maintaining an employee's existing pay point. The tribunal found that the employees, on comparison with the male comparators, were at a relative or comparative particular disadvantage by the amalgamation and the application of the pay protection policy. Having found indirect sex discrimination, the tribunal held that the employer had not made out the defence of objective justification. It rejected the employer's contentions that it had legitimate aims of preventing the employees or their comparators suffering a reduction in pay and retaining their skills and experience. The tribunal considered that the discriminatory effect might have been reduced by the 'red circling' of the pay of those on higher pay points. Alternatively, it considered that the discriminatory effect could have been eliminated by assimilation of the junior role into the new post. The tribunal found that the employer's arguments on justification were not strong in light of the reasonable alternatives available to it. The employer's appeal succeeded on the ground that the employment tribunal had not been entitled to make a finding of prima facie indirect discrimination and that the immediate cause of the disparity in pay had been nothing to do with gender. The Employment Appeal Tribunal went on to consider the issue of objective justification in case it was wrong on the prima facie discrimination issue. It concluded that protecting the pay of employees affected by restructuring was, in principle, a legitimate aim and that it had been a legitimate aim in the present case. The Appeal Tribunal also found that the pay protection policy was legitimate. It criticised the suggested alternatives of assimilation and 'red circling' and, in particular, could not see how assimilation was relevant to the question of whether the resulting disparity could be justified. The employees appealed. *Held*, Mummery LJ dissenting, the employment tribunal appeared to have accepted the employer's stated aims but to have rejected them as being legitimate. The employment tribunal had not asked itself the right question and had been wrong in law in rejecting the employer's aims as legitimate ones. Further, despite having rejected the employer's aims as legitimate, the employment tribunal went on to consider the question of proportionality. The Appeal Tribunal was correct to reject the employment tribunal's suggestion of red circling and assimilation. The Appeal Tribunal had been well equipped to assess whether any issue meriting remission arose and its decision to substitute conclusions had been within its discretion. Accordingly, the appeal would be dismissed.

Haq v Audit Commission [2012] EWCA Civ 1621, [2012] IRLR 206 (Court of Appeal: Mummery and Lewison LJJ and Sir Mark Waller).

872   Sex discrimination—employment—equal pay and treatment—surrogacy leave—
       entitlement to leave equivalent to maternity or adoption leave

An employee was employed as a postprimary school teacher, pursuant to terms and conditions of employment determined by a government department, which was responsible for her pay. She had a rare condition which had the effect that, although she had healthy ovaries and was fertile, she had no uterus and so could not support a pregnancy. In 2008 and 2009, the employee and her husband opted for surrogacy and turned to a specialist agency in California. In vitro-fertilisation treatment took place in Ireland, with egg transfer to the surrogate mother occurring in California. The employee travelled to California in order to be present at the birth of the child. As a matter of Californian law, the employee and her husband were considered the baby's parents and the surrogate mother was not identified on the child's birth certificate. The employee with, the help of her husband, had been taking care of the child since the birth. They returned with their baby to Ireland, a member state in which surrogacy arrangements were unregulated. The terms and conditions of the employee's employment included a right to paid maternity leave and adoptive leave. When either kind of leave was taken by a teacher employed subject to those terms and conditions, the payment in respect of such leave was, in the majority of cases, disbursed in part by the government department, and the balance paid by the Department of Social Protection in the form of maternity benefit. Since she had not been pregnant and could not give birth to a child, the employee was unable to satisfy the statutory requirements for taking maternity leave. Nor was she in a position to qualify for adoptive leave since she had not adopted a child born through surrogacy. In February 2010, the employee had made an application to the government department for leave equivalent to adoptive leave. That application had been refused on the ground that she had not satisfied the requirements laid down by the existing maternity or adoptive leave schemes. In November 2010, the employee brought an action against the government department before the Equality Tribunal. She claimed that she had been the subject of discriminatory treatment on the grounds of gender, family status and disability, that the government department had failed to reasonably accommodate her as a person with a disability, and that the government department had refused to provide her with paid leave equivalent to maternity or adoptive leave, although she had undergone in vitro fertilisation treatment. The Equality Tribunal stayed the proceedings and sought a preliminary ruling from the Court of Justice for the European Union. It sought to ascertain whether: (i) European Parliament and Council Directive (EC) 2006/54, in particular arts 4 and 14, were to be interpreted as meaning that a refusal to provide paid leave equivalent to maternity leave or adoptive leave to a female worker who as a commissioning mother had had a baby through a surrogacy arrangement constituted discrimination on grounds of sex and, if not, whether that Directive was valid in the light of art 3 of the TEU, arts 8, 157 of the TFEU and arts 21, 23, 33 and 34 of the Charter of Fundamental Rights of the European Union ('the Charter'); and (ii) whether Council Directive (EC) 2000/78, interpreted if necessary in the light of the United Nations Convention on the Rights of Persons with Disabilities ('the UN Convention'), should be understood as meaning that a refusal to provide paid leave equivalent to maternity leave or adoptive leave to a female worker who was unable to bear a child and who had availed of a surrogacy arrangement constituted discrimination on the ground of disability and, if not, whether that Directive was valid in the light of art 10 TFEU, arts 21, 26 and 34 of the Charter and the UN Convention. *Held*, (1) Directive 2006/54, in particular arts 4 and 14, should be interpreted as meaning that a refusal to provide paid leave equivalent to maternity leave to a female worker who as a commissioning mother had had a baby through a surrogacy arrangement did not constitute discrimination on grounds of sex. Further, the situation of such a commissioning mother as regards the grant of adoptive leave was not within the scope of that Directive. Accordingly, it was not necessary to examine the validity of that Directive in the light of the various provisions of the TEU, TFEU and the Charter. (2) Directive 2000/78 should be interpreted as meaning that a refusal to provide paid leave equivalent to maternity leave or adoptive leave to a female worker who was unable to bear a child and who had availed of a surrogacy arrangement did not constitute discrimination on the ground of disability. Further, the validity of that Directive could not be assessed in the light of the UN Convention, but that Directive should, as far as possible, be interpreted in a manner that was consistent with that Convention.

Case C-363/12 *Z v A Government Department* [2014] All ER (D) 175 (Mar) (ECJ: Grand Chamber).

873 Sex discrimination—employment—equal pay and treatment—justification for difference in pay

The employees were female civil servants assigned to clerical duties in the Irish police force. They considered that they were engaged in work equivalent to that of male police officers also assigned to clerical duties in specific posts reserved for members of the police. The employees brought equal pay proceedings. The court found that there was prima facie indirect pay discrimination, but that the discrimination was justified. The employees appealed. On a reference for a preliminary ruling, questions arose as to the interpretation of the EC Treaty art 141 and Council Directive (EEC) 75/117 (on the approximation of the laws of the member states relating to the application of the principle of equal pay for men and women). *Held*, the EC Treaty art 141 and Directive 75/117 had to be interpreted as meaning employees performed the same work or work to which equal value could be attributed if, taking account of a number of factors such as the nature of the work, the training requirements and the working conditions, they could be considered to be in a comparable situation, which was a matter for the national court to ascertain. In relation to indirect pay discrimination, it was for the employer to establish objective justification for the difference in pay between the workers who considered that they were discriminated against and the comparators. The employer's justification for the difference in pay, which was evidence of a prima facie case of gender discrimination, had to relate to the comparators who, on account of the fact that their situation was described by valid statistics which covered enough individuals, did not illustrate purely fortuitous or short-term phenomena, and which, in general, appeared to be significant. The interests of good industrial relations might be taken into consideration by the national court as one factor among others in its assessment of whether differences between the pay of two groups of workers were due to objective factors unrelated to any discrimination on grounds of sex and were compatible with the principle of proportionality.

Case C-427/11 *Kenny v Ministry for Justice, Equality and Law Reform* [2013] IRLR 463 (ECJ: Third Chamber).

EC Treaty art 141 now TFEU art 157.

874   Sex discrimination—employment—equal pay and treatment—work of equal value—same employment

Scotland

The claimants were classroom assistants, support for learning assistants and nursery nurses employed in the defendant local authority's schools. Their individual contracts specified the particular school at which they were based and also stated that they might be required to work at other locations. The posts were predominantly held by women. The claimants brought an equal pay claim against the defendant, using as their comparators a variety of manual workers employed by the defendant, including groundsmen, refuse collectors, refuse drivers and a leisure attendant. The comparators were based at various depots in the area, from which they would go out to do their work in a variety of locations. Although some of their work was done at schools, they were not based there. Their individual contracts of employment specified the depot at which they were based and that they might be required to work at other locations. A pre-hearing review was held in order to determine whether the appellants were in the same employment as the comparators within the meaning of the Equal Pay Act 1970 s 1(6). The tribunal decided that the employees were not in the same employment. In coming to that conclusion, the tribunal adopted an approach in which it considered the adjustments that might be made to the comparators' terms and conditions of employment in the unlikely event that they were transferred to the claimants' workplace. The claimants appealed, submitting that the tribunal's approach was wrong in law. *Held,* the common terms and conditions referred to in s 1(6) were not those of, on the one hand, the female applicants and, on the other hand, their claimed comparators. They were, on the one hand, the terms and conditions under which the male comparators were employed at different establishments from the women and, on the other hand, the terms and conditions under which those male comparators were or would be employed if they had been employed at the same establishment as the women. It was no answer to say that no such male comparators ever would be employed, on those or any other terms, at the same establishment as the women. Otherwise, it would be far too easy for an employer so to arrange things that only men worked in one place and only women in another. Some very different jobs which were not or could not be carried out in the same workplaces might nevertheless be rated as equivalent or assessed as having equal value. The effect of the deemed equality clause was to modify the relevant term of the woman's contract so as not to be less favourable than a term of a similar kind in the contract under which the man was employed or to include a beneficial term in her contract if she had none. Further, the object of the 'same employment' test was to weed out those cases in which geography played a significant part in determining what those terms and conditions were. Applying those principles, the claimants were in the same employment as the chosen comparators. Accordingly, the appeal would be allowed.

North v Dumfries and Galloway Council [2013] UKSC 45, [2013] 4 All ER 413 (Supreme Court: Lord Hope DP, Lady Hale, Lord Wilson, Lord Reed and Lord Hughes SCJJ). Decision of Inner House [2011] CSIH 2, [2011] IRLR 239 (2011 Abr para 878) reversed.

1970 Act s 1(6) replaced by Equality Act 2010 s 79(2)–(4).

875   Sex discrimination—employment—redundancy—criteria for selection—performance review—person returning from maternity leave

See Case C-7/12 *Riezniece v Zemkopibas minisrija*, para 1042.

876   Sex discrimination—employment—unfair pay arrangements—application to strike out

Two female employees were employed as port assistants. They brought a claim against their employer, alleging that they were entitled to be paid the same as output clerks, one of whom was male, for performing like work. The employees conceded that they did not seek to contend that they had been directly discriminated against. The employer applied to strike out the claim, contending that the employees could not hope to establish indirect discrimination because the available pool had simply been far too small to amount to providing significant statistics which would compel a tribunal to conclude that there had been a systematic disadvantage to women as a group. The employees had not identified any provision, criterion or practice. Therefore, the employees had no hope of success before the tribunal. The judge refused the application, having considered that the employees had not conceded that the employer had provided a defence, under the Equality Act 2010 s 69, namely that there had been a material factor which had been the cause of the disparity in pay. On the employer's appeal, it fell to be determined whether the tribunal judge had erred in exercising her discretion to refuse the employer's application to strike out the claim. *Held*, the starting point was for the employer to show that the difference between the men's pay and the woman's pay was because of a material factor. Where a pay disparity arose for examination, it was not sufficient for an employer to show why one party was paid as one party was. The statute required an explanation for the difference, which inevitably involved considering why the claimants were paid as they were, on the one hand, and separately, why the comparator was paid as he was. Discrimination claims in particular should not be struck out where they involved a core disputed fact. In the circumstances, the judge had completely identified that the employees had not conceded the reasons advanced by the employer. Therefore, there remained a prima facie case of discrimination. It had to be answered on the facts. It followed that the decision which the judge had reached had been one which had been within her discretion and she had not erred in law. Accordingly, the appeal would be dismissed.

Wallace v Calmac Ferries Ltd [2013] All ER (D) 242 (Dec) (Employment Appeal Tribunal: Langstaff J presiding). *Nelson v Carillion Services Ltd* [2003] EWCA Civ 544, [2003] IRLR 428 (2003 Abr para 955) considered.

877   **Sexual orientation discrimination—employment—occupational pension scheme—supplementary retirement pension**

See Case C-147/08 *Romer v Freie und Hansestadt Hamburg*, para 1981.

878   **Sexual orientation discrimination—hoteliers—religious beliefs—refusal to let double-bedded rooms to unmarried couples**

The defendants were devout Christians who ran a hotel. They had a policy of only allowing heterosexual married couples to have double rooms. Single and twin rooms were available to any person regardless of marital status or sexual orientation. The claimants were a homosexual couple who went to stay at the hotel. On arrival, they were informed that the double rooms were for married couples only. The claimants stated that they were in a civil partnership. The defendants confirmed that they did not believe in civil partnerships, that marriage was only between a man and woman and that they could not honour the booking. The claimants were refunded their deposit. Proceedings were commenced by the claimants. They claimed that they had been subjected to unlawful discrimination on account of sexual orientation. It was found that the hotel policy amounted to direct discrimination within the meaning of the Equality Act (Sexual Orientation) Regulations 2007, SI 2007/1263, reg 3(1). The defendants' appeal was dismissed. On their further appeal, *held*, Lord Neuberger P and Lord Hughes dissenting in part, reg 3(4) provided that people who were married and people who were civil partners were to be regarded as similarly situated. If followed that the policy amounted to direct discrimination on the grounds of sexual orientation and was therefore unlawful. There was great difficulty in seeing how discriminating between a married and a civilly-partnered person could be anything other than direct discrimination on the grounds of sexual orientation. At the time of the hearing, marriage was only available between a man and a woman and civil partnership was only available between two people of the same sex. The principal purpose of each institution was to provide a legal framework within which loving, stable and committed adult relationships could flourish. The criterion of marriage or civil partnerships was indissociable from the sexual orientation of those who qualified to enter it. Further, there was an exact correspondence between the advantage conferred and the disadvantage imposed in allowing a double bed to the one and denying it to the other. With regard to justification, to permit someone to discriminate on the grounds that he did not believe that persons of homosexual orientation should be treated equally with persons of heterosexual orientation would be to create a class of people who were exempt from the discrimination legislation. Further, reg 14 contained a carefully tailored exemption for religious organisations and ministers of religion from the prohibition of both direct and indirect discrimination on the grounds of sexual orientation. That strongly suggested that the purpose of the 2007 Regulations was to go no further than that in catering for religious objections. Finally, in respect of the Human Rights Act 1998, sexual orientation was a core component of a person's identity which required fulfilment through relationships with others of the same orientation. The courts should be slow to accept that prohibiting hotel keepers from discriminating against homosexuals was a disproportionate limitation on their right to manifest their religion. The defendants could not get round the fact that United Kingdom law prevented them from acting as they had. The reasons for holding that the denial of a double-bedded room could not be justified under reg 3(3)(d) were equally relevant to the question of whether the limitation on the defendants' right to manifest their religion had been a proportionate means of achieving a legitimate aim. Accordingly, the appeal would be dismissed.

Bull v Hall [2013] UKSC 73, [2014] 1 All ER 919 (Supreme Court: Lord Neuberger P, Lady Hale DP, Lord Kerr, Lord Hughes and Lord Toulson SCJJ). Decision of Court of Appeal [2012] EWCA Civ 83, [2012] 2 All ER 1017 (2012 Abr para 935) affirmed.

The defendant ran a bed and breakfast business from her house. Of the seven bedrooms at the house, three were let to guests. Because of her Christian beliefs, the defendant sought to restrict the sharing of double bedrooms to heterosexual, preferably married, couples. She neither allowed couples of the same sex to share a double room nor knowingly allowed an unmarried heterosexual couple to do so. The claimants were a homosexual couple who were not in a civil partnership. The first claimant contacted the defendant about booking a double room, She offered him the same and the first claimant sent a cheque for the deposit. On their arrival, the defendant told the claimants that there was a problem as they had booked a double room. She made it clear that she would not accommodate them because she did not like the idea of two men sharing a bed. She refunded the deposit and the claimants left. Had two separate rooms been available, the defendant would have allowed the claimants to stay but in separate bedrooms. The claimants alleged that they had been unlawfully discriminated against on the ground of their sexual orientation contrary to the Equality Act (Sexual Orientation) Regulations 2007, SI 2007/1263. The recorder held that there had been such unlawful discrimination. On the defendant's appeal, an issue arose as to whether the defendant's house was a 'boarding house or similar establishment' within the meaning of reg 4(2)(b). *Held*, there was no reason to hold that 'board' had to include more than one meal per day. The normal meaning of the word was the provision of accommodation and some food which was prepared, served and cleared away by the provider. Further, a bed and breakfast establishment was similar to a hotel and boarding house in that accommodation was provided for varying periods of time and the guests received at least one meal per day; some hotels and boarding houses provided full or half board, but many only provided bed and breakfast. There was no policy reason why Parliament would have intended to protect individuals from discrimination on grounds of sexual orientation in relation to the provision of half board, that was bed, breakfast and one other meal, but not in relation to the provision of bed and breakfast accommodation. Regulation 4(2)(b) was concerned with protecting the rights of guests staying in commercial accommodation, not just the rights of those who had breakfast plus one other meal. The recorder had been correct to find that a bed and breakfast establishment was capable of falling within the meaning of the term 'boarding house' in the 2007 Regulations. Even if the defendant did not provide accommodation in a boarding house, in the alternative, the accommodation was in a 'similar establishment' within the meaning of reg 4(2)(b). The recorder had been correct to reject the defendant's interpretation of the exception contained in reg 6(1). Both the recorder and the present court were bound to follow the decision in *Bull v Hall* and hold that there had been unlawful direct discrimination on the ground of sexual orientation. Had the present court not been bound to hold that there had been direct discrimination against the claimants, it would have held that the defendant had indirectly discriminated against a homosexual couple on the ground of their sexual orientation by having applied a policy which put them at a disadvantage as compared with a heterosexual couple and which the defendant could not reasonably justify by reference to matters other than the claimants' sexual orientation. Accordingly, the appeal would be dismissed.

Black v Wilkinson [2013] EWCA Civ 820, [2013] All ER (D) 108 (Jul) (Court of Appeal: Lord Dyson MR, Arden and McCombe LJJ). *Bull v Hall* [2012] EWCA Civ 83, [2012] 2 All ER 1017 (2012 Abr para 935) (affd [2013] UKSC 73, [2014] 1 All ER 919 (see above)) criticised.

2007 Regulations replaced by Equality Act 2010.

879   Victimisation—employment—duty of tribunal to consider complaint separately

An employee, who was of Pakistani origin, worked for his employer, a local authority, as a housing benefits officer. He also worked on a voluntary basis for the same employer as a canvasser for electoral services. The employee was subject to disciplinary proceedings in relation to various incidents, including his involvement in an alleged forgery of canvass forms. The employee was eventually made redundant. He brought a claim before an employment tribunal asserting that his dismissal was not on the ground of redundancy, but was actually for prohibited reasons, namely that he had made protected disclosures and had been harassed and subjected to less favourable treatment on racial grounds. The tribunal rejected the claim and the employee appealed, submitting that the tribunal had not dealt adequately with his specific allegation that he had been victimised within the meaning of the Equality Act 2010 s 27. *Held*, although the tribunal could have dealt separately and distinctly with the heads of direct discrimination, harassment and victimisation rather than rolling them together, it was sufficiently plain that it did consider the acts which were said to be complaints of discrimination. It concluded that they had no express relationship to race. It therefore concluded that, if any act was to be proved to have been done by the employer in response to those complaints, it would not amount to victimisation under either the Race Relations Act 1976 or the 2010 Act. The present decision should not be taken as any general endorsement of the view that, where an employee complained of discrimination, he had not yet said enough to bring himself within the scope of s 27. However, the tribunal was entitled to reach the decision it did, since the employee on unchallenged evidence had been invited to say that he was alleging racial discrimination. Instead of accepting that invitation, he had stated, in effect, that his complaint was rather of unfair treatment generally. The tribunal said enough in its decision, taken as a whole, to justify its conclusion that the employee had no reasonable prospect of success in a claim for victimisation for having raised a complaint relating to racial discrimination. Accordingly, the appeal would be dismissed.

Durrani v Ealing LBC [2013] All ER (D) 218 (Sep) (Employment Appeal Tribunal: Langstaff J presiding).

880   Victimisation—employment—post-employment victimisation—poor reference following issue of equality proceedings

An employee was employed by the first defendant employer company. The second defendant was a director of the company. The employee was dismissed on the ground that he was aged over 65. He issued proceedings alleging unfair dismissal and age discrimination. The employer gave the employee, who was looking for alternative employment, a very poor reference. The employee believed that the reason for the reference was because he had issued proceedings and he presented a further claim alleging victimisation contrary to the Equality Act 2010. An employment tribunal upheld the claims of unfair dismissal and age discrimination. It found that the reason for the bad reference had been that the employee was pursuing tribunal proceedings. However, it held that 'post-employment victimisation' was not unlawful under the 2010 Act. The Employment Appeal Tribunal affirmed the tribunal's decision on the victimisation issue. However, in separate proceedings two months later, it found in *Onu* that the 2010 Act did prohibit acts of victimisation committed against a former employee. On the employee's appeal, it fell to be determined whether the 2010 Act applied to post-employment victimisation. Consideration was given to ss 39, 40, 83 and 108 and to Council Directive (EC) 2000/43 (implementing the principle of equal treatment between persons irrespective of racial or ethnic origin), Council Directive (EC) 2000/78 (establishing a general framework for equal treatment in employment and occupation) and Parliament and Council Directive (EC) 2006/54 (on the implementation of the principle of equal opportunities and equal treatment of men and women in matters of employment and occupation (recast)). *Held*, post-termination victimisation was proscribed by the 2010 Act. The apparent failure of the Act to proscribe post-termination victimisation was a drafting error. Firstly, when the Act had been drafted, the existing state of the law had been that post-termination victimisation was unlawful. The draftsman would have been, and Parliament could be taken to have been, well aware of that history. Secondly, there was no indication that the government, in promoting the Act, had intended to change the law by withdrawing, even if only with regard to victimisation, the protection previously enjoyed by former employees. The Act's purpose, although not formally a consolidating statute, was to re-state with some clarifications and enhancements where necessary, existing protections against discrimination (including victimisation and harassment). Thirdly, the explanatory notes to the Act stated that post-termination victimisation was intended to be proscribed, albeit by (unidentified) 'victimisation provisions' other than s 108. Fourthly, if post-termination victimisation were not proscribed, the United Kingdom would be in breach of its obligations as a matter of EU law. Finally, no rational basis had been suggested for treating post-termination victimisation differently from post-termination discrimination and harassment. Given the obligation under EU law to proscribe post-termination victimisation, the only question was whether it was 'possible' to imply words into the Act which achieved that result. The answer was that it was; the implication of such a provision would not only be consistent with the fundamental principles of the Act but in fact represented what the draftsman had intended. Given the tribunal's finding of fact that the second defendant had given the reference that he had because the employee was pursuing tribunal proceedings, the victimisation claim succeeded and the case would be remitted to the tribunal for the assessment of compensation. Accordingly, the appeal would be allowed.

Jessemey v Rowstock Ltd [2014] EWCA Civ 185, [2014] All ER (D) 237 (Feb) (Court of Appeal: Maurice Kay VP, Ryder and Underhill LJJ). *Onu v Akwiwu* [2013] IRLR 523, EAT (para 864), considered. Decision of Employment Appeal Tribunal [2013] IRLR 439 reversed.

ECCLESIASTICAL LAW
Halsbury's Laws of England (5th edn) vol 34 (2011) paras 1–1201

Articles
For articles relating to this title please refer to the Table of Articles at the beginning of the Abridgment.

881 Church minister—contract of employment—existence of contract
See *President of the Methodist Conference v Preston*, para 1003.

882 Clergy—discipline appeal rules
The Clergy Discipline Appeal (Amendment) Rules 2013, SI 2013/1921 (in force on 1 February 2014), amend the 2005 Rules, SI 2005/3201, by (1) making provision in relation to applications for leave to appeal and permission to appeal out of time and the making of representations as to the suitability of a proposed member of the appellate court; and (2) revising prescribed forms.

883 Clergy—discipline rules
The Clergy Discipline (Amendment) Rules 2013, SI 2013/1917 (in force on 1 February 2014), amend the 2005 Rules, SI 2005/2022, and make provision in relation to (1) the non-disclosure to a respondent to a complaint of the contact details of the complainant or of the maker of a statement in support; (2) the postponement of the resolution of complaints, where appropriate, to await the outcome of police or other investigations; (3) delaying the notification of a complaint to a respondent in exceptional circumstances; (4) the making of representations where the imposition of a penalty by consent has been proposed; (5) time limits in which representations may be made as to the suitability of a proposed member of the tribunal; (6) the pronouncement of determinations or penalties in the event of the death or incapacity of the chair of the tribunal; (7) the suspension of priests, deacons, bishops and archbishops following conviction for a criminal offence or inclusion on a barred list; (8) notices, and notifications to others, of suspension; (9) applications for the extension of the two-year period for the imposition of a penalty; and (10) the disposal by the President of Tribunals of any application, appeal or request. A number of amendments to prescribed forms are also made.

884 Clergy Discipline (Amendment) Measure 2013
The Clergy Discipline (Amendment) Measure 2013 amends the Clergy Discipline Measure 2003. The Measure received the royal assent on 26 March 2013 and came into

899   Apprenticeships—existing vocational specifications—transitional provision

The Apprenticeships (Transitional Provision for Existing Vocational Specifications) (Wales) Order 2013, SI 2013/1202 (in force on 23 June 2013), specifies the existing vocational specifications which are to be treated as if they were apprenticeship frameworks issued under the Apprenticeships, Skills, Children and Learning Act 2009 s 19(1). The existing vocational specifications are to be treated as being issued on 23 June 2013 and as being withdrawn on 28 June 2013. The 2013 Order specifies, for each of the existing vocational specifications, the qualification that is to be treated as the competencies qualification, and the level and apprenticeship sector that is to be treated as being stated in the deemed framework.

900   Apprenticeships—standards—specification—England

The Apprenticeships (Modifications to the Specification of Apprenticeship Standards for England) Order 2013, SI 2013/575 (in force on 6 April 2013), provides for the document entitled 'Specification of Apprenticeship Standards for England (SASE)', published by the Secretary of State on 20 January 2011, to have effect with the modifications contained in the document entitled 'Specification of Apprenticeship Standards for England (SASE)', published by the Secretary of State on 7 March 2013.

901   Apprenticeships, Skills, Children and Learning Act 2009—commencement

The Apprenticeships, Skills, Children and Learning Act 2009 (Commencement No 4) (Wales) Order 2013, SI 2013/1100, brings into force, on 10 May 2013, ss 2, 7–10, 18–22, 28–31, and, in relation to Wales only, ss 11, 12, 39.

The Apprenticeships, Skills, Children and Learning Act 2009 (Commencement No 6) Order 2013, SI 2013/975, brings into force, on 31 May 2013, ss 145 and 146, and a repeal in Sch 16.

For a summary of the Act, see 2009 Abr para 1187. See also the commencement table in the title STATUTES AND LEGISLATIVE PROCESS.

902   Education and Skills Act 2008—commencement

The Education and Skills Act 2008 (Commencement No 9 and Transitory Provision) Order 2013, SI 2013/1204, brings into force (1) on 28 June 2013, ss 1 (in part), 2–8, 10–14, 16–18, 39(1), (2), 62(1), (2), (5), (6), 64(1), (2), (5), 66; and (2) on 26 June 2015, s 1 (so far as not already in force). Transitory provision is also made. For a summary of the Act, see 2008 Abr para 1267. See also the commencement table in the title STATUTES AND LEGISLATIVE PROCESS.

903   Education and training—duty to participate

The Duty to Participate in Education or Training (Miscellaneous Provisions) Regulations 2013, SI 2013/1205 (in force on 28 June 2013), make provision in relation to the duty of young people, under the Education and Skills Act 2008 Pt 1 (ss 1–67), to participate in education or training until the age of 18 or, if earlier, the attainment of a level 3 qualification. The 2013 Regulations, in particular, (1) specify the qualifications and descriptions of qualifications which comprise a level 3 qualification; (2) set out the types of education provided otherwise than at a school, or training, which are to be treated as full-time for the purposes of the 2008 Act; (3) define 'normal weekly working hours'; (4) provide that persons who work at least 40 hours each fortnight or who are serving members of the armed forces are to be treated as working for at least 20 hours each week and therefore being in full-time occupation; (5) make provision in relation to the date on which a relevant period, during which a person should fulfil the duty to participate in education or training, ends; (6) make provision in relation to the calculation and attribution of hours of guided learning within a relevant period; and (7) modify the 2008 Act Pt 1 Ch 1 (ss 1–8) in relation to serving members of the armed forces.

904   Education (Wales) Measure 2011—commencement

The Education (Wales) Measure 2011 (Commencement No 2) Order 2013, SI 2013/2090, brings ss 22–25 into force on 22 August 2013. For a summary of the Measure, see 2011 Abr para 931. See also the commencement table in the title STATUTES AND LEGISLATIVE PROCESS.

905   Further education—student support—eligibility—person ordinarily resident—
       unlawful residence

The claimant was a Nigerian national who arrived in the United Kingdom on a visitor's visa. The visa expired but the claimant remained in the United Kingdom as an overstayer. The claimant's application for leave to remain was refused by the Secretary of State. However, the Asylum and Immigration Tribunal allowed her appeal and she was granted discretionary leave to remain. The claimant was accepted on a degree course. She applied to the Student Loans Company for financial assistance and her application was accepted. The university enrolled the claimant as an overseas student. That led to judicial review proceedings, which resulted in a consent order that the university should treat the claimant as 'a person with leave to remain' under the Education (Fees and Awards) (England) Regulations 2007, SI 2007/779. When the claimant's status as an overstayer came to light, her student grant payments were cancelled on the ground that she did not have the required period of ordinary residence because, for part of the relevant period, her presence in the United Kingdom had been unlawful. The claimant's appeal was unsuccessful. The Secretary of State subsequently confirmed the decision to revoke assistance, determining that the claimant did not meet the qualification criteria for assistance under the Education (Student Support) Regulations 2009, SI 2009/1555, as she had not been 'ordinarily resident' in the United Kingdom for the period of three years preceding the first day of the first academic year of study for the purposes of reg 5(1)(c). The claimant sought judicial review of the decision. Her application was refused, the judge holding that ordinary residence could not be based on a period of unlawful residence. The claimant appealed, submitting that the judge had erred in concluding that unlawful residence could not be or count towards ordinary residence. Consideration was given to previous authority that a person could not rely on his unlawful residence in a country as constituting ordinary residence. *Held*, there had been no error on the part of the judge. The obiter dicta in *Shah v Barnet LBC* clearly explained the rationale for implying a requirement of lawfulness into the residence on which 'ordinary residence' was based. That rationale had been accepted as implicit in successive sets of regulations. The draftsman of the 2009 Regulations had to be taken as having intended to import that settled understanding of the phrase 'ordinarily resident'. Accordingly, the appeal would be dismissed.

  R (on the application of Arogundade) v Secretary of State for Business, Innovation and Skills [2013] EWCA Civ 823, [2013] All ER (D) 177 (Jul) (Court of Appeal: Longmore and McCombe LJJ and Sir Stanley Burnton). *Shah v Barnet LBC* [1983] 2 AC 309, [1983] 1 All ER 226, HL (1982 Abr para 1001), applied. Decision of Robin Purchas QC [2012] EWHC 2502 (Admin), [2012] All ER (D) 52 (Sep) (2012 Abr para 959) affirmed

  2009 Regulations replaced by Education (Student Support) Regulations 2011, SI 2011/1986.

906   Further education—student support—European institutions—Wales

The Education (European Institutions) and Student Support (Wales) Regulations 2013, SI 2013/765 (in force on 23 April 2013), replace the 2011 Regulations, SI 2011/736, and provide for financial support for eligible students ordinarily resident in Wales undertaking postgraduate courses at the graduate school for international relations established by Johns Hopkins University at Bologna and the College of Europe.

907   Governors—annual reports—Wales

The National Curriculum (Amendments relating to Educational Programmes for the Foundation Phase and Programmes of Study for the Second and Third Key Stages) (Wales) Regulations 2013, SI 2013/437 (in force in part on 1 May 2013 and in part on 1 September 2013), amend (1) the School Governors' Annual Reports (Wales) Regulations 2011, SI 2011/1939, so as to require the governing body of a maintained school to publish, in its annual report, the most recent literacy and numeracy comparative information in relation to the school's performance in the literacy and numeracy tests; (2) the Head Teacher's Report to Parents and Adult Pupils (Wales) Regulations 2011, SI 2011/1943, so as to require the head teacher of a maintained school to report to parents on the results of (a) the end of phase tests in the foundation phase in the final year the child is in the foundation phase; (b) the literacy and numeracy tests; (3) the School Information (Wales) Regulations 2011, SI 2011/1944, so as to require governing bodies of maintained schools to publish in the school prospectus the most recent literacy and numeracy comparative information in relation to the school's performance in the literacy and numeracy tests; and (4) the School Performance Information (Wales) Regulations 2011, SI 2011/1963, so as to require the governing body of a maintained school to include in the information provided to Welsh Ministers and local authorities the results of the literacy and numeracy tests.

908   Healthy Eating in Schools (Wales) Measure 2009—commencement

The Healthy Eating in Schools (Wales) Measure 2009 (Commencement) Order 2013, SI 2013/1985, brings into force (1) ss 1–3, 5–11 on 2 September 2013; and (2) s 4 on 8 August 2013. For a summary of the Measure, see 2009 Abr para 1206. See also the commencement table in the title STATUTES AND LEGISLATIVE PROCESS.

909   Her Majesty's Chief Inspector of Education, Children's Services and Skills—fees and frequency of inspections

See para 220.

910   Higher education—student fees—England

See para 913.

911   Higher education—student fees, awards, qualifying course and persons—Wales

The Education (Student Fees, Awards, Qualifying Courses and Persons) (Wales) Regulations 2013, SI 2013/1792 (in force on 1 September 2013), further amend the Education (Fees and Awards) (Wales) Regulations 2007, SI 2007/2310, and the Student Fees (Qualifying Courses and Persons) (Wales) Regulations 2011, SI 2011/691, by (1) adding a reference to St-Barthélemy, following European Council Decision (EU) 2010/718, which changed the status of St-Barthélemy from one of the outermost regions of the European Union to an overseas country or territory; and (2) removing the requirement for non-EU family members of EU nationals to have been ordinarily resident in the EEA for the three years immediately preceding the start of their course. In consequence of the amendments, those family members will qualify for home fee status if the EU national from whom they derive their right of residence satisfies the two conditions that (a) the person is either not a United Kingdom national, or is a United Kingdom national who has exercised an EU law right of free movement, and (b) the person has been ordinarily resident in the EEA for the three years immediately preceding the first day of the first academic year of his family member's course.

912   Higher education—student support—child in need—duty of local authority

See *R (on the application of Kebede) v Newcastle City Council*, para 183.

913   Higher education—student support—England

The Education (Student Support and European University Institute) (Amendment) Regulations 2013, SI 2013/1728 (in force in part on 1 August 2013 and in part on 1 September 2013), further amend (1) the Education (Student Support) Regulations 2011, SI 2011/1986, so as to increase elements of the student support package and introduce new fee loan caps for eligible students studying at an institution in England or Wales who are undertaking (a) an academic year of certain courses where they are participating in the Erasmus action scheme of the European Union for the mobility of university students; (b) a period of study at an overseas institution; or (c) a sandwich course; and (2) the Education (Student Support) (European University Institute) Regulations 2010, SI 2010/447, by removing, from provision for determining the taxable income of a student's partner, certain references to ordinary residence in the United Kingdom or another EEA state or Switzerland.

The Education (Fees and Student Support) (Amendment) Regulations 2013, SI 2013/3106 (in force in part on 15 January 2014 and in part on 1 August 2014), further amend (1) the 2011 Regulations above (a) in order to make it clear that the Secretary of State has the power to suspend or revoke the designation of full-time, distance learning, part-time or postgraduate courses which have previously been designated by the Secretary of State for student support purposes; and (b) in relation to the periods of previous study which are taken into account when calculating fee loan entitlement; (2) the Higher Education (Higher Amount) (England) Regulations 2010, SI 2010/3020, and the Higher Education (Basic Amount) (England) Regulations 2010, SI 2010/3021, in order to align, with the maximum fee loan amounts in the 2011 Regulations, the maximum fee caps for students undertaking sandwich work placement years, overseas study years, Erasmus study and work placement years.

914 Higher education—student support—Wales

The Education (Student Support and European Institutions) (Wales) Regulations 2013, SI 2013/1965 (in force on 30 August 2013), amend the Assembly Learning Grants and Loans (Higher Education) (Wales) (No 2) Regulations 2011, SI 2011/886, the Education (Student Support) (Wales) Regulations 2012, SI 2012/3097 (replaced by SI 2013/3177 below), and the Education (European Institutions) and Student Support (Wales) Regulations 2013, SI 2013/765 (see para 906), so as to refer to universal credit and the new council tax reduction schemes alongside references to existing benefits.

The Education (Student Support) (Wales) Regulations 2013, SI 2013/3177 (in force on 10 January 2014), replace the 2012 Regulations, SI 2012/3097, so as to provide for financial support for students who are ordinarily resident in Wales taking designated higher education courses in respect of academic years beginning on or after 1 September 2014, and (1) make provision (a) concerning eligibility; (b) for applications for support; (c) time limits for applications; and (d) concerning the information that must be provided by applicants; (2) provide for fee support in the form of grants for fees and fee loans; (3) make provision (a) for grants for living costs including grants for travel for certain categories of eligible student; and (b) for loans for living costs; (4) set out general provisions relating to loans; (5) make provision for college fee loans, which are loans in respect of the college fees payable by a qualifying student to a college or permanent private hall of the University of Oxford or to a college of the University of Cambridge in connection with attendance of a qualifying student on a qualifying course; (6) continue to make provision for the means-testing of students taking designated full-time courses; and (7) make provision (a) for payment of grants and loans; (b) for support to students who are undertaking designated distance learning courses; (c) for support for part-time courses; and (d) for postgraduate students with disabilities.

915 Higher Education Funding Council for Wales—functions

The Higher Education Funding Council for Wales (Supplementary Functions) Order 2013, SI 2013/1733 (in force on 31 August 2013), confers supplementary functions on the Higher Education Funding Council for Wales relating to (1) the payment of a new fee grant to higher education institutions; (2) the recovery of overpayments of such grant; and (3) requesting and receiving information connected to the payment of the new fee grant.

916 Learning and skills—regulated qualifications—meaning

The Apprenticeships, Skills, Children and Learning Act 2009 (Consequential Amendments to Part 1 of the Education and Skills Act 2008) Order 2013, SI 2013/1242 (in force on 24 May 2013), amends the Education and Skills Act 2008 as a consequence of provisions in the Apprenticeships, Skills, Children and Learning Act 2009 Pt 7 (ss 127–174). The 2013 Order, in particular, (1) alters the meaning of 'level 3 qualification' so that references to prescribed external qualifications and external qualifications of a prescribed description are instead to prescribed qualifications and qualifications of a prescribed description; and (2) changes the meaning of 'relevant training or education' and 'sufficient relevant training or education' by replacing references to accredited qualifications with references to regulated qualifications.

917   Local curriculum—operation—Wales

The Operation of the Local Curriculum (Wales) Regulations 2013, SI 2013/1793 (in force on 1 September 2013), provide for the application of various provisions of education-related legislation in relation to pupils and students following courses of study for the purpose of the local curriculum provided at a school or institution other than their own.

918   Local education authority—duty of care—duty to pupil—delegation of duty

See *Woodland v Essex CC*, para 1904.

919   Maintained schools—government—governing body—clerk—Wales

The Government of Maintained Schools (Clerk to a Governing Body) (Wales) Regulations 2013, SI 2013/2127 (in force on 20 September 2013), make provision in relation to clerks to governing bodies of maintained schools in Wales so as to (1) require the local authority which maintains the school to provide the governing body with a suitable person to appoint as a clerk, meaning either a governor support officer or a person who has completed the clerk training; (2) require the authority to provide a clerk within 16 weeks of being requested by the governing body to do so, and empower the authority to charge a fee to cover the cost of providing the clerk; (3) require the training of a clerk to be completed satisfactorily within one year of appointment; (4) provide that, if the clerk has not completed the training in accordance with the stipulated requirements, the governing body must remove the clerk from office; and (5) provide that a clerk who is removed from office may be reappointed only when the training has been completed.

920   Maintained schools—recoupment—adjustment between local authorities—England

The Inter-authority Recoupment (England) Regulations 2013, SI 2013/492 (in force on 1 April 2013), make provision for recoupment between local authorities where a person belonging to the area of one authority in England is educated by another authority in England or Wales. SI 1994/3251 is amended.

921   National Curriculum—assessment arrangements—key stage 2—England

The Education (National Curriculum) (Key Stages 1 and 2 Assessment Arrangements) (England) (Amendment) Order 2013, SI 2013/1513 (in force on 20 June 2013), further amends (1) the Education (National Curriculum) (Key Stage 2 Assessment Arrangements) (England) Order 2003 Order, SI 2003/1038, so as to (a) omit provisions relating to single level tests and to the English writing test; (b) introduce a new biennial test in science; and (c) make provision for moderation of teacher assessment in writing and for determination by the Secretary of State; (2) the Education (National Curriculum) (Key Stage 1 Assessment Arrangements) (England) Order 2004, SI 2004/2783, so as to (a) provide for its application to maintained nursery schools that have pupils aged six; (b) alter the definition of 'core subject topics' so as to include the attainment targets in science and mathematics; (c) require teacher assessments to determine overall levels as well as levels against each attainment target; (d) provide that a phonics check must be carried out in respect of those pupils who were not assessed the previous year; and (e) make provision for the Secretary of State to make a determination in relation to a pupil's phonics check.

922   National Curriculum—assessment arrangements—key stage 1—England

See para 921.

923   National Curriculum—assessment arrangements—new qualification—award—
       judicial review

A new set of GCSE English qualifications were awarded for the first time by four different awarding organisations under the supervision of the first defendant statutory regulator. The pupils who sat the examination at the beginning of the year received more C grades than those who sat the examination in the summer and the applicants issued proceedings for judicial review against the second and third defendant awarding organisations and the first defendant, seeking to have the summer examination papers assessed in accordance with the boundaries applying to the examination sat by pupils at the beginning of the year. The applicants contended that the defendants' conduct had been so conspicuously unfair as to amount to an abuse of power, that the defendants had failed to give effect to the legitimate expectation engendered by statements to the effect that grading standards would be the same irrespective of when the assessment had been completed, that the defendants had acted irrationally in failing to treat all candidates alike and subjecting them to different assessment standards, that the defendants had acted unlawfully in treating the reported predicted number of C grades as though it was a binding principle, that the way in which the third defendant sought to bring their marks into line with the tolerance limits amounted to an arbitrary and unprincipled manipulation of unit grade boundaries to protect its reputation and, in determining not to follow the marking scheme of the earlier examinations and choosing instead to let higher standards apply in the summer examinations, the defendants had failed to carry out the public sector equality duty under the Equality Act 2010 s 149. The second and third defendants contended that, since they were non-governmental bodies providing services for reward under private law contracts, they were not amenable to judicial review and that the public sector equality duty was irrelevant when it came to assessing performance. *Held*, there had been no improper fettering of the awarding organisations' discretion by the first defendant, merely a proper concern that they should only depart from the tolerance limits in circumstances where they could provide sufficient justification. That was a perfectly legitimate principle to apply to ensure that there was broad consistency in standards year on year. As to whether the applicants had a legitimate expectation that grading standards would be the same, the applicants had not been able to point to any clear and unequivocal assurance of that kind. The failure to make public a relevant criterion could not create any positive assurance so as to engage the doctrine of legitimate expectation. Moreover, the examiners in the summer examinations made assessments which they thought fairly reflected the standard of the assessment and, in the light of the fuller information then available to them, their judgments had been more accurate and more reliable than the earlier assessments. Wider concerns about creating unfairness as between those qualifying in different years, and the need to retain the value of the qualification, strongly militated against applying the grades from the beginning of the year to the summer assessments. It followed that there had been no unfairness, conspicuous or otherwise. In relation to whether the third defendant had been arbitrary in its boundary fixing, while concerns about its reputation had always been present in discussions, there had been a genuine belief that it had been legitimate for the unit concerned to bear the weight of the adjustment. Moreover, as to whether the second and third defendants were amenable to judicial review, the argument that it was pointless to proceed against them because they were under the control of the first defendant and had been effectively obliged to act as they had done, might be a defence to the claim, but it was not a justification for denying the court jurisdiction to consider it. Further, the public sector equality duty had plainly been wholly irrelevant in the context. Accordingly, the application would be dismissed.

R (on the application of Lewisham LBC) v Assessment and Qualifications Alliance [2013] EWHC 211 (Admin), [2013] All ER (D) 228 (Feb) (Queen's Bench Division: Elias LJ and Sharp J).

924   National Curriculum—assessment arrangements—reading and numeracy—Wales

The Education (National Curriculum) (Assessment Arrangements for Reading and Numeracy) (Wales) Order 2013, SI 2013/433 (in force on 1 May 2013), sets out the assessment arrangements for reading and numeracy for pupils who attend schools maintained by a local authority in Wales, other than those which are established in hospitals, and, in particular, (1) requires head teachers to make arrangements for the administration and marking of the English- and Welsh-medium National Reading Tests and the National Numeracy Test; (2) requires head teachers to make a statement confirming that tests have been administered and marked; (3) makes provision for the monitoring of tests by local authorities; and (4) empowers the Welsh Ministers to investigate matters brought to their attention which relate to the accuracy or correctness of test results.

925   National Curriculum—attainment targets and programmes of study—England

The Education (National Curriculum) (Attainment Targets and Programmes of Study) (England) Order 2013, SI 2013/2232 (in force on 1 September 2014), makes provision for a new National Curriculum from 2014 by giving effect to the Framework Document, published by the Department for Education on 11 September 2013, which contains new programmes of study and attainment targets for core and other foundation subjects at all four key stages.

926   National Curriculum—disapplication—England

The National Curriculum (Exceptions for First, Second, Third and Fourth Key Stages) (England) Regulations 2013, SI 2013/1487 (in force on 1 September 2013), replace the 2012 Regulations, SI 2012/1926, and (1) make provision for the National Curriculum for England to be disapplied, with exceptions, for pupils in the 2013–14 school year; the exceptions are for the core subjects, which are mathematics, English and science, for the first key stage and for the third and fourth years of the second key stage; and (2) provide for the programmes of study for the core subjects to be disapplied for the fourth key stage for the 2014–15 school year.

927   National Curriculum—educational programmes—foundation phase and programmes of study—keys stages 2 and 3—Wales

The National Curriculum (Educational Programmes for the Foundation Phase and Programmes of Study for the Second and Third Key Stages) (Wales) Order 2013, SI 2013/434 (in force on 1 September 2013), gives legal effect to additional educational programmes for the language, literacy and communication skills and mathematical development areas of learning in the foundation phase, and gives legal effect to the additional programmes of study in English, Welsh and mathematics in the second and third key stages.

928   National Curriculum—languages—England

The Education (National Curriculum) (Languages) (England) Order 2013, SI 2013/2230 (in force on 1 September 2014), sets out the meaning of a 'foreign language' for the purposes of the Education Act 2002 s 84 and provides that (1) in relation to the second key stage, a foreign language means any foreign language; and (2) in relation to the third key stage, a modern foreign language means any modern foreign language. SI 2006/1766 is revoked.

929   National Curriculum—requirements—England

The Education (Amendment of the Curriculum Requirements) (England) Order 2013, SI 2013/2092 (in force on 1 September 2014), amends the Education Act 2002 by substituting computing for information and communication technology as a foundation subject for the first, second, third and fourth key stages.

The Education (Amendment of the Curriculum Requirements for Second Key Stage) (England) Order 2013, SI 2013/2093 (in force on 1 September 2014), amends the Education Act 2002 by providing for a foreign language as a foundation subject for the second key stage and enabling foreign languages to be specified in an order made by the Secretary of State for this purpose.

930   Private educational institution—immigration—sponsor licence—revocation

See R (on the application of Manchester College of Accountancy and Management) v Secretary of State for the Home Department, para 1432; and R (on the application of Warnborough College Ltd) v Secretary of State for the Home Department, para 1431.

931   Pupil—attendance—failure to secure regular attendance—penalty notice scheme— England

The Education (Penalty Notices) (England) (Amendment) Regulations 2013, SI 2013/757 (in force on 1 September 2013), further amend the 2007 Regulations, SI 2007/1867, by providing that (1) the amount of the penalty is (a) £60, if paid within 21 days of receipt of the notice; and (b) £120, if paid within 28 days of receipt of the notice; and (2) proceedings for the offence to which the notice relates may not be instituted within 28 days of receipt of the notice.

932   Pupil—attendance—failure to secure regular attendance—penalty notice scheme—
       Wales

The Education (Penalty Notices) (Wales) Regulations 2013, SI 2013/1983 (in force on
2 September 2013), provide for the operation of the penalty notice scheme in respect of
failure to secure the regular attendance of registered pupils at school under the Education
Act 1996 s 444A. The 2013 Regulations, in particular, (1) set out the matters to be
contained in penalty notices; (2) prescribe the level of penalties and what constitutes
evidence of their payment or non-payment; (3) provide that penalties must be paid within
42 days of receipt of a penalty notice to discharge the recipient's liability for the offence to
which the notice relates; (4) specify the local authorities to which penalties must be paid;
(5) prescribe 42 days as the period during which proceedings for offences to which penalty
notices relate may not be instituted; (6) set out the circumstances in which penalty notices
may be withdrawn; (7) prescribe the persons who have authority to issue penalty notices;
(8) require (a) a local code of conduct for the issue of penalty notices to be drawn up and
consulted on; and (b) the issue of notices to comply with the local code; (9) require (a) the
provision of copies of penalty notices to the local authorities to which payment must be
made; and (b) the keeping of records of notices by local authorities and the provision of
information in respect of notices to the Welsh Ministers; and (10) prescribe how penalty
notices are to be served and how sums received by local authorities are to be spent.

933   Pupil—career guidance—compulsory provision—relevant age

The Careers Guidance in Schools Regulations 2013, SI 2013/709 (in force on 1 September
2013), (1) provide that, for the purposes of the Education Act 1997 s 42A, independent
careers guidance must be provided to pupils from school years 8 to 13; and (2) disapply, in
respect of pupils over compulsory school age, the requirement for careers guidance to
include information on options concerning 16 to 18 education or training.

934   Pupil—individual pupil information—prescribed persons—England

The Education (Individual Pupil Information) (Prescribed Persons) (England) (Amendment)
Regulations 2013, SI 2013/1193 (in force on 28 June 2013), further amend the
2009 Regulations, SI 2009/1563, so as to (1) omit reference to the British Educational
Communications and Technology Agency; (2) prescribe various bodies in respect of schools
designated as having a religious character; and (3) set out a category of person carrying out
specified activities and who require individual pupil information for the purpose of
promoting the education or well-being of children in England.

935   Pupil—individual pupil information—Wales

The Education (Information About Individual Pupils) (Wales) (Amendment)
Regulations 2013, SI 2013/3137 (in force on 13 January 2014), further amend the
2007 Regulations, SI 2007/3562, so as to require a governing body to provide to a local
authority (1) additional information to that which it is already required to provide in
relation to permanent exclusion of pupils; and (2) information in relation to fixed period
exclusions of pupils.

936   Pupil—pupil information—England

The Education (Pupil Information and School Performance Information) (Miscellaneous
Amendments) (England) Regulations 2013, SI 2013/3212 (in force on 12 February 2014),
further amend (1) the Education (Pupil Information) (England) Regulations 2005,
SI 2005/1437, so as to remove the requirement (a) for a head teacher to include assessment
or attainment information for the third key stage in the annual report to parents; and (b) for
the governing body of a maintained school, or a local authority, to include assessment
information for the third key stage in the record it transfers to another school when a pupil
ceases to be registered at the former school and becomes registered at the latter; and (2) the
Education (School Performance Information) (England) Regulations 2007, SI 2007/2324, by
removing the requirement for the governing body of a maintained school, or the proprietor
of an academy, city technology college or city college for the technology of the arts, to
provide pupil assessment information for the third key stage to the local authority or the
Secretary of State.

937   Pupil—pupil information—Wales

See para 907.

938   Pupil—registration—England

The Education (Pupil Registration) (England) (Amendment) Regulations 2013, SI 2013/756 (in force on 1 September 2013), further amend the 2006 Regulations, SI 2006/1751, so as to (1) prohibit the proprietor of a maintained school from granting leave of absence to a pupil except where an application has been made in advance and the proprietor considers that there are exceptional circumstances relating to the application; and (2) require the name of a pupil to be deleted from the school's admissions register where the pupil ceases to be of compulsory school age before the school next meets and either the pupil, where he is 18, or his parent has indicated that he will no longer attend the school or where the pupil does not meet the academic entry requirements for the school's sixth form.

939   School Standards and Organisation (Wales) Act 2013

The School Standards and Organisation (Wales) Act 2013 reforms the powers of local authorities and the Welsh Ministers to intervene in the conduct of schools maintained by local authorities that are causing concern, reforms the powers of the Welsh Ministers to intervene in the exercise of education functions by local authorities, provides for school improvement guidance, reforms the statutory arrangements for the organisation of maintained schools, provides for Welsh in education strategic plans, and makes miscellaneous provision in relation to maintained schools. The Act received the royal assent on 4 March 2013 and came into force in part on 5 March 2013. Further provisions came into force on and between 1 April 2013 and 3 December 2013: SI 2013/1000, SI 2013/1800, SI 2013/3024. The remaining provisions come into force on a day or days to be appointed. For details of commencement, see the commencement table in the title STATUTES AND LEGISLATIVE PROCESS.

Part 1 (s 1) Introduction
Section 1 provides an overview of the key provisions of the Act.

Part 2 (ss 2–37, Sch 1) Standards

Chapter 1 (ss 2–20, Sch 1) Intervention in conduct of maintained schools
Section 2 sets out the eight grounds for intervention by a local authority or the Welsh Ministers in a maintained school. Section 3 provides that if one or more of grounds one to six set out in s 2 exist the local authority may give a warning notice to the governing body of a school and specifies what information a warning notice must contain. The circumstances where the powers to intervene in a maintained school may be exercised by a local authority are set out in s 4. Section 5 gives a new power for a local authority to direct the governing body of a school to make arrangements or enter into a contract for the provision of advisory services or to collaborate in accordance with the Education (Wales) Measure 2011 s 5(2), so as to improve the school's performance. The 2013 Act s 6 replaces the School Standards and Framework Act 1998 s 16 and provides local authorities with a power to appoint additional governors to the governing body of a maintained school. The 2013 Act s 7 replaces the intervention power in the 1998 Act s 16A so as to provide local authorities with a power to appoint a specially constituted governing body in place of the existing governors at a school where the local authority has a power to intervene. A power for local authorities to suspend a school's right to a delegated budget if a local authority has the power to intervene in the school is granted: 2013 Act s 8. Section 9 gives a general power for local authorities to issue such directions to the governing body or head teacher of a school it maintains as it thinks appropriate and to take any other steps when one or more of the grounds for intervention exist. Section 10 sets out the circumstances in which the Welsh Ministers may give a formal warning notice to a maintained school. The circumstances where the powers to intervene in a maintained school may be exercised by the Welsh Ministers are laid out in s 11. Sections 12–14 provide mirror powers for the Welsh Ministers to intervene to those of the local authority contained in ss 5–7. Section 15 replaces the intervention power in the 1998 Act s 18B and provides the Welsh Ministers with the power to issue directions relating to the federation of schools. The intervention power in s 19 is replaced and the Welsh Ministers are provided with the power to direct the closure of

a school if they have the power to intervene on the basis of ground eight (school requiring special measures): 2013 Act s 16. Section 17 makes a mirror power in respect of the Welsh Ministers to that of the local authority in s 9. Section 18 introduces Sch 1 which makes further provision in relation to interim executive boards (constituted following a direction under s 7 or s 14); it deals with the transition from a normally constituted body to one consisting of interim executive members, and also the transition from a governing body consisting of interim executive members back to a normally constituted governing body (general power to give directions and take steps). Section 19 provides that a head teacher or governing body of a school must comply with a direction given to them by a local authority or the Welsh Ministers under Pt 2 Ch 1. Section 20 empowers the Welsh Ministers to issue guidance to local authorities in relation to the exercise of their functions under Pt 2 Ch 1.

Chapter 2 (ss 21–31) Intervention in local authorities
Section 21 sets out the grounds for intervention that must exist for the Welsh Ministers to intervene in a local authority. Section 22 provides that if one or more of the three grounds set out in s 21 exist, the Welsh Ministers may issue a warning notice to the local authority and specifies what information a warning notice must contain. Section 23 specifies the circumstances where the powers to intervene in a local authority may be exercised by the Welsh Ministers. A power for the Welsh Ministers to direct the local authority to obtain advisory services from a third party is granted by s 24. There is a power for Welsh Ministers to direct a local authority to use the services of a third party to carry out its functions: s 25. Section 26 allows the Welsh Ministers to direct that a local authority's functions are carried out by the Welsh Ministers or by a person nominated by the Welsh Ministers. Section 27 enables the Welsh Ministers, when issuing directions under s 25 or s 26, to include directions that relate to any of the local authority's education functions, and not just those functions to which the powers to intervene relate. Where the power to intervene exists, s 28 provides a general power to give directions to a local authority and take steps in relation to it. By virtue of s 29, a local authority, or an officer of an authority, subject to a direction or instruction under Pt 2 Ch 2 must comply with it. Under s 30, local authorities and governing bodies must assist with the action required to comply with directions. Section 31 sets out rights of access in connection with the carrying out of directions.

Chapter 3 (ss 32–37) Rationalisation of school places
Section 32 defines the term 'school authority' to mean a local authority, governing body or head teacher of a maintained school in Wales. Section 33 provides a power for the Welsh Ministers to issue guidance to school authorities setting out how they are to improve the standards of education in schools. Section 34 sets out the procedure the Welsh Ministers must follow before issuing school improvement guidance. Section 35 places a duty on school authorities to comply with guidance issued. A policy statement issued under s 35 must set out how the local authority or governing body proposes that functions should be exercised differently from the course set out in the school improvement guidance and the authority's or the body's reasons for proposing that different course: s 36. By virtue of s 37, where the Welsh Ministers consider that the alternative course of action set out in a school authority's policy statement is not likely to improve educational standards they may issue a direction to the school authority requiring it to comply with the guidance.

Part 3 (ss 38–83) School organisation

Chapter 1 (ss 38, 39) School organisation code
Section 38 creates a requirement for the Welsh Ministers to issue and publish a code (or codes) on school organisation ('the Code') with which the persons listed at s 38 must act in accordance if the Code requires them to do so. The procedure that the Welsh Ministers must follow before issuing the Code is set out in s 39.

Chapter 2 (ss 40–56) School organisation proposals
A new community school, voluntary school or community special school may be established in Wales only in accordance with Pt 3: s 40. Sections 41–44, Sch 2 give local authorities the power to make proposals to: (1) establish a community, voluntary, maintained nursery, or community special school; (2) discontinue a community, maintained nursery, voluntary, foundation, or community special school; (3) make a regulated alteration to a community, maintained nursery, or community special school; (4) make a regulated alteration to increase

or reduce capacity at a voluntary or foundation school that does not have a religious character; (5) make a regulated alteration to open or close a school's sixth form at a voluntary or foundation school, with the consent of the Welsh Ministers. The governing body of a community school may make proposals for the school to become a voluntary aided school or a voluntary controlled school: s 45. Under s 46, a maintained school within one of the categories set out in the 1998 Act s 20(1) may become a school within another of those categories only in accordance with the 2013 Act Pt 3. By virtue of s 47, a school's change of category in accordance with proposals made under s 45 is not to be taken as authorising or requiring any change in the character of the school. Section 48 requires that school organisation proposals are consulted on and published; the Code will set out requirements for consultation and how and when proposals are to be published. Section 49 enables any person to object in writing to proposals within 28 days of the publication date (known as 'the objection period'), and requires proposers to publish a summary of the objections together with their responses within 28 days of the end of the objection period. Proposals published under s 48 require approval under s 50 if the proposals affect sixth form education or the proposals have been made by a proposer other than the relevant local authority and an objection has been made by that authority in accordance with s 49 and has not been withdrawn in writing before the end of 28 days beginning with the end of the objection period. Under s 51, proposals published under s 48 require approval if they do not require approval under s 50, they have been made by a proposer other than the relevant local authority and an objection to the proposals has been made in accordance with s 49 and has not been withdrawn in writing before the end of 28 days beginning with the end of the objection period. Section 52 provides that a proposer must send to the Welsh Ministers proposals ('proposals B') it has made if it considers that they are related to proposals requiring approval under s 50 ('proposals A') and the proposer has not determined whether to implement proposals B under s 53 before the Welsh Ministers approve or reject proposals A. Where any proposals published under s 48 do not require approval under s 50 or s 51, the proposer must determine whether the proposals should be implemented: s 53. Section 54 provides that where a local authority has determined to approve or reject proposals, or determined to implement its own proposals to which there was an objection, the proposals may be referred to the Welsh Ministers for their approval by those bodies set out in s 54. Section 55 requires that proposals which have been approved, or the proposer has determined should be implemented, must be implemented in the form in which they were approved or determined, and in accordance with Sch 4 for change of category proposals, or in accordance with Sch 3 for every other type of proposal. Section 56 provides interpretation for Pt 3 Ch 2.

Chapter 3 (ss 57–63) Rationalisation of school places
The Welsh Ministers may direct a local authority to exercise its powers to make proposals to establish, alter or discontinue schools and direct the governing body of a foundation or voluntary school maintained by the authority to exercise its powers to make proposals to alter its school: s 57. Section 58 provides that proposals made in accordance with a direction under s 57 may not be withdrawn without the consent of the Welsh Ministers. Where the Welsh Ministers have made a direction under s 57 and either proposals have been published in accordance with the direction, or the time allowed under the direction for the publication of the proposals has expired, the proposals must be published in accordance with the code issued under s 38 for the time being in force: s 59. In accordance with s 60, any person may object to proposals published under s 59. Section 61 provides that if objections have been made in accordance with s 60, then, unless all objections so made have been withdrawn in writing within the 28 days referred to in s 60, the Welsh Ministers must cause a local inquiry to be held. Section 62 provides that where a local inquiry has been held, the Welsh Ministers may, after considering the report of the person appointed to hold the inquiry: (a) adopt, with or without modifications, or determine not to adopt any of the proposals made by the Welsh Ministers and considered by the inquiry; (b) approve, with or without modifications, or reject any other proposals which were referred to the inquiry; (c) make further proposals under s 59. By virtue of s 63, proposals adopted or approved by the Welsh Ministers under s 62 have effect as if they had been approved by the Welsh Ministers under s 50 after having been made by the local authority under its powers to make

proposals to establish, alter or discontinue schools, or in the case of proposals to alter a foundation or voluntary school, by the governing body under its powers to make proposals to alter its school.

Chapter 4 (ss 64–70) Regional provision for special educational needs
Section 64 provides the meanings of 'regional provision' and 'special education functions'. The Welsh Ministers may direct local authorities to consider whether they would be able to carry out their special education functions, in respect of children with the special educational needs specified in the direction, more efficiently or effectively if regional provision were made: s 65. The Welsh Ministers may give directions for the purpose of securing that regional provision is made in relation to the areas of those authorities: s 66. Under s 67, proposals made in accordance with a direction under s 66 may not be withdrawn without the consent of the Welsh Ministers. Section 68 provides that the Welsh Ministers may make any proposals that could have been made in accordance with the direction. By virtue of s 69 any person may object to proposals published under s 68. After considering any objections made in accordance with s 69, the Welsh Ministers may adopt the proposals with or without modifications, or determine not to adopt the proposals: s 70.

Chapter 5 (ss 71–77) Proposals for restructuring sixth form education
Section 71 gives the Welsh Ministers powers to restructure sixth form education. Before publishing proposals made under s 71, the Welsh Ministers must consult on the proposals in accordance with the code issued under s 38 for the time being in force: s 72. Under s 73, after the end of 28 days, the Welsh Ministers must determine whether to adopt the proposals, with or without modifications, or withdraw the proposals. By virtue of s 74, the proposals must be implemented in the form in which they were adopted. Proposals to establish a school must be implemented by the local authority that it is proposed will maintain the school: s 75. Under s 76, where a local authority is required to provide a site for a foundation or voluntary controlled school, Sch 3 para 7 (provision of site and buildings for foundation or voluntary controlled school) applies as it applies in the circumstances mentioned. Section 77 provides consequential amendments to inspection reports on sixth form education.

Chapter 6 (ss 78–83) Miscellaneous and supplemental
Section 78 allows proposals to establish a new school to include the establishment of the school as a federated school; a federated school is a school which is part of a group of schools with a single governing body. Section 79 prevents the establishment of a school in England which would be maintained by a local authority in Wales. Section 80, which re-enacts and updates the 1998 Act s 30, enables the governing body of a foundation or voluntary school, following the procedure required by the 2013 Act s 80, to discontinue the school by serving two years' notice on the Welsh Ministers and local authority. Section 81, which re-enacts the 1998 Act s 32, allows the Welsh Ministers to direct a local authority to discontinue (without the need for proposals under the 2013 Act s 44) a community special school if they consider it expedient to do so in the interests of health, safety or welfare of pupils. Section 82 deals with transitional exemption orders for the purposes of the Equality Act 2010. The 2013 Act s 83 provides interpretation of Pt 3.

Part 4 (ss 84–87) Welsh in education strategic plans
Section 84 sets out what a Welsh education strategic plan should contain and imposes a duty on all local authorities to prepare a plan, keep it under review and revise it if necessary. Each local authority is required to submit its plan to the Welsh Ministers for approval: s 85. Under s 86, the Welsh Ministers are empowered to make regulations requiring local authorities to assess parental demand for Welsh-medium provision in certain circumstances. Welsh Ministers have powers under s 87 to make regulations about matters such as the form and content of a plan, its timing and duration, keeping the plan under review, consultation and submission of the plan for approval to the Welsh Ministers and its publication.

Part 5 (ss 88–96) Miscellaneous schools functions
Section 88 requires a local authority to provide breakfasts free of charge on each school day for pupils at a primary school it maintains if the governing body of the school has made a written request to the authority for breakfasts to be provided and 90 days have passed since the authority received the request. Transitional provision is made by s 89. Provision for the interpretation of ss 88, 89 is made by s 90. With regard to the power to charge for school

meals, s 91 repeals the requirement that any charge made for the provision of milk, meals and other refreshments in a school must be the same for every person for the same quantity of the same item. Section 92 requires a local authority to make reasonable provision for an independent counselling service in respect of health, emotional and social needs for specified categories of persons. Section 93 enables the Welsh Ministers to obtain information from a local authority about its independent counselling service. Section 94 provides that a governing body must hold a meeting if the following four conditions are met: (i) it receives a petition requesting a meeting from whichever is the lower of the parents of 10 per cent of registered pupils, or the parents of 30 registered pupils; (ii) the meeting is for the purpose of discussing a matter relating to the school; (iii) that there will be no more than three such meetings in a school year; and (iv) that there are enough school days left in the school year in which to hold the meeting. As a consequence of the provision on parents' meetings in s 94, by virtue of s 95, governing bodies of maintained schools are no longer required to hold an annual parents' meeting.

Part 6 (ss 97–101) General

Section 97 provides for the making of orders and regulations, and s 98 deals with general interpretation and contains an index of defined expressions. Section 99, Sch 5 provide for minor and consequential amendments. Section 100 deals with commencement and s 101 with short title and the inclusion of the 2013 Act as one of the Education Acts.

Amendments, repeals and revocations

The list below, which is not exhaustive, mentions repeals and amendments which are or will be effective when the Act is fully in force.

The following provisions of the following Acts and Measures are amended or repealed or added: Education Reform Act 1988 ss 198, 219; Diocesan Boards of Education Measure 1991 ss 3, 7; Further and Higher Education Act 1992 s 58; Education Act 1996 ss 5, 409, 484, 496, 497, 512ZA, 512A, 533, 560; Education Act 1997 ss 29, 43; Teaching and Higher Education Act 1998 s 19; School Standards and Framework Act 1998 ss 14–19A, 20, 21, 28–35, 49, 51A, 62, 82, 89C, 101, 103, 127, 142, 143, Schs 1A, 3, 6–8, 22; Learning and Skills Act 2000 ss 33P, 83, 126, Schs 7, 7A, 9; Education Act 2002 ss 19, 33–37, 55–59, 64, 72, 97, 111, 116N, 129, 153, 154, 191–193, Schs 1, 5, 6, 9, 10, 21; Children Act 2004 ss 50, 50A; Education Act 2005 ss 28, 31, 41–43, 44A–44F, 45, 46, 68–71, 103, 114, Sch 9; Education and Inspections Act 2006 ss 54, 58, 87, Schs 3, 7, 17; National Health Service (Wales) Act 2006 Sch 1; Childcare Act 2006 s 29; Learner Travel (Wales) Measure 2008 s 24; Apprenticeships, Skills, Children and Learning Act 2009 s 205, Sch 14; Learning and Skills (Wales) Measure 2009 s 44; Healthy Eating in Schools (Wales) Measure 2009 ss 8, 11; Equality Act 2010 s 87, Sch 11; Education (Wales) Measure 2011 ss 8, 13, 16, 18, 20, 21, 26–30; Welsh Language (Wales) Measure 2011 Sch 6; Education Act 2011 s 35.

940   Schools—admissions—admission appeals arrangements—Wales

The Education (Admission Appeals Arrangements) (Wales) (Amendment) Regulations 2013, SI 2013/2535 (in force on 1 January 2014), amend the 2005 Regulations, SI 2005/1398, so as to (1) enable appeal panels to consider whether admission arrangements are unlawful because they do not comply with either the School Standards and Framework Act 1998 or the mandatory provisions of any school admissions code; (2) allow a panel to uphold an appeal, where a child is refused a place at school on the basis that to admit the child would breach the statutory limit on infant class size unless a relevant measure was taken to avoid that breach, if it is satisfied that either the child would have been offered a place if the relevant admission arrangements had been properly implemented, or if they had been lawful, or if the panel is satisfied that the decision of the admission authority was unreasonable; and (3) provide that allowances that may be paid to panel members are to reflect the rates applicable to community councillors under the Local Government (Wales) Measure 2011 Pt 8 (ss 141–160).

941   Schools—admissions—admission arrangements—variation—Wales

The School Admissions (Variation of Admission Arrangements) (Wales) Regulations 2013, SI 2013/1140 (in force on 8 July 2013), prescribe the circumstances in which an admission authority may vary the admission arrangements it has determined for a particular school year, so that an admission authority may vary, without further procedures or approval from the Welsh Ministers, the admission arrangements which it has determined for any relevant age group where such a variation is necessary to give effect to the School Admissions Code.

942   Schools—admissions—Code of Practice—appointed day—Wales

The School Admissions Code (Appointed Day) (Wales) Order 2013, SI 2013/1659 (made on 3 July 2013), appoints 8 July 2013 as the day on which the School Admissions Code, issued under the School Standards and Framework Act 1998 ss 84 and 85, comes into force. The Code applies in relation to Wales in respect of admissions to the school year 2014–15 and subsequent years.

943   Schools—admissions—common offer date—Wales

The School Admissions (Common Offer Date) (Wales) Regulations 2013, SI 2013/1144 (in force on 8 July 2013), prescribe (1) 1 March or, in any year when 1 March is not a working day, the next working day, as the date on which decisions in relation to secondary school admissions are to be communicated to parents; and (2) 16 April or, in any year when 16 April is not a working day, the next working day, as the date on which decisions in relation to primary school admissions are to be communicated to parents.

944   Schools—admissions—School Admission Appeals Code—appointed day—Wales

The School Admission Appeals Code (Appointed Day) (Wales) Order 2013, SI 2013/3141, appoints 1 January 2014 for the coming into force of the School Admission Appeals Code, issued under the School Standards and Framework Act 1998 ss 84, 85 by the Welsh Ministers. The Code replaces the School Admission Appeals Code which came into force on 15 July 2009.

945   Schools—attendance—failure to secure regular attendance—penalty notice—Wales

The Anti-Social Behaviour Act 2003 (Amendment to the Education Act 1996) (Wales) Order 2013, SI 2013/1657 (in force on 3 July 2013), amends the Education Act 1996 ss 444A and 444B, which provide for a penalty notice for failure to secure the regular attendance at school of a registered pupil, so that they apply to Wales as well as to England.

946   Schools—establishment and discontinuance

The School Organisation (Establishment and Discontinuance of Schools) Regulations 2013, SI 2013/3109 (in force on 28 January 2014), prescribe various matters relating to proposals for the establishment and discontinuance of schools pursuant to the provisions contained in the Education and Inspections Act 2006 Pt 2 (ss 6A–32). The 2013 Regulations, in particular, (1) prescribe (a) the interval after which a date may be set for proposals in response to a competition notice to be sent to the local authority; (b) the information to be contained in a competition notice published by a local authority inviting proposals for the establishment of a foundation, voluntary or foundation special school (other than one providing education suitable only to the requirements of persons above compulsory school age), or an academy; (c) the information that must be contained in proposals for the establishment of a new school made pursuant to a competition notice; (d) the manner in which details of proposals which a local authority has received in response to a competition notice must be published, the requirement to make copies of proposals available, and also those bodies to which copies of proposals should be sent; (e) the information to be contained in proposals for the establishment with the consent of the Secretary of State (i) by a local authority, of a new community or community special school, or a new foundation or foundation special school, (other than one providing education suitable only to the requirement of persons above compulsory school age); or (ii) by other persons, of a new foundation, voluntary or foundation special school, other than one providing education suitable only to the requirements of persons above compulsory school age; (f) the information that must be contained in proposals for the establishment (i) by a local authority, of a new maintained nursery school, or a new foundation or foundation special school providing education suitable only to the requirements of persons above compulsory school age; or (ii) by any persons, of a new foundation, voluntary or foundation special school which is to provide education suitable only to the requirements of persons above compulsory school age, is to replace an independent school that is not an academy, a city technology college or city college for the technology of the arts, or, in the case of a new foundation special school, is to replace a non-maintained special school; (g) the manner in which the details of proposals made pursuant to the 2006 Act ss 10 and 11 that it has received or made itself must be published by the local authority; (h) the requirement to make copies available; (i) those bodies to which copies of proposals should be sent; (j) the information that must be contained in proposals made, either by a local authority or the governing body, to discontinue a maintained school; (k) the manner in which the details of proposals to discontinue a school that the local authority has received or made itself must be published by the local authority; (l) the requirement to make copies available; and (m) those bodies to which copies of proposals must be sent; (2) provide for the making of objections or comments to the local authority in relation to published proposals and for the time within which they may be made; (3) prescribe (a) in relation to proposals the period within which a local authority must determine whether to give approval; (b) the period within which a local authority must make a determination in relation to proposals to discontinue a school where there have been no objections to the proposals or any objections made have all been withdrawn; (c) the events that may be specified in a conditional approval; (d) the time within which the local authority must refer matters to the adjudicator; (e) the time within which requests made by a relevant person must be made, and the time within which such requests must be referred to the adjudicator; (f) the period of time within which related proposals must be referred to the adjudicator; (g) the persons who must be notified of a particular decision; and (h) the information that must be contained in proposals that the original proposals should not be implemented and the manner of publication of such proposals; (4) require the local authority to refer to the adjudicator certain proposals, and specify the time within which they must be made, where the initial decision was made by the adjudicator; (5) prescribe cases that must be referred to the adjudicator, the time within which such referrals must be made and the persons who must be consulted before proposals are modified or a later date for a conditional approval is set; (6) make provision for references to the adjudicator by relevant persons following a particular determination by a local authority; and (7) make certain modifications in relation to proposals to establish schools in an area outside the area of the relevant local authority. SI 2007/1288 is revoked. SI 2007/1355, SI 2007/3464, SI 2009/1556, SI 2009/2984, SI 2010/1941 and SI 2012/956 are amended.

947   Schools—finance—England

The School and Early Years Finance (England) Regulations 2013, SI 2013/3104 (in force on 1 January 2014), make provision for the financial arrangements of local authorities in relation to the funding of maintained schools and providers of prescribed early years provision in England, for the financial year 2014–15 and, in particular, (1) define the non-schools education budget, the schools budget, central expenditure and the individual schools budget; (2) require local authorities to determine budget shares for schools maintained by them and amounts to be allocated in respect of early years provision in their area, in accordance with the appropriate formulae; (3) impose a minimum funding guarantee and requirements in relation to local authorities' schemes; and (4) revoke the School Finance (England) Regulations 2012, SI 2012/335.

948   Schools—free lunches—transfer of functions

See para 958.

949   Schools—free lunches and milk—universal credit—England

The Free School Lunches and Milk (Universal Credit) (England) Order 2013, SI 2013/650 (in force on 29 April 2013), provides, for the purposes of the Education Act 1996 s 512ZB, that where a person or his parent is in receipt of universal credit on or after 29 April 2013, he is within s 512ZB(4), and, therefore, eligible for free school lunches and milk when a request has been made by him, or on his behalf, that these be provided free of charge.

950   Schools—free lunches and milk—universal credit—Wales

The Free School Lunches and Milk (Universal Credit) (Wales) Order 2013, SI 2013/2021 (in force on 6 September 2013), provides, for the purposes of the Education Act 1996 s 512ZB, that where a person or his parent is in receipt of universal credit on or after 6 September 2013, he is within s 512ZB(4) and, therefore, eligible for free school lunches and milk when a request has been made by him, or on his behalf, that these be provided free of charge.

951   Schools—governance—annual reports—Wales

The School Governors' Annual Reports (Wales) (Amendment) Regulations 2013, SI 2013/1561 (in force on 18 July 2013), amend the 2011 Regulations, SI 2011/1939, in consequence of the coming into force of the School Standards and Organisation (Wales) Act 2013 s 94, which imposes a duty on the governing body of a school to hold a meeting following a petition by parents. The 2013 Regulations, in particular, (1) require a copy of the school governors' report to be provided free of charge to parents unless an exception from such requirement applies; (2) add to the list of those exceptions; and (3) require a governing body to include in its annual report certain information relating to its duty to hold a parents' meeting.

952   Schools—governance—roles, procedure and allowance—England

The School Governance (Roles, Procedures and Allowances) (England) Regulations 2013, SI 2013/1624 (in force on 1 September 2013), set out procedures which must be adopted by all maintained schools and, in particular, (1) make provision for the roles of governing body and head teacher; (2) deal with the appointment, functions and removal of officers from the governing body; (3) provide for meetings and proceedings of governing bodies; (4) set out provisions relating to the establishment and proceedings of committees of governing bodies; and (5) enable allowances to be paid to governors and associate members. The 2013 Regulations apply, with modifications, to governing bodies of federations and apply in part to management committees of pupil referral units. SI 2000/2122, SI 2003/523 and SI 2003/1377 are revoked. SI 2003/1962, SI 2007/2978, SI 2007/2979, SI 2012/1035 are amended.

The School Governance (Roles, Procedures and Allowances) (England) (Amendment) Regulations 2013, SI 2013/2688 (in force on 14 November 2013), amend SI 2013/1624 above so as to (1) reintroduce a requirement for reports or other papers to be considered at meetings of governing bodies and meetings of committees of governing bodies to be circulated seven days in advance of such meetings; and (2) enable governing bodies to approve alternative arrangements for members of committees of governing bodies to participate or vote at meetings of the committee, including but not limited to by telephone or video conference.

953   Schools—healthy eating in schools—nutritional standards and requirements—Wales

The Healthy Eating in Schools (Nutritional Standards and Requirements) (Wales) Regulations 2013, SI 2013/1984 (in force on 2 September 2013), which replace the Education (Nutritional Standards for School Lunches) (Wales) Regulations 2001, SI 2001/1784, apply to local authorities and governing bodies of maintained schools that provide food and drink to pupils of maintained schools, whether on school premises or not, and to other persons on school premises. The 2013 Regulations set out the types of food and drink which may, and may not, be provided during the school day and define the nutrient content of school lunches and, in particular, (1) set out exemptions; (2) specify the requirements which must be met where school breakfast is provided; (3) impose requirements where school lunch is provided to pupils in nursery schools or to other persons on the premises of a nursery school in cases where school lunch does not comply with the requirements which apply in primary and secondary schools; (4) set out the requirements and nutritional standards which must be met where school lunch is provided; (5) set out requirements relating to food which must, or must not, be provided as part of school lunch in primary and secondary schools; (6) require a calculation to be made for a school or group of schools to ensure that the correct amount of energy and nutrients is contained in an average school lunch; (7) prescribe requirements that must be satisfied in relation to drinks; and (8) require food provided at times other than school breakfast or school lunch, such as at break times, to comply with specified requirements.

provide for (1) the circumstances in which a local authority is required to carry out a Welsh medium education assessment and the questions and information to be included in such an assessment; (2) the duration of a Welsh in education strategic plan; (3) the form and content of the plan; (4) the date for submission of the plan to the Welsh Ministers for approval; (5) the date on which the plan must be published; (6) the manner of publication of the local authority's plan; (7) the persons and bodies which a local authority must consult on the draft plan; and (8) the date by which the plan must be reviewed and who must be consulted.

976 Youth leisure-time activities—transfer of functions

The Transfer of Functions (Youth Leisure-time Activities) Order 2013, SI 2013/1721 (in force on 7 August 2013), transfers, from the Secretary of State to the Minister for the Cabinet Office, certain functions, under the Education Act 1996 s 507B, relating to the duty of local authorities to secure leisure-time activities for young persons.

ELECTIONS AND REFERENDUMS

Halsbury's Laws of England (5th edn) vol 37 (2013) paras 1–338, vol 38 (2013) paras 339–526, vol 38A (2013) paras 527–910

Articles

For articles relating to this title please refer to the Table of Articles at the beginning of the Abridgment.

977 Candidate—election expenses—disability-related expenses—exclusion

The Representation of the People (Election Expenses Exclusion) Order 2013, SI 2013/688 (in force on 22 March 2013), amends the Representation of the People Act 1983 so as to exempt, from regulation as election expenses, expenditure by or on behalf of disabled candidates which is designed to reduce the effect of barriers in seeking elected office which are faced by such candidates as a consequence of their disability, provided that any such expenditure has been defrayed or reimbursed by a grant from the Access to Elected Office for Disabled People Fund and has been incurred in accordance with the terms of that grant.

978 Candidate—selection—procedure—lawfulness

The applicant was a Member of the European Parliament, representing the defendant political party. The candidates for European parliamentary elections were chosen by the defendant by ballot from among the persons selected by a body called the National Selection Panel. The applicant was not one of the candidates selected by the panel for a forthcoming election. He brought proceedings against the defendant seeking an injunction preventing it from carrying out a ballot of its membership with a view to selecting candidates for the election. He submitted that there was an implied term in the defendant's rules that the assessment of potential candidates for election to the European Parliament would be conducted (1) fairly, as between the potential candidates; (2) by reference to objective criteria; (3) in such a manner that each potential candidate would in interview be given such an opportunity to address issues that might materially influence the assessment of his suitability for election; and (4) in such a manner that the criteria were applied, and the assessment conducted, in the same manner in respect of each potential candidate. He submitted that that implied term was necessary to give business efficacy to the arrangements for the selection of candidates or on the ground of obviousness. *Held*, the court had to be very wary of finding itself in the position where it started to control part of the ongoing democratic political process in the country. On the evidence, it was not clear that the applicant had established any breach of the implied terms that he pleaded or, if he had, what the consequences of that breach were. He had not come anywhere near to establishing that he would or ought to have been selected, had the process been any different. It was quite impossible to argue that there ought to be a duty to put to a candidate everything that might conceivably be held against him at the end of the day. What the selection process had been meant to achieve was a comparative assessment of all the candidates. If a duty of natural justice was to be read into the process, then every candidate presumably ought to have a free rein to comment on other candidates' comparative weaknesses, which was clearly not, or not claimed to be, the case. What had happened in the present case did not give rise to a serious argument that the applicant had been the victim of a breach of contract or other wrong. The balance of convenience fell very much in favour of allowing the proposed ballot to proceed. Accordingly, the claim would be dismissed.

Nattrass v UK Independence Party [2013] EWHC 3017 (Ch), [2013] All ER (D) 111 (Oct) (Chancery Division: Purle J).

979   Elector—right to vote—disenfranchisement—prisoners—human rights

The appellants in two cases were convicted murderers who were serving prison sentences. The appellants brought separate judicial review claims challenging the lawfulness of the legal prohibition on prisoners voting in United Kingdom and European parliamentary elections. They sought to rely on their right under the European Convention on Human Rights First Protocol art 3 to participate in free elections. The claims and subsequent appeals were dismissed and, in their conjoined appeal, they submitted that the court should apply the decisions of the European Court of Human Rights in *Hirst v United Kingdom* (No 2) and *Scoppola v Italy* (No 3), in which it had been established that a blanket ban on prisoner voting was disproportionate. They further contended that EU law recognised a right to vote, in terms equalling or exceeding the right arising under the Convention First Protocol art 3. *Held*, it was not appropriate for the court to refuse to apply the principles established by the decisions in *Hirst* and *Scoppola* consistently with the way in which they had been understood and applied in those cases. Even if a claimant came within the scope of the Human Rights Act 1998, that did not necessarily mean that he was entitled to any particular relief. A declaration of incompatibility was a discretionary remedy, and the incompatibility of the prohibition on prisoners voting in the United Kingdom with the Convention had previously been the subject of a declaration of incompatibility and was, at the present time, under active consideration by Parliament. In those circumstances, there was no point in making a further declaration of incompatibility. With regard to the second of the appellants' contentions, there was nothing in EU law that could entitle them to complain in respect of their inability to vote in parliamentary elections. Eligibility to vote was a matter for national parliaments, one of considerable national interest. There was no sign that the European Commission had ever sought to involve itself in or take issue with voting eligibility in member states or specifically with the restrictions on voting eligibility that applied in a number of such states. Furthermore, the provisions that the European treaties contained concerning individual voting rights were notably limited in scope. They related to the core treaty concerns of equality between nationals or Union citizens and freedom of movement within the EU. It followed that EU law did not incorporate any right to vote paralleling that recognised by the European Court of Human Rights in its case law or any other individual right to vote that was engaged or on which, if engaged, the appellants were able to rely. Accordingly, the appeals would be dismissed.

R (on the application of Chester) v Secretary of State for Justice; McGeoch v The Lord President of the Council [2013] UKSC 63, 2013 SLT 143, [2013] All ER (D) 174 (Oct) (Supreme Court: Lady Hale DP, Lords Hope, Mance, Kerr, Clarke, Sumption and Hughes SCJJ). Application 74025/01 *Hirst v United Kingdom* (No 2) (2004) 16 BHRC 409, ECtHR (2004 Abr para 1127); and Application 126/05 *Scoppola v Italy* (No 3) (2012) Times, 12 June, ECtHR (2012 Abr para 2195), considered. Decision of Court of Appeal [2010] EWCA Civ 1439, [2010] All ER (D) 219 (Dec) (2010 Abr para 1116) affirmed.

980   Electoral registration—absent voters—fresh signatures

The Elections (Fresh Signatures for Absent Voters) Regulations 2013, SI 2013/1599 (in force on 21 June 2013), modify (1) for a limited period, the provisions of the Representation of the People (England and Wales) Regulations 2001, SI 2001/341, which relate to the mandatory signature refresh for absent voters for parliamentary and local government elections, so that an absent voter who would otherwise be requested to provide a new example of his signature in January 2014 will instead be requested to do so between 1 August 2013 and 19 August 2013; and (2) in terms corresponding to those under head (1), the European Parliamentary Elections Regulations 2004, SI 2004/293, in relation to absent voters for European parliamentary elections.

981 Electoral registration—absent voters—provision of information regarding proxies

The Representation of the People (Provision of Information Regarding Proxies) Regulations 2013, SI 2013/3199 (in force on 10 June 2014), enable registration officers to require other registration officers to provide information about whether a person, whom an absent voter wishes to appoint as his proxy, has or will have an entry in a register of parliamentary or local government electors maintained by that officer, so as to ensure that the appointment complies with the relevant provisions of the Representation of the People Act 2000.

982 Electoral registration—annual canvass—postponement

The Electoral Registration (Postponement of 2013 Annual Canvass) Order 2013, SI 2013/794 (in force on 27 March 2013), (1) postpones, for 2013, the annual canvass conducted under the Representation of the People Act 1983 s 10(1); (2) requires the canvass to be conducted between 1 October 2013 and 17 February 2014, in relation to England, and between 1 October 2013 and 10 March 2014 in relation to Wales; (3) modifies the 1983 Act so as to provide that (a) where a returned canvass form is treated as an application for registration, the application is to be treated as having been made on the date on which the form was received by the registration officer, rather than on 15 October 2013; and (b) in order to remain registered, an elector must be resident at the conclusion of the canvass, instead of on 15 October 2013, at the address in respect of which they are registered; (4) specifies dates by which registration officers are required to publish revised versions of their registers; and (5) makes consequential provision.

983 Electoral registration—electoral registers—disclosure

The Electoral Registration (Disclosure of Electoral Registers) Regulations 2013, SI 2013/760 (in force on 27 March 2013), (1) require registration officers to disclose to the Lord President of the Council a copy of the electoral registers maintained by them and any other related information; (2) enable the Lord President to specify the format and means of disclosure; (3) authorise the Lord President to disclose any information received from a registration officer to the Secretary of State, who may then compare the information with information already held and disclose the results of the comparison back to the Lord President; (4) provide that disclosed information may not be shared with any other person except (a) to verify information relating to a registered person; (b) to ascertain the names and addresses of people who are not registered but are entitled to be; (c) to identify people who are registered but are not entitled to be; and (d) for the purpose of any civil or criminal proceedings; (5) provide that it is an offence to disclose information in breach of the regulations; and (6) require information to be processed in accordance with any requirements imposed by the Lord President.

984 Electoral registration—individual registration—transitional provisions

The Electoral Registration and Administration Act 2013 (Transitional Provisions) Order 2013, SI 2013/3197 (in force in part on 11 September 2014 and in part on 19 September 2014), contains transitional provisions relating to the introduction of individual elector registration in Great Britain and, in particular, (1) shortens the period immediately before commencement in which applications for registration in Scotland may be determined; (2) requires each electoral registration officer ('ERO') in Great Britain to check whether each person with an entry on an electoral register is entitled to remain registered; (3) makes provision about the information an ERO must verify for the purpose of confirming entitlement to remain registered and the process for determining such entitlement; (4) provides for the disclosure of the information and its comparison with data held by the Secretary of State for Work and Pensions; (5) specifies the evidence which supports a person's entitlement to remain registered; (6) makes the disclosure of the information, except for the purposes of confirmation or for the purposes of any civil or criminal proceedings, a criminal offence; (7) requires an ERO to give notice in writing of a person's entitlement to remain registered; (8) empowers EROs to use the verification procedure in relation to people whose entries on the register were carried forward at the conclusion of the final old canvass; (9) prescribes the period within which invitations to register must be given to existing electors in 2014; (10) provides for the first new canvass in Scotland to be delayed, and as a consequence, for the revised version of the register in

Scotland to be published on 28 February 2015; (11) prescribes the period within which canvass forms must be given for the second new canvass throughout Great Britain; (12) makes provision about invitations to register in relation to existing electors that EROs are required to give; (13) requires the ERO to send a second invitation if no response is received to the first invitation and a third invitation if no response is received to the second invitation and makes provision for visits to an address in order to encourage the person concerned to make a new application for registration; (14) makes provision about requirements to make an application for registration by a specified date; (15) sets out the level of the civil penalty for failure to make an application for registration by a specified date; (16) requires an ERO to give a person notice in writing of the civil penalty; (17) prescribes the form and content of the civil penalty notice; (18) provides for payment, enforcement and cancellation of a civil penalty and for reviews of, and appeals against, a civil penalty; (19) prescribes the manner in which an ERO must notify an absent voter that his entry has been removed from the register; and (20) enables EROs to find out whether a proxy for an absent voter is registered in another officer's registers.

985   Electoral Registration and Administration Act 2013

The Electoral Registration and Administration Act 2013 makes provision about the registration of electors and the administration and conduct of elections. The Act received the royal assent on 31 January 2013 and came into force in part on that day and on 31 March 2013. Further provisions came into force between 25 March 2013 and 23 April 2013: SI 2013/219, SI 2013/702, SI 2013/969. The remaining provisions come into force on a day or days to be appointed. For details of commencement, see the commencement table in the title STATUTES AND LEGISLATIVE PROCESS.

Part 1 (ss 1–13) Individual electoral registration in Great Britain
Section 1 requires a registration officer to enter a person in an electoral register where that person has applied for registration, the application meets the prescribed requirements and the person appears to the registration officer to be entitled to be registered, and requires registration officers to have regard to any guidance given by the minister (ie the Lord President of the Council or the Secretary of State) about determining applications to register. Section 1 introduces Sch 1 which specifies when a registration officer must alter the name or address of an elector, or remove the name or address from a register. Section 2, Sch 2 empower the minister to make regulations enabling a system to be established for the verification of the eligibility of applicants and registered electors in Great Britain, and for verification that applicants are the person they claim to be, and enable regulations to be made authorising or requiring a person to disclose to another person information that will assist a registration officer to verify information that an individual has provided in a new application for registration. A person is eligible for appointment as a proxy if he is registered in an electoral register: s 3. Registration officers are required, by virtue of s 4, to carry out an annual canvass to ascertain the names and addresses of persons entitled to be registered. Section 5 requires registration officers to give invitations to register to unregistered persons of whom they are aware and empowers a registration officer to impose a civil penalty on a person who fails to comply with a requirement to make an application for registration. Section 5 also introduces Sch 3, which makes further provision about such civil penalties. The date by which the Boundary Commissions must submit their reports about review of boundaries is changed from a date before 1 October 2013 to a date in September 2018: s 6. Section 7 empowers the minister to put in place alternative arrangements to assist registration officers to find out the names and addresses of people who are entitled to be registered but are not registered, or who are registered but are not entitled, and a power to abolish, amend and reinstate the annual canvass. The Electoral Commission must prepare a report if the minister consults it about a proposal so to amend, abolish or reinstate the annual canvass, or so to make alternative arrangements: s 8. The minister may implement pilot schemes temporarily amending or abolishing the annual canvass (s 9) and may implement pilot schemes, in relation to a particular area and for a particular time, for the purpose of testing how changes to any electoral registration provision would work in practice (s 10). Orders made under a power in Pt 1 must be laid before Parliament and approved by each House before they are made: s 11. Section 12 provides for interpretation. Section 13, Schs 4 and 5 make amendments and transitional provision.

Part 2 (ss 14–23) Administration and conduct of elections etc
Section 14 provides for the dissolution of Parliament 25 working days before the next general election, and for by-elections to take place between 17 and 19 working days after the last day for delivery of nomination papers, so as to provide for an extended electoral timetable. Section 15 allows a poll at a parish or community council election to be held on the same date as the poll at a parliamentary or European parliamentary general election. Provision is made by s 16 for the alteration of electoral registers pending elections, so as to enable a person to be entered on an electoral register in sufficient time to be sent a postal ballot. By virtue of s 17, local authorities must review, at least once every five years, every polling place and every polling district. Section 18 empowers the Secretary of State, on a recommendation by the Electoral Commission, to withhold or reduce a returning officer's fee for reasons of poor performance. Section 19 allows voters waiting in, or queuing at, a polling station at close of poll for the purpose of voting to be issued with ballot papers and vote despite the time of close of poll having passed. Provision is made by s 20 allowing a candidate standing on behalf of more than one party at a parliamentary election to request that the ballot paper contain against the candidate's particulars a registered emblem of one of those parties. Section 21 allows police community support officers to be admitted to vote at any polling station in their constituency or electoral area if they are prevented from voting at their own polling station by reason of their employment on the day of the poll. Section 22 provides for a power to specify in regulations the circumstances in which, following close of poll in a parliamentary or local government election, an electoral registration officer must notify a person that his postal ballot paper has been rejected. Section 23 repeals powers to establish the co-ordinated online record of electors.

Part 3 (ss 24–28) Final provisions
Section 24 makes financial provision and s 25 is interpretational. Section 26 deals with extent, s 27 with commencement and s 28 with short title.

Amendments, repeals and revocations
The list below, which is not exhaustive, mentions repeals and amendments which are or will be effective when the Act is fully in force.
  Specific provisions of a number of Acts are amended or repealed. These include: Representation of the People Act 1983 ss 7, 7A, 7C, 9, 9A–9E, 10, 10ZB–10ZE, 10A, 13, 13A, 13AB, 13B, 13BB, 15, 18C, 29A, 40, 49, 54, 56, 201, Schs ZA1, 1, 2, 4; Representation of the People Act 1985 ss 2, 16, 29; Parliamentary Constituencies Act 1986 s 3; Political Parties, Elections and Referendums Act 2000 s 20A; Representation of the People Act 2000 Schs 1, 6; Electoral Administration Act 2006 ss 1–8, 77, Sch 1; Political Parties and Elections Act 2009 ss 28–37; Fixed-term Parliaments Act 2011 s 3, Sch 1; Parliamentary Voting System and Constituencies Act 2011 ss 11, 14.

986   European parliamentary elections—appointed day of poll

The European Parliamentary Elections (Appointed Day of Poll) Order 2013, SI 2013/2063 (in force on 2 September 2013), appoints 22 May 2014 as the day of the poll for the next election of members of the European Parliament.

987   European parliamentary elections—general provisions

The European Parliamentary Elections (Amendment) Regulations 2013, SI 2013/2876 (in force on 1 January 2014), make miscellaneous changes to the law governing European parliamentary elections in order to transpose Council Directive (EU) 2013/1, which makes amendments to Council Directive (EC) 93/109 (laying down detailed arrangements for the exercise of the right to vote and stand as a candidate in elections to the European Parliament for citizens of the European Union residing in a member state of which they are not nationals). The 2013 Regulations, in particular, (1) further amend the 2004 Regulations, SI 2004/293, so as to (a) revise the requirement for a declaration to be made by a candidate who is a citizen of another member state; (b) remove the requirement for such a candidate to provide a certificate from the member state of nationality; (c) make changes to the time by which nomination documents must be submitted; (d) require the Secretary of State to notify another member state that one of its nationals has made a declaration and to ask if that person has been deprived of the right to stand as a candidate in that member state; (e) provide that, if information is received showing that the candidate has been so deprived, the candidate's nomination may be declared invalid or the candidate may be removed from the party's list; (f) provide that, if the information is received after the publication of the statement of parties and candidates standing nominated, the candidate and votes for the candidate may be disregarded for the purposes of allocating seats; (g) make changes consequential on changes to criminal justice legislation in Gibraltar; (h) allow the fee payable to a returning officer or local returning officer to be reduced because of inadequate performance; (i) amend the maximum amounts of fines that may be imposed in Gibraltar on conviction of certain offences; (j) require the Secretary of State to respond to a request from another member state for information about a United Kingdom national who is standing as a candidate at a European parliamentary election in that member state; (k) replace or amend various forms and notices used by voters at European parliamentary elections; (l) enable a police community support officer to enter a polling station in England and Wales on the same terms as a constable; (m) allow a voter to vote if he is in a polling station or in a queue outside the polling station at 10pm on polling day; (n) require a local returning officer to check the personal identifiers (date of birth and signature) on every returned postal voting statement against the identifiers held on file; (o) require a registration officer to notify a voter that his vote has been rejected because the personal identifiers on the postal voting statement could not be verified, and enable the registration officer to request the voter to provide a fresh signature; (p) repeal obsolete transitional provisions relating to postal and proxy voting; (q) allow a voter to apply for a proxy voting arrangement after 5pm on the sixth day before the date of the poll (an emergency proxy vote) on grounds relating to occupation, service or employment; (r) require postal ballot papers to be sent out as soon as it is practicable to do so; (s) make consequential provision and provision for how an application to change an absent voting arrangement is to be dealt with when a postal vote has already been sent out; and (t) provide for the statement of postal ballot papers to be forwarded by the local returning officer to the registration officer; (2) amend the European Parliamentary Elections Act 2002 so as to (a) transpose a change to Directive 93/109 about the types of decision that may disqualify a person from standing as a candidate at a European parliamentary election; and (b) replace the reference to a 'criminal law or civil law decision' with a reference to a 'judicial decision or an administrative decision that can be subject to a judicial remedy'; and (3) further amend the European Parliamentary Elections (Franchise of Relevant Citizens of the Union) Regulations 2001, SI 2001/1184, so as to transfer, from the Lord Chancellor to the Lord President of the Council or the Secretary of State, the duty to maintain a list of representatives of other member states to whom certain information must be sent.

988   European parliamentary elections—returning officers

The European Parliamentary Elections (Returning Officers) Order 2013, SI 2013/2064 (in force on 20 August 2013), replaces the 2008 Order, SI 2008/1914, and designates returning officers at European parliamentary elections for the electoral regions of England, Wales and Scotland.

989   Local elections—electoral register—false votes—corrupt and illegal practices

The defendant was elected by a narrow majority to a borough council. The claimant, a candidate for an opposing party, commenced proceedings claiming that the defendant had caused false names to be entered on the electoral register of the ward, made up of people who did not reside at the addresses stated or who did not exist at all. The claimant further contended that the defendant had harvested the postal votes of people genuinely resident in the ward and entitled to be registered to vote by intercepting and using their votes. Moreover, the claimant submitted that the defendant had used his connections in the Asian Muslim community of the ward to control voting and that voting reflected internal politics between factions in the community, rather than the politics of the political parties, and had been organised along familial lines. It fell to be determined whether (1) corrupt practices had occurred and were sufficiently widespread so as to justify a finding of general corruption; (2) applying the civil standard of proof, the corruption could reasonably be supposed to have affected the result of the election; and (3) applying the criminal standard of proof, the defendant, either by himself or his agents, had been guilty of corrupt practices contrary to the Representation of the People Act 1983. *Held*, on the evidence, there had been a high proportion of postal votes to personal votes in the ward. There had also been abnormally high turnout figures, well beyond the natural expectations of a keenly-contested election. Viewing the properties as a whole, there was no doubt that false registration and false votes, both personal and postal, had been widespread in the ward. The evidence was overwhelming that the frauds had been perpetrated by the defendant's team of close relatives and associates. Applying the criminal standard of proof, the widespread corruption could be reasonably supposed to have affected the result of the election. The defendant was, by himself and by his agents, guilty of corrupt practices contrary to the 1983 Act. It followed that the election of the defendant would be declared avoided by corrupt or illegal practices. Accordingly, the claim would be allowed.

Ali v Bashir [2013] EWHC 2572 (QB), [2013] All ER (D) 24 (Nov) (Queen's Bench Division: Commissioner Mawrey QC).

990 Local elections—ordinary day of elections

The Local Elections (Ordinary Day of Elections in 2014) Order 2013, SI 2013/2277 (in force on 7 September 2013), (1) changes the date of local elections in England in 2014, so that it is the same as the date of the European parliamentary elections in that year; (2) provides that the retirement date of any councillors due to retire in 2014 is to be determined in accordance with the new election date, while that of any councillors coming into office in 2014 is to be unaffected by the change of ordinary day; and (3) extends (a) in relation to local elections in England, the period during which it is not necessary to hold a by-election prior to the ordinary day of elections, so that in relation to elections in 2014, the period will last for the six months immediately before the date of the poll at the European parliamentary general election held in 2014; (b) the date by which joint authorities in England must hold their annual meetings until 31 August 2014, so that they may be held after any elections which may affect their composition; (c) the date by which annual parish meetings in parishes which are having ordinary elections to the parish council in 2014 must take place to 31 July 2014; and (d) the date by which the London Fire and Emergency Planning Authority must hold its annual meeting until 31 August 2014 so that it may be held after any election which may affect its composition.

991 Local Government (Democracy) (Wales) Act 2013

See para 1797.

992 National Assembly for Wales—electoral registration—absent voters—fresh signatures

The National Assembly for Wales (Representation of the People) (Fresh Signatures for Absent Voters) Order 2013, SI 2013/1514 (in force on 20 June 2013), (1) modifies, for a limited period, the National Assembly for Wales (Representation of the People) Order 2007, SI 2007/236, in line with the transitional arrangements for the implementation of individual electoral registration under the Electoral Registration and Administration Act 2013; and (2) modifies the provisions relating to the mandatory signature refresh for absent voters so that an absent voter who would otherwise be requested to provide a new example of his signature in January 2014 will instead be requested to do so between 1 and 19 August 2013.

993 Parliamentary elections—eligibility to vote—British citizen resident overseas—human rights

The applicant was a British national who had left the United Kingdom to live in Italy. By virtue of the Representation of the People Act 1983 s 1, British citizens residing overseas for less than 15 years were permitted to vote in parliamentary elections in the United Kingdom. The applicant did not meet the 15-year criterion and was therefore not entitled to vote. The applicant complained to the European Court of Human Rights, submitting that the 1983 Act s 1 contravened the right to participate in free elections under the European Convention on Human Rights First Protocol art 3. The applicant contended that no time limit should be imposed on the right of EU citizens resident abroad to vote in their country of origin while they retained the nationality of that country. *Held*, the rights bestowed by the First Protocol art 3 were not absolute. For a measure to be deemed compatible with the right to vote, the conditions to which the right to vote was made subject could not curtail the right to such an extent as to impair its very essence and deprive it of its effectiveness. The measure had to be imposed in pursuit of a legitimate aim and the means employed could not be disproportionate. The restriction in the present case pursued the legitimate aim of confining the parliamentary franchise to those citizens with a close connection with the United Kingdom and who would therefore be most directly affected by its laws. If the applicant returned to live in the United Kingdom, his right to vote as a resident would be restored. In those circumstances it could not be said that the restriction had impaired the very essence of the applicant's rights. The central question, therefore, concerned the proportionality of the restriction imposed. Problems were posed by migration in terms of political participation in countries of origin and residence. However, allowing non-residents to vote for 15 years after leaving the country was not an unsubstantial period of time. Having regard to the significant burden which would be imposed if the United Kingdom were required to ascertain in every application to vote by a non-resident whether the individual had a sufficiently close connection to the country, the general measure in the present case promoted legal certainty and avoided problems of arbitrariness and inconsistency inherent in weighing interests on a case-by-case basis. Accordingly, the application would be dismissed.

Application 19840/09 *Shindler v United Kingdom* [2013] All ER (D) 239 (May) (European Court of Human Rights).

994   Political Parties and Elections Act 2009—commencement

The Political Parties and Elections Act 2009 (Commencement No 6) Order 2013, SI 2013/99, brings into force (1) on 22 January 2013, s 27(1), (2), (4); and (2) on 1 January 2014, s 27(4). For a summary of the Act, see 2009 Abr para 1299. See also the commencement table in the title STATUTES AND LEGISLATIVE PROCESS.

995   Referendum—local authority—council tax increase—England

See para 1749.

996   Representation of the people—general provisions

The Representation of the People (England and Wales) (Description of Electoral Registers and Amendment) Regulations 2013, SI 2013/3198 (in force in part on 19 December 2013 and in part on 6 April 2014), further amend the 2001 Regulations, SI 2001/341, so as to implement the Electoral Registration and Administration Act 2013. The 2013 Regulations, in particular, (1) prescribe the form and content of applications under the Representation of the People Act 1983 s 10ZC or 10ZD; (2) confer on the Electoral Commission the function of designing the paper application form; (3) prescribe the information which must be included in the paper application form; (4) provide that applications may be made online through the individual electoral registration digital service; (5) empower an electoral registration officer to accept applications through assisted means, either by telephone or in person; (6) make provision for cases where certain information is not available or where a registration officer considers that additional evidence is necessary to verify the identity of a person; (7) make provision relating to service electors and overseas electors; (8) deal with the processing of information, including the retention and deletion of information; (9) provide that an offence is committed if certain information is disclosed; (10) include additional orders and injunctions for the purpose of an application for an anonymous entry in the electoral register; (11) provide for the annual canvass, including requirements for the design of the annual canvass form and the manner in which forms must be given; (12) prescribe the steps a registration officer must take when no information is received in response to a form; (13) provide for invitations to apply for registration and the steps to be taken by a registration officer to encourage a person to make an application for registration; (14) set out the conditions under which a registration officer may require a person to apply for registration; (15) provide for the imposition of a civil penalty where a person fails to comply with a requirement to make an application for registration by a specified date; (16) specify details of the requirements of notice of the penalty, the payment, enforcement and cancellation of the penalty and the review of and appeals against a penalty; (17) allow a voter to apply for a proxy voting arrangement after 5pm on the sixth day before the date of the poll on grounds relating to occupation, service or employment; (18) provide that, notwithstanding the deadline otherwise provided for, an application to cancel or change an absent vote may not be made after a postal vote has been returned; (19) make provision about cancellation of postal ballot papers, requiring postal voters to provide fresh signatures

Furthermore, the tenth defendant would be vicariously liable to the claimant for the fraudulent conduct of the thirteenth defendant in using his account, which he had a right to use honestly and which he had been authorised to use to place bets. Moreover, for the same reason, the second defendant would be liable to compensate the claimant for the loss suffered as a result of fraud carried out by the third defendant on her account. In relation to the manifest error clause, the claimant was entitled as against the second and tenth to twelfth defendants to amend the opening level of each relevant bet to that which it believed would have been fair and reasonable at the time it was entered had the false dividend not been fraudulently entered by the first defendant. However, as against the thirteenth defendant, the claimant would not be entitled to amend the relevant bets as the version of the manifest error clause which applied to him had not reserved to the claimant an unqualified right to amend the terms of any bet containing or based on a manifest error. Judgment would be given accordingly.

IG Index plc v Colley [2013] EWHC 478 (QB), [2013] All ER (D) 99 (Mar) (Queen's Bench Division: Stadlen J).

1005   Contract of employment—frustration—disability—reasonable adjustments

An employee was employed as a site manager for his employer in a role which required a high level of mobility. He suffered a severe and disabling stroke. Although there was no contractual obligation to pay sick pay, the employer paid the employee full pay for the following three months. The employee did not contact the employer to say that he anticipated a return to work. Eleven months after the employee had suffered the stroke, the employer wrote to him, enclosing a cheque for his accrued holiday pay and his P45, and confirming the end of his employment. The employer subsequently explained that the reason for the termination of the employee's contract was capability on medical grounds. The employee commenced proceedings in an employment tribunal for unfair dismissal, breach of contract and disability discrimination. The tribunal had before it a doctor's report which found that the employee's mobility was still substantially affected and dexterity in his left hand was markedly reduced. The tribunal dismissed the claims, holding that the employee's contract had been frustrated by operation of law and that the employer had not discriminated against him. The employee appealed, arguing that there was no room for the doctrine of frustration once a duty to make reasonable adjustments arose; and that the tribunal had failed to deal with his submission that the employer, by failing to carry out any form of capability procedure and by dismissing the employee without any procedure, had treated him unfavourably for a reason arising from his disability. Held, it was established law that the doctrine of frustration applied to contracts of employment, even where those contracts were terminable on short notice. In the case of a disabled person, before the doctrine of frustration could apply, there was an additional factor which the tribunal had to consider over and above other factors identified in the relevant authorities, namely, whether the employer was in breach of a duty to make reasonable adjustments. While there was something which it was reasonable to expect an employer to have to do in order to keep the employee in employment, the doctrine of frustration could have no application. The tribunal had considered whether the employer was in breach of the duty to make reasonable adjustments and found that it had not been. The tribunal had applied the correct test and its conclusion could not be impugned. On the facts, the tribunal had not dealt with the employee's submission that the employer had treated him unfavourably by failing to carry out any form of capability procedure and by dismissing him without any form of inquiry or procedure. It was arguable that this had been unfavourable treatment and that it had been because of something arising in consequence of his disability. Findings were required as to whether the employer had behaved as it had because of something arising in consequence of the employee's disability, whether it had amounted to unfavourable treatment and whether it had been justified. Accordingly, the appeal would be allowed in respect of the issue concerning discrimination arising out of disability and the matter would be remitted to the same tribunal for its consideration; the appeal would be dismissed in all other respects.

Warner v Armfield Retail & Leisure Ltd [2013] All ER (D) 260 (Oct) (Employment Appeal Tribunal: Judge David Richardson presiding).

1006   Contract of employment—non-remunerative benefits—continuation after retirement—senior trade union official

The defendant had been employed by the claimant trade union in a number of senior roles, including president, but had since retired from the organisation. When he became president, his contract of employment stated that the claimant would pay the rent on a London property, fuel allowance, costs of security and accountancy advice for the defendant. The arrangement dated back approximately 30 years when the defendant assumed the position and negotiated an arrangement for the claimant to cover the cost of the rent of his flat rather than to buy one outright and retain the benefit of it after the death of the defendant and his widow. The defendant also owned a house outside London. Its security costs were paid by the claimant. There were a number of purported contractual restatements of these benefits over the years, some drafted by the defendant himself and passed to the claimant's accounts section. As the defendant approached retirement he sought clarity on the claimant's obligations to continue with these payments, on which the claimant demurred. *Held*, the surrounding circumstances and subsequent history both supported the view that having the claimant pay the rent on the flat was not a replacement for the custom of purchasing a house for its presidents, but was a facility to enable a president to do his job in London. Moreover, the defendant had been too closely involved in drafting the contracts regarding the flat, which raised an issue of agency. The claimant's executive committee had never approved those contracts, so when the defendant retired, the contract that appeared to bind the claimant was not effective. With regard to the issue of fuel, there was no evidence that the committee decision was intended to create a distinct right beyond the putting of national officials in the same position as area officials regarding concessionary coal. Similarly, while it was reasonable to assume that the accountancy charges would be paid during the defendant's term of employment, there was no basis on which any such obligation could continue following his retirement. However, on the evidence, the agreement to pay for the security system at the house could not be taken to be limited to the defendant's employment. It was unrealistic to think that any security threat to the defendant would instantly end once he retired and the claimant had to have contemplated that risks against the defendant would continue after his retirement, although they might diminish. However, despite the absence of a continuing obligation to pay rent, the claimant's claim for equitable compensation could not succeed. There was no evidence that any of the signatories to the agreements had acted in breach of any fiduciary duty to the claimant while acting as agents for the defendant. It followed that the claimant was entitled to declarations regarding the issues of the flat, the fuel allowance and the accountancy costs, but would not be able to claim equitable compensation for the rent already paid. Judgment would be given accordingly.

National Union of Mineworkers v Scargill [2012] EWHC 3750 (Ch), [2013] All ER (D) 197 (Feb) (Chancery Division: Underhill J). *Amalgamated Investment and Property Co Ltd v Texas Commerce International Bank plc* [1982] QB 84, [1981] 3 All ER 577, CA (1981 Abr para 1084), distinguished.

1007   Contract of employment—terms of employment—grievance meeting—right to be accompanied at grievance hearing

A number of employees raised grievances with their employer who invited them to attend grievance meetings. The employees asked to be accompanied by a third party who was an elected official of a union. The employer declined to allow the third party to accompany the employees and, in consequence, each employee instead sought the assistance of a colleague. The employees found the outcome of the meetings unsatisfactory and appealed. At the appeal hearings, the colleague was replaced by an elected union official, who was not the third party. The employees brought proceedings, submitting that the employer breached the Employment Relations Act 1999 s 10 by refusing to allow the third party to accompany them to the meetings. The tribunal decided that the third party came within s 10(3) and that, when the employer originally rejected him, it had been in potential breach of s 10, but that because the employees had chosen another companion they waived the potential breach. The employees appealed. *Held*, the employer breached the employees' right to be accompanied at the grievance hearings by not allowing their chosen union official to accompany them. With regard to the right to be accompanied at the disciplinary or grievance hearings under s 10, the choice of companion did not have to be reasonable.

Parliament legislated for the choice to be that of the worker, subject only to the safeguards set out in s 3 as to the identity or the class of persons who might be available to be a companion. The tribunal erred in finding that the employees waived their rights to their chosen companion by choosing another companion after the employer rejected their first choice. The statutory prohibition on waiver was found in the Employment Rights Act 1996 s 203 and there was no reason to depart from the decision in *Secretary of State for Employment v Deary*, which established the principle that it was not open to an employer or an employee to waive a statutory requirement through an express or implied agreement. Accordingly, the appeals would be allowed.

Toal v GB Oils Ltd [2013] IRLR 696 (Employment Appeal Tribunal: Mitting J presiding). *Secretary of State for Employment v Deary* [1984] IRLR 180, EAT (1984 Abr para 940), considered.

1008 Contract of employment—terms of employment—overtime payments

An employee was employed as an HGV driver. His contract of employment provided for (1) regular hours of work of up to 52 hours per week; (2) a discretionary meal allowance; (3) payment for hours in excess of normal working hours at the normal rate of pay; and (4) a discretionary payment for hours worked in excess of normal working hours at an enhanced rate. The employee was dismissed and he brought a claim in an employment tribunal alleging unfair dismissal and arrears of pay in respect of overtime worked but not paid for and non-payment of the meal allowance. At the hearing, the employee gave no evidence in respect of the meal allowance claim. The tribunal allowed the claim for unfair dismissal, but dismissed the claims for the meal allowance and arrears of pay. The employee appealed. *Held,* (1) it was settled law that (a) the starting point was the contract of employment; (b) if the contract of employment entitled the employee at least to consideration of the exercise of a discretion, it would be a breach of that contract not to consider its exercise; (c) where a discretion was said to be exercisable only on some prior facts having been established, there could be no question factually of any award becoming payable unless those factual pre-conditions were satisfied; (4) if the discretion had been exercised, then the exercise might be reviewed; (5) if the discretion had not been exercised then the employee was entitled to be put into the position in which he would have been if the contract had been fully and properly performed; (6) in such a situation the employer would have given proper consideration to the exercise of the discretion; (7) the task in assessing compensation for the breach therefore, was to ask what that employer, acting neither irrationally nor perversely would have decided to pay the employee. The effect of the employee's contract was that, if it was shown that an employee had worked beyond the 52 hours averaged across the working year, he was entitled to be paid the ordinary rate for the job for those additional hours and he might at the discretion of the employer be entitled to an enhanced rate for those hours. The tribunal had not determined what had been in dispute before it, which had been whether the employee had worked more than 52 hours per week. There was no resolution by the tribunal of the factual issues. Since the question of whether the employee had been entitled to be paid at the normal rate for additional hours depended entirely on whether he had worked those additional hours, and no finding had been made, the present tribunal was in no position to say that the decision which the tribunal had come to had been inevitably right. Therefore, the appeal in respect of the arrears of pay would be allowed and the matter remitted to the same tribunal for re-determination. (2) In respect of the meal allowance, that issue had depended on evidence that the meal allowance had been due and payable. The employee had given no such evidence at the hearing. The tribunal could only have come to the conclusion that the claim had not been established. Accordingly, the appeal in respect of the meal allowance would be dismissed.

Czarnecki v Choice Textiles Ltd [2013] All ER (D) 77 (Sep) (Employment Appeal Tribunal: Langstaff J presiding). *Driver v Air India Ltd* [2011] EWCA Civ 986, [2011] IRLR 992 (2011 Abr para 1029) considered.

1009 Contract of employment—terms of employment—remuneration—training post paying less than hospital position

An employee was a doctor specialising in oral and maxillo-facial surgery, who had originally trained as a dentist. She worked in a hospital as a trust grade doctor in oral surgery. She left that employment and was offered a training post with the employer, an NHS trust, that being a necessary step for the employee to qualify as a consultant. The pay in the new post was less than that offered by the hospital. The contractual terms relevant to the post were in the NHS Terms and Conditions of Service for Hospital Medical and Dental staff and Doctors in Public Health Medicine and the Community Health Service (England and Wales). Pay in the post was determined in relation to the number of half-days or sessions worked. Each session was three and a half hours long. The employee brought proceedings against the employer, contending that there had been an unlawful deduction from her wages contrary to the Employment Rights Act 1996 Pt 2 (ss 13–27). She argued that she was entitled to the basic hourly rate that she had received at the hospital for the time she had spent working with the employer. The employer argued that the employee's pay protection should be limited to five sessions per week, which was the maximum time she would have been able to work when working at the hospital. An employment tribunal held that the employer's view was to be preferred. On the claimant's appeal, the Employment Appeal Tribunal held that the employee was entitled to payment protection, but limited her protection to five sessions, which was the maximum that she could have worked in her previous post. On the employer's appeal, the Court of Appeal decided that the view of the employment tribunal was to be preferred. The employee appealed. *Held,* the issue had to be approached by applying ordinary principles of construction. The object was to ascertain the intention of the parties by examining the words they used and giving them their ordinary meaning in their contractual context. It was disturbing that a condition designed to confer important rights on employees should be so obscure. The condition was clearly not well drafted, and required reconsideration. The critical words were 'the practitioner shall ... continue to be paid on the incremental point the practitioner has reached in ... her previous appointment'. The 'incremental point' was clearly a reference to the relevant point in the scale for the practitioner's grade. Since, in the employee's case, that point was expressed in terms of sessional rates, some means had to be found to convert those rates into a form which could be applied to the different terms of her training post, in which her periods of work were measured in hours, rather than in sessions. The most obvious way of doing that was by conversion of the sessional rates to hourly rates. Although it was potentially counter-intuitive that those rates were not limited in some way by reference to the number of sessions that were, or could have been, worked in the former post, there was nothing in the wording of the terms that could be relied on to support such a limitation. The terms, elsewhere, simply confirmed that no distinction was to be made in the application of the rates between part-time and full-time practitioners. The reasoning and conclusion of the employment appeal tribunal would be restored, along with its order. Accordingly, the appeal would be allowed.

Verma v Barts and the London NHS Trust [2013] UKSC 20, [2013] IRLR 567, [2013] All ER (D) 176 (Apr) (Supreme Court: Lord Hope DP, Lord Walker, Lady Hale, Lord Sumption and Lord Carnwath SCJJ). Decision of Court of Appeal [2011] EWCA Civ 1129, [2011] All ER (D) 128 (Oct) reversed.

1010   Contract of employment—terms of employment—termination—duty of confidentiality

See *Vestergaard Frandsen A/S v Bestnet Europe Ltd*, para 421.

1011   Contract of employment—variation—adverse change clause—bonus

The contracts of employment of employees of a bank incorporated the bank employee handbook, one clause of which gave the employer power unilaterally to vary those contracts by notice in writing. After the employer was taken over, an effort was made to reduce running costs in view of adverse trading conditions. Promises were made that the bonus pool would not be affected but, in the employee bonus letters, the employer introduced an adverse conditions clause stating that the actual amount payable would be kept under review. An extraordinary meeting of the employer's board decided to reduce the bonus by 90 per cent, and, in some cases, to not pay a bonus at all. The employees issued proceedings claiming sums due as bonuses. It fell to be determined (1) whether the announcement had created a binding obligation on the employer to pay the employees; and (2) whether the introduction of the material adverse conditions clause had amounted to a breach of the implied duty of mutual trust and confidence inherent to contracts of employment. The judge rejected the employer's submissions that there had been no intention to create legal relations in a dispute between individuals in order to preclude, as the case may be, the application of the national provision which is not in conformity with that Directive. Since the French Labour Code was adopted to implement Directive 2002/14, art 27 of the Charter is applicable to the instant case. It is clear from the wording of art 27 that, for it to be fully effective, it must be given more specific expression in EU or national law. It is not possible to infer from the wording of art 27 of Directive 2002/14 or from the explanatory notes to art 27 that art 3(1), as a directly applicable rule of law, lays down and addresses to the member states a prohibition on excluding from the calculation of the staff numbers in an undertaking a specific category of employees initially included in the group of persons to be taken into account in that calculation. In this connection, the facts of the case may be distinguished from those which gave rise to *Kucukdeveci* in so far as the principle of non-discrimination on grounds of age at issue in that case, laid down in art 21(1) of the Charter, was held to be sufficient in itself to confer on individuals an individual right which they may invoke as such. Accordingly, art 27 of the Charter cannot, as such, be invoked in a dispute, such as that in the main proceedings, in order to conclude that the national provision which is not in conformity with Directive 2002/14 should not be applied. That finding cannot be called into question by considering art 27 of the Charter in conjunction with the provisions of Directive 2002/14, given that, since that article by itself does not suffice to confer on individuals a right which they may invoke as such, it could not be otherwise if it is considered in conjunction with Directive 2002/14. (4) The French Labour Code could not have been interpreted in conformity with Directive 2002/14. The obligation on a national court to refer to the content of a directive when interpreting and applying the relevant rules of domestic law is limited by general principles of law and it cannot serve as the basis for an interpretation of national law contra legem. Such a limitation had existed in relation to the French law. Accordingly, art 27 of the Charter, by itself or in conjunction with the provisions of Directive 2002/14, had to be interpreted to the effect that, where a national provision implementing Directive 2002/14, such as art L1111–3 of the French Labour Code, is incompatible with EU law, that article of the Charter cannot be invoked in a dispute between individuals in order to disapply that national provision.

Case C-176/12 *Association de Médiation Sociale v Union Locale des Syndicats* [2014] IRLR 310 (ECJ: Grand Chamber). Case C-555/07 *Kucukdeveci v Swedex GmbH & Co KG* [2010] IRLR 346, ECJ (2010 Abr para 961), considered.

1042   Maternity leave—right to return to same job—redundancy—assessment exercise

The applicant was employed in Latvia as a principal adviser in a legal affairs department. Shortly after returning from 18 months' parental leave, her post was abolished. The defendant employer carried out an assessment, which involved comparing the performance of the applicant and a colleague who was employed in the same job. The applicant's latest performance review predated her parental leave. As her rating in that review was lower than her colleague's score in the latest review, the defendant notified the applicant that her employment was being terminated. She subsequently accepted a position in another department, but shortly afterwards that post was also abolished. The applicant brought proceedings challenging the decision to terminate her employment, submitting that the manner in which her performance had been assessed was unlawful. Her claim was rejected. On her appeal, a preliminary ruling was sought as to whether European law should be interpreted as precluding a situation where, as part of an assessment of workers in the context of abolition of public officials' posts due to national economic difficulties, a female worker who had taken parental leave was assessed in her absence on the basis of the last annual performance appraisal done before she took parental leave, using new criteria, while workers who had remained in active service were assessed on the basis of a more recent period. *Held*, European law should be interpreted as precluding such a situation. The national court should ensure that the assessment encompassed all workers liable to be concerned by the abolition of the post, that it was based on criteria which were absolutely identical to those applying to workers in active service and that the implementation of those criteria did not involve the physical presence of workers on parental leave. European law also precluded a situation where a female worker who had been transferred to another post at the end of her parental leave following that assessment was dismissed due to the abolition of that new post, where it had not been impossible for the employer to allow her to return to her former post or where the work assigned to her had not been equivalent or similar and consistent with her employment contract or employment relationship because, at the time of the transfer, the employer had been informed that the new post had been due to be abolished, which it was for the national court to verify.

Case C-7/12 *Riezniece v Zemkopibas minisrija* [2013] IRLR 828 (ECJ: Fourth Chamber).

1043   National minimum wage—general provisions

The National Minimum Wage (Amendment) Regulations 2013, SI 2013/1975 (in force on 1 October 2013), further amend the 1999 Regulations, SI 1999/584, so as to (1) increase, from £6·19 to £6·31 per hour, the rate of the national minimum wage for workers who are aged 21 or over; (2) increase, from £4·98 to £5·03 per hour, the rate for workers who are aged 18 or over (but not yet aged 21); (3) increase, from from £3·68 to £3·72 per hour, the rate for workers who are under the age of 18; (4) increase, from £2·65 to £2·68 per hour, the rate paid to apprentices within the first 12 months of their employment or engagement under certain government arrangements, or who are under the age of 19; and (5) increase, from £4·82 to £4·91 for each day that accommodation is provided, the accommodation amount which is applicable where an employer provides a worker with living accommodation.

1044   Parental leave—contract variation—employed agency workers

The Parental Leave (EU Directive) Regulations 2013, SI 2013/283 (in force on 8 March 2013), amend (1) the Employment Rights Act 1996 s 80F, so as to extend the right to request a contract variation to employed agency workers who are returning to work from a period of parental leave; and (2) the Maternity and Parental Leave etc Regulations 1999, SI 1999/3312, so as to increase a qualifying employee's entitlement to parental leave in respect of an individual child from 13 weeks to 18 weeks, and to require the Secretary of State to review and report on the operation and effect of provisions concerning parental leave at least every five years.

1045   Parental leave—entitlement—increase

See 1044.

1046   Paternity leave—entitlement—employee father—refusal on ground of mother's self-employed status

An employee covered by the Spanish state social security scheme had a son with a mother who was self-employed and covered by an occupational scheme that was independent of the state scheme. The mother's scheme provided for maternity allowance, but not maternity leave. The employee requested 10 weeks' paternity leave following the six weeks' compulsory leave that the mother had to take under national law. His request was refused on the ground that under national law the right to leave was a right of mothers who were covered by the state scheme and that a father did not have his own autonomous right to leave. Since the mother was not covered by the state scheme, she did not herself have a primary right to maternity leave, meaning that the employee was not entitled to paternity leave. On a reference for a preliminary ruling in proceedings challenging the refusal, issues arose as to the interpretation of Council Directive (EEC) 92/85 (on the introduction of measures to encourage improvements in the safety and health at work of pregnant workers and workers who have recently given birth or are breastfeeding) and Council Directive (EEC) 76/207 (on the implementation of the principle of equal treatment for men and women as regards access to employment, vocational training and promotion, and working conditions). *Held*, Directives 92/85 and 76/207 did not preclude a national measure which provided that the father of a child, who was an employed person, was entitled, with the consent of the mother, who was also an employed person, to take maternity leave for the period following the compulsory leave of six weeks which the mother had to take after childbirth except where her health would be at risk, whereas a father of a child who was an employed person was not entitled to take such leave where the mother of his child was not an employed person and was not covered by a state social security scheme.

Case C-5/12 *Montull v Instituto Nacional de la Seguridad Social* [2013] IRLR 976 (ECJ: Fourth Chamber).

1047   Protected disclosure—detriment—post-termination disclosure

An employee brought claims of direct race discrimination, harassment and victimisation against his employer. He sought to rely on a letter to the employer and a report to the Legal Complaints Service, both dated after the termination of the employment, as protected disclosures. Allegations of forgery and dishonesty subsequently made by the employer against the employee led to the employee being investigated by the Solicitors Regulatory Authority. It was accepted, following the decision in *Relaxion*, that a complaint under the Employment Rights Act 1996 s 47B in respect of protected disclosures could rely on post-termination detriment to complete the statutory tort. Accordingly, the only question that fell to be determined was whether the protected act might occur after the termination of the relevant employment. The tribunal answered that question in the negative and on that basis declined jurisdiction to consider the complaint under s 47B. The employee appealed. *Held*, since the detriment had to occur and be causatively linked to the protected disclosure, it followed that it had to come later in time and since the detriment might arise post-termination, there was no warrant for limiting the disclosure temporally to the duration of the employment. Nor was there any force in the employer's reference to use of the present tense in ss 43A–43C. Those provisions were concerned only with the quality of the disclosures when they were made, not with the temporal point which was raised in the present case. It followed that as a matter of pure construction of the statute, post-termination disclosures might be relied on if they led to detrimental treatment, which was an issue yet to be determined in the present case. That was also in line with the legislative purpose of protection for whistleblowers and was entirely consistent with the authority previously referred to, save for *Fadipe*, which was no longer to be followed. Accordingly, the appeal would be allowed.

Onyango v Berkeley (t/a Berkeley Solicitors) [2013] IRLR 338 (Employment Appeal Tribunal: Judge Peter Clark presiding). *Post Office v Adekeye* [1997] IRLR 105, CA; *Relaxion Group plc v Rhys-Harper; D'Souza v Lambeth LBC; Jones v 3M Healthcare Ltd* [2003] UKHL 33, [2003] 4 All ER 1113 (2003 Abr para 963); and *Woodward v Abbey National plc* [2006] EWCA Civ 822, [2006] 4 All ER 1209 (2006 Abr para 1248) considered. *Fadipe v Reed Nursing Personnel* [2001] EWCA Civ 1885, [2005] ICR 1760, [2001] All ER (D) 23 (Dec) disapproved.

1048   Public interest disclosure—prescribed persons

The Public Interest Disclosure (Prescribed Persons) (Amendment) Order 2013, SI 2013/2213 (in force in part on 1 October 2013 and in part on 6 April 2014), further amend the 1999 Order, SI 1999/1549, so as to (1) reflect changes made to policing governance arrangements by the Police Reform and Social Responsibility Act 2011; (2) add health and social care professional regulatory bodies to the list of prescribed persons; (3) make changes to existing entries for certain health and social care regulators; and (4) expand the description of matters in respect of which the Civil Aviation Authority is prescribed.

1049   Redundancy—collective redundancies—employer's duty to consult—authority of representatives

Owing to financial pressure, an employer decided that it needed to vary the contracts of employment of its staff. After considerable discussion between the management and the workforce, the vast majority of the employees agreed to the variation. The employer wrote to those employees who had not returned signed new contracts to advise them that it would enter into collective consultation in relation to its proposal to terminate their contracts and offer re-engagement on the new terms and conditions. Such action constituted dismissal on the ground of redundancy, and hence triggered the consultation duties in the Trade Union and Labour Relations (Consolidation) Act 1992 s 188. The employees brought a claim before an employment tribunal, submitting that the employer had failed to fulfil its consultation obligations under s 188. The tribunal found that, by recognising that the alternative to varying contracts might involve redundancy and by entering into a collective consultation relating to re-engagement of affected employees, the employer had satisfied the requirements of s 188. On the employees' appeal, they submitted that (1) the appropriate representatives had not had the authority of the affected employees to consult with a view to reaching agreement on their behalf; and (2) there had not been discussion of the three matters specifically referred to in s 188(2). *Held*, whether the appropriate representatives had had the authority of those affected by the proposals to consult with a view to reaching agreement on their behalf was a matter which could not be determined by the present court. The question of appropriateness depended on a finding of fact as to authority, which the present court was in no position to make. In relation to the second ground of appeal, the tribunal had not been clear whether there had been any discussion about the three matters specifically referred to in s 188(2). The tribunal had considered it the burden of the employee rather than the employer to raise matters for discussion. It might be that the communications read together constituted sufficient compliance, albeit in more than one written document. It seemed that the employer had not realised till late in the process, if at all, that it had been bound by the obligations under s 188. There might well be a case for supposing that the employer's fault had been accidental, and that standing back the employer had sought to involve many of its employees in discussions about entering a new contract. Against that background, there was much to be said for a negotiated or mediated settlement between the parties. Accordingly, the appeal would be allowed in part.

Kelly v Hesley Group Ltd [2013] IRLR 514 (Employment Appeal Tribunal: Langstaff J presiding).

1050　Redundancy—collective redundancies—general provisions

The Trade Union and Labour Relations (Consolidation) Act 1992 (Amendment) Order 2013, SI 2013/763 (in force on 6 April 2013), relates to the implementation of Council Directive (EC) 1998/59 (on the approximation of the laws of the member states relating to collective redundancies) and amends provisions relating to collective redundancies in the Trade Union and Labour Relations (Consolidation) Act 1992. The 2013 Order, in particular, (1) reduces, from 90 to 45, the minimum number of days which must elapse before the first dismissal may take effect in cases where the employer is proposing to dismiss 100 or more employees as redundant within a period of 90 days or less; (2) reduces, from 90 to 45 days, the minimum period of notice which the employer must give to the Secretary of State, before the first dismissal takes effect, in cases where the employer is proposing to dismiss 100 or more employees as redundant within a period of 90 days or less; and (3) excludes the expiry of fixed term contracts from the provisions dealing with collective redundancies but the expiry of a fixed term contract will not be excluded from such provisions if the employer is proposing to dismiss the employee as redundant and the dismissal will take effect before the point at which it was agreed in the contract that it would expire.

1051　Redundancy—collective redundancies—pay—redundancy policy—incorporated terms—enhanced payment

The employees were employed at a plant which produced engine valves. The plant had an advisory council on which management and employees were represented, but there was no recognised trade union. The human resources manager presented to the advisory council a redundancy policy which made provision for employees to receive enhanced payments over and above statutory requirements and the policy was signed on behalf of management and the advisory council. Employees were provided with a document which contained certain details of the terms and conditions of employment as required by the Employment Rights Act 1996 s 1 and made reference to the employee handbook, although there was no general statement that terms and conditions were to be found in the handbook. The handbook provided that, in the event of redundancies, the redundancy policy would be implemented. There was pressure at the plant for union recognition and, in order to resist that pressure, the human resources manager wrote open letters to all employees giving a guarantee that the existing redundancy policy would remain until the end of the next pay deal and that the redundancy policy negotiations would not take place until a specified date. The company subsequently decided to close the plant and a decision was made at the highest level that no enhanced payments were to be made. The employees brought proceedings to enforce the entitlement under the redundancy policy to an enhanced payment as a contractual term. The employment tribunal dismissed the claim, finding that there was no express term that the redundancy policy was incorporated into the contracts of employment and stating that the terms and conditions did not refer to the redundancy policy. Moreover, the tribunal considered whether the policy was incorporated by implication and concluded, giving consideration to the factors set out in *Albion Automotive Ltd v Walker*, that there was no implied term. The employees appealed. *Held,* the employee handbook was capable of being a source of contractual obligation and the tribunal ought to have considered it. With regard to the tribunal's conclusion that the employees could not have had a reasonable expectation that payment would have been made, the employer agreed the policy with the advisory council and made it the subject of an express promise in the employee handbook. That begged the question of how an employer, having acted in that way, could sensibly have denied that its employees had a reasonable expectation that payment would have been made in accordance with the promise. In considering that matter, the tribunal had not referred to the express promise in the handbook to implement the policy. Further, the tribunal placed no weight on the promise confirming that the policy would remain in its entirety and stay as it was until renegotiated. Those promises served to confirm that employees did indeed have a reasonable expectation that payment would have been made unless and until the policy was renegotiated. They expressly confirmed the conclusion which any reasonable employee would have had from reading the employee handbook and the redundancy policy. Accordingly, the appeal would be allowed.

Allen v TRW Systems Ltd [2013] IRLR 699 (Employment Appeal Tribunal: Judge David Richardson presiding). *Carmichael v National Power plc* [1999] 4 All ER 897, HL (1999 Abr para 1494), applied. *Albion Automotive Ltd v Walker* [2002] EWCA Civ 946, [2002] All ER (D) 170 (Jun); and *Keeley v Fosroc International Ltd* [2006] EWCA Civ 1277, [2006] IRLR 961 considered.

1052   Redundancy—duty to consult—breach—dismissals at one establishment

The Trade Union and Labour Relations (Consolidation) Act 1992 s 188(1) provides that, where an employer is proposing to dismiss as redundant 20 or more employees at one establishment within a period of 90 days or less, the employer is to consult about the dismissals all the persons who are appropriate representatives of any of the employees who may be affected by the proposed dismissals or may be affected by measures taken in connection with those dismissals.

The proceedings concerned an appeal by the claimants in two sets of proceedings relating to breach of the duty to consult over mass redundancies by two businesses. The employment tribunal in each set of proceedings decided that the claimants' claims for breach of the duty to consult over the redundancies would succeed and made protective awards for failure to consult in advance of the redundancies. However, it was also concluded that those made redundant in establishments where fewer than 20 workers had been dismissed were excluded from the decisions. On the claimants' appeal, it fell to be determined whether the duty to consult was owed when 20 employees were dismissed or when 20 employees were dismissed in any one establishment. The claimants, in submitting their first and second contentions, argued that in order to comply with Council Directive (EC) 98/59 (on the approximation of the laws of member states relating to collective redundancies), the 1992 Act s 188(1) ought to be interpreted as requiring the employer to consult where it proposed to dismiss as redundant 20 or more employees, whether at one or more establishments, or at one establishment, to mean the whole of the relevant retail business, rather than each of its individual stores. Alternatively, in their third contention, the claimants submitted that the words 'at one establishment' ought to be deleted from s 188(1). *Held,* applying the principles set down in *Coleman v EBR Attridge Law LLP,* the court was entitled to construe s 188(1) so that it complied with the obligation under Directive 98/59. If necessary, the court would accept the claimants' second contention. However it would go further, since the claimants' third contention made the point more clearly and simply so that it could be applied without detailed consideration of the added fact sensitive dimension. It followed that the words 'at one establishment' ought to be deleted from the 1992 Act s 188(1) as a matter of construction pursuant to the court's obligations to apply the purpose of Directive 98/59. If the court was going too far in adopting the claimants' second or third contention, then it would adopt the first contention so as to give effect to the purpose in *Rockfon A/S v Specialarbejderforbundet i Danmark.* Moreover, there was a further proposition which was literal and which did not invoke EU principles. In each of the two appeals, the employer had one establishment at which there had been 20 dismissals. Once over that threshold in that one establishment, the obligation to consult was triggered for all the dismissals, extending protection even to a shop with only one dismissed employee, since the staff in the smaller workplaces would be affected employees. Accordingly, the appeals would be allowed.

Usdaw v Ethel Austin Ltd (in administration); Usdaw v Unite the Union [2013] IRLR 686 (Employment Appeal Tribunal: Judge McMullen QC presiding). *Coleman v EBR Attridge Law LLP* [2010] IRLR 10, EAT (2009 Abr para 1139), applied. Case C-449/93 *Rockfon A/S v Specialarbejderforbundet i Danmark* [1996] IRLR 168, ECJ (1996 Abr para 3388), considered.

1053   Redundancy—duty to consult—employee engaged under fixed-term contract

Scotland
The University of Stirling, like other universities, traditionally employed a significant number of employees in both academic and non-academic posts on fixed-term contracts ('FTCs'). The University and College Union brought proceedings against the university in relation to four test case university employees whose FTCs were not renewed, but allowed to expire by the effluxion of time. Dr Harris had been employed for a research project dependent on outside funding; Dr Doyle had been employed to deliver three specific undergraduate modules; Ms Fife had been employed to provide maternity leave cover and thereafter for three short terms limited in time; and Dr Kelly had been employed to provide sick leave cover. The litigation related to the obligation, imposed by s 188 of the Trade Union and Labour Relations (Consolidation) Act 1992 in the event of an employer proposing to dismiss as redundant 20 or more employees at an establishment, to consult about the dismissals with appropriate representatives of the employees. The union argued that the test case employees should have counted towards the threshold figure. At a pre-hearing review, the employment tribunal defined the preliminary issue for determination as whether the test case employees had been dismissed as redundant within the meaning of s 195 of the 1992 Act. Section 195(1) provided so far as material that references to dismissal as redundant were references to dismissal 'for a reason not related to the individual concerned'. The employment tribunal thought that the expression 'for a reason not related to an individual' was not clear and unambiguous. It considered that it was inevitable that the reason for a dismissal, even a dismissal by reason of redundancy, would relate to the individual concerned. It concluded therefore that for a dismissal to be excluded from the duty to consult, the required relationship between the individual and the reason for dismissal had to be a close and direct one with a reason personal to the individual, such as the employee's conduct or capability, being identified rather than the employee's job or the employer's need to have work done. It found that the test cases had fallen within the class of cases in respect of which there was a duty to consult. The Employment Appeal Tribunal upheld an appeal by the university. It found that in all four cases at least one of the reasons for dismissal had related to the fact that the employee had agreed to accept that the contract under which they were employed would have come to an end at a particular time or on the occurrence of a particular event. It concluded that that was a reason for the dismissals that had indeed related to the individuals concerned and that, having regard to the terms of s 195 of the 1992 Act, the dismissals were excluded from the ambit of s 188. The union appealed. *Held*, the employees whose fixed-term contracts had expired by the effluxion of time had not been dismissed as redundant under s 195; the dismissals had been excluded from the ambit of s 188. Section 195(1) must be understood by reference to the ordinary English meaning of the words used in the statute. There is nothing unclear or ambiguous about the expression 'a reason not related to the individual concerned'. The resolution of the issue of whether employees have been dismissed as redundant within the meaning of s 195 requires the determination of, first, a question of pure fact (what was the reason or reasons for the dismissal?) and, second, a question of mixed fact and law (having regard to the proper construction of s 195(1), was the reason for the dismissal or, if more than one, a reason for the dismissal, not related to the individual concerned?). The difficult question is the mixed question of fact and law. Non-renewal of a FTC may constitute dismissal as redundant, but then again, it may not. In the present case, the tribunal had never properly considered, as it should have done, what the reasons were for dismissal in the particular cases before it and whether the conditions set by s 195(1) of the 1992 Act had been met. Properly considered, the employer's reason for dismissal in each of the test cases (that the employee had agreed that the contract would come to an end) had related to the individuals. It had been specific to each of them. It had to do with their particular circumstances and their particular decisions, for example to undertake certain limited teaching duties or to provide cover during the maternity or sick leave of another employee. It had to do with the individual

employee's own approach to their employment with the university. The 'reason for dismissal' was the fact that the employee had entered into a FTC and that reason was related to the individual employees. Accordingly, the appeal would be dismissed.

University of Stirling v University and College Union [2014] CSIH 5, [2014] IRLR 287 (Inner House). Decision of Employment Appeal Tribunal [2012] IRLR 266 (2012 Abr para 1096) affirmed.

1054 Redundancy—redundancy payments—continuity of employment—local government service

The Redundancy Payments (Continuity of Employment in Local Government, etc) (Modification) (Amendment) Order 2013, SI 2013/1784 (in force on 19 August 2013), further amends the 1999 Order, SI 1999/2277, so as to add police authorities established under the Police Act 1996 s 3 and the Metropolitan Police Authority established under the 1996 Act s 5B to the list of local government employers with whom employment may constitute relevant service for the purposes of redundancy.

1055 Restraint of trade—restrictive covenant—enforceability—reasonableness

See *Cavendish Square Holdings BV v Makdessi*, para 785.

1056 Settlement agreements—code of practice

The Employment Code of Practice (Settlement Agreements) Order 2013, SI 2013/1665 (made on 4 July 2013), appoints 29 July 2013 as the day on which the Code of Practice on Settlement Agreements comes into effect. The Code of Practice provides guidance on the implications of the Employment Rights Act 1996 s 111A, which provides for evidence of negotiations about ending the employment relationship on agreed terms to be inadmissible as evidence in any subsequent unfair dismissal claim.

1057 Surrogacy leave—entitlement to leave equivalent to maternity or adoption leave

See Case C-363/12 *Z v A Government Department*, para 872.

1058 Trade union—listing of trade unions—entry in the list

A union applied to the certification officer for Trade Unions and Employers Associations under the Trade Union and Labour Relations (Consolidation) Act 1992 s 3 to have its name entered in the list of trade unions. The appellant was described as the union's general secretary. He was also a director of a company, which was set up to represent workers for a fee at meetings with employers. The union was to share premises and office equipment with the company. The appellant wrote to the certification officer that the union was unable to effectively and adequately negotiate on behalf of workers who had suggested that the company could negotiate better working conditions for them and that in some cases the union was unable to attend any internal disciplinary hearings because it was not a trade union. The union had no members at the time of the application, but the certification considered the application on the basis that the union did exist as an organisation and did have members. The certification officer found that the appellant was the prime mover behind both the company and the union, both of which were to provide representation for workers. It noted that if the appellant were to have been asked to represent a worker in a disciplinary hearing, then it was not clear whether that worker would have been channelled to the company or the proposed union given the close connection between the two. It found that the principal purpose for the proposed creation of the union had been to take advantage of accreditation to further the commercial interests of the company or its directors, and did not include the regulation of relations between workers and employers as required by the definition of a trade union in s 1. The appellant appealed. *Held*, the certification officer had not erred in refusing to certify the union as a trade union. The question of whether an organisation fitted the description in s 1(a) was a question of fact. The principal purposes referred to were not the purposes as declared or set out in a rule book or statement of aims and objectives or similar document unless they were factually the principal purposes of that organisation. In any case in which the certification officer decided the purposes did not include the regulation of relations between workers and employers, he could not certify the organisation as a trade union. The regulation of relations was between groups, workers on the one hand and employers or employers' associations on the other. Therefore, an organisation which did not include such a purpose but which existed to provide representation at hearings internal to the employer would not, purely by reason of that alone, be a trade union. There would be nothing of the collective about it. Section 3(3) was framed in the present tense. The 'organisation is a trade union', were words which looked not to what would be at some future date. They did not anticipate what it was contended would be the situation next week or next month. In the present case, there were facts from which the certification officer could conclude that the union was not within the definition in s 1. One of the central difficulties in the purported union's case was that much of the case related to undertakings, assurances and assertions as to how matters might have operated in the future but the question of whether an organisation was a trade union could not have been answered by answering a different question as to whether it would or it might have been reasonable to think it would have become a trade union. Accordingly, the appeal would be dismissed.

Akinosun v The Certification Officer [2013] IRLR 937 (EAT: Langstaff J presiding).

1059 Transfer of undertaking—contract of employment—collective agreement—agreement made after transfer

The claimants were local government employees who were transferred to a private sector company under the Transfer of Undertakings (Protection of Employment) Regulations 1981, SI 1981/1794. That company was taken over by another private sector employer, the defendant, and the claimants' contracts of employment transferred over to it under the 1981 Regulations. The contracts provided that the claimants' terms and conditions would be set according to collective agreements negotiated from time to time through a national council, which included representatives of local authority employers and trade unions. After the first transfer, the claimants were awarded pay increases. The defendant increased pay in line with a council pay settlement without acknowledging liability to do so. As a private sector employer, it could not belong to the council or be represented by it. A dispute arose as to whether the defendant was bound to increase pay in line with council settlements. Proceedings were brought by the claimants, who claimed that the contractual term providing that their pay would be set in accordance with council settlements was protected by the 1981 Regulations, with the result that the defendant was obliged to raise pay in line with the settlements. Regulation 6 provided that, where there was a collective agreement at the time of transfer made by or on behalf of the transferor with a trade union in respect of an employee whose contract of employment was preserved by reg 5(1) the agreement, after the transfer, had the effect as if made by or on behalf of the transferee with that trade union, and therefore anything done under it after the transfer, was to be deemed to have been done by or in on relation to the transferee. The national court decided to stay the proceedings and refer to the European Court of Justice the question of to what extent a transferee was bound by a collective agreement made after the expiry of an agreement that was in force at the date of the transfer. *Held*, a dynamic clause referring to collective agreements negotiated and agreed after the date of transfer of the undertaking concerned that were intended to regulate changes in working conditions in the public sector was liable to limit considerably the room for manoeuvre necessary for a private transferee to make such adjustments and changes. In such a situation, the clause was liable to undermine the fair balance between the interests of the transferee in its capacity as employer and those of the employees. It followed that a member state was precluded from providing, in the event of a transfer of an undertaking, that dynamic clauses referring to collective agreements negotiated and adopted after the date of transfer were enforceable against the transferee, where that transferee did not have the possibility of participating in the negotiation process of such collective agreements concluded after the date of the transfer.

Case C-426/11 *Alemo-Herron v Parkwood Leisure Ltd* [2013] IRLR 744 (ECJ: Third Chamber). For earlier related proceedings see *Parkwood Leisure Ltd v Alemo-Herron* [2011] UKSC 26, [2011] 4 All ER 800 (2011 Abr para 1062).

1981 Regulations replaced by Transfer of Undertakings (Protection of Employment) Regulations 2006, SI 2006/246.

1060   Transfer of undertaking—protection of employment—transfer of public health
        staff

The Transfer of Undertakings (Protection of Employment) (Transfers of Public Health Staff)
Regulations 2013, SI 2013/278 (in force on 1 April 2013), provide for the treatment of
persons employed by various public bodies in public health activity, who are to transfer to
the Department of Health, so that such employees will be treated in a similar way to those
employees to whom the Transfer of Undertakings (Protection of Employment)
Regulations 2006, SI 2006/246, apply, and, in particular, (1) provide for the effect on
contracts of employment; (2) make provision in relation to pensions; and (3) ensure a
transfer is treated as a relevant transfer.

1061   Transfer of undertaking—relevant transfer—unfair dismissal—economic, technical
        or organisational reasons

The first respondent company, which owned a professional football club, went into
administration. The administrator sought to sell the club as a going concern as it had few or
no assets that could be realised for the benefit of its creditors. Agreement was reached for
sale of the company to the second respondent consortium. The decision was taken to make
the majority of the administrative staff redundant and to proceed with the sale of the more
valuable players. The four appellants were administrative employees of the employer who
were identified as staff who could be made redundant. They were given letters of dismissal
by the administrator. The sale of the club was agreed. The appellants brought proceedings
for unfair dismissal. They submitted that the effect of the Transfer of Undertakings
(Protection of Employment) Regulations 2006, SI 2006/246, regs 4 and 7 was that their
dismissals had been for a reason connected with the sale of the club and had been
automatically unfair because they were for a reason that was not an economic, technical or
organisational reason entailing changes in the workforce, and, by reason of that, the liability
of the employer in respect of their unfair dismissal had transferred. An employment tribunal
found that the appellants had not transferred under the 2006 Regulations. It determined
that the reason for the dismissals had not been the transfer itself, but a reason connected
with the transfer. The tribunal accepted the administrator's evidence that the reason for the
dismissals had been that he had run out of money, and unless staff costs were reduced the
company would go into liquidation. On the appellants' appeal, the Employment Appeal
Tribunal decided that the dismissals had not been for an economic, technical or
organisational reason because they had not been for the purpose of continuing the business
but had been with a view to sale or acquisition. On that basis, the liability for the various
claims had passed to the second respondent. The respondents appealed. *Held*, the Appeal
Tribunal was mistaken in its finding that the employment tribunal had fallen into legal error.
The employment tribunal had been justified in distinguishing between the administrator's
reason for having implemented the dismissals and his ultimate objective, namely the early
sale of the club which had to be achieved in time for the commencement of the following
season. The administrator had needed to reduce the wage bill in order to continue running
the business and to avoid liquidation. The employment tribunal's conclusion on that had not
been surprising. While the non-playing staff were being reduced so as to enable the club to
carry on, the players had been retained, as had sufficient other staff to enable the club to
remain in business rather than sink into liquidation. The dismissals had unquestionably
entailed changes to the workforce. It followed that it had been permissible for the
employment tribunal to have concluded that there had been an economic, technical or
organisational reason, specifically an economic reason, for the dismissals. Accordingly, the
appeal would be allowed.
    Kavanagh v Crystal Palace FC Ltd [2013] EWCA Civ 1410, [2014] 1 All ER 1033 (Court
of Appeal: Maurice Kay VP, Beatson and Briggs LJJ).

1062   Unfair dismissal—capability—ill health—long-term sick leave

Scotland

BS had been employed by Dundee City Council for 35 years. In September 2008, he visited
his general practitioner and was signed off work, initially with nervous debility and
thereafter with depression and anxiety. He had a series of meetings with occupational
health, which produced a series of reports saying that he was unfit and would be absent for
eight more weeks, but that it might be less than that. He was repeatedly signed off work by

his GP. In August 2009, the council met with BS. It set him a date to return to work of 14 September 2009 and said that if he did not return to work on that date then consideration would be given to his dismissal. He was told that there would be a review appointment with occupational health prior to his return. On 11 September 2009, BS attended an assessment with a consultant occupational health physician, Dr Spencer, who stated that his health was improving, that he expected that he would be able to return to work within the next one to three months and that he would be happy for him to return to work when his GP issues a final certificate. BS did not return to work on 14 September 2009, as he was still sick. He attended a further appointment with his GP and was signed off for a further four weeks. The council arranged a meeting to take place on 23 September 2009 and informed him that further consideration was to be given to terminating his employment. At the meeting, BS stated he was not any better since the last meeting. The council dismissed BS on the basis that he was unlikely to return in either the short term or the foreseeable future. He brought proceedings against the council for unfair dismissal. An employment tribunal held that the council had shown that the reason for dismissal was ill health which affected BS's capability for performing his work and that capability was a potentially fair reason for dismissal under s 98(2) of the Employment Rights Act 1996. Accordingly, it moved on to the critical question of reasonableness under s 98(4). It held that no reasonable employer would have dismissed BS only nine days after receiving the indication from Dr Spencer that he expected BS to return in one to three months. It found that, in the absence of medical evidence to support its belief that BS was unlikely to return in the short term or the foreseeable future and in circumstances where the only medical evidence suggested a return within one to three months, the council had not had reasonable grounds for its belief. It held that, in circumstances where there was an inconsistency between BS's understanding of his condition and the medical advice, no reasonable employer would have disregarded the medical advice and gone ahead and dismissed an employee with 35 years' service without first clarifying the true medical position. Occupational health could have contacted BS's GP about, for example, when a final certificate might have been issued. The Employment Appeal Tribunal allowed the council's appeal, remitting the case to a freshly constituted employment tribunal to determine whether the council could reasonably have been expected to wait longer before dismissing BS. BS appealed. *Held*, three important themes emerged from the authorities. Firstly, in a case where an employee had been absent from work for some time owing to sickness, the critical question was whether in all the circumstances any reasonable employer would have waited longer before dismissing the employee. Secondly, there was a need to consult the employee and take their views into account. This was a factor that could operate either for or against dismissal. Thirdly, there was a need to take steps to discover the employee's medical condition and their likely prognosis, but this merely required the obtaining of proper medical advice; it did not require the employer to pursue detailed medical examination; all that the employer was required to do was to ensure that the correct question was asked and answered. While length of service would often be relevant in misconduct cases, in cases involving dismissal on the ground of ill-health its relevance was not quite so clear cut. In an appropriate case, however, it might show that the employee in question was a good and willing worker with a good attendance record, someone who would do their utmost to get back to work as soon as they could. The critical question in every case was whether the length of the employee's service, and the manner in which they worked during that period, yielded inferences that indicated that they were likely to return to work as soon as they could. In the present case, firstly, the tribunal had failed to directly address the question of whether in all the circumstances any reasonable employer would have waited longer before dismissing BS. It had made reference to relevant factors such as the availability of temporary staff, that BS was no longer being paid a salary, and that the council was a large organisation. Against those considerations and the administrative and occupational health costs, however, it had been necessary to set the unsatisfactory situation of having an employee on very lengthy sick leave. In such a case it clearly had to have been open to the employer to have brought the employment to an end. Secondly, it had not given adequate weight to BS's own views about his ability to return to work. His own evidence did not suggest that he was in a position to return to work in the immediate future – that was a factor that should have been weighed against Dr Spencer's report. As to the third issue, the obtaining of adequate medical advice, the tribunal had attached great importance to the views expressed by Dr Spencer and indicated that no reasonable employer, given those views, would have dismissed the appellant without further investigation of his medical state. However, on the facts, Dr Spencer's report was to the effect that BS's health was improving and he expected that BS would be able to return to work within one to three months. BS's subjective view, however, was that he was not improving. Against that background, it was difficult to see how further medical advice could have clarified matters. The council had had a medical opinion, and they had to balance that against BS's own view. For that reason, the tribunal had attached too much importance to the need to obtain a further medical opinion; that question was rather whether a reasonable employer, in view of Dr Spencer's report, the continuing note from the GP, and BS's own views, would have waited longer, or whether the decision to dismiss was within the range of reasonable responses open to such an employer. That issue was not squarely faced by the tribunal. With regard to length of service, the tribunal had not addressed the proper question, but had merely treated length of service as a factor that in itself was automatically relevant. The case would be remitted to the original tribunal reconsider those four issues. Accordingly, the appeal would be allowed.

   BS v Dundee City Council [2013] CSIH 91, [2014] IRLR 131 (Inner House).

1063   Unfair dismissal—compensation—award—limit

The Unfair Dismissal (Variation of the Limit of Compensatory Award) Order 2013, SI 2013/1949 (in force on 29 July 2013), amends the Employment Rights Act 1996 so as to limit the compensatory award in an unfair dismissal claim to whichever is the lower of £74,200 or the weekly pay, multiplied by 52, of the employee concerned. Transitional provision is also made.

1064   Unfair dismissal—compensation—post-dismissal conduct

An employee who worked as a teacher was dismissed by his employer, a local authority, on the ground of misconduct. He brought a successful unfair dismissal claim against the employer. The compensation award included a substantial sum in respect of pension loss. Following the remedy hearing, the employee was convicted of assaulting a former pupil. The employer applied for a review of the tribunal's decision on remedy, submitting that the employee would have been dismissed following his conviction for assault. The tribunal revoked the element of the award in respect of pension loss. However, at a further hearing, the tribunal reinstated the original remedy judgment in respect of pension loss, holding that, in the light of the decision in *Soros v Davison*, it was not appropriate to take post-termination conduct into account. On the employer's appeal, it contended that the tribunal had erred by refusing to look at the witness statement of a certain witness and to allow the employer to make submissions by reference to it. *Held*, on the facts, the employee's conviction for assault and sentence of a term of imprisonment might have substantially reduced his pension loss and a tribunal determining the proper compensatory award in the case would plainly have been entitled to take into account that evidence. The employer had been entitled to refer to the witness statement in question and the tribunal had unfairly refused to look at it. It followed that the employer was unfairly prevented from making any effective submissions in relation to the witness statement. There had been no justification for the tribunal adopting such an approach. The tribunal also made no reference to the employee's evidence when assessing the employer's contention that the employee's employment would have ended before he reached the age of 65. The tribunal had incorrectly suggested that there had been no evidence to support the employers' submissions in that regard. Accordingly, the appeal would be allowed.

   Bates v Cumbria CC [2013] All ER (D) 165 (Aug) (Employment Appeal Tribunal: Supperstone J presiding). *Soros v Davison* [1994] IRLR 264, EAT (1994 Abr para 1256), distinguished.

1065   Unfair dismissal—constructive dismissal—change in terms of employment— removal of obligation to provide work

Scotland

The employees were welders in the railway and construction industry. Their employer suffered a serious downturn in business and rescinded their terms and conditions of employment. The employer notified the employees that their guaranteed minimum weekly salary would be abolished and that they would be employed on the basis that it would engage them whenever they were required, but had no obligation to engage them at all. The new terms included a provision that, if the claimants were given no work for two months, the employer would give them their P45s. The employees resigned and claimed constructive dismissal. The employment tribunal found that they were unfairly dismissed. The employer's appeal succeeded on the basis that the dismissals were fair because the employer had good business reasons for its decision and had not appreciated the change of status it would cause. On appeal by the employees, *held*, (1) the employment tribunal failed to consider properly whether the employer's ignorance of the law was excusable and, if it was, whether that was a decisive consideration or one outweighed by other factors. (2) The Appeal Tribunal did not take a correct approach to its assessment of the employment tribunal's reasoning. In relation to the fairness of the dismissals, the Appeal Tribunal appeared to have considered that if the tribunal's reasoning on the point was flawed, the only possible outcome was to substitute a finding that the dismissals were fair. That was plainly wrong. The tribunal's task was to reach a view on the issue of fairness by considering the whole facts and circumstances having regard to equity and the substantial merits of the case. The employer's lack of awareness of the legal consequences of its action was only one element in that process. The tribunal also drew attention to the substantive fairness of the employer's changes. Its central concern was the destructive effect that the change imposed on the employees' statutory rights. The Appeal Tribunal did not consider that aspect of the case. A further aspect of the case that might have been a relevant consideration was that, even if the employer was right in thinking that the employees would have retained their status as employees, they would still have faced the possibility of having to keep themselves available for work for up to two months without receiving either work or pay, and then being dismissed. The Appeal Tribunal should have remitted the matter to the tribunal for further consideration. Accordingly, the appeal would be allowed.

Docherty v SW Global Resourcing Ltd [2013] CSIH 72, [2013] IRLR 874 (Inner House). Decision of Employment Appeal Tribunal [2012] IRLR 727 (2012 Abr para 1113) reversed.

1066   Unfair dismissal—disciplinary proceedings—dismissal of employees consequent to second disciplinary proceedings—reasonableness of dismissal

A number of employees who were social workers employed by the employer local authority had been found to be at fault in the way in which they had dealt with the case of a child who had died as a result of a chronic lack of care and abuse displayed by his mother and two men. The child had been subject to a child protection plan and on the child protection register. The first employee had been a team leader responsible for a number of social workers, including the second employee. The latter had had specific responsibility for the child. The employees had been disciplined under the employer's simplified disciplinary procedure and given a written warning. Following the conviction of the perpetrators of the abuse, the Secretary of State for Education issued a direction that required the employer to appoint a person to the statutory position of Director of Children's Services who was to consider staffing issues that had arisen from the case. That investigation included an examination of the role played by social service staff, including the employees, notwithstanding that they had already been disciplined. Consequently, fresh disciplinary proceedings were instituted against the employees. Both employees were summarily dismissed for gross misconduct. Their appeals were dismissed and they appealed further. *Held*, in the employment context the disciplinary power was conferred on the employer by reason of the hierarchical nature of the relationship. The purpose of the procedures was not to allow a body independent of the parties to determine a dispute between them. Typically it was to enable the employer to inform himself whether the employee had acted in breach of contract or in some other inappropriate way and if so, to determine how that should affect future relations between them. The employer had a duty to act fairly and procedures were designed to achieve that objective. If a process was judicial and gave rise to a binding adjudication, it involved determining rights in the same way as a court did. The critical question was not the formality of the procedures, but rather whether they operated independently of the parties such that it was appropriate to describe their function as an adjudication between the parties. The fact that the simplified procedure was so far removed from any kind of adjudicative process reinforced the conclusion that the doctrine of res judicata was inapplicable. Even if the doctrine of abuse of process were applicable, it did not provide an automatic bar to a second disciplinary process provided that it would not be abusive or oppressive to take that step. Moreover, the burden was on the party asserting organisation of working time, relating to the administration of annual leave in their application to workers employed in agriculture. In particular, the regulations (1) have the effect that the provisions for a worker employed in agriculture in England in relation to the date on which the worker's leave year begins and notice of leave year no longer apply; and (2) provide a saving in relation to the employment of a worker employed in agriculture in England before 1 October 2013 the effect of which is that those same provisions continue to apply on and after that date in relation to that employment.

1075   Working time—paid annual leave—additional leave—sickness—leave not taken—entitlement to carry forward

The Working Time Regulations 1998, SI 1998/1833, reg 13(1) provides that a worker is entitled to four weeks' annual leave in each leave year. A worker is entitled in each leave year to a period of additional leave of 1·6 weeks: reg 13A(1), (2). A relevant agreement may provide for any such additional leave to be carried forward into the leave year immediately following the leave year in respect of which it is due: reg 13A(7).

An employee suffered a stroke and was unable to return to work. He had taken 11 days holiday out of his entitlement for the year and none for the following year, when he resigned. Although the employee had not requested holiday pay or to carry over holiday during the year in which he suffered his stroke, in the following year he wrote to his employer seeking any holiday pay that was due to him in respect of both years. The employer did not make any payment and the employee brought proceedings in an employment tribunal against the employer for holiday pay accruing in both years pursuant to the 1998 Regulations regs 13, 13A. The tribunal found that his entitlement to statutory holidays was 28 days in each year and that payment should have been made for holidays accrued in both years. The employer appealed. *Held*, the tribunal had erred in finding that the claimant had been entitled to have been paid in respect of additional leave in relation to the time he was off sick in the first leave year, as there had been no relevant agreement between him and the employer entitling him to carry that leave into the subsequent year. The entitlement to four weeks' annual leave under reg 13 implemented the minimum period of entitlement to leave specified by European Parliament and Council Directive (EC) 2003/88 art 7. It was established that a compatible reading of the 1998 Regulations reg 13 required that provision to be construed to allow a worker who had been unable to take his entitlement to leave under reg 13 due to illness to carry it over to the next leave year. However, there was no reason to apply such a construction to a national provision allowing annual leave in addition to that required by Directive 2003/88, such as the 1998 Regulations reg 13A. By virtue of reg 13A(7), the entitlement to carry forward additional annual leave only applied when a relevant agreement so provided. The tribunal had not found that there was any relevant agreement, and so the employee had not been entitled to carry forward his entitlement to additional leave. Accordingly, the appeal would be allowed.

Sood Enterprises Ltd v Healy [2013] IRLR 865 (Employment Appeal Tribunal: Lady Stacey presiding). Case C-337/10 *Neidel v Stadt Frankfurt Am Main* [2012] IRLR 607, ECJ (2012 Abr para 1135), considered. *Leeds NHS Primary Care Trust v Larner* [2012] EWCA Civ 1034, [2012] 4 All ER 1006 (2012 Abr para 1136) distinguished.

ENERGY AND CLIMATE CHANGE

Halsbury's Laws of England (5th edn) vol 42 (2011) paras 1–296, vol 43 (2011) paras 297–760, vol 44 (2011) paras 761–1224.

Articles

For articles relating to this title please refer to the Table of Articles at the beginning of the Abridgment.

1076   Climate change agreements—administration

The Climate Change Agreements (Administration) (Miscellaneous Amendments) Regulations 2013, SI 2013/508 (in force on 31 March 2013), amend the 2012 Regulations, SI 2012/1976, so as to (1) provide that the base year for a greenfield facility is the 12-month period starting on the date of an underlying climate change agreement, with the measurement of emissions in terms of tonnes of carbon dioxide equivalent; (2) provide that the buy-out fee in a climate change agreement is to be calculated by reference to emissions of tonnes of carbon dioxide equivalent; and (3) revise the calculation of financial penalties in respect of target units which include greenfield sites if the penalty notice is served within the 12-month period starting on the date of an underlying climate change agreement.

1077　Climate change agreements—eligible facilities

The Climate Change Agreements (Eligible Facilities) (Miscellaneous Amendments) Regulations 2013, SI 2013/505 (in force on 31 March 2013), amend the 2012 Regulations, SI 2012/2999, so as to provide that (1) until 31 May 2014, if, at the time it falls to be determined whether a facility is eligible to be covered by a climate change agreement, the operator of the facility has insufficient data available on the supply or use of reckonable energy by the installation for the previous 12-month period in order to determine the intended supply or use of reckonable energy by the installation, the intended supply or use of reckonable energy by the installation must instead be estimated by the administrator; and (2) until the later of 31 May 2014 or the day which is one year following the date of an underlying agreement, if it falls to be determined whether a greenfield facility is eligible to be covered by a climate change agreement, the administrator must estimate the intended supply or use of reckonable energy by the installation.

1078　Climate change levy—exemption—combined heat and power stations

The Climate Change Levy (Combined Heat and Power Stations) (Amendment) Regulations 2013, SI 2013/232 (in force on 1 April 2013), amend the 2005 Regulations, SI 2005/1714, so as to provide, for the purposes of calculating the quantitative limit up to which electricity produced in a partly exempt combined heat and power station may be supplied exempt from climate change levy, for supplies to a utility or for a domestic or non-business use of a charity to be disregarded, but to require the electrical equivalent of any mechanical output of the station produced otherwise than for the purpose of generating electricity to be included.

1079　Climate change levy—general provisions

The Climate Change Levy (General) (Amendment) Regulations 2013, SI 2013/713 (in force on 1 April 2013), further amend the 2001 Regulations, SI 2001/838, so as to (1) entitle a registrable person who has overpaid the carbon price support rate of climate change levy on a deemed supply to reclaim the overpayment; (2) provide that a quantity of a commodity is not to be the subject of a deemed supply under the Finance Act 2000 Sch 6 para 24A if it is the subject of a taxable supply; (3) set out the calculation for determining the extent to which a quantity of fossil fuels (other than oil) delivered to a combined heat and power station is referable to the production of electricity in the station for the purposes of the 2006 Act Sch 6 paras 24A, 24B, provide for a compulsory review of the calculation and provide for tax credits and further deemed supplies in cases where the quantity determined in accordance with the calculation is subsequently found to be too high or too low; (4) provide that, for the purposes of the deemed self-supply of electricity produced from taxable commodities, electricity must not be treated as produced from taxable commodities if those commodities (other than electricity) are not the subject of a deemed taxable supply; (5) impose a civil penalty for failure to carry out a compulsory review under head (3); and (6) revise the climate change levy relief formula in consequence of a change to the rate of reduced rate supplies of electricity (but not for reduced rate supplies of other taxable commodities).

The Climate Change Levy (General) (Amendment No 2) Regulations 2013, SI 2013/1716 (in force on 1 August 2013), further amend the 2001 Regulations above so that fuels used in a combined heat and power station to produce mechanical outputs of the station are not treated as being referable to the production of electricity and are therefore not subject to the carbon price support rate of climate change levy.

1080　Electricity—applications for consent

The Electricity (Applications for Consent) Amendment (England and Wales) Regulations 2013, SI 2013/495 (in force on 6 April 2013), further amend the information; (5) enable the Authority to conduct investigations; (6) empower the Authority to summon and hear, require the production of reports by skilled persons and enter premises under a warrant; (7) enable the court to deal with failures to comply with certain requirements of the Authority as if the defaulter were in contempt; (8) create offences of hindering an investigation and knowingly or recklessly providing false or misleading information in the course of an investigation; (9) allow an injunction to be made where the court is satisfied that a person is failing to comply with a specified requirement of the Regulation; (10) make provision for restitution where a person has accrued profits or caused loss or other adverse effect by failing to comply with a specified requirement of the Regulation; (11) empower the Authority to impose either a financial penalty of such amount as it considers appropriate or a statement of censure if a person has failed to comply with a specified requirement, and require the Authority to produce and publish a statement of policy with respect to penalties, to which it must have regard when exercising that power; (12) enable the court to impose a penalty where the Authority has applied for an injunction or restitution order; (13) make provision in relation to warning notices and decision notices, which must be given by the Authority when exercising its power to require restitution or to impose a penalty or statement of censure, and in relation to the Authority's procedures in respect of such notices; (14) make provision for the publication of notices and details concerning them; (15) confer rights on third parties who may be prejudiced by warning notices or decision notices given by the Authority; (16) set out the Authority's obligation to allow the recipient of a warning notice or decision notice to have access to certain Authority material; (17) make provision in relation to references to the Upper Tribunal made in respect of certain decisions; (18) make provision as to offences by bodies corporate, proceedings for offences and jurisdiction and procedure in respect of offences; (19) contain miscellaneous provisions relating to disclosure and the protection of information; and (20) require the Secretary of State to review the regulations and to publish a report containing the conclusions of the review.

1087   Electricity—overhead lines—development consent

The Planning Act 2008 (Nationally Significant Infrastructure Projects) (Electric Lines) Order 2013, SI 2013/1479 (in force on 18 June 2013), amends the Planning Act 2008 by specifying two new categories of electric line installation which are no longer considered to be nationally significant infrastructure projects and which are therefore subject to the development consent process prescribed by the Electricity Act 1989 s 37.

1088   Electricity—property schemes—transitional period—extension

The Electricity (Extension of Transitional Period for Property Schemes) Order 2013, SI 2013/968 (in force on 19 May 2013), extends, by a period of 12 years to 19 May 2025, the transitional period specified in the Electricity Act 1989 Sch 2A para 5(2).

1089   Electricity—registers

The Gas and Electricity (Registers) (Revocation) Order 2013, SI 2013/1420 (in force on 12 July 2013), revokes the Gas (Register) Order 1988, SI 1988/159, which prescribed the hours during which the register maintained under the Gas Act 1986 s 36 was to be kept open for public inspection and the fees payable for the supply of copies or extracts from the register, and the Electricity (Register) Order 1990, SI 1990/194, which made similar provision in relation to the register maintained under the Electricity Act 1989 s 49.

1090   Electricity—renewable obligation

The Renewables Obligation (Amendment) Order 2013, SI 2013/768 (in force on 1 April 2013), further amends the 2009 Order, SI 2009/785, which imposes an obligation on all electricity suppliers to produce, by a specified day, a certain number of renewables obligation certificates in respect of each megawatt hour of electricity that each supplies during a specified period known as an obligation period. The 2013 Order, in particular, (1) adds new definitions for different types of generating capacity, 'advanced fuel', 'combustion unit' and 'qualifying power output' and revises the definitions of 'energy crops' and 'total installed capacity'; and revises the definition of 'regular biomass' to exclude all 'advanced fuels'; (2) expands the definition of biomass to include all fossil derived bioliquids; (3) removes a limit on the certificates issued for co-firing that suppliers may submit in each obligation period; it also adds a limit on the certificates issued for electricity generated using bioliquids that suppliers may submit in each obligation period; (4) adds corrosion control and fouling reduction to the uses of fossil fuel or waste that are permitted ancillary purposes; (5) prevents certificates from being issued in respect of electricity generated from landfill gas unless the electricity meets certain conditions; (6) removes the minimum gross calorific value requirements applying to liquid fuels produced by means of pyrolysis; and sets rules for how renewable output is to be apportioned between generating capacity accredited or installed during different obligation periods and where electricity is generated in different ways; (7) excludes all advanced fuels from the scope of the 2009 Order; (8) changes the provisions for determining the amount of electricity that must be generated by a generating station in order to be eligible for a certificate depending on the way in which it has been generated ('bands'); (9) adds some new bands, to remove some existing bands and to amend the definitions of some existing bands; (10) sets out the levels of support for the bands applying to generating capacity accredited, and additional capacity added, before 1 April 2013; (11) sets out the levels of support for the bands applying to generating capacity accredited, and additional capacity added on or after 1 April 2013; (12) replaces the provisions for determining the amount of electricity which is eligible for a higher level of support by virtue of being generated by a qualifying combined heat and power generating station, and for determining what that higher level of support should be; (13) sets (a) the level of support for electricity generated from high-range co-firing in the 2013–14 obligation period; (b) the level of support for electricity generated from co-firing of regular bioliquid and from low-range co-firing in the 2013–14 and 2014–15 obligation periods; and (c) the level of support for low-range co-firing of energy crops supplied under contracts made before 7 September 2012; (14) sets the level of support for microgenerators; (15) sets out the circumstances in which certain offshore wind generating stations will be entitled to 1.5 certificates per megawatt hour; (16) sets out the circumstances in which electricity generated by certain wave and tidal stream generating stations will be entitled to five certificates per megawatt hour; (17) enables the Gas and Electricity Markets Authority to treat a notification by the operator of a generating station as sufficient evidence that the energy content of the biomass burned in a combustion unit makes up less than 50 per cent of the energy content of all of the energy sources burned in that unit; (18) implements, in relation to the renewables obligation, Commission Decision (EU) 2011/13 on certain types of information about biofuels and bioliquids to be submitted by economic operators to member states; and (19) enables generating stations to submit a request to the Authority to be registered as grace period generating stations, and so obtain the levels of support available to generating stations accredited on 31 March 2013; requests may be submitted only in respect of stations first commissioned on or after 1 April 2013 and in respect of which an application for accreditation is made on or before 30 September 2013; the request must be accompanied by various documents, including a declaration that the station would have been commissioned on or before 31 March 2013 if the grid connection or certain radar works had been completed by the date specified in the agreement for the grid connection or the radar works.

1091　Electricity—supply from photovoltaic installation—value added tax

See Case C-219/12 *Finanzamt Freistadt Rohrbach Urfahr v Unabhangiger Finanzsenat Außenstelle Linz*, para 2513.

1092　Electricity—wayleave—felling and lopping of trees—applications—charges

The Electricity (Necessary Wayleaves and Felling and Lopping of Trees) (Charges) (England and Wales) Regulations 2013, SI 2013/1986 (in force on 1 October 2013), (1) specify the charge payable for an application for a necessary wayleave or a reference for an order for the felling or lopping of trees or shrubs; (2) specify the charge payable for the time incurred by an inspector appointed by the Secretary of State to consider the application under the Electricity (Necessary Wayleaves and Felling and Lopping of Trees) (Hearing Procedures) Rules 2013, SI 2013/1987 (see PARA 1093); and (3) specify the charge payable for the inspector's travel and subsistence incurred in attending a pre-hearing meeting, oral hearing or site inspection under the 2013 Rules. The charges differ in relation to England and to Wales; a charge of £1,000 per day applies to applications relating to England, and a charge of £742 per day applies to applications relating to Wales, or to England and Wales.

1093   Electricity—wayleave—felling and lopping of trees—applications—hearing procedures

The Electricity (Necessary Wayleaves and Felling and Lopping of Trees) (Hearing Procedures) (England and Wales) Rules 2013, SI 2013/1987 (in force on 1 October 2013), replace the Electricity (Compulsory Wayleaves) (Hearings Procedure) Rules 1967, SI 1967/450, and set out the written representations procedure and oral hearing procedure to be followed in respect of applications, made pursuant to the Electricity Act 1989 Sch 4, for necessary wayleaves and for orders for the felling or lopping of trees or shrubs. In particular, the rules (1) specify the criteria which determine whether the written representations procedure or the oral hearing procedure applies; (2) in relation to the written representations procedure, make provision as to statements of evidence, the submission of further representations and the appointment of an inspector, who may request further information from any party, to consider relevant evidence; (3) in relation to the oral hearing procedure, provide for (a) the appointment of an inspector to conduct the hearing; (b) notification of the hearing date; (c) the holding of pre-hearing meetings where appropriate; (d) exchange of statements of evidence in advance of the hearing; and (e) the procedure for the hearing; (4) empower inspectors to carry out site inspections in certain circumstances; (5) require inspectors to report to the Secretary of State in writing following the conclusion of any written representations procedure or oral hearing; (6) empower the Secretary of State, after receipt of such a report, to require the written representations procedure or oral hearing procedure to be invoked or re-opened; (7) make provision in relation to decisions of the Secretary of State, including decisions made after further representations from the parties have been invited and taken into account; and (8) make provision in relation to extensions of time and the service of notices and documents.

1094   Energy Act 2011—commencement

The Energy Act 2011 (Commencement No 2) Order 2013, SI 2013/125, brings into force on 28 January 2013 ss 23–28 and, so far as they are not already in force, ss 1, 2, 4, 5, 7–9, 11(2), 12, 13, 14(1)–(5), (9) and 29. For a summary of the Act, see 2011 Abr para 1103. See also the commencement table in the title STATUTES AND LEGISLATIVE PROCESS.

1095   Energy Act 2013

The Energy Act 2013 makes provision for the setting of a decarbonisation target range and duties in relation to it, for reforming the electricity market for purposes of encouraging low carbon electricity generation or ensuring security of supply, for the establishment and functions of the Office for Nuclear Regulation and about the government pipe-line and storage system and rights exercisable in relation to it. The Act also makes provision about the designation of a strategy and policy statement, about domestic supplies of gas and electricity, for extending categories of activities for which energy licences are required, for the making of orders requiring regulated persons to provide redress to consumers of gas or electricity, about offshore transmission of electricity during a commissioning period, for imposing fees in connection with certain costs incurred by the Secretary of State and about smoke and carbon monoxide alarms. The Act received the royal assent on 18 December 2013 and came into force in part on that day and on 18 February 2014. The remaining provisions come into force on a day or days to be appointed. For details of commencement, see the commencement table in the title STATUTES AND LEGISLATIVE PROCESS.

Part 1 (ss 1–4) Decarbonisation
Section 1 imposes a duty on the Secretary of State to ensure that, once a decarbonisation target range has been set, the carbon intensity of the electricity generation sector in the United Kingdom does not exceed the maximum level permitted by that decarbonisation target range. The Secretary of State must take into account specified matters when setting or amending a decarbonisation target range: s 2. Section 3 requires the Secretary of State to lay a report before Parliament, as soon as reasonably practicable after making a decarbonisation order, setting out proposals and policies for meeting a decarbonisation target range that has been set. Section 4 defines 'carbon intensity of electricity generation in the United Kingdom'.

Part 2 (ss 5–66) Electricity Market Reforms

Chapter 1 (s 5) General considerations
Section 5 requires the Secretary of State to take account of the government's obligations under the Climate Change Act 2008 to meet the 2050 target and to stay within carbon budgets, the duty to meet any decarbonisation target range once this has been set, the need to ensure security of electricity supplies, the likely cost to consumers in the parts of the United Kingdom affected by the decision he is taking and the United Kingdom's obligation to meet European Union targets on the use of energy from renewable sources.

Chapter 2 (ss 6–26) Contracts for Difference
The Secretary of State's power to make regulations about contracts for difference ('CFD') is provided for by s 6. Section 7, Sch 1 empower the Secretary of State to designate a company or a public authority, with its consent, to act as the counterparty for the CFD. A person so designated has a duty to comply with the regulations and any direction made under these provisions: s 8. Section 9 requires the Secretary of State, when making regulations under s 6, to include provision requiring electricity suppliers in Great Britain and Northern Ireland to make payments to the CFD counterparty so that the body has sufficient funds to make the totality of the payments to generators that are required under CFD contracts. The Secretary of State has powers to issue a direction to the CFD counterparty to offer a CFD to eligible generators in accordance with provisions set out in regulations (s10) and to issue and, from time to time, revise, standard terms for the CFD (s 11). Section 12 sets out how the national system operator is to notify the CFD counterparty of an allocation decision, and s 13 specifies the process by which the Secretary of State may make provision setting out detailed rules about the CFD allocation process. Section 14 sets out how the CFD counterparty must act on a notification from the system operator to offer a CFD contract, and s 15 enables the CFD counterparty to agree modifications to the standard terms with generators. The Secretary of State has power under s 16, when making provision under ss 12–15, to make further provision enabling calculations and determinations to be made by such persons and in accordance with such procedure as is specified. Regulations may require the CFD counterparty to make payments to suppliers (s 17), may make provision about the allocation of sums between generators by the CFD counterparty in circumstances where the supplier obligation is not large enough to meet all of its obligations in full (s 18), may make provision to ensure that information and advice required to make the scheme work is provided to the bodies requiring it at appropriate points (s 19), and may confer functions on the Authority to provide advice to and make determinations for the parties to CFDs (s 20). Regulations under s 21 may make provision requiring the CFD counterparty to enter into arrangements or to offer contracts for purposes connected to a CFD, or to specify things that the CFD counterparty may, must, or may not, do. Section 22 provides for the enforcement by the Authority in Great Britain of the obligations of suppliers under regulations made under Pt 2 Ch 2 as if they were relevant requirements. Section 23 enables the Secretary of State to make regulations setting out a limit on the cost of the scheme, and also includes powers for the Secretary of State to instruct the national system operator that the maximum cost has been reached and prevent it from giving a notification to the CFD counterparty if the Secretary of State believes it may cause the maximum cost to be breached. The Secretary of State must consult licensed suppliers in Great Britain and Northern Ireland, the national system operator, the Authority, the Department of Enterprise, and Trade and Investment in Northern Ireland before making or amending secondary legislation: s 24. In exercising their regulatory controls over the CFD counterparty, neither the Secretary of State nor the national system operator is to be regarded as managing or controlling the CFD counterparty in such a way that would class them as a shadow director or principal to the CFDs: s 25. Section 26 sets out the Secretary of State's powers to modify transmission and distribution licences, the standard conditions of such licences and documents maintained in accordance with conditions of such licences, and to allow the CFD counterparty to be provided with services.

Chapter 3 (ss 27–43) Capacity Market
Section 27 enables the Secretary of State to make electricity capacity regulations about the provision of capacity to meet the demands of consumers for the supply of electricity in Great Britain. Such regulations may make provision about capacity agreements: s 28. The Secretary of State may make provision in electricity capacity regulations for the determination on a competitive basis, through capacity auctions run by the national system

operator, of who may be a capacity provider: s 29. In the event that a settlement body is appointed to administer capacity payments and capacity incentives, s 30 enables regulations to require electricity suppliers or capacity providers to make payments to the settlement body for certain ancillary purposes. The Secretary of State may make provision in electricity capacity regulations to confer functions on the Authority or the national system operator (s 31) and may make provision to impose other requirements, in addition to those particularly associated with capacity agreements, on licence holders, persons carrying out functions under the capacity market and any other person who is, or has ceased to be, a capacity provider (s 32). By virtue of s 33, the Secretary of State may make provision in electricity capacity regulations for the provision and publication of information. The Secretary of State may make capacity market rules, which may contain any provision that may be made by electricity capacity regulations except for specified matters: s 34. Section 35 applies when electricity capacity regulations made under the power in s 27 relate to the provision of capacity which is created by reducing demand for electricity, and enables the Secretary of State to confer functions on a person or body for the purposes of, for example, administering an electricity demand reduction regime. The Secretary of State may make provision in electricity capacity regulations and capacity market rules about enforcement and the resolution of disputes, including conferring functions on any public body or any other person: s 36. The Secretary of State may make licence modifications under s 37 for the purposes of the capacity market. Section 38 makes provision for the amendment by regulations of certain enactments. Section 39 provides that the Electricity Act 1989 ss 3A–3D, which set out the principal objective and general duties of the Secretary of State and the Authority in relation to electricity supply, apply to the functions of the Authority under or by virtue of the 2013 Act Pt 2 Ch 3. Section 40 sets out how the Secretary of State may use the powers to make regulations and the process that must be followed, and s 41 sets out the procedures to be followed in making capacity market rules. Section 42 makes further provision for capacity market rules to make the additional changes required to enable them to function. Section 43 enables the Secretary of State to spend money on an electricity demand reduction pilot programme, and adds a statutory reporting requirement for any pilot schemes.

Chapter 4 (s 44) Investment contracts
Section 44 introduces Sch 2 which makes further provision about investment contracts.

Chapter 5 (ss 45–48) Conflict of interest and contingency arrangements
The Secretary of State may modify the conditions of existing electricity licences and codes for the purposes of imposing business separation measures between system operation functions, or one or more individual system operation functions, and other functions: s 45. Under s 46, the Secretary of State has power to transfer the delivery functions for the CFD and capacity market schemes and those relating to investment contracts ('EMR functions') to a new delivery body in certain situations. Section 47, Sch 3 allow the transfer of a functions order to provide the alternative delivery body with the power to require fees to be paid in relation to any EMR functions it carries out. The special administration regime for the national system operator is extended by s 48 to include its EMR functions.

Chapter 6 (ss 49–54) Access to markets etc
Section 49 enables the Secretary of State to modify electricity generation and supply licences and to amend electricity industry codes to facilitate participation and promote liquidity in the wholesale electricity market. The Secretary of State may modify the conditions of electricity supply licences and related industry codes for the purpose of facilitating investment in electricity generation by means of a power purchase agreement ('PPA') scheme: s 50. Section 51 enables the Secretary of State to make regulations in connection with any modifications made under s 50 for or in connection with a PPA scheme. General restrictions on disclosure of information are extended by s 52 to ss 50, 51, and s 53 requires the Secretary of State and the Authority to apply the principal objective to comply with certain general duties when exercising functions so far as they relate to a PPA scheme. Section 54 sets out additional provisions that apply to both ss 49 and 50 and clarifies how these licence modification powers may be exercised.

Chapter 7 (ss 55, 56) The renewables obligation: transitional arrangements
The Secretary of State has power under s 55 to make a renewables obligation closure order, and s 56 enables him to make an order requiring the Authority, the Secretary of State or a CFD counterparty to purchase GB certificates which have been issued to generators in respect of renewable electricity.

Chapter 8 (ss 57–62) Emissions performance standard
Section 57, Sch 4 place a limit on the amount of carbon dioxide that a fossil fuel plant may emit within a year. A fossil-fuel plant that is equipped with carbon capture and storage ('CCS') will be exempt from the emissions limit duty for a period of three years starting from the date when a complete CCS system is ready for use: s 58. Section 59 confers power on the Secretary of State to suspend or modify the emissions limit duty on fossil fuel plant located in Great Britain, and sets out the circumstances in which the power to suspend or modify the emissions limit duty arises. Section 60, Sch 5 impose a duty on the appropriate national authority to make arrangements for monitoring compliance with, and enforcement of, the emissions limit duty. Section 61 provides for the interpretation of terms in ss 57–62, and s 62 provides for the making of regulations under ss 57–62.

Chapter 9 (ss 63–66) Miscellaneous
Section 63 empowers the Secretary of State to make provision in CFD regulations, capacity market regulations or regulations relating to investment contracts to limit the national system operator's liability to pay damages if a civil claim was brought against it in respect of its role, or a particular element of its role, as the delivery body for the CFD and capacity market schemes and in relation to investment contracts. Further detail about the licence and industry code modification powers relating to CFD, the capacity market, conflicts of interest, access to markets, and investment contracts are provided for by s 64. Section 65 makes minor amendments to other legislation to ensure the coherence of electricity law, and s 66 requires the Secretary of State to carry out a review of much of Pt 2, as soon as is reasonably practicable five years after royal assent, and report the conclusions to Parliament.

Part 3 (ss 67–118) Nuclear Regulation

Chapter 1 (ss 67–73) The ONR's purposes
Section 67 sets out each of the ONR's purposes, s 68 defines the ONR's nuclear safety purposes, s 69 defines the ONR's non-nuclear or 'conventional' health and safety purposes, and s 70 sets out the ONR's nuclear security purposes. Section 71 relates to one of the areas of the ONR's nuclear security purposes, namely ensuring the security of sensitive nuclear information in the United Kingdom. Section 72 sets out the ONR's purposes relating to nuclear safeguards. Section 73 defines 'radioactive material' by reference to various international transport agreements that cover the transport of goods by road, rail and inland waterway, and being consistent with those agreements ensures that all preparatory processes to transport, such as loading, packaging and delivery, are part of the ONR's remit.

Chapter 2 (ss 74–76) Nuclear Regulations
Section 74, Sch 6 empower the Secretary of State to make nuclear regulations generally subject to the negative resolution procedure for the purposes of nuclear safety, nuclear security, nuclear safeguards and transport purposes. Section 75 elaborates on the power to create offences within nuclear regulations, and s 76 provides that breaches of duties imposed by nuclear regulations and relevant statutory provisions will not give rise to a claim for breach of statutory duty, irrespective of whether such breach also constitutes an offence.

Chapter 3 (s 77) Office for Nuclear Regulation
Section 77, Sch 7 establish the Office for Nuclear Regulation ('ONR') as a body corporate, and provide for its constitution and for the appointment and remuneration of its staff and members.

Chapter 4 (ss 78–101) Functions for the ONR
Section 78 imposes a general duty on the ONR to do whatever it considers appropriate for its purposes. The ONR may issue, revise or withdraw codes of practice, which give practical guidance about the requirements of the relevant statutory provisions: s 79. Provision is made by s 80 for a code of practice issued or revised by the ONR to be subject to a parliamentary process akin to the negative resolution procedure. Section 81 enables the ONR to submit proposals to the Secretary of State or the Health and Safety Executive for a

number of different types of secondary legislation. A duty is imposed on the ONR by s 82 to make adequate arrangements to enforce relevant statutory provisions, for example to employ sufficient inspectors and to ensure they are adequately resourced or, where the ONR makes arrangements for another person to carry out the ONR's functions on its behalf, that the person makes suitable arrangements and suitable financial provision. Section 83, Sch 8 enable the ONR to appoint inspectors to inspect, investigate breaches of, and otherwise carry into effect, the relevant statutory provisions. The ONR may, or may authorise another person to, investigate and produce a special report on certain defined matters: s 84. Section 85 confers power on the ONR the power to arrange for an inquiry to be held, where it considers it necessary or desirable for any of its purposes. The ONR may make payments to anyone who holds an inquiry under s 85 or an assessor who assists in such an inquiry: s 86. Section 87 imposes a duty on the ONR to make such arrangements as it considers appropriate for the dissemination of information, for example to industry and the public, that is relevant to its purposes. The ONR may undertake research, or arrange for someone else to carry out research, in relation to any matter connected with its purposes: s 88. Under s 89, the ONR has a duty to provide certain information or advice if it is requested to do so by a relevant authority, and s 90 permits the ONR, by agreement, to perform functions of ministers of the Crown, government departments and other public authorities, regardless of whether those functions fall within the ONR's purposes. Section 91 allows the ONR to provide services or facilities to any person for the ONR's purposes, and s 92 enables the Secretary of State to make directions to the ONR. Section 93 requires the ONR to do such things as it considers are best calculated to ensure compliance by the United Kingdom or to enable or facilitate compliance by a minister of the Crown, with the safeguards obligations. The ONR is required to seek consent from the Secretary of State before it issues certain communications relating to both the ONR's nuclear security policy and the government's national security policy: s 94. By virtue of s 95, the ONR may delegate any of its functions to any person, subject to obtaining the Secretary of State's consent. The ONR and the Health and Safety Executive are required by s 96 to enter into arrangements, and to maintain, review and revise them from time to time, in order to ensure mutual co-operation and the exchange of information about their functions. The ONR may by notice require a person to provide it with any information needed by it for the purposes of carrying out its functions, and a refusal or failure to comply with such a notice is a criminal offence: s 97. Section 98 enables the Commissioners for Her Majesty's Revenue and Customs to provide the ONR or an inspector appointed by it with information about imports regardless of whether information has been requested. An officer of Revenue and Customs may seize any imported article or substance and detain it for the purpose of facilitating the ONR or an inspector to carry out any function under the relevant statutory provisions: s 99. Section 100, Sch 9 prohibit the disclosure of protected information otherwise than in accordance with specific gateways. Section 101 enables the Secretary of State to make provision for fees to be payable in connection with the performance of the ONR's functions under the relevant statutory provisions and under certain regulations made under the Anti-terrorism, Crime and Security Act 2001.

Chapter 5 (ss 102–118) Supplementary
Sections 102–108, Schs 10–12 provide for supplementary matters, including staff and property transfers, provision relating to criminal offences under Pt 3 and minor and consequential amendments to existing legislation.

Part 4 (ss 119—130) Government pipe-line and storage system
Section 119 defines 'the government pipe-line and storage system' which the Secretary of State may maintain and use, or any part of it, for any purpose for which it is suitable (s 120). For the purpose of exercising a right conferred by s 120, the Secretary of State may enter any land on or under which the government pipe-line and storage system is situated or any land held with that land. A warrant may be issued under s 122 to authorise entry on to land in the exercise of a right conferred by s 121, if necessary using reasonable force. The rights conferred by provisions of ss 120, 121, 125 are not subject to any enactment requiring the registration or recording of interests in, charges over or other obligations affecting land but they bind any person who is at any time the owner or occupier of the land: s 123. The Secretary of State must pay compensation to a person who proves that the value of a relevant interest in land to which that person is entitled is depreciated by the creation of rights by ss 120, 121, 125: s 124. The Secretary of State may sell, lease or

transfer the government pipe-line and storage system or any part of it and transfer any right or liability relating to the system or any part of it, subject to any appropriate conditions: s 125. Section 126 modifies the application of certain provisions of the Pipe-lines Act 1962 to the government pipe-line and storage system. Nothing in the 2013 Act Pt 4 affects any other rights of the Secretary of State in relation to the government pipe-line and storage system: s 127. Section 128 repeals certain legislation, and s 129, Sch 13 enable the Secretary of State to dissolve the Oil and Pipelines Agency. Section 130 provides for the application of Pt 4 to the Crown.

Part 5 (ss 131–138) Strategy and policy statement
The Secretary of State has power under s 131 to designate a strategy and policy statement, the strategic priorities in which the Authority has a duty under s 132, with exceptions specified in s 133, to have regard. Section 134 imposes a duty on the Secretary of State to review the statement every five years, and s 135 sets out the procedural requirements for preparing and designating a statement. Section 136 provides that the principal objective and general duties in relation to gas supply found in the Gas Act 1986 ss 4AA–4B apply to the Secretary of State when determining the policy outcomes under the 2013 Act Pt 5. Section 137 amends the Utilities Act 2000 in relation to the Authority's reporting requirements. The 2013 Act s 138 repeals provisions under which the existing social and environmental guidance is issued.

Part 6 (ss 139–151) Consumer protection and miscellaneous

Chapter 1 (ss 139–145) Consumer protection
The Secretary of State has powers under s 139 to amend the licence conditions for suppliers of gas and electricity, with regard to the tariffs they offer domestic customers and the information they must provide. Section 140 requires the Secretary of State to undertake a consultation ahead of making any licence modifications under s 139 and ensures that any such modifications are carried forward into subsequent licences granted by the Authority. The principal objective and the general duties of the Secretary of State under existing legislation also apply to the functions given to the Secretary of State under s 139 or 140: s 141. Consequential amendments are made by s 142 to existing legislation to provide for consistency with ss 139 and 140. Section 143 extends the scope of energy-related activities that may be made subject to the licence regime governed by the Authority. Section 144, Sch 14 enable the Authority to impose requirements on a regulated person to pay compensation to consumers of gas or electricity if the person has contravened certain conditions or requirements thereby causing loss, damage or inconvenience. Section 145 imposes a duty on the Secretary of State to set a new objective for addressing fuel poverty in England.

Chapter 2 (ss 146–151) Miscellaneous
Under s 146, the Secretary of State may increase, from 5 megawatts to 10 megawatts, the specified maximum capacity of installations eligible for the Feed-in Tariffs scheme. An exception is created by s 147 to the prohibition on participating in the transmission of electricity without a licence for a person who participates in offshore transmission activity during a commissioning period in certain circumstances. Section 148 confers power on the Secretary of State to charge fees for services provided in the exercise of energy resilience powers in Great Britain, and s 149 makes provision for fees in respect of decommissioning and clean-up of nuclear sites. Under s 150, the Secretary of State may make regulations which introduce a requirement for landlords of residential properties to install smoke and/or carbon monoxide alarms in properties they rent out and to make checks to ensure that any such alarms remain in proper working order. The Secretary of State is required by s 151 to carry out a review of the consumer redress and decommissioning fees provisions in Pt 6, as soon as reasonably practicable five years after such provisions come into force and to report his conclusions to Parliament.

Part 7 (ss 152–157) Final
Section 152 deals with interpretation of the Act, s 153 makes provision in respect of transfer schemes, s 154 deals with financial provisions, and ss 155–157 deal with the extent, commencement, and the short title, of the Act.

mechanism, which was the previous mechanism restricting access to the scheme if the forecast for total expenditure reached a certain point; and (6) add expenditure provisions for the purposes of new calculations.

The Renewable Heat Incentive Scheme (Amendment) (No 2) Regulations 2013, SI 2013/2410 (in force on 24 September 2013), further amend the 2011 Regulations above by (1) extending the renewable heat incentive scheme to cleaning and drying carried on otherwise than in a building; (2) imposing a requirement for combined heat and power plants and plants generating heat from solid biomass to have an applicable renewable heat incentive emission certificate; (3) making provision for renewable heat incentive emission certificates; (4) introducing new metering requirements for new accreditations; (5) allowing accredited renewable heat incentive installations to be moved to a new location; (6) revising the ongoing obligations in relation to emissions from biomass; (7) providing for the calculation of periodic support payments for plants to which the new metering requirements apply; (8) making new provision relating to the disregarding of heat loss, or the calculation of heat loss in certain circumstances; and (9) altering provision made in relation to enforcement.

The Renewable Heat Incentive Scheme (Amendment) (No 3) Regulations 2013, SI 2013/3179 (in force on 13 December 2013), further amend the 2011 Regulations so as to (1) set out the circumstances in which certain values in the formula used for the purposes of calculating the initial tariff payable in respect of accredited renewable heat incentive installations for which a renewable heat incentive certificate is one of the eligibility criteria will be zero; (2) set lower thresholds in relation to the tests concerning growth in forecast expenditure that are used to determine whether and by how much a tariff will be reduced in a particular tariff period; and (3) require testing of emissions of oxides of nitrogen and of particulate matter to be carried out in accordance with specified standards or requirements.

1115   Renewable transport fuel obligations

The Renewable Transport Fuel Obligations (Amendment) Order 2013, SI 2013/816 (in force in part on 9 April 2013 and in part on 15 April 2013), further amends the 2007 Order, SI 2007/3072, so as to transpose, in part, European Parliament and Council Directive (EC) 98/70 on the quality of petrol and diesel fuels. The 2013 Order, in particular, (1) sets out the meaning of 'not operating at sea'; (2) adds definitions of 'gas oil' and 'low sulphur gas oil' and revises the definition of 'relevant hydrocarbon oil'; (3) ensures that the total volume of fuel supplied to the United Kingdom that must come from a renewable source is not increased by fuel for the additional end uses being brought with the scope of the 2007 Order; (4) imposes an obligation on fuel suppliers to ensure that a certain percentage of the fuel they supply is made up of renewable transport fuel; (5) brings fuel for the additional end uses within the meaning of 'eligible oil'; (6) introduces a presumption that certain types of fuel which pass the duty point on or after 15 April 2013 will be taken to constitute relevant hydrocarbon oil; (7) provides that fuel for the additional end uses counts towards discharging a supplier's renewable transport fuel certificate obligation but this does not apply for calculations that occur on or after 15 April 2013 in relation to fuel that passed the duty point before that date; (8) provides that fuel for the additional end uses counts as fuel for which renewable transport fuel certificates must be issued; and (9) provides for an unpaid civil penalty, along with interest on the penalty, to be enforceable as a civil debt.

ENVIRONMENTAL QUALITY AND PUBLIC HEALTH

Halsbury's Laws of England (5th edn) vol 45 (2010) paras 1–575; vol 46 (2010) paras 576–1081

Articles

For articles relating to this title please refer to the Table of Articles at the beginning of the Abridgment.

1116   Antarctic Act 2013

The Antarctic Act 2013 makes provision consequential on the Protocol on Environmental Protection to the Antarctic Treaty Annex VI and amends the Antarctic Act 1994. The

2013 Act received the royal assent on 26 March 2013 and came into force in part on that day and on 26 May 2013. The remaining provisions come into force on a day to be appointed. For details of commencement, see the commencement table in the title STATUTES AND LEGISLATIVE PROCESS.

Part 1 (ss 1–13) Environmental emergencies
Section 1 requires those who organise activities carried out in Antarctica, where those activities are connected with the United Kingdom, to take reasonable, prompt and effective response action in relation to any environmental emergency arising directly or indirectly from those activities. By virtue of s 2, a party who takes response action under the Protocol Annex VI, in respect of an environmental emergency, is able, in the event that the person causing the emergency fails to take reasonable, prompt and effective response action, to recover its costs from the person in question. Under the 2013 Act s 3, where the organiser of the activities which gave rise, directly or indirectly, to an environmental emergency in Antarctica fails to take reasonable, prompt and effective response action, and no response action is taken by any party to the Protocol Annex VI, the amount that reasonable, prompt and effective response action would have cost becomes a liability which the organiser of the activities is liable to pay to the Antarctic Environmental Liability Fund. The 2013 Act s 4 introduces the Schedule, which sets out the limits to the amounts recoverable under ss 2 and 3. By virtue of s 5, an organiser of activities in Antarctica is required, where those activities are connected to the United Kingdom, to take reasonable preventative measures designed to reduce the risk of environmental emergencies arising from those activities and their potential adverse impact. Organisers of activities in Antarctica are required by s 6 to secure adequate insurance cover or other financial security for the costs of taking any response action required by s 1 and any liability which may be incurred under s 2 or 3. Under s 7, the organisers of activities in Antarctica, which are connected to the United Kingdom, are required to inform the Secretary of State promptly of any environmental emergency of which they become aware as a result of the carrying out of those activities, it being immaterial whether the activities gave rise to the emergency. By virtue of s 8, the Secretary of State may, by notice, require specific and detailed information from those organising activities connected with the United Kingdom in Antarctica in the event that those activities appear to the Secretary of State to have, directly or indirectly, caused an environmental emergency or an incident which has the potential to cause an adverse impact on the environment of Antarctica. A person organising activities as an employee of another person, in the course of service in the regular forces or in the course of service or undertaking training or duties in the reserve forces, is excluded by s 9 from criminal and civil liability under Pt 1. Section 10 provides that Pt 1 binds the Crown, except as otherwise expressly provided. Section 11 makes provision relating to offences. By virtue of s 12, the exercise of any delegated powers by way of an order under Pt 1 is required to be subject to annulment in pursuance of a resolution of either House of Parliament. Section 13 deals with interpretation.

Part 2 (ss 14–18) Miscellaneous and final
Section 14 extends the scope of the offences that prohibit United Kingdom nationals from harming Antarctic fauna and flora, introducing non-native species into Antarctica and entering restricted areas without a permit to cover non-United Kingdom nationals on a British expedition and enables the Secretary of State to grant a permit for an activity otherwise prohibited to a non-United Kingdom national on a British expedition for the purposes of education or scientific research. Under s 15, the Secretary of State may grant a new form of permit in respect of conservation or repair work of designated historic sites and monuments. Section 16 makes provision in relation to the conservation of animals and plants in Antarctica. Section 17 deals with Northern Ireland and s 18 with extent, commencement and the short title.

Amendments, repeals and revocations
The list below, which is not exhaustive, mentions amendments which are or will be effective when the Act is fully in force.

Specific provisions of a number of Acts are amended. These include: Antarctic Act 1994 ss 7–12.

1117   Detergents

The Detergents (Amendment) Regulations 2013, SI 2013/1244 (in force on 30 June 2013), amend the 2010 Regulations, SI 2010/740, in implementation of European Parliament and Council Regulation (EC) 259/2012, in respect of the use of phosphates and other phosphorus compounds in consumer laundry detergents and consumer automatic dishwasher detergents, so that (1) it is an offence to place on the market a consumer laundry detergent which contains phosphorus in excess of a prescribed weight, rather than a prescribed proportion; and (2) the Secretary of State is required to review the 2010 Regulations and to publish a report containing the conclusions of the review and specify the appropriate enforcement agency in relation to the new offence.

1118   Energy efficiency—energy savings—eligible buildings

The Energy Efficiency (Eligible Buildings) Regulations 2013, SI 2013/3220 (in force in part on 15 January 2014 and in part on 5 June 2014), transpose European Parliament and Council Directive (EU) 2012/27 on energy efficiency and, in particular, (1) set an energy savings target to be achieved in eligible buildings owned and occupied by central government; (2) require the Secretary of State to report to the European Commission, on an annual basis, the amount of energy savings achieved in each year of the reporting period; (3) impose a duty on the Secretary of State and the Welsh Ministers to encourage public bodies to adopt energy efficiency plans; and (4) require the Secretary of State to review the operation and effect of the regulations and to publish a report containing the conclusions of the review.

1119   Energy efficiency—schemes—home energy—Wales
See para 1388.

1120   Enterprise and Regulatory Reform Act 2013
See para 414.

1121   Environmental assessment—scope of EU legislation—Command Paper—proposed high speed rail network
See *HS2 Action Alliance Ltd v Secretary of State for Transport*, para 2121.

1122   Environmental information—access to information—European Commission—exceptions to disclosure
See Case T-111/11 *Client Earth v European Commission*, para 423.

1123   Environmental information—costs—proceedings not prohibitively expensive—test
See *R (on the application of Edwards) v Environment Agency (No 2)*, para 280.

1124   Environmental information—freedom of information—exempt information
See *R (on the application of Evans) v A-G*, para 470.

1125   Environmental protection—air pollution—reduction in emissions—failure to comply

European Parliament and Council Directive (EC) 2008/50 (on ambient air quality and clearer air for Europe) art 13 requires member states to ensure that levels of nitrogen dioxide in ambient air do not exceed the prescribed limit. Where conformity with the limit values for nitrogen dioxide cannot be achieved by the deadline, a member state may postpone the deadline by a maximum of five years on condition that an air quality plan is established in accordance with art 23: art 22.

The appellant submitted that pursuant to Directive 2008/50 art 22(4) the government was obliged to put to the European Commission a plan for reducing nitrogen dioxide to levels below the limit values. Further, the appellant sought a declaration that the United Kingdom was in breach of an obligation to comply with nitrogen dioxide limit values provided for in art 13. The government contended that its obligation was to reduce nitrogen dioxide to comply with the limit values, something which it accepted that it had not done.

Consideration was given to TFEU art 258. Although the appellant's submissions centred on Directive 2008/50 art 22(4), the court considered the issue mainly in relation to art 22(1). The judge declined to grant any relief and the appellant's appeal was unsuccessful. On the appellant's further appeal, *held*, the fact that the breach had been conceded was not a sufficient reason for declining to grant a declaration, where there were no other discretionary bars to the grant of relief. Such an order was appropriate both as a formal statement of the legal position, and also to make clear that, regardless of arguments about the effect of arts 22, 23, the way was open to immediate enforcement action at national or European level. The other issues raised difficult issues of law, the determination of which required the guidance of the European Court of Justice, and on which accordingly, as the final national court, a reference was obligatory. The following questions appeared appropriate to refer to the European Court of Justice: (1) where in a given zone or agglomeration conformity with the limit values for nitrogen dioxide could not be achieved by the deadline specified in Annex XI, was a member state obliged pursuant to Directive 2008/50 to seek postponement of the deadline in accordance with art 22; (2) if so, in what circumstances, if any, might a member state be relieved of that obligation; (3) if the answer to (1) was no, to what extent, if at all, were the obligations of a member state which had failed to comply with art 13, and had not made an application under art 22, affected by art 23; (4) in the event of non-compliance with art 13, and in the absence of an application under art 22, what, if any, remedies should a national court provide as a matter of European law in order to comply with art 30 and/or TFEU art 4 or 19. As to the present proceedings, the relevant breach of art 13 had been clearly established. Accordingly, the declaration would be granted.

R (*on the application of ClientEarth*) *v Secretary of State for the Environment, Food and Rural Affairs* [2013] UKSC 25, [2013] All ER (D) 15 (May) (Supreme Court: Lord Hope DP, Lord Mance, Lord Clarke, Lord Sumption and Lord Carnwath SCJJ). Decision of Court of Appeal [2012] EWCA Civ 897, [2012] All ER (D) 150 (Aug) reversed.

1126 Environmental protection—chemicals—EU legislation—enforcement

See para 504.

1127 Environmental protection—gaseous and particulate pollutants—agricultural and forestry tractors

The Agricultural or Forestry Tractors (Emission of Gaseous and Particulate Pollutants) and Tractor etc (EC Type-Approval) (Amendment) Regulations 2013, SI 2013/3171 (in force on 28 January 2014), further amend (1) the 2002 Regulations, SI 2002/1891, so as to (a) give effect to changes to the flexibility scheme brought about by European Parliament and Council Directive (EU) 2011/72 in relation to tractor engines and tractors and the application of emission stages to narrow-track tractors brought about by European Parliament and Council Directive (EU) 2011/87; (b) require the Secretary of State to review the operation and effect of the 2002 Regulations and publish a report within five years after the 2013 Regulations come into force and within every five years after that; (c) substitute a new table showing the appropriate stage for each category of engine; and (d) give effect to the changes brought about by Directive 2011/72 with regard to the operation of flexibility schemes in the United Kingdom, in particular as a consequence of the substitution by that directive of a revised Council Directive (EC) 2000/25 Annex IV; and (2) the Tractor etc (EC Type-Approval) Regulations 2005, SI 2005/390, so as to update definitions of 'separate directive' and 'the Tractor Type Approval Directive'.

1128 Environmental protection—gaseous and particulate pollutants—non-road mobile machinery

The Non-Road Mobile Machinery (Emission of Gaseous and Particulate Pollutants) (Amendment) Regulations 2013, SI 2013/1687 (in force on 31 July 2013), further amend the 1999 Regulations, SI 1999/1053, so as to implement amendments which have been made to European Parliament and Council Directive (EC) 97/68, on the approximation of the laws of the member states relating to measures against the emission of gaseous and particulate pollutants from internal combustion engines to be installed in non-road mobile machinery. In particular, the regulations (1) update the definition of Directive 97/68; (2) make provision to ensure that replacement spark ignition and compression ignition

1143 Pollution—prevention and control—environmental permits

The Environmental Permitting (England and Wales) (Amendment) Regulations 2013, SI 2013/390 (in force in part on 27 February 2013, in part on 7 January 2014 and in part on 1 January 2016), further amend the 2010 Regulations, SI 2010/675, so as to transpose European Parliament and Council Directive (EU) 2010/75 (on industrial emissions). In particular, the regulations (1) insert a new provision whereby the requirement for an environmental permit will not apply to certain activities until 7 July 2015; (2) make provision for incidents and accidents in accordance with arts 7 and 8; (3) provide for a new defence in relation to the requirement to hold a permit where an application for a permit is made by the specified date; (4) implement changes introduced by Directive 2010/75 Annex 1; (5) delete certain activities which are not included in Directive 2010/75 and change the description of existing activities; (6) provide for the insertion into permits of a deemed provision in relation to incidents and accidents; (6) make provision regarding new waste incineration and co-incineration plants from 27 February 2013 and to existing waste incineration plants and waste co-incineration plants from 7 January 2014; (7) make provision relating to solvent emission activities; (8) insert new provisions relating to new large combustion plants from 27 February 2013 and to existing large combustion plants from 1 January 2016; (9) make provision relating to new installations producing waste titanium dioxide from the 27 February 2013 and to new installations producing waste titanium dioxide from 7 January 2014; and (10) make provision for changes to the classification of certain activities and for those which cease to be covered.

The Environmental Permitting (England and Wales) (Amendment) (No 2) Regulations 2013, SI 2013/766 (in force on 26 April 2013), further amend (1) the 2010 Regulations, SI 2010/675, so as to (a) replace the definition of Council Directive (EC)1999/31 (on the landfill of waste) so as to take account of the amendments made by Council Directive (EU) 2011/97; (b) enable the regulator to exercise its functions so as to permit the storage of liquid waste in accordance with European Parliament and Council Regulation (EC) 1102/2008 (on the banning of exports of metallic mercury and certain mercury compounds and mixtures and the safe storage of metallic mercury); and (c) impose obligations to send copies of environmental permits and safety assessments to the Secretary of State; and (2) the Control of Major Accident Hazards Regulations 1999, SI 1999/743, to bring sites used for the storage of metallic mercury pursuant to Regulation 1102/2008 art 3(1)(b) within the scope of application of the regulations.

1144 Pollution—prevention and control—merchant shipping—limits—revocation

The Merchant Shipping (Prevention of Pollution) (Limits) (Revocation) Regulations 2013, SI 2013/3042 (in force on 31 March 2014), revoke the 1996 Regulations, SI 1996/2128, as amended, which defined the limits of the zone beyond the territorial sea around the United Kingdom and the Isle of Man in which jurisdiction was exercisable in order to prevent pollution by discharges from ships. They are superseded by the declaration of an exclusive economic zone under the Marine and Coastal Access Act 2009 s 41 by the Exclusive Economic Zone Order 2013, SI 2013/1361 (see para 1103).

1145 Pollution—prevention and control—offshore combustion installations

The Offshore Combustion Installations (Pollution Prevention and Control) Regulations 2013, SI 2013/971 (in force on 19 May 2013), replace the 2001 Regulations, SI 2001/1091, in implementation of European Parliament and Council Directive (EU) 2010/75 on industrial emissions. The 2013 Regulations, in particular, (1) make provision for their periodic review by the Secretary of State; (2) require a permit to operate an offshore combustion installation; (3) set out the procedure to be followed by an operator of an offshore combustion installation wishing to make an application to the Secretary of State for a permit; (4) require the Secretary of State to make publicly available applications for permits; (5) require certain applications for a permit, or for a variation of a permit, to be notified to other member states, Iceland and Norway; (6) set out the matters which the Secretary of State must take into account before granting or refusing an application for a permit; (7) make provision in relation to the communication and publication of a decision to grant or refuse a permit; (8) provide that conditions may be included in a permit, including the imposition of emission limit values which are less strict than those set out in Directive 2010/75; (9) prohibit the imposition of conditions in respect of greenhouse gas emissions, except where required to ensure that no significant local pollution is caused; (10) enable an operator to apply to vary the conditions in a permit and prescribe the matters which the Secretary of State must take into account before deciding whether to approve or refuse such an application; (11) require the Secretary of State to review the conditions in a permit and prescribe the matters which must be taken into account on a review; (12) make provision for the procedures by which variations to permits are brought into effect; (13) make provision in relation to the revocation, surrender and assignment of permits; (14) require the Secretary of State to consult with another member state where the operation of a combustion installation in that state is likely to have significant negative effects on the areas of the sea in which offshore combustion installations require a permit; (15) require the Secretary of State to maintain a public register; (16) allow the Secretary of State to charge fees for certain matters in accordance with a charging scheme; (17) empower the Secretary of State to require persons to provide information to enable the performance of his functions and to monitor compliance with Directive 2010/75; (18) require operators to give notice of certain matters to the Secretary of State; (19) provide for the appointment of inspectors to assist the Secretary of State in the performance of his functions, grant powers to those inspectors and clarify when information obtained by inspectors may be admissible evidence in proceedings; (20) require the Secretary of State to have environmental inspection plans and programmes, prescribe the frequency of inspections and require publicly available reports to be prepared after an inspection; (21) provide for enforcement and prohibition notices, appeals in relation to relevant decisions, offences, penalties and the form of notices; (22) make transitional provision; and (23) provide that no requirement to make environmental information publicly available extends to information which the Secretary of State would be entitled to refuse to make available under the Environmental Information Regulations 2004, SI 2004/3391.

1146   Pollution—prevention and control—oil pollution—legislation—revocation

The Marine Pollution and Merchant Shipping (Revocation) Regulations 2013, SI 2013/2944 (in force on 31 December 2013), revoke the Oil in Navigable Waters (Transfer Records) Regulations 1957, SI 1957/358, the Oil in Navigable Waters (Records) Regulations 1972, SI 1972/1929, the Merchant Shipping (Safety Convention) (Transitional Provisions) Regulations 1981, SI 1981/584, and the Prevention of Oil Pollution Act 1971 (Application of Section 1) Regulations 1984, SI 1984/1684, all of which are spent or have been superseded.

1147   Pollution—prevention and control—water—nitrate vulnerable zones—England

The Nitrate Pollution Prevention (Amendment) and Water Resources (Control of Pollution) (Silage, Slurry and Agricultural Fuel Oil) (England) (Amendment) Regulations 2013, SI 2013/1001 (in force on and between 17 May 2013 and 16 May 2014), further amend (1) the Nitrate Pollution Prevention Regulations 2008, SI 2008/2349, so as to (a) provide for revised designations of areas of land identified as nitrate vulnerable zones for the purposes of Council Directive (EEC) 91/676, concerning the protection of waters against pollution caused by nitrates from agricultural sources; (b) introduce new exemptions from certain aspects of the rules for greenhouse crops and low intensity grassland farming; (c) create an exception to the limit on the total amount of nitrogen in organic manure which may be spread on any given hectare where certified green compost or certified green/food compost is applied at specified volumes over specified periods; (d) make provision in respect of derogations which may be granted to grassland farmers; (e) make changes concerning the introduction of non-livestock organic manure to the requirements relating to the total nitrogen spread on a holding where certain crops are grown and extend the list of crops subject to these controls; (f) allow the application of nitrogen to grass grown for dehydration or for the production of chlorophyll; (g) prohibit the application of organic manure the nitrogen content of which is not established in accordance with prescribed methods; (h) enable specified types of organic manure to be spread nearer to water where precision spreading equipment is used; (i) extend the closed period for spreading organic manure; (j) clarify provisions relating to the exemption for organic holdings and the period during which the spread of manufactured nitrogen fertiliser is prohibited; (k) reduce, from 50 to 30 cubic metres, the amount of slurry which may be spread following the end of the closed period; and (l) make further provision in relation to temporary field sites; and (2) the

Water Resources (Control of Pollution) (Silage, Slurry and Agricultural Fuel Oil) (England) Regulations 2010, SI 2010/639, so as to require persons proposing to build or improve storage facilities for slurry, silage or fuel oil to notify the Environment Agency 14 days before construction work commences.

The Nitrate Pollution Prevention (Designation and Miscellaneous Amendments) Regulations 2013, SI 2013/2619 (in force on 18 November 2013), further amend the 2008 Regulations above so as to (1) provide for revised designations of areas of land identified as nitrate vulnerable zones for the purposes of Directive 91/676 above; (2) require the Environment Agency to refuse an application for a grassland derogation where the applicant has been found to be in breach of derogation conditions and where there is no further possibility of a successful appeal against conviction, enforcement notice or penalty; (3) make minor changes in relation to the calculation of total nitrogen spread for horticultural crops and the equipment which may be used to spread nitrogen fertiliser; and (4) clarify the requirements for fertiliser plans relating to both phosphate and nitrate fertilisers which must be met by farmers benefiting from a derogation.

1148   Pollution—prevention and control—water—nitrate vulnerable zones—Wales

The Nitrate Pollution Prevention (Wales) Regulations 2013, SI 2013/2506 (in force on 25 October 2013), replace the 2008 Regulations, SI 2008/3143, and continue to implement Council Directive (EEC) 91/676, concerning the protection of waters against pollution by nitrates from agricultural sources. The 2013 Regulations, in particular, (1) designate nitrate vulnerable zones and establish an appeals procedure against designation; (2) impose annual limits on the amount of nitrogen from organic manure that may be applied or spread in a holding in a nitrate vulnerable zone; (3) establish requirements relating to the amount of nitrogen to be spread on a crop, and require an occupier to plan in advance how much nitrogen fertiliser will be spread; (4) require an occupier to provide a risk map of a holding and impose conditions on how, where and when to spread nitrogen fertiliser; (5) establish closed periods during which it is prohibited to spread nitrogen fertiliser; (6) impose requirements as to the storage of nitrogen fertiliser, and require storage capacity for manure produced on a holding during a specified period; (7) specify which records must be kept; (8) require the Welsh Ministers to review the regulations within set time scales; and (9) make provision in relation to enforcement, offences and penalties.

1149   Pollution—prevention and control—water—silage, slurry and agricultural fuel oil—England

See para 1147.

1150   Site waste management plans—England—revocation

See para 1135.

1151   Smoke control areas—authorised fuels—England

The Smoke Control Areas (Authorised Fuels) (England) (No 2) Regulations 2013, SI 2013/2111 (in force on 1 October 2013), replace the Smoke Control Areas (Authorised Fuels) (England) Regulations 2013, SI 2013/447, and add one further fuel to the list of authorised fuels for the purposes of the Clean Air Act 1993 Pt III (ss 18–29) (smoke control areas). SI 2013/447 replaced the 2012 Regulations, SI 2012/2281, and added three further fuels to the list.

1152   Smoke control areas—authorised fuels—Wales

The Smoke Control Areas (Authorised Fuels) (Wales) (Amendment) Regulations 2013, SI 2013/562 (in force on 3 April 2013), further amend the 2008 Regulations, SI 2008/3100, by adding eight new fuels to the list of authorised fuels.

1153   Smoke control areas—exempted fireplaces—England

The Smoke Control Areas (Exempted Fireplaces) (England) Order 2013, SI 2013/462 (in force on 6 April 2013), replaces the 2012 Order, SI 2012/2282, and exempts specified fireplaces from the provisions of the Clean Air Act 1993 s 20 which prohibits, subject to certain conditions, smoke emissions in smoke control areas.

The Smoke Control Areas (Exempted Fireplaces) (England) Order 2013, SI 2013/2112 (in force on 1 October 2013), replaces SI 2013/2112 so as to exempt, subject to certain conditions, further specified fireplaces from the provisions of the Clean Air Act 1993 s 20.

The Smoke Control Areas (Exempted Fireplaces) (England) (No 2) (Amendment) Order 2013, SI 2013/3026 (in force on 25 December 2013), amends SI 2013/2112 so as to exempt an additional fireplace.

1154   Smoke control areas—exempted fireplaces—Wales

The Smoke Control Areas (Exempted Fireplaces) (Wales) Order 2013, SI 2013/561 (in force on 1 April 2013), replaces the 2012 Order, SI 2012/244, and exempts specified fireplaces from the provisions of the Clean Air Act 1993 s 20, which prohibits, subject to certain conditions, smoke emissions in smoke control areas.

1155   Waste—collection—separate collection—EU requirements

The Waste (England and Wales) Regulations 2011, SI 2011/988, reg 13(4) provides that the duties in reg 13 apply where separate collection (1) is necessary to ensure that waste undergoes recovery operations in accordance with European Parliament and Council Directive (EC) 2008/98 arts 4 and 13 and to facilitate or improve recovery; and (2) is technically, environmentally and economically practicable.

The 2011 Regulations transposed the relevant provisions of Directive 2008/98 to the extent that it required the separate collection of paper, metal, plastic and glass from 2015. The claimants, who were all involved in the commercial recycling of waste into new products, issued judicial review proceedings contending that, by importing a restriction based on necessity, the 2011 Regulations reg 13(4)(a) did not properly implement Directive 2008/98. However, they conceded that, if the necessity requirement was incorporated, then it had been properly transposed by the 2011 Regulations reg 13. The defendants, together with various interested parties who were responsible for the collection and disposal of waste in England and Wales or who represented workers in that field, argued that Directive 2008/98 art 10(2) required separate collection of waste only where necessary and practicable, contending that the word 'where' in art 10(2) should be interpreted to mean 'if'. *Held*, the obligations under art 11(1) had been properly transposed into domestic law by the 2011 Regulations reg 13. As a matter of construction, it was overwhelmingly more likely that the word 'where' in Directive 2008/98 art 10(2) was equivalent to 'if'. The interpretation of art 11(1) was unambiguously clear: the obligation to set up separate collection of paper, metal, plastic and glass from 2015 was restricted by both the practicality and necessity requirements that also restricted the obligation in art 10(2) to collect separately for the purposes of recovery. That was also generally concordant with the objectives and aims of Directive 2008/98, and general European law principles. Accordingly, the claim would be dismissed.

R (on the application of UK Recyclate Ltd) v Secretary of State for the Environment, Food and Rural Affairs [2013] EWHC 425 (Admin), [2013] All ER (D) 100 (Mar) (Queen's Bench Division: Hickinbottom J).

1156   Waste—controlled waste—disposal—lack of licence—confiscation order

See *R v Morgan*, para 2278.

1157   Waste—electrical and electronic equipment

The Waste Electrical and Electronic Equipment Regulations 2013, SI 2013/3113 (in force on and between 1 January 2014 and 1 January 2019), replace the 2006 Regulations, SI 2006/3289, as amended, and transpose the main provisions of Council Directive (EU) 2012/19, on waste electrical and electronic equipment. The 2013 Regulations, which apply to different categories of electrical and electronic equipment at different times, subject to exceptions, (1) impose obligations on producers who place electrical and electronic equipment on the market in relation to financing the costs of the collection, treatment, recovery and environmentally sound disposal of waste electrical and electronic equipment; (2) allow for exemptions from those obligations in respect of producers registered with approved producer compliance schemes; (3) impose obligations on the operator of an approved producer compliance scheme in relation to (a) the registration, or notification to should have regard to expert evidence both as to the general principles or legal framework which would govern the case under foreign law and as to how a court in the foreign jurisdiction would apply those principles or framework to the facts of the case. The claimant's application for summary judgment had to fail. The first defendant had a good arguable case that the Canadian judgment would not be treated as res judicata against it under the law of Canada. The first defendant had shown that it had a good arguable defence to the claimant's claim, by reference to the law of Canada. A trial would be necessary for the differences between the views of expert witnesses to be explored in detail before the court could form a concluded view as to whether that defence was established. Applying settled law, there was no privity of interest between the Canadian group sued in the Canadian action and the first defendant in relation to the Canadian judgment. Therefore, no issue estoppel arose by reference to any such privity between the Canadian group and the claimant. The law as regards the position of an assignee of personal property where there was pending litigation was settled. The assignee was not bound by later judgment in the litigation between the assignor and a third party. Applying settled law, in relation to assignments of personal property, as opposed to real property, the assignee was not bound by any later judgment obtained against the defendant in the proceedings. The Berne Convention did not provide for complete harmonisation by states party to the Convention of all aspects of the law relating to copyright. Accordingly, the application would be dismissed.

Seven Arts Entertainment Ltd v Content Media Corpn plc [2013] EWHC 588 (Ch), [2013] All ER (D) 197 (Mar) (Chancery Division: Sales J). *Powell v Wiltshire* [2004] EWCA Civ 534, [2005] QB 117, [2004] 3 All ER 235 (2004 Abr para 1260) applied. *Johnson v Gore Wood & Co (a firm)* [2002] 2 AC 1, [2001] 1 All ER 481, HL (2002 Abr para 2543), considered.

EXPLOSIVES

Halsbury's Laws of England (5th edn) vol 47 (2014) paras 601–757

1166   Identification and traceability

The Identification and Traceability of Explosives Regulations 2013, SI 2013/449 (in force in part on 5 April 2013 and in part on 5 April 2015), replace the 2010 Regulations, SI 2010/1004, and implement Commission Directive (EC) 2008/43 (setting up a system for the identification and traceability of explosives for civil uses). The 2013 Regulations, in particular, (1) exclude specified explosives from the scope of regulation; (2) impose requirements on manufacturers, importers and distributors of explosives as to the marking of the explosives with a unique identification; (3) require manufacturers of explosives and importers of explosives manufactured in a country that is not an EEA state to apply to the Health and Safety Executive for the attribution of a code for the manufacturing site; (4) impose record-keeping requirements on persons who manufacture, import, distribute, acquire or keep explosives, and provide for exceptions for employees and individuals acquiring explosives for personal use; (5) require the Secretary of State to review their operation and effect; (6) provide for enforcement; and (7) provide for their application to the acquisition or keeping of explosives on specified premises outside Great Britain.

1167   Pyrotechnic articles—safety

The Pyrotechnic Articles (Safety) (Amendment) Regulations 2013, SI 2013/1950 (in force on 30 August 2013), implement European Parliament and Council Directive (EU) 2013/29 on the harmonisation of the laws of the member states relating to the making available on the market of pyrotechnic articles, and amend the 2010 Regulations, SI 2010/1554, as regards the provisions in Directive 2013/29, relating to the prohibition on use of detonative explosives in the manufacture of categories P1, P2, T2 pyrotechnic articles and category F4 fireworks except on certain conditions.

EXTRADITION
Halsbury's Laws of England (5th edn) vol 47 (2014) paras 451–600

Articles
For articles relating to this title please refer to the Table of Articles at the beginning of the Abridgment.

1168   Designated territories
The Extradition Act 2003 (Amendment to Designations) Order 2013, SI 2013/1583 (in force on 1 July 2013), further amends (1) the Extradition Act 2003 (Designation of Part 1 Territories) Order 2003, SI 2003/3333, so as to designate Croatia as a Part 1 territory for the purposes of the Extradition Act 2003; and (2) the Extradition Act 2003 (Designation of Part 2 Territories) Order 2003, SI 2003/3334, by (a) omitting references to Croatia; (b) designating the Republic of Korea as a Part 2 territory; (c) designating the Republic of Korea for the purposes of specified provisions of the 2003 Act, in order to set the evidential requirements made of that country when it makes an extradition request to the United Kingdom and the matters which a judge must take into account when deciding an extradition request from that country; and (d) adding India to the list of territories specified for the purpose of s 74(11)(b).

1169   European arrest warrant—surrender procedures—execution—right to be heard by judicial authority issuing warrant
Judicial authorities in Germany issued European arrest warrants for the arrest of the appellant in Romania. The appellant did not consent to his surrender and brought proceedings opposing the execution of the warrants. Questions arose as to whether Council Framework Decision 2002/584 on European arrest warrants, read in the light of the Charter of Fundamental Rights of the European Union arts 47 and 48, which guaranteed the right to an effective remedy and to a fair trial, the presumption of innocence and respect for the right of defence, and the European Convention on Human Rights art 6, which guaranteed the right to be heard, had to be interpreted as meaning that the executing judicial authorities could refuse to execute a European arrest warrant issued for the purposes of conducting a criminal prosecution on the ground that the issuing judicial authorities had not heard the requested person before the arrest warrant had been issued. *Held*, member states were in principle obliged to act on a European arrest warrant and could refuse to execute such a warrant only in the cases of mandatory non-execution and in the cases of optional non-execution listed in the Framework Decision. An obligation for the issuing judicial authorities to hear the requested person before a European arrest warrant was issued would inevitably lead to the failure of the very system of surrender provided for by the Framework Decision and, consequently, prevent the achievement of the area of freedom, security and justice, in so far as such an arrest warrant had to have a certain element of surprise, in particular in order to stop the person concerned from taking flight. In any event, the European legislature had ensured that the right to be heard would be observed in the executing member state in such a way as not to compromise the effectiveness of the European arrest warrant system. It followed that the Framework Decision had to be interpreted as meaning that the executing judicial authorities could not refuse to execute a European arrest warrant issued for the purposes of conducting a criminal prosecution on the ground that the requested person was not heard in the issuing member state before that arrest warrant was issued.
   Case C-396/11 *Criminal proceedings against Radu* [2013] QB 1031, [2013] All ER (EC) 410 (ECJ: Grand Chamber).

1170   European arrest warrant—surrender procedures—member states—ground for non-execution
The Spanish High Court authorised the extradition to Italy of the applicant to face trial in relation to two European arrest warrants issued. The applicant had fled Italy after being released on bail. The district court ruled that the applicant had failed to make appearance in court and directed that notice should in future be given to the lawyers who had been chosen and appointed by him. The applicant was sentenced in absentia to ten years' imprisonment

for bankruptcy fraud. The Italian Supreme Court dismissed the appeal lodged by the applicant's lawyers. That same month, the Italian public prosecutor's office issued a European arrest warrant for execution of the sentence. The applicant was arrested by Spanish police and opposed his surrender to Italian authorities. The applicant's surrender to Italian authorities was authorised by the High Court in order for him to serve the sentence. The applicant successfully petitioned for constitutional protection against the order. The first section of the constitutional court suspended enforcement of the order. The plenary chamber of the constitutional court decided that it would examine the petition. The referring court pointed out that a decision of a Spanish judicial authority to consent to extradition to countries which, in cases of very serious offences, allowed convictions in absentia without making the surrender conditional on the convicted party being able to challenge the same in order to safeguard his rights of defence, gave rise to an 'indirect' infringement of the requirements deriving from the right to a fair trial. The referring court further pointed out that the precedent was also applicable to the system of surrender established by Framework Decision 2002/584 because art 5(1) contemplated the possibility that the execution of a European arrest warrant issued for the execution of a sentence imposed in absentia ought to be subject to the condition that the issuing judicial authority should furnish guarantees to ensure that the person requested would have an opportunity to apply for a retrial. The referring court held that the difficulty arose from the fact that Framework Decision 2009/299 had repealed Framework Decision 2002/584 art 5(1) and introduced art 4a which precluded a refusal to execute the European arrest warrant issued for the purpose of executing a custodial sentence if the person did not appear in person at the trial resulting in the decision where the person concerned had given a mandate to a legal counsellor to defend him at the trial, and was indeed defended by that counsellor at the trial. The question to be decided was whether Framework Decision 2002/584 precluded Spanish courts from making the applicant's surrender conditional on the right to have the conviction reviewed. The referring court decided to stay the proceedings and to refer certain questions to the European Court of Justice for a preliminary ruling. *Held*, (1) art 4a(1) should be interpreted as precluding the executing judicial authorities, in the circumstances specified in that provision, from making the execution of a European arrest warrant issued for the purposes of executing a sentence conditional on the conviction rendered in absentia being open to review in the issuing member state. (2) Article 4a(1) did not disregard either the right to an effective judicial remedy and to a fair trial or the rights of the defence guaranteed by the Charter of Fundamental Rights of the European Union arts 47, 48(2). It followed that Framework Decision 2002/584 art 4a(1) was compatible with the requirements under the Charter arts 47, 48(2). (3) It was settled law that, by virtue of the principle of European Union law, which was an essential feature of the EU legal order, rules of national law could not be allowed to undermine the effectiveness of EU law on the territory of that state. Allowing a member state to avail itself of art 53 to make the surrender of a person convicted in absentia conditional on the conviction being open to review in the issuing member state in order to avoid an adverse effect on the right to a fair trial and the rights of the defence guaranteed by the constitution of the executing member state, by casting doubt on the uniformity of the standard of protection of fundamental rights as defined in that framework decision, would undermine the principles of mutual trust and recognition which that decision purported to uphold and would, therefore, compromise the efficacy of that framework decision. Accordingly, art 53 had to be interpreted as not allowing a member state to make the surrender of a person convicted in absentia conditional on the conviction being open to review in the issuing member state, in order to avoid an adverse effect on the right to a fair trial and the rights of the defence guaranteed by its constitution.

Case C-399/11 *Melloni v Ministerio Fiscal* [2013] QB 1067, [2013] All ER (EC) 475 (ECJ: Grand Chamber).

1171   European arrest warrant—validity—particulars of sentence—cumulative sentence

The Extradition Act 2003 s 2(6)(e) provides that a European arrest warrant must include the particulars of the sentence which has been imposed under the law of the category 1 territory in respect of the offence, if the person has been sentenced for the offence.

The defendant had been found guilty of various offences of dishonesty or violence in his native Poland, and a European arrest warrant was raised by the claimant court in Poland that specified the offences he was charged with and their indicative sentences. At the time the warrant was made out, the defendant was facing further criminal charges in the United Kingdom and the extradition proceedings were adjourned pending the outcome of the English proceedings. Meanwhile, the defendant applied to the claimant to have his sentences aggregated, as was permissible under Polish law, and, in due course, his original sentence of 45 months was reduced to a cumulative sentence of 22 months. When the defendant came before the court for extradition it was argued that the warrant no longer gave the correct particulars required by the 2003 Act s 2(6)(e) because the only relevant sentence was now the cumulative sentence. For that reason, the defendant argued that the warrant had become invalid, or the court should exercise its inherent jurisdiction not to proceed with the extradition on the ground that it no longer gave proper, fair or accurate particulars. *Held*, category 1 territories enjoyed mutual trust and recognition by the requested state of the authority of the requesting state. For this reason, the validity of the warrant depended on whether the prescribed particulars were to be found in it, and not on whether they were correct. Validity was not a transient state; a warrant was either valid or not, and did not change over time from one to the other. The safeguard against an unjustified extradition where there might be a factual error in the warrant was twofold. Firstly, the receiving court might request further information from the issuing authority under the Framework Decision art 15.2, which was receivable as evidence under the 2003 Act s 202 on the same basis as the warrant itself. Secondly, the English court retained an inherent right (as the executing court) to ensure that its process had not been abused. That jurisdiction was exceptional and was not to be used as an indirect way of mounting a contentious challenge to the factual or evidential basis for the conduct alleged in the warrant, as this was an issue for the requesting court. The warrant was undoubtedly valid at the point of issue and, moreover, the information in the warrant about the original sentences did not cease to be true when the cumulative sentence was passed. So long as the composite offence exceeded the four-month minimum sentence necessary to be an extradition offence this reduction did not change the substance of the request. It followed that the warrant was valid, but the proceedings would be dismissed under s 43(4) because the defendant had voluntarily returned. Judgment would be given accordingly.

Zakrzewski v Regional Court in Lodz, Poland [2013] UKSC 2, [2013] 2 CMLR 877, [2013] All ER (D) 147 (Jan) (Supreme Court: Lord Neuberger P, Lord Sumption, Lord Kerr, Lord Clarke and Lord Wilson SCJJ). *Criminal Court at the National High Court, First Division v Murua* [2010] EWHC 2609 (Admin), [2010] All ER (D) 85 (Oct) (2010 Abr para 1265); and *Pilecki v Circuit Court of Legnica, Poland* [2008] UKHL 7, [2008] 4 All ER 445 (2008 Abr para 1476) applied. *Assange v Swedish Prosecution Authority* [2012] UKSC 22, [2012] 4 All ER 1249 (2012 Abr para 1211) considered. Decision of Lloyd Jones J [2012] EWHC 173 (Admin), [2012] 1 WLR 2248, [2012] All ER (D) 99 (Feb) (2012 Abr para 1212) affirmed on other grounds.

1172　　Extradition hearing—appeal—European arrest warrant—information contained in warrant

The claimant was a Polish national. He was arrested in England and served with a European arrest warrant issued in Poland in relation to offences of what were described as fraud and forgery of administrative documents. Later, his extradition was ordered. On appeal by the claimant, *held*, the particulars given in the warrant had been inadequate. They could not fairly be said to describe the circumstances of the offence or the degree of the claimant's participation. While they claimed the claimant had swindled a company, no details had been given of the form of the swindle or of what the alleged criminal conduct had consisted. Therefore, the warrant would be quashed. Accordingly, the appeal would be allowed.

Morawski v Regional Court in Wloclawek, Poland [2012] EWHC 4102 (Admin), [2013] All ER (D) 27 (Apr) (Queen's Bench Division: Underhill J). *Sandi v Craiova Court, Romania* [2009] EWHC 3079 (Admin), [2009] All ER (D) 297 (Nov), DC (2009 Abr para 1468); *Hewitt v First Instance and Magistrates' Court Number One of Denia, Spain; Woodward v First Instance and Magistrates' Court Number One of Denia, Spain* [2009] All ER (D) 234 (Apr), DC (2009 Abr para 1473); and *Ektor v National Public Prosecutor of Holland* [2007] All ER (D) 109 (Dec), EAT, applied.

apply to small authorised AIFMs; (6) make provision regarding external valuers appointed by AIFMs, the delegation of functions by an AIFM and the liability of depositaries appointed for alternative investment funds managed by AIFMs subject to full authorisation; (7) make provision for where an AIF managed by an AIFM subject to full authorisation holds a significant proportion of the shares in, or acquires control of, a private company or an issuer of traded securities, and imposes requirements about the provision of information to the company or issuer, shareholders, employees and employees; (8) require approval by the Financial Conduct Authority or the giving of notification to it before AIFMs and investment firms may market alternative investment funds in certain circumstances; (9) provide for the procedure by which approval may be obtained or notification given, and the consequences of marketing without meeting the requirements; (10) give the Financial Conduct Authority various duties and powers which arise out of Directive 2011/61, relating mainly to the provision of information to the European Securities and Markets Authority and to regulators in other EEA states; (11) extend the application of various provisions in the Financial Services and Markets Act 2000; (12) make provision for the transition to the new regime for existing AIFMs and the alternative investment funds managed by them, and for depositaries of alternative investment funds; (13) require the Treasury to review the operation and effect of the regulations within five years and within every five years thereafter; and (14) bring into effect amendments to specified primary and secondary legislation.

The Alternative Investment Fund Managers (Amendment) Regulations 2013, SI 2013/1797 (in force in part on 22 July 2013 and in part on a day or days to be appointed), implement provisions of European Parliament and Council Directive (EU) 2011/61 (on alternative investment fund managers) and amend the principal 2013 Regulations above. In particular, the regulations (1) provide that the management of alternative investment funds is considered to take place in the United Kingdom where managers from outside the EEA have the United Kingdom as their member state of reference and the funds managed are either EEA funds or are marketed in the EEA; (2) prescribe that such managers, and United Kingdom managers of funds outside the EEA, have access to the procedure by which United Kingdom managers may manage or market EEA funds in other EEA states; (3) apply the regime for authorisation or registration of United Kingdom managers of alternative investment funds to managers from outside the EEA that have the United Kingdom as their member state of reference; (4) make provision relating to the managing and marketing of alternative investment funds by United Kingdom managers to managers from outside the EEA that become authorised or registered in the United Kingdom; (5) provide that the separate national regime permitting managers from outside the EEA and United Kingdom managers of funds from outside the EEA to market their funds in the United Kingdom is retained as an alternative to the regime in head (3); (6) revoke the separate national regime for managers from outside the EEA and United Kingdom managers of funds from outside the EEA to market their funds in the United Kingdom, with the result that from that point all managers of alternative investment funds managing United Kingdom funds or marketing funds in the United Kingdom must be authorised in the United Kingdom or in another EEA state; (7) preserve the ongoing obligations of managers from outside the EEA that have marketed funds under those separate national regimes; (8) empower the Financial Conduct Authority or the Prudential Regulation Authority to make rules to implement the relevant provisions without complying with various procedural requirements imposed under the Financial Services and Markets Act 2000, including the obligation to consult on a draft of the rules before making them; and (9) provide that if the Financial Conduct Authority or the Prudential Regulation Authority makes such rules, an equivalent consultation must be carried out before the rules come into force, unless the rules are revoked before they come into force. An error in the Financial Services and Markets Act 2000 (EEA Passport Rights) Regulations 2001, SI 2001/2511, is also rectified.

1183   Banking—bank—account—payment—fund transfer

The claimant company was a customer of the defendant bank. He gave instructions to the defendant to pay a supplier. The claimant's instruction was given on one of the defendant's standard clearing house automated payment system transfer forms. On the form, the claimant instructed the defendant to pay out of its business account the standard sum to an account with another bank. The claimant stated the necessary sort code and account number for the supplier account and stated the supplier name. The form contained an acceptance by the claimant that no responsibility was attached to the defendant for any loss caused by 'delays, interruptions or errors in transmission of payment' which were not directly due to negligence on the part of the defendant. Information given to the claimant about the receiving account had been false. The claimant had been the victim of a fraud. Proceedings were commenced by the claimant seeking a declaration that it was entitled to have its account re-credited. The claimant submitted that the other bank had had no authority to accept the payment on behalf of the supplier because that was not the name of the customer who held the account with the sort code and account number stated in the transfer form. Therefore, no valid acceptance of the payment was ever given and the other bank ought to have rejected the transfer and returned the funds, with the effect that the claimant's instructions to the defendant to make payment to the supplier was not carried out and it was entitled, therefore, to have the money back. In defence, the defendant asserted that normal banking practice was to process payments on the basis of the payee's account number and sort code and not the name of the payee. Both the claimant and the defendant made applications for summary judgment. *Held*, the instruction had been to pay a sum of money to the beneficiary by transfer to the account number and sort code specified. Although the identity of the beneficiary was important to the claimant, the evidence was that transfers did not operate in such a way that the beneficiary's name formed part of the identifier which determined the destination of the payment. There was no requirement in the rules that the beneficiary's name had to be included, and in practice, transfers were processed without reference to it. The evidence was unequivocal that the identity of the beneficiary was irrelevant to the way in which the payment was processed. It was the destination account number and sort code that mattered. The manner in which the transfer worked was that a receiving bank which was able to match the account number and sort code to one of its accounts would be expected to credit that account with money and send a 'logical acknowledgment' back to the paying bank to indicate acceptance of the payment. At that point, the payment was complete. Therefore, the claimant's argument that the payment was not completed would be rejected. In addition, the transfer was one which the defendant had undertaken to carry out on terms of the transfer form, which had included the express acknowledgment by the claimant that no responsibility was attached to the defendant. There would be judgment for the defendant on the claimant's claim. The claimant's application for summary judgment would be dismissed. Judgment would be given accordingly.

Tidal Energy Ltd v Bank of Scotland plc [2013] EWHC 2780 (QB), [2013] All ER (D) 214 (Sep) (Queen's Bench Division: Havelock-Allan QC).

1184   Banking—bank—duty of care—negligent mis-statement

The claimants carried on business together in partnership. For that purpose they had loans with the defendant bank. Following a meeting with the defendant, the claimants were told that an interest rate swap would be a good idea. The meeting was followed by the defendant sending a letter which enclosed the defendant's terms of business. In due course, the claimants entered into an interest rate swap with the defendant. The documents provided by the defendant stated that early termination of the swap could attract break costs. At the time of swap, the defendant was governed by the Conduct of Business Rules promulgated by the Financial Services Authority pursuant to the Financial Services and Markets Act 2000. The 2000 Act s 150 provided that a contravention of a rule was actionable at the suit of a private person who has suffered loss. The Rules stated that a 'firm' could not make a personal recommendation of a transaction to a private customer unless it had taken reasonable steps to ensure that the customer had understood the nature of the risks involved. In the circumstances, both the defendant and the claimants thought it was a reasonable view that interest rates would decrease in the short term and thereafter rise. That did not occur, and rates fell to an all-time low, with the result that the claimants were worse off than they would have been had they not entered into the swap. The claimants sought early termination of the swap, which the defendant stated would attract a break cost. That prompted the claimants to issue proceedings claiming that the defendant had mis-sold the swap. It was found that the defendant had given no recommendation or advice for the swap, that the defendant had not assumed an advisory duty of care before the meeting and that no such duty had arisen as a result of anything said by the defendant at the meeting. The judge assumed that the defendant owed the claimants a duty to take care when making statements in circumstances in which it had known or ought to have known that the claimants would have relied on its skill and judgment. He went on to state that the Rules comprised a duty to give information unless without it a relevant statement made within the context of the assumption of responsibility was misleading. The judge found that the duty imposed by the Rules to take reasonable steps to ensure that the counterparty to a transaction understood its nature was well outside any notion of a duty not to mis-state. Therefore, he did not regard the content of the defendant's common law duty in relation to the accuracy of its statements as in any relevant manner informed by the content of the Rules, although the judge had been prepared to recognise that, had the bank undertaken an advisory duty, the content of the duty would have been in part informed by the content of the Rules. The judge dismissed the claim. On appeal by the claimants, *held*, the claimants' submissions had amounted to saying that the mere existence of the Rules had given rise to a co-existence duty of care at common law. However, it was no answer to the question of what feature of the statutory duty, if there was a relevant statutory duty, had given rise to a co-extensive duty of care at common law to assert that the defendant was undertaking a regulated activity in circumstances where a failure to comply with the Rules had been likely to cause loss. Therefore, the defendant had not owed the claimants a common law duty of care which had involved taking reasonable care to ensure that they had understood the nature of the risks involved in entering into the swap transaction. The defendant had not crossed the line which had separated, on the one hand, the activity of giving information about selling a product and, on the other hand, the activity of giving advice. There was neither justification nor a need for the imposition of a common law duty independent of but co-extensive with the remedy provided by statute. Accordingly, the appeal would be dismissed.

Green v Royal Bank of Scotland [2013] EWCA Civ 1197, [2014] Bus LR 168, [2013] All ER (D) 86 (Oct) (Court of Appeal: Richards, Hallett and Tomlinson LJJ).

1185   Banking—bank—duty of care—party to inter-creditor deed

The claimant companies loaned money to a company (the 'borrower') for the purposes of investing in a property portfolio. The defendant bank, which had also provided finance, subsequently reorganised the funding by creating a tiered financing structure which involved a number of interrelated agreements, including a loan facility agreement and an inter-creditor deed which governed the relationship between the various lenders at the different tiers in the structure. For this purpose the defendant acted as the borrower's agent at the junior mezzanine ('B1') level. The borrower raised concerns with the defendant concerning its financial performance, before defaulting on the loan and entering into receivership. The claimants brought proceedings against the defendant in its capacity as the borrower's agent, alleging that the defendant had failed in its duty to inform the claimants about events of default, had failed to disclose relevant financial material received from the borrower, namely a business plan and cashflow spreadsheet, and had made negligent misstatements to the claimants in order to gain their consent to the rolling-up of interest payments on the loan at the lower ('B2') level. The claimants contended that, had the defendant complied with its duties, they would have been able to take action to avoid the resulting losses. *Held*, the defendant had not breached its duty in failing to notify the claimants. As the borrower's agent, the defendant owed no relevant duties to the claimants beyond what could be found in the agreement and the inter-creditor deed. The defendant had not become aware of any default event and no general term imposing an obligation on the defendant as agent to pass on relevant information to the claimants regarding financial performance could be implied into the agreement or deed. Moreover, the agreement conferred discretion on the defendant to consider any document put forward by the borrower as its annual budget in order to decide whether to approve it as such. Once approved, the borrower would be obliged to provide the defendant with sufficient copies for onward transmission to the lenders. However, the borrower had not put forward the documentation as its annual budget and the defendant did not therefore become subject to any obligation to pass it on to the claimants. The defendant was simply not under any implied obligation to pass on any financial information received from the borrower to the claimants. Nor was the defendant under an implied obligation to consider, on its own initiative, what additional information should be sought from the borrower regarding its financial condition. Such obligations were inconsistent with the scheme of the agent's duties as set out in the agreement and the specific information provision requirements. Also, while the defendant had provided a materially inaccurate and misleading account of the facts, the scope of the duty assumed by the defendant was limited to the proposal for the claimants to consent to the roll-up of the B2 interest. The defendant had assumed merely an obligation to exercise reasonable care to protect the claimants against such loss as they might suffer by reason of giving their consent. The claimants had suffered no such loss, and the defendant's breach of its duty therefore had no relevant impact on the claimants. Accordingly, the application would be dismissed.

Torre Asset Funding Ltd v Royal Bank of Scotland plc [2013] EWHC 2670 (Ch), [2013] All ER (D) 27 (Sep) (Chancery Division: Sales J).

1186　Banking—bank—duty to exercise reasonable care and skill—breach of duty

See *Deutsche Bank AG v Sebastian Holdings Inc*, para 529.

1187　Banking—bank—facility agreement—governing law—conflict of laws

See *Mauritius Commercial Bank Ltd v Hestia Holdings Ltd*, para 453.

1188　Banking—bank—freezing order—cross-undertaking in damages

Proceedings were commenced by the Financial Services Authority against three defendants on the basis that (1) the first defendant company was promoting the sale of shares without being authorised to do so and without an approved prospectus, contrary to the Financial Services and Markets Act 2000 ss 21, 85; (2) the second and third defendants were knowingly engaged in that activity; and (3) the second defendant was an unauthorised person carrying on regulated activities in breach of s 19. The first defendant had six bank accounts at a bank. Prior to issuing the proceedings, the Authority obtained without notice an injunction freezing the defendants' assets under s 380(3) or the Senior Courts Act 1981 s 37(1). The bank was subsequently notified of the order and the injunction was continued at a hearing on notice. In the injunction, the Authority gave undertakings to the court. The Court of Appeal ordered a cross-undertaking, the effect of which was to preserve the Authority's undertaking in respect of costs incurred by third parties but to eliminate any requirement that the Authority give an undertaking in respect of losses incurred by third parties. The bank appealed. The issue was whether and, if so, in what circumstances the Authority should, as a condition of obtaining a freezing injunction under the 2000 Act s 380(3) or the 1981 Act s 37(1), be required to give to the court a cross-undertaking in damages in favour of third parties affected by the injunction. *Held*, there was no general rule that a body like the Authority should be required to give a cross-undertaking in damages in favour of a third party affected by a freezing injunction. No cross-undertaking should be required unless circumstances appeared that justified a different position. In private litigation, a claimant acted in its own interests and had a choice whether to commit its assets and energies to doing so. If it sought interim relief which might, if unjustified, cause loss or expense to the defendant, it was usually fair to require the claimant to be ready to accept responsibility for the loss or expense. There was no general rule that the Authority should be required to give a cross-undertaking, in respect of loss suffered either by the defendants or by third parties. There was no distinction to be drawn between a cross-undertaking intended to protect a defendant or a third party. There was however a distinction to be drawn between a cross-undertaking in respect of costs and a cross-undertaking in damages. The rationale that public authorities should be able to enforce the law without being inhibited by the fear of cross-claims and of exposing financially the resources allocated by the state for their functions, applied with particular force to any open-ended cross-undertaking in respect of third party loss. It did not apply in the same way to a cross-undertaking in respect of third party expense. The Authority had been acting under its express power to seek injunctive relief conferred by the 2000 Act s 380(3). It had been acting in fulfilment of its public duties in ss 3–6 to protect the interests of the United Kingdom's financial system, to protect consumers and to reduce the extent to which it was possible for a business being carried on in contravention of the general prohibition against being used for a purpose connected with financial crime. In the circumstances, there was no reason to move away from the starting position that the Authority should not have to give any cross-undertaking in order to obtain an injunction under s 380(3). Accordingly, the appeal would be dismissed.

to the national financial information unit could not relieve those institutions of their obligation to supply the required information to the financial information unit in the member state in whose territory they were situated, in compliance with art 22.

Case C-212/11 *Jyske Bank Gibraltar Ltd v Administración del Estado* [2013] All ER (EC) 731 (ECJ: Third Chamber).

1205   Financial Services Act 2012—commencement

The Financial Services Act 2012 (Commencement No 1) Order 2013, SI 2013/113, appoints (1) 24 January 2013, for the coming into force of (a) for all purposes, ss 7–9, 48 (in part), 49–52, 57, 64, 67, 83, 93, 94, 119(1), (2), Schs 20, 21; (b) for the purposes of making regulations or orders, ss 4 (in part), 6 (in part), 11 (in part), 12 (in part), 15 (in part), 27, 29, 30, 33, 35 (in part), 37 (in part), 38 (in part), 41 (in part), 43 (in part), 110, 112, 114(1) (in part), Schs 7, 8–10 (in part), 12 (in part), 18 (in part); and (c) for limited purposes, ss 4, 6, 11, 12, 14–16, 18, 19, 24, 27, 29, 33, 35, 37–43, 45, 65, 66, 80, 84–87, 114, Sch 18 (in part); and (2) 19 February 2013, for the coming into force, for certain purposes, of ss 1, 4–6.

The Financial Services Act 2012 (Commencement No 2) Order 2013, SI 2013/423, brings into force, so far as not already in force (1) on 27 February 2013, Sch 4 (for certain purposes); and (2) on 1 April 2013, ss 1–6, 10–48, 53–56, 58–63, 65, 66, 68–82, 84–92, 95, 97, 103, 104–107, 110–112, 114, and Schs 1–19.

The Financial Services Act 2012 (Commencement No 3) Order 2013, SI 2013/651, brings into force, on 19 March 2013, for certain purposes, ss 17, 18 and Sch 11 para 28.

For a summary of the Act, see 2012 Abr para 1243. See also the commencement table in the title STATUTES AND LEGISLATIVE PROCESS.

1206   Financial services and markets—advice—duty of care—breach of duty

The claimant was a Saudi national who was married to a member of one of Saudi Arabia's richest families. Following her divorce, she received a capital sum in addition to yearly payments for expenses. She invested in structured notes, most through the first defendant and the rest through the second defendant, virtually all leveraged by loans from a bank. Following the collapse of various banks, and the collapse in the equities and fixed interest markets, the value of the notes that the claimant had purchased dropped significantly. Consequently, the bank made margin calls which the claimant failed to meet. The claimant brought a claim against the defendants alleging that, in breach of statutory duty under the Financial Services and Markets Act 2000 s 150, they had failed properly to explain the risks of the transactions and to satisfy themselves as to the suitability of the investments. The claimant contended that the bank and the second defendant had failed to explain that the structured notes that she had purchased with money lent by the bank would be pledged to it as collateral for the loans, that the bank was entitled to require her to provide additional collateral in the shape of margin calls if the value of the notes dropped and that if she did not provide such margin calls within the time scale stipulated, her notes could be sold with the consequent loss of some or all of her capital. Accordingly, she claimed the losses she allegedly incurred by investing in the notes. She contended that she was an inexperienced investor and had relied on her advisers to inform her of the risk. The defendants contended that she had been told of the risks involved in investing in high yields, that she had caused her own losses by failing to put up margin when she could have done, and that she had failed to heed earlier advice to sell the notes, which would have protected her against margin calls being made. It fell to be determined whether the defendants had acted in breach of statutory, contractual or tortious common law duty as alleged by the claimant. Consideration was given to the impact of the change in the 'LTV ratio', namely, the inter-relationship between the aggregate of the loans and the security provided, on the losses suffered by the claimant. *Held,* on the facts, neither the bank nor the second defendant were in breach of statutory duty, contractual or tortious common law duty. The claimant's evidence on critical conflicts of evidence was not credible. The risks in leveraged investment and structured notes had been explained to her, both in documents and orally. The cause of the loss was not only the unforeseeable collapse of the market and change in the LTV ratios required by the bank, but more particularly the claimant's own extraordinary and unreasonable decision not to meet a margin call when she was well able to do so after ignoring advice to sell more notes. Accordingly, the claim would be dismissed.

Al Sulaiman v Credit Suisse Securities (Europe) Ltd [2013] EWHC 400 (Comm), [2013] All ER (D) 27 (Mar) (Queen's Bench Division: Cooke J).

1207 Financial services and markets—capital requirements—general

The Capital Requirements Regulations 2013, SI 2013/3115 (in force on 1 January 2014), implement in part a package of European Union legislation known as 'CRD4' concerned with the authorisation of credit institutions and the prudential rules applicable to credit institutions and investment firms. In particular, the regulations (1) designate the competent authorities for the purposes of European Parliament and Council Directive (EU) 2013/36 on access to the activity of credit institutions and the prudential supervision of credit institutions and investment firms and European Parliament and Council Regulation (EU) 575/2013 on prudential requirements for credit institutions and investment firms; (2) impose (a) obligations on the Prudential Regulation Authority and the Financial Conduct Authority in relation to cooperation and co-ordination with other competent authorities and the European Supervisory Authorities; and (b) obligations on the Prudential Regulation Authority and the Financial Conduct Authority regarding disclosure of information and notifications required under Directive 2013/36; (3) make provision (a) on how the Prudential Regulation Authority or the Financial Conduct Authority must act when it is the consolidating supervisor of a group of credit institutions or investment firms; (b) about the exercise of supervision by the Prudential Regulation Authority and the Financial Conduct Authority, in particular in relation to own funds, specific liquidity requirements, employee remuneration and diversity practices; (c) concerning permissions under Regulation 575/2013; and (d) for the procedural aspects of the exercise of this discretion; (4) extend the criminal offence established by the Financial Services and Markets Act 2000 s 398 to requirements imposed by or under Regulation 575/2013, directly applicable regulations made under Directive 2013/36 or Regulation 575/2013, or the 2013 Regulations; and (5) make various amendments to primary and secondary legislation. SI 2006/3221 is revoked.

1208 Financial services and markets—capital requirements—reporting

The Capital Requirements (Country-by-Country Reporting) Regulations 2013, SI 2013/3118 (in force on 1 January 2013), implement European Parliament and Council Directive (EU) 2013/36 (on access to the activity of credit institutions and prudential supervision of credit institutions and investment firms) art 89. Specifically, the regulations (1) impose obligations on institutions in the United Kingdom to annually publish information on a consolidated basis relating to their activities in the United Kingdom and those of their establishments in other countries; (2) establish an interim reporting obligation which must be met by 1 July 2014 which requires only part of the information to be reported; (3) prescribe that global systemically important institutions must report certain information to the European Commission and Her Majesty's Revenue and Customs; (4) provide that where institutions are part of a group they are able to choose to meet their obligations to make information public by the parent undertaking publishing it for the entire group; (5) prescribe that where an institution has already complied with art 89 in another European Economic Area state, or the information relating to it has been published in the United Kingdom for the purposes of the regulations, it is to be treated as complying with the regulations provided it publishes where the information can be obtained; and (6) specify that a breach of the regulations will be enforced by the Prudential Regulation Authority in respect of institutions authorised by it and the Financial Conduct Authority in respect of all other institutions.

1209 Financial services and markets—client money pool—administration

A company carried on business as broker-dealers in financial markets throughout the world. Its subsidiary company acted as a broker-dealer in commodities, fixed income securities, equities, foreign exchange, futures and options. Administrators were appointed to the subsidiary. The Financial Services Authority's Handbook of Rules and Guidance required investment firms to segregate money received from, or held for, their clients and to hold it on trust for them. In certain circumstances, including the administration or liquidation of the firm, the money held for clients had to be distributed among the clients, pro rata, according to their entitlements. The value of a client's entitlement for distribution purposes was to be established as at the date when the obligation arose, the primary pooling event. The administrators sought the court's direction as to the proper approach to be taken in assessing client entitlement. *Held*, there was clear authority that the amount of the client money entitlement of each client was to be ascertained by reference to their individual client balances and client equity balances as determined in accordance with the Handbook, subject to the one modification that set-off between the two balances was to be mandatory, not voluntary. The liquidation value or hindsight principle was not applicable to the determination of claims to client money for the purposes of distribution under the Handbook.

Re MF Global UK Ltd (*in special administration*) [2013] EWHC 92 (Ch), [2013] WLR (D) 30, [2013] All ER (D) 221 (Jan) (Chancery Division: David Richards J). *Re Lehman Bros International* (*Europe*) (*in administration*) [2012] UKSC 6, [2012] 3 All ER 1 (2012 Abr para 1245) considered.

1210   Financial services and markets—conglomerates and other financial groups

The Financial Conglomerates and Other Financial Groups (Amendment) Regulations 2013, SI 2013/1162 (in force on 10 June 2013), implement, in part, European Parliament and Council Directive (EU) 2011/89 in relation to the supplementary supervision of financial entities in a financial conglomerate. In particular, the regulations (1) amend the 2004 Regulations, SI 2004/1862, by updating the definition of the financial conglomerates directive and references to the Financial Services and Markets Act 2000 Pt 12 (ss 178–192); (2) amend the Capital Requirements Regulations 2006, SI 2006/3221, by adding references to mixed financial holding companies in various definitions, so as to amend the requirement on the regulators to provide essential information to other relevant competent authorities, and to enable the competent authorities of all regulated entities within a group to participate in colleges of supervisors; and (3) amend certain definitions in the Financial Services and Markets Act 2000 and the Financial Services and Markets Act 2000 (Disclosure of Confidential Information) Regulations 2001, SI 2001/2188.

1211   Financial services and markets—consultation with home state regulators

The Financial Services and Markets Act 2000 (Exercise of Powers under Part 4A) (Consultation with Home State Regulators) Regulations 2013, SI 2013/431 (in force on 1 April 2013), prescribe circumstances in which the appropriate regulator must consult with the home state regulator when giving permission under the 2000 Act Pt 4A (ss 55A–55Z4) in response to an application made by a person who is connected with certain EEA firms. First, the appropriate regulator must consult the home state regulator unless the permission relates only to a relevant activity. Second, the appropriate regulator must consult the home state regulator when varying permission unless the permission relates only to a 'relevant activity' or where the effect of the variation is to give permission for the purposes of a single market directive other than the one for the purposes of which the existing permission was granted.

1212   Financial services and markets—EEA passport rights

The Financial Services and Markets Act 2000 (EEA Passport Rights) (Amendment) Regulations 2013, SI 2013/439 (in force on 1 April 2013), amend the 2001 Regulations, SI 2001/2511, so as to (1) prescribe the cases in which the Financial Conduct Authority must give the Prudential Regulation Authority copies of notices relating to the exercise of rights by EEA firms under single market directives to establish a branch in the United Kingdom; and (2) require the Financial Conduct Authority and the Prudential Regulation Authority to notify each other when an EEA firm or a non-United Kingdom firm exercising other Treaty rights qualifies for authorisation under the Financial Services and Markets Act 2000.

1213   Financial services and markets—enforcement—transitional provision

The Financial Services Act 2012 (Transitional Provisions) (Enforcement) Order 2013, SI 2013/441 (in force on 1 April 2013), makes transitional provision in relation to the coming into force of various provisions of the 2012 Act that amend the Financial Services and Markets Act 2000. The provisions in question relate to (1) the imposition of penalties and disciplinary measures concerning the performance of controlled functions; (2) disciplinary powers connected with (a) the contravention of listing rules; (b) failures by auditors to comply with trust scheme rules; and (c) contraventions by recognised clearing houses and recognised investment exchanges; (3) the exercise of powers over EEA firms exercising passporting rights under various single market directives; (4) persons disqualified from being the auditor of, or acting as the actuary for, an authorised person or class of authorised person; (5) injunctions and restitution; (6) the treatment of notices made by the Financial Services Authority as being imposed by the Prudential Regulation Authority and/or the Financial Conduct Authority; (7) the publication of warning notices; and (8) the prosecution of offences.

1214   Financial services and markets—financial collateral arrangements—default on facility agreement—appropriation of shares—terms of relief

British Virgin Islands
By a facility agreement, the respondent agreed to lend the first appellant a sum, secured on the first appellant's shareholding in a telecoms company and on the second appellant's shareholding in the first appellant, those shareholdings providing control of Turkey's largest mobile telephone company, to be repaid in four equal annual instalments plus interest. An event of default occurred under the facility agreement, entitling the respondent to declare the whole outstanding loan immediately repayable and, following a default in repayment of the accelerated loan, the respondent appropriated the charged shares to itself. The board decided that relief against forfeiture should be available to the appellants in relation to the appropriation on appropriate conditions and invited submissions as to the basis and terms on which relief ought to be granted. The appellants submitted that it would only be proper for the board to exercise its discretion to determine the basis and conditions of relief by requiring payment of the amount of the debt, together with appropriate interest and costs, but that what was appropriate was not necessarily determined by what the facility agreement would have provided had the loan continued unpaid and that account should be taken of the fact that the loan was due and about to be repaid at the time of the appropriation, the respondent's aim in fact being to forestall repayment and to convert its charges into ownership of shares, and that repayment had been tendered and rejected by the respondent. The respondent contended that the board's discretion was limited to granting the appellants an extension of time by which the terms of the facility agreement had to be performed in full and to imposing on the appellants additional conditions. It fell to be determined whether the grant of relief in respect of the appropriation was tied ineluctably to a conclusion or condition according to which the loan was to be treated as having remained unpaid from the date of the appropriation or whether a discretion existed to adopt a different approach if required by exceptional circumstances. *Held*, to insist on an axiomatic and unchallengeable assumption that the appellants would, instead of repaying the loan, have continued remorselessly in breach of every repayment obligation, made no payment at all and incurred default interest for six years would be unjustified and unconscionable and conflict with the general aim of equity in giving relief. There was considerable attraction in a result which had the effect of broadly restoring the respondent to the position in which it would have been but for its refusal to accept the tender, including default interest, as opposed to a result based on the unreal hypothesis of nothing happening, save continuous defaults, for the past six years. It followed that the respondent should be viewed as having had and rejected the opportunity to receive payment in full. The tender, coupled with the opening and maintenance of an interest earning escrow account for the following three years, should prevent interest running. Thereafter, the respondent should receive interest, but that should not be on the basis that the appellants remained in default. Rather, the essential reason why the loan remained unpaid could be identified as having been the respondent's rejection of the full repayment then tendered. It followed that relief against appropriation of the shares should be available to the appellants on condition that they pay to the respondent within 60 days of the date of the judgment a redemption sum plus interest accruing between the date of the judgment and the date of payment. Judgment would be given accordingly.

Cukurova Finance International Ltd v Alfa Telecom Turkey Ltd [2013] UKPC 20, [2013] All ER (D) 14 (Aug) (Privy Council: Lord Neuberger, Lord Mance, Lord Kerr, Lord Clarke and Lord Sumption).

recognised pursuant to, the provisions of Regulation 648/2012; (2) amend the Companies Act 1989 to implement and facilitate the provisions on segregation and portability of accounts in Regulation 648/2012 arts 39 and 48; (3) amend the Financial Services and Markets Act 2000 (Recognition Requirements for Investment Exchanges and Clearing Houses) Regulations 2001, SI 2001/995, so as to (a) disapply the requirements relating to clearing houses in relation to recognised central counterparties; and (b) provide that the requirements of Regulation 648/2012 must be met in order for a body to gain recognition as a recognised central counterparty, together with certain additional requirements; (4) designate the Bank of England as the competent authority under Regulation 648/2012 for central counterparties; (5) grant powers to the Financial Conduct Authority to obtain information; (6) give the Financial Conduct Authority power to impose penalties for contravening Regulation 648/2012; (7) make provision with regard to applications and notifications to the Financial Conduct Authority under Regulation 648/2012; (8) give the Bank of England enforcement powers in relation to requirements in Regulation 648/2012 art 31; (9) make provision to enable the European Securities and Markets Authority to gain access to telephone and data traffic records and make on-site inspections so that it may carry out its obligations under Regulation 648/2012 Title 6; (10) make various consequential amendments; and (11) provide for the 2013 Regulations to be reviewed before 1 April 2018 and subsequently at intervals of not more than five years.

The Financial Services and Markets Act 2000 (Over the Counter Derivatives, Central Counterparties and Trade Repositories) (No 2) Regulations 2013, SI 2013/1908 (in force in part on 26 August 2013, in part on 1 February 2014 and in part on 1 May 2014), further implement certain provisions of Regulation 648/2012 above and make provision in connection with the implementation of Commission Delegated Regulation (EU) 149/2013, regarding regulatory technical standards on indirect clearing arrangements, the clearing obligation, the public register, access to a trading venue, non-financial counterparties and risk mitigation techniques for over the counter derivatives not cleared by a central counterparty. In particular, the regulations (1) amend the Companies Act 1989 in order to facilitate the segregation of indirect client accounts at a clearing member and the transfer of indirect client accounts on the failure of a client providing indirect clearing services; (2) further amend the 2001 Regulations, SI 2001/995 above so as to require (a) clearing houses which provide clearing services without doing so as a central counterparty to maintain recovery plans specifying the steps they will take in order to maintain the continuity of their exempt activities if such continuity is threatened; and (b) clearing houses which act as central counterparties to (i) have in place effective arrangements for the allocation of losses arising for reasons other than member default; (ii) have in place plans for maintaining the provision of certain specified services when the continuity of service provision is threatened; and (iii) include in their default rules provision allocating losses that arise as a result of member default and which are not covered by the relevant provision in Regulation 648/2012; (3) amend the principal 2013 Regulations above in order to (a) give the Financial Conduct Authority the power to obtain information from third country entities for which it has supervisory responsibilities; (b) empower the Authority to direct the manner of making and content of reports to be made to it under Regulation 149/2013; (c) confer on the Authority the power to publish a statement of censure as an alternative to imposing a penalty for certain contraventions of Regulation 648/2012 or its implementing legislation; and (d) require the Bank of England to give notice before removing a member of the board of directors of a recognised central counterparty and to give a person so removed, and the counterparty concerned, the right to refer the matter to the Upper Tribunal; and (4) alter the implementation of a provision of European Parliament and Council Directive (EC) 2004/39, on markets in financial instruments, so that that provision does not apply to overseas investment exchanges.

1227 Financial services and markets—qualifying European Union provisions

The Financial Services and Markets Act 2000 (Qualifying EU Provisions) Order 2013, SI 2013/419 (in force on 1 April 2013), identifies the directly applicable provisions of European Union law which are specified as qualifying provisions and directly applicable provisions for the purposes of various provisions of the Financial Services and Markets Act 2000. In particular, the order (1) specifies provisions of EU law for general purposes including ss 1A and 2A and the functions of the Prudential Regulation Authority and s 168;

(2) sets out provisions of EU law for the purposes of disciplinary measures imposed under Pt 14 (ss 204A–211) and specifies which of the Financial Conduct Authority or the Prudential Regulations Authority is responsible for taking disciplinary action in relation to each specified provision of EU law; (3) specifies provisions of EU law for purposes connected with the regulation of clearing houses and investment exchanges under Pt 18 (ss 285–313); (4) makes provision for the purposes of the powers under Pt 25 (380–386) to obtain injunctions or provide for restitution; and (5) specifies provisions of EU law for the purposes of the fee-raising powers of the Financial Conduct Authority, the Prudential Regulation Authority and the Bank of England under the 2000 Act.

The Financial Services and Markets Act 2000 (Qualifying EU Provisions) (No 2) Order 2013, SI 2013/3116 (in force on 1 January 2014), specifies (1) European Parliament and Council Regulation (EC) 1060/2009 on credit rating agencies arts 4(1), 5a, 8b, 8c, 8d and 25a, European Parliament and Council Regulation (EU) 575/2013 on prudential requirements for credit institutions and investment firms and any directly applicable regulation made under Regulation 575/2013 or European Parliament and Council Directive (EU) 2013/36 on the access to the activity of credit institutions and the prudential supervision of credit institutions and investment firms as qualifying EU provisions for the purposes of various provisions of the Financial Services and Markets Act 2000; and (2) which of the Financial Conduct Authority or the Prudential Regulation Authority is responsible for taking disciplinary action in relation to each specified provision of EU law.

1228   Financial services and markets—regulated activities—activities regulated by the Prudential Regulation Authority

The Financial Services and Markets Act 2000 (PRA-regulated Activities) Order 2013, SI 2013/556 (in force in part on 8 March 2013 and in part on 1 April 2013), specifies, for the purposes of the Financial Services and Markets Act 2000, which regulated activities are 'PRA-regulated activities' and so are the regulated activities which are subject to prudential regulation by the Prudential Regulation Authority ('PRA'), rather than the Financial Conduct Authority. The regulations (1) provide that (a) the activities of accepting deposits and effecting or carrying out contracts of insurance; (b) acting as a managing agent at Lloyd's; (c) arranging by the Society of Lloyd's of contracts of insurance written at Lloyd's; and (d) dealing in investments as principal, to the extent designated by the PRA, are PRA-regulated activities; (2) set out the criteria which must be applied by the PRA in designating persons under head (1)(d); (3) set out the procedure the PRA must follow when designating a person; (4) require the PRA to keep under review designations; (5) enable the PRA to withdraw a designation and set out the procedure for withdrawal; (6) provide that a designation ceases to have effect if the person concerned ceases to have permission to carry on the activity of dealing in investment as principal; (7) require the PRA to prepare and issue a statement of its policy in relation to designation, the review of designations and the withdrawal of designations; (8) set out the procedure that the PRA must follow in preparing a statement of policy; and (9) make transitional provision.

1229   Financial services and markets—regulated activities—additional activities

The Financial Services and Markets Act 2000 (Regulated Activities) (Amendment) Order 2013, SI 2013/655 (in force on 2 April 2013), further amends the 2001 Order, SI 2001/544, so as to specify new regulated activities. In particular, the order specifies the activities of providing information in relation to and administering a specified benchmark, and (1) adjusts the definition of a consumer in order that consumer protection objective applies with regard to the new regulated activities and so that those affected by the carrying on of the new regulated activities may benefit from the provisions of the Financial Services and Markets Act 2000 to protect consumers; (2) specifies the new regulated activities and set out the specified benchmarks; (3) provides for a Pt 4A permission to be deemed to be extended to those firms which immediately before 2 April 2013 were already carrying on the activity of providing information to the administrator of a specified benchmark that was required for the determination of that benchmark and who already had a Pt 4 permission; (4) provides for an interim permission to be granted to persons wishing to undertake administering, analysing or determining activities; (5) enables the Financial Conduct

Authority to modify amongst other things, its rules in their application to persons with an interim permission; and (6) sets out the application of the 2000 Act to persons with an interim permission.

The Financial Services and Markets Act 2000 (Regulated Activities) (Amendment) (No 2) Order 2013, SI 2013/1881 (in force on and between 26 July 2013 and 1 April 2014), sets out additional activities which are to be treated as 'regulated activities' for the purposes of the Financial Services and Markets Act 2000. Specifically, the order (1) specifies the following new regulated activities: (a) credit broking; (b) operating an electronic system in relation to lending; (c) debt adjusting; (d) debt-counselling; (e) debt-collecting; (f) debt administration; (g) entering into a regulated credit agreement; (h) entering into a regulated consumer hire agreement; (i) providing credit information services; and (j) providing credit references; (2) makes transitional provisions regarding the new regulated activities; (3) sets out requirements relating to information which certain persons who are not authorised persons who carry on credit broking must comply with; (4) repeals provisions of the Consumer Credit Act 1974 which relate to the licensing of consumer credit activities; (5) makes consequential amendments to certain Acts and related transitional provision; and (6) implements European Parliament and Council Directive (EC) 2008/48 art 21 (on credit agreements). In addition, the order further amends the Consumer Credit (Agreements) Regulations 1983, SI 1983/1555, the Financial Services and Markets Act 2000 (Carrying on Regulated Activities By Way of Business) Order 2001, SI 2001/1177, the Financial Services and Markets Act 2000 (Exemption) Order 2001, SI 2001/1201, the Financial Services and Markets Act 2000 (Appointed Representatives) Regulations 2001, SI 2001/1217, the Financial Services and Markets Act 2000 (Rights of Action) Regulations 2001, SI 2001/2256, the Consumer Credit (Early Settlement) Regulations 2004, SI 2004/1483, the Financial Services and Markets Act 2000 (Financial Promotion) Order 2005, SI 2005/1529, the Consumer Credit (Information Requirements and Duration of Licenses and Charges) Regulations 2007, SI 2007/1167, the Financial Services and Markets Act 2000 (Ombudsman Scheme) (Consumer Credit Jurisdiction) Order 2007, SI 2007/383, the Financial Services and Markets Act 2000 (Controllers) (Exemption) Order 2009, SI 2009/774, the Consumer Credit (Disclosure of Information) Regulations 2010, SI 2010/1013, and the Consumer Credit (Agreements) Regulations 2010, SI 2010/1014.

1230 Financial services and markets—regulated activities—carrying on regulated activity—permission and approval—transitional provision

The Financial Services Act 2012 (Transitional Provisions) (Permission and Approval) Order 2013, SI 2013/440 (in force on 1 April 2013), makes transitional provision in relation to the coming into force of various provisions of the 2012 Act that amend the Financial Services and Markets Act 2000. The provisions in question relate to (1) permission to carry on regulated activities; (2) the approval for a person to perform functions which are specified in rules made by a regulator; (3) the authorisation of Lloyd's to undertake certain regulated activities; and (4) the authorisation of EEA firms exercising rights to establish a branch or provide services in the United Kingdom under certain single market directives relating to financial services or under other EU Treaty rights.

1231 Financial services and markets—regulated activities—carrying on regulated activity—threshold conditions

The Financial Services and Markets Act 2000 (Threshold Conditions) Order 2013, SI 2013/555 (in force on 1 April 2013), amends the threshold conditions that must be satisfied by a person seeking to carry out regulated activities under the 2000 Act. The revised conditions reflect the abolition of the Financial Services Authority and the creation of the Financial Conduct Authority and the Prudential Regulation Authority as joint financial regulators.

1232 Financial services and markets—regulated activities—carrying on without authorisation—contracts of insurance—extended warranty contracts

The appellants' businesses consisted of selling and performing extended warranty contracts under which, in consideration of a periodic payment, they contracted to repair or, if necessary, replace satellite television dishes, digital boxes and associated equipment. They undertook only to provide benefits in kind; there was no contractual obligation to pay money. The proceedings were conducted on the footing that, at common law, the contracts were contracts of insurance. The appellants were not authorised under the Financial Services and Markets Act 2000 to carry on any kind of insurance business. The Financial Services Authority sought orders to wind up the appellants in the public interest, pursuant to s 367(1)(c), on the ground that each of them was 'carrying on, or has carried on, a regulated activity in contravention of the general prohibition' which provided that no person might carry on a regulated activity unless he was either an authorised or an exempt person under s 19. Of relevance to the proceedings was the Financial Services and Markets Act 2000 (Regulated Activities) Order 2001, SI 2001/544, Sch 1 Pt I para 16(b) which concerned 'miscellaneous financial loss' including contracts insuring against risk of loss to the insured attributable to their incurring unforeseen expense, as well as any other kind of risk not covered by other provisions. The 2001 Order was made to give effect to Council Directive (EEC) 92/49, which amended Council Directive (EEC) 73/239 on the co-ordination of laws, regulations and administrative provisions relating to the taking up and pursuit of the business of direct insurance other than life assurance. The appellants appealed against orders for their winding up, contending that the classes of business in Directive 73/239 Annex did not extend to contracts of insurance that provided benefits in kind. *Held*, there was no material distinction, when determining whether a contract fell within class 16, between a contract which provided only for repair or replacement and one which also provided an indemnity for costs actually incurred by the insured. In each case, the risk covered was essentially the same; it was the possibility of the equipment breaking down or malfunctioning. A contract which provided only for repair and replacement, and not for payment of any indemnity, therefore fell within class 16(b) or if not within that class then within class 16(c), as set out in the 2001 Order Sch 1 Pt I para 16. Furthermore, it was clear that Directive 73/239 was concerned only to prescribe what kinds of business national law had to regulate and not what other kinds of business it might regulate. Still less was it concerned with the legislative technique that member states might employ to regulate other kinds of business to which Directive 73/239 ex hypothesi did not apply. It was clear that the object of Directive 73/239 had been to impose certain uniform principles of authorisation and regulation on insurance business in the standard classes but not on any business falling outside those classes. Even if the Annex classes 1–17 were confined to insurance of the relevant descriptions providing pecuniary benefits, there was nothing to prevent the United Kingdom from legislating to regulate insurance of those descriptions irrespective of whether they provided benefits in cash or kind or both. The extended warranty agreements which the appellants had made in the course of their business fell within class 16, and the contracts were of a kind which required their business to be authorised. Accordingly, the appeal would be dismissed.

Re Digital Satellite Warranty Cover Ltd [2013] UKSC 7, [2013] 1 All ER (Comm) 625 (Supreme Court: Lord Neuberger P, Lady Hale, Lord Mance, Lord Clarke and Lord Sumption SCJJ). Decision of Court of Appeal [2011] EWCA Civ 1413, [2012] 2 All ER (Comm) 38 (2011 Abr para 1215) affirmed.

1233　　Financial services and markets—regulated activities—prohibition order

The applicant acted as an insurance broker for general insurance contracts, including household and motor insurance and commercial insurance for businesses. He received approval from the respondent, the Financial Services Authority, to undertake those activities through his company. He was acquitted of various charges of fraud but the respondent commenced its own investigation into the applicant and his firm and subsequently removed the applicant's permission to conduct regulated activities. The respondent served a warning notice on the applicant and sent him a decision notice which stated that it had decided to impose a penalty for breaches of statements in the respondent's Statements of Principle and Code of Conduct for Approved Persons; and to make a prohibition order pursuant to the Financial Services and Markets Act 2000 s 56 to prevent him from carrying out any function in relation to an regulated activity carried on by any authorised person, exempt person or exempt professional firm. In its decision letter, the respondent stated that its decision had been made on five grounds. The applicant denied all the allegations against him and raised a limitation defence to certain of the grounds for the imposition of a penalty under s 66. On the applicant's reference of the decision notice to the Upper Tribunal, it fell to be determined whether the respondent had known of any of the relevant misconduct or had information from which the misconduct could reasonably be inferred within the specified period, which was two years earlier than the issue of the warning notice. *Held*, for time to start running for the purposes of s 66(4), it was not necessary that the respondent had the full picture that would justify the issue at that stage of a warning notice. Although the respondent might only take action under s 66(1) if it appeared to it that the relevant person was guilty of misconduct, the limitation period started to run from an earlier time, when the respondent knew or had information from which the misconduct could reasonably be inferred. The respondent, however, should have sufficient knowledge of the particular misconduct, or such knowledge should be capable of being reasonably inferred, to justify an investigation. Mere suspicion was not enough and there was no general impression that misconduct might have taken place. A mere allegation or assertion unsupported by evidence would be unlikely to be regarded as sufficient to amount to knowledge of misconduct or as information from which it would be reasonable for the respondent to have inferred misconduct, although it might be expected to give rise to further inquiry. Knowledge of an allegation of misconduct was not the same as knowledge of the misconduct. Where the respondent became aware of more than one act of misconduct of which a particular person appeared to be guilty, the time limit operated separately in respect of each. The respondent might not take action in respect of misconduct of which it had known or which could reasonably be inferred more than two, subsequently three, years before the issue of a warning notice. The respondent had not known of any of the misconduct to which the reference related and, prior to that time, the respondent had no information from which such misconduct could reasonably have been inferred. It followed that there was no limitation impediment to any of the actions taken by the respondent under s 66. The principal purpose of a financial penalty was to promote high standards of regulatory conduct by deterring persons who had committed breaches from committing further breaches, and helping to deter other persons from committing similar breaches, as well as demonstrating generally the benefits of compliant business. As the applicant had demonstrated a serious case of lack of integrity, the making of false statements and failure to deal with the respondent in an open and co-operative manner, there was no doubt that a substantial financial penalty should be imposed. In all the circumstances, the penalty imposed by the respondent on the applicant had been appropriate. In the light of the applicant's lack of integrity in the performance of his controlled function, there was no doubt that he was not a fit and proper person to perform functions in relation to a regulated activity carried on by an authorised person. The only appropriate order was to prohibit the applicant from performing any function in relation to any regulated activity carried on by any authorised person, exempt person or exempt professional firm. Accordingly, the reference would be dismissed.

Jeffery v Financial Conduct Authority [2013] All ER (D) 85 (Jul) (Upper Tribunal: Judge Roger Berner presiding).

1234   Financial services and markets—regulated market—prohibition order— procedure—discontinuance of proceedings

See *Hobbs v Financial Conduct Authority (formerly the Financial Services Authority)*, para 1235.

1235   Financial services and markets—regulation—procedure—discontinuance of proceedings—notice of discontinuance

The applicant was a proprietary trader who conducted trading on the London International Financial Futures and Options Market. Following an investigation by the respondent Financial Conduct Authority into the applicant's trading, the respondent decided that his conduct had constituted market abuse and that he had lied during the investigation in attempting to explain his conduct. The respondent imposed a prohibition order on him pursuant to the Financial Services and Markets Act 2000 s 56 on the ground that he was not a fit and proper person to perform functions in relation to a regulated market. The respondent served the applicant with a decision notice in accordance with s 57(3) and (4). He referred the matter to the Upper Tribunal (Tax and Chancery Chamber) which found that the respondent had not made out its case that the applicant had engaged in market abuse or that he was not a fit and proper person, and so directed the respondent to discontinue its action against him. The respondent published the result on its website, noting that it would discontinue its action against the applicant. Five days later, it removed the sentence that it would discontinue its action. The respondent was subsequently given permission to appeal against the Upper Tribunal's decision. The issues were whether the respondent had discontinued its proceedings against the applicant with the result that it was not entitled to pursue its appeal, and, if so, whether it had been incumbent on the tribunal to address the question of whether the applicant's conduct, namely his lying as found by the tribunal, had rendered him unfit and lacking propriety. *Held*, the communication of a decision to take no further action, by way a notice of discontinuance, was an intrinsic part of the process. Parliament had specified to whom and how notice was to be given, in s 389 and by the Financial Services and in the Markets Act 2000 (Service of Notices) Regulations 2001, SI 2001/1420. A statement on the respondent's website, not addressed in any way to the person to whom the decision notice was addressed, was not sufficient notice of a decision to take no further action for the purposes of the 2000 Act so as it render it irrevocable. The Upper Tribunal had therefore erred in finding that the respondent was bound by a decision to discontinue. The matters which a person subject to a decision notice was entitled to refer to the Upper Tribunal under s 57 included the facts and evidence referred to in the decision notice on the basis of which the respondent concluded that the person in question was not a fit and proper person and that a prohibition order was appropriate. This was for two reasons. First, the Upper Tribunal's consideration of a reference was not ordinary civil litigation. There was a public interest in ensuring that persons who were not fit and proper persons to perform functions in relation to a regulated activity were precluded from doing so. Second, if the Upper Tribunal incorrectly restricted its determination, it might be difficult for the respondent to rely on the excluded facts in future in assessing, for example, whether the applicant was a fit and proper person, or should be granted an authorisation he sought to engage in a regulated activity. It had therefore been incumbent on the Upper Tribunal to address the question whether, even if the applicant was not guilty of market abuse, his lying during the course of the investigation demonstrated that he was not a fit and proper person. It had erred in law in failing to do so. Accordingly, the appeal would be allowed.

Hobbs v Financial Conduct Authority (formerly the Financial Services Authority) [2013] EWCA Civ 918, [2013] All ER (D) 365 (Jul) (Court of Appeal: Rimer and Ryder LJJ and Sir Stanley Burnton). Decision of Upper Tribunal [2012] All ER (D) 369 (Nov) (2012 Abr para 1252) reversed.

1236 Financial services and markets—securities—undertakings for collective investment in transferable securities—contractual scheme

The Collective Investment in Transferable Securities (Contractual Scheme) Regulations 2013, SI 2013/1388 (in force on 6 June 2013), provide for the formation of undertakings for collective investment ('UCITS') constituted in accordance with contract law, and for the authorisation and supervision of contractual schemes by the Financial Conduct Authority ('FCA'). The regulations (1) define 'contractual scheme' and 'contractual scheme deed'; (2) provide that the operator of a co-ownership scheme has authority to acquire, manage and dispose of scheme property, and for that purpose to enter into contracts on behalf of the participants in the scheme; (3) provide that, in order to be authorised, a scheme must meet specified requirements, including a requirement that the scheme must not allow units in the scheme to be issued to anyone other than specified persons; (4) extend to authorised contractual schemes the power which the FCA has under the Financial Services and Markets Act 2000 ss 247 and 248 to make rules in relation to authorised unit trust schemes; (5) make provision about the contracts and the rights and liabilities of the participants in an authorised co-ownership scheme; (6) limit their liability for debts incurred under, or in connection with, contracts which the operator is authorised to enter into on their behalf; (7) provide for the segregation of the liabilities of participants in sub-schemes (where a co-ownership scheme is constituted as an umbrella co-ownership scheme); (8) provide for the alteration of authorised contractual schemes, including the replacement of the operator or the depositary and the conversion of a UCITS which is a feeder UCITS into a UCITS which is not a feeder UCITS; (9) provide for the revocation of an authorisation order made for a contractual scheme; (10) confer intervention powers on the FCA and on the court on application by the FCA, including powers exercisable where a master UCITS which has one or more feeder UCITS which are authorised contractual schemes is wound up, merges with another UCITS or is divided into two or more UCITS; (11) amend the Stock Transfer Act 1963 so that provision for the simplified transfer of securities applies to the transfer of units of an authorised contractual scheme; (12) amend the Corporation Tax Act 2010 so that no charge to corporation tax arises in relation to a co-ownership scheme; (13) amend the Limited Partnerships (Forms) Rules 2009, SI 2009/2160, by substituting the form which is required to be used for registering changes to limited partnerships; (14) modify the Limited Partnerships Act 1907 in relation to a limited partnership which is a partnership scheme for which an authorisation order under the Financial Services and Markets Act 2000 has been made; (15) provide for winding up insolvent contractual schemes; (16) provide for winding up a stand-alone co-ownership scheme or a sub-scheme of an umbrella co-ownership scheme by the court as if it were an unregistered company; (17) limit the liability of the general partner of an insolvent authorised partnership; (18) modify the application to authorised contractual schemes of the Law of Property Act 1925, to allow such transfers to be made by electronic communication; (19) make transitional provision in relation to depositaries of authorised contractual schemes; and (20) require the Treasury to review the operation and effect of the provisions and publish a report within five years after they come into force and within every five years after that.

1237 Financial services and markets—terrorist financing—restrictions on dealings with foreign banks—lawfulness

Pursuant to the Counter-Terrorism Act 2008 Sch 7, the defendant made the Financial Restrictions (Iran) Order 2009, SI 2009/2725. The 2009 Order was in force for a year and directed all persons operating in the financial sector not to enter into or continue to participate in, any transaction or business relationship with two companies, one of which was the claimant bank. It was made on account of the claimant's alleged connection with Iran's nuclear weapons and ballistic missile programmes. The 2009 Order effectively shut down the claimant's operations in the United Kingdom and those of its English incorporated subsidiary bank. Under the 2008 Act s 63, the claimant issued proceedings to set aside the 2009 Order. That application and subsequent appeal were dismissed. The claimant appealed further. As a preliminary issue to the appeal, the Supreme Court considered whether it was possible for it to adopt a closed material procedure and, if so, whether the circumstances were appropriate to do that. It concluded in the affirmative on both questions. *Held*, Lord Hope and Lord Reed dissenting, Lord Neuberger, Lord Dyson and Lord Carnwath dissenting in part, the defendant's direction under the 2008 Act which had led to the making of the 2009 Order had been unlawful. The essential question raised by the subjective grounds was whether the interruption of commercial dealings with the claimant's United Kingdom financial markets had borne some rational and proportionate relationship to the statutory purpose of hindering the pursuit by Iran of its weapons programmes. The distinction between the claimant and other Iranian banks which had been at the heart of the case put to Parliament had been an arbitrary and irrational distinction and the measure as a whole had been disproportionate. That was because, once it was found that the problem was not specific to the claimant, but was an inherent risk of banking, the risk posed by the claimant's access to those markets was no different from that posed by the access which comparable banks had continued to enjoy. The defendant had not explained why it was necessary to eliminate the claimant's business in order to achieve the objective of the 2008 Act. It might be that other Iranian banks had not been found to number among their clients entities involved in Iran's nuclear and ballistic missile programmes, but it followed from the fact that that was a problem inherent in the conduct of international banking business that they were as likely to do so as the claimant. Further, the defendant's direction which had designated the claimant had been unlawful for want of prior notice to it or any procedure enabling it to be heard in advance of the 2009 Order being made. Unless the 2008 Act had expressly or impliedly excluded any relevant duty of consultation, it was obvious that fairness in the circumstances had required that the claimant should have had an opportunity to make representations before the defendant's direction had been made. That the direction had been made by statutory instrument did not change the fact that there would have been every reason, in the absence of practical difficulties, to say that the defendant had had a duty to give prior notice to the claimant and to hear what it had had to say. The decision of the defendant to make the direction would be set aside and the 2009 Order would be quashed. Accordingly, the appeal would be allowed.

Bank Mellat v HM Treasury [2013] UKSC 39, [2013] All ER (D) 172 (Jun) (Supreme Court: Lord Neuberger P, Lord Hope DP, Lady Hale, Lord Kerr, Lord Clarke, Lord Dyson, Lord Sumption, Lord Reed and Lord Carnwath SCJJ). *Wiseman v Borneman* [1971] AC 297, [1969] 3 all ER 275, HL; *Lloyd v McMahon* [1987] AC 625, [1987] 1 All ER 1118, HL (1987 Abr para 1598); *R v Secretary of State for the Home Department, ex p Doody* [1994] 1 AC 531, [1993] 3 All ER 92, HL; *R (on the application of Daly) v Secretary of State for the Home Department* [2001] UKHL 26, [2001] 2 AC 532, [2001] 3 All ER 433, HL; *R v Shayler* [2002] UKHL 11, [2003] 1 AC 247, [2002] 2 All ER 477 (2002 Abr para 880); and *R (on the application of Aguilar Quila) v Secretary of State for the Home Department; R (on the application of Bibi) v Secretary of State for the Home Department* [2011] UKSC 45, [2012] 1 AC 621, [2012] 1 All ER 1011 (2011 Abr para 1484) applied. Decision of Court of Appeal [2011] EWCA Civ 1, [2012] QB 101, [2011] 2 All ER 802 (2011 Abr para 1223) reversed.

1238   Financial services and markets—transitional provision

The Financial Services Act 2012 (Transitional Provisions) (Miscellaneous Provisions) Order 2013, SI 2013/442 (in force in part on 25 March 2013 and in part on 1 April 2013), makes transitional provision in relation to the coming into force of various provisions of the 2012 Act that amend the Financial Services and Markets Act 2000. The provisions in question relate to (1) the annual reports of the Financial Conduct Authority and the Prudential Regulation Authority; (2) the Consumer and Practitioner Panels; (3) the control of business transfers; (4) appeals to the Upper Tribunal; (4) information gathering and investigation powers; (5) control over authorised persons; (6) the scheme manager of the Financial Services Compensation Scheme; (7) recognised clearing houses and recognised investment exchanges; (8) Lloyd's of London; (9) insolvency; (10) complaints; (11) amendments to the Companies Act 1989 relating to recognised clearing houses; (12) references to European legislation; and (13) the making of rules by the Bank of England.

1239   Financial Services (Banking Reform) Act 2013

The Financial Services (Banking Reform) Act 2013 makes further provision about banking and other financial services, including provision about the Financial Services Compensation Scheme, for the amounts owed in respect of certain deposits to be treated as a preferential debt on insolvency, about payment systems and securities settlement systems, about the accounts of the Bank of England and its wholly owned subsidiaries, and in relation to persons providing claims management services. The 2013 Act received the royal assent on 18 December 2013 and came into force in part on that day and on 18 February 2014. The remaining provisions come into force on a day or days to be appointed. For details of commencement, see the commencement table in the title STATUTES AND LEGISLATIVE PROCESS.

Part 1 (ss 1–12) Ring-fencing
Section 1 requires the Prudential Regulation Authority ('PRA'), when acting in relation to ring-fencing matters, to further its general objective of promoting the safety and soundness of PRA-authorised persons, by exercising its functions so as to protect the continuity of core services. Under s 2, the Financial Conduct Authority ('FCA') is provided with a new continuity objective which is applicable only if a core activity is not regulated by the PRA and accordingly falls under the remit only of the FCA. By virtue of s 3, the PRA may by direction require the FCA to refrain from specified action if in the opinion of the PRA that action may threaten the continuity of core services provided in the United Kingdom. Section 4 defines 'ring-fenced body' for the purposes of the Financial Services and Markets Act 2000, as any United Kingdom institution which carries on at least one core activity for which it has been given a Pt 4A permission under the Financial Services and Markets Act 2000; building societies are excluded from the definition, and the Treasury has the power to exclude other institutions from the definition by order. The PRA is required by the 2013 Act s 5 to make an annual report on the way in which ring-fenced bodies comply with the ring-fencing provisions. Section 6, Sch 1 make provision for ring-fencing transfer schemes. Section 7 enables the Treasury to ensure that building societies are subject to restrictions equivalent to those applying to ring-fenced bodies in the Financial Services and Markets Act 2000 Pt 9B (ss 142A–142Z1), or in rules or orders made under Pt 9B. By virtue

1241 Financial Services Compensation Scheme—negligent mortgage advice—assessment of compensation

The claimant sought advice from a mortgage broker regulated by the Financial Services Authority. Following the broker's advice, the claimant remortgaged her home by redeeming the existing repayment mortgage and taking out a new, larger interest-only mortgage with a longer term. She used the balance to invest in a property in Spain as advised by the broker, on the basis that the income and capital from the investment would service and pay off the new mortgage. The value of the Spanish property subsequently fell to almost zero as a result of a collapse in the Spanish property market. The claimant sought compensation from the defendant, which administered the Authority's compensation scheme. The defendant decided that the claimant was eligible for compensation on the ground that she had received negligent mortgage advice. However, in calculating the compensation payable, the defendant said that it could only compensate for losses that arose directly from the mortgage advice and not for the capital released from the new mortgage that was used to invest in the Spanish property. On the defendant's appeal against the claimant's successful application for judicial review of that decision, it fell to be determined if the defendant was entitled to ignore the part played by the investment in the Spanish property when assessing compensation. *Held*, the central question was whether the broker's breach of duty was characterised as giving bad advice in relation to a mortgage or giving bad advice in relation to an investment in land. Although it might be said that the advice related to both kinds of transaction, the defendant admitted liability on the grounds that the broker was in breach of the relevant code of conduct because the interest-only mortgage was unsuitable for the claimant. The mortgage was unsuitable not because the claimant could not meet the monthly interest payments, but because she had no prospect of paying back the loan if her investment failed to live up to expectations. The broker's bad advice in relation to the mortgage was given to the claimant in her capacity as a borrower and exposed her to a risk which later came about, and which caused her to lose capital and her home. Although the extent of the loss might have been unforeseen, the nature of the risk, and therefore the kind of loss likely to occur if it happened, was clear. Consequently, the loss suffered by the claimant flowed from the broker's bad advice in relation to mortgaging her home. In assessing compensation solely by reference to the additional costs incurred by the claimant in connection with the interest-only mortgage, the defendant proceeded on a false basis. Accordingly, the appeal would be dismissed.

Emptage v Financial Services Compensation Scheme Ltd [2013] EWCA Civ 729, [2013] All ER (D) 144 (Jun) (Court of Appeal: Moore-Bick, Sullivan and Underhill LJJ). Decision of Haddon-Cave J [2012] EWHC 2708, [2012] All ER (D) 109 (Oct) (2012 Abr para 1262) affirmed.

1242 Guarantee—guarantor—event of default—liability

The claimant bank provided banking and financial services in accordance with Islamic law. It claimed, against the second to fourth defendants, in respect of a debt, which it contended was due under a restructuring agreement, entered into after the claimant had discovered that it had been the victim of a long-standing fraud, following an event of default. The agreement provided that it represented the entire understanding and agreement. The second to fourth defendants were guarantors under the agreement. It was alleged that monies which had been misappropriated from the claimant, pursuant to the fraud, were paid to a special purpose vehicle ('P') of which the second and third defendants were shareholders. The lease of land held by P was the principal security provided to the claimant under the agreement. The fifth defendant was one of the companies through which the fraud had allegedly been perpetrated and the principal counterparty to the agreement and to which judgment in default was obtained against. The first defendant was a Bahraini company beneficially owned by the second defendant. It was contended by the claimant that events of default had occurred under the agreement which led to the acceleration by the claimant of repayment of sums due, with the result that the second to fourth defendants were jointly and severally liable. In respect of P, the event of default on which the claimant relied was the failure of P to perform its obligation to make mandatory prepayment. The claimant also contended that it was entitled to trace monies applied, in breach of fiduciary duty, into shares in another company ('A'), which was owned by the first defendant, and over which the claimant asserted a proprietary interest. The defendants counterclaimed. *Held*, it was settled that the party seeking rectification had to show that the parties had a common continuing intention in respect of a particular matter in the instruments to be rectified. Further, that there was an outward expression of accord, the intention continued at the time of the execution of the instrument sought to be rectified, and by mistake, the instrument did not reflect that common intention. In the circumstances, the case for rectification failed. The agreement gave rise to a contractual estoppel, precluding the defendants from asserting that something outside the four corners of the agreement had contractual effect. None of the requirements which had to be satisfied before rectification would be ordered even begun to be satisfied by the defendants. Further, there had been nothing untoward in the claimant having sought legal advice as to whether there had been an event of default and, if there had, in serving notice to cure the default and then, if the default was not cured, seeking to enforce against security available under the agreement. Far from that being a breach of the agreement, the claimant had relied on the provisions of the agreement intended to give it protection. There was no question of the claimant failing to perform its obligations under the agreement prior to the time when it served notices of default. The court was satisfied that the claimant had not been in breach of any duty owed to the defendants, whether they were merely guarantors or also principal debtors. It had been under no duty to the defendants to sell the security once it went into possession. With respect to the shares in A, nothing in the agreement precluded the claimant from advancing a proprietary claim against a disclosed proceeds asset, which included those shared. The shares in A were held on trust for the claimant. The counterclaims would be dismissed. Judgment would be given accordingly.

Dubai Islamic Bank PJSC v PSI Energy Holding Co BSC [2013] EWHC 3781 (Comm), [2013] All ER (D) 79 (Dec) (Queen's Bench Division: Flaux J) *China and South Sea Bank Ltd v Tan* [1990] 1 AC 536, [1989] 3 All ER 839, PC (1989 Abr para 1046); *Re Hampshire Land Co* [1896] 2 Ch 743; and *Matchbet Ltd v Openbet Retail Ltd* [2013] EWHC 3067 (Ch), [2013] All ER (D) 150 (Oct) applied.

1243   Guarantee—guarantor—liability—variation of guarantee

The claimant was an industrial and provident society that operated for the benefit of its members, which were companies in the construction industry. The claimant negotiated framework agreements with suppliers with whom its members could place orders. The claimant paid the supplier and the members paid the claimant. The two defendants owned equal shares in a member ('the member') of the claimant. Concerned about the member's financial situation, the claimant obtained joint and several personal guarantees from the defendants. The member subsequently traded over its credit limit. The second defendant resigned as a director of the member and left the company with an agreement that the first defendant would buy his shares. The second defendant did not, however, revoke his guarantee. The member failed to bring its trading within its credit limit, which was duly increased by the claimant. During the following year, a substantial part of the member's debt was attributable to an associated company which had been set up by, and was wholly owned by, the first defendant. The member became insolvent during the course of the following year, and it subsequently went into creditors' voluntary liquidation. The claimant, which was one of its creditors, successfully issued proceedings seeking payment by the defendants under their personal guarantees. The second defendant appealed, submitting that the successive increases to the member's credit limit and the repeated breaching of the credit limit, and the claimant's acceptance of liability to pay suppliers for orders placed by the associated company, amounted to non-consensual material variations to the contract between the claimant and the member which had the effect of discharging his liability under the guarantee. *Held*, it was clear that the judge had embarked, in an orthodox way, on the exercise of interpreting the guarantee and had given cogent reasons for having concluded that it was a conventional 'all moneys' guarantee that was in no manner intended to be linked to, or limited by, the then credit limit that applied to the trading arrangements between the claimant and the member. Had the parties intended that the second defendant's liability would be limited to the initial credit limit that the member had been given, then the guarantee would have said so. Further, it did not appear to have been suggested at trial, let alone found by the judge, that the circumstances in which the member had incurred liabilities to the claimant for the supply of goods to the associated company had been other than part of a proper trading relationship between the parties. On the face of it, all of the liabilities incurred by the member to the claimant had been properly incurred in the course of its business, and the second defendant had proved no case at the trial that they had not been. It followed that the guarantee had been engaged, and, accordingly, the appeal would be dismissed.

National Merchant Buying Society Ltd v Bellamy [2013] EWCA Civ 452, [2013] All ER (D) 69 (May) (Court of Appeal: Longmore, Rimer and Kitchin LJJ). Decision of Nicholas Strauss QC [2012] All ER (D) 325 (Jul) (2012 Abr para 1267) affirmed.

1244 Market abuse—qualifying investments—derivatives trading

The Financial Services and Markets Act 2000 s 118(1), (5) defines 'market abuse' as behaviour that (1) occurs in relation to qualifying investments admitted to trading on a prescribed market, or qualifying investments in respect of which a request for admission to trading on such a market has been made; and (2) consists of effecting transactions or orders to trade (otherwise than for legitimate reasons and in conformity with accepted market practices on the relevant market) which (a) give, or are likely to give, a false or misleading impression as to the supply of, or demand for, or as to the price of, one or more qualifying investments; or (b) secure the price of one or more such investments at an abnormal or artificial level.

The defendant decided that the claimant, a Canadian company with no place of business in the United Kingdom, had committed market abuse in breach of the 2000 Act s 118. The defendant believed that the claimant had systematically and deliberately engaged in a form of manipulative trading activity known as 'layering' in relation to shares traded on the London Stock Exchange. A person engaged in layering attempted to move the price up in order to benefit from a sale at a high price, then attempted to move it down in order to buy again, but at a lower price, and typically repeated the process several times. It was undisputed that traders located in various countries around the world, referred to as 'dealers', placed orders for contracts for differences ('CFDs') using the claimant's facilities with the United Kingdom subsidiaries of two large American financial institutions. The CFDs were placed in relation to shares quoted on the Exchange. As the dealers placed their CFD orders, the American institutions hedged them by placing orders of their own, to buy or sell (depending on the nature of the CFD) an equivalent quantity of the shares. As the American institutions provided direct market access, the dealers were able to see the Exchange order book in 'real time' and were therefore also able to track the movements in the price of the shares. Almost all of the dealers' orders were cancelled (if not previously executed) within a very short time, usually measured in seconds, of their being placed, and the hedging orders, which were cancelled as the CFDs were cancelled, likewise survived for very short periods. In proceedings brought by the claimant challenging the defendant's decision, the claimant contended that the dealers' activities did not involve 'qualifying investments admitted to trading on a prescribed market' within the meaning of s 118 because the CFDs had not been in shares but in synthetic products, in other words derivatives rather than securities, even though the underlying securities had been shares listed on the Exchange. *Held*, it was not possible to avoid liability for conduct which otherwise fell within s 118(5) by arguing that an unwitting intermediary had come between the supposed abuser and the market. Anyone dealing on an exchange who was not a member of that exchange necessarily had to deal through an intermediary, whether a broker or, as in the present case, a member which had offered direct market access. If the claimant had placed orders for shares, rather than for CFDs, with a broker who had been a member of the Exchange, it was obvious that it could not argue that its orders were outwith s 118(5) because they had been placed by an unwitting broker. There was no material difference in the outcome when the placing of an order for a CFD, as the person placing that order knew and intended, resulted in the placing of a corresponding order for the underlying shares. It followed that derivatives trading might fall within the scope of s 118(5). For the same reasons, the claimant's argument that it had been the American institutions which had placed the orders was unsustainable. Judgment would be given accordingly.

7722656 Canada Inc (formerly t/a Swift Trade Inc) v Financial Services Authority [2013] All ER (D) 266 (Feb) (Upper Tribunal: Judge Colin Bishopp presiding).

1245 Multi-national development banks—Asian Development Bank—further payments

The Asian Development Bank (Tenth Replenishment of the Asian Development Fund) Order 2013, SI 2013/1771 (in force on 11 July 2013), approves the making of payments on behalf of the government of the United Kingdom of sums not exceeding £200m as a further contribution to the resources of the Asian Development Fund in accordance with the specified arrangements. In addition, the order approves the redemption of non-interest-bearing and non-negotiable notes issued by the Secretary of State in payment of the further contributions.

1246 Multi-national development banks—Caribbean Development Bank—contribution

The Caribbean Development Bank (Eighth Replenishment of the Unified Special Development Fund) Order 2013, SI 2013/3175 (in force on 12 December 2013), approves the making of a payment on behalf of the government of the United Kingdom to the Caribbean Development Bank of a sum not exceeding £36m as the contribution of the government of the United Kingdom to the eighth replenishment of the resources of the Special Development Fund (Unified) of the bank in accordance with arrangements made with it pursuant to the Resolution entitled 'Resolution of Contributors to the Special Development Fund of the Caribbean Development Bank (SDF8)' adopted by the Board of Directors of the bank on 21 March 2013.

1247 Mutual societies—functions

The Financial Services Act 2012 (Mutual Societies) Order 2013, SI 2013/496 (in force on 1 April 2013), provides for functions of the Financial Services Authority relating to mutual societies to be exercisable by the Financial Conduct Authority and the Prudential Regulation Authority.

1248 National Savings Stock Register

The National Savings Stock Register (Amendment) Regulations 2013, SI 2013/416 (in force on 6 April 2013), further amend the 1976 Regulations, SI 1976/2012. Specifically, the regulations (1) alter the definition of 'new stock' to include variable interest stock; (2) set out the conditions under which variable interest stock is subscribed for to include provision that the Treasury may amend at any time the conditions under which the variable interest stock was subscribed for; (3) make minor amendments to the requirements to issue records to take account of the fact that variable interest stock does not offer a fixed rate of interest for a term; (4) provide for the manner in which interest is to accrue on a daily basis on variable interest stock; (5) omit provisions concerning when and where warrants issued by the Director of Savings are payable; (6) provide that only a person aged 16 or over may subscribe for new stock; and (7) make provision to allow those persons who are under 16 years of age and who already hold stock to continue to do so, and for the management of such stock.

1249 Payment of penalties—amounts received—payment to the Treasury

The Payment to Treasury of Penalties Regulations 2013, SI 2013/429 (in force on 1 April 2013), provide that amounts received by the regulator by way of penalties imposed under the Money Laundering Regulations 2007, SI 2007/2157, the Transfer of Funds (Information on the Payer) Regulations 2007, SI 2007/3298, the Regulated Covered Bonds Regulations 2008, SI 2008/346, the Payment Services Regulations 2009, SI 2009/209, the Electronic Money Regulations 2011, SI 2011/99, the Recognised Auction Platforms Regulations 2011, SI 2011/2699, and the Payments in Euro (Credit Transfers and Direct Debits) Regulations 2012, SI 2012/3122, is to be paid by the regulator to the Treasury. Sums received by the Treasury are to be paid into the Consolidated Fund.

1250 Regulated activities—performance of regulated activities—Financial Services Authority—disciplinary proceedings—appropriate tribunal

The claimant was the group finance director of a bank which undertook an unsuccessful rights issue. The defendant, which was the former statutory regulator of the financial services industry, issued a preliminary investigation report which stated that the claimant had failed to comply with his duty to exercise due skill, care and diligence in managing the business of the firm for which he was responsible in his controlled functions. The defendant's regulatory decisions committee issued a formal warning notice to the claimant proposing to impose a penalty against him. The claimant made submissions to the committee at an oral hearing, but the committee proceeded to issue a decision notice informing the claimant that the defendant had decided to impose a financial penalty. The claimant issued a claim for judicial review of the decision on the ground that the defendant had failed to give adequate reasons for its decision, contrary to the Financial Services and Markets Act 2000 s 388, because it had not specifically addressed each of the individual submissions that he had made to the committee. The defendant was of the view that the decisions were adequate, but that, in any event, the claimant should have brought his challenge by way of referral to the Upper Tribunal pursuant to s 67(7). The judge held that, since the jurisdiction of the Upper Tribunal was to consider the matter afresh, it had no power to require the defendant to give reasons for its decision and so had no power to remedy the particular breach of duty complained of. A reference to the Upper Tribunal was therefore not a suitable or convenient means of determining the issue between the parties. On that basis, the judge granted the application for judicial review and quashed the decision notice. The defendant appealed. *Held*, only in exceptional cases would the court entertain a claim for judicial review if there was an alternative remedy available to the applicant. The purpose of establishing the defendant to regulate the financial services industry and associated markets had been to place responsibility for ensuring the maintenance of high standards in the hands of an expert body. Therefore, it was not surprising that the statutory scheme included provision for disputes relating to decisions taken by the defendant in the exercise of its regulatory functions to be referred to an expert tribunal. The opportunity to refer an investigation that had culminated in a disputed decision notice to the Upper Tribunal for a full rehearing formed an integral part of the statutory scheme. It would have been surprising if Parliament had intended that disputes relating to the procedure adopted by the defendant should be reviewed by the courts, save in the most exceptional cases. Viewed in the context of the statutory scheme as a whole, the real issue had been whether the claimant's conduct had fallen short of what had been expected of him. To quash the decision notice and remit the matter to the committee would not have advanced the resolution of that issue but would simply have caused delay. This was not a case in which it could be said that the claimant could obtain by judicial review a remedy of real importance which had not otherwise been available to him. Accordingly, the appeal would be allowed.

   R (on the application of Willford) v Financial Services Authority [2013] EWCA Civ 677, [2013] All ER (D) 114 (Jun) (Court of Appeal: Pill, Moore-Bick and Black LJJ).

1251   Regulated activities—performance of regulated activities—Financial Services Authority—disciplinary proceedings—private hearing

See *R (on the application of Willford) v Financial Services Authority*, para 901.

1252   United Kingdom Green Investment Bank—designation

The Enterprise and Regulatory Reform (Designation of the UK Green Investment Bank) Order 2013, SI 2013/2880 (in force on 7 November 2013), designates the United Kingdom Green Investment Bank for the purposes of the Enterprise and Regulatory Reform Act 2013 ss 3–6.

FIRE AND RESCUE SERVICES

Halsbury's Laws of England (5th edn) vol 51 (2013) paras 1–200

1253   Fire and rescue services—college trading fund—revocation

The Fire Services College Trading Fund (Revocation) Order 2013, SI 2013/490 (in force on 1 April 2013), revokes the 1992 Order, SI 1992/640, so that the trading fund established by the 1992 Order ceases to exist.

1254   Fire and rescue services—inspector—appointment—Wales

The Fire and Rescue Services (Appointment of Inspector) (Wales) Order 2013, SI 2013/3155 (in force on 12 December 2013), replaces the 2011 Order, SI 2011/2721, and appoints a named individual as an inspector pursuant to the Fire and Rescue Services Act 2004 s 28(1).

1255   Fire safety—building regulations—Wales

See para 116.

1256   Fire safety—enforcement of fire safety duty—offence—defence

The defendant, who was the sole director of a company, owned a hotel. A fire on the premises was started by a guest in one of the bedrooms carelessly disposing of a lighted cigarette. The company, which was the 'responsible person' for the purposes of the Regulatory Reform (Fire Safety) Order 2005, SI 2005/1541, art 3, was charged with six offences with regard to its fire safety duties. The defendant was also charged with six offences under art 32(8). The defence case at trial was that the defendant and company had taken all reasonable precautions and had exercised all due diligence. However, in summing up the case against the defendant, the judge did not direct the jury about that defence. He concluded that, if the jury could be satisfied to the criminal standard that the defendant was guilty of neglect, connivance or consent, it could not then be open to them to conclude that he had exercised all due diligence. No point was taken as to the wording of art 32(8) or about the indictment. The company was convicted on all counts against it and the defendant was convicted of all counts against him. The defendant appealed against conviction. *Held,* the judge had expressly decided not to place the statutory defence before the jury. Before considering it, the jury would have had to be satisfied, to the criminal standard of proof, that the defendant had consented to, or connived at, the commission of the offences by the company, or that the company's offences had been attributable to his neglect. How could the jury on the one hand be sure that there had been such consent, connivance or neglect and, on the other hand, consider that the defendant could prove that he had exercised that due diligence. It was a defence which had only been available if and when the jury had been sure that there had been consent, connivance or neglect. If they had been sure of that, the issue of due diligence could not possibly arise. Article 32(8) did not create its own offence. Within art 32(3)–(7), there was no provision for a penalty for a breach of art 32(8). There were prescribed penalties for all other offences. That went to confirm that art 32(8) did not create its own offence. The defendant had been wrongly charged. So far as the company had been concerned, taking the first count, the offence was created by a combination of arts 9(1) and 32(1)(a). They had been correctly pleaded in the indictment. So far as the defendant was concerned on the associated count, the offence was created by a combination of arts 9(1) and 32(8) and it should have been so charged and particularised. That was the way indictments were drafted in practice when the Crown relied on the Health and Safety at Work etc Act 1974 s 37(1) in order to prosecute a director. It was settled law that, when an indictment was a nullity, the error was incurable and, whatever the merits, a conviction based on it could not stand. Conversely, even where there had been a material irregularity in the drafting of the indictment, where the error constituted what had been described as mislabelling, the conviction might well be safe subject to any unfairness occasioned to the defendant by reason of the error. Whether it was unsafe had to be a question of fact and degree. In the circumstances, the reference to the 2005 Order art 32(8) in the statement of offence in the counts had not rendered the indictment a nullity so far as concerned the defendant. The error in the statement of offence had been one of labelling rather than a substantive error. The indictment was not a nullity. It had been defective but the defect occasioned neither unfairness nor prejudice. Accordingly, the appeal would be dismissed.

R v Wilson [2013] EWCA Crim 1780, [2014] 1 Cr App Rep 127, [2013] All ER (D) 18 (Nov) (Court of Appeal: Gross LJ, MacDuff J and Judge Elgan Edwards). *R v Ayres* [1984] AC 447, [1984] 1 All ER 619, HL (1984 Abr para 550); and *R v Mohammed* [2004] EWCA Crim 678, [2004] All ER (D) 540 (Mar) applied.

1257   Firefighters—occupational and personal pension schemes—England

The Firefighters' Pension Scheme (Amendment) (England) Order 2013, SI 2013/703 (in force on 1 April 2013), further amends the Firefighters' Pension Scheme 1992, set out in the Firemen's Pension Scheme Order 1992, SI 1992/129, by (1) providing a different rate for pension contributions payable by members of the Firefighters' Pension Scheme that increase according to the amount of pensionable pay which the member receives; and (2) creating a new band of pensionable pay so that those firefighters who earn more than £15,000 and up to and including £21,000 will pay a lower rate than those earning more than £21,000 and up to and including £30,000.

The Firefighters' Pension Scheme (Amendment) (No 2) (England) Order SI 2013, 2013/1392 (in force on 1 July 2013), further amends the 1992 Scheme above, by (1) amending provision concerning retirement on grounds of efficiency or disablement; (2) removing the requirement for a chief fire officer to obtain the permission of the fire and rescue authority ('authority') before retiring; (3) amending the formula for the calculation of pension where a person is entitled to an ill-health award or deferred pension and benefits from the entitlement to two pensions; (4) clarifying that only pensionable service with an English authority count towards the long-service increment additional pension benefit; (5) extending additional pension benefit to cover (a) payments to reward additional skills and responsibilities outside the requirements of the firefighter member's duties under the contract of employment but which are within the wider functions of the job; (b) any additional pay received while on temporary promotion or while temporarily carrying out the duties of a higher role; and (c) any non-consolidated performance related payment; (6) amending the method of uprating additional pension benefit for the long-service increment and continuing professional development; (7) conferring on authorities a discretion to permit the commutation of a pension for a lump sum in certain cases, and requiring an authority which exercises this discretion to make a transfer into the Firefighters' Pension Fund of an amount equal to the increase in the commuted lump sum; (8) making provision in relation to a child's allowance; (9) updating provisions concerning the reckoning of service for purposes of awards; (10) amending provision relating to the calculation of average pensionable pay; (11) providing that payments which are not within the definition of pensionable pay, other than additional pension benefits payable for long service or in respect of a firefighter's continual professional development, remain pensionable only while the firefighter continues to receive them; (12) updating provision concerning aggregate pension contributions for the purposes of awards; (13) enabling the review of medical opinion where there is new evidence; (14) making changes to the appeals procedure; (15) removing a deferred member's entitlement to the early payment of a deferred pension where he has become capable of undertaking regular employment; (16) amending an authority's power to abate a firefighter member's pension; (17) requiring an authority to transfer into the Firefighters' Pension Fund an amount equal to the amount of pension paid to a person in respect of whom the authority chooses not to exercise its discretion to withdraw or abate the permitted amount of the individual's pension; and (18) amending the powers of the board of medical referees.

The Firefighters' Pension Scheme (England) (Amendment) (No 2) Order 2013, SI 2013/1393 (in force on 1 July 2013), further amends the 2006 Order, SI 2006/3432, to (1) ensure that those who took up employment as a firefighter before 6 April 2006 and were either not eligible to be a member of the Firefighters' Pension Scheme 1992, or made an election not to pay pension contributions required by that Scheme, are treated as a firefighter member of the Scheme when automatically enrolled into the Scheme; (2) clarify which pensionable service can count for the additional pension benefit: long service increment; (3) extend additional pension benefit so that it covers (a) payments to reward additional skills and responsibilities outside the requirements of the firefighter member's duties under the contract of employment but which are within the wider functions of the job; (b) any additional pay received while on temporary promotion or while temporarily carrying out the duties of a higher role; and (c) any non-consolidated performance related payment; (4) change the method of uprating additional pension benefit for the long service increment and continuing professional development from the retail price index to an index in accordance with the Pensions (Increase) Act 1971; (5) revise the definition of 'pensionable pay' to include payments which are pensionable under additional pension benefit, and provide that payments which are not within the definition of pensionable pay, or additional pension benefits payable for long service or in respect of a firefighter's continual professional development, should remain pensionable while the firefighter continues to receive them; (6) exclude additional pension benefit payments from the payments treated as final pensionable pay; (7) require a fire and rescue authority to transfer into the Firefighters' Pension Fund an amount equal to the amount of pension paid to a person in respect of whom the authority chooses not to exercise its discretion to withdraw or abate the permitted part of that individual's pension; (8) enable the board of medical referees to reconsider its decision where the parties agree that it has made a material error of fact; and (9) enable an authority to recover some or all of the expenses of the board where the appellant has withdrawn an appeal or requested the date for an interview or examination to be cancelled or postponed less that 22 working days before the date appointed.

The Firefighters' Pension Scheme (Amendment) (No 3) (England) Order 2013, SI 2013/2125 (in force on 1 October 2013), further amends the 1992 Scheme above so as to (1) provide a right for certain persons, in respect of pensions in payment and pensions which may become payable in respect of persons who have ceased to be in service or have died, to elect that any amendments made by SI 2013/1393 above which place them in a worse position do not apply to them; and (2) correct errors made in SI 2013/1393.

1258　Firefighters—occupational and personal pension schemes—Wales

The Firefighters' Pension Scheme (Wales) (Contributions) (Amendment) Order 2013, SI 2013/735 (in force on 1 April 2013), further amends the New Firefighters' Pension Scheme (Wales), set out in the 2007 Order, SI 2007/1072, so as to (1) insert the word 'percentage' to clarify the meaning of a provision amended by the Firefighters' Pension Scheme (Wales) (Contributions) (Amendment) Order 2012, SI 2012/972; (2) provide a different rate for pension contributions payable by members of the Scheme to provide a different rate for pension contributions payable by members of the Scheme which increases according to the amount of pensionable pay which the member receives; and (3) create a new band of pensionable pay so that those firefighters who earn more than £15,000 and up to an including £21,000 will pay a lower rate than those earning more than £21,000.

The Firefighters' Pension (Wales) Scheme (Contributions) (Amendment) Order 2013, SI 2013/736 (in force on 1 April 2013), further amends the Firefighters' Pension (Wales) Scheme, set out in the 1992 Order, SI 1992/129, so as to provide different rates for pension contributions payable by members of the Scheme which increase according to the amount of pensionable pay which the member receives. In addition, the order creates a new band of pensionable pay so that those firefighters who earn more than £15,000 and up and including £21,000 will pay a lower rate than those earning more than £21,000.

The Firefighters' Pension Scheme (Wales) (Amendment) Order 2013, SI 2013/1577 (in force on 1 August 2013), further amends the 2007 Order, SI 2007/1072, so as to ensure that the New Firefighters' Pension Scheme (Wales) complies with the requirements prescribed by the Pensions Act 2008 and the Occupational and Personal Pension Schemes (Automatic Enrolment) Regulations 2010, SI 2010/772, with regards to arrangements the employer must make in respect of automatic enrolment and automatic re-enrolment of a jobholder in a qualifying scheme. In addition, the order also ensures that the Scheme complies with other arrangements prescribed by the 2008 Act and the 2010 Regulations by which a jobholder or a worker can join and/or leave a qualifying pension scheme.

FISHERIES AND AQUACULTURE

Halsbury's Laws of England (5th edn) vol 51 (2013) paras 201–600

1259　Common fisheries policy—traceability requirements—labelling—England

See para 1264.

1260　Common fisheries policy—traceability requirements—labelling—Wales

See para 1265.

1261　Sea fishing—fishery limits—legislation—revocation

The Fishery Limits (Revocation) Order 2013, SI 2013/3163 (in force on 31 March 2014), revokes the Fishery Limits Order 1997, SI 1997/1750, and the Fishery Limits Order 1999, SI 1999/1741, which are superseded by the declaration of an Exclusive Economic Zone under the Marine and Coastal Access Act 2009 s 41.

FOOD AND DRINK

Halsbury's Laws of England (5th edn) vol 51 (2013) paras 601–950

Articles

For articles relating to this title please refer to the Table of Articles at the beginning of the Abridgment.

1262 Contaminants in food—England

The Contaminants in Food (England) Regulations 2013, SI 2013/2196 (in force on 31 October 2013), replace the 2010 Regulations, SI 2010/2228, so as to provide for the execution and enforcement of Commission Regulation (EC) 1881/2006, on maximum levels for contaminants in foodstuffs, and Commission Regulation (EC) 124/2009, on maximum permitted levels for certain feed additives which may occur in food. In particular, the regulations (1) provide that it is an offence to (a) place on the market specified foods containing erucic acid in excess of permitted levels; (b) place on the market certain foods containing contaminants of any kind specified, and at levels exceeding those specified, in the Commission Regulations; (c) use food containing contaminants in excess of those permitted by Regulation 1881/2006 as ingredients in the production of certain foods; (d) mix foods which contain contaminants in excess of the levels prescribed in the Commission Regulations with foods which do not; (e) mix foods to which Regulation 1881/2006 relates and which are intended for direct consumption, or as food ingredients, with foods to which that Regulation relates and which are intended to be sorted or otherwise treated prior to consumption; (f) detoxify by chemical treatment food containing mycotoxins in excess of the limits specified in Regulation 1881/2006; (g) fail to observe particular labelling requirements for certain groundnuts, other oilseeds, derived products thereof and cereals; and (h) place on the market or mix certain foods containing specified coccidiostats and histomonstats in excess of prescribed limits; (2) make provision in relation to penalties, enforcement and competent authorities; (3) apply, with modifications, specified provisions of the Food Safety Act 1990 for the purposes of the regulations; and (4) require the Food Standards Agency to review the operation and effect of the regulations and to publish a report containing the conclusions of the review. SI 1966/1073, SI 1977/691 and SI 1982/264 are revoked. SI 2013/264 is amended.

1263 Contaminants in food—Wales

The Contaminants in Food (Wales) Regulations 2013, SI 2013/2493 (in force on 31 October 2013), replace the 2010 Regulations, SI 2010/2394, and provide for the execution and enforcement of Commission Regulation (EC) 1881/2006, on maximum levels for contaminants in foodstuffs, and Commission Regulation (EC) 124/2009, on maximum permitted levels for certain feed additives which may occur in food. In particular, the regulations (1) provide that it is an offence to (a) place on the market specified foods containing erucic acid in excess of permitted levels; (b) place on the market certain foods containing contaminants of any kind specified, and at levels exceeding those specified, in the Commission Regulations; (c) use food containing contaminants in excess of those permitted by Regulation 1881/2006 as ingredients in the production of certain foods; (d) mix foods which contain contaminants in excess of the levels prescribed in the Commission Regulations with foods which do not; (e) mix foods to which Regulation 1881/2006 relates and which are intended for direct consumption, or as food ingredients, with foods to which that Regulation relates and which are intended to be sorted or otherwise treated prior to consumption; (f) detoxify by chemical treatment food containing mycotoxins in excess of the limits specified in Regulation 1881/2006; (g) fail to observe particular labelling requirements for certain groundnuts, other oilseeds, derived products thereof and cereals; and (h) place on the market or mix certain foods containing specified coccidiostats and histomonstats in excess of prescribed limits; (2) make provision in relation to penalties, enforcement and competent authorities; and (3) apply, with modifications, specified provisions of the Food Safety Act 1990 for the purposes of the regulations. SI 1966/1073, SI 1977/691 and SI 1982/264 are revoked. SI 2013/479 is amended.

1264   Fish—labelling—England

The Fish Labelling Regulations 2013, SI 2013/1768 (in force on 2 September 2013), (1) designate the Secretary of State as the competent authority (a) to draw up and publish the list of commercial designations of fish species accepted in the United Kingdom pursuant to Council Regulation (EC) 104/2000 art 4(2) on the common organisation of the markets in fishery and aquaculture products; (b) for the purposes of Commission Regulation (EC) 2065/2001 art 2(1), laying down detailed rules for the application of Regulation 104/2000 as regards informing consumers about fishery and aquaculture products; and (2) enforce in England the consumer information requirements of Regulations 104/2000 and 2065/2001, and the traceability requirements of Council Regulation (EC) 1224/2009 establishing a Community control system for ensuring compliance with the rules of the common fisheries policy, by (a) applying the Food Safety Act 1990 s 10 with modifications so that an authorised officer of an enforcement authority can serve an improvement notice on an operator who fails to comply with the consumer information requirements or traceability requirements; (b) applying s 37 with modifications so that an operator can appeal against service of an improvement notice to the First-tier Tribunal; (c) applying s 39 to enable the First-tier Tribunal to either cancel or affirm an improvement notice; (d) requiring operators to keep records of information specified in Council Regulation (EC) 1224/2009 art 58(4), and creating an offence of failure to comply with that requirement; (e) applying certain other provisions of the 1990 Act with consequential modifications; (f) providing that each food authority must execute and enforce these provisions in its area; and (g) requiring the Secretary of State to review the operation and effect of the provisions and publish a report within five years after they come into force and within every five years after that.

1265   Fish—labelling—Wales

The Fish Labelling (Wales) Regulations 2013, SI 2013/2139 (in force on 26 September 2013), enforce in Wales (1) the consumer information requirements of Council Regulation (EC) 104/2000, on the common organisation of the markets in fishery and aquaculture products; (2) Commission Regulation (EC) 2065/2001, laying down detailed rules for the application of Regulation 104/2000 as regards informing consumers about fishery and aquaculture products; and (3) the traceability requirements of Council Regulation (EC) 1224/2009, establishing a Community control system for ensuring compliance with the rules of the common fisheries policy. In particular, the regulations (a) set out the consumer information requirements and the traceability requirements; (b) apply the Food Safety Act 1990 s 10, with modifications, so that an authorised officer of an enforcement authority can serve an improvement notice on an operator who fails to comply with the consumer information requirements or traceability requirements; (c) apply s 37, with modifications, so that an operator can appeal against service of an improvement notice to a magistrates' court; (d) apply s 39 to enable the court to either cancel or affirm an improvement notice; (e) require operators to keep records of information specified in Regulation 1224/2009 art 58(4), and create an offence of failing to comply with that requirement; (f) apply certain other provisions of the 1990 Act, with consequential modifications; and (g) provide that each food authority in Wales must execute and enforce the requirements in its area.

1266   Food additives—enzymes—England

See para 1268.

1267   Food additives—enzymes—Wales

See para 1269.

1268   Food additives—general—England

The Food Additives, Flavourings, Enzymes and Extraction Solvents (England) Regulations 2013, SI 2013/2210 (in force on 31 October 2013), provide for the execution and enforcement of (1) European Parliament and Council Regulation (EC) 2065/2003, on smoke flavourings used, or intended for use, in or on foods; (2) European Parliament and Council Regulation (EC) 1332/2008, on food enzymes; (3) European Parliament and Council Regulation (EC) 1333/2008, on food additives; and (4) European Parliament and

Council Regulation (EC) 1334/2008, on flavourings and certain food ingredients with flavouring properties for use in and on foods. The regulations also implement European Parliament and Council Directive (EC) 2009/32 on extraction solvents used in the production of foodstuffs and food ingredients. In particular, the regulations (a) provide that it is an offence to contravene the European Parliament and Council Regulations, or to use or place on the market a product which contravenes specified requirements of those Regulations; (b) empower, in the case of certain types of non-compliance relating to labelling, an authorised officer of an enforcement authority to serve a compliance notice requiring specified steps to be taken; (c) create an offence of failing to comply with a compliance notice; (d) allow a person served with a compliance notice to appeal to a magistrates' court; (e) specify the circumstances in which controls on extraction solvents do not apply; (f) define what constitutes a permitted extraction solvent; (g) prohibit the use of extraction solvents, other than permitted extraction solvents, in the production of food; (h) prohibit the placing on the market of an extraction solvent which is not a permitted extraction solvent or which is not accompanied by certain information on its packaging, container or label; (i) designate the Food Standards Authority as the competent authority for the purposes of applications for authorisation of a smoke flavouring; (j) make provision in relation to penalties and enforcement; (k) provide that, where food is certified as being food which it is an offence to place on the market, it will be treated for the purposes of the Food Safety Act 1990 s 9 as failing to comply with food safety requirements; (l) apply, with modifications, specified provisions of the 1990 Act for the purposes of the regulations; and (m) require the Food Standards Agency to review the operation and effect of the regulations and to publish a report containing the conclusions of the review. SI 1993/1658, SI 2005/464, SI 2007/2266, SI 2011/258, SI 2011/1456, SI 2011/1738 and SI 2012/1155 are revoked. SI 1996/1499, SI 2009/3235 and SI 2010/2817 are amended. SI 2009/3238 is further amended.

1269   Food additives—general—Wales

The Food Additives, Flavourings, Enzymes and Extraction Solvents (Wales) Regulations 2013, SI 2013/2591 (in force on 31 October 2013), provide for the execution and enforcement of (1) European Parliament and Council Regulation (EC) 2065/2003, on smoke flavourings used, or intended for use, in or on foods; (2) European Parliament and Council Regulation (EC) 1332/2008, on food enzymes; (3) European Parliament and Council Regulation (EC) 1333/2008, on food additives; and (4) European Parliament and Council Regulation (EC) 1334/2008, on flavourings and certain food ingredients with flavouring properties for use in and on foods. The regulations also implement European Parliament and Council Directive (EC) 2009/32 on extraction solvents used in the production of foodstuffs and food ingredients. In particular, the regulations (a) provide that it is an offence to contravene the European Parliament and Council Regulations, or to use or place on the market a product which contravenes specified requirements of those Regulations; (b) empower, in the case of certain types of non-compliance relating to labelling, an authorised officer of an enforcement authority to serve a compliance notice requiring specified steps to be taken; (c) create an offence of failing to comply with a compliance notice; (d) allow a person served with a compliance notice to appeal to a magistrates' court; (e) specify the circumstances in which controls on extraction solvents do not apply; (f) define what constitutes a permitted extraction solvent; (g) prohibit the use of extraction solvents, other than permitted extraction solvents, in the production of food; (h) prohibit the placing on the market of an extraction solvent which is not a permitted extraction solvent or which is not accompanied by certain information on its packaging, container or label; (i) designate the Food Standards Authority as the competent authority for the purposes of applications for authorisation of a smoke flavouring; (j) make provision in relation to penalties and enforcement; (k) provide that, where food is certified as being food which it is an offence to place on the market, it will be treated for the purposes of the Food Safety Act 1990 s 9 as failing to comply with food safety requirements; and (l) apply, with modifications, specified provisions of the 1990 Act for the purposes of the regulations. SI 1993/1658, SI 2005/1350, SI 2007/2315, SI 2011/655, SI 2011/1450 and SI 2012/1198 are revoked. SI 1996/1499 and SI 2009/3378 are further amended. SI 2009/3377 and SI 2010/2922 are amended.

1270   Food hygiene—general—England

The Food Safety and Hygiene (England) Regulations 2013, SI 2013/2996 (in force on 31 December 2013), replace the Food Hygiene (England) Regulations 2006, SI 2006/14, and provide for the execution and enforcement of (1) European Parliament and Council Regulation (EC) 178/2002, laying down the general principles and requirements of food law, establishing the European Food Safety Authority and laying down procedures in matters of food safety; (2) European Parliament and Council Regulation (EC) 852/2004, on the approval of establishments producing sprouts; (3) European Parliament and Council Regulation (EC) 853/2004, laying down specific hygiene rules for food of animal origin; (4) European Parliament and Council Regulation (EC) 854/2004, laying down specific rules for the organisation of official controls on products of animal origin intended for human consumption; (5) Commission Regulation (EC) 2073/2005, on microbiological criteria for foodstuffs; and (6) Commission Regulation (EC) 2075/2005, laying down specific rules on official controls for Trichinella in meat. In particular, the regulations (a) create certain presumptions that, for the purposes of the regulations, specified food is intended for human consumption; (b) designate the Food Standards Agency as the competent authority, except where it has delegated competence; (c) make provision for the availability of enforcement measures against food business operators in the form of hygiene improvement notices, hygiene prohibition orders, hygiene emergency prohibition notices and orders, remedial action notices and detention notices; (d) make provision in relation to offences which arise from the act or default of some other person; (e) set out defences of due diligence and in relation to non-compliant food which is destined for export; (f) provide for the procurement and analysis of samples; (g) confer powers of entry on authorised officers of a food authority or of the Food Standards Agency; (h) create offences of obstructing an officer and contravening, or failing to comply with, specified provisions of the EC Regulations and specify penalties for offences; (i) impose a time limit for bringing prosecutions; (j) provide that, in relation to certain potential contraventions, no offence is committed if certain conditions are met; (k) make provision in relation to offences by bodies corporate; (l) set out a right of appeal against a decision of an officer of an enforcement authority to serve a hygiene improvement notice or a remedial action notice, or to refuse to issue a certificate confirming that the health risk condition no longer exists in relation to a food business; (m) apply, with a modification, the Food Safety Act 1990 s 9; (n) provide for the issue by the Secretary of State to food authorities of codes of recommended practice; (o) confer protection on enforcement officers acting in good faith; (p) provide for the revocation or suspension of the appointment or designation of specified officials; (q) provide that, where an enforcement officer has certified that any food has not been produced, processed or distributed as required, it is to be treated for the purposes of s 9 as failing to comply with food safety requirements; (r) make provision in connection with the service of documents; (s) give effect to requirements relating to (i) bulk transport in sea-going vessels of liquid oils or fats and the bulk transport by sea of raw sugar; (ii) temperature control; (iii) the direct supply by a producer of small quantities of meat from poultry or lagomorphs slaughtered on the farm; (iv) restrictions on the sale of raw milk intended for direct human consumption; and (v) the special health mark to be applied in the case of animals that have undergone emergency slaughter; (t) make a consequential amendment to the 1990 Act; and (u) require the Food Standards Agency to carry out a periodic review of the operation and effect of the regulations. SI 1998/1277, SI 1998/1284, SI 1998/1673, SI 2010/534 and SI 2012/1742 are revoked. SI 2004/3279 and SI 2009/3255 are further amended. SI 2011/1197 and SI 2013/2952 are amended.

1271   Food hygiene—general—Wales

The Food (Miscellaneous Amendments) (Wales) Regulations 2013, SI 2013/3049 (in force on 1 January 2014), (1) implement Commission Regulation (EU) 1079/2013 laying down transitional measures for the application of European Parliament and Council Regulation (EC) 853/2004 and European Parliament and Council Regulation (EC) 854/2004 by further amending the Food Hygiene (Wales) Regulations 2006, SI 2006/31, to extend transitional measures until 31 December 2016, by omitting the definition of and references to Commission Regulation (EC) 1162/2009, which is being repealed, and adding references to Regulation 1079/2013 and Commission Implementing Regulation (EU) 702/2013 on transitional measures for the application of European Parliament and Council Regulation

1303   Dangerous substances—biocidal products—fees and charges

The Biocidal Products (Fees and Charges) Regulations 2013, SI 2013/1507 (in force on 1 September 2013), make provision for the charging regime in relation to European Parliament and Council Regulation (EU) 528/2012 concerning the making available on the market and use of biocidal products. In particular, the regulations (1) make provision for the functions of a specified member state to be performed by the competent authority; (2) enable the competent authority to charge fees, at a daily rate, for work carried out within the scope of Regulation 528/2012 and the Biocidal Products (Appointment of Authorities and Enforcement) Regulations 2013, SI 2013/1506 (see para 1302), relating to applications for the authorisation and mutual recognition of biocidal products, the approval of active substances and permits and notifications under specific conditions; (3) provide for an annual charge to be paid to the competent authority by persons placing biocidal products on the market in respect of costs incurred by or on behalf of the competent authorities, associated with any work carried out within the scope of Regulation 528/2012 that cannot be attributed to an individual application; (4) require anyone liable to pay the annual charge to notify the competent authority, or a person designated by the competent authority, of certain specified information, subject to stated exceptions; and (5) omit provision that enabled fees to be charged in respect of the evaluation of biocidal product authorisation applications submitted before 1 September 2013, and allow the annual charge to be recovered in respect of the period from 1 April 2013 to 31 August 2013.

1304   Dangerous substances—notification and marking of sites

The Health and Safety (Miscellaneous Repeals, Revocations and Amendments) Regulations 2013, SI 2013/448 (in force on 6 April 2013), make repeals, revocations and amendments to legislation relating to Health and Safety using powers under the Health and Safety at Work Etc Act 1974. In particular, the regulations (1) repeal the Celluloid and Cinematograph Film Act 1922, which contained provision for the regulation of the storage of Raw Celluloid and Cinematographic film; (2) revoke the Construction (Head Protection) Regulations 1989, SI 1989/2209 and amend the Personal Protective Equipment at Work Regulations 1992, SI 1992/2966, so that all of the provisions of the latter apply to the regulation of the wearing of suitable head protection by persons engaged in construction work; (3) make amendments to the Dangerous Substances (Notification and Marking of Sites) Regulations 1990, SI 1990/304, as a consequence of the revocation of the Notification of Installations Handling Hazardous Substances Regulations 1982, SI 1981/1357, so as to bring Ammonium Nitrate and mixtures containing Ammonium Nitrate where the nitrogen content exceeds 15.75 per cent of the mixture by weight above a prescribed quantity within the ambit of the 1990 Regulations' notification regime; the amendment to the 1990 Regulations requires that dutyholders notify the fire and rescue services where such substances are kept on their premises; and (4) make amendments to the Workplace (Health, Safety and Welfare) Regulations 1992, SI 1992/3004, as a consequence of the revocation of the Shipbuilding and Ship-repairing Regulations 1960, SI 1960/1932; the effect of two provisions from the 1960 Regulations is retained by the consequential amendment so that the requirement for dutyholders to provide adequate lighting and safe access for workers on ships that are in a shipyard or harbour for the purposes of construction, repair or maintenance activities is preserved.

The Health and Safety (Miscellaneous Revocations and Amendments) Regulations 2013, SI 2013/1512 (in force in part on 1 October 2013 and in part on 6 April 2014), make revocations and amendments relating to health and safety using powers under the Health and Safety at Work etc Act 1974. In particular, the regulations (1) further amend the Health and Safety (First-aid) Regulations 1981, SI 1981/917, so as to remove the requirement for the Health and Safety Executive to approve the training and qualifications of appointed first aid personnel; (2) further amend the Work at Height Regulations 2005, SI 2005/735, so as to provide that special provision for people working at height while engaged in dock operations remain. SI 1988/1655 is revoked.

1305   Employer—breach of statutory duty—civil liability

The Health and Safety at Work etc Act 1974 (Civil Liability) (Exceptions) Regulations 2013, SI 2013/1667 (in force on 1 October 2013), (1) create a right of action in relation to a breach of the prohibition in the Employment Rights Act 1996 s 72(1) to the extent that the breach causes damage; (2) provide that new and expectant mothers, including agency workers, will continue to have a right of action in civil proceedings in relation to breaches of the Management of Health and Safety at Work Regulations 1999, SI 1999/3242, regs 16–17A to the extent that the breach causes damage; and (3) require the Secretary of State to review the regulations and publish a report setting out the conclusions of the review every five years starting from 1 October 2018. SI 2006/438 is revoked.

1306   Employer—breach of statutory duty—duty to maintain work equipment—contributory negligence

The claimant was the sole director and shareholder of the defendant company which specialised in servicing vehicles. Day-to-day management of the defendant's workshop was delegated to an experienced mechanic. While assisting the mechanic on a vehicle elevated on a hydraulic ramp, the claimant's finger was severed. He issued proceedings against the defendant seeking damages through its insurer. It was found that the defendant had been in breach of its obligations under the Provision and Use of Work Equipment Regulations 1998, SI 1998/2306, reg 5(1) to ensure that the equipment, namely the ramp, was maintained in an efficient state, in efficient working order and in good repair. The defect in the ramp's compressor had been causative of the accident and, therefore, there was primary liability on the part of the defendant. However, the judge found that the claimant, who had given no consideration to health and safety matters in the workshop, had been responsible for the breach and, therefore, 100 per cent contributorily negligent. On appeal by the claimant, *held*, where a director/claimant had paid no attention whatsoever to health and safety issues, and had abrogated his responsibilities as owner and director, he would be in breach of his duty qua director under the Companies Act 2006 s 174(2)(a). The fact that the claimant had not been a mechanic or skilled in operating a workshop, and that there had been other people who had been more closely involved in the setting up and day-to-day running of the workshop, did not mean that he could satisfy the standard required in s 174. Therefore, the claimant had been a wrongdoer and had fallen within the common law principle that a person could not derive any advantage from his own wrong. That common law proposition was applicable where the director/claimant had paid no attention whatsoever to health and safety issues and had abrogated his responsibilities as owner and director. The claimant could not assert that the defendant had not proved that it had done all that it could have done to ensure compliance when it had only been through the claimant's acts that the defendant could have acted. In the circumstances, the claimant was also the director. Although the defendant's duty under the 1998 Regulations was absolute, whereas the claimant's duty under the 2006 Act was to exercise reasonable care, skill and diligence, the damages payable by the claimant to the defendant would have been the same as those which the claimant would have been able, in principle, to recover from the defendant. In addition, the application of s 174 had not involved the piercing of the corporate veil since the breach that was relevant was breach of the different and personal duty the claimant owed to the defendant qua director under s 174. The claimant was not personally liable for breach of the absolute obligation in the 1998 Regulations reg 5(1); he was personally liable for his breach of the qualified duty to exercise reasonable care as contained in the 2006 Act s 174. Therefore, the judge's decision would be upheld, albeit for different reasons. Accordingly, the appeal would be dismissed.

Brumder v Motornet Service and Repairs Ltd [2013] EWCA Civ 195, [2013] 3 All ER 412 (Court of Appeal: Ward, Longmore and Beatson LJJ). *Boyle v Kodak Ltd* [1969] 2 All ER 439, HL; and *Ginty v Belmont Building Supplies Ltd* [1959] 1 All ER 414 applied.

1307   Employer—breach of statutory duty—safe place of work—boat used in course of employment

See *Cairns v Northern Lighthouse Board*, para 2322.

1308   Employer—breach of statutory duty—suitability of work equipment

The claimant was a professional jockey. While riding in a steeplechase at a course managed by the defendant company, his horse stumbled as it landed from jumping over a hurdle. The claimant fell and sustained a fractured pelvis and a head injury. Both the nature of the fall and the injuries were unusual. As a licensed course, the defendant had to comply with general instructions issued by the British Horseracing Authority. The claimant sought damages from the defendant, relying largely on the Provision and Use of Work Equipment Regulations 1998, SI 1998/2306, reg 4, which required work equipment to be so constructed or adapted as to be suitable for the purpose for which it was provided. The claimant contended that the hurdle had been placed too close to the perimeter railing, which was itself unyielding and insufficiently padded. The claim was dismissed although the judge held that an accident of the kind that had occurred had been possible and in that sense foreseeable and that both the hurdle and the guard rail were suitable equipment for the purpose for which they had been used or provided. He further held that the layout of the hurdle and rail were likely to be suitable if, in the view of those with knowledge and experience of racing, a layout was not thought likely to be a cause of danger. On the claimant's appeal, questions arose as to whether the judge had been correct to use the concept of reasonable foreseeability in the classic common law manner when assessing liability under the 1998 Regulations; whether the judge's use of the word 'likely' had unacceptably diluted the concept of reasonable foreseeability in any event; and (3) whether the defendant and its staff could truly be the best indication of what disposition of hurdle and fence was suitable. *Held*, a breach of the 1998 Regulations could give rise to criminal liability. On their true construction, they were to be regarded as giving rise to a form of liability which was a stricter liability than at common law. It would be wrong to dilute the liability aspect of the 1998 Regulations when questions of the degree of fault could always be taken into account in sentencing. The judge had been wrong to import the common law phrase of 'reasonable foreseeability' into reg 4, and then dismiss the claim on the basis that the way in which the claimant had been injured was very unusual. An accident of the kind that had happened to the claimant, while not at all likely, was possible and in that sense foreseeable. It was for the defendant to show that it had been due to unforeseeable circumstances beyond his control or to exceptional events, the consequences of which could not be avoided. The defendant was unable to do that. Apart from the fact that it had not pleaded such circumstances or events, it was difficult to see what unforeseeable circumstances or exceptional events could be relied on and an unusual fall could not be considered to be either. Even if it could, the circumstances of the fall could not be said to be beyond the control of the defendant. The defendant could not show that, if further precautions had been taken, the claimant would inevitably have suffered the injury that he had done. Accordingly, the appeal would be allowed.

Hide v The Steeplechase Co (Cheltenham) Ltd [2013] EWCA Civ 545, [2014] 1 All ER 405 (Court of Appeal: Longmore, McFarlane and Davis LJJ).

1309   Employer—duty of care—healthcare—sharp instruments

The Health and Safety (Sharp Instruments in Healthcare) Regulations 2013, SI 2013/645 (in force on 11 May 2013), impose duties on employers in the healthcare sector to protect employees from injuries caused by medical sharps and (1) provide that the regulations apply to both a healthcare employer and healthcare contractor; (2) confine the application of requirements imposed by the regulations on healthcare contractors to particular circumstances; (3) establish the extent to which the requirements imposed apply to a healthcare contractor, such that those requirements only apply in so far as the healthcare contractor is able to control the relevant activities of the relevant employee; (4) provide for the use and disposal of medical sharps; and (5) require (a) an employer to provide information, developed in cooperation with representatives, and training to employees at risk of injury caused by medical sharps; (b) an employer to record, investigate and take measures to prevent the recurrence of an injury to an employee caused by a medical sharp where notified; (c) an employer to take immediate steps to ensure that employees who have been exposed to a biological agent as a result of such an injury receive medical attention and treatment, and to consider providing the employee with counselling; (d) employees to notify any incident at work which results in that employee suffering an injury from a medical sharp to their employer or person responsible for health and safety; and (e) the Secretary of State to review the operation and effect of the regulations and to publish a report within five years after they come into force and within every five years after and, following a review, to consider whether the regulations should remain as they are, or be revoked or amended.

1310   Legislation—application outside Great Britain

The Health and Safety at Work etc Act 1974 (Application outside Great Britain) Order 2013, SI 2013/240 (in force on 6 April 2013), replaces the 2001 Order, SI 2001/2127, which applied the Health and Safety at Work etc Act 1974 ss 1–59, 80–82 to certain premises and activities in the territorial sea adjacent to Great Britain and to areas designated under the Continental Shelf Act 1964. In particular, the order (1) provides that the application of the prescribed provisions to certain premises or activities within the territorial sea or a designated area now extends to gas importation and storage within a gas importation and storage zone; and (2) extends the application of the prescribed provisions to underground coal gasification production in the territorial sea and to designated areas.

1311   Railways—safety

See para 1300.

1312   Reporting of injuries, diseases and dangerous occurrences

The Reporting of Injuries, Diseases and Dangerous Occurrences Regulations 2013, SI 2013/1471 (in force on 1 October 2013), which replace the 1995 Regulations, SI 1995/3163, require responsible persons to notify, and subsequently report to, relevant enforcing authorities by approved means in relation to fatal and certain non-fatal work-related accidents, specified diseases contracted by persons at work and certain specified dangerous occurrences. In particular, the regulations (1) define, with exceptions, a responsible person as the employer of an employee involved in an accident or dangerous occurrence, or diagnosed with a reportable disease, or the person controlling the place in which an accident or dangerous occurrence takes place; (2) identify reportable accidents arising out of or in connection with work and provide that specified dangerous occurrences are reportable; (3) identify diseases which are reportable in specified circumstances; (4) describe situations in which deaths, losses of consciousness or certain injuries in connection with gas are reportable by the gas worker involved in the distribution, filling, import or supply of that gas; (5) require responsible persons to keep a record of reportable incidents which contains specified particulars; (6) prohibit the disturbance of the site of a reportable incident occurring at a mine, quarry or offshore workplace until certain steps have been taken, unless such disturbance is necessary on safety grounds; (7) set out restrictions on the application of the regulations; (8) clarify that parallel requirements do not apply more than once where the same incident gives rise to more than one requirement; (9) provide that, where proceedings are brought for failing to comply with a requirement of the regulations, it is a defence to prove that the failure to comply arose from a lack of awareness of the circumstances giving rise to the requirement; (10) empower the Health and Safety Executive and, in certain circumstances, the Office of Rail Regulation to grant individual certificates of exemption from any requirement of the regulations to any person or class of persons; (11) make consequential amendments to a variety of enactments; (12) provide for the application of the regulations outside Great Britain in accordance with the provisions of the Health and Safety at Work etc Act 1974 (Application Outside Great Britain) Order 2013, SI 2013/240; and (13) require the Secretary of State to review the regulations and to publish a report containing the conclusions of the review. SI 2012/199 is revoked.

HEALTH SERVICES

Halsbury's Laws of England (5th edn) vol 54 (2008) paras 1–836

Articles

For articles relating to this title please refer to the Table of Articles at the beginning of the Abridgment.

1313   Charges—dental services—England

See paras 1315, 1339, 1340.

1314   Charges—dental services—Wales

See paras 1320, 1339, 1340.

responsibility of the group. However, the group still has responsibility for commissioning accident and emergency services for all persons if present in the group's area.

The National Health Service Commissioning Board and Clinical Commissioning Groups (Responsibilities and Standing Rules) (Amendment) Regulations 2013, SI 2013/2891 (in force in part on 16 December 2013 and in part on 1 April 2014), further amend the 2012 Regulations, SI 2012/2996, so as to (1) require NHS England and clinical commissioning groups to carry out an assessment for NHS continuing healthcare before issuing a delayed discharge notice to a local authority in respect of a patient; (2) enable NHS England and clinical commissioning groups to rely on recommendations of NHS trusts in relation to NHS continuing healthcare; (3) remove the disqualification from review panel membership in respect of persons who provide commissioning support for clinical commissioning groups, or who work for organisations which do so; (4) make provision in relation to personal health budgets and their management; (5) impose a duty on NHS England and clinical commissioning groups to be in a position to commission NHS continuing healthcare or continuing care for children by means of a personal health budget; (6) enable enforcement powers to be conferred on Monitor in relation to specified provisions of the 2012 Regulations; (7) remove the exemption previously applied to mental health services from certain obligations relating to choice; and (8) provide that, where certain requirements are satisfied, a clinical commissioning group is responsible for commissioning NHS continuing healthcare services for a person who it places in a care home or independent hospital in the area of a local health board.

1334   National Health Service—clinical negligence scheme—England

The National Health Service (Clinical Negligence Scheme) Amendment Regulations 2013, SI 2013/497 (in force on 1 April 2013), which apply in relation to England only, amend the 1996 Regulations, SI 1996/251, so as to (1) enable a number of additional bodies to be eligible to participate in the Clinical Negligence Scheme; (2) include as liabilities to which the Scheme applies certain additional liabilities incurred by sub-contractors which provide National Health Service services and certain additional liabilities incurred by certain bodies whose membership of the Scheme had been terminated as a result of insolvency; (3) enable the Secretary of State to terminate the membership of the Scheme of a member which is a non-National Health Service body and provides National Health Service services under arrangements made with the National Health Service Commissioning Board, a clinical commissioning group or a Special Health Authority with immediate effect if that member becomes insolvent or the member is no longer an eligible body; (4) permit a member to terminate its membership of the Scheme by means of seven months rather than 12 months' written notice; (5) change some of the deadlines by which notifications of payments must be made, and by which payments must be made, under the Scheme; and (6) enable the Secretary of State to agree with a member that that member can make a payment prior to terminating its membership of the Scheme determined by the Secretary of State to be sufficient to cover liabilities which have been incurred prior to its membership terminating but have not yet fallen to be met.

1335   National Health Service—commissioning services—National Health Service Commissioning Board

See para 1358.

1336   National Health Service—constitution—revision

The National Health Service (Revision of NHS Constitution—Principles) Regulations 2013, SI 2013/317 (in force on 1 April 2013), substitute the first, third, fourth and fifth guiding principles contained in the NHS Constitution.

1337   National Health Service—cross-border healthcare

The National Health Service (Cross-Border Healthcare) Regulations 2013, SI 2013/2269 (in force on 25 October 2013), implement the provisions of European Parliament and Council Directive (EU) 2011/24 on the application of patients' rights in cross-border healthcare and, in particular, (1) require the Secretary of State, in relation to England, and the Welsh Ministers, in relation to Wales, to designate a suitable person or body as national contact point; (2) require each national contact point to (a) make specified information available or accessible to patients from other member states seeking to access healthcare in England or Wales and to NHS patients seeking to obtain healthcare services in another member state; (b) co-operate with other national contact points and the EU Commission; and (c) consult organisations representing patients, health providers and insurers; (3) amend the National Health Service Act 2006 and the National Health Service (Wales) Act 2006 so as to (a) set out the conditions for reimbursement of qualifying EEA expenditure; (b) clarify which services are subject to the condition of prior authorisation; (c) provide for limitations which may be imposed on reimbursement and NHS charges which may be deducted; (d) make separate provision in relation to Iceland, Liechtenstein and Norway; and (e) make provision in relation to applications for prior authorisation, setting out when authorisation must be granted and when it may be refused; (4) require the National Health Service Commissioning Board, a clinical commissioning group or a local health board to make available to patients information about their rights and entitlements; (5) restrict the amount which may be charged to patients from other member states for the provision of certain NHS services; (6) provide for an exemption from charges for NHS healthcare provided to a person who is an insured person, or a family member of an insured person, and who is resident in a member state other than the United Kingdom but for whom the United Kingdom is the competent member state under European Parliament and Council Regulation (EC) 883/2004, on the co-ordination of social security systems; and (7) require the Secretary of State to review the operation and effect of the regulations and to publish a report containing the conclusions of the review. SI 2013/261 is amended.

The Welsh Ambulance Services National Health Service Trust (Establishment) (Amendment) Order 2013, SI 2013/2729 (in force on 22 October 2013), further amends the 1998 Order, SI 1998/678, so as to designate the Welsh Ambulance Services National Health Service Trust as the national contact point in relation to Wales for the purposes of the provision of information to patients and duties in relation to co-operation and consultation under European Parliament and Council Directive 2011/24 above.

1338   National Health Service—direct payments

The National Health Service (Direct Payments) (Repeal of Pilot Schemes Limitation) Order 2013, SI 2013/1563 (in force on 1 August 2013), repeals the National Health Service Act 2006 ss 12A(6) and 12C(1)–(4) so that direct payments for healthcare may be made available across England and not just in pilot schemes.

The National Health Service (Direct Payments) Regulations 2013, SI 2013/1617 (in force on 1 August 2013), make provision for the making of direct payments for health care to secure the provision of certain health services under the National Health Service Act 2006 by a clinical commissioning group, the National Health Service Commissioning Board, a local authority or the Secretary of State, or in the case of a clinical commissioning group or the Board, under any other enactment, and (1) specify (a) the persons to, or in respect of whom, direct payments may be made; and (b) the persons excluded from direct payments; (2) provide for the nomination of a person to receive direct payments on a patient's behalf; (3) specify the requirements in accordance with which direct payment must be made; (4) set out the requirements in relation to the preparation of a care plan for a patient; (5) provide for the provision of information, advice or support in connection with the making of a direct payment; (6) set out (a) the conditions that apply to the making of a direct payment; and (b) the conditions to be complied with by the patient and any representative or nominee; (7) make provision in relation to the amount of a direct payment; (8) provide for the monitoring and review of direct payments and the repayment, recovery and stopping of direct payments; and (9) amend the NHS Bodies and Local Authorities Partnership Arrangements Regulations 2000, SI 2000/617, providing for the making of direct payments to be an NHS function for the purposes of partnership arrangements under the 2000 Regulations. SI 2010/1000 is revoked.

The National Health Service (Direct Payments) (Amendment) Regulations 2013, SI 2013/2354 (in force on 14 October 2013), amend the principal 2013 Regulations, SI 2013/1617, above so as to require a health body to reconsider a decision (1) not to make a direct payment to a person; (2) not to include a particular service in a care plan; or (3) to reduce the amount paid by way of direct payments, and to give reasons for any decision reached on reconsideration. Provision is also made in order to allow, in very limited circumstances, an individual living in the same household, a family member or a friend to be paid to provide care using part of a patient's direct payment.

1339   National Health Service—general dental services—charges

The National Health Service (Primary Dental Services) (Miscellaneous Amendments to Charges) Regulations 2013, SI 2013/711 (in force in part on 31 March 2013 and in part on 1 April 2013), (1) amend the National Health Service (Primary Dental Services) (Miscellaneous Amendments and Transitional Provisions) Regulations 2013, SI 2013/364 (see para 1340), and the National Health Service (Charges for Drugs and Appliances), (Dental Charges) and (Travel Expenses and Remission of Charges) (Amendment) Regulations 2013, SI 2013/475 (see para 1315), so as to correct drafting errors; and (2) further amend the National Health Service (Dental Charges) Regulations 2005, SI 2005/3477, by introducing a new dental charge of £18 for an interim care course of treatment which includes certain components provided where patients are receiving treatment under a Capitation and Quality Scheme 2 Agreement. Transitional provision is also made.

See para 1340.

1340   National Health Service—general dental services—contracts

The National Health Service (Primary Dental Services) (Miscellaneous Amendments and Transitional Provisions) Regulations 2013, SI 2013/364 (in force on 1 April 2013), make amendments in consequence of the transfer of primary dental services contracts and agreements to the National Health Service Commissioning Board from primary care trusts and in consequence of the abolition of strategic health authorities and primary care trusts on the coming into force of the Health and Social Care Act 2012 ss 33 and 34. The 2013 Regulations, in particular, (1) further amend the National Health Service (General Dental Services Contracts) Regulations 2005, SI 2005/3361, so as to provide for the transfer of general dental services contracts from primary care trusts to the National Health Service Commissioning Board, the abolition of primary care trusts and as a consequence of amendments made to the National Health Service Act 2006 Pt 5 (99–114A); (2) reflect changes to the 2006 Act s 102 by the 2012 Act s 203 which provide that limited liability partnerships may enter general dental services contracts; (3) require the terms of a general dental services contract to be varied in a case where the contractor and the National Health Service Commissioning Board elect to enter into a Capitation and Quality Scheme 2 Agreement; (4) make provision relating to notice provisions specific to a contract with a limited liability partnership and to take account of limited liability partnerships; (5) reflect limited liability partnerships in patient information leaflets; and (5) make transitional provisions in respect of general dental services contracts which are transferred from primary care trusts to the National Health Service Commissioning Board; (6) further amend the National Health Service (Personal Dental Services Agreements) Regulations 2005, SI 2005/3373, so as to mirror amendments made to the General Dental Services Contracts 2005 Regulations, apart from amendments relating to changes made to the 2006 Act s 108 by the 2012 Act s 204(2)(c), (d) which substitute qualifying bodies with dental corporations, companies limited by shares and limited liability partnerships, in relation to bodies that can enter personal dental services agreements; and (7) further amend the National Health Service (Dental Charges) Regulations 2005, SI 2005/3477, so as to (a) provide for an additional charge to be known as a Band 1A charge of £17·50 which applies where an interim care course of treatment is provided to persons who receive primary dental services under the Capitation and Quality Scheme 2; and (b) set out the components of a Band 1A course of treatment.

1341   National Health Service—general medical services—contracts—prescription of drugs

The National Health Service (General Medical Services Contracts) (Prescription of Drugs etc) (Amendment) Regulations 2013, SI 2013/2194 (in force on 1 October 2013), further amend the 2004 Regulations, SI 2004/629, so as to make changes to the restrictions on the National Health Service supplying drugs for the treatment of erectile dysfunction to clarify that any such drug may also be ordered for any patient for the purpose of treating a medical condition, other than erectile dysfunction, if it is considered an appropriate treatment for that condition.

1342   National Health Service—general medical services—contracts—prescription of drugs—Wales

The National Health Service (General Medical Services Contracts) (Prescription of Drugs Etc) (Wales) (Amendment) Regulations 2013, SI 2013/683 (in force on 12 April 2013), further amend the 2004 Regulations, SI 2004/1022, so as to add further circumstances in which certain drugs may be ordered under Sch 2.

1343   National Health Service—hospital—closure—lawfulness of decision—legitimate expectation

The defendants were clinical commissioning groups which had decided to implement prior decisions to close the accident and emergency department (the 'A&E') of a particular hospital. The claimant local authority sought permission to seek judicial review of that decision, submitting that (1) the defendants had created a substantive expectation either as to the actual primary care services to be in place before closure or as to an identifiable level of such services, from which it would be an abuse of power for them to depart; and (2) any such departure comprised a proposal for a substantial variation in the provision of the health service in the claimant's area, such that the defendants had to consult the claimant under the Local Authority (Public Health, Health and Wellbeing Boards and Health Scrutiny) Regulations 2013, SI 2013/218, reg 23 before acting on it, which they had not. *Held*, it was settled law that the initial burden lay on an applicant to prove the legitimacy of his expectation. That meant that, in a claim based on a promise, the claimant had to prove the promise, and that it had been clear, unambiguous and devoid of relevant qualification. If he wished to reinforce his case by saying that he relied on the promise to his detriment, then obviously he had to prove that too. Once those elements had been proved by the claimant, the onus shifted to the authority to justify the frustration of the legitimate expectation. It was for the authority to identify any overriding interest on which it relied to justify the frustration of the expectation. It would then be a matter for the court to weigh the requirements of fairness against that interest. In the present case, the claim based on substantive or procedural legitimate expectation could not succeed. Both ways of putting the case came up against the same barrier: the requirement for the claimant to point to a promise which had been clear, unambiguous and devoid of relevant qualification, and which had been broken. The National Health Service had not promised that the A&E would remain open until all the primary care improvements in the area argued for by the claimant had been carried out; nor had it made the same promise with the alternative of yet further consultation. With regard to the claimant's second submission, the decision under challenge was not a new one. It represented the implementation of earlier decisions, which had been the subject of widespread consultation. Therefore, it had not represented a proposal for the substantial development of the health service in the area or for substantial variation in the provision of such services so as to bring the requirement under reg 23 into play. It followed that the claimant had no arguable case for judicial review, and, accordingly, the application would be dismissed.

R (on the application of Enfield LBC) v Barnet Clinical Commissioning Group [2013] EWHC 3496 (Admin), [2013] All ER (D) 279 (Nov) (Queen's Bench Division: Bean J).

1344   National Health Service—licence exemptions

The National Health Service (Licence Exemptions, etc) Regulations 2013, SI 2013/2677 (in force on 1 April 2014), make provision in relation to the licensing of providers of health care services for the purposes of the Health and Social Care Act 2012 Pt 3 Ch 3 (ss 81–114) by (1) making provision in relation to the persons to be regarded as providing a health care service for the purposes of the licensing regime established by Pt 3 Ch 3; (2) clarifying that no exemption from the requirement for providers of health care services to hold a licence to provide such services is to apply to an NHS foundation trust; (3) exempting from the requirement to hold a licence (a) NHS trusts; (b) providers of medical services under the National Health Service Act 2006 Pt 4 (ss 83–98A); (c) providers of dental services under Pt 5 (ss 99–114A); (d) for a limited period, providers of NHS Continuing Healthcare or

NHS funded nursing care; (e) persons who do not carry on an activity which requires them to be registered with the Care Quality Commission; and (f) persons whose applicable turnover for the last business year is less than £10m; and (4) providing for exemptions to be subject to conditions and to be withdrawn in certain circumstances, including where one or more of those conditions is no longer met.

1345   National Health Service—licensing and pricing

The National Health Service (Licensing and Pricing) Regulations 2013, SI 2013/2214 (in force on 5 September 2013), make provision in relation to certain matters to be prescribed for the purposes of the Health and Social Care Act 2012 Pt 3 Ch 3 (ss 81–114) and Ch 4 (ss 115–127) and, in particular, prescribe (1) percentages for the purposes of the objection percentage and the share of supply percentage; (2) which services are relevant for the purposes of the share of supply percentage; (3) how a relevant licence holder's share of supply is to be calculated; (4) how turnover is to be calculated for the purposes of s 105(4); and (5) who is a relevant provider for the purposes of ss 118, 120 and 121 and Sch 12.

1346   National Health Service—licensing criteria—approval

The National Health Service (Approval of Licensing Criteria) Order 2013, SI 2013/2960 (in force on 1 April 2013), makes provision in relation to the licensing of providers of a health care service for the purpose of the National Health Service under the Health and Social Care Act 2012 Pt 3 Ch 3 (ss 81–114).

1347   National Health Service—ophthalmic services—universal credit—Wales

The National Health Service (Welfare Reform Consequential Amendments) (Wales) Regulations 2013, SI 2013/684 (in force on 12 April 2013), further amend the National Health Service (General Ophthalmic Services) Regulations 1986, SI 1986/975, in consequence of the introduction of universal credit by the Welfare Reform Act 2012. Similar amendments are also made to the National Health Service (Optical Charges and Payments) Regulations 1997, SI 1997/818. In addition, the regulations also further amend the National Health Service (Travelling Expenses and Remission of Charges) (Wales) Regulations 2007, SI 2007/1104, as a result of the introduction of universal credit by the 2012 Act, the abolition of council tax benefit, the introduction of personal independence payment by the 2012 Act and the introduction of the armed forces independence payment by the Armed Forces and Reserve Forces (Compensation Scheme) Order 2011, SI 2011/517.

1348   National Health Service—optical charges—payments

The National Health Service (Optical Charges and Payments) Regulations 2013, SI 2013/461 (in force in part on 1 April 2013 and in part on 29 April 2013), consolidate and revoke the 1997 Regulations, SI 1997/818. In particular, the regulations (1) provide for a charge to be made for the supply of glasses or contact lenses; (2) prescribe for a voucher to be issued to an eligible person in respect of the cost of a sight test and for an ophthalmic practitioner to use that voucher in part payment of the cost of the test; (3) provide for the issue of a voucher to an eligible person in respect of the cost of supply of an optical appliance and for the supplier to use the voucher in whole or part payment of the cost of supply; (4) specify that receipt of universal credit is a ground for eligibility for a voucher during the period April to October 2013; (5) allow the issue of a replacement voucher where a voucher had been lost or destroyed; (6) set out that the Secretary of State must issue a notice of entitlement to the family of certain eligible persons; (7) provide for a voucher to be issued in respect of the replacement or repair of an optical appliance, and for the supplier to use the voucher in whole or part payment of the cost of the repair or replacement; (8) set out the circumstances in which payments to a supplier must cease and also make provision for a supplier to have a right of appeal to the First-tier Tribunal against any notice given by the Secretary of State that no further payments may be made; (9) make provision for the Secretary of State to apply to the Tribunal for a stop order and for the review of notices or stop orders; (10) allow a payment to be made to a person who paid for the supply, repair or replacement of an optical appliance despite being entitled to a voucher; (11) prescribe National Health Service trusts and National Health Service foundation trusts for the purposes of the National Health Service Act 2006 s 180(6A); and (12) make transitional provisions.

The National Health Service (Optical Charges and Payments) (Amendment) Regulations 2013, SI 2013/1856 (in force on 1 November 2013), amend the principal 2013 Regulations above so as to remove the possibility of certain claims for payment being made to the Secretary of State.

See para 1354.

1349   National Health Service—optical charges—payments—Wales

The National Health Service (Optical Charges and Payments) (Amendment) (Wales) Regulations 2013, SI 2013/543 (in force on 1 April 2013) amend the 1997 Regulations, SI 1997/818, which provide for payments to be made by means of a voucher system in respect of costs incurred by certain categories of persons in connection with sight tests and the supply, replacement and repair of optical appliances, so as to (1) make reference to an increase in the NHS sight test fees of 1 per cent; (2) increase the redemption value of a voucher issued towards the cost of replacement of a single contact lens and increase the maximum contribution by way of voucher to the cost of a repair of a frame; (3) increase the value of vouchers issued towards the cost of the supply and replacement of glasses and contact lenses, increase the additional values for vouchers for prisms, tints, photochromic lenses and special categories of appliances and increase the value of vouchers issued towards the cost of the repair and replacement of optical appliances; and (4) make transitional provision in relation to vouchers accepted or used on or before 31 March 2013.

1350   National Health Service—optical charges—Wales

See para 1347.

1351   National Health Service—performers lists—England

The National Health Service (Performers Lists) (England) Regulations 2013, SI 2013/335 (in force on 1 April 2013), replace the 2004 Regulations, SI 2004/585. Specifically, the regulations (1) require the National Health Service Commissioning Board to prepare, maintain and publish performers lists of medical, dental and ophthalmic practitioners; (2) provide for applications for inclusion in a performers list and for their consideration; (3) allow for applications for readmission after removal following a conviction where the conviction is overturned; (4) provide for decisions on applications and for the refusal of applications in certain circumstances; (5) allow for the deferral of decisions in specified circumstances; (6) set out requirements with which a practitioner on a performers list must comply; (7) provide for a practitioner's entry in a performers list to be subject to conditions and for the consequences of failure to comply with such conditions; (8) prescribe for the suspension of practitioners in certain circumstances and make provision about payments to such practitioners during the period of suspension; (9) provide for removals from performers lists and reviews and appeals; (10) make provision for notifications about decisions under the regulations; (11) provide for amendment of, or withdrawal from, performers lists; (12) set out restrictions on withdrawal from the performers lists; (13) make provision about disclosure of information; (14) make provision about medical registered practitioners; (15) specify who may perform primary medical services, primary dental services or primary ophthalmic services and that, save for specified exceptions, a practitioner must satisfy certain requirements and be included in the relevant performers list in order to do so; (16) provide for the contents of each performers list; (17) prescribe additional information to be provided by an applicant for each performers list; (18) provide for additional grounds for refusal in the case of each list to those required by head (4); (19) set out additional grounds for removal from each performers list to those set out in head (9); and (20) make provision for approval for the purposes of the ophthalmic performers list of ophthalmic medical practitioners. The regulations also make transitional and savings provisions.

1352   National Health Service—personal dental services—agreements

See para 1340.

1353   National Health Service—primary medical services—general provisions

The National Health Service (Primary Medical Services) (Miscellaneous Amendments and Transitional Provisions) Regulations 2013, SI 2013/363 (in force on 1 April 2013), further amend the National Health Service (General Medical Services Contracts) Regulations 2004, SI 2004/291, in consequence of the transfer of the General Medical Services contracts from primary care trusts to the National Health Service Commissioning Board, and the abolition of primary care trusts and their areas. Minor amendments are made as a consequence of amendments to the National Health Service Act 2006 Pt 4 (ss 83–98A) by the Health and Social Care Act 2012 s 202(1). The 2013 Regulations (1) ensure that a contractor under its contractual terms is not required to provide essential services during any period in respect of which the Care Quality Commission has suspended the contractor as a service provider; (2) provide that contracts are to contain a term requiring a contractor to be a member of a clinical commissioning group and require a contractor to appoint one individual to act on its behalf; (3) omit provisions relating to the Patient Choice Scheme; (4) provide for a new Patient Choice Extension Scheme; (5) make provision in relation to electronic prescriptions which are required as a consequence of the National Health Service information technology infrastructure changes which include the electronic system that enables the transmission of digitally signed prescriptions and prescription messages to dispensing contracts; (6) add new provisions in consequence of the newly established Special Health Authority known as Health Education England; (7) make provision in consequence of chiropodists and podiatrists and physiotherapists being able to be recorded on the register as independent prescribers; (8) provide for the abolition of local involvement networks and the establishment of Local Healthwatch organisations in accordance with the Local Government and Public Involvement in Health Act 2007 s 222(2A); (9) make provision in respect of General Medical Services Contracts which are transferred from primary care trusts to the National Health Service Commissioning Board; (10) further amend the National Health Service (Personal Medical Services Agreements) Regulations 2004, SI 2004/627, so as to mirror amendments made to the 2004 Regulations, SI 2004/291; (11) further amend the National Health Service (General Medical Services Contracts) (Prescription of Drugs etc) Regulations 2004, SI 2004/629, so as to omit the entry for Cyanocobalamin Tablets from the list of drugs that may be ordered in respect of specified persons in certain circumstances, and in respect of the circumstances in which Oseltamivir and Zanamivir may be ordered for a person as part of an antiviral distribution service as a consequence of the abolition of primary care trusts, the establishment of the National Health Service Commissioning Board and Public Health England and the public health functions of local authorities; and (12) further amend the Primary Medical Services (Sales of Goodwill and Restrictions on Sub-contracting) Regulations 2004, SI 2004/906, in consequence of the abolition of primary care trusts and strategic health authorities.

1354   National Health Service—primary ophthalmic services—general

The National Health Service (Primary Ophthalmic Services) (Miscellaneous Amendments and Transitional Provisions) Regulations 2013, SI 2013/365 (in force in part on 1 April 2013 and in part on 29 April 2013), further amend the General Ophthalmic Services Contracts Regulations 2008, SI 2008/1185, as a consequence of the transfer of functions relating to primary ophthalmic services to the National Health Service Commissioning Board from primary care trusts, and the abolition of strategic health authorities and primary care trusts. The 2013 Regulations, in particular, (1) make transitional provisions in respect of General Ophthalmic Service contracts; (2) provide that where a contractor or ophthalmic practitioner tests the sight of a patient with diabetes or glaucoma there is no longer a need to notify the patient's doctor of the test results; (3) further amend the Primary Ophthalmic Services Regulations 2008, SI 2008/1186, so as to include receipt of universal credit as a ground for eligibility for a sight test during the period April to October 2013; and (4) further amend the National Health Service (Charges for Appliances) Regulations 1974, SI 1974/284, by including reference to the National Health Service Commissioning Board.

The National Health Service (Primary Ophthalmic Services) (Miscellaneous Amendments) Regulations 2013, SI 2013/2555 (in force on 1 November 2013), further amend the 2008 Regulations, SI 2008/1186 above and the National Health Service (Optical Charges and Payments) Regulations 2013, SI 2013/461 (see para 1348), so as to extend eligibility for

NHS sight tests and payment vouchers to recipients, and certain family members of recipients, of universal credit between 1 November 2013 and 5 April 2014.

1355 National Health Service—travelling expenses—remission of charges

The National Health Service (Travel Expenses and Remission of Charges) (Amendment) Regulations 2013, SI 2013/1600 (in force in part on 1 August 2013, in part on 1 September 2013, and in part on 1 November 2013), further amend the 2003 Regulations, SI 2003/2382, so as to provide that the young students' bursary and the independent students' bursary, both paid on behalf of the Scottish Ministers by the Student Awards Agency for Scotland, are to be disregarded from the assessment of an eligible student's income when determining whether the student is entitled to benefits under the 2003 Regulations. However, if an eligible student has a student loan, that loan is to be taken into account when determining whether the student is entitled to benefits under the 2003 Regulations, unless it is a hardship loan. Further, eligible students who are paid student loans but are not in receipt of the maximum amount potentially payable to people studying on their course are treated as if they were paid that maximum amount for the purposes of determining their income when determining whether they are entitled to benefits under the 2003 Regulations. In addition, the regulations deal with amendments relating to students who are eligible for assistance from the Welsh Ministers. Maintenance grants payable by the Welsh Ministers and which are not taken into account in certain student loans calculations are to continue to be disregarded from the assessment of a student's income when determining whether they are entitled to benefits under the 2003 Regulations. The regulations also provide for persons who are in receipt of an award of universal credit for the period beginning on 1 November 2013 and ending on 5 April 2014 to be entitled to full remission of certain National Health Service charges and payment of certain NHS travel expenses without making a claim.

1356 National Health Service—travelling expenses—remission of charges—Wales

See paras 1347, 1355.

1357 National Health Service Commissioning Board—duties in relation to clinical commissioning groups—specified date

The National Health Service (General Duties of the National Health Service Commissioning Board in Relation to Clinical Commissioning Groups–Specification of Date) Order 2013, SI 2013/124 (made on 23 January 2013), specifies 31 March 2013 for the purposes of the National Health Service Act 2006 s 14A, which sets out the general duties of the National Health Service Commissioning Board in relation to clinical commissioning groups.

1358 National Health Service Commissioning Board—general provisions

The National Health Service and Public Health (Functions and Miscellaneous Provisions) Regulations 2013, SI 2013/261 (in force on 1 April 2013), provide for a range of matters relating to the functions of the National Health Service Commissioning Board and clinical commissioning groups ('CCGs'). The regulations, in particular, (1) make provision in relation to the exercise of the Secretary of State's European Union health functions by the Board and CCGs; (2) provide that certain functions of the Secretary of State in relation to the reimbursement of the cost of services provided in another EEA state and to authorisation for treatment in another member state are to be exercised by the Board; (3) impose duties on the Board as to procedures in relation to applications for reimbursement of costs of services and prior authorisation; (4) impose requirements as to the form and content of the Board's determination of such an application; (5) set out requirements on a CCG in relation to the provision of information to the Board in connection with applications made under head (3); (6) make provision in relation to notifications of birth and deaths; (7) provide that the Board, a local authority whose area includes the whole or part of a registrar of births and deaths sub-district, and any CCG whose area coincides with or includes the whole or part of the registrar's sub-district are relevant bodies to whom the registrar of births and deaths must furnish particulars of births or deaths entered in a register of births or deaths kept for the registrar's sub-district; (8) make provision for the furnishing to the relevant bodies of the particulars entered by registrars in the register of births and deaths; (9) set out the identities of the persons to

and for conditional inclusion in pharmaceutical lists, for fitness reasons; (12) provide that, where the NHSCB decides to grant an application subject to permissible fitness conditions, and these conditions are not appealed against or are upheld on appeal, the applicant has to decide within a set timetable whether he wishes to withdraw the granted application; (13) make provision for determinations as to whether an area is a controlled locality or a reserved location, and in particular by providing that such determinations may only take place once every five years unless there is a substantial change of circumstances in the intervening period, and by imposing additional requirements in relation to routine applications from retail pharmacy businesses to locate pharmacy premises in a controlled locality; (14) specify the procedure applicable to pharmaceutical list applications and related appeals; (15) provide that an NHS general practitioner who has, or whose practice has, a registered patient list may provide dispensing services only if (a) the patients to whom he could provide dispensing services have applied to him for such services; (b) he has been granted premises approval for the medical practice premises from which he wishes to dispense; and (c) he has been granted outline consent in relation to the area to whose residents he wishes to dispense; (16) authorise the delay in decisions to grant outline consent and premises approval being given effect, to allow for the processing of outstanding pharmacy applications and to mitigate the effects on other providers of pharmaceutical services locally; (17) provide that, once included on a dispensing doctor list maintained by the NHSCB and so permitted to provide dispensing services, dispensing doctors must comply with prescribed terms of service; (18) require dispensing doctors to discontinue the provision of such services if the conditions that led to the grant of their entitlement to dispense no longer apply, subject to arrangements for possible postponement of the discontinuation; (19) specify the circumstances in which outline consent and premises approval may lapse, such as where it has been more than six months since any drug or appliance was dispensed under the arrangements with the dispensing doctor; (20) outline the procedures for dealing with medical practices which relocate or amalgamate; (21) set out the conditions that are to be imposed on chemists as part of their terms of service with the NHSCB, which include requirements relating to co-operation with the NHSCB over the local resolution of disputes; (22) provide that, where a dispute between a chemist and the NHSCB cannot be resolved under the local dispute resolution procedures, the chemist faces the possibility of a breach or remedial notice, as a part of which payment may be withheld; (23) provide that, in certain cases, repeated failures to comply with terms of service, or failures with particularly serious consequences, may lead to the removal of a chemist's business premises from the relevant pharmaceutical list; (24) prescribe procedures for dealing with fitness issues of chemists on pharmaceutical lists; (25) provide that, where fitness sanctions are imposed, relevant information must be disseminated to other bodies, such as the devolved administrations and the General Pharmaceutical Council, which may need to consider taking action, and to other persons who are entitled to request the information; (26) provide for the publication of the Drug Tariff; (27) specify the Secretary of State as the determining authority for reimbursement referable to the cost of drugs and appliances, and the NHSCB as the determining authority for other remuneration; (28) link dispensing doctors' remuneration to what their entitlement is or would be under a general medical services contract; (29) make provision for overpayments and refunds of prescription charges; (30) empower the Secretary of State to make a separate determination of remuneration applicable to chemists who are suspended from a pharmaceutical list, either during an investigation or pending an appeal, for fitness reasons; (31) provide, in relation to local pharmaceutical services ('LPS') schemes, that (a) before commissioning services under the standard form of LPS scheme, the NHSCB may designate an area of a Health and Wellbeing Board, premises or descriptions of premises, which allows the deferral of routine applications for the duration of the designation, facilitating the commissioning of local pharmaceutical services at the location in question; (b) the review and cancellation of designations are subject to prescribed procedures; (c) where the NHSCB enters into the standard form of LPS scheme, the scheme is (unless the contractor objects) an NHS contract; (d) only contractors demonstrating certain fitness requirements may become parties to such schemes; (e) persons proposing to enter into such schemes must first send the NHSCB information about their fitness to be parties to them; (f) proposals for the standard form of LPS scheme that may proceed for development must be notified by the NHSCB to interested parties; (g) if a contractor, on entering into the standard form of LPS scheme, gives up a right to be on a pharmaceutical list, it may be given a right of return; (h) LPS pilot schemes may be NHS contracts in certain prescribed circumstances; and (i) unless a pilot LPS scheme terminates for a reason relating to the fitness of the provider to be a provider of pharmaceutical services, the scheme premises and the contractor are included in a pharmaceutical list; (32) allow applications for services to be made on behalf of some patients by duly authorised persons; (33) delegate certain functions of the Secretary of State to the National Health Service Litigation Authority; (34) make transitional provision dealing with the abolition of primary care trusts; and (35) make various consequential amendments and revocations.

1370   Pharmaceutical services—Wales

The National Health Service (Pharmaceutical Services) (Wales) Regulations 2013, SI 2013/898 (in force on 10 May 2013), replace the 1992 Regulations, SI 1992/662, and govern the provision of pharmaceutical services as part of the National Health Service under the National Health Service (Wales) Act 2006 Pt 7 (ss 80–103). In particular, the regulations (1) require each local health board to prepare and maintain for its area pharmaceutical lists of NHS pharmacists and NHS appliance contractors, and dispensing doctor lists of doctors, who undertake to provide pharmaceutical services from premises in the area; (2) set out the terms of service for inclusion in a pharmaceutical or dispensing doctor list, on which persons included in those lists undertake to provide pharmaceutical services as part of the NHS; (3) make provision for the determination by a local health board of whether a particular locality within its area is, by virtue of its rural nature, a controlled locality or part of a controlled locality, and for a right of appeal against any such determination; (4) set out the types of applications which may be made in respect of inclusion in or amendment to pharmaceutical lists, the tests which a local health board must apply in order to determine such applications and rights of appeal against determinations; (5) specify the applications which doctors can make in order to be able to fulfil the conditions on which they can then make arrangements with a local health board to provide pharmaceutical services to eligible patients in controlled localities, the procedures that a local health board must follow in determining such applications and rights of appeal against determinations; (6) make provision for the deferral or refusal of inclusion in a pharmaceutical list on fitness grounds as well as for conditional inclusion and removal; and (7) deal with payments to NHS pharmacists and NHS appliance contractors.

1371   Primary care trusts—abolition—consequential amendments

The Health and Social Care Act 2012 (Consequential Amendments) Order 2013, SI 2013/594 (in force on 1 April 2013), amend the Vehicle Excise and Registration Act 1994, the Education Act 1996, the Audit Commission Act 1998, the Local Government Act 2000, the Local Government and Public Involvement in Health Act 2007, and the Welfare Reform Act 2012 in consequence of the Health and Social Care Act 2012. In particular, the order (1) removes reference to primary care trusts; (2) reflects the establishment of the National Health Service Commissioning Board and clinical commissioning groups; (3) specifies those bodies as 'partner authorities'; and (4) makes clinical commissioning groups subject to the Audit Commission Act 1998.

The Health and Social Care Act 2012 (Consequential Amendments) (No 2) Order 2013, SI 2013/2341 (in force on 1 November 2013), makes minor amendments in consequence of the coming into force of the Health and Social Care Act 2012. Specifically, the order amends (1) the Disabled Persons (Services, Consultation and Representation) Act 1986, in order to reflect the fact that the provision and commissioning of health services in England is now conferred on a number of different bodies rather than the Secretary of State, and in order to clarify the way in which services are provided in Wales; (2) the Community Care (Delayed Discharges etc) Act 2003, by adding the National Health Service Commissioning Board and clinical commissioning groups to the definition of 'NHS body' for the purposes of that Act; and (3) the National Health Service Act 2006, so as to reflect the abolition of primary care trusts by the 2012 Act.

1372   Public health—local authority functions

The Local Authority (Public Health, Health and Wellbeing Boards and Health Scrutiny) Regulations 2013, SI 2013/218 (in force on 1 April 2013), make provision in relation to Health and Wellbeing Boards established under the Health and Social Care Act 2012 s 194, local authority public health functions and review and scrutiny of the local health service by local authorities. In particular, the regulations (1) modify provisions in primary legislation relating to a committee appointed under the Local Government Act 1972 s 102 in so far as those provisions relate to Health and Wellbeing Boards and provide that certain provisions do not apply to Health and Wellbeing Boards; (2) enable certain functions of Health and Wellbeing Boards to be carried out by a sub-committee of a Health and Wellbeing Board and for functions of Health and Wellbeing Boards under the 2012 Act s 196(2) to be carried out by a sub-committee of the Board or an officer of the local authority; (3) make provisions for the 1972 Act s 102(2) to apply subject to the 2012 Act s 194(2)–(9) and allow a Health and Wellbeing Board to appoint a sub-committee to advise the Board; (4) disapply the 1972 Act s 104(1) in so far as that provision relates to Health and Wellbeing Boards, a sub-committee of such a Board, or a joint-committee of two or more such Boards so as to remove the restrictions which would prevent certain local authority officers from being members of Health and Wellbeing Boards; (5) provide that head (4) does not apply in so far as it relates to the 1972 Act s 80(1)(b) and (d); (6) enable all members of Health and Wellbeing Boards to vote in a s 102 committee meeting unless the local authority directs otherwise; (7) disapply the political balance requirements as set out in the Local Government and Housing Act 1989 ss 15 and 16 and Sch 1 in so far as those provisions relate to Health and Wellbeing Boards, a sub-committee of such a Board of a joint sub-committee of two or more such Boards; (8) make provision for the weighing and measuring of children in attendance at schools under arrangements provided for by local authorities; (9) prescribe personal information relating to children participating in a weighing and measuring exercise can be disclosed to the person carrying out the weighing and measuring exercise; (10) set out the conditions subject to which children may be weighed and measured and provide that the resulting information and any personal information relating to the children concerned may be processed where those conditions are met; (11) make provision for parents to have an opportunity to opt-out their child from the National Child Measurement Programme; (12) provide that a local authority may disclose information resulting from a weighing and measuring exercise, and personal information relating to the children concerned, for the purposes of research, monitoring, audit or the planning of services or for any purpose connected with public health; (13) allow for the disclosure of information resulting from the weighing and measuring exercise about an individual child to the child's parents, or to a health professional, with a view to the information being used to help the child concerned to improve its health; (14) require local authorities to forward specified information resulting from the weighing and measuring exercise together with personal information relating to the children concerned to the Health and Social Care Information Centre; (15) provide that the information may be further processed by the Information Centre for the purposes of surveillance, research, monitoring, audit or the planning of health services and for onward disclosure to the Department of Health, local authorities or any other person, subject to certain conditions; (16) require any person carrying out functions in relation to weighing and measuring or in relation to the processing of information, to have regard to guidance issued by the Secretary of State; (17) enable a local authority to review and scrutinise matter relating to the planning, provision and operation of the health service in its area; (18) set out duties that apply where a matter is referred to a local authority by a Local Healthwatch organisation or a representative of such an organisation; (19) empower a local authority to make reports and recommendations to certain National Health Service bodies and certain providers of health services on matters reviewed or scrutinised by it and impose duties on those persons to respond where the local authority so requests; (20) enable a committee, sub-committee or other local authority to make reports and recommendations to the first local authority; (21) set out information which must be included in a report or recommendation; (22) deal with consultation of local authorities by responsible persons on proposals for substantial developments of the health service or for substantial variations in the provision of the health service; (23) set out proposals to which the duty to consult under head (22) does not apply; (24) enable the Secretary of State to give Direction to the Board and the Board to give Directions to a clinical commissioning group in relation to proposals on which the local authority has reported to the Secretary of State; (25) impose duties on responsible persons to provide a local authority with information about the planning, provision and operation of health services in the area of the authority as it may reasonably require to discharge its health scrutiny functions; (26) enable a local authority to make arrangements for the discharge of its health scrutiny functions by an overview and security committee of its or of another local authority in certain circumstances; (27) disapply, in relation to health scrutiny functions of local authorities, various provisions of the 1972 Act s 101 which relate to arrangements by a local authority for the discharge of its functions by a committee, sub-committee or officer of the authority or by another local authority; (28) enable local authorities to appoint a joint committee for the discharge of health scrutiny functions and require local authorities to do so in certain circumstances; (29) empower a county council to arrange for members of an overview and scrutiny committee of its district councils to be appointed to their own overview and scrutiny committee; and (30) enable the Secretary of State to direct local authorities to make arrangements for the discharge of their health scrutiny functions by overview and scrutiny committees, joint overview and scrutiny committees or to make arrangements for co-option. In addition, the regulations amend the Community Right to Challenge (Expressions of Interest and Excluded Services) (England) Regulations 2012, SI 2012/1313, so as to (a) set out additional services which are excluded from a right whereby certain bodies may submit an expression of interest in providing or assisting in providing services on behalf of specified authorities in the exercise of any of those relevant authorities' functions in relation to England; and (b) provide that specified services are excluded from the right only until 1 April 2014, while other services are excluded from the right from the date on which the exclusion takes effect until 1 April 2016. SI 2002/3048 is revoked.

The Local Authorities (Public Health Functions and Entry to Premises by Local Healthwatch Representatives) Regulations 2013, SI 2013/351 (in force on 1 April 2013), make provision for the steps to be taken by local authorities in exercising certain public health functions and the making and recovering of charges in respect of certain steps taken in the service of their public health functions. Specifically, the regulations (1) impose duties on local authorities to exercise prescribed public health functions of the Secretary of State and to take prescribed steps in exercise of public health functions of their own, including the duty as to the improvement of public health; (2) require local authorities to provide for the weighing and measuring of certain children in their area by reference to the age of the children and the type of school which they attend; (3) make provision for health checks, including the dissemination of information about dementia to older persons and that particular information to be recorded for every person at the time of an assessment; (4) require local authorities to provide, or make arrangements to secure the provision of open access sexual health services in their area; (5) prescribe that head (4) does not extend to offering services to those persons undergoing sterilisation or vasectomy procedures or for treating or caring for persons infected with Human Immunodeficiency Virus; (6) set out a duty on local authorities to provide or make arrangements to secure the provision of a public health advice service to any clinical commissioning group in their area, the purpose of which is to assist clinical commissioning groups in relation to their powers and duties to commission health services for the persons for whom they have responsibility; (7) impose a duty on local authorities to provide information and advice to certain persons and bodies within their area in order to promote the preparation of, or participation in, health protection arrangements against any threat to the health of the local population, including infectious disease, environmental hazards and extreme weather events; (8) make provision for a local authority to make and recover charges in respect of certain steps taken in the exercise of its duty as to health improvement; (9) specify that charges are not permitted in respect of things which are not provided at the request of, or with the agreement of the person concerned, or in respect of steps taken to improve an individual's health; (10) provide that the power does not apply in respect of anything which the local authority is required to do in exercise of its public health functions; (11) impose a duty of certain providers of health and social care services requiring them to allow authorised representatives of Local Healthwatch organisations or Local Healthwatch contractors to enter and view certain premises owned or controlled by them and to allow those authorised representatives to observe the carrying-on of certain activities on those premises; (12) set out the duty imposed on providers of health and social care services; and (13) provide that while an authorised representative is on premises owned or controlled by a services-provider, the authorised representative must not compromise the provision of care services or the privacy of or dignity of any person. SI 2008/915 is revoked.

1390   Homeless persons—duty of local authority to provide accommodation—intentional homelessness—allocation policy

A local housing authority accepted a full duty to secure that suitable accommodation was available for the occupation by the respondent under the Housing Act 1996 s 193(2) due to homelessness. The authority accepted that the respondent's father, a man in his sixties with some health problems, and the respondent's sister, aged 14, were entitled to be accommodated with the respondent under its housing duty. The family was accommodated in a three bedroom house under a private sector leasing scheme. The authority asked the family to move to two units on the same floor of a hostel separated by a few yards, with the father living separately. The respondent refused the offer as unsuitable. The authority confirmed that the offer was considered to be suitable and that its housing obligation to the respondent had come to an end. The respondent appealed on the basis that, under s 176, it was not lawful for the authority to purport to discharge its duty to secure accommodation for the respondent by providing separate accommodation for her father. The appeal was dismissed at first instance but allowed on appeal. The authority appealed. *Held*, the word 'accommodation', in itself, was neutral. It was not, in its ordinary sense, to be equated with 'unit of accommodation'. It was no abuse of language to speak of a family being 'accommodated' in two adjoining flats. The limitation, if any, had to be found in the words 'available for occupation ... together with' the other members of his family. The statutory test would be satisfied by a single unit of accommodation in which a family could live together. However, it might also be satisfied by two units of accommodation, if they were so located that they enabled the family to live 'together' in practical terms. Accommodation, whether in one unit or two, would not be 'suitable' unless it enabled the fundamental objective of the 1996 Act, which was to ensure that families could 'live together', to be achieved. It was settled law that one of the main purposes of the 1996 Act was to secure that, when accommodation was provided for a homeless person by the authority, it should be made available for all the members of his family together. Further, no specific standard of 'accommodation' had been laid down by Parliament. It had plainly, and wisely, placed no qualifying adjective before the word 'accommodation'. What was properly to be regarded as accommodation was a question of fact to be decided by the authority. On the proper construction of s 176, the original order would be restored. Accordingly, the appeal would be allowed.

Sharif v Camden LBC [2013] UKSC 10, [2013] 2 All ER 309 (Supreme Court: Lord Hope DP, Lord Walker, Lady Hale, Lord Kerr and Lord Carnwath SCJJ). Decision of Court of Appeal [2011] EWCA Civ 463, [2011] All ER (D) 221 (Apr) (2011 Abr para 1334) reversed.

1391   Homeless persons—duty of local authority to provide accommodation—priority need—person with learning difficulties—assistance from relative

The Housing Act 1996 s 189(1)(c) provides that a person who is vulnerable as a result of old age, mental illness or handicap or physical disability or other special reason, or with whom such a person resides or might reasonably be expected to reside, has a priority need for accommodation.

The claimant applied to the defendant local housing authority for housing assistance. It was common ground that the claimant suffered learning difficulties which affected his ability to cope with daily living, and that he relied on his brother for daily personal support. A reviewing officer decided that the claimant was eligible for housing assistance, but that he was not in priority need for the purposes of the 1996 Act s 189(1)(c) because he received assistance from his brother and, in a homeless situation, he would not suffer injury or detriment or be less able to fend for himself than the ordinary street homeless person. The claimant brought proceedings challenging that decision, contending that the defendant had misdirected itself in law when assessing his vulnerability by reference not just to his personal disabilities but also to the support available to him from his brother. The claim was dismissed, the judge ruling that there was nothing in s 189(1)(c) or any other statutory provision that precluded consideration of the provision by another person of support and assistance for the purpose of assessing vulnerability. The claimant appealed, submitting that the policy of the legislation was to provide support for all of the members of a household where one of them was in priority need. *Held*, the assessment process under s 189 was not a purely theoretical one, but an intensely fact-sensitive and practical one. An important part of the assessment involved a judgment as to the harm or detriment which might befall the applicant once he was made homeless. Parliament had specified the qualifying categories in s 189. Those which required only that the primary facts were established did not involve any assessment of cause and effect nor, therefore, any comparison between the ability of the applicant and the average homeless person to cope with the effects of homelessness. The distinction between the two groups was a consequence of Parliament's decision to create a presumption of priority need in some circumstances but not in others. The fact that, for some categories, no judgment of the effect of the qualifying factor on the applicant's ability to cope with homelessness was required, did not inform the question of what facts were relevant to the assessment of vulnerability in the other category. It followed that a reviewing officer was not required to make an assessment of vulnerability in isolation from the applicant's known personal circumstances. Those personal circumstances might in any case serve to emphasise the applicant's vulnerability or to demonstrate that, despite the existence of the qualifying reason, the applicant was not vulnerable. Accordingly, the appeal would be dismissed.

Hotak v Southwark LBC [2013] EWCA Civ 515, [2013] All ER (D) 172 (May) (Court of Appeal: Moore-Bick, Richards and Pitchford LJJ).

1392　　**Homeless persons—duty of local authority to provide accommodation—priority need—provision of accommodation pending review**

The claimant was an Iranian national who was granted asylum in the United Kingdom. He suffered from depression, panic attacks, insomnia and back and leg pains. The defendant local authority provided him with local housing allowance, which funded his housing with a private sector landlord. Because the claimant's landlord wished to recover a higher rent for the property, the claimant was given notice to quit. Shortly before the claimant's accommodation was to end he lodged a claim for homelessness accommodation with the defendant. In support of his application, he provided a report from his doctor stating that, due to his medical condition, the claimant was finding it difficult to cope and would need help and support with his daily needs. The claimant was interviewed by a caseworker. At the end of a relatively short interview, the caseworker printed off, signed and handed to the claimant a written decision under the Housing Act 1996 s 184. The decision informed the claimant that he was homeless and eligible for assistance, but did not have a priority need. Soon after, the claimant requested a review of that decision and, in light of the claimant's imminent homelessness, he asked the defendant to exercise its discretion to provide him with interim accommodation pending the review decision. The defendant refused the claimant's application for the exercise of discretion under s 188 to provide him with interim accommodation, and informed the claimant that its priority need decision had been referred to the defendant's review team. On review, the defendant upheld the s 184 decision. The claimant applied for judicial review of the s 184 decision rejecting him as being vulnerable and in priority need. He was granted a without notice order requiring the defendant to secure suitable accommodation for him pending determination of the claim for judicial review. It fell to be determined whether permission should be granted and whether the injunction should be continued. *Held*, the claimant had a highly arguable case for demonstrating that no inquiry under s 184 had ever been conducted and that, perversely, the inquiry was screened out by the adverse screening decision. The decision had failed to take account any of the inquires that s 184 envisaged as being required on the facts of a case such as the instant. None of those matters were considered, or sufficiently considered, by the defendant and, therefore, the clamant had good prospects of showing that the decision was flawed. If the s 184 decision was flawed and susceptible to challenge, it followed that the claimant had good prospects of showing that the defendant was in breach of its duty under s 188(1) in not providing him with interim accommodation pending the provision of a lawful s 184 decision. The claimant had provided significant additional information to the defendant following the s 184 decision, but none of that information had been assessed by appropriate inquiries. It followed that, in light of the original apparently flawed s 184 decision, the decision taken by the defendant in refusing the claimant interim accommodation pending the review was highly arguably flawed since it had made no assessment of the merits of the claimant's case that he was vulnerable on mental health and other grounds. The claimant had good prospects of success in obtaining a judicial review of the defendant's interim accommodation decision. In those circumstances, it was clear that the claimant had been correct in seeking an interim injunction requiring the defendant to provide interim accommodation. Therefore, the interim injunction would be continued until a review was available. Judgment would be given accordingly.

R (on the application of IA) v Westminster City Council [2013] EWHC 1273 (QB), [2013] All ER (D) 355 (May) (Queen's Bench Division: Judge Anthony Thornton QC).

1393   Houses in multiple occupation—excluded buildings—specified educational establishments—England

The Houses in Multiple Occupation (Specified Educational Establishments) (England) Regulations 2013, SI 2013/1601 (in force on 1 August 2013), replace the 2012 Regulations, SI 2012/249, and specify educational establishments, for the purposes of the Housing Act 2004 Sch 14 para 4, which are not houses in multiple occupation.

1394   Housing and Regeneration Act 2008—commencement

The Housing and Regeneration Act 2008 (Commencement No 3 and Transitional, Transitory and Saving Provisions) (Wales) Order 2013, SI 2013/1469, brings into force, on 10 July 2013, in relation to Wales, ss 318, 321(1) (in part) and certain repeals in Sch 16. Transitional, transitory and saving provisions are also made. For a summary of the Act, see 2008 Abr para 1712. See also the commencement table in the title STATUTES AND LEGISLATIVE PROCESS.

1395   Housing benefit

See WELFARE BENEFITS AND STATE PENSIONS.

1396   Housing renewal grants—armed forces independence payment—Wales

The Housing Renewal Grants (Amendment) (Wales) (No 2) Regulations 2013, SI 2013/3138 (in force on 29 January 2014), further amend the 1996 Regulations, SI 1996/2890, so as to deal with the impact of armed forces independence payment on means testing for receipt of disabled facilities grants. In particular, the regulations make amendments (1) concerning the reduction of assessed income to take account of child care payments; (2) concerning the entitlement to certain premiums where disabled persons or members of their household are in receipt of armed forces independence payment; and (3) to disregard armed forces independence payment in calculating income other than earnings.

1397   Housing renewal grants—general

See para 2665.

1398   Housing renewal grants—personal independence payments—Wales

The Housing Renewal Grants (Amendment) (Wales) Regulations 2013, SI 2013/552 (in force on 1 April 2013), further amend, in relation to Wales only, the 1996 Regulations, SI 1996/2890, so as to introduce personal independence payments, which replace Disability Living Allowance in respect of persons between the ages of 16 and 64.

1399   Local authority housing—accommodation for person in need of care and attention—asylum seeker—entitlement

The claimant arrived in the United Kingdom and claimed asylum because of fear of persecution in Iran on account of his sexual orientation. His claim was refused. He became homeless and, following a suicide attempt, was admitted as a patient at the mental health unit of a hospital. He was discharged from the hospital and diagnosed as suffering from depression and post-traumatic stress disorder. At the material time, the claimant was independent in all self-care needs. The defendant local authority informed the claimant that it had decided that he was not in need of care and attention for the purpose of the National Assistance Act 1948 s 21(1)(a), under which a local authority had a duty to make arrangements for providing residential accommodation for persons aged 18 or over who by reason of age, illness, disability or any other circumstances were in need of care and attention which was not otherwise available to them. However, the defendant did provide support for the claimant including weekly meetings with the care co-ordinator to monitor the claimant's condition. The claimant's application for judicial review of the decision that he was not in need of care and attention was allowed and the defendant appealed. *Held*, if the concept of care and attention were isolated from the overall context of s 21(1)(a), the term could be given an artificially wide scope and could lead to absurd results. What was involved in providing 'care and attention' had to take some colour from its association with the duty to provide residential accommodation. Clearly, it could not be confined to that species of care and attention that could only be delivered in residential accommodation of a specialised kind but the fact that accommodation had to be provided for those who were deemed to need care and attention strongly indicated that something well beyond mere monitoring of an individual's condition was required. In the circumstances, the defendant's assessment could not be regarded as irrational. It had been entitled to take the view that it had taken and, accordingly, the appeal would be allowed.

R (on the application of L) v Westminster City Council [2013] UKSC 27, [2013] 1 WLR 1445, [2013] All ER (D) 94 (May) (Supreme Court: Lord Neuberger P, Lady Hale, Lord Mance, Lord Kerr and Lord Carnwath SCJJ). Decision of Court of Appeal [2011] EWCA Civ 954, [2012] 1 All ER 935 (2011 Abr para 1346) reversed.

1400   Local authority housing—right to transfer from local authority landlord—England

The Housing (Right to Transfer from a Local Authority Landlord) (England) Regulations 2013, SI 2013/2898 (in force on 5 December 2013), set out the procedure which must be followed where a tenant group wishes to serve a notice on an authority proposing that it should dispose of particular land used for housing purposes to a private registered provider of social housing. In particular, the regulations (1) require authorities to have regard to guidance given by the Secretary of State; (2) set out the conditions which a tenant group must satisfy in order to be eligible to serve a proposal notice; (3) prescribe the contents of proposal notices; (4) provide for the agreement of extensions of time; (5) require any communication under the regulations to be in writing; (6) enable an arbitrator to be appointed by agreement between an authority and a tenant group or, in default of such agreement, by the Secretary of State; (7) make provision in relation to the service, acceptance and rejection of proposal notices; (8) enable an authority to request a determination from the Secretary of State as to whether a proposed transfer will have a significant detrimental effect on the provision of housing services or regeneration in the authority's area; (9) make provision for the carrying out of feasibility studies and set out authorities' duties in relation to such studies; (10) require an authority to enter into, and agree a timetable for, a development stage once a feasibility study has been accepted, or found by an adjudicator to have been wrongly rejected; (11) require an authority to consult with tenants and to ballot secure and introductory tenants as to whether a transfer should proceed; (12) provide that a transfer may only proceed with the consent of the Secretary of State; and (13) set out the procedure which must be followed where a determination is sought from the Secretary of State.

1401   Mobile Homes (Wales) Act 2013

See para 1670.

1402   Prevention of Social Housing Fraud Act 2013

The Prevention of Social Housing Fraud Act 2013 creates offences and makes other provision relating to subletting and parting with the possession of social housing, and makes provision about the investigation of social housing fraud. The Act received the royal assent on 31 January 2013 and came into force in part on that day. The remaining provisions came into force in relation to England on 15 October 2013, and in relation to Wales on 5 November 2013: SI 2013/2622, SI 2013/2861. For details of commencement, see the commencement table in the title STATUTES AND LEGISLATIVE PROCESS.

Section 1 makes it an offence for a tenant to sublet the whole or part of a dwelling house let under a secure tenancy in breach of an express or implied term of the tenancy, while ceasing to occupy the dwelling house, where the tenant either knows that the conduct is in breach of the tenancy or acts with dishonesty. Section 2 creates equivalent offences in the case of a tenant of an assured tenancy under which the landlord is a private registered provider of social housing or a registered social landlord and which is not a shared ownership lease. Proceedings for an offence created by s 1 or 2 not including dishonesty, which are summary-only offences, may be brought within six months of the date on which

refugee status and it was proposed that such an application should be refused, the requirement to co-operate with an applicant imposed on a member state by art 4(1) required the administrative authorities of the member state to supply the applicant with the results of such an assessment before a decision was finally made so as to enable him to address those aspects of the proposed decision that suggested a negative result. *Held,* the requirement that the member state co-operate with an applicant for asylum could not be interpreted as meaning that, where a foreign national requested subsidiary protection status after he had been refused refugee status and the competent national authority was minded to reject the second application, the authority was obliged to inform the applicant that it proposed to reject his application and notify him of the arguments on which it intended to base its rejection, so as to enable him to make known his views in that regard. However, in the case of a system such as that established by Irish legislation, a feature of which was that there were two separate procedures, one after the other, for examining applications for refugee status and applications for subsidiary protection, it was for the national court to ensure observance of the applicant's fundamental rights and of the right to be heard in the sense that the applicant should be able to make known his views before the adoption of any decision that did not grant the protection requested. In such a system, the fact that the applicant had already been heard when his application for refugee status had been examined did not mean that such procedural requirement might be dispensed with in the procedure relating to the application for subsidiary protection.

Case C-277/11 *MM v Minister for Justice, Equality and Law Reform, Ireland* [2012] All ER (D) 284 (Nov) (ECJ: First Chamber).

1406   Asylum—appeal—legitimate need to control immigration—appellant's right to private and family life

The appellant and his wife were both citizens of the Republic of Congo. He entered the United Kingdom illegally and was granted temporary admission. His subsequent claim for asylum, along with his wife's, was refused. The wife's appeal under the European Convention on Human Rights art 8 was dismissed while the appellant's appeal against the refusal of his asylum claim was refused. Later, the appellant submitted further representations which asserted that there had been a change in circumstances because the family unit had been in the United Kingdom for several years and had established a family and private life which should be respected under art 8. The defendant stated that the representations did not qualify the appellant for asylum or humanitarian protection and he did not merit a grant of limited leave to enter or remain in the United Kingdom. The decision letter found that the appellant had established a private life and a family life in the United Kingdom and that his removal would interfere with that. However, it concluded that interference would be in accordance with the law and in pursuit of the legitimate aim of maintaining effective immigration control. In considering the proportionality of the interference, the decision referred to the family's unlawful residence and the fact that the appellant and his wife had established their family life in the United Kingdom in the full knowledge that they both had no legal right to reside in the United Kingdom and could be removed at any time. The conclusion was that there was no evidence of any family ties in the United Kingdom other than the wife and children, who would be removed to the Republic of Congo with him, thus preserving family life. Therefore, the application was dismissed. The appellant appealed. *Held,* there had not been a failure by the defendant to consider the best interests of the children in the art 8 proportionality exercise. The status of well-being of the children as a primary consideration did not require the defendant in every case to consider the children's best interests first and then to address other considerations which might outweigh those interests. There was nothing that barred the official who acted for the defendant from considering the various issues, including the proportionality exercise under art 8, before drafting the decision letter. It was important to read the decision letter as a whole and to analyse the substance of the decision. It was a misreading of the letter to assert that the defendant had made a decision on proportionality before addressing the well being of the children. The consideration of the children's best interests had been, as the decision had stated, a primary consideration in the proportionality exercise. Further, there was nothing wrong with a template decision letter that provided for the statement of the defendant's conclusion to be followed by her reasoning, What was important was that the interests of the children had to be at the forefront of the decision-makers' mind. In the circumstances, there was no lack of clarity in the defendant's findings on the children's best interests or any indication that there had not been a careful examination of those interests. The decision letter had set out the defendant's conclusions briefly, but that did not give rise to an inference that there had not been careful consideration. It was not necessary for the defendant to record and deal with every piece of evidence in her decision letter. There was not such a strong case for the children that their interest in remaining in the United Kingdom could have outweighed the considerations on which the decision-maker had relied in striking the balance in the proportionality exercise. Accordingly, the appeal would be dismissed.

Zoumbas v Secretary of State for the Home Department [2013] UKSC 74, [2014] 1 All ER 638 (Supreme Court: Lady Hale DP, Lord Kerr, Lord Reed, Lord Toulson and Lord Hodge SCJJ). *ZH (Tanzania) v Secretary of State for the Home Department* [2011] UKSC 4, [2011] 2 AC 166, [2011] 2 All ER 783 (2011 Abr para 1480); and *HH v Deputy Prosecutor of the Italian Republic, Genoa; PH v Deputy Prosecutor of the Italian Republic, Genoa; F-K (FC) v Polish Judicial Authority* [2012] UKSC 25, [2013] 1 AC 338, [2012] 4 All ER 539 (2012 Abr para 1209) applied.

1407　Asylum—appeal—member state responsible—safe third country—unaccompanied minors

The first applicant, an Eritrean national, arrived in the United Kingdom and lodged an application for asylum. Having established that she had already lodged an application for asylum in Italy, the United Kingdom authorities requested the Italian authorities to take the first applicant back in accordance with Council Regulation (EC) 343/2003 (establishing the criteria and mechanisms for determining the member state responsible for examining an asylum application lodged in one of the member states by a third-country national). The Italian authorities agreed to do so but the first applicant was not transferred to Italy and she challenged the legality of the transfer. The Home Secretary decided, pursuant to art (2), to examine the first applicant's application for asylum and she was subsequently granted refugee status. The Home Secretary invited the first applicant to withdraw her action but she declined to do so. The second applicant, also an Eritrean national, arrived in the United Kingdom and lodged an application for asylum. Having established that the second applicant had already lodged an application for asylum in Italy, the United Kingdom authorities requested the Italian authorities to take her back, which they agreed to do. The second applicant was transferred to Italy. She brought an action before the High Court challenging the legality of her transfer to Italy. Following a decision taken by the High Court, the second applicant was able to return to the United Kingdom. The Home Secretary subsequently decided, pursuant to art 3(2), to examine the application for asylum lodged by the second applicant. She was granted refugee status, but declined to withdraw her action. The third applicant, an Iraqi national, arrived in the United Kingdom and claimed asylum. Since the third applicant had acknowledged that he had already lodged an asylum application in the Netherlands, the Netherlands authorities were requested to take him back, which they agreed to do. The Home Secretary ordered that the third applicant be transferred to the Netherlands but, after the third applicant brought an action before the High Court, it was decided not to carry out the transfer. The Home Secretary had since agreed to examine the third applicant's application for asylum on the basis of art 3(2). The High Court dismissed the applications. On the applicants' appeals, a question arose as to the interpretation of art 6(2) on the criteria and mechanisms for determining the member state responsible for examining an asylum application lodged in one of the member states by a third country. *Held*, in interpreting a provision of European Union law it was necessary to consider not only its wording, but also the context in which it occurred and the objectives pursued by the rules of which it was part. With regard to the context of art 6(2), it should be noted that the expression 'first lodged his application' used in art 5(2) had not been repeated in art 6(2). Further, art 6 referred to the member state 'where the minor has lodged his application for asylum', whereas art 13 expressly stated that the first member state with which the application for asylum was lodged was to be responsible for examining it. Assuming that the EU legislature had intended to designate, in art 6(2), the first member state as responsible, that would have been expressed in the same precise terms as in art 13. Further, art 6(2) should also be interpreted in light of its objective, which was to focus particularly on unaccompanied minors, as well as in light of the main objective, which was to guarantee effective access to an assessment of the applicant's refugee status. Since unaccompanied minors formed a category of particularly vulnerable persons, it was important not to prolong more than was strictly necessary the procedure for determining the member state responsible, which meant that, as a rule, unaccompanied minors should not be transferred to another member state. Article 6(2) could not be interpreted in such a way that it disregarded the fundamental rights set out in the Charter of Fundamental Rights of the European Union art 24(2), whereby in all actions relating to children the child's best interests were to be a primary consideration. Regulation 343/2003 art 6(2) should be interpreted as meaning that, where an unaccompanied minor with no member of his family legally present in the territory of a member state had lodged asylum applications in more than one member state, the member state in which that minor was present after having lodged an asylum application there was to be designated the member state responsible.

Case C-648/11 *R (on the application of MA v Secretary of State for the Home Department* [2014] All ER (EC) 181 (ECJ: Fourth Chamber).

1408 Asylum—appeal—remittal—adverse findings of credibility

The appellants were citizens of Zimbabwe whose applications for asylum had been rejected on the basis that they were not credible witnesses. They appealed. Determination of their appeals was stayed pending the decision of the Supreme Court in *RT (Zimbabwe) v Secretary of State for the Home Department*. The core decision in *RT* was to the effect that there was no basis for treating differently a person who had no political beliefs, but who, in order to avoid persecution, would be obliged to pretend that he did, from a person who did have active political beliefs and who, in order to avoid persecution, would be obliged to conceal them. *Held*, a finding of lack of credibility was capable of being of real relevance in deciding whether an appeal should be remitted. There was not in itself any unfairness, conspicuous or otherwise, such as justified a refusal to remit because the appeal would be decided, on remittal, in the light of the restated country guidance. In making the decision whether to remit an appeal, it was appropriate to ask whether, on the then current evidence and findings, the appeal in question would in any event be bound to succeed and, even if it would not be bound to succeed, to ask whether it would be unjust in all the circumstances to remit. Accordingly, applying those principles and those laid down in *RT* to the circumstances of each appellant, the appeals would be remitted for redetermination.

SS (Zimbabwe) v Secretary of State for the Home Department [2013] EWCA Civ 237, [2013] All ER (D) 266 (Mar) (Court of Appeal: Pill and Davis LJJ and Warren J). *RT (Zimbabwe) v Secretary of State for the Home Department; KM (Zimbabwe) v Secretary of State for the Home Department* [2012] UKSC 38, [2013] 1 AC 152, [2012] 4 All ER 843 (2012 Abr para 1421) applied.

1409 Asylum—application—priority to applicants of specified nationalities— compatibility with EU law

On a reference for a preliminary ruling in appeals against the dismissal of asylum applications made by Nigerian nationals in Ireland, it has been held that Council Directive (EC) 2005/85 art 23(3), (4) on minimum standards on procedures in member states for granting and withdrawing refugee status does not preclude a member state from examining by way of prioritised or accelerated procedure, in compliance with the basic principles and guarantees set out in Ch II (arts 6–22), certain categories of asylum applications defined on the basis of the criterion of the nationality or country of origin of the applicant.

Case C-175/11 *HID v Refugee Applications Comr* [2013] 2 CMLR 809, [2013] All ER (D) 74 (Feb) (ECJ: Second Chamber).

1410 Asylum—application—withdrawal—member state responsible

The applicants were a mother and her two children who had arrived in Sweden from their native Kosovo and claimed asylum. As the applicants possessed a valid French visa, the defendant migration board decided that, pursuant to Council Regulation (EC) 343/2003 art 9(2), France was the member state responsible for examining the asylum applications. The defendant therefore requested the French authorities to take charge of the applicants under art 16(1)(a). Before the French authorities had replied to the request, the applicants withdrew their asylum applications and sought permission to reside in Sweden on the ground that the first applicant was married to a Swedish national. The French authorities were not alerted to that development, and, in due course, accepted responsibility for the applicants. The defendant subsequently refused the applications for residence permits and asylum and decided to transfer the applicants to France pursuant to art 19. The applicants brought proceedings challenging that decision. The Swedish court allowed the claim, ruling that, at the time of the decision, the conditions for applying Regulation 343/2003 had not been met since the applicants had withdrawn their asylum applications. On the defendant's appeal, a preliminary ruling was sought as to whether Regulation 343/2003 had any application in such circumstances. *Held*, the European Union legislature had not expressly ruled on the situation of where an asylum seeker had withdrawn his sole asylum application without having also lodged an asylum application in at least one other state. Although arts 4(5) and 16(3) determined, in principle exhaustively, the situations in which the obligations on the member state responsible for examining an asylum application to take charge of or take back an applicant who had lodged an asylum application in another member state might cease, and although art 5(2) stipulated that the responsible member state was to be determined on the basis of the situation obtaining when the asylum seeker first lodged his application with a member state, those provisions presupposed the existence of an asylum application which the responsible member state had to examine, was in the process of examining or on which it had already taken a decision. It followed that the withdrawal of an asylum application within the terms of art 2, which had occurred before the member state responsible for examining that application had agreed to take charge of the applicant, had the effect that Regulation 343/2003 could no longer be applicable and it was for the member state within the territory of which the application had been lodged to take the decisions required as a result of that withdrawal.

Case C-620/10 *Migrationsverket v Kastrati* [2013] 1 WLR 1 (ECJ: Fourth Chamber).

1411   Asylum—asylum seeker—assessment of age—local authority—duty to provide
          assistance

See R (*on the application of Kadri*) *v Birmingham City Council*, para 184.

1412   Asylum—asylum seeker—country guidance—status of United Nations Refugee
          Agency report

In the first of two appeals, it fell to be determined whether the level of indiscriminate violence in the five central governorates of Iraq had created such a risk of serious harm as to confer a right of humanitarian protection pursuant to Council Directive (EC) 2004/83 (on minimum standards for the qualification and status of third country nationals or stateless persons as refugees or as persons who otherwise need international protection and the content of the protection granted) art 15(c). In the second appeal, it fell to be considered whether, even if there was a real risk of serious harm in parts of Iraq controlled by the government in Baghdad there could be relocation to other parts of Iraq. The second appeal was determined before the first, which relied on the findings in the second appeal in relation to country guidance with respect to humanitarian protection. *Held*, there was no justification for conferring a presumptively binding status on United Nations Refugee Agency reports merely because of their source. The court had to assess all the evidence affording such weight to different pieces of evidence as it saw fit. No principle of international or domestic law dictated any different approach. It was settled law that the considerable respect which the courts had afforded the report was entirely consistent with the conventional view that questions of weight were for the court. Further, there had been evidence that a sponsor was not required in order to register with the local security office, certainly not in all circumstances. Even if a sponsor had been required, the evidence had suggested that, in practice, it was of little significance. In practical terms, it might fairly be said that residence could be effected without a sponsor. There was some confusion resulting from the way in which the Upper Tribunal had summarised its conclusions on the issue of relocation. However, looking at the decision as a whole, the Upper Tribunal had been entitled to conclude that, in general, relocation was possible in a different part of Iraq. Even if there was any formal requirement for a sponsor, it was not likely to pose any practical difficulties. Where sponsors were necessary, they could readily be found, and it was very exceptional for anyone to be removed from the region if they could not. It would have been necessary for the court to consider whether the appellants would have been at risk on return if the return had been feasible. However, the Upper Tribunal had not been required to ask itself the hypothetical question of what would have happened on return if that had simply not been possible for one reason or another. Therefore, there had been no obligation on the Upper Tribunal to determine the issue of the European Convention on Human Rights art 3 status. Accordingly, the appeals would be dismissed.

HF (Iraq) v Secretary of State for the Home Department [2013] EWCA Civ 1276, [2013] All ER (D) 275 (Oct) (Court of Appeal: Maurice Kay VP, Elias and Fulford LJJ).

1413   Asylum—asylum seeker—detention—determination of age

The appellant, an Afghan national, arrived in the United Kingdom concealed in a lorry. On his arrest, he said that he was aged 14 and claimed asylum. Local authority social workers carried out an age assessment and concluded that the appellant was aged over 19. That conclusion was reported to the respondent. In turn, the appellant was granted temporary admission and released from immigration detention. His asylum claim was refused and the respondent made a decision to remove him as an illegal entrant. The First-tier Tribunal dismissed the appellant's appeal, the immigration judge being satisfied that he was aged over 18. Soon after, the appellant's solicitors alleged that the original age assessment had not complied with *R (on the application of B) v Merton LBC*. There was a period of delay in carrying out a fresh age assessment. Meanwhile, the appellant was detained under the Immigration Act 1971 Sch 2 para 16 and removal directions were set. The appellant issued proceedings seeking to bring an application for judicial review. A fresh age assessment, which stated that it was in accordance with *Merton* guidance, accepted that the appellant was aged 17. That assessment was accepted by the respondent. The appellant, by consent, withdrew his application for permission to apply for judicial review on terms that the local authority agreed to treat him as a child under the Children Act 1989. The application for judicial review continued as against the respondent, but was dismissed. The appellant was granted permission to appeal on the ground that it was arguable that the lawfulness of the respondent's decision should be assessed on the basis that, whatever the understanding at the time, the appellant had been a child and should have been treated as such, including not being removed from the United Kingdom and not being detained pending removal. The appeal was dismissed. It was found that the application of the Borders, Citizenship and Immigration Act 2009 s 55 did not depend on whether the appellant had subsequently been found to be a child but on whether the statutory detention power had permitted his detention at the time it had taken place. The appellant's detention had been in accordance with those provisions. He had been in law an adult and outside the reach of s 55. On his further appeal, *held*, s 55 and the 1989 Act s 20 contained the same definition of children, but their structure and language were very different. Under the 2009 Act s 55, the respondent had a direct and a vicarious responsibility. She had direct responsibility under s 55(1) for making arrangements for a specified purpose, namely to see that immigration functions were discharged in a way which had regard to the need to safeguard and promote the welfare of children. She had a vicarious responsibility for any failure by an immigration officer to have regard to the guidance given by the respondent or to the welfare principle. In order to safeguard and promote the welfare of children, the respondent had to establish proper systems for arriving at a reliable assessment of a person's age. Section 55 was not inconsistent with the European Convention on Human Rights art 5. The arrangements made by the respondent under s 55 included the published policies. In the circumstances, there had been no breach of s 55. There was no basis for finding that there had been a failure by any official to follow the relevant guidance. Therefore, the exercise of the detention power under the 1971 Act had not been unlawful. Accordingly, the appeal would be dismissed.

R (on the application of AA) v Secretary of State for the Home Department [2013] UKSC 49, [2013] All ER (D) 117 (Jul) (Supreme Court: Lord Neuberger P, Lord Clarke, Lord Wilson, Lord Carnwath and Lord Toulson SCJJ). *AAM (a child acting by his litigation friend, FJ) v Secretary of State for the Home Department* [2012] EWHC 2567 (QB), [2012] All ER (D) 175 (Sep) disapproved. Decision of Court of Appeal [2012] EWCA Civ 1383, [2012] All ER (D) 296 (Oct) affirmed.

1414   Asylum—asylum seeker—detention—non-suspensive appeals process

The claimant was a Jamaican national. He came to the United Kingdom but overstayed his one-month visa and claimed asylum on the ground that he had suffered persecution in

Jamaica as he was a homosexual. Following his initial interview, the claimant was detained by the defendant Secretary of State under the non-suspensive appeals process. The claimant's asylum claim was dismissed as the defendant did not consider the claimant was a homosexual. The claimant appealed. He remained in detention as his appeal was allocated to the fast-track process. While he was in detention, the claimant applied for judicial review of the decision to include Jamaica in the designated list of countries contained in the Nationality, Immigration and Asylum Act 2002 s 94(4) and of the decision to detain him. On the day the claimant's appeal was due to be heard, the decision was taken to take his appeal out of the fast-track process and he was released from detention. At the hearing, it was common ground that Jamaica was a deeply homophobic society and that homosexuals were routinely reviled and attacked with no protection from the authorities. The defendant contended that, as the lesbian, gay, bisexual and transgender people in Jamaica represented a small minority of the population, it could not properly be said that there was in general in Jamaica no serious risk of persecution of persons entitled to reside there. In respect of the designation decision, the judge found that it could not be said that no reasonable person could have failed to find that the risk of persecution affected such a significant proportion of the population as to be 'serious' within the meaning of s 94(5)(a) and the claim failed. It was also found that the claimant's detention had been lawful. The claimant appealed. *Held*, Moore-Bick LJ dissenting in part in respect of the designation decision, the proper approach for the defendant in considering the inclusion of Jamaica in the list in s 94(4) would have been to assume a figure at the top of the postulated range. Therefore, ten per cent of the population had to be taken to be at risk. Bearing in mind the proportion of the populace affected, the fact that the entirety of that sector was at risk and the failure of the state to offer sufficient protection, even making full allowance for the margin of appreciation to be afforded to the defendant, she had not been entitled to conclude that there was in general in Jamaica no serious risk of persecution of persons entitled to reside there. A state in which there was a serious risk of persecution for an entire section of the community, defined by sexual orientation and substantial in numbers, was not a state where there was no general risk of persecution. It did not follow from the absence of risk to the much larger heterosexual community that, in general, there was no serious risk in the terms of s 94(5)(a) where an entire section of the community of significant size and defined by its immutable characteristics, was at serious risk of systematic persecution. In the circumstances, the interviewing officer at the initial interview had made no attempt by means of supplementary questions to ensure that the kind of detailed assessment required by the defendant's policy had been carried out. Therefore, the defendant had not complied with her own policy. Furthermore, it should have been obvious to anyone who considered the claimant's claim with care that the decision had not been a simple one because of the difficulty of ascertaining where the truth lay. No reasonable person could have been satisfied at the time of the claimant's detention that a fair and sustainable determination of his claim could have been made within a period of two weeks. Accordingly, the appeal would be allowed.

R (on the application of JB (Jamaica)) v Secretary of State for the Home Department [2013] EWCA Civ 666, [2014] 2 All ER 91 (Court of Appeal: Pill, Moore-Bick and Black LJJ). Decision of Nicholas Paines QC [2012] EWHC 1660 (Admin), [2012] All ER (D) 237 (May) (2012 Abr para 1415) reversed.

1415　Asylum—asylum seeker—removal to safe third country—prohibition on removal on humanitarian grounds

Council Regulation (EC) 343/2003 art 15(1) provides that any member state, even where it is not responsible under the criteria set out in the Regulation, may bring together family members, as well as other dependent relatives, on humanitarian grounds, and in this case that member state must, at the request of another member state, examine the application for asylum of the person concerned. In cases in which the person concerned is dependent on the assistance of the other on account of a new-born child, serious illness or severe handicap, member states should normally keep or bring together the asylum seeker with another relative present in the territory of one of the member states: art 15(2).

The applicant, a third country national, entered Poland and applied for asylum there. Before her application had been determined, the applicant travelled to Austria and joined her son, who had refugee status there, along with his spouse and their children. She then lodged an application for asylum in Austria. The Austrian authorities accepted that the applicant's daughter-in-law was dependent on her because the daughter-in-law had a new-born baby and suffered from a serious illness and handicap. However, they took the view that Poland was responsible for examining the applicant's asylum application and the Polish authorities agreed to take her back without making a request to the Austrian authorities. The Austrian authorities rejected her application for asylum. It fell to be determined whether a member state which was not the member state primarily responsible under the criteria set out in Council Regulation (EC) 343/2003, but was a member state where the applicant had a daughter-in-law and grandchildren who were in need of care which the applicant was willing and able to give, could automatically become the responsible state on humanitarian grounds and, if so, whether that remained the case where the first member state had not made a request pursuant to art 15(1). *Held*, while art 15(1) afforded the member states extensive discretion with regard to deciding to 'bring together' family members and other dependent relatives on humanitarian grounds, art 15(2) restricted that power in such a way that, where the relevant conditions were satisfied, the member states 'normally keep together' the asylum seeker and another member of his family. The objective of art 15(2) of bringing together family members where necessary on humanitarian grounds was attained both where the asylum seeker was dependent on a relative present in the second member state and, conversely, where that relative was dependent on the asylum seeker. Unlike art 15(1), which referred to 'family members', a term defined in art 2(i) which did not cover a daughter-in-law or grandchildren, art 15(2) referred to 'another relative'. Taking into account the humanitarian purpose of art 15(2), the concept of 'other relatives' referred to in art 15(2) was necessarily wider than 'family members', and included a relative with whom the asylum seeker had family ties and was a person to whom the asylum seeker could actually provide assistance. A member state could derogate from the obligation to 'normally' keep together the asylum seeker and other relative only if an exceptional situation had arisen, so that where dependency under art 15(2) was established, the member state became responsible for examining the application for asylum. Once such a situation of dependence had been proven, the responsible authorities could not ignore its existence, so the making of a request by the first member state became redundant. In those circumstances, the second member state would have become the responsible member state and so would have to inform the member state previously responsible.

Case C-245/11 *K v Bundesasylamt* [2013] 1 WLR 833, [2012] All ER (D) 137 (Nov) (ECJ: Grand Chamber).

1416 Asylum—asylum seeker—victim of human trafficking—identification of victims

See *R (on the application of Atamewan) v Secretary of State for the Home Department*, para 2169.

1417 Asylum—refugee—identity documents—improper intention—availability of defence

The defendants had entered or left the United Kingdom while attempting to rely on a false passport or a false travel document issued under the Geneva Convention relating to the Status of Refugees 1951 relating to the status of refugees. The passport or travel document was a forgery or it related to a different person. Each of the defendants was charged with the offence of possession of an identity document with improper intention, either contrary to the Identity Cards Act 2006 s 25(1) or the Identity Documents Act 2010 s 4. None of the solicitors representing the defendants raised the fact that each defendant had a potential defence to the charge by virtue of the Immigration and Asylum Act 1999 s 31 or if they did raise s 31 it was to state that no defence was available. Therefore, each pleaded guilty. They subsequently appealed against conviction. *Held*, a s 31 defence contained a number of elements. First, the defendant had to provide sufficient evidence in support of his claim to refugee status to raise the issue and thereafter the burden fell on the prosecution to prove to the criminal standard that he was not a refugee unless an application by the defendant for asylum had been refused, when the legal burden would rest on him to establish on a balance of probabilities that he was a refugee. Second, if the prosecution failed to disprove that the defendant was a refugee, it then fell to the defendant to prove on the balance of probabilities that he had not stopped in any country in transit to the United Kingdom for more than a short stopover or, alternatively, that he could not reasonably have expected to be given protection under the Convention in countries outside the United Kingdom in which he stopped. If so, he had presented himself to the authorities in the United Kingdom 'without delay', unless it was explicable that he had not presented himself during a short stopover in the United Kingdom when travelling through to the nation where he had intended to claim asylum. Further, he had good cause for his illegal entry or presence in the United Kingdom and he had made a claim for asylum as soon as was reasonably practicable after his arrival in the United Kingdom, unless it was explicable that he had not presented himself during a short stopover in the United Kingdom when travelling through to the nation where he had intended to claim asylum. Third, the requirement that the claim for asylum had to be made as soon as was reasonably practicable did not necessarily mean at the earliest possible moment. Fourth, the fact that a refugee stopped in a third county in transit was not necessarily fatal and might be explicable, the refugee had some choice as to where he might properly claim asylum. Finally, the requirement that the refugee demonstrated 'good cause' for his illegal entry or presence in the United Kingdom would be satisfied by him showing he was reasonably travelling on false papers. There was an obligation on those representing defendants charged with an offence of possession of an identity document with improper intention to advise them of the existence of a possible s 31 defence if the circumstances and instructions generated the possibility of mounting that defence. If a defendant's representatives failed to advise him about the availability of that defence, on appeal to the court, the court would assess whether the defence would quite probably have succeeded. In the defendants' cases, if they had raised the s 31 defence, it would quite probably have succeeded. Therefore, in each case, a clear injustice had been done and the convictions would be quashed. Judgment would be given accordingly.

R v Mateta [2013] EWCA Crim 1372, [2014] 1 All ER 152 (Court of Appeal: Leveson and Fulford LJJ and Spencer J). R v Asfaw [2008] UKHL 31, [2008] 1 AC 1061, [2008] 3 All ER 775; R v Boal [1992] QB 591, [1992] 3 All ER 177 (1992 Abr para 1185), CA; R v Makuwa [2006] EWCA Crim 175, [2006] All ER (D) 324 (Feb) (2007 Abr para 439); R v Abdalla; R v MV; R v Mohamed; R v Nofallah [2010] EWCA Crim 2400, [2010] All ER (D) 181 (Oct); and R v Sadighpour [2012] EWCA Crim 2669, [2012] All ER (D) 138 (Dec) applied.

1418   Asylum—refugee—Refugee Convention—exclusion from protection—membership of terrorist organisation

The Geneva Convention relating to the Status of Refugees 1951 does not apply to any person with respect to whom there are serious reasons for considering that (1) he has committed a serious non-political crime outside the country of refuge prior to his admission to that country as a refugee (art 1F(b)); (2) he has been guilty of acts contrary to the purposes and principles of the United Nations (art 1F(c)).

The claimant, an Algerian citizen, had travelled to France on business. While he was in France, he was convicted in Algeria in his absence in connection with the bombing of an airport. He was subsequently convicted in France of being a member of an association or group formed with a view to preparing acts of terrorism and sentenced to two years' imprisonment. After serving his sentence, the claimant travelled to the United Kingdom and applied for asylum. The Secretary of State refused his application for asylum on the grounds that the claimant was excluded from the protection of the Geneva Convention by virtue of art 1F(b) and (c). The Asylum and Immigration Tribunal confirmed the decision on the basis that, in the light of the findings of the French court, there were serious reasons for considering that the claimant fell within art 1F. The claimant appealed. Held, in reaching its decision for the purposes of art 1F(c), the tribunal had followed authority to the effect that voluntary membership of an organisation whose aims, methods and activities were exclusively terrorist in nature created a presumption that the person was personally and knowingly involved in the crimes in question. However, that authority had been disapproved subsequent to the tribunal's decision and so, by applying that presumption, the tribunal had erred in law. While the facts found by the French court were sufficient for the purpose of convicting the claimant of membership of a terrorist group, they did not enable the tribunal to determine his personal involvement and role in the grouping. The words 'serious crime' in art 1F(b) were ordinary words and should be given their ordinary universal meaning. Although 'serious' was an ordinary word, it had shades of meaning and the appropriate colour was given by the context in which the word was used. The context was that the crime which the refugee had committed had to be serious enough to justify the withholding of the protection he would otherwise have enjoyed as a person having a well-founded fear of persecution. Even if the tribunal had considered the seriousness of the claimant's offence in the context of the appropriate threshold of seriousness for the purpose of art 1F(b), it would have done so in the context of its conclusions in respect of art 1F(c), which had been reached by the application of a since discredited presumption. Accordingly, the appeal would be allowed.

AH (Algeria) v Secretary of State for the Home Department [2012] EWCA Civ 395, [2012] 1 WLR 3469, [2012] All ER (D) 09 (Apr) (Court of Appeal: Ward, Rix and Sullivan LJJ). *R (on the application of JS (Sri Lanka)) v Secretary of State for the Home Department* [2010] UKSC 15, [2011] 1 AC 184, [2010] 3 All ER 881 (2010 Abr para 1601); and *DD (Afghanistan) v Secretary of State for the Home Department* [2010] EWCA Civ 1407, [2010] All ER (D) 140 (Dec) (2010 Abr para 1599) followed. Cases C-57/09 and C-101/09 *Bundesrepublik Deutschland v B* [2010] All ER (D) 96 (Nov), ECJ, considered.

1419   British nationality

See BRITISH NATIONALITY.

1420   European Union (Croatian Accession and Irish Protocol) Act 2013

See para 469.

1421   Immigration—application—cost recovery fees

The Immigration and Nationality (Cost Recovery Fees) Regulations 2013, SI 2013/617 (in force on 6 April 2013), replace, with modifications, the 2012 Regulations, SI 2012/813, and specify fees for applications, services and processes in connection with immigration and nationality in cases where the amount of the fee does not exceed the administrative costs incurred by the Secretary of State in relation to the application, service or process concerned. In particular, the regulations specify fees for (1) applications for limited leave to remain in the United Kingdom; (2) applications for entry clearance into the United Kingdom; (3) the transfer of conditions, immigration employment documents, travel documents (other than passports), transit visas, registration certificates and residence cards; (4) applications for biometric immigration documents and the process used to take a record of biometric information; (5) applications for sponsor licences and for changing sponsor; (6) services and processes related to immigration and nationality, including (a) the arrangement of citizenship ceremonies; (b) the administration of citizenship oaths; (c) the supply of certified copies; (d) the amendment of certificates of registration or naturalisation as a British citizen; (e) the reconsideration of applications for registration or naturalisation as a British citizen; and (f) the issuing of action plans; (7) documents relating to travel or entry into the United Kingdom, Commonwealth countries, British Overseas Territories and the Channel Islands.

1422   Immigration—application—fees

The Immigration and Nationality (Fees) (Amendment) Order 2013, SI 2013/249 (in force on 8 February 2013), amend the 2011 Order, SI 2011/445, so as to add (1) the provision of optional arrangements for processing of immigration and nationality applications, the provision of optional services for sponsors, and the administration of tests for the purposes of the immigration rules, to the list of applications, services and processes in relation to which the Secretary of State is able to charge a fee; and (2) the processes for recording biometric information for the purposes of the Immigration (Biometric Registration) Regulations 2008, SI 2008/3048, reg 8(2)(d) to the list of applications, services and processes in relation to which the Secretary of State is able to charge a fee.

The Immigration and Nationality (Fees) Regulations 2013, SI 2013/749 (in force on 6 April 2013), replace the 2012 Regulations, SI 2012/971, and specify fees in cases where the amount of the fee either exceeds the administrative costs incurred by the Secretary of State or reflects the costs related to other applications, services or processes relating to immigration or nationality. In particular, the regulations (1) prescribe fees relating to applications (a) for limited and indefinite leave to remain in the United Kingdom; (b) for entry clearance to enter the United Kingdom; (c) for entry clearance or leave to remain made under the points-based system; (d) for sponsor licenses; (e) in connection with nationality; and (f) made outside the United Kingdom for entry clearance to enter the Channel Islands; (2) specify the fees payable for various services and processes, including the provision of premium services for sponsors, the expedited processing of applications for leave to remain, the processing of applications for limited leave to remain made under the super premium service and the provision of services by the United Kingdom Border Agency outside office hours; and (3) provide that any application which attracts a specified fee is not validly made unless it is accompanied by that fee.

1423 Immigration—deportation—appeal—Special Immigration Appeals Commission— procedure

The appellant was regarded by the United Kingdom as an exceptionally high risk terrorist. The respondent Secretary of State sought to deport him to Jordan under the Immigration Act 1971 s 5(1). The appellant had been twice convicted in his absence in Jordan of terrorist offences, and he faced a retrial in Jordan if returned. The appellant maintained that the convictions had been based on the statements of co-defendants and had been obtained by torture. The European Court of Human Rights upheld the appellant's challenge against the lawfulness of the respondent's proposal to deport the appellant. It held that there was a real risk that the appellant's retrial would amount to a flagrant denial of justice if he were deported to Jordan. In extensive discussions between the United Kingdom and Jordan, the latter made it clear that it would do everything in its power to ensure that a retrial was fair. On that basis, the respondent refused to revoke the earlier deportation order. The appellant appealed to the Special Immigration Appeals Commission before which the respondent submitted that there was no longer a real risk of a flagrant denial of justice if the claimant were to face a retrial in Jordan. The Commission identified as the issue for determination whether, under Jordanian law, there was a real risk that the impugned statements would be admitted as probative of the appellant's guilt at his retrial. With regard to Jordanian law, the respondent submitted that, because of the number of possible outcomes of a retrial, the risk that the impugned statements would be admitted probatively was small. The Commission acknowledged that there were a number of possible outcomes, but concluded that the respondent had not established that, on a retrial, there was no real risk that the impugned statements would be admitted probatively against the appellant. The appeal was allowed and the respondent appealed. *Held*, if the Commission had intended to have said that the burden of proof to a high standard had to be on the prosecution in all cases, it would have said so but it had explained instead why, on the facts, the only way of eliminating a real risk that the impugned statements would be admitted as evidence at the retrial would have been to place the burden of proof on the prosecution to a high standard to show that the impugned statements would not be admitted. That had been an assessment that the Commission had been entitled to make. The focus of the case before the Commission had been on whether there was a real risk that the impugned statements would be adduced in evidence at a retrial. In light of that, it had been common ground before the Commission that, if it were shown that there was a real risk that the statements would be admitted as evidence, it would follow that there was a real risk that there would be a flagrant denial of justice. In adopting that approach, the Commission had made no error of law. Further, the Commission had not failed to have regard to the combined effect of the two possible ways in which the evidence might properly have been excluded under Jordanian law. Since the Commission had decided that the relevant law in relation to both matters was so uncertain, the only conclusion it could properly have reached had been that there was a real risk that evidence obtained by torture would be admitted. In any event, the Commission had not approached the question of whether there was a real risk that the impugned statements would be admitted in a narrow way. The Commission had dealt fully with all the matters which realistically bore on the question of whether the impugned statements would be adduced in evidence. At the forefront of those were the two critical questions of Jordanian law and there was no challenge to the way in which the Commission had dealt with them. Also, the Commission had dealt with the possible outcomes suggested by the respondent in so far as there was an evidential basis for having done so. The Commission could not be criticised for having failed to deal explicitly with mere speculative possibilities. Accordingly, the appeal would be dismissed.

not been accepted as a matter of principle because the decisions were based on various assumptions which had not been challenged in the evidence that appeared to have been put forward in each of those cases. Those decisions might be overruled by the Supreme Court. If those assumptions, or at least some of them, had been shown by evidence not to have been applicable, the result in each of those cases might well have been different. It was therefore open to the claimant to seek to show that the assumptions were inapplicable given the facts and circumstances of the case. All the assumptions which had supported the findings in the cases relied on by the defendant to show that the refusal rate of 20 per cent provided a mandatory and fixed percentage which was not susceptible to revision in any of the respects contended for by the claimant were challenged by the claimant and it was clear that the grounds which relied on those challenges had reasonable prospects of success. The claimant would be granted permission to challenge the defendant's refusal decision on all the grounds contended for. Accordingly, the application would be allowed.

R (on the application of Warnborough College Ltd) v Secretary of State for the Home Department [2013] EWHC 1510 (Admin), [2013] All ER (D) 78 (Jun) (Queen's Bench Division: Anthony Thornton QC). *R (on the application of New London College Ltd) v Secretary of State for the Home Department* [2012] EWCA Civ 51, [2012] All ER (D) 25 (Feb) considered.

1432 Immigration—education—sponsor licence—revocation—reasonableness

The claimant, a private educational institution, held a Tier 4 (General) Student sponsor licence issued by the United Kingdom Border Agency. The licence enabled it to issue a confirmation of acceptance for studies to students who wished to study in the United Kingdom. The licence was suspended and soon after revoked. Five areas of complaint were identified in the revocation letter, namely attendance records, students who failed to enrol, non-compliance with a previous action plan, student assessment, and reporting duties. In respect of the attendance records the defendant had obtained witness statements from former members of staff in which they made allegations of improper conduct. The claimant sought judicial review of the decisions to suspend and subsequently revoke its licence. *Held*, the defendant had been entitled to conclude that the claimant had not been properly monitoring its students' attendance. Her determination of the issue had not been unlawful by reason of any unfairness in the procedure adopted by her to investigate the complaint. The other four reasons for revoking the claimant's sponsor licence had each been raised with the claimant on previous occasions and in the letter of suspension. The defendant had been entitled to reach the conclusions that she had. Further, there had been no unfairness in the investigation into those matters and the decision to revoke the licence had been made in accordance with the defendant's stated policy and guidance. Overall, the procedure by which the decisions had been taken to suspend and revoke the claimant's licence had not been unlawful, unreasonable or unfair. Accordingly, the application would be dismissed.

R (on the application of Manchester College of Accountancy and Management) v Secretary of State for the Home Department [2013] EWHC 409 (Admin), [2013] All ER (D) 04 (Mar) (Queen's Bench Division: Supperstone J). *Associated Provincial Picture Houses Ltd v Wednesbury Corpn* [1948] 1 KB 223, [1947] 2 All ER 680, CA, applied.

1433 Immigration—entry—indefinite leave to remain—refusal—spouse of national of another member state

The claimant was a Zimbabwean national. She arrived in the United Kingdom on a visitor's visa, but remained illegally following its expiry. She met a Spanish national, who had begun working in the United Kingdom over ten years ago. He had ceased to work because of ill health. At that time, he became entitled to permanently reside in the United Kingdom under Commission Regulation (EEC) 1251/70 (on the right of workers to remain in the territory of a member state after having been employed in that state) art 2(1)(b). Regulation 1251/70 was replaced by Council Directive (EC) 2004/38 (on the right of citizens of the European Union and their family members to move and reside freely within the territory of the member states), which introduced a new right in art 16(1) to permanently reside in the United Kingdom following a period of five years' permanent residence. The right to reside under Regulation 1251/70 art 2(1) was replaced by Directive 2004/38 art 17(1)(b). The claimant married the Spanish national. After his death, she claimed asylum. The defendant refused the claim. The First-tier Tribunal dismissed the appeal. A judge ordered a reconsideration of the claimant's appeal as it was arguable that, on her marriage, she fell within the Immigration (European Economic Area) Regulations 2006, SI 2006/1003, reg 15(1)(d). The Upper Tribunal upheld the decision and the claimant appealed. *Held*, (1) a worker who had continuously resided within the United Kingdom for four years and eleven months and who had a two-year period of continuous residence prior to retirement through incapacity would nonetheless be entitled, based on his two years residence prior to retirement, to avail himself of the rights afforded by Directive 2004/38 art 17, notwithstanding that his rights had originally been acquired under Regulation 1251/70. It had to follow that his family members, who were residing with the worker as at that date, were also entitled to continue to enjoy, pursuant to Directive 2004/38 art 17, the rights of permanent residence which they had originally acquired under Regulation 1251/70. That position clearly could not change simply because a month later the worker arguably acquired a further right of permanent residence pursuant to Directive 2004/38 art 16 on completion of a continuous period of five years' residence. In the present case, the correct analysis was (a) the claimant's husband's right of permanent residence had originally been acquired under Regulation 1251/70 art 2(1)(b); (b) the circumstances of that acquisition had satisfied the relevant description in Directive 2004/38 art 17(1); and (c) for the purposes of art 17(3), he was to have been regarded as somebody who had acquired the right of permanent residence under art 17(1). Therefore, as at the date of his marriage to the claimant, the Spanish national had fallen to be regarded as a person falling within art 17(1). (2) There was nothing in the wording of Directive 2004/38 art 17(3) which suggested any temporal pre-condition as to the date on which a person became a family member of the worker. The only condition was that the family member had to be residing with the worker who had acquired the right of permanent residence on the basis of art 17(1). In the present case, as at the date of her marriage, the claimant had acquired a permanent right of residence in the United Kingdom pursuant to art 17(3), on the grounds that her husband had acquired the right of permanent residence under art 17(1). Accordingly, the appeal would be allowed.

RM (Zimbabwe) v Secretary of State for the Home Department [2013] EWCA Civ 775, [2013] CMLR 1185, [2013] All ER (D) 11 (Jul) (Court of Appeal: Longmore and Gloster LJJ and Sir Robin Jacob).

1434   Immigration—exclusion—Special Immigration Appeals Commission—power

The claimant Tunisian national's claim for asylum in the United Kingdom was outstanding at the time when he was extradited to Italy. The defendant Secretary of State informed the claimant that he had been excluded from the United Kingdom, with no right of appeal, on the ground that his presence was not conducive to the public good for reasons of national security. The claimant sought judicial review of the exclusion direction, of the failure to determine his asylum application, of the failure to re-admit him to the United Kingdom and of the failure to accept responsibility for determining his asylum claim. A special advocate was appointed and the matter was listed for hearing. The defendant applied to vacate the hearing on the basis that the claimant had open to him, pursuant to the Justice and Security Act 2013, a new route to challenge her decision to exclude him by way of application to the Special Immigration Appeals Commission. The defendant informed the claimant that the exclusion certification had the effect of terminating his judicial review proceedings and invited him to apply to the Commission to challenge his exclusion. It was found that the clear parliamentary intention behind s 15 was that, where a person had been excluded from the United Kingdom on grounds of the public good, in reliance on information which in the defendant's opinion should not be made public for national security or similar reasons, a challenge to the exclusion direction had to be advanced in the Commission if the defendant had certified the direction. Consequently, existing judicial review proceedings were terminated without any court order or residual jurisdiction in the court. The claimant had an alternative means of challenging the exclusion direction elsewhere. On appeal by the claimant, *held*, the 2013 Act did not preclude an application to the court by way of judicial review in relation to an exclusion direction made and certified after the day on which s 15 had come into force. In relation to a direction made before the commencement date of s 15, the 2013 Act did not empower the defendant to effect the automatic termination of existing juridical review proceedings by a certificate made after the commencement day. The Special Immigration Appeals Commission Act 1997 s 2C provided that, where a direction was visa under the Tier 1 class of post-study work which allowed the United Kingdom to retain the most able non-European international graduates who had studied in the United Kingdom with a view to their moving on promptly to skilled work. The claimant was offered work with a university which made it a condition of her taking up her employment that she have leave to be in the United Kingdom on a visa which was not dependent on a certificate of sponsorship so that she would have to seek to recategorise her status. If her husband were to be successful in his outstanding application, then the claimant would fall into the category of 'Partner of a Relevant Points Based System Migrant'. The claimant was advised that, in order to take this option, she would have to return to China and make her application there pursuant to the Statement of Changes in Immigration Rules (HC Paper (1993–94) no 395) para 319C(h)(i). The claimant argued that the requirement was unlawful and sought a declaration to that effect. Compliance with para 319C(h)(i) resulted in the claimant being separated from her husband for two months which, she contended, was contrary to her rights under the European Convention on Human Rights art 8 as a disproportionate interference with her family and private life. *Held*, applying established case law, it would be rare, except in particular cases, that the immigration priorities of the state were such as to give rise to a proportionate answer to art 8 rights to family life where the requirement of the Immigration Rules para 319C(h)(i) was engaged. The aptness of the requirement in para 319C(h)(i) to reflect the obligations arising under the Convention art 8 had to be adjudicated on with reference to a proper interpretation of the wording of the requirement itself. The application of the blanket requirement to leave the country imposed by the Immigration Rules para 319C(h)(i) was unsustainable. It was not a bar to the application that the claimant had not pursued the alternative remedies relied on by the Secretary of State and also on the facts, the claimant's Convention art 8 rights had been engaged and infringed. She was in a loving marriage and had no real option but to endure separation from her new husband for two months. The Immigration Rules para 319C(h)(i), as presently worded, should continue to form part of the Immigration Rules. There would be no formal declaration on the matter. It was not the function of the court to redraft the rules but the Secretary of State would in future face difficulties in enforcing the requirement as presently worded in all but a small number of cases in which the Convention art 8 was engaged. Whether to keep the Immigration Rules para r 319C(h)(i) in a limited form or to drop it altogether was a matter for the Secretary of State but it could not lawfully be applied to the claimant in the case.

R (on the application of Zhang) v Secretary of State for the Home Department [2013] EWHC 981 (Admin), [2013] All ER (D) 225 (Apr) (Queen's Bench Division: Turner J). *R (on the application of Chikwamba) v Secretary of State for the Home Department* [2008] UKHL 40, [2009] 1 All ER 363 (2008 Abr para 1802) applied. *R (on the application of Ekinci) v Secretary of State for the Home Department* [2003] EWCA Civ 765, [2003] All ER (D) 215 (Jun); and *R (on the application of Mdlovu) v Secretary of State for the Home Department* [2008] EWHC 2089 (Admin), [2008] All ER (D) 20 (Oct) considered.

1444 Immigration—leave to remain—child—assistance with university fees—duty of local authority

See *R (on the application of Kebede) v Newcastle City Council*, para 183.

1445 Immigration—leave to remain—extension—refusal—removal directions

Three appeals before the Supreme Court raised issues as to the respective duties of the respondent Secretary of State and the First-tier Tribunal on an appeal against refusal of an application to vary leave to enter or remain under the Immigration Act 1971. It fell to be determined whether the respondent's failure to issue a removal direction at the same time as the decision to refuse leave to remain was not only unlawful in itself, but had undermined the validity of the previous decision to refuse leave to remain. Further, whether the conclusion of the Court of Appeal in *AS (Afghanistan) v Secretary of State for the Home Department* had been correct and finally when balancing the demands of fair and firm immigration control against the disruption to the family or private life of a person if removed for non-compliance with the Statement of Changes in Immigration Rules (HC Paper (1993–94) no 395), whether the nature and degree of the non-compliance was significant or whether the degree of failure to meet the requirements of the Rules might be relevant in the proportionality balance. *Held*, the powers to issue removal directions under the Immigration and Asylum Act 1999 s 10 and the Asylum and Nationality Act 2006 s 47 were merely powers. Their statutory purpose was as part of the armoury available to the respondent for the enforcement of immigration control. Any extra protection to an appellant was incidental. Neither section could be read as imposing an obligation to make a direction in any particular case, still less as providing any link between failure to do so and the validity of a previous immigration decision. Exercise of the power to direct removal was likely to involve both public cost and personal hardship or indignity. The respondent did not thwart the policy of the 2006 Act if she proceeded in the first instance on the basis that unlawful overstayers should be allowed to leave of their own volition. In the circumstances, it followed that the respondent had been under no duty to issue removal directions at the time of the decision to refuse leave to remain, and the actual decision was not invalidated by the failure to have done so. Further, the Nationality, Immigration and Asylum Act 2002 s 85(2) was to be construed as imposing a duty on the First-tier Tribunal to consider any potential ground of appeal raised in response to a notice served under s 120, even if it was not directly related to the issues considered by the respondent in the original decision. That approach had gained some support from the scheme of the 1971 Act s 3C, under which the initial application for leave to remain, if made in time, could later be varied to include wholly unrelated grounds without turning it into a new application or prejudicing the temporary right to remain given by s 3C. Thus, the identity of the application depended on the substance of what was applied for, rather than on the particular grounds or rules under which the application was initially made. That broad approach was to be preferred. It was more consistent with the coherence of that part of the 2002 Act and echoed the effect of the notice served under s 120 which urged applicants to raise any additional ground at that stage, on pain of not being able to do so later. Furthermore, although the context of the Rules might be relevant to the consideration of proportionality, that could not be equated with a formalised 'near-miss' or 'sliding scale' principle. A near-miss under the Rules could not provide substance to a human rights case which was otherwise in merit. In the circumstances, the near-miss argument had been advanced in the same form before the Court of Appeal. Even if well-founded, it had not been available since no separate human rights grounds had been advanced. Therefore, the issue as to whether the First-tier Tribunal or the Upper Tribunal would have been obliged to consider them, and to what effect, had not arisen. Accordingly, the appeals would be dismissed.

Patel v Secretary of State for the Home Department; Anwar v Secretary of State for the Home Department; Alam v Secretary of State for the Home Department [2013] UKSC 72, [2014] 1 All ER 1157 (Supreme Court: Lord Mance, Lord Kerr, Lord Reed, Lord Carnwath and Lord Hughes SCJJ). *Huang v Secretary of State for the Home Department; Kasmiri v Secretary of State for the Home Department* [2007] UKHL 11, [2007] 2 AC 167, [2007] 4 All ER 15 (2007 Abr para 1777) applied. *AS (Afghanistan) v Secretary of State for the Home Department; NV (Sri Lanka) v Secretary of State for the Home Department* [2009] EWCA Civ 1076, [2010] 2 All ER 21 approved. *R (on the application of Mirza) v Secretary of State for the Home Department* [2011] EWCA Civ 159, [2011] All ER (D) 245 (Feb) (2011 Abr para 1486); *Sapkota v Secretary of State for the Home Department* [2011] EWCA Civ 1320, [2011] All ER (D) 141 (Nov) overruled. Decisions of Court of Appeal [2012] EWCA Civ 960, [2012] All ER (D) 336 (Jul); and [2012] EWCA Civ 741, [2012] 4 All ER 94 (2012 Abr para 1455) affirmed.

1446   Immigration—leave to remain—marriage—age requirement—policy—refusal of leave—right to private and family life

The court heard three applications for judicial review relating to amendments made to the Immigration Rules (HC Paper (1993–94) no 395) by the defendant. The first claimant was a national of Lebanon who had been granted limited leave to remain in the United Kingdom as a refugee. He lived with his nephew and he married by proxy in Lebanon. The second claimant was a British citizen of Pakistani origin. He married a Pakistani woman who lived in Kashmir and they had five children, four of whom were resident in the United Kingdom and the youngest of whom lived with his mother. The third claimant was a British citizen of Pakistani origin who married a Pakistani national who lived in Pakistan. The claimants challenged the requirements with respect to (1) the setting of the minimum income level to be provided by the sponsor; (2) the requirement of a certain sum before savings could be said to contribute to rectify an income shortfall; (3) the use of a 30-month period for forward income projection, as opposed to a 12-month period that could be applied in a borderline case of ability to maintain; (4) the disregard of reliable evidence of undertakings of third party support effected by deed and supported by evidence of ability to fund; and (5) the disregard of the spouse's own earning capacity during the 30-month period of initial entry. The defendant contended that any interference with the right to respect for family life was necessary and proportionate to the legitimate aim. *Held*, in previous authority, the Supreme Court had found that a refusal of the Secretary of State to allow foreign spouses to reside in the United Kingdom with British citizens with whom they had recently entered into a consensual marriage represented an interference with respect for their family life. Further, refugees were in a different position from foreigners generally, because they were unable to reside in their country of nationality. British citizens were also in a different position from foreign sponsors generally because they had an independent right to reside in their own country. The Immigration Rules did not forbid the claimants from residing in the United Kingdom or from marrying anyone they chose. However, it would be difficult to exercise the associated right to found a family if there were serious obstacles to matrimonial cohabitation. It was clear that a rule restricting the admission of a spouse was an interference with family life. British nationality was of importance because, if the spouse could not obtain admission under the Immigration Rules and the citizen sponsor wanted to enjoy family life and matrimonial cohabitation following marriage, he would have to leave the country of nationality in order to do so. That was a serious interference with the right of residence. The measures both had a legitimate aim and were rationally connected with the aim. The claimants had failed to demonstrate that the Immigration Rules were unlawfully discriminatory, taking the European Convention on Human Rights arts 8, 14 together. Further, the requirements were not unlawful on the basis that they made no overriding accommodation for the best interests of children affected by the immigration decisions. In principle, it was not unreasonable to expect more funds to be available where children who were not British citizens were coming to the United Kingdom in addition to a spouse. However, although there might be sound reasons in favour of some of the individual requirements, when applied to recognised refugees or British citizens, the combination of more than one of the requirements was so onerous as to be an unjustified and disproportionate interference with a genuine spousal relationship. Most strikingly, to prevent a couple from having any regard to the future earning capacity of the spouse to be admitted for the first 30 months of the residence, was both irrational and manifestly disproportionate. The Immigration Rules were capable of leading to a result compatible with art 8 and they should be left undisturbed. Claims of individual violations should be examined in the context of an application when the relevant facts could be established. There was substantial merit in the contention that the interference represented by the combination of the requirements in the family life of the claimants on the assumed facts was disproportionate and unlawful. Accordingly, the applications would be allowed.

MM v Secretary of State for the Home Department [2013] EWHC 1900 (Admin), [2013] All ER (D) 96 (Jul) (Queen's Bench Division: Blake J). *R (on the application of Aguilar Quila) v Secretary of State for the Home Department; R (on the application of Bibi) v Secretary of State of the Home Department* [2011] UKSC 45, [2012] 1 All ER 1011 (2011 Abr para 1484) considered.

1447   Immigration—leave to remain—post-study work migrant—application made before qualification obtained

Each of the four claimants had applied for leave to remain in the United Kingdom under the Tier 1 (Post-Study Work) provisions of the Points Based System of the Statement of Changes in Immigration Rules (HC Paper (1993–94) no 395). Each claimant had obtained the requisite recognised bachelor or post-graduate degree. However, by virtue of the Immigration Rules Appendix A, eligibility was also dependent on an applicant applying for leave to remain within 12 months of his qualification being awarded. The claimants had received notification of their qualification only after they had submitted their applications for leave to remain. The defendant refused the claimants' applications on that ground. The claimants' appeals against the defendant's decisions were allowed by the First-tier Tribunal, which ruled that the claimants had needed to have been notified of their qualification only by the time that the defendant had come to make her decision on their applications. The decision was affirmed on appeal and the defendants appealed further. *Held*, there was no room under the Points Based System for a near miss. Viewed as a whole, qualification required strict compliance with the requirement to make the application within the period of 12 months from the time when the qualification was obtained. The claimants could not score the required number of points because they had made their applications before they had obtained their qualifications. On a true construction of Appendix A, the claimants could not have scored the points they needed. No subsequently obtained evidence could have cured that defect. Accordingly, the appeal would be allowed.

Raju v Secretary of State of the Home Department [2013] EWCA Civ 754, [2013] All ER (D) 232 (Jun) (Court of Appeal: Moses, Kitchin and Floyd LJJ).

1448   Immigration—leave to remain—post-study work migrants—degree requirement—holder of professional qualification

The claimants had successfully passed examinations at the professional level of the Association of Chartered Certified Accountants ('ACCA'). They each applied for leave to remain in the United Kingdom as a Tier 1 (Post-Study Work) Migrant. Their applications were refused by the defendant on the ground that the ACCA qualification did not satisfy the 'attributes' requirement of the Statement of Changes in Immigration Rules (HC Paper (1993–94) no 395). The relevant part of the Immigration Rules stated that the purpose of the post-study work route to leave to remain was to encourage international graduates who had studied in the United Kingdom to stay on and do skilled or highly skilled work. The claimants brought judicial review proceedings challenging the defendant's decisions. According to the Immigration Rules para 245FD(c), an applicant was required to have a minimum of 75 points under the provisions of Appendix A, which required that an applicant had been awarded a United Kingdom recognised bachelor or postgraduate degree. The defendant contended that the claimants' qualification was not a recognised degree. The claimants submitted that the word 'recognised' enlarged the ambit of the word 'degree' to include a qualification which was equivalent to a degree. *Held*, the relevant rule was quite clear, whether read alone or side by side with the policy guidance. Quite simply, the applicant had to hold a degree, and the ACCA qualification was not a degree. There was no ambiguity. The purpose of the word 'recognised' was to qualify the word 'degree' so as to make clear that the degree had to be one which was recognised for the purposes of the Education Reform Act 1988 and not one which involved any criminal offence. In any case, even if the court was mistaken in that view, there was nothing at all in the policy guidance which resolved any alleged ambiguity in the Immigration Rules in favour of the claimants. Nor did the policy guidance relax or widen in any way at all the requirements in the rules. Rather, the relevant parts of the policy guidance served merely to repeat and fortify that only a degree awarded by a recognised body with degree-awarding powers would suffice and that professional qualifications would not, no matter how high-level and prestigious they were. Accordingly, the applications would be dismissed.

R (on the application of Syed) v Secretary of State for the Home Department; R (on the application of Ahmed) v Secretary of State for the Home Department [2013] EWHC 984 (Admin), [2013] All ER (D) 212 (Apr) (Queen's Bench Division: Holman J).

This decision has been affirmed on appeal: [2014] EWCA Civ 196, [2014] All ER (D) 27 (Mar).

1449   Immigration—leave to remain—removal directions—judicial review—legal aid

See *Rrapaj v Director of Legal Aid Casework*, para 1680.

1450   Immigration—leave to remain—variation—removal directions—time when decision takes effect

The Immigration (Continuation of Leave) (Notices) Regulations 2006, SI 2006/2170, reg 2 provides that, for the purpose of the Immigration Act 1971 s 3C, an application for variation of leave is decided when notice of the decision has been given in accordance with regulations made under the Nationality, Immigration and Asylum Act 2002 s 105, or, where no such notice is required, when notice of the decision has been given in accordance with the 1971 Act s 4(1).

The defendant issued a decision which contained both a refusal of the claimant's application for variation of his leave to remain in the United Kingdom and directions for his removal from the United Kingdom under the Immigration, Asylum and Nationality

basis that her son, born in Northern Ireland, had Irish citizenship and was an EU citizen. The petition was dismissed. She made an application for the court to make a reference to the European Court of Justice for a preliminary ruling on whether the Secretary of State's refusal to grant her a residence card was illegal having regard to the TFEU art 20. *Held*, the law set out in *Ruiz Zambrano v Office National de l'Emploi (ONEm)* did not apply to the applicant's situation and the reasoning there could not be read or even have possibly been intended to extend a right of residence to a parent in a country which was not both the place of residence and the country of nationality of her dependent child. *Zambrano* was intended to prevent the removal of an EU citizen from the territory of the EU as a whole and it was not enough that the applicant could show that her child might need to leave the member state in which he resided if she was not given residence. Rather she needed to show that any refusal to allow her to reside would require the child to leave the EU as a whole. On a correct interpretation of European law there was no ambiguity; no question arose from *Zambrano* which would mean that European law might be held to confer a right of residence on a person in the applicant's situation and therefore, it was unnecessary to seek a preliminary ruling. Accordingly, the application would be refused.

Z v Secretary of State for the Home Department [2013] CSIH 16, 2013 SLT 794 (Inner House). Case C-34/09 *Ruiz Zambrano v Office National de l'Emploi (ONEm)* [2012] QB 265, [2011] All ER (EC) 491, ECJ (2011 Abr para 2484), considered.

1462   **Immigration—right of residence—permanent residence—parent of child receiving education**

The applicants, a mother and son, both of Nigerian nationality, arrived in the United Kingdom. They obtained a right of residence, respectively as the spouse of a national of member state employed in the territory of another member state and as the minor child or dependent of that person, those rights of residence expiring on a specified date. During her period of residence, the mother worked on a part-time self-employed basis, so that she had a monthly income. She paid taxes and national insurance contributions. The son had been in full-time education since arriving in the United Kingdom. On the date when the request for a preliminary ruling was lodged at the European Court of Justice, he had been formally admitted to the University of Edinburgh to study for a doctorate. He had intended to live in Edinburgh for the period of his studies. The Secretary of State refused the application made by the applicants for a right of permanent residence in the United Kingdom pursuant to the European Parliament and Council Directive (EC) 2004/38. The mother's marriage was ended by divorce. The First-tier Tribunal (Immigration and Asylum Chamber) dismissed the applicants' appeal. The tribunal decided that the applicants had not proved that the member of their family who was a European Union citizen had exercised in the United Kingdom rights stemming from the EC Treaty in the period at issue. The court further rejected the applicants' arguments that, first, the mother had acquired a retained right of residence after her divorce and, secondly, that their fundamental right to respect for private and family life had been infringed by the refusal. In the appeal brought before the referring court against that decision, the applicants raised for the first time an argument based on Council Regulation (EEC) 1612/68 art 12 (on freedom of movement for workers within the Community). A preliminary ruling was sought as to the conditions which should be met by a parent of a child who was more than 21 years old and who had obtained access to education on the basis of art 12 if that parent was to continue to be entitled to a right of residence; and whether periods of residence in a host member state that were completed by family members of an EU citizen who were not nationals of a member state solely on the basis of art 12, where the conditions of entitlement to a right of residence under Directive 2004/38 were not satisfied, might be taken into consideration for the purpose of the acquisition by those family members of a right of permanent residence. *Held,* the parent of a child who had reached the age of majority and who had obtained access to education on the basis of Regulation 1612/68 art 12 might continue to have a derived right of residence under art 12 if that child remained in need of the presence and care of that parent in order to be able to continue and to complete his education, which it was for the referring court to assess, taking into account all the circumstances of the case before it. Periods of residence in a host member state which were completed by family members of an EU citizen who were not nationals of a member state solely on the basis of art 12, where the conditions laid down for entitlement to a right of residence under Directive 2004/38 were not satisfied, might not be taken into consideration for the purposes of acquisition by those family members of a right of permanent residence under Directive 2004/38.

Case C-529/11 *Alarape v Secretary of State for the Home Department* [2013] All ER (D) 129 (May) (ECJ: Second Chamber).

1463   Immigration—right to reside—dependant of non-EEA national

The appellant, a Brazilian citizen, had lived in Brazil in the same household as his aunt who was also a Brazilian citizen. The aunt had been the main breadwinner of the household and the appellant had been dependent on her. The aunt married a man who held duel Brazilian and Italian nationality. The aunt and her husband never lived together in Brazil so that the appellant was not part of the husband's household in Brazil. The husband moved to the United Kingdom and was followed by the aunt and the appellant, who was then aged 15. The aunt was issued with a residence card as the spouse of a European citizen. The appellant returned to Brazil. He then returned to the United Kingdom on a visitor's visa but he overstayed. He lived with the aunt and her husband. The applicant's application for a residence card was refused on the ground that the applicant failed to meet the criteria set out in the Immigration (European Economic Area) Regulations 2006, SI 2006/1003, reg 8, which defined 'extended family member'. It was accepted that the husband was a European national exercising treaty rights in the United Kingdom, but the appellant had failed to establish that, prior to his arrival in the United Kingdom, he had been residing with or been dependent on the husband. The appellant's appeal was dismissed on the ground that he had neither been a member of the household of, nor dependent on, the husband in Brazil before coming to the United Kingdom. On the appellant's further appeal, *held*, reg 8(2)(a) was specific in requiring that a person was residing in a country other than the United Kingdom and was dependent on the European national or was a member of his household. The requirements of reg 8(2)(a) were then expressly incorporated into reg 8(2)(c). In the circumstances, the appellant did not meet the requirements of reg 8(2)(c). Before coming to the United Kingdom, he had been neither dependent on nor a member of the husband's household. The appellant was both a dependant of, and a member of, the aunt's household, but she was not herself a European national. Accordingly, the appeal would be dismissed.

Soares v Secretary of State for the Home Department [2013] EWCA Civ 575, [2013] 3 CMLR 847, [2013] All ER (D) 229 (May) (Court of Appeal: Longmore, McFarlane and Davis LJJ).

1464   Immigration—right to reside—EEA national—extended family member

The claimants were citizens of Nigeria who were present in the United Kingdom illegally. They had arrived on separate dates over the course of a two-year period. A Dutch national with whom they had formerly lived in Nigeria, and to whom they claimed to be related, subsequently entered the United Kingdom. Relying on the Immigration (European Economic Area) Regulations 2006, SI 2006/1003, reg 8, the claimants applied for residence cards on the basis of their connection with the Dutch national, who was providing them with financial support. Their applications and subsequent appeals were dismissed, but, on their further appeals, the Upper Tribunal ruled that the requirements of reg 8 had been met. The Secretary of State appealed, submitting that reg 8(2)(c) required the arrival of an applicant to be broadly contemporaneous with the arrival of the European Union citizen on whom he was dependent. As the claimants had arrived in the United Kingdom between 12 and 21 months before the Dutch national, the Secretary of State contended that the requirement had not been met. Consideration was given to Council Directive (EC) 2004/38 art 3(2), and to the ruling in Case C-83/11 *Secretary of State for the Home Department v Rahman. Held*, while *Rahman* established the need for a situation of dependence in the country from which the applicant came, and a situation of dependence at the date of the application, it was not to be read as laying down a requirement that the dependency at the date of the application had to be dependency in the country from which the applicant came, such that a relative who had been dependent throughout could not qualify if he had arrived in the host member state many months before the EU citizen and the making of the application. The court had ruled that the requirement of dependency in the country from which the applicant had come did not refer to the country in which the EU citizen resided before settling in the host member state, but to the country from which the family member came. When the court said that the situation of dependence had to exist in that country at the time when he applied to join the EU citizen on whom he was dependent, it was adopting a formulation appropriate to the particular circumstances of the case (where the applications were made by persons outside the host member state) rather than laying down a principle of universal applicability. The court could not have intended to exclude from the scope of art 3(2) persons who had arrived in the host member state before the EU citizen and before making their applications. The claimants all came within the ambit of the 2006 Regulations reg 8. Accordingly, the appeals would be dismissed.

Aladeselu v Secretary of State for the Home Department [2013] EWCA Civ 144, [2013] All ER (D) 03 (Mar) (Court of Appeal: Pill, Richards and Davis LJJ). Case C-83/11 *Secretary of State for the Home Department v Rahman* [2012] 3 CMLR 1315, [2012] All ER (D) 48 (Sep), ECJ (2012 Abr para 1463), considered.

1465 Immigration—right to reside—third-country national—parent and child residing in different member states

See Case C-40/11 *Iida v Stadt Ulm*, para 2688.

1466 Immigration—Special Immigration Appeals Commission—procedure

The Special Immigration Appeals Commission (Procedure) (Amendment) Rules 2013, SI 2013/2995 (in force on 28 November 2013), further amend the 2003 Rules, SI 2003/1034, so as to ensure that the 2003 Rules provide procedures for application for review and on the use of closed material proceedings in relation to such applications.

1467 Immigration—Tier 4 sponsor licence—unlawful delegation of powers

In the first appeal, the respondent Secretary of State revoked the appellant's Tier 4 general sponsor licence. The respondent introduced a new status for Tier 4 sponsoring institutions known as Highly Trusted Sponsor status. The appellant in the second appeal had become a licensed sponsor and applied for Highly Trusted Sponsor status. That application was rejected and it was found that it could not be a licensed sponsor at all. Both appellants appealed, challenging the lawfulness of the Tier 4 Sponsor Guidance issued by the respondent. They contended that the guidance concerning the qualification for entry clearance and leave to remain, had constituted an unlawful delegation to the sponsoring institutions of the respondent's powers to control entry into or stay in the United Kingdom. It was further contended that, so far as the guidance contained mandatory requirements for sponsors, it had to be laid before Parliament under the Immigration Act 1971 s 3(2). As that had not occurred, the respondent had acted unlawfully in making decisions affecting the sponsors by reference to the guidance. *Held*, it was correct that, when the points-based system had been introduced for Tier 4 migrants, a number of matters on which students had previously been required to satisfy immigration officers or the respondent, such as a bona fide intention to study, had to be examined by the sponsoring institution as a condition of being entitled to issue a confirmation of acceptance for studies. However, leave to enter or remain continued to be the responsibility of immigration officers and the respondent, who retained the last word in each individual case by virtue of the general grounds of refusal. The grant of a confirmation by an educational institution was not tantamount to leave to enter or remain. It was strong, but not conclusive evidence of some of the matters which were relevant on the migrant's application for leave to enter or remain. Further, properly construed, s 3(2) did not apply to all rules, but only to those which related to the practice to be followed in the administration of the 1971 Act for regulating the entry into and stay in the United Kingdom of persons required by the 1971 Act to have leave to enter. In the circumstances, the mandatory criteria for the award and retention of a sponsor licence were rules. However, subject to one reservation, they were not rules calling for compliance by the migrant as a condition of his obtaining leave to enter or remain. The guidance was wholly concerned with the position of the sponsor. That was not a technical or adventitious distinction. The reservation arose out of the cross-reference to the guidance in the Immigration Rules (HC Paper (1993–94) no 395). Since the guidance was liable to be changed without parliamentary scrutiny at the discretion of the respondent, the Immigration Rules could not lawfully incorporate anything which constituted a rule that, if not satisfied, would lead to the migrant being refused leave to enter or remain. However, none of the sections of the guidance incorporated by reference to the Immigration Rules raised the bar against migrants any higher than the Immigration Rules themselves had. The criteria for sponsoring licensing contained in the guidance had not fallen within the 1971 Act s 1(4) or 3(2) and had not fallen to be laid before Parliament. Furthermore, the statutory power of the respondent to administer the system of immigration control necessarily had to extend to a range of ancillary and incidental administrative powers not expressly spelt out, including the vetting of sponsors. The respondent had not transgressed any of the Immigration Rules by operating a system of approved Tier 4 sponsors. Accordingly, the appeals would be dismissed.

R (on the application of New London College Ltd) v Secretary of State for the Home Department; R (on the application of West London Vocational Training College) v Secretary of State for the Home Department [2013] UKSC 51, [2013] All ER (D) 211 (Jul) (Supreme Court: Lord Hope DP, Lord Clarke, Lord Sumption, Lord Reed and Lord Carnwath SCJJ). *R (on the application of Alvi) v Secretary of State for the Home Department* [2012] UKSC 33, [2012] 4 All ER 1041 (2012 Abr para 1457); and *R (on the application of Munir) v Secretary of State for the Home Department* [2012] UKSC 32, [2012] 4 All ER 1025 (2012 Abr para 1453) applied. Decision of Court of Appeal [2012] EWCA Civ 51, [2012] All ER (D) 25 (Feb) affirmed.

1468   Immigration—trafficking people for exploitation—information society services

See para 673.

1469   Immigration—worker registration scheme—application for certificate—authorised employer

The claimant, who was a Polish national, arrived in the United Kingdom and commenced work with the first employer. Pursuant to a worker registration scheme established under the Accession (Immigration and Worker Registration) Regulations 2004, SI 2004/1219, the claimant was entitled to apply for state benefits provided he complied with certain requirements, including that he worked for an authorised employer, which was satisfied if, during a one month period beginning on the date on which the claimant began work, he applied for and received a registration certificate authorising him to work for the employer. A number of months after commencing his employment with the first employer, the claimant applied for a registration certificate, which was subsequently issued. The claimant then worked for the second employer and a certificate was also issued for that period. At the end of his employment with the second employer, the claimant became unemployed. He applied for income-based job seekers allowance, but his application was refused on the ground that he had not been legally working in the United Kingdom for twelve months or more for an authorised employer because the certificate that had initially been issued had been issued on a date later than one month after the commencement of his employment, and the period for the purposes of the 2004 Regulations would not be backdated to the beginning of his employment. The claimant challenged the decision and the Upper Tribunal determined that a person was not working for an authorised employer unless he had, at the time when the work was performed, received a valid registration certificate in respect of that employment. The claimant appealed, submitting that, pursuant to reg 8(8), a certificate required the date that the worker began working for the employer to be included on the face of the certificate, the inclusion of which would have been misleading to third parties relying on the contents of the certificate unless the effect of the certificate was to have retrospective effect back to the date of the commencement of employment. *Held*, a certificate under the scheme did not have the effect of validating, including retrospectively, the whole period of the employment identified on the certificate. It only validated the period of such employment following the date of receipt of the certificate by the worker. On the claimant's argument, any retrospectivity would have been confined to that part of the prior period when, under the ordinary intended workings of reg 7, the employer was not an authorised employer because the one-month period during which the claimant should have applied and obtained a certificate had expired. The retrospectivity that was involved had therefore been a selective one directed at filling the gap created by the claimant's failure to comply with the intended scheme of reg 7. Neither the scheme of the 2004 Regulations as a whole, nor the wording of reg 7(2)(c) supported a selective retrospectivity from reg 7(2)(c). It followed that the tribunal had been correct to find that the claimant had not been legally working during the period between the expiry of the first month of his employment and the subsequent receipt by him of his registration certificate. Accordingly, the appeal would be dismissed.

Szpak v Secretary of State for Work and Pensions [2013] EWCA Civ 46, [2013] All ER (D) 147 (Feb) (Court of Appeal: Pill, Hughes and Rimer LJJ).
SI 2004/1219 revoked: SI 2011/544.

1470   Justice and Security Act 2013

See para 475.

INCOME TAXATION

Halsbury's Laws of England (4th edn) vol 23(1) (Reissue) paras 1–950, vol 23(2) (Reissue) paras 951–1836

Articles

For articles relating to this title please refer to the Table of Articles at the beginning of the Abridgment.

1471   Assessment—appeal—late appeal—reasonable excuse—approach of First-tier Tribunal

The Revenue wrote to the taxpayer's accountant (the 'second accountant') informing it that it intended to issue PAYE assessments in relation to the taxpayer. In the letter the Revenue raised queries about certain documents that the taxpayer had failed to supply concerning some of its employees. In the second accountant's reply to the Revenue, it stated that the documents related to a period when the taxpayer had engaged a different accountant (the 'first accountant'), and the taxpayer had been unsuccessful in obtaining those documents from the first accountant. The taxpayer failed to appeal against the assessments within the 30-day time limit, and a statutory demand was subsequently made to the taxpayer in respect of unpaid tax. The second accountant requested that the demand be set aside or postponed, explaining that it had been unable to provide the information to the inspectors as the matter had been dealt with by the taxpayer's previous accountant. The second accountant also submitted a late appeal to the Revenue and requested a review of the case. The Revenue refused permission to bring a late appeal. The taxpayer's application to the tribunal for permission to make a late appeal was dismissed. On appeal against that decision, *held*, it was well established that, on an application to bring a late appeal, the tribunal should consider all material factors, including the reasons for the delay, whether there would be prejudice to the Revenue if the taxpayer was permitted to appeal out of time, and whether there would be demonstrable injustice to the taxpayer if permission was not given. It was apparent from an examination of its individual findings that the tribunal had directed its attention almost exclusively to the question of whether the taxpayer had had a reasonable excuse for failing to make an appeal within the proper time limits. It had done so because it had perceived that to be the correct question as a matter of law. In so doing the tribunal had been in error. The tribunal should have approached the issue as one of discretion. It should have conducted a balancing exercise, taking into account all the relevant factors and circumstances. Those factors should have included the arguable merits of the taxpayer's case. The focus given by the tribunal to the question of reasonable excuse ignored the submissions on merits. It had not needed to reach any conclusion on the taxpayer's substantive case, but it had needed to consider whether that case had any arguable merit in order that that factor could be taken into account as part of the balancing exercise. Accordingly, the appeal would be allowed.

O'Flaherty v Revenue and Customs Comrs [2013] UKUT 161 (TCC), [2013] STC 1946 (Upper Tribunal: Judge Roger Berner presiding).

1472   Assessment—appeal—objection to production of documents—legal professional privilege

The Revenue opened an inquiry into the taxpayer's self-assessment. Subsequently, the Revenue issued him with a notice to provide information and documents under the Finance Act 2008 Sch 36 para 1. The taxpayer lodged an appeal against the notice. It was claimed that the documents were subject to legal professional privilege and were not reasonably required for the purpose of the inquiry. The taxpayer applied under the Information Notice:

Resolution of Disputes as to Privileged Communications Regulations 2009, SI 2009/1916, reg 5(5) to claim privilege over two documents, an engagement letter between the taxpayer and his solicitors and a report in relation to the trust arrangements prepared by the solicitors. *Held*, the taxpayer's submission that engagement letters were, by their nature, subject to privilege would be rejected. A client engagement letter was not in general subject to privilege. Nevertheless those parts of the letter which had set out the legal advice for which the solicitors had been retained were subject to privilege. With regard to the report, it largely comprised legal advice. It was therefore subject to privilege and did not fall to be disclosed. A schedule to the report contained a statement of the solicitors' opinion of an aspect of law and/or proposed law. As a schedule to a report giving legal advice to the taxpayer, it should necessarily been seen as a part of that advice given to him by the solicitors. It was therefore subject to privilege. A further schedule contained a note of a meeting between a representative of the solicitors, a barrister and a representative of an external body. The note did not record the giving of legal advice, it merely recorded a discussion of the legal position and by itself was not subject to privilege. However, the concern was that if privilege was not extended to it as an annex to the report in the present case, its disclosure would identity the subject matter of the legal advice given by the solicitors to the taxpayer in the report. For that reason, although the note itself was not subject to privilege, it was similarly covered by privilege in the present context. In relation to other schedules, those were copies of information published by other bodies. By themselves they were not subject to privilege. Nevertheless, the concern was that to order their disclosure, as they were schedules to the privileged report, would identify the subject matter on which the solicitors had given legal advice to their client. For that reason, the privilege to which the report was subject extended to its schedules and in that context they were not disclosable. Judgment would be given accordingly.

Behague v Revenue and Customs Comrs [2013] UKFTT 596 (TC), [2014] WTLR 187, [2013] All ER (D) 120 (Nov) (First-tier Tribunal: Judge Mosedale).

1473 Capital allowances—first-year tax credits

The Capital Allowances (First-year Tax Credits) Order 2013, SI 2013/464 (in force on 28 March 2013), extends to 31 March 2018 the period during which relevant first-year expenditure must be incurred in respect of which a first-year tax credit may be claimed.

1474 Capital allowances—plant and machinery—energy-saving plant and machinery

The Capital Allowances (Energy-saving Plant and Machinery) (Amendment) Order 2013, SI 2013/1763 (in force on 7 August 2013), further amends the 2001 Order, SI 2001/2541, by updating the definitions of 'Energy Technology Criteria List' and 'Energy Technology Product List'.

1475 Capital allowances—plant and machinery—environmentally beneficial plant and machinery

The Capital Allowances (Environmentally Beneficial Plant and Machinery) (Amendment) Order 2013, SI 2013/1762 (in force on 7 August 2013), amends the 2003 Order, SI 2003/2076, by updating the definitions of 'Water Technology Criteria List' and 'Water Technology Product List' and adding 'greywater recovery and reuse equipment' to the descriptions of the environmentally beneficial plant and machinery technology classes.

1476 Capital allowances—plant and machinery—film—production costs

A partnership agreement was executed and the taxpayer was formed for the purpose of producing a film. The total budget of the film was agreed as part of the partnership agreement which included a sum of deferred revenue expenditure. A company entered into a number of production team contracts with cast, crew and other service providers, each of which provided for a mixture of fixed payments and further sums. In all cases, the production team contract was between the individual member of the production team and the company, and in each case, the fixed amount was to be paid by instalments during the period for which he had been obliged to provide services. The further sums were expressed as pre-agreed amounts of net income, when fully received from the sales agent subject to an overall limit applicable to each individual. Residue of the proceeds of exploitation of the film was dealt with as producer's profits and belonged to those who had agreed to share in that residue. The company was free to assign the benefit of any contractual undertaking in its favour. However, it could not, by assignment or otherwise, override the rights of the individual members of the production team to deferred cast and crew amounts, if any. The rights to those amounts would have belonged to those individuals from the moment they had signed up and performed the services specified in their production team contracts. Later, the taxpayer entered into a production and financing agreement with the company, the effect of which was to transfer ownership of the completed film to the taxpayer and to grant it exclusive rights to exploit the film. Services of the cast and crew, as required by the individual production team contracts, had been performed and the individuals' particular right to payment of their deferred cast and crew amounts would therefore have become the property of those individuals. Work on the film continued after the end of the tax year, but the film was not released until some time later. A copy of the taxpayer's financial statement for the relevant tax year recorded a large tangible fixed asset value. In its tax return, the taxpayer claimed relief under the Finance (No 2) Act 1997 s 48 for film production costs, comprising an amount by way of deferred cast and crew amounts. Later, the Commissioners for Her Majesty's Revenue and Customs issued a closure notice of its inquiry into the tax return, reducing the taxpayer's loss to the amount actually contributed to the taxpayer. On appeal by the taxpayer, *held*, nothing had displaced the obligations in the production team contracts assumed by the company to account to the individual members of the production team for their shares of net income as and when exploitation proceeds came through the pipeline. Nor could the production and financing agreement be read as showing that the taxpayer had assumed those liabilities. There was no ambiguity in that agreement and no aberration in the language that called for a different interpretation. The words of exclusion in the agreement covered the deferred cast and crew amounts that would belong to the individual members of the production team as and when successful exploitation of the film took place, and the company would remain contractually bound to those individuals to account to them for their respective deferred cast and crew amounts. Further, no term could be implied in the agreement that passed the obligation in respect of the deferred cast and crew amounts to the taxpayer. No such implication was required to make the arrangements embodied in the agreement effective. Furthermore, the agreement excluded the taxpayer's responsibility for deferred cast and crew amounts. The disputed amount, representing the aggregate of the deferred cast and crew amounts, had not been capital expenditure by the partnership on the production of the film for the purposes of the 1997 Act. Accordingly, the appeal would be dismissed.

Re Alchemist (Devil's Gate) Film Partnership [2013] UKFTT 157 (TC), [2013] All ER (D) 215 (Mar) (First-tier Tribunal: Sir Stephen Oliver QC).

Finance (No 2) Act 1997 s 48 repealed: Finance Act 2006 Sch 26.

1477 Capital allowances—research and development—loss relief

A company registered in Jersey and an English company entered into a limited partnership agreement which established the taxpayer. Certain partners became parties to that agreement by adherence agreements made on the same day. They were required to pay their capital contributions two days later. On the same day, the taxpayer reached agreement with a company to provide administrative services to it. Soon after, the taxpayer entered into a research agreement with the English company under which it agreed to undertake research and development for the taxpayer. On the same day, the English company agreed a research sub-contract with a third company to undertake research and development of vaccines, with any intellectual property being vested in the taxpayer. The third company assigned the benefit of four identified patent applications and inventions to the English company in pursuance of that agreement. In turn, the English company assigned to the taxpayer the benefit of the same identified patent applications and inventions. The taxpayer and the English company concluded a licence agreement under which the taxpayer granted licences to the English company for up to 70 years to use or deal with any products incorporating or based on any of the patents or other intellectual property arising from the vaccine research. In consideration, the English company agreed to pay guaranteed non-refundable licence fees to the taxpayer. The taxpayer claimed a large amount of loss relief in respect of research and development capital allowances incurred. It further claimed 70 per cent of the total fee which had been paid to the Jersey company on the basis that it was a payment of a revenue nature incurred as an expense of its trade. Some time later, the Revenue issued a closure notice to the taxpayer, concluding that the taxpayer had not been carrying on a trade in the United Kingdom or at all. Alternatively, it had not incurred expenditure qualifying for relief under the Capital Allowances Act 2001 s 437 or had not incurred expenditure deductible in computing the profits of a trade. For a successful claim to be made by the individual partners, the conditions for a claim for research and development allowance had to be met as did the conditions for claiming sideways loss relief as set out in the Income and Corporation Taxes Act 1988 ss 380–384A, 391. Pursuant to s 381, one of the partners claimed losses, of which over half were to be carried back to previous years. He further claimed for loan interest relief pursuant to s 353 within the scope of s 362 in respect of the loan he had taken out to help finance his capital contribution to the taxpayer. Later, the Revenue informed him of a check on his self-assessment return and he was notified that his claim was reduced to zero. His claim for loan interest was also refused. The taxpayer appealed. *Held*, there was no contention that any capital had been recovered by any partner from the taxpayer during the relevant period. It followed that the partner had been entitled to relief only to the extent that the sums he had contributed as capital to the partnership had been used for the purposes of the trade. They were allowable to the extent that they had been used to fund the partner's share of the research sub-contract with the third company and incidental expenses. Therefore, the appeal would be allowed to the limited extent that the partners might claim research and development allowances in respect of their appropriate shares of the total sums incurred by them in funding the third company to conduct relevant research and development. They were further entitled to interest under s 362 for their loans to the extent that those loans had been used for trading income. Accordingly, the appeal would be allowed in part.

Re Partners of the Vaccine Research Ltd Partnership [2013] UKFTT 073 (TC), [2013] All ER (D) 342 (Feb) (First-tier Tribunal: Judge David Williams presiding).

1988 Act ss 362, 380–384A, 391 replaced by provisions of Income Tax Act 2007.

1478   Capital securities—taxation

The Taxation of Regulatory Capital Securities Regulations 2013, SI 2013/3209 (in force on 1 January 2014), make provision in relation to the taxation of new types of regulatory capital security issued to meet the requirements of Commission Directive (EU) 36/2013 and Commission Regulation (EU) 575/2013 by (1) providing (a) that regulatory capital securities represent loan relationships for the purposes of the Corporation Tax Acts, subject to special rules in respect of the issuer of such securities and, in the case of a connected company, the holder of the security; (b) that a regulatory capital security is treated as a normal commercial loan; (c) that a payment in respect of a regulatory capital security is not a distribution but is income under the Income Tax (Trading and Other Income) Act 2005 Pt 4 Ch 2 (ss 369–381); (d) a specific exception from the duty to deduct tax from yearly interest in the Income Tax Act 2007 ss 874 and 889; and (e) an exemption from stamp duties; (2) making provision in relation to anti-avoidance; (3) disapplying the exceptions from the duty to deduct tax from yearly interest in the 2007 Act ss 878 and 885; (4) making consequential amendments to the Loan Relationship and Derivative Contracts (Disregard and Bringing into Account of Profits and Losses) Regulations 2004, SI 2004/3256; and (5) making consequential repeals.

1479   Car and van fuel benefit—appropriate percentage

The Van Benefit and Car and Van Fuel Benefit Order 2013, SI 2013/3033 (in force on 31 December 2013), amends the Income Tax (Earnings and Pensions) Act 2003 ss 150(1), 155(1)(b) and 161(b). Specifically, the order (1) increases the figure in s 150(1) to £21,700 for the tax year 2014–15 and subsequent tax years; (2) increases the figure in s 155(1) to £3,090 for the tax year 2014–15 and subsequent tax years; and (3) increases the figure in s 161(b) to £581 for the tax year 2014–15 and subsequent tax years.

1480   Car fuel benefit—appropriate percentage

See para 1479.

1481   Commissioners of Customs and Excise—exercise of functions

See para 648.

Accounting Practice ('UK GAPP'). In those accounts the taxpayer had showed, within shareholders' funds on its balance sheet, certain redeemable preference shares issued shortly before the end of that year at a value which corresponded to the net proceeds of their issue. The preference shares had been divided into four classes and each class had been referenced to a particular bond owned by the taxpayer ('the relevant assets'). The relevant assets had been loan relationships and had been recognised at their full value as assets in the taxpayer's balance sheet as at 31 December 2004. The taxpayer resolved to adopt the use of International Financial Reporting Standards ('IFRS') in place of UK GAAP with effect from 1 January 2005. Following the adoption of IFRS the preference shares were classified as liabilities of the taxpayer and both the preference shares and 95 per cent of the relevant assets were de-recognised in the taxpayer's balance sheet. Those de-recognitions had reflected differences between the closing balances on the balance sheet as at 31 December 2004 and the opening balances as at 1 January 2005. The taxpayer claimed that in those circumstances the effect of the 1996 Act Sch 9 para 19A was to allow a debit in the 2005 year to reflect the difference between the carrying value of the relevant assets in the balance sheet as the end of the 2004 year and the carrying value of the relevant assets recognised as at 1 January 2005. The taxpayer claimed to bring into account in the 2005 year a loan relationship debit. The Commissioners for Her Majesty's Revenue and Customs amended the taxpayer's corporation tax return for the 2005 year, disallowing the loan relationship debit claimed by the taxpayer. The taxpayer appealed. *Held*, following the adoption of IFRS in the taxpayer's accounts for the 2005 year, in the opening balances as at 1 January 2005, 95 per cent of the relevant assets had been de-recognised and the linked preference shares had ceased to be recognised. In consequence, there had been a difference between the accounting value of a debit in the 2004 and 2005 accounting periods in so far as accounting de-recognition of assets was concerned. Accordingly, the conditions in Sch 9 para 19A applied and the identified difference was required to be brought into account in the 2005 year in accordance with Sch 9 para 19A(3). On the evidence, one of the taxpayer's purposes in issuing the preference shares had been that the taxpayer would dispose of the relevant assets as part of a general policy of conducting an orderly disposal of its remaining assets. Once that tax avoidance purpose had been achieved, after the end of the 2004 year, that had been the only 'main purpose' of the taxpayer's retention of the legal title to the relevant assets. At no time during the 2005 year had the taxpayer had a tax avoidance purpose as a purpose for being party to the loan relationships constituted by the relevant assets. The 'times' during the 2005 year when the taxpayer's purposes for being a party to the relevant assets had included a tax avoidance purpose, as the main or one of the main purposes for being a party to the relevant assets and, by the same token, the 'times' during the 2005 year when the taxpayer's said purposes had not included such a tax avoidance purpose, should be considered and were highly relevant in carrying out the just and reasonable apportionment required by Sch 9 para 13(1). Carrying out that exercise, at all 'times' during the 2005 year, the taxpayer's purposes for being a party to the relevant assets had not included a tax avoidance purpose as the main or one of the main purposes for its being a party to the relevant assets. Therefore, no part of the debit under Sch 9 para 19A debit fell to be excluded from the debits falling to be brought into account by the taxpayer for the 2005 year. Accordingly, the appeal would be allowed.

Fidex Ltd v Revenue and Customs Comrs [2013] UKFTT 212 (TC), [2013] All ER (D) 89 (May) (First-tier Tribunal: Judge John Walters QC presiding).

1996 Act Sch 9 paras 13, 19A replaced by Corporation Tax Act 2009 ss 315–318, 441, 442.

1492 Corporation tax—capital allowances—plant and machinery—leasing of overseas ships

The Capital Allowances Act 2001 s 123(1) provides that a ship is used for a qualifying purpose at any time when it is let on charter in the course of a trade which consists of or includes operating ships by a person who is (a) resident in the United Kingdom or carries on the trade there; and (b) is responsible for navigating and managing the ship throughout the period of the charter and for defraying (i) all expenses in connection with the ship throughout that period; or (ii) substantially all such expenses other than those directly incidental to a particular voyage or to the employment of the ship during that period.

A Japanese company with a United Kingdom subsidiary won a tender to acquire and operate two vessels to transport natural gas under a time charter. The taxpayer leased the vessels to two specially formed Cayman Islands companies. Under the leases, the risk of having to bear additional costs and the hope and expectation of receiving the value of the vessels at the end of the primary period was vested in two further companies, which granted charters to the subsidiary for a defined period. During the construction of the vessels, it was realised that increases in their manning costs would result in the subsidiary suffering substantial losses once they were delivered. The subsidiary re-organised its business and the Revenue amended the taxpayer's corporation tax return on the basis that the taxpayer was not entitled to claim capital allowances in respect of its expenditure on the vessels. The taxpayer appealed successfully against the amendment. On appeal by the Revenue, an issue arose as to the construction of the 2001 Act s 123(1). *Held*, the words 'substantially all' suggested 'nearly all'. It did not matter that costs were, to an insubstantial extent, defrayed by someone other than the ship operator. The contrast between the reference to 'all expenses' in s 123(1)(b)(i) and the reference to 'substantially all ... expenses' in s 123(1)(b)(ii) tended to confirm that something less than all would suffice in the context of s 123(1)(b)(ii). Every word of an enactment had to be presumed to have been put there for a purpose. Whichever way 'substantially' was construed, there was no situation in which s 123(1)(b)(i) would apply but s 123(1)(b)(ii) would not. It was not inherently implausible that Parliament had thought it good enough for a ship operator to defray nearly all the expenses in question rather than every single one. Accordingly, the appeal would be dismissed.

Lloyds TSB Equipment Leasing (No 1) Ltd v Revenue and Customs Comrs [2013] UKUT 368 (TCC), [2014] STC 191 (Upper Tribunal: Newey J and Judge Howard Nowlan).

1493   Corporation tax—computation—loan relationships—credits and debits brought into account

The Finance Act 1996 s 84(1)(a) provides that the credits and debits to be brought into account in the case of any company in respect of its loan relationships are the sums which, in accordance with an authorised accounting method and when taken together, fairly represent, for the accounting period in question, all profits, gains and losses of the company, including those of a capital nature, which arise to the company from its loan relationships and related transactions. 'Profits, gains and losses arising to a company' does not include any amounts required to be transferred to the company's share premium account (s 84(2)(a)), but does include any profits, gains or losses which are carried to or sustained by any other reserve maintained by the company (s 84(2)(b)).

It has been held, on an appeal by a taxpayer against a notice of amendment in relation to its corporation tax return, that the purpose of the 1996 Act s 84(2)(a) is clear. On the issue by a company of shares at a premium, the amount or value of that premium is required to be transferred to the share premium account and, in broad terms, it is treated as paid up share capital of the company with the attendant restrictions limiting reduction of share capital. The important point, in the context of the loan relationship rules, is that the amount of the profit comprising the premium bears little or no relationship to any profit inherently arising from the terms of the loan relationship itself, or even arising from the dealing in the loan relationship. It is for that reason that it is excluded from the profits to be treated as a credit for loan relationship purposes and so excluded from the tax charge. It follows from that purpose that s 84(2)(a) relates to those circumstances where the amount required to be transferred to the share premium account is the profit arising by reason of the shares being issued at a premium, and it is that profit, so arising, which is excepted from the profits and gains giving rise to credits to be brought into the tax charge.

Vocalspruce Ltd v Revenue and Customs Comrs [2013] UKUT 276 (TCC), [2013] STC 2261 (Upper Tribunal: Proudman J and Judge Edward Sadler).
1996 Act s 84(1), (2) now Corporation Tax Act 2009 ss 293(1), (3), 307(3).

1494   Corporation tax—computation—profits—deductions—payments made wholly and exclusively for trade

The taxpayer company was a fishing, fish processing, fish wholesaling and fish retailing business. It was wholly owned by an individual and a family trust, and was controlled by a second individual whose state of mind amounted to the state of mind of the taxpayer. The taxpayer made payments to a rugby club which it treated as deductible amounts in its accounts under the heading 'Advertising and Marketing'. The club was in severe financial difficulty and the second individual bought shares in the taxpayer in order to keep the club going. It was common ground that the second individual obtained significant influence in the community through being the club's major sponsor in a way which could not be achieved by simply participating as a director. The second individual acquired more shares but some years later, having achieved what he wanted for the taxpayer, told the club that he was reducing his sponsorship payments. In the relevant period, the taxpayer had advertised its brand on players' shirts and the club's website. A particular benefit to the taxpayer as a result of making the sponsorship payments was that it made it easier to obtain bank funding for the taxpayer's expansion. The taxpayer sought to exclude the payments it had made to the club from the computation of its profits for the purposes of corporation tax. The Income and Corporation Taxes Act 1988 s 74(1)(a) precluded the deduction of expenditure which had not been 'wholly and exclusively laid out or expended for the purposes of the trade'. The taxpayer appealed against assessments to corporation tax made by the Commissioners for Her Majesty's Revenue and Customs on the basis that it should be allowed to deduct payments made to the club from the computation of profits. The First-tier Tribunal decided that improving the financial position of the club had been a conscious purpose in the mind of the second individual and therefore the taxpayer. It concluded that the sums paid by the taxpayer to the club for purposes such as increasing the club's player budget were not deductible for the purposes of corporation tax. On appeal by the taxpayer, *held*, the First-tier Tribunal had been correct. A necessarily inherent objective or result of some activity carried on for another reason did not mean that the activity automatically had two purposes in the relevant sense which would prevent the expenditure from being deductible. The real question was whether that was what the First-tier Tribunal had found on the facts. The judge clearly had in mind the question whether the fact that it could be said that helping the club had been a means to an end had made helping the club consequential and incidental. The judge had not accepted that they had been. He had made a clear finding that the second individual's and, therefore, the taxpayer's, subjective intentions had included improving the club's position. It was a finding that had plainly been open to the First-tier Tribunal to make on the evidence. The second individual's conscious purpose of improving the club's financial position had been so that the taxpayer's commercial interests would be furthered in consequence. Both purposes had been in view and therefore the payments had not been wholly and exclusively for the purposes of the taxpayer's trade. Accordingly, the appeal would be dismissed.

Interfish Ltd v Revenue and Customs Comrs [2013] UKUT 336 (TCC), [2014] STC 79 (Upper Tribunal: Birss J). *Okolo v Revenue and Customs Comrs* [2012] UKUT 416 (TCC), [2013] STC 906 applied.

1988 Act s 74(1)(a) now Corporation Tax Act 2009 s 54(1)(a).

1495 Corporation tax—contract for differences—definition

The Corporation Tax Act 2009, Section 582 (Contract for Differences) (Amendment) Order 2013, SI 2013/3218 (in force on 31 December 2013), amends the definition of 'contract for differences' in the Corporation Tax Act 2009 s 582 so as to extend it to a new type of contract introduced by the Energy Act 2013.

1496 Corporation tax—deductions—loan interest—different treatment of non-residents—free movement of capital

The taxpayer was a Portuguese company whose share capital was held mostly by a Belgian company. The remaining shares were held by an American company. The taxpayer and the American company entered into a loan agreement pursuant to which the taxpayer had the use of a line of credit. The taxpayer took the view that the interest payable under the loan was tax deductible. However, Portuguese tax law restricted the deduction of interest connected with debts exceeding a specified debt to equity ratio. That restriction did not apply where the lender was resident in the European Union. On that basis, the Portuguese tax authority refused to allow the taxpayer to make the deduction. The taxpayer brought proceedings challenging that decision, claiming that the law in question contravened the right under TFEU art 63 to the free movement of capital. The national court decided to stay the proceedings and refer to the European Court of Justice for a preliminary ruling the question of whether art 63 should be interpreted as precluding rules of a member state which provided that, where interest applied to the part of an overall debt categorised as excessive had been paid by a resident company to a lending company established in a non-member country with which the borrowing company had special relations, it was not deductible as an expense for the purposes of determining taxable profit, but where such interest was paid to a resident lending company with which the borrowing company has special relations, it was deductible for those purposes. *Held*, art 63 prohibited measures that were of such a kind as to discourage non-residents from making investments in a member state or discourage that member state's residents from doing so in other states. Any such restriction had to be appropriate for ensuring the attainment of the objective in question and not go beyond what was necessary to attain that objective. In the present case, the relevant provisions of the Portuguese tax code went beyond what was necessary in order to attain their objective. The term 'special relations' encompassed situations that did not necessarily involve the lending company of a non-member country holding shares in the resident borrowing company. Where there was no such shareholding, the effect of the method for calculating the excess indebtedness was that any credit arrangement between those two companies fell to be regarded as excessive. It followed that art 63 should be interpreted as precluding rules of the specified kind in circumstances where, if the lending company established in a non-member country did not have a shareholding in the resident borrowing company, they nevertheless presumed that the overall debt owed by the borrowing company formed part of an arrangement designed to avoid the tax normally payable.

Case C-282/12 *Itelcar – Automoveis de Aluguer Lda v Fazenda Publica* [2013] All ER (D) 114 (Oct) (ECJ: Fourth Chamber).

1497　　Corporation tax—direct internal taxation—merger between parent company and
　　　　non-resident subsidiary—deduction of subsidiary's losses—freedom of
　　　　establishment

The TFEU art 49 prohibits restrictions on freedom of establishment of nationals of the EU, and art 54 provides for companies formed pursuant to the law of a member state and having their registered office, central administration or principal place of business within the EU, the right to exercise their activity in the member state concerned through a subsidiary, a branch or an agency in the same way as natural persons.

The applicant was a Finnish undertaking with a subsidiary in Sweden. Following trading losses, the subsidiary ceased trading. The applicant planned to merge with the subsidiary whose assets, liabilities and residual obligations would be transferred to the applicant which would then no longer have a subsidiary or permanent establishment in Sweden. The applicant sought an advance decision from the Finnish tax authority as to whether, once the merger had been effected, the applicant would be able to deduct the subsidiary's losses in accordance with Finnish law. The authority decided that, as the subsidiary's losses had been ascertained pursuant to Swedish tax law, they could not fall within the scope of Finnish law. In proceedings in which the applicant challenged the authority's decision, a Finnish court decided that, if a resident company absorbed a Finnish company, it could deduct from tax the Finnish company's losses under the conditions set out in Finnish law on income tax, provided that the operation had not been carried out for the sole purpose of obtaining a tax advantage. No indication was given as to the conditions under which a deduction could be made if the company absorbed was situated in another member state. It fell to be determined whether the Finnish law contained a restriction on freedom of establishment and, if so, whether the restriction might be regarded as justified by the need for member states to preserve a balanced allocation of their power to impose taxes and to guard against the risks of the double use of losses and tax avoidance. *Held*, the TFEU arts 49 and 54 did not preclude national legislation under which a parent company merging with a subsidiary established in another member state that had ceased activity could not deduct from its taxable income the losses incurred by that subsidiary in respect of the tax years prior to the merger, while that national legislation allowed such a possibility when the merger was with a resident subsidiary. Such national legislation was none the less incompatible with EU law if it did not allow the parent company the possibility of showing that its non-resident subsidiary had exhausted the possibilities of taking those losses into account and that there was no possibility of their being taken into account in its state of residence in respect of future tax years either by itself or by a third party. Further, freedom of establishment did not as a matter of principle imply the application of a particular law to the calculation of the merged subsidiary's losses taken over by the parent company, in an operation such as that at issue. On the other hand, EU law precluded those methods of calculation being such as to constitute an obstacle to freedom of establishment. It followed that, in principle, the calculation of the losses of the non-resident subsidiary taken over by the parent company should not lead to unequal treatment compared with the calculation which would have been made in a similar case for the taking over of the losses of a resident subsidiary. However, that question could not be addressed in an abstract and hypothetical manner, but should be necessary on a case-by-case basis.

Case C-123/11 *Proceedings brought by A Oy* [2013] STC 1960 (ECJ: Fourth Chamber).

1498   Corporation tax—group relief—losses incurred by subsidiaries in other member states—'no possibilities' test

The present case involved a group litigation against the Revenue and Customs Commissioners concerning the availability of cross-border group relief from corporation tax for United Kingdom resident companies. It had been decided in *Marks & Spencer plc v Halsey (Inspector of Taxes)* that the relief was available in the case of a simple corporate group structure on the basis of the 'no possibilities' test. Under that test, the relief would be available if the foreign subsidiary had exhausted the possibilities available in its state of residence for setting the losses against current or past profits, and there was no possibility for the losses to be taken into account in the foreign subsidiary's state of residence in future periods. An appeal by the Revenue to the Supreme Court was pending, including on the issue of the correct interpretation of the 'no possibilities' test. In the present case, the taxpayers sought a reference to the European Court of Justice for a preliminary ruling on the question whether such claims for cross-border group relief could in principle be made in various forms of corporate group structure which differed from the simple structure. They were concerned that the Supreme Court might not provide definitive guidance on the interpretation of the no possibilities test and that there would be further delay in the resolution of the group structure questions if they were not immediately referred to the European Court of Justice. The Revenue contended that as the taxpayers had failed to answer its inquiries in respect of the no possibilities test, the underlying facts had not been established and a reference was premature. *Held*, given the huge amounts of tax potentially recoverable by the taxpayers, the Revenue had been entitled to require full replies to its requests for information on the 'no possibilities' test before it agreed to a joint referral to the European Court of Justice on the group structure issues. It appeared that, with goodwill and co-operation on both sides, it should be possible both for the taxpayers to provide full information about the no possibilities test in representative test cases, and for the same or other test cases to be brought before the First-tier Tribunal by the most convenient route in order to resolve the group structure issues. The application was both premature and procedurally questionable and, accordingly, would be dismissed.

Group Register of the Loss Relief Group Litigation Order v Revenue and Customs Comrs [2013] EWHC 205 (Ch), [2013] All ER (D) 129 (Feb) (Chancery Division: Henderson J). Case C-446/03 *Marks & Spencer plc v Halsey (Inspector of Taxes)* [2006] All ER (EC) 255, ECJ (2005 Abr para 3231); and *Marks & Spencer plc v Revenue and Customs Comrs* [2011] EWCA Civ 1156, [2012] STC 231 (2011 Abr para 1515) considered.

The taxpayer was a leading retailer in the United Kingdom, with subsidiaries in Germany and Belgium. The subsidiaries began to incur losses and they were eventually dissolved following liquidation. The taxpayer sought cross-border group relief in respect of the losses sustained by the subsidiaries. A dispute arose between the taxpayer and the Revenue as to the date at which the determination of whether group relief was available should be made. The matter came to trial, and the court, applying the 'no possibilities' test, ruled that group relief had to be applied at the date at which the group relief claim was made. The Revenue appealed, submitting that the correct approach was to apply group relief at the end of the accounting period in which the losses crystallised. *Held*, entitlement to cross-border relief was to be examined on the basis of the circumstances existing at the date of the claim. The question for inquiry was whether the taxpayer had been able to show, on the basis of the circumstances known at the date when it made its claim, that there had been no possibility of the losses in question being utilised in the member state of the surrendering company in any accounting period prior to the date of the claim and no possibility of such utilisation in the accounting period in which the claim was made or in any future accounting periods. In the present case, what the taxpayer had been doing could be attributed to the fact that the subsidiaries had ceased trading six years earlier, and had not been exercising an option to choose where to seek relief for the losses that had been incurred nor to seek freely from one year to the next the tax scheme applicable to those subsidiaries' losses. There was no reason to think that what the taxpayer had done had to be seen as a threat to the balanced allocation of taxing powers. Accordingly, the appeal would be dismissed.

Marks & Spencer plc v Revenue and Customs Comrs [2013] UKSC 30, [2013] 3 All ER 835 (Supreme Court: Lord Neuberger P, Lord Hope DP, Lord Mance, Lord Reed and Lord Carnwath SCJJ). Decision of Court of Appeal [2011] EWCA Civ 1156, [2012] STC 231 (2011 Abr para 1515) affirmed.

1499   Corporation tax—insurance companies—transitional provision

The Insurance Companies (Amendment to Schedule 17 to the Finance Act 2012 (Transitional Provision)) Regulations 2013, SI 2013/2244 (in force on 30 September 2013), amend the Finance Act 2012 Sch 17 to correct a mismatch between the transitional provisions for the corporate tax regime for insurance companies established by the 2012 Act and rules for the transfer of insurance business so that amounts derived from items that have been taken into account for tax purposes by a transferor company but which have been disregarded under the transitional provisions as excluded items cannot be brought into account again by a transferee company following a transfer of insurance business.

1500   Corporation tax—intangibles relief—acquisition of interest in limited liability partnership

The taxpayer company decided to increase its interest in a limited liability partnership ('the associate partnership'). As a result, the parties entered into a new limited liability partnership agreement. For accounting periods prior to the date of the agreement, the taxpayer's interest had been recognised in its accounts as an investment. However, following the agreement, the accounts showed the associate partnership as a subsidiary undertaking and not as goodwill. The consolidated group accounts for the period showed goodwill relating to the purchase calculated as the difference between the total consideration paid and the fair value of members' capital purchased, to be amortised over seven years. The taxpayer's calculation of profits for corporation tax purposes treated the purchase of a controlling interest in the associate partnership as an acquisition of goodwill. On that basis, the taxpayer claimed relief under the Finance Act 2002 Sch 29 for the relevant part of the accounting period. The Revenue rejected the claim and the taxpayer appealed, submitting that, by virtue of the Income and Corporation Taxes Act 1988 s 118ZA, which required that relief under the 2002 Act Sch 29 should be available if it would have been available had the associate partnership been a general partnership and not an LLP, an LLP and its members should be treated in the same way for corporation tax purposes as a general partnership. *Held*, the associate partnership was an LLP carrying on a trade, profession or other business with a view to profit and, therefore, was to be treated as a partnership for corporation tax purposes. It followed that the interests in the associate partnership acquired by the taxpayer were to be treated as interests in a partnership for corporation tax purposes. Such interests were excluded from Sch 29 by Sch 29 para 76(1)(c), but they were brought back within Sch 29 by Sch 29 para 76(3) if they were treated for accounting purposes as representing an interest in an intangible fixed asset of the associate partnership. The uncontested expert evidence was that the assets of the associate partnership were not the taxpayer's assets for accounting purposes and that the taxpayer could not include those assets in its own accounts, but should show its interest as an investment in a subsidiary undertaking. It followed that Sch 29 para 76(3) could not save the taxpayer's interests in the associate partnership from being excluded from Sch 29 by Sch 29 para 76(1)(c). The fact that, if the associate partnership was a general partnership, it would have been appropriate for the taxpayer to treat its acquisition of a controlling interest for accounting purposes as an acquisition of the underlying goodwill which the taxpayer could proportionally consolidate in its accounts, did not assist the taxpayer in the actual circumstances of the associate partnership being an LLP. It followed that the taxpayer had not been entitled to intangibles relief under Sch 29 in respect of its acquisition of the interest. Accordingly, the appeal would be dismissed.

Armajaro Holdings Ltd v Revenue and Comrs [2013] UKFTT 571 (TC), [2013] All ER (D) 41 (Nov) (First-tier Tribunal: Judge Greg Sinfield presiding).

1988 Act s 118ZA now Corporation Tax Act 2009 s 1273. 2002 Act Sch 29 para 76 now 2009 Act s 807.

1501   Corporation tax—investment trusts—approval of companies

The Investment Trust (Approved Company) (Tax) (Amendment) Regulations 2013, SI 2013/1406 (in force on 28 June 2013), amend the 2011 Regulations, SI 2011/2999, so as to (1) make changes in relation to the amount that an investment trust is permitted to retain in respect of an accounting period; and (2) include a new measure of the maximum amount where the investment trust has accumulated revenue losses brought forward from previous accounting periods and where the investment trust is required to retain income by virtue of a restriction imposed by law.

1502   Corporation tax—novation of swaps—closure notice—novation of interest-rate swap with company in same group

The Finance Act 2002 had replaced the swaps regime of the Finance Act 1994 with a somewhat modified regime, the new regime coming into force in relation to companies for their first accounting period to commence after 1 October 2002. The taxpayer company made a novation of an 'in the money' fixed/floating interest-rate swap to another company in the same corporate group (the 'sister company') in return for a premium. In relation to that transaction, the taxpayer's accounting period commenced after 1 October 2002 and the sister company's accounting period commenced before that date. The taxpayer's intention was that that mismatch, taken together with an effective rollover rule introduced by the 2002 Act Sch 26 para 28, which was designed to disregard novations between group companies, would result in the premium paid for the novation falling out of charge in the hands of the taxpayer while the sister company, which was taxed in relation to swaps on a 'mark to market' basis, would inherit no tax liability under the novation. The Revenue opened inquiries into the taxpayer's tax returns. They considered that the effective rollover rule of Sch 26 para 28 did not apply in relation to the novation and that the taxpayer should simply be taxed on the amount of the premium. The Revenue then mistakenly issued what appeared to be closure notices, the effect of which would be to complete their inquiries. After the letters in question had been sent for printing, but prior to their being posted, a Revenue officer dealing with the case e-mailed the taxpayer and indicated that the closure notices had been issued in error. The taxpayer appealed, contending that the mistaken issuance of the two closure notices precluded the Revenue from making any adjustments to its tax returns and, alternatively, that the effective rollover rule in Sch 26 para 28 had not applied to the novation. *Held*, a closure notice was a notice issued to inform the taxpayer that the Revenue had completed its inquiries. The notices sent by the Revenue could not be construed to have served that function in view of the fact that the taxpayer had been informed that those notices had been issued in error before they had been posted. Accordingly, it could not be said that the taxpayer had been notified that the Revenue's inquiries had been completed, and so it had been entitled to challenge the treatment of the novation. It was clear that so far as Sch 26 para 28(1) and (2) were concerned, those provisions aptly referred to the situation of the taxpayer and the sister company in relation to the novation. However, Sch 26 para 28(3) governed what had to be done when a transaction was effected by the parties covered by Sch 26 para 28(1) and (2). Schedule 26 para 28(3) did not apply disjunctively to the transferor and the transferee, but required the two companies to be treated in a clearly matching manner. Therefore, even on a literal interpretation, let alone a purposive construction, the direction had been to calculate the tax of the two companies together in a manner that had simply not been possible on the facts of the novation in the present case. Further, it would have been contrary to the manifest intention of Parliament to strain the language to enable it to be relied on by just one party to the transaction when it had been clearly inapplicable to the other. In those circumstances, Sch 26 para 28(3) had not applied at all to the novation and the taxpayer was liable to tax on the premium. Accordingly, the appeal would be dismissed.

Bristol & West plc v Revenue and Customs Comrs [2013] UKFTT 216 (TC), [2013] All ER (D) 49 (Nov) (First-tier Tribunal: Judges Nowlan and Lousada). *Tower Mcashback LLP v Revenue and Customs Comrs* [2011] UKSC 19, [2011] 3 All ER 171 (2011 Abr para 1503) followed.

2002 Act Sch 26 para 28 now Corporation Tax Act 2009 ss 625–627.

1503   Corporation tax—profits from patents—EEA rights

The Profits from Patents (EEA Rights) Order 2013, SI 2013/420 (in force on 1 April 2013), specifies rights to which the Corporation Tax Act 2010 Pt 8A (ss 357A–357GE) applies, lists the EEA states which can grant such rights and describes the rights by reference to the process under which they are granted.

1504   Corporation tax—unauthorised unit trusts

See para 1524.

1505   Deductions—computation of profits—trade expenses—accommodation costs

The taxpayer, who was a professional actor, deducted certain expenses relating to accommodation in his income tax self-assessment, including expenses for the taking on of a tenancy while performing in a musical. The Commissioners for Her Majesty's Revenue and Customs decided that the taxpayer was not entitled, under the Income Tax (Trading and Other Income) Act 2005 s 34(1)(a), to deduct those expenses, but the First-tier Tribunal allowed the taxpayer's appeal against the Commissioners' decision on the basis that the taxpayer was not seeking a home. The Commissioners appealed on the ground that the First-tier Tribunal had not considered, or considered properly, whether the taxpayer had a dual purpose in incurring the expenditure in order to meet his ordinary needs for warmth and shelter, as well as for his stated business purpose. *Held,* it was settled law that a distinction had to be drawn between an expense that was necessary to enable a profession to be carried out, and that which was wholly and exclusively incurred for the purposes of that profession. The exclusivity limb of the wholly and exclusively test entailed examining whether the expenditure in question had a dual purpose. If the expenditure was not solely for a business purpose, it would not be deductible. However, expenditure on items that, outside a business context, simply met ordinary needs could be regarded as having solely a business purpose. The First-tier Tribunal focused purely on the issue as to whether, in taking on the tenancy, the taxpayer had been seeking a home. Therefore, it was clear that the First-tier Tribunal had deliberately not considered the question as to whether the shelter and warmth that inevitably followed from arranging accommodation had been anything more than incidental to the business purpose that the taxpayer had in mind. The facts found had not inevitably led to a conclusion that there had been a dual purpose. The tribunal was unable to conclude that the application of the correct legal test would inevitably result in the expenditure not being deductible. It was necessary to establish on a subjective basis what had been in the taxpayer's mind when he entered into the tenancy agreement. Not having the taxpayer before the tribunal, it was unable to carry out that exercise and it was properly a matter for the First-tier Tribunal. Accordingly, the appeal would be allowed.

Revenue and Customs Comrs v Healy [2013] UKUT 0337 (TCC), [2014] STC 384 (Upper Tribunal: Judge Timothy Herrington and Judge John Clark). *MacKinlay (Inspector of Taxes) v Arthur Young McClelland Moores & Co* [1990] 2 AC 239, [1990] 1 All ER 45, HL (1989 Abr para 1243); *Prior (Inspector of Taxes) v Saunders* [1993] STC 562 (1993 Abr para 1500); and *McLaren v Mumford (Inspector of Taxes)* [1996] STC 1134 (1996 Abr para 1688) applied.

1506   Double taxation relief—foreign withholding tax—maximum amount

See Case C-168/11 *Beker v Finanzamt Heilbronn*, para 2710.

1507   Double taxation relief—taxes on income—Albania

The Double Taxation Relief and International Tax Enforcement (Albania) Order 2013, SI 2013/3145 (in force on a date to be notified in the London Gazette), contains an agreement between the governments of the United Kingdom and the Republic of Albania for the avoidance of double taxation and the prevention of fiscal evasion with respect to taxes on income and capital gains.

1508   Double taxation relief—taxes on income—Brunei Darussalam

The Double Taxation Relief and International Tax Enforcement (Brunei Darussalam) Order 2013, SI 2013/3146 (in force on a date to be notified in the London Gazette), contains an agreement and a protocol which further amend an agreement, scheduled to the

becoming a bad leaver, his becoming a good leaver, or as a result of an exit. The taxpayer surrendered his shares to the employer and received a large payment. The employer deducted income tax and national insurance contributions from the sum. The employee filed his self-assessment income tax return declaring the income from his surrender of the shares, but claiming a deduction of the same amount, thereby reducing his chargeable income to nil and resulting in a refund claim. He declared a capital gain in respect of his disposal of the shares in his return. The Commissioners for Her Majesty's Revenue and Customs opened an inquiry into the taxpayer's return and, on the basis that they considered that the taxpayer had been negligent in making his self-assessment return, imposed a penalty on him pursuant to the Taxes Management Act 1970 s 95. The taxpayer appealed against the tax assessment and the penalty imposed on him. The issue was whether the gain made by the taxpayer on a disposal of shares in that tax year had been taxable as employment income or whether it had been chargeable, as the taxpayer contended, to capital gains tax. The relevant statutory provisions applied where an employee acquired a beneficial interest in shares as a director or employee of the company and the interest was acquired on terms that made it 'only conditional'. *Held*, the deed dealt with circumstances in which the taxpayer had been required to transfer his shares as a 'bad leaver'. The Income Tax (Earnings and Pensions) Act 2003 s 424(2) appeared to exclude the deed from having the result that the taxpayer's shares had been, for that reason alone, 'only conditional'. However, the other provisions of the deed had the effect that the taxpayer's shares had been 'only conditional'. It provided that where a shareholder was a 'good leaver' then the shareholder would transfer the shares. The deed further provided that a shareholder, as a 'good leaver' should be paid a specified amount, with the effect that the taxpayer's shares were conditional shares for the purposes of s 424. In relation to the clause dealing with the situation of an exit, a shareholder was paid the same amount as under the 'good leaver' clause except that there was no discount. There was no evidence that the amount payable to a shareholder would be equal to or in excess of market value so that the taxpayer had failed to establish that the second limb of the definition of conditional shares contained in s 424(1)(b) had not been satisfied. Both clauses were part of a document other than the articles of association of the employer with the result that the exception to s 424(1) contained in s 424(2)(b) did not apply. The requirement that the shareholder should transfer its shares in the specified circumstances had been binding unless and until the discretion was exercised. There was no evidence that a director had exercised that discretion. The taxpayer's tax return had been negligently made. His accountants had seemed either reluctant or unable to engage with the Commissioners in correspondence in relation to the relevant provisions of the 2003 Act. The application of the provisions of the 2003 Act had simply been overlooked by the taxpayer and his advisers, notwithstanding the terms of the guidance contained in the remittance advice. Accordingly, the appeal would be dismissed.

Stratton v Revenue and Customs Comrs [2013] UKFTT 578 (TC), [2013] All ER (D) 175 (Nov) (First-tier Tribunal: Judge Brannan presiding).

1520   Employment income—exemptions—childcare vouchers and employer contracted childcare

The Income Tax (Exempt Amount for Childcare Vouchers and for Employer Contracted Childcare) Order 2013, SI 2013/513 (in force on 6 April 2013), amends the Income Tax (Earnings and Pensions) Act 2003 ss 270A(6ZA) and 318A(6A) by increasing, from £22 to £25, the maximum weekly amount of childcare vouchers and directly contracted childcare that can be subject to tax relief.

1521   Enterprise management incentives—share option agreement—termination of employment—repayment of investment—compromise agreement

The taxpayer was invited to enter into a share option agreement as an incentive to join a company. He agreed to purchase an option for a specified sum. The taxpayer's employment was subsequently terminated by mutual consent. The taxpayer believed that the company had agreed to repay the amount paid for the option. A compromise agreement was subsequently reached, but the agreement did not state whether it included the amount paid for the option. In his income tax return for the relevant year, the taxpayer omitted the option investment, which he understood to be tax exempt as a redundancy payment. After deciding that the sum included the option repayment, the taxpayer then submitted an amended tax return. The company refused to give the Revenue a breakdown of the sum paid to the taxpayer under the compromise agreement, and on that basis the Revenue concluded that no part of the sum represented the repayment of the option. The taxpayer appealed against that decision, submitting that he would not have signed the compromise agreement if it had not included the repayment of his investment. The Revenue argued that it was not obliged to examine the prior negotiations between the parties when interpreting an agreement. *Held,* the Revenue had a duty to attempt to identify the parties' intentions when making an agreement, although that duty was not identical to that of a court construing a contract. Although the Revenue had been unable to ascertain from the company what the individual component sums had been under the compromise agreement, that did not mean that it was obliged to look at the agreement alone without more. It did not require any distortion of the terms of the compromise agreement to conclude that it comprised a sum in respect of the option agreement as well as a sum in respect of the abrupt termination of the taxpayer's contract of employment. It was inconceivable that the taxpayer would have signed an agreement that did not reflect the fact that he had invested a large sum of money in the option, given that the agreement precluded him from taking any separate action in respect of the option. In the circumstances, the option payment was included in the total sum paid under the compromise agreement. Accordingly, the appeal would be allowed.

Johnson v Revenue and Customs Comrs [2013] UKFTT 242 (TC), [2013] All ER (D) 52 (Jun) (First-tier Tribunal: Judge Jill Gort presiding).

1522   Exemption—base of employer—free movement of workers

See Case C-544/11 *Petersen v Finanzamt Ludwigshafen*, para 2692.

1523   Exemption—monitoring schemes relating to vulnerable persons

The Income Tax (Monitoring Schemes Relating to Vulnerable Persons) Order 2013, SI 2013/1133 (in force on 10 June 2013), amends the Income Tax (Earnings and Pensions) Act 2003 s 326A so as to (1) add an exemption from income tax for the fee for the up-dating service of the Disclosure and Barring Service where those fees are paid or reimbursed by an employer; and (2) provide an exemption from income tax for the fee for criminal record certificates and enhanced criminal record certificates in circumstances where an application is made at the same time as an application to the up-dating service and the fee is paid or reimbursed by an employer.

1524   Exemption—unauthorised unit trusts

The Unauthorised Unit Trusts (Tax) Regulations 2013, SI 2013/2819 (in force in part on 1 November 2013 and in part on 6 April 2014), make provision about the treatment of trustees or unit holders of unauthorised unit trusts for the purposes of income tax, corporation tax and capital gains tax and, in particular, (1) define an exempt unauthorised unit trust and set out the conditions a trust must meet to be an exempt unauthorised unit trust in a period of account; (2) make provision in relation to the process of approval as an exempt unauthorised unit trust; (3) provide that gains accruing to an exempt unauthorised unit trust are not chargeable gains for the purposes of the Taxation of Chargeable Gains Act 1992; (4) set out provisions concerning the taxation of income of exempt unauthorised unit trusts; (5) deal with the charge to tax on unit holders of an exempt unauthorised unit trust; (6) provide for relief for trustees of an exempt unauthorised unit trust; (7) make miscellaneous provision relating to the treatment of exempt unauthorised unit trusts; (8) define a non-exempt unauthorised unit trust as an unauthorised unit trust which is not an exempt unauthorised unit trust; (9) deal with the tax treatment of non-exempt unauthorised unit trusts; (10) set out transitional provision in relation to exempt unauthorised unit trusts and non-exempt unauthorised unit trusts; and (11) make consequential amendments to primary and secondary legislation.

1525   Extra-statutory concessions—enactment

The Enactment of Extra-Statutory Concessions Order 2013, SI 2013/234 (in force on 1 March 2013), enacts an existing HMRC extra-statutory concession in so far as it applied to stamp duty, and amends statutory provisions inserted by the 2010 Order, SI 2010/157, and the 2011 Order, SI 2011/1037. In particular, the 2013 Order (1) replaces the Taxation of Chargeable Gains Act 1992 s 248B(1), (2) so as to amend the method for the calculation of roll-over relief where there is an exchange of interests in land for which provision is made under ss 248A–248D; these amendments are made so that ss 248A–248D enact the extra-statutory concession as originally intended; (2) replaces the term 'compromise' with 'settlement' and removes the definition of compromise agreement in the Income Tax (Earnings and Pensions) Act 2003 s 413A which relieves the payment of certain legal costs from the charge to income tax in s 403; (3) enacts extra-statutory concession C10 as it was applied in practice by HMRC to stamp duty; and (4) adds the Finance Act 1930 ss 42A, 42B and the Finance Act 2003 Sch 7 paras 2A, 2B, so as to provide (a) that the 1930 Act s 42 (relief from transfer stamp duty in case of transfer of property as between associated companies) and the 2003 Act Sch 7 para 2 (restrictions on availability of group relief) will not apply, prior to various contingencies occurring, in relation to certain types of agreement regulating the affairs of two or more members of a joint venture company carrying on a commercial activity; and (b) that the 1930 Act s 42 and the 2003 Act Sch 7 para 2 do not apply, prior to a default or other event which allows the mortgagee to exercise his rights against the mortgagor, if shares or securities in a company are used as a security under a mortgage in certain situations.

1526 Finance Act 2013

See para 2149.

1527 Income or capital receipt—compensation—loss of investment bonus

A hedge fund, which operated under the umbrella of a company, was transferred by the company to a Luxembourg bank. The taxpayer, the fund manager, who had been the company's employee, became an employee of the bank whose directors agreed to pay the taxpayer an investment bonus as consideration for introducing particular business to the bank. The bank made the taxpayer redundant without paying him the bonus. Legal proceedings brought by the taxpayer against the bank were settled out of court, the bank agreeing to pay compensation to the taxpayer for the loss of the bonus in addition to the redundancy payment he had already received. The taxpayer treated the compensation payment as a capital receipt. The Commissioners for Her Majesty's Revenue and Customs issued a closure notice treating the compensation payment as chargeable to income tax. The taxpayer appealed. *Held*, the taxpayer had not established that the bonus was intended by the parties to be the purchase price of a particular hedge fund vehicle model or any other identifiable competitive intangible asset such as to render the bonus a capital receipt nor was it the case that the taxpayer sold to the bank an intangible asset consisting of customer relationships which he 'owned' personally, having built them up over a number of years. That was because, on the evidence, it appeared that, following the transfer of the fund from the company to the bank, the position of the bank was materially the same as that of the company prior to the transfer, and the role of taxpayer within that structure was materially the same as it was previously. The only material difference was that the manager of the fund was subsequently the bank rather than the company. Ultimately, the nature of the bonus had to be ascertained from the particular facts and circumstances of the case, including the wording of the letter providing for the terms on which the bonus would be paid. On a proper reading, the letter indicated that neither the bank nor the taxpayer or the company regarded the investment bonus as payment for purchase of the division of the company. On consideration of the evidence as a whole, the proper conclusion was that the bonus was a reward for the part played by the taxpayer in enabling the bank to acquire the hedge fund business from the company. It was not a capital sum and, accordingly, the appeal would be dismissed.

Manduca v Revenue and Customs Comrs [2013] UKFTT 234 (TC), [2013] All ER (D) 48 (Nov) (First-Tier Tribunal: Judges Staker and Gable). *Jarrold (Inspector of Taxes) v Boustead; McInnes (Inspector of Taxes) v Large; McInnes (Inspector of Taxes) v Simms* [1964] 3 All ER 76, CA, considered. *Hose v Warwick (Inspector of Taxes)* (1946) 27 TC 459, CA, distinguished.

1528 Individual savings accounts

The Individual Savings Account (Amendment) Regulations 2013, SI 2013/267 (in force on 6 April 2013), further amend the 1998 Regulations, SI 1998/1870, by increasing the overall annual subscription limits for ISAs, including junior ISA accounts. In particular, the 2013 Regulations increase the overall annual subscription limit (1) from £5,640 to £5,760, for ISA accounts held by qualifying individuals aged 16 or over but less than 18; (2) from £11,280 to £11,520, for ISA accounts held by all other qualifying individuals; and (3) from £3,600 to £3,720, for junior ISA accounts.

The Individual Savings Account (Amendment No 2) Regulations 2013, SI 2013/623 (in force on 5 April 2013), further amend the 1998 Regulations above so as to (1) secure that no tax disadvantage accrues to savers who are certified to their ISA account manager by Royal Bank of Scotland Group as having held an account affected by a technical incident within that group during the period 19 June to 6 July 2012 (to 22 July 2012 for Ulster Bank), who as a result withdrew sums from their cash ISAs in that period, and who later in the tax year re-subscribed up to the same total amount in a cash account held with the same ISA manager; and (2) revoke the duty on an ISA account manager at the start of a tax year to give account investors notice about not subscribing to another ISA of the same type in that tax year, and about not exceeding the ISA subscription limits.

The Individual Savings Account (Amendment No 3) Regulations 2013, SI 2013/1743 (in force on 5 August 2013), further amend the 1998 Regulations so as to (1) update the definitions of 'EEA Agreement' and 'EEA State' in light of changes to the membership of the EEA and in order to ensure consistency with definitions in other enactments; (2) expand the definition of 'bulk transfer of accounts' to include a bulk transfer of accounts pursuant to an insurance business transfer scheme or a banking business transfer scheme under the Financial Services and Markets Act 2000 Pt VII (ss 103A–117); (3) allow, subject to certain conditions being met, a subscription to be made to an account following a bulk transfer of accounts sanctioned by the court under Pt VII, without the need for a fresh application to be made by an ISA investor; and (4) include as qualifying investments shares in a company which are admitted to trading on a recognised stock exchange in the European Economic Area.

1529   Information—production of documents—third party notice—request by foreign tax authority—relevant foreign tax

The Finance Act 2008 Sch 36 para 63(1)(m) provides that 'tax' includes 'relevant foreign tax'. 'Relevant foreign tax' means any tax which is imposed under the law of a territory in relation to which arrangements having effect by virtue of the Finance Act 2006 s 173 have been made and which is covered by the arrangements: 2008 Act Sch 36 para 63(4)(b).

The Australian Taxation Office applied to Her Majesty's Commissioners for Revenue and Customs for assistance in accordance with the exchange of information procedure under the Double Taxation Relief (Taxes on Income) (Australia) Order 2003, SI 2003/3199, art 27. An officer of the Revenue was empowered by the 2008 Act Sch 36 para 2 to require a person to provide information for the purposes of checking a person's tax position ('a third party notice'). Such arrangements were made in relation to the signatory countries to the Organisation for Economic Co-operation and Development Convention on Mutual Assistance in Tax Matters ('the OECD Convention'). Australia became a signatory of the OECD Convention, which entered into force in respect of Australia on 1 December 2012. The Commissioners applied for the First-tier Tribunal's approval to the giving of those third party notices. The day before the application came before the tribunal, the Commissioners received representations from solicitors acting for a number of taxpayers whose affairs were the subject of the inquiries. In accordance with usual practice, the hearing was ex parte and the taxpayers had not been informed where or when the hearing would take place. The tribunal approved all of the third party notices. The taxpayers challenged the tribunal's jurisdiction in respect of the Australian Taxation Office's request for third party notices, contending that prior to 1 December 2012 Australian tax was not a 'relevant foreign tax'. Further, they submitted that their preclusion from taking any part in the proceedings constituted a violation of their rights under the European Convention on Human Rights. *Held*, the mere existence of the exchange of information procedure in the 2003 Order would not be sufficient to constitute 'arrangements' within the meaning of the 2008 Act Sch 36 para 63(4)(b). To be within that provision, the arrangements should have effect by virtue of the 2006 Act s 173. If the arrangements already had effect, as they did in the case of the 2003 Order, by virtue of the Income and Corporation Taxes Act 1988 s 788, there was no room for them also to have effect under the 2006 Act s 173. However, the draftsman had clearly been aware of the fact that the OECD Convention was not to be signed by all relevant countries at the same time, and that it would come into effect over an extended period. Therefore, to deal with the lacuna that would otherwise arise, deeming provisions had been inserted in the form of ss 173(8)–(10). In particular, s 173(8), (10)(a) provided that any provisions which were included in an Order in Council made under the 1988 Act s 788, were in force immediately before the passing of the 2006 Act, and could have been included in an Order in Council under s 173 had the Order in Council been made after that time, had effect after that time as if included in an Order in Council under s 173. This covered the provisions in the 2003 Order dealing with the exchange of information procedure. Those provisions therefore had effect as if they had been included in an Order in Council under the 2006 Act s 173, and were treated as having effect by virtue of s 173. Australian taxes within those arrangements were accordingly within the scope of 'relevant foreign tax' for the purpose of the 2008 Act Sch 36 at all relevant times. Although a taxpayer had no right of appeal against an approval of a third party notice, a taxpayer in respect of whose tax affairs an information notice was approved could seek judicial review. Such a review was not in the nature of an appeal on a point of law but could consider both the law and the underlying facts. It therefore could not be said that the procedure under Sch 36 contravened the taxpayer's right to a fair trial or deprived the taxpayer of an effective remedy under the European Convention on Human Rights.

Ex p certain taxpayers [2012] UKFTT 765 (TC), [2013] All ER (D) 34 (Mar) (First-tier Tribunal: Judge Roger Berner). *Deutsche Morgan Grenfell Group plc v IRC* [2006] UKHL 49, [2007] 1 All ER 449 (2006 Abr para 2458) applied. Application 18497/03 *Ravon v France* (unreported), ECtHR, distinguished.

1988 Act s 788 replaced by Taxation (International and Other Provisions) Act 2010 ss 2–6, 18, 20, 134.

1530 International tax compliance—international agreements—implementation—United States of America

The International Tax Compliance (United States of America) Regulations 2013, SI 2013/1962 (in force on 1 September 2013), give effect to the agreement reached between the United Kingdom and the United States of America to improve international tax compliance and to implement FATCA (the provisions known as the Foreign Account Tax Compliance Act in the United States Hiring Incentives to Restore Employment Act) (London, 12 September 2012) (Cm 8445).

1531 International tax enforcement—Albania

See para 1507.

1532 International tax enforcement—Brunei Darussalam

See para 1508.

1533 International tax enforcement—Guernsey

The International Tax Enforcement (Guernsey) Order 2013, SI 2013/3154 (in force on a date to be notified in the London Gazette), contains an exchange of letters and an agreement which amend an agreement, scheduled to the Double Taxation Relief and International Tax Enforcement (Guernsey) Order 2009, SI 2009/3011, between the United Kingdom and Guernsey for the exchange of information relating to tax matters.

1534 International tax enforcement—India

See para 1510.

1535 International tax enforcement—Isle of Man

See para 1511.

1536 International tax enforcement—Jersey

The International Tax Enforcement (Jersey) Order 2013, SI 2013/3151 (in force on a date to be notified in the London Gazette), contains an exchange of letters and an agreement which amend an agreement, scheduled to the Double Taxation Relief and International Tax

Enforcement (Jersey) Order 2009, SI 2009/3012, between the United Kingdom and Jersey for the exchange of information relating to tax matters.

1537 International tax enforcement—Marshall Islands

The International Tax Enforcement (Marshall Islands) Order 2013, SI 2013/3153 (in force on a date to be notified in the London Gazette), contains an agreement between the governments of the United Kingdom and the Republic of the Marshall Islands for the exchange of information relating to tax matters.

1538 International tax enforcement—mutual assistance—tax debts pre-dating mutual assistance arrangements

The first taxpayer company, incorporated in the British Virgin Islands, was owned and controlled by a South African based businessman. The first taxpayer was found to be liable to the South African tax authority for substantial taxes for the 1998–2000 years of assessment. The South African tax authority maintained that when the owner had learned that it was investigating the first taxpayer's tax affairs, he had procured the transfer of its assets to the second taxpayer company. A substantial deposit was credited to a bank account in London in the name of the second taxpayer. Following the coming into force of a protocol amending the double taxation treaty between the United Kingdom and the Republic of South Africa which made provision for mutual assistance in the collection of taxes, and which had effect pursuant to the Finance Act 2006 s 173, the South African tax authority made a request to the Commissioners for Her Majesty's Revenue and Customs for assistance in the collection of the tax debt. The Commissioners sought judgment against the first taxpayer in respect of the tax debt and relief against both taxpayers under the Insolvency Act 1986 Pt XVI (ss 423–425) with a view to making the deposit available for satisfying the tax debt. The taxpayers unsuccessfully applied for an order striking out the claim. The taxpayers appealed. *Held*, the protocol had effect in respect of requests for assistance in the collection of taxes made on or after the date of entry into force of the protocol, irrespective of when the liability to those taxes arose. There was no unfairness in permitting the enforcement of pre-existing tax liabilities and the 2006 Act s 173 authorised the making of international tax enforcement arrangements in relation to tax liabilities which had arisen before that section had come into force. Prior to the amendment to the tax treaty made by the protocol, the revenue rule prohibited the enforcement by the South African tax authority of South African tax liabilities in the United Kingdom. However, the revenue rule had always been liable to be abrogated by treaty and the taxpayer could have had no legitimate expectation that the rule would not be abrogated in the future. Moreover, the revenue rule had not existed for the benefit or protection of taxpayers. Its basis lay in relationships between sovereign states and its abrogation, therefore, could not be regarded as an injustice to a party seeking to resist enforcement of a tax liability. Accordingly, the appeal would be dismissed.

Ben Nevis (Holdings) Ltd v Revenue and Customs Comrs [2013] EWCA Civ 578, [2013] STC 1579 (Court of Appeal: Jackson, Lloyd Jones and Floyd LJJ). Decision of Judge Pelling QC [2012] EWHC 1807 (Ch), [2012] STC 2157 (2012 Abr para 1502) reversed.

1539 International tax enforcement—Norway

See para 1513.

1540 International tax enforcement—Panama

See para 1514.

1541 International tax enforcement—Spain

See para 1515.

1542 Joint assessment—married couple—tax advantage—freedom of establishment

A German national ('I') and a Belgian national ('G') were married with two children and lived in Belgium. Although under national law, spouses were in principle to be taxed jointly, for two years they had completed separate tax returns in Belgium, without stating that they were married. I, who worked in Germany and earned all his income there, had not mentioned any taxable income in Belgium or any dependents. In contrast, G, who was employed in Belgium, had declared mortgage interest, two dependent children and childcare costs. Those tax returns had given rise to three disputes brought before the national court. The first dispute concerned one tax year, for which the Belgian tax authorities had initially determined the amount of tax payable solely in G's name. The authorities had subsequently issued a correction notice stating that G and I would be taxed jointly and determining a new amount of tax payable on the basis of their respective incomes. Following complaints by G and I in respect of that correction notice, the amount of tax to be levied was determined in their joint names, an amount against which they brought proceedings before the national court. The second dispute concerned the following tax year. The third dispute concerned the advantage for dependent children in the form of a tax free allowance for which I qualified in Germany. In that respect, I had been taxed as an individual, namely without entitlement to the joint tax regime to which married taxpayers who were not permanently separated and who were liable to tax in Germany while residing in another member state were entitled under German national law. It was apparent that the German tax authorities had refused to accept that I had qualified for that tax regime. The action brought by I against that refusal was dismissed by the German court. The national court stated that the assessment of G and I together complied with the law. The court further raised the issue as to whether the method of calculation of the tax payable in Belgium complied with European Union law. Joining the various disputes, the national court referred for a preliminary ruling a question as to the interpretation of TFEU art 49. *Held*, art 49 was to be interpreted as precluding the application of the tax legislation of a member state which had the effect that a couple residing in that member state and earning income both in that member state and in another member state did not in fact receive a specific tax advantage, by reason of the rules for offsetting it, where that couple would receive the tax advantage if the member of the couple earning the higher income had not earned his entire income in another member state.

Case C-303/12 *Imfeld v Belgium* [2013] All ER (D) 202 (Dec) (ECJ: Fifth Chamber).

1543   Loan relationships and derivative contracts—profits and losses—disregard and bringing into account

The Loan Relationships and Derivative Contracts (Disregard and Bringing into Account of Profits and Losses) (Amendment) Regulations 2013, SI 2013/2781 (in force on 21 November 2013), further amend the 2004 Regulations, SI 2004/3256, so as to (1) add definitions of 'Additional Tier 1 instrument' and 'deferred shares'; and (2) extend the matching provisions to deferred shares issued by building societies and Additional Tier 1 instrument to the extent that they are accounted for as equity instruments in accordance with generally accepted accounting practice.

1544   Natural Resources Body for Wales—transfer scheme—tax consequences

See para 1919.

1545   Offshore funds—general provisions

The Offshore Funds (Tax) (Amendment) Regulations 2013, SI 2013/661 (in force at 3 pm on 20 March 2013), further amend the 2009 Regulations, SI 2009/3001, to clarify the application of the charge to tax where the interest in the offshore fund which is disposed of was acquired in consequence of an exchange or scheme of reconstruction to which the Taxation of Chargeable Gains Tax 1992 s 135 or 136 applied.

The Offshore Funds (Tax) (Amendment No 2) Regulations 2013, SI 2013/1411 (in force on 28 June 2013), further amend the 2009 Regulations above by (1) specifying how the reportable income of a fund for a reporting period is to be calculated in the case of funds which do not operate equalisation arrangements; (2) making provision in relation to the information to be provided in the report to participants in respect of the amount of any excess treated as additional distributions made to participants in the fund, and in relation to how those amounts to be reported are to be determined; (3) reversing the order in which equalisation amounts reduce actual distributions and amounts treated as additional distributions; and (4) making various minor and consequential amendments.

The Offshore Funds (Tax) (Amendment No 3) Regulations 2013, SI 2013/1770 (in force on 7 August 2013), further amend the 2009 Regulations so as to provide that an annual payment made to a participant in an offshore fund is not a qualifying annual payment for the purposes of the Income Tax Act 2007 Pt 15 Ch 6 (ss 898–905) if certain conditions are met. The 2013 Regulations also reapply tax withholding provisions in certain cases where the condition requiring the person making the payment to have reasonable grounds for believing that the participant is not resident in the United Kingdom is met but in fact the participant or, in the case of a trust, the beneficial owner is not resident in the United Kingdom.

The Temporary Non-Residence (Miscellaneous Amendments) Regulations 2013, SI 2013/1810 (in force on 12 August 2013), further amend the Pensions Schemes (Taxable Property Provisions) Regulations 2006, SI 2006/1958, and the 2009 Regulations so that their temporary non-residence rules accord with the new statutory residence test, introduced by the Finance Act 2013, which includes a new test for temporary non-residence by virtue of which, where an individual has a period of temporary non-residence, certain events will be treated as taking place in the year the individual returns to the United Kingdom and will thus be taxable in the United Kingdom.

See para 1547.

1546   Offshore income—penalties—designation of territories

The Penalties, Offshore Income etc (Designation of Territories) (Amendment) Order 2013, SI 2013/1618 (in force on 24 July 2013), amends the 2011 Order, SI 2011/976, so as to reclassify certain territories from category 2 territories to category 1, and from category 3 territories to category 2.

1547   Ordinary residence—removal of references

The Income Tax (Removal of Ordinary Residence) Regulations 2013, SI 2013/605 (in force on 6 April 2013), amend, by removing references to being 'ordinarily' resident, (1) in relation to a person's liability to income tax for the tax year 2013–14 or any subsequent tax years, the Income Tax (Entertainers and Sportsmen) Regulations 1987, SI 1987/530, the Individual Savings Account Regulations 1998, SI 1998/1870, and the Offshore Funds (Tax) Regulations 2009, SI 2009/3001; (2) in relation to a scheme chargeable payment treated as made in the tax year 2013–14 or any subsequent tax years, the Pensions Schemes (Taxable Property Provisions) Regulations 2006, SI 2006/1958; and (3) in relation to interest distributions made on or after 6 April 2014, and in relation to the making of declarations on or after 6 April 2014, the Investment Trusts (Dividends) (Optional Treatment as Interest Distributions) Regulations 2009, SI 2009/2034.

1548   Pay As You Earn—general provisions

The Income Tax (Pay As You Earn) (Amendment) Regulations 2013, SI 2013/521 (in force in part on 6 April 2013 and in part on 6 April 2014), further amend the 2003 Regulations, SI 2003/2682, by (1) allowing Her Majesty's Revenue and Customs ('HMRC') to use PAYE coding to collect the new high income child benefit charge; (2) closing to all employers, other than care and support employers, from 6 April 2013, the simplified deduction scheme and, with effect from the tax year 2014–15, closing the scheme to all employers; (3) making provision for relevant lump sum payments where the pension payer does not know which code is to be applied to the payment and the pension scheme is not already in payment; (4) changing the code that is applied to relevant lump sum payments to pensioners in cases where the pension payer is unaware of the code to be applied to the payment; (5) making further provision in relation to the provision of real time information to the Commissioners for Her Majesty's Revenue and Customs on or before the making of a payment to an employee; (6) excluding certain employers from becoming RTI employers; (7) making provision for the situation where Form P45 Part 3 is not available to an employer; (8) taking into account the introduction of employment and support allowance and amending the periods of time set out in Form P46 Statements A, B and C, one of which must be given by an employee who is a seconded expatriate; (9) omitting provision for a penalty to be charged if the return containing information about the final payment for the tax year 2012–13 was not delivered; (10) providing for exceptions from the requirement to deliver information on or before the making of a payment; (11) requiring an employer who makes a notional payment to deliver information regarding the payment no later than 14 days after the end of the tax month in which the payment is made; (15) extending the time limit and the categories of employers who are not required to deliver information regarding a payment on or before making a payment to an employee so that specified employers, including those employers whom HMRC has directed are unable to file using an approved method of electronic communications, are for the tax year 2013–14 entitled to file in accordance with provisions not relating to real time information employers; (16) expanding the information which an employer must provide when making a return which includes details of information omitted from an earlier return; (17) requiring an employer who has failed to make a return of information to provide the information in the next return for the tax year in question; and if by 20 April following the tax year the information has not been included in such a return, requiring the employer to report the information; and making provision for special penalties to apply if the return has not been made before 20 May following the end of the tax year to which the information relates; (18) requiring an employer to notify the date of cessation of a PAYE scheme; (19) providing for the situation where an employer has failed to make a return during the tax year; (20) providing for a return sent to HMRC after 19 April to be treated as if it were sent in respect of the final tax period of the tax year to which it applies; and (21) revising the data that employers are required to include on a return to HMRC when making a relevant payment to an employee. Consequential amendments are also made to SI 2012/822, including new data items to be submitted by an employer who becomes a real time employer on or after 6 April 2013.

The Income Tax (Pay As You Earn) (Amendment No 2) Regulations 2013, SI 2013/2300 (in force on 6 October 2013), further amend the 2003 Regulations above in relation to relevant payments made in the period beginning on 6 October 2013 and ending on 5 April 2014, by requiring an employer which employs no more than 49 employees at the commencement date to deliver specified information to HMRC by the end of the tax month in which a payment is made to an employee, rather than on or before making such a payment.

1549   Profits—services provided through company—services provided prior to company's incorporation

The taxpayer acquired a company that was in receivership and a new company was formed to take over its business and assets. The new company appointed the taxpayer as a consultant to develop the business and provide strategic advice. She intended to provide consultancy services through a company, though this company was not formed until after the contract for the consultancy services had been drawn up. An invoice from the taxpayer's company in respect of the consultancy services was tabled and approved. As the taxpayer's company still had not been incorporated the consultancy fee was paid to the new company's solicitors to hold for the taxpayer's company. The taxpayer's company was incorporated in Guernsey and the consultancy fee was paid to it. The taxpayer's company reported the consultancy fee as income in its accounts and United Kingdom corporation tax return. The Revenue considered that the consultancy fee fell to be taxed as the taxpayer's self-employed trading income and raised two protective discovery assessments. The taxpayer appealed against those assessments. *Held*, the substance and commercial effect of the arrangements had been that the taxpayer would never be entitled to payment of the consultancy fee. She had to incorporate a company, it had been within her power to do so and she had eventually done so. Payment of the consultancy fee was made between the companies. There was never any intention that the taxpayer would have any entitlement as an individual to the fee. If the substance and commercial effect of the arrangements had been as stated, then generally accepted accounting practice would not require the taxpayer to recognise the consultancy fee as her income. Accordingly, the appeal would be allowed.
  Re Hepburn [2013] UKFTT 445 (TC), [2013] All ER (D) 29 (Sep) (First-tier Tribunal: Judge Gordon Reid presiding).

1550   Rate limits and allowances—indexation

The Income Tax (Indexation) Order 2013, SI 2013/3088 (made on 5 December 2013), applies in relation to the tax year 2014–15 and replaces certain rate limits and allowances specified in the Income Tax Act 2007 with increased amounts calculated by reference to the increase in the retail prices index.

1551   Relief—dividend relief—restriction on relief—free movement of capital

The pension scheme in issue had been an exempt approved scheme. Nearly three quarters of the investments of the pension scheme were in equities. Some were investments in companies resident in the United Kingdom, and some were in companies resident in the European Union and elsewhere. Pursuant to the Income and Corporation Taxes Act 1988 s 231(1), a United Kingdom-resident company receiving a qualifying distribution from another resident company was entitled to a tax credit: the total of the distribution and the tax credit was called franked investment income ('FII'). However, by virtue of s 246C, a United Kingdom-resident company receiving a distribution from a non-resident company was not entitled to a tax credit and the income did not qualify as FII. Where a United Kingdom-resident company received FII, under s 241 it was liable to pay advanced corporation tax ('ACT') in relation to its own dividends only to the extent that those dividends and the ACT referable to them exceeded the FII. A company was entitled to set off ACT paid in respect of a qualifying distribution during an accounting period against its mainstream corporation tax liability. Subsequently, the ACT system was abolished. For companies with brought-forward surplus ACT, a 'shadow ACT' system was introduced which allowed companies to access their surplus ACT in an amount similar to the relief allowable previously. The trustees of the pension scheme brought claims before the First-tier Tribunal against the Revenue for payable tax credits claiming that the disallowance effected by s 246C breached their rights to free movement of capital. The tribunal decided that the absence of a tax credit, by reason of s 246C, constituted a breach of the EC Treaty art 56 which was not justified. However, on limitation points, the Taxes Management Act 1970 s 43 had specified a time limit of six years for claims to receive payable tax credits so that the claims had been properly rejected by the Revenue on the basis that they had been submitted out of time. The trustees appealed and the Revenue cross-appealed in relation to foreign dividend income. *Held*, although direct taxation did not fall within the scope of the legislative powers of the European Union regarding the internal market, national tax legislation should be compatible with EC law. The following principles could be derived from case-law: firstly, any legislative provision which tended to discourage the exercise of an investor's rights under the EC Treaty art 56 was a breach of the right to free movement of capital afforded by that provision; secondly, any such legislative provision was also in breach of art 56 because as a consequence the securities of companies in which investment might be made on a cross-border basis were less attractive to investors residing in the member state where the restrictive provision was to be found in that member state's tax legislation; thirdly, where the tax legislation provided a tax credit in respect of the dividends that an investor received from a company established in the member state in which he was resident, such tax credit being provided as a means of avoiding double taxation on profits which were liable to corporation tax at the company level and were then distributed as a dividend, the provision of a tax credit to such an investor who had made an investment in the securities of a company established in another member state of an amount calculated by reference to the underlying corporation tax paid by the latter company would preclude any breach of art 56 and did not affect the cohesion of the first member state's tax system; and fourthly, the overarching principle that led to those conclusions was that situations which were objectively comparable should not suffer unequal treatment. In the present case, the pension scheme's situation was an internal situation in the sense that it made its investment in a United Kingdom incorporated company but not 'wholly internally' in the sense that the income of that company was substantially derived from investments made overseas. Where the pension scheme made an investment in a multinational company, there was a cross-border movement of capital that was made by the pension scheme which happened through two transactions, firstly, its investment in the multinational, and secondly, the investment of the funds raised by the multinational in the overseas subsidiaries. Consequently, the absence of a tax credit for a foreign dividend income by virtue of the application of the 1988 Act s 246C did not arise in a wholly internal situation. It followed that the provisions of s 246C denying the pension scheme a tax credit on payment of a foreign dividend income amounted to an infringement of its rights pursuant to the Treaty art 56. Accordingly, the concept of 'effective fiscal supervision' of the foreign tax could not be engaged at all. Once the 1988 Act s 246C was disapplied, there was nothing more which needed to be done: s 231 could be given effect to according to its terms. There was no justification for concluding that an exempt taxpayer such as the pension scheme should not be entitled to the full tax credit in the same way as a fully taxable person. The absence of a

intervals. Fourth, while interest accrued from day to day, or at other fixed intervals, it did not have to be paid at any intervals; it might not become payable until the principal became repayable. Fifth, what the return was called was not determinative of its nature. Sixth, the mere fact that the payment by way of interest might be aggregated with a payment of a different nature did not 'denature' the payment that was interest. In the present case, it was plain that the additional payment had been in law capable of being 'interest', and the First-tier Tribunal had made no error of law in characterising it as such. The return described as 'a premium' bore all the characteristics of a payment of interest: it had been paid by reference to an underlying debt, at a stipulated rate, calculated by reference to time elapsed, and it accrued daily. Accordingly, the appeal would be dismissed.

Pike v Revenue and Customs Comrs [2013] UKUT 225 (TCC), [2013] STC 2042 (Upper Tribunal: Norris J and Judge Roger Berner). *Davies (Inspector of Taxes) v Premier Investment Co Ltd* [1945] 2 All ER 681; *Re Euro Hotel (Belgravia) Ltd* [1975] 3 All ER 1075; *Willingale (Inspector of Taxes) v International Commercial Bank Ltd* [1978] AC 834, [1978] 1 All ER 754, HL (1978 Abr para 1604); and *Chevron Petroleum (UK) Ltd v BP Petroleum Development Ltd* [1981] STC 689 (1981 Abr para 1601) applied.

1996 Act Sch 13 paras 2, 3 repealed: Finance Act 2003 Sch 39 paras 2, 5, Sch 43 Pt 3(16); Income Tax (Trading and Other Income) Act 2005 Sch 1 para 490, Sch 3.

1557 Relief—television programmes—British programmes—qualification and certification

The Cultural Test (Television Programmes) Regulations 2013, SI 2013/1831 (in force on 13 August 2013), introduce points-based cultural tests for television programmes in order to determine whether a programme may be certified as a 'British programme' for tax relief purposes. The regulations also prescribe the particulars and evidence that must be provided to the Secretary of State in support of an application for certification.

1558 Return—annual tax on enveloped dwellings

The Annual Tax on Enveloped Dwellings (Returns) Regulations 2013, SI 2013/1844 (in force on 12 August 2013), provide (1) the Commissioners for Her Majesty's Revenue and Customs with the authority to prescribe the form and content of an annual tax on enveloped dwellings return; (2) for the delivery of returns and the provision of information by electronic communication; and (3) for the validation of an electronic communication and incorporation of an electronic validation process.

1559 Return—inaccurate return—penalty—employee's failure to declare severance payment

The Finance Act 2007 Sch 24 para 1 provides that a penalty is payable by a taxpayer where a tax return he gives to the Revenue contains an inaccuracy which amounts to or leads to an understatement of his liability to tax and the inaccuracy is careless or deliberate.

The taxpayer's employment was terminated in accordance with the terms of a compromise agreement. The agreement provided for his employer to make a severance payment to him. The payment was expressed to be compensation for the early termination of the taxpayer's employment and comprised an ex gratia sum of £110,000 and a contribution to the taxpayer's pension fund. The taxpayer completed a short form self-assessment tax return in which he did not disclose the payment. The Revenue's notes on how to complete the return stated that a short form return was not to be used if a taxpayer received a lump sum from his employer unless it was a redundancy payment below £30,000. The employer made a return to the Revenue in respect of the payment. The taxpayer was assessed to income tax on the payment and the Revenue imposed a penalty under the 2007 Act Sch 24 para 1. The taxpayer's appeal against the penalty was dismissed. On further appeal, *held*, on the facts, when the taxpayer made his return he should, on any reasonable basis, have considered that the severance payment was, at the very least, possibly taxable. Even if he had any lingering doubts, the notes accompanying the return should have prompted him to make a full self-assessment return including the payment, or at least to indicate that he had received a payment but did not consider it was liable to tax. In the terms of Sch 24 para 1, the taxpayer's return contained an inaccuracy which led to an understatement of his liability to tax. The inaccuracy was careless because it was due to the taxpayer's failure to take reasonable care. He failed to take reasonable care because he knew, or should reasonably have known, that there was at least a possibility that the payment was liable to tax. Accordingly, the appeal would be dismissed.

Harding v Revenue and Customs Comrs [2013] UKUT 575 (TCC), [2013] All ER (D) 301 (Nov) (Upper Tribunal: Judge Colin Bishopp and Judge Edward Sadler).

1560   Return—incorrect return—penalty—standard of proof

The taxpayer was the owner of a restaurant business. The Revenue, pursuant to the Taxes Management Act 1970 s 95(1)(a), issued a penalty determination against the taxpayer on the basis that he had negligently submitted incorrect returns. The penalties were calculated, pursuant to s 95(2), on the basis of 50 per cent of the difference between the amount of tax originally paid by the taxpayer and the amount of tax which it had been determined should have been paid. The taxpayer appealed to the General Commissioners who determined that, on the facts, they were satisfied beyond reasonable doubt that there had been a negligent submission but, applying the same standard of proof, the Revenue had failed to prove beyond reasonable doubt that there had been understated profits. The Revenue appealed against that decision on the ground that the General Commissioners had wrongly applied the criminal standard of proof. The appeal was allowed on the ground that the appropriate standard of proof for penalty proceedings under the 1970 Act was the civil and not the criminal standard of proof and that such conclusion was not affected by the European Convention on Human Rights art 6. The matter was remitted and determined by the First-tier Tribunal. The tribunal considered that there had been a period of unreasonable delay caused by the length of time that it had taken the clerk to the General Commissioners to state a case for the High Court, a period of nearly two years. However, it determined that it had no discretion under s 100(2)(b)(iii) to reflect that delay by way of an adjustment to the penalty on the ground that the power of reduction arose only if the tribunal considered that the amount of the penalty itself was incorrect. The tribunal upheld part of the penalty determination made by the Revenue. The taxpayer appealed and the Revenue cross-appealed against the tribunal's decision that the delay in the proceedings had been unreasonable. *Held*, the application of the civil standard of proof to penalty proceedings under the 1970 Act was in accordance with domestic law. There was no link with any conduct which was criminal in nature for domestic purposes, and to which the criminal standard ought properly to be applied. In those circumstances it was the civil standard which applied. The tribunal had been correct to find that the applicable standard of proof was that of the balance of probabilities. The power of the tribunal to adjust the penalty was not constrained to the making of a reduction only in circumstances where the tribunal considered that the amount of the penalty itself was incorrect. Part of the purpose of a penalty was to punish the conduct of the person concerned. Factors which went to the appropriate level of punishment were not confined to matters of calculation, nor to factors which the Revenue decided were appropriate to take into account. If a breach of the reasonable time requirement was established after the event, then the appropriate remedy might be a public acknowledgment of the breach and a reduction in the penalty. The tribunal was not confined to a review of the arithmetic and the extent of the mitigation allowed by the Revenue. The tribunal was entitled, and indeed required, to consider all the material circumstances. The delays in the relevant period had been unreasonable. Accordingly, the appeal would be allowed and the cross-appeal would be dismissed.

Khawaja v Revenue and Customs Comrs [2013] UKUT 0353 (TCC), [2014] STC 150 (Upper Tribunal: Judge Roger Berner and Judge Tim Herrington). *A-G's Reference* (No 2 of 2001) [2003] UKHL 68, [2004] 1 All ER 1049 (2003 Abr para 703); and *R v Briggs-Price* [2009] UKHL 19, [2009] 4 All ER 594 (2009 Abr para 2587) applied. *Revenue and Customs Comrs v Khawaja* [2008] EWHC 1687 (Ch), [2008] STC 2880 (2008 Abr para 1910) followed. *Gale v Serious Organised Crime Agency* [2011] UKSC 49, [2012] 2 All ER 1 (2011 Abr para 755) distinguished.

1561   Return—late return—penalty—Construction Industry Scheme—power of court to cancel penalty

The taxpayer was fined for failing to file on time numerous monthly returns due under the Construction Industry Scheme ('CIS'). An offer by the Revenue to reduce the penalties was rejected by the taxpayer, who decided to bring proceedings challenging the fines. The taxpayer contended that he had made each CIS return on time, and that he had not received a significant number of the Revenue's penalty notices. He also submitted that his right to peaceful enjoyment of his possessions under the European Convention on Human Rights First Protocol art 1 had been breached. The First-tier Tribunal ruled that the taxpayer had not had a reasonable excuse for the late delivery of his returns and that the penalty notices had been validly issued. However, the Tribunal determined that the amounts levied by the Revenue had been excessive within the meaning of the Taxes Management Act 1970 s 100B(2) and decided to reduce them pursuant to s 100B(3). It decided that it was permitted on human rights grounds to read the word 'incorrect' in s 100B(2)(a)(iii) in such a way as to include penalties which were disproportionate. The Revenue appealed against that decision, arguing that the Tribunal lacked jurisdiction to reduce the amount of the penalties imposed. *Held*, the control of the Revenue's exercise of their discretion under s 102 to mitigate penalties by judicial review resulted in a guarantee that Convention rights would be respected. All of the penalties at issue had been properly imposed in accordance with the legislation as construed according to ordinary canons of construction. The taxpayer's right of appeal did not extend to penalties that were 'incorrect' merely by virtue of being disproportionate and in purported breach of the taxpayer's rights under the Convention. Once the taxpayer's appeal had been determined by the Tribunal, the Revenue had to consider the application of the 1970 Act s 102. If the taxpayer considered that the penalties, once they had been mitigated, were not proportionate and infringed his rights, he might challenge the Revenue's decision by seeking to bring judicial review. There was no scope for the application of the Convention since the scheme of the legislation was compliant with the Convention. Since the Tribunal itself had no judicial review powers, the application for judicial review had to be commenced in the Administrative Court. Accordingly, the appeal would be allowed.

Revenue and Customs Comrs v Bosher [2013] UKUT 579 (TCC), [2014] STC 617 (Upper Tribunal: Warren J presiding).

1562   Return—set-off—carrying back of relief into preceding year—power of set-off

The taxpayer had carried on business as a self-employed hirer and supplier of plant and machinery and he was registered for value added tax in that capacity. He was also a director of a civil engineering company, receiving a salary, and had investment income. He filed self-assessment tax returns with the assistance of accountants. He disclosed substantial taxable earnings from his employment, self-employment and investments, and some chargeable gains. Disregarding the taxpayer's claims for relief, tax and Class 4 national insurance contributions were due for payment. The taxpayer entered into certain transactions which resulted in a loss when shares he had acquired became of negligible value. That loss crystallised shortly before he submitted his tax return. The taxpayer contended that the loss was available by way of relief against his tax liability, and that the relief might be 'carried back' so as to be offset against the tax due in accordance with the Income Tax Act 2007 s 132. The following tax year, the taxpayer entered into a partnership venture, allegedly suffering a trading loss, again seeking to carry back the relief to the preceding year but on that occasion in accordance with s 64. The Commissioners for Her Majesty's Revenue and Customs maintained that both of the losses were achieved by the use of tax avoidance schemes which had not achieved their purpose. In respect of the first and second claims, various adjustments were made to the taxpayer's account with the Revenue, reflecting payments he had made, credits for the claimed relief which had been made as he had submitted his returns, and reversals of those credits as the Revenue had decided to inquire into or reject the claims. The Revenue made inquiries into the first and second claims pursuant to s 9A and consequently removed or cancelled the credit the second claim had generated. The taxpayer's VAT return for an accounting period was a repayment return. The Revenue accepted that the return was correct and that a repayment was due, subject only to the Revenue's right of set-off pursuant to the Finance Act 2008 s 130. The taxpayer sought judicial review of the Revenue's decision. *Held*, in each case, the taxpayer had made a claim for year two relief in his year one return. It would be very strange if, against the background of an invitation by the Revenue to make a claim accepted by a taxpayer intending to do just that, it should be determined nevertheless that what he had done could not amount to the making of a claim. Further, if what the taxpayer had entered on the return form had not amounted to a claim, it was difficult to see what other description might be attached to it. His purpose in doing so had been to secure the accelerated relief which had been available to him only by the invocation of the Taxes Management Act 1970 Sch 1A para 4(1), and in compliance with that provision, the Revenue had given him the relief he had claimed. Its subsequent withdrawal of the relief, in exercise of the power in Sch 1A para 4(3), followed on its opening of an inquiry in accordance with Sch 1A para 5(1). However, in *Cotter* it was decided that only an inquiry under s 9A could be opened into a claim contained in a return. Notwithstanding the fact that Sch 1A had been engaged, the inquiry mechanism of Sch 1A para 5(1) had not been, with the consequence that the inquiry that the Revenue had purported to open had been invalid and the condition on which Sch 1A para 4(3) power might be exercised had not been satisfied. Consequently, there had been no valid exercise of the power, and correspondingly no debit on the taxpayer's account against which the VAT credit due to him might be set off. Accordingly, the application would be allowed.

R (on the application of Rouse) v Revenue and Customs Comrs [2013] UKUT 383 (TCC), [2013] All ER (D) 189 (Aug) (Upper Tribunal: Warren J presiding). *Revenue and Customs Comrs v Cotter* [2012] EWCA Civ 81, [2012] STC 745 (2012 Abr para 1531) considered.

1563　Returns and information—partnership statement—trade losses—amendment of statement

The taxpayer, which was a limited liability partnership, entered into a contract for the purchase of three commercial properties. No suitable tenants were found for the properties and they were sold at a loss. In its partnership tax returns the taxpayer recorded the loss as loss from trade. The Commissioners for Her Majesty's Revenue and Customs opened inquiries into the taxpayer's tax returns and issued closure notices to the taxpayer, which concluded that the Commissioners were not satisfied that the taxpayer carried on a trade in the relevant period and that the losses were in fact property income losses. The Commissioners amended the taxpayer's partnership tax return accordingly but in a letter to the taxpayer did not cite which statutory provision that amendment had been made under. On appeal, the taxpayer contended that the losses in question were trading losses as, at the time it bought the properties, its intention had been to improve the value of the properties by securing tenants and then sell the properties on within a period of three to six months. The Commissioners contended that the taxpayer's intention had been to continue to hold the properties once tenants had been secured in order to receive rental income. The lack of an intention to trade had been consistent with the way the taxpayer compiled its balance sheets and completed its tax returns for the relevant years. Consequently, the losses had not been trading losses but losses attributable to the taxpayer's United Kingdom property business. The taxpayer further contended that, even if the Commissioners were right that the losses had been United Kingdom property business losses instead of trading losses, the Revenue had no statutory basis to amend the taxpayer's tax return under either the Taxes Management Act 1970 ss 29 or 30B. *Held*, the taxpayer's argument that there was no statutory basis for the amendment accorded with the plain words of s 30B, it was consistent with the drafting of other provisions where specific mention was made when losses were intended to be included, and it was not inconsistent with the underlying purpose of the provision. On that basis, s 30B did not apply so as to provide a basis for the Commissioner's stated amendment. It followed that the amendment was ineffective and the appeal in relation to the amendment of the partnership statement would be allowed. Moreover, it was settled law that in order to determine whether the taxpayer had been carrying on a trade or whether its activities constituted a United Kingdom property business within the meaning given in the Income Tax (Trading and Other Income) Act 2005 s 264, certain factors were relevant. However, there was no comprehensive list of all relevant matters, nor was any one of them decisive in all cases. Further, it was settled law that the tribunal should look to ascertain the intention of the taxpayer at the time the properties had been acquired. The evidence relating to the approach taken to the preparation of the tax returns and balance sheets weighed, albeit in a limited way, in the Commissioner's favour. However, the combination of the evidence submitted on the taxpayer's behalf and the evidence provided by the contemporaneous documents more than outweighed the point taken in the Commissioner's favour. On balance, the taxpayer's intention had been to trade in the properties not hold onto them to earn rental income from them. The available evidence did not suggest that intention had changed during the period up to the eventual sale of the properties. Accordingly, the appeal would be allowed.

Albermarle 4 LLP v Revenue and Customs Comrs [2013] UKFTT 083 (TC), [2013] All ER (D) 41 (May) (First-tier Tribunal: Judge Swami Raghavan).

1564   Small charitable donations—administration

The Small Charitable Donations Regulations 2013, SI 2013/938 (in force on 19 April 2013), provide for the administration of top-up claims, top-up payments and overpayments under the Small Charitable Donations Act 2012. Specifically, the regulations (1) apply, with modifications, the provisions of the Taxes Management Act 1970 Sch 1A for the purposes of making and giving effect to top-up claims and amendments, inquiring into top-up claims, completing inquiries and amending claims by closure notice and appealing against any such amendments; (2) provide that, for the purposes of top-up claims, where an offence involving serious fraud in relation to a top-up claim is suspected, ss 20BA and 20BB apply; (3) empower Her Majesty's Revenue and Customs to obtain information and documents in order to check that a charity has complied with the 2012 Act in relation to a top-up claim and in order to establish whether there has been an overpayment under s 10; (4) prescribe, that in relation to an individual who in the course of business assists a charity in connection with a top-up claim, the information and penalty provisions in the Finance Act 2012 Sch 38 apply; (5) provide for notice of an assessment to be given to a charity by an officer of Her Majesty's Revenue and Customs; (6) make provision for an appeal against an assessment; (7) prescribe that, for the purposes of collecting and recovering an overpayment which is due and payable, the 1970 Act Pt VI (ss 60–70A) applies; (8) provide for interest to be charged on unpaid overpayments, applying and incorporating the interest charging provisions on late payment of amounts payable to Her Majesty's Revenue and Customs in the Finance Act 2009 ss 101, 103 and Sch 53; (9) provide that, for the purposes of a charity making a top-up claim, the tax penalty provisions in the Finance Act 2007 Sch 24 apply with modification; (10) provide for publication of the details of a charity, its managers or trustees, who have incurred one or more penalties under Sch 24 in relation to a top-up claim; (11) set out the requirements of an application by the new charity for Her Majesty's Revenue and Customs to certify; (12) provide for an election as to which is the relevant old charity which has been taken over and at least two of them have equal gift aid claim histories; (13) provide for notification by Her Majesty's Revenue and Customs of its decision on the application and for appeals to the tribunal in the case of a refusal by Her Majesty's Revenue and Customs to certify; and (14) make provision for the administrative provisions for tax in the 1970 Act ss 108(1) and 113–115A and Sch 3A, in relation the form of documents, their delivery, service and electronic lodgment, to apply for the purposes of a top-up claim, a top-up payment and an overpayment.

1565   Tax avoidance schemes—descriptions of arrangements

The Tax Avoidance Schemes (Prescribed Descriptions of Arrangements) (Amendment) Regulations 2013, SI 2013/2595 (in force on 4 November 2013), further amend the 2006 Regulations, SI 2006/1543, in relation to aspects of the confidentiality hallmarks and to replace the redundant pensions hallmark with a new hallmark relating to employment income provided through third parties. Specifically, the regulations (1) clarify when arrangements which a promoter might wish to keep confidential from either Her Majesty's Revenue and Customs, or other promoters, must be disclosed; (2) extend the circumstances in which a user must disclose arrangements; and (3) replace the redundant pensions hallmark with the employment income provided through third parties hallmark and remove a redundant revocation provision.

The Annual Tax on Enveloped Dwellings Avoidance Schemes (Prescribed Descriptions of Arrangements) Regulations 2013, SI 2013/2571 (in force on 4 November 2013), prescribe arrangements which enable, or might be expected to enable, any person to obtain a tax advantage in relation to annual tax on enveloped dwellings and which must, except where falling within the list of excluded arrangements, be notified to Her Majesty's Revenue and Customs under the Finance Act 2004 Pt 7 (ss 306–319).

1566   Tax avoidance schemes—employment bonus—composition of bonus—exemption from income tax

The taxpayer company ran a community pharmacy shop. The taxpayer was owned and run by a qualified pharmacist and his wife. The pharmacist received advice on how to extract value from the taxpayer in a tax-efficient manner. He used a scheme which involved the taxpayer subscribing for shares in another company, the transfer of those shares subject to a forfeiture restriction to himself, his transfer of the shares to another company and various other steps. To that effect the taxpayer subscribed for shares in a special purpose vehicle at a substantial premium. The taxpayer transferred those shares to the pharmacist. The taxpayer's advisors had received advice that if employment-related securities were shares of a particular class in a company, all of the shares of that class had been acquired either for no payment or for a payment less than their market value, and the company was employee controlled by virtue of the employment-related securities then, when the restriction came to an end or was lifted, there would be no income tax charge. Value in the shares could be realised by selling the shares or liquidating the company, although the owner of the shares would potentially be subject to a capital gains tax charge. It was announced that changes would be made to the Income Tax (Earnings and Pensions) Act 2003 Pt 7 (ss 417—554). The changes gave rise to concerns by the taxpayer's advisers that the original planning would not have the effect that had been intended and further steps were taken. The pharmacist transferred his shares in the special purpose vehicle to an unlimited liability company which had been incorporated four months before the transfer. That was said to have been a sale and to be a transfer to an associated company such that there was no chargeable event for the purposes of s 427(3). The taxpayer guaranteed payment of the price of those shares to the pharmacist. In turn, the unlimited company transferred the beneficial interest in the shares in the special purpose vehicle back to the taxpayer by declaration of a dividend in specie of shares in the special purpose vehicle and declared that it held the shares in it on trust for the taxpayer. The taxpayer then borrowed money from the special purpose vehicle which it then used to discharge the debt due to the pharmacist, the guarantee having been triggered. Both the special purpose vehicle and the unlimited liability company were dissolved. It was not in dispute that those arrangements amounted to a scheme designed to minimise or avoid tax or that the bonus paid to the pharmacist was a reward for services. The taxpayer's case was that the bonus amounted to an award of securities that was not subject to income tax pursuant to s 420. However, the Revenue took the view that the pharmacist had been rewarded with money which was taxable as earnings. Consequently, the Revenue made a determination against the taxpayer under the Income Tax (Pay As You Earn) Regulations 2003, SI 2003/2682, reg 80 and a notice of decision under the Social Security (Transfer of Functions, etc) Act 1999 s 8. The taxpayer challenged the determination. *Held*, the transaction which had taken place amounted to an artificial contrived scheme, whose essence had been to pay money. The transaction was one which it had been the intention of Parliament to exclude from the regime of the 2003 Act Pt 7. The shares in the special purpose vehicle could be regarded as a vehicle for payment of cash. Steps which had followed the taxpayer's decision that it would pay the pharmacist a bonus disclosed no commercial purpose. It followed that the scheme amounted to a bonus of money rather than shares and was therefore subject to income tax. On that basis, the money had also counted as earnings for National Insurance contribution purposes. Accordingly, the appeal would be dismissed.

　　LM Ferro Ltd v Revenue and Customs Comrs [2013] UKFTT 463 (TC), [2013] All ER (D) 103 (Nov) (First-tier Tribunal: Judge Raghavan presiding).

1567　　Tax avoidance schemes—information

The Tax Avoidance Schemes (Information) (Amendment, etc) Regulations 2013, SI 2013/2592 (in force on 4 November 2013), further amend the 2012 Regulations, SI 2012/1836, so as to (1) extend the regime to arrangements which enable, or might be expected to enable, any person to obtain a tax advantage in relation to annual tax on enveloped dwellings; (2) prescribe what information must be provided under new disclosure obligations introduced to the Finance Act 2004 Pt 7 (ss 306–319), and by when this information must be provided; and (3) make transitional provision for arrangements arising between 31 January 2013 and 3 November 2013.

1568　　Tax consequences—public bodies—BRB (Residuary) Limited

See para 2117.

1569   Tax credits—entitlement—dividends from company established in other member state

See Case C-262/09 *Meilicke v Finanzamt Bonn-Innenstadt*, para 2706.

1570   Tonnage tax—training requirements

The Tonnage Tax (Training Requirement) (Amendment) (No 2) Regulations 2013, SI 2013/2245 (in force on 1 October 2013), further amend the 2000 Regulations, SI 2000/2129, so as to (1) provide that, in respect of each eligible officer trainee for whom training is required to be provided, there is to be an increase, from £1,092 to £1,176, in the amount payable for each month during a relevant four-month period, commencing on or after 1 October 2013, in which the training commitment of a company or group provides for payment in lieu of training or the company or group does not provide training in accordance with the training commitment; (2) provide that, where a company or group is treated as having failed to meet its training commitment and the higher rate of payment applies, the basic rate used to calculate the higher rate is increased from £1,020 to £1,094; and (3) revise the definitions of 'EEA Agreement' and 'EEA state' by substituting the definitions for those terms which are set out in the Interpretation Act 1978. SI 2013/5 is revoked.

1571   Trusts (Capital and Income) Act 2013

See para 2482.

INFORMATION TECHNOLOGY LAW

Halsbury's Laws of England (5th edn) vol 57 (2012) paras 501–694

Articles

For articles relating to this title please refer to the Table of Articles at the beginning of the Abridgment.

1572   Computer program—patentability

See *Lantana Ltd v Comptroller General of Patents, Designs and Trade Marks*, para 1953.

1573   Computer software—copyright—infringement—partnership property

See *Coward v Phaestos Ltd*, para 578.

1574   Database right—infringement—qualifying databases

The claimants claimed to own a sui generis database right, as protected by Council Directive (EC) 96/9. The database included live data about football matches in various leagues, a section called 'football live', which was updated by analysts attending every match and reporting results to their central information centre. The second defendant owned and maintained its own very large database of sport statistics, part of which pulled data from the claimant's database. The first defendant was a bookmaker that paid a fee for the use of the second defendant's information. Customers accessed the second defendant's site through a pop-up box packaged as the first defendant's gambling service, but that process temporarily downloaded a larger image of the claimant's data to the user's computer and displayed at least some of it. After the claim was brought this practice continued, although less of the claimant's data was used. The judge found that the claimants had a qualifying database, but held that the data that was extracted from it was insufficient to found a claim. On appeal, the issues for determination were: (1) whether football live was a database which qualified for protection under art 7; (2) whether the United Kingdom-based users of the first defendant's website were infringers pursuant to art 7; (3) whether either or both defendants had been joint tortfeasors with the customers; and (4) whether there was a defence of infringement of the right to freedom of expression under the European Convention on Human Rights art 10. *Held*, there was a sui generis right in the football live database for the purposes of Directive 96/9 art 7. The established test for ascertaining whether what was extracted had amounted to a substantial part of a database was a qualitative issue that depended on the scale of the investment in obtaining verification of what had been extracted. The claimant had made a very significant investment into its data and, accordingly, the judge's conclusion concerning the pre-defence data could not be faulted. However, the judge had erred in his findings concerning the post-defence data. It was not relevant whether that data could be collected at virtually no additional cost. What mattered was the investment which in fact had gone into collecting the data. Furthermore, it was difficult to see how the data could be collected without having someone at each ground watching and communicating when each goal was scored. The provider of a website was a joint tortfeasor with a United Kingdom user of that website if the inevitable consequence of access to that site by the user was infringement by that user. Indeed, the website provider's very purpose in providing the website was to cause or procure acts which would amount in law to an infringement by any United Kingdom user of it. Both defendants were targeting United Kingdom customers, the first defendant to attract to and keep customers on its website while the second defendant had received money for assisting in that endeavour. The customer was made to infringe if he used the pop-up box at all, the second defendant was extracting a substantial part of the claimant's football live database without having paid, and the first defendant was paying the second defendant for that data. In those circumstances, the Convention art 10 did not justify the commercial piracy at issue. Accordingly, the appeal would be allowed in part.

Football Dataco Ltd v Stan James plc [2013] EWCA Civ 27, [2013] 2 CMLR 932, [2013] All ER (D) 61 (Feb) (Court of Appeal: Lloyd and Lewison LJJ and Sir Robin Jacob J). Case C-203/02 *British Horseracing Board Ltd v William Hill Organisation Ltd* [2005] IP & T 407, ECJ; and *Unilever plc v Gillette (UK) Ltd* [1989] RPC 583 applied. Decision of Floyd J sub nom *Football Dataco Ltd v Sportradar GmbH* [2012] EWHC 1185 (Ch), [2012] 3 CMLR 427, [2012] All ER (D) 121 (May) (2012 Abr para 1546) reversed in part.

1575   Email—messages sent to commercial agent—principal's right to message after termination of agreement

See *Fairstar Heavy Transport NV v Adkins*, para 420.

1576   Internet—copyright—infringement—music downloads—file sharing website

See *EMI Records Ltd v British Sky Broadcasting Ltd*, para 576.

1577   Internet—copyright—internet service provider—injunction to restrain customers accessing website

See *Football Association Premier League Ltd v British Sky Broadcasting Ltd*, para 583.

1578   Internet—copyright—streaming of television broadcasts

See Case C-607/11 *ITV Broadcasting Ltd v TVCatchup Ltd*, para 577.

1579   Internet—copyright—website indexing films available to download—authorising acts of infringement—proprietary injunction

See *Twentieth Century Fox Film Corpn v Harris*, para 580.

1580   Internet—publication—breach of injunction—contempt of court

See *A-G v Harkins; A-G v Liddle*, para 521.

1581   Internet—publication—libel—absence of control over content

See *Tamiz v Google*, para 847.

1582   Internet—publication—website operators—defamation

See para 838.

1583   Internet—search engine—keyword advertising—trade mark infringement

See *Interflora Inc v Marks and Spencer plc*, para 2406.

1584   Internet—social networking site—cyberbullying—legal proceedings—right of victim to anonymity

See AB (*by her litigation guardian CD*) *v Bragg Communications Inc*, para 425.

1585   Internet—website—use of domain and metatags—prohibition on misleading and comparative advertising

See Case C-657/11 *Belgian Electronic Sorting Technology NV v Peelaers*, para 512.

INHERITANCE TAXATION

Halsbury's Laws of England (4th edn) vol 24 (Reissue) paras 401–800

Articles

For articles relating to this title please refer to the Table of Articles at the beginning of the Abridgment.

1586   Assessment—tax-free allowance—non-resident—free movement of capital

See Case C-181/12 *Welte v Finanzamt Velbert*, para 2708.

1587   Avoidance schemes—information

See para 1567.

1588   Exempt transfers and reliefs—business property relief—relevant business property—business of holding investments—office letting business

The appellants were trustees of a settlement, the principal asset in the settlement being a commercial building which was divided into units that were let to tenants for between one and five years. The units were intended to offer flexible office space for computer, media and high technology businesses and a number of services and facilities were provided to the tenants, including the services of a cafe, gym, cycle arch, wi-fi, portage, 24 hour access, meeting rooms, media events, outdoor screens for viewing football matches and film shows and an art gallery area. The appellants sought inheritance tax business property relief in respect of the settlement but the Commissioners for Her Majesty's Revenue and Customs refused relief on the basis that none of the property was relevant business property for the purposes of the Inheritance Tax Act 1984 s 104, the business consisting mainly of making or holding investments which was excluded under s 105(3). The appellants appealed, contending that sufficient services were provided to the tenants of the property so that it ought not to be classified as an investment business. *Held,* the degree of services required to take a business out of the mainly holding of investment category was not stated in law. Consideration would be given to the main or preponderant activities of the business, assets and the source of income over a reasonable period. The business must be looked at as a whole and consideration given to all relevant factors to decide if it was mainly an investment, including the level of profit from the activities, turnover, employees, use of assets and time required for management. It was a question of degree and proportion. When the non-investment activities in relation to the property were looked at closely, the conclusion was that they were primarily concerned with increasing the return from the building. The appellants had sought to do this by providing a flexible management, shorter leases and tenants who could provide café facilities, a gym and a hair dressing salon among others. Moreover, the income from the cycle rack and gallery as well as the coffee shop, hairdressing salon and gym was all rental income. It was accepted that the business was actively managed and there was a different relationship between the management and the tenants, but the services which were not investment related were not sufficient to tip the balance in favour of obtaining business property relief. Accordingly, the appeal would be dismissed.

The Trustee of David Zetland Settlement v Revenue and Customs Comrs [2013] UKFTT 284, [2013] WTLR 1065 (First-tier Tribunal: Judge K Khan).

1589   Exempt transfers and reliefs—business property relief—relevant business property—holiday letting business

The Inheritance Tax Act 1984 s 105(3) provides that a business or interest in a business is not relevant business property if the business consists wholly or mainly of making or holding investments.

At the date of her death the testatrix owned a 25 per cent beneficial interest in a bungalow which, in the two years preceding her death, had been used for the purposes of a holiday letting business carried on for gain. The testatrix's executors claimed that her interest in the property had consisted of 'a business or interest in a business' within the 1984 Act s 105(1)(a) and so was 'relevant business property' which qualified for business property relief from inheritance tax. This contention was not accepted by Her Majesty's Commissioners for Revenue and Customs, who issued a notice of determination to the effect that the testatrix's interest in the property was excluded from the definition of 'relevant business property' by s 105(3) as the holiday letting business was mainly a business of holding investments. The executors appealed against the notice to the First-tier Tribunal. In allowing the appeal, the tribunal took the view that the services provided to holidaymakers had gone well beyond those which an intelligent businessman would regard as consisting of an investment, and considered that the non-investment services had been of such a nature and extent that the business had not been 'mainly' one of holding the property as an investment. The Commissioners appealed. *Held*, the statutory test of holding an investment was not a term of art, and should be given the meaning that would be given by an intelligent businessman. Where a landowner derived income from land he would be treated as having a business of holding an investment notwithstanding that in order to obtain the income he carried out incidental maintenance and management work, found tenants and granted leases. The relevant test was not the degree or level of activity, but rather the nature of the activities which were carried out. It was settled law that the provision of additional services and facilities was not to be regarded as part of the maintenance of the property as an investment, and that their characterisation as services was unaffected by the fact that no separate charge had been made for them. In any normal case, an actively managed property would still fall within the exception in s 105(3) because the 'mainly' condition would still be satisfied. On the basis of its findings of primary fact, the only conclusion which it had been reasonably open to the tribunal to draw had been that the business in question had been mainly that of holding the property as an investment. The services provided had all been of a relatively standard nature, and they had all been aimed at maximising the income which the family could obtain from the short term holiday letting of the property. Accordingly, the appeal would be allowed.

Revenue and Customs Comrs v Lockyer [2013] UKUT 50 (TCC), [2013] STC 976 (Upper Tribunal: Henderson J). *Weston (executor of Weston) v IRC* [2000] STC 1064 (2000 Abr para 1879); and *IRC v George* [2003] EWCA Civ 1763, (2003) 75 TC 735, [2004] STC 147 (2003 Abr para 1597) applied. *Martin (Moore's Executors) v IRC* [1995] STC (SCD) 5 considered. Decision of First-tier Tribunal [2012] UKFTT 51 (TC) reversed.

1590   Finance Act 2013

See para 2149.

INSURANCE

Halsbury's Laws of England (5th edn) vol 60 (2011) paras 1–807

Articles

For articles relating to this title please refer to the Table of Articles at the beginning of the Abridgment.

1591   Consumer Insurance (Disclosure and Representations) Act 2012—commencement

The Consumer Insurance (Disclosure and Representations) Act 2012 (Commencement) Order 2013, SI 2013/450, brings ss 2–11 and Schs 1, 2 into force on 6 April 2013. For a summary of the Act, see 2012 Abr para 1562. See also the commencement table in the title STATUTES AND LEGISLATIVE PROCESS.

1592   Insurance broker—duty of care—delay in remission of funds—calculation of losses

The claimant was the successor to Lloyd's syndicates writing non-life insurance business. A settlement agreement was concluded as the culmination of a long process of reconstruction and renewal, which was intended to bring an end to the extensive litigation resulting from market turmoil. The defendant was added as a party to the settlement agreement by way of a brokers' agreement. The claimant contended that the defendant had breached its duties to remit certain funds it had recovered reasonably promptly and brought an action against the defendant in contract, tort and restitution. A number of preliminary issues fell to be determined. *Held*, the defendant's contractual and restitutionary duty was an absolute duty and not merely a duty to exercise due diligence. Unless it could be said that the duty of care was inconsistent or excluded by contract, a duty of care had been owed to the syndicates. There was no reason why an absolute contractual duty should not coexist comfortably with a duty in tort to exercise reasonable care. The losses suffered by the syndicates were to be measured by reference to the cost of borrowing in the market. The effect of the settlement agreement had been that the defendant's cross-claims had been waived and could not be asserted by way of set off. However, if and to the extent that any equitable set off in favour of the defendant had arisen, it had not operated automatically to extinguish or reduce the syndicates' claims at the time when the cross-claims had arisen. Judgment would be given accordingly.

Equitas Ltd v Walsham Bros & Co Ltd [2013] EWHC 3264 (Comm), [2013] All ER (D) 358 (Oct) (Queen's Bench Division: Males J).

1593   Insurance company—taxation—corporation tax—transitional provision

See para 1499.

1594   Legal expenses insurance—after the event policy—order for costs—recoverability

See *Hawksford Trustees Jersey Ltd v Stella Global UK Ltd (No 2)*, para 270.

1595   Legal expenses insurance—before the event policy—insured's wish to instruct own lawyer—refusal of cover

The applicant took out legal expenses insurance with Reaal Schadeverzekeringen NV (Reaal). The insurance contract provided that DAS Nederlandse Rechtsbijstand Verzekeringsmaatschappij NV (DAS) was the company responsible for providing legal assistance cover. That contract also provided that cases were to be dealt with by DAS's own staff. However, if, according to the contract or in DAS's opinion, a case should be delegated to external counsel, the insured person had the right to instruct a lawyer or legal practitioner of his own choosing. In the case in the main proceedings, the applicant wished to bring legal proceedings against his former employer in order to claim damages on the ground of unfair dismissal. To that end, he intended to be assisted by a lawyer of his choosing and to have the costs of legal assistance covered by his legal expenses insurer. DAS had indicated its agreement to such legal proceedings being brought, but considered that the contract entered into by the applicant did not provide, in such a case, cover for the costs of legal assistance provided by a lawyer chosen by the insured person. DAS indicated that it was prepared to provide legal assistance to the applicant only through one of its own employees, who was not a lawyer. In accordance with Netherlands law, in the proceedings which the applicant wished to bring against his former employer, legal assistance was not compulsory. Following DAS's refusal to cover the costs of assistance provided by a lawyer chosen by the applicant, the applicant unsuccessfully requested the court hearing applications for interim relief in Amsterdam to order DAS to bear those costs. Relying on Council Directive (EEC) 87/344 art 4(1) (on the co-ordination of laws, regulations and administrative provisions relating to legal expenses insurance), the Court of Appeal, Amsterdam, upheld that court's decision. The applicant contested that judgment before the Supreme Court of the Netherlands (the referring court). That court took the view that the analysis of the various linguistic versions of art 4(1) provided substantive support for the view that, if judicial or administrative proceedings were brought, the contract terms should always offer the insured person the right freely to choose his legal representative. The referring court considered that the reply which it was called on to give in the case in the main proceedings could have certain social consequences, since, if such an interpretation of art 4(1) was to be accepted, that would inevitably lead to an increase in insurance premiums, probably of a considerable amount. In those circumstances, the referring court decided to stay proceedings and to refer certain questions to the Court of Justice of the European Union (the Court) for a preliminary ruling. By its questions, the referring court asked, in essence (1) whether art 4(1)(a) should be interpreted as meaning that it precluded a legal expenses insurer which stipulated in its insurance contracts that legal assistance would in principle be provided by its employees from also providing that the costs of legal assistance provided by a lawyer or legal representative chosen freely by the insured person would be covered only if the insurer took the view that the handling of the case should be sub-contracted to an external lawyer; and (2) whether the answer to question 1 would differ depending on whether or not legal assistance was compulsory under national law in the inquiry or proceedings concerned. *Held*, (1) according to the Court's case-law, freedom of choice, within the terms of art 4(1), did not mean that member states were obliged to require insurers, in all circumstances, to cover in full the costs incurred in connection with the defence of an insured person, on condition that that freedom was not rendered meaningless. That would be the case if the restriction imposed on the payment of those costs had to render de facto impossible a reasonable choice of representative by the insured person. In any event, it was for the national courts, if an action was brought before them in that regard, to determine whether or not there was any such restriction. Further, the contracting parties remained free to agree cover for a higher level of legal assistance costs, possibly against payment of a higher premium by the insured person. Article 4(1)(a) should be interpreted as precluding a legal expenses insurer which stipulates in its insurance contracts that legal assistance would in principle be provided by its employees from also providing that the costs of legal assistance provided by a lawyer or legal representative chosen freely by the insured person would be covered only if the insurer took the view that the handling of the case should be sub-contracted to an external lawyer. (2) Since the right freely to choose a representative was of general application and was obligatory in nature, and secondly, the Directive, as was apparent in particular from recital 11 in the preamble and art 4(1)(a), did not make the right to choose a representative and the scope of that right subject to national rules on legal representation, such national rules could not affect the answer given to the first question. The answer to question 1 would not differ depending on whether or not legal assistance was compulsory under national law in the inquiry or proceedings concerned.

Case C-442/12 *Sneller v DAS Nederlandse Rechtsbijstand Verzekeringsmaatschappij NV* [2014] Bus LR 180, [2013] All ER (D) 101 (Nov) (ECJ: Eighth Chamber).

1596   Liability insurance—employer's liability—insurance period—indemnity— apportionment

The claimant company was an insured party under an employer's liability policy with the defendant insurer. The policy provided that, if any employee sustained 'any bodily injury or disease caused during the period of insurance and arising out of and in the course of his employment', the defendant would indemnify the claimant the sums for which the claimant was liable. The claimant and its predecessor had employed an employee for 27 years for the final six years of which the policy was in place. The claimant had been insured for the earlier period under an employer's liability policy with a different insurer. After leaving his employment with the claimant, the employee was diagnosed as suffering from mesothelioma. His claim for negligence against the claimant was settled before the employee's death. The claimant sought an indemnity from the defendant for the settlement sum. It fell to be determined whether the claimant was entitled to an indemnity from the defendant for the entirety of its outlay in respect of the employee's claim, or whether the claimant was only entitled to a contribution from the defendant reflecting that part of its outlay corresponding to the proportion which the policy period bore to the whole period of the employee's exposure to asbestos. It was held that the claimant's right of indemnity had been limited to the proportion of the period of the employee's employment by the claimant for which it was insured by the defendant. The claimant appealed. *Held*, it was settled law that when an employee contracted mesothelioma as a result of being exposed to asbestos fibres or dust at work, his cause of action rested on the fact that he had contracted the disease. The mesothelioma itself was the damage and it was that damage that was the gist of the cause of action, not that the employee had been tortiously exposed to the risk of mesothelioma. For the purpose of the insurance, mesothelioma was 'sustained' or 'contracted' when the process that led to the disease was initiated as a result of the tortious exposure of the employee to the asbestos fibres. If an employer was liable to his employee for his employee's mesothelioma following a tortious exposure to asbestos created during an insurance period, then, for the purposes of the insuring clause in the employer's liability policy, the disease was 'caused' within the insurance period because it was sufficient that there was a 'weak' or 'broad' causal link between the exposure to the asbestos during the insurance policy and the employee's eventual contraction of the mesothelioma. Once the causal link was fulfilled, then the employer would have proved that the mesothelioma was caused during any period of insurance. The employee had been employed for the whole of the period by the claimant and its predecessor. Therefore, for the purposes of the insuring clause, the mesothelioma which he contracted might have been 'sustained' in the course of his employment by the claimant. It had followed from the wording of the policy that the defendant had been liable to indemnify the claimant for the whole of the damages paid out by the claimant in respect of the employee's claim for damages for contracting mesothelioma, not just a proportion worked out by reference to the period during which the claimant had been covered by policies for which the defendant had been responsible. Once it was accepted that exposure during any policy period had met the causal requirement for the employer's liability to the claimant, to withhold part of that indemnity from the employer on account of its conduct in other years would have been to deprive the employer of insurance coverage for which it had paid. There was a sufficient causal link between the employee's exposure to asbestos during the years when the claimant had been insured by the defendant and his contraction of mesothelioma, for the claimant to have been legally liable for causing his disease, and the claimant had had a contractual right of indemnity under the policy against that liability. The fact that the employee's exposure to asbestos during the rest of his employment was also an effective cause of the disease was irrelevant to the claimant's right to indemnity on the wording of the policy. The policy would have required a special clause to limit the scope of the indemnity in such circumstances. Accordingly, the appeal would be allowed.

International Energy Group Ltd v Zurich Insurance plc UK Branch [2013] EWCA Civ 39, [2013] 3 All ER 395 (Court of Appeal: Maurice Kay VP, Toulson and Aikens LJJ). *Fairchild v Glenhaven Funeral Services Ltd; Fox v Spousal (Midlands) Ltd; Matthews v Associated Portland Cement Manufacturers (1978) Ltd* [2002] UKHL 22, [2003] 1 AC 32, [2002] 3 All ER 305 (2002 Abr para 1545); and *Durham v BAI (Run Off) Ltd (in scheme of arrangement)* [2012] UKSC 14, [2012] 3 All ER 1161 (2012 Abr para 1572) applied. *Barker v Corus UK Ltd; Murray v British Shipbuilders (Hydrodynamics) Ltd; Patterson v Smiths Dock Ltd* [2006] UKHL 20, [2006] 2 AC 572, [2006] 3 All ER 785 (2006 Abr para 2075); and *Sienkiewicz v Greif (UK) Ltd; Willmore v Knowsley MBC* [2011] UKSC 10, [2011] 2 AC 229, [2011] 2 All ER 857 (2011 Abr para 1912) considered.

1597   Marine insurance—collision—causation—constructive total loss

A vessel suffered damage during a voyage. It had moved while at anchor, resulting in the anchor being dragged, and had grounded itself. It was agreed between the parties that the third officer of the vessel ('G'), had been negligent in allowing it to drift on the current that had grounded it. The vessel was refloated and reached port a number of days later. Damage was discovered as a result of the grounding and, after expert assessment of the vessel, the claimant owners served on the defendant underwriters a notice of abandonment, stating that they considered that the cost of repairs to the hull or the hull and engine would exceed the insured value of the vessel. The defendants instructed their own experts to examine the vessel. They declined the notice, but agreed that the claimants should be treated as if proceedings had been issued when it was given. Later, the claimant agreed to sell the vessel for scrap. The claimants commenced proceedings, seeking to claim under the insurance. *Held*, the claimants had established that the grounding had been a fortuity and that, as a matter of common sense, the grounding or the fact that the current grounded the vessel as it had done, was a proximate cause of the damage. The causal impact of G's negligence had not been so potent in terms of efficiency as to displace the proximate causes of the damage and the events that he had not prevented, which were the action of the current and the grounding itself. Damage to the vessel had been caused by a peril of the seas covered by the policies. Further, the vessel would have been an actual total loss if it had been physically or

destination or any intervening point. Violation of the warranty rendered the reinsurance policy void. The original policy contained a similar provision. One of the scheduled vessels under the original policy sailed into the eye of a typhoon and the captain gave the order to abandon ship. Before departure, he had a severe weather bulletin in his. The vessel capsized and only 32 of the 851 passengers and crew on board survived. The claimants sought a declaration that the departure of the vessel constituted a breach of the warranty so that they were not liable as the reinsurers of the defendant in respect of the loss of and/or damage to the cargo on the vessel occurring by reason of the typhoon. There was evidence that the captain had intended to follow a usual route, but would depart from it if the weather had become extremely bad before the latest point when the vessel could take an alternate route. *Held*, if a scheduled vessel had sailed from a port where there had been a typhoon or storm warning, the warranty had been breached. If it had been the parties' intention to prohibit a scheduled vessel from departing only when the circular had prohibited or advised against it, they could have easily so provided and the fact that they had not told strongly against the defendant's construction, even though the circular was part of the contractual background. Therefore, the first limb of the warranty had been breached and, in consequence, the reinsurance policy had been avoided. The second limb of the warranty had also been breached. The captain had intended to follow the usual route, but would depart from it if the weather had become really bad before the latest point when the vessel could take the alternate route. If followed that the usual route had been the intended route for the purpose of the second limb. The policy of the warranty had been 'safety first' and a route intended to be taken, subject only to the possibility of a change of course if the weather was going to be bad, was the intended route for the purpose of the second limb. The warranty had been breached, the reinsurance policy had been avoided and the claimants would be entitled to a declaration to that effect. Accordingly, the claim would be allowed.

Amlin Corporate Member Ltd v Oriental Assurance Corpn [2013] EWHC 2380 (Comm), [2014] 1 All ER (Comm) 415 (Queen's Bench Division: Field J).

1601   Motor insurance—repairs—cost—reasonableness

See *Coles v Hetherton*, para 791.

1602   Motor insurance—requirement to produce evidence

The Motor Vehicles (Third Party Risks) (Amendment) Regulations 2013, SI 2013/2904 (in force on 16 December 2013), further amend the 1972 Regulations, SI 1972/1217, by removing the requirement to produce evidence of motor insurance or comparable surety when applying for a vehicle excise licence. A similar amendment relating to visitors to Great Britain is made to the Motor Vehicles (International Motor Insurance Card) Regulations 1971, SI 1971/792.

1603   Property insurance—riot damage—claim against police authority

See *Mitsui Sumitomo Insurance Co (Europe) Ltd v The Mayor's Office for Policing and Crime; Royal and Sun Alliance plc v Mayor's Office for Policing and Crime; Lace International Ltd v Mayor's Office for Policing and Crime*, para 2067.

1604   Reinsurance—contract of reinsurance—claims control clause—breach

The defendant insurers entered a contract for reinsurance with the claimant reinsurers. A claim control clause was included in the contract which stated that it was a condition precedent to any liability under the reinsurance that the claimant had the right to control all negotiations, adjustments, and settlements in connection with such loss or losses. The contract also stated that no settlement or compromise would be made and no liability admitted without the prior approval of the claimant. The defendants were notified of a claim by the insured in respect of damage and loss. They notified the claimant. The claimant contended that it was not liable under the contract, as the defendants had committed various breaches of the clause by a telephone call negotiation, a memo providing internal approval of the telephone call, a letter, and an email. It fell to be determined whether the defendants had breached the clause. *Held*, on the true construction of the contract, there had been no breach of the claim control clause, as there had been no negotiations, still less any agreement, during the telephone call, and the internal approval in the memo had no legal effect as between the parties. Further, there had been no 'settlement', 'compromise' nor 'admission of liability' during the telephone call. The memo, letter and email could not, without more, have constituted a settlement, compromise, or admission of liability. There had been no breach by the defendants of the clause and they were not barred from pursuing their claim against the claimant under the contract. Judgment would be given accordingly.

Beazley Underwriting Ltd v Al Ahleia Insurance Co [2013] EWHC 677 (Comm), [2013] Lloyd's Rep IR 561, [2013] All ER (D) 286 (Mar) (Queen's Bench Division: Eder J). *Royal and Sun Alliance Insurance plc v Dornoch Ltd* [2005] EWCA Civ 238, [2005] 1 All ER (Comm) 590 (2005 Abr para 1904) applied.

1605   Reinsurance—contract of reinsurance—construction—'follow the settlements' clause

Insurance claims were made as a result of loss incurred due to severe flooding in Thailand. The insurance companies against whom the claims were made were reinsured under a facultative reinsurance under which various reinsurers, including the claimant company, agreed to reinsure part of the losses. The claimant purchased from the defendant company a facultative excess of loss reinsurance (the 'retrocession'). The claimant paid its share of the settlement sum, and then sought to recover its share of the losses excess from the defendant. The defendant denied liability. In the course of the proceedings, preliminary issues arose relating to the interpretation of the retrocession, and in particular the 'follow the settlements' clause. *Held*, reinsurance contracts were to be construed by adopting the same principles applicable to the construction of commercial contracts. The general approach was to consider what a reasonable person, having all the background knowledge which would have been available to the parties at the time of contracting, would have understood themselves to be agreeing in using the language in the contract. If there were two possible constructions of a document or term, a court was entitled to prefer the construction which was more consistent with business or commercial sense. By contrast, where the parties had used unambiguous language, the court had to apply it. In the context of proportional reinsurance in which the reinsured ceded a share of the risk to the reinsurer, it would frequently be inferred that it was the intent of the parties that the insurance and reinsurance were to be back-to-back. In the case of non-proportional reinsurance contracts, such as a retrocession, there was, however, no presumption that the reinsurance contract was intended to be back-to-back with the underlying insurance contract. In the present case, on the true and proper construction of the retrocession, and the follow the settlements clause in particular, the defendant had agreed to follow the settlements (excluding without prejudice and ex gratia payments) of the insured companies under the master policy and/or the local policy respectively. The burden on the claimant was to show that the claim was one which arguably fell within the terms of the retrocession as a matter of law. On the assumption that the insured company had acted in an honest, proper and businesslike manner in concluding the original settlement, the defendant was bound by a determination as to the construction and application of the aggregation provisions in the master policy and/or (if different) whether the losses were consequent on or attributable to one source or original cause. Judgment would be given accordingly.

Tokio Marine Europe Insurance Ltd v Novae Corporate Underwriting Ltd [2013] EWHC 3362 (Comm), [2013] All ER (D) 67 (Nov) (Queen's Bench Division: Hamblen J).

1606   Reinsurance—contract of reinsurance—construction—meaning of 'loss arising out of one event'

The claimant and the defendant insurance companies were parties to reinsurance contracts which became the subject of claims brought against four airlines following the '9/11' hijackings of four aeroplanes in the United States. Liability for the property and business interruption claims flowing from the hijackings was allocated in different amounts between the four airlines. Each of the claims under ten inward reinsurances was settled on the basis that the attacks on each of the two towers of the World Trade Centre were separate events. The relevant reinsurance contracts were subject to London Standard Wording which provided that the term 'each and every loss' was to be understood to mean 'each and every loss or accident or occurrence or series thereof arising out of one event'. Some of the inwards contracts were written on a 'one event' basis, while others were written on an 'each aircraft', 'each insured' or 'one event' basis at the discretion of the reinsured. All of the inwards claims to the defendant were settled on a two event basis. The claimant contended that its liability under the outward reinsurances was on a one event basis. The matter was referred to arbitration, and it fell to be determined whether the losses sustained by the defendants on the ten reinsurance contracts had been caused by one or more occurrences or series of occurrences 'arising out of one event'. The tribunal concluded that the losses which arose on the inward reinsurances had been caused by two separate occurrences arising out of separate events. The claimant appealed, submitting that, instead of confining its analysis to whether the attacks on the World Trade Centre constituted one event, the tribunal had wrongly focused on, and had been wrongly influenced by, its conclusion as to the number of loss events arising out of the hijackings of all four flights. *Held*, the tribunal had made no error of law in reaching its conclusion that the insured losses caused by the attacks arose out of two events and not one. It had accurately identified the applicable law pursuant to which it had undertaken an exercise of judgment. Accordingly, the appeal would be dismissed.

Aioi Nissay Dowa Insurance Co Ltd v Heraldglen Ltd [2013] EWHC 154 (Comm), [2013] 2 All ER (Comm) 231 (Queen's Bench Division: Field J).

1607   Reinsurance—contract of reinsurance—entitlement to indemnity

A major worldwide pharmaceutical group was insured by the claimant insurer under a liability insurance policy. The defendant specialised in the provision of high level or catastrophe excess of loss insurance and reinsurance. It agreed to reinsure the claimant for a 50 per cent share in respect of insurance provided by the claimant under the policy which provided for the insured to be indemnified for damages on account of personal injury and that damages would include defence costs. The group manufactured, marketed and sold an anti-psychotic drug in the United States and Canada. Claims against the group alleged that the drug had caused users of the drug personal injury. The claimant settled claims presented by the group for legal costs incurred in defending the claims and for settlements reached in respect of the claims against the group. The claimant also indemnified other companies in the group in respect of the legal costs incurred in defending the claims. The claimant sought indemnification by the defendant pursuant to the reinsurance contracts in respect of all sums the claimant had paid in respect of settlements and defence costs. The defendant denied that it was liable to indemnify the claimant. Preliminary issues arose as to the construction of the underlying insurance policy between the group and the claimant. *Held*, the general principle was that liability insurance provided an indemnity against actual established liability, as opposed to mere allegations. English cases established, consistently, that the insured under a liability insurance policy would need to establish actual legal liability to a third party claimant before it could recover from the insurer, unless the particular language used in the policy clearly provided to the contrary. The insured was only entitled to an indemnity under the policy where it demonstrated that it was under an actual legal liability, namely where the insured had entered into a settlement. That meant that the insured had to show, on a balance of probabilities, that it would have been liable for the claim in question, on the basis of the correct application of the system of law governing the claim to the evidence properly analysed. The insured was only entitled to an indemnity for defence costs where it established that it was or would have been liable for the claim in question. The parties had expressed the intention that defence costs should only be recoverable in circumstances where what might be described as 'traditional' damages were recoverable, not that there should be free-standing coverage for such defence. Judgment would be given accordingly.

Astrazeneca Insurance Co Ltd v XL Insurance (Bermuda) Ltd [2013] EWHC 349 (Comm), [2013] 2 All ER (Comm) 97 (Queen's Bench Division: Flaux J). *Re Hooley Hill Rubber and Chemical Co Ltd and Royal Insurance Co Ltd* [1920] 1 KB 257, CA, applied. *Yorkshire Water Services Ltd v Sun Alliance & London Insurance Ltd* [1997] 2 Lloyd's Rep 21 (1996 Abr para 1774); *Commercial Union Assurance Co plc v NRG Victory Reinsurance Ltd; Skandia International Insurance Corpn v NRG Victory Reinsurance Ltd* [1998] 2 All ER 434, CA (1998 Abr para 1926), considered.

INTERNATIONAL RELATIONS LAW

Halsbury's Laws of England (5th edn) vol 61 (2010) paras 1–600

Articles

For articles relating to this title please refer to the Table of Articles at the beginning of the Abridgment.

1608   Antarctic Act 2013

See para 1116.

1609   Asylum

See IMMIGRATION AND ASYLUM.

1610   Consular fees

The Consular Fees (Amendment) Order 2013, SI 2013/535 (in force on 6 April 2013), further amends the 2012 Order, SI 2012/798, so as to replace the table of general consular fees, by adding a fee for making a search in (1) the consular register of births, deaths and marriages or civil partnerships where the number or date of entry is not provided; and (2) the naturalisation, registration or renunciation records kept by a consular officer.

The Consular Fees (Amendment) (No 2) Order 2013, SI 2013/1720 (in force on 1 August 2013), further amends the 2012 Order above by replacing the table of consular fees relating to passport services.

The Consular Fees (Amendment) Regulations 2013, SI 2013/762 (in force on 6 April 2013), further amend the 1981 Regulations, SI 1981/476, so as to allow for consular fees to be paid in sterling by debit or credit card at the discretion of a consular officer. Payment may still be made in currency circulating at the place of payment.

1611   European Union—asset-freezing—Belarus

The Belarus (Asset-Freezing) Regulations 2013, SI 2013/164 (in force on 21 February 2013), make provision relating to the enforcement of Council Regulation (EC) 765/2006 concerning restrictive measures in respect of Belarus, and (1) define a designated person as any person named in Regulation 765/2006 Annex I; (2) provide (a) prohibitions against dealing with the funds or economic resources of a designated person or making funds or economic resources available, directly or indirectly, to or for the benefit of, a designated person; (b) an exception to the prohibitions where a frozen account is credited for a permitted reason; and (c) a licensing procedure to enable funds and economic resources to be exempted from the prohibitions; (3) make it an offence to breach any of the prohibitions or to seek to circumvent them; and (4) make provision about penalties, proceedings and who, in relation to bodies corporate and other bodies, may be prosecuted for an offence. SI 2012/1509 is revoked.

1612   European Union—asset-freezing—Libya

The Libya (Asset-Freezing) (Amendment) Regulations 2013, SI 2013/2071 (in force on 13 September 2013), further amend the 2011 Regulations, SI 2011/605, to give effect to Council Regulation (EU) 488/2013, which amends an existing exemption to the asset-freezing provisions in Council Regulation (EC) 204/2011 (concerning restrictive measures in view of the situation in Libya) to permit the crediting of funds, by any person, to frozen accounts in specified circumstances when the payments are due under judicial, administrative or arbitral liens, judgments or decisions.

1613   European Union—financial sanctions—North Korea

The Democratic People's Republic of Korea (European Union Financial Sanctions) Regulations 2013, SI 2013/1877 (in force on 16 August 2013), replace the Democratic People's Republic of Korea (Asset-Freezing) Regulations 2011, SI 2011/1094, and provide for the enforcement of Council Regulation (EC) 329/2007 concerning restrictive measures against the Democratic People's Republic of Korea ('North Korea'). In particular, the 2013 Regulations (1) prohibit dealing with the funds or economic resources of designated persons or making funds or economic resources available to or for the benefit of designated persons; (2) provide an exception to the prohibitions of making funds available to or for the benefit of designated persons; (3) set out a licensing procedure to enable funds and economic resources to be exempted from prohibitions; (4) prohibit credit or financial institutions from establishing certain relationships with North Korean credit or financial institutions and opening representative offices or establishing branches in North Korea; (5) prohibit the making of agreements for or on behalf of North Korean credit or financial institutions to establish representative offices, branches or subsidiaries in the European Union; (6) prohibit certain North Korean credit or financial institutions from acquiring or extending an ownership interest in credit or financial institutions; (7) prohibit the sale or purchase of North Korean public bonds to or from the North Korean government or its public bodies, its central bank, or certain other persons, entities or bodies linked to North Korea; (8) provide for offences, penalties, proceedings and specify who, in relation to bodies corporate and other bodies, may be prosecuted for offences; and (9) provide for the gathering and disclosure of information.

1614   European Union—financial sanctions—suspension—Zimbabwe

See para 2389.

1615   European Union—financial sanctions—Syria

The Syria (European Union Financial Sanctions) (Amendment) Regulations 2013, SI 2013/877 (in force on 7 May 2013), further amend the 2012 Regulations, SI 2012/129, so as to (1) provide that payments made to Syrian Arab Airlines for the sole purpose of evacuating citizens of the European Union and their family members from Syria will not contravene asset freezing restrictions; and (2) permit the crediting of funds to frozen accounts when payments are due under judicial, administrative or arbitral decisions rendered or enforceable in a member state.

The Syria (European Union Financial Sanctions) (Amendment No 2) Regulations 2013, SI 2013/1876 (in force on 16 August 2013), further amend the 2012 Regulations above so as to except anything under the authority of a licence granted by the Treasury from the prohibitions on credit institutions opening a new bank account with any Syrian credit or financial institution, opening a new representative office in Syria and establishing a new branch or subsidiary in Syria.

1616   European Union—restrictive measures—freezing of economic resources—inclusion of individual on list—challenge

The applicant's name was added to the United Nations Sanctions Committee list established by United Nations Security Council Resolution 1267 on the situation in Afghanistan, on the basis that he had allegedly raised funds on behalf of, and held a senior position in, the Libyan Islamic Fighting Group. The applicant's name was therefore added to the list of persons and entities whose funds and other economic resources would be frozen under Council Regulation (EC) 881/2002. The applicant brought an action before the General Court of the European Union for the annulment of Regulation 881/2002 in so far as it applied to him. Before the hearing could take place, the applicant's name was removed from both of the lists. For that reason, a declaration was made by the General Court that the action for annulment had become devoid of purpose and that there was no longer any need to adjudicate on that point. The applicant appealed against that decision, submitting that the General Court had erred in law in holding that the action had become devoid of purpose. *Held*, the restrictive measures adopted under Regulation 881/2002 had substantial negative consequences and a considerable impact on the rights and freedoms of the persons concerned, including the suspicion by the public of such a person as being associated with a terrorist organisation. In the light of the circumstances of the case and, in particular, the extent of the damage to the applicant's reputation resulting from his inclusion on the EU list, his interest in bringing proceedings continued to exist for the purpose of seeking annulment of Regulation 881/2002 in so far as it concerned him and of securing, should his action be upheld, his rehabilitation and, thus, some form of reparation for the non-material harm suffered by him. The General Court had erred in inferring from the removal of his name that the applicant had obtained full satisfaction and that his action for annulment was no longer such as to procure him an advantage. It followed that the General Court had erred in law in holding that he lacked an interest in bringing proceedings and that there was no longer any need to adjudicate on his action. Accordingly, the appeal would be allowed.

  Case C-239/12P *Abdulrahim v European Council and European Commission* [2013] 3 CMLR 1101, [2013] All ER (D) 01 (Jul) (ECJ: Grand Chamber).

1617   European Union—restrictive measures—overseas territories—Iran

The Iran (Restrictive Measures) (Overseas Territories) (Amendment) Order 2013, SI 2013/786 (in force on 7 May 2013), further amends the 2011 Order, SI 2011/2989, in implementation of Council Decision (CFSP) 2012/810, so as to allow the governor of a specified territory to authorise the sale, supply, transfer or export to Iran of equipment which may be used for internal repression, or to authorise the provision of technical assistance, brokering services, financing or financial assistance in relation to such equipment, where the equipment is intended solely for the protective use in Iran of personnel of the European Union and its member states.

The Iran (Restrictive Measures) (Overseas Territories) (Amendment) (No 2) Order 2013, SI 2013/1444 (in force on 11 July 2013), amends the 2012 Order, SI 2012/1756, so as to give effect to Council Decision (EU) 2012/635, which amends the European Union sanctions regime adopted in response to concerns about Iran's nuclear programme. In particular, the order (1) introduces, in the specified United Kingdom Overseas Territories, new prohibitions on the sale, supply, transfer and export of certain key technology and software, natural gas, graphite and raw or semi-finished materials; (2) prohibits the provision of brokering services, financing, or financial assistance in respect of the goods specified in head (1); (3) imposes restrictions on credit and financial institutions in the United Kingdom Overseas Territories in respect of making transfers to, or receiving transfers from, Iranian credit and financial institutions and bureaux de change; and (4) prohibits the provision of services to Iranian vessels, and the provision of vessels to store or transport oil or petroleum products for Iranian persons or entities.

The Hydrocarbons (Temporary Management Scheme) Regulations 2013, SI 2013/1329 (in force on 30 June 2013), implement Council Regulation (EU) 267/2012 art 43a, which empowers a member state to authorise activities related to the exploration for, or exploitation of, hydrocarbons undertaken pursuant to a licence for such exploration or exploitation issued to a person against whom restrictive measures have been imposed. The 2013 Regulations establish a framework of duties, restrictions, powers and procedures (a 'temporary scheme') in respect of hydrocarbons interests that relate to a licence granted under the Petroleum Act 1998 s 3 or the Petroleum (Production) Act 1934 s 2 where that licence is held by a listed person (a 'restricted licence'). A temporary scheme may be applied to hydrocarbons interests where that is necessary to avoid or remediate environmental damage or to prevent permanent destruction of the value of the restricted licence. Under a temporary scheme, the Secretary of State may, on behalf of a restricted person, carry out various activities in relation to that person's hydrocarbons interests ('temporary management activities') and exercise certain management powers in order to do so. Persons who deal with the Secretary of State in the exercise of the management powers may request a notice from the Secretary of State that their dealing is authorised for the purposes of Regulation 267/2012 art 43a. The Secretary of State may take control of contracts entered into by the listed person which relate to restricted interests or enter into contracts on behalf of the listed person. Transactions of moneys are permitted and the management powers include the power to set up bank accounts ('temporary management accounts') to effect such transactions. Bank accounts may also be set up to hold funds or effect transactions in relation to the decommissioning of restricted interests. The Secretary of State is required to provide a periodic report every six months to the listed person that in summary form includes a description of the temporary management activities undertaken and the balances held in any temporary management accounts or decommissioning accounts. To the extent that the information is held by the Secretary of State, a periodic report must include such information as a listed person may require in order to deal with tax which may arise in respect of the temporary management activities. Provision is also made for a temporary scheme to end.

1618   European Union—restrictive measures—overseas territories—Syria

The Syria (Restrictive Measures) (Overseas Territories) (Amendment) Order 2013, SI 2013/1719 (in force on 7 August 2013), further amends the 2012 Order, SI 2012/1755, in order to give effect to changes to the sanctions measures adopted by the European Union, by (1) widening the power of the governor of a specified territory, with the consent of the

Secretary of State, to license the sale, supply, transfer or export of arms and related items and equipment which might be used for internal repression; and (2) adding new exemptions to the asset freezing provisions.

The Syria (Restrictive Measures) (Overseas Territories) (Amendment) (No 2) Order 2013, SI 2013/2598 (in force on 6 November 2013), further amends the 2012 Order above in implementation of Council Regulation (EU) 697/2013, so as to allow the governor of a specified territory, with the consent of the Secretary of State, to grant a licence authorising specified activities relating to the importation of crude oil and petroleum products from Syria, the financing of certain enterprises and the opening by credit or financial institutions of new bank accounts or new representative offices in Syria.

1619   Foreign Compensation Commission—winding up

The Foreign Compensation Commission (Winding Up) Order 2013, SI 2013/236 (in force on 29 March 2013), winds up the Foreign Compensation Commission established under the Foreign Compensation Act 1950 s 1(1) and makes provision for the transfer of its property, rights and liabilities to the Secretary of State.

1620   Foreign judgments—enforcement

See CONFLICT OF LAWS.

1621   International organisations—International Fund for Agricultural Development— funding

The International Fund for Agricultural Development (Ninth Replenishment) Order 2013, SI 2013/3230 (in force on 19 December 2013), (1) approves the making of a payment on behalf of the government of the United Kingdom to the International Fund for Agricultural Development ('the Fund') of a sum not exceeding £51,132,720, such payment to be made pursuant to arrangements made between the government and the Fund in accordance with Resolution No 166/XXXV on the Ninth Replenishment of the Fund's Resources adopted by the Governing Council on 23 February 2012; and (2) provides for the redemption of non-interest-bearing and non-negotiable notes issued by the Secretary of State pursuant to those arrangements.

1622   Privileges and immunities—diplomatic privilege—immunity from legal proceedings—claims by employees

The first employer was a member of the diplomatic staff of the Saudi Arabian mission in the United Kingdom and the second employer was his wife. The employees were employed by the employers as domestic staff at the official diplomatic residence of the first employer. Both employees claimed that they had been subject to racial discrimination and harassment, had unauthorised deductions made from their wages and had not been provided with a statement of particulars of employment and an itemised pay statement. They also claimed to have been trafficked. The employers sought to claim immunity under the Diplomatic Privileges Act 1964. An employment tribunal found that the employers could not invoke diplomatic immunity and that it could not consider the trafficking allegations as they were too remote for the tribunal to consider. The employers appealed and the employees cross-appealed against the decision in respect of the trafficking allegations. *Held*, the employment of another person by a diplomat to provide personal services to him while engaged in his mission might be regarded as a function of the mission. The employment of a domestic worker who performed no task outside the diplomat's home, had such little connection with the functions of the diplomat's mission that it would fall at the end of the spectrum which was outside the proper scope of 'official functions', and it followed that such act of employing such a person was unlikely to be an act performed in the exercise of those functions as such. A clear distinction might fall between that and the case of someone performing such services, and that of someone such as a personal assistant, whose job in replying to correspondence and managing the diary, travel arrangements and the like of the diplomat would suggest employment towards the opposite end of the spectrum. In the circumstances, applying those principles, if the employment of either employee had began regarded as within the scope of 'commercial activity', that activity would not have been within the scope of the first employer's official functions as a diplomat. Therefore, unless the

1964 Act had to yield the effect of the Human Rights Act 1998, a plea of diplomatic immunity would have to be given effect. The employment tribunal had not given full justice to the purpose of diplomatic immunity. Since there had been no modification of the Vienna Convention applicable to diplomatic immunity as had been the case with state immunity, and since diplomatic immunity was wider reaching than state immunity, there had been no warrant for holding that the restriction of access in the circumstances had been disproportionate. The tribunal had neither sufficiently nor precisely identified the legitimate aim of diplomatic immunity against the achievement of which the interference had to be balanced. It had erred in law in taking the seriousness of the claim into account. Since that had led directly to the conclusion on the claim for immunity, it had been a material error. On the facts, the balance to be struck was that between the legitimate aims of diplomatic immunity as against the interest of employees, in a class of those who did not occupy a strategic role and would not as a matter of course have access to sensitive information, in being able to litigate claimed breaches of their employment rights. The Vienna Convention defined the limited exceptions to the former. The aim was legitimate. The interference with the right otherwise conferred by the European Convention on Human Rights art 6 was in accordance with the 1964 Act. Although the interference with the right was complete, there was a sound basis in principle for that. Therefore, it was not possible to conclude that the plea was a breach of the Convention art 6. With regard to the trafficking allegations, the tribunal had no power and therefore no right to consider them. Accordingly, the appeals would be allowed and the cross-appeal would be dismissed.

Al-Malki v Reyes [2013] IRLR 929 (Employment Appeal Tribunal: Langstaff J presiding).

1623 Privileges and immunities—state immunity—exception—arbitration

See *London Steam Ship Owners Mutual Insurance Association Ltd v Kingdom of Spain*, para 58.

1624 Privileges and immunities—state immunity—immunity from suit—embassy employees—breach of employment law

The State Immunity Act 1978 s 4(1) provides that a state is not immune as respects proceedings relating to a contract of employment between the state and an individual where the contract was made in the United Kingdom or the work is to be wholly or partly performed there. Section 4(1) does not apply if, at the time the proceedings are brought, the individual is a national of the state concerned, or at the time when the contract was made the individual was neither a national of the United Kingdom nor habitually resident there, or the parties to contract have otherwise agreed in writing: s 4(2).

The employees were employed in the United Kingdom at their employers' embassies. In the first case, the employee brought a claim in an employment tribunal for unfair dismissal, non-payment of the national minimum wage, unpaid wages and holiday and for a breach of the Working Time Regulations 1988, SI 1988/1833. It was found that the first employer was immune from suit as the 1978 Act s 16 could not be interpreted to permit a claim. In the second case, the employee brought a claim for unfair dismissal, arrears of pay and holiday pay, race discrimination and harassment, and for a breach of the 1988 Regulations. It was found that the second employer was immune from suit under the 1978 Act ss 4(2) and 16 and that neither provision could be interpreted to permit a claim. The employees appealed. *Held*, in the circumstances, given the factual findings of the tribunals, to render the employees' employment disputes amenable to a decision of the court would not appear to interfere with any public governmental function of those states. The principles on which state immunity was based did not out-balance the importance of access to court for employees with functions such as those of the employees. The converse was so. Therefore, the starting point was that there had been a breach of the European Convention on Human Rights art 6 in so far as the 1978 Act s 16 was applied. Further, the parliamentary intent expressed in the 1978 Act was to confer immunity, and the scheme was to do so generally, subject to specific exceptions. It was framed so as to provide a careful, detailed and clear pattern. A danger of the court altering the width of one exception viewed in isolation was to affect the overall balance struck by the legislature while lacking its panoramic vision across the whole of the landscape. The essential principle and scope of the 1978 Act was that it intended to restrict a right of access to the court in a situation in which that would otherwise be available. Where Parliament had set out a clear list of those in respect of whom a plea of immunity would fail, and those in respect of whom it would succeed, it would cross the critical line between interpretation and legislation to alter the list by removing one category from the 'yes' camp, so as to place it in the 'no' camp. Given that the overall approach was deliberately to limit access to justice in certain cases, there was no proper interpretive scope for allowing the criteria defined. The decision of the judges in respect of the interpretation issue would be upheld. It was established law that, where a fundamental principle of European Union law was concerned, the courts would disapply a provision of domestic law which stood in its way. Therefore, the Employment Appeal Tribunal was bound to find that, so far as the first claim in respect of the 1988 Regulations was concerned, and so far as the second claim for racial discrimination and harassment and breaches of the 1988 Regulations was concerned, the provisions of the 1978 Act ss 4(2) and 16 were to be disapplied. Accordingly, the appeals would be allowed to that extent.

Benkharbouche v Embassy of the Republic of Sudan; Janah v Libya [2013] IRLR 918 (Employment Appeal Tribunal: Langstaff J presiding). *Ghaidan v Godin-Mendoza* [2004] UKHL 30, [2004] 2 AC 557, [2004] 3 All ER 411 (2004 Abr para 1757) applied.

1625   Privileges and immunities—state immunity—immunity from suit—members of
        sovereign's family forming part of household

The third and fifth defendants were members of the family of the king of Saudi Arabia. The third defendant was a senior member of the Saudi royal family and a close confidante of the king. However, the third defendant had his own household and lived separately from the king. The fifth defendant was the third defendant's son. The claimant company brought an unfair prejudice petition under the Companies Act 2006 against the third and fifth defendants in relation to the affairs of the first defendant, an English company. The petition was challenged by the third and fifth defendants. They asserted sovereign immunity on the ground that, within the meaning of the State Immunity Act 1978 s 20(1)(b), they were each members of the family of the king and formed 'part of his household'. The judge found that it would be possible for an adult member of a sovereign's family exercising royal or presidential constitutional and representational functions to be regarded in some circumstances as a member of the sovereign's household, even though he lived apart from the sovereign, but that would be rare and limited to the case of a person broadly exercising the sovereign's functions in a full-time capacity. Therefore, the judge found that, although s 20(1)(b) focused on the sovereign's family, an heir to the throne or a regent undertaking the offices of state on behalf of the sovereign could be regarded as part of the household. However, the judge found that the third and fifth defendants had failed to discharge the burden of proving that they were part of the king's household. The third and fifth defendants appealed. *Held*, there was no interpretational basis for giving the phrase 'members of his family forming part of his household' in s 20(1)(b) a wider meaning in relation to heads of state than in relation to diplomats. The practice of the United Kingdom government in regard to the conferral of diplomatic immunity on family members of an ambassador's household by the Convention on Diplomatic Relations (Vienna, 18 April 1961; TS19 (1965), Cmnd 2565) art 37 was to treat members of the family forming part of the household as including the spouse, civil partner and minor children of the diplomat. Parliament had chosen to define its extension to close members of the head of state's family in the 1978 Act s 20 by precisely the same formula as had been used in the Convention for the same purposes in relation to diplomats. The essence of the mechanism by which the 1978 Act grafted a form of personal immunity on the immunity ratione materiae already conferred on heads of state by the 1978 Act was, precisely and without any specific relevant modification, by reference to diplomatic immunity, and it was clear that Parliament did not think s 20 used the household concept more widely in relation to heads of state than to diplomats. In the circumstances, the third defendant was neither a child of, nor a dependant relative of, the king. On the contrary, he was a substantial businessman in his own right. The fifth defendant was even further outside the household of the king. Accordingly, the appeal would be dismissed.

Apex Global Management Ltd v Fi Call Ltd [2013] EWCA Civ 642, [2013] 4 All ER 216 (Court of Appeal: Maurice Kay V-P, Richards and Briggs LJJ). *R v Bow Street Metropolitan Stipendiary Magistrate, ex p Pinochet Ugarte (No 3)* [2000] 1 AC 147, [1999] 2 All ER 97, HL (1999 Abr para 1730); and *Aziz v Aziz* [2007] EWCA Civ 712, [2008] 2 All ER 501 (2007 Abr para 1596) applied. Decision of Vos J [2013] EWHC 587 (Ch), [2013] All ER (D) 202 (Mar) affirmed.

1626   Restrictive measures—overseas territories—Burma

The Burma (Sanctions) (Overseas Territories) Order 2013, SI 2013/1447 (in force on 11 July 2013), gives effect, in specified overseas territories, to sanctions in respect of Burma applied by the European Union in Council Decision (EU) 2013/184. In particular, the order revokes sanctions in respect of Burma except for the embargoes on the supply of arms and related material and equipment which might be used for internal repression, together with the prohibition on the provision of technical assistance and military assistance related to such goods. SI 2009/3008, SI 2012/2596 are revoked.

1627   Restrictive measures—overseas territories—Guinea

The Guinea (Sanctions) (Overseas Territories) Order 2013, SI 2013/244 (in force on 12 March 2013), gives effect in specified overseas territories to sanctions in respect of the Republic of Guinea adopted by the European Union in Council Decision (CFSP) 2010/638. In particular, the order (1) prohibits the making available of funds and economic resources to persons or entities identified as responsible for violent repression in Guinea on 28 September 2009; (2) freezes funds and economic resources owned or controlled by such persons or entities; (3) prohibits the sale or supply to Guinea, or for use in Guinea, of arms and related material and equipment which might be used for internal repression; (4) prohibits the supply of technical assistance, training, financial and other specified forms of assistance; (5) empowers the governor of any specified overseas territory to grant a licence authorising an activity which would otherwise be prohibited by the order; (6) requires governors to publish and maintain lists of designated persons and restricted goods; and (7) makes provision in relation to penalties and criminal proceedings.

1628   Restrictive measures—overseas territories—Zimbabwe

The Zimbabwe (Sanctions) (Overseas Territories) (Suspension and Amendment) Order 2013, SI 2013/1446 (in force on 11 July 2013), amends the 2012 Order, SI 2012/2753, so as to suspend financial sanctions provisions and make minor corrections.

1629   United Nations—restrictive measures—overseas territories—Libya

The Libya (Restrictive Measures) (Overseas Territories) (Amendment) Order 2013, SI 2013/3160 (in force on 8 January 2014), gives effect, in specified overseas territories, to measures adopted by the United Nations Security Council. Specifically, the order provides that states no longer require the approval of the United Nations Sanctions Committee before selling, supplying or transferring arms or assistance to Libya where such activity is solely for the benefit of the Libyan Government for security or disarmament purposes. In addition, states no longer have to notify the United Nations Sanctions Committee when selling, supplying or transferring to Libya non-lethal military equipment or related technical assistance when it is intended solely for humanitarian or protective use. The order also specifies a new exemption introduced in respect of the frozen accounts of European Union listed persons. These persons can now benefit from, or make, payments in accordance with judicial or administrative decisions or liens where such decisions or liens become enforceable after the persons were listed.

1630   United Nations—sanctions—overseas territories—Liberia—revocation

The United Nations Sanctions (Overseas Territories) (Revocations) Order 2013, SI 2013/237 (in force on 12 March 2013), revokes the Sierra Leone (United Nations Sanctions) (Overseas Territories) Order 2000, SI 2000/1822, the Liberia (United Nations Sanctions) (Overseas Territories) Order 2001, SI 2001/946, the Liberia (United Nations Sanctions) (Overseas Territories) (No 2) Order 2001, SI 2001/1867, and the Liberia (United Nations Sanctions) (Overseas Territories) (Amendment) Order 2003, SI 2003/1876.

1631   United Nations—sanctions—overseas territories—North Korea

The Democratic People's Republic of Korea (Sanctions) (Overseas Territories) (Amendment) Order 2013, SI 2013/1718 (in force on 7 August 2013), amends the 2012 Order, SI 2012/3066, so as to give effect in specified overseas territories to additional sanctions against the Democratic People's Republic of Korea ('North Korea') adopted by the United Nations Security Council in resolution 2094 (2013). The order (1) prohibits banks and financial institutions established in North Korea from opening branches, acquiring a joint venture, establishing correspondent banking relationships, or maintaining correspondent banking relationships in certain circumstances; and (2) introduces restrictions on the sale or purchase of gold, precious metals, diamonds and North Korean bonds, and the movement of North Korean bank notes.

The Democratic People's Republic of Korea (Sanctions) (Overseas Territories) (Amendment) (No 2) Order 2013, SI 2013/2599 (in force on 6 November 2013), further amends 2012 Order above by extending the application of sanctions to persons, entities or bodies specified in Council Regulation (EU) 696/2013 Annex Va.

1632   United Nations—sanctions—overseas territories—Sierra Leone—revocation

See para 1630.

1633   United Nations—sanctions—overseas territories—Somalia

The Somalia (Sanctions) (Overseas Territories) (Amendment) Order 2013, SI 2013/1443 (in force on 11 July 2013), amends the 2012 Order, SI 2012/3065, so as to reflect changes to the arms embargo introduced in United Nations Security Council Resolution 2093 (2013) and the implementation of the changes by the European Union. Specifically, the order alters provision for Governors of Overseas Territories to licence certain activities in line with exemptions under the sanctions regime.

JUDICIAL REVIEW

Halsbury's Laws of England (5th edn) vol 61 (2010) paras 601–800

Articles

For articles relating to this title please refer to the Table of Articles at the beginning of the Abridgment.

1634   Alternative remedy—decision of county court—care proceedings—care order

A local authority obtained an emergency protection order in respect of a child and removed him from the care of the claimant, his mother, placing him with foster carers. A final care order was made and the claimant appealed. The claimant also sought judicial review of the decision, but the application was refused as being without merit. The authority subsequently sought permission to restrict or extinguish contact between the claimant and the child and submitted that no application should be made by the claimant in respect of the child without the court's permission. The claimant did not oppose the applications and an order was made pursuant to the Children Act 1989 s 91(14) requiring the mother to seek the permission of the court before making any further application in connection with the care proceedings. The claimant applied for leave to apply to discharge the care order and for contact with the child, but her application was refused. The claimant sought permission to apply for judicial review of the decision, contending that there had been breaches of her rights, under the European Convention on Human Rights arts 6 and 8, to a fair trial and to respect for her family life. *Held*, with respect to the claim under art 6, there had been no realistic prospect of making a suggestion that there had been an unfair trial. The trial had been fair. A comprehensively unfocused submission had been made in relation to art 8 so that there had been no properly arguable art 8 point in the case whatsoever. It was very sad for the claimant, at a personal level, to have the child taken into care, and for other consequential orders to have been made within the family proceedings. However, it had always be remembered that the paramount concern of the family court was the welfare of the child. There was a more than adequate appellate process open to the claimant to have challenged decisions and orders made by a judge sitting in the county court. The claimant had not availed herself of that process. The route of appeal, provided permission was given, was to the Court of Appeal and not to seek judicial review of the county court decision. It followed that judicial review was not open to the claimant as there was an obvious alternative remedy. In any event, as far as the court could see, there could in fact be no challenge to the decision. There had been no error of law or other irregularity that would have given rise to a realistic prospect of success of any appeal. Accordingly, the application would be refused.

R (on the application of CB) v Sheffield CC [2013] EWHC 2766 (Admin), [2013] All ER (D) 21 (Nov) (Queen's Bench Division: Judge Jeremy Richardson QC).

1635 Alternative remedy—decision of Financial Services Authority—performance of regulated activities

See *R (on the application of Willford) v Financial Services Authority*, para 1250.

1636 Application—parties—interested party—inquest—properly interested person

An inquest was held by the defendant coroner into the death of a man who was suspected of working for the United Kingdom intelligence agencies. The deceased's family, together with various domestic and international authorities, were accorded the status of 'properly interested persons' in the inquest. The claimant Secretary of State requested public interest immunity in respect of a number of documents relating to the case. The defendant allowed the claim in respect of some of the material. The claimant sought judicial review of that part of the defendant's decision rejecting public interest immunity. He contended that there was no rule that the properly interested persons should be interested parties, and therefore entitled to bring judicial review proceedings, as they were not parties to the inquest and would not be directly affected by the judicial review. CPR 54.1(2)(f) defined 'interested party' for the purpose of judicial review claims as any person, other than the claimant and defendant, who was directly affected by the claim. It fell to be determined whether the properly interested persons in the inquest were interested parties capable of participating in the judicial review proceedings. *Held*, to be directly affected by something within the meaning of CPR Pt 54 meant to be affected without the intervention of any intermediate agency. Applying the plain and natural meaning of CPR 54.1(2)(f), the properly interested persons in the present case were interested parties in the judicial review. The quashing of the defendant's decision would mean that they would not receive the material which the defendant had decided had been relevant and necessary for a proper inquest. They could not exercise their rights in relation to it. They could not make submissions regarding it in pre-inquest hearings. They could not examine any witness regarding it. That would be a direct consequence of the claim for judicial review. However, there were cogent reasons why, in the particular circumstances of the case, they should not be added as interested parties. The very unusual circumstances of the case had not required, as a matter of justice, that matters which had been properly dealt with by the defendant by way of the public interest immunity process, because of sensitivities relating to matters of the national interest, should be dealt with differently in the present proceedings. Judgment would be given accordingly.

Secretary of State for Foreign and Commonwealth Affairs v Assistant Deputy Coroner for Inner North London [2013] EWHC 1786 (Admin), [2013] All ER (D) 269 (Jun) (Queen's Bench Division: Goldring and Treacy LJJ and Mitting J).

1637 Legitimate expectation—health services—closure of hospital

See *R (on the application of Enfield LBC) v Barnet Clinical Commissioning Group*, para 1343.

1638 Natural justice—fair hearing—bias—apparent bias—judge's previous association with expert witness—application for recusal

The claimant sought the revocation of a supplementary protection certificate in the name of the defendant on the ground that the patent on which the certification was based was invalid due to obviousness. An order was made giving directions for the trial of the claim, including that the trial should be listed on an expedited basis before the judge. During the course of a hearing of a number of applications made by the parties, an exchange took place between the claimant and the judge during which the judge stated that one of the expert witness's was known to him and had been one of his supervisors at university. The defendant requested that the judge recuse himself from hearing the claim on the basis that his past connection with the expert gave rise to a real possibility of apparent bias, as the fair-minded and informed observer would conclude that there was a real possibility of the judge being subconsciously biased in his assessment of the expert's evidence by reason of his past association with him. That request was opposed by the claimant both on the merits and on the ground of waiver. *Held*, the overall context of the present case was that of a claim for patent revocation, which was a specialist area involving the application of a sophisticated body of law to highly technical facts. The observer would appreciate that, because it was a specialist field, it was one in which many of the participators were known to each other. The judge was well acquainted with most of the barristers, and many of the solicitors, who conducted litigation in the Patents Court. It was also not uncommon for experts to act in more than one case. Moreover, the observer would appreciate that all experts were obliged to assist the court by providing objective, unbiased opinions on matters within their expertise, that the expert's primary role would be to educate the court and what would matter would not be his opinion, but the objective reasons he gave for his opinions, and that the expert was an eminent scientist and an experienced expert witness. It followed from those considerations that there was unlikely to be any issue as to the expert's credibility. The fair-minded and informed observer would note that a little over 30 years had passed since the judge's association with the expert, and would appreciate that, as a supervisor supervising a student, the expert had some measure of authority over the judge, but that, as a judge assessing a witness, the judge would have a considerable measure of authority over the expert. Taking all those factors into account, the fair-minded and informed observer would not conclude that there was a real possibility of the judge being subconsciously biased in his assessment of the expert's evidence by reason of his past association with him. Moreover, the defendant had been aware of the fact that the trial had been listed before the judge, of the judge's connection with the expert and the real possibility, but not the certainty, that the expert would be called as a witness by the claimant. The defendant did not notify the claimant, or the court, that it would have an apprehension of apparent bias in that event. Nevertheless, the defendant could not be said to have waived its right to object at that stage since it had not been certain that the expert would be called. However, it was clear that, after the date that the claimant's intentions to call the expert had been confirmed, the defendant's actions were voluntary and it had all the information it needed. Although the court had sympathy with the proposition that the defendant could and should have raised its objection at an earlier date than it had, in the end the court was not persuaded that the defendant's actions had been sufficiently unequivocal as to amount to a waiver. Accordingly, the application would be dismissed.

Resolution Chemicals Ltd v H Lundbeck A/S [2013] EWHC 3160 (Pat), [2013] All ER (D) 287 (Oct) (Chancery Division: Arnold J). *Porter v Magill; Weeks v Magill* [2001] UKHL 67, [2002] 2 AC 357, [2002] 1 All ER 465 (2001 Abr para 2107); *Helow v Secretary of State for the Home Department* [2008] UKHL 62, [2009] 2 All ER 1031 (2008 Abr para 141); and *JSC BTA Bank v Ablyazov* [2012] EWCA Civ 1551, [2013] 1 WLR 1845, [2012] All ER (D) 327 (Nov) (2012 Abr para 1633) applied.

1639　Natural justice—fair hearing—bias—wasted costs order—application for recusal

The appellant was a firm of solicitors which formerly represented the claimants in an action. The respondents were the defendants in that action. The claimants' proceedings had begun in Ethiopia where they had held an investment in an undertaking. They claimed that they had been deprived of that investment by a false case which the respondents had raised against them. Judgment was given against the claimants and appeals left the judgments almost unchanged. Subsequently, the claimants acquired new evidence and brought a claim for compensation in the English courts. The respondents sought to stay the case on the basis that there was an insufficient link with England and Wales to found jurisdiction. The only question in issue was whether the claimants would obtain a fair trial in Ethiopia. The claimants' Ethiopian law expert gave evidence during the case. The expert reports did not comply with CPR 35. The judge held that (1) the expert's duties and his potential exposure if his evidence was given recklessly or negligently had not been explained to him by the appellant; (2) it was plain that he had not understood the consequences that might flow personally to him; and (3) the fault lay entirely with the appellant. The defendants applied for a wasted costs order against the appellant on the grounds that it ought to have withdrawn from the case in light of the defects in the Ethiopian law evidence. The appellant applied to the judge for an order that he recuse himself from hearing that application. The judge refused to recuse himself. The judge gave judgment on the application to make a stage 1 wasted costs order, finding that the appellant ought not to have associated itself with the litigation. The judge then went on to give directions for the stage 2 hearing. The appellant appealed against the judge's refusal to recuse himself, and his stage 1 wasted costs order. *Held*, (1) judicial recusal occurred when a judge decided that it was not appropriate for him to hear a case listed to be heard by him. A judge might recuse himself when a party applied to him to do so. A judge had to step down in circumstances where there appeared to be bias. If a fair-minded and informed observer, having considered the facts, would conclude that there had been a real possibility that the judge had been biased, the judge had to recuse himself. In almost every case, the judge who heard the substantive application would be the right judge to deal with consequential issues as to costs, even if he made findings adverse to a party in the course of reaching his conclusion. However, there could always be exceptions. The present case was an exceptional case and there had been apparent bias stemming from the facts of the case which meant that the judge ought to have recused himself from hearing the wasted costs application. That conclusion was reached principally for the following reasons: (a) the judge's criticism had not been necessary to enable him to evaluate the expert's evidence; (b) the judge's failure to leave the door open for the possibility of some explanation when he had not heard evidence from the appellant gave rise to an impression of bias; and (c) there was no doubt that the criticisms had been of high gravity for a solicitor, which made them extreme. (2) It was established law that a court might make a wasted costs order against a party's legal representative for payment of costs incurred by the applicant as a result of the improper, unreasonable or negligent act or omission of the representative. At stage 1 of such an application, the applicant for the order had to show cause that there was a strong case for the respondent legal representative to answer. At stage 2, the court would decide whether the grounds were made out and whether it was just to make the order sought. In the present case, the test that a stage 1 order ought to have been made had not been met. It was apparent that any decision as to whether the requirements for a stage 1 order were met had to be made on the totality of the material. The appellant admitted breaches of CPR 35. The appellant did not invite the judge to disregard the passages in the expert's reports that had gone beyond his proper role as an expert witness. There had been no misdirection by the judge. On causation, it had to be a question of fact capable of being proved whether the claimants would have continued without professional representation. They would have been pursuing complex claims in a jurisdiction with which they had not been familiar. On that basis, the court could infer that it was inevitable if a sufficient case was shown that some costs must have been incurred, even if not the totality of the costs of the action which the defendants claimed. The appellant had sought a direction from the court that no further application ought to be made because no order could be made. That test had not been met. Whether such an application ought to be made was a matter for the respondents and not the court. The recusal appeal would be allowed with the consequence that the stage 1 wasted costs order would be set aside. However, the application on the stage 1 wasted costs appeal that no further stage 1 wasted costs application should be made, would be dismissed. Judgment would be given accordingly.

Mengiste v Endowment Fund for the Rehabilitation of Tigray; Rylatt Chubb v Endowment Fund for the Rehabilitation of Tigray [2013] EWCA Civ 1003, [2013] 5 Costs LR 841, [2013] All ER (D) 116 (Aug) (Court of Appeal: Arden, Patten and McFarlane LJJ). *Porter v Magill, Weeks v Magill* [2001] All ER (D) 181 (Dec) applied.

1640 Natural justice—fair hearing—right to be heard—absence of lay member

The claimant, who was a chartered accountant and member of the defendant, a professional body, was faced with disciplinary proceedings alleging that he had committed an act or default likely to bring discredit to the defendant or the profession. A six-day hearing took place before a disciplinary tribunal consisting of two professional members and a lay member. On the fourth day of the hearing, when the claimant was giving his oral evidence, the lay member of the panel stated that he could sit no longer than 5 pm on that day. The parties were asked whether they agreed to the lay member leaving while the hearing continued, and the lay member reading the transcript of the claimant's oral evidence given after he had left, and returning to the proceedings when the tribunal sat again. The parties agreed to that course. The lay member was present for the final day of the hearing and the tribunal ultimately gave a decision adverse to the claimant. The claimant challenged the tribunal's decision on the ground that the procedure which it had adopted, by allowing the lay member to be absent during the hearing and return to be involved with the final decision, amounted to a breach of the rules of natural justice, and that the breach was not waived. The judge decided that there had been a breach of the rules of natural justice, but that breach had been waived by the claimant's agreement, which was voluntary, informed and unequivocal, to the procedure. The claimant appealed. *Held,* a breach of the rules of natural justice of the kind that was said to have occurred was at most an irregularity that could be waived. Indeed, if there had been an agreement to the procedure adopted, there was no breach at all of the relevant rule of natural justice. Once one looked at the circumstances, it was odd to say that the tribunal had acted in breach of the rules of natural justice when all the parties had agreed to the course that was to be taken. Waiver was more naturally used in respect of something that was definitely a breach when it occurred but was later agreed not to matter, and the question of whether there was no breach of the rules of natural justice by virtue of the parties' agreement or that there was a breach of the rules of natural justice but that it had been waived was a mere matter of words. However, both the question of whether there was an agreement which meant that there was no breach of the rules of natural justice, and the question of whether, granted there was a breach of the rules of natural justice that breach had been waived, had to be answered in the affirmative. The judge had been wrong to find that there had been a breach of natural justice and that breach had been waived. Rather, there was no beach of the rules of natural justice in the circumstances. Accordingly, the appeal would be dismissed.

R (on the application of Hill) v Institute of Chartered Accountants in England and Wales [2013] EWCA Civ 555, [2014] 1 WLR 86, [2013] All ER (D) 279 (May) (Court of Appeal: Longmore, Beatson and Underhill LJJ). *Ahsan v Carter* [2005] EWCA Civ 990, [2005] ICR 1817, [2005] All ER (D) 419 (Jul) (2005 Abr para 1388) applied.

1641   Procedural fairness—consultation—high-speed rail link

See *HS2 Action Alliance Ltd v Secretary of State for Transport,* para 2121.

1642   Procedural fairness—consultation—litigation funding—reform—Secretary of State engaging in discussions with only one interested group

The payment and receipt of referral fees in personal injury cases was banned by virtue of the Legal Aid, Sentencing and Punishment of Offenders Act 2012 ss 56–60 as part of the government's reform of 'no win no fee' conditional fee agreements. One of the effects of the provisions was to reduce the fixed costs for small value personal injuries claims. The reforms had been made clear in advance to relevant groups and there had been some discussions concerning the amount of the reduction to fixed costs. The Prime Minister met with representatives from the insurance industry, following which communications were sent between the government and the insurance industry. Subsequently, the provisions and effects of the 2012 Act were made public. The applicant sought judicial review of the Secretary of State's decision to implement the reforms. It claimed that the Secretary of State had, by engaging in meetings and communications with members of the insurance industry, undertaken a process of consultation, and that that consultation exercise had been flawed by the non-inclusion of other relevant stakeholders. *Held,* on a proper analysis of the events, including the relevant meetings and communications, it had been clear that the process adopted had not been one of consultation. The discussions carried out had been no more than negotiating what the reduction in fixed costs would be. The government had already made its decision that there would be a ban on referral fees and there had been no doubt about its position in that regard. However, it could not be inferred that a consultation exercise had been carried out merely from the fact that the government had had discussions with an interested party. In the absence of a consultation exercise, the government had been entitled talk to an interested party without entering discussions simultaneously with other stakeholders. Accordingly, the application would be dismissed.

R (on the application of Association of Personal Injury Lawyers) v Secretary of State for Justice [2013] EWHC 1358 (Admin), [2013] All ER (D) 11 (Mar) (Queen's Bench Division: Elias LJ and Cranston J).

1643   Procedural fairness—consultation—reinterment of remains of monarch

The first defendant Secretary of State granted the second defendant, a university, a licence for the removal of human remains from a particular site. Two human skeletons were excavated from the site, one of which was identified as being that of a British monarch who lived during the fifteenth century. The second defendant then made plans for the reinterment of the remains in a different location. The claimant company, which was a campaigning organisation representing a group of collateral descendants of the monarch in question, sought permission to bring judicial review proceedings challenging (1) the decision of the first defendant to grant the licence without consulting, or requiring the second defendant to consult, as to how or where the remains should be appropriately reinterred in the event that they were found; (2) the first defendant's decision not to revisit the grant of the licence once it became clear that the second defendant would not carry out an appropriate consultation; and (3) the second defendant's decision to begin to make arrangements for the reinterment of the remains. The defendant resisted the application, asserting that (a) the claimant had been guilty of unreasonable delay in bringing the claim; (b) the claimant lacked standing to bring the claim; and (c) the claim was not arguable on its merits. *Held*, there had been good reasons for an immediate challenge not being brought to the first defendant's decision to grant the licence. It had been clear that there could be no guarantee that the remains had been those of the monarch until DNA results had been obtained. Once the identification had been made, those seeking to challenge the decisions had taken steps to garner support, obtain legal advice and organise their challenge. In all the circumstances, those supporting the claimant had acted with reasonable promptness and could not reasonably be criticised for lodging the challenge just within the three-month deadline. The claimant also had sufficient interest and standing to bring the present proceedings, both on conventional principles and in the unusual circumstances of the case, which involved the discovery of the proven remains of a former monarch. Further, the merits of the claimant's challenge were clearly arguable, in particular, the propositions that (i) there had been a legitimate expectation that the first defendant would, prior to granting a licence, consult widely on how and where the remains should be appropriately reinterred; (ii) the category of appropriate consultees was potentially very wide; (iii) the first defendant's duty to consult had been non-delegable and, in any event, it could not properly be delegated to a party or licensee who had not been independent or had had a personal interest in the outcome, such as the second defendant; (iv) the first defendant had failed to carry out any, or any proper, consultation regarding the reinterment of the remains prior to issuing the licence; (v) the first defendant had failed thereafter to revisit his decision to grant the licence; and (vi) the second defendant, as a responsible public body, should not have begun making arrangements for the reinterment of the remains prior to an appropriate consultation being carried out. Accordingly, the application would be allowed.

   R (on the application of the Plantagenet Alliance Ltd) v Secretary of State for Justice [2013] All ER (D) 143 (Aug) (Queen's Bench Division: Haddon-Cave J).

1644   Proceedings—fees

See para 601.

1645   Refusal to initiate prosecution—review—realistic prospect of conviction

See *R (on the application of F) v DPP*, para 662.

JURIES

Halsbury's Laws of England (5th edn) vol 61 (2010) paras 801–900

Articles

For articles relating to this title please refer to the Table of Articles at the beginning of the Abridgment.

1646   Defamation Act 2013

See para 840.

1647   Juror—bias—complaint by some jurors against other jurors—effect on integrity of trial

The defendants were part of an extended family which originated from the Irish travelling community. They were accused of offences which included conspiracy to hold a person in servitude, assault occasioning actual bodily harm, holding a person in servitude and requiring forced labour. During the course of the trial, the judge received a note from a member of the jury which stated that 'throughout the trial and especially since we were given a room, it has become quite obvious that certain jurors, not all, are quite anti-traveller/prejudiced'. The judge did not discharge the jury but gave the relevant directions. The defendants were convicted. On their appeals against conviction, *held*, the receipt of any communication by a juror or jurors complaining of possible irregularities by or among the other jurors demanded rapid and close attention. It behoved the judge to decide whether the integrity of the trial process had been irretrievably damaged or whether the trial could continue notwithstanding the complaints. Depending on the individual facts, it might be appropriate for the judge to discharge the jury as a whole, or one or more individual members of it, or to continue with the trial, with any necessary direction or warning sufficient to deal with the specific problem. A member of a jury finding himself in a minority might not bring a trial to a halt by writing a measured letter to a judge complaining of irregularities by the other members of the jury. In the circumstances, the judge had not been bound to discharge the jury because of the letter, however troublesome its contents, signed by one juror. Equally, it would have been inappropriate for him to try and conduct an investigation into what had been happening in the jury room. The judge had handled the problem presented to him impeccably, and his assessment of the integrity of the jury had been amply justified. In the context of alleged jury bias, there was no reason to doubt the safety of the guilty verdicts returned by the jury. Accordingly, the appeals would be dismissed.

R v C [2013] EWCA Crim 368, [2013] Crim LR 854, [2013] All ER (D) 55 (Apr) (Court of Appeal: Lord Judge CJ, Simon and Irwin JJ).

1648   Juror—contempt of court—intention to interfere with administration of justice— juror posting message and conducting research on internet

See *A-G v Davey; A-G v Beard*, para 524.

1649   Juror—unconscious bias—discharge of jury

The defendant grew up in Iran and was educated in the United Kingdom. He returned to Iran to help his father who founded an Iranian company. The defendant returned to the United Kingdom and became involved with an English company of which he became the managing director. The English company began as a procurement handling company for the Iranian company supplying electrical switchgear for use in industry. The defendant, through the English company, was charged with attempting to export restricted goods, namely electrical switchgear, contrary to the Customs and Excise Management Act 1979 s 68(2). On the second day of the defendant's trial, the judge was passed a note from one of the jurors. The note stated that the juror was afraid that his professional endeavours might have an effect on his view of the case. The juror's role meant that he was confronted with the supervision of similar export transactions to the one covered in the case. There had been several details that would have entailed automatic rejection of the transaction on compliance grounds at the juror's place of work. The juror had found it difficult to forget about specific details of the case that, at least in his professional environment, were definite warnings. The judge was asked to consider whether the concerns raised by the juror were of no effect to the fairness of the process for the defendant. Counsel for the defence submitted that there was a strong indication of bias, a danger of some contamination with other jurors having already occurred, and that situation could not be cured by a robust direction to the jury. It was submitted that the whole jury had to be discharged. The judge found that the fact the juror had brought the information to the court's attention in the most careful and fair-minded way dispelled any possibility that he was biased and the case had to be tried on the evidence given in the courtroom and not on any other evidence. He ordered the case to carry on. The defendant was convicted of being knowingly concerned in an attempt to export prohibited or restricted goods contrary to s 68(2). The defendant appealed against conviction. *Held*, although the juror had not been biased against the defendant, that did not resolve the question of whether a fair minded and informed observer would have concluded that there had been a real possibility of unconscious bias. The judge's direction that the case had to be tried on the evidence given in the courtroom and not on other evidence had been correct but it was insufficient in the context of a full understanding of the contents of the note and the underlying possible risk of unconscious bias inherent within it. The juror's special knowledge and experience was directly related to the issue which had arisen for decision in the trial. In the juror's professional knowledge and experience, his unconscious prejudice had been that there were definite warnings and there would have been automatic rejection of the transaction such that the defendant's actions would have been prohibited. That issue had not been addressed in either the decision to permit the juror to remain on the jury or in the direction to the whole jury once a decision had been taken to permit the juror to remain on the jury. Therefore, due to the real possibility of unconscious jury bias a fair trial had not been possible and the safety of the conviction could not be sustained. Accordingly, the appeal would be allowed and the conviction quashed.

R v Pouladian-Kari [2013] EWCA Crim 158, [2013] Crim LR 510, [2013] All ER (D) 314 (Feb) (Court of Appeal: Lord Judge CJ, Wyn Williams and Globe JJ).

1650   Trial—jury—irregularities—juror acquainted with defendant—safety of conviction
See *R v Taylor*, para 679.

1651   Trial—jury—irregularities—juror contacting defendant—safety of conviction
See *R v Lewis*, para 680.

1652   Trial—jury—irregularities—protocol—Crown Court
The President of the Queen's Bench Division has issued a *Protocol (jury irregularities in the Crown Court)* [2013] 1 Cr App Rep 286, on 19 November 2012.

1. A jury irregularity is anything that may prevent a juror, or the whole jury, from remaining faithful to their oath or affirmation as jurors to 'faithfully try the defendant and give a true verdict according to the evidence'. Anything that compromises the jury's independence, or introduces into the jury's deliberations material or considerations extraneous to the evidence in the case, may impact on the jurors' ability to remain faithful to their oath or affirmation.

During the course of the trial
2. Any irregularity relating to the jury should be drawn to the attention of the trial judge in the absence of the jury as soon as it is known.

3. Irregularities take many forms: some may clearly appear to be contempt by a juror, for example, searching for material about the defendant on the internet; others may appear to be an attempt to intimidate or suborn a juror; on other occasions, for example, where there has been contact between a juror and a defendant, it may not be clear whether it may be a contempt or an attempt at intimidation. The judge may also be made aware of friction between individual jurors.

4. Difficult situations do arise and, although the trial process must not be delayed unduly, the trial judge may wish to consult with the Registrar of Criminal Appeals. Contact details for the Registrar and the Criminal Appeal Office are given at the end.

5. When an irregularity is drawn to the attention of the trial judge, the judge should consider whether the juror(s) concerned should be isolated from the rest of the jury if that has not already been done by the usher. If it appears that a juror has improperly obtained information, consideration should be given as to the risk that the information has already been shared with other members of the jury or that the information could be shared if the jury remain together.

6. The judge should consult with the advocates and invite submissions. This should be in open court in the presence of the defendant(s) unless there is good reason not to do so.

7. The trial judge should try to establish the basic facts of what has occurred. This may involve questioning individually the juror(s) involved. Unless there is good reason, again this should be in open court in the presence of the defendant(s). However, if there is suspicion about the defendant's conduct in the irregularity then the hearing should take place with all parties represented, but in the defendant's absence. The hearing should be held in court sitting in chambers, not in the judge's room. If there is any suspicion of tampering, the defendant ought to be taken into custody, if not already.

8. The judge's inquiries should be directed towards ascertaining whether the juror(s) can remain faithful to their oath or affirmation; the trial judge should not inquire into the

deliberations of the jury. The inquiry should only be to ascertain what has occurred and what steps should be taken next. It may be appropriate for the judge to ask the juror(s) whether they feel able to continue and remain faithful to their oath or affirmation.

9. In the light of the basic facts as they appear to be, the trial judge may invite further submissions from the advocates, including on what should be said to the jurors, and take time to reflect on the appropriate course of action. The judge may consider the stage the trial has reached and in cases of potential bias whether a fair minded and informed observer would conclude that there was a real possibility that the juror or jury would be biased. Judges should be alert to attempts by defendants or others to obstruct or thwart the trial process.

10. In relation to the conduct of the trial, the trial judge may:

(a) Take no action and continue the trial. If so, the judge should consider giving some explanation to the jurors to reassure them that nothing untoward has happened that need concern them.

(b) Continue the trial but, if appropriate, give a reminder to the jury, tailored to the requirements of the case, that their verdict is a decision of the whole jury as a body and that they should give and take and try to work together. It is, in every case, essential that no undue pressure is exerted on the jury.

(c) Discharge the juror(s) concerned and continue the trial if sufficient jurors remain. The minimum number required to continue is nine: Juries Act 1974 s 16(1). Consideration must be given as to what to say to the remaining jury members when one or more have been discharged and to the juror(s) on discharge. The juror(s) must be warned not to discuss the circumstances with anyone and it may be necessary to discharge the juror(s) from current jury service.

(d) Discharge the whole jury and re-list the trial. Again the jury should be warned not to discuss the circumstances with anyone. Consideration should be given to discharging them from current jury service. If the jury has been discharged and there is a danger of jury tampering in the new trial, the Crown may make an application under the Criminal Justice Act 2003 s 44 at a preliminary hearing for a trial without a jury if jury protection measures would be insufficient.

(e) If the judge is satisfied that jury tampering has taken place, discharge the jury and continue the trial without a jury (s 46(3)), or discharge the jury and order that a new trial take place without a jury (s 46(5)).

11. Contempt by jurors should generally be dealt with by the Attorney General; however it may be appropriate for the trial judge to deal with a very minor and clear contempt in the face of the court admitted by the juror. The procedure in such a case is provided for in CrimPR Pt 62. If, after the preliminary inquiry, it appears to the trial judge that someone may be in contempt and it is not appropriate for the trial judge to deal with it, or that a criminal offence may have been committed, an investigation by the police may be appropriate to clarify the factual position or to gather evidence.

12. Before the name(s) and address(es) of any juror(s) are provided to the police or the police are requested to take any action, the approval of the Court of Appeal (Criminal Division) (the 'CA(CD)') to the release of information must be obtained. The court manager, on behalf of the trial judge, should contact the Registrar of Criminal Appeals setting out the position neutrally and seeking the approval of the CA(CD) to release the names and addresses of the juror(s) to the police. The initial approach may be by telephone, but the information must be provided in writing; e-mail is acceptable.

13. The Registrar will put the application before the Vice-President of the CA(CD) or a judge of the CA(CD) nominated by the Vice-President to consider approval. The Court of Appeal judge will consider the application and, if approval is granted, may also give directions as to the scope of the investigation. It may be that any investigation is made in stages. The Registrar will also inform the Attorney General's Office, who may allocate a lawyer and assist the police in the direction of the investigation.

14. Where there is to be an investigation by the police, it will be necessary to act expeditiously to obtain witness statements whilst memories are still fresh. Such statements may be required for criminal or contempt proceedings. Police investigating the matter must pay scrupulous regard to the Contempt of Court Act 1981 s 8.

15. When the investigation is complete, the police should report to the Attorney General through the allocated AGO lawyer. If it appears that a criminal offence may have been committed, the Attorney General will hand the file to the Crown Prosecution Service; if a contempt may have taken place, the Attorney General will decide whether or not to instigate proceedings in the Divisional Court.

After verdicts have been returned

16. A trial judge has no jurisdiction in relation to inquiries about jury irregularities that come to light after the end of the trial. A trial will be considered to have concluded for these purposes when a jury has delivered all verdicts or has been discharged from giving all verdicts on all defendants in the trial. In *R v Thompson* [2010] EWCA Crim 1623, [2011] 2 All ER 83, (2010) 2 Cr App Rep 27 (2010 Abr para 1843) the Lord Chief Justice, Lord Judge said:

'Much more difficult problems arise when after the verdict has been returned, attention is drawn to alleged irregularities. This may take the form of a complaint from a defendant, or his solicitors, or in a very few cases it may emerge from one or more jurors, or indeed from information revealed by the jury bailiff. It is then beyond the jurisdiction of the trial judge to intervene. Responsibility for investigating any irregularity must be assumed by this court. In performing its responsibilities, it is bound to apply the principle that the deliberations of the jury are confidential. Except with the authority of the trial judge during the trial, or this court after the verdict, inquiries into jury deliberations are 'forbidden territory' (per Gage LJ in *R v Adams* [2007] EWCA Crim 1, [2007] 1 Cr App Rep 34, [2007] All ER (D) 25 (Jan) (2007 Abr para 1916).'

17. If information about a jury irregularity comes to light during an adjournment after verdict but before sentence, then the trial judge should be considered functus officio in relation to the jury matter, not least because the jury will have been discharged. The trial judge should inform the Registrar of Criminal Appeals about the information. Unless there is a good reason not to do so, the trial judge should proceed to sentence.

18. If at any stage after trial, a juror contacts the trial judge about the trial, that communication should be referred to the Registrar of Criminal Appeals to consider what steps may be appropriate. The Registrar may seek the direction of the Vice-President of the CA(CD) or a judge of the CA(CD) nominated by the Vice-President.

19. If the communication suggests any issue of contempt or criminal offence, the Registrar will inform the Attorney General. If it appears to suggest a possible ground of appeal, the defendant's legal representatives will be informed. Where it raises no issues of legal significance (for example, a general complaint about the verdict from a dissenting juror or expressions of doubt or second thoughts,) the Registrar will respond to the communication explaining that no action is required.

20. If the prosecution become aware of an irregularity which might form a basis for an appeal then they should notify the defence in accordance with their duties to act fairly and assist in the administration of justice: *R v Makin* [2004] EWCA Crim 1607, [2004] All ER (D) 259 (Jun).

21. If the defence become aware of an irregularity which would found an arguable ground of appeal, whether they are informed directly or via the prosecution or the Registrar of Criminal Appeals, they may wish to lodge a notice and grounds of appeal. The defence should be mindful of the provisions of the Contempt of Court Act 1981 s 8.

22. If an application for leave to appeal is received with grounds relating to a jury irregularity then the Registrar may refer the case to the full court to consider whether the court would wish to direct the Criminal Cases Review Commission to conduct an investigation in to the irregularity under the Criminal Appeal Act 1968 s 23A and the Criminal Appeal Act 1995 s 5(1).

23. An investigation may be directed before or after leave is granted: Criminal Appeal Act 1968 ss 23A, 23A(1)(aa).

24. If the Court directs that an investigation should take place, directions will be given as to the scope of the investigation. The Criminal Cases Review Commission will report back to the court. Copies of the report or other appropriate information are provided to the parties and the court either refuses leave or grants leave and subsequently hears the appeal.

Contact details

Master Egan QC

The Registrar of Criminal Appeals Royal Courts of Justice Strand London WC2A 2LL

Secretary to the Registrar:

Penny Donnelly Tel: 0207 947 6103 E-mail: penny.donnelly@hmcts.x.gsi.gov.uk

Criminal Appeal Office, General Office

Tel: 0207 947 6011 E-mail: criminalappealoffice.generaloffice@hmcts.x.gsi.gov.uk

1653   Trial—jury—selection—discharge after juror found to be incompetent—random selection of new juror

The Juries Act 1974 s 11(1) provides that the jury to try an issue before a court must be selected by ballot in open court from the panel, or part of the panel, of jurors summoned to attend at the time and place in question. No judgment after verdict is to be stayed or reversed by reason that the provisions of the 1974 Act about the summoning or impanelling of jurors, or the selection of jurors by ballot, have not been complied with if objection is not taken at, or as soon as practicable after, the time it occurs: s 18(1)(a), (2).

The jury in the defendant's trial was discharged after it became clear that one of the 12 jurors lacked sufficient proficiency in English to ensure that justice would be achieved in the case. The 12 jurors had been randomly selected from a panel of 15 jurors in waiting. The judge decided that the 11 remaining jurors should be re-sworn and a twelfth juror randomly selected from the remaining three jurors in waiting. Counsel for the prosecution queried whether the entire jury should be reselected from the 14 remaining jurors, but the judge concluded that the course he proposed was technically correct since all of the persons forming the jury had been selected at random. On his appeal against conviction, the defendant submitted that the manner in which the jury had been empanelled contravened the 1974 Act s 11(1). A further issue arose as to whether the defendant's appeal was defeated by s 18. *Held*, since the original jury had been discharged, the fact that it had been selected by ballot was irrelevant to the question of whether the jury which tried the defendant had been selected by ballot for the purposes of s 11(1). It followed that 11 of the jurors who tried the defendant had been pre-selected so that the jury which tried the defendant had not been selected by ballot, in contravention of s 11(1). However, as the defence had not raised any objection at the time to the course adopted by the judge, s 18 precluded him from relying on appeal on a breach of s 11. Accordingly, the appeal would be dismissed.

R v M [2012] EWCA Crim 2056, [2013] 1 WLR 958 (Court of Appeal: Lord Judge CJ, Mackay and Sweeney JJ).

LANDFILL TAX

Halsbury's Laws of England (5th edn) vol 61 (2010) paras 901–1010

1654   Annual landfill tax liability—maximum credit

The Landfill Tax (Amendment) Regulations 2013, SI 2013/658 (in force on 1 April 2013), further amend the 1996 Regulations, SI 1996/1527, so as to (1) provide that the maximum credit a landfill site operator can claim against annual landfill tax liability, in respect of qualifying contributions made, is changed from 5·6 per cent to 6·8 per cent for contribution years beginning on or after 1 April 2013; and (2) update references to the Charities Act 1993 s 72 with references to the Charities Act 2011 s 178.

1655   Finance Act 2013

See para 2149.

LANDLORD AND TENANT

Halsbury's Laws of England (5th edn) vol 62 (2012) paras 1–694, vol 63 (2012) paras 695–1296, vol 64 (2012) paras 1297–2024

Articles

For articles relating to this title please refer to the Table of Articles at the beginning of the Abridgment.

1656   Assured and protected tenancies—student lettings—England

The Assured and Protected Tenancies (Lettings to Students) (Amendment) (England) Regulations 2013, SI 2013/38 (in force on 11 February 2013), further amend the 1998 Regulations, SI 1998/1967, so that Student Union Lettings Ltd is specified for the purpose of the Housing Act 1988 Sch 1 para 8 instead of University of Leicester Students' Union; the amendment is to reflect the fact that letting services previously provided by University of Leicester Students' Union are now being undertaken by Student Union Lettings Ltd, a joint venture between University of Leicester Students' Union and University of De Montfort Students' Union.

The Assured and Protected Tenancies (Lettings to Students) (Amendment) (England) (No 2) Regulations 2013, SI 2013/1461 (in force on 8 July 2013), further amend the 1998 Regulations above to provide that UPP (Broadgate Park) Limited, UPP (Clifton) Ltd and UPP (Nottingham) Ltd are specified for the purpose of the Housing Act 1988 Sch 1 para 8.

1657   Covenant—covenant to repair—breach—damages—value of reversion

After a lease ended, the landlord discovered that the tenant had left the property in a very poor condition despite the lease having contained comprehensive repair obligations. After repairs were completed, the landlord issued proceedings against the tenant seeking to recover the cost of the work. The conventional way of calculating the diminution in value of a landlord's reversion caused by a tenant's breaches of his repair obligations was by valuing the reversion in the state in which it actually was at the end of the lease and comparing that value with the value of the reversion in the state in which it should have been at the end of the lease. The tenant challenged some aspects of alleged liability and some of the landlord's calculations of loss. At trial, the judge found that, if the tenant had left the property in the state in which it ought to have been left, the landlord would not have carried out the works that it had. He directed himself to answer questions as to (1) the scope of the tenant's obligations under the covenants; (2) the reasonable cost of putting the building back into the condition in which it should have been if there had been sufficient performance by the tenant of those obligations; and (3) the tenant having failed to make sufficient performance of its obligations, the difference between the value of the building in its actual condition at the expiry of the leases and the condition that it should have been in if there had been sufficient performance by the tenant of its obligations. According to the judge's calculations, the diminution in value exceeded the cost of the necessary work, with the result that the Landlord and Tenant Act 1927 s 18, which limited damages to the diminution in value of the landlord's reversion, did not apply. The judge concluded that the amount of the diminution in value was to be inferred from the costs of the repairs reasonably necessary to make good the loss caused by breaches of covenant, there being no satisfactory evidence that it was any lower amount. The judge therefore awarded the landlord the cost of the necessary works, plus various incidental items. The tenant appealed against the assessment of the value of the reversion. *Held*, there had been no error in the judge's reasoning or in his conclusion. On the judge's findings, if the tenant had left the building in the state in which it ought to have been left, the landlord would not have carried out the works that it had. Further, the judge's finding had been that the work that the landlord had in fact carried out had been, with some exceptions, the work that the tenant ought to have carried out in order to put the building into the condition in which it ought to have been handed back. Accordingly, the appeal would be dismissed.

Sunlife Europe Properties Ltd v Tiger Aspect Holdings Ltd [2013] EWCA Civ 1656, [2013] All ER (D) 163 (Dec) (Court of Appeal: Longmore, Lewison and Floyd LJJ).

1658   Lease—forfeiture—notice—breach of covenant—identification of breach in notice

The respondents owned the freehold of premises and the appellant owned the leasehold. The lease contained covenants, including the first covenant not to use the premises or permit the premises to be used for any purpose whatsoever other than as a self-contained private dwelling for residential purposes only, and the second covenant not to assign, underlet or part with or share possession of occupation of part only of the premises. The respondents brought proceedings under the Commonhold and Leasehold Reform Act 2002 s 168, relying on multiple occupation and the absence of a licence, and stating that the appellant was in breach by virtue of sub-letting the premises. The first judge found that there had been a breach of the covenants on the basis that the appellant used the premises on a commercial basis for lodging students, but made no reference to sub-letting or any tenancy. The respondents served notice under the Law of Property Act 1925 s 146 and proceedings for possession were commenced. The appellant applied for relief from forfeiture. At the hearing before the second judge, the appellant conceded that no defence to the claim for forfeiture had been filed and the breaches were incapable of remedy. The second judge found that the covenants had been breached by the sub-letting for reward and declared that the appellant's lease was forfeited. The appellant appealed against the order of the second judge on the grounds that the forfeiture notice failed to identify the breaches determined by the first judge and the way the matter had proceeded before the second judge had been on the basis of a concession by the appellant that the breaches were incapable of remedy, which had been wrongly made. *Held*, with respect to the second covenant, to the extent that the second judge based himself on the appellant's own evidence, in particular with reference to sub-letting, that had been wrong and had not reflected the fact that the appellant's case changed throughout her various witness statements and that it had clearly been arguable that she had not been using the term 'sub-letting' in any technical legal sense. What was critical for the purposes of the second covenant was the reference in the forfeiture notice to the fact that the appellant allegedly sub-let the premises to students. There had been a reference to the first judge's findings and that reference had been incorrect. What the respondent's had to do had been to rely more precisely on what the exact findings and conclusions made by the first judge had been. On that basis, any reasonable recipient of the notice would have believed that the finding of the first judge had been that there had been a breach of the second covenant by dint of sub-letting alone. Further, there had been nothing that the appellant could reasonably and properly have done to remedy the breach and it might have been for that reason that she applied for relief against forfeiture, rather than seeking to take any other or additional point. With respect to the first covenant, it was clear that, whatever the appellant had done, she had been in breach of that covenant. On any fair reading of the forfeiture notice, the position had been clear. It had been alleged that the premises, including part of the premises, had been sub-let to students, thus operating them as a business. It had been that which had been said to be the breach of the first covenant and that allegation had been inextricably linked with the facts relied on, namely, the sub-letting, which were not the correct facts. It followed that the appellant had not known what she had needed to do to rectify the matter. Furthermore, it would not have been sufficient merely to have stated that the appellant, in breach of the first covenant, had been using the premises other than for residential purposes. Accordingly, the appeal would be allowed.

Anders v Haralambous [2013] EWHC 2676 (QB), [2013] All ER (D) 174 (Sep) (Queen's Bench Division: Jay J). *Akici v LR Butlin Ltd* [2005] EWCA Civ 1296, [2006] 2 All ER 872 applied.

1659   Lease—option to extend—freeholder disputing right to exercise option—rule against perpetuities

The freehold of a property was subject to a lease for a term of 80 years registered in the name of an association. One flat in the property was subject to an underlease registered to the first defendant. The first defendant charged the underlease by way of legal mortgage to a building society to secure repayment of a loan. The first defendant extended the flat by the creation of an additional floor and roof terrace. Subsequently, the additional floor only was regularised by a deed supplemental to the underlease, confirming that the addition formed part of the demised premises and was held on the same terms as the underlease. The first defendant and his brother, the second defendant, were registered as the proprietors and, therefore, the head lessors of the freehold of the property. By deed, the defendants as freeholders granted the first defendant as lessee an option to extend the underlease, which extended to the freeholders' and lessees' successors in title. Subsequently, the building society, having taken possession of the flat, sold the residue of the term created by the underlease, as chargee, to the claimant and his wife, who were duly registered as proprietors of the underlease. The association and the claimant executed a deed of variation to include the roof terrace in the premises demised by the underlease. The defendants were not parties to the deed of variation. Some years later, the claimant was registered as the sole proprietor of the underlease. The claimant then gave notice to exercise the option to extend. The defendants refused to grant the extension lease on the ground that the option was void for perpetuity as it did not comply with the Perpetuities and Accumulations Act 1964 s 9. The claimant sought an order for specific performance of the option, which the judge made. The defendants appealed on the basis that the claimant was not successor in title to the first defendant as underlessee. They contended that the first defendant held title under the surrender and re-grant effected by the deed supplemental to the underlease, and the claimant held title under the surrender and re-grant effected by the deed of variation, and they were different titles. It fell to be determined whether the claimant was a successor in title to the first defendant. *Held*, in the case of s 9(1)(a), the interest to be granted had to be 'reversionary' on a lease. Accordingly, the successor had to be a successor to the original lessee in respect of the same title, namely that lease. The claimant was not a successor in title to the first defendant as underlessee. Until the execution of the deed of variation, the legal right to the roof terrace had been vested in the association. There had been no grant by the association to either the first defendant or the claimant between the time of the construction of the roof terrace to the execution of the deed of variation to pass that right to either of them. Under the option and s 9(1)(a), it was necessary that the title should be that in existence as at the date of the option or its grant. In the case of the option, it was to be 'an extension' of the lease. There was no basis on which a surrender and re-grant could be excepted from that requirement as a matter of construction of either the option or s 9(1)(a). Accordingly, the appeal would be allowed.

Souglides v Tweedie [2012] EWCA Civ 1546, [2013] Ch 373, [2012] All ER (D) 83 (Dec) (Court of Appeal: Sir Andrew Morritt C, Rix and Patten LJJ). Decision of Newey J [2012] EWHC 561 (Ch), [2012] 3 All ER 189 (2012 Abr para 1647) reversed.

1660   Lease—service charge—costs incurred—management company

The claimant was the registered leaseholder of a flat in a development which included a communal leisure centre with a swimming pool. The defendant company was a management company which was party to the claimant's lease. When the defendant started managing the development, it was told by the developer that the gas supply to the swimming pool was supplied by an energy company. The defendant sent meter readings to the energy company which generated invoices which the defendant paid from payments made to it by the tenants of the development. The defendant was notified that another supplier, rather than the energy company, had been supplying the gas to the swimming pool and demanded payment for the period of the claimant's lease. The defendant charged the tenants an amount in respect of the gas as part of the service charge. The claimant paid such amount under protest and issued proceedings against the defendant. The proceedings were transferred to the Leasehold Valuation Tribunal which held that the cost of the gas charge had been incurred for the purposes of the Landlord and Tenant Act 1985 s 20B when the gas had been supplied. The defendant's appeal succeeded on the basis that, although a liability to pay had arisen when the gas had been supplied, the cost of the gas charge had not been incurred until the cost had been paid or an invoice for payment had been issued. The claimant appealed, submitting that the effect of the decision was to undermine and defeat the aim of the 1985 Act of protecting tenants from demands for expenditure of which they were not sufficiently warned to set aside provision. Consideration was given to ss 18 and 19. *Held*, in the circumstances, there was an obvious difference between a liability to pay and the incurring of costs. That difference was recognised in the 1985 Act. It was significant that 'relevant costs' were defined in s 18(2) as 'the costs or estimated costs incurred or to be incurred' and were not defined as 'the liability or estimated liability for costs'. Further, s 19(2) provided strong support for the view that costs were incurred only when they were paid or when an invoice was submitted. A liability had to crystallise before it became a cost.

Costs were not incurred within the meaning of ss 18, 19, 20B on the mere provision of services or supplies to the landlord or management company. Accordingly, the appeal would be dismissed.

Burr v OM Property Management Ltd [2013] EWCA Civ 479, [2013] 1 WLR 3071, [2013] All ER (D) 76 (May) (Court of Appeal: Lord Dyson MR, Elias and Patten LJJ).

1661   Lease—service charge—qualifying works—consultation requirements—dispensation

The Landlord and Tenant Act 1985 s 20ZA(1) provides that where an application is made to a leasehold valuation tribunal for a determination to dispense with all or any of the consultation requirements, the tribunal may make the determination if satisfied that it is reasonable to dispense with the requirements.

The claimant was the freehold owner and landlord of flats leased by the defendants. The claimant informed the defendants that it intended to carry out major works on the building. Four tenders for the works were received, but only one of the tenderer's priced specifications were provided to the defendants at that stage of the statutory consultation process. That tenderer was ultimately awarded the contract for the proposed works. The defendants applied to a leasehold valuation tribunal for a determination of the service charges payable under their respective leases. The tribunal held that the claimant had failed to comply with the Service Charges (Consultation Requirements) (England) Regulations 2003, SI 2003/1987, in respect of works. It was common ground that the extent, quality and cost of the works had been in no way affected by the landlord's failure to comply with the consultation requirements under the 2003 Regulations. During the course of the hearing, the claimant proposed a significant deduction from the sums claimed as compensation for any prejudice suffered, but this was rejected by the defendants. The tribunal declined to conclude that it was reasonable to dispense with the consultation requirements, holding that the financial effects of the grant or refusal of the application for dispensation on the landlord or tenant were irrelevant, and so made no order for dispensation under the 1985 Act s 20ZA(1). Consequent to the tribunal's refusal to dispense with the consultation requirements, pursuant to the statutory scheme, the claimant's recovery from the defendants was capped. The decision was affirmed on appeal and the claimant appealed further. *Held*, Lord Hope and Lord Wilson dissenting, the purpose of the consultation requirements was to ensure that tenants were protected from paying for inappropriate works or paying more than would be appropriate. The issue on which a tribunal should focus when entertaining an application by a landlord under s 20ZA(1) had to be the extent, if any, to which the tenants were prejudiced in either respect by the failure of the landlord to comply with the consultation requirements. In a case where it was common ground that the extent, quality and cost of the works were in no way affected by the landlord's failure to comply with the consultation requirements, dispensation should not be refused solely because the landlord had seriously breached, or departed from, the consultation requirements. The financial consequences to the landlord of the grant or refusal of dispensation were not a relevant consideration. Adherence to the consultation requirements was not an end in itself, and the dispensing jurisdiction was not a punitive or exemplary exercise. In the absence of clear words precluding a tribunal imposing terms, a tribunal could impose conditions on the grant of a dispensation under s 20(1)(b), including that the landlord paid the tenants' reasonable costs incurred in connection with the landlord's application under s 20ZA(1). The essential question was whether the tenants would suffer relevant prejudice as a result of the landlord's failure if dispensation were granted unconditionally. In so far as they would suffer relevant prejudice, the tribunal should, at least in the absence of some good reason to the contrary, effectively require the landlord to reduce the amount claimed as service charges to compensate the tenants fully for that prejudice. As the tenants' complaint was that they had been deprived of the opportunity to have their voices heard, they had an obligation to identify what they would have said. In the present case, there had been no evidence before the tribunal that the defendants had suffered relevant prejudice worth as much as the deduction offered by the claimant. In those circumstances, the tribunal ought to have decided that the claimant's application for a dispensation should have been granted on terms that the defendants' aggregate liability to pay for the works be reduced by the amount of that deduction. Accordingly, the appeal would be allowed.

Daejan Investments Ltd v Benson [2013] UKSC 14, [2013] 2 All ER 375 (Supreme Court: Lord Neuberger P, Lord Hope DP, Lord Clarke, Lord Wilson and Lord Sumption SCJJ).

Decision of Court of Appeal [2011] EWCA Civ 38, [2011] 1 WLR 2330, [2011] All ER (D) 224 (Jan) (2011 Abr para 1685) reversed.

1662   Lease—surety—licence to alter premises

The claimant was the freehold proprietor and lessor of commercial premises (the premises) under a lease entered into in 1981 (the lease). The lease was entered into by the claimant's predecessor in title (PAT) and the lessee (the lessee) as tenant. The lease provided for general repairs, restrictions and rent, and, by cl 14(e) placed restrictions upon the lessee from altering or adding to the premises. The lease also provided for the provision of a surety, pursuant to which, the defendant company became the surety of the lessee. In 1987, PAT and the lessee entered into a licence (the licence), which gave the lessee permission to execute works of alteration and extension to the premises. By cl 4(a) of the licence, all of the covenants, conditions and obligations contained in the lease were applicable to the works and to the premises in their altered state. The works permitted by the licence included the construction of an opening in a wall to the premises, the construction of a new garden centre, alterations to the layout of the car park and the erection of a high security boundary. The defendant was not a party to the licence. In 2011, the lessee went into administration and was subsequently dissolved. The claimant gave notice to the defendant that, as surety, it was responsible for the rental and all other sums owing under the terms of the lease. The defendant asserted that it was released from the further performance of its obligations by reason of the variation of the lease and the enlargement of its obligations under it brought about by the licence. The claimant issued proceedings seeking to enforce the defendant's obligations as surety under the lease. The defendant submitted that the lessee had carried out the works upon the grant of the licence, and the works had become part of the demised premises and, therefore, subject to the covenants and conditions of the lease. Each of the obligations under the lease, including obligations to replace fixtures and fittings, and to keep the interior and exterior windows and premises clean, had been enlarged and rendered more onerous by the effect of the licence and the execution of the works under it. Accordingly, applying *Holme v Brunskill* the defendant submitted that it had been released from its obligations. The claimant submitted that the licence had not been a variation of the lease, but had been a concession; a permission that had been given notwithstanding the lease. *Held,* it was settled law that a surety was discharged if the creditor agreed with the principal debtor to vary the terms of the contract guaranteed, unless it was self-evident that the variation was insubstantial or one which could not be prejudicial to the guarantor. Under that rule, the court did not examine whether or not there was actual prejudice or damage, it had to be self-evident that that was the case, or that the variation was not substantial. A surety was discharged entirely where the risk upon the creditor increased. It was for the claimant to show that there had been no variation which was not insubstantial or that such variation that existed was one which could not be prejudicial to the surety. In the instant case, it could not properly be said that the works carried out under the licence had been of a type already contemplated in the lease; they were of a different order and magnitude. Nothing in the rent clauses nor in the definition of the demised premises compelled a different reading. On any plain reading of the two instruments, the works had amounted to a new garden centre being built, thus, only by varying the lease had it been possible to have done the works under the licence. It made no difference to the character of the permission that it was a one-off licence; a variation to the original promises made had been required unless there was to have been a plain breach of the covenant in cl 14(1)(e) not to alter. There was no flexibility in the lease. It was no answer to say that the defendant, as surety, had not been bound by the licence because it had not itself executed it. The licence engaged the obligations of the lessee under the lease, and the question was whether that might increase the lessee's exposure and, therefore, that of the defendant. It had been self-evident that where there had been substantial alterations that had increased the bulk of the structures on the land, there had inevitably been an increase in the scope of the repairing obligations, and the increase of burdens upon the lessee would necessarily have increased the risk of default and the burden on the defendant. It could not be the case that the defendant's duty to guarantee the lessee's obligations to repair under the lease had remained in place, but the licence which clearly also bound the lessee and had incorporated a duty to repair the newly built parts of the premises had been of no potential effect upon the defendant. Therefore, the defendant was discharged from liability. Accordingly, the claim would be dismissed.

Topland Portfolio No 1 Ltd v Smiths News Trading Ltd [2013] EWHC 1445 (Ch), [2014] 1 P & CR 20, [2013] All ER (D) 74 (Jun) (Chancery Division: Judge Foster QC). *Holme v Brunskill* (1878) 3 QBD 495, CA considered.

1663   Leasehold enfranchisement—house—conversion into house in breach of covenant—right to rely on breach to acquire freehold

The present proceedings concerned a two-storey property on a parade of shops. The ground floor was a shop. The first floor had been used as a store room for the adjoining shop and was not internally accessible from the property. The claimants had become the registered proprietors of the property under a 99 year lease which had originally been granted in the 1930s. The opening between the first floor of the property and the neighbouring property had been bricked up rendering the first floor of the property accessible only from the exterior of the rear of that property. The claimants applied to the defendant freeholder/lessor for consent to convert the first floor of the property into a self-contained residential flat. Consent was refused. There were a number of grounds for the refusal, including the defendant's wish to avoid the application of the Leasehold Reform Act 1967 and the Leasehold Reform, Housing and Urban Development Act 1993. Despite that refusal, the claimant carried out the conversion works. Subsequently, the claimants granted an assured shorthold tenancy of that flat. The claimants gave notice in writing to the defendant of their intention to acquire the freehold of the property pursuant to the 1967 Act. In a counter-notice, the defendant denied that entitlement. The claimants served a notice of claim to the freehold under the 1967 Act. The defendant disputed that claim and alleged breach of covenant by the claimants in reliance on the claimants having carried out the first floor conversion works in breach of the lease, which contained a covenant against alterations. The defendant also relied on that alleged breach as a ground for disentitling the claimants from purchasing the freehold of the property. The judge declared that the claimants were not entitled to acquire the freehold of the property. The claimants appealed. *Held*, (1) on the evidence, the judge had not applied the wrong legal test. What mattered for the purposes of the present appeal was that the answer that had been given by the judge had been amply supported by the evidence and had in law been reasonably justified by the arguments relied on. The property had been neither adapted for residential use at the date when the lease had begun nor had it ever been used as such until the recent conversion works, which had been completed shortly before the claimants had given notice under the 1967 Act. The first floor of the property had been a subsidiary part of the building and there was no connecting access from the commercial unit on the ground floor to the first floor flat. The judge had been entitled to place the use of the first floor relied on as at the date of the notice, on which the claimants had placed such emphasis, into the proper setting of the use of it under the lease during the preceding 70 plus years. (2) The judge had not been wrong to find that the covenant in the lease had been broken by the carrying out of the conversion works without the defendant's consent. He had been entitled to find that the work had amounted to an alteration to the plan of the property. (3) As a general rule, it would be unacceptable if a person were entitled to enforce a right to acquire property compulsorily by deliberately doing something that was necessary to found the claim, which act was wrongful between him and the person against whom he sought to enforce that right. When a right of that kind was based on a statute, the question would be whether the language of the relevant provision, construed in the context of the purpose and scheme of the legislation, and applied to the circumstances of the particular case, had made that right available to the person who sought to enforce it. The judge had found that the claimants had carried out those unauthorised conversion works in order to qualify for the right to acquire the freehold. As a matter of statutory construction it could not have been intended by Parliament to give the lessee the right to enfranchise by making, in breach of covenant, the very adaptation of the building for living in that was necessary for him to exercise the right. Accordingly, the appeal would be dismissed.

    Henley v Cohen [2013] EWCA Civ 480, [2013] 2 P & CR 201, [2013] All ER (D) 36 (May) (Court of Appeal: Mummery, Hallett and Leveson LJJ). *Day v Hosebay Ltd; Howard de Walden Estates Ltd v Lexgorge Ltd* [2012] UKSC 41, [2012] 4 All ER 1347 (2012 Abr para 1651) considered.

1664   Leasehold enfranchisement—house—meaning of 'house'

The Leasehold Reform Act 1967 s 2(1) provides that 'house' includes any building designed or adapted for living in and reasonably so called, notwithstanding that the building is not structurally detached, or was or is not solely designed or adapted for living in, or is divided horizontally into flats or maisonettes; where a building is divided horizontally, the flats or other units into which it is so divided are not separate houses, though the building as a whole may be, and where a building is divided vertically the building as a whole is not a house though any of the units into which it is divided may be.

A tenant was granted a lease of a property which comprised a basement, ground floor and five upper floors. There had been minor alterations to the internal layout over the years so that, at the relevant time, the building comprised three retail units, which made up seven per cent of its total area, and eight self-contained flats. The tenant served a notice contending that it was entitled to acquire the freehold under the lease. In proceedings before the court, an issue arose as to whether the property constituted a 'house' within the meaning of the 1967 Act s 2(1). It was common ground that the building had been designed or adapted for living in, and that it was divided horizontally into flats or maisonettes. The judge ruled that the property did not fall within the definition in s 2(1). On the claimant's appeal, *held*, the judge had been correct in her determination that the question was not whether it was possible to call a building 'a house', but whether it was reasonable to do so. In the case of a building predominantly used for residential purposes, whether it could reasonably be called a house would depend primarily on its external and internal physical character and appearance. The structure and use of the building in the present case had hardly changed since it was first erected. The clear consensus of judicial opinion was that a purpose-built block of flats could not reasonably be called a house. There was the added feature that the property was not a wholly residential building but also included three shops. Simply as a matter of ordinary language, the property could not have reasonably been called a house at the time when the claimant had served its notice. In the absence of very unusual factors, a building constructed, laid out and used as a block of substantial self-contained flats throughout its 120 years of existence could not reasonably be called a house. Accordingly, the appeal would be dismissed.

Earl Cadogan v Magnohard Ltd [2012] EWCA Civ 594, [2013] 1 WLR 24, [2012] All ER (D) 47 (May) (Court of Appeal: Lord Neuberger MR, Longmore and Lewison LJJ).

1665   Leasehold enfranchisement—valuation—development value—exclusion

The first respondent was the owner of a freehold property which comprised four floors and a basement and was laid out as three flats, which were each held under a separate underlease. There was also an overriding lease of flat three which was interposed between the headlease and the tenant of flat three. The second respondent was the owner of the overriding lease and the tenant of flat three. A statutory notice of a claim to exercise the right to collective enfranchisement under the Leasehold Reform, Housing and Urban Development Act 1993 Pt 1 (ss 1–103) was issued by the tenants of flats one and two. The appellant was the nominee purchaser for the participating tenants. It was common ground that there was potential to develop the roof space above flat three so as to provide a fourth floor for the property and extend the flat and that the value of the property as a house was far greater than the aggregate value of the individual flats. The value of the property as a house could only be realised by uniting in one person the headlease and the overriding lease. Before the Leasehold Valuation Tribunal, the appellant contended that the hope of realising the property's development value should be ignored in fixing the price to be paid for the intermediate leases and that where only one of the intermediate leases was acquired, a discount should be applied to the price of that lease. That contention was rejected and the appellant's appeal was also dismissed. The Upper Tribunal adopted a hypothetical two stage open market sale approach and found that the development value had to be taken into account and that in the event that only one of the intermediate leases was acquired a discount of five per cent was appropriate. The appellant further appealed. *Held*, it could be said that there was no obvious part of the social policy underlying the 1993 Act to confer on tenants of flats in a building not only the right to acquire the freehold and intermediate leases, but to do so at a price which ignored completely the value attributable to development value if those interests or some of them had been vested in the same person. Therefore, it was not appropriate to extend the express scope of Sch 6 para 3(1) so as to exclude the Upper Tribunal's hypothetical two stage open market sale of the intermediate leases to the same purchaser. The Upper Tribunal had been perfectly entitled to postulate what inquiries the reasonably prudent buyer would have made of whichever of them would have been the potential second seller and what the reaction would have been. What inquiries the purchaser would have made and what answers would have been received were partly matters of fact and partly expert evidence. What would have been the valuation consequence of those matters was a matter for expert evidence. None of those issues raised an issue of law. Accordingly, the appeal would be dismissed.

Cravecrest Ltd v Trustees of the Will of the Second Duke of Westminster [2013] EWCA Civ 731, [2013] 4 All ER 456 (Court of Appeal: Sir Terence Etherton, Rimer and McCombe LJJ). *Day v Hosebay Ltd; Howard de Walden Estates Ltd v Lexgorge Ltd* [2012] UKSC 41, [2012] 4 All ER 1347 (2012 Abr para 1651) applied.

1666   Mobile homes—gipsy and traveller sites—Wales

The Housing and Regeneration Act 2008 (Consequential Amendments to the Mobile Homes Act 1983) (Wales) Order 2013, SI 2013/1722 (in force on 10 July 2013), which applies in relation to Wales only, makes amendments to the Mobile Homes Act 1983. In particular, the 2013 Order (1) provides that the right of an occupier to apply to the court or a tribunal if the owner fails to provide a written statement is disapplied for occupiers of transit pitches on local authority gipsy and traveller sites in Wales; and (2) provides that the right of a party to the agreement to apply to the court or a tribunal as to the terms of the agreement within six months of it being made or of the written statement being given is disapplied for transit pitches in Wales.

The Mobile Homes Act 1983 (Amendment of Schedule 1 and Consequential Amendments) (Wales) Order 2013, SI 2013/1723 (in force on 10 July 2013), (1) amends the Mobile Homes Act 1983 Sch 1 so as to apply certain implied terms relating to agreements for transit and permanent pitches on local authority gipsy and traveller sites to Wales; (2) amends the Mobile Homes (Commissions) Order 1983, SI 1983/748, the Residential Property Tribunal Procedures and Fees (Wales) Regulations 2012, SI 2012/531, and the Mobile Homes (Written Statement) (Wales) Regulations 2012, SI 2012/2675, in consequence of changes under head (1); and (3) extends the jurisdiction of residential property tribunals to matters arising as a result of amendments made to the 1983 Act.

1667   Mobile homes—pitch fee review notice—prescribed form—England

The Mobile Homes (Pitch Fees) (Prescribed Form) (England) Regulations 2013, SI 2013/1505 (in force on 26 July 2013), prescribe the form of the document that must accompany a pitch fee review notice served by a site owner under the Mobile Homes Act 1983 proposing an increase in the pitch fee for a mobile home.

1668   Mobile homes—selling and gifting—England

The Mobile Homes (Selling and Gifting) (England) Regulations 2013, SI 2013/981 (in force on 26 May 2013), make detailed provision in relation to the selling and gifting of mobile homes and the assignment of agreements. In particular, the regulations (1) prescribe the information and documents which the occupier of a mobile home must provide to a prospective purchaser before a sale can be completed; (2) prescribe the information which an occupier must provide to a site owner in cases where the occupier proposes to assign, by sale or gift, an agreement which is not a new agreement; (3) set out forms to be used in the provision of information to prospective purchasers and site owners; (4) prescribe certain types of evidence which may be supplied, as constituting 'relevant evidence', to a site owner by an occupier who wishes to give a mobile home and assign an agreement to a member of their family; (5) set out the grounds on which a site owner may apply to a tribunal for an order preventing an occupier from selling or gifting a mobile home and from assigning an agreement; (6) prescribe the maximum amount of commission payable to a site owner by a new occupier on the sale of a mobile home; (7) specify procedural requirements which parties must comply with in connection with the assignment of an agreement and the payment of commission; (8) provide that any rules made by a site owner before the regulations come into force which relate to the management or conduct of the site will cease to have effect 12 months after the regulations come into force; and (9) provide that any rule relating to the sale of a mobile home which is made by a site owner before the regulations come into force has no effect in relation to specified matters.

The Mobile Homes Act 2013 (Saving Provisions) (England) Order 2013, SI 2013/1168 (in force on 26 May 2013), makes savings provisions in connection with the coming into force of the Mobile Homes Act 2013 s 10 so as to provide that, where, before that provision comes into force, an occupier of a mobile home has served a request on a site owner for the approval of a person to whom the occupier wishes to sell or gift the mobile home, the transaction may proceed under the existing statutory provisions if the occupier so wishes.

1669 Mobile Homes Act 2013

The Mobile Homes Act 2013 amends the law relating to mobile homes. The Act received the royal assent on 26 March 2013 and came into force in part on 26 May 2013 and 1 April 2014. The remaining provisions come into force on a day to be appointed. For details of commencement, see the commencement table in the title STATUTES AND LEGISLATIVE PROCESS.

Section 1 allows local authorities to charge fees in relation to the licensing of 'relevant protected sites' in England, principally permanent caravan sites, and to enable them to recover the costs incurred in operating licensing schemes. In particular, local authorities may charge relevant protected site application fees, annual fees, fees for applications for alteration of the conditions attached to the site licence and fees for applications for consent to the transfer of a site licence. Section 2 confers a discretion on a local authority in England when deciding whether to issue a site licence authorising the use of the land as a relevant protected site and empowers the Secretary of State to make regulations relating to such a local authority's exercise of its discretion to issue and to transfer a site licence. In the case of a site in England, an appeal against a condition attached to a site licence is to be brought to a residential property tribunal rather than a magistrates' court: s 3. Existing provisions concerning compliance notices are replaced by s 4 in relation to relevant protected sites in England. Provision is made by s 5 empowering a local authority in England to carry out works on a site where an occupier of land is convicted of failure to take steps required by a compliance notice, and to take emergency action if it appears to the authority that, as a result of the occupier's failure to comply with a condition attached to the site licence, such action is necessary to remove an imminent risk of serious harm to the health and safety of any person who is or may be on the land. Section 5 also empowers local authorities to impose a charge on the occupier of land to recover expenses connected with action it has taken and makes provision dealing with appeals. Section 6 deals with procedural aspects of appeals, specifying when compliance notices and expenses demands become operative and provides for the recovery of expenses by local authorities. Residential property tribunals have power under s 7 to make directions requiring the payment of money by one party to the proceedings to another by way of compensation, damages or otherwise. Section 8 makes provision relating to the management of relevant protected sites in England. In particular, s 8 confers powers on the Secretary of State to make regulations providing that the occupier or person appointed by the occupier to manage the site is a fit and proper person and requiring local authorities to establish a register of fit and proper persons, and makes provision for inclusion in such a register and for the removal of persons from a register. In the case of a protected site in England (other than a gipsy and traveller site) for which there are site rules, each of the rules is to be an express term of each agreement between the site owner and the mobile home occupier that relates to a pitch on the site: s 9. Section 9 also empowers the Secretary of State to make regulations about the procedure to be followed by a site owner who is proposing to make new site rules or to vary or delete existing site rules. Section 10 entitles the occupier of a mobile home in England to sell or give it to a member of the occupier's family and to assign the agreement to the purchaser or donee without the approval of the site owner. By virtue of s 11, when a site owner serves a pitch fee review notice on an occupier of a mobile home in England proposing to increase the pitch fee, the site owner is required to provide the occupier with an accompanying document which meets certain prescribed requirements. Section 12 deals with offences, in particular, by providing that the owner of a protected site in England, or his agent, commits an offence if, during the subsistence of a residential contract, the owner or agent knowingly or recklessly provides information or makes a representation to a person which is false or misleading in a material respect. Section 13 increases from level 4 to level 5 on the standard scale the fine for an occupier of land in England who commits the offence of causing or permitting any part of the land to be used as a caravan site without holding a site licence, and increases from level 1 to level 4 on the standard scale the fine for a person wilfully obstructing any person exercising the power of entry or entering land in England by authorisation of a warrant. In relation to land in England, where a body corporate commits an offence under the Caravan Sites and Control of Developments Act 1960 and it is proved that the offence was committed with the consent or connivance of an officer of the body corporate, or the offence was attributable to neglect on the part of this person, then the officer is guilty of the offence as well as the body corporate: 2013 Act s 14. Section 15 deals with commencement, transitional, transitory and saving provision, extent and short title.

Amendments, repeals and revocations
The list below, which is not exhaustive, mentions repeals and amendments which are or will be effective when the Act is fully in force.
    Specific provisions of a number of Acts are amended or repealed. These include: Caravan Sites and Control of Development Act 1960 ss 1(2), 3(2A), (5A)–(5F), (7), (8), 5A, 7(1A), 8(1B), 9A–9I, 10(1A)–(1F), 10A, 12A–12E, 26(5), 26A; Caravan Sites Act 1968 s 3(1), (1A), (1AA), (1B); Mobile Homes Act 1983 ss 2C, 2D, Sch 1 Pt 1 Ch 2 paras 7A–7C, 8, 8A–8C, 9, 17–20, 25A, Sch 1 Pt 3 para A1; Housing Act 2004 s 230(5ZA), Sch 13 paras 3, 8.

1670   Mobile Homes (Wales) Act 2013

The Mobile Homes (Wales) Act 2013 reforms and restates the law relating to mobile home sites in Wales. The Act received the royal assent on 4 November 2013 and came into force in part on 5 November 2013. The remaining provisions come into force on a day or days to be appointed. For details of commencement, see the commencement table in the title STATUTES AND LEGISLATIVE PROCESS.

Pt 1 (ss 1–3) Introduction
Section 1 summarises the main provisions of the Act. Definitions of 'regulated site', 'protected site' and 'local authority gipsy and traveller site' are provided by s 2, Sch 1, and s 3 defines 'owner'.

Pt 2 (ss 4–39) Licensing of Mobile Homes etc
Section 4 provides an overview of Pt 2, which restates with significant changes provision formerly made in relation to Wales by the Caravan Sites and Control of Development Act 1960. Under the 2013 Act s 5, using land as a regulated site without a site licence is an offence punishable with a fine at level 5 on the standard scale. The requirements for site licence applications to local authorities are specified by s 6. Section 7 sets out the timescale for issuing a licence, and provides for a right of appeal to a residential property tribunal against a decision not to issue a licence. A licence may be issued for a period of up to five years from the date the licence comes into operation, unless it is revoked: s 8. A local authority is entitled under s 9 to attach certain types of conditions when it issues a site licence. For the purposes of s 9, the Welsh Ministers are empowered by virtue of s 10 to specify model standards with respect to the layout of the site and the provision of facilities, services and equipment for regulated sites. Local authorities have a duty to consult the fire and rescue authorities when considering the conditions to attach to a site licence: s 11. Section 12 sets out an applicant's right of appeal to a residential property tribunal against any condition that is attached to a site licence. Under s 13, a local authority may vary the conditions attached to a site licence at any time. A licence holder may appeal to a residential property tribunal against any alteration of the conditions of the licence or any refusal to vary the conditions: s 14.
    Section 15 provides that, where an owner of land is failing or has failed to comply with a site licence condition, a local authority may give the owner a fixed penalty notice or a compliance notice. The information to be included in a fixed penalty notice is set out in s 16. Where it appears to a local authority that an owner of land is failing to comply with a licence condition, the local authority is empowered by s 17 to serve a compliance notice on the owner. Pursuant to s 18, an owner of land who has been served with a compliance notice which has become operative under s 24 commits an offence if he fails to take the steps set out in the notice within the specified time period. Section 19 provides for a power to demand expenses where a compliance notice has been served under s 17. Under s 20, where

a site owner is convicted of an offence of failing to comply with the steps specified in a compliance notice, the local authority may take steps required by the compliance notice, and any further action it considers appropriate, to ensure the relevant condition is complied with. A local authority is empowered by s 21 to take emergency action in certain situations, and has the power to demand expenses where action has been taken under s 20 or 21: s 22. By virtue of s 23, an appeal may be brought in relation to a decision of a local authority under s 17, 21 or 22. Section 24 sets out when a compliance notice or expenses demand becomes operative. Provision is made by s 25 for the recovery of expenses demanded under s 19 or 22.

Under s 26, a site licence is revoked where the licence holder dies, where the licence holder ceases to be the owner of the land, or where the land covered by a licence ceases to be used as a regulated site. A licence holder has a duty pursuant to s 27 to surrender a licence for alteration when required to do so by the local authority which issued it. Section 28 introduces a new 'fit and proper person' requirement that applies to a person who manages a regulated site. In deciding whether a person is such a person, a local authority must have regard to all matters it considers appropriate: s 29. Under s 30, a local authority is permitted to appoint an interim manager of a regulated site if certain specified conditions are met. The terms of appointment of an interim manager are prescribed by s 31. Section 32 provides any authorised officer or agent of a local authority with power to enter a regulated site if there are reasonable grounds for entry. Where a site is unlicensed, the occupier of the mobile home may apply pursuant to s 33 to a residential property tribunal for a repayment order. It is an offence contrary to s 34 to make a false or misleading declaration or other statement, or to provide false or misleading information knowing or believing it to be false or misleading, under Pt 2. The Welsh Ministers may issue guidance to local authorities on the performance of their functions under Pt 2: s 35. Section 36 allows local authorities to charge fees under s 6 or 13. Under s 37, local authorities must keep a register of site licences that is available for public inspection. By virtue of s 38, Pt 2 does not apply to Crown land. Section 39 defines various terms used in Pt 2.

Pt 3 (ss 40–47) Protection from Eviction
Section 40 provides that the protection offered by Pt 3 applies in relation to any licence or contract under which a person is entitled (1) to station a mobile home on a protected site and occupy it as the person's residence; or (2) if the mobile home is stationed on the protected site by another, to occupy it as the person's residence. Under s 41, the notice of termination contained in a residential contract must be for at least four weeks. It is an offence to withdraw or withhold services or facilities reasonably required for the occupation of a mobile home: ss 42, 43. The circumstances in which a court can suspend the enforcement of an order it has made to evict the occupier from a site for a period not exceeding 12 months are specified in s 44. Section 45 makes supplementary provision in relation to s 44. Under s 45, proceedings for an offence under Pt 3 may be instituted by any local authority. Definitions of 'occupier' and 'residential contract' are made by s 47 for the purposes of Pt 3.

Pt 4 (ss 48–55) Mobile Home Agreements
By virtue of s 48, Pt 4 applies to any agreement under which a person is entitled to station a mobile home on a protected site, and to occupy the mobile home as the person's only or main residence. Before making an agreement to which Pt 4 applies, an owner of a protected site must give to the proposed occupier under the agreement a written statement in a prescribed form: s 49. Section 50, Sch 2 set out the terms to be implied in any agreement to which Pt 4 applies. Under s 51, the Welsh Ministers may by order amend Sch 2 as they consider appropriate. Where site rules apply to a protected site (with the exception of local authority gipsy and traveller sites), such rules are to be express terms of the pitch agreement between the site owner and the mobile home occupier: s 52. Section 53 provides for a mobile home agreement to be passed to another on the death of a party to the agreement. Procedural provision relating to the resolution of disputes under Pt 4 is made by s 54, and s 55 defines terms used in Pt 4.

Pt 5 (ss 56, 57) Powers of Local Authorities
Section 56 sets out the power of a local authority to provide mobile homes sites on land within its area. Section 57, Sch 3 allow local authorities to prohibit the stationing of mobile homes on common land.

Pt 6 (ss 58–65) Supplementary and General
Section 58, Sch 4 make consequential amendments, and s 58, Sch 5 make transitional provisions and savings. Provision for the liability of a corporate body for offences is made by s 59. Section 60 defines 'mobile home', s 61 defines 'qualifying residents' association', and s 62 defines further terms. Section 63 deals with the making of secondary legislation, s 64 deals with commencement, and s 65 specifies the short title.

1671   Possession—order—impact of human rights—Ministry of Defence accommodation

The claimant had been married to a member of the armed forces and she and her children were provided with residential accommodation by the defendant. The claimant's husband resigned from the army, but the defendant continued to allow the claimant to stay in her home on compassionate grounds as a temporary measure until she could obtain housing from the local authority. The claimant was wheel-chair bound and her two children had either mental or physical health problems. One of the claimant's children had a child, who also developed health problems. The defendant commenced possession proceedings. The claimant resisted the claim on the basis that her eviction from the premises would be an unjustified interference with her rights under the European Convention on Human Rights art 8. As the law then stood, a residential occupier's rights under art 8 could not be prayed in aid by way of defence to the unqualified right of a property owner to possession. An order for possession was made but then stayed and the claimant made a homelessness application. In the meantime, judgment was given in *Manchester City Council v Pinnock (No 2)*, which determined that, in order for domestic law to be compatible with the Convention art 8, a court which was asked to make an order for possession of a person's home at the suit of a local authority had to have the power to assess the proportionality of making the order and, therefore, to consider a defence based on an alleged breach of the occupant's rights under art 8. A written ministerial submission made by the Deputy Chief Executive of Defence Estates recommended the eviction of the claimant and her family. The minister decided that there should be possession and, therefore, the defendant obtained a writ of possession. The claimant sought judicial review of the decision. The judge found that the minister's decision had not been unlawful. The claimant appealed. *Held*, the criticisms of the lawfulness of the decision-making process which led to the defendant obtaining a warrant for the possession of the premises were ill-founded. The decision to enforce the possession order had been lawful. In the absence of special circumstances, the owner of property would only be in a position to seek a writ of possession after the occupant's rights under art 8 had been exhausted, either because they had not been prayed in aid during the possession proceedings, or because they had been raised, but rejected, as a defence. Generally, an attempt to relitigate the art 8 issue at the enforcement stage, or to litigate it for the first time when it could and should have been raised as a defence in the possession proceedings, would be an abuse of process by the occupier. However, there would be exceptional cases where raising the rights under art 8 at the enforcement stage would not be an abuse, for example, where there was a fundamental change in the occupant's personal circumstances after the making of the possession order but before its enforcement. The claimant had vigorously pursued her rights under art 8 during the possession proceedings, but, as the law then stood, they afforded her no defence. The judge had carried out a careful and sympathetic analysis of the consequences for the claimant and her family of the threatened eviction. The judge had recognised that it was the authority rather than the defendant which had had the statutory function of dealing with the housing needs of the claimant arising from her homelessness and her own and her family's medical difficulties, and that there had been nothing in the evidence to show that the authority would have fallen short of a full discharge of that responsibility. Where Parliament had allocated the responsibility for addressing the rights under art 8 to a particular public authority, the taking of steps by another public authority with no such responsibility, which would have the effect of placing on the responsible authority the burden of addressing those rights, would be a very powerful form of legitimate aim. The challenge made by the claimant under art 8 to the enforcement of the possession order would fail. Accordingly, the appeal would be dismissed.

    R (on the application of JL) v Secretary of State for Defence [2013] EWCA Civ 449, [2013] HLR 359, [2013] All ER (D) 30 (May) (Court of Appeal: Arden, Sullivan and Briggs LJJ). *Manchester City Council v Pinnock (No 2)* [2011] UKSC 6, [2011] 2 AC 104,

[2012] 2 All ER 586 (2012 Abr para 1403) applied. Decision of Judge Simler QC [2012] EWHC 2216 (Admin), [2012] All ER (D) 370 (Jul) affirmed.

1672   Prevention of Social Housing Fraud Act 2013
See para 1402.

1673   Rent—rent arrears—penalty clause in tenancy agreement—lawfulness under European law
See Case C-488/11 *Brusse v Jahani BV*, para 509.

1674   Rent—rent assessment committee—transfer of functions—England
See para 612.

1675   Secure tenancy—joint tenancy—wife serving notice to terminate tenancy—order for possession against husband
The appellant and his wife were joint tenants of the respondent's property under a secure weekly tenancy. The wife moved out of the property and gave notice to the respondent purporting to terminate the tenancy. The respondent refused the appellant's request to transfer the tenancy into his sole name and issued possession proceedings. In making an order for possession, the judge followed *Monk* and found that where a notice to quit was served by one of two joint tenants, the notice was effective to determine the tenancy. On appeal, the appellant submitted that the rule in *Monk* breached his rights under the European Convention on Human Rights art 8 and the First Protocol to the Convention art 1. *Held*, the appellant was aiming to obtain a tenancy of a three-bedroom family house for himself in place of the joint tenancy that the respondent originally granted. In those circumstances, there seemed to be more of an interference with the respondent's enjoyment of its possessions than an interference by the respondent with the possessions of the appellant. The Convention art 8 was not engaged. *Monk* laid down a substantive rule of property and contract law under which one joint tenant had the right to serve notice unilaterally terminating a periodic joint tenancy. The wife exercised her right. There was nothing in the rule that was an interference by her or by the respondent with respect to the appellant's home. The First Protocol art 1 was also not engaged. The rule in *Monk* was a proprietary and contractual legal right inherent in the joint tenancy granted by the respondent and the notice given by the wife was in exercise of her right as a joint tenant. Therefore there was no interference by her or by the respondent with the enjoyment of the appellant's possessions. His relevant possession was an interest in a joint tenancy that was, in its very nature, terminable unilaterally by the wife or by the respondent. The respondent's role regarding the rule in *Monk* was simply as the recipient of the notice given to it by the wife, and it did nothing in relation to the termination of the tenancy that could possibly have been described as an interference by it with the peaceable enjoyment of the property by the appellant. Accordingly, the appeal would be dismissed.
   Sims v Dacorum BC [2013] EWCA Civ 12, [2013] HLR 178, [2013] All ER (D) 172 (Jan) (Court of Appeal: Mummery and Etherton LJJ and Sir Scott Baker). *Hammersmith and Fulham LBC v Monk* [1992] 1 AC 478, [1992] 1 All ER 1, HL (1991 Abr para 1495), applied.

1676   Secure tenancy—possession—conditional order—guidance
The defendant had lived her whole life in the same three-bedroom property of which the claimant local authority was the freehold owner. It had granted a weekly tenancy to the defendant's late father a number of years previously. Following his death, the tenancy transferred to the defendant's late mother. From the commencement of the Housing Act 1980, the mother had enjoyed a secure tenancy. After the death of her mother, the defendant succeeded to the tenancy by virtue of the Housing Act 1985 ss 87 and 89. The claimant formed the view that allowing the defendant to remain in the property on her own was not an efficient use of its resources and it assisted the defendant to complete a registration form for the allocation of a new property. She was categorised as being of a high level of priority with an urgent need to move and became entitled to bid for a one-bedroom property. However, she refused to bid for alternative accommodation as she did not want to

leave her property. The claimant served notice on the defendant seeking possession of the property under the 1985 Act Sch 2 and a claim for possession was issued. The recorder made an order for possession of the property conditional on an offer of alternative suitable accommodation being made to the defendant. The defendant appealed. *Held*, the recorder had directed herself correctly as to the relevant principles, had properly considered the evidence before her, had identified the material considerations and weighed them with great care in arriving at her conclusion. In accordance with s 84(2)(c), the court could not make an order for possession, whether conditional or otherwise, unless it was satisfied that suitable accommodation would be available when it was to take effect. Further, there was no requirement that an offer of accommodation be made before the date of the hearing of the application for the possession order or that the accommodation was available at the date of that hearing. Instead, the court had to be satisfied that suitable accommodation would be available when the order took effect. Furthermore, the court would need to be satisfied that those requirements were fulfilled on the basis of the evidence before it at the hearing at which the possession order was made. Finally, there was nothing in the legislation which said that the court had to be satisfied that the requirements were fulfilled by reference to a particular property. If, in the particular circumstances of the case and having regard to the matters set out in Sch 2 Pt IV para 2, the court was satisfied that accommodation having particular characteristics would be reasonably suitable to meet the needs of the tenant and his family and that such accommodation would become available then the court had jurisdiction to make a possession order which would not take effect until such accommodation had in fact become available. It might not always be appropriate to make a conditional order whenever a local housing authority sought possession. The court had to consider whether such an order was necessary and appropriate in the circumstances of the case, or whether justice would be better served by adjourning the final determination of the application until a particular property had been identified. A conditional order normally had to include a time limit within which the local authority had to make the suitable accommodation available, and a provision that if it failed to do so the order would lapse. The recorder had had jurisdiction to make a conditional order for possession in the form that she had. Accordingly, the appeal would be dismissed.

Reading BC v Holt [2013] EWCA Civ 641, [2013] HLR 536, [2013] All ER (D) 67 (Jun) (Court of Appeal: Arden and Kitchin LJJ and Sir David Keene).

1677   **Secure tenancy—possession—order—tenant remaining as tolerated trespasser— temporary transfer to different property**

The claimant was granted a secure tenancy of a flat (the 'first flat') by the defendant local authority. A possession order was subsequently made in respect of the first flat, which had the effect of terminating the secure tenancy. However, the claimant remained in occupation as a tolerated trespasser. The claimant was later moved to a temporary flat (the 'second flat') to enable the defendant to undertake repairs to the first flat. The work ended up taking significantly longer than estimated, so the parties entered into a 'decant agreement', described as a temporary secure tenancy agreement, under which the claimant was to reoccupy the first flat when it was again suitable for occupation. For the next seven months, during which time the claimant went into arrears of rent in respect of the second flat, the parties disputed whether the works on the first flat were complete. The defendant then commenced successful possession proceedings in respect of the second flat, but the possession warrant was suspended on terms. After the first flat again became habitable, the claimant attempted to resume possession but was removed from occupation. The defendant's stated policy was that, where a person was displaced for more than 12 months, the decant became permanent. On that basis, the second flat had become the claimant's permanent home. The first flat was subsequently let to a different tenant. The claimant issued proceedings seeking to be restored to occupation of the first flat, submitting that her claim had priority over that of the new tenant. The judge decided that the claimant was not a tenant of the first flat and, since entering into the decant agreement, the only tenancy the claimant had had was of the second flat. The claimant appealed. *Held*, in the absence of any evidence that the decant agreement had been entered into on the basis of a mistake by either side, the assumption was that the parties had had a full grasp of the relevant history but had nevertheless been evincing a combined intention that, as from the moment of the decant agreement, the claimant was to be recognised as having the status of a secure tenant of the first flat. That recognition had been reflected in the recital to the agreement. Although the defendant had been in error in that respect, that consideration would not stand in the way of achieving what the parties had plainly intended to achieve. That was how the reasonable man would interpret the decant agreement. It followed that, on the signing of the decant agreement, the claimant had become a secure tenant of the first flat, and, following her removal to the second flat, had remained a tenant of the first flat. Accordingly, the appeal would be allowed.

Francis v Brent Housing Partnership Ltd [2013] EWCA Civ 912, [2013] All ER (D) 348 (Jul) (Court of Appeal: Laws, Rimer and Beatson LJJ).

1678   Unlawful eviction—secure tenant—damages—valuation

The Housing Act 1988 s 28(1) provides that the basis for the assessment of damages referred to in s 27(3) is the difference in value, determined as at the time immediately before the residential occupier ceased to occupy the premises in question as his residence, between (a) the value of the interest of the landlord in default determined on the assumption that the residential occupier continues to have the same right to occupy the premises as before that time; and (b) the value of that interest determined on the assumption that the residential occupier has ceased to have that right.

The claimant was a secure tenant of the defendant local authority. He occupied a one-bedroom flat which formed part of a purpose-built building. Under the terms of the tenancy agreement, the claimant was required to notify the authority of any absence from the property for more then eight weeks. For a period of five months the claimant visited Ghana. He continued to pay his rent by standing order during the time, but did not notify the defendant of his absence. The defendant gained forcible entry to the property and cleared out the claimant's possessions and prepared the property for re-letting. A replacement occupant prepared to take an introductory tenancy was found one day before the claimant's return. The re-letting was completed two days after the claimant's return. On his return, the claimant attempted to contact the defendant, but his message did not reach those responsible for the grant of new introductory tenancies until it was too late. Efforts to reinstate the claimant's tenancy of the property came to nothing. The claimant issued proceedings alleging unlawful eviction and seeking damages for the wrongful disposal of his possessions. By the time of the trial, damages for the loss of his possession had been agreed and, subject to liability, common law damages for unlawful eviction were agreed. The defendant's valuer had concluded that the claimant's rights had had no adverse effect on the value of the defendant's interest because a private purchaser would pay the same for a building with one flat subject to an assured tenancy as would be paid for it with the flat vacant. However, the claimant's valuer assumed that the purchaser should be deemed to take the building subject to an on-going secure tenancy of the flat, and advised that that would depreciate the value of the building. It was common ground that if liability for statutory damages was established pursuant to the Housing Act 1988 ss 27 and 28, then the appropriate amount for statutory damages should be either the depreciated value of the building or nil. The judge concluded that it had to be assumed that the claimant's rights were for all purposes to be deemed to be those of a secure tenant, even after a hypothetical sale to a private landlord. Consequently, the claimant was awarded statutory damages. On appeal by the defendant, *held*, the vulnerability of the claimant's secure tenancy to becoming downgraded into an assured shorthold tenancy on an open market sale to the highest bidder was inherent in the nature of his rights. That was because on an open market sale, the highest bidder was likely to be a private rather than local authority landlord due to the depressing effect on the value of the block to anyone whose status meant that the claimant would continue to be a secure tenant. The judge's error had been to conclude that a valuation which had taken full account of the conversion of the claimant's rights on any sale from those of a secure tenant to those of an assured tenant was such as to ignore the nature of the right to occupy the premises immediately before the eviction took place. The claimant's rights of occupation had, from the very grant of his secure tenancy, been vulnerable to being downgraded on a sale by the defendant to a private landlord. It had been a vulnerability inherent in the nature of his rights. The landlord in default was the owner of the relevant interest to be valued at the date prescribed by s 28(1). It was nonetheless an interest to be valued by reference to the valuer's assessment of the best price which it could reasonably be expected to obtain in the open market, on the specific assumptions set out in s 28. Therefore, the agreed common law damages for unlawful eviction would be substituted for the statutory damages that had been awarded by the judge. Accordingly, the appeal would be allowed.

Loveridge v Lambeth LBC [2013] EWCA Civ 494, [2013] 3 All ER 261 (Court of Appeal: Arden, Briggs LJJ and Sir Stanley Burnton).

LEGAL AID

Halsbury's Laws of England (5th edn) vol 65 (2008) paras 1–300

Articles

For articles relating to this title please refer to the Table of Articles at the beginning of the Abridgment.

1679   Armed forces independence payment—general provisions

See para 2583.

1680   Civil proceedings—asylum claim—removal directions—exclusion

The claimants were illegal entrants to the United Kingdom. Italy, France and Malta accepted responsibility for considering their asylum claims substantively and their claims were accordingly certified under the Asylum and Immigration (Treatment of Claimants etc) Act 2004 Sch 3 paras 4 and 5 and removal directions were set. On their applications for legal aid in respect of judicial review proceedings, it fell to be determined whether they were challenging the certifying decisions under the 2004 Act or the removal directions, which were excluded from the scope of civil legal services under the Legal Aid, Sentencing and Punishment of Offenders Act 2012 Sch 1 Pt 1 para 19(6)(a). *Held,* there was an important difference between what might be two contemporaneous decisions, that was an immigration decision that someone whose asylum claim had already been certified on third country grounds was to be removed by way of removal directions and the decision to set removal directions for that removal, not sensibly distinguishable from the removal directions themselves. It was the second decision that was excluded from scope by Sch 1 Pt 1 para 19(6). Further, Sch 1 Pt 1 para 19(7) clearly covered the refusal to treat further representations as a fresh asylum claim. There was no reason to give a restricted meaning to the clear words 'no right to appeal', since decisions limiting the right of appeal in asylum cases were within scope anyway. Where there was a restricted right of appeal, arising from judicially reviewable certifying decisions, those certifying decisions were either in scope generally or excepted from exclusions. Certain of the applications could be read as for funding to challenge the removal directions. Those applications would be dismissed. One of the applications for which funding was sought could only be discerned from counsel's advice, which clearly provided that it was a challenge to the decision to set removal directions. The advice sought funding for a challenge to the decision to set removal directions, which was not sensibly distinguishable from the removal directions themselves. That application would also be dismissed. The application for funding to challenge the certifying decision would be allowed.

Rrapaj v Director of Legal Aid Casework [2013] EWHC 1837 (Admin), [2013] All ER (D) 48 (Jul) (Queen's Bench Division: Ouseley J).

1681   Civil proceedings—connected matters

The Civil Legal Aid (Connected Matters) Regulations 2013, SI 2013/451 (in force on 1 April 2013), prescribe the civil legal services which may be made, and the circumstances in which they may be made, available in connection with the provision of services described in the Legal Aid, Sentencing and Punishment of Offenders Act 2012 Sch 1 Pt 1 paras 1–45 so that, where an individual qualifies for civil legal services, further services may be made available to the individual in connection with those services, where the purpose of the further services is to identify the proposed defendant or respondent, so that matters otherwise excluded from the scope of legal aid may be funded because of their connection with matters which are within the scope of legal aid.

1682   Civil proceedings—costs

The Civil Legal Aid (Costs) Regulations 2013, SI 2013/611 (in force on 1 April 2013), make provision about costs orders in civil proceedings in favour of or against a legally aided party and, in certain circumstances, against the Lord Chancellor. In particular, the regulations (1) make exceptions to the general principle of cost protection in relation to certain forms of civil legal aid and in certain family proceedings; (2) make provision in relation to the periods to which cost protection applies and when it comes to an end; (3) set out the grounds on which a costs order might also be made against the Lord Chancellor where civil legal aid has been provided to a party to proceedings; (4) make provision in relation to the procedure, determination and enforcement of costs orders against a legally aided party and the Lord Chancellor; and (5) set out the principles to be applied when a costs order or a costs agreement is made in favour of a legally aided party to proceedings.

The Legal Aid, Sentencing and Punishment of Offenders Act 2012 (Consequential, Transitional and Saving Provisions) (Amendment) Regulations 2013, SI 2013/621 (in force on 1 April 2013), amend SI 2013/534 (see PARA 1703) and (1) make transitional provision in relation to the application of the Civil Legal Aid (Costs) Regulations 2013 above in respect of the application of cost protection where a party receives certain funded services under the Access to Justice Act 1999 and goes on to receive legal aid under the Legal Aid, Sentencing and Punishment of Offenders Act 2012 in connection with the same proceedings; and (2) make provision to enable funded services under the 1999 Act to be taken into account for the purpose of determining costs payable by the Lord Chancellor to a non-legally aided party. The Damages-Based Agreements Regulations 2013, SI 2013/609 (see PARA 313), are also amended in relation to the information required to be given before an agreement is made in an employment matter so as to refer to arrangements made for the purposes of the 2012 Act Pt 1 (ss 1–43) instead of to the Community Legal Service.

1683   Civil proceedings—eligibility for legal aid—financial resources and payment for
        services

The Civil Legal Aid (Financial Resources and Payment for Services) Regulations 2013, SI 2013/480 (in force on 1 April 2013), make provision about the rules the Director of Legal Aid Casework must apply to determine whether an individual's financial resources are such that the individual is eligible for civil legal services under the Legal Aid, Sentencing and Punishment of Offenders Act 2012 Pt 1 (ss 1–43). The regulations, in particular, (1) provide a general delegation power to enable functions of the Director under the regulations to be exercisable by, or by employees of, a person authorised by the Director; (2) set out the general rules for making a determination about an individual's financial resources; (3) provide for the exceptions to the rule that the Director must determine whether an individual's financial resources are such that the individual is eligible for civil legal services; (4) prescribe the eligibility limits for disposable income, disposable capital and gross income, and the cases in which it is possible to waive these limits; (5) set out the process for making a determination in respect of an individual's financial resources, including the requirement for the individual whose eligibility is being determined to provide information, the calculations which the Director must undertake, and the powers to amend determinations or make further determinations in the light of new information; (6) set out the rules for calculating income and capital; and (7) set out the requirements for paying contributions towards the cost of civil legal services.

The Civil Legal Aid (Financial Resources and Payment for Services) (Amendment) Regulations 2013, SI 2013/753 (in force on 1 April 2013), amend the principal 2013 Regulations above to give effect to the Hague Convention of 23 November 2007 on the International Recovery of Child Support and other forms of Family Maintenance. The effect of the amendments is that (1) family help (higher) or legal representation are available for cases where the 2007 Hague Convention art 17(b) applies without being subject to a means test; and (2) legal help, family help (lower), family help (higher) and legal representation are available for a matter where a creditor makes an application concerning maintenance obligations towards a person under the age of 21, arising from a parent-child relationship.

1684   Civil proceedings—legal persons—financial resources and payment for services

The Legal Aid (Financial Resources and Payment for Services) (Legal Persons) Regulations 2013, SI 2013/512 (in force on 1 April 2013), make provision for determining the financial eligibility of legal persons for civil and criminal legal aid.

The Legal Aid (Financial Resources and Payment for Services) (Legal Persons) (Amendment) Regulations 2013, SI 2013/754 (in force on 1 April 2013), amend the principal 2013 Regulations above so as to give effect to the Hague Convention of 23 November 2007 on the International Recovery of Child Support and other forms of Family Maintenance. The effect of the amendments is that (1) family help (higher) or legal representation are available for applications under the Hague Convention art 10(1)(a) or (b), without being subject to a means test, where the legal person previously received legal aid for the matter in the State of origin; and (2) legal help, family help (lower), family help (higher) and legal representation are available, without being subject to a means test, for applications concerning maintenance obligations towards a person under the age of 21, arising from a parent-child relationship.

1685   Civil proceedings—merits criteria

The Civil Legal Aid (Merits Criteria) Regulations 2013, SI 2013/104 (in force on 1 April 2013), make provision for the criteria which the Director of Legal Aid Casework must apply when determining whether an individual or legal person qualifies for civil legal services under the Legal Aid, Sentencing and Punishment of Offenders Act 2012 Pt 1 (ss 1–43). In particular, the regulations (1) enable functions of the Director under the regulations to be exercisable by, or by employees of, a person authorised by the Director; (2) make provision for how the prospects of success of a case are to be assessed and when a case is of significant wider public interest; (3) set out the reasonable private paying individual test; (4) set out the proportionality test; (5) set out how the regulations apply to an application for civil legal services; (6) make provision for the forms of civil legal services to which different merits tests apply and define the different forms of civil legal services; (7) make provision in relation to which form of civil legal services is appropriate in certain cases; if an individual qualifies for more than one form of civil legal services the Director must decide which form of civil legal services is most appropriate in all the circumstances of the case; (8) make provision for the general merits criteria, which apply in the absence of provision to the contrary; (9) make provision for the application of the merits criteria in cases which are described in more than one paragraph of the 2012 Act Sch 1 Pt 1 and in cases in relation to which civil legal services are available under s 10; and (10) make provision for the specific merits criteria, which apply to certain cases which fall with the description of specified paragraphs of Sch 1 Pt 1 and for the criteria which apply in relation to applications by legal persons for civil legal services.

The Civil Legal Aid (Merits Criteria) (Amendment) Regulations 2013, SI 2013/772 (in force on 1 April 2013), amend the principal 2013 Regulations above, so as to amend the criteria which the Director of Legal Aid Casework must apply in relation to determinations for legal representation in relation to public law claims. The amendment gives the Director the express power to grant legal aid for public law claims even where other court or tribunal proceedings have not been pursued if the Director considers that such proceedings would not provide the remedy which the individual requires.

The Civil Legal Aid (Merits Criteria) (Amendment) (No 3) Regulations 2013, SI 2013/3195 (in force on 1 January 2014), further amend the 2013 Regulations to provide specific merits criteria for a judicial review of a transfer decision within the meaning of European Parliament and Council Regulation (EU) 604/2013 establishing the criteria and mechanisms for determining the member states responsible for examining an application for international protection lodged in one of the member states by a third-country national or a stateless person.

1686   Civil proceedings—preliminary proceedings

The Civil Legal Aid (Preliminary Proceedings) Regulations 2013, SI 2013/265 (in force on 1 April 2013), specify the proceedings which are not to be regarded as preliminary for the purposes of the Legal Aid, Sentencing and Punishment of Offenders Act 2012 Sch 1 Pt 4 para 5(1)(b), by virtue of which, where a paragraph of Sch 1 Pt 1 describes services that consist of, or include, services provided in relation to proceedings, the description is to be treated as including services provided in relation to preliminary or incidental proceedings. The 2013 Regulations provide that proceedings under the Tribunals, Courts and Enforcement Act 2007 s 11(4)(a), under which the First-tier Tribunal may grant permission to appeal to the Upper Tribunal on application by a party, are not to be regarded as preliminary to proceedings for which civil legal services may be provided under the 2012 Act Sch 1 Pt 1 para 8 so that, in cases relating to welfare benefits, applications to the First-tier Tribunal for permission to appeal against a decision of the First-tier Tribunal to the Upper Tribunal are not within the general scope of civil legal aid.

1687 Civil proceedings—remuneration

The Civil Legal Aid (Remuneration) Regulations 2013, SI 2013/422 (in force on 1 April 2013), make provision about the payment by the Lord Chancellor to persons who provide civil legal services under arrangements made for the purposes of the Legal Aid, Sentencing and Punishment of Offenders Act 2012 Pt 1 (ss 1–43). The fees and rates set out in the regulations are subject to definitions and payment schemes contained in contracts made between the Lord Chancellor and a provider of civil legal services, the relevant contract in any particular case being the contract which governs the provision of civil legal services for which the claim for remuneration relates. The regulations do not apply to the payment of remuneration under contracts awarded as part of a pilot which provides for remuneration by way of one or more standard fees. Nor do the majority of the provisions in the regulations apply to contracts which have been awarded after competitive tendering as to price has taken place.

The Civil Legal Aid (Remuneration) (Amendment) Regulations 2013, SI 2013/2877 (in force on 2 December 2013), amend the principal regulations above so as to (1) provide for remuneration of barristers in independent practice and for enhancement, in exceptional circumstances, of the rates payable; (2) remove the table of rates and fees relating to legal representation in non-fast track proceedings before the Immigration and Asylum Chamber of the Upper Tribunal where permission has been granted, thereby ensuring that remuneration for such representation is payable at the same rate as representation in all other immigration and asylum cases which constitute controlled work, other than those to which escape fees apply; (3) set out the rates and fees to be paid to experts; and (4) make special provision in relation to certain experts in clinical negligence cerebral palsy cases.

1688 Civil proceedings—scope

The Legal Aid, Sentencing and Punishment of Offenders Act 2012 (Amendment of Schedule 1) Order 2013, SI 2013/748 (in force on 1 April 2013), amends the Legal Aid, Sentencing and Punishment of Offenders Act 2012 Sch 1, which sets out the scope of civil legal aid. In particular, the order (1) adds new provision so that civil legal services are available in relation to an appeal on a point of law to the High Court, the Court of Appeal and Supreme Court relating to a council tax reduction scheme; (2) amends the definition of domestic violence to cover incidents, or patterns of incidents, of controlling and coercive behaviour; (3) provides that civil legal services are available in relation to an application under the Hague Convention of 23 November 2007 on the International Recovery of Child Support and other forms of Family Maintenance art 10, provided that the individual previously received legal aid in the State of origin; (4) provides that civil legal services will also be available to an individual for proceedings in England and Wales in relation to recognition and enforcement of a maintenance decision where the individual makes a request directly to a competent authority for recognition and enforcement of the decision if the individual previously received legal aid in the state of origin; and (5) adds a new exclusion for civil legal services provided in relation to judicial review of an enactment, decision, act or omission.

1689 Civil proceedings—statutory charge

The Civil Legal Aid (Statutory Charge) Regulations 2013, SI 2013/503 (in force on 1 April 2013), (1) make provision about the statutory charge which arises, under the Legal Aid, Sentencing and Punishment of Offenders Act 2012 s 25(1), over money and other property preserved or recovered by a legally aided party in civil proceedings and over costs payable to the legally aided party by another party to the proceedings; (2) make provision about the calculation and operation of the charge and make exceptions to it; (3) determine when the charge is in favour of the Lord Chancellor or a provider of civil legal services; (4) make provision about when the charge may be waived in specified circumstances; (5) make provision about the enforcement of the charge, including the obligations on providers and the Lord Chancellor in relation to the transfer, retention and payment of money, including costs, which is subject to the charge; (6) provide for the enforcement of the charge by the Lord Chancellor, providers and the legally aided party; and (7) make provision for postponement of the charge and the payment of interest.

1690 Criminal proceedings—advice, assistance and representation—choice of representative

See para 1699.

1691 Criminal proceedings—advice, assistance and representation—remuneration

The Criminal Legal Aid (Remuneration) Regulations 2013, SI 2013/435 (in force on 1 April 2013), make provisions for the funding and remuneration of advice, assistance and representation made available under the Legal Aid, Sentencing and Punishment of Offenders Act 2012 ss 13, 15 and 16. The 2013 Regulations, in particular, (1) deal with the manner in which fees are to be claimed, determined and paid and include provisions permitting interim payments and payments for expert services; (2) provide for an appeal mechanism to challenge, in certain circumstances, the appropriate officer's determination of the fees payable to a litigator or an advocate; (3) deal with the redetermination of fees by an appropriate officer, appeals from the appropriate officer to a costs judge and appeals from the costs judge to the High Court; (4) set out the graduated fees and fixed fees payable to advocates for proceedings in the Crown Court; (5) set out the fees payable to solicitors and other appropriately qualified persons for proceedings in the Crown Court; (6) set out the manner in which fees are to be claimed, determined and paid in proceedings in the Court of Appeal; (7) set out the rates payable for proceedings in a magistrates' court and certain other work to which the 2010 Standard Crime Contract applies; and (8) set out the fees and rates payable to experts.

The Criminal Legal Aid (Remuneration) (Amendment) Regulations 2013, SI 2013/2803 (in force on 2 December 2013), amend the 2013 Regulations above so as to (1) reduce fees for very high cost criminal trials; (2) reduce fees and rates paid to expert witnesses; and (3) provide that fixed fee representation can no longer be claimed in respect of prisoners challenging their treatment in prison.

1692 Criminal proceedings—contempt of court—entitlement to legal aid

An order was made against the defendant and persons unknown, restraining them from using certain land for residential purposes without the express grant of planning permission. The claimant local authority contended that the defendant had been made aware of the order and was living on the land for residential purposes in breach of the order. The claimant commenced proceedings for contempt against the defendant and her estranged partner but the proceedings were adjourned. The defendant had been endeavouring to obtain legal representation for the contempt hearing. She had encountered difficulties in processing an application with the interested party for legal aid. There was uncertainty as to whether the contempt proceedings should be classified as civil proceedings, where an application for exceptional funding had to be made to the director of the interested party, or criminal proceedings, where any application had to be made to the court. It fell to be determined whether the court should make an order granting legal aid representation in favour of the claimant. *Held*, the Legal Aid, Sentencing and Punishment of Offenders Act 2012 s 16(1) required that representation for the purpose of criminal proceedings was to be available to an individual if he was a specified individual. Regulations made under s 19(1) were designed to facilitate the discharge of that duty, rather than define or restrict it. If there were to be any conflict between the regulation and the primary statute, the latter would prevail. Any conflict could be avoided by reading the Criminal Legal Aid (Determination by a Court and Choice of Representative) Regulations 2013, SI 2013/614, reg 5 (see PARA 1699) as requiring an order to be made when the court proceeded under reg 6 or 7, but not preventing the court making an order in other cases where an application under reg 4 had been made. The source of the court's duty in determining other cases was the scheme of the 2012 Act itself and the provisions of the Criminal Legal Aid (General) Regulations 2013, SI 2013/9 (see PARA 1696). In the circumstances, the proceedings for which legal representation was sought were criminal proceedings within the meaning of the 2012 Act. The defendant was a specified individual within the meaning of s 16(1) and representation was to be available. The relevant authority for determining whether representation was to be granted was the High Court. That application had been made and SI 2013/9 reg 21 provided that such representation was in the public interest. Therefore, an order granting legal aid in favour of the defendant would be made.

King's Lynn and West Norfolk Council v Bunning [2013] EWHC 3390 (QB), [2013] All ER (D) 108 (Nov) (Queen's Bench Division: Blake J).

1693 Criminal proceedings—contribution orders

The Criminal Legal Aid (Contribution Orders) Regulations 2013, SI 2013/483 (in force on 1 April 2013), (1) make provision in relation to the liability of individuals who are in receipt of representation under the Legal Aid, Sentencing and Punishment of Offenders Act 2012 s 16 to make a payment in connection with the provision of such representation, based on an assessment of the financial resources of the individual; (2) provide that the functions of the Lord Chancellor and the Director of Legal Aid Casework under the 2013 Regulations may be exercised by, or by an employee of, a person authorised for that purpose by the Lord Chancellor or the Director; (3) make provision in relation to payments by individuals who are in receipt of representation under the 2012 Act s 16 for the purpose of Crown Court trials; (4) make provision in relation to payments by individuals who are in receipt of representation under s 16 for the purpose of appeals to the Crown Court; and (5) make provision in relation to the enforcement of an obligation to make a payment imposed under s 23 for the payment of services.

The Criminal Legal Aid (Contribution Orders) (Amendment) Regulations 2013, SI 2013/2792 (in force on 27 January 2014), amend the 2013 Regulations above, so as to provide that an individual will be liable to make a payment under the 2013 Regulations in relation to representation in the Crown Court under the Legal Aid, Sentencing and Punishment of Offenders Act 2012 s 16 only where the Director has determined that the individual is eligible for legal aid in respect of those proceedings.

1694 Criminal proceedings—eligibility for legal aid—financial resources

The Criminal Legal Aid (Financial Resources) Regulations 2013, SI 2013/471 (in force on 1 April 2013), make provision in relation to the circumstances in which an individual's financial resources are such that they are eligible for criminal legal aid under the Legal Aid, Sentencing and Punishment of Offenders Act 2012 Pt 1 (ss 1–43) so as to (1) enable the functions of the Director of Legal Aid Casework under the regulations to be exercised by, or by an employee of, a person authorised for that purpose by the Director; and (2) make provision in relation to the financial eligibility of an individual (a) for advice and assistance provided under the 2012 Act s 15; and (b) for representation provided under s 16.

The Criminal Legal Aid (Financial Resources) (Amendment) Regulations 2013, SI 2013/2791 (in force in part on 2 December 2013 and in part on 27 January 2014), amend the principal regulations above by removing references to cases in which a prisoner wishes to challenge his treatment in prison, to reflect the fact that legal aid is no longer available in such cases. The regulations also set out new financial eligibility criteria for individuals who apply for legally aided representation in Crown Court proceedings, such that an individual with a disposable annual income of £37,500 or more will not be eligible for legal aid, subject to any review of such a determination.

1695 Criminal proceedings—funding—very high cost cases

The Criminal Defence Service (Very High Cost Cases) (Funding) Order 2013, SI 2013/2804 (in force on 2 December 2013), (1) makes provision in relation to very high cost cases which are the subject of a contract made between the Legal Services Commission and members of the Very High Cost Case Contract (Crime) Panel and dated 14 January 2008, as amended on 13 November 2008, 15 December 2008 and 5 May 2009, or a 2010 VHCC contract, so as to provide for new, reduced fees payable for work done pursuant to any Task List agreed between a member of the Panel or a provider under a 2010 VHCC contract and the

Lord Chancellor; and (2) amends the 2007 Order, SI 2007/1174, so as to provide for the rates applicable to advocates who are not members of the Panel.

1696   Criminal proceedings—general provisions
The Criminal Legal Aid (General) Regulations 2013, SI 2013/9 (in force on 1 April 2013), make provision for determinations in relation to whether an individual qualifies for criminal legal aid under the Legal Aid, Sentencing and Punishment of Offenders Act 2012 Pt 1 (ss 1–43). The 2013 Regulations, in particular, make provision (1) authorising the functions of the Lord Chancellor or the Director of Legal Aid Casework to be exercised by, or by an employee of, a person authorised for that purpose by the Lord Chancellor or Director; (2) for the making of determinations in relation to individuals who are arrested and held in custody; (3) about the proceedings which constitute criminal proceedings in addition to those already listed in the 2012 Act s 14; (4) for the making and withdrawal of determinations about advice and assistance for criminal proceedings; (5) for determinations about representation for criminal proceedings and for the withdrawal of such determinations; (6) in relation to proceedings which are or are not to be regarded as incidental to criminal proceedings; (7) about the circumstances in which the interests of justice test set out in s 17 (qualifying for representation) is taken to be met; (8) enabling an individual to apply for a review of a determination by the Director that the interests of justice do not require representation to be made available; (9) for appeals by individuals who are dissatisfied with a review; and (10) for the application of the 2013 Regulations to legal persons.

The Criminal Legal Aid (General) (Amendment) Regulations 2013, SI 2013/2790 (in force in part on 2 December 2013 and in part on 27 January 2014), amend the principal regulations above so as to (1) restrict the provision of advice and assistance regarding an individual's sentence to cases that relate to the calculation of the total period of time that an individual must serve in custody before either being entitled to release by the Secretary of State or becoming eligible for consideration by the Parole Board for a release direction; (2) restrict the provision of advice and assistance in prison law cases to disciplinary hearings in prisons or young offender institutions where the proceedings engage the European Convention on Human Rights art 6(1) or where the governor has exercised his discretion to allow advice and assistance in relation to the hearing; (3) restrict the provision of advice and assistance in proceedings before the Parole Board to those proceedings where the Board has the power to direct the individual's release; (4) provide that, where the Director of Legal Aid Casework makes a determination that an individual is financially eligible for legal aid in magistrates' courts proceedings, he must also make a determination that the individual is eligible for legal aid in the Crown Court in relation to those proceedings; and (5) require the Director to consider the application for legal aid in the Crown Court of an individual determined to be financially ineligible for legal aid in relation to proceedings in a magistrates' court where the proceedings continue in the Crown Court other than on appeal.

1697   Criminal proceedings—legal persons—financial resources and payment for services
See para 1684.

1698   Criminal proceedings—motor vehicle orders
The Criminal Legal Aid (Motor Vehicle Orders) Regulations 2013, SI 2013/1686 (in force on 30 July 2013), make provision about the enforcement of an obligation to make a payment under the Criminal Legal Aid (Contribution Orders) Regulations 2013, SI 2013/483 (see PARA 1693), in connection with the provision of representation to the individual in criminal proceedings, and authorise a court to make motor vehicle orders in respect of an individual for the purpose of enabling certain sums required to be paid under SI 2013/483 to be recovered from the individual, where those sums are overdue. SI 2013/1686, in particular, (1) provides that the functions of the Lord Chancellor may be exercised by, or by an employee of, a person authorised for that purpose by the Lord Chancellor; (2) makes provision in connection with clamping orders; (3) provides for the application for a clamping order and the making of the order; (4) makes provision for the clamping and removal to storage of a motor vehicle subject to an order; (5) concerns the release of a motor vehicle subject to an order; (6) makes provision for a vehicle sale order

and the making of the order; (7) provides for the release of a motor vehicle subject to an order; (8) concerns the sale of a motor vehicle and make provision about the proceeds of sale; and (9) makes provision in connection with the charges that may be imposed in connection with motor vehicle orders and the recovery of such charges.

1699 Criminal proceedings—qualifying for legal aid—determinations

The Criminal Legal Aid (Determinations by a Court and Choice of Representative) Regulations 2013, SI 2013/614 (in force on 1 April 2013), make provision for determinations by a court under the Legal Aid, Sentencing and Punishment of Offenders Act 2012 Pt 1 (ss 1–43) in relation to whether an individual qualifies for criminal legal aid, and in relation to the right of an individual who qualifies for legal aid to select a representative of his own choice. In particular, the regulations (1) make provision in relation to the power of the Crown Court, High Court and Court of Appeal to make a determination as to whether an individual qualifies for representation for criminal proceedings; (2) make provision about the form and content of applications for a determination, the requirements placed on courts in making such determinations and about the withdrawal of a determination; (3) make general provision about when a relevant court may make a determination; (4) specify the types of provider (persons who have entered into arrangements with the Lord Chancellor to provide legal aid under the 2012 Act Pt 1) that an individual may select to represent him in criminal proceedings; (5) require co-defendants to select the same provider unless there is, or is likely to be, a conflict of interest; (6) specify the circumstances in which an individual may change providers; (7) provide that, where an individual has a determination withdrawn and there is a subsequent determination in respect of the same proceedings, the individual must select the same provider unless the relevant court considers that there are good reasons not to do so; (8) make general provision that an individual in criminal proceedings before a magistrates' court may not select an advocate, but provide that in certain specified circumstances a Queen's Counsel or more than one advocate may be selected by the individual; (9) make general provision that an individual in criminal proceedings before a court other than the magistrate's court may select only a single junior advocate, but provide that, in specified circumstances, the relevant court may permit a Queen's Counsel or more than one advocate to be selected by the individual; (10) specify which judges sitting in the relevant court may permit an individual to select a Queen's Counsel or more than one advocate; (11) provide that an individual may not in any circumstances select more than one Queen's Counsel; (12) provide that, in determining whether an individual should be able to select a Queen's Counsel or more than one advocate, the relevant court may require a written opinion about appropriate representation from an advocate already assigned to the case; (13) provide that, in certain limited circumstances, the Director may permit an individual to select a Queen's Counsel or a Queen's Counsel with one junior advocate; and (14) provide that individuals may not select junior advocates if they can adequately be represented by noting juniors.

The Criminal Legal Aid (Determinations by a Court and Choice of Representative) (Amendment) Regulations 2013, SI 2013/2814 (in force on 2 December 2013), amend the 2013 Regulations above so as to (1) enable the court to make a determination permitting a defendant who qualifies for legal aid to instruct multiple advocates if the court is satisfied that the defendant will be prejudiced, or is likely to be prejudiced, if he is not represented by two or more advocates in circumstances in which the prosecution has two or more advocates; and (2) provide that, in the Crown Court, the trial judge may make a determination in relation to multiple counsel or Queen's counsel or, if a trial judge has not been assigned, the resident judge may make such a determination.

1700 Criminal proceedings—recovery of defence costs orders

The Criminal Legal Aid (Recovery of Defence Costs Orders) Regulations 2013, SI 2013/511 (in force on 1 April 2013), (1) provide that, where an individual receives legal aid for representation under the Legal Aid, Sentencing and Punishment of Offenders Act 2012 Pt 1 (ss 1–43) in relation to criminal proceedings before any court other than a magistrates' court or the Crown Court, the court hearing the proceedings must, at the conclusion of the proceedings and unless an exception applies, make a determination, to be recorded in a document known as a recovery of defence costs order, requiring the individual to pay some or all of the cost of his representation; (2) provide that the functions of the Director of Legal

Aid Casework or the Lord Chancellor under the 2013 Regulations may be exercised by, or by an employee of, a person authorised for that purpose by the Director or the Lord Chancellor; (3) provide that a court may make a determination, to be recorded by the court in a recovery of defence costs order, that an individual must pay some or all of the cost of his representation; (4) set out the circumstance in which a court may not make such a determination; (5) make provision for the assessment of financial resources; (6) make provision in relation to the provision of information; and (7) make provision for the enforcement of a recovery of defence costs order by the Lord Chancellor.

1701   Disclosure of information

The Legal Aid (Disclosure of Information) Regulations 2013, SI 2013/457 (in force on 1 April 2013), make provision (1) for providers of services under the Legal Aid, Sentencing and Punishment of Offenders Act 2012 Pt 1 (ss 1–43) to disclose information notwithstanding the usual rules of privilege regarding the disclosure of client information; and (2) to prevent the disclosure of certain information for the purposes of the investigation and prosecution of offences.

1702   Information about financial resources

The Legal Aid (Information about Financial Resources) Regulations 2013, SI 2013/628 (in force on 1 April 2013), (1) prescribe additional information that the relevant authority (in practice, the Director of Legal Aid Casework) may request from a relevant Northern Ireland Department and the Commissioners under the Legal Aid, Sentencing and Punishment of Offenders Act 2012 s 22 for the purposes of facilitating a determination about an individual's financial resources for the purpose of legal aid; (2) specify the particular benefits in relation to which an individual's benefit status may be requested; and (3) prescribe cases in which an individual's benefit status includes the amount of a prescribed benefit an individual is receiving, and where the benefit consists of a number of elements, what those elements are and how much the individual is receiving in respect of each element of the benefit.

The Legal Aid (Information about Financial Resources) (Amendment) Regulations 2013, SI 2013/2726 (in force on 24 October 2014), amend the principal 2013 Regulations above so as to (1) enable the relevant authority (in practice, the Director of Legal Aid Casework) to request from the Driver and Vehicle Licensing Agency register information as to whether an individual is the registered keeper of a vehicle identified by a particular Vehicle Registration Mark, and if so, any particulars contained in the register in relation to that Vehicle Registration Mark; and (2) provide that armed forces independence payment is a prescribed benefit.

1703   Legal aid scheme—replacement—consequential, transitional and saving provisions

The Legal Aid, Sentencing and Punishment of Offenders Act 2012 (Consequential, Transitional and Saving Provisions) Regulations 2013, SI 2013/534 (in force on 1 April 2013), make transitional and saving provisions, and consequential amendments to secondary legislation, in connection with the replacement of the legal aid scheme by the provisions of the Legal Aid, Sentencing and Punishment of Offenders Act 2012 Pt 1 (ss 1–43). The regulations make provision about the treatment of legal aid applications made before 1 April 2013 when the 2013 Act Pt 1 comes into force.

1704   Legal Aid, Sentencing and Punishment of Offenders Act 2012—commencement

The Legal Aid, Sentencing and Punishment of Offenders Act 2012 (Commencement No 5 and Saving Provision) Order 2013, SI 2013/77, brings into force (1) on 19 January 2013, s 48 and, for the purpose only of exercising any power to make orders, regulations or rules of court, ss 44, 45 (so far as not already in force), 46; and (2) on 1 April 2013, ss 44–46 (so far as not already in force) and 47. A saving provision is also made.

The Legal Aid, Sentencing and Punishment of Offenders Act 2012 (Commencement No 6) Order 2013, SI 2013/453, brings into force (1) on 4 March 2013, ss 38(2), 58, 60 and Sch 4; (2) on 1 April 2013, Pt 1 (ss 1–43) (so far as not already in force, except s 19(4)), ss 56, 57, 59, Schs 1–3, 5; and (3) on 8 April 2013, ss 88, 132–138, Schs 23, 24.

solicitor's responsibilities was derived from his retainer. It was right that he was under no general obligation to expend time and effort on issues outside the scope of his retainer. But if, in the course of doing that for which he was retained, a solicitor became aware of a risk, or a potential risk, to his client which it was reasonable to assume the client did not know about, it was the solicitor's duty to inform the client. The standard expected of a solicitor in the performance of that duty was to be assessed against the reasonably competent practitioner having regard to the standards normally adopted in his profession. A solicitor who did not follow the guidance contained within the Law Society's Conveyancing Handbook, was not exercising reasonable care. It was not an excuse for a solicitor to say that he did not know his client's intentions, it was up to him to find out. It was the duty of a solicitor to ask the client appropriate questions designed to ensure that the solicitor was aware of the client's relevant circumstances and intentions, and that the client had all the relevant information and understood the legal consequences. In the circumstances, the defendant was in breach of duty in failing to give proper advice as to the planning status of the property. However, as the full position with regards to the status of the property for planning purposes did not emerge until a later time, the claimant was already too committed to the purchase, and also under too much pressure of time to have backed out of the purchase and therefore on the balance of probabilities, it would not have done so. The claimant succeeded on breach of duty but failed on causation. Judgment would be given accordingly.

AW Group Ltd v Taylor Walton [2013] EWHC 2610 (Ch), [2013] All ER (D) 10 (Oct) (Chancery Division: Judge Hodge QC). Credit Lyonnais SA v Russell Jones & Walker (a firm) [2002] EWHC 1310 (Ch), [2002] All ER (D) 19 (Jul) (2002 Abr para 2832) applied.

1721 Solicitor—negligence—advice on undertakings

Two individuals were shareholders and holders of convertible loan notes issued by the claimant company. They gave undertakings not to exercise the conversion rights conferred by the loan notes issued to them, which entitled them to convert the loans made by them to the claimant into shares therein. The undertakings were expressed to be irrevocable. The claimant brought a claim for damages for professional negligence against the defendant firm of solicitors in respect of the undertakings. It was claimed that a solicitor and partner in the defendant firm, had acted in breach of retainer and negligently in advising that the undertakings were no longer irrevocable, and that it was in the best interests of the claimant to compromise with the individuals by paying out a sum to them in satisfaction of their loan notes. Held, none of the claims for breach of retainer or negligence made by the claimant against the defendant had been established or made out. Neither the solicitor nor the defendant had acted in breach of the terms of his/their retainer or negligently in respect of the advice given to the claimant prior to the entry by the claimant into the deed of settlement. Further, the solicitor had not fallen below the requisite standard to be expected of him, or acted in breach of the terms of his retainer or negligently, in failing to advise the claimant not to make payments of the sum or to recall the same, and in not seeking advice from counsel at that stage. In respect of the alternative case, the claim under that head was not made out for the simple reason that the relevant construction of the undertakings did not accord with the true subjective intention of the parties thereto. It was never actually intended by the relevant party that the undertakings given should be truly irrevocable in the sense that they would continue to be irrevocable even if the claimant failed to pay the two sums due. Accordingly, the claim would be dismissed.

Petrocapital Resources plc v Morrison and Foerster (UK) LLP [2013] EWHC 2682 (Ch), [2013] All ER (D) 57 (Sep) (Chancery Division: Mark Cawson QC). Investors' Compensation Scheme Ltd v West Bromwich Building Society; Investors' Compensation Scheme Ltd v Hopkin & Sons (a firm); Alford v West Bromwich Society; Armitage v West Bromwich Building Society [1998] 1 All ER 98, HL; and Chartbrook Ltd v Persimmon Homes Ltd [2009] UKHL 38, [2009] AC 1101, [2009] 4 All ER 677 (2012 Abr para 635) applied.

LICENSING AND GAMBLING

Halsbury's Laws of England (5th edn) vol 67 (2008) paras 1–546, vol 68 (2008) paras 547–800

Articles

For articles relating to this title please refer to the Table of Articles at the beginning of the Abridgment.

1722 Alcohol—minimum pricing—lawfulness—Scotland—freedom of trade

See *Scotch Whisky Association v Lord Advocate*, para 492.

1723 Betting—gaming machine—multi-terminal machine—value added tax on takings

See *Revenue and Customs Comrs v Rank Group plc* para 2484.

1724 Bookmaker—duty of care to employee—existence of duty—robbery causing psychiatric injury

See *Nicholls v Ladbrokes Betting & Gaming Ltd*, para 1906.

1725 Finance Act 2013

See para 2149.

1726 Gambling—company providing services—trade mark—infringement—name

See *Société Anonyme des Bains de Mer et du Cercle des Etrangers à Monaco v Anglofile International Ltd t/a Monte Carlo Entertainment*, para 2409.

1727 Gambling—Gambling Commission and National Lottery Commission—merger

The Public Bodies (Merger of the Gambling Commission and the National Lottery Commission) Order 2013, SI 2013/2329 (in force in part on 1 October 2013 and in part on 2 October 2013), abolishes the National Lottery Commission and makes provision for the transfer of its functions, property, rights and liabilities to the Gambling Commission.

1728 Gambling—horserace betting levy—betting exchanges

The Betting, Gaming and Lotteries Act 1963 s 55 defines 'bookmaker' as any person other than the Totalisator Board who (1) whether on his own account or as servant or agent to any other person, carries on, whether occasionally or regularly, the business of receiving or negotiating bets or conducting pool betting operations; or (2) by way of business in any manner holds himself out, or permits himself to be held out, as a person who receives or negotiates bets or conducts such operations.

The defendant statutory board was required pursuant to the 1963 Act to assess and collect horserace betting levy. The defendant accepted legal advice that persons who entered into betting transactions through a betting exchange, if they did so in the course of their business, were not bookmakers within the meaning of the 1963 Act so that customers of such exchanges were not required to pay the levy imposed by the 1963 Act. The essential feature of a betting exchange was that, whereas traditional bookmakers sought to generate profit by setting odds so that the amount they paid to winners was less than the stake they reclaimed from losers, the betting exchange generated revenue by charging commission on the winnings of successful customers. The claimant challenged the defendant's decision by way of judicial review, submitting that customers of betting exchanges received bets so that they fell within the definition of 'bookmaker' in s 55. The application was dismissed and the claimant appealed against that decision. *Held*, the statutory scheme distinguished between bookmakers, on whom the levy might be imposed, and their customers, who placed bets, on whom no levy could be imposed. It was not possible to do away with that distinction and say that the customers were also bookmakers. To regard those whose bets were matched on an exchange as persons who received bets was inconsistent with the division made in s 55 between those who made bets and those who received them. The user of the exchange made bets no less than the punters who made bets with the traditional bookmaker. The customer of a betting exchange never knew, when he entered a bet, whether he was offering odds or taking the odds of another customer. No customer could know, when he placed the bet, whether he was offering a bet or accepting a bet. It would be entirely arbitrary, therefore, on a construction which equated acceptance with receipt, whether the customer was making a bet or receiving a bet. The concept of acceptance thus provided no sensible means of identifying those who were bookmakers in any particular transaction. Accordingly, the appeal would be dismissed.

R (on the application of William Hill Organisation Ltd) v Horserace Betting Levy Board [2013] EWCA Civ 487, [2013] 3 All ER 297 (Court of Appeal: Maurice Kay VP, Moses and Davis LJJ). Decision of Stanley Burnton LJ [2012] EWHC 2039 (Admin), [2013] 1 All ER 109 (2012 Abr para 1693) affirmed.

1729   Gaming—gaming duty—rate—banker's profits

The Finance Act 1997 s 11(1), (2) provides that the amount of gaming duty charged on premises for a relevant accounting period is calculated by applying a specified rate of duty to the specified part of the gross gaming yield in that period from the premises. The gross gaming yield from premises in an accounting period consists of the aggregate of the gaming receipts for that period from those premises and, where a provider of the premises is banker in relation to any dutiable gaming taking place on the premises in that period, the banker's profits for that period from that gaming: s 11(8). The banker's profits from any gaming are the amount by which the value of the stakes staked with the banker in any such gaming exceeds the value of the prizes provided by the banker to those taking part in such gaming: s 11(10).

The taxpayer casino operated three incentive schemes for high value potential customers. The first provided a commission to a player proportional to the amount of his cash chips staked. The second and third provided percentage rebates on losses incurred by a player. The taxpayer claimed that the commission paid on chips staked had to be treated as reducing the value of the stakes, or alternatively as a prize for taking part in the gaming; and the rebates allowed on losses had to be treated as prizes provided by the banker to those taking part in the gaming. The Commissioners for Her Majesty's Revenue and Customs rejected these claims and the taxpayer appealed. *Held*, the value in money or money's worth of the stakes staked was the face value of the chip. Staking a chip was the same as staking money and the value in money of the chip was its face value. The stake was the amount risked in connection with the game; it was the value of that stake which was put at risk in the game. In the present case, the value put at risk in the game was not altered by reference to any commission the player received under the cash chip agreement. The taxpayer's contention that the substitution of the words 'winnings paid' in the 1997 Act s 11(10) by 'prizes provided' had extended the meaning of the provision so as to allow deduction of commissions and rebates could not be accepted. If it had been intended that the prizes to which s 11(10) referred had been intended to include the crediting of money or the crediting of an account then the 2007 Act would have said so explicitly. The 2007 Act had enlarged the concept of prizes for the purposes of remote gaming but had not done so for the purposes of the duty on premises under that Act. Accordingly, the appeal would be dismissed.

Aspinalls Club Ltd v Revenue and Customs Comrs [2013] EWCA Civ 1464, [2014] STC 602 (Court of Appeal: Moses, Black and Gloster LJJ). Decision of Upper Tribunal [2012] UKUT 242 (TCC), [2012] STC 2124 (2012 Abr para 1698) affirmed.

1730   Gaming—gaming duty—rate—payments on account

The Gaming Duty (Amendment) Regulations 2013, SI 2013/1819 (in force on 1 October 2013), further amend the 1997 Regulations, SI 1997/2196, so as to change provision which deals with the amount of payments on account; they substitute a new Table reflecting changes to the bands of gross gaming yield for gaming duty made by the Finance Act 2013 s 183, and will apply in the case of payments on account of gaming duty for any quarter that ends on or after 31 October 2013.

1731   Licensing—club premises certificate—forms and applications

See para 1732.

1732   Licensing—premises licence—forms and applications

The Licensing Act 2003 (Forms) (Amendment) Regulations 2013, SI 2013/432 (in force on 21 March 2013), further amend the Licensing Act 2003 (Premises licences and club premises certificates) Regulations 2005, SI 2005/42, by substituting the forms prescribed for the making of (1) an application to vary a premises licence; (2) an application for a minor variation to a premises licence or club premises certificate; and (3) an application to vary a club premises certificate.

1733   Licensing—premises licence—variation—application to vary—amendment of application

A bar consisted of a basement and ground floor area with a ground floor entrance. The operator of the bar applied to vary its premises licence to permit it to extend its hours and to create two separate venues, one on the ground floor and one in the basement, with a new basement entrance. The application was advertised and objections to the proposals to extend the hours and to create the new entrance were received from the local licensing authority and local residents. No objections were made to the division of the premises into two venues. After the deadline for representations had passed, the operator sought to amend its application to omit the extension of hours and the creation of the new entrance. A resident objected to the revised plans on the basis of noise, but indicated that, if suitable conditions were applied to the licence, he would no longer object. The authority granted the amended application with two additional conditions attached to the licence. The resident's appeal was dismissed and he appealed further. *Held*, in respect of an application to vary a licence, a licensing authority was limited to rejecting the application, in whole or in part, and/or to modifying the conditions of the licence to accommodate the variation in the context of the licence as a whole. Given the power of an authority to reject part of an application or to modify the licence conditions, it was open to an applicant to indicate to the authority and anyone who made relevant representations that he no longer wished to pursue part of his application, or that he was willing to agree to a modification of the licence conditions to cater for the concerns expressed. While that might be presented as an amendment to the application to vary, it did not amount to a formal amendment to the application. The issue in the present case was whether the authority was entitled to grant the variation of the licence on the basis of the original application without requiring the operator to submit a new application or at least requiring the amended application to be re-advertised. On the facts, the original licence undoubtedly allowed the ground floor entrance to be used for public access to the premises. The amended application involved a change of business that resulted in a change of intensity of use of the entrance. However, that did not require a variation of the licence to enable the operator lawfully to use the entrance for public access to the basement. After the amended application was submitted, the only variation proposed by the operator related to the internal structure and layout of the premises, in respect of which no representations were made and about which neither the resident nor anyone else had complained. The authority was lawfully entitled to make its decision and, accordingly, the appeal would be dismissed.

Taylor v Manchester City Council [2012] EWHC 3467 (Admin), [2013] 2 All ER 490 (Queen's Bench Division: Hickinbottom J).

1734   Licensing—regulated entertainment—authorisation

The Licensing Act 2003 (Descriptions of Entertainment) (Amendment) Order 2013, SI 2013/1578 (in force on 27 June 2013), amends the Licensing Act 2003 so as to provide that indoor sporting events and performances of plays or dances do not comprise regulated entertainment requiring authorisation if the audience does not exceed a specified number, the entertainment takes place between 8am and 11pm and, in relation to dance performances, the entertainment is not relevant entertainment within the meaning of the Local Government (Miscellaneous Provisions) Act 1982 Sch 3 para 2A. The order also clarifies that a contest, exhibition or display which combines boxing or wrestling with one or more martial arts is licensable under the 2003 Act as a boxing or wrestling entertainment rather than as an indoor sporting event.

1735   Licensing—sex establishment—licence fee—charge for costs of enforcement of licensing regime—lawfulness

See *R (on the application of Hemming (t/a Simply Pleasure Ltd)) v Westminster City Council*, para 2270.

1736   National Lottery—New Parks for People (England) Joint Scheme—authorisation—England

The New Parks for People (England) Joint Scheme (Authorisation) Order 2013, SI 2013/1098 (in force on 1 June 2013), authorises the New Parks for People (England) Joint Scheme until 31 May 2025 and sets out the specified matters in respect of the new scheme as required by the National Lottery etc Act 1993 Sch 3A para 3.

1737   Olympic Lottery Distributor—dissolution

The Olympic Lottery Distributor (Dissolution) Order 2013, SI 2013/207 (in force on 1 April 2013), dissolves the Olympic Lottery Distributor and (1) provides for the transfer of the property, rights and liabilities of the Distributor immediately before 1 April 2013 to the Secretary of State for Culture, Media and Sport; and (2) makes related provision for the preparation and audit of the Distributor's final accounts and the preparation of its final report.

LIEN

Halsbury's Laws of England (5th edn) vol 68 (2008) paras 801–900

Articles

For articles relating to this title please refer to the Table of Articles at the beginning of the Abridgment.

1738   Contractual lien—shipowner's lien—general average contribution—refusal to deliver cargo

See *Metall Market OOO v Vitorio Shipping Co Ltd; The Lehmann Timber*, para 140.

LIMITATION PERIODS

Halsbury's Laws of England (5th edn) vol 68 (2008) paras 901–1241

Articles

For articles relating to this title please refer to the Table of Articles at the beginning of the Abridgment.

1739   Expiry—discretion to extend—human rights claim—personal injuries

See *Bedford v Bedfordshire CC*, para 2167.

1740   Expiry—discretion to extend—personal injury—guidance

The claimant injured his back on a training course in the course of his employment with the defendant. He issued a claim form against the defendant, but his then solicitors failed to serve it prior to the expiry of the three-year limitation period for commencing personal injury actions. The claimant's application for an extension of time for service was refused. He instructed new solicitors, issued and served a new claim form, and applied to disapply the limitation period. In refusing the application, the judge cited *McDonnell* to the effect that it should not be easy for the claimant, who had failed to serve proceedings in time, to commence a second action and obtain a disapplication of the limitation period. On appeal, the claimant submitted that the judge was wrong to apply *McDonnell* as it was inconsistent with *Aktas*, which was to be preferred. *Held*, it was settled law that, on an application to disapply the three-year time limit in personal injury cases, the basic question to be asked was whether it was fair and just in all the circumstances to expect the defendant to meet the claim on the merits, notwithstanding the delay in commencement. The length of the delay was important not so much for itself as for the effect it had. The extent to which the defendant was disadvantaged in his investigation of the claim or the assembly of evidence in respect of the issues of both liability and quantum needed to be addressed. However, it was also important to consider the reasons for the delay. There was no conflict between *McDonnell* and *Aktas*. *McDonnell* said that it should not be easy to obtain a disapplication of the time limit, whereas in *Aktas* practitioners were reminded that it should not be too difficult either. Neither *McDonnell* nor *Aktas* remotely questioned the settled guidance. Accordingly, the appeal would be dismissed.

Davidson v Aegis Defences Services (BVI) Ltd [2013] EWCA Civ 1586, [2014] 2 All ER 216 (Court of Appeal: Longmore, McFarlane and Vos LJJ). *Cain v Francis; McKay v Hamlani* [2008] EWCA Civ 1451, [2009] QB 754, [2009] 2 All ER 579 (2009 Abr para 2072) applied. *McDonnell v Walker* [2009] EWCA Civ 1257, [2009] All ER (D) 259 (Nov); *Aktas v Adepta; Dixie v British Polythene Industries plc* [2010] EWCA Civ 1170, [2011] QB 894, [2011] 2 All ER 536 (2010 Abr para 1952) considered.

1741   Expiry—discretion to override time limits—burden of proof

The claimant began work for the defendant married couple as a forester and gardener. The work involved, on occasion, the use of noisy equipment. The claimant's employment by the defendants ended. The claimant attended a periodic health check arranged by his new employer at which he was informed that he might be suffering from noise-induced industrial hearing loss. The claimant was referred to hospital, which arranged for the claimant to be fitted with a hearing aid and to receive hearing therapy. The claimant attended a review appointment at which the doctor recorded that the claimant had tinnitus and hearing loss following noise exposure at work. The claimant instructed a firm of solicitors to pursue a claim for personal injuries sustained during his employment by the defendants. The defendants denied liability and asserted that the claim was barred under the Limitation Act 1980 s 11. The question of limitation was tried as a preliminary issue. The district judge held that the claimant's date of knowledge for the purposes of s 14 was when his solicitor had advised him that he could bring a claim, within the three-year limitation period. A circuit judge allowed the claimant's appeal on the basis that his date of knowledge had been when he had undergone a health check, and therefore outside the limitation period. The judge further held that the claimant had a particularly heavy burden to satisfy the court under s 33 that it should exercise its discretion and allow the action to proceed after such a long delay and, in the circumstances, that it was not appropriate to exercise that discretion. The claimant appealed. *Held*, there was no doubt that if a claimant commenced proceedings out of time and asked the court, in the exercise of its discretion under s 33, to disapply ss 11, 11A or 12, then the burden was on the claimant to persuade the court by evidence and argument that such a direction was appropriate. Such a claimant was seeking the indulgence of the court and such indulgence was exceptional, in the sense that the claimant was seeking an exemption from the normal consequences of failing to commence proceedings within the limitation period. Once it was established which party had the burden in relation to a particular issue, it was not helpful to discuss in the abstract whether that burden was a heavy one or a light one. How difficult or easy it was for the claimant to discharge the burden would depend on the facts of the particular case. All that could be said in relation to s 33 at a level of generality was that the burden was on the claimant. The judge, in stating that the claimant had a 'particularly heavy burden' to satisfy the court under s 33 had applied the wrong test. He ought simply to have said that the burden was on the claimant. Since the judge had applied the wrong test, it fell to the present court to re-exercise the discretion conferred by s 33. The task of the court was to weigh up the prejudice to the claimant if his claim was barred by s 11 and the prejudice to the defendant if the action was allowed to proceed despite having been started out of time. In the circumstances, the prejudice to the defendants under the second limb outweighed the prejudice to the claimant under the first limb. Accordingly, the appeal would be dismissed.

Sayers v Lord Chelwood [2012] EWCA Civ 1715, [2013] 2 All ER 232 (Court of Appeal: Arden, Jackson and Kitchin LJJ). *AB v Ministry of Defence* [2012] UKSC 9, [2012] 3 All ER 673 (2012 Abr para 1715) applied.

1742   Possession of land—adverse possession—mistake in land register—rectification

See *Parshall v Hackney*, para 2129.

1743   Time from which period runs—construction contract—breach—adjudicator's decision—payment in compliance with decision

See *Aspect Contracts (Asbestos) Ltd v Higgins Construction plc*, para 112.

LOCAL GOVERNMENT FINANCE

Halsbury's Laws of England (5th edn) vol 70 (2012) paras 1–516

Articles

For articles relating to this title please refer to the Table of Articles at the beginning of the Abridgment.

1744   Accounts and audit—Wales

The Accounts and Audit (Wales) (Amendment) Regulations 2013, SI 2013/217 (in force on 1 March 2013), further amend the 2005 Regulations, SI 2005/368, so as to provide that, instead of police authorities, police and crime commissioners and chief constables are subject to the requirement to prepare a statement of accounts.

1745   Calculation of budgetary requirements—Wales

The Local Authorities (Alteration of Requisite Calculations) (Wales) Regulations 2013, SI 2013/216 (in force on 28 February 2013), which apply to the financial year beginning on 1 April 2013, amend the Local Government Finance Act 1992 so as to (1) exclude (a) expenditure to be charged to a business improvement district revenue account from the expenditure that a billing authority must aggregate under s 32(2); and (b) business improvement district levy or financial contributions made by a person under the Local Government Act 2003 s 43 and sums payable by the Welsh Ministers under s 31 in respect of an authority's council tax reduction scheme from the income that the authority must aggregate under the 1992 Act s 32(3); (2) provide (a) that an authority is expressly required to take into account any expenditure it expects to incur in the year in repaying grants or redistributed non-domestic rates; and (b) that an authority is expressly required to take into account payments of redistributed non-domestic rates and grants that it expects to receive for an earlier financial year; (3) ensure that the amounts of redistributed non-domestic rates and revenue support grant excluded from the budget requirement calculation in ss 32, 33 relate only to such amounts payable under the respective local government reports for a particular year; and (4) provide that (a) a major precepting authority is expressly required to take into account any expenditure that it expects to incur in the year in repaying grants or redistributed non-domestic rates; (b) an authority is expressly required to take into account payments of redistributed non-domestic rates and grants that it expects to receive for an earlier financial year; and (c) major precepting authorities must take into account any floor funding received from the Secretary of State for a financial year when making the required calculation for that year.

1746   Capital finance and accounting—England

The Local Authorities (Capital Finance and Accounting) (England) (Amendment) Regulations 2013, SI 2013/476 (in force in part on 31 March 2013 and in part on 1 April 2013), further amend the 2003 Regulations, SI 2003/3146, so as to (1) provide for the calculation of the sub-liability, which forms part of the poolable amount; (2) permit local authorities to use capital receipts received on or after 1 April 2012 to make back payments of equal pay costs; (3) extend, until and including 31 March 2018, the ability of local authorities to defer charging liabilities for back payments following unequal pay to a revenue account until the date on which a back payment must actually be paid; and (4) describe the dwellings to which head (1) relates.

The Local Authorities (Capital Finance and Accounting) (England) (Amendment) (No 2) Regulations 2013, SI 2013/1751 (in force on 13 August 2013), further amend the 2003 Regulations above by amending the definitions of 'sub-liability' and the value of 'F'.

1747   Council tax—administration and enforcement—England

The Council Tax (Administration and Enforcement) (Amendment) (England) Regulations 2013, SI 2013/590 (in force on 10 April 2013), further amend the 1992 Regulations, SI 1992/613, in relation to Wales, by (1) taking into account penalties under the Council Tax Reduction Schemes (Detection of Fraud and Enforcement) (England) Regulations 2013, SI 2013/501 (see PARA 1760), which relate to local council tax reduction schemes introduced through the Local Government Finance Act 2012; and (2) prescribing the purposes for which information may be supplied to a qualifying person, the purposes for which such information may be used by such a person and the purposes for which it may be supplied to another qualifying person.

1748   Council tax—administration and enforcement—Wales

The Council Tax (Administration and Enforcement) (Amendment) (Wales) Regulations 2013, SI 2013/62 (in force in part on 7 February 2013 and in part on 1 April 2013), enable the Council Tax Reduction Schemes and Prescribed Requirements (Wales) Regulations 2012, SI 2012/3144, to be taken into account in the billing and enforcement of council tax. Specifically, the regulations (1) enable a billing authority, unless a hard copy is requested, to supply the information required to be supplied with a council tax demand notice by publishing that information on a website; (2) prevent billing authorities from sharing information supplied under the Local Government Finance Act 1992 Sch 2 para 15B or the Welfare Reform Act 2012 s 131 with other authorities under the Council Tax (Administration and Enforcement) Regulations 1992, SI 1992/613; and (3) provide for a person to request to pay their council tax in twelve monthly instalments rather than ten.

The Council Tax (Administration and Enforcement) (Amendment No 2) (Wales) Regulations 2013, SI 2013/570 (in force in part on 1 April 2013 and in part on 29 April 2013), further amend the 1992 Regulations above in relation to Wales, by (1) adding definitions of 'council tax offences', 'detection of fraud regulations' and 'universal credit'; (2) setting out the purposes for which a Revenue and Customs official may supply information relating to council tax to a qualifying person, the other purposes this information may be used for, and the purposes for which this information can be supplied to another qualifying person; (3) providing for the collection of penalties imposed in accordance with the Council Tax Reduction Schemes (Detection of Fraud and Enforcement) (Wales) Regulations 2013, SI 2013/588 (see PARA 1761); (4) making changes consequential on the introduction of universal credit; and (5) permitting the collection of penalties imposed in accordance with the Council Tax Reduction Schemes (Detection of Fraud and Enforcement) (Wales) Regulations 2013 as outstanding liabilities on death.

1749   Council tax—approval of increases—referendums—England

The Local Authorities (Conduct of Referendums) (Council Tax Increases) (England) (Amendment) Regulations 2013, SI 2013/409 (in force on 26 February 2013), amend the 2012 Regulations, SI 2012/444, so as to make changes (1) to the question to be asked in a referendum held in accordance with the Local Government Finance Act 1992 Pt 1 Ch 4ZA (ss 52ZA–52Z); and (2) to the form of ballot paper used in the referendum to reflect the revised wording of the referendum question.

The Local Authority (Referendums Relating to Council Tax Increases) (Date of Referendum) (England) Order 2013, SI 2013/2862 (in force on 6 December 2013), specifies 22 May 2014 as the latest date in the financial year beginning 1 April 2014 by which a billing authority may hold a referendum on an increase in the relevant basic amount of council tax for that financial year.

1750   Council tax—collection funds—England

The Local Authorities (Funds) (England) (Amendment) Regulations 2013, SI 2013/2974 (in force on 20 December 2013), further amend the 1992 Regulations, SI 1992/2428, so as to provide that (1) agreed variations to precept payments in a financial year where a billing authority estimates that there will be a deficit to the collection fund for that year as a result of a council tax reduction scheme are properly taken into account in the formulae for calculating how the surplus or deficit estimates are to be shared among or borne between a billing authority and its relevant major precepting authorities; and (2) billing authorities repay precept payment variations where there is no surplus or deficit in the collection fund at the point at which the surplus and deficit calculations are made.

1751   Council tax—demand notices—England

The Council Tax and Non-Domestic Rating (Demand Notices) (England) (Amendment) Regulations 2013, SI 2013/694 (in force on 18 April 2013), which apply in relation to

England only, further amend the 2003 Regulations, SI 2003/2613, so as to substitute the explanatory notes in Pts 1 and 3 and the additional paragraph to be included in the notes for rural settlement authorities in Pt 2.

1752   Council tax—demand notices—Wales

The Council Tax (Demand Notices) (Wales) (Amendment) Regulations 2013, SI 2013/63 (in force on 7 February 2013), further amend the 1993 Regulations, SI 1993/255, so as to take into account the introduction of local council tax reduction schemes in accordance with the requirements of the Council Tax Reduction Schemes and Prescribed Requirements (Wales) Regulations 2012, SI 2012/3144. In particular, the regulations (1) ensure that demand notices refer to reductions where relevant; and (2) provide for a new statement to be included on a demand notice where a reduction under a local council tax reduction scheme applies, explaining the amount of the reduction, the reason for it and the possible consequences of failing to comply with duties to notify the billing authority of relevant charges in circumstances.

1753   Council tax—discount disregards—England

The Council Tax (Additional Provisions for Discount Disregards) (Amendment) (England) Regulations 2013, SI 2013/725 (in force on 8 April 2013), further amend the 1992 Regulations, SI 1992/552, so as to change the requirements which must be fulfilled by care workers under the 1992 Regulations so that care workers providing care to a person who is entitled to an attendance allowance at any rate or the highest or middle rate of the care component of a disability living allowance under the Social Security Contributions and Benefits Act 1992 fulfil the requirements necessary to be disregarded for the purposes of the Local Government Finance Act 1992 s 11.

1754   Council tax—discount disregards—Wales

The Council Tax (Discount Disregards) (Amendment) (Wales) Order 2013, SI 2013/638 (in force in part on 8 April 2013 and in part on 29 April 2013), amends the 1992 Order, SI 1992/548, which prescribes that, to be disregarded for the purposes of council tax discounts, a severely mentally impaired person must be in receipt of a qualifying benefit, (1) so that the daily living component of personal independence payment is included within the definition of a qualifying benefit; and (2) so as to include universal credit, which comprises an amount paid to a person due to that person's limited capability for work or limited capability for work and work related activity, within the definition of a qualifying benefit.

The Council Tax (Discount Disregards) (Amendment No 2) (Wales) Order 2013, SI 2013/1048 (in force on 24 May 2013), further amends the 1992 Order above so as to provide that persons in receipt of armed forces independence payment are disregarded for the purposes of council tax discounts.

The Council Tax (Additional Provisions for Discount Disregards) (Amendment) (Wales) Regulations 2013, SI 2013/639 (in force on 8 April 2013), further amend the 1992 Regulations, SI 1992/552, so as to (1) change the conditions which must be fulfilled by care workers under the 1992 Regulations so that care workers providing care to a person entitled to an attendance allowance at any rate or the highest or middle rate of the care component of a disability living allowance under the Social Security Contributions and Benefits Act 1992 fulfil the requirements necessary to be disregarded for the purposes of the Local Government Finance Act 1992 s 11; and (2) amend the requirements of the 1992 Regulations so that care workers providing care to a person entitled to the standard or enhanced rate of the daily living component of a personal independence payment under the Welfare Reform Act 2012 fulfil the requirements necessary to be disregarded for the purposes of the 1992 Act s 11.

The Council Tax (Additional Provisions for Discount Disregards) (Amendment No 2) (Wales) Regulations 2013, SI 2013/1049 (in force on 24 May 2013), further amend the 1992 Regulations above so as to provide that care workers providing care to a person entitled to armed forces independence payment are disregarded for the purposes of council tax discounts.

1755   Council tax—Greater London Authority—consolidated council tax requirement—
        procedure
See para 1808.

1756   Council tax—liability—definition of dwelling—England
See para 1779.

1757   Council tax—reduction schemes—annexes—England
The Council Tax (Reductions for Annexes) (England) Regulations 2013, SI 2013/2977 (in
force on 1 April 2013), which apply in relation to England only, prescribe a 50 per cent
reduction in the amount of council tax payable for people living in annexes provided that
they are related to the person liable to pay the council tax of the main dwelling, and for
those people living in dwellings with annexes which are unoccupied provided they are using
those annexes as part of their main residence.

1758   Council tax—reduction schemes—consultation—lawfulness
The Local Government Finance Act 1992 Sch 1A para 3(1) provides that, before making a
council tax reduction scheme, a billing authority must, in the following order (1) consult
any major precepting authority which has power to issue a precept to it; (2) publish a draft
scheme in such manner as it thinks fit; and (3) consult such other persons as it considers are
likely to have an interest in the operation of the scheme. Having made a scheme, the
authority must publish it in such manner as the authority thinks fit: Sch 1A para 3(3).
    The government decided to abolish council tax benefit and replace it with council tax
reduction schemes that were locally determined by each billing authority under the 1992 Act
s 13A. The defendant local authority approved its officers' recommendation that it consult
with the Greater London Authority in respect of its scheme. The defendant subsequently
published its draft scheme and commenced a consultation exercise which ran for almost
three months. An explanatory document was delivered to all council tax benefit claimant
households in the defendant's area, was published on the defendant's website, and was
prominently displayed at the defendant's main offices and other locations such as libraries
and citizens advice bureaus. It was also discussed at various forums. During the course of
the consultation exercise, the government announced a transitional grant scheme which
made additional funding available to those authorities whose council tax reduction schemes
met certain criteria. Details of the transitional scheme were contained in a circular and were
published on the Department for Communities and Local Government website. The
defendant accepted the recommendation in the officers' reports and in due course made its
scheme. The claimant applied for judicial review of the defendant's decision to make its
scheme, contending that (1) the consultees had not been provided with sufficient
information to enable them to appreciate that there were alternatives to the draft scheme;
and (2) the defendant should have told consultees about the transitional scheme and asked
them if they wished to make any, or further, responses in the light of the availability of that
scheme. The application was dismissed and, on the claimant's appeal, *held*, unlike some
statutory provisions which provided for a more open-textured consultation process, Sch 1A
para 3(1) prescribed a sequential process in which a draft scheme was prepared, and the
defendant then consulted, not the council tax payers as a whole, or all of its inhabitants who
were in receipt of its services, but only those persons who were likely to have an interest in
the operation of the draft scheme. In that statutory context, fairness had not required the
defendant in the consultation process to mention other options which it had decided not to
incorporate into its published draft scheme; much less had it required that the consultation
document contain an explanation as to why those options were not incorporated into the
draft scheme. In any event, the present case was not one in which the failure to mention the
three options in the consultation document might have had the consequence that the
decision-maker would have failed to appreciate their existence. A holistic approach ought to
be adopted where a new factor emerged during the course of the consultation process.
Relevant factors included, in addition to the nature and significance of the new material,
such matters as the extent to which the new material was in the public domain, thereby
affording consultees the opportunity to comment on its relevance to the proposal the subject
of the consultation, and the practical implications, including cost and delay, of further
consultation. While the transitional scheme was plainly relevant, it was not a change of such

significance that the defendant would have been bound to draw it to the attention of what would, inevitably have been a much broader category of consultees than the current council tax benefit claimant households in its area. Accordingly, the appeal would be dismissed.

R (*on the application of Stirling*) *v Haringey LBC* [2013] EWCA Civ 116, [2013] LGR 251 (Court of Appeal: Sir Terence Etherton C, Sullivan and Pitchford LJJ).

1759   Council tax—reduction schemes—default scheme—Wales

The Council Tax Reduction Schemes (Default Scheme) (Wales) Regulations 2013, SI 2013/3035 (in force on 28 November 2013), set out a default scheme in relation to council tax reduction. In particular, the regulations (1) provide the procedure for reduction applications and appeals; (2) specify the classes of person entitled and not entitled to a reduction under the scheme; (3) set out matters relevant to determining eligibility for a reduction and the amount of reduction under the scheme; (4) prescribe how income and capital of the applicant and others is treated in calculating eligibility for a reduction, including in cases where an applicant or partner has an award of universal credit; (5) provide for the application of the scheme to students; (6) provide for extended reductions in certain circumstances; (7) set out the period of entitlement and how a change in circumstances affects any reduction; (8) provide for the making of an application for a reduction; (9) set out the time within which an authority must make its decision on the application and provide for notification of the decision; (10) make provision about the award or payment of a reduction; and (11) set out the matters which must be included within notifications.

1760   Council tax—reduction schemes—detection of fraud and enforcement—England

The Council Tax Reduction Schemes (Detection of Fraud and Enforcement) (England) Regulations 2013, SI 2013/501 (in force in part on 7 March 2013 and in part on 20 March 2013), make provision for powers to require information, the creation of offences and powers to impose penalties in connection with council tax reduction schemes. In particular, the regulations (1) provide that a billing authority may grant an authorisation to an individual to exercise the powers conferred on an authorised officer; (2) enable authorised officers to require information from specified persons for the purpose of preventing, detecting and securing evidence of the commission, whether by particular persons or more generally, of offences connected with an application for or award of a reduction under a council tax reduction scheme; (3) enable a billing authority to require the persons specified to enter into arrangements under which authorised officers are allowed access to electronic records; a billing authority may require a person to enter into such arrangements where it appears that facilities exist under which access to those records is being provided or is capable of being provided; in addition, the records must contain or be likely to contain information about a matter relevant to the purpose of preventing, detecting and securing evidence of the commission (whether by particular persons or more generally) of offences connected with an application for or award of a reduction under a council tax reduction scheme; (4) provide that it is an offence intentionally to delay or obstruct an authorised officer in the exercise of any of the powers to require information; it is also an offence for a person to refuse or fail (without reasonable excuse) to comply with a requirement to enter into arrangements for access to electronic records, or to provide information when required to do so; (5) create an offence of making a statement or representation which is known to be false for the purpose of obtaining a reduction under a council tax reduction scheme; it is also an offence for a person to provide or knowingly cause or allow to be provided a document or information which that person knows to be false in a material particular, for that purpose; (6) create an offence where there has been a change of circumstances which a person knows affects his entitlement to a reduction, and the person fails to give a notice of the change as required by an authority's scheme by virtue of the Council Tax Reduction Schemes (Prescribed Requirements) (England) Regulations 2012, SI 2012/2885 or the Council Tax Reduction Schemes (Default Scheme) (England) Regulations 2012, SI 2012/2886; it is also an offence to cause or allow a person to fail to give this notification; (7) make provision for offences under the regulations committed by bodies corporate; (8) set out the time limit for commencing proceedings for an offence under the regulations; (9) enable a billing authority to invite a person to agree to pay a penalty as an alternative to prosecution for an offence relating to the award of a reduction under a council tax reduction scheme which a person was not entitled to, or an offence relating to an act or omission which could have resulted in such an award; and (10) enable a billing authority to impose a penalty of £70 on a person in circumstances such as where a person negligently makes an incorrect statement in connection with an application for a reduction under a council tax reduction scheme or where a person fails to notify a change of circumstances when required to do so under a scheme.

1761   Council tax—reduction schemes—detection of fraud and enforcement—Wales

The Council Tax Reduction Schemes (Detection of Fraud and Enforcement) (Wales) Regulations 2013, SI 2013/588 (in force in part on 13 March 2013 and in part on 26 March 2013), make provision for the creation of offences and for powers to require information and to impose penalties in connection with council tax reduction schemes and the default scheme. In particular, the regulations (1) provide that a billing authority may grant an authorisation to an individual to exercise the powers conferred on an authorised officer under the regulations; (2) enable officers authorised under the regulations to require information from specified persons for the purpose of preventing, detecting and securing evidence of the commission of offences connected with an application for or award of a reduction under a council tax reduction scheme or the default scheme; (3) enable a billing authority to require the persons specified in the regulations to enter into arrangements under which authorised officers are allowed access to electronic records; such arrangements may be required where it appears to a billing authority that facilities exist under which access to those records is being provided or is capable of being provided and the records contain or are likely to contain information about a matter relevant to the purpose of preventing, detecting and securing evidence of the commission of offences connected with an application for or award of a reduction under a council tax reduction scheme or the default scheme; (4) provide that it is an offence intentionally to delay or obstruct an authorised officer in the exercise of any power under the regulations to require information; it is also an offence for a person to refuse or fail, without reasonable excuse, to comply with a requirement to enter into arrangements for access to electronic records, or to provide information when required to do so; (5) create an offence of making a statement or representation which is known to be false for the purpose of obtaining a reduction under a council tax reduction scheme or the default scheme; it is also an offence to provide or knowingly cause or allow to be provided a document or information which is false for that purpose; (6) create an offence where there has been a change of circumstances which a person knows affects that person's entitlement to a reduction, and that person fails to give notice of a change as required by an authority's council tax reduction scheme or the default scheme; it is also an offence to cause or allow a person to fail to give this notification; (7) create an offence where a person dishonestly makes a false statement or representation for the purpose of obtaining a reduction under a council tax reduction scheme or the default scheme; it is also an offence dishonestly to provide or cause or allow to be provided a document or information which is false for that purpose; (8) create an offence where there has been a change of circumstances which a person knows affects that person's entitlement to a reduction, and that person dishonestly fails to give notice of a change as required by an authority's council tax reduction scheme or the default scheme; it also provides that it is an offence dishonestly to cause or allow a person to fail to give this notification; (9) make provision for offences under the regulations committed by bodies corporate; (10) set out the time limit for commencing proceedings for an offence under the regulations; (11) enable a billing authority to invite a person to agree to pay a penalty as an alternative to prosecution for an offence relating to the award of a reduction under a council tax reduction scheme to which a person was not entitled, or an offence relating to an act or omission which could have resulted in such an award; and (12) enable a billing authority to impose a penalty of £70 on a person in circumstances such as where a person negligently makes an incorrect statement in connection with an application for a reduction under a council tax reduction scheme or the default scheme or where a person fails to notify a change of circumstances when required to do so under such a scheme.

1762   Council tax—reduction schemes—prescribed requirements—England

The Council Tax Reduction Schemes (Prescribed Requirements) (England) (Amendment) Regulations 2013, SI 2013/3181 (in force on 13 January 2014), further amend the

2012 Regulations, SI 2012/2885, in order to (1) provide that the rights of a jobseeker under those regulations are not to be treated as a right to reside for the purposes of entitlement under a council tax reduction scheme; (2) update a provision clarifying when a person has leave to remain in the United Kingdom such that he is not required to show habitual residence; (3) provide that persons in receipt of certain income-related benefits, together with nationals of Croatia who are subject to and treated as workers under the worker authorisation scheme, are not required to show habitual residence; (4) provide that persons subject to immigration control are eligible for a reduction where they are persons who benefit from the European Convention on Social and Medical Assistance or the European Social Charter; (5) increase certain of the figures which are used in calculating whether a person is entitled to a reduction and, if so, the amount of that reduction; (6) provide that a non-dependant deduction will not be made in respect of a member of the armed forces away on operations; and (7) provide for the disregard, when assessing an applicant's capital, of certain payments made by local government for welfare purposes, certain arrears of universal credit and payments made to annuitants of the Equitable Life Assurance Company.

1763 Council tax—reduction schemes—prescribed requirements—Wales

The Council Tax Reduction Schemes and Prescribed Requirements (Wales) Regulations 2013, SI 2013/3029 (in force on 28 November 2013), require each billing authority in Wales to make a scheme specifying the reductions which are to apply to amounts of council tax payable by persons, or classes of person, considered to be in financial need. In particular, the regulations (1) make provision about scheme requirements in relation to billing authorities in Wales, including classes of person, reductions and scheme procedural requirements; (2) prescribe classes of persons who must be included in an authority's scheme; (3) specify classes of person who must not be included in an authority's scheme; (4) prescribe the matters that must be included in an authority's scheme in relation to pensioners; (5) set out the rules relevant to determining the eligibility of pensioners for a reduction and the amount of reduction under a scheme; (6) set out how income and capital of pensioners is to be treated in calculating eligibility for a reduction; (7) prescribe the matters that must be included in an authority's scheme in relation to persons who are not pensioners; (8) set out the rules relevant to determining the eligibility of non-pensioners for a reduction and the amount of reduction under a scheme; (9) specify how income and capital of non-pensioners is to be treated in calculating eligibility for a reduction, including in cases where a non-pensioner or partner has an award of universal credit; (10) provide for the application of the scheme to students; and (11) prescribe the matters that must be included in an authority's scheme in respect of all applicants.

1764 Council tax—reduction schemes—prescribed requirements and default scheme—Wales

The Council Tax Reduction Schemes (Prescribed Requirements and Default Scheme) (Wales) (Amendment) Regulations 2013, SI 2013/112 (in force on 23 January 2013), amend the Council Tax Reduction Schemes and Prescribed Requirements (Wales) Regulations 2012, SI 2012/3144, and the Council Tax Reduction Schemes (Default Scheme) (Wales) Regulations 2012, SI 2012/3145, so as to increase, from 90 per cent to 100 per cent, the maximum amount of council tax reduction a person can receive under an authority's scheme, and increase certain of the figures which are used in calculating whether a person is entitled to a reduction, and the amount of that reduction. The up-rated figures relate to adjustments made to the maximum amount of reduction a person can receive to take account of adults living in the dwelling who are not dependants of the applicant, and the amount against which an applicant's income is compared in order to determine the amount of reduction to which the applicant is entitled.

1765 Council tax—reduction schemes—transitional provision—England

The Council Tax Reduction Schemes (Transitional Provision) (England) Regulations 2013, SI 2013/215 (in force on 6 March 2013), make transitional provision in relation to the commencement of schemes specifying the reductions which are to apply to amounts of council tax payable by persons, or classes of person, whom the authority considers are in financial need.

1766   Council tax—reduction schemes—transitional provision—Wales

The Council Tax Reduction Schemes (Transitional Provisions) (Wales) Regulations 2013, SI 2013/111 (in force on 23 January 2013), set out the transitional provisions that will apply to persons who are in receipt of, or who have made an application for, council tax benefit when the reduction schemes set out in the Council Tax Reduction Schemes and Prescribed Requirements (Wales) (Regulations) 2012, SI 2012/3144, come into force on 1 April 2013.

1767   Council tax—valuation lists—alteration of lists and appeals—England

The Council Tax (Alteration of Lists and Appeals) (England) (Amendment) Regulations 2013, SI 2013/467 (in force on 1 April 2013), amend the 2009 Regulations, SI 2009/2270, so as to introduce a new restriction on alteration to the valuation band applicable to a dwelling in relation to which a lease under a rent-a-roof or similar scheme for the installation of solar panels or other micro-generation plants has been granted or transferred on sale.

1768   Growth and Infrastructure Act 2013

See para 2022.

1769   Local authority—contractors—powers—England

The Local Authorities (Contracting Out of Tax Billing, Collection and Enforcement Functions) (Amendment) (England) Order 2013, SI 2013/502 (in force on 7 March 2013), amends the 1996 Order, SI 1996/1880, so as to make provision to enable billing authorities to authorise contractors to give notification of a decision about an application for a reduction of council tax, determining whether the payment of a reduction should be made, payment of such a reduction and collecting penalties under the Council Tax Reduction Schemes (Detection of Fraud and Enforcement) (England) Regulations 2013, SI 2013/501 (see PARA 1760).

1770   Local authority—contractors—powers—Wales

The Local Authorities (Contracting Out of Tax Billing, Collection and Enforcement Functions) (Amendment) (Wales) Order 2013, SI 2013/695 (in force on 23 March 2013), amends the 1996 Order, SI 1996/1880, so as to make provision to enable billing authorities to authorise contractors to give notification of a decision about an application for a reduction of council tax, determining whether the payment of a reduction should be made, payment of such a reduction and collecting penalties under the Council Tax Reduction Schemes (Detection of Fraud and Enforcement) (Wales) Regulations 2013, SI 2013/588 (see PARA 1761).

1771   Local authority—finance—calculation of budgetary requirements—library services

The mayor of the respondent local authority decided to make changes that would have affected fourteen of the libraries in the area. The full council wished to retain the existing level of service and it passed an amendment to the budget which had been presented for approval by the mayor. The amendment did not pass the mayor's proposal for a reduction in the library services and instead allocated the money to achieve a full retention of library services. Following the passing of the amendment, the mayor said that he would not spend the full budget as per the amendment. The applicant sought judicial review of the mayor's decision, seeking a declaration that he had acted unlawfully in refusing to implement the budget amendment determined by the full council. The application was dismissed on the basis that the mayor's decision had been neither contrary to the budget nor contrary to a 'plan or strategy' within the meaning of the Local Authorities (Functions and Responsibilities) (England) Regulations 2000, SI 2000/2853, Sch 4. The applicant appealed. Consideration was given to the Local Government Act 2000 ss 9C, 9D and the Local Government Finance Act 1992 s 31A(1), (2). *Held*, s 31A(2)(a) gave the full council no power to interfere with the executive function of the mayor, except where the mayor proposed to exercise the function in a way that was contrary to, or not wholly in accordance with the respondent's budget or contrary to a plan or strategy adopted or approved by the respondent. That required determining whether a matter would incur expenditure in excess of that for which budget approval had been given by the full council. The 2000 Regulations Sch 4 para 2 provided that the determination of a matter was not the responsibility of the executive if it was minded to determine the matter contrary to, or not wholly in accordance with the respondent's budget. Thus, the full council was not permitted to micro-manage the respondent's functions and interfere with the executive functions of the mayor. The full council could not require the mayor to expend money in a particular way, or, unless he proposed to act in a way contrary to the plans and strategies reserved to the full council, to expend money on a particular function. The language of 'plan or strategy', read in the context of the 2000 Regulations, denoted something that operated at a general level. It could not embrace any and every decision that might be taken on an individual issue. If it did, it would undermine the basic distinction between executive and non-executive functions which lay at the heart of the 2000 Act. The full council might, in certain respects, set the policy framework for the respondent, but its detailed implementation was a matter for the executive. The mayor's budget proposals in relation to the library services had not comprised a plan or strategy. Accordingly, the appeal would be dismissed.

R (on the application of Buck) v Doncaster MBC [2013] EWCA Civ 1190, [2013] LGR 847 (Court of Appeal: Lord Dyson MR, McCombe and Gloster LJJ).

1772   Rating—non-domestic rating—central rating list—England

The Central Rating List (England) (Amendment) Regulations 2013, SI 2013/408 (in force on 1 April 2013), further amend the 2005 Regulations, SI 2005/551, by removing two companies from the list of persons designated in relation to electricity distribution and electricity meter hereditaments.

The Central Rating List (England) (Amendment) (No 2) Regulations 2013, SI 2013/2887 (in force on 13 December 2013), which have effect from 1 April 2013, further amend the principal regulations above by making an alteration to the provisions dealing with long-distance pipeline hereditaments in order to reflect a change in ownership of a pipeline.

1773   Non-domestic rating—contributions—Wales

The Non-Domestic Rating Contributions (Wales) (Amendment) Regulations 2013, SI 2013/3046 (in force on 31 December 2013), further amend the 1992 Regulations, SI 1992/3238, by substituting Sch 4 which makes provision for adult population figures.

1774   Non-domestic rating—demand notices—England

See para 1751.

1775   Non-domestic rating—designated areas

The Non-Domestic Rating (Designated Areas) Regulations 2013, SI 2013/107 (in force on 18 February 2013), (1) designate the areas in relation to which a proportion of the non-domestic rating income is to be disregarded in certain calculations; (2) specify that the designations take effect on 1 April 2013 and have effect for a period of 25 years; and (3) provide for the calculation of the proportion of non-domestic rating income that is to be disregarded.

1776   Non-domestic rating—local retention—general and collection funds

The Local Government Finance Act 2012 (Consequential Amendments) Order 2013, SI 2013/733 (in force on 27 March 2013), amends the Local Government Finance Act 1992 and the Greater London Authority Act 1999 in consequence of changes made by the Local Government Finance Act 2012 to the way in which income from non-domestic rates is distributed. In particular, the 2013 Order (1) amends the provisions of the 1992 Act which govern the manner in which billing authorities are required to calculate their council tax requirements as a result of the new local retention scheme, so that transfers between the general fund and the collection fund are accounted for correctly in the calculations; and (2) amends both Acts so as to (a) insert definitions of 'locally retained non-domestic rates'; (b) change the definition of 'local government finance report'; and (c) substitute references to 'redistributed non-domestic rates' with references to 'locally retained non-domestic rates'.

1777 Non-domestic rating—local retention—levy and safety net

The Non-Domestic Rating (Levy and Safety Net) Regulations 2013, SI 2013/737 (in force on 27 March 2013), make provision for the calculation of safety net payments due to, or levies payable by, an authority or pool of authorities under the system of locally retained non-domestic rates established by the Local Government Finance Act 1988 Sch 7B. In particular, the 2013 Regulations (1) prescribe the manner in which retained rates income is to be calculated for different types of authority; (2) specify business rates baselines and baseline funding levels for specified authorities; (3) prescribe the method of calculation of an authority's individual levy rate and safety net threshold; (4) allow authorities to request safety net payments on account from the Secretary of State and make provision for the manner in which such payments are to be made; (5) set out the circumstances in which the Secretary of State must make a safety net payment, calculated in a prescribed manner, to an authority; and (6) set out the circumstances in which an authority must make a levy payment, calculated in a prescribed manner, to the Secretary of State.

1778 Non-domestic rating—rates retention—England

The Non-Domestic Rating (Rates Retention) Regulations 2013, SI 2013/452 (in force on 1 March 2013), provide for the payment by billing authorities of a proportion of their non-domestic rating income to the Secretary of State ('the central share'). In particular, the regulations (1) define 'non-domestic rating income' as an estimate of the aggregate of amounts that will be charged and credited to a billing authority's income and expenditure account with respect to non-domestic rates in each year; (2) provide for an amount to be deducted from the central share payment where rates relief has been granted in a prescribed area and for the deduction to be shared with major precepting authorities in specified circumstances; (3) require billing authorities to pay a proportion of their non-domestic rating income to major precepting authorities; (4) require a billing authority to pay to a county council an amount that is disregarded in respect of a hereditament because it falls within a designated class if the council was the planning authority for the purposes of determining the application that led to the hereditament falling within that class; (5) provide for the transfer of a billing authority's share of its income, plus an amount for its costs of collection and disregarded and deducted amounts, to the authority's general fund; (6) require billing authorities to carry out further calculations at the end of the year, to have the calculations certificated, and to make adjustments so that if they have made provision for bad or doubtful debt that is disallowed by the auditor that carries out the certification, they must carry the cost rather than it being shared with the Secretary of State and the major precepting authorities; (7) provide for the reconciliation of differences between amounts notified at the start of the year and certified amounts; (8) provide for the calculation of surpluses and deficits on collection funds; and (9) set out when payments are to be made and the consequences of late payment.

1779 Non-domestic rating—rating lists—definition of 'domestic property'—England

The Non-Domestic Rating and Council Tax (Definition of Domestic Property and Dwelling) (England) Order 2013, SI 2013/468 (in force on 1 April 2013), amends the definition of (1) 'domestic property' in the Local Government Finance Act 1988 s 66 (property which is not subject to non-domestic rates) so as to include property used for the purpose of small-scale energy generation using sustainable technologies such as solar and wind ('micro-generation'); and (2) 'dwelling' in the Local Government Finance Act 1992 s 3 (meaning of dwelling for the purposes of assessing liability to council tax) so as to exclude property used for the purpose of micro-generation except in so far as it forms part of a larger property which is itself a dwelling.

1780 Non-domestic rating—renewable energy projects—England

The Non-Domestic Rating (Renewable Energy Projects) Regulations 2013, SI 2013/108 (in force on 18 February 2013), designate classes of hereditaments in relation to which a billing authority may disregard an amount of non-domestic rating income for the purpose of certain calculations concerning local retention of non-domestic rates. In particular, the regulations (1) make general provision for certificates by valuation officers; (2) designate (a) new renewable power stations; (b) existing renewable power stations; (c) renewable power stations created from hereditaments under head (2)(b); (d) energy from waste plants;

(e) hereditaments which generate electricity, but are primarily used for other purposes; and (f) cables and sub-stations associated with offshore generating plants as classes of hereditaments in relation to which a proportion of non-domestic rating income is to be disregarded; (3) give effect to the designations as of 1 April 2013; and (4) provide for the calculation of the amounts to be disregarded for the purpose of calculations under the rates retention scheme.

1781   Non-domestic rating—single hereditament—separate floors in building—two floors under separate leases

Under two separate leases, the respondent firm of accountants occupied the second and sixth floors in an eight-storey office building. The appellant, a valuation officer, was of the view that, under the General Rate Act 1967 s 115, which provided that 'hereditament' meant property which was or might become liable to a rate, being a unit of such property which was, or would fall to be, shown as a separate item in the valuation list, each level or floor was a separate unit of property and should be entered as a separate hereditament. The Valuation Tribunal rejected this argument, finding that there was a link between the floors that was essential to the efficiency of the working of the respondent's overall service-provision business. The function carried out at the two levels was sufficiently integrated to be essential to the effective business as a whole. On appeal by the appellant, it was determined that the fact that the floors were in the same occupation for the purposes of the occupying firm was by itself a significant pointer. It was concluded that the proper approach was to treat the floors occupied within the building by the same occupier as a single hereditament. On further appeal by the appellant, *held*, the determination did not appear to involve any departure from established principles. It had expressly adopted a physical test and, accepting that floors of office premises were in the same occupation for the purposes of the occupying firm, had not espoused the further functional connection between parts. A physical test to floors within a single building had been applied. On the facts, which were likely to be similar to those in many other office blocks, the second and sixth floors in the occupation of the respondent could not legitimately be distinguished on practical grounds or in terms of the value of the occupation. Flexibility in applying a physical or geographical test was acceptable and its application did not permit a distinction, on physical grounds, between the second and sixth floors. To constitute a single hereditament, the floors did not have to constitute a physical cube. A commonsense assessment had rightly led to the conclusion that floors two and six in the block constituted a single hereditament. Accordingly, the appeal would be dismissed.

Woolway v Mazars LLP [2013] EWCA Civ 368, [2013] All ER (D) 206 (Apr) (Court of Appeal: Pill, Tomlinson and Kitchin LJJ). *Gilbert v S Hickinbottom & Sons Ltd* [1956] 2 QB 40, [1956] 2 All ER 101, CA, applied.

1967 Act repealed: Local Government Finance Act 1988 Sch 13 Pt I.

1782   Non-domestic rating—small business rate relief—England

The Non-Domestic Rating (Small Business Rate Relief) (England) (Amendment) Order 2013, SI 2013/15 (in force on 11 February 2013), amends the 2012 Order, SI 2012/148, so as to provide for a continued temporary increase in the level of small business rate relief for the financial year beginning on 1 April 2013.

1783   Non-domestic rating—small business rate relief—Wales

The Non-Domestic Rating (Small Business Relief) (Wales) (Amendment) Order 2013, SI 2013/371 (in force on 16 March 2013), further amends the 2008 Order, SI 2008/2770, so as to extend the provision for an increase in the level of small business rate relief for specified categories of ratepayer to 31 March 2014.

1784   Non-domestic rating—transitional protection payments—England

The Non-Domestic Rating (Transitional Protection Payments) Regulations 2013, SI 2013/106 (in force on 18 February 2013), deal with the calculation of payments to and by billing authorities where their income from rates varies as a result of the operation of transitional arrangements on periodic revaluations of non-domestic hereditaments ('transitional protection payments'). In particular, the regulations provide for (1) the calculation of the rating income an authority would be deemed to have received if transitional arrangements were not in place; (2) the calculation of the actual income the authority has received net of transitional protection; and (3) the making of payments on account of transitional protection payments in the course of the year to which they relate on the basis of estimated figures, and the making of reconciliation payments at the end of the year if the estimated figures differ from certified final amounts.

1785   Valuation Tribunal for England—council tax and rating appeals—procedure

The Valuation Tribunal for England (Council Tax and Rating Appeals) (Procedure) (Amendment) Regulations 2013, SI 2013/465 (in force on 1 April 2013), further amend the 2009 Regulations, SI 2009/2269, by (1) conferring on the Valuation Tribunal for England power to delegate its function of striking out cases in certain circumstances; (2) providing for the use of information supplied to the Tribunal under certain data-sharing powers; (3) prescribing the method for initiating an appeal under the Local Government Finance Act 1992 s 16 and the particulars required to be included in the notice of appeal; (4) providing that written reasons in such an appeal need only be given on request; (5) making provision for the quashing of penalties; and (6) providing for an extended period of appeal to the High Court in certain cases.

1786   Valuation Tribunal for Wales—council tax and rating appeals—procedure

The Valuation Tribunal for Wales (Wales) (Amendment) Regulations 2013, SI 2013/547 (in force on 1 April 2013), amend the 2010 Regulations, SI 2010/713, so as to (1) provide (a) that the Valuation Tribunal may deal with appeals in relation to council reduction schemes; and (b) for the minimum and maximum number of members that may be appointed to the Tribunal; (2) make changes to the information that must be provided to the Tribunal on an application for a council tax appeal; (3) enable the Tribunal to strike out an appeal where a billing authority has awarded the maximum possible reduction in council under its council tax reduction scheme or under the scheme that applies in default; (4) provide that information supplied in pursuance of regulations made under the Welfare Reform Act 2012 s 131 is admissible as evidence before the Tribunal in council tax appeals; and (5) enable the Tribunal to conduct hearings relating to council tax in private where it is in the interests of justice to do so.

LOCAL GOVERNMENT

Halsbury's Laws of England (5th edn) vol 69 (2009) paras 1–879

Articles

For articles relating to this title please refer to the Table of Articles at the beginning of the Abridgment.

1787   Business improvement districts—England

The Business Improvement Districts (England) (Amendment) Regulations 2013, SI 2013/2265 (in force on 7 October 2013), amend the 2004 Regulations, SI 2004/2443, so as to enable two or more billing authorities to make Business Improvement District Arrangements in respect of a business improvement district which spans authority boundaries. In particular, the regulations (1) establish that two or more billing authorities may make joint Business Improvement District Arrangements covering areas comprising all or part of the area of each of the authorities concerned; (2) clarify the procedures to be followed where a billing authority draws up the proposals; and (3) correct certain provisions.

1788   Employment—redundancy payments—continuity of employment—relevant service

See para 1054.

1789   Family absence—conditions—Wales

The Family Absence for Members of Local Authorities (Wales) Regulations 2013, SI 2013/2901 (in force on 5 December 2013), which apply in relation to Wales only, prescribe the conditions that members of local authorities must satisfy to be entitled to a period of family absence. In particular, the regulations (1) make provision relating to maternity absence; (2) prescribe the conditions that a member must satisfy to be entitled to a period of maternity absence; (3) make provision for the start of maternity absence, variation of the intended start, duration, bringing to an end and cancellation; (4) set out the conditions as to the relationship with a child or the child's mother and responsibility for the upbringing for that child required for a member to be entitled to newborn absence; (5) make provision for duration of newborn absence, when absence may be taken, cancellations of absence and the start date of a period of newborn absence; (6) prescribe the conditions that a member must satisfy to be entitled to a period of adopter's absence; (7) make provision for the duration of adopter's absence, when absence may be taken, the start date of a period of adopter's absence and cancellation; (8) prescribe the conditions that a member must satisfy to be entitled to a period of new adoption absence; (9) set out the relationship requirements between a member and a child's adopter and that the member must have responsibility for the upbringing of a child; (10) make provision for the duration of new adoption absence, when absence may be taken, cancellation and the start date of a period of new adoption absence; (11) prescribe the conditions to be satisfied for a member to be entitled to a period of parental absence; (12) set out the notification requirements and evidence to be produced to the head of democratic services, where required; (13) provide for the duration of absence, when absence may be taken, cancellation, bringing parental absence to an end and the start date of a period of parental absence; and (14) make provision relating to record keeping duties to inform cancellation of family absence by the local authority, complaints and standing orders relating to members whilst taking a period of family absence.

1790   Local authority—discharge of functions—duty to consult—change in circumstances

See *R* (*on the application of Stirling*) *v Haringey LBC*, para 1758.

1791   Local authority—executive arrangements—functions and responsibilities—Wales

The Local Authorities (Executive Arrangements) (Functions and Responsibilities) (Wales) (Amendment) Regulations 2013, SI 2013/2438 (in force on 22 October 2013), further amend the 2007 Regulations, SI 2007/399, by adding functions in respect of the approval or determination of school organisation proposals under the School Standards and Organisation (Wales) Act 2013 s 51 or 53 to the list of functions which may, but need not, be the responsibility of a local authority's executive.

The Local Authorities (Executive Arrangements) (Functions and Responsibilities) (Wales) (Amendment No 2) Regulations 2013, SI 2013/2902 (in force on 5 December 2013), further amend the 2007 Regulations above by adding functions in respect of powers to promote or oppose private bills, pursuant to the Local Government (Democracy) (Wales) Act 2013 ss 52 and 53, and in respect of family absence of local authority members, pursuant to the Family Absence for Members of Local Authorities (Wales) Regulations 2013, SI 2013/2901 (see PARA 1789), to the list of functions which cannot be the responsibility of a local authority's executive.

1792   Local authority—failures in family proceedings—wasted costs order

See *HB v PB*, para 212.

1793   Local authority—functions—Council of the Isles of Scilly

The Isles of Scilly (Functions) (Review and Scrutiny) Order 2013, SI 2013/643 (in force on 1 April 2013), provides for the Council of the Isles of Scilly to exercise the local authority power to appoint one or more committees as its overview and scrutiny committee or committees. In particular, the order provides for the Council to exercise functions under the Local Government Act 2000 s 9JA(1) and certain functions of the Local Authorities (Committee System) (England) Regulations 2012, SI 2012/1020, of a local authority operating a committee system. SI 2004/1412 is revoked.

1794   Local authority—functions and responsibilities—England

The Local Authorities (Functions and Responsibilities) (England) (Amendment) Regulations 2013, SI 2013/2190 (in force on 1 October 2013), further amend the

2000 Regulations, SI 2000/2853, in respect of the existing functions exercised by local authorities under the Licensing Act 2003 and new functions exercised by such authorities in relation to the late night levy requirements under the Police Reform and Social Responsibility Act 2011 Pt 2 Ch 2 (ss 125–139).

1795 Local authority—overview and scrutiny committee—Wales

The Local Authorities (Joint Overview and Scrutiny Committees) (Wales) Regulations 2013, SI 2013/1050 (in force on 24 May 2013), permit two or more local authorities to appoint a joint overview and scrutiny committee to make reports or recommendations to any of the authorities or their executives about matters affecting their areas. In particular, the regulations make provision (1) for the appointment by two or more local authorities ('the appointing authorities') of a joint overview and scrutiny committee to exercise functions of making reports and recommendations to any of the authorities or their executives on any matter which affects the whole or part of the area of each of the appointing authorities and is also not an excluded matter, which is a matter falling within the remit of a local authority's crime and disorder committee; (2) requiring the appointing authorities to enter into an agreement, and making provision about the contents of the agreement; (3) about membership of a joint overview and scrutiny committee, sub-committees of a joint overview and scrutiny committee, and the chair of a joint overview and scrutiny committee and any sub-committees; (4) about access to meetings and documentation; (5) about termination of membership of a joint overview and scrutiny committee on ceasing to be a member of the authority; (6) that any member or co-opted member of any of the appointing authorities may not be a member of a joint overview and scrutiny committee for the period of suspension; (7) about co-option of members on to a joint overview and scrutiny committee; (8) about references of matters to a joint overview and scrutiny committee or sub-committee; (9) about responses to reports or recommendations of a joint overview and scrutiny committee and about the publication of reports, recommendations and responses; (10) about the notification to designated persons of reports and recommendations of the joint overview and scrutiny committee; and (11) about the exclusion of exempt and confidential information from published reports, recommendations and responses to reports and recommendations.

1796 Local authority—public health functions—general

See para 1372.

1797 Local Government (Democracy) (Wales) Act 2013

The Local Government (Democracy) (Wales) Act 2013 makes provision as to the constitution and functions of the Local Democracy and Boundary Commission for Wales and various provision relating to local government. The Act received the royal assent on 30 July 2013 and came into force in part on that day and on 30 September 2013. The remaining provisions come into force on a day or days to be appointed. For details of commencement, see the commencement table in the title STATUTES AND LEGISLATIVE PROCESS.

Part 1 (s 1) Overview
Section 1 provides an overview of the main provisions of the 2013 Act and what it seeks to achieve.

Part 2 (ss 2–20) Local Democracy and Boundary Commission for Wales
Section 2 renames the Local Government Boundary Commission for Wales as the Local Democracy and Boundary Commission for Wales ('the Commission') and s 3 provides that the Commission is not a Crown body. The members of the Commission are the chair, deputy chair and up to three others, to be appointed on such terms and conditions as determined by the Welsh Ministers (s 4), and they hold and vacate office in accordance with their terms and conditions of appointment (s 5). Pursuant to ss 6, 7, the quorum for meetings of the Commission is three, it may regulate its own procedure, and it may have a seal for use on documents. The Welsh Ministers must appoint and decide on the terms and conditions of a chief executive of the Commission following consultation with the Commission: s 8. Section 9 enables the Commission to employ staff and to decide on their remuneration and terms and conditions, and ss 10, 11 enable the Commission to appoint expert advisers to

assist in the exercise of their functions and assistant commissioners to assist in the conduct of reviews of local government areas and electoral arrangements and to chair local inquiries.

The Commission may do anything which facilitates or is conducive or incidental to the exercise of its functions, but is not allowed to borrow money, acquire land or property (except with ministerial consent) or form or promote companies: s 12. Section 13 provides that the Commission may delegate its functions relating to reviews of local government areas or arrangements or local inquiries to individual members or assistant commissioners, without negating the Commission's overall responsibility for the performance of those functions. By virtue of s 14, the Commission must comply with any direction given by the Welsh Ministers and the Welsh Ministers may vary or revoke a direction by issuing a subsequent direction. Section 15 specifies that funding for the Commission will be provided through grants made by the Welsh Ministers, and under s 16 the Welsh Ministers must designate an accounting officer from the Commission's staff with responsibilities in relation to the Commission's financial arrangements. The Commission must establish an audit committee to keep under review its financial affairs and corporate governance: s 17. Pursuant to s 18, the audit committee must include at least two commissioners and at least one lay member. The Commission is required by s 19 to prepare an annual statement of accounts for each financial year, which must be sent to the Welsh Ministers and the Auditor General for Wales and laid before the National Assembly for Wales ('the Assembly'). Before the end of November after the end of each financial year, the Commission must also submit an annual report of its activities during that year to the Welsh Ministers, who must lay a copy of the report before the Assembly: s 20.

Part 3 (ss 21–49) Arrangements for local government

Chapter 1 (ss 21, 22) Duties to monitor local government arrangements
By virtue of s 21, the Commission must keep local government arrangements under review. County councils and county borough councils ('principal councils') must keep the communities in their areas and the electoral arrangements of such communities under review, and must report on these matters at least once every 10 years: s 22.

Chapter 2 (ss 23–28) Area reviews
The Commission may review counties or county boroughs ('principal areas') and make proposals to the Welsh Ministers: s 23. The Commission must also conduct a review of any principal areas affected by a new towns order made by the Welsh Ministers under the New Towns Act 1981: s 24. Provision is also made for the review of community boundaries by principal councils and the Commission (ss 25, 26), and for the review by the Commission of counties preserved for certain administrative purposes and for local government boundaries that lie beneath the sea and do not adjoin another local government boundary (ss 27, 28).

Chapter 3 (ss 29–33) Electoral arrangements reviews
Pursuant to s 29, the Commission must conduct an electoral review of each principal area at least every 10 years, but it cannot make recommendations or publish a report in the nine months before an ordinary council election. The matters to which the Commission must have regard in considering whether to make recommendations for changes to electoral arrangements for a principal area are set out in s 30. Provision is made for the review of electoral arrangements for communities by principal councils and the Commission by ss 31, 32, and the matters to which principal councils and the Commission must have regard in considering changes to electoral arrangements are set out in s 33.

Chapter 4 (ss 34–36) Procedure for local government reviews
Prior to starting a local government review, the Commission or the principal council conducting the review ('the reviewing body') must notify specified mandatory consultees that a review is about to take place: s 34. Pursuant to s 35, the reviewing body must consult with the mandatory consultees and carry out such investigations as it considers appropriate. The procedure for reporting on a review is provided by s 36.

Chapter 5 (ss 37–44) Implementation following review
Section 37 provides that, on receiving a report on boundary changes from the reviewing body, the Welsh Ministers may by order implement any recommendation, with or without modification, or decide to take no action in light of the report. Provision for the implementation of community boundary changes and changes to community electoral arrangements is made by ss 38, 39. An order made by the Welsh Ministers, the Commission or a principal council following a review may make such consequential provision as they

feel necessary: s 40. The Welsh Ministers may also, under s 41, make regulations providing for incidental and consequential matters for the purposes of giving full effect to review orders. Section 42 provides that any transfers of staff must not result in a deterioration of the terms and conditions of the transferred staff, s 43 enables the Welsh Ministers, the Commission or a principal council to vary or revoke a review order and correct mistakes, and s 44 deals with transitional arrangements as to property and finance.

Chapter 6 (ss 45–47) Other provision relevant to local authority boundaries
If, as part of a boundary review, a change of police area boundaries appears appropriate, the Commission may under s 45 recommend that the Secretary of State makes such change by order. Section 46 provides that communities which border the sea extend to the low water mark of the shore and that any accretion from the sea forms part of the community and county bordering on the shore. The Welsh Ministers may by order vary a local government area boundary as a result of an alteration in water course following consultation with the Commission: s 47.

Chapter 7 (ss 48, 49) Miscellaneous provision
The Welsh Ministers may give directions to the Commission and principal councils in relation to reviews of local government areas and electoral arrangements, and the Commission and principal councils must, when conducting reviews or implementing recommendations, have regard to any relevant guidance that the Welsh Ministers have issued: s 48. The Commission or a principal council may organise a local
inquiry associated with any review they are conducting, and the Welsh Ministers or a principal council may arrange for a local inquiry when considering making an order varying or revoking a previous order: s 49.

Part 4 (s 50) Reviews of public body membership
The Welsh Ministers may by virtue of s 50, following consultation, direct the Commission to review the membership of specified public bodies.

Part 5 (ss 51–69) Other changes to local government
Principal councils may, pursuant to s 51, appoint a presiding member and a deputy presiding member to carry out the functions of a council chairman. Sections 52–54 enable principal councils to promote private bills either in Parliament or the Assembly, enable local authorities to oppose private bills, and prevent local authorities from paying any of their members for acting as counsel or agents in promoting or opposing a bill. Under ss 55–57, community councils must publish specified information, public notices, agendas and public reports for forthcoming meetings electronically. Registers of the interests of members of certain bodies must also be published electronically: s 58. Section 59 provides that, unless principal councils make different provision, at least 30 per cent of the total number of members at a remotely attended council meeting must be present at the main meeting place for the meeting to be quorate. The scope of a local authority democratic services committee is broadened by s 60 so that, if requested by an authority, it can review anything relevant to the support and advice made available to elected members and their terms and conditions.

Section 61 provides that an audit committee of a local authority is one to which the rules of political balance apply, and s 62 enables the Independent Remuneration Panel ('the Panel'), when considering entitlement to a particular payment, to set a limit on the number of councillors who may receive it. Section 63 empowers the Panel to make recommendations to authorities about their policies in relation to the salaries of their chief executive officers and any proposed changes to those salaries. The Welsh Ministers may add to the public bodies whose remuneration must be considered by the Panel: s 64. Section 65 changes the date by which the Panel must produce their annual report from 31 December to the 28 February, s 66 varies the consultation times on draft supplementary reports by the Panel, and s 67 provides that the Panel may require local authorities to publish details of any income received by their members from specified public bodies. Relevant authorities may establish joint standards committees (s 68), and regulations may be made relating to the monitoring officer or standards committee of one authority being able to refer a matter to the standards committee of another authority (s 69).

Part 6 (ss 70–76, Schs 1–3) Miscellaneous and general provision
Under s 70, the Welsh Ministers may by order make changes to other legislation if they are necessary to give effect to the provisions of the 2013 Act. Section 71 sets out the procedure for the making of orders and regulations by the Welsh Ministers and s 72 deals with

interpretation. Section 73, Schs 1, 2 contain minor and consequential amendments and repeals, and ss 74–76 deal with ongoing reviews and other savings, commencement, and the short title of the Act.

Amendments, repeals and revocations
The list below, which is not exhaustive, mentions repeals and amendments which are or will be effective when the Act is fully in force.

Specific provisions of a number of Acts and Measures are added, substituted, amended or repealed. These include: Local Government Act 1972 ss 24A, 24B, 25, 30, 31, 70, 73, 74, 76, 80, 83, 112, 232, 239, 246, Sch 12; Police Act 1996 s 1; Local Government Act 2000 ss 53, 54, 73, 81, 106; Public Services Ombudsman (Wales) Act 2005 Sch 3; Local Government (Wales) Measure 2011 ss 4, 11A, 19, 82, 142, 143A, 144, 147, 148, 151; Police Reform and Social Responsibility Act 2011 s 72; Welsh Language (Wales) Measure 2011 Sch 6; Local Government Byelaws (Wales) Act 2012 Sch 2.

1798   Local government finance

See LOCAL GOVERNMENT FINANCE.

1799   Local government pension scheme

The Local Government Pension Scheme Regulations 2013, SI 2013/2356 (in force in part on 1 November 2013 and in part on 1 April 2014), introduce a new local government pension scheme, which is to come into existence on 1 April 2014 and replace the local government pension scheme constituted by the Local Government Pension Scheme (Benefits, Membership and Contributions) Regulations 2007, SI 2007/1166, and the Local Government Pension Scheme (Administration) Regulations 2008, SI 2008/239. In contrast to the previous scheme, which was a final salary pension scheme in which unreduced benefits were payable to members from the age of 65, the Scheme provides for members to accrue pension on a career average revalued earnings basis and for unreduced benefits to be payable from their state pension age. The regulations set out provisions relating to benefits, membership and contributions, and in particular, (1) set out the rules for eligibility for membership and the different categories of member; (2) set out the rules for contributions and include provision known as the '50/50' option, which enables members to elect to pay half the usual rate of contribution and to accrue benefits at half the usual rate; (3) make provision for the purchase of additional benefits; provision is also made for the payment or crediting of contributions during absences from work and for the calculation of an assumed level of pensionable pay during such absences; (4) provide for the creation and maintenance of pension accounts; and (5) provide for the payment of benefits to members and their survivors. Further, the regulations set out provisions relating to the administration of the Scheme, and in particular, (a) provide for management of the Scheme including the obtaining of actuarial valuations and the calculation of employer contributions; (b) provide for the making and notification of decisions and for challenges to those decisions, and for the supply of relevant information to enable decisions to be taken; (c) set out provisions for forfeiture of benefits; (d) set out provisions relating to transfers between funds; (e) contain definitions; (f) set out who can be Scheme employers and make provision relating to admission agreements between employers who are not listed and administering authorities; and (g) set out who must maintain a fund for the Scheme, and is thus an administering authority, and contain provision identifying who is the appropriate administering authority for the employees of any particular Scheme employer.

The Local Government Pension Scheme (Management and Investment of Funds) (Amendment) Regulations 2013, SI 2013/410 (in force on 1 April 2013), amend the 2009 Regulations, SI 2009/3093, by increasing, from 15 per cent to 30 per cent, the maximum proportion of a local government pension fund which can be invested in contributions to partnerships.

1800   Localism Act 2011—commencement

The Localism Act 2011 (Commencement No 2 and Transitional Provisions) Order 2013, SI 2013/722, brings ss 180(1) (for certain purposes), (2) and (3), 181, 182 into force in relation to England on 1 April 2013. Transitional provision is also made.

The Localism Act 2011 (Commencement No 9) Order 2013, SI 2013/797, brings into force (1) on 6 April 2013, so far as not already in force, Schs 9–12; and (2) on 1 October 2013, Sch 5. The Localism Act 2011 (Commencement No 7 and Transitional, Saving and Transitory Provisions) Order 2012, SI 2012/2029, is amended.

The Localism Act 2011 (Commencement No 3) Order 2013, SI 2013/2931, brings s 122 into force, so far as it is not already in force, on 17 December 2013.

For a summary of the Act, see 2011 Abr para 1784. See also the commencement table in the title STATUTES AND LEGISLATIVE PROCESS.

1801   Modification of enactments—Wales

The Local Government (Wales) Measure 2011 (Modification of Enactments and other Provisions) Order 2013, SI 2013/3005 (in force on 27 November 2013), which applies in relation to Wales only, makes modifications to enactments which are considered appropriate in connection with the Local Government (Wales) Measure 2011. In particular, the order (1) omits the Local Government and Public Involvement in Heath Act 2007 Sch 3 paras 23, 24 and 25; (2) omits a council manager from the list of persons contained in the Definition of Independent Visitors (Children) Regulations 1991, SI 1991/892, considered to be connected to a local authority and not regarded as independent of the authority; (3) modifies the Standards Committees (Wales) Regulations 2001, SI 2001/2283, regs 2, 8 and 9 so as to omit provision about alternative arrangements; (4) omits provisions regarding alternative arrangements from the Parent Governor Representatives and Church Representatives (Wales) Regulations 2001, SI 2001/3711, regs 2, 3 and 11; (5) modifies the Local Authorities (Executive Arrangements) (Discharge of Functions) (Wales) Regulations 2002, SI 2002/802, regs 2, 5 and 12 so as to omit provision about mayor and council manager executive arrangements and alternative arrangements; (6) makes saving provision with respect to local authorities operating alternative arrangements which are required under the 2011 Measure s 35 to operate instead a form of executive arrangements in accordance with Sch 1; (6) substitute reference in the Local Authorities (Executive Arrangements) (Functions and Responsibilities) (Wales) Regulations 2007, SI 2007/399, to the Local Government Act 1972 (a) s 27D for reference to s 28; and (b) s 27F or s 27H for reference to s 29A; and (7) alters the Local Authorities (Miscellaneous Provisions) Order 1979, SI 1979/1123, so as to substitute reference to s 24F or 27H for reference to s 29.

1802   Public Audit (Wales) Act 2013

The Public Audit (Wales) Act 2013 makes provision reforming audit arrangements in Wales, continuing the office of Auditor General for Wales, creating a new body to be known as the Wales Audit Office and providing for the Auditor General to audit local government bodies in Wales. The Act received the royal assent on 29 April 2013 and the following provisions came into force on that date: ss 30, 35, 36. Sections 1, 8 (for certain purposes), 10, 12, 13 (for certain purposes), 14–16, 17(2), (3) (for certain purposes), 18 (for certain purposes), 20 (for certain purposes), 24–28, 29(1), (2), (3)(b),(c), (4), 31–33, Sch 1 paras 1–3 (for certain purposes), 4–13, 26 (for certain purposes), 27, 28, 29(1), 30, 31, 32 (for certain purposes), Sch 2 paras 1, 2, 5–14, Sch 3 paras 4, 13, Sch 4 para 79(2) (for certain purposes) came into force on 4 July 2013 and the remaining provisions come into force on 1 April 2014: SI 2013/1466. For details of commencement, see the commencement table in the title STATUTES AND LEGISLATIVE PROCESS.

Introduction
Section 1 provides an overview of the provisions of the 2013 Act.

Part 1 (ss 2–12) Auditor General for Wales

Chapter 1 (ss 2–7) The Office of Auditor General for Wales
Section 2 provides for the office of the Auditor General to continue. Under s 3, the Auditor General holds office until the end of the term for which he has been appointed unless he is relieved of the appointment by Her Majesty on request, relieved of the appointment because Her Majesty is satisfied that he is no longer capable of performing the duties because of medical reasons and is also incapable for such reasons of requesting to be relieved of office, or removed from the post by Her Majesty because of misbehaviour. The grounds on which

a person would be disqualified from being an Auditor General are set out by s 4. Section 5 prescribes the restrictions around future employment, office-holding or provision of services that apply to persons who have been appointed as the Auditor General but who no longer hold the office. By virtue of s 6, the person for the time being holding the office of Auditor General continues, by the name of that office, to be a corporation sole. Section 7 requires the Welsh Assembly to make remuneration arrangements for an Auditor General.

Chapter 2 (ss 8–12) Auditor General's functions
Section 8 maintains and enhances the independence of the Auditor General in the exercise of his functions. Under s 9, the Auditor General is provided with a general power to do anything which facilitates, or is incidental or conducive to, the exercise of his functions. By virtue of s 10, the Auditor General must issue a code of practice which embodies the best professional practice to be adopted in the carrying out of his functions relating to the examining of any accounts or statement of accounts in accordance with any enactment, carrying out, undertaking or promoting value for money studies or examinations, and as provided for in various provisions of the Government of Wales Act 1998, the Public Audit (Wales) Act 2004 and the Government of Wales Act 2006 Sch 8. The 2013 Act s 11 provides for the Auditor General to be the statutory auditor of the accounts of all local government bodies in Wales. Under s 12, the Welsh Ministers are required to consult the Wales Audit Office before making an order providing for certain functions of the Welsh Ministers to be transferred to or exercised on their behalf by the Auditor General.

Part 2 (ss 13–27) The Wales Audit Office and its relationship with the Auditor General

Chapter 1 (ss 13–15) The Wales Audit Office
Section 13, Sch 1 establish the Wales Audit Office. Sections 14 and 15 provide that the Wales Audit Office may do anything that facilitates or is incidental or conducive to the exercise of its functions, but must aim to carry out its functions efficiently and cost-effectively.

Chapter 2 (ss 16–27) Relationship between the Auditor General and the Wales Audit Office
Section 16 provides that the Auditor General is the chief executive of the Wales Audit Office, but not an employee of it, and gives effect to Sch 2, which makes further provision about the relationship between the Auditor General and the Wales Audit Office. Under s 17, the Wales Audit Office must monitor and may advise the Auditor General in respect of his functions. By virtue of s 18, the functions of the Auditor General may be carried out by an employee of the Wales Audit Office or a person providing services to the Wales Audit Office, provided the employee or person is authorised to do so in a scheme of delegation and agrees to comply with the Auditor General's code of audit practice. Section 19 enables the Wales Audit Office to make arrangements to receive administrative, professional or technical services that it or the Auditor General may need to carry out their respective functions. The Auditor General and the Wales Audit Office must jointly prepare an estimate for each financial year of all of the income and expenditure of the Wales Audit Office: s 20. Section 21 requires the Wales Audit Office, as the budget-holder, to provide resources to the Auditor General as required by the Auditor General so he can carry out his functions. Under s 22, the Wales Audit Office may borrow money, by way of an overdraft or otherwise, to meet a temporary excess of expenditure. Section 23 enables the Wales Audit Office to charge fees for audit-related functions carried out by the Auditor General, and any services provided by the Auditor General, in accordance with a scheme for charging fees prepared by the Wales Audit Office. By virtue of s 24, the Wales Audit Office must identify the enactments enabling it to charge a fee in accordance with any prescribed amount or any scale of fees as the case may be. Sections 25–27 make provision in relation to an annual plan that must be jointly prepared by the Auditor General and the Wales Audit Office, setting out the planned work for both the Auditor General and the Wales Audit Office, the resources available, and which may become available to the Wales Audit Office, and how those resources are to be used to achieve their planned work.

Part 3 (ss 28–36) Miscellaneous and general
Section 28 provides authority for the Assembly to make provision as to how the functions set out in the 2013 Act falling to the Assembly are to be exercised. By virtue of s 29, any compensation to a third party for a breach of a duty by an Auditor General appointed under the 2013 Act, a person providing services to the Auditor General or the Wales Audit Office,

the Wales Audit Office's former or current members or employees is to be charged on and paid from the Welsh Consolidated Fund. Section 30 makes general provision about powers that enable subordinate legislation to be made and s 31 makes general provision in respect of powers to issue directions. Section 32 deals with interpretation. Section 33 gives effect to Schedule 3, which makes transitional provision, and s 34 gives effect to Schedule 4, which makes various minor and consequential amendments. Section 35 deals with commencement and s 36 with the short title.

Amendments, repeals and revocations
The list below, which is not exhaustive, mentions amendments which are or will be effective when the Act is fully in force.

Specific provisions of a number of Acts are amended. These include: Government of Wales Act 1998 s 146A; Public Audit (Wales) Act 2004 ss 13, 16.

1803 Public Service Pensions Act 2013

See para 2001.

1804 Regulatory enforcement—enforcement action

The Co-ordination of Regulatory Enforcement (Enforcement Action) (Amendment) Order 2013, SI 2013/2286 (in force on 1 October 2013), amends the 2009 Order, SI 2009/665, so as to provide that action taken by a local authority pursuant to or in connection with the exercise of functions under the Gambling Act 2005 Pt 4 (ss 45–64) will also constitute 'enforcement action'. In addition, the order provides that the requirements of the Regulatory Enforcement and Sanctions Act 2008 s 28(1)–(4), for a local authority to notify the primary authority before taking enforcement action and not to take the proposed action if so directed by the primary authority, do not apply to the making of emergency prohibition orders or the service of notice of emergency remedial action under the Housing Act 2004 Pt 1 (ss 1–54).

1805 Regulatory enforcement—sanctions

The Regulatory Enforcement and Sanctions Act 2008 (Amendment of Schedule 3) Order 2013, SI 2013/2215 (in force on 1 October 2013), further amends the Regulatory Enforcement and Sanctions Act 2008 Sch 3, adding legislation to the list in Sch 3, so that provisions of the added legislation, and of any secondary legislation made under a newly specified Act, will constitute 'relevant enactments' for the purposes of the definition of a 'relevant function' of a local authority in England or Wales which applies for the purposes of the 2008 Act Pts 1 (ss 1–21), 2 (ss 22–35).

1806 Sustainable communities—parish councils

The Sustainable Communities (Parish Councils) Order 2013, SI 2013/2275 (in force on 14 October 2013), specifies parish councils, which includes town councils, as another class of person who can make proposals under the Sustainable Communities Act 2007.

LONDON GOVERNMENT

Halsbury's Laws of England (5th edn) vol 71 (2013) paras 1–400

1807 City of London (Various Powers) Act 2013

The City of London (Various Powers) Act 2013 amends the provision for the control of street trading in the City of London, and makes provision relating to city walkways. The Act received the royal assent on 18 December 2013 and came into force on that day. Sections 1, 2 provide for citation and interpretation. Section 3 amends the City of London (Various Powers) Act 1987 concerning temporary street trading by amending and adding various definitions and by making provision for the granting of a temporary licence which permits a temporary licence holder to carry on street trading. The City of London (Various Powers) Act 1965 s 13(1) is consequentially amended as a result of the provision made by the 2013 Act s 3: s 4. Section 5 amends the 1987 Act s 16, which provides for offences and penalties in respect of unauthorised street trading so as to include the provision of a temporary licence. The penalties for unlicensed street trading in s 16(3) are increased from level 2 to level 3: s 6. Section 7 provides for enforcement and makes provision for (1) seizure; (2) the return of seized articles or things; (3) the forfeiture of seized article or things by court; (4) compensation for seizure; (5) the seizure of perishable articles or things; (6) seizure of motor vehicles; (7) disposal orders; (8) provision of information by the Corporation; and (9) training. Section 8 makes provision with regards to charges for licensed street traders, and s 9 makes provision for training outside business premises where an occupier of a business, under certain conditions, will be treated as not engaging in street trading. Section 10 amends the City of London (Various Powers) Act 1967 so as to make provision for charges in respect of resolutions, and offences for parking on city walkways.

1808 Greater London Authority—consolidated council tax requirement—procedure

The Greater London Authority (Consolidated Council Tax Requirement Procedure) Regulations 2013, SI 2013/3178 (in force on 17 January 2014), modify the Greater London Authority Act 1999 so as to require the Mayor of London to prepare and present, in relation to the financial year beginning on 1 April 2014, a draft consolidated budget to the London Assembly on or before 10 February 2014 for the purposes of the procedure for determining the Greater London Authority's consolidated council tax requirement.

1809 Greater London Authority—specified activities

The Greater London Authority (Specified Activities) Order 2013, SI 2013/973 (in force on 20 May 2013), specifies the management and exploitation of land on a commercial basis with a view to the realisation of a profit in connection with the Greater London Authority's housing, regeneration and economic development functions as activities which must, by virtue of the Greater London Authority Act 1999 s 34A, be carried on through a taxable body.

1810 Growth and Infrastructure Act 2013

See para 2022.

1811 London Local Authorities and Transport for London Act 2013

The London Local Authorities and Transport for London Act 2013 confers further powers on local authorities in London and on Transport for London. The 2013 Act received the royal assent on 18 December 2013 and came into force in part on 18 February 2014. The remaining provisions come into force on a day or days to be appointed. For details of commencement, see the commencement table in the title STATUTES AND LEGISLATIVE PROCESS.

Section 1 deals with citation and commencement, s 2 with interpretation and s 3 with the appointed day. Section 4 brings the powers of London authorities under the Public Health Act 1961 s 45 and the Road Traffic Regulation Act 1984 s 74, regarding the attachment of street lamps and traffic signs to buildings, in line with the City Corporation by disapplying the consent provisions as they apply in London, except in relation to the Common Council of the City of London. The 2013 Act s 5 makes provision in relation to the notice that must be served on the relevant owner of a building before a London authority begins work to affix an attachment or a traffic sign to that building. By virtue of s 6, provision is made in relation to London enabling the highway authority to recover expenses reasonably incurred in making good damage to a highway maintainable at the public expense which was damaged by or in consequence of any works on land adjacent to the highway. Section 7 deals with interpretation. Under s 8, a relevant highway authority may, for the purposes of identifying who is responsible for paying a penalty charge in relation to a builder's skip, require the relevant person to provide them with the name and address of the owner of the skip. Section 9 makes provision for the payment of a penalty charge in relation builders' skips where certain requirements have not been complied with. Section 10 makes provision in relation to requirements as to the lighting and guarding of builders' skip. By virtue of s 11, if a builder's skip is found by a relevant highway authority to be deposited on a highway in Greater London and the skip is not lighted or covered in accordance with the conditions of a permission under the Highways Act 1980 s 139, was deposited without a permission having been obtained or is not properly lighted during the hours of darkness, the highway authority may themselves light, cover or mark the skip or cause it to be lighted, covered or marked. The 2013 Act s 12 provides that, where a penalty notice has been served in relation to a penalty charge, an authorised officer of the relevant highway authority or a person acting under his direction may fix an immobilisation device to the builder's skip concerned while it remains in the place where it was found. Section 13 makes provision in relation to the release of an immobilised builder's skip and s 14 deals with appeals in relation to immobilisation. Section 15 provides that, any person who opens, closes or otherwise operates or interferes with a relevant barrier without lawful excuse is to be guilty of an offence and liable, on summary conviction, to a fine not exceeding level three on the standard scale. By virtue of s 16, a London authority may provide and operate charging apparatus or grant a person permission to provide or operate charging apparatus for electrically powered motor vehicles in any public off-street car park under its management and control or on any highway for which they are responsible. Under s 17, a London authority is not to exercise any power conferred by s 16 unless they have first published a notice. Section 18 provides that a London authority is not to exercise any power conferred by s 16 unless they have consulted any authority other than themselves who are a local planning authority and an authorised person is not to provide or operate charging apparatus in accordance with a permission given unless the authorised person has consulted any authority who are a local planning authority for the area to which the proposed permission relates. By virtue of s 19, a person is to be guilty of an offence and liable on summary conviction to a fine not exceeding level three on the standard scale if he uses charging apparatus in contravention of a sign displayed on the apparatus which indicates that the apparatus is not to be used for any purpose other than charging a vehicle and that it is an offence to so use the apparatus. Section 20 makes consequential amendments to the London Local Authorities and Transport for London Act 2008.

Amendments, repeals and revocations
The list below, which is not exhaustive, mentions repeals and amendments which are or will be effective when the Act is fully in force.
    Specific provisions of a number of Act are amended or repealed. These include: London Local Authorities and Transport for London Act 2008 ss 6, 7(2).

1812   Planning—urban development—London Thames Gateway—dissolution
See para 2019.

MAGISTRATES
Halsbury's Laws of England (5th edn) vol 71 (2013) paras 401–800

1813   Family proceedings
See CHILDREN AND YOUNG PERSONS.

1814   Local justice areas—reorganisation
The Local Justice Areas Order 2013, SI 2013/1777 (in force in part on 30 August 2013 and in part on 1 January 2014), further amends the 2005 Order, SI 2005/553, and makes provision for (1) a new local justice area named Leicestershire and Rutland to replace the existing local justice areas of (a) Ashby-de-la-Zouch and Market Bosworth; (b) Leicester, Market Harborough and Lutterworth; and (c) Loughborough, Melton, Belvoir and Rutland; (2) a new local justice area named Lincolnshire to replace the existing local justice areas of East Lincolnshire, South Lincolnshire and West Lincolnshire; and (3) a new local justice area named South and East Cheshire to replace the existing local justice areas of Macclesfield and South Cheshire.

The Local Justice Areas (No 2) Order 2013, SI 2013/1878 (in force in part on 30 August 2013 and in part on 1 January 2014), amend the 2005 Order, SI 2005/554, so as to provide for the new local justice area named Black Country to replace the existing local justice areas of Dudley and Halesowen, Sandwell, Walsall and Aldridge and Wolverhampton. It also provides for the new local justice area named Birmingham and Solihull to replace the existing local justice areas of Birmingham and Solihull, Coventry and Warwickshire to replace the existing local justice areas of Coventry District and Warwickshire and Nottinghamshire to replace the existing local justice areas of Mansfield and Worksop and Nottingham and Newark.

1815 Magistrates' courts—conviction—simple and aggravated offence—same set of facts

The victim, a taxi driver, admitted two of the claimant's friends to his taxi. Subsequently, the claimant approached the taxi and got in with a lit cigarette. The victim asked the claimant to exit the taxi, but he refused and used racially abusive language. The claimant then kicked out at the victim when he opened the car door and an argument ensued, during which the claimant used more racist language. The claimant's pre-trial plea of guilty to the simple offence of causing fear or provocation of violence pursuant to the Public Order Act 1986 s 4 was rejected by the prosecution. At trial, the racial element of the aggravated offence of causing racially aggravated fear or provocation of violence pursuant to the Crime and Disorder Act 1988 s 31(1)(a) was proved, but the claimant was convicted of both the simple and aggravated offences. The claimant applied for judicial review of that decision. *Held*, where both a simple and aggravated charge arose out of the same facts, it was not open to a magistrates' court to convict a defendant of both offences. A person's criminal record ought to reflect what they had done and the magistrates' court's practice of convicting in such circumstances of two offences in respect of a single wrong offended that basic principle. The lesser charge should be adjourned before conviction and, in the event of a successful appeal against the aggravated offence, a conviction on the lesser offence might thereafter be recorded. There existed no practical difficulty which could override the basic principle of justice. In the circumstances, the claimant's double conviction had been wrong in principle. He stood convicted of two offences for a single wrong and that was unfair and disproportionate. Therefore, the conviction on the lesser charge would be quashed.

    R (on the application of Dyer) v Watford Magistrates' Court [2013] EWHC 547 (Admin), (2013) 177 JP 265 (Queen's Bench Division: Laws LJ and Hickinbottom J). *R v Greater Manchester Coroner, ex p Tal* [1985] QB 67, [1984] 3 All ER 240, DC, applied.

1816 Magistrates' courts—fees

The Magistrates' Courts Fees (Amendment) Order 2013, SI 2013/1409 (in force on 1 July 2013), further amends the 2008 Order, SI 2008/1052, by (1) increasing certain fees that are payable in magistrates' courts by the cumulative rate of inflation since those fees were last increased; (2) harmonising certain fees with the amounts payable in civil and family proceedings in county courts and the High Court for the same application; and (3) merging certain fees for supervision orders and care orders.

MARKETS

Halsbury's Laws of England (5th edn) vol 71 (2013) paras 801–922

1817 City of London (Various Powers) Act 2013

See para 1807.

MATRIMONIAL AND CIVIL PARTNERSHIP LAW

Halsbury's Laws of England (5th edn) vol 72 (2009) paras 1–541, vol 73 (2009) paras 542–1042

Articles

For articles relating to this title please refer to the Table of Articles at the beginning of the Abridgment.

1818 Ancillary relief—financial provision—husband declared bankrupt—concealment of assets

The parties were husband and wife. The husband had become extremely wealthy prior to the breakdown of the marriage. Later, he was made bankrupt, and he remained an undisclosed bankrupt. In the course of proceedings, which had run for several years, there had been a considerable struggle to secure full and frank disclosure from the husband. He failed to provide answers to questionnaires drafted by the wife and, later, he was committed to prison for contempt of court. Very substantial costs had been amassed by the wife while the husband had acted in person throughout. Considerable expert evidence had been adduced. The wife made an application for a full range of financial remedies against the husband. Those included an application for an order pursuant to *Hadkinson* to prevent the husband from participating in the final hearing given that he had been found to be in contempt of court. *Held*, as to whether the husband lied, it was necessary to decide whether he had done so deliberately. If the husband had lied, it was necessary to assess whether there had been an 'innocent' explanation for those lies that did not support the wife's case that he had hidden assets. If the court was satisfied that there was no such explanation, the lies could be taken into account in an assessment of his case that he was penniless and hopelessly bankrupt. While the *Hadkinson* jurisdiction did apply in family cases and there would be occasions where it was proportionate to make such an order, such an order would not be made in the circumstances. While the wife was entitled to be aggrieved at the husband's contempt of court, and that contempt had to be considered when deciding where the truth lay, and while the court expected and required its order to be obeyed, it would not be right to restrict the husband's participation in the hearing. There was clearly an important role for the taking of oral evidence before a final hearing. However, it ought not to be an unfocused, wide-ranging trawl through the evidence without findings of fact being made at the conclusion of the hearing. Generally, it would only be a proper use of court resources if it led to specific findings of fact that became res judicata so that the issues needed not be revisited at the final hearing, or if it was part of an exercise in obtaining pre-trial discovery of documents where the witness was asked to give evidence by way of an explanation of the document or how it came into his possession. The case had fallen foul of almost every part of the requirement that cases be dealt with justly. Even though the husband's affairs had been exceptionally complicated, the case had not been dealt with proportionally at any stage. The wife had been able to spend a large amount in funding whilst the husband had been in person virtually throughout. There had been no saving of expense in the case. It was difficult to see how a number of preliminary hearings followed by a final hearing could possibly be a fair allocation of the court's limited resources on one case. It followed that in such cases, there should be rigorous control on the amount spent, in particular on expert evidence. Further, the obligation on the husband was to be full, frank and clear in his disclosure. Although the wife had raised many unfounded issues, the husband had misled the court as to his finances to a very considerable extent. The wife was therefore entitled to half of his undisclosed assets. Judgment would be given accordingly.

Young v Young [2013] EWHC 3637 (Fam), [2013] All ER (D) 313 (Nov) (Family Division: Moor J). *Re Holliday (a bankrupt), ex p Trustee of the Property of the Bankrupt v Bankrupt* [1981] Ch 405, [1980] 3 All ER 385, CA; *Baker v Baker* [1996] 1 FCR 567, CA (1996 Abr para 1104); and *Hellyer v Hellyer* [1997] 1 FCR 340, CA (1997 Abr para 1309), applied. *Hadkinson v Hadkinson* [1952] 2 All ER 567, CA, considered.

1819   **Ancillary relief—financial provision—lump sum order—husband owner and controlling mind of company**

In ancillary relief proceedings by a wife, questions arose concerning the position of a number of companies belonging to a group which had been found to be wholly owned and controlled by the husband and which were joined as additional respondents to the wife's application for ancillary relief. The judge concluded that, in applications for financial relief ancillary to a divorce, a wider jurisdiction to pierce the corporate veil was available under the Matrimonial Causes Act 1973 s 24. He ordered the husband to procure the transfer to the wife of the relevant properties, in partial satisfaction of a lump sum order and directed the respondent companies to execute such documents as might be necessary to give effect to the transfer of those properties. On appeal by the respondents, the Court of Appeal criticised the practice to treat assets of companies substantially owned by one party to the marriage as available for distribution under s 24, provided that the remaining assets of the company were sufficient to satisfy its creditors. It was found that the practice was beyond the jurisdiction of the court unless the corporate personality of the company was being abused for a purpose which was in some relevant respect improper or, on the particular facts of the case, it could be shown that an asset legally owned by the company was held in trust for the husband. Therefore, the judge should not have made the order. The wife appealed. *Held*, the judge had been correct to decline to find that there had been relevant impropriety, which would enable him to pierce the corporate veil. The husband had acted improperly in many ways. However, the problem was that the legal interest in the properties was vested in the respondents and not in the husband. They had been vested in the respondents long before the marriage had broken up. Whatever the husband's reasons for organising things in that way, there was no evidence that he had been seeking to avoid any obligation which was relevant. The piercing of the corporate veil could not be justified by reference to any general principles of law. If there was no justification as a matter of general legal principle for piercing the corporate veil, it was impossible to say that a special and wider principle applied in matrimonial proceedings by virtue of s 24(1)(a). The judge had been entitled to take account of the husband's ownership and control of the respondents and his unrestricted access to their assets in assessing what his resources were for the purposes of the 1973 Act. However, the judge had not been entitled to order the respondents' assets to be transferred to the wife in satisfaction of the lump sum order simply by virtue of s 24(1)(a). It was not in doubt that the object of s 24(1)(a) was to achieve a proper division of the assets of the marriage but it did not follow that the courts would stop at nothing in their pursuit of that end. There was nothing in the 1973 Act and nothing in its purpose or broader social context to indicate that the legislature had intended to authorise the transfer by one party to the marriage to the other of property which was not his to transfer. It followed that the only basis on which the respondents could be ordered to convey the properties to the wife was that they belonged to the husband by virtue of the particular circumstances in the properties vested in them. On the facts, it was a fair inference that the main reason for the respondents' failure to co-operate was to protect the properties. That suggested that the proper disclosure of the facts would reveal them to have been held beneficially by the husband. A declaration would be made that the properties were held on trust for the husband and the relevant part of the order would be restored so far as it required the respondents to transfer them to the wife. Accordingly, the appeal would be allowed.

Prest v Petrodel Resources Ltd [2013] UKSC 34, [2013] 2 AC 415, [2013] 4 All ER 673 (Supreme Court: Lord Neuberger P, Lord Walker, Lady Hale, Lord Mance, Lord Clarke, Lord Wilson and Lord Sumption SCJJ). *Nokes v Doncaster Amalgamated Collieries Ltd* [1940] AC 1014, [1940] 3 All ER 549, HL; *R v IRC, ex p TC Coombs & Co* [1991] 2 AC 283, [1991] 3 All ER 623, HL (1991 Abr para 1375); *Gilford Motor Co Ltd v Horne* [1933] Ch 935, CA; and *Ben Hashem v Al Shayif* [2008] EWHC 2380 (Fam), [2009] 1 FLR 115 applied. *VTB Capital plc v Nutritek International Corpn* [2012] EWCA Civ 808, [2012] 2 BCLC 437 criticised. Decision of Court of Appeal [2012] EWCA Civ 1395, [2012] All ER (D) 293 (Oct) (2012 Abr para 1811) reversed.

1820   Ancillary relief—financial provision—maintenance payments—contempt of court—committal

The parties were a divorced couple. The husband was ordered to pay periodical payments to the wife for their joint lives, or until her re-marriage, or further order. It was common ground that, over a nine year period the husband had not made any payment under that order, despite numerous attempts by the wife at enforcement. The husband was arrested under a warrant and taken to the magistrates' court. It appeared that the husband was, at that time, living at his mother's home and claimed to be without income, capital or other assets. The judge recorded that the wife was proceeding under the Maintenance Orders Act 1958 s 3 and the Magistrates' Courts Act 1980 s 98. She noted that, before committing the husband to prison, she had to be sure that there had been wilful refusal or culpable neglect and that that was ongoing. It was found that the husband was not a credible or reliable witness, that there had been an ongoing, wilful refusal to pay maintenance, that he had made no attempt to make any payment when he had been on benefits or when he had received income and the judge was highly suspicious as to his then current income and assets and was uncertain as to whether he had an income or capital or assets at the time of the hearing. The husband was committed to prison for non-payment of an order for periodical payments. On appeal by the husband, *held*, the Debtors Act 1869 s 5 and the Family Procedure Rules 2010, SI 2010/2955, in particular r 33.14, governed and circumscribed the power to commit to prison for default in payment of maintenance in the High Court and county court. However, the 1869 Act s 5 did not directly apply to magistrates' courts or family proceedings courts. The Administration of Justice Act 1970 s 11 precluded exercise of the power to commit to prison under the 1869 s 5 by a magistrates' court. Consistent with that, the provisions of the 2010 Rules Pt 33 (rr 33.1–33.25) in relation to judgment summonses did not directly apply to magistrates' courts or family proceedings courts. However, r 2.1(2)(a) provided that nothing in the 2010 Rules was to be construed as purporting to apply to proceedings in a magistrates' court which were not family proceedings within the meaning of the 1980 Act s 65. Section 65 listed proceedings which were classed as 'family proceedings', none of which included the 1958 Act s 3 nor the 1980 Act s 93. The decision to commit had been based on flawed and ultimately unlawful reasoning. The judge had not ordered, or apparently thought fit to order, that the proceedings before her that day should have been treated as family proceedings for the purposes of the 1980 Act. Therefore, she had not directly been operating under, or bound to apply, the provisions of the 2010 Rules Pt 33. It was one thing when the court was deciding whether to make a maintenance order, or the level of that order, to take into account current or likely earning capacity. It would be intolerable if a person was liable to be imprisoned on an argument that he ought to be earning more. It was scarcely more tolerable to imprison someone on an argument that, although in fact he was not earning, and had no income, he could and should be earning. Those sorts of considerations were far too speculative a foundation for the ultimate and grave sanction of imprisonment. On the evidence, the only matter of which the judge had been sure had been that the husband had 'earning potential' which he had chosen not to exercise or maximise. That was not a sufficient, justifiable or lawful basis for imprisoning anyone. Accordingly, the appeal would be allowed.

Constantinides v Constantinides [2013] EWHC 3688 (Fam), [2013] All ER (D) 336 (Nov) (Family Division: Holman J).

1821　　Ancillary relief—financial provision—maintenance pending suit—provision of legal fees—appeal—return of sums paid under order

A wife was granted a maintenance pending suit order, which included a sum for past fees incurred by her solicitors on account and a sum for future estimated fees of the proceedings. The husband applied to the judge for permission to appeal against the order. The application was refused but the judge granted the husband an extension of time in which to apply for permission to appeal. The husband filed his application for permission to appeal and the application was adjourned to an oral hearing with the appeal to follow if permission was granted. The Court of Appeal allowed the husband's appeal and set aside the order and the husband applied for the repayment of the sums paid to the wife. The wife contended that the sums paid under the order had been properly applied to the costs and disbursements incurred in the proceedings and that, on settled authority, there was no basis on which she should be ordered to repay those sums. *Held*, the case was plainly distinguishable from the authorities on which the wife relied in that the case had not been one in which the wife failed at trial on the substantive issues in the ancillary relief proceedings, but had failed with regard to the order itself. It had been plain that, had the husband's challenge to the order been determined earlier, soon after the date when it was ordered that permission to appeal would be determined at an oral hearing with appeal to follow if granted, then the two instalment payments which had still been due at that date would not have been paid. It had been necessary to look realistically and determine when the wife's solicitors had been on notice that the instalment payments had been conditional on the wife's success in the appeal. The wife had known from the outset that an appeal had been under way, had been intended and had been planned from the application made to the judge for permission to appeal. The solicitors had also been on notice following the grant of an extension of time by the judge for the husband to issue an application for permission to appeal, and it had been even clearer when the application was adjourned for an oral hearing. It followed that, from an early stage the wife's solicitors had to ask themselves whether the future conduct of the litigation on behalf of the wife had been risk free. It was fair to say that the husband could have applied for a stay of the order pending his attempts to obtain permission to appeal, but it was likely that the application would have been refused in light of the function and purpose of the order itself. Therefore, in the circumstances, the husband had been entitled to an order for the return of the sums paid under the order from the date on which it had been apparent that the security provided by the order had been vulnerable to appeal, in particular when the husband filed his application for permission to appeal. Accordingly, the appeal would be allowed.

Wyatt v Vince [2013] EWCA Civ 934, [2013] All ER (D) 109 (Jun) (Court of Appeal: Thorpe, Jackson and Tomlinson LJJ). *A v A* (*maintenance pending suit: provision for legal costs*) [2001] 1 WLR 605, [2001] 1 FCR 226 (2000 Abr para 1259) considered. *Moses-Taiga v Taiga* [2005] EWCA Civ 1013, [2008] 1 FCR 696; and *M v M* [2009] EWCA Civ 1427, [2010] 1 FLR 1413 distinguished.

1822   Ancillary relief—financial provision—property—charging order—judgment debtor

A husband was the beneficial owner of a property that represented the only asset available to him in the jurisdiction. The legal owner of the property was a company incorporated in the British Virgin Islands. At around the same time as his marriage disintegrated, the husband transferred the single share in the company to a third party, who entered into an agreement to sell the company to the intervener. The wife learnt that the husband had, or might have, disposed of the property. She obtained an injunction to prevent the company and the husband from dealing with the property. The wife informed the intervener that an injunction had been granted but the intervener proceeded with the transaction on the basis that the injunction prohibited a disposition by the company or the husband, but did not affect the sale to him by the third party. The wife applied under the Matrimonial and Family Proceedings Act 1984 s 23(2)(b) to set aside the transactions on the grounds that the first had been a sham and that both had been entered into with the intention of defeating her claim to financial relief. The judge found that, as the intervener had known of the existence and nature of the dispute between the parties, his defence under s 23(6) had not been made out. The judge exercised his discretion and set the transaction aside and ordered the husband to indemnify the intervener against all expenses and costs. The intervener issued proceedings against the husband under the indemnity. He obtained judgment in default of defence and an interim charging order over the property was made in his favour. His application for a charging order absolute was dismissed. On appeal by the intervener, *held*, the interests of the judgment creditor had to be respected, except to the extent that it was necessary to override them in order to make appropriate provision for the wife and any minor children. Since the existence of the discretion to set aside the transaction between the intervener and the third party had turned on the need to strike a fair balance between the interests of the wife and those of the intervener, it was understandable why the judge had regarded the application for a charging order as an attempt to undo the earlier judgment. The equity in the property had been insufficient to satisfy the judgment debt and, if the application were successful, its effect for practical purposes would be the same as the transfer to him of the company. Nonetheless, the judge's characterisation of the application had been unduly harsh because, rather than being simply a transferee of the company with notice of the wife's claim, the intervener had become a judgment creditor and, as such, he had been entitled to expect the court to enable him to enforce his rights. Further, the judge had also been wrong to describe the intervener's application as an abuse of process. It was not suggested that he had obtained that judgment by collusion and in those circumstances he had been entitled to enlist the assistance of the court in his attempt to enforce it. In having regard to all the circumstances of the case, the court could not properly ignore the wider financial needs of the wife and children beyond that of accommodation. In the circumstances of the sale of the property, the intervener had been the author of his own misfortune and that undermined any expectation he might otherwise have had as a judgment creditor that the court would make an order to enable him to recover the losses incurred as a result. That was all the more so in circumstances where the wife and her children would be likely to suffer a degree of hardship if a charging order were made in his favour. The interests of justice would not be served by making a charging order absolute over the property on any terms in favour of the intervener. Accordingly, the appeal would be dismissed.

Kremen v Agrest [2013] EWCA Civ 41, [2013] 2 FCR 181 (Court of Appeal: Sir Terence Etherton C, Thorpe and Moore-Bick LJJ). Decision of Mostyn J [2012] EWHC 45 (Fam), [2012] 2 FCR 472 (2012 Abr para 1815) affirmed in part.

1823   Ancillary relief—financial provision—transfers of money—set aside

See *W v H*, para 85.

1824   Ancillary relief—financial provision—wife seeking financial support—breach of court orders

See *Young v Young*, para 517.

1825   Ancillary relief—proceedings—freezing order—order breaching relevant principles—application for continuation of order

A wife obtained an ex parte freezing order against her husband having earlier filed divorce proceedings. The without notice freezing order prevented the husband from dealing with a property in Spain and further assets. The freezing order failed to specify important information. In her affidavit in support, the wife stated that she had obtained copies of documents from her husband's briefcase, from a filing cabinet and also documents which the husband had either left lying around or which he had placed in the rubbish bin. The husband sued the wife for breach of confidence and misuse of private information. In an affidavit in those proceedings the wife admitted that she had accessed the husband's safe. She sought the continuation of the freezing order. *Held*, the court gave guidance on the relevant principles. Firstly, the court had a general power to preserve specific tangible assets in specie where they were the subject matter of the claim. Such an order did not necessarily require application of all the freezing order principles and safeguards, although it was open to the court to impose them. Secondly, for a freezing order in a sum of money which was capable of embracing all of the respondent's assets up to the specified figure it was essential that all the principles and safeguards were scrupulously applied. Thirdly, whether the application was made under the Supreme Court Act 1981 or the Matrimonial Causes Act 1973, the applicant had to show an unjustified dealing with assets, which would include threats by the respondent giving rise to the conclusion that there was a solid risk of dissipation of assets to the applicant's prejudice. Fourthly, the sources of information and belief had to be clearly set out. Fifthly, where the application for a freezing order was made ex parte the applicant had to show that the matter was one of exceptional urgency. Short informal notice had to be given to the respondent unless it was essential that he was not made aware of the application. Cases where no notice at all could be justified were very rare indeed. The order of the court should record on its face the reason why it was satisfied that no or short notice was given. Sixthly, where no notice, or short informal notice, was given the applicant was fixed with a high duty of candour. Breach of that duty would likely lead to a discharge of the order. Seventhly, where no notice, or short informal notice was given the safeguards assumed critical importance. The safeguards were set out in the standard examples for freezing and search orders. If an applicant sought to disapply any safeguard the court had to be made unambiguously aware of that and the departure had to be clearly justified. The giving of an undertaking in damages, whether to the respondent or to an affected third party, was an almost invariable requirement; release had to be clearly justified. Standard examples of freezing and search orders were appended to the judgment. In the present case, the application for the ex parte freezing order had been fatally flawed in numerous respects: (1) the wife had seriously breached her duty of candour in not mentioning that she had accessed the husband's safe illegitimately; (2) she had failed to provide sufficient evidence of an unjustified dealing by the husband with his assets which had given rise to a serious risk of dissipation to her prejudice; (3) the order had frozen personal assets of the husband in a vast sum in the face of specific evidence from the wife that he had no such assets; (4) there had been no explanation to the court why it was a case of exceptional urgency justifying no, not even short, notice; (5) there had been no explanation to the court why the key safeguards had not been applied, in particular the right of the husband to have money on which to live, to pay his costs, and to conduct his business; and (6) there had been a failure to offer undertakings in damages notwithstanding that they were required by the rules. Accordingly, the freezing order had to be discharged. Further, as to whether the injunction should be re-granted, the wife's defaults had not been confined to a breach of the duty of candour. Weighing up all her conduct, she had forfeited the right to the exercise of the court's discretion to re-grant an injunction. The husband's presentation had not supplied the evidence of a present unjustified dealing by him with his assets giving rise to a risk of dissipation to the wife's prejudice. All the arrangements mentioned in the husband's affidavit had been done long ago as part of his desire to keep his business and other activities as secret as possible. The wife had at all times been well aware of that. Accordingly, the injunction would not be re-granted.

UL v BK (freezing orders: safeguards: standard examples) [2013] EWHC 1735 (Fam), [2013] All ER (D) 277 (Jun) (Family Division: Mostyn J). *Arena Corpn Ltd (in provisional liquidation) v Schroeder* [2003] All ER (D) 199 (May) applied. *Harrow LBC v Johnstone* [1997] 1 All ER 929, HL; *Roche v Roche* [1981] 11 Fam Law 243, CA; *Imerman v Tchenguiz* [2010] EWCA Civ 908, [2011] Fam 116, [2011] 1 All ER 555 (2010 Abr para 2007); *National Commercial Bank Jamaica Ltd v Olint Corpn Ltd* [2009] UKPC 16, [2009] 1 WLR 1405; *Shipman v Shipman* [1991] FCR 628 (1991 Abr para 883); *Wade v Wade* [2003] All ER (D) 38 (Apr); *ND v KP (ex p application)* [2011] EWHC 457 (Fam), [2011] 2 FLR 662, [2011] All ER (D) 24 (May) (2011 Abr para 342); and *O'Farrell v O'Farrell* [2012] EWHC 123 (QB), [2013] 1 FLR 77, [2012] All ER (D) 09 (Feb) considered.

1826   Ancillary relief—proceedings—striking out—abuse of process—delay in commencing proceedings

The Family Procedure Rules 2010, SI 2010/2055, r 4.4(1) provides that, except in specified proceedings, the court may strike out a statement of case if it appears that (a) the statement of case discloses no reasonable grounds for bringing or defending the application; or (b) the statement of case is an abuse of the court's process or is otherwise likely to obstruct the just disposal of the proceedings.

When the parties married, they had neither assets nor income. The wife gave birth to their only child shortly before the marriage and she also had a daughter from a previous relationship, whom the husband accepted into the family. The parties separated four years later, still without assets or income, and were subsequently divorced. Twenty-six years after the separation, the wife applied for financial relief. By this time, the husband had built a company worth millions of pounds. He applied for the proceedings to be struck out under the 2010 Rules r 4.4. The judge proceeded on the basis that r 4.4(1)(a) caught cases which failed for want of jurisdiction, whereas r 4.4(1)(b) better fitted the husband's fundamental attack, which rested on the wife's inordinate delay and the prejudice to the husband that would arise were the case permitted to go to trial. The judge ruled that the potential for prejudice to the wife in being prevented from bringing her case was such that the husband's application had to be dismissed. The husband appealed. *Held*, the judge fell into error in his construction of r 4.4 and approached his essential task too narrowly. It was not apt simply to ask whether the delay was inordinate and, if so, whether the prejudice to the husband was greater than the prejudice to the wife. The judge had to have regard to all relevant considerations within the history and exercise his case management powers not just to protect against the greater prejudice but also to make economic use of the resources of the court. Although there was no statutory bar to bringing a claim for financial relief after a divorce, the court should not allow either party to a former marriage to be harassed by claims for financial relief that were issued many years after the divorce and had no real prospect of success. It was an abuse of the court's process to bring such proceedings, and the present case was a classic example of such abuse. However, an application to strike out under 4.4(1)(b) would only succeed in rare and exceptional cases. Under no circumstances should parties start making applications to strike out merely on the grounds that the other side's case was weak or unlikely to succeed. Accordingly, the appeal would be allowed.

Wyatt v Vince [2013] EWCA Civ 495, [2013] 1 WLR 3525, [2013] 3 FCR 1 (Court of Appeal: Thorpe, Jackson and Tomlinson LJJ).

1827   Civil partnership—formation—approved premises

The Marriages and Civil Partnerships (Approved Premises) (Amendment) Regulations 2013, SI 2013/2294 (in force on 7 October 2013), further amend the 2005 Regulations, SI 2005/3168, by adding the United Reformed Church to the table specifying the person whose consent must be obtained for the approval of the use of the premises for the holding of civil marriage ceremonies.

1828   Civil partnership—formation—procedure—immigration control

The Immigration (Procedure for Formation of Civil Partnerships) (Amendment) Regulations 2013, SI 2013/227 (in force on 7 March 2013), amend the 2011 Regulations, SI 2011/2679, so as to update the list of registration authorities specified for the purposes of the requirement to give notice to a specified authority where a civil partnership is to be formed and a party to the civil partnership is subject to immigration control.

1829   Civil partnership—registration abroad—certificates

The Civil Partnership (Registration Abroad and Certificates) (Amendment) Order 2013, SI 2013/2872 (in force on 1 January 2014), further amends the 2005 Order, SI 2005/2761, by removing the requirement for registration officers to transmit certificates of overseas relationships to the Registrar General.

1830   Divorce—financial provision—allegation of fraudulent agreement—reliance on claims

A wife petitioned for divorce alleging that her husband had conspired with his friend, who was an investor in the husband's investment management company, to execute an agreement which they backdated and which had the effect of transferring three-quarters of his wealth to the friend for the purpose of removing from the powers of the court the majority of her and the husband's shared fortune. The friend sued the husband under the agreement. That led to a default judgment in the friend's favour, after the husband had declined to dispute the friend's entitlement to the money claimed. The wife originally applied to set aside the judgment, but came to a compromise with the husband whereby her application to set aside the judgment would be dismissed. However, the compromise did not involve the wife abandoning her claims that the agreement had been the result of collusive fraud and that its true date had been a number of years after originally dated. During the course of financial remedy proceedings it fell to be determined whether the wife was barred by operation of the doctrine of res judicata from asserting in the impending financial remedy proceedings that the agreement was either the product of collusive fraud between the husband and the friend, or, if not actually fraudulent, was formed at the date suggested. *Held*, the withdrawal by a consent order, which had not yet been made, dismissing the application by the wife of her claim to set aside the friend's default judgment in proceedings between her and the friend, had not given rise to estoppel in proceedings for a financial remedy between the husband and wife. It could not be argued that the husband would be unjustly harassed were the wife to be allowed to pursue her contention in the financial remedy proceedings as to the date of formation of the agreement simply because the overall compromise provided for a dismissal by consent of the wife's claim for a set-aside against the friend. The husband was a party to the consent order and the order specifically recorded the wife's contentions. It was absurd to argue that the husband would be the subject of abusive harassment were the wife to be allowed to put forward her case. Therefore, the wife was not estopped from seeking a finding as to the date on which the agreement was formed at the final trial in support of her add-back argument. Further, it was an established principle that where a party had disposed of assets in circumstances where there was clear evidence it had amounted to dissipation, with a wanton element in that dissipation, then those assets could be added back or re attributed to the pool of divisible assets subject to dispute. However, that technique should be applied very cautiously, and only where the dissipation was demonstrably wanton. In the circumstances, the parties' arguments would have to be tested by close cross-examination and scrutiny of documents. There was no justification to decide on a proleptic basis that the wife's arguments of financial misconduct had no realistic prospect of success and to strike them out. Judgment would be given accordingly.

BP v KP (financial remedy proceedings: res judicata) [2013] EWHC 2995 (Fam), [2013] All ER (D) 307 (Feb) (Family Division: Mostyn J). *Henderson v Henderson* (1843) 3 Hare 100; and *BJ v MJ (financial remedy: overseas trusts)* [2011] EWHC 2708 (Fam), [2012] 1 FLR 667 applied.

1831   Divorce—post-nuptial settlement—variation of settlement

A husband and wife separated after over 30 years of marriage. Of the couple's assets a substantial sum was held in a post-nuptial settlement trust created after they married. That trust owned several companies. There were a total of 11 beneficiaries of the trust at the time of the proceedings. The wife applied for a variation of the settlement under the Matrimonial Causes Act 1973 s 24(1)(c). Subsequently, the trustees of the trust and all the companies were joined as parties. No application was made for joinder, and neither the husband, nor the trustees nor the companies had any notice of the application to join. An application to be dis-joined was made by the companies. *Held*, there was no good reason why either the trustees or the companies had been joined. Quite apart from the failure to comply with the prescribed procedure, neither limb of the Family Procedure Rules 2010, SI 2010/2955, r 9.26B was engaged. The substantive application for variation did not require the joinder of the proposed new parties in order that it could be effectually resolved. There was no separate dispute between the wife and either the trustees or the companies which it would be desirable to determine alongside the variation application. There was no evidence that enforcement of any variation order would be better achieved if the trustees or companies were joined. Therefore, the companies succeeded on their application to be dis-joined. Applying established principles, the court was required to have regard to the interests of the other beneficiaries when exercising its powers as well as to the fact that the creation of the trust was plainly an agreed part of the financial architecture of the marriage. The wife agreed that the object of the trust was to benefit all members of the family. On the other hand the assets of the trust were the product of the joint endeavour of the parties each making the fullest possible contribution in their different ways and were quintessentially matrimonial property. The fairest way of balancing those two considerations was not to allow the full value of the trust as matrimonial property. On the facts the entire structure comprised a variable post-nuptial settlement and the court was empowered to deal directly with, and to make orders in respect of, the trust assets owned by the companies. Subject to the question of need, the matrimonial property ought to be divided equally. Judgment would be given accordingly.

DR v GR (financial remedy: variation of overseas trust) [2013] EWHC 1196 (Fam), (2013) 16 ITELR 281 (Family Division: Mostyn J).

1832   Family Procedure Rules

See para 209.

1833   Family proceedings—fees

The Family Proceedings Fees (Amendment) Order 2013, SI 2013/1407 (in force on 1 July 2013), further amends the 2008 Order, SI 2008/1054, by increasing certain fees that are payable in family proceedings in England and Wales in the senior courts and county courts by the cumulative rate of inflation since those fees were last increased. The order also harmonises certain fees with the amounts payable in the senior courts, county courts and magistrates' courts for the same application and merges certain fees in relation to proceedings for divorce or dissolution of a civil partnership, a care or supervision order or a detailed assessment.

1834   Family proceedings—procedure—evidence—witnesses who do not speak English—preparation of evidence—guidance

The following general guidance has been given about the way in which evidence from witnesses who do not speak English should be prepared. (1) An affidavit or statement by a non-English-speaking witness must be prepared in the witness's own language before being translated into English. This is implicit from *Practice Direction—Written Evidence* PD 22A para 8.2. (2) There must be clarity about the process by which a statement has been created. In all cases, the statement should contain an explanation of the process by which it has been taken: for example, face-to-face, over the telephone, by Skype or based on a document written in the witness's own language. (3) If a solicitor has been instructed by the litigant, he should be fully involved in the process and should not subcontract it to the client. (4) If presented with a statement in English from a witness who cannot read or speak English, the solicitor should question its provenance and not simply use the document as a proof of evidence. (5) The witness should be spoken to wherever possible, using an interpreter, and a draft statement should be prepared in the native language for them to read and sign. If the solicitor is fluent in the foreign language then it is permissible for him to act in the role of the interpreter. However, this must be made clear either within the body of the statement or in a separate affidavit. (6) A litigant in person should where possible use a certified interpreter when preparing a witness statement. (7) If the witness cannot read or write in their own native language, the interpreter must carefully read the statement to the witness in his own language and set this out in the translator's jurat or affidavit, using the words provided by *Practice Direction—Written Evidence* PD 22A Annexes 1 or 2. (8) Once the statement has been completed and signed in the native language, it should be translated by a certified translator who should then either sign a jurat confirming the translation or provide a short affidavit confirming that he has faithfully translated the statement. (9) If a witness is to give live evidence either in person or by video-link, a copy of the original statement in the witness's own language and the English translation should be provided to them well in advance of the hearing. (10) If a statement has been obtained and prepared abroad in compliance with the relevant country's laws, a certified translation of that statement must be filed together with the original document.

NN V ZZ [2013] EWHC 2261 (Fam), [2013] All ER (D) 21 (Oct) (Family Division: Jackson J).

1835   Marriage—capacity to marry—vulnerable adult—marriage valid according to foreign law
See *Sandwell MBC v RG*, para 1877.

1836   Marriage—foreign marriage—domicile and certificates
The Foreign Marriage (Amendment) Order 2013, SI 2013/2875 (in force on 1 January 2014), further amends the 1970 Order, SI 1970/1539, by removing the test of domicile in respect of the parties to a consular marriage, with the result that parties to such a marriage will elect under which United Kingdom jurisdiction they wish to be married, rather than jurisdiction being determined by where the parties are domiciled. The order also removes the requirement for British consular officers to transmit certificates of foreign marriages to the Registrar General.

1837   Marriage—procedure—immigration control
The Immigration (Procedure for Marriage) (Amendment) Regulations 2013, SI 2013/226 (in force on 7 March 2013), amend the 2011 Regulations, SI 2011/2678, so as to update the list of registration districts specified for the purposes of the requirement to give notice to the superintendent registrar of a specified district where a marriage is to be solemnised on the authority of certificates issued by a superintendent registrar and a party to the marriage is subject to immigration control.

1838   Marriage—registered building—place of meeting for religious worship—Church of Scientology
See *R (on the application of Hodkin) v Registrar General of Births, Deaths and Marriages*, para 891.

1839   Marriage (Same Sex Couples) Act 2013
The Marriage (Same Sex Couples) Act 2013 makes provision for the marriage of same sex couples in England and Wales, about gender change by married persons and civil partners, about consular functions in relation to marriage, for the marriage of armed forces personnel overseas, for permitting marriages according to the usages of belief organisations to be solemnised on the authority of certificates of a superintendent registrar, for the review of civil partnership and for the review of survivor benefits under occupational pension schemes. The Act received the royal assent on 17 July 2013 and came into force in part on that day. Further provisions came into force on and between 31 October 2013 and 3 June 2014: SI 2013/2789, SI 2014/93. The remaining provisions come into force on a day or days to be appointed. For details of commencement, see the commencement table in the title STATUTES AND LEGISLATIVE PROCESS.

Part 1 (ss 1–11) Marriage of same sex couples in England and Wales
Section 1 provides that marriage of same sex couples is lawful. Section 2 protects individuals and religious organisations who do not wish to conduct or participate in a religious marriage ceremony on the ground that it is a marriage of a same sex couple. Section 3 replaces the Marriage Act 1949 s 26 and further authorises certain marriages of same sex couples by civil ceremony. The 2013 Act s 4, Sch 1 add the 1949 Act s 26A, the effect of which is to authorise religious marriage ceremonies of same sex couples in certified places of worship where the relevant religious organisation has opted in and registered the place of worship to solemnise marriages of same sex couples. The 2013 Act s 5 adds the 1949 Act

s 26B so as to make certain kinds of marriage available to same sex couples, subject to the relevant opt-in procedure being followed. The 2013 Act s 6 amends the 1949 Act ss 68, 70 and adds s 70A so as to make provision for the registration of military chapels for the solemnisation of marriages of same sex couples through religious ceremonies, except in accordance with the rites of the Church of England or the Church in Wales. The 2013 Act s 7 amends the Marriage (Registrar General's Licence) Act 1970 s 1 so as to provide that a marriage of a same sex couple according to religious rites or usages may not be solemnised unless the relevant governing authority has given written consent to marriages of same sex couples according to those religious rites or usages. The 2013 Act s 8 sets out a procedure by which the Church in Wales can choose to allow marriages of same sex couples to take place according to its rites. The parties to an England and Wales civil partnership may convert their civil partnership into a marriage under a procedure established by regulations made by the Secretary of State: s 9. A marriage under the law of any part of the United Kingdom, other than England and Wales, or the law of any country or territory outside the United Kingdom, is not prevented from being recognised under the law of England and Wales only because it is the marriage of a same sex couple: s 10, Sch 2. By virtue of s 11, Schs 3, 4, in the law of England and Wales, marriage has the same effect in relation to same sex couples as it has in relation to opposite sex couples.

Part 2 (ss 12–16) Other provisions relating to marriage and civil partnership
Section 12, Sch 5 make provision so as to enable couples to remain married following one or both parties obtaining gender recognition, if both parties to the marriage wish the marriage to continue. Section 13, Sch 6 repeal the Foreign Marriage Act 1892. The Secretary of State must arrange for a review of whether an order should be made permitting marriages according to the usages of belief organisations to be solemnised on the authority of certificates of a superintendent registrar and if so, what provision should be included in the order: 2013 Act s 14. Under s 15, the Secretary of State must arrange for the operation and future of the Civil Partnership Act 2004 in England and Wales to be reviewed and for a report on the outcome of the review to be produced and published. Pursuant to the 2013 Act s 16, the Secretary of State must arrange for a review, in relation to occupational pension schemes, relevant differences in survivor benefits and the costs, and other effects, of securing that relevant differences in survivor benefits are eliminated by the equalisation of survivor benefits.

Part 3 (ss 17–21) Final provisions
Section 17, Sch 7 set out transitional and consequential provision. Section 60 provides transitional, transitory or saving provision. Any power of the Secretary of State or Lord Chancellor to make an order or regulations under the 2013 Act is exercisable by statutory instrument: s 18. Section 19 provides interpretation. Section 20 deals with extent and s 21 with short title and commencement.

Amendments, repeals and revocations
The list below, which is not exhaustive, mentions repeals and amendments which are or will be effective when the Act is fully in force.
    Specific provisions of a number of Acts are amended, added or repealed. These include: Marriage Act 1949 ss 3, 25–26B, 27D, 28A, 41–44D, 45A, 46, 48, 49A, 68–70, 75, 78, 80A, Sch 4; Marriage (Registrar General's Licence) Act 1970 ss 1, 2, 13A; Matrimonial Causes Act 1973 ss 1, 11, 12; Domicile and Matrimonial Proceedings Act 1973 ss 5, 6, Sch A1; Public Order Act 1986 s 29JA; Social Security Contributions and Benefits Act 1992 s 48; Pension Schemes Act 1993 ss 8, 17, 24D, 37, 38A, 47, 84, 99, Sch 3; Civil Partnership Act 2004 s 213; Gender Recognition Act 2004 ss 1–4B, 5B, 6–8, 10, 11A, 11B, 21, 22, 25, Sch 3; Constitutional Reform Act 2005 Sch 7; Human Fertilisation and Embryology Act 2008 ss 35, 40, 42, 46; Equality Act 2010 s 23, Schs 3, 9.

1840   Presumption of Death Act 2013
See para 2138.

MEDICAL PRODUCTS AND DRUGS
Halsbury's Laws of England (5th edn) vol 75 (2013) paras 1–555

Articles
For articles relating to this title please refer to the Table of Articles at the beginning of the Abridgment.

1841　Controlled drugs—management and use—supervision

The Controlled Drugs (Supervision of Management and Use) Regulations 2013, SI 2013/373 (in force on 1 April 2013), contain measures relating to arrangements underpinning the safe management and use of controlled drugs in England and Scotland. Specifically, the regulations (1) prescribe a number of commissioners and providers of health care as designated bodies, which are the bodies required to appoint controlled drugs accountable officers ('CDAOs'); (2) provide for some small independent hospitals to be exempt from the designated body obligations; (3) make provision for who may be appointed as CDAOs, how they may be removed from office and the national lists that are to be kept of them; (4) set out the core functions of CDAOs; (5) provide for the establishment of local intelligence networks for the sharing of information about individuals who are engaged in activities that involve, or may involve, the management or use of controlled drugs; (6) prescribe that local networks are led by the CDAOs of the National Health Service Commissioning Board in England and Health Boards in Scotland, and they draw their membership, at the invitation of the local lead CDAO, from the bodies prescribed as responsible bodies; (7) make provision for co-operation between responsible bodies, and in relation to the handling of, and acting on, shared information; (8) enable the Care Quality Commission, Healthcare Improvement Scotland and the General Pharmaceutical Council to obtain information from particular persons engaged in relevant activities; and (9) set out an information management provision to prevent the inappropriate handling of information received by designated bodies and responsible bodies. SI 2006/3148 is revoked.

1842　Controlled drugs—misuse—dangerous drugs

The Misuse of Drugs (Amendment) (England, Wales and Scotland) Regulations 2013, SI 2013/176 (in force on 26 February 2013), further amend the 2001 Regulations, SI 2001/3998, so as to (1) add 2-((dimethylamino)methyl)-1-(3-hydroxyphenyl)cyclohexanol, commonly known as O-desmethyltramadol, to the list of controlled drugs; (2) add new categories of synthetic cannabinoids to the list of controlled drugs; (3) add 2-(ethylamino)-2-(3-methoxyphenyl)cyclohexanone, commonly known as methoxetamine, and other compounds related to ketamine and phencyclidine to the list of controlled drugs; and (4) have the effect that an ester or ether of O-desmethyltramadol is not specified in the list of controlled drugs.

1843　Controlled drugs—misuse—designation

The Misuse of Drugs (Designation) (Amendment) (England, Wales and Scotland) Order 2013, SI 2013/177 (in force on 26 February 2013), further amends the 2001 Order, SI 2001/3997, so as to (1) add Order 2-((dimethylamino)methyl)-1-(3-hydroxyphenyl)cyclohexanol, commonly known as O-desmethyltramadol, new categories of synthetic cannabinoids and 2-(ethylamino)-2-(3-methoxyphenyl)cyclohexanone, commonly known as methoxetamine, and other compounds related to ketamine and phencyclidine to the list of controlled drugs to which the Misuse of Drugs Act 1971 s 7(4) applies; and (2) provide that an ester or ether of O-desmethyltramadol is not designated as a drug to which s 7(4) applies. Section 7(3) requires regulations to be made to allow the use for medical purposes of the drugs which are subject to control under the 1971 Act. Section 7(3) does not apply to any drug designated by order under s 7(4) as a drug to which s 7(4) is to apply.

The Misuse of Drugs (Designation) (Amendment No 2) (England, Wales and Scotland) Order 2013, SI 2013/624 (in force on 10 April 2013), further amends the 2001 Order above by excluding the cannabis-based medicine 'Sativex' from the list of controlled drugs to which the Misuse of Drugs Act 1971 s 7(4) applies.

The Misuse of Drugs (Amendment No 2) (England, Wales and Scotland) Regulations 2013, SI 2013/625 (in force on 10 April 2013), further amends the 2001 Order in order to distinguish cannabis-based medicine 'Sativex' from cannabis in its raw form, and to impose record-keeping requirements in relation to the possession and destruction of Sativex.

1844   Controlled drugs—misuse—temporary class drug

The Misuse of Drugs Act 1971 (Temporary Class Drug) Order 2013, SI 2013/1294 (in force on 10 June 2013), specifies certain substances and products as drugs subject to temporary control under the Misuse of Drugs Act 1971 s 2A(1), and provides that specified regulations apply to those substances and products.

The Misuse of Drugs Act 1971 (Amendment) Order 2013, SI 2013/239 (in force on 26 February 2013), further amends the 1971 Act Sch 2, which specifies drugs which are subject to control as Class B drugs under the 1971 Act, so as to (1) add 3, 2-((dimethylamino)methyl)-1-(3-hydroxyphenyl)cyclohexanol, commonly known as O-desmethyltramadol, to Sch 2; (2) add new categories of synthetic cannabinoids; (3) adds 2-(ethylamino)-2-(3-methoxyphenyl)cyclohexanone, commonly known as methoxetamine, and other compounds related to ketamine and phencyclidine; 2-(ethylamino)-2-(3-methoxyphenyl)cyclohexanone was a substance specified under s 2A as a drug subject to temporary control by virtue of the Misuse of Drugs Act 1971 (Temporary Class Drug) Order 2012, SI 2012/980, and ceases to be subject to such temporary control on the coming into force of the order; and (4) have the effect that any ester or ether of the substances specified in the new provisions are to be controlled as Class B drugs.

1845   Medical products—medical devices

The Medical Devices (Amendment) Regulations 2013, SI 2013/2327 (in force on 21 October 2013), further amend the 2002 Regulations, SI 2002/618, in implementation of Commission Regulation (EU) 207/2012, on electronic instructions for use of medical devices, and Commission Regulation (EU) 722/2012, relating to active implantable medical devices and medical devices manufactured utilising tissues of animal origin. Specifically, the regulations make provision in order to (1) ensure the enforcement in the United Kingdom of requirements directly imposed, under the Commission Regulations, on manufacturers who adopt electronic labelling of medical devices and on manufacturers of medical devices which utilise tissue of animal origin; (2) remove national requirements which duplicate directly applicable requirements under Regulation 722/2012; (3) reflect changes in membership of the European Union; and (4) require the Secretary of State, by 31 December 2019, to review the 2002 Regulations and to publish a report containing the conclusions of the review. SI 2003/1697 and SI 2012/1426 are amended.

1846   Medical products—products for human use—fees

The Medicines (Products for Human Use) (Fees) Regulations 2013, SI 2013/532 (in force in part on 1 April 2013 and in part on a day to be appointed), replace with amendments the 2012 Regulations, SI 2012/504, and make amendments to the Medicines for Human Use (Clinical Trials) Regulations 2004, SI 2004/1031. The regulations make provision for the fees payable under the Medicines Act 1971 and other fees payable in respect of EU obligations relating to marketing authorisations, licences and certificates and registrations in respect of medicinal products for human use. The fees prescribed in the regulations are revised on an annual basis and based on an assessment of the costs associated with a range of licensing requirements and functions. In general, the regulations provide for an increase in all medicines fees to reflect the higher costs for the Medicines and Healthcare Products Regulatory Agency in carrying out related regulatory activities. In particular, the regulations also (1) provide for capital fees to be payable in connection with (a) pre-application meetings; (b) applications for, or variations to, authorisations, manufacturer's licences, wholesale dealer's licences, clinical trial authorisations, broker's registrations, active substance registrations, traditional herbal registrations and certificates permitting the export of medicinal products; (c) assistance in obtaining or renewing marketing authorisations in other EEA States; (d) the assessment of labels and leaflets; (e) renewals of certain manufacturer's licences; and (f) inspections; (2) provide new fees in relation to brokers of medicinal products and persons who import, manufacture or distribute an active substance; (3) provide new fees in relation to persons who provide a pharmacovigilance service; (4) simplify the fees payable for clinical trial authorisations; (5) reduce the fees payable by new manufacturers of simple substances that also serve as active pharmaceutical ingredients; (6) make minor technical changes to variations of marketing authorisations implementing Commission Regulation (EC) 1234/2008; (7) provide for periodic fees in connection with authorisations, registrations and licences; (8) provide for fees in relation to homoeopathic medicinal products; and (9) deal with the time for payment and waiver or refund of both capital and periodic fees in specified circumstances.

1847 Medical products—products for human use—marketing authorisations—refusal—grounds for refusal

Pursuant to European Parliament and Council Regulation (EC) 726/2004, the applicant, a French company, applied for a marketing authorisation in relation to a medicinal product used to treat serious liver disorders. The European Commission issued a draft decision and then a final Implementing Decision declining to grant the authorisation, stating that the conditions for making the grant had not been satisfied. The applicant brought proceedings seeking an annulment of that decision, submitting that the following conclusions made by the Commission were manifestly incorrect: (1) that well established medicinal use of cholic acid had not been proved; (2) that the bibliographical data had to be comprehensive and the concept of exceptional circumstances could not be relied on; and (3) that granting the authorisation would undermine the objectives of European Parliament and Council Regulation (EC) 1901/2006 and the protection of innovation. *Held*, the French legislature had excluded cholic acid-based hospital preparations from the provisions of European Union legislation on medicinal products for human use. It was common ground that there was no medicinal product on the market capable of treating the liver disorders in question, which were likely to lead rapidly to the death of any person who was diagnosed with those disorders. It followed that, in the present case, the cholic acid-based hospital preparations had complied with the conditions laid down in European Parliament and Council Directive (EC) 2001/83 art 5(1), a finding which was not undermined by any of the Commission's arguments. The Commission had therefore been wrong to conclude that the use of cholic acid as a hospital preparation had not constituted well established medicinal use. With respect to the issue of documentation, Directive 2001/83 provided for the possibility of an authorisation being granted even where information was missing, where the demonstration of an acceptable level of safety and/or efficacy could be supported. In the present case, justification had been given for the absence of such documentation and cholic acid had been used in accordance with art 5. It followed that the relevant conditions had been met. The Commission had also been wrong to conclude that granting an authorisation in the present case would undermine the objectives of Regulation 1901/2006. Accordingly, the application would be allowed.

Case T-301/12 *Laboratoires CTRS v European Commission* [2014] All ER (EC) 300 (EGC: Fifth Chamber).

1848 Medical products—products for human use—marketing authorisations—requirement

Marketing authorisation was granted by the European Commission to the claimant for a therapeutic product ('L'). One of the therapeutic indications specifically mentioned in the marketing authorisation for L was treatment of wet age-related macular degeneration ('AMD'). L was distributed in perforable vials, each vial being supplied with a syringe authorised for that use, a filter cannula and an injection cannula. According to the instructions for health professionals, L should be drawn up from the vial using the syringe and filter cannula supplied with the vial. The filter cannula placed on the syringe should then be replaced by an injection cannula and the contents of the syringe should be discarded until the syringe contained only the recommended dose of the product. An injection into the eye might then be given. A third party, which was not a party to the proceedings, was the holder of a marketing authorisation for a product ('A') that covered therapeutic indications connected to the treatment of various metastatic cancers. In Germany, A was used, on a doctor's prescription, in the treatment of AMD, since it had already been used for that purpose before L had been authorised and since at that time there had been no medicinal products specifically for the treatment of AMD. As in other member states, A continued to be used in ophthalmology because it cost substantially less than L. The defendant company prepared, using the content of the medicinal products A and L, syringes which contained only the dose necessary for an injection on the basis of the dose prescribed by a doctor. According to the defendant, pharmacies placed orders only when patients produced prescriptions to that effect. Proceedings were brought by the claimant seeking an order that the defendant cease commercial activity of that kind, which amounted to acts of unfair competition. In support of its action, the claimant asserted that the activity of filling ready-to-use syringes with doses of the unmodified medicinal product further required a marketing authorisation, in particular because the active substances in A and L had been developed by means of recombinant DNA technology and were also obtained using hybridoma and monoclonal antibody methods. The defendant contended that a marketing authorisation was not required for the procedures it carried out, since the process of producing the medicinal product had already been completed at the time when it re-packages it, then distributed it in the form of ready-to-use syringes. The national court decided to stay the proceedings and to refer a question to the European Court of Justice for a preliminary ruling. It fell to be determined whether activities such as those at issue required a marketing authorisation under European Parliament and Council Regulation (EC) 726/2004 (laying down Community procedures for the authorisation and supervision of medicinal products for human and veterinary use and establishing a European Medicines Agency) art 3(1), and, if not, whether those activities remained subject to European Parliament and Council Directive (EC) 2001/83 (on the Community code relating to medicinal products for human use). *Held*, activities such as those at issue, provided that they did not result in a modification of the medicinal product concerned and were carried out solely on the basis of individual prescriptions calling for processes of such a kind, a matter which fell to be determined by the national court, did not require a marketing authorisation under Regulation 726/2004 art 3(1) but remained subject to Directive 2001/83.

Case C-535/11 *Novartis Pharma GmbH v Apozyt GmbH* [2013] All ER (D) 127 (Apr) (ECJ: Fourth Chamber).

1849   Medical products—products for human use—wholesalers, manufacturer, etc

The Human Medicines (Amendment) Regulations 2013, SI 2013/1855 (in force on 20 August 2013) amend the 2012 Regulations, SI 2012/1916, so as to (1) make changes to provisions relating to manufacturers or wholesalers of medicinal products, marketing authorisations and traditional herbal registrations; (2) add provisions relating to (a) brokers of medicinal products; (b) importers, manufacturers or distributors of active substances; and (c) the sale at a distance of medicinal products; (3) make consequential amendments related to active substances; (4) make changes so that brokers of medicinal products and importers, manufacturers and distributors of active substances can apply for certain decisions to be reviewed on oral representations; (5) make provision in relation to information requirements for registration in relation to active substances; (6) provide sanctions for breaches of obligations and requirements imposed by Commission Implementing Regulation (EU) 520/2012; (7) enable physiotherapist independent prescribers and podiatrist independent prescribers to mix, sell or supply certain types of prescription only medicines; (8) provide that, where a licence holder wishes to make oral representations to the licensing authority, a fee is payable by the licence holder; and (9) ensure that regulations related to inspections, sampling and seizure and the review of provisions can be applied in relation to new provisions for brokers, the importation, manufacture and distribution of active substances and the sale of medicines to the public at a distance.

The Human Medicines (Amendment) (No 2) Regulations 2013, SI 2013/2593 (in force on 11 November 2013), further amend the 2012 Regulations above so as to implement European Parliament and Council Directive (EU) 2012/26. In particular, the 2013 Regulations (1) ensure that changes made to European Parliament and Council Regulation (EC) 726/2004 by Directive 2012/26 are enforceable in the United Kingdom; (2) transpose changes made to European Parliament and Council Directive (EC) 2001/83 arts 23a and 123 by Directive 2012/26 in so far as they apply to marketing authorisations, homeopathic certificates of registration and traditional herbal registrations; (3) transpose changes made to Directive 2001/83 art 107i; (4) require the Secretary of State to carry out a review of the 2012 Regulations regs 73, 82, 113 and 142; and (5) prescribe that an operator or commander of an aircraft or an operator of train is able to sell or supply general sale medicinal products.

1850   Medical products—sale and marketing

The Medical Devices (Fees Amendment) Regulations 2013, SI 2013/525 (in force on 1 April 2013), further amend the 2002 Regulations, SI 2002/618, so as to increase the amounts of certain fees to cover the expertise required from external consultants in considering clinical investigations, further to the expansion of the definition of a medical device and consequent scope.

1851   Plastic surgery and cosmetic treatments—provision of medical care—value added tax—exemption

See Case C-91/12 *Skatteverket v PFC Clinic AB*, para 2494.

1852   Veterinary medicines

The Veterinary Medicines Regulations 2013, SI 2013/2033 (in force on 1 October 2013), replace the 2011 Regulations, SI 2011/2159, and make provision for the authorisation, manufacture, classification, distribution and administration of veterinary medicinal products, thereby implementing (1) Council Directive (EEC) 90/167, laying down the conditions governing the preparation, placing on the market and use of medicated feedingstuffs in the Community; (2) Commission Directive (EEC) 91/412, laying down the principles and guidelines of good manufacturing practice for veterinary medicinal products; and (3) European Parliament and Council Directive (EC) 2001/82, on the Community code relating to veterinary medicinal products. The regulations also provide for the enforcement of (a) European Parliament and Council Regulation (EC) 178/2002, laying down the general principles and requirements of food law, establishing the European Food Safety Authority and laying down procedures in matters of food safety, in so far as it applies to veterinary medicinal products used in feedingstuffs; (b) European Parliament and Council Regulation (EC) 1831/2003, on additives for use in animal nutrition, in so far as it applies to veterinary medicinal products used in feedingstuffs; (c) European Parliament and Council Regulation (EC) 882/2004, on official controls performed to ensure the verification of compliance with feed and food law, animal health and animal welfare rules, in so far as it applies to veterinary medicinal products used in feedingstuffs; (d) European Parliament and Council Regulation (EC) 183/2005, laying down requirements for feed hygiene, in so far as it applies to veterinary medicinal products used in feedingstuffs; and (e) European Parliament and Council Regulation (EC) 470/2009, laying down Community procedures for the establishment of residue limits of pharmacologically active substances in foodstuffs of animal origin. In particular, the regulations (i) require a veterinary medicinal product to have a marketing authorisation granted by the Secretary of State before being placed on the market and make provision for the grant of a marketing authorisation; (ii) require a veterinary medicinal product to be manufactured by a person holding a manufacturing authorisation and make provision for the grant of such an authorisation; (iii) regulate the supply and possession of veterinary medicinal products and introduce new classifications of such products; (iv) provide that a veterinary medicinal product may only be administered as specified in its marketing authorisation or, in the case of administration by a veterinary surgeon, where specified exceptions apply; (v) impose controls in relation to (A) bringing a veterinary medicinal product into the United Kingdom; (B) advertising; (C) wholesale dealing; and (D) medicated feedingstuffs and feedingstuffs containing specified additives; (vi) make provision in relation to exemptions, fees and record keeping; (vii) establish the Veterinary Products Committee; (viii) set out the appeals procedure to be followed in specified circumstances; (ix) make provision in relation to enforcement, offences and penalties; and (x) require the Secretary of State to review the regulations, except for the provisions relating to fees, and to publish a report containing the conclusions of the review. SI 2012/2711 is revoked.

MEDICAL PROFESSIONS

Halsbury's Laws of England (5th edn) vol 74 (2011) paras 1–980

Articles

For articles relating to this title please refer to the Table of Articles at the beginning of the Abridgment.

1853 Abortion—medical termination—religious objection—midwives

Scotland

The Abortion Act 1967 s 4(1) provides that no person is under any duty, whether by contract or by any statutory or other legal requirement, to participate in any authorised treatment for the termination of pregnancy to which he has a conscientious objection.

The appellants were labour ward co-ordinators who provided clinical leadership and operational management for the delivery of the midwife service within the labour ward and obstetric theatre. They were not involved directly in the carrying out of any medical procedures. The appellants objected on religious grounds to abortion, and brought judicial review proceedings claiming that the 1967 Act s 4(1) entitled them to refuse to delegate to, supervise or support staff in the provision of nursing care to patients undergoing medical termination of pregnancy. The judge decided that the word 'treatment' in s 4(1) meant activities which directly brought about termination, and the word 'participate' meant 'taking part in', but did not extend to all those involved in the chain of causation. On that basis, the judge ruled that, since the appellants were not being required to play any direct part in bringing about the termination of pregnancy, they did not have a right of conscientious objection under s 4(1). The judge also stated that the 1967 Act was concerned only with authorising action which would previously have been criminal, and that the right under s 4(1) would not extend to terminations authorised under s 1(1)(b) or (c). On the appellants' appeal against that decision, *held*, the 1967 Act authorised not only a medical termination, but also any part of the treatment which was given for that end purpose. It followed that the right of conscientious objection under s 4(1) should also extend to the whole process of treatment relating to the termination of pregnancy. Legislation which dealt with such matters should be interpreted in a way which allowed individuals to be true to their beliefs while remaining respectful of the law. The right of conscientious objection in s 4 was provided solely to respect the strong moral and religious convictions on abortion which it was recognised that many people possessed. The only situation in which the exemption would not arise was where s 1(1)(b) applied and the real purpose of the procedure was to save life or prevent serious permanent injury rather than effect a termination. Accordingly, the appeal would be allowed.

Doogan v Greater Glasgow and Clyde Health Board [2013] CSIH 36, (2013) 132 BMLR 39 (Inner House). Decision of Outer House [2012] CSOH 32, (2012) 125 BMLR 40 (2012 Abr para 1845) reversed.

1854 General Medical Council—fitness to practise

The General Medical Council (Fitness to Practise and Constitution of Panels and Investigation Committee) (Amendment) Rules Order of Council 2013, SI 2013/815 (in force on 8 May 2013), further amend (1) the General Medical Council (Fitness to Practise) Rules 2004, SI 2004/2608, so as to (a) make provision for the postponing of fitness to practise hearings by an appointed case manager; (b) remove the requirement to notify a practitioner when a complaint is closed on the ground that it does not raise a question of impairment under the Medical Act 1983 s 35C(2); (c) provide that documentary evidence may be admitted before the Investigation Committee without a requirement for the Committee to consider whether such evidence is desirable to enable it to discharge its functions; (d) require the Committee or a Fitness to Practise or Interim Orders Panel to accept witness statements as evidence-in-chief unless the parties agree, a case manager directs, or the Committee or Panel decide otherwise; (e) introduce an express power for a case manager to issue a direction to permit evidence-in-chief by way of oral evidence; (f) provide that notice must be given where a party intends to apply to the Committee or Panel for a witness to give evidence-in-chief orally; (g) permit a case manager to issue a direction for two or more allegations against one or more practitioners to be listed for consideration together at the same hearing; (h) provide that any such direction is to be taken into account by the Committee or Panel when considering the exercise of their power of joinder; (i) remove the requirement, at the start of a hearing, for the particulars of the allegation against the practitioner to be read out; (j) introduce a requirement for the Chair of the panel to ask if the presenting officer wishes to apply for the particulars to be amended and to consider any such application accordingly; (k) provide that the practitioner may make submissions after the Council has presented its evidence that there is insufficient evidence to find some or all of the facts proved and that the hearing should proceed no further as a result; (l) make changes to (i) the formal requirements for notices of hearing before an Interim Orders Panel; and (ii) the procedure for cancellation of fitness to practise hearings to provide that cancellation of decisions are to be made by a case examiner in place of a member of the Committee; (m) provide (i) that, on the resumption of an adjourned Committee or Panel hearing, if a panellist will not be present who was present prior to the adjournment or a panellist will be present who was not present prior to the adjournment, the Committee or Panel may issue such directions as they consider necessary in the interests of justice about the stage at which the hearing is to be resumed and any special procedure which must be followed; and (ii) that the proviso for circumstances in which a subsequent panel considers, on legal advice, that a preliminary legal issue has been wrongly decided is sibstituted with a provisio that reconsideration of the issue can take place in circumstances in which the Committee or Panel consider that there has been a material change in circumstances and it is in the interest of justice to do so, or where it is otherwise in the interests of justice to do so; (n) remove the rule which prohibits a Committee or Panel from admitting evidence which would not be admissible in criminal proceedings in England unless the Committee or Panel are satisfied that their duty of making due inquiry into the case before them makes its admission desirable; (o) make provision for applications to a Committee or Panel for oral evidence to be given by means of video link or telephone link; and (p) remove the requirement for the secretary to a Committee or Panel to record and publish the panel's decision and places the obligation on the panel to record the decision itself; and (2) the General Medical Council (Constitution of Panels and Investigation Committee) Rules 2004, SI 2004/2611, so as to (a) make provision enabling panellists to sit on review hearings before a Panel or restoration hearings, or to act both as a case manager and panellist in a case, notwithstanding the rule which provides that no panellist is to sit on the substantive hearing of a case which the panellist has previously considered or adjudicated on in another capacity; and (b) clarify that a quorum of a Panel or the Committee is to be three panellists, including the Chair, of whom at least one must be a medical panellist and at least one must be a lay panellist.

1855　General Medical Council—registration—overseas qualification—validity

The claimant was a qualified pharmacist who wished to qualify as a doctor. He identified a medical course, offered by a university which was a listed institution in the World Health Organisation Directory and had some affiliation with a United Kingdom-based college. The claimant wanted to obtain clarification from the defendant, the General Medical Council, that it recognised and accepted the primary medical qualification provided by the university with a view to him obtaining eligibility for taking the Professional Linguistics Assessment Board examination, which was a competency and linguistics examination which had to be taken when a primary medical qualification was granted outside the European Economic Area as a precondition to being registered with the defendant and commencement of foundation training as a junior doctor. The defendant stated that it accepted the qualification from the university and that it would entitle a student to sit the Professional Linguistics Assessment Board exam. The claimant proceeded to enrol on the course. Before the claimant had completed his studies, the defendant adopted a new definition and criteria of what was an 'acceptable overseas qualification' for the purposes of the Medical Act 1983 s 21B(2). The criteria included that the qualification had not to have involved study where more than 50 per cent of the study was undertaken outside the country that awarded the qualification, and also had not to have involved a programme of study where more than 25 per cent of the study was distance-learning. The claimant was required to take the Professional Linguistics Assessment Board examination and needed to register provisionally with the defendant which informed him that his qualification was not an acceptable overseas qualification because he had not undertaken at least 50 per cent of the standard course of study in the country which awarded the qualification. The claimant applied for judicial review of the defendant's decision. *Held*, the duty imposed on the defendant by s 23B(1)(a) to identify qualifications which were acceptable to it to enable an applicant to progress, enabled the defendant to specify minimum criteria which had to be satisfied in respect of a particular qualification before it would be an acceptable overseas qualification. In specifying such criteria, the defendant had not fettered its discretion. Further, it was not irrational for the defendant to insist on a requirement that went to ensure to a significant degree that the awarding institution had a proper degree of control and supervision over the period of study looked at as a whole nor was the criteria rendered irrational by their lack of transitional provisions, which might have been adopted to cater for those who might have commenced studies abroad towards becoming a doctor in the United Kingdom. In any event, the defendant had been entitled to change the criteria for educational requirements with immediate effect if it had considered that it was appropriate to bring in the necessary changes with such immediacy. In the circumstances, the requirement for 50 per cent of the study to take place in the country that awarded the primary medical qualification fell far short of being irrational. Furthermore, the criteria had a perfectly rational basis and had been intended generally to protect the public and could not be regarded as disproportionate. There was no representation as to the future, or that the defendant would not change the criteria for acceptable overseas qualifications in the future. Accordingly, the application would be dismissed.

R (on the application of Patel) v General Medical Council [2012] EWHC 2120 (Admin), (2013) 128 BMLR 146, [2012] All ER (D) 327 (Jul) (Queen's Bench Division: Hickinbottom J). *Associated Provincial Picture Houses Ltd v Wednesbury Corpn* [1947] 2 All ER 680 applied.

1856   General Optical Council—fitness to practise—rules

The General Optical Council (Fitness to Practise) Rules Order of Council 2013, SI 2013/2537 (in force on 1 April 2014), approves Rules which replace the rules scheduled to the 2005 Order of Council, SI 2005/1475, and which make provision for the procedures to be followed in the General Optical Council's fitness to practise proceedings. In particular, the rules (1) set out the procedure for the investigation of complaints of allegations of impairment of a registrant's fitness to practise; (2) provide for the initial consideration and referral of allegations by the registrar and prescribe the circumstances in which the registrar may or must refer a registrant directly to the Fitness to Practise Committee; (3) make provision in relation to the notification of an allegation to a registrant, the process for investigation and the making of comments on the allegation by the registrant and the maker of the allegation; (4) set out the procedure by which an assessment of an individual registrant's health or performance may be directed by either the Investigation Committee or the Fitness to Practise Committee; (5) allow the Investigation Committee or the Fitness to Practise Committee to draw such inference as seems appropriate where the registrant has failed to co-operate with the assessment process; (6) prescribe the process for the consideration of allegations by case examiners; (7) set out the process for the consideration by the Investigation Committee of an allegation referred to it by the case examiners or where that committee has directed an assessment; (8) empower the Investigation Committee to direct a warning to be given; (9) provide for case examiners to review a decision to refer, or not to refer, an allegation to the Fitness to Practise Committee; (10) make provision in relation to the notification to a registrant of an application for an interim order and for the conduct of the interim order hearing; (11) make provision for various matters relating to hearings of the Fitness to Practise Committee, including representation of parties, proceedings in the absence of a registrant, joinder of allegations and the holding of public hearings; (12) set out rules of procedure relating to substantive and procedural hearings of the Fitness to Practise Committee; (13) provide that the civil standard of proof applies in relation to any facts alleged by the Council, on which the burden of proof rests; (14) allow the Fitness to Practise Committee to admit any evidence it considers fair and relevant to the case, regardless of whether such evidence would be admissible in a court of law; (15) make provision as to witnesses, vulnerable witnesses and for the Fitness to Practise Committee to be advised by a legal adviser, clinical adviser or specialist adviser; (16) require the Fitness to Practise Committee to consider and reach separate decisions, supported by reasons, on whether the facts of an allegation are proved, whether it is minded to conclude that alleged grounds of impairment are established, whether it finds a registrant's fitness to practise to be impaired and, if so, the appropriate sanction which is to be imposed; (17) set out the procedure for the imposition of an immediate order for suspension or conditions after the Fitness to Practise Committee has made a substantive decision, as well as for the revocation of an existing interim order; (18) provide for a declaration to be made by the Fitness to Practise Committee where it has decided that an individual registrant's fitness to practise, or a business registrant's fitness to carry on business, is not impaired; (19) deal with the notification and disclosure of the outcome of investigations and hearings; (20) enable the

Fitness to Practise Committee to summarily assess the costs of any party to a substantive or review hearing, other than a review of an interim order, and to order any party to pay all or part of the costs or expenses of the other party; (21) set out the procedure which applies in relation to review hearings; and (22) make provision in relation to voting procedures, record keeping and the service of documents.

1857   General Osteopathic Council—register of osteopaths—fees

The General Osteopathic Council (Application for Registration and Fees) (Amendment) Rules Order of Council 2013, SI 2013/1026 (in force on 1 May 2013), approves Rules of the General Osteopathic Council which further amend the Rules scheduled to the 2000 Order of Council, SI 2000/1038, so as to reduce the fees payable for entry to, retention on and restoration to the register of osteopaths.

1858   Health and Care Professions Council—constitution

The Health Professions Council (Constitution) (Amendment) Order 2013, SI 2013/3004 (in force on 1 January 2014), amends the 2009 Order, SI 2009/1345, by changing its title so as to reflect the renaming of the Health Professions Council as the Health and Care Professions Council. The order also reduces the constitution of the Council from 20 to 12 and its quorum from 11 to 7.

1859   Health care professionals—European qualifications—accession of Croatia

The European Qualifications (Health Care Professions) (Croatia Accession Amendment) Regulations 2013, SI 2013/3036 (in force on 31 December 2013), implement, in part, the Treaty concerning the Accession of the Republic of Croatia to the European Union, insofar as it amends European Parliament and Council Directive (EC) 2005/36 on the recognition of professional qualifications. In particular, the regulations amend the Medical Act 1983 s 17, the Postgraduate Medical Education and Training Order of Council 2010, SI 2010/473, the Dentists Act 1984 Sch 2, the European Primary and Specialist Dental Qualifications Regulations 1998, SI 1998/811, the European Nursing and Midwifery Qualifications Designation Order of Council 2004, SI 2004/1766, and the Pharmacy Order 2010 (Approved European Pharmacy Qualifications) Order 2010, SI 2010/1620, so as to transpose special provision for the recognition of professional qualifications held by member state nationals where training commenced in the former Yugoslavia before 8 October 1991, or where the qualifications were awarded by the former Yugoslavia before that date, and which are now attested by Croatia as being valid qualifications under Directive 2005/36, into United Kingdom law.

1860   Human tissue—removal for testing—approval—persons having capacity to consent

The applicant doctor had been driving home when she saw the body of the deceased, lying motionless on the pavement. The deceased was seriously injured and had bled profusely. The applicant performed emergency first aid on the deceased but she died at the scene. In the course of the resuscitative efforts, the applicant's hands became covered with the deceased's blood. On her return home, the applicant noticed that she had a number of abrasions on her hands, probably caused by the alcohol hand wash which she used in her work. She was anxious about the risk of being infected with a blood-borne disease and commenced a course of prophylactic antiretroviral medication. The drugs, which had the potential to cause long-term harm, left the applicant feeling extremely unwell. The applicant wished to establish whether there was any risk that she had been contaminated by any serious blood-borne illness. The second respondent coroner, into whose custody the deceased's body had been placed, was contacted and asked for his co-operation in obtaining samples of the deceased's blood or tissue for testing. The coroner, who had no free-standing power to permit the sampling or testing, had no objection to a blood sample being taken and tested, provided that appropriate authorisation had been given. The police were able to trace a family member, a cousin of the deceased's mother. The cousin confirmed that the deceased's parents lived abroad and were not yet aware of her death. He stated that he was the deceased's closest relative in the United Kingdom and gave his consent to the taking of a blood sample. The applicant sought declarations in the High Court regarding the lawfulness of the sampling and testing. Consideration was given to the requirements of the Human

Tissue Act 2004. *Held,* in the circumstances it was not reasonably practicable to seek the consents of the deceased's parents for the removal or use of blood or tissue within the time available in accordance with s 27(8). Further, the cousin was a person in a 'qualifying relationship' within the definition of s 3(6)(c) and s 27(4)(h), for the purposes of giving consent to the removal, storage and use of samples of the deceased's blood or human tissue. Furthermore, the coroner had indicated his agreement to the removal and testing of the relevant material, subject to the consent obtained from the qualifying person. Accordingly, that opened the gateway for the exercise of the court's discretion under the inherent jurisdiction to authorise the removal, storage and use of the deceased's human tissue samples. In the circumstances, the court had little hesitation in granting the relief sought. The applicant's request only arose because she had undertaken an act of great humanity in attempting to save the deceased's life. If testing were not to be undertaken, the applicant would live for the foreseeable future in a state of profoundly anxious uncertainty as to whether she had contracted a serious, life-threatening illness. That would doubtless affect not only her personal well-being, but also her ability to treat other patients. Further, the applicant was suffering the harmful side-effects of the antiretroviral medication. Judgment would be given accordingly.

CM v Executor of the Estate of E (deceased) [2013] EWHC 1680 (Fam), [2013] 2 FLR 1410, [2013] Fam Law 964 (Family Division: Cobb J).

1861 Human Transplantation (Wales) Act 2013

The Human Transplantation (Wales) Act 2013 makes provision concerning the consent required for the removal, storage and use of human organs and tissue for the purpose of transplantation. The 2013 Act received the royal assent on 10 September 2013 and came into force in part on that day. The remaining provisions come into force on a day or days to be appointed. For details of commencement see the commencement table in the title STATUTES AND LEGISLATIVE PROCESS.

The 2013 Act s 1 summarises the main provisions of the 2013 Act. By virtue of s 2, the Welsh Ministers must promote transplantation as a means of improving the health of the people of Wales, provide information and increase awareness about transplantation, inform the public of the circumstances in which consent to transplantation activities is deemed to be given in the absence of express consent, and ensure that the resources available to local health boards include the specialist skills and competencies required for the purposes of the 2013 Act. Section 3 provides that consent, either expressed or deemed, is required in order to carry out a transplantation activity. Section 4 introduces the concept of deemed consent and sets out the possible exceptions to its application. The meaning of consent in relation to a transplantation activity for excepted adults is set out by s 5. Provision is made by s 6 for the arrangements that apply to children and young people aged under 18 who die in Wales. By virtue of s 7, the Welsh Ministers may make regulations specifying excluded relevant material and express consent is required in relation to transplantation involving any such specified material. Section 8 provides that a person may appoint a representative or representatives to give consent to any of the activities set out in s 3. Section 9 makes provision in relation to circumstances where a living adult lacks capacity to consent to donation and no decision is in force. By virtue of s 10, it is a criminal offence in Wales to undertake the transplantation activities set out in s 3 without consent. Section 11 makes provision in relation to offences committed by a body corporate. By virtue of s 12, no proceedings for an offence may be instituted except by or with the consent of the Director of Public Prosecutions. Section 13 makes it lawful to retain the body of a deceased person and preserve organs in the body which may be suitable for transplantation, while the issue of consent to the use of organs is resolved. Under s 14, anything done for the purposes of the functions of a coroner, or under his authority, is exempt from the requirements of the 2013 Act and, before acting on authority under s 3 or 13, if a body or relevant material is or may be required for the purposes of the functions of a coroner, the coroner's consent is required. The Human Tissue Authority is required by s 15 to issue a code of practice which includes practical guidance and standards. Section 16 makes consequential and incidental amendments to the Human Tissue Act 2004 and the 2013 Act s 17 makes consequential amendments to the Wills Act 1837 to reflect the 2013 Act in cases where someone makes provision for an appointed representative in a will. Section 18 defines what is meant by the material removed from the body for the purpose of transplantation. Section 19 deals with interpretation, s 20 with the making of orders and regulations, s 21 with commencement and s 22 with the short title.

Amendments, repeals and revocations
The list below, which is not exhaustive, mentions amendments which are or will be effective when the Act is fully in force.
Specific provisions of a number of Acts are amended. These include: Human Tissue Act 2004 ss 1, 6, 8, 15, 36, 43, 52, 58, 60, Schs 2, 5; Wills Act 1837 s 1.

1862   Medical practitioner—disciplinary proceedings—disciplinary committee—gross misconduct—fairness of hearing

The claimant was employed by the defendant NHS trust as a forensic psychiatrist. Allegations were made that the claimant had breached patient confidentiality by discussing a patient in front of other passengers on a train. A case investigator, appointed by the defendant, produced a report which concluded that the claimant had breached patient confidentiality on more than one occasion amounting to a serious breach of the General Medical Council's guidelines. Concerns were also raised in relation to the claimant's inability to communicate effectively with colleagues and patients. The case manager notified the claimant that the conduct allegations amounted to allegations of gross misconduct and would be referred to a disciplinary panel. The claimant sought an injunction to restrain the defendant from proceeding. The judge held that the claimant had been entitled as a matter of contract to have the breach of confidentiality matter determined in a way which was not under a charge of gross misconduct for which she was dismissible. The judge granted the injunction and declaration sought and the defendant appealed. The appeal was allowed and the claimant appealed. *Held,* the procedures, which the national policy framework envisaged and which the defendant had set out in policies, did not give the case investigator a power to determine the facts. The aim of the procedure was to have someone, who could act in an objective and impartial way, investigate the complaints identified by the case manager to discover if there was a case of a capability issue and/or misconduct. The case investigator gathered relevant information by interviewing people and reading documents. In many cases, the case investigator would not be able to resolve disputed issues of fact. Where a practitioner admitted that she had behaved in a certain way, the case investigator could more readily make findings of fact. If the case investigator were to conclude that there was no prima facie case of misconduct, there would normally be no basis for the case manager to decide to convene a conduct panel. If, however, the report recorded evidence which made such a finding by the case investigator perverse, the case manager would not be bound by that conclusion. Where the case investigator's report made findings of fact or recorded evidence capable of amounting to misconduct, the case manager might decide to convene a conduct panel. The Court of Appeal had been correct in deciding that the case manager would have been entitled to take the view that there had been evidence which could have amounted to serious misconduct and that he could properly have convened a conduct panel on that basis. However, there had been a number of irregularities in the proceedings against the claimant that rendered the convening of the conduct panel unlawful. The defendant had breached its contract with the claimant in treating the matters as gross misconduct for which she could be dismissed. Also the case manager had broken the contract by referring to the conduct panel charges which were not grounded in a previous report. It would be unlawful for the defendant to proceed with the disciplinary procedure and the court should grant the relief sought. Accordingly, the appeal would be allowed.
West London Mental Health NHS Trust v Chhabra [2013] UKSC 80, [2014] 1 All ER 943 (Supreme Court: Lady Hale DP, Lord Kerr, Lord Reed, Lord Hughes and Lord Hodge SCJJ). Decision of Court of Appeal [2013] EWCA Civ 11, [2013] IRLR 398 reversed.

1863   Medical practitioner—disciplinary proceedings—professional misconduct—five-year time limit—extension—exceptional circumstances

The applicant was a consultant obstetrician and gynaecologist. He was the subject of a complaint to the police lodged by his former wife alleging that he had touched his 15-year-old step-daughter in a sexually inappropriate manner. The matter was investigated and found to be 'malicious'. The health authority responsible for the applicant's employment decided not to refer the allegations to the General Medical Council ('GMC').

Over 21 years later, the applicant was the subject of a fresh allegation. Once again the concerns were not substantiated. This time the applicant's employer referred the matter to the GMC. The GMC was informed by the police that the case had been closed with no further action. However, the GMC's registrar decided that it was necessary to undertake further investigations before making a final decision under the General Medical Council (Fitness to Practice) Rules 2004 r 4(5). The assistant registrar decided to waive the five-year rule on the basis that there was a public interest in the allegation being investigated by the GMC. The GMC conducted a preliminary investigation that included taking detailed statements from the applicant's step-daughter and his ex-wife. The applicant sought judicial review of the decision to waive the five-year rule. *Held*, the five-year rule provided a distinct and free-standing safeguard which set a general prohibition against the pursuit of long-delayed complaints. It provided only for very limited 'exceptional' circumstances in which such complaints might proceed. In the event of a wrong decision there was no satisfactory remedy later in the proceedings. The registrar had to be satisfied that there were circumstances in the case which could fairly be described as 'exceptional circumstances' and that proceeding with the case was in the public interest, in those exceptional circumstances. Although a reasonable amount of time had to be allowed to pursue complaints, the policy underlying the rule was that practitioners should not be pursued by stale complaints. The registrar's decision had to identify the public interest and the exceptional circumstances pertinent to the particular allegations under consideration. The assistant registrar's decision to waive the 'five-year rule' was fundamentally flawed and wrong for each of three reasons: first, the earlier allegations were found to be without foundation; second, the health authority had decided not to refer the matter to the GMC; and third, the later allegation was not substantiated. Accordingly, the application would be allowed.

R (on the application of D) v General Medical Council [2013] EWHC 2839 (Admin), [2013] All ER (D) 202 (Sep) (Queen's Bench Division: Haddon-Cave J). *R (on the application of Peacock) v General Medical Council* [2007] EWHC 585 (Admin), [2007] All ER (D) 294 (Feb); and *R (on the application of Gwynn) v General Medical Council* [2007] EWHC 3145 (Admin), [2007] All ER (D) 448 (Nov) applied.

1864   Medical practitioner—disciplinary proceedings—professional misconduct— investigating committee—evidence challenging allegation

The claimant, who was a registered mental health nurse, was employed as part of a youth offending service. Allegations were made against him that he acted improperly towards the mother of a patient and his employer carried out a disciplinary procedure and summarily dismissed him. The claimant's case was referred to the defendant regulatory body, which informed him that the investigating committee of the regulatory body had received an allegation and would be carrying out an investigation. The claimant made concessions in regard to some allegations, but denied others. An interim hearing took place before the committee, which directed itself that it was not required to weigh up evidence, but had only had to be satisfied that, from the information in front of it, there was a prima facie case requiring consideration of an interim order. The committee suspended the claimant for a period of 18 months and, on appeal, the judge concluded that an order of suspension had been unnecessary, and that an order imposing conditions on his practice as a nurse had been sufficient and appropriate. The claimant appealed, submitting that the hearing before the committee engaged his rights under the European Convention on Human Rights arts 6, 8 and, accordingly, fairness required that he should have been given the opportunity to give evidence addressing the substance of the allegations against him, which the committee prevented him from doing. *Held*, notwithstanding that rights under the Convention were engaged, fairness did not require the claimant to have the opportunity to give evidence for the committee, when determining whether to make an interim order, to consider the truth of the allegations made against him. The statutory function of the committee was its duty to determine whether to make an interim order and, for that purpose, it had to decide whether, on the basis of the allegation and evidence against the claimant, including any admission by him, it was satisfied that an order was necessary for the protection of the public, or otherwise in the public interest or in the interests of the claimant himself. The committee had to permit both parties to make their submissions on the need for an interim order, and, for that purpose, it had to consider the nature of the evidence on which the allegation made was based. The committee might receive and assess the evidence on the effect of an interim order on the claimant and the claimant was entitled to give evidence on that. He might also give evidence to establish that the allegation was manifestly unfounded or manifestly exaggerated. However, the committee was not otherwise required to hear his evidence as to whether the substantive allegation against him was well-founded. That was a matter for the substantive hearing of the allegation. It followed that the hearing before the committee had been fair and had not infringed the claimant's Convention rights. Accordingly, the appeal would be dismissed.

Perry v Nursing and Midwifery Council [2013] EWCA Civ 145, (2013) 135 BMLR 61 (Court of Appeal: Hughes and Davis LJJ and Sir Stanley Burnton). *GMC v Hiew* [2007] EWCA Civ 369, [2007] 4 All ER 473 (2007 Abr para 2102); *R* (*on the application of Wright*) *v Secretary of State for Health* [2007] EWCA Civ 999, [2008] QB 422, [2008] 1 All ER 886 (2007 Abr para 2793); *General Medical Council v Shiell* [2006] EWHC 3025 (Admin), [2006] All ER (D) 425 (Nov); and Application 17056/06 *Micallef v Malta* (2009) 28 BHRC 31, ECtHR, considered.

1865   Medical practitioner—disciplinary proceedings—professional misconduct—
        suspension—doctor continuing to provide clinical care

The appellant was a doctor who operated a cosmetic surgery business. A female patient attended the appellant's surgery with a view to undergoing cosmetic surgery. The appellant examined the patient and referred her to a breast augmentation surgeon. Later the same month, the appellant was suspended from the medical register for previous acts of misconduct. Despite that suspension, the appellant nevertheless saw the patient again as a joint consultant with the surgeon, and was present during an operation performed by the surgeon. The patient also attended the appellant's surgery following post-operative problems and was seen by the appellant. The respondent charged the appellant with providing clinical care and treatment to the patient that was in breach of the suspension order and not in the best interests of the patient. The fitness to practise panel found that the charge had been proved on the grounds that (1) the appellant had not informed the patient of his suspension, and his presence at the joint consultation must have left a clear, uncorrected impression that he had remained the patient's treating doctor in terms of her future after-care; (2) the appellant had offered an emergency phone number to the patient, had remained in possession of that mobile phone and had answered it during the period of his suspension; and (3) while the appellant claimed to have examined the patient only visually, the reality of the situation was that he had been conducting an examination in connection with the patient's clinical care and, in all the circumstances, the appellant had held himself out as a doctor providing clinical care and treatment to the patient during his suspension. On that basis, the panel made a further suspension order in relation to the appellant. The appellant appealed against that decision, submitting that he had done nothing in relation to the patient that he had not been entitled to do under the Medical Act 1983, as his involvement, actions and interactions with the patient had not involved any activities for which, as a matter of law, medical registration was required under the 1983 Act. *Held*, it was clear from the terms of ss 41A(11), 41C(1) that the legal effect of an order of suspension was that a registered medical practitioner was to be treated as not being registered and his licence to practice was withdrawn for the duration of his suspension. It followed that the privileges conferred by the 1983 Act were no longer available to suspended doctors. It was not open to a doctor who was suspended from the register to provide clinical care and treatment to a patient in his capacity as a registered medical practitioner. The appellant had treated the patient while giving the impression that he was still registered and licensed to practice. It did not matter that the appellant might, in theory, have informed the patient that he had in fact been suspended and had sought her prior consent to him continuing to treat her notwithstanding his suspension. The fact was that he had not done so. It followed that the panel had been right to find that, in providing clinical care and treatment to the patient while continuing to assume the mantle of a registered medical practitioner, the appellant had clearly been in breach of his suspension order. Accordingly, the appeal would be dismissed.

Dutta v General Medical Council [2013] EWHC 132 (Admin), (2013) 132 BMLR 212 (Queen's Bench Division: Haddon-Cave J).

1866   Medical practitioner—fitness to practise—responsible officers

The Medical Profession (Responsible Officers) (Amendment) Regulations 2013, SI 2013/391 (in force on 1 April 2013), further amend the 2010 Regulations, SI 2010/2841, so as to (1) change the definition of 'NHS body'; (2) alter the duty to nominate a responsible officer; (3) enable the Secretary of State to nominate a responsible officer to the National Health Service Commissioning Board where it has failed to appoint a sufficient number of responsible officers; (4) make further connections between designated bodies and medical practitioners; (5) alter the connection between private hospitals and medical practitioners with practising privileges so that the connection is only made where the medical practitioner is treating patients in the hospital; (6) make provision where a medical practitioner is a member of more than one body so that the medical practitioner is connected to the body with which he has been a member for the longest period; (7) make provision for the Board to determine the division of responsibilities; (8) prescribe the connections between designated bodies and medical practitioners who are responsible officers; (9) impose additional responsibilities on responsible officers in England; (10) require responsible officers to have regard to guidance given by the Board in relation to responsible officers duties in respect of language knowledge; (11) replace references to primary care trusts with references to the Board; (12) omit references to strategic health authorities; (13) provide that ambulance trusts will only be required to appoint a responsible officer if they employ one or more medical practitioners and have a connection with a medical practitioner; (14) add local education and training boards and the Pathology Delivery Board as designated bodies; (15) prescribe organisations which are engaged in providing the services of medical practitioners to work as resident medical officers in independent hospitals, and organisations which provide medical defence services to medical practitioners in respect of claims for medical negligence or professional misconduct as designated bodies; (16) provide that ambulance trusts, the British College of Aesthetic Medicine, and the Faculty of Homeopathy have been prescribed as designated bodies; and (17) substitute the NHS Purchasing and Supply Agency's national framework agreement with the new Framework Agreement for the supply of medical locums.

1867   Medical practitioner—negligence—duty of care—incorrect diagnosis

Almost two months after the claimant was born, he began suffering from shortness of breath, drowsiness and an unwillingness to feed. A doctor at his medical practice examined him and diagnosed colic. Three days later the claimant's mother contacted the out-of-hours contact service at the practice. The call was referred to the defendant doctor, who advised the claimant's mother to bring the claimant in for a further examination. The defendant also diagnosed colic. Two days later the claimant was admitted to hospital where he was found to have acute bacterial meningitis. He was treated with antibiotics, but the illness left him with learning and development difficulties and significant gross motor difficulties. The claimant's mother issued clinical negligence proceedings on the claimant's behalf against the defendant. The allegation was that the defendant ought to have referred her son and that, had she done so, the claimant would have been prescribed antibiotics immediately which would have had the effect of preventing the development of meningitis. The judge heard evidence from the claimant's parents and the medical professionals who had treated the claimant in the days before the relevant consultation. He was also shown the contemporaneous medical records. He found that, due to discrepancies between the mother's account and the contemporaneous records, the mother's account could not be relied on. The experts were agreed that, if the defendant's notes were accurate and the mother's recollection was not, then breach of duty was ruled out. The judge ruled that, although the earlier prescription of antibiotics would have prevented the development of bacterial meningitis, the defendant had not acted negligently in declining to make a hospital referral. The claimant appealed. *Held*, the judge came to a clear conclusion about the consultation with the defendant, and there was no material error in his approach or findings. He had the advantage of seeing and hearing the controversial witnesses giving their evidence. The form of meningitis which the claimant contracted was rare, but the history of symptoms as presented to the defendant was very common. The judge had been entitled to make a finding that there had been no negligence. Accordingly, the appeal would be dismissed.

Doy (a child by his litigation friend Joanne Doy) v Gunn [2013] EWCA Civ 547, [2013] All ER (D) 79 (May) (Court of Appeal: Maurice Kay VP, Moses LJ and Sir Stanley Burnton).

1868   Medical practitioner—registration—overseas qualification—validity

The claimant decided that he wanted to qualify as a doctor with a view to practising medicine. He identified a course offered by a university in St Kitts and Nevis. Pre-clinical studies were by way of distance-learning and two months studying in St Kitts. Clinical rotations were to take place in a number of hospitals in England. Before embarking on the course, the claimant obtained clarification from the defendant that it accepted the primary medical qualification ('PMQ') from the university and that it would entitle him to sit the competency and linguistics examinations which had to be taken when a PMQ was granted outside the European Economic Area. The claimant proceeded to enrol on the course. The defendant adopted a new definition and criteria of what was an acceptable overseas qualification for the purposes of the Medical Act 1983 s 21B(2), which included a revised definition that an acceptable PMQ was one which had not involved a course of study undertaken wholly or substantially outside the country that awarded the PMQ and which had not involved following a course of study undertaken wholly or substantially by correspondence. The defendant amended the criteria and definition of what was an acceptable overseas qualification and informed the claimant that his PMQ was not an acceptable overseas qualification because he had not undertaken at least 50 per cent of the standard course of study in the country which awarded the qualification. The claimant's application for judicial review of the decision was dismissed and he appealed. *Held*, the judge had been right to find that it had been the intention of Parliament that the defendant should set minimum criteria which an applicant had to meet before he could be registered and that that was what the defendant had done. There had not been an unlawful fettering of discretion by the defendant. The judge had been correct to conclude that the retrospective change in the criteria had not been irrational. However, in the circumstances, it had not been open to the defendant to go back on the assurance that it had given the claimant. He had expressly and repeatedly drawn attention to the fact that he had planned to undertake the course by distance learning. In turn, he had received a clear, unequivocal and unqualified assurance from the defendant, the effect of which had been that if he completed the course in a reasonable time the qualification would be recognised by the defendant. The 1983 Act did not in the circumstances exclude the operation of the principle of legitimate expectation. It was for the defendant to prove that its refusal to honour its assurance had been justified in the public interest. It appeared that, in amending the criteria, the defendant had not given consideration to whether it had been necessary to introduce the new rules with immediate effect or to the consequences of doing so. That in itself seemed sufficient to lead to the conclusion that the decision to apply the later amended criteria to the claimant should be quashed. It had not been open to the defendant to change its policy without having adopted some transitional provision that would cater for the claimant's case. There was no sufficient public interest which outweighed the unfairness to the claimant of refusing to honour the assurance that had been given to him and to refuse to recognise his qualification. Accordingly, the appeal would be allowed.

R (on the application of Patel) v General Medical Council [2012] EWCA Civ 1938, [2013] All ER (D) 287 (Mar) (Court of Appeal: Lord Dyson MR, Lloyd and Lloyd Jones LJJ). *Associated Provincial Picture Houses Ltd v Wednesbury Corpn* [1948] 1 KB 223, [1947] 2 All ER 680, CA; *R (on the application of Bhatt Murphy (a firm) v Independent Assessor; R (on the application of Niazi) v Secretary of State for the Home Department* [2008] EWCA Civ 755, [2008] All ER (D) 127 (Jul) (2008 Abr para 980); and *R v Board of Inland Revenue, ex p MFK Underwriting Agencies Ltd* [1990] 1 All ER 91, DC (1989 Abr para 1188), applied. Decision of Hickinbottom J [2012] EWHC 2120 (Admin), 128 BMLR 146 reversed.

1869   Nursing and Midwifery Council—disciplinary proceedings—decision to strike off register—appeal—time limit

The claimants were both nurses who had sought to bring an appeal against a disciplinary decision of the defendant regulatory council under the Nursing and Midwifery Order 2001, SI 2002/253, art 29(9). Both claimants sought to appeal outside of the 28-day time limit. The judge found that both appeals were time-barred. On appeal by the claimants, *held*, it was established that, where a right of appeal was provided, it had to be compliant with the European Convention on Human Rights art 6 and that the rights enshrined in art 6 might be subject to limitations but that such limitations were not to restrict or reduce the access left to the individual in such a way or to such an extent that the very essence of the right was impaired. Although there were differences between extradition appeals and appeals in disciplinary or regulatory cases, they were not sufficient to leave the pre-existing line of authority untouched by *Pomiechowski v Poland*. To take the absolute approach in such circumstances would have been to allow the time limit to impair the very essence of the statutory right of appeal. If the Convention art 6 required the 2001 Order art 29 to be read to the extent necessary to give it legal effect, it had to be to the minimum extent necessary to secure compliance with the Convention. Such discretion was only to arise in exceptional circumstances and where the appellant personally had done all that he could to bring the appeal timeously. Therefore, although the absolute approach could no longer be said to be invariable, the scope for departure from the 28-day limit was extremely narrow and it did not extend to the cases of either of the claimants. Accordingly, the appeal would be dismissed.

R (on the application of Adesina) v Nursing and Midwifery Council [2013] EWCA Civ 818, [2013] All ER (D) 112 (Jul) (Court of Appeal: Maurice Kay VP, Patten and Floyd LJJ). Application 18139/91 *Tolstoy Miloslavsky v United Kingdom* (1995) 20 EHRR 442, ECtHR (1995 Abr para 1567); and *Lukaszewski v District Court in Torun, Poland; R (on the application of Halligen) v Secretary of State for the Home Department* [2012] UKSC 20, [2012] 4 All ER 667 (2012 Abr para 1227) applied. Decision of Hickinbottom J [2012] EWHC 2615 (Admin), [2012] All ER (D) 153 (Oct) (2012 Abr para 1859) affirmed.

1870   Qualifications—European qualifications—recognition

See para 2698.

MENTAL HEALTH AND CAPACITY

Halsbury's Laws of England (5th Edition) vol 75 (2013) paras 556–1016

Articles

For articles relating to this title please refer to the Table of Articles at the beginning of the Abridgment.

1871   Court of Protection—jurisdiction—habitual residence

The applicant was the daughter of an 88-year-old lady. She had three siblings. The old lady was habitually resident in England and Wales, and lived in her own house with a mixture of family and other support and care. The first two siblings were the old lady's financial attorneys under an enduring power of attorney. The first sibling moved the old lady to Scotland, initially to his own house but, shortly after, to a care home located within the responsibility of the respondent local authority. The respondent applied for a welfare guardianship order under Scottish law. That application was made on the basis that, although the old lady was not habitually resident in Scotland, she was present there and it was urgent that the application be dealt with. On that basis, the Scottish courts had jurisdiction. In turn, a welfare guardianship order appointing the respondent's chief social work officer as the old lady's welfare guardian with powers in relation to her personal welfare. Proceedings were commenced by the applicant seeking an order from the Court of Protection for the return of the old lady. The respondent responded with an application under the Court of Protection Rules 2007, SI 2007/1744, r 87, for a declaration that the Court of Protection had no jurisdiction to hear the applicant's application, the old lady being no longer habitually resident in England. Alternatively, the respondent submitted that the Court of Protection ought to decline to exercise any jurisdiction it might have had. *Held*, habitual residence was, in essence, a question of fact to be determined having regard to all the circumstances of the particular case. Habitual residence could in principle be lost and another habitual residence acquired on the same day. In the case of an adult who lacked the capacity to decide where to live, habitual residence could, in principle, be lost and another habitual residence acquired without the need for any court order or other formal process, such as the appointment of an attorney or deputy. In that case, the doctrine of necessity applied. Put shortly, what the doctrine of necessity required was a decision taken by a relative or carer which was reasonable, arrived at in good faith and taken in the best interests of the assisted person. There was nothing in the Mental Capacity Act 2005 to displace that approach. Sections 4 and 5 pre-supposed that such actions were not unlawful. In the circumstances, there had been no kidnapping. There had not been some high-handed action undertaken for some ulterior motive. On the contrary, it had been something reasonably and sensibly undertaken by, or in agreement with, three of the old lady's children in what they had seen as her best interests. In addition, the old lady had been in Scotland for some time and had settled in her care home. Therefore, she was not habitually resident in England. Further, there was nothing, either in the 2007 Rules r 87 or elsewhere, which either expressly or implicitly circumscribed the ability of the Court of Protection to apply the doctrine of forum non conveniens. On the contrary, r 87 was plainly apt to enable the Court of Protection to decline to exercise jurisdiction in an appropriate case on the ground of forum non conveniens. In determining how to exercise its discretion under r 87(1)(b), the Court of Protection was not required to treat the individual's best interests as determinative. When it was considering a question of forum conveniens, or forum non conveniens, it was deciding not what should be done 'for and on behalf of' the individual concerned, it was deciding only which court should make those decisions. In the circumstances, Scotland was the forum conveniens and there were no special circumstances requiring the Court of Protection nonetheless to assume jurisdiction. Therefore, an order under r 87(1)(a) would be made. Judgment would be given accordingly.

JO v GO [2013] EWHC 3932 (COP), [2014] WTLR 337, [2013] All ER (D) 151 (Dec) (Court of Protection: Sir James Munby P). ZH v Metropolitan Police Commissioner [2012] EWHC 604 (Admin), [2012] All ER (D) 134 (Mar) (para 1872); and R (on the application of Cornwall Council) v Secretary of State for Health [2012] EWHC 3739 (Admin), [2013] LGR 197 approved. Spiliada Maritime Corp v Cansulex Ltd, the Spiliada [1987] AC 460, [1986] 3 All ER 843, HL (1986 Abr para 2027); Re F [1990] 2 AC 1, [1989] 2 All ER 545, HL; Re A (children) (jurisdiction: return of child) [2013] UKSC 60, [2013] All ER (D) 66 (Sep) (para 179) applied.

1872　Forcible restraint—police—lawfulness of detention

The claimant was a severely autistic and epileptic young man who suffered from learning disabilities and could not communicate by speech. At the age of 16 he was taken by his carers to the local swimming baths. During the visit, he made his way to the poolside where he became fixated by the water and did not move. After about 30 minutes, the police were called by the pool manager. When the police arrived, the claimant was still standing by the side of the pool. Within the next few minutes, the officers had caused him to jump into the pool. He was removed from the water by lifeguards and police officers. He was then forcibly restrained on his back by the side of the pool by five officers. After he had been placed in handcuffs and leg restraints, he was taken to a police van and detained in the cage at the back of the van. He remained there until he was released to one of his carers. As a result of his autism, he had an aversion to being touched in an unfamiliar way and would not have understood what was happening to him. The agreed medical evidence was that he experienced an acute level of psychological suffering and as a result of the incident suffered from post-traumatic stress syndrome and an exacerbation of his epilepsy. It was accepted by the defendant Police Commissioner that the officers had not sought advice from the claimant's carers as to how to deal with him. The claimant brought a claim for damages against the defendant. He contended that the police had failed to comply with the duty to make reasonable adjustments to the application of their usual control and restraint policies in order to accommodate his disabilities and had thereby unlawfully discriminated against him contrary to the Disability Discrimination Act 1995. He further contended that his detention and restraint amounted to breaches of the European Convention on Human Rights arts 3, 5 and 8. The judge upheld all his claims and awarded the claimant damages. On appeal by the defendant, held, in relation to the claimant's entry into the pool, the judge had been entitled to conclude that the officers had not acted in the best interests of the claimant. The judge's decision had not removed from the officers their operational discretion or imposed an obligation on officers to speak to any carer present whatever the circumstances. Whether it was practicable and appropriate to consult a carer before taking action would always be fact-sensitive. Therefore, the judge had been entitled to find that the officers had not reasonably believed that their actions had been in the best interests of the claimant when they had proceeded to lift him out of the water. Furthermore, in view of his finding that it had been practicable and appropriate to consult the carers before lifting the claimant out of the pool and that, had they done so, the need to restrain him would probably have been avoided, the judge had been entitled to conclude that the officers had not reasonably believed that it was in the best interests of the claimant to restrain him. In any event, the Mental Capacity Act 2005 s 5 defence to the claim in relation to the restraint had been rejected by the judge because neither of the two conditions set out in the 1995 Act s 6(2), (3) had been satisfied. Those findings were unimpeachable and had been fatal to a best interests defence to the claim in relation to the restraint of the claimant after he was lifted out of the water. Furthermore, the judge had been entitled to find that the threshold of the Convention art 3 had been crossed. The police officers had made serious errors which had led them to treat a vulnerable young man in a way which had caused him great distress and anguish. Accordingly, the appeal would be dismissed.

ZH v Metropolitan Police Comr [2013] EWCA Civ 69, [2013] 3 All ER 113 (Court of Appeal: Lord Dyson MR, Richards and Black LJJ).

1873   Mental capacity—lack of capacity—capacity to consent to cohabitation—person having capacity to marry

The Mental Capacity Act 2005 s 2(1) provides that a person lacks capacity in relation to a matter if at the material time he is unable to make a decision for himself in relation to the matter because of an impairment of, or a disturbance in the functioning of, the mind or brain. For the purposes of s 2, a person is unable to make a decision for himself if he is unable to understand the information relevant to the decision, to retain that information, to use or weigh that information as part of the process of making the decision, or to communicate his decision: s 3(1).

The appellant, who had significant learning difficulties, married a man who was serving a long-term prison sentence for serious sexual offences. Concerned about the appellant's welfare, the respondent local authority obtained a declaration from the Court of Protection that, although the appellant had had capacity to marry and to understand the obligations of marriage, she did not have the capacity to decide whether to cohabit with her husband on his release. The Court decided that the appellant was impaired for the purposes of the 2005 Act s 2(1) and was unable to understand the potential risks and their importance to her decision within the meaning of s 3(1). The appellant appealed against that decision, submitting that the judge had erroneously applied a person-specific test that focused on her capacity to decide to resume cohabitation with a particular individual, rather than an act-specific approach that focused on whether she had capacity to cohabit with any person. Held, the test for capacity was decision-specific, rather than person- or act-specific. Although the specific identity of any particular spouse was irrelevant to determining capacity to marry, the factual context of the proposed marriage had to be taken into consideration in order to arrive at a meaningful conclusion about capacity. It followed that the reference in s 3(1)(a) to 'information' included information that was specifically relevant to the particular parties involved. There was an understandable and justified professional concern to protect a vulnerable woman who had formed a close relationship with her husband, but the 2005 Act had to be applied with clarity and care to ensure that the court did not erode the autonomy of the individual. The court's jurisdiction was not founded on professional concern about the outcome of an individual's decision; it could only 'protect' if mental capacity was lacking. The judge had approached the statutory scheme as though ss 2(1) and 3(1) were separate tests, rather than affording central prominence to s 2(1). The judge should have stated expressly the evidential basis on which he found that the appellant did not have capacity to understand the risks which her husband presented. If the appellant had capacity to marry, then, in the absence of clear and cogent evidence to the contrary, she had to be taken as having capacity to decide to perform the terms of the marriage contract. The judge should also have explained how and why the appellant's mental impairment did not rob her of capacity in other aspects of her life, yet caused her to be unable to live with her husband. It followed that the judge had not given the explanations required by s 2(1) and his decision had to be set aside. Accordingly, the appeal would be allowed in part.

PC (by her litigation friend the Official Solicitor) v A Local Authority [2013] EWCA Civ 478, [2013] All ER (D) 71 (May) (Court of Appeal: Richards, McFarlane and Lewison LJJ).

1874　Mental capacity—lack of capacity—ill-treatment of person lacking capacity—directions to jury—conviction unsafe

See *R v Turbill; R v Broadway*, para 635.

1875　Mental capacity—lack of capacity—neglect of person lacking capacity—actus reus of offence

The deceased had been a resident of a nursing home. He had suffered from vascular dementia and lived in a unit for residents with mental conditions. The defendant nurse was in charge of the unit when a healthcare assistant notified her that the deceased was ill. The defendant examined him and sought the second opinion of another nurse on duty. They agreed that the deceased's breathing was shallow and his pulse faint. The defendant called the deceased's son to inform him that the deceased was ill and asked him what he wanted to be done. The son informed the defendant and the other nurse that, as he was in the United States of America, he could not assist them. The defendant then called the emergency services and asked for an ambulance. A clinical adviser from the emergency services called back and spoke to the defendant who stated that the deceased had stopped breathing and had died. The clinical adviser asked the defendant if anyone was conducting cardiopulmonary resuscitation ('CPR'). The defendant stated that this was not allowed at the nursing home. The clinical adviser repeated the question a number of times and, each time, the defendant provided the same response and, at one point, stated that the nursing home did not have the equipment to carry out CPR. The ambulance arrived seven minutes later and the head of the paramedic team examined the deceased and pronounced him dead. A subsequent post-mortem determined that the deceased had contracted pneumonia, which had led to respiratory arrest and then to cardiac arrest. The defendant was interviewed by police and criminal proceedings were commenced. The defendant pleaded not guilty to a charge of wilful neglect of a person who lacked capacity contrary to the Mental Capacity Act 2005 s 44. In his directions, the judge informed the jury that if they concluded that the defendant decided not to administer CPR because she could not bring herself to do so, that would not be an answer to enable the jury to state that the defendant had not acted wilfully. The defendant was found guilty and appealed, contending that the judge had failed to direct the jury properly in relation to the correct meaning of 'neglect' and 'wilful'. She relied on the Children and Young Persons Act 1933 s 1 which provided that if any person who had attained the age of 16 years and had responsibility for any child or young person under that age, wilfully assaulted, ill-treated, neglected, abandoned, or exposed him, or caused or procured him to be assaulted, ill-treated, neglected, abandoned, or exposed, in a manner likely to cause him unnecessary suffering or injury to health then that person would be guilty of a misdemeanour. *Held*, the parties to the proceedings had accepted that there had been a notice in the deceased's room to the effect that he should not be resuscitated; proper medical practice had required that CPR should have been administered to the deceased in the circumstances; and the standard practice of the nursing home had been to provide CPR. The 2005 Act s 44 did not have similar qualifying words to the 1933 Act s 1 such that the actus reus of the offence under the 2005 Act s 44 was complete if a nurse or medical practitioner neglected to do that which should have been done in the treatment of the patient. Section 44 had to be construed according to the obvious meaning of the wording. It had been significant that the judge had found that the defendant had decided not to administer CPR. That the defendant had taken a conscious decision had been an entirely appropriate reference and a correct direction by the judge. There had been no misdirection in law. Accordingly, the appeal would be dismissed.

　　R v Patel [2013] All ER (D) 216 (May) (Court of Appeal: Jackson LJ, Thirlwall J and Judge Goldstone QC). *R v Sheppard* [1981] AC 394, [1980] 3 All ER 899, HL (1980 Abr para 582), not followed.

1876　Mental capacity—lack of capacity—neglect of person lacking capacity—ambit of offence

The Mental Capacity Act 2005 s 44(1)(a), (2) provides that a person ('D') who has the care of a person ('P') who lacks, or whom D reasonably believes to lack, capacity is guilty of an offence if he ill-treats or wilfully neglects P.

　　It has been held, on an appeal by a mental health nurse against a conviction of neglecting an elderly person who lacked capacity contrary to the 2005 Act s 44, that the purpose of s 44 was clear. Those who are in need of care are entitled to protection against ill-treatment or wilful neglect. Ill-treatment and wilful neglect within s 44 are distinct offences. The question whether those in need of care have been so neglected must be examined in the context of the 2005 Act ss 1–3, which provide that, to the greatest extent possible, their autonomy should be respected. The evidential difficulties when the offence of neglect is charged do not make it legally uncertain. Section 44 makes it an offence for an individual responsible for the care of someone who lacks the capacity to care for himself to ill-treat or wilfully to neglect that person. Those in care who still enjoy some level of capacity for making their own decisions are entitled to be protected from wilful neglect which impacts on the areas of their lives over which they lack capacity. However, s 44 does not create an absolute offence. Actions or omissions, or a combination of both, which reflect or are believed to reflect the protected autonomy of the individual do not constitute wilful neglect. Where, therefore, a jury concludes that a carer may have been motivated by the wish or sense of obligation to respect the autonomy of the person in his care, any area of apparent neglect so motivated is not wilful for the purposes of the offence.

R v Nursing [2012] EWCA Crim 2521, [2013] 1 All ER 1139 (Court of Appeal: Lord Judge CJ, Simon and Wilkie JJ).

1877 Mental capacity—lack of capacity—person married abroad—best interests

The defendant was a 38-year-old Sikh man who had lived most of his life in the United Kingdom. He had moderate learning difficulties, was of low intelligence and could exhibit challenging behaviour. The medical prognosis was that his condition was likely to be lifelong with little or no prospect of improvement. He lived in accommodation provided and staffed by the claimant local authority. It was common ground that the defendant lacked the capacity to make a range of decisions as to where to reside, his care package, his contact with others, and certain other matters. The defendant was taken to the Punjab, where he participated in a marriage ceremony arranged by the parents of the two participants. The marriage had formal validity under local law, although at that point the wife was unaware of the defendant's behavioural problems. The couple moved back to England, where the defendant remained in local authority accommodation with his wife's consent. The claimant contended that a declaration should be made that it was in the best interests of the defendant that his marriage be annulled. The claimant submitted that, on the assumption that the defendant had been domiciled in England at the date of the marriage, and that under the law of England he had lacked capacity to contract a marriage, then the marriage should be annulled in his interests. Consideration was given to the Mental Capacity Act 2005 s 4. *Held*, it was not likely that the defendant would ever have capacity in relation to the matter for the purposes of s 4(3). So far as reasonably practicable, he had participated in the decisions by means of his interviews with medical professionals, his solicitor, an independent social worker and with the judge so that the requirements of s 4(4) were satisfied. So far as they were ascertainable, the defendant's wishes and feelings were to remain married. It was difficult to ascertain his beliefs and values, but he did have some awareness of being a Sikh. If he had had the capacity to contract the marriage, it did not seem likely that he would have wished to bring shame and ostracism on his wife by divorcing her or seeking to annul their marriage. He could not gain the support, pleasures and benefits of a marriage as normally understood, but he did gain some pleasure and benefit from the marriage and relationship. His best interests did not require or justify that the marriage be annulled. Judgment would be given accordingly.

Sandwell MBC v RG [2013] EWHC 2373 (COP), [2013] All ER (D) 55 (Aug) (Court of Protection: Holman J).

1878 Mental capacity—lack of capacity—provision of nutrition and hydration against adult patient's will—inherent jurisdiction

The patient, an Iranian citizen, arrived in the United Kingdom on a six-month visa to study English. He made a number of unsuccessful asylum applications, following which the Border Agency confiscated his passport, to be returned on the condition that he returned to Iran. The patient was taken into the applicant NHS trust's hospital under the Mental Health Act 1983 s 136. After his release, he went on hunger strike in an attempt to recover his passport. He was admitted to hospital, received treatment and was discharged but continued his hunger strike. He was readmitted with a variety of consequential physical problems.

Psychiatrists formed the view that the patient did not have the capacity to refuse nutrition and hydration, and that he should be rehydrated against his will if necessary. The patient was detained under s 3. The applicant sought declaratory relief that the patient lacked capacity to litigate, and to make decisions in respect of his nutrition and hydration and that it was lawful for it to administer artificial nutrition and hydration. *Held*, the patient was suffering from a delusional disorder as a result of which he lacked capacity both to litigate and to make decisions about nutrition, hydration and associated treatment. The patient's delusional disorder had impaired the functioning of his brain by affecting his ability to use or weigh up information relevant to his decision whether to accept nourishment. Therefore, declarations as to lack of capacity would be made. It was in the patient's best interests for the court to make an order that permitted the forcible administration of artificial nutrition and hydration but the court would decline to make a declaration that artificial nutrition and hydration could be administered to the patient under the 1983 Act. His physical disorder was, in part, a consequence of his mental disorder, but it was not obviously a manifestation or a symptom of a mental disorder. The course proposed by the Official Solicitor involved reading into the Mental Capacity Act 2005 s 16A a provision that would have the effect of fundamentally altering its clear meaning. The consequences of the proposed reading in of words in s 16A had not been fully identified. However, the court retained power under its inherent jurisdiction to make a declaration and order authorising the treatment of an incapacitated adult on the grounds that it was in the patient's best interests. In the circumstances, where the court was under an operational duty under the European Convention on Human Rights art 2 to protect the patient, it would make a declaration under its inherent jurisdiction that it would be lawful for the applicant to provide the patient with artificial nutrition and hydration, and to use reasonable force and restraint for that purpose. Judgment would be made accordingly.

A NHS Trust v Dr A [2013] EWHC 2442 (COP), [2013] All ER (D) 07 (Sep) (Court of Protection: Baker J). *Re F* [1990] 2 AC 1, [1989] 2 All ER 545, HL; *Airedale NHS Trust v Bland* [1993] AC 789, [1993] 1 All ER 821, HL (1992 Abr para 1770); *St George's Healthcare NHS Trust v S; R v Collins, ex p S* [1999] Fam 26, [1998] 3 All ER 673, CA (1998 Abr para 2207); *Re A (medical treatment: male sterilisation)* [2000] 1 FCR 193, CA (2000 Abr para 2239); and *A Local Authority v DL* [2012] EWCA Civ 253, [2013] Fam 1, [2012] 3 All ER 1064 (2012 Abr para 1875) applied.

1879 Mental capacity—lasting and enduring powers of attorney

The Lasting Powers of Attorney, Enduring Powers of Attorney and Public Guardian (Amendment) Regulations 2013, SI 2013/506 (in force on 1 April 2013), further amend the 2007 Regulations, SI 2007/1253, so as to (1) substitute a period of four weeks for the existing six week period that must elapse between the date of the latest notice by which the Public Guardian notifies the donor or donees (as appropriate) of a lasting power of attorney ('LPA') that an application to register has been received, and the date on which the LPA is registered; (2) substitute a three week period for a five week period during which a donee or donor of the power, or a named person, must give notice of objection to registration to the Public Guardian; (3) substitute a period of three weeks for the current five week period in which a person who wishes to make an application to the court objecting to registration must do so; (4) introduce a new basis on which a security given by a deputy to the Public Guardian in respect of the discharge of his or her functions can be discharged; (5) amend the forms of instrument for the property and financial LPA or the health and welfare LPA, to reflect the change in the time periods made by the regulations; (6) make amendments to the forms prescribed for the purposes of providing notice of intention to apply for registration of an LPA, and notice of receipt of application for such registration; and (7) make transitional provision.

1880 Mental capacity—medical treatment—adult patient—best interests

The respondent, who suffered from a lifelong learning disability, was assessed as having a mental age of between six and nine years. He lived with his parents and achieved a modest measure of autonomy in his day-to-day life and was in a long standing and loving relationship with the third party, who also suffered from a learning disability and lived with her parents. The third party became pregnant by the respondent and had a child. There were legitimate concerns that the respondent might not have capacity to consent to sexual relations and protective measures were put in place to ensure that the respondent and the third party were not left alone and that the respondent was supervised at all times. The respondent was clear that he did not want any more children and that the events had caused him considerable distress. Moreover, the respondent's parents formed the view that the best way, in his interests, to achieve the respondent's wish not to have any more children and to restore as much independence as possible to him was by his having a vasectomy. The applicant, an NHS Trust, applied for a number of declarations in respect of the respondent and the Official Solicitor was invited to act as the respondent's litigation friend as he had been deemed to lack capacity to act on his own behalf in the proceedings. An independent psychiatric report prepared under instruction from the Official Solicitor concluded that the respondent's best interests lay in a vasectomy being carried out. During the time between the making of the application and the hearing, work was undertaken with the respondent to assist him to acquire capacity to enter into sexual relations and, by the time of the hearing, the respondent was considered to have the capacity to consent to sexual relations, although it was accepted by all parties that he did not have capacity to consent to contraception and would not gain the necessary capacity. It fell to be determined whether it was in the respondent's best interests for the court to grant the declarations requested. *Held,* on the evidence and in all the circumstances it was overwhelmingly in the respondent's best interests to undergo a vasectomy. First, his relationship with the third party was enduring and loving and was very important to him. The relationship had been sexual in the past and the parties to that relationship would like, and should be permitted, to resume that sexual relationship. The respondent had been unequivocal and consistent in his wish not to have any more children, which could only be ensured by the respondent having a vasectomy. If another child were born, not only would the respondent be deeply distressed but a removal of the child from the third party would very likely result in the breakdown of the relationship. Secondly, the respondent's only other consistently held view was that he wanted to live at home with his parents. His parents had been deeply distressed by the child's birth and their distress had a significant impact on the respondent's own emotional comfort and well-being. It was not unreasonable to expect that if the parents did not have reassurance that the respondent had the benefit of effective contraception then the level of independence that they would believe was in his best interests for him to be afforded would be compromised. Thirdly, the consequences that followed from the third party's pregnancy had been very serious for the respondent and resulted in his losing, for a period, all autonomy. It was the entitlement and in the best interests of any person with significant disabilities that they were given such support as would enable them to be as much an integral part of society as could reasonably be achieved. The respondent's desire not to have any more children was undoubtedly a magnetic factor which carried considerable weight, but allowing the respondent to resume his long term relationship with the third party and restoring his lost skills and independence were as important, if not more so, when determining his best interests. Accordingly, the application would be allowed.

A NHS Trust v DE (appearing by his litigation friend the Official Solicitor) [2013] EWHC 2562 (Fam), [2013] 3 FCR 343, [2013] All ER (D) 137 (Aug) (Court of Protection: Eleanor King J). *Re A (medical treatment: male sterilisation)* [2000] 1 FCR 193, CA (2000 Abr para 2239); and *K v A Local Authority* [2012] EWCA Civ 79, [2012] 1 FCR 441 (2012 Abr para 1876) applied.

1881   Mental capacity—parent of child in care proceedings—appointment of Official Solicitor—right to fair hearing

See Application 38245/08 *RP v United Kingdom*, para 2171.

1882   Mental Health (Discrimination) Act 2013

The Mental Health (Discrimination) Act 2013 makes further provision about discrimination against people on the grounds of their mental health. The Act received the royal assent on 28 February 2013 and came into force in part on that day and on 28 April 2013. The remaining provision came into force on 15 July 2013: SI 2013/1694. For details of commencement see the commencement table in the title STATUTES AND LEGISLATIVE PROCESS.

The 2013 Act s 1 repeals the Mental Health Act 1983 s 141, thereby removing the rule that MPs and members of the devolved assemblies lose their seats if they are detained under the 1983 Act for more than six months. Amendments consequential on the repeal of s 141 are made by the 2013 Act Sch 1, which is given effect by s 1. Section 1 also abolishes any common law provision which disqualifies a person from membership of the House of Commons on the grounds of mental illness. By virtue of s 2, persons voluntarily receiving regular treatment for a mental health disorder, but who are not resident in a hospital or similar institution, are not excluded from jury service. Section 3 revokes certain provisions providing for the termination of a company director's appointment by reason of his mental health. Section 4 deals with commencement, extent and short title.

Amendments, repeals and revocations
The list below, which is not exhaustive, mentions repeals and amendments which are or will be effective when the Act is fully in force.
  Specific provisions of a number of Acts are amended or repealed. These include: Juries Act 1974 s 1, Sch 1; Mental Health Act 1983 s 141.

1883   **Mental health review tribunal—powers—restricted patient—conditions of excessive security**

Scotland
The appellant was charged with committing rape, assault and breach of the peace. He was subsequently acquitted of all charges on the ground of insanity. He was made the subject of orders under which he was detained at a hospital. Subsequently, the appellant applied to the Mental Health Tribunal for Scotland for an order under the Mental Health (Care and Treatment) (Scotland) Act 2003 s 264(2) for a declaration that he was being detained under conditions of excessive security and specifying a period during which the duties under s 264(3), (5) should be performed. Although the appellant had been subject to the lowest level of security at the state hospital, he was found to continue to pose some risk of sexual violence. The best way of managing that risk could only be determined following his undertaking and completing a course of psychological treatment for sexual offending. The tribunal identified that decision-making under s 264(2) involved two stages. Concerning stage one, it concluded that the appellant had not been required to be detained under conditions of special security that could be provided in a state hospital. The tribunal found that the appellant could be managed within a medium secure hospital, although only subject to considerable restrictions until he had completed a course of treatment for sexual violence. At stage two, the tribunal had had regard to s 1. It referred to the importance of providing the maximum benefit to the patient and to the 'least restrictive option'. Due to the risk he posed to women, the appellant would be required to be subjected to restrictions on his movements in a medium secure hospital at a greater extent to that to which he was subjected at the state hospital unless such treatment was successfully completed. The tribunal refused the application. The appellant's appeal was dismissed and it appealed further. *Held*, if a tribunal reached a conclusion favourable to a patient's application at stage one, it had then to exercise its discretion whether to grant the application in accordance with s 1 and in accordance with the policy underlying s 264. If a patient did not require to be detained under conditions of special security available only in a state hospital, that approach should lead to the granting of the application unless in the particular circumstances there was some good reason to refuse it. However, it would also be wrong to say that it was only in exceptional circumstances that an application should be refused at stage two. Indeed, 'exceptional circumstances' could not be a legal test: circumstances could be described as exceptional only by reference to a criterion, rather than exceptionality being a criterion in itself. Risk was plainly relevant at each stage of the decision-making process. The tribunal had been entitled to have regard to the increased risk to women that might result from transfer to a medium secure hospital where there would be female patients. Its finding that the risk to women posed by the appellant in the setting of a medium secure hospital, prior to completion of an appropriate treatment course, would necessitate his being made subject to restrictions which would be greater than those to which he had been subjected to in the state hospital, had been plainly relevant to its assessment. The tribunal had been correct to consider one aspect of the issue of risk at stage one, namely, the necessity for security arrangements available only in a state hospital, and other aspects at stage two, namely, the risk to female patients in a medium secure hospital, and the implications of that risk for restrictions on the appellant's freedom in that setting, and consequently for the appellant's mental health. When a tribunal was taking a decision under s 264(2), the unavailability of accommodation for the patient at another hospital where he

could be detained in appropriate conditions did not preclude the granting of the application. The tribunal's focus had been on the availability of the most suitable treatment for the appellant's particular needs in the state hospital and in a medium secure hospital, the likelihood of his accepting appropriate treatment in each of those settings. Although the tribunal might have given a fuller explanation of its factual findings in relation to those matters, its approach to them had not involved any error of law. The reasons given by the tribunal dealt with the critical issues sufficiently to enable the parties and the court to understand why the application had been refused. In the light of the matters to which the tribunal had referred when reaching its conclusions, all of which had been relevant, its decision could not be regarded as unreasonable. Accordingly, the appeal would be dismissed.

G (AP) v Scottish Ministers [2013] UKSC 79, [2013] All ER (D) 166 (Dec) (Supreme Court: Lady Hale DP, Lord Wilson, Lord Sumption, Lord Reed and Lord Hodge SCJJ). Decision of Inner House [2011] CSIH 55, 2012 SC 138 affirmed.

1884 Patient—benefits—employment and support allowance

See R (on the application of MM) v Secretary of State for Work and Pensions, para 853.

1885 Patient—detention—compulsory detention—failure to consult nearest relative—lawfulness

The Mental Health Act 1983 s 139(1) provides that no person is to be liable to any civil or criminal proceedings in respect of any act purporting to be done in pursuance of the 1983 Act unless the act was done in bad faith or without reasonable care. No civil proceedings are to be brought against any person in any court in respect of any such act without the leave of the High Court: s 139(2).

The claimant was a 43-year-old woman who suffered from chronic obsessive compulsive disorder. She had repeatedly told health care professionals not to consult her family about her condition. An approved social worker employed by the defendant local authority applied for the claimant to be admitted to hospital for treatment. In the application, the social worker made a note to the effect that, as the claimant had suggested that her parents had sexually abused her, it was not reasonably practicable to consult her father, who was her nearest relative. According to the claimant, while a warrant was being executed by the police to enter her property, she shouted to those around to call her parents. The social worker denied that, but admitted that, on arriving at hospital, the claimant told one of the nursing staff that she wished to speak to her father. The claimant applied for leave to bring proceedings under the 1983 Act s 139 against the defendant, submitting that her admission and detention were unlawful because her nearest relative had not been contacted and given the opportunity to object, and the defendant had acted in bad faith or failed to take reasonable care in the circumstances. She also sought a declaration that s 139 was incompatible with the European Convention on Human Rights. Held, even if the 1983 Act s 139 did affect the claimant's rights under the Convention art 6, such an interference was justified when read in conjunction with art 14 because the protection of carers from being harassed by litigation was a legitimate objective. The present case was one in which it was appropriate to take the patient at her word, since she had repeatedly instructed local authority staff not to involve her family. She had even obtained legal advice about possible breaches of patient confidentiality, and it had been correct to take her comments seriously. Evidence from the defendant's witnesses was that they had considered that involving the claimant's father would be likely to cause the claimant distress, and whether other practitioners would have taken a different view was irrelevant as the test was subjective and a matter of professional judgment. It followed that it was not reasonably practicable for the defendant to consult the claimant's father before applying for the claimant's admission to hospital for treatment, and, accordingly, the application would be dismissed.

TW v Enfield LBC (Secretary of State for Health intervening) [2013] EWHC 1180 (QB), (2013) 132 BMLR 227 (Queen's Bench Division: Bean J).

1886 Patient—detention—compulsory detention—review—time limit—human rights

The claimant, who suffered from schizophrenia, was detained under the Mental Health Act 1983 s 2. Pursuant to s 66(1)(a), she had a right to apply to the First-tier Tribunal within 14 days for a review of her detention. The Tribunal was then obliged to arrange a hearing within seven days of receiving the application. The claimant's completed application form was sent to the relevant NHS trust eleven days after the date of her detention, but the form was not faxed to the Tribunal for a further four days owing to the office being closed over New Year. Officials in the Tribunal's office deemed the application to be out of time. Two days later, the claimant ceased to be detained under s 2 but became detained for treatment under s 3 so that she was entitled to make a separate application to the Tribunal under s 66(1)(b), to which no time limit applied. The claimant's solicitors wrote to the Secretary of State asking him to exercise his discretion under s 67(1) to refer the claimant to the Tribunal. The Secretary of State decided that the 14-day time limit could not be extended on the ground of a public holiday, and advised the claimant to make a separate application under s 3. In judicial review proceedings, the claimant questioned the decision of the Secretary of State declining to refer the case under s 67, and, the conduct of the NHS trust allegedly contravening the claimant's right under the European Convention on Human Rights art 5(4) to have the lawfulness of her detention decided speedily by a court. The claim and an appeal were dismissed and, on the claimant's further appeal, *held*, art 5(4) prescribed no more than that a patient should have the entitlement to take proceedings to have the lawfulness of his detention decided speedily by a court. Given the existence of the claimant's right under the 1983 Act s 3, the risk of a breach would arise only if and when her first application had failed, and her circumstances had changed sufficiently to make a second application realistic. The Secretary of State had not promised to make a reference at that stage, and s 67 gave him no power to commit himself in that way. All he could do was to agree to consider the use of that power if and when it became necessary. However, that discretion would be underpinned by his duty to avoid a breach of the Convention art 5(4). The issue had not been the existence of the right, but how speedily it might be exercised and whether it was as advantageous, as might have been the case if the claimant's original application had been accepted. Accordingly, the appeal would be dismissed.

R (on the application of Modaresi) (FC) v Secretary of State for Health [2013] UKSC 53, [2013] All ER (D) 277 (Jul) (Supreme Court: Lord Neuberger P, Lady Hale, Lord Wilson, Lord Sumption and Lord Carnwath).

1887 Patient—medical treatment—payment by patient for treatment

The claimant had a long psychiatric history and suffered from a major depressive disorder and compulsive neurosis. He was detained under the Mental Health Act 1983 s 3 in a locked unit at a clinic. After he complained of chest pains, he was taken to hospital, from where he absconded. He was subsequently located and, while being transported by ambulance back to the clinic, he jumped or fell from the back of the ambulance and sustained a severe head injury. The claimant, by his brother and litigation friend, brought proceedings for personal injury against the defendant NHS trust. The defendant accepted liability for the claimant's fall from the ambulance and his resultant injury and the claim moved to a determination of quantum. A preliminary issue arose as to whether the defendant could be made responsible for the costs of care or treatment during the claimant's detention under the 1983 Act. It was held that a patient with funds to command would have opportunities to increase the options available to the authorities to improve the standard of his care and treatment. On the defendant's appeal, it fell to be determined whether an involuntary patient detained in a mental hospital under the provision of the 1983 Act could pay privately for his care or treatment, or whether such a possibility was denied the patient by the provisions of the 1983 Act or public policy. *Held*, there was nothing inherent in the structure or wording of the 1983 Act or the National Health Service Act 2006, and nothing by way of public policy to exclude absolutely the possibilities of detained patients, or their family or others holding responsibility for looking after their assets, paying for or contributing in part to the cost of their treatment or care. Detained patients who were being looked after by an NHS authority would have most, if not all, of their costs funded by the state. Even in their case, it might be possible, as in the case of any patient within the NHS system, to purchase additional care or treatment facilities without running into the principle of free provision and the limitations on the exceptions to that principle. Responsible clinicians might recommend treatment or care which the NHS was not under a duty to provide because the treatment or care went beyond its statutory duty. There seemed to be no reason in statute or public policy why there should be an absolute bar on the provision of facilities, recommended by or consistent with the recommendations of the responsible clinician, which might be available at a price, within or without the NHS system. It followed that there was nothing in public policy or otherwise that prevented the claimant from paying for his own care or treatment. Accordingly, the appeal would be dismissed.

Coombs v North Dorset NHS Primary Care Trust [2013] EWCA Civ 471, [2013] All ER (D) 250 (Apr) (Court of Appeal: Rix, Aikens and Black LJJ). Decision of Judge Platts [2012] EWHC 521 (QB), [2012] All ER (D) 42 (Apr) affirmed.

1888   Patient—medical treatment—withdrawal of treatment—patient lacking mental capacity—patient's best interests

The Mental Capacity Act 2005 s 1(5) provides that an act or decision made for or on behalf of a person who lacks capacity must be done or made in his best interests.

Following treatment for cancer, the respondent was left with a stoma in his left iliac region and a colostomy bag was fitted. Some years later, he was admitted to the applicant hospital where he acquired an infection that caused his health to deteriorate severely and his organs to fail. He was placed on ventilator support. The applicant, pursuant to the 2005 Act, sought an order that it would be lawful, in the event of the respondent's clinical deterioration, for it to withhold specific treatment. The applicant believed that it was not in the best interests of the respondent for the applicant to administer invasive treatment. The respondent's family opposed the application as they considered that, although the respondent could not speak, he had communicated and shown positive expressions when the family had visited him. They hoped that the respondent would recover and return home. The judge concluded that the treatment administered to the respondent by the applicant could not be said to be futile. Although the judge found the burdens to have been great, he held that they had to be weighed against the benefits of a continued existence. Further, he held that, in terms of recovery, recovery did not mean a return to full health, but a resumption of a quality of life that the respondent would regard as worthwhile. The judge held that it would not be right to validate, in advance, the withholding of any treatment in all circumstances. The applicant's appeal against that decision was allowed and, following the death of the respondent, his family appealed. *Held*, cases under the 2005 Act were not about a general power to order how the doctors should treat their patient. The court had no greater powers than the patient would have if he were of full capacity. It was settled law that the court could not require the health authority to follow a particular course of treatment. What the court could do was to withhold consent to treatment of which it disapproved and it could express its approval of other treatment proposed by the authority. The court's role was to decide whether a particular treatment was in the best interests of a patient who was incapable of making the decision for himself. The starting point was a strong presumption that it was in a person's best interests to stay alive. However, there were cases where it would not be in a patient's best interests to receive life-sustaining treatment. In considering the best interests of a patient, decision-makers had to: (1) look at his welfare in the widest sense, not just medical but social and psychological; (2) consider the nature of the medical treatment in question, what it involved and its prospects of success; (3) consider what the outcome of that treatment for the patient was likely to be; (4) try and put themselves in the place of the individual patient and ask what his attitude to the treatment was or would be likely to be; and (5) consult others who were looking after him or interested in his welfare. In the present case, the judge at first instance had been correct in his approach. The court disagreed with the statements of principle in the Court of Appeal where they differed from those of the judge at first instance. Thus it was setting the goal too high for the Court of Appeal to say that treatment was futile unless it had a real prospect of curing or at least palliating the life-threatening disease or illness from which the patient was suffering. In respect of the suggestion in the Court of Appeal, that the test of the patient's wishes and feelings was an objective one, namely what the reasonable patient would think, the court disagreed. The purpose of the best interests test was to consider matters from the patient's point of view. However, on the basis of the fresh evidence which was before it, the Court of Appeal had been correct to allow the appeal and make the declarations they had. There had been such a significant deterioration in the respondent's condition that the prospect of his regaining even his previous quality of life appeared very slim. Therefore, the Court of Appeal had reached the right result but for the wrong reasons. Accordingly, the appeal would be dismissed.

Aintree University Hospitals NHS Foundation Trust v James [2013] UKSC 67, 2014] 1 FCR 153, [2013] All ER (D) 339 (Oct) (House of Lords: Lord Neuberger P, Lady Hale DP,

Lord Clarke, Lord Carnwath and Lord Hughes SCJJ). Decision of Court of Appeal [2013] EWCA Civ 65, [2013] 131 BMLR 124 reversed.

1889   Patient—restricted patient—discharge—extra-statutory recommendation—duties of First-tier Tribunal

The appellants in two conjoined appeals were restricted patients subject to hospital and restriction orders under the Mental Health Act 1983 following their convictions for criminal offences. Pursuant to ss 72 and 73, a restricted patient had to be absolutely discharged if the First-tier Tribunal was not satisfied that appropriate medical treatment was available for him. The First-tier Tribunal had a statutory discretion in the case of an unrestricted patient to recommend the grant of leave of absence or transfer to another hospital with a view to facilitating his discharge on a future date. The appellants' applications for extra-statutory recommendations as to their care or treatment were rejected by the First-tier Tribunal. Their appeals against those decisions were dismissed by the Upper Tribunal, which also refused the appellants permission to bring judicial review proceedings in respect of the First-tier Tribunal's determinations. On the appellants' appeals, they submitted (1) that they had had a legitimate expectation, enforceable as a matter of public law, that the First-tier Tribunal would make a recommendation; and (2) if it was suggested to the First-tier Tribunal that leave or transfer was, on the facts, a part of treatment, that had to be listened to and findings made, and that amounted to the very exercise which the First-tier Tribunal would undertake if it received submissions for a recommendation. *Held*, if the appellants had any expectation, it was a procedural one, namely that the First-tier Tribunal would entertain submissions as to whether a recommendation should be made and take such submissions properly into account in deciding what to do. However, there was no evidence of a promise or practice for allowing representations or conferring procedural rights with regard to the making of such representations or submissions. The proposal for an extra-statutory recommendation plainly involved no exercise of a statutory function. What the appellants had sought had been an enforceable right to put before the First-tier Tribunal a class of case that it had had no statutory duty or authority to entertain. Further, the First-tier Tribunal had fulfilled its duties under ss 72 and 73. The express cases of the appellants in the First-tier Tribunal had been to seek non-statutory recommendations. Any suggestion that the First-tier Tribunal had not properly considered what might constitute 'treatment' for the purpose of s 72(1)(b) was to raise a new factual case which the First-tier Tribunal could not have been obliged to consider for itself. If the First-tier Tribunal was faced with a contention and with evidence that leave or transfer was a necessary part or desirable or available part of the patient's treatment, that was something which it had to consider pursuant to ss 72 and 73. However, that was not what had happened in the present cases. Accordingly, the appeals would be dismissed.

C v Birmingham and Solihull Mental Health NHS Trust; F v Birmingham and Solihull Mental Health NHS Trust [2013] EWCA Civ 701, [2013] All ER (D) 238 (Jun) (Court of Appeal: Laws, Rimer and Beatson LJJ).

1890   Public Guardian—fees

The Public Guardian (Fees, etc) (Amendment) Regulations 2013, SI 2013/1748 (in force on 1 October 2013), further amend the 2007 Regulations, SI 2007/2051, so as to (1) permit the Public Guardian to remit or reduce certain prescribed fees where a relevant person is in receipt of universal credit under the Welfare Reform Act 2012; and (2) reduce (a) from £130 to £110, the fee for an application to register an enduring, or a lasting, power of attorney; and (b) from £65 to £55, the fee for a repeat application to register a lasting power of attorney.

MINES, MINERALS AND QUARRIES

Halsbury's Laws of England (5th edn) vol 76 (2013) paras 1–700

Articles

For articles relating to this title please refer to the Table of Articles at the beginning of the Abridgment.

MISREPRESENTATION

Halsbury's Laws of England (5th edn) vol 76 (2013) paras 701–872

Articles

For articles relating to this title please refer to the Table of Articles at the beginning of the Abridgment.

1891   Fraud—fraudulent trading—spread betting transactions—company's clients participating in fraud of employee

See *IG Index plc v Colley*, para 1004.

MISTAKE

Halsbury's Laws of England (5th edn) vol 77 (2010) paras 1–100

Articles

For articles relating to this title please refer to the Table of Articles at the beginning of the Abridgment.

MORTGAGE

Halsbury's Laws of England (5th edn) vol 77 (2010) paras 101–800

Articles

For articles relating to this title please refer to the Table of Articles at the beginning of the Abridgment.

1892   Legal charge—subrogation—marshalling

See *Szepietowski v National Crime Agency*, para 1162.

1893   Legal charge—subrogation—marshalling—exception to 'common debtor' rule

See *Highbury Pension Fund Management Co (a Liberian company) v Zirfin Investments Ltd*, para 1163.

1894   Mortgage broker—negligent advice—Financial Services Compensation Scheme— assessment of compensation

See *Emptage v Financial Services Compensation Scheme Ltd*, para 1241.

1895   Mortgagee—power of sale—duties—breach

The claimants were companies in the same group. The first two claimants were the holding companies of two companies which had borrowed, by way of mortgage, from the first defendant company in order to purchase a number of aircraft. The aircraft were then leased to a third company. In a second transaction, three more aircraft were purchased by a fourth company through funding by the first defendant. The fourth company was also part of the same group as the claimants. The aircraft purchased by the fourth company were newer and there was substantial equity, over and above the amounts advanced by the first defendant, providing for cross-collateralisation in respect of the amounts owing to the first defendant on the original purchase. The fourth claimant was entitled to the balance of any proceeds left after payment of sums due to the first defendant in respect of the aircraft purchased by the fourth company. When the third company filed for insolvency, the first defendant's power of sale arose in respect of the original purchase and an auction was held. The aircraft were purchased by the first defendant at a price approved by the second defendant company, transferred on an inter-company basis to the second defendant and leased to another airline. The first defendant put the original aircraft into effectively good as new condition for the lease and charged the net cost to the mortgage account for the borrowers. As a result, the outstanding balance in the mortgage account, which was substantially in arrears, was set off/cross-collateralised against the equity in the aircraft purchased by the fourth company. The claimants alleged breach of duty. *Held*, there had been a breach of duty to the borrowers by the first defendant. Under settled principles, it had not necessarily been impossible for the second defendant to have advanced its determination to purchase the original aircraft for the purposes of lending to the airline provided that the first defendant could show that the correct value had been obtained. The auction had been something of a charade. As a special purchaser, the first defendant would have paid more than the market price. That was what and should have occurred. As the onus was on the first defendant to show what would have occurred had proper steps been taken to obtain the proper market value, then a greater sum would have been credited to the mortgage account in respect of the original aircraft than the price which the first defendant had bid in the auction. The first defendant had owed a duty not to have gone through the half-hearted exercise of the auction. The difference between the price obtained in breach of duty for the original aircraft and the best price that had been reasonably obtainable had not fallen within an acceptable margin of error such that the first defendant had acted reasonably. Further, the first defendant had known that the residual balance after satisfaction of the sums owing to it under the fourth company cross-collateralised equity passed down to the fourth claimant. On the evidence, there had been a wilful misconduct on the part of the first defendant. The second defendant had known that the first defendant had owed a duty to the borrowers and that the second defendant had known that, or had been reckless as to whether, the first defendant had thereby owed a duty to the fourth claimant, the breach of which the second defendant had procured. Furthermore, the first and second defendants had been liable for conspiracy to the relevant standard of proof. There had been a breach of duty by the first defendant owed to the borrowers and the fourth claimant and the procurement of such a breach by the second defendant. There had been deliberate loss which the first and second defendants had known and intended to be caused by the unlawful acts to the borrowers and the fourth claimant as the residual beneficiary. Accordingly, the application would be allowed.

Alpstream AG v PK Airfinance Sarl [2013] EWHC 2370 (Comm), [2014] 1 All ER (Comm) 441 (Queen's Bench Division: Burton J). *Tse Kwong Lam v Wong Chit Sen* [1983] 3 All ER 54, PC (1983 Abr para 2378); *Kuwait Oil Tanker Co SAK v Al Bader* [2000] 2 All ER (Comm) 271, CA (2000 Abr para 3146); *Meretz Investments NV v ACP Ltd* [2007] EWCA Civ 1303, [2008] Ch 244, [2007] All ER (D) 156 (Dec) (2007 Abr para 2865); and *Bank of Tokyo-Mitsubishi UFJ Ltd v Baskan Gida Sanayi Ve Pazarlama As* [2009] EWHC 1276 (Ch), [2009] All ER (D) 308 (Jun) applied.

NATIONAL CULTURAL HERITAGE

Halsbury's Laws of England (5th edn) vol 77 (2010) paras 801–1117

Articles

For articles relating to this title please refer to the Table of Articles at the beginning of the Abridgment.

1896   Libraries—legal deposit libraries—non-print works

The Legal Deposit Libraries (Non-Print Works) Regulations 2013, SI 2013/777 (in force on 6 April 2013), provide for the Legal Deposit Libraries Act 2003, under which works published in print in the United Kingdom are delivered to deposit libraries, to be extended to work published in a medium other than print, that is, work published on line or off line; there is an exemption for existing micro-businesses and new businesses. In particular, the regulations (1) contain definitions of expressions used in the regulations; (2) provide that in relation to certain regulations, the expression 'deposit library' includes reference to the Faculty of Advocates; (3) provide that for a specified period ('the exemption period') certain regulations do not apply in relation to non-print work where the person who publishes the work does so in the course of a business and that business is an existing micro-business or a new business; a charity which trades will fall within the meaning of 'in the course of a business' whether or not it is carrying out trading activities with a view to profit; (4) provide that once the exemption period has ended the automatic entitlement of the British Library Board to delivery of off line work within one month of publication does not apply to any work that was subject to the exemption; (5) provide that once the exemption period has ended, the British Library Board may request delivery, along with the other deposit libraries, of off line work that was subject to the exemption; (6) explain what is meant by 'micro-business'; (7) explain what is meant by 'existing micro-business', and what is meant by 'new business'; (8) provide that a person, or number of persons, starts a new business when he begins to carry on a business during the period starting on the commencement date and ending on 31 March 2014; (9) define when a business is not to be regarded as a 'new business'; in the vast majority of cases there will be no question about whether a new business has started as no business will have existed before and so this test will be satisfied; the definition of a new business provides that a business will not be a new business if a person has at any time in the six months before the start of the business carried on another business consisting of most of the activities of which the most recent business consists; this is to exclude a business which ceases and then restarts or restructures itself in circumstances where it is not actually a new business; (10) have the effect that a business which does cease and restart will continue to qualify as a new business if the earlier business was a new business; (11) provide that a business is not a 'new' business if a person carries it on as a result of a transfer; that happens when a person begins to carry on the business on another person ceasing to carry on the activities of which it consists or mostly consists in consequence of arrangements involving the person and the other person; so a business will not count as a new business if: (a) there is a transfer of activities of an existing business from one person to another; (b) those activities constitute all or most of the activities of the business to which the transfer is made, and (c) there is an arrangement for the transfer between the parties; (12) provide that a person is to be taken, for the purposes of head 11, to begin to carry on a business on another person ceasing to carry on such activities if the business begins to be carried on by a person otherwise than in partnership on such activities ceasing to be carried on by persons in partnership; (13) provide that a person is to be taken, for the purposes of head 11, to begin to carry on a business on another person ceasing to carry on such activities if the person, or number of persons, is a partnership which begins to carry on the business on such activities ceasing to be carried on: (a) by a person or persons otherwise than in partnership; (b) by a partnership not consisting only of all the persons constituting the persons, or number of persons; or (c) partly as mentioned in head (a) and partly as mentioned in head (b); (14) have the effect that a business will continue to qualify as a new business after a transfer (within the meaning of head 11) if the business before it was transferred was also a new business; (15) provide that a person will not be starting a new business if (a) before beginning to carry on a business, he enters into arrangements under which he may at any time during the relevant period carry on, as part of the business, activities carried on by another person, and (b) the business would have been prevented by head 11 from being a new business if the person had been undertaking the activities at the time he started his business, and the other person at that time had ceased to carry them on; the intended effect of this provision is that a person will be not be carrying on a new business if, before beginning to carry on a business, the person enters into arrangements that mean that at some point after the person's business has started that person may undertake activities carried on by another business and, had the person been undertaking those activities at the time the business was started, that person's business would not have been a new business; (16) define the exemption period in relation to an existing micro-business and a new business; (17) explain how the number of employees of a business is calculated; (18) explain what is meant by 'employees of a business'; (19) explain what is meant by 'employee'; (20) provide that the expression 'commencement date' means the date on which the regulations come into force; (21) prescribe a description of non-print work for the purposes of the 2003 Act s 1(4); the description is based on the manner by which the work is published, specifically, work published on line and work published off line; (22) provide that the prescribed description does not include certain works, namely works consisting only or predominantly of a sound recording or film or both, work which contains personal data and which is only made available to a restricted group of persons, or work which was published before the regulations were made; (23) set out the description of work that is prescribed for the purposes of the 2003 Act s 10(5)(a); (24) make provision, for the purposes of the 2003 Act s 2(2)(b), for the medium in which a work should be delivered in circumstances where substantially the same work is published in more than one medium; (25) provide that where substantially the same work is published in print and non-print media, the work should be delivered in print unless the publisher and the deposit library agree that delivery should be in a non-print medium; the non-print medium in which the work is delivered must be one in which the work is published; (26) provide that where substantially the same work is published in more than one non-print medium, the medium of delivery is the medium agreed by the deposit library and the publisher or in the absence of agreement, that decided by the publisher; (27) provide for the entitlement of the deposit libraries to a copy of work published off line; (28) provide that the British Library Board is automatically entitled to a copy of work published off line within one month of the work being published; (29) provide that the other deposit libraries are entitled on request to delivery of off line work; (30) provide for the entitlement of the deposit libraries to a copy of work published on line; (31) provide that each deposit library is entitled to delivery of a copy of the on line work it requests and that any such request must be made in accordance with head 32 or 33; (32) provide that a request may be made pursuant to an agreement between the publisher and the deposit library as to the method by which work requested under the agreement will be delivered; the method agreed between the publisher and the deposit library regarding the delivery of on line work may, but need not, include web harvesting; if on line material is delivered pursuant to such an agreement, it must be delivered within one month of the request, and the request must be in writing; (33) provide that where no agreement of the kind referred to in head 32 is in place, a request must be made by way of web harvester software sent from an IP address of the deposit library to the IP address hosting the work; (34) provide that the work requested under head 33 must be delivered by electronic means and by automated response to the request by the web harvester; overall, the effect is that unless there is in place an agreement of the kind referred to in head 32, the request and delivery of prescribed on line works is achieved by a deposit library's collecting such work through the use of web harvester software; in relation to works that are not immediately accessible to a web harvester because they are behind a login facility, the regulations provide that the request by the web harvester will be treated as a request for the works behind the login facility provided that the deposit library has given the publisher at least one month's written notice before making the request; (35) provide that the deposit library must use any login details provided by the publisher in making a request for works behind a login facility; (36) provide that in relation to off line work, and on line work delivered pursuant to an agreement under head 32, the publisher must also deliver to the deposit library a copy of any computer program or other information required to access the work, and a copy of any manual that accompanies the published work; (37) define in relation to an on line work what is meant by 'published in the United Kingdom'; (38) provide that this definition is also the prescribed manner in which the publication of a work on the internet, or a person publishing it there, is connected with the United Kingdom for the purposes of the 2003 Act s 10(5)(b); (39) provide that a deposit library may transfer or lend relevant material to other deposit libraries; (40) provide that a deposit library may use relevant material in order to review or maintain the relevant material, or for the purposes of the deposit library's own non-commercial research; (41) provide that the National Library of Scotland may permanently transfer off line legal publications to the Faculty of Advocates and may transfer or lend on line legal publications to the Faculty of Advocates; (42) provide that in each deposit library the same relevant material may only be displayed on one computer terminal at any one time; (43) provide that at least seven days must elapse from delivery of on line material to a deposit library before a reader may view it; (44) allow a copyright or database right owner in relation to relevant material to request a deposit library to withhold reader access to that material for periods of up to three years provided that the deposit library is satisfied that reader access during this period would, or would be likely to, unreasonably prejudice the interests of the requestor; subsequent requests may be made in relation to the same relevant material, and a subsequent request may extend an earlier request; (45) provide for a deposit library to make and supply accessible copies of relevant material for use by visually impaired persons provided that accessible copies are not otherwise commercially available; the terms 'accessible copy' and 'visually impaired' have the same meanings as in the Copyright, Designs and Patents Act 1988 s 31F; (46) provide that only one reader may use an accessible copy of the same relevant material at the same time; (47) make provisions in relation to intermediate copies, which are necessarily made during the production of accessible copies, and impose certain requirements on deposit libraries in connection with making accessible copies; (48) provide for a deposit library to make and supply a copy of relevant material to a person provided that the conditions specified are met; (49) provide for what is meant by 'similar' and 'related' in relation to the requirements of persons requesting copies; (50) provide for the circumstances in which, and the purposes for which, a deposit library may rely on a signed declaration by a person in relation to a request for a copy of relevant material; (51) impose certain requirements on the supply of a copy of relevant material under heads 48–50; (52) provide that, in certain circumstances, a deposit library may copy or adapt relevant material for the purposes of preservation; (53) provide that a deposit library may destroy relevant material or copies or adaptations of relevant material but must keep at least one copy of the relevant material; and (54) contain the form of the declaration to be signed by persons requesting a copy of relevant material under heads 48–50.

1897 Libraries—Registrar of Public Lending Right—abolition

See para 1897.

NEGLIGENCE

Halsbury's Laws of England (5th edn) vol 78 (2010) paras 1–100

Articles

For articles relating to this title please refer to the Table of Articles at the beginning of the Abridgment.

1898 Contributory negligence—road accident—intoxicated pedestrian—reasonable action of driver

The parties were involved in an accident on a pedestrianised road through a city centre, at a traffic light intersection late at night. The claimant, who was intoxicated, approached the defendant's car while it was stationary, blocked the path of the defendant and dropped his trousers. At some point the defendant drove his car forward, trying to avoid the claimant, but knocking him down and causing the claimant brain and knee injuries. The claimant brought a claim in damages against the defendant. He contended that he was struck by the defendant's car as it moved off, causing him to fall and hit his head on the kerb, and that his knee was injured by the car's bumper impacting it or by the car driving over him. The defendant's case was that the claimant fell to the ground and sustained his head injury before any contact with the defendant's car had occurred and, unaware that the claimant was lying in the road, he then ran over the claimant. *Held*, the evidence suggested that the defendant had deliberately, but not maliciously, driven towards the claimant under the mistaken impression that he had moved. However, this did not rob the defendant of primary liability for the accident. While the claimant had no business to cause an obstruction in the road and was acting in an anti-social manner, it was incumbent on the defendant not to drive away until it was safe to do so without risk of injuring the claimant. His priority should have been to observe the claimant's movements, and to wait until the claimant was safely clear of his car before moving forward. The claimant had to take some responsibility for his actions, having deliberately placed himself in the road in front of the defendant's car and remained there, while his drunken condition and state of attire hampered his ability to move freely and at a normal speed out of the path of the defendant's car. In the circumstances liability would be apportioned 80 per cent to the defendant and 20 per cent to the claimant. Judgment would be given accordingly.

Ayres v Odedra [2013] EWHC 40 (QB), [2013] All ER (D) 114 (Jan) (Queen's Bench Division: Swift J). *Eagle v Chambers* [2003] EWCA Civ 1107, [2003] All ER (D) 411 (Jul) (2003 Abr para 1980) applied. *Lee North v TNT Express (UK) Ltd* [2001] EWCA Civ 853, [2001] All ER (D) 358 (May) distinguished.

1899 Duty of care—accountant—tax advice—person with non-domiciled status

The claimant sold his shareholding in a company, resulting in a large capital gains tax liability. On the advice of a third party, he entered into a capital redemption plan, which ultimately failed and caused him to incur tax penalties and interest payments. The claimant issued proceedings against the defendant, his accountant, submitting that its advice about the reduction in his tax liability had been negligent. In particular, he contended that the defendant should have advised him, as a person not domiciled in the United Kingdom, to enter into a bearer warrant scheme rather than the capital redemption plan, or at least to consult a tax adviser specialising in the tax affairs of non-domiciled persons. *Held*, the defendant had had a contractual duty or concurrent tortious duty to advise the claimant of his non-domiciled status, and that such a status carried with it potentially significant tax advantages. It also had a contractual duty or concurrent tortious duty to advise the claimant, especially in the light of his large potential tax liability, that he should take tax advice from a firm of accountants or tax advisers who specialised in advising individuals who had or might have non-domiciled status. Moreover, on the evidence, any reasonably competent accountant holding himself out as having expertise in advising non-domiciled persons would not have recommended the capital redemption plan to the claimant. The plan had been much more risky and costly than the bearer warrant scheme. Accordingly, the application would be allowed.

Mehjoo v Harben Barker (a firm) [2013] EWHC 1500 (QB), [2013] All ER (D) 132 (Jun) (Queen's Bench Division: Silber J).

1900   Duty of care—accountant—valuation—professional negligence—expert witness

See *Caribbean Steel Co Ltd v Price Waterhouse*, para 300.

1901   Duty of care—bank—negligent advice—collapse of market

See *Al Sulaiman v Credit Suisse Securities (Europe) Ltd*, para 1206.

1902   Duty of care—bank—negligent mis-statement—interest rate swap agreement

See *Green v Royal Bank of Scotland*, para 1184.

1903   Duty of care—breach of duty—credit rating agency—failure to ensure accuracy of personal information

See *Smeaton v Equifax plc*, para 427.

1904   Duty of care—education authority—delegation of duty—injury to pupil—accident in swimming pool

The appellant attended a swimming lesson with her school class. At some point during the lesson, the appellant got into difficulties and was found hanging vertically in the water. She was resuscitated but suffered a serious hypoxic brain injury. The school she attended was the responsibility of the fourth defendant, the local education authority. The swimming pool was run by the fifth defendant, a different local authority. The swimming lessons had been provided by the second defendant, an independent contractor who employed both the swimming teacher and the third defendant, a life guard, who had been on duty that day. The appellant issued proceedings contending that the fourth defendant had owed a non-delegable duty of care to her. The judge struck out that part of the claim, finding that that assertion was, on the pleaded facts, bound to fail. The appellant appealed. The application to strike out was upheld. The appellant appealed further. *Held*, there were two categories of case in which a non-delegable duty had been held to have arisen. The first was where the defendant employed an independent contractor to perform some function which was either inherently hazardous or liable to become so in the course of his work. The second category comprised cases where the common law imposed a duty on the defendant which had three characteristics: (1) the duty arose not from the negligent character of the act itself but because of an antecedent relationship between the defendant and the claimant; (2) the duty was a positive duty to protect a particular class of persons against a particular class of risks, and not simply a duty to refrain from acting in a way that forseeably caused injury; and (3) the duty was by virtue of that relationship personal to the defendant. It was established that there were a number of defining features which characterised non-delegable duty of care cases, namely: (a) the claimant was a patient or a child, or for some other reason was especially vulnerable or dependent on the protection of the defendant against the risk of injury; (b) there was an antecedent relationship between the claimant and the defendant, independent of the negligent act or omission itself, which placed the claimant in the actual custody, charge or care of the defendant, and from which it was possible to impute to the defendant the assumption of a positive duty to protect the claimant from harm, and not just a duty to refrain from conduct which would forseeably damage the claimant; (c) the claimant had no control over how the defendant chose to perform those obligations; (d) the defendant had delegated to a third party some function which was an integral part of the positive duty which he had assumed towards the claimant; and the third party was exercising, for the purpose of the function thus delegated to him, the defendant's custody or care of the claimant and the element of control that went with it; and (e) the third party had been negligent in the performance of the function assumed by the defendant and delegated by the defendant to him. The responsibilities of fee-paying schools were already non-delegable because they were contractual, and the possibility of contracting out of them was limited by legislation. In that particular context, there seemed to be no reason why the absence of consideration should lead to a different result when comparable services were provided by a public authority. The fourth defendant had assumed a duty to ensure that the appellant's swimming lessons were carefully conducted and supervised, by whomever they might get to perform those functions. The swimming lessons occurred in school hours in a place where the school had chosen to carry out that part of its functions. The teaching and the supervisory functions of the school, and the control of the appellant, had been delegated by the school to the second defendant and through her to the swimming teacher, and probably to the third defendant as well, to the extent necessary to enable them to give swimming lessons. The alleged negligence occurred in the course of the functions which the school assumed an obligation to perform and delegated to its contractors. It had to follow that if the latter had been negligent in performing those functions and the appellant had been injured as a result, the fourth defendant was in breach of duty. The judge's order striking out the allegation of a non-delegable duty would be set aside. Accordingly, the appeal would be allowed.

Woodland v Essex CC [2013] UKSC 66, [2013] All ER (D) 252 (Oct) (Supreme Court: Lady Hale DP, Lord Clarke, Lord Wilson, Lord Sumption and Lord Toulson SCJJ). Decision of Court of Appeal [2012] EWCA Civ 239, [2012] PIQR P178, [2012] All ER (D) 75 (Mar) (2012 Abr para 1904) reversed.

1905 Duty of care—employer—disciplinary proceedings—fair treatment

See *Yapp v Foreign and Commonwealth Office*, para 1001.

1906 Duty of care—existence of duty—bookmaker—robbery causing psychiatric injury to employee

The claimant was an employee of the defendant bookmakers, which was robbed while the claimant was working. The front entrance to the store was equipped with a magnetic lock, although it was not in use at the time of the robbery. The claimant was not physically injured but sustained psychiatric injury and commenced proceedings against the defendant seeking damages for personal injury caused by the defendant's negligence and breach of statutory duty. The judge found that the defendant had been negligent and in breach of its statutory duty in failing to carry out a risk assessment for the store, establish a satisfactory policy as to the circumstances in which the magnetic lock should be used, require that the magnetic lock be operated after the hours of darkness, and install proper lighting so that staff could see persons who were seeking to enter the shop. The judge further decided that, if the defendant had avoided the specified failures, the robbery probably would not have occurred. On the defendant's appeal, it fell to be determined whether the evidence justified a finding that the defendant ought to have put in place a policy of operating the magnetic lock as a vetting procedure in the hours of darkness at the store. *Held*, on the evidence, the judge had not been justified in concluding that a reasonably prudent employer would have imposed a policy of using the magnetic lock at the store in the hours of darkness. The judge had been offered no evidence by the claimant as to the standards adopted by a reasonably prudent employer in the industry. The judge had fallen into the error of substituting his own view as to the standards which ought to have prevailed. It followed that it had not been a breach of duty by the defendant to leave the use of the magnetic lock after dark at the store to the discretion of the manager. Accordingly, the appeal would be allowed.

Nicholls v Ladbrokes Betting & Gaming Ltd [2013] EWCA Civ 1963, [2013] All ER (D) 145 (Jul) (Court of Appeal: Jackson, Tomlinson and Floyd LJJ). *Robb v Salamis (M & I) Ltd* [2006] UKHL 56, [2007] 2 All ER 97 (2006 Abr para 1449); *Allison v London*

Underground Ltd [2008] EWCA Civ 71, [2008] IRLR 440 (2008 Abr para 1619); and *Baker v Quantum Clothing Group* [2011] UKSC 17, [2011] 4 All ER 223 (2011 Abr para 1278) considered.

1907　Duty of care—medical practitioner—incorrect diagnosis

See *Doy* (*a child by his litigation friend Joanne Doy*) *v Gunn*, para 1867.

1908　Duty of care—solicitor

See LEGAL PROFESSIONS.

1909　Duty of care—third party—local authority—lack of statutory duty

The defendant was the proprietor of a farm which offered a range of recreational activities on an agricultural theme intended to be particularly attractive for families with young children. The farm became the source of a very serious outbreak of E. coli. The claimants, who were young children who visited the farm and subsequently became seriously ill, issued claims for compensation in respect of their injuries. It was alleged that the defendant was liable on a number of grounds, including negligence, occupiers' liability and breach of statutory duty. The defendant denied liability, and brought claims against the third parties, who were the Health Protection Agency and the relevant local authority. She contended that the third parties were liable to the claimants in respect of the same damage as the defendant and sought an indemnity or contribution under the Civil Liability (Contribution) Act 1978 s 1. The defendant's claims were subsequently struck out by the master on the application of the third parties. On the defendant's appeal, *held*, if a statutory duty had not given rise to a private right to sue for breach, the duty could not create a duty of care that would not have been owed at common law if the statute was not there. If the policy of the statute was not consistent with the creation of a statutory liability to pay compensation for damage caused by a breach of the statutory duty, the same policy would exclude the use of the statutory duty in order to create a common law duty of care that would be broken by a failure to perform the statutory duty. Further, if a public body failed to provide a benefit which it was under a duty or had a power to provide, then no action in negligence would lie against it unless brought within the context of a genuinely private law claim arising out of an assumption or attachment of liability. It would be wrong to hold that the third parties could be held to owe a blanket duty of care to those foreseeably likely to suffer injury, loss or damage as a result of their omissions, even if such omissions could be shown to have been irrational. Further, the third parties had not assumed a private law duty of care in the particular circumstances of the case. Accordingly, the appeal would be dismissed.

　Furnell v Flaherty [2013] EWHC 377 (QB), [2013] All ER (D) 25 (Mar) (Queen's Bench Division: Turner J).

1910　Duty of care—valuers and surveyors

See BUILDING CONTRACTS.

1911　Nervous shock—secondary victim—post-traumatic stress—relevant incident

The claimant's mother was injured in an accident at work as a result of the admitted negligence of the defendant, her employer. The mother suddenly and unexpectedly collapsed and died at home in consequence of the injuries she had sustained in the accident. The claimant had not witnessed the accident but she did witness her mother's death and suffered significant post-traumatic stress disorder. In proceedings against the defendant, it was found that the claimant was entitled as a matter of law to claim damages from the defendant as a secondary victim of the accident. The defendant appealed. *Held*, the decision that the death of the mother was the relevant event for the purposes of deciding the proximity question was wrong. The claimant would have been able to recover damages as a secondary victim if she had suffered shock and psychiatric illness as a result of seeing her mother's accident. She could not recover damages for the shock and illness that she suffered as a result of seeing her mother's death shortly after the accident. If the original decision was right, the claimant would have been able to recover damages for psychiatric illness even if her mother's death had occurred months, and possibly years, after the accident. That suggested that the concept of proximity to a secondary victim could not reasonably be stretched that far. The effect of such approach was potentially to extend the scope of liability to secondary victims considerably further than had been done previously. The courts had been astute, by means of strict control mechanisms, to confine the right of action of secondary victims. Those same policy reasons militated against further substantial expansion. That ought only to be done by Parliament. Accordingly, the appeal would be allowed.

Taylor v A Novo (UK) Ltd [2013] EWCA Civ 194, [2014] QB 150, [2013] All ER (D) 167 (Mar) (Court of Appeal: Lord Dyson MR, Moore-Bick and Kitchin LJJ). *Taylor v Somerset Health Authority* (1993) 16 BMLR 63 approved. *Walters v North Glamorgan NHS Trust* [2002] EWCA Civ 1792, [2002] All ER (D) 87 (Dec); and *Gali-Atkinson v Seghal* [2003] EWCA Civ 697, (2003) 78 BMLR 22 distinguished.

NUISANCE

Halsbury's Laws of England (5th Edn) vol 78 (2010) paras 101–300

Articles

For articles relating to this title please refer to the Table of Articles at the beginning of the Abridgment.

1912   High hedges—park land—anti-social behaviour—line of trees

The applicant, who owned residential property that backed onto park land owned by the defendant local authority, complained to the defendant that trees growing in the park at the rear of his property constituted high hedges for the purposes of the Anti-Social Behaviour Act 2003 s 66. The defendant rejected the applicant's complaint, stating, in its first decision letter, that it would not be taking any further action because the trees were not considered to be a hedge for the purposes of the 2003 Act. The applicant challenged the decision and, by its second decision letter, the defendant stated that its decision that the trees were not a hedge had been correct in fact and law, the hedge comprised five separate trees, there was no growth in the essential two metre zone as measured from ground level on the defendant's side and the trees were in fact individual trees which formed an edge to woodland in that part of the park. The applicant challenged the defendant's decision by way of judicial review, submitting that, in determining whether the trees had been a hedge, the defendant erred in law by applying a test that there was no growth in the essential two metre zone. Moreover, the applicant argued that the lines of trees that were on the edge of woodland were not excluded from the 2003 Act. *Held*, the defendant erred by disqualifying a growth from being a high hedge by its finding that there had been an absence of foliage in the so-called two metre zone measured from ground level. The consideration of the absence of foliage below the two metre line could not logically have contributed to an overall assessment under s 66. Accordingly, that had not supplied a legally good reason for finding that trees had not constituted a hedge, nor as feeding any relevant consideration into the requirements of s 66. However, in approaching a group of trees of the sort in the present case, proximity, as well as the extent to which they were in a straight line and their positioning vis-à-vis other trees, had to be factored in. It was open to a decision-maker to decide that something was not a line of trees within the meaning of 66, weighing up the factors of alignment, proximity and relationship to other trees and bearing in mind that, while s 66 was supplying its own definition of a high hedge, it was there for the purpose of enabling decision-makers to identify a hedge. The defendant's decisions adequately recorded a conclusion that the trees complained of did not amount to a line of trees within the meaning of the 2003 Act. Accordingly, the claim would be dismissed.

R (on the application of Castelli) v Merton LBC [2013] EWHC 602 (Admin), [2013] All ER (D) 33 (Apr) (Queen's Bench Division: Judge Nicholas Paines QC).

OIL AND GAS TAXATION

Halsbury's Laws of England (5th edn) vol 78 (2010) paras 301–500

1913   Additionally-developed oil fields

The Additionally-developed Oil Fields Order 2013, SI 2013/2910 (in force on 1 April 2013), specifies the conditions that a project carried out in an oil field must satisfy in order for that oil field to be an additionally-developed oil field for the purposes of the Corporation Tax Act 2010 Pt 8 Ch 7 (ss 333–357). The order also amends the 2010 Act so as to specify the time at which a company having an interest in an additionally-developed oil field is entitled to field allowance and in order to prescribe the method by which the total field allowance for an additionally-developed oil field is to be calculated.

1914　　Finance Act 2013
See para 2149.

OPEN SPACES AND COUNTRYSIDE
Halsbury's Laws of England (5th edn) vol 78 (2010) paras 501–800

Articles
For articles relating to this title please refer to the Table of Articles at the beginning of the Abridgment.

1915　　Access to the countryside—conclusive maps—review—England
The Countryside and Rights of Way Act 2000 (Review of Maps) (England) Regulations 2013, SI 2013/514 (in force on 6 April 2013), amend the Countryside and Rights of Way Act 2000 s 10(2) by (1) extending, from 10 to 15 years, the time limit within which Natural England must undertake the first review of conclusive maps prepared under the 2000 Act showing all registered common land and all open country in England (excluding inner London); and (2) extending, from 10 to 20 years, the time limit within which Natural England must undertake any subsequent review.

1916　　Access to the countryside—maps—England
The Access to the Countryside (Maps) (England) Regulations 2013, SI 2013/1798 (in force on 1 October 2013), replace the Access to the Countryside (Maps in Draft Form) (England) Regulations 2001, SI 2001/3301, the Access to the Countryside (Provisional and Conclusive Maps) (England) Regulations 2002, SI 2002/1710, and the Access to the Countryside (Correction of Provisional and Conclusive Maps) (England) Regulations 2003, SI 2003/1591. In particular, the regulations (1) require Natural England to retain conclusive maps issued by the Countryside Agency in electronic form and provide for the inspection of such maps; (2) provide for the inspection and supply of reduced scale maps; and (3) require maps retained in electronic form to be capable of reproduction in printed form.

1917　　Natural habitats—conservation—application for planning permission
See R (on the application of Prideaux) v Buckinghamshire CC, para 2041.

1918　　Natural Resources Body for Wales—functions
The Natural Resources Body for Wales (Functions) Order 2013, SI 2013/755 (in force on 1 April 2013), modifies and transfers to the Natural Resources Body for Wales ('the Body') the Welsh devolved functions of the Environment Agency ('the Agency') and the Forestry Commissioners ('the Commissioners') and nearly all the functions of Countryside Council for Wales ('the Council'), transfers certain licensing functions of the Welsh Ministers relating to the environment to the Body, and transfers the powers of the Commissioners to make subordinate legislation in relation to Wales to the Welsh Ministers. In particular, the order (1) amends the Natural Resources Body for Wales (Establishment) Order 2012, SI 2012/1903, so as to (a) place duties on the Body relating to nature conservation, access, recreation and co-operation; (b) confer on the Body powers to enter into agreements with local authorities and public bodies, provide advice or assistance to others, undertake or commission research and institute criminal proceedings in England and Wales; (c) revise provisions relating to directions to the Body by the Welsh Ministers and the Secretary of State; (d) give the Body power to charge for work; and (e) require the Body to adopt a scheme for the publication of information about permitting decisions and to notify the Welsh Ministers of certain permit applications; (2) amends specified primary and secondary legislation by omitting references to the Council, substituting references to the Body for

existing references to the Commissioners, the Council, the Agency and the Welsh Ministers, and substituting references to the Welsh Ministers for certain references to the Commissioners; (3) provides that certain references in local enactments to the Council, the Commissioners and the Agency are to be read as references to the Body; (4) abolishes the Council and makes related repeals; and (5) abolishes the Environment Protection Advisory Committee and the regional and local fisheries advisory committee established for Wales and makes related repeals. Transitional and saving provision is also made.

1919   Natural Resources Body for Wales—transfer scheme—tax consequences

The Natural Resources Body for Wales (Tax Consequences) Order 2013, SI 2013/489 (in force on 1 April 2013), deals with the tax consequences of a transfer scheme made under the Public Bodies Act 2011 s 23 transferring property, rights and liabilities from the Countryside Council for Wales to the Natural Resources Body for Wales.

1920   Recreational land—allotments—land managed by parish council—power to sell surplus land

See *Snelling v Burstow Parish Council*, para 8.

PARLIAMENT

Halsbury's Laws of England (5th edn) vol 78 (2010) paras 801–1101

Articles

For articles relating to this title please refer to the Table of Articles at the beginning of the Abridgment.

PARTNERSHIP

Halsbury's Laws of England (5th edn) vol 79 paras 1–300

Articles

For articles relating to this title please refer to the Table of Articles at the beginning of the Abridgment.

1921   Insolvency

See COMPANY AND PARTNERSHIP INSOLVENCY.

1922   Limited liability partnerships—registration of charges

The Limited Liability Partnerships (Application of Companies Act 2006) (Amendment) Regulations 2013, SI 2013/618 (in force immediately after the amendments made by the Companies Act 2006 (Amendment of Part 25) Regulations 2013, SI 2013/600 (see para 351), come into force), amend the 2009 Regulations, SI 2009/1804, so as to revise the application of provisions concerning the registration of charges in the Companies Act 2006 Pt 25 Ch A1 (ss 859A–859Q) to limited liability partnerships, consequent on the amendment of those provisions by SI 2013/600. The 2006 Act Pt 26 Ch A1 provides for a single scheme for the registration of company charges applicable to all United Kingdom registered companies irrespective of the place of incorporation.

1923   Property—computer software—copyright—infringement

See *Coward v Phaestos Ltd*, para 578.

PATENTS AND REGISTERED DESIGNS

Halsbury's Laws of England (5th edn) vol 79 paras 301–800

Articles

For articles relating to this title please refer to the Table of Articles at the beginning of the Abridgment.

1924   Patent—concurrent proceedings—European Patent Office—application for stay of proceedings

The claimant company was the owner of a European patent which related to a method of controlling access to the random access channel in a wireless telecommunications network. The claimant alleged that the defendants had infringed the patent and proceedings ensued. The result was that a trial was fixed in relation to technical issues in the Patents Court. Running parallel to the present proceedings were opposition proceedings commenced in the European Patents Office ('EPO') by the defendants, seeking revocation of the patent. The defendants applied for a stay of the present proceedings until a final decision of the EPO on the opposition proceedings, including any appeal. The judge applied the guidelines applicable when the Patents Court was exercising its discretion to grant a stay on the ground that there were parallel proceedings pending in the EPO contesting the validity of the patent as set out in *Glaxo Group Ltd v Genentech Inc.* In the circumstances, applying the *Glaxo* guidance, the judge refused to grant the stay with the effect that the trial of the technical issues in the present proceedings would proceed. The defendants appealed. *Held*, the *Glaxo* guidance had required some revision in the light of *Virgin Atlantic Airways Ltd v Zodiac Seats UK Ltd (formerly Contour Aerospace Ltd)*, but should not be swept away altogether. In the light of the observations in *Virgin*, the *Glaxo* guidance as to the Patents Court's discretion to grant stays on the ground that there were parallel proceedings pending in the EPO contesting the validity of the patent would be recast as follows: (1) the discretion, which was very wide indeed, should be exercised to achieve the balance of justice between the parties having regard to all the relevant circumstances of the particular case; (2) the discretion was of the Patents Court, not of the Court of Appeal. The Court of Appeal would not be justified in interfering with a first instance decision that accorded with legal principle and had been reached by taking into account all the relevant, and only the relevant, circumstances; (3) although neither the European Patents Convention nor the Patents Act 1977 contained express provisions relating to automatic or discretionary stay of proceedings in national courts, they provided the context and conditioned the exercise of the discretion; (4) the possibility of concurrent proceedings contesting the validity of a patent granted by the EPO was inherent in the system established by the European Patents Convention. It also had to be remembered that national courts exercised exclusive jurisdiction on infringement issues; (5) if there were no other factors, a stay of the national proceedings was the default option. There was no purpose in pursuing two sets of proceedings simply because the European Patents Convention allowed for it; (6) it was for the party resisting the grant of the stay to show why it should not be granted. Ultimately it was a question of where the balance of justice lay; (7) one important factor affecting the exercise of the discretion was the extent to which refusal of a stay would irrevocably deprive a party of any part of the benefit which the concurrent jurisdiction of the EPO and the national court was intended to confer. Thus, if allowing the national court to proceed might allow the patentee to obtain monetary compensation which was not repayable if the patent was subsequently revoked, that would be a weighty factor in favour of the grant of a stay. It might, however, be possible to mitigate the effect of that factor by the offer of suitable undertakings to repay; (8) the Patents Court judge was entitled to refuse a stay of the national proceedings where the evidence was that some commercial certainty would be achieved at a considerably earlier date in the case of the United Kingdom proceedings than in the EPO. It was true that it would not be possible to attain certainty everywhere until the EPO proceedings were finally resolved, but some certainty, sooner rather than later, and somewhere, such as in the United Kingdom, rather than nowhere, was, in general, preferable to continuing uncertainty everywhere; (9) it was permissible to take account of the fact that resolution of the national proceedings, while not finally resolving everything, might, by deciding some important issues, promote settlement; (10) an important factor affecting the discretion would be the length of time that it would take for the respective proceedings in the national court and in the EPO to reach a conclusion. That was not an independent factor, but needed to be considered in conjunction with the prejudice which any party would suffer from the delay, and lack of certainty, and what the national proceedings could achieve in terms of certainty; (11) the public interest in dispelling the uncertainty surrounding the validity of monopoly rights conferred by the grant of a patent was also a factor to be considered; (12) in weighing the balance it was material to take into account the risk of wasted costs, but that factor would normally be outweighed by commercial factors concerned with early resolution; and (13) the hearing of an application for a stay was not to become a mini-trial of the various factors affecting its grant or refusal. The parties' assertions needed to be examined critically, but at a relatively high level of generality. In the present case, there was nothing in the revisions to the *Glaxo* guidance which was of any real materiality to the judge's evaluation of the factors that he had taken into account. The court would not be justified in interfering with his exercise of discretion. Accordingly, the appeal would be dismissed.

Ipcom GMBH & Co KG v HTC Europe Co Ltd [2013] EWCA Civ 1496, [2013] All ER (D) 234 (Nov) (Court of Appeal: Patten, Rafferty and Floyd LJJ). *Virgin Atlantic Airways Ltd v Zodiac Seats UK Ltd* [2013] UKSC 46, [2013] 4 All ER 715 (para 1931) applied. *Glaxo Group Ltd v Genentech Inc* [2008] EWCA Civ 23, [2008] Bus LR 888, [2008] All ER (D) 282 (Jan) (2008 Abr para 2279) considered. Decision of Roth J [2013] EWHC 2880 (Ch), [2013] All ER (D) 235 (Sep) affirmed.

1925 Patent—infringement—construction of claim

The claimant brought an action for infringement of a European patent entitled 'Tilting device for a seat back'. The patent was concerned with a folding mounting bracket for fitting to the backrest of a seat. The defendant manufactured devices of a similar nature, which were to be folded to the horizontal, but they contended that there were three reasons the products in suit were outside the scope of claim 1 of the patent. The issue to be decided was whether the defendant's products infringed the patent. The defendant relied on three non-infringement points. First, claim 1 required that the surface of the housing was adapted to bear against a complementary surface of the rod. The defendant contended that the natural meaning of the word 'complementary' was that the two shapes should be essentially identical and that it was not intended to have anything to do with the relationship between the surfaces of the locking pin and the notch. Second, the defendant contended that it installed its devices in its seats so that the backrest fell forwards whereas the patent had a specific embodiment installed in a seat so that the backrest dropped to the horizontal in a backwards direction. Third, the defendant contended that its devices did not, as the patent did, allow their seat backs to be lifted without interruption from the locking mechanism. *Held*, (1) although, in principle, it was necessary to construe the claims of a patent independently of any alleged infringement, it was a waste of effort to contemplate the precise construction of all the integers which had not been put in issue. The fact that a defendant was doing something in a particular way should not influence the court in deciding whether the claim on its true construction covered that or not. The defendant's device would lack a notch of the kind required by claim 1 and for that reason it would not infringe. The defendant's first non-infringement point succeeded in relation to all the defendant's devices, whether greased or not. (2) The claimant's contention that claim 1 covered the device per se, irrespective of the manner in which it was actually built into a seat was accepted. The second non-infringement point failed. (3) The defendant's device with grease on it was a different device from the device without grease. One had the characteristic required by claim 1; the other did not. The third non-infringement point succeeded in relation to the defendant's devices if ungreased, but it failed in relation to the devices when greased. Judgment would be given accordingly.

Scopema Sarl v Scot Seat Direct Ltd [2013] EWPCC 32, [2013] All ER (D) 152 (Sep) (Patents County Court: Alastair Wilson QC).

1926 Patent—infringement—copy of design—damages

The claimant company owned a European patent, which applied to a form of loading platform used in the construction industry. The work of the rolling platform had previously been carried out using fixed platforms, which were a less sophisticated equivalent. The invention was a form of improved rolling platform. Following the grant of the application, the claimant hired out both fixed and rolling platforms. The defendant companies were competitors of the claimant. They purchased a rolling platform for export from the claimant and arranged for the design to be copied, following which they hired out their own product similar to the claimant's. That came to the attention of the claimant, and correspondence followed. During the correspondence the defendant made undertakings not to infringe the claimant's patent, and gave figures for the amount of infringement that had occurred. Those figures were much lower than the true quantities. The claimant subsequently brought a claim, seeking damages for patent infringement. *Held*, the only source of non-infringing platforms had been a company in Australia. The relevant customers had only been aware of the claimant and the defendant as a source of platforms. Had customers of the infringing platforms not been able to hire infringing products from the defendant, it was likely that they would have sourced those platforms from the claimant. Customers who had purchased infringing platforms from the defendant, had they not been able to do so, would have hired platforms from the claimant. On the evidence, with regard to the question of whether the defendant's hire of infringing platforms had caused the claimant to lose hires of fixed platforms, the fraction of the defendant's fixed hires that could truly be said to have been hired together with a rolling platform was negligible. It was fair to say that none of the defendant's fixed platform hire business was lost to the claimant. The claimant would not have incurred extra costs, had they hired platforms to the defendant's customers. Further, with regard to the question of whether the claimant could claim for services provided to the defendant's customers had they gone to the claimant, the losses contended for were direct and foreseeable, and hence could be recovered by the claimant. In the circumstances, it was plain that the defendant had knowingly infringed the claimant's patent. They had had notice. However, although the later letter had been an attempt to mislead the claimant, it had been written three years after the infringing acts, and had nothing to do with the damage actually caused. To award damages for the letter would be to punish the defendant. The concept of awarding damages for moral prejudice would not extend to the current circumstances. Instead, it was a matter to be taken into account when awarding costs. Judgment would be given accordingly.

Xena Systems Ltd v Cantideck [2013] EWPCC 1, [2013] All ER (D) 159 (Jan) (Patents County Court: Judge Birss QC).

1927   Patent—infringement—costs—bringing in third party

The proceedings involved a number of communications companies, including the claimant company, the defendant company, the defendant company in the counterclaim and an intervening company. In the course of the proceedings, the parties identified a 'confidential club' of individuals to include counsel and experts. That group included a German lawyer external to the claim and a director of the defendant. They had given an undertaking as to confidentiality. The issue arose as to whether the intervening company and the defendant should pay the costs of the application in so far as the intervening company was brought into the proceedings. Further issues arose as to the nature of the undertaking as to confidentiality that the lawyer and the director ought to give, and whether it should be given directly to intervening interested parties, including the intervening company. *Held*, with regard to costs, the order that had been made had not been an order for third party disclosure, but the analogy of the position of a respondent to an application for third party disclosure was reasonably close. The intervening company had done no more than to attempt to maintain, so far as possible, the privacy of its licence agreement and had been entirely reasonably in the approach it had taken. The defendant should pay the costs of the intervening company's intervention. Given the overall background, the lawyer's position as an external lawyer and the fact that he would not normally be required to give any such undertaking, it would be inappropriate to have a concrete form of undertaking. It did not seem right for the court to lay down in advance that the lawyer should not be involved in such negotiations or consideration. The giving of an undertaking in the form sought would potentially interfere with a legitimate activity in each of the categories proposed, although there might be many aspects of those activities on which the confidential information would have no bearing at all. Additional undertakings proposed were both unnecessary and excessive. Given that the intervening parties were among the class of persons having an interest in the confidential information that was protected by the undertakings given by the parties, it would be logical to make it express that it was given in favour of the intervening parties as well. Judgment would be given accordingly.

Nokia Oyj (Nokia Corpn) v Ipcom GmbH & Co Kg [2013] EWHC 407 (Pat), [2013] All ER (D) 213 (Mar) (Chancery Division: Floyd J).

1928   Patent—infringement—infringement by making of patented product—meaning of making

The Patents Act 1977 s 60(1)(a) provides that, subject to certain exceptions, a person infringes a patent for an invention if, but only if, while the patent is in force and where the invention is a product, he in the United Kingdom makes, disposes of, offers to dispose of, uses or imports the product or keeps it whether for disposal or otherwise.

It has been held, on an appeal by a company found liable for infringement of a patent concerning intermediate bulk carriers pursuant to the 1977 Act s 60(1)(a), that the word 'makes' must be interpreted contextually and has to be approached bearing in mind the following considerations: (1) the word must be given a meaning which, as a matter of ordinary language, it could reasonably bear; (2) it is not a term of art and, like many English words, does not have a precise meaning; (3) it will inevitably be a matter of fact and degree in many cases whether an activity involves making an article; (4) the word must be interpreted in a practical way, by reference to the facts of the particular case; (5) there is a need for clarity and certainty for patentees and others, and for those advising them; (6) the word applies to patents for all sorts of products, from machinery to chemical compounds; (7) the need to protect the patentee's monopoly while not stifling reasonable competition must be borne in mind, at least as part of the background; (8) the word must be interpreted bearing in mind that the precise scope of a claim might be a matter almost of happenstance in the context of the question whether the alleged infringer makes the claimed product; (9) where there is a decision of the House of Lords or the Supreme Court on the meaning of the word, it cannot be departed from save for very good reasons; and (10) particularly given that s 60 is one of the sections mentioned in s 130(7) (interpretation), it must be interpreted bearing in mind that it was included in a provision that is intended to be part of a scheme that applies in many other jurisdictions.

Schutz Ltd v Werit (UK) Ltd [2013] UKSC 16, [2013] IP & T 321, [2013] All ER (D) 114 (Mar) (Supreme Court: Lord Neuberger P, Lord Walker, Lady Hale, Lord Mance and Lord Kerr). Decision of Court of Appeal [2011] EWCA Civ 1337, [2011] All ER (D) 198 (Nov) (2011 Abr para 1942) reversed.

1929   Patent—infringement—injunction—invalid patent—pending appeal as to validity

The defendant owned European patents that covered the use of a drug for the treatment of osteoporosis. In respect of one of the patents, it also had a supplementary protection certificate. The claimant commenced revocation proceedings against the patents because it was minded to market its own generic product. Before the revocation proceedings had come to trial, but after the trial date had been fixed, the claimant obtained a marketing authorisation for the acid for osteoporosis. The defendant wrote to the claimant seeking undertakings not to sell the acid or to infringe its patents. The claimant gave a partial undertaking. The defendant again wrote to the claimant requesting confirmation that, if any of the patents were held valid following trial, the claimant would undertake not to launch its acid in the United Kingdom. The judge found the patents to be invalid on the ground that they were not entitled to their claimed priority date and, therefore, were rendered invalid by an intervening prior publication. The defendant was granted permission to appeal. The claimant informed the defendant that it intended to launch its product following expiry of the supplementary protection certificate. The defendant commenced infringement proceedings. The judge declined to grant the injunction sought. The defendant appealed. *Held*, the principles which applied to the grant of an interim injunction pending appeal where the claimant had lost at first instance were (1) the court had to be satisfied that the appeal had a real prospect of success; (2) if the court was so satisfied, it would not usually be useful to attempt to form a view as to how much stronger the prospects of appeal were, or to attempt to give weight to that view in assessing the balance of convenience; (3) it did not follow automatically from the fact that an interim injunction had been, or would have been, granted pre-trial that an injunction pending appeal should be granted; (4) the grant of an injunction was not limited to the case where its refusal would render an appeal nugatory;

and (5) as in the case of the stay of a permanent injunction which would otherwise be granted to a successful claimant, the court should endeavour to arrange matters so that the Court of Appeal was best able to do justice between the parties once the appeal had been heard. The judge's approach had not been correct. Once he was satisfied that the appeal had real prospects of success, he should have gone on to consider the balance of hardships in accordance with established principles. Further, it was not a case where it could be said that there was substantial unfairness in declining to give the claimant the right to rely on the judgment pending appeal if the other considerations would otherwise have justified an injunction. The trial date for the revocation proceedings was set without recourse to any expedition. In order to have caused the trial date to be scheduled sufficiently far in advance of the expiration of the special protection certificate for an appeal to have been accommodated before that date, one of the parties would have had to apply to the court for expedition. It could not be said that the defendant should have taken any steps to apply for expedition before it became aware of the marketing authorisation. Until that time, it would not have been able to say that there was any commercial urgency from its point of view. Even after that time, the defendant was unaware of the claimant's actual launch plans. Further, the way to market for a generic manufacturer was not clear until all arguable objections from the patentee had been eliminated. If the generic manufacturer allowed the trial of the action at first instance to coincide with the intended launch date, he ran the risk that a successful appeal could get in the way even if judgment at first instance was given in his favour. It was also wrong to suggest that the parties were proceeding to trial on the tacit understanding that the decision at first instance on the validity of the patents would determine the claimant's freedom to sell the product covered by its marketing authorisation after expiry of the special protection certificate. The present case was one in which the court should grant an injunction pending the appeal to restrain the sale of the claimant's product. The unquantifiable damage to the defendant outweighed that to the claimant. Consequently, an injunction would be granted until final judgment in the appeal or further order. Accordingly, the appeal would be allowed.

Novartis AG v Hospira UK Ltd [2013] EWCA Civ 583, [2013] IP & T 810 (Court of Appeal: Lewison, Kitchin and Floyd LJJ). Decision of Birss J [2013] EWHC 1285 (Pat), [2013] All ER (D) 177 (May) reversed.

1930 Patent—infringement—injunction—threat to infringe patent

The first claimant company was the patentee and proprietor of a supplementary protection certificate and the second claimant was the exclusive licensee. The patent and certificate related to a non-nucleoside reverse transcriptase inhibitor used in the control of HIV infections. A positive opinion was issued by the Committee for Medical Products for Human Use on the grant of a marketing authorisation for a generic efavirenz product to the defendant companies. That authorisation was granted soon after. The defendants' long term plan had a preliminary limiting marketing date of one day after the expiry of the claimants' certificate. The claimants believed that there was a risk that the defendants were going to launch its product in the United Kingdom before the certificate expired and, after correspondence between the parties, proceedings were commenced. *Held*, the objective position had been that there was real risk that the defendants could launch the product before the expiry of the certificate. It had been reasonable for the claimants to raise the matter in correspondence. The defendants' actual intentions had been tolerably clear. Despite the preliminary limiting marketing date, the possibility of launching in the United Kingdom before expiry of the certificate had been under active consideration as a result of the timing of the opinion from the Committee for Medical Products for Human Use. The option that the defendants had been actively considering had been to launch at risk, in other words to sell the product without the claimants' permission. It followed that the defendants had actively considered the option of committing an act of patent infringement, which would have been unlawful, would have interfered with the claimants' legal right and would have inflicted serious damage on the patentee. The probability that an injunction would be required to prevent the defendants from infringing had been sufficiently strong to justify legal proceedings. Therefore, the action had been justified. An injunction would be granted to restrain the defendants from infringing the patent and certificate. Accordingly, the claim would be allowed.

Merck Sharp Dohme Corpn v Teva Pharma BV [2013] EWHC 1958 (Pat), [2013] All ER (D) 106 (Jul) (Chancery Division: Birss J). *Hooper v Rogers* [1975] Ch 43, [1974] 3 All ER 417, CA (1974 Abr para 1759), applied.

1931   Patent—infringement—proceedings—subsequent ruling of European Patent Office—res judicata

The claimant brought proceedings alleging that the defendant had infringed its European patent in a seating system and passenger accommodation unit used in long-haul aircraft. The defendant counterclaimed for revocation of the patent and challenged the validity of the patent before the European Patent Office. A judge ruled that the defendant had not infringed the patent, and shortly afterwards the Opposition Division of the European Patent Office upheld the patent. The claimant appealed to the Court of Appeal against the former ruling, and the defendant appealed to a technical board of appeal against the latter ruling. The Court of Appeal allowed the claimant's appeal, deciding that the patent was valid and had been infringed by the defendant's product. The defendant applied for a stay of the English proceedings pending their application for permission to appeal to the Supreme Court and the outcome of their appeal to the board. Applying previous authority, the Court of Appeal refused the application on the ground that, having made a final determination in the claimant's favour, its decision was res judicata, irrespective of whether the board subsequently amended the patent. The Court of Appeal subsequently declared that the patent was valid and had been infringed, and directed an inquiry as to damages. In advance of any such inquiry, the board amended the patent, with the effect that, by virtue of the Patents Act 1977 s 77, the patent was to be treated as limited accordingly with retrospective effect from the date of grant. The defendant's application for the discharge of the order for an inquiry was declined on the ground that it was the mechanism for working out the effect of the court's decision that the patent was valid and that the matter was res judicata. The defendant appealed against that decision. *Held*, cause of action estoppel was absolute only in relation to points actually decided on the earlier occasion, and was sufficiently flexible not to preclude the raising of essential points which had not been decided in the earlier proceedings. A question of res judicata in a patent case could not be correctly considered without proper regard to the Patents Act 1977 and the European Patent Convention, pursuant to which the revocation or amendment of a patent applied retrospectively to the date of grant. Although res judicata barred an alleged infringer from relying on arguments relating to validity or infringement which had been determined in English proceedings, it did not prevent the assertion that the patent had, as a matter of fact, been revoked or amended. In relying on that fact, the defendant had made no challenge to the conclusions reached by the Court of Appeal and did not seek to relitigate or raise a point which the Court of Appeal had already determined. The consequence of the retrospective amendment was to remove all claims held by the Court of Appeal to infringe the unamended patent. It would be wrong to prevent alleged infringers of the patent from invoking in later proceedings a subsequent revocation or amendment so as to avoid liability. It followed that the defendant was entitled to rely on the amendment in answer to the claim for damages in the inquiry. Accordingly, the appeal would be allowed.

Virgin Atlantic Airways Ltd v Zodiac Seats UK Ltd [2013] UKSC 46, [2014] AC 160, [2013] 4 All ER 715 (Supreme Court: Lord Neuberger P, Lady Hale, Lords Clarke, Sumption and Carnwath SCJJ). *Poulton v Adjustable Cover and Boiler Block Co* [1908] 2 Ch 430, 25 RPC 661, CA; and *Coflexip SA v Stolt Offshore MS Ltd (No 2)* [2004] EWCA Civ 213, [2004] IP & T 611 (2004 Abr para 1256) overruled. Decision of Court of Appeal [2009] EWCA Civ 1062, [2009] All ER (D) 235 (Oct) (2009 Abr para 2315) reversed.

1932   Patent—infringement—right to sue—exclusive licensee

The claimant company brought patent infringement proceedings against the defendant, a manufacturer of heated hair rollers. The defendant counterclaimed alleging wrongful threats of patent infringement. Several issues arose, including whether, in relation to the infringement action, the claimant had status to bring the claim. It purported to sue as an exclusive licensee pursuant to the Patents Act 1977 s 67(1). The question arose as to whether it was relevant that the patentee was continuing to deal in patented goods, and whether there was a basis for concluding that such dealings were inconsistent with the claimant having the legal right to exclusivity. In relation to the threats action, it fell to be determined whether three letters sent by the defendants in that action, one of which was from the defendants' solicitors and specifically mentioned patent infringement, could be considered to be groundless threats of infringement proceedings under s 70. *Held*, a patentee might carry on dealing in patented goods consistently with the grant of an exclusive licence. There was a licence which was not said to be a sham, and which on its face complied with ss 67 and 120(7). Whether the patentee was continuing to deal in patented goods was irrelevant, and, in any case, there was no basis for concluding that any such dealings were in any way inconsistent with the claimant having the legal right to exclusivity. It followed that the claimant was an exclusive licensee and was entitled to sue. With regard to the threats point, individually, some of the features of the letter in question lacked cogency, and by themselves would not constitute a threat. However, taken as a whole, the letter did clearly convey a threat. It was an urgent letter from solicitors that specifically spoke of patent infringement. The ordinary reader would have understood that the thrust of the letter was that some consequence was intended to follow, and that consequence could really only be proceedings for patent infringement. In the circumstances, each of the communications complained about amounted to an actionable threat under s 70. Judgment would be given accordingly.

SDL Hair Ltd v Next Row Ltd; Master Distributor Ltd v SDL Hair Ltd [2013] EWPCC 31, [2013] All ER (D) 185 (Jun) (Patents County Court: Richard Meade QC presiding).

1933   Patent—infringement—threat—nature of threat—letter from solicitor

See *SDL Hair Ltd v Next Row Ltd; Master Distributor Ltd v SDL Hair Ltd*, para 1932.

1934   Patent—infringement—validity of patent—construction of claim by skilled person

The defendant company held a patent which disclosed and claimed the use of particular agents called human vascular endothelial growth factor antagonists for the treatment of non-cancerous (non-neoplastic) diseases which were characterised by excessive blood vessel growth (neovascularisation or angiogenesis). The claimant companies sought revocation of the patent on the grounds of lack of novelty, obviousness and insufficiency and a declaration of non-infringement in respect of a product developed by the first claimant and which the second claimant wished to sell in the United Kingdom for the treatment of neovascular age-related macular degeneration. The defendant counterclaimed for infringement. The judge found that the claims of the patent were novel, inventive and sufficient and, therefore, all attacks on the patent were dismissed. The defendants appealed. *Held*, the judge's analysis could not be faulted. It was not suggested by any party that the claim had not required any therapeutic effect. It clearly had, and the judge had so found. However, it had not required a medicament which would cure or even treat all aspects of a disease and it had not required treatment of those aspects of a disease which were independent of angiogenesis. Further, it was clear that the judge had construed the claims entirely correctly as requiring the achievement of a therapeutic effect, and he had duly applied that construction when considering novelty. In respect of obviousness, the judge had not erred in considering the prospects of success and had weighted all the various matters in an entirely proper manner. There was no doubt that the judge had correctly interpreted the claims as requiring therapeutic efficacy and he had approached the issue of obviousness on that basis. In the circumstances, he had been right to reject all the allegations of insufficiency. It followed that he had been right to reject the allegation that the invention was obvious because it had not worked and solved no technical problem. Accordingly, the appeal would be dismissed.

Regeneron Pharmaceuticals Inc v Genentech Inc; Bayer Pharma AG v Genentech Inc [2013] EWCA Civ 93, [2013] IP & T 619 (Court of Appeal: Longmore, Moses and Kitchin LJJ). Decision of Floyd J [2012] EWHC 657 (Pat), [2012] All ER (D) 24 (Jun) (2012 Abr para 1948) affirmed.

1935   Patent—infringement—validity of patent—lack of priority

In proceedings alleging the infringement of a patent relating to the functioning of mobile communications systems, a question arose as to whether the priority document gave the skilled person enough information in respect of two particular features of the patent. *Held*, regarding priority, it was necessary for the court to (1) read and understand, through the eyes of the skilled person, the disclosure of the priority document as a whole; (2) determine

1949   Patent—supplementary protection certificate—irregularity

The proceedings concerned the acquisition of supplementary protection certificates ('SPCs') for medical products. An SPC was filed by the appellant fund with regard to a patent that was due to expire a number of years later. To obtain the SPC, it was necessary to pay a fee within a time limit, as prescribed by the Patents Act 1977. The regime for the grant of SPCs in respect of medicinal products was first established by Council Regulation (EC) 1768/92 concerning the creation of a complementary protection certificate for medicinal products. An applicant was not required to take a certificate for the whole period permitted by Regulation 1768/92. He could elect to take the certificate for a shorter period and, if he did so, he would only pay a fee in respect of those years for which he had elected. The appellant granted a licence to a third party company to pay its various fees. That company failed to pay the fee within the required period, but attempted to pay it shortly before the patent was to expire. Owing to the wrong system being used, the payment was rejected. Consequently, the SPC lapsed on the date of expiry of the patent. The hearing officer and, on appeal, the Chancery Division, found that the appellant had failed to pay the fees within the time limit and therefore the SPC had never come into effect. The appellant appealed that decision. *Held*, in considering whether the rules imposed a regime for the payment of annual fees, it was important to have in mind that an SPC might be granted some time before it was due to take effect. Further, the maximum term of each SPC would vary from certificate to certificate and would depend on the date on which the application for the basic patent was filed and the date of the first authorisation to place the product on the market in the European Union, subject to the requirement that the duration of the certificate could not exceed five years from the date on which it took effect. Further, an applicant was not required to take a certificate for the whole period permitted by Regulation 1768/92. He could elect to take the certificate for a shorter period and, if he did so, he would only pay a fee in respect of those years for which he had elected. Thus far, the prescribed fee could properly be described as an annual fee. It was calculated by reference to the number of years for which a certificate was to have effect. With regard to the impact of the Patents Rules 2007, SI 2007/3291, r 116, which provided that the fee had to be paid before the SPC took effect, the appellant's submissions confused the nature of the fee and the date on which the liability to pay it arose. The fee did not cease to be an annual fee because the rule imposed an obligation to pay it in advance. Nor did the fee cease to be an annual fee because the rules imposed an obligation to pay it all at once. Provided the fee was paid within the prescribed period, the SPC would automatically take effect on the day after expiry of the patent. The answer to the construing of the 1977 Act s 128B lay in the wording of s 128B. That defined the SPCs to which it applied as including certificates issued under Regulation 1768/92. There could be no doubt that the SPC was subject to the 1977 Act s 128B. The SPC would not be granted. Accordingly, the appeal would be dismissed.

Tulane Education Fund v Comptroller General of Patents [2013] EWCA Civ 890, [2013] BUS LR 1225, [2013] All ER (D) 317 (Jul) (Court of Appeal: Sir Terence Etherton C, Kitchin and Underhill LJJ). Decision of Roger Wyand QC [2012] EWHC 932 (Pat), [2012] All ER (D) 16 (May) (2012 Abr para 1960) affirmed.

1950   Patent—supplementary protection certificate—structural definition of active ingredient

The applicant brought an action for a declaration that any supplementary protection certificate ('SPC'), relying for its legal basis on the respondent's patent and based on a marketing authorisation for a medicinal product containing the respondent's antibody, would be invalid. It argued that the antibody was not covered by a basic patent within the meaning of European Parliament and Council Regulation (EC) 469/2009 art 3 (concerning the SPC for medicinal products), in so far as the respondent's patent was too broadly drafted for it to be possible for the antibody to be regarded as being specified. Consequently, according to the applicant, in order for an SPC to be granted on the basis of the respondent's patent, the patent would have to contain a structural definition of the active ingredients and the claims would have to be significantly more specific. A preliminary ruling was sought as to whether art 3(a) should be interpreted as meaning that, in order for an active ingredient to be regarded as 'protected by a basic patent in force', the active ingredient should be identified in the claims of the patent by a structural formula, or whether the active ingredient might also be considered to be protected where it was covered by a functional formula in the patent claims. *Held*, in light of the objective of Regulation 469/2009, the refusal of an SPC application for an active ingredient which was not specifically referred to by a patent relied on in support of such an application might be justified in circumstances such as those at issue and as observed by the applicant where the holder of the patent in question had failed to take any steps to carry out more in-depth research and identify his invention specifically, making it possible to ascertain clearly the active ingredient which might be commercially exploited in a medicinal product corresponding to the needs of certain patients. In such a situation, if an SPC were granted to the patent holder, even though that patent holder had not made any investment in research relating to that aspect of his original invention, that would undermine the objective of Regulation 469/2009. Article 3(a) should be interpreted as meaning that, in order for an active ingredient to be regarded as 'protected by a basic patent in force' within the meaning of art 3(a), it was not necessary for the active ingredient to be identified in the claims of the patent by a structural formula. Where the active ingredient was covered by a fundamental formula in the claims of a patent, art 3(a) did not preclude, in principle, the grant of an SPC for that active ingredient, on condition that it was possible to reach the conclusion on the basis of those claims, interpreted in light of the description of the invention that the claims related, implicitly but necessarily and specifically, to the active ingredient in question, which was a matter to be determined by the national court.

Case C-493/12 *Eli Lilly and Co Ltd v Human Genome Sciences Inc (No 2)* [2014] IP & T 101 (ECJ: Third Chamber).

1951   Patent—supplementary protection certificate—validity

The applicant brought proceedings challenging the validity of a supplementary protection certificate ('SPC'). In support of its application, it contended, that a SPC obtained by the respondent was invalid, in so far as the combination of ingredients was not protected by the basic patent within the meaning of European Parliament and Council Regulation (EC) 469/2009 art 3(a) since the combination was not expressly specified or identified in the wording of any of the claims of the patent. It was also argued that the SPC was invalid in light of art 3(c), given that the 'product' had already been the subject of an initial SPC. A preliminary ruling was sought as to whether, on the basis of a patent protecting an innovative active ingredient and marketing authorisation ('MA') for a medicinal product containing that ingredient as the single active ingredient, the holder of the patent had already obtained an SPC for that active ingredient, art 3(c) should be interpreted as precluding the holder of the patent from obtaining, on the basis of the same patent but an MA for a different medicinal product containing that active ingredient in combination with another active ingredient which was not protected by the patent, a second SPC relating to that combination of active ingredients. *Held*, the basic objective of Regulation 469/2009 was to compensate for the delay to the marketing of what constituted the core inventive advance which was the subject of the basis patent. In light of the need to take into account all the interests at stake if it was accepted that all subsequent marketing of that active ingredient in conduction with an unlimited number of other active ingredients, not protected as such by the basic patent but simply referred to in the wording of the claims of the patent in the general terms, conferred entitlement to multiple SPCs, that would be contrary to the requirements to balance the interests of the pharmaceutical industry and those of public health as regards the encouragement of research within the European Union by the use of SPCs. It followed that, in such a situation, art 3(c) precluded a patent holder from obtaining, on the basis of one and the same basic patent, more than one SPC in connection with the active ingredient, since such SPCs would in fact be connected, wholly or in part, with the same product. On the other hand, if the subject of a new basic patent within the meaning of art 1(c) consisted of an innovative active ingredient in respect of which an SPC had already been granted and another active ingredient not protected as such by the patent in question, the new patent, in so far as it covered a totally separate innovation, could confer entitlement to an SPC for that new combination which was subsequently placed on the market. In circumstances, where, on the basis of a patent protecting an innovative active ingredient and an MA for a medicinal product containing that ingredient as the single active ingredient, the holder of that patent had already obtained an SPC for that active ingredient entitling him to oppose the use of that active ingredient, either alone or in combination with other active ingredients, art 3(c) should be interpreted as precluding that patent holder from obtaining a second SPC relating to that combination of active ingredients.

Case C-443/12 *Actavis Group PTC EHF v Sanofi* [2014] IP & T 189 (ECJ: Third Chamber).

1952   Patent—unitary patent—co-operation between member states—enhanced co-operation—competence of European Council

The applicants were two European Union member states who sought annulment of Council Decision (EU) 2011/167, which authorised enhanced cooperation in the area of the creation of unitary patent protection. The applicants submitted that (1) the European Council lacked competence to establish the enhanced co-operation in question; (2) by authorising the enhanced co-operation, the Council had circumvented the requirement of unanimity laid down by TFEU art 118(2) and had brushed aside their objections to the European Commission's proposal on the language arrangements for the unitary patent, which amounted to a misuse of powers; and (3) the condition that the decision authorising enhanced co-operation should be adopted as a last resort had been breached. *Held*, (1) although it was true that rules on intellectual property were essential in order to maintain competition undistorted on the internal market, they did not constitute 'competition rules' for the purpose of TFEU art 3(1)(b). The competences conferred by art 118 fell within an area of shared competences for the purpose of TFEU art 4(2). It followed that the Council had the authority to authorise the enhanced co-operation in question. (2) The Council had decided that the unitary patent and its language arrangements could not be established by the EU as a whole within a reasonable period. By no means did that constitute circumvention of the requirement of unanimity laid down in art 118(2), or, indeed, exclusion of those member states that did not join in making requests for enhanced co-operation. The contested decision did not amount to misuse of powers, but rather, having regard to its being impossible to reach common arrangements for the whole EU within a reasonable period, contributed to the process of integration. (3) In accordance with the EU Treaty art 20(2), the Council should not authorise enhanced co-operation, except as a last resort, when it had established that the objectives of such co-operation could not be attained within a reasonable period by the EU as a whole. The EU's interests and the process of integration would, quite clearly, not be protected if all fruitless negotiations could lead to one or more instances of enhanced co-operation, to the detriment of the search for a compromise enabling the adoption of legislation for the EU as a whole. Accordingly, the application would be dismissed.

Case C-274/11 *Spain v European Council* [2013] All ER (EC) 874 (ECJ: Grand Chamber).

1953   Patent—validity—exclusions from patentability—invention—computer program— technical contribution

The appellant made an application for a patent relating to a method for retrieving data from a remote computer using machine-readable instructions contained in emails. A hearing officer acting for the respondent found that the application was excluded on the basis that there was no technical effect outside of the two computers, and neither the computer nor the connecting network operated in a new way, so that the invention was a computer program within the meaning of the Patents Act 1977 s 1(2)(c). The appellant appealed, submitting that the invention could be regarded as providing four technical effects which showed that the contribution made by the invention was technical in nature and not within the exclusions on patentability. Those technical effects were (1) the telecommunications messages were generated by computers forming part of a telecommunications network, and transmitted from one computer to another over the network; (2) one computer remotely controlled the processing performed by another via a telecommunications network; (3) the result of the remote control was the transmission of files and information from the remote computer over the telecommunications network to the local computer; and (4) the remote control and transmission was achieved in a manner which did not require a continuous connection between the two computers. *Held*, the first and third technical effects involved communication between two computers over the internet. At the priority date, that was entirely conventional and could not form part of anything contributed by the invention. With regard to the second claimed technical effect, to say that one computer remotely controlled another was not a fair characterisation. All that was happening was that one computer was sending an email message to another. The fourth claimed technical effect, which was said to have solved the problem of the need for continuous connections described in the patent, failed to deal with the technical issues. It used email and thereby avoided the technical problems of continuous communication altogether. If a thing was not solving the technical problem but only circumventing it, then that thing could not be said to have taken any technical character from the problem. In substance, the claim related to computer software running on conventional computers connected by a conventional network. The task the software performed moved data from one computer to another using a conventional technique for carrying out that task, namely email. The context in which that arose was that accessing remote computers via continuous connections could be problematic, but that was not a technical solution to those problems; it avoided them, but did so using a conventional technique. Accordingly, the appeal would be dismissed.

Lantana Ltd v Comptroller General of Patents, Designs and Trade Marks [2013] EWHC 2673 (Pat), [2013] All ER (D) 37 (Sep) (Chancery Division: Birss J).

1954   Patent—validity—exclusions from patentability—invention—computer program—touch-screen interface

The claimant company owned a patent relating to computer devices with touch-sensitive screens which were capable of responding to more than one touch at a time. The first claim of that patent related to the method for handling touch events on a multi-touch device. Specifically, the claim related to the method of selectively sending one or more touch events, each touch event describing a received touch, to one or more of the software elements associated with the one or more views at which a touch was received based on the valued of the multi-touch and exclusive touch flags. The claimant issued proceedings alleging that the defendant company had infringed the patent in its own mobile phones. The defendant contended that the patent was invalid. The judge decided that the patent was invalid because it related to computer programmes as such and because it was obvious. The claimant appealed against that decision. *Held*, the court had to consider whether the invention made a technical contribution to the known art, with the rider that novel or inventive purely excluded subject matter did not count as a technical contribution. In considering whether the invention might be regarded as solving a problem which was essentially technical, the following signposts were useful: (1) whether the claimed technical effect had a technical effect on a process which was carried on outside the computer; (2) whether the claimed technical effect operated at the level of the architecture of the computer; (3) whether the claimed technical effect resulted in the computer being made to operate in a new way; (4) whether a program made a computer a better computer in the sense of running more efficiently and effectively as a computer; and (5) whether the perceived problem was overcome by the claimed invention as opposed to being merely circumvented. The problem which the present invention sought to address was how to deal with multiple touches in multi-touch enabled devices. The judge had erred in concluding that the first claim of the patent related to a computer program as such. The problem which the patent addressed was essentially technical. Also, the solution to the problem lay in a method which concerned the basic internal operation of the device and applied irrespective of the particular application for which the device was being used and the application software that it ran for that purpose. It was fair to say that that solution was embodied in software, but an invention which was patentable in accordance with conventional patentable criteria did not become unpatentable simply because a computer program was used to implement it. Further, a practical benefit of the invention was that it presented a new and improved interface to application programmers and made it easier for them to write application software for the multi-touch device. The device was, in a real practical sense, an improved device, not because it ran different application programs, but because it was easier for programmers to use. It followed that the invention did make a technical contribution to the art, which contribution did not lie in excluded matter. However, in certain respects the patent was obvious. Accordingly, the appeal would be allowed in part.

HTC Europe Co Ltd v Apple Inc; Apple Inc v HTC Europe Co Ltd [2013] EWCA Civ 451, [2013] All ER (D) 49 (May) (Court of Appeal: Richards, Lewison and Kitchin LJJ). *Aerotel Ltd v Telco Holdings Ltd; Re Macrossan's Application* [2006] EWCA Civ 1371, [2007] 1 All ER 225 (2006 Abr para 2126) applied.

1955   Patent—validity—obviousness—inventive step—anti-malarial drug

The defendant was the registered proprietor of a European patent relating to an anti-malarial pharmaceutical composition ('the composition'). The inventive step in the claim was a combination of two chemicals in a specified ratio. The composition was the most successful anti-malarial prophylactic in the United Kingdom. The claimants wished to sell a generic version of the composition. There was no dispute that the products proposed by the claimants would infringe the patent if it was valid. The claimants sought revocation of the patent, alleging that it was invalid on the ground of obviousness. They contended that the patent was part of the common general knowledge of the clinical pharmacologist. They relied on two items of prior art that did not disclose the ratio of the constituent chemicals. *Held*, viewed without any knowledge of the alleged invention as claimed, the question was whether the differences between the product and prior art constituted steps which would have been obvious to the person skilled in the art. What mattered was whether the invention was technically obvious, not whether it was commercially obvious. The court was satisfied that the defendant's patent for treating malaria was common general knowledge. The skilled team would have concluded that the combination of chemicals was worth pursuing. There was an urgent need for new anti-malarials, and the prior art relied on disclosed a combination which showed promising results. It would have been straightforward to carry out a larger trial. The skilled team would have expected to achieve similar cure rates in such a trial. It followed that the patent was invalid for obviousness. Accordingly, the application would be allowed.

   Glenmark Generics (Europe) Ltd v The Wellcome Foundation Ltd [2013] EWHC 148 (Pat), [2013] All ER (D) 95 (Feb) (Chancery Division: Arnold J).

1956   Patent—validity—obviousness—test of obviousness

The claimants brought proceedings in which they alleged that a European patent in respect of sustained release formulations of an anti-psychotic drug marketed by the defendant was obvious. The judge considered that the skilled person to whom the patent was addressed was a team of people, comprising a clinician, a pharmacologist, a formulation scientist and a pharmacokineticist. The defendant argued that the patent was not obvious and that, at the priority date, no dosage form of the drug had been approved or was on the market and that it was inventive to think of what the patent provided in the light of the problems alleged to exist. The judge found that the claimants were correct as to obviousness and that the patent lacked inventive step. On its appeal, the defendant contended that the judge erred in identifying the roles of the different members of the notional skilled team at different stages in the notional project; and in adopting an impermissible analysis in the sense of taking suggested modifications to a piece of prior art and then proceeding step-by-step to find something obvious in the claim that would have led the skilled addressee to have concerns over the development and effectiveness of a sustained release formulation of the drug and would have put a skilled person off from actual trial in detail. *Held*, the judge's description of the notional skilled person as a team was accurate and realistic. The notional team would include a clinician and a formulator, whose roles at different stages would overlap and interact. The analysis performed by the judge was the permissible one of addressing in a structured way the various reasons advanced by the defendant as to why the sustained release formulation would not have been done. Accordingly, the appeal would be dismissed.

   Hexal AG v AstraZeneca AB [2013] EWCA Civ 454, [2013] All ER (D) 247 (Apr) (Court of Appeal: Sir Terence Etherton, Mummery and McFarlane LJJ).

1957   Registered design—EU design—infringement—prior use of similar design

The claimant manufactured and sold a child's ride-on suitcase under a trade mark. The defendant imported and sold a similar product under a different name, whose design was admittedly inspired by that of the claimant's. The claimant contended that the defendant had infringed the following intellectual property rights: (1) the European Union registered design; (2) design rights in a number of designs relating to the product; (3) the copyright in the artwork for the packaging; and (4) the copyright in a safety notice which appeared on the packaging. At trial, the defendant conceded claim (4), but disputed claims (1)–(3). In relation to claim (1), the defendant contended that, if the scope of protection of the registered design was broad enough to encompass its product, it was invalid over an earlier design. Consideration was given to Council Regulation (EC) 6/2002 (on EU designs) arts 4–6 and to the Copyright, Patents and Designs Act 1988 s 213(2). *Held*, by virtue of Regulation 6/2992 arts 4–6, a registered design had to be novel and have individual character having regard to any design, which had been made available to the public. Any disclosure which made the design public in any part of the world would suffice. That was subject to two exceptions: obscure disclosures and confidential disclosures. On the facts, the defendant had infringed the registered design. Despite the differences between the defendant's product and the registered design, the overall impression the defendant's product created had shared the slimmer, sculpted, sophisticated, modern appearance, prominent ridge and horn-like handles and clasps looking like the nose and tail of an animal which were present in the registered design, but which were absent from the earlier design. Moreover, neither the defendant's product nor the registered design had anything like the handle which was a prominent feature of the earlier design. The 1988 Act s 213(2) defined design for the purposes of design right as meaning the design of any aspect of the shape or configuration of an article. Any aspect extended to any aspect of the shape or configuration that was discernible or recognisable. In order for design right to subsist, a design had to be original in the copyright sense of having originated with the author, and not being copied by the author from another. The test for originality in relation to a design which had been improved over an antecedent design for a product was whether sufficient skill, effort and aesthetic judgment had been expended on the new design to make it original compared to the old design. Configuration bore a wider meaning than shape, and included the relative arrangement of parts or elements of an article. The correspondences between the two artworks, such as they were, were insufficient to amount to a reproduction of a substantial part of the claimant's artwork. On the facts, the defendant had infringed the claimant's design right. In all the circumstances, the defendant had not infringed the copyright in the claimant's safety notice. Judgment would be given accordingly.

Magmatic Ltd v PMS International Ltd [2013] EWHC 1925 (Pat), [2013] All ER (D) 164 (Jul) (Chancery Division: Arnold J).

1958   Registered design—EU design—protection by utility model—invalidation proceedings—evidence

The defendant company filed an application with the Hungarian Patent Office for registration of an industrial design, and an application for protection by means of a utility model was subsequently filed successfully. The claimant sought the invalidation of the protection of the utility model concerned on the ground of lack of novelty and underlying inventive step. The protection of the utility model was confirmed. The defendant then filed a further application for invalidation of the disputed utility model, seeking to rely on new patent specifications not adduced in the earlier proceedings. The application for invalidation was rejected without reference to the new specifications adduced. The defendant appealed, requesting that account be taken of all the documents produced and stated that protection by utility model secured for its proprietor exclusive rights comparable to those conferred by a patent. It fell to be determined whether, in view of the requirements of European Parliament and Council Directive (EC) 2004/48 arts 2(1) and 3(2), European Union law required that, in judicial proceedings relating to an application for invalidation of the protection of a utility model, the court was bound (1) by the claims and other statements made by the parties and was entitled to order of its own motion the production of any evidence that it might deem necessary; (2) by an administrative decision made in relation to an application for invalidation or by the findings of fact in that decision; and (3) to re-examine evidence which had already been submitted in connection with a previous application for invalidation. *Held*, an invalidation procedure was specifically available to a person who, without being the proprietor of an intellectual property right, disputed the protection of a utility model granted to the proprietor of the corresponding rights. Consequently, such a procedure was not intended to ensure, for the purposes of the relevant provisions, that proprietors of intellectual property rights were protected. Indeed, that procedure did not involve infringement of an intellectual property right, whether (a) as regards the person who initiated that procedure, since, not being the proprietor of such a right, he could not, by definition, be subject to any infringement of that right; or (b) as regards the proprietor of a right to which that procedure related, since an action which was brought against him and disputed, in law, the existence of his intellectual property right could not, by definition, be categorised as an infringement. It followed that the relevant provisions were not intended to govern the various aspects of an invalidation procedure such as that at issue in the main proceedings. It followed that, in so far as arts 2(1) and 3(2) were not applicable to an invalidation procedure such as that at issue in the main proceedings, those provisions did not preclude the court being bound in the three ways identified.

Case C-180/11 *Bericap Zarodastechnikai Bt v Plastinova 2000 Kft* [2013] All ER (D) 264 (Feb) (ECJ: Third Chamber).

1959   Registered design—EU design—validity—individual character—informed user

Pursuant to Council Regulation (EC) 6/2002, the applicant company applied to the defendant for registration of a European design relating to corkscrews. A challenge was made to registration on the basis that the design was not new and lacked individual character. The defendant's Cancellation Division upheld the challenge, ruling that the overall impression produced by the contested design was no different to that produced by an earlier design in the light of the many similarities between them, such as the appearance of the curved handle, the element made up of two plates fixed together with a pin in an identical position, and the small blade located in an identical position. The Cancellation Division further stated that those similarities fell to be assessed in the same way whether the devices were open or closed. In rejecting the applicant's appeal against that decision, the defendant's Third Board of Appeal stated that the informed user of the design was a private individual and a professional who used the products covered by that design, and found that the designer had enjoyed a high degree of freedom. Although such devices should, as a matter of necessity, have certain functional parts, they might, according to the Board, be designed and put together in a number of ways. The Board found that the two designs at issue had non-functional elements in common, namely the design of the handle and the positioning of the small blade, and, as a result, they did not produce a different overall impression on the informed user. The applicant brought proceedings seeking annulment of that decision. It submitted that the Board had erred in its findings relating to the informed user of the design and the degree of freedom enjoyed by the designer. *Held*, the Board had correctly identified the informed user as a person who, without being an expert in industrial design, was aware of what the market offered and the basic features of the product. An informed user knew the various designs which existed in the sector concerned, possessed a certain degree of knowledge with regard to the features which those designs normally included, and, as a result of his interest in the products concerned, showed a relatively high degree of attention when he used them. The Board had also been correct to find, in essence, that the designer's degree of freedom with regard to a corkscrew was high. The designer's degree of freedom in developing his design was established by the constraints of the features imposed by the technical function of the product or an element of it, or by statutory requirements applicable to the product. Those constraints resulted in a standardisation of certain features, which would thus be common to the designs applied to the product concerned. If the designer enjoyed a high degree of freedom in developing a design, that reinforced the conclusion that the designs which did not have significant differences produced the same overall impression on the informed user. In the present case, the design and shape of the handle and the position of the relevant features were not dictated by requirements of functionality. The general appearance of the corkscrew was not therefore determined by the existence of technical constraints and might vary considerably. Accordingly, the application would be dismissed.

Case T-337/12 *El Hogar Perfecto del Siglo XXI, SL v Office for Harmonisation in the Internal Market (Trade Marks and Designs)* [2014] IP & T 114 (EGC: Sixth Chamber).

1960   Registered design—EU design—validity—use of distinctive sign

Council Regulation (EC) 6/2002 art 25(1)(e) (on EU designs) provides that an EU design may be declared invalid if a distinctive sign is used in a subsequent design, and EU law or the law of the member state governing that sign confers on the right holder of the sign the right to prohibit such use.

A registered EU design was declared invalid pursuant to Regulation 6/2002 art 25(1)(e). In an action brought by the proprietor of the design seeking annulment of a decision confirming the declaration of invalidity, an issue arose as to the interpretation of the concept of use in art 25(1)(e). *Held*, it was apparent from the case law that the ground for invalidity specified in art 25(1)(e) did not necessarily pre-suppose a full and detailed reproduction of an earlier distinctive sign in a subsequent EU design. Even if the contested design lacked certain features of the sign in question or had different, additional features, there might be use of that sign, particularly where the omitted or added features were of secondary importance. Accordingly, the action would be dismissed.

Case T-55/12 *Su-Shan Chen v Office for Harmonisation in the Internal Market (Trade Marks and Designs) (OHIM)* [2013] All ER (D) 74 (May) (EGC: Seventh Chamber).

1961   Registered design—legislation—application to Isle of Man

The Registered Designs (Isle of Man) Order 2013, SI 2013/2533 (in force on 11 November 2013), replaces the 2001 Order, SI 2001/3678, and extends to the Isle of Man, with modifications, the Registered Designs Act 1949 and certain provisions of the Copyright, Designs and Patents Act 1988 which relate to registered designs.

1962   Registered design—protection of industrial property—Convention countries

The Designs (Convention Countries) (Amendment) Order 2013, SI 2013/539 (in force on 6 April 2013), further amends the 2007 Order, SI 2007/277, so as to fulfil the international obligation on the United Kingdom as a member of the World Trade Organisation. Specifically, the order declares that Samoa and Vanuatu are convention countries for the purposes of the Registered Designs Act 1949.

PERPETUITIES AND ACCUMULATIONS

Halsbury's Laws of England (5th edn) vol 80 paras 1–200

1963   Rule against perpetuities—perpetuity period—start date—pre-emption rights— option to purchase land in specified circumstances

See *Cosmichome Ltd v Southampton City Council*, para 2127.

PERSONAL AND OCCUPATIONAL PENSIONS

Halsbury's Laws of England (5th edn) vol 80 paras 201–800

Articles

For articles relating to this title please refer to the Table of Articles at the beginning of the Abridgment.

1964   Automatic enrolment—earnings trigger—qualifying earnings band

The Automatic Enrolment (Earnings Trigger and Qualifying Earnings Band) Order 2013, SI 2013/667 (in force on 6 April 2013), (1) amends (a) the amount of earnings that a jobholder must receive before an employer is subject to the duty imposed by the Pensions Act 2008 s 3 in relation to that jobholder; (b) the amount of earnings a jobholder must receive before an employer is subject to the duty imposed by s 5 in relation to that jobholder; and (c) the amounts in s 13 used in determining a person's qualifying earnings; and (2) specifies rounded figures for the purposes of ss 3, 5 and 13; the amounts are in relation to a pay reference period of 12 months.

1965   European parliamentary pensions—United Kingdom representatives

The European Parliamentary (United Kingdom Representatives) Pensions (Amendment) Order 2013, SI 2013/481 (in force on 29 March 2013), further amends the 1994 Order, SI 1994/1662, by (1) providing for new rates at which United Kingdom representatives to the European Parliament ('representatives') contribute to the pension scheme set out in the 1994 Regulations; (2) allowing representatives to change their membership category; (3) amending the definitions of the membership categories; and (4) providing for the collection of the additional contributions from representatives whose contribution rate increases consequent to the changes made by the regulations.

married, not permanently separated, pensioner if (1) in the member state concerned, marriage was reserved to persons of different gender and existed alongside a registered life partnership such as that provided for by the domestic law on registered life partnerships, which was reserved to persons of the same gender; and (2) there was direct discrimination on the ground of sexual orientation because, under national law, that life partner was in a legal and factual situation comparable to that of a married person as regards that pension. It was for the referring court to assess the comparability, focusing on the respective rights and obligations of spouses and persons in a registered life partnership, as governed within the corresponding institutions, which were relevant, taking account of the purpose of and the conditions for the grant of the benefit in question.

Case C-147/08 *Romer v Freie und Hansestadt Hamburg* [2011] All ER (D) 212 (May) (ECJ: Grand Chamber).

1982 Occupational pension schemes—revaluation

The Occupational Pensions (Revaluation) Order 2013, SI 2013/2913 (in force on 1 January 2014), specifies the necessary revaluation percentages for the purpose of the revaluation on or after 1 January 2014 of benefits under occupational pension schemes, as required by the Pension Schemes Act 1993 s 84, Sch 3. The order also provides that it is not necessary to specify a lower revaluation percentage for revaluation periods which start before 1 January 2009.

1983 Pension Protection Fund—levy ceiling and compensation cap

The Pension Protection Fund and Occupational Pension Schemes (Levy Ceiling and Compensation Cap) Order 2013, SI 2013/105 (in force in part on 14 March 2013, in part on 31 March 2013 and in part on 1 April 2013), specifies the levy ceiling and the amount of the compensation cap for use in relation to the Pension Protection Fund in the financial year beginning on 1 April 2013. SI 2012/528 is revoked.

1984 Pension Protection Fund—miscellaneous amendments

The Pension Protection Fund, Occupational and Personal Pension Schemes (Miscellaneous Amendments) Regulations 2013, SI 2013/627 (in force in part on 29 March 2013 and in part on 30 March 2013), amend (1) the Pension Protection Fund (Review and Reconsideration of Reviewable Matters) Regulations 2005, SI 2005/669, so as to change, from two months to 28 days, the time within which an eligible person may make an application for an internal review of a decision by the Board of the Pension Protection Fund; (2) the Pension Protection Fund (Compensation) Regulations 2005, SI 2005/670, so as to give members the ability to postpone the payment of compensation and allow credit members to apply for early payment of compensation; (3) the Pension Protection Fund (Valuation) Regulations 2005, SI 2005/672, so that the market rate used to calculate the value of protected liabilities is the best value rate available in the market and the valuations of scheme assets which are contribution notices and orders reflect the actual payments received; (4) the Pension Protection Fund (General and Miscellaneous Amendments) Regulations 2006, SI 2006/580, so that the Board may discharge all of its liabilities in respect of money purchase benefits to a member by making a small lump sum payment, provided that the value of such benefits does not exceed £2,000; (5) the Pension Protection Fund (Pension Compensation Sharing and Attachment on Divorce etc) Regulations 2011, SI 2011/731, so as to make provision for the postponement of compensation by pension compensation credit members; (6) the Personal and Occupational Pension Schemes (Pensions Ombudsman) Regulations 1996, SI 1996/2475, so as to update the statutory references to matters which are excluded from the Ombudsman's jurisdiction; (7) the Pension Protection Fund (Partially Guaranteed Schemes) (Modification) Regulations 2005, SI 2005/277, so as to provide that the Board is not able to make a determination in respect of partially guaranteed schemes under the Pensions Act 2004 Act; (8) the Occupational Pension Schemes (Employer Debt) Regulations 2005, SI 2005/678, so as to exclude, for employer debt purposes, determinations under the 2004 Act s 143; and (9) the Pension Protection Fund (Provision of Information) Regulations 2005, SI 2005/674, so that the Board is required to provide members with information on postponement of compensation.

1985   Pension rights—employment—part-time work—less favourable treatment

See *O'Brien v Ministry of Justice*, para 1013.

1986   Pension schemes—company pension schemes—determination of schemes

The case concerned the status of nine schemes or arrangements which created, or purported to create, pension schemes. It involved two claims. The two claimants had been appointed by the defendant Pensions Regulator, as independent trustees. The claimant in the first claim was appointed as trustee for one of the schemes and the claimant in the second claim was appointed as trustee for the other eight schemes. Following their appointment, the claimants asked the court to determine whether the schemes in question fulfilled were 'occupational pension schemes' within the meaning of the Pension Schemes Act 1993 s 1. *Held*, on the true construction of the language of the schemes, all of them had the purpose of providing benefits to, or in respect of, people with service in employments of a description or for that purpose and also for the purpose of providing benefits to, or in respect off, other people. As such they fulfilled the purpose test in the definition of an 'occupational pension scheme' in s 1(1). Further, each of the schemes, by reason of the fact that the founder was a limited company which had a director at the point in time when the relevant scheme was established and, in the case of each scheme, the director was in an employment of the description concerned, the founder test in s 1(2)(a) was satisfied.

PI Consulting (Trustee Services) Ltd v The Pensions Regulator; Dalriada Trustees Ltd v Nidd Vale Trustees Ltd [2013] EWHC 3181 (Ch), [2013] All ER (D) 232 (Oct) (Chancery Division: Morgan J).

1987   Pension schemes—overseas pension schemes—recognised overseas pension schemes—requirements

The Registered Pension Schemes and Overseas Pension Schemes (Miscellaneous Amendments) Regulations 2013, SI 2013/2259 (in force on 14 October 2013), make provision relating to registered pension schemes, recognised overseas pension schemes and qualifying recognised overseas pension schemes ('QROPS'). In particular, the regulations further amend (1) the Pension Schemes (Categories of Country and Requirements for Overseas Pension Schemes and Recognised Overseas Pension Schemes) Regulations 2006, SI 2006/206, so as to exempt certain overseas pension schemes from a specified requirement relating to the availability of tax relief; (2) the Pension Schemes (Information Requirements for Qualifying Overseas Pension Schemes, Qualifying Recognised Overseas Pension Schemes and Corresponding Relief) Regulations 2006, SI 2006/208, so as to (a) impose a five-yearly re-notification requirement on QROPS; (b) specify additional information which must be provided in relation to payments made by a QROPS and extend that obligation to payments made by former QROPS; (c) provide that the information requirement in relation to transfers made by a QROPS extends to transfers made by former QROPS; (d) prescribe the information to be provided on cessation of a QROPS; (e) extend to former QROPS, with a limitation, the existing obligation on QROPS to correct and update information which has been provided to Her Majesty's Revenue and Customs ('HMRC') and revise the time limits within which such information must be corrected and updated; and (f) apply a modified version of the penalties regime in the Finance Act 2008 Sch 36 Pt 7 to the scheme manager of a former QROPS in respect of information requirements imposed on former QROPS; and (3) the Registered Pension Schemes and Overseas Pension Schemes (Electronic Communication of Returns and Information) Regulations 2006, SI 2006/570, by extending the range of information which a QROPS may submit electronically and so as to permit the electronic submission of specified information by former QROPS. The regulations also amend the Registered Pension Schemes etc (Information) (Prescribed Descriptions of Persons) Regulations 2010, SI 2010/650, so that HMRC is not required to serve two identical information notices on the scheme manager of a QROPS or former QROPS. Transitional provision is also made.

1988   Pension schemes—pension rates—reduction

The Registered Pension Schemes (Reduction in Pension Rates, Accounting and Assessment) (Amendment) Regulations 2013, SI 2013/1111 (in force on 31 May 2013 but having effect, in part, from 6 April 2013), further amend (1) the Registered Pension Schemes (Accounting and Assessment) Regulations 2005, SI 2005/3454, so as to require a scheme administrator making a return under the Finance Act 2004 s 254 to include the tax year to which an annual allowance charge relates; and (2) the Pension Schemes (Reduction in Pension Rates) Regulations 2006, SI 2006/138, so as to provide that a pension may be reduced, without ceasing to be a scheme pension, where an individual's annual allowance charge has been satisfied by the scheme administrator.

1989 Pension schemes—registered pension schemes—lifetime allowance—transitional protection—notification

The Registered Pension Schemes and Relieved Non-UK Pension Schemes (Lifetime Allowance Transitional Protection) (Notification) Regulations 2013, SI 2013/1741 (in force on 12 August 2013), provide how individuals may give notice to Her Majesty's Revenue and Customs that they intend to rely on fixed protection 2014 (protection from the lifetime allowance charge for those who may already have built up pension savings in the expectation that the lifetime allowance would remain at the current level of £1,500,000 pursuant to the Finance Act 2013 Sch 22 Pt 1) and make provision for supplementary and incidental matters. In particular, the regulations (1) make provision about giving that notice, its form and contents; (2) provide that if HMRC accept a notice they must issue a certificate; (3) set out the circumstances in which HMRC may refuse to accept a notice; (4) set out how the individual may appeal against that decision; (5) require that individuals inform HMRC if incorrect information has been given in a notice, or an event occurs which means that the individual is no longer entitled to rely upon the transitional protection; (6) set out the circumstances in which, following acceptance of a notice, HMRC may replace or revoke a certificate; (7) set out how the individual may appeal against replacement or revocation; and (8) deal with the preservation of documents.

1990 Pension schemes—relieved non-United Kingdom pension schemes—lifetime allowance—transitional protection—general

The Registered Pension Schemes and Relieved Non-UK Pension Schemes (Lifetime Allowance Transitional Protection) (Amendment) Regulations 2013, SI 2013/1740 (in force on 12 August 2013), amend the Finance Act 2011 so as to (1) extend transitional protection in relation to the lifetime allowance to relieved members of relieved non-United Kingdom pension schemes who are not also members of a registered pension scheme; (2) apply relevant provisions in relation to transitional protection to relieved non-United Kingdom pension schemes with effect from 6 April 2013; (3) provide that certain increases in the value of an individual's rights are ignored for the purposes of determining if there has been a benefit accrual and calculating the value of such an accrual; (4) ensure that, in relation to certain schemes, increases in value which result from revaluations under relevant statutory provisions are ignored for the purposes of calculating a benefit accrual; and (5) clarify that references to a relieved non-United Kingdom pension scheme or a relieved member of such a scheme are to be read in accordance with the provisions of the Finance Act 2004 which apply lifetime allowance provisions to members of overseas pension schemes. The regulations also amend the Registered Pension Schemes (Lifetime Allowance Transitional Protection) Regulations 2011, SI 2011/1752, by setting 5 April 2014 as the deadline for a relieved member of a relieved non-United Kingdom pension scheme to serve a notice of intention to rely on the transitional protection provisions.

1991 Pension schemes—relieved non-UK pension schemes—lifetime allowance—transitional protection—notification

See para 1989.

1992 Pension schemes—retirement benefit scheme—cessation of approval—charge to tax—date of cessation

The Income and Corporation Taxes Act 1988 s 591D(7)(b) provides that the reference in s 591C(1) to an approval of a retirement benefit scheme ceasing to have effect is a reference to the approval of the scheme being withdrawn under section 591B(1), and any reference in s 591C to the date of the cessation of the approval of the scheme must be construed accordingly.

It has been held, on an appeal by the administrators of a retirement benefit scheme against assessments to income tax under the 1988 Act s 591C issued on cessation of the Revenue's approval of the scheme, that the words 'construed accordingly' in s 591D(7)(b) mean construed in accordance with s 591B(1). Section 591B(1) includes reference both to the withdrawal of approval taking place by the service of a notice, and to the date on which the withdrawal took effect which was to be specified in the notice. Therefore, in relation to a withdrawal by notice pursuant to s 591B(1), the reference in s 591C to the date of the cessation of the approval of the scheme must be taken to be a reference to the date on which the withdrawal of approval took effect.

John Mander Pension Scheme Trustees Ltd v Revenue and Customs Comrs [2013] UKUT 51 (TCC), [2013] STC 1453 (Upper Tribunal: Vos J).

1988 Act ss 591B–591D repealed: Finance Act 2004 Sch 42 Pt 3.

1993   Pensions Act 2011—commencement

The Pensions Act 2011 (Commencement No 4) Order 2013, SI 2013/585, brings into force, on 13 March 2013, s 22 (so far as not already in force), Sch 4 paras 1 (so far as not already in force), 21–36. For a summary of the Act, see 2011 Abr para 1991. See also the commencement table in the title STATUTES AND LEGISLATIVE PROCESS.

1994   Pensions regulator—codes of practice—reporting late payment of contributions—appointed day

The Pensions Act 2004 (Codes of Practice) (Reporting Late Payment of Contributions) Appointed Day Order 2013, SI 2013/2316, appoints 20 September 2013 as the day for the coming into effect of the Pensions Regulator Code of practice no. 5: Reporting late payment of contributions to occupational pension schemes: Second issue, and the Pensions Regulator Code of practice no. 6: Reporting late payment of contributions to personal pension schemes: Second issue.

1995   Pensions regulator—financial support direction—contribution notice—limit on amount specified or recovered

The applicants were the administrators of a number of companies in a corporate group. They applied for directions as to the potential liabilities of those companies to make payments to or for the benefit of the group's pension scheme. The appointment of administrators constituted a relevant event under the Pensions Act 1995 s 75, giving rise to a liability to pay to the trustees of the scheme an amount equal to its share of the deficit in the scheme as at the date of the appointment of the administrators. The Pensions Regulator issued a number of contribution notices under the Pensions Act 2004 to other companies in the group to provide financial support for the scheme. A question arose as to whether, on the proper construction of the relevant statutory provisions, there was any limit on the aggregate amount which might be specified in or recovered under two or more contribution notices issued in respect of the same non-compliance with a financial support direction. *Held*, the Regulator had the power to issue a financial support direction where he was of the opinion that it was reasonable to impose the requirements of the direction on that person. The Regulator was given wide discretionary powers to determine whether and to whom financial support directions should be issued, to decide whether to approve the financial support proposed in response to financial support directions and to decide whether and to whom contribution notices should be issued. The Regulator had a wide discretion as to amounts to be specified in each contribution notice and, where the same amount was specified in two or more notices, whether to provide for the liability to be joint and several. In the event of non-compliance with a financial support direction, the Regulator had the power, under s 47(2), to issue a contribution notice. The Regulator was required by law to exercise his powers reasonably, having regard to the objectives under s 5(1). Section 100 required the Regulator, in determining whether to exercise any regulatory function relevant to the present case, to have regard to the interests of the generality of the members of the scheme in question and to the interests of such persons as appeared to the Regulator to be directly affected by the proposed exercise of its powers. In considering the interests of an insolvent target, the Regulator had to take account of the inability of the target to pay its debts in full. Additionally, there were imposed on the Regulator express requirements to have regard to all relevant matters, including the financial circumstances of potential targets of a financial support direction or contribution notices. Having regard to the relevant provisions of the 2004 Act, contribution notices might be issued under s 47 to more than cost cap, and sets out how this cap should be set, measured and operated. Section 13 provides for the setting of the rate of employer contributions in defined benefits schemes with a pension fund. Under s 14, scheme regulations must require scheme managers for defined benefit schemes to provide active pension scheme members with benefit information statements. The Treasury is empowered by s 15 to direct schemes to publish information or to provide information to the Treasury, and to specify how and when that information is to be published or produced. The Secretary of State is entitled to make regulations requiring scheme managers to keep specified records: s 16. Section 17 and Sch 4 make provision about the regulatory responsibility of the Pensions Regulator in relation to the governance and administration of public service schemes. By virtue of s 18, benefits may not be provided under existing pension schemes (as defined in Sch 5) in relation to service after the closing date for the scheme. Provision is made by s 19 and Sch 6 for the closure or restriction of existing injury and compensation schemes. Section 20 gives effect to Sch 7, which sets out the final salary link that applies to past service in those final salary schemes restricted under s 18.

Responsible authorities are obliged by s 21 to consult those likely to be affected before making or changing scheme regulations. Section 22 sets out the process to be followed in the event that a responsible authority wishes to make changes to the new public service pension schemes that impact on certain protected elements of the scheme. The procedure to be followed when retrospective provisions are included within scheme regulations proposed by the relevant authority is prescribed by s 23. Section 24 sets out the legislative procedures which apply to the making of scheme regulations. Under s 25, schemes may be extended to persons who are not in the main categories of persons in public service specified in s 1. Scheme managers and employers are permitted by s 26 to make payments towards the provision of pensions and other benefits that are not delivered through a scheme made under s 1 for persons who could have access to such schemes. Section 27 gives effect to Sch 8, which makes consequential and minor amendments to primary legislation. By virtue of s 28, certain regulations made under the Superannuation Act 1972 s 7 are to have effect as if they were scheme regulations made under the 2013 Act s 1. Section 29 gives effect to Sch 9, which amends the 1972 Act to extend access to schemes made under the 2013 Act s 1. Sections 30, 31 and Sch 10 allow the public authorities responsible for certain existing public body schemes to establish new pension schemes for staff or office-holders where it is not possible for those persons to become members of one of the major schemes established under s 1, and specify the provisions of the 2013 Act which apply to such schemes. Under s 32, an existing public body pension scheme may be reformed to include a provision that the normal pension age and deferred pension age of members of the scheme is to be the same as their state pension age. Section 33 and Sch 11 amend the pension arrangements for future incumbents of the offices of Prime Minister, Lord Chancellor and the Speaker of the House of Commons. By virtue of s 34, where a scheme under the Constitutional Reform and Governance Act 2010 Sch 6 para 12 or 16 links the normal pension age under the scheme to state pension age, the scheme can provide for a change in the normal pension age in consequence of the link to apply to benefits that have accrued as well as other benefits under the scheme. The 2013 Act s 35 amends the European Parliament (Pay and Pensions) Act 1979 s 4 so that, if a pension scheme in respect of European Parliament representatives links the normal pension age under the scheme to the state pension age, the scheme can provide for benefits that have accrued under the scheme to be subject to the link. The Secretary of State is required to carry out a review of how the provisions of the 2013 Act s 10 are likely to affect members of the Ministry of Defence Police and the Defence Fire and Rescue Service: s 36. Section 37 deals with interpretation, and technical provision relating to the making of regulations is made by s 38. Section 39 makes financial provision and s 40 deals with extent. Section 41 deals with commencement, and s 42 specifies the short title.

Amendments, repeals and revocations
The lists below, which are not exhaustive, mention repeals and amendments which are or will be effective when the Act is fully in force.

The following Act is repealed in full: Lord Chancellor's Pension Act 1832.

Specific provisions of a number of Acts are amended or repealed. These include: Pensions (Increase) Act 1971 Sch 2; Parliamentary and other Pensions Act 1972 ss 31, 36, 37;

Superannuation Act 1972 s 1; European Parliament (Pay and Pensions) Act 1979 s 4; Pensions Act 2004 ss 17, 71–73, 90; Constitutional Reform and Governance Act 2010 Sch 6.

2002 Registered pension schemes—accounting and assessment

See para 1988.

2003 Registered pension schemes—authorised payments

The Registered Pension Schemes (Authorised Payments) (Amendment) Regulations 2013, SI 2013/1818 (in force on 12 August 2013), amend the 2009 Regulations, SI 2009/1171, so as to clarify that incentive payments and age-related rebates paid by the Commissioners of Her Majesty's Revenue and Customs and 'minimum payments' made by employers to registered pension schemes and recovered from employees are 'member's contributions' for the purpose of the limit on part refund payments relating to short service.

2004 Registered pension schemes—lifetime allowance—transitional protection—general

See para 1990.

2005 Registered pension schemes—provision of information

The Registered Pension Schemes (Provision of Information) (Amendment) Regulations 2013, SI 2013/1742 (in force on 12 August 2013), further amend the 2006 Regulations, SI 2006/567, so as to reflect amendments to the Finance Act 2004 Pt 4 (ss 149–284) which reduce, with effect from the tax year 2014–15, the pensions lifetime allowance from £1·5m to £1·25m and the annual allowance from £50,000 to £40,000. In particular, the regulations (1) add a definition and references relating to transitional protection; (2) require a scheme administrator to provide Her Majesty's Revenue and Customs with additional information where there is a recognised transfer to a qualifying recognised overseas pension scheme, or where the scheme administrator is required to provide a member with a pensions savings statement because the annual allowance for the relevant tax year has been exceeded in that scheme; (3) require a member of a registered pension scheme who wishes to rely on transitional protection to provide a specified reference number to the scheme administrator; and (4) require a member of a registered pension scheme to give additional information to the scheme administrator when making a request for a recognised transfer.

See para 1987.

2006 State pensions

See WELFARE BENEFITS AND STATE PENSIONS.

2007 Superannuation—employments and offices—specification

The Superannuation (Specification of Employments and Offices) Regulations 2013, SI 2013/1564 (in force on 18 July 2013), (1) prescribe, for the purposes of the Superannuation Act 1972 s 1A(4)(a), employment or offices where the individual appointed to that employment or office was a member, or eligible to be a member, of a scheme under s 1 by virtue of s 1(4) prior to the appointment; (2) prescribe, for the purposes of s 1A(4)(a), employment or offices which ceased to be of a kind mentioned in s 1(4) before 21 June 2006 where persons serving in the employment or office continued after the employment or office ceased to be of a kind mentioned in s 1(4) to be treated by the Minister for the Civil Service as if they were members of a scheme under s 1; and (3) set out information which must be included in the list produced for the purposes of s 1(4A).

2008 Teachers—pensions

See EDUCATION.

PERSONAL PROPERTY
Halsbury's Laws of England (5th edn) vol 80 paras 801–875

Articles

For articles relating to this title please refer to the Table of Articles at the beginning of the Abridgment.

PLANNING
Halsbury's Laws of England (5th edn) vol 81 (2010) paras 1–618, vol 82 (2010) paras 619–1034, vol 83 (2010) paras 1035–1656

Articles

For articles relating to this title please refer to the Table of Articles at the beginning of the Abridgment.

2009   Community infrastructure levy

The Community Infrastructure Levy (Amendment) Regulations 2013, SI 2013/982 (in force on 25 April 2013), further amend the 2010 Regulations, SI 2010/948, so as to (1) allow preparatory work to be done by the Mayor of London to prepare a charging schedule in anticipation of a mayoral development corporation ('MDC') becoming the charging authority for an area in Greater London; (2) make transitional provision for when an MDC becomes, or ceases to be, a charging authority; (3) make provision for when the Mayor of London makes a transfer scheme under the Localism Act 2011 s 216 in relation to an MDC; (4) clarify that development granted permission by a community right to build order could be liable to the community infrastructure levy ('CIL'); (5) place a duty on charging authorities to pass some CIL funds to local councils where some or all of a chargeable development takes place in an area for which there is a parish or community council; (6) set out the proportion of the CIL raised in relation to a development that the duty applies to; (7) set out how the duty applies where the charging authority accepts a land payment; (8) set out a default provision for when payments are to be made to local council in the absence of an agreement with the charging authority; (9) empower the charging authority to recover funds from the local council if the local council have misapplied the CIL by not using it to support the development of its area or by using it for another purpose; (10) provide that the duty does not apply where a chargeable development (or part of a development) takes place in an area for which there is not a parish or community council, in which case the charging authority has wider spending powers in relation to those parts of its area for which there is not a parish or community council; (11) ensure that the neighbourhood funding element of the CIL will not impact on the relationship between the CIL and agreements reached under the Town and Country Planning Act 1990 s 106; (12) impose new reporting requirements on charging authorities and local councils; and (13) revise the operation of surcharges so that they are not treated as CIL for the purposes of the requirement to pass funds to parish or community councils.

2010   Development—consent—electric lines
See para 1087.

2011   Development—control over development—certificate of lawful use—material change of use

The applicant company entered into two agreements with the respondent local planning authority under the Town and Country Planning Act 1990 s 106. In each agreement, the applicant accepted restrictions on the kinds of goods that could be sold from retail units in an out-of-town retail shopping park developed by it. The planning purpose and practical effect of the agreed restrictions was that the units should only be used for the retail of bulky goods and were qualified by standard form provisos to cover subsequent planning events. It was agreed that the use restrictions on goods would not prohibit or limit the right to develop any part of the centre site in accordance with any subsequent planning permission granted after the date of the agreements. The applicant obtained a succession of individual planning permissions for building operations on a number of units. Such permissions imposed no use condition expressly restricting the kinds of goods that could be sold from the altered units. The applicant relied on the subsequent permissions for building operations, the language and context of the provisos and the provisions of s 75(2) and (3) as releasing the altered units from the agreed goods restrictions. It applied to the respondent for certificates of lawful development pursuant to s 191 for unrestricted A1 retail use of the units. The application was refused and the applicant's application for judicial review of the decision was dismissed. It was decided that the later planning permissions did not grant permission for a change of use of the altered units, that s 75(2) and (3) did not apply so as to permit a material change of use of the units, that there was no new planning chapter, and that the provisos in the s 106 agreements were not triggered by the later permissions. The applicant appealed that decision. *Held*, the judge had reached the correct overall conclusions and he had correctly applied those conclusions to the facts. The later permission had been granted for operational building works only. They had been neither for, not had involved, a material change of use in the units. Section 75 had not applied to the later planning permissions because they had not been granted for a material change of use of the units. Section 75(2) had not applied because the later permissions had not specified the purpose for which the relevant unit be used. They had related to building works and not to the use of the units or to specified purposes. Section 75(3) had not applied because the later permissions, in the absence of a specified purpose, had not been granted for a material change of use of the units. Further, the later planning permissions had not opened a new planning chapter in the history of the units. They had been for physical alterations for their improvement and had not involved any material change from the then existing restricted use to unrestricted use. Furthermore, the later permissions had not triggered the operation of the provisos to the s 106 agreements so as to have released the units from the restrictions. The provisos had only ceased to apply if the applicant had had the right to develop the units in a sense relevant to a material change of use. The subsequent permissions had only been granted for building works, which had not involved a change of use and had been compatible with the continuation of the existing restricted use. Therefore, the applicant had not had the right to develop within the meaning of the provisos. If that was correct, the provisos had not been triggered, the agreed restrictions had remained and they had applied to the altered units as they had applied to the unaltered units. Accordingly, the appeal would be dismissed.

Peel Land and Property Investments plc v Hyndbum BC [2013] EWCA Civ 1680, [2013] All ER (D) 193 (Dec) (Court of Appeal: Tomlinson and Davis LJJ and Sir John Mummery).

2012   Development—development management procedure—England

The Growth and Infrastructure Act 2013 (Local Development Orders) (Consequential Provisions) (England) Order 2013, SI 2013/2879 (in force on 9 December 2013), further amends the Town and Country Planning (Development Management Procedure) (England) Order 2010, SI 2010/2184, and the Town and Country Planning (Environmental Impact Assessment) Regulations 2011, SI 2011/1824, as a consequence of the removal, by the Growth and Infrastructure Act 2013, of the Secretary of State's powers to intervene in local development orders before they are adopted by local planning authorities. Transitional and saving provision is also made.

The Town and Country Planning (Development Management Procedure) (England) (Amendment) Order 2013, SI 2013/1238 (in force on 25 June 2013), further amends the 2010 Order above so as to (1) reduce the number of types of application for planning permission which must be accompanied by a design and access statement; (2) provide for a right of appeal against a failure to determine a planning permission application where the applicant considers that the local authority requires particulars or evidence which do not meet specified requirements; (3) expand the list of consultations in relation to which the duty to respond, under the Planning and Compulsory Purchase Act 2004 s 54, applies; and (4) remove the requirement on local authorities to include in a decision notice both a summary of reasons for any grant of permission and a summary of the policies and proposals in the development plan which are relevant to the decision to grant permission.

The Town and Country Planning (Development Management Procedure) (England) (Amendment No 2) Order 2013, SI 2013/2136 (in force on 1 October 2013), which applies in relation to England only, further amends the 2010 Order above so as to enable certain minor commercial appeals to be considered through the expedited written representations procedure. It sets out the time limits for submitting such an appeal, and the related publicity requirements. In addition, the order alters art 33 so as to (1) provide that applicants will be required to submit a greater amount of information with their appeal forms; (2) prescribe that applicants will also have to send copies of the specified documents to the local planning authority; and (3) empower the Secretary of State to determine which procedure will be used to determine the appeal under the Town and Country Planning Act 1990 s 319A.

The Town and Country Planning (Development Management Procedure and Section 62A Applications) (England) (Amendment) Order 2013, SI 2013/2932 (in force on 17 December 2013), further amends the 2010 Order above and the Town and Country Planning (Section 62A Applications) (Procedure and Consequential Amendments) Order 2013, SI 2013/2140 (see para 2017), so as to apply the compulsory pre-application consultation duty, under the Town and Country Planning Act 1990 s 61W, to relevant applications for planning permission in respect of any development involving an installation for the harnessing of wind power for energy production where the development involves the installation of more than two turbines or where the hub height of any turbine exceeds 15 metres. The order also sets out the particulars which must accompany a relevant application for planning permission which is subject to the duty to carry out pre-application consultation.

The Town and Country Planning (Development Management Procedure and Section 62A Applications) (England) (Amendment No 2) Order 2013, SI 2013/3194 (in force on 13 January 2014), further amends the 2010 Order above so as to provide that (1) the Secretary of State, rather than the local planning authority, is to publish the form of application for planning permission consisting of the winning and working of oil or natural gas by underground operations, including exploratory drilling; and (2) in relation to an application for planning permission of that nature, the applicant is not required to notify the owners of land where the land in question is solely to be used for underground operations. The order also further amends SI 2013/2140 above by making equivalent provision as described in head (2) in relation to applications for planning permission made directly to the Secretary of State, in accordance with the 1990 Act s 62A.

2013   Development—environmental impact assessment—development not directly connected with management of protected site—effect on integrity of site

Council Directive (EEC) 92/43 (on the conservation of natural habitats and of wild fauna and flora) art 6(3) provides that any plan or project not directly connected with or necessary to the management of a site of Community importance ('SCI') but likely to have a significant effect on it, either individually or in combination with other plans or projects, is subject to appropriate assessment of its implications for the SCI in view of its conservation objectives. In the light of the conclusions of the assessment, and subject to specified provisions, the competent national authorities must agree to the plan or project only after having ascertained that it will not adversely affect the integrity of the site concerned and, if appropriate, after having obtained the opinion of the general public: art 6(3).

The respondent granted development consent for a bypass scheme which was planned to cross an SCI. The respondent stated in its decision that the development would not have unacceptable effects on the environment and would be in accordance with the proper planning and sustainable development of the area. The applicant sought judicial review of the decision on the ground that the respondent had erred in its interpretation of Directive 92/43 art 6 in concluding that the effect of the scheme on the SCI would not constitute an adverse effect on the integrity of the site. The application was dismissed and the applicant appealed. On a reference for a preliminary ruling on the interpretation of art 6(3), *held*, art 6(3) had to be interpreted as meaning that a plan or project not directly connected with or necessary to the management of an SCI would adversely affect its integrity if it was liable to prevent the lasting preservation of the constitutive characteristics of the SCI that were connected to the presence of a priority natural habitat whose conservation was the objective justifying the designation of the SCI in accordance with Directive 92/43. The precautionary principle was applicable for the purposes of that appraisal.

  Case C-258/11 *Sweetman v An Bord Pleanala* [2013] 3 CMLR 404, [2013] All ER (D) 96 (Apr) (ECJ: Third Chamber).

2014　Development—general permitted development—England

The Town and Country Planning (General Permitted Development) (Amendment) (England) Order 2013, SI 2013/1101 (in force on 30 May 2013), further amends the Town and Country Planning (General Permitted Development) Order 1995, SI 1995/418, so as to (1) add a definition of 'article 1(6A) land'; (2) allow (a) larger home extensions to be built until 30 May 2016; and (b) schools to build a higher boundary fence or wall adjacent to a highway, provided it does not create an obstruction which is likely to be a danger for highway users; (3) increase the size of floor space in business premises which may change use from 235 square metres to 500 square metres; (4) add (a) a temporary new permitted development right consisting of a change of use of a building and land within its curtilage to a use as a dwellinghouse from use as an office; (b) a new permitted development right that enables various types of building to change use to use as a state-funded school, subject to the approval of the local planning authority regarding transport and highways, noise impacts and contamination; (c) a new permitted development right that allows reversion to the previous use; and (d) a new permitted development right which allows existing agricultural buildings to change use to a flexible use falling within a specified class; (5) set out the procedure to be followed where a developer is required to apply to the local planning authority for prior approval; (6) add a new temporary permitted development right allowing any building within a certain specified class to change use as a state-funded school for a single period of one academic year; (7) introduce a temporary right which increases the permitted development right to erect, extend or alter industrial and warehouse premises from 25 per cent of gross floor space or 100 square metres, whichever is lesser, to 50 per cent or 200 square metres; (8) set out permitted development rights in relation to developments by electronic communications code operators; (9) provide that, in relation to art 1(5) land, the construction, installation or replacement of telegraph poles, cabinets or lines for fixed-line broadband services will not require prior approval for a five year period; (10) give buildings which qualify for the right to change temporarily to school use the benefit of existing permitted development rights which allow schools to carry out building works, including the erection, extension or alteration of buildings and the provision of hard surfaces, subject to various conditions and limitations; and (11) provide (a) a temporary right which increases the permitted development right to extend or alter an office building from 25 per cent of gross floor space or 50 square metres, whichever is the lesser, to 50 per cent or 100 square metres; and (b) a temporary right which increases the permitted development right to extend or alter a shop, catering, professional or financial services establishment from 25 per cent of gross floor space or 50 square metres, whichever is the lesser, to 50 per cent or 100 square metres.

The Town and Country Planning (General Permitted Development) (Amendment) (No 2) (England) Order 2013, SI 2013/1868 (in force on 21 August 2013), further amends the 1995 Order above so as to (1) make provision to allow existing freestanding masts to be altered or replaced to become masts up to 20 metres high and up to a third wider than the existing mast, but not on art 1(5) land nor on a site of special scientific interest, and subject to prior approval on other land by virtue of Class A para A.2(4); (2) allow larger dish antennas and more antenna systems to be attached to certain buildings and structures; (3) permit up to three additional dish antennas and three non-dish antennas, subject to size limits, to be attached to existing electronic communications apparatus attached to buildings or structures on art 1(5) land; (4) clarify that current size limits for radio equipment housing are in one case cumulative and in another case applicable to single development proposals; (5) make provision to allow up to two of a new of sort of antenna to be attached to buildings and other structures, as long as they are not on a site of special scientific interest; (6) insert a new version of Class para A.2(4); (7) clarify that where Class A gives planning permission for the development of electronic communications apparatus, that permission extends to certain development ancillary to, and reasonably required for, the purpose of that apparatus; and (8) make consequential amendments.

The Town and Country Planning (General Permitted Development) (Amendment) (England) (No 3) Order 2013, SI 2013/2147 (in force on 1 October 2013), further amends the 1995 Order above so as to provide that (1) demolition of certain unlisted buildings in conservation areas is not permitted development; and (2) demolition of a scheduled monument or listed building is permitted development, but is not subject to the conditions relating to the demolition of buildings.

The Town and Country Planning (General Permitted Development) (Amendment) (England) (No 4) Order 2013, SI 2013/2435 (in force on 1 October 2013), further amends the 1995 Order above so as to provide that demolition of the whole or any part of any gate, fence, wall or other means of enclosure, where such demolition is 'relevant demolition' for the purposes of the Town and Country Planning Act 1990 s 196D, is not permitted development for the purposes of the 1995 Order. Such demolition will require planning permission.

2015 Development—general permitted development—Wales

The Town and Country Planning (General Permitted Development) (Amendment) (Wales) Order 2013, SI 2013/1776 (in force on 30 September 2013), further amends the 1995 Order, SI 1995/418, by making changes to the permitted development rights in relation to (1) the enlargement, improvement or alteration of a dwellinghouse (Class A); (2) the enlargement of a dwellinghouse consisting of an addition or alteration to its roof (Class B); (3) any other alteration to the roof of a dwellinghouse (Class C); (4) the provision within the curtilage of any building, enclosure, pool or container (Class E); and (5) the provision within the curtilage of a hard surface (Class F). The previous Class G (erection or provision within the curtilage of a container) is subsumed within the new Class E. A new Class G confers permitted development rights in relation to the installation, alteration or replacement of a chimney. Class H (installation, alteration or replacement of a microwave antenna) is amended to provide for when an antenna is treated as visible from a highway.

2016 Development—planning obligation—modification and discharge—England

The Town and Country Planning (Modification and Discharge of Planning Obligations) (Amendment) (England) Regulations 2013, SI 2013/147 (in force on 28 February 2013), further amend, in relation to England, the 1992 Regulations, SI 1992/2832, so as to (1) prescribe a period of one month, beginning from a specified date, after which applications to modify or discharge planning obligations entered into on or before 6 April 2010 can be made; and (2) prevent that provision from applying if an earlier application could be made under the default period set out by the Town and Country Planning Act 1990 s 106A(4)(b).

2017 Development—planning permission—application to Secretary of State—procedure—England

The Town and Country Planning (Section 62A Applications) (Procedure and Consequential Amendments) Order 2013, SI 2013/2140 (in force on 1 October 2013), which applies in relation to England only, sets out the procedures in connection with applications, made pursuant to the Town and Country Planning Act 1990 s 62A, for planning permission for major development which are submitted directly to the Secretary of State. In particular, the order (1) makes provision as to content and procedure in relation to the making of planning applications and reserved matter applications under s 62A, including the requirement for a design and access statement; (2) requires an applicant to serve a notice on the owner of land to which an application relates; (3) requires the Secretary of State to notify the relevant local planning authority where an application has been made, and the authority to provide information to the Secretary of State in relation to the land to which the application relates; (4) makes provision for the publication of applications by both the Secretary of State and the relevant local planning authority; (5) imposes a duty on the Secretary of State to consult the relevant local planning authority and certain statutory consultees in relation to an application, and requires substantive replies to be provided within 21 days; (6) provides that the Secretary of State is to make available on his website copies of any representations made; (7) prescribes the time period within which the Secretary of State must determine an application and sets down requirements as to publication of the decision; and (8) requires the Secretary of State to notify the Mayor of London where an application in relation to land in Greater London concerns a development of potential strategic importance, and specifies the criteria which the Mayor must apply when calling in such an application. SI 2011/1824 is further amended.

See para 2012.

2018   Development—stopping up of highway—objection—time limit

The claimant was the owner of property with the benefit of a right of way over a residential street. The owner of a doctors' surgery on the same street wished to develop the surgery and adjoining properties. The surgery owner was granted planning permission to do so, but because of the existence of public rights of way in the street, he was required to apply for a stopping-up order under the Town and Country Planning Act 1990 s 247. Pursuant to s 252, the defendant gave notice of the application, which commenced the 28-day period during which objections could be raised. No objections were raised and the defendant made a stopping-up order in relation to the street. Under s 287(4), an application could be made to question the validity of a stopping-up order within six weeks of the date on which the notice required by s 252 was first published ('the relevant date'). The claimant issued a claim dated one day after the relevant date seeking to challenge the order. The defendant submitted that there was an absolute requirement that a claimant challenging a decision made pursuant to s 247 did so within the prescribed time limit, regardless of whether there was potentially a flaw in the decision being challenged. *Held*, it was established law that even if there was substance to a complaint that the process involved in the decision of a public authority was flawed, the validity of the decision would stand unless challenged in accordance with properly laid down time limits under a particular statutory provision. In the present case, the claimant did not challenge the defendant's decision within the stipulated time period. He was out of time, and he faced an absolute time bar to the bringing of the proceedings. The court had no discretion to override the time limit that was provided by s 287(4). Accordingly, the claim would be dismissed.

Eatessami v Department of Transport [2012] EWHC 4002 (Admin), [2013] All ER (D) 192 (Feb) (Queen's Bench Division: Judge Wood QC).

2019   Development—urban development area—London Thames Gateway—dissolution

The London Thames Gateway Development Corporation (Dissolution) Order 2013, SI 2013/110 (in force on 24 January 2013), provides for the dissolution of the London Thames Gateway Development Corporation on 28 February 2013.

2020   Enforcement notice—appeal—time limit

An appeal under the Town and Country Planning Act 1990 s 174(2)(e) against an enforcement notice may be brought on the ground that copies of the notice were not served as required by s 172.

The claimant was the owner and occupier, together with his wife, of a barn. The local planning authority served two enforcement notices in respect of the barn. Each notice was stated to take effect at a specified time unless an appeal was made against it. To comply with the requirements of the 1990 Act s 172(3)(b), which required service of a notice to take place not less than 28 days before the date specified in it as the date on which it was to take effect, the notices would have needed to be served, at the latest, on a particular date. However, they were served on the claimant two days after that date. The claimant wished to appeal against the notices and instructed a planning consultant. The consultant claimed that the appeal notices were sent with guaranteed next day delivery. To have complied with the requirements of s 174(3), it would have been necessary for the consultant to have posted the appeal notices before the intervening bank holiday, or to have sent them electronically or to have delivered them by hand on the day he sent them by post. As he did not do so, the appeal notices were served out of time. The planning inspectorate stated that it had no power to extend the time in which an appeal could be brought or to waive s 174(3). The authority refused to reissue fresh enforcement notices in order to give the claimant an opportunity to appeal. In judicial review proceedings, the claimant challenged the validity of the notices. *Held*, interpreting s 174(2)(e) in the context of the legislative scheme as a whole, the words had to be given a narrower meaning. The legislation would not comply with the European Convention on Human Rights art 6(1) in a case where an enforcement notice had not been served in time causing the recipient to issue his appeal out of time, where the only means available to him to challenge the validity of the notice would be to appeal in time. An enforcement notice was a strong thing as a failure to comply with it led to very serious consequences. The right to appeal against an enforcement notice was a central part of the statutory scheme and gave an owner an opportunity to be heard and to object to the validity of the notice before its enforcement. Since the statute was capable of interpretation in such a way as to avoid an unreasonable result, it ought to be so interpreted. Therefore, the notices would be quashed. Accordingly, the claim would be allowed.

R (on the application of Stern) v Horsham DC [2013] All ER (D) 32 (May) (Queen's Bench Division: Leggatt J.

2021   Enterprise and Regulatory Reform Act 2013

See para 414.

2022   Growth and Infrastructure Act 2013

The Growth and Infrastructure Act 2013 makes provision in connection with facilitating or controlling the provision or use of infrastructure, the carrying-out of development, and the compulsory acquisition of land; about when rating lists are to be compiled; and about the rights of employees of companies who agree to be employee shareholders. The Act received the royal assent on 25 April 2013 and came into force in part on that day. Further provisions came into force on and between 9 May 2013 and 9 December 2013: s 35; SI 2013/1124, SI 2013/1488, SI 2013/1766, SI 2013/2143, SI 2013/2878. The remaining provisions come into force on a day or days to be appointed. For details of commencement, see the commencement table in the title STATUTES AND LEGISLATIVE PROCESS.

Section 1, Sch 1 provide applicants for planning permission with the option to apply directly to the Secretary of State if a local planning authority has been designated as not performing adequately in determining planning applications. Sections 2, 3 extend the powers of the Secretary of State to award costs between the parties at planning appeals and certain other planning proceedings, to recover his own costs from the parties, and to award costs between the parties at compulsory purchase order inquiries. Pursuant to s 4, the Secretary of State may provide in a development order that gives planning permission for change of use that the local planning authority or the Secretary of State may approve certain matters relating to the new use of the land. Such an order may provide, as respects permitted development within the curtilage of a dwelling in England, that the local planning authority may consider the impact of the development on the amenity of neighbouring properties: s 4. Pursuant to s 5, the powers in England for the Secretary of State to intervene in and reject local development orders and the requirement on local planning authorities to report on them are replaced by a new requirement that, where a local planning authority in England adopts a local development order, it must submit a copy of the order to the Secretary of State after the order is adopted. Under s 6, the legislative framework that governs what local planning authorities can request in support of a planning application is amended to ensure that such requests are reasonable and relate to matters that are likely to be material planning considerations.

Section 7, Sch 2 provide for applications and appeals to modify or discharge the affordable housing elements of planning obligation agreements to make developments viable, and s 8 removes an anomaly whereby general consents for the disposal of land by local authorities can be given under the Local Government Act 1972 for less than best consideration but cannot be given under the Town and Country Planning Act 1990 where land is held for planning. The need to promote economic growth is added by the 2013 Act s 9 as another consideration to be taken into account by the Secretary of State in making regulations about conditions and restrictions on the application of the electronic communications code. Section 10, Sch 3 change the regime of fixed reviews of mineral planning permissions every 15 years to give mineral planning authorities in England local discretion over when reviews are required, subject to the proviso that the interval between any two reviews cannot be shorter than under the present regime.

Sections 11, 12 enable the stopping up or diversion of highways and public paths to commence before planning permission has been granted in all cases. The process for landowners to make statements and declarations to counter rights of way claims is aligned with the equivalent process in relation to town and village greens (s 13), and the period within which a town or village green application can be made after the requisite 20 years of recreational use as of right has ceased is reduced from two years to one year (s 14). By virtue of s 15, landowners are permitted to deposit a map and statement to protect their land from registration as a town or village green, while permitting access to the land. Section 16, Sch 4 exclude the right to apply to register land as a town or village green on the occurrence of specified events, and s 17 permits regulations to prescribe more flexible fees in relation to applications for registration of common land and town or village greens.

Section 18 removes the requirement for developers or operators to give written notice to the Secretary of State of proposals to establish or convert electricity generating stations to be fuelled by natural gas or petroleum. Pursuant to s 19, licences for gas transporters may contain specified conditions requiring them to make payments to other persons holding such licences. Sections 20, 21 provide powers to vary consents for energy infrastructure projects and to make associated directions deeming planning permission to be granted where such variation occurs. Where projects are granted consent under legislation prior to the Planning Act 2008 and the consent concerned has been varied or replaced under that prior legislation, the 2013 Act s 22 makes it clear that development consent under the 2008 Act is not required. The 2013 Act s 23 removes certain consent and certification requirements under the 2008 Act, the 2013 Act s 24 repeals provisions under the 2008 Act applying special parliamentary procedure where land belonging to a local authority or a statutory undertaker is compulsorily acquired, and the 2013 Act s 25 modifies special parliamentary procedure in specified cases. By virtue of s 26, the scope of the planning regime for nationally significant infrastructure under the 2008 Act is amended to include significant commercial and business development. Under the 2013 Act s 27, procedural provisions regarding new roads and streetworks do not apply to development consent orders for nationally significant highways projects that authorise the charging of tolls if they also authorise other road user charging. Section 28 gives the Mayor of London power to delegate his decisions on whether to call-in planning applications of potential strategic importance for his own determination and to delegate decisions on whether to grant permission in cases where an application has been called-in.

Section 29 postpones the date on which the next non-domestic rating lists in England must be compiled from 1 April 2015 to 1 April 2017, and s 30 enables the Welsh Ministers to make an order postponing the date on which the new non-domestic rating lists in Wales must be compiled from 1 April 2015 to 1 April 2016, 2017, 2018, 2019 or 2020. Section 31 creates a new employment status of employee shareholder under which an employee shareholder agrees to have different employment rights to employees and receives fully paid up shares of a minimum of £2,000 in the employing company or its parent company.

Section 32 deals with the making of orders, s 33 enables the Secretary of State to make consequential amendments, and s 34 contains financial provision. Section 35 deals with commencement and s 36 with short title and extent.

Amendments, repeals and revocations
The list below, which is not exhaustive, mentions repeals and amendments that will be effective when the Act is fully in force.

Specific provisions of the following Acts are amended or repealed: Statutory Orders (Special Procedure) Act 1945 ss 1, 1A, 3, 4–7, 9A, 11; Harbours Act 1964 s 44; Energy Act 1976 ss 14, 19; Highways Act 1980 s 31; Acquisition of Land Act 1981 ss 5, 17, 18, 27, Sch 3; New Towns Act 1981 Sch 4; Gas Act 1986 s 7B; Local Government Finance Act 1988 ss 41, 52, 54A, 143; Electricity Act 1989 ss 36C, 106, Sch 16; Town and Country Planning Act 1990 ss 2A–2C, 5, 58–60, 61B, 62, 62A–62C, 70A, 70B, 76C–76E, 78, 90, 106–106C, 233, 253, 257, 259, 284, 303, 319A, 320, 322, 322A, 322B, 323, 333, Schs 4A, 6, 16; Water Industry Act 1991 Sch 11; Water Resources Act 1991 Sch 19; Transport and Works Act 1992 s 12; Tribunals and Inquiries Act 1992 s 9; Environment Act 1995 Sch 14; Employment Rights Act 1996 ss 47G, 48, 104G, 108, 205A, 236; Greater London Authority Act 1999 s 38; Countryside and Rights of Way Act 2000 Sch 6; Communications Act 2003 s 109; Planning and Compulsory Purchase Act 2004 s 59; Commons Act 2006 ss 15, 15A–15C, 24, 59, Sch 1A; Planning Act 2008 ss 33, 35, 35ZA, 35A, 127–129, 131, 132, 137, 138, 144, 232, 237A, Schs 2, 12; Localism Act 2011 s 141, Sch 22.

2023   Infrastructure planning—business or commercial projects—prescribed description

The Infrastructure Planning (Business or Commercial Projects) Regulations 2013, SI 2013/3221 (in force on 18 December 2013), provide that the description of a business, commercial project or proposed project is prescribed for the purposes of the Planning Act 2008 s 35(2)(a)(ii), and that such a project (1) consists wholly or mainly of either or both of the following: (a) the construction of buildings or facilities for use for the purposes of one or more of the matters in the Schedule; (b) the winning and working of minerals in, on or under land; and (2) does not include (a) the winning or working of peat, coal, oil or gas; or (b) the construction of one or more dwellings.

2024   Infrastructure planning—Infrastructure Planning Commission—applicant—fees

The Infrastructure Planning (Fees) (Amendment) Regulations 2013, SI 2013/498 (in force on 6 April 2013), further amend the 2010 Regulations, SI 2010/106, by providing that any day during the examination period is a relevant day, subject to stated exceptions, for the purpose of calculating the final payment for the handling of an application for development consent.

2025   Infrastructure planning—nationally significant infrastructure projects—highways and railways

The Highway and Railway (Nationally Significant Infrastructure Project) Order 2013, SI 2013/1883 (in force on 25 July 2013), amends the Planning Act 2008 so as to provide that (1) highway-related development falls within the scope of s 14(1)(h), so as to represent nationally significant infrastructure, only where the development consists of construction, alteration or improvement of a highway falling within the cases set out in s 22(2), (3) and (5); (2) construction or alteration of a highway falls within s 14(1)(h) only where the highway will be, or is, in England, the Secretary of State will be, or is, the highway authority and the area of development exceeds the limit values in s 22(4); (3) improvements to a highway fall within s 14(1)(h) only where the highway is wholly in England, the Secretary of State is the highway authority and the improvement is likely to have a significant environmental effect; (4) highway-related development is exempted from being a nationally significant infrastructure project where any order listed in s 33(4) has been made before 1 March 2010 and where a further order is needed; (5) the construction of a railway falls within s 14(1)(k) only if the railway, when constructed, includes a continuous stretch of track of more than two km in length on land that either was not railway operational land immediately before the construction work began or else was acquired for the purpose of constructing the railway; (6) the alteration of a railway falls within s 14(1)(k) only if the alteration includes the laying of a continuous stretch of track of more than two km in length on land that either was not railway operational land immediately before the alteration work began or else was acquired for the purpose of the alteration; and (7) the construction or alteration of a railway does not fall within s 14(1)(k) to the extent that the construction or alteration is on the operational land of a railway undertaker (unless that operational land was acquired for the purpose of the construction or alteration of the railway).

2026   Infrastructure planning—prescribed consultees and interested parties

The Infrastructure Planning (Prescribed Consultees and Interested Parties etc) (Amendment) Regulations 2013, SI 2013/522 (in force on 6 April 2013), amend various pieces of secondary legislation relating to major infrastructure by (1) removing bodies which no longer exist; (2) removing certain other bodies; (3) replacing bodies where other bodies have taken over functions or where a body has changed its name; (4) revising the circumstances in which certain bodies are to be contacted; and (5) adding certain new bodies.

2027   Infrastructure planning—prescription of consent requirements

The Infrastructure Planning (Miscellaneous Prescribed Provisions) (Amendment) Regulations 2013, SI 2013/520 (in force on 6 April 2013), further amend the 2010 Regulations, SI 2010/105, so that certain specified consents prescribed for the purposes of the Planning Act 2008 s 150(1) are prescribed in respect of Wales only.

2028   Local planning authorities—functions—Isles of Scilly

See para 2047.

2029   Mobile Homes Act 2013

See para 1669.

2030   Mobile Homes (Wales) Act 2013

See para 1670.

2031   Neighbourhood area—designation—exclusion of site

The claimant, a residents' association, applied to the defendant local authority for designation as a neighbourhood forum with regard to a neighbourhood area which included existing residential development in the locality, a Royal Air Force site and a sports centre. The defendant decided in principle to approve a recommendation excluding the Royal Air Force site and the sports centre from the neighbourhood area for the claimant neighbourhood forum pursuant to the Town and Country Planning Act 1990 s 61G. The claimant challenged the defendant's failure to take into account the purpose of the 1990 Act. The parties agreed that the legislative purpose in introducing the neighbourhood planning provisions into the 1990 Act was to enable neighbourhood forums which reflected the community in question to make neighbourhood plans guiding development in their neighbourhood area within a strategic planning context. *Held*, s 61G(5) required the defendant, in determining an application for a neighbourhood area, to consider whether the area proposed was appropriate. The decision given to the defendant was a wide one. The exercise of discretion turned on the specific factual and policy matrix that existed in the individual case at the time the determination was made. In the circumstances, the defendant had properly had regard to the specific circumstances existing at the time when the decision was made to designate a neighbourhood area which excluded the Royal Air Force site and the sports centre. Accordingly, the claim would be dismissed.

R (on the application of Daws Hill Neighbourhood Forum) v Wycombe DC [2013] EWHC 513 (Admin), [2013] All ER (D) 166 (Mar) (Queen's Bench Division: Supperstone J).

This decision has been affirmed on appeal: [2014] EWCA Civ 228, [2014] All ER (D) 83 (Mar).

2032   Neighbourhood planning—referendums

The Neighbourhood Planning (Referendums) (Amendment) Regulations 2013, SI 2013/798 (in force on 6 April 2013), amend the 2012 Regulations, SI 2012/2031, so as to make provision for the conduct of additional business referendums held under the Town and Country Planning Act 1990 Sch 4B para 12(4). In particular, the regulations (1) insert definitions of 'business referendum' and 'residential referendum'; (2) provide that information must be published in connection with a referendum and a business referendum in a designated business area not fewer than 56 days before the date it is held; (3) modify the formula for referendum expenses where there is a business referendum; (4) make provision so that a business referendum cannot be combined with any other election or referendum (including the residential neighbourhood planning referendum ('corresponding residential referendum'); (5) provide that a business referendum must be held on the same day as the corresponding residential referendum; (6) correct an error and make the correct provision for the mode by which a legal challenge may be brought in relation to a referendum held under the 1990 Act Sch 4B para 14; (7) set out the rules for the business voting register, in particular, making provision for obtaining data from the business rates records held by local authorities, sending out invitations to register, compilation, publication and supply of the business voting register, alteration of the business voting register and appeals; (8) set out the rules which apply to the conduct of business referendums; these rules are based closely on the rules for conduct of referendums; and (9) set out the election legislation which is to apply to business referendums, and how that legislation is modified, namely the Representation of the People Act 1983, Representation of the People Act 2000, Political Parties, Elections and Referendums Act 2000 and the Electoral Administration Act 2006.

2033   Planning permission—appeals—hearings and inquiries procedure—England

The Town and Country Planning (Hearings and Inquiries Procedure) (England) (Amendment) Rules 2013, SI 2013/2137 (in force on 1 October 2013), further amend the Town and Country Planning (Inquiries Procedure) (England) Rules 2000, SI 2000/1624, the Town and Country Planning Appeals (Determination by Inspectors) (Inquiries Procedure) (England) Rules 2000, SI 2000/1625, and the Town and Country Planning (Hearings Procedure) (England) Rules 2000, SI 2000/1626, so as to revise the procedure for hearings and inquiries held in relation to most planning appeals. In particular, the rules (1) amend the procedure to take account of the introduction of the draft statement of common ground and the full statement of case; (2) provide that the appellant is no longer required to send the

Secretary of State an additional copy of his full statement of case for the Secretary of State to forward to the local planning authority; (3) change the timings for certain stages in the procedure for inquiries determined by inspectors and hearings so that the local planning authority has one week less to notify relevant third parties an appeal has been made and one week less to submit its full statement of case, and all parties have one week less to agree a statement of common ground; (4) provide for inquiries determined by inspectors and hearings to be held sooner where practicable, and bring forward the date of inquiries determined by inspectors by four weeks and for hearings by two weeks; and (5) exclude the changes in relation to (a) circumstances where the Secretary of State issues a national security direction; (b) urgent Crown development; (c) type A or B appeals within the meaning of the Town and Country Planning (Development Management Procedure) (England) Order 2010, 2010/2184, for appeals relating to development substantially the same as development in respect of which an enforcement notice has been served; and (d) any appeal transferred out of the expedited written representations procedure.

2034   Planning permission—appeals—written representations procedure—England

The Town and Country Planning (Appeals) (Written Representations Procedure and Advertisements) (England) (Amendment) Regulations 2013, SI 2013/2114 (in force on 1 October 2013), further amend the Town and Country Planning (Appeals) (Written Representations Procedure) (England) Regulations 2009, SI 2009/452, so as to (1) expand the scope of the written representations procedure for householder appeals to cover the determination of advertisement consent and minor commercial appeals; and (2) reduce the time for certain stages in the procedure for other appeals and make consequential changes to the operation of that procedure when the Mayor of London is involved. Consequential amendments are also made to the Town and Country Planning (Control of Advertisements) (England) Regulations 2007, SI 2007/783.

2035   Planning permission—applications—major developments—hearings—England

The Town and Country Planning (Section 62A Applications) (Hearings) Rules 2013, SI 2013/2141 (in force on 1 October 2013), regulate the procedure to be followed for hearings caused by the Secretary of State to be held before he or an inspector determines applications for planning permission for major developments made directly to the Secretary of State under the Town and Country Planning Act 1990 s 62A. In particular, the rules provide for (1) the use of electronic communications and service of documents; (2) the fixing of the date for hearings and the notification of the date, time and place of the hearing and of the name of the inspector holding the hearing; (3) the publication of pre-hearing reports by the Secretary of State; (4) the admission of the public to hearings and for persons attending to report on the proceedings to be afforded reasonable facilities for making their report; (5) appearances at hearings; (6) the procedure at a hearing; (7) site inspections; and (8) the procedure after a hearing.

2036   Planning permission—applications—major developments—written representations—England

The Town and Country Planning (Section 62A Applications) (Written Representations and Miscellaneous Provisions) Regulations 2013, SI 2013/2142 (in force on 1 October 2013), provide for applications for planning permission for major developments made directly to the Secretary of State under the Town and Country Planning Act 1990 s 62A that are to be determined by way of written representation instead of a hearing. In particular, the regulations (1) provide for the use of electronic communications and service of documents; (2) prescribe which developments are 'major developments' under the 1990 Act s 62A; (3) prescribe the period within which the Secretary of State must determine which procedure an application under s 62A is to follow; and (4) set out the procedure for determining relevant applications on the basis of written representations.

2037   Planning permission—applications, requests and site visits—fees—England

The Town and Country Planning (Fees for Applications, Deemed Applications, Requests and Site Visits) (England) (Amendment) Regulations 2013, SI 2013/2153 (in force on 1 October 2013), amend the 2012 Regulations, SI 2012/2920, so as to (1) set out how the fee for pre-application advice is calculated in relation to applications for planning permission and for approval of reserved matters by the Secretary of State under the Town and Country Planning Act 1990 s 62A; (2) provide that the fee for applications under the 1990 Act s 62A is to be paid to the Secretary of State and is to be the same as the fee the applicant would have paid had the application been made to a local planning authority; (3) provide that there is no fee for submitting an application for planning permission in respect of the demolition of certain buildings in a conservation area; (4) provide that a fee paid by an applicant in respect of an application for planning permission or for the approval of reserved matters is to be refunded where the local planning authority (or the Secretary of State in relation to an application made under s 62A) fails to determine the application within 26 weeks unless the time for determination of the application has been extended by agreement; and (5) provide that the fee for an application for prior approval relating to development which involves the making of any material change in the use of buildings or other land is £80, but that no fee is payable where a planning application for the same site is submitted at the same time by the same person.

2038   Planning permission—change of use—material change—adequacy of reasons

An interested party operated a family farm containing a parcel of land which was in use as agricultural land. The site was in a Green Belt area. The interested party applied for planning permission for a change of use, including use of the land as a 20 pitch caravan and camping site and for residential use of a manager's mobile home. The planning officer noted that the change of use was an inappropriate development in the Green Belt area and that it could only be justified in very special circumstances. However, the defendant local authority approved the application in full and granted, subject to a number of conditions, planning permission for change of use from an agricultural field to a 20-pitch caravan and camping site. The claimant, a local resident, challenged the decision on the basis that there was a failure to give adequate reasons and that, as the decision refused, at least in part, to follow the recommendation of the planning officer, a fuller summary of reasons was necessary. The interested party contended that the reasons were not inadequate or, alternatively that, even if the reasons were inadequate, the defendant's decision should not be quashed, but the appropriate remedy rather was an order for reasons to be given or for a declaration of breach of the statutory duty to give reasons. *Held*, only summary reasons were required for the grant of permission. When considering whether summary reasons were adequate, it was necessary to have regard to the surrounding circumstances of the case in question. Where members of the local planning authority followed the recommendation of a planning officer to grant permission, then a relatively brief summary of reasons might well be sufficient. On the other hand, where the members granted permission contrary to the advice of a planning officer to refuse it, a fuller summary of reasons might well be necessary or appropriate. Further, in such a case, the reasons should also contain a summary explanation of the reasons why members disagreed with the reasoning in the officer's report that led to that recommendation. The normal remedy for failure to provide adequate reasons was to quash the underlying substantive decision. Alternative remedies included an order for a statement of the reasons or a declaration that the authority had breached its statutory duty to provide summary reasons. Quashing the underlying substantive decision might be refused where it was clear that, on reconsideration, the substantive decision would be the same. In circumstances where the planning officer had given detailed reasons for concluding that very special circumstances had not existed and where he had effectively reached that conclusion on two distinct occasions, it was a case where fuller summary reasons were necessary. On a consideration of all relevant material, it was not possible for the interested party, or indeed any relevant third party, to ascertain from the reasons given for the decision whether the defendant had properly interpreted or applied the very special circumstances test and the considerations which it had or had not taken into account. It followed that the defendant's decision would be quashed. Accordingly, the application would be allowed.

R (on the application of Wildie) v Wakefield Metropolitan DC [2013] EWHC 2769 (Admin), [2013] All ER (D) 146 (Sep) (Queen's Bench Division: Stephen Morris QC). *R (on the application of Siraj) v Kirklees Metropolitan Council* [2010] EWCA Civ 1286, [2010] All ER (D) 205 (Oct) applied.

2039   Planning permission—decision of local planning authority—Green Belt land—
        policy—very special circumstances

The second defendant, a local authority, refused to grant the claimant company outline
planning permission for the construction of 116 dwellings, a 72-bed care home, new road
access, two tennis courts and an open space on a site in the Green Belt. An inspector
appointed by the first defendant, the Secretary of State, dismissed the claimant's appeal
under the Town and Country Planning Act 1990 s 78. The claimant applied for an order
quashing the inspector's decision under s 288, contending that, on a proper understanding
of the National Planning Policy Framework read as a whole, a shortfall between objectively
identifiable housing need and the housing that could be provided on deliverable housing
sites identified by the second defendant was capable of being a very special circumstance
and, where such a contention was relied on, the second defendant and, on appeal, the
inspector were required to start by identifying the full housing needs of the relevant area on
the basis of the best and most up-to-date evidence available. The judge ruled that the
inspector had erred in law. The proper approach was to assess need, then identify the
unfulfilled need having regard to the supply of specific deliverable sites, and then to decide
whether fulfilling the need clearly outweighed the harm which would be caused to the Green
Belt. The judge therefore quashed the inspector's decision. On the second defendant's
appeal, *held*, it was not for the inspector on a s 78 appeal to carry out some sort of local
plan process as part of determining the appeal so as to arrive at a constrained housing
requirement figure. An inspector in that situation was not in a position to carry out such an
exercise in a proper fashion, since it was impossible for any rounded assessment similar to
the local plan process to be done. That process was an elaborate one involving many parties
who were not present at or involved in the s 78 appeal. It followed that, in agreement with
the judge, the inspector had erred by adopting such a constrained figure for housing need. It
led her to find that there was no shortfall in housing land supply in the district when, using
the correct policy approach, she should have concluded that there was such a shortfall.
However, the crucial question for the inspector in such a case was not whether there was a
shortfall in housing land supply but rather whether very special circumstances had been
demonstrated to outweigh the Green Belt objection. One of the considerations to be
reflected in the decision in that regard was likely to be the scale of the shortfall in housing
land supply. But there were other factors as well. It was not impossible for an inspector to
take into account the fact that such broader, district-wide constraints existed. The Green
Belt might come into play both in that broader context and in the site-specific context where
it was the trigger for the requirement that very special circumstances be shown. That was an
approach which took proper account of the need to read the framework as a whole. It
followed that the inspector had gone wrong in using a quantified figure for the five-year
housing requirement which departed from the approach in the Framework. Accordingly, the
appeal would be dismissed.

Hunston Properties Ltd v St Albans City and District Council [2013] EWCA Civ 1610,
[2013] All ER (D) 122 (Dec) (Court of Appeal: Maurice Kay VP and Ryder LJJ and
Sir David Keene). Decision of Judge Pelling QC sub nom *Hunston Properties Ltd v
Secretary of State for Communities and Local Government* [2013] EWHC 2678 (Admin),
[2013] All ER (D) 70 (Sep) affirmed.

2040   Planning permission—development—specific deliverable sites—inclusion of
        strategic sites—consideration of separate planning decision

The claimant developer applied to a local planning authority, the interested party, for
permission to build a number of houses. An issue arose in relation to the proposal as to
whether there was a supply of specific deliverable sites sufficient to provide five years worth
of housing against the first interested party's relevant housing requirements, with an
additional buffer of five per cent to ensure choice and competition in the market for land, as
required by the National Planning Policy Framework para 47. The claimant's proposal was
referred to the first inspector, who was appointed by the defendant Secretary of State, and
the interested party contended that the strategic sites included in its draft core strategy and
annual monitoring report should be included when determining the supply of deliverable
sites over the next five years. The claimant contended that they should be excluded. After
the hearing, two decisions by the second inspector were promulgated in relation to certain
other sites, which determined, in materially identical terms, that strategic sites should be

excluded from consideration of the supply of deliverable sites. The claimant requested that, notwithstanding that the inquiry had closed, the decisions by the second inspector should be taken into account by the first inspector as they dealt with the same policy area relevant to the claimant's proposal. The first inspector found against the claimant and included the strategic sites. No reference was made in the first inspector's decision to the second inspector's decisions and no further information or reason was given to explain why those decisions had not been considered. The claimant challenged the first inspector's decision under the Town and Country Planning Act 1990 s 288. *Held,* there must have been a real possibility that considering the second inspector's decisions would have led the first inspector to a different conclusion. Although it would have been his decision and he would have been entitled to disagree with the second inspector's conclusion, before doing so he would have been obliged to have regard to the importance of consistency and to give his reasons for departure from his decision. Further, there was no evidential basis on which it could have been said that it was disproportionate or contrary to the wider interests of justice for the second inspector's decisions to have been taken into account and there was no information to support the suggestion that the second inspector's decisions had been received too late to have been considered by the first inspector. The first inspector failed to exercise his discretion properly and, had he carried out his exercise properly, he should have concluded that the considerations that weighed in favour of admitting the second inspector's decisions outweighed those that had weighed in favour of excluding them. Furthermore, the first inspector acknowledged the existence of objections and identified that it had been for him to decide what weight he should attach to the sites having been allocated. He identified as a reason for including the sites that they had been identified by the interested party in the course of the development of the emerging core strategy. He acknowledged the weakness inherent in that process but had come to a planning judgment that sufficient weight could be given to the evidence in favour of inclusion so that the sites could be included in the absence of other, specific, evidence that they could not have included. Having interpreted the National Planning Policy Framework footnote 11 correctly, the first inspector had been entitled to reach the conclusions that he reached on the materials he considered and the reasons which he had given. Judgment would be given accordingly.

Wainhomes (South West) Holdings Ltd v Secretary of State for Communities and Local Government [2013] EWHC 597 (Admin), [2013] All ER (D) 23 (Apr) (Queen's Bench Division: Stuart-Smith J).

2041   Planning permission—grant of permission—lawfulness—ecological impact

The defendant local authority applied for planning permission to construct a waste facility. The planning proposal involved the construction of an access road to the facility, the construction of which would adversely affect the habitat of three protected species. There were also four sites of special scientific interest within close proximity of the proposed access road. The defendant considered seven alternative access proposals, and took into consideration an ecological management plan which provided a single point of reference for all ecological mitigation, compensation and enhancement measures. Natural England, which was the body responsible for enforcing the Conservation of Habitats and Species Regulations 2010, SI 2010/490, which implemented Council Directive (EC) 92/43, had originally objected to the planning proposal, but later granted derogation licences in respect of the protected species. Planning permission was eventually granted by the defendant in relation to the facility, subject to a number of conditions intended to mitigate ecological impact. The claimant issued judicial review proceedings challenging the grant of planning permission, contending that it was unlawful on the grounds that there had been a failure to (1) comply with the requirements of Directive 92/43; (2) apply the government's planning policy for nature conservation; and (3) provide adequate reasons for the grant of planning permission. *Held,* it was the function of Natural England to enforce compliance with Directive 92/43 by prosecuting those who committed offences contrary to its provisions. The 2010 Regulations reg 9(5) made it the defendant's duty simply to have regard to those provisions. Regulation 9(5) did not require a planning authority to carry out the assessment that Natural England had to make when deciding whether there would be a breach of Directive 92/43 or whether a derogation should be permitted and a licence granted. A planning authority was not expected to supervise the performance by Natural England of that responsibility or to take on the responsibility itself. It followed that the defendant had discharged its duty under the 2010 Regulations reg 9(5) with no less rigour than had been required to comply with established law. With regard to the claimant's second objection, it was an established principle that judicial review did not provide an opportunity to contest the merits of a planning authority's decisions. Questions of planning judgment and weight were not for the court but for the planning decision-maker. The second part of the claim was an attack on the expert judgment of Natural England and the views of the defendant's own ecological expert and planning officers. It was impossible on the facts and the evidence to conclude that the judgment was either unreasonable or contrary to government policy. On the facts, the claimant's third objection also failed. The summary reasons provided by the defendant had been terse but not unlawful. Even if the summary reasons had fallen short of what was required, the court would have found that nobody had suffered substantial prejudice. Accordingly, the claim would be dismissed.

  R (on the application of Prideaux) v Buckinghamshire CC [2013] EWHC 1054 (Admin), [2013] All ER (D) 25 (May) (Queen's Bench Division: Lindblom J).

2042   **Planning permission—Green Belt—change of use**

The claimant applied to its local planning authority for planning permission to develop a caravan and camping site. The site was located wholly in designated Green Belt land, and the development involved a change in use of that land from agricultural use to the intended use. The authority considered the National Planning Policy Framework ('NPPF') and decided to reject the application on the basis that the proposed change of use would constitute inappropriate development, that therefore very special circumstances were required to be demonstrated before the proposed development could be permitted, and that such circumstances did not exist because the harm to the Green Belt that would be caused by the development was not clearly outweighed by the material considerations in favour of the scheme. The claimant appealed against that decision, but a planning inspector decided that the authority's conclusions had been correct. On the claimant's further appeal, it contended that (1) the inspector had been wrong to conclude that a change of use from agricultural use to outdoor sport and recreation was inevitably inappropriate development and thus not to be permitted in the absence of very special circumstances being demonstrated; and (2) the inspector had failed to have regard to the NPPF policy that significant weight should be given to the need to support economic growth through the planning system. *Held*, the effects of the NPPF paras 87, 89 and 90, when read together, was that all development in the Green Belt was inappropriate unless it was either development falling within one or more of the categories set out in para 90 or was the construction of a new building or buildings that came or potentially came within one of the exceptions referred to in para 89. A change of use falling within one of the categories identified in para 90 of the NPPF was in principle capable of being appropriate. The real issue, therefore, was whether development in the form of a material change of use outside the categories identified in para 90 had to, by definition, be inappropriate development, or whether such a change of use had to be considered on its merits. The forms of development other than those falling within para 90 that were capable of being appropriate referred back to the exceptions listed in para 89, which was exclusively concerned with a particular form of operational development being the construction of new buildings. It did not apply and was not expressed to apply to any other form of development. It followed that, when paras 87, 89 and 90 were read together, as they ought to be, the meaning was clear. Development in the Green Belt was inappropriate, and thus could be permitted only in very special circumstances, unless it fell within one of the exceptions identified in para 89 and 90. The second ground of the challenge was also misplaced. It was clear that the inspector had accorded weight to the economic benefits of what was proposed. It was apparent, when the decision letter was considered, that the inspector had carried out the evaluation of the effect of the various material considerations relevant to the appeal that he had been required to carry out. Accordingly, the appeal would be dismissed.

  Fordent Holdings Ltd v Secretary of State for Communities and Local Government [2013] EWHC 2844 (Admin), [2013] All ER (D) 247 (Sep) (Queen's Bench Division: Judge Pelling QC). *Europa Oil and Gas Ltd v Secretary of State for Communities and Local Government* [2013] EWHC 2643 (Admin), [2013] All ER (D) 352 (Jul) applied.

2043　Planning permission—listed buildings and conservation areas—appeals—England

The Planning (Listed Buildings and Conservation Areas) (Amendment No 2) (England) Regulations 2013, SI 2013/2115 (in force on 1 October 2013), further amend the 1990 Regulations, SI 1990/1519, so as to (1) require specified appellants against decisions under the regulations to submit their full statement of case, a statement of what procedure they think should be used to consider their appeal and, where relevant, a draft statement of common ground with their appeal form; (2) require such appellants to send copies of these documents and the notice of appeal to the local planning authority as well as the Secretary of State; and (3) change the starting point of the period within which an appeal must be made from within six months of receipt of a decision notice to within six months of the date of the notice.

2044　Planning permission—listed buildings and conservations areas—applications—design and access statements—England

The Planning (Listed Buildings and Conservation Areas) (Amendment) (England) Regulations 2013, SI 2013/1239 (in force on 25 June 2013), further amend the 1990 Regulations, SI 1990/1519, so as to set out the content which is required for design and access statements which accompany applications made under the 1990 Regulations. The regulations also (1) remove the requirement for design and access statements to explain the principles and concepts that have been applied to the scale, layout, and appearance of the works to be carried out; and (2) remove the requirement for a design and access statement to explain how features which ensure access to the building will be maintained, with the effect of streamlining the content required in all applications for listed building consent.

2045　Planning permission—listed buildings and conservation areas—conservation area consent—abolition—consequential provision—England

The Enterprise and Regulatory Reform Act 2013 (Abolition of Conservation Area Consent) (Consequential and Saving Provisions) (England) Order 2013, SI 2013/2146 (in force on 1 October 2013), amends a number of enactments as a consequence of the abolition, by the Enterprise and Regulatory Reform Act 2013, of the system of conservation area consent as it applies to buildings in conservation areas in England. SI 1990/1519, SI 1997/420, SI 2000/1624, SI 2000/1625, SI 2000/1626, SI 2000/2853, SI 2002/2682, SI 2002/2683, SI 2002/2684, SI 2002/2685, SI 2002/2686 and SI 2005/598 are further amended. SI 2005/205 is amended.

2046　Planning permission—listed buildings and conservation areas—demolition of buildings in conservation areas—England

The Town and Country Planning General (Amendment) (England) Regulations 2013, SI 2013/2145 (in force on 1 October 2013), further amend the 1992 Regulations, SI 1992/1492, so as to provide for the Secretary of State to determine applications for planning permission made by an interested local planning authority for the development of land which relates solely to the demolition of an unlisted building in a conservation area and set out the procedure to be followed on such applications.

2047　Planning permission—listed buildings and conservation areas—Isles of Scilly

The Town and Country Planning (Isles of Scilly) Order 2013, SI 2013/2148 (in force on 2 October 2013), replaces the Planning (Listed Buildings and Conservation Areas) (Isles of Scilly) Order 1990, SI 1990/2237, and the 2005 Order, SI 2005/2085. In particular, the order (1) incorporates changes arising as a result of the abolition of conservation area consent; and (2) provides for the exercise of planning functions in the Isles of Scilly by the Council of the Isles of Scilly, subject to specified exceptions, adaptations and modifications.

2048　Planning permission—withdrawal—compensation—England

The Town and Country Planning (Compensation) (England) Regulations 2013, SI 2013/1102 (in force on 30 May 2013), replace the 2012 Regulations, SI 2012/749, and prescribe (1) certain types of development permitted by development order for the purposes of the Town and Country Planning Act 1990 s 108(2A), (3C); (2) the manner in which planning permission granted by development order is to be withdrawn; (3) the manner of publication of notice of withdrawal; and (4) the maximum period of such notice in respect of permissions granted by (a) a development order; (b) a local development order; and (c) a neighbouring development order.

2049   Public path orders—stopping up or diversion orders—England

See para 1386.

2050   Regional planning—strategies—revocation—England

The Regional Strategy for Yorkshire and Humber (Partial Revocation) Order 2013, SI 2013/117 (in force on 22 February 2013), revokes the regional strategy for Yorkshire and Humber, subject to a specified exception.

The Regional Strategy for the South East (Partial Revocation) Order 2013, SI 2013/427 (in force on 25 March 2013), revokes the regional strategy for the South East, subject to a specified exception.

The Regional Strategy for the East Midlands (Revocation) Order 2013, SI 2013/629 (in force on 12 April 2013), revokes the regional strategy for the East Midlands.

The Regional Strategy for the North East (Revocation) Order 2013, SI 2013/635 (in force on 12 April 2013), revokes the regional strategy for the North East.

The Regional Strategy for the West Midlands (Revocation) Order 2013, SI 2013/933 (in force on 20 May 2013), revokes the regional strategy for the West Midlands.

The Regional Strategy for the North West (Revocation) Order 2013, SI 2013/934 (in force on 20 May 2013), revokes the regional strategy for the North West.

The Regional Strategy for the South West (Revocation) Order 2013, SI 2013/935 (in force on 20 May 2013), revokes the regional strategy the South West.

2051   Temporary stop notice—prescribed circumstances—England

The Town and Country Planning (Temporary Stop Notice) (England) (Revocation) Regulations 2013, SI 2013/830 (in force on 4 May 2013), revoke the 2005 Regulations, SI 2005/206.

POLICE AND INVESTIGATORY POWERS

Halsbury's Laws of England (5th edn) vol 84 (2013) paras 1–431, vol 84A (2013) paras 432–800.

Articles

For articles relating to this title please refer to the Table of Articles at the beginning of the Abridgment.

2052   Crime and Courts Act 2013

The Crime and Courts Act 2013 establishes and makes provision about the National Crime Agency, abolishes the Serious Organised Crime Agency and the National Policing Improvement Agency, makes provision about the judiciary and the structure, administration, proceedings and powers of courts and tribunals, makes provision about deferred prosecution agreements, makes provision about border control and makes provision about drugs and driving. The Act received the royal assent on 25 April 2013 and came into force in part on that day and on 26 April 2013. Further provisions came into force on and between 8 May 2013 and 1 February 2014: SI 2013/1042, SI 2013/1682, SI 2013/1725, SI 2013/2200, SI 2013/2349, SI 2013/2981, SI 2013/3176. Sections 34–39 come into force at the end of the period of one year beginning with the day on which a body is established by royal charter with the purpose of carrying on activities relating to the recognition of independent regulators of relevant publishers. The remaining provisions come into force on a day or days to be appointed. For details of commencement, see the commencement table in the title STATUTES AND LEGISLATIVE PROCESS.

Part 1 (ss 1–16) The National Crime Agency

Section 1, Sch 1 establish the National Crime Agency, which is to consist of the National Crime Agency officers. Section 2 enables the Secretary of State to make provision about National Crime Agency counter-terrorism functions. In accordance with s 3, the Secretary of State must determine strategic priorities for the National Crime Agency. Section 4 provides that the Director General of the National Crime Agency has the power to decide which particular operations are to be mounted by National Crime Agency officers and how such operations are to be conducted and Sch 2 makes provision about the framework document, which deals with ways in which the National Crime Agency is to operate. By virtue of s 5, the chief officer of a United Kingdom police force or a United Kingdom law enforcement agency may perform a task if the Director General requests the person to perform it. The Director General must make arrangements for publishing information about the exercise of National Crime Agency functions and other matters relating to the National Crime Agency and publish information in accordance with those arrangements: s 6. Under s 7, a person may disclose information to the National Crime Agency if the disclosure is made for the purposes of the exercise of any National Crime Agency function. Section 8 amends the Children Act 2004 ss 11, 28 so as to provide that the National Crime Agency has a duty to ensure that its functions are discharged having regard to the need to safeguard and promote the welfare of children and the 2013 Act Sch 4 provides that the Secretary of State may make regulations requiring equipment used by the National Crime Agency to satisfy requirements as to design and performance. The Director General has, in relation to any customs matter, the same powers as the Commissioners for Her Majesty's Revenue and Customs: s 9. Under s 10, the Director General may designate any other National Crime Agency officer as a person having the powers and privileges of a constable, the powers of an officer of Revenue and Customs, or the powers of an immigration officer. Section 11, Sch 6 set out provision regarding inspections and complaints concerning the National Crime Agency. Section 12 gives effect to Sch 7, which applies to disclosures made for the purposes of the criminal intelligence function. A person must not induce the Director General or any National Crime Agency officer designated under s 10 to withhold services as a National Crime Agency officer: s 13. By virtue of s 14, the Secretary of State may provide for the establishment, maintenance and operation of procedures for the determination of the rates of pay and allowances to be applied to the Director General and to the National Crime Agency. Section 15, Sch 8 abolish the Serious Organised Crime Agency and the National Policing Improvement Agency. Section 16 provides interpretation for Part 1.

Part 2 (ss 17–50) Courts and justice
Section 17, Schs 9–11 amend the County Courts Act 1984 to provide for the establishment of a single county court and for the establishment of the family court. By virtue of the 2013 Act s 18, Sch 12 youth courts are to have jurisdiction to grant gang-related injunctions. Section 19 amends the Legal Aid, Sentencing and Punishment of Offenders Act 2012 s 102 so as to vary designations of authorities responsible for remanded young persons. The 2013 Act s 20, Sch 13 provide for there to be no more than the equivalent of 12 full-time judges of the Supreme Court and make provision about their selection, contain provisions to facilitate greater diversity among judges and amend provisions about membership of the Judicial Appointments Commission. The Lord Chief Justice's deployment responsibility includes responsibility for the maintenance of appropriate arrangements for the deployment to tribunals of judiciary deployable to tribunals and the deployment to courts in England and Wales of judiciary deployable to such courts: s 21. Section 22 makes provision for the transfer of immigration or nationality judicial review applications. The Senior Courts Act 1981 s 44 ceases to have the effect of conferring jurisdiction on judges of the High Court sitting as Visitors to the Inns of Court: 2013 Act s 24. Section 25 amends the Tribunals, Courts and Enforcement Act 2007 Sch 12 to provide a power to use reasonable force, but not against the person, to enter commercial premises to enforce High Court and county court debts pursuant to a writ or warrant of control. Under s 26, provision is made in order (1) to enable the recovery of charges for some or all of the administrative costs of collecting or pursuing criminal financial penalties from offenders who have defaulted on that sum; and (2) to facilitate the performance of the functions of fines officers by staff provided under contract. Section 27 amends the Courts Act 2003 to enable the Secretary of State, a Northern Ireland department and Her Majesty's Revenue and Customs to share social security and finances information with Her Majesty's Courts and Tribunals Service for the purpose of facilitating the making of a decision by a court or a fines officer as to whether to make an attachment of earnings order or an application for benefits deductions

against the offender, or of facilitating the making of such an order or application. The 2013 Act s 28 allows the disclosure of social security information to a relevant person who wants social security information in connection with deciding a fee-remission application. Section 29 amends the Constitutional Reform Act 2005 s 48 so as to make the President of the Supreme Court responsible for the appointment of the Chief Executive of the Supreme Court instead of the Lord Chancellor. The 2013 Act s 30 adds the Constitutional Reform Act 2005 ss 51A–51E so as to provide for Supreme Court security officers who will operate in any building where the business of the Supreme Court or the judicial committee of the Privy Council is carried on. The 2013 Act s 31 disapplies the provisions in the Contempt of Court Act 1981 s 9 relating to the prohibition on sound recording and the subsequent broadcasting of any such recordings. The 2013 Act s 32 enables the making and use of films and other recordings of proceedings. Scandalising the judiciary is abolished as a form of contempt of court under the common law of England and Wales: s 33. Exemplary damages may not be awarded against the defendant in respect of the claim if the defendant was a member of an approved regulator at the material time: s 34. Section 35 sets out the relevant considerations for the court when it is deciding whether to award exemplary damages under s 34. The amount of exemplary damages must not be more than the minimum needed to punish the defendant for the conduct complained of and the amount must also be proportionate to the seriousness of the conduct: s 36. Under s 37, in deciding whether to award exemplary damages under s 34 or the amount of such damages to award, the court must take account of any settlement or compromise by any persons of a claim in respect of the conduct. Any liability of two or more persons for exemplary damages awarded under s 34 is several: s 38. Section 39 provides that aggravated damages may be awarded against the defendant only to compensate for mental distress and not for purposes of punishment. Section 40 governs the awards of costs where a relevant claim is made against a person ('the defendant'), the defendant was a relevant publisher at the material time and the claim is related to the publication of news-related material. 'Relevant publisher' means a person who in the course of a business publishes news-related material which is written by different authors and which is to any extent subject to editorial control: s 41. Section 42 provides other interpretative provisions. Section 43 deals with the use of force in self-defence at a place of residence. Section 44, Sch 16 make provision about community orders, restorative justice, community requirements in suspended sentence orders, compensation orders and fines. Provision about deferred prosecution agreements is made by s 45, Sch 17. Under s 46, a restraint order must be made subject to an exception enabling relevant legal aid payments to be made. Section 47 allows the Secretary of State to make regulations about the making of relevant legal aid payments from property subject to a restraint order. Section 48, Sch 18 provide that the High Court in England and Wales and the Court of Session in Scotland have the power to make orders in respect of property, wherever that property is situated and in respect of a person wherever that person is domiciled, resident or present. Section 49 introduces Sch 19 which makes provisions about orders and warrants including provision for obtaining evidence overseas, in connection with civil recovery investigations. Section 50 gives effect to Sch 20 which amends the Extradition Act 2003 to provide a new forum bar to extradition.

Part 3 (ss 51–61) Miscellaneous and general
The 2013 Act s 51 amends the Nationality, Immigration and Asylum Act 2002 to reinstate race discrimination as a ground of appeal against an immigration decision. The 2013 Act s 52 amends the 2002 Act s 88A and the Immigration, Asylum and Nationality Act 2006 s 4, so as to remove full rights of appeal for persons refused a visa for a family visit to the United Kingdom. The 2013 Act s 53 adds the Nationality, Immigration and Asylum Act 2002 ss 92(2A), 97B, so as to provide for a certification power for the Secretary of State to remove the application of the in-country right of appeal provisions under certain circumstances. Under the 2013 Act s 54, the Secretary of State may remove an appellant's in-country right of appeal if the Secretary of State certifies that the removal of the appellant, prior to the appellant's appeal against a deportation order being exhausted, would not breach the United Kingdom's obligations under the European Convention on Human Rights. The 2013 Act s 55, Sch 21 make provision so as to extend the list of officers who can authorise applications to interfere lawfully with property and wireless telegraphy. Section 56, Sch 22 introduce an offence of driving, attempting to drive or being in charge of a motor vehicle with a specified controlled drug in the blood or urine in excess of the specified limit for that drug. Section 57 makes the use of insulting words and behaviour no

longer a criminal offence. Orders and regulations made by the Secretary of State or Lord Chancellor under the 2013 Act are to be made by statutory instrument: s 58, Sch 23. Section 59 sets out consequential amendments. Section 60 provides transitional, transitory or saving provision. Section 61 deals with short title, commencement and extent and Sch 24 provides that certain National Crime Agency provisions do not extend to Northern Ireland.

Amendments, repeals and revocations
The list below, which is not exhaustive, mentions repeals and amendments which are or will be effective when the Act is fully in force.
　　Specific provisions of a number of Acts are amended, added or repealed. These include: Magistrates' Courts Act 1980 ss 75A, 85, 139, 139A; Contempt of Court Act 1981 s 9; Senior Courts Act 1981 ss 31A, 44; Public Order Act 1986 ss 5, 6; Road Traffic Act 1988 ss 5A, 11, 195; Road Traffic Offenders Act 1988 Sch 2; Police Act 1997 s 93; Regulation of Investigatory Powers Act 2000 s 32; Police Act 2002 s 26C; Proceeds of Crime Act 2002 ss 41, 47A, 282A, 378, 459, Sch 7A; Nationality, Immigration and Asylum Act 2002 ss 84, 88A, 92, 97A, 97B, 99; Courts Act 2003 ss 36A, 111, Sch 5; Constitutional Reform Act 2005 ss 48, 51A–51E; Tribunals, Courts and Enforcement Act 2007 ss 12, 13, 20; Education and Skills Act 2008 s 56; Criminal Justice and Immigration Act 2008 s 76; Policing and Crime Act 2009 ss 43, 48, 49, Sch 12; Legal Aid, Sentencing and Punishment of Offenders Act 2012 s 102.

2053　Data-gathering powers—Her Majesty's Revenue and Customs—relevant data

The Data-gathering Powers (Relevant Data) (Amendment) Regulations 2013, SI 2013/1811 (in force on 1 September 2013), amend the 2012 Regulations, SI 2012/847, so as to (1) specify data relating to credit and debit card payments taken by retailers which merchant acquirers and similar bodies must provide to an officer of Her Majesty's Revenue and Customs on receipt of a data-holder notice under the Finance Act 2011 Sch 23; and (2) correct technical errors in provisions relating to interest payments made by deposit-holders.

2054　Duty of care—protection from physical injury—time taken to attend scene of incident

See *Sarjantson v Humberside Police Chief Constable*, para 2193.

2055　Elected local policing bodies—specified information

The Elected Local Policing Bodies (Specified Information) (Amendment) Order 2013, SI 2013/1816 (in force on 12 August 2013), further amends the 2011 Order, SI 2011/3050, so that (1) an elected local policing body must publish quarterly information about the allowances paid to relevant office holders (ie police and crime commissioners, the Mayor of London in his capacity as the holder of the Mayor's Office for Policing and Crime, and their deputies) in respect of expenses incurred in the exercise of the body's functions; and (2) where an elected local policing body pays, for its relevant office holders, for travel, accommodation or food and drink with a value of £500 or less, and does so by purchasing the services directly rather than reimbursing expenses incurred by the relevant office holders, information in relation to all such expenditure must be published quarterly.

2056　Independent Police Complaints Commission—forces maintained otherwise than by police authorities

The Independent Police Complaints Commission (Forces Maintained Otherwise than by Local Policing Bodies) Order 2013, SI 2013/1779 (in force on 16 August 2013), replaces the 2004 Orders, SI 2004/672, and provides that procedures which are similar to the Police Reform Act 2002 Pt 2 (ss 9–29), and to subordinate legislation made under Pt 2, are to be established and maintained in relation to the Ministry of Defence Police and the British Transport Police Force constables.

2057　Independent Police Complaints Commission—investigation—conduct of interviews

The Police (Complaints and Conduct) Regulations 2013, SI 2013/281 (in force on 7 March 2013), make provision in relation to the Independent Police Complaints Commission's power, under the Police Reform Act 2002 Sch 3 para 19F, to require serving officers to attend for interview in relation to investigations carried out or managed by the Commission. In particular, the regulations, which do not apply in relation to an interview of a person in connection with an investigation into that person's alleged misconduct, (1) require an investigator to give written notice to a serving officer of an interview; (2) make provision for the agreement and notification of the date, time and place of an interview; (3) require an investigator to provide a serving officer, in advance of an interview, with such information as the investigator considers to be appropriate to enable the officer to prepare for the interview; (4) require a serving officer to attend an interview; (5) enable a serving officer to be accompanied at an interview; and (6) prescribe the bodies of constables, whose officers and members of staff can also be required to attend an interview.

2058 Independent Police Complaints Commission—investigation—report—finding that officer had acted unlawfully—ambit of Commission's powers

A police officer stopped a motorist for allegedly driving in excess of the speed limit. An altercation erupted and the officer arrested the motorist for a public order offence. During the altercation, the officer used incapacitant spray, struck the motorist with his police baton and handcuffed him. The motorist's mother made a complaint to the claimant police force. The complaint was referred to the Independent Police Complaints Commission ('the Commission'), which issued a report upholding the complaint and concluding that there was a case to answer in respect of an alleged breach of the standards of professional behaviour. It also clearly set out that the Commission's view was that the arrest was unlawful and the officer had acted unlawfully. The claimant brought judicial review proceedings, seeking to quash the report on the basis that it had exceeded the lawful ambit, which was to find if there was a case to answer. *Held*, the purpose of a Commission report was to inform the police disciplinary body or Crown Prosecution Service whether a charge should be brought. It was for those bodies and not the Commission to exercise that judgment. An expression of opinion was necessarily called for which fell short of conclusive determination and was consistent with deciding whether there was sufficient evidence to place a police officer before a disciplinary panel for its decision. The language used in the report amounted to a suggestion of determination, rather than opinion. It had considered the lawfulness of the arrest and concluded that the officer had acted unlawfully and that the arrest had been unlawful. The Commission had been justified in recording factual matters adverse to the officer, but to go further using the language of determination, rather than recommendation, had been outside the lawful boundaries of its statutory responsibility. It followed that the report could not stand. Accordingly, the application for judicial review would be allowed.

R (on the application of the Chief Constable of the West Yorkshire Police) v Independent Police Complaints Commission [2013] EWHC 2698 (Admin), [2013] All ER (D) 137 (Sep) (Queen's Bench Division: Judge Jeremy Richardson QC). *R (on the application of Reynolds) v Independent Police Complaints Commission* [2008] EWCA Civ 1160, [2009] 3 All ER 237 (2008 Abr para 2342); and *R (on the application of Allatt) v Chief Constable of Nottinghamshire Police* [2011] EWHC 3908 (Admin) applied.

2059 Independent Police Complaints Commission—National Crime Agency— complaints and misconduct

The National Crime Agency (Complaints and Misconduct) Regulations 2013, SI 2013/2325 (in force on 7 October 2013), provide for the basis on which the Independent Police Complaints Commission has oversight of complaints and other matters relating to the conduct of a National Crime Agency officer ('NCA officer'), including the Director General of the National Crime Agency. The regulations (1) contain a definition of the appropriate authority, which performs a number of investigative functions under the framework established by the regulations; the appropriate authority is ordinarily the Permanent Secretary to the Home Office or the Director General of the National Crime Agency; their respective role is determined by the nature of the complaint or other matter which is being investigated; (2) contain provision which sets out the broad basis on which the Commission has oversight of complaints and misconduct relating to the NCA, and in particular, (a) make provision to apply specific sections of the Police Reform Act 2002 Pt 2 (ss 9–29) with modifications; (b) set out the general functions of the Commission and the reporting requirements which apply to it; (c) define the matters which may be the subject of an investigation under the regulations (a complaint, conduct matter or death or serious injury matter); (d) set out the general duties of the appropriate authority, payment for assistance (for example in a case where the police assists with an investigation), the provision of information by the NCA to the Commission and requirements in relation to onward disclosure of such information and the inspection of NCA premises by the Commission; and (e) make provision for keeping complainants and other interested persons informed about investigations, and include provision about the manner in which these requirements are fulfilled and exceptions to them; (3) contain provision about the handling of complaints, and in particular, impose duties to preserve evidence, handling and recording of complaints, the cases in which complaints are referred to the Commission and the handling of complaints by the appropriate authority; there are prescribed appeal rights in certain cases; (4) contain provision about the handling of conduct matters, and in particular, impose duties in relation to the identification and recording of conduct matters, preservation of evidence and the cases in which conduct matters are referred to the Commission; (5) contain provision about the handling of death or serious injury matters, and in particular, impose duties to record death or serious injury matters and preserve evidence and the reference of death or serious injury matters to the Commission and its corresponding duties on a referral to it; (6) contain provision governing the basis on which the Commission determines the form of an investigation in a matter referred to it, ranging from investigations carried out by the appropriate authority on its own behalf or supervised or managed by the Commission to investigations carried out by the Commission itself; there is also provision governing the appointment of investigators and the processes which apply in specific cases (for example withdrawn complaints or the resumption of an investigation following the conclusion of relevant criminal proceedings); they also contain provision governing a special procedure which applies in a case in which a conduct matter is revealed during the course of the investigation of a complaint, the Commission's powers to interview witnesses, restrictions on certain proceedings during an investigation and an accelerated procedure in cases where gross misconduct is identified during an investigation into a complaint or conduct matter; there is also provision governing the discontinuance of an investigation and the procedure in cases where a conduct matter is revealed during an investigation into a death or serious injury matter; (7) set out the basis governing the submission of investigation reports, the actions which the Commission or the appropriate authority are required to take, the prescribed appeal rights in relation to an investigation and the availability of a review or reinvestigation following an appeal; the duties on the appropriate authority with respect to disciplinary proceedings (for example following recommendations made by the Commission) and the information which is required to be provided to complainants about such proceedings are set out; and (8) contain provision about a number of general matters including appeal processes and which person may hear an appeal.

2060   Interception of communications—communication in course of transmission—voicemail—message saved by recipient on voicemail facility

The Regulation of Investigatory Powers Act 2000 s 1(1) provides that it is an offence for a person intentionally and without lawful authority to intercept any communication in the course of its transmission by means of a public telecommunication system. The times while a communication is being transmitted by means of a telecommunication system must be taken to include any time when the system by means of which the communication is being, or has been, transmitted is used for storing it in a manner that enables the intended recipient to collect it or otherwise to have access to it: s 2(7).

Allegations were made that the appellants, who worked as editors or journalists for a newspaper, had intercepted mobile telephone voicemail messages. They were charged with conspiring to intercept communications in the course of their transmission without lawful authority, contrary to the 2000 Act s 1(1). The appellants sought to have the charges dismissed at a preparatory hearing. It was held that s 2(7) extended the concept of transmission to include the period when the transmission system stored the communication in a manner that enabled the intended recipient to collect it or otherwise have access to it, irrespective of whether the intended recipient had previously accessed it. On appeal, *held*, s 2(7) was clearly intended to extend the scope of the course of transmission. There was no justification for limiting the extension to periods of transient storage prior to receipt by the intended recipient. The statutory wording made it entirely clear that the course of transmission might continue notwithstanding that the voicemail message had already been received and read by the intended recipient. Accordingly, the appeal would be dismissed.

R v Coulson [2013] EWCA Crim 1026, [2013] 4 All ER 999 (Court of Appeal: Lord Judge CJ, Lloyd Jones LJ and Openshaw J). *R v Effik* [1995] 1 AC 309, [1994] 3 All ER 458, HL (1994 Abr para 803), considered.

2061 Interception of communications—covert surveillance—authorisation—likely acquisition of matters subject to legal professional privilege

See *R v Turner*, para 715.

2062 Interception of communications—surveillance camera systems—Code of Practice

The Protection of Freedoms Act 2012 (Code of Practice for Surveillance Camera Systems and Specification of Relevant Authorities) Order 2013, SI 2013/1961 (in force on 12 August 2013), (1) brings into force a Code of Practice for surveillance camera systems, which the Secretary of State is required to prepare, pursuant to the Protection of Freedoms Act 2012 s 29(1); and (2) specifies the relevant authorities which are under a statutory duty to have regard to the Code.

2063 National Crime Agency Remuneration Review Body

The National Crime Agency (Remuneration Review Body) Regulations 2013, SI 2013/1958 (in force on 29 August 2013), (1) establish the National Crime Agency Remuneration Review Body, make provision for its constitution and governance, and require it to produce a report in relation to any matter referred to it; and (2) provide that, before determining rates of pay and allowances for officers, of a lower grade than deputy director, who have been designated with one or more powers under the Crime and Courts Act 2013 s 10(1) (power of Director General of the National Crime Agency to designate any other NCA officer as a person having one or more of the powers and privileges of a constable, the powers of an officer of Revenue and Customs or an immigration officer), the Secretary of State must refer the matter to the National Crime Agency Remuneration Review Body and consider its report.

2064 National Policing Improvement Agency—abolition—consequential provisions

See para 740.

2065 Police and Justice Act 2006—commencement

The Police and Justice Act 2006 (Commencement No 16) Order 2013, SI 2013/592, brings into force on 8 April 2013, so far as it is not already in force, s 17(1), (2) (in part), (3), (4). For a summary of the Act, see 2006 Abr para 2245. See also the commencement table in the title STATUTES AND LEGISLATIVE PROCESS.

2066 Police authority—powers—application for breach of court order—forced marriage protection order

See *Bedfordshire Police Constabulary v RU*, para 519.

2067 Police authority—riot damage—compensation—liability

The Riot (Damages) Act 1886 s 2(1) provides that, where a house, shop, or building in a police area has been injured or destroyed, or the property therein has been injured, stolen, or destroyed, by any persons riotously and tumultuously assembled together, compensation is to be paid out of the police fund of the area to any person who has sustained loss by such injury.

During a night of widespread rioting in a city, a warehouse containing goods belonging to an electronics company was looted and set alight by a gang of approximately 25 youths. The warehouse and its contents were destroyed. The first and second claimants, who were the company's insurers, sought compensation under the 1886 Act from the defendant, the statutory body responsible for the oversight of the relevant local police authority. The third claimant, who was the owner of certain stock held in the warehouse, also sought compensation from the defendant for uninsured losses. Preliminary issues arose as to whether (1) the losses claimed by the claimants arose out of the injury to, or the destruction of, a house, shop or building, or injury to, theft or the destruction of any property therein, by any persons riotously and tumultuously assembled together, within the meaning of s 2(1);

and (2) consequential losses, including loss of profit and loss of rent, were in principle recoverable pursuant to s 2(1) and (2), and if so, on what basis. *Held*, on the evidence, the offenders had been 'persons riotously and tumultuously assembled together' within the meaning of s 2(1). A person of reasonable fortitude would have feared for his personal safety. The raid on the warehouse had clearly been organised before, although not in a systematic way. Further, there had undoubtedly been a perceived or palpable threat of rioting in the vicinity of the warehouse. The behaviour of the group from the time that they had been gathering had been such that the police ought to have been aware of their presence and could have prevented the incident which had eventually occurred. Further, the use of petrol bombs evidenced wanton violence towards the property damaged or destroyed. Such violence was a hallmark of riotous and tumultuous behaviour and was a paradigm example of the situation where victims of the damage and destruction would qualify for compensation under the 1886 Act. With regard to the second issue, on the correct construction of the 1886 Act as a whole, the compensation payable was limited to physical damage to the relevant premises or property in it and did not extend to consequential losses such as loss of profit or loss of rent. The compensation was analogous to insurance generally and other such compensation schemes, and, being so, there was nothing surprising or alarming in the compensation provided excluding consequential losses. There was no basis for suggesting that the approach of the court ought somehow to be different from that of the compensation authority. It followed that consequential losses were not in principle recoverable pursuant to s 2(1), at least as a freestanding head of claim. Judgment would be given accordingly.

Mitsui Sumitomo Insurance Co (Europe) Ltd v The Mayor's Office for Policing and Crime; Royal and Sun Alliance plc v Mayor's Office for Policing and Crime; Lace International Ltd v Mayor's Office for Policing and Crime [2013] EWHC 2734 (Comm), [2014] 1 All ER 422 (Queen's Bench Division: Flaux J).

2068   Police authority—special police services—entitlement to payment—football stadium—area outside stadium

Under the Police Act 1996 s 25(1), the chief officer of police of a police force may provide, at the request of any person, special police services at any premises or in any locality in the police area for which the force is maintained, subject to the payment to the local policing body of charges.

The claimant football club requested the defendant police force to provide, both before and after football matches, police services within the club's stadium and in areas immediately outside the stadium that were owned or controlled by the club. It fell to be determined whether services provided in the area outside the immediate environs of the stadium on land neither owned nor controlled by the club (this area was described as the 'extended footprint' of the club) were special services for which the defendant could charge the claimant. *Held*, the provision of policing services at football matches on private land at the request of a football club would usually be special police services except where the police were summoned to deal with actual or imminent violence. Of the four factors suggested in *Harris v Sheffield United Football Club Ltd*, the question of whether services were provided on public or private land was plainly of central importance to whether they were special police services where those services were provided in order to promote the maintenance of law and order. The fact that there was actual or imminent violence at private premises might well indicate that the provision of police services at those premises for law and order purposes was in performance of the general police duty and not special police services. However, attendance at private premises just in case there was an outbreak of violence was likely to be special police services. On the other hand, policing provided in a public place in order to protect persons and property, even where there was no actual or imminent threat of violence, would usually be in discharge by the police of their ordinary public duty. Professional football matches attended by thousands of members of the public were essentially public events. The question whether the provision of services placed a particular strain on resources was unlikely to shed much light on whether those services were special. The focus on who benefited from the police service might be a relevant part of the analysis of whether the service provided fell within the scope of a police officer's ordinary duties. If the police operation was conducted predominantly for the protection of the public at large, that was a factor which pointed strongly against the services being special but the benefit test ought not be regarded as determinative or even necessarily of great weight in all cases. To consider ex post facto whether the services provided by the police benefited the general public or particular groups or individuals was too narrow an approach since it overlooked the fact that there was a real public interest in the police maintaining law and order. The policing of the extended footprint on match days was provided in order to maintain law and order and protect life and property in a public place. The law and order services provided by the defendant in the extended footprint were not different in principle from the law and order services which they provided in any other public place.

Leeds United Football Club v Chief Constable of West Yorkshire Police [2013] EWCA Civ 115, [2014] QB 168, [2013] 2 All ER 760 (Court of Appeal: Lord Dyson MR, Moore-Bick and McCombe LJJ). *Glasbrook Bros Ltd v Glamorgan CC* [1925] AC 270, HL; and *Harris v Sheffield United Football Club Ltd* [1987] 2 All ER 838, CA (1987 Abr para 1960), applied. *West Yorkshire Police Authority v Reading Festival Ltd* [2006] EWCA Civ 524, [2006] 1 WLR 2005, [2006] All ER (D) 40 (May) (2006 Abr para 2248); and *Chief Constable of Greater Manchester Police v Wigan Athletic AFC Ltd* [2007] EWHC 3095 (Ch), [2007] All ER (D) 394 (Dec) considered. Decision of Eady J [2012] EWHC 2113 (QB), [2012] All ER (D) 261 (Jul) (2012 Abr para 2090) affirmed.

2069   Police Federation—central committees—members—election

The Police Federation (Amendment) Regulations 2013, SI 2013/3189 (in force on 31 January 2014), further amend the 1969 Regulations, SI 1969/1787, so as to ensure that members of the central committees of the Federation are elected from among the members of the relevant branch boards, regardless of whether any particular branch board member is a delegate to the central conference in question.

2070   Police officer—chief constable—suspension—lawfulness

The claimant was the temporary chief constable for his area. The defendant was the police and crime commissioner for the relevant county and therefore the appropriate authority for complaints and conduct matters related to the office of chief constable under the Police Reform Act 2012 and the Police (Complaints and Misconduct) Regulations 2012, SI 2012/1204. The claimant had acted as 'police friend' at a colleague's employment tribunal proceedings to speak on behalf of his colleague and provide support at the hearing. Going beyond that role, the claimant approached a member of the constabulary to arrange a without prejudice meeting between his colleague and the officers involved. The solicitor in attendance prepared a note of that meeting, raising concerns about the actions that the claimant had taken in discussing a possible racial discrimination claim and suggested that he had overstepped his role in those proceedings. The note was copied to the defendant and formed the basis for the claimant's suspension by the defendant. The claimant applied for a review of the defendant's decision to suspend him on the grounds that it unlawful and/or irrational, and that it denied him due process. The defendant argued that the case turned on rationality, and that the decision to suspend the claimant had been rational and in the public interest. *Held*, reg 10(4) provided that there should be no suspension unless the public interest required that the officer be suspended. The court had to bear in mind that the defendant had been appointed by statute to be the primary decision-maker on questions of public interest in the manner required by reg 10(4), and the court ought not to interfere unless it was satisfied that the defendant's decision was irrational or perverse. The assessment of the defendant's decision had to be made by reference to the material he had available to him and which he should have examined. For that reason it was remarkable that there was no mention of the claimant's character or reputation anywhere in the decision documents or the suspension letter. His unblemished service should have been taken into account when considering the likelihood that he had engaged in a dishonest enterprise and, because it was a factor that tended to suggest that the claimant was unlikely to have done so, it should also have been taken into account when considering suspension. The defendant had treated his preferred interpretation of what the attendance letter said as the only possible interpretation of events. Moreover, the defendant failed to undertake any consideration of the likelihood or lack of likelihood that his interpretation of the attendance letter would be proved correct, and that the claimant would be found to have acted in a fundamentally dishonest manner. For that reason, even if the defendant addressed the public interest criterion correctly, he based it on an inadequate and unjustifiable assessment of the state of the case as it stood before him. Accordingly, the application would be allowed.

R (*on the application of Rhodes*) *v Lincolnshire Police and Crime Comr* [2013] EWHC 1009 (Admin), [2013] All ER (D) 232 (May) (Queen's Bench Division: Stuart-Smith J).

2071   Police officer—code of conduct—complaints

The Police (Complaints and Misconduct) (Old Cases) Regulations 2013, SI 2013/1778 (in force on 9 August 2013), modify the application of the Police Reform Act 2002 Pt 2 (ss 9–29) and any provision made under it to a matter in relation to which the Independent Police Complaints Commission has made a declaration under s 28A(1) or (4). In particular, the regulations amend the 2012 Regulations, SI 2012/1204, so as to (1) require the appropriate authority to refer a complaint to the Commission if that complaint is the subject of a direction; (2) provide that the appropriate authority must refer a conduct matter to the Commission if that matter is the subject of a direction; and (3) prescribe that the 2012 Regulations will apply as if they contained a further provision which (a) requires that a complaint, conduct matter or death or serious injury matter is treated as, and recorded as, a new matter regardless of whether it had come to the attention of the appropriate authority before, on or after 22 November 2012; (b) provides that exceptions in the 2002 Act from the duty to notify or record a complaint do not apply to a complaint which is the subject of a direction; and (c) makes provision which modifies the 2002 Act to the effect that a person who has previously been the subject of a disciplinary procedure in relation to certain conduct cannot, as a result of the Commission given a direction, become subject to a further disciplinary procedure in relation to the same conduct.

2072   Police officer—dismissal—special constable—failure to follow statutory procedure—judicial review—claim brought out of time

The claimant was dismissed from his position as a special constable with the defendant police force. In the course of his dismissal, he was not dealt with under the misconduct procedures set out in the Police (Conduct) Regulations 2008, SI 2008/2864. The following month, he attended a meeting with one of the defendant's officers at which he was informed that he would not be reinstated. Four months after that meeting, the claimant's solicitors wrote to the defendant asking for an explanation of the full grounds for the claimant's dismissal. Six months later, the claimant issued judicial review proceedings seeking an order quashing the defendant's decision to dismiss him. It was common ground that the claim was brought out of time. It fell to be determined whether the claimant should be permitted to bring the claim out of time, whether the 2008 Regulations applied in his case, and whether it was appropriate to make an order quashing the defendant's decision. *Held*, Parliament could not have intended that, in a case of misconduct which led to a dismissal, a police force could choose to bypass the 2008 Regulations, which had been specifically issued to lay down appropriate procedures and safeguards for police officers, including special constables, in cases of misconduct. It was plain from the terms of the letter dismissing the claimant that a decision had been taken to dispense with his services. He had not retired, he had been dismissed. It was clear that the 2008 Regulations applied and that the claimant's dismissal had not been in accordance with the procedures laid down therein. It followed that the dismissal had been unlawful and there was no defence to the claim. Further, there was a good reason why, notwithstanding the delay, the claim should have been allowed to proceed. There was no remedy other than an order quashing the defendant's decision that could provide the claimant with the opportunity to clear his name. Accordingly, the application would be allowed.

R (*on the application of Monger*) *v Chief Constable of Cumbria Police* [2013] EWHC 455 (Admin), [2013] All ER (D) 16 (Apr) (Queen's Bench Division: Supperstone J).

SI 2008/2864 replaced by Police (Conduct) Regulations 2012, SI 2012/2632.

2073   Police officer—forcible restraint—lawfulness—autistic and epileptic young adult

See *ZH v Metropolitan Police Comr*, para 1872.

2074   Police officer—misconduct in public office—conviction

See *R v Dizaei*, para 704.

2075   Police officer—powers—fingerprints and DNA samples—requirement to provide non-intimate sample

The claimant had been convicted of unlawful act manslaughter and, later, he had been convicted of kidnapping. Those convictions rendered him liable to have taken from him, without his consent, a non-intimate sample pursuant to the Police and Criminal Evidence Act 1984 s 63(3B)(a), (3BA)(a). Later, the claimant was visited at his home by a police officer and handed a letter, informing him that he was requested to consent to the taking of a non-intimate sample or he would be required to attend a police station. He did not consent. Soon after, the claimant's solicitors wrote a pre-action protocol letter challenging the decision. The claimant was then notified that his appointment at the police station had been made. In turn, the claimant filed his claim form for judicial review together with his witness statement, seeking an order quashing the decision, a declaration that the decision was unlawful and damages. A detective inspector gave his authorisation for the taking of the sample as necessary to assist in the prevention or detection of crime and made a requirement that the claimant should attend a police station for the purpose of taking a non-intimate sample a few weeks later. In the judicial review proceedings, the claimant contended that, by the original decision, the defendant chief constable had unlawfully required him to attend a police station for the purpose that a non-intimate sample could be taken without his consent on the grounds that a fair balance had to be struck between his right to respect for his private life under the European Convention on Human Rights art 8 and the public interest in the legitimate aim of the prevention of disorder or crime. It was also contended that the original decision had failed to comply with the statutory pre-condition that authorisation should be given by a police officer of the rank of inspector before the requirement was made and before the requirement was made to provide a non-intimate sample, the defendant was bound, in order to ensure fairness and/or to render the demand proportionate, to provide him with the opportunity to make representations, which the defendant had failed to do. *Held*, the demand in the defendant's letter had been unlawful because it had been made without prior authorisation by a police officer of the rank of inspector or above, contrary to the 1984 Act Sch 2A para 11(2). The requirement to provide a non-intimate sample for the purpose of producing a DNA profile for comparison with crime scene profiles had constituted an interference with the claimant's right under the Convention art 8(1). However, the absence of specific grounds for suspicion had not rendered the requirement disproportionate. The detective inspector had been correct to conclude that his requirement of the claimant to provide a sample had been proportionate. He had been fully justified in concluding that the public interest in the detection of crime had outweighed the limited interference with the claimant's private life. By the time the detective inspector had made the later decision, the claimant had submitted his witness statement in support of his claim that the interference with his private life by means of a requirement to provide a sample had been unlawful. The claimant's evidence had been considered by the detective inspector before he had made his decision. The resolution of the dispute depended on the assessment of facts which had been largely undisputed and which the claimant had had a full opportunity to address. It had not been demonstrated that the claimant's rights under art 8 had not been properly protected. Accordingly, the application would be dismissed.

R (on the application of R) v A Chief Constable [2013] EWHC 2864 (Admin), [2014] 1 Cr App Rep 222, [2013] All ER (D) 207 (Sep) (Queen's Bench Division: Pitchford LJ and Hickinbottom J).

2076   Police officer—powers—search and seizure—lawfulness—lack of warrant

Five police officers arrested the claimant, searched his home and took him to a police station, where he was further detained by a custody officer. The police did not inform the claimant that they lacked a search warrant. The claimant sought damages from the defendant for unlawful arrest, the unlawful search of his home and his further detention at the police station. He contended that the search of his home was unlawful as he had not been perceived to be dangerous within the meaning of the Police and Criminal Evidence Act 1984 s 32(2)(b). The defendant chief constable contended that a search warrant had not been required because the claimant had been lawfully arrested for an indictable offence away from a police station. *Held*, the search of the claimant's home, purportedly carried out under s 32(2)(b), could not be characterised as unlawful merely because the claimant had not been perceived to be dangerous. Moreover, the requirement of 'necessity', as laid down by Parliament in s 24(4), had not, on any realistic interpretation of the word, been met. In the circumstances, there had been no rational basis for rejecting alternative procedures. There had simply been no solid grounds to suppose that the claimant would suddenly start to hide or destroy evidence, or that he would make inappropriate contacts. There had been only the theoretical possibility that he might do so. There had been no justification for bypassing all the usual statutory safeguards involved in obtaining a warrant. As the original arrest had been unlawful, the subsequent detention could not be regarded in itself as lawful simply because the custody officer had not had the same information laid before him. The custody officer's reasons for detention could not cure any defect in the original arrest. The claimant would be entitled to an award of compensation, in accordance with the conventional scale, to cover the arrest, search and period of detention. Accordingly, the claim would be allowed.

Lord Hanningfield v Chief Constable of Essex Police [2013] EWHC 243 (QB), [2013] 1 WLR 3632, [2013] All ER (D) 185 (Feb) (Queen's Bench Division: Eady J).

2077   Police officer—promotion

The Police (Promotion) (Amendment) Regulations 2013, SI 2013/1780 (in force on 19 August 2013), further amend the 1996 Regulations, SI 1996/1685, so as to allow a police constable who is on temporary promotion to the rank of sergeant while undertaking a work-based assessment for substantive promotion to that rank, and who is taking part in the High Potential Development Scheme, to undertake the initial written examination for promotion to the rank of inspector.

2078   Police officer—recommendations—qualification

The Police (Amendment) Regulations 2013, SI 2013/2793 (in force on 25 November 2013), further amend the 2003 Regulations, SI 2003/527, so as to implement certain recommendations of the Independent Review of Police Officer and Staff Remuneration and Conditions. In particular, the regulations (1) from April 2013, provide that an additional qualification should be added to the list required for appointment to a police force; (2) enable police officers to be seconded to organisations outside policing for a period not exceeding five years; (3) provide for the return to the police service of former non-probationary officers at the rank they last held; and (4) provide that returning officers should be subject to a probationary period of six months.

2079   Police pensions

The Police Pensions (Amendment) Regulations 2013, SI 2013/487 (in force on 1 April 2013), further amend the Police Pension Regulations 1987, SI 1987/257, and the Police Pensions Regulations 2006, SI 2006/3415, in order to increase the rates of contribution payable by members of the specified police pension schemes. In addition, the regulations further amend the Police Pension Regulations 1987, SI 1987/3057, so as to correct an error relating to early payment of a police pension.

2080   Police pensions—liabilities—accounting practices

The Police Reform and Social Responsibility Act 2011 (Transitional Provision) Order 2013, SI 2013/2319 (in force on 31 March 2014), modifies the Police Reform and Social Responsibility Act 2011, with the effect that chief constables and the Commissioner of Police of the Metropolis are treated as though they were subject to specified local government enactments concerning accounting practices, particularly the charging of expenditure to a revenue account. The purpose of the modifications, which cease to have effect on the coming into force of amendments to the 2011 Act which have the same effect, is to ensure that staff pension liabilities are treated in accordance with accepted practices in the accounts of chief constables and the Commissioner.

2081   Regulation of investigatory powers—covert human intelligence sources—relevant sources

The Regulation of Investigatory Powers (Covert Human Intelligence Sources: Relevant Sources) Order 2013, SI 2013/2788 (in force on 1 January 2014), introduces a notification and prior approval regime in relation to certain categories of Covert Human Intelligence

Sources, as well as an enhanced authorisation regime. In particular, the order (1) defines a 'relevant source'; (2) modifies the Regulation of Investigatory Powers Act 2000 s 43(3) in relation to a 'long term authorisation' and defines what it is and how it is calculated; (3) provides that only once a relevant source has been authorised for a period of 12 months in total in relation to the same investigation or operation does any subsequent authorisation become a long term authorisation; (4) disregards from the calculation of a long term authorisation periods in respect of which authorisations were granted orally or by a person whose authority to act is confined to urgent cases and periods more than three years prior to the intended date of authorisation; (5) modifies the definition of 'a long term authorisation' by reducing the period of 12 months to 3 months in respect of authorisations involving access to legally privileged material, so as to provide consistency with the authorisation periods in the Regulation of Investigatory Powers (Covert Human Intelligence Sources: Matters Subject to Legal Privilege) Order 2010, SI 2010/123; (6) contains provisions requiring notification of authorisations to and prior approval of certain authorisations from an ordinary surveillance commissioner; (7) requires notice to be given (although not necessarily in advance) of the grant of an authorisation for a relevant source, save where the authorisation is for the grant or renewal of a long term authorisation, and sets out the particulars to be provided; (8) provides that prior approval must be sought from an ordinary surveillance commissioner in respect of the grant or renewal of a long term authorisation and sets out the criteria to be applied, both in respect of any request for approval and the commissioner's decision; (9) creates an appeal mechanism where a request for prior approval is refused; and (10) creates an enhanced authorisation regime both in relation to the conduct or use of relevant sources and the long term authorisation of the same. The order also amends the 2010 Order so as to prescribe the offices, positions and ranks of those within the Home Office who can authorise activity for the purposes of the 2000 Act ss 28, 29 following the abolition of the UK Border Agency.

2082   Regulation of investigatory powers—covert human intelligence sources—undercover police officer—sexual relationships

In the first of two claims, a police officer had infiltrated a group of political activists, and had embarked on a sexual relationship with two members of the group. In the second claim, a different police officer had had sexual relationships with three members of a group of environmental activists. In each case, the officer had used the relationships to gather intelligence and/or for personal gratification. It was accepted that the claimants would not have slept with the officers had they known their true identity. The claimants brought proceedings against the defendant police commissioner, submitting that the activities of the officers contravened their rights under the European Convention on Human Rights arts 3 and 8, and involved the commission of the torts of deceit, misfeasance in public office, assault and negligence. They also argued that the covert establishment or maintenance by a police officer of an intimate relationship with another person for the purpose of obtaining information or access to information was incapable of being authorised under the Regulation of Investigatory Powers Act 2000 Pt II (ss 26–48). The claimants further contended that the Investigatory Powers Tribunal had no jurisdiction to determine the tort claims. The judge held that the alleged conduct was conduct to which Pt II applied so that the tribunal had jurisdiction to decide the human rights claims. In the interests of justice, the judge also stayed the tort claims pending the determination of the human rights claims by the tribunal. On the claimants' appeal, it fell to be determined (1) whether the establishing or maintaining of a personal or other relationship by a covert human intelligence source within the meaning of s 26(8)(a) was conduct to which Pt II applied; and (2) whether the judge had erred in staying the proceedings concerning the tort claims. *Held*, the phrase 'personal or other relationship' in s 26(8)(a) formed part of the definition of the type of conduct which could be authorised under s 27 and which, if it was carried out in challengeable circumstances, might be the subject of human rights proceedings before the tribunal under s 65. In its plain and ordinary meaning it included intimate sexual relationships. If the expression 'personal relationship' could not be understood as encompassing an intimate sexual relationship then the tribunal would be the sole forum for dealing with claims for breaches of Convention rights that arose from non-sexual relationships established or maintained by covert human intelligence sources, but it would not have jurisdiction to deal with claims for breaches of Convention rights that arose from sexual relationships. That was absurd and the courts should be slow to impute such absurdity to Parliament. Parliament had clearly intended that human rights proceedings about the establishing or maintaining of relationships by undercover police officers should be determined only by the tribunal. It followed that the tribunal had jurisdiction to determine the human rights claims made by the claimants. With regard to the stay, the judge's decision had been flawed and plainly wrong. The legislation gave no priority to the tribunal proceedings. The issues raised by the claims were acknowledged to be novel and difficult. They seemed likely to give rise to numerous issues of fact on both liability and damages. Those were matters which the ordinary litigation process was apt to resolve and which could be fairly resolved by the High Court, at least on the evidence that had been before the judge. It was difficult to see how a decision of the tribunal would assist in resolving procedural issues that arose in the court proceedings. Accordingly, the appeal would be allowed in part.

AJA v Metropolitan Police Comr; AKJ v Metropolitan Police Comr [2013] EWCA Civ 1342, [2014] 1 WLR 285, [2013] All ER (D) 46 (Nov) (Court of Appeal: Lord Dyson MR, Maurice Kay VP and Sharp LJ).

2083   Regulation of investigatory powers—intrusive surveillance—covert recordings in police vehicle

See *R v Plunkett*, para 698.

2084   Search and seizure—search warrant—validity—execution

The violent aftermath of earlier student and trade union demonstrations formed part of the background to the policing of the royal wedding. There was concern, but no direct evidence, that anarchist groups would attempt to cause disruption on the day of the wedding with acts of criminality and serious disorder. During the previous disorders, squats had been used as convergence centres and there was concern that individuals might be gathering at those squats to disrupt the wedding. A covert surveillance operation did not reveal evidence of the suspects but did reveal a pattern of behaviour indicating that the squats were being used as an exchange or dealing points for stolen goods. The defendant was granted four search warrants authorising it to enter the premises to search for listed categories of stolen property and the decision was taken to execute the warrants based on the suspected criminal activity at the squats and the fact that the premises were being used by people likely to be planning or involved in criminal activity on the day of the wedding. When the warrant was executed, a large number of people were seen to run to another nearby premises, of which the police had previously been unaware. An emergency search warrant was obtained, the premises raided and some equipment believed to be stolen was seized along with several toothbrushes. A large number of anti-monarchy flyers promoting disruption to the wedding were also found and samples seized. The claimants were arrested on suspicion of conspiracy to cause a public nuisance but the Crown Prosecution Service decided that there was insufficient evidence for a prosecution. The claimants issued judicial review proceedings contending that the execution of the search warrants had been unlawful. The court dismissed the appeal and the claimants appealed, submitting that the circumstances of the case led inexorably to the conclusion that the dominant purpose behind the execution of the warrants had been to effect preventative action in relation to the apprehended disruption of the wedding and not to advance a criminal investigation into the theft or handling of property. *Held,* while there had been a relationship between the suspects, the preventative action in relation to the wedding, the criminality observed or reasonably suspected during surveillance, the obtaining of the search warrants and the execution of the warrants, that relationship did not compel a conclusion that the preventative action had been the dominant motive at all stages. The lawfully obtained search warrants had been executed for the purpose for which they had been obtained, namely the recovery of stolen goods which, as a result of the surveillance, the officers had every reason to believe were in the premises. That the searches had been carried out in accordance with the authorisations was incontrovertible. The timing of the execution of the warrants had been the result of an operational decision which had been conditioned by a desire to maximise security gains but which had not meant that the dominant purpose of the search itself had been anything other than that which had been authorised by the lawfully obtained warrants. Accordingly, the appeals would be dismissed.

R (on the application of Pearce) v Metropolitan Police Comr [2013] EWCA Civ 866, [2013] All ER (D) 226 (Jul) (Court of Appeal: Maurice Kay VP, Patten and Fulford LJJ).

The first claimant was a practising solicitor and a partner in the second claimant solicitors' firm. The third claimant was another firm of solicitors. Two search warrants were issued against all three claimants in respect of the first claimant's home and the professional premises of the second and third claimants at the request of the first defendant Chief Constable of the British Transport Police. The claimants sought to quash the warrants having regard to the Police and Criminal Evidence Act 1984 s 15, which provided that the issue of a search warrant and an entry or search of premises under a warrant was unlawful unless it complied with ss 15, 16. It was conceded that the first warrant had been wrongly issued. The second warrant issued was challenged on the basis that it was sought for wider purposes than disclosed on its face. In relation to the warrant issued in respect of the third claimant, the grounds of challenge were that the application should have been for a production order and not a warrant since Sch 1 para 14(d) was not satisfied, the execution of the warrant was unnecessary and the second defendant Crown Court was misled. Further there was a judicial failure to give reasons when granting the warrants. *Held*, an applicant for a warrant had to give full and frank disclosure. Schedule 1 para 4 required the person against whom the order was sought to produce to a constable, for the constable to take away, or give the constable access to, the particular material to which the application made related, in both cases no later than seven days from the date of the order, or at the other end of such longer period as specified in the order. In relation to the warrant issued in respect of the second claimant, it was clear that the purpose of the warrant was to go far beyond what had been expressly stated on it and, in fact, it had been seeking many more documents. Given the terms of s 15(1), the warrant was unlawful and had to be quashed. In relation to the warrant issued in respect of the third claimant, it was clear from the facts that Sch 1 para 14(d) had not been satisfied. Further at the time that the warrant for the search of the third claimant's premises was executed, the officers of the first defendant had not known whether the file they had seized contained the material 'for which this warrant applies' or whether the search at the second claimant's premises had not located it. So neither of the conditions for the execution of the warrant against the third claimant had been fulfilled at the time it had in fact been executed. Each of the three warrants had to be quashed and accordingly, the applications would be granted.

R (on the application of S) v Chief Constable of the British Transport Police [2013] EWHC 2189 (Admin), [2014] 1 All ER 268 (Queen's Bench Division: Aikens LJ and Silber J).

2085 Terrorism—counter-terrorism powers—power to stop, search and detain— compliance with human rights

The appellant, a French national resident in the United Kingdom, was subjected to an examination by the police under the Terrorism Act 2000 Sch 7 following a visit to her husband, who was being held in custody in France in relation to terrorist offences. It was made clear to her that she was not under arrest or suspected of being a terrorist. She refused to answer a number of questions in the course of the examination. At the conclusion of the examination, she was cautioned and reported for the offence of failing to comply with her duties under Sch 7 by refusing to answer the questions put to her. She was charged with wilfully failing to comply with a duty under Sch 7. She pleaded guilty following a ruling by the judge that he had no power to stay the proceedings as an abuse of process. On her appeal, it fell to be determined whether the powers under Sch 7 were compliant with the European Convention on Human Rights arts 6 and 8. *Held*, the powers under the 2000 Act Sch 7 were the United Kingdom's first line of defence against the entry of terrorists and there was a continuing need for such powers. Those powers were an aspect of port and border control rather than of a criminal investigation. Their underlying purpose was to protect the public from terrorism, having regard to its international character. The exercise of the powers was subject to a number of statutory limitations. The absence of reasonable suspicion was explicable and justifiable. The powers could only be exercised for the purpose of determining whether a traveller at a port, airport or border area appeared to be or had been concerned with the acts of terrorism and there was an objective justification for the focus on those places. In the circumstances, such interference as there had been with the appellant's rights under the Convention art 8 occasioned by exercise of the powers under the

2000 Act Sch 7 were justified. The questions asked had been rationally connected to the statutory purpose of the powers and in no way disproportionate. Further, although not expressed, there was an implied privilege against self-incrimination under the Convention art 6. Where a person's Convention rights were potentially engaged the correct temporal starting point for considering whether those rights had been breached was the moment as from which he was charged. If art 6 was engaged, while the gravity of the security context could not, by itself, justify extinguishing the very essence of the privilege against self-incrimination, it was plain that not every statutory interference with the privilege would violate an individual's rights under art 6. In the circumstances, the examination of the appellant under the 2000 Act Sch 7 had not been an inquiry preparatory to criminal proceedings. It had been an inquiry relating to border control with the specific public interest of safeguarding society from the risk of terrorism. Therefore, the appellant's rights under the Convention art 6 had not been engaged by the examination. Accordingly, the appeal would be dismissed.

Beghal v DPP [2013] EWHC 2573 (Admin), [2013] All ER (D) 214 (Aug) (Queen's Bench Division: Gross, Swift and Foskett LJJ).

2086   Terrorism—prevention—power to detain terrorist suspect—examination of material retained from suspect

The claimant was the partner of a journalist who wrote stories for newspapers relating to mass surveillance programmes by the United States and United Kingdom governments. The claimant regularly assisted his partner in his journalistic work and was doing so when he was stopped by police in the international transit area of a United Kingdom airport in exercise of powers under the Terrorism Act 2000 Sch 7. The claimant was detained for nine hours, during which time he was questioned and his laptop, telephone and other items were taken and retained. He sought an interim injunction to stop the defendants examining the retained material or informing third parties of its contents before a full hearing of his claim. The claimant submitted that to allow the defendants to investigate the material would defeat the primary purpose of his claim, which was to protect the confidentiality of the journalistic material seized and the identity of journalistic sources. The defendants submitted that the balance of the risk of injustice came down decisively against the interim relief sought by the claimant. *Held*, to exclude from the prohibition of inspection and disclosure any inspection and disclosure for the purposes of a criminal investigation and use in criminal proceedings was too broad. If the defendants prevailed at the full interim relief hearing, they would be able to undertake those activities. It had not been shown that it was necessary for them to do so before that time. However, inspection for the purpose of considering whether the claimant fell within the definition of 'terrorist' in s 40(1)(b) and more generally for the purpose of protecting national security ought to be permitted pending the full interim relief hearing. The reason for this exception was simply to allow the police to continue, for a relatively short period, to perform a central and important task that Parliament had laid on them. Notwithstanding the competing interests, the public interest in the investigation, detection and prosecution of those who were reasonably suspected to be terrorists plainly justified the specific and relatively short exception. It was significant that one of the exceptions in the Contempt of Court Act 1981 s 10 to the protection of journalistic sources and the European Convention on Human Rights art 10(2) was where the interests of national security required disclosure. Further, while the argument that any denial or limitation of relief would make future success by the claimant a pyrrhic victory had force in respect of a denial of any such relief pending the substantive hearing, given the volume of the material that would not be so in the period until the matter could be properly determined by the court. Finally, to preclude the defendants from continuing to inspect the material would run the risk that they would be handicapped in developing their case at the full hearing. Judgment would be given accordingly.

R (on the application of Miranda) v Secretary of State for the Home Department [2013] EWHC 2609 (Admin), [2013] All ER (D) 191 (Aug) (Queen's Bench Division: Beatson LJ and Parker J).

2087   Terrorism—suspect—detention and questioning—right to presence of solicitor

On arriving at an airport, the claimant was stopped by police officers for examination pursuant to the Terrorism Act 2000 Sch 7. The claimant provided the officers with basic information about himself, but asked to speak to a solicitor before answering further questions. The claimant was permitted to speak to a solicitor by telephone, but not in private. The claimant was served with TACT 1 and 2 notices, which formed the two annexes to the Code of Practice for Examining Officers and set out the rights accorded to those detained and examined. The TACT 2 form stated that consultation with a solicitor was allowed 'in person, in writing or on the telephone'. The claimant was detained and questioned before his solicitor arrived. The claimant sought judicial review of the conduct of the police, submitting that (1) once detained, he had had a right to consult the solicitor in person before and during his interview; and (2) there had been a breach of his right to liberty under the European Convention on Human Rights art 5. *Held*, there was no doubt that the claimant had had the right to consult a solicitor before being interviewed. The examining officers had had no power to question the claimant after he had requested the presence of the solicitor and prior to the solicitor's arrival. The questioning had, therefore, been unlawful. The detainee had the choice of whether he wished to consult a solicitor in person, in writing or on the telephone. That right could be exercised at any time during the period of detention and might be exercised repeatedly, although not in a manner which frustrated the proper purpose of the examination. A reasonable delay to await the arrival of a solicitor might be required, but the detainee was not entitled to exercise that right in such a way as to frustrate the proper purpose of the examination. It followed that the claimant was entitled to a declaration that the conduct of the officers had been unlawful, though there was no evidence that the unlawful questioning had caused the claimant any loss or any adverse consequences. Also, although the questioning of the claimant had been unlawful, that had not made his detention unlawful. He had no domestic cause of action in false imprisonment since, if the officers had awaited the arrival of a solicitor, the claimant would have been detained longer. He had suffered no loss. Putting the same point in terms of art 5(1)(b), he had been lawfully detained in order to secure the fulfilment of his obligation to answer questions put to him pursuant to the 2000 Act. Accordingly, the application would be allowed.

R (on the application of Elosta) v Metropolitan Police Comr [2013] EWHC 3397 (Admin), [2014] 1 WLR 239, [2013] All ER (D) 70 (Nov) (Queen's Bench Division: Bean J).

PORTS AND HARBOURS

Halsbury's Laws of England (5th edn) vol 85 (2012) paras 1–190

Articles

For articles relating to this title please refer to the Table of Articles at the beginning of the Abridgment.

2088   Marine Navigation Act 2013

See para 2319.

2089   Ports—port authority—land held by port authority for statutory purposes—registration as town or village green

See *R (on the application of Newhaven Port and Properties Ltd) v East Sussex CC*, para 339.

2090   Ports—port security

See para 2325.

POSTAL SERVICES

Halsbury's Laws of England (5th edn) vol 85 (2012) paras 201–307

2091   Postal services—universal postal service

The Postal Services (Universal Postal Service) (Amendment) Order 2013, SI 2013/3108 (in force on 31 December 2013), amends the 2012 Order, SI 2012/936, so as to (1) remove unused defined terms; (2) change the way in which the term 'working day' is used, and limit its use to the calculation of routing times; (3) apply limitations set out in the Postal Services Act 2011 s 33(1), (3) to postal packets in relation to all the services described in the 2012 Order; (4) amend the description of the 'priority' and 'standard' services to require Certificates of Posting to be provided free of charge and to omit the prohibition of tracking; (5) set limits of size for postal packets required to be conveyed as part of the 'return to sender' service; (6) change the descriptions of outgoing international services; (7) amend requirements relating to services for the blind and partially sighted by removing requirements to provide free of charge registered items, requiring Certificates of Posting to be provided free of charge and removing provisions which allowed a charge to be made for international services to certain territories; (8) amend the definition of 'redirection services' to cover any addressee; and (9) set limits of size for postal packets in relation to certain services.

2092　Royal Mail—occupational pension scheme—construction—increase in pension
See *Royal Mail Group Ltd v Evans*, para 1975.

2093　Special administration regime—postal administration regime
The Postal Administration Rules 2013, SI 2013/3208 (in force on 31 January 2014), set out the procedure for the postal administration process under the Postal Services Act 2011 Pt 4 (ss 68–88). In particular, the rules (1) set out the procedure for applying for a postal administration order; (2) specify the initial steps to be taken in postal administration proceedings; (3) govern the conduct of creditors and company meetings; (4) make provision relating to an application to court for authority to dispose of property subject to a security; (5) provide for the priority of expenses of the postal administration; (6) make provision relating to distribution to creditors, including provision as to proving debts and quantifying claims; (7) prescribe how the remuneration of a postal administrator is to be fixed by the court; (8) set out the arrangements for ending a postal administration; (9) specify the requirements and procedures for replacing a postal administrator; (10) specify the court procedure and practice for postal administration; (11) make provision for the use of proxies at creditors' or members' meetings; (12) set out the provisions for examination of persons where an application to court has been made by the postal administrator; (13) prescribe the forms that are to be used in postal administration proceedings; and (14) specify details of the punishment of offences under the rules.

PRISONS AND PRISONERS
Halsbury's Laws of England (5th edn) vol 85 (2012) paras 401–595

Articles
For articles relating to this title please refer to the Table of Articles at the beginning of the Abridgment.

2094　Offender Management Act 2007—commencement
The Offender Management Act 2007 (Commencement No 6) Order 2013, SI 2013/1963, brings ss 28 and 29 into force on 6 January 2014. For a summary of the Act, see 2007 Abr para 2414. For details of commencement, see the commencement table in the title STATUTES AND LEGISLATIVE PROCESS.

2095　Parole Board—release or recall of prisoners—provision of advice to Secretary of State—exclusion of untried material
The claimant was sentenced to seven years' imprisonment plus an extended licence period of three years, under the Powers of Criminal Courts (Sentencing) Act 2000 s 85. The sentence was imposed in relation to two different sets of offences, the first concerning possession of firearms and ammunition; and the second concerning possession of a large number of indecent images of children on his computer. The claimant was released on licence but was subsequently recalled to prison. The claimant's case was considered by the Parole Board. A series of further risk assessment reports were placed before the Board which was considering re-release in an updated dossier prepared by the Secretary of State. The updated dossier

included untried material consisting of a case summary prepared by the Crown Prosecution Service prior to the claimant's Crown Court trial containing additional allegations, prosecution witness statements from the police and a report from a forensic psychologist. No indictment was ever pursued in relation to the allegations and the claimant was not convicted of any offence in connection with them. The claimant sought to exclude the untried material from the final dossier of material to be taken into account by the Board in deciding whether to release him on licence. On his appeal against the dismissal of his application for judicial review of the decision not to exclude the untried material, *held*, the Criminal Justice Act 2003 s 239(3) did not require that the panel deciding the case had always to consider all documents supplied to the Board by the Secretary of State. There was no reason why s 239(3) had to be read so as to prevent the Board having a power, in a rare case where it might be necessary, to make arrangements whereby a document might be excluded from the dossier prepared for the panel making the recommendation to the Secretary of State, provided a member or panel of the Board considered all documents given to the Board by the Secretary of State. It followed that the documents supplied by the Secretary of State ought not in every case be subject to analysis by a legally qualified member of the Board, or a panel of legally qualified members. That would be unnecessary as well as wasteful of time and resources. Given the powers available to the panel, the court would not assume that it was improper for the panel members to proceed. Judgment would be given accordingly.

R (on the application of McGetrick) v Parole Board [2013] EWCA Civ 182, [2013] 3 All ER 636) (Court of Appeal: Pill, Toulson and Tomlinson LJJ). Decision of Queen's Bench Divisional Court [2012] EWHC 882 (Admin), [2012] All ER (D) 39 (Apr) reversed in part.

2096   Prison staff—misconduct in public office—prison nurse—prison/health officer

See *R v Cosford*, para 651.

2097   Prisoner—Category A prisoner—progression to lower category—ability to demonstrate reduced risk—duty of Secretary of State

The claimant was serving a life sentence with a minimum term of 25 years for the murder of a police officer. At the time of the murder, the claimant had been under the influence of alcohol and other substances. On his account, he had never been able to recall either the murder itself or the events surrounding it. However, he had accepted responsibility for the murder. He had remained a Category A prisoner throughout his time in prison and had completed a number of rehabilitative programmes. The claimant brought proceedings seeking judicial review of what he alleged to be the continuing failure of the defendant Secretary of State to provide him with the means to demonstrate reduced risk so that he could progress to a lower security category while in prison. It was contended that he was unable to undertake to take the necessary programmes since he had been found to be unsuitable, partly on the basis of his inability to recall the offence. *Held*, the defendant was under a public law duty to provide indeterminate sentence prisoners with the means by which they could demonstrate, at or around the expiry of their sentences, that their risk had reduced sufficiently to enable their release. That duty included life sentence prisoners. A breach of the duty occurred when there was a failure to provide the appropriate systems and resources covering matters such as reports and rehabilitative courses. Breach of the duty did not confer on a particular prisoner a right to a remedy in his particular case, although the upshot of a prisoner demonstrating a breach might be a ready improvement in how he was treated within the prison system. There was a separate and well-accepted public law duty on the defendant to act rationally and to take into account relevant factors, while disregarding irrelevant matters. That duty applied to making choices in relation to the allocation of resources for rehabilitative programmes. The threshold was high. However, it would be a breach of that duty to require a prisoner to demonstrate a type of progress to a reduction of risk which was effectively impossible for him to perform. The duty could not be interpreted as an absolute obligation to make a prisoner ready for release when his tariff expired. In the circumstances, the defendant was in breach of its public law duty to act rationally in the provision of courses or other means by which he could demonstrate reduced risk. The reality was that it was impossible for the claimant to demonstrate a reduction in risk. First, he could not remember the details surrounding the murder. Secondly, the murder had been the claimant's only use of extreme violence, so the requirement that he addressed his use of extreme violence before progressing to conditions of lower security had to refer to the murder. Thirdly, there were no rehabilitative courses available to the claimant enabling him to address his use of extreme violence. Fourthly, while rehabilitative programmes were not the only means by which the claimant could address his extreme violence, the fact was that the defendant had failed to provide any other means by which he could demonstrate a reduced risk. There was no practical consideration in the evidence of how the claimant might progress should his recall of the murder events remain a blank. If the defendant believed that one to one work with a psychologist to address extreme violence was the best way forward, it was irrational for him not to have taken practical steps to explore its potential. By failing to unfold the steps by which he could evidence a reduction in the risk of extreme violence, the defendant was acting irrational and in breach of his public law duty. Accordingly, the claim would be allowed.

R (on the application of Weddle) v Secretary of State for Justice [2013] EWHC 2323 (Admin), [2013] All ER (D) 201 (Aug) (Queen's Bench Division: Cranston J). R (on the application of James) v Secretary of State for Justice; R (on the application of Lee) v Secretary of State for Justice; R (on the application of Wells) v Secretary of State for Justice [2009] UKHL 22, [2010] 1 AC 553, [2009] 4 All ER 255 (2009 Abr para 2416);and R (on the application of Wells) v Parole Board; R (on the application of Walker) v Secretary of State for the Home Department [2007] EWHC 1835 (Admin), [2008] 1 All ER 138, DC (2007 Abr para 2421), distinguished.

2098   Prisoner—damage to property—compensation requirement

The Prison and Young Offender Institution (Amendment) Rules 2013, SI 2013/2462 (in force on 1 November 2013), further amend the Prison Rules 1999, SI 1999/728, so as to (1) require governors or adjudicators to impose a requirement on a prisoner to pay compensation for destroying or damaging prison property where that prisoner has been found guilty at an adjudication of causing the destruction or damage; (2) limit any compensation ordered to the cost of the destruction or damage and provide that it must not, in any event, exceed £2,000; (3) provide that a compensation requirement ceases to have effect two years after its imposition, regardless of whether the prisoner has paid the full amount due; (4) enable a prisoner to seek a review of an amount ordered to be paid under a compensation requirement and allow a reviewer to vary the amount payable; (5) provide that, where a compensation requirement has been imposed by a governor, the Secretary of State may reduce the amount to be paid; (6) empower a governor to debit money due under a compensation requirement from any money held by the prison for the prisoner in order to recover the amount payable, provided that the prisoner is not left with less than £5 in his prison account; (7) provide for the continued enforcement of any compensation requirement imposed on a young offender on his becoming detained in a prison; and (8) enable the directors or governors of contracted out prisons to exercise those powers exercisable by prison governors. Similar amendments are also made to the Young Offender Institution Rules 2000, SI 2000/3371.

2099   Prisoner—life sentence—indeterminate sentence—transfer to open prison—lawfulness of policy

Two separate applications were ordered to be heard together as test cases concerning the transfer of indeterminate sentence prisoners ('ISPs') from closed prisons to open prisons. In determining the intake of prisoners, prisons had been expressly forbidden to apply allocation criteria which excluded ISPs or limited the number of ISPs they would hold, except where such criteria had been expressly authorised. Due to difficulties in effecting moves for ISPs into open conditions, new arrangements were made by the Secretary of State under which ISPs whose tariff had expired should be prioritised over pre-tariff ISPs because they had served the punitive part of their sentence and would be eligible for release once the Parole Board was satisfied that they could safely be released. The applicants were pre-tariff ISPs who had been identified as being eligible for transfer to open conditions in advance of their release from custody. However, due to delays in their transfer, the applicants had not been able to demonstrate a reduction in the risk that they presented prior to consideration of their release by the board. They were both transferred before their tariffs expired. The applicants commenced judicial review proceedings of the Secretary of State's policy,

PUBLISHING

Halsbury's Laws of England (5th edn) vol 85 (2012) paras 701–764

Articles

For articles relating to this title please refer to the Table of Articles at the beginning of the Abridgment.

2109   Internet—publication on internet—libel—absence of control over content

See *Tamiz v Google*, para 847.

2110   Newspaper—publication of photographs—famous person—right to privacy

See *Rocknroll v News Group Newspapers Ltd*, para 2215.

2111   Publication of book—licence agreement—entitlement to royalties

The claimant was the chief executive officer of two publishing companies. The first of those companies entered into a written licence with the defendant company that permitted the defendant to repackage a particular edition of a wildlife book. The licence also provided for the split of royalties between the components of the combined book and gift product. The claimant brought proceedings against the defendant for breach of contract in connection with the alleged entitlement to royalties under the licence. The action related to a series continuity publication which was packaged by the defendant, and which, through the first company, reused some copyright material belonging to the claimant's second company. It fell to be determined (1) whether any elements of the fixed packaging costs paid by the publisher of the wildlife book directly to the defendant, in addition to the royalty specifically referred to in the licence, was or should be treated as a royalty or profit which the claimant was entitled to share; (2) whether it was proper for the defendant to deduct picture costs from the expressly agreed royalty before making payment to the first company; and (3) whether there was any interest owing to the claimant by the defendant. *Held*, on the correct construction of the licence, the claimant was entitled only to a proportion of royalties in the strict sense. Picture costs were to be deducted from the royalty payments, although the claimant was entitled to an account of the sums said to have been expended on picture costs. There had been no intention sufficient to satisfy the prerequisites for a rectification of the licence. Further, no fiduciary relationship existed between the parties and the defendant did not therefore owe any fiduciary duties to the first company. There had been no misrepresentation on the part of the defendant that induced the first company to enter into the licence and there was no collateral contract as alleged nor was the claimant entitled to interest to the extent that payments under the licence had been made late. Judgment would be given accordingly.

Morse v Eaglemoss Publications Ltd [2013] EWHC 1507 (Ch), [2013] All ER (D) 58 (Jun) (Chancery Division: Proudman J).

13/1191.

2112   Reports of judicial proceedings—exclusion of press from proceedings—care proceedings—risk to lives of subjects of proceedings

See *Re Al-Hilli (children: reporting restrictions)*, para 2206.

2113   Reports of judicial proceedings—reporting restrictions—anonymity of party— child victim of cyberbullying

See *AB (by her litigation guardian CD) v Bragg Communications Inc*, para 425.

2114   Reports of judicial proceedings—reporting proceedings—criminal proceedings— child not directly concerned in proceedings

See *R (on the application of A) v Lowestoft Magistrates' Court*, para 204.

RAILWAYS AND TRAMWAYS
Halsbury's Laws of England (5th edn) vol 86 (2013) paras 1–537

Articles
For articles relating to this title please refer to the Table of Articles at the beginning of the Abridgment.

2115 High Speed Rail (Preparation) Act 2013
The High Speed Rail (Preparation) Act 2013 authorises expenditure in preparation for a high speed railway transport network. The Act received the royal assent on 21 November 2013 and came into force on that day.

Section 1 authorises the Secretary of State, with the approval of the Treasury, to incur expenditure in preparation for a high speed railway transport network, including preparation for (1) the construction of any railway line and any other infrastructure proposed to be included at any time in the network; and (2) the provision of services as part of the network. The Secretary of State must, pursuant to s 2, prepare a report on such expenditure in relation to each financial year and lay each report before Parliament as soon as is reasonably practicable after the end of the financial year to which it relates. Section 3 deals with extent, commencement and short title.

2116 Public bodies—BRB (Residuary) Limited—abolition
The Public Bodies (Abolition of BRB (Residuary) Limited) Order 2013, SI 2013/2314 (in force on 1 October 2013), (1) transfers the statutory functions of BRB (Residuary) Limited to the Secretary of State and Network Rail (Asset) Limited; (2) abolishes BRB (Residuary) Limited; (3) provides for the removal of BRB (Residuary) Limited's name from the register of companies; (4) makes consequential amendments to the Transport Act 1968 in relation to functions transferred to the Secretary of State under the order in relation to bridges carrying highways over railways; and (5) amends the Public Bodies Act 2011 Sch 1 so as to repeal the entry in relation to BRB (Residuary) Limited.

2117 Public bodies—BRB (Residuary) Ltd—tax consequences
The BRB (Residuary) Limited (Tax Consequences) Order 2013, SI 2013/2242 (in force on 30 September 2013), deals with the tax consequences of a transfer scheme made under the Public Bodies Act 2011 s 23 transferring property, rights and liabilities from BRB (Residuary) Ltd ('BRB') to the Secretary of State for Transport, London & Continental Railways Ltd ('LCR'), Network Rail Infrastructure Ltd or Rail Safety and Standards Board Ltd. In particular, the 2013 Order provides (1) that, for the purposes of the Taxation of Chargeable Gains Act 1992, a disposal under a relevant transfer to LCR or to the Secretary of State is to be treated as being for a consideration such that no gain or loss accrues to BRB; (2) that, where consideration is given by Network Rail Infrastructure Ltd in respect of a relevant transfer, the disposal is to be treated as made for an amount equal to the value of that consideration and, where no such consideration is given, it is treated as made for nil consideration; (3) for continuity of treatment in relation to any allowances or charges under the Capital Allowances Act 2001 which relate to part of BRB's property business transferred to LCR by a relevant transfer; (4) for the transfer of losses, for corporation tax purposes, in respect of unrelieved losses incurred by BRB in relation to part of BRB's property business transferred to LCR by a relevant transfer; (5) for provisions made in the accounts of BRB and LCR in relation to property, rights or liabilities transferred by a relevant transfer; (6) for continuity of treatment, for corporation tax purposes, in the case of a relevant transfer transferring loan relationships to LCR; and (7) that stamp duty is not chargeable on an instrument making or executing a relevant transfer to LCR.

2118 Public bodies—Railway Heritage Committee—abolition
The Public Bodies (Abolition of the Railway Heritage Committee) Order 2013, SI 2013/64 (in force in part on 1 April 2013 and in part on 2 April 2013), abolishes the Railway Heritage Committee and transfers its functions, under the Railway Heritage Act 1996, relating to the designation and disposal of historically significant railway records and artefacts to the Board of Trustees of the Science Museum. The 2013 Order, in particular,

(1) abolishes the Committee and transfers its functions to the Board of Trustees and amends the Railway Heritage Act 1996 so that the provision, which provides for the establishment of a committee is repealed and all references in the 1996 Act to the Committee are replaced with references to the Board of Trustees; (2) revokes the Railway Heritage Scheme Order 2005, SI 2005/2905, which gave effect to the Railway Heritage Scheme; and (3) makes consequential amendments to the Parliamentary Commissioner Act 1967, the Freedom of Information Act 2000, the Public Bodies Act 2011 and the Freedom of Information (Additional Public Authorities) Order 2010, SI 2010/937.

2119   Railway—construction—decision to build rail link—lawfulness of decision

See HS2 Action Alliance Ltd v Secretary of State for Transport, para 2121.

2120   Railway—interoperability

The Railways (Interoperability) (Amendment) Regulations 2013, SI 2013/3023 (in force on 1 January 2014), amend the 2011 Regulations, SI 2011/3066, by updating the definition of European Parliament and Council Directive (EC) 2008/57, on the interoperability of the rail system within the Community, so as to take account of recent amendments to it and by including accessibility in the factors which the competent authority must take into account when deciding whether a project or type of project is for the renewal or upgrading of structural subsystems within the context of the interoperability regime.

2121   Railway—proposed high speed network—scope of EU legislation—hybrid bill—requirement for public consultation

The defendant proposed the construction of a new high speed rail network between London and the West Midlands and potentially beyond, and a formal consultation process was initiated. Following consideration of the consultation responses, the defendant presented to Parliament a command paper which explained that the high speed rail network would be built in two phases and that a modified Parliamentary hybrid bill procedure would be used to obtain development consent. Various applications for judicial review were made in relation the proposal, including a claim that the defendant failed to re-consult a consortium of local authorities in respect of further reports commissioned on the alternative of enhancing an existing main line that the consortium put forward in its consultation response and which the defendant later rejected. On appeal against the refusal of the applications, held, Sullivan LJ dissenting, the command paper did not fall within the scope of European Parliament and Council Directive (EC) 2001/42 (on the assessment of the effects of certain plans and programmes on the environment) because it did not have such an influence on Parliament's decision-making process as to amount to a plan or programme which set the framework for future development consent. Parliament was not obliged to comply with the command paper or even to have regard to it in reaching its decision on whether to give consent to the development. Nor was it appropriate or possible for the court to assess the degree of influence the command paper was likely to have as a matter of fact on Parliament's decision-making process. Even if it were constitutionally appropriate for the court to assess the likely degree of influence, the court was not equipped to make such an assessment. The modified hybrid bill procedure was capable of giving the public an opportunity to participate effectively in the environmental decision-making process. European Parliament and Council Directive (EU) 2011/92 (on the assessment of the effects of certain public and private projects on the environment) envisaged that the objectives pursued by the directive were, in principle, capable of being met by a legislative process. The non-disclosure of the reports did not make the consultation unfair and unlawful. In the circumstances, fairness did not require an opportunity to be given to the consortium to comment on the reports before the defendant reached the decisions set out in the command paper. The reports did not contain information that was needed by consultees before they were in a position to address the issues. Accordingly, the appeals would be dismissed.

HS2 Action Alliance Ltd v Secretary of State for Transport [2013] EWCA Civ 920, [2013] PTSR 1194, [2014] All ER (D) 291 (Jul) (Court of Appeal: Lord Dyson MR, Richards and Sullivan LJJ). Decision of Ouseley J sub nom R (on the application of Buckinghamshire CC) v Secretary of State for Transport [2013] EWHC 481 (Admin), [2013] All ER (D) 185 (Mar) affirmed.

This decision has been affirmed on appeal: [2014] UKSC 3, [2014] 2 All ER 109.

2122　Railway—railway byelaws—railway assets—exclusion

The Railway Byelaws Amendment Order 2013, SI 2013/3269 (in force on 18 January 2014), further amends the national Railway Byelaws made by the Strategic Rail Authority in 2005 by excluding from the scope and application of those byelaws railway assets owned by or under the management of Merseyrail Electrics Ltd 2002.

2123　Railway—safety—accessibility—non-interoperable rail systems—exemption

The Rail Vehicle Accessibility (Non-Interoperable Rail System) (London Underground Victoria Line 09TS Vehicles) Exemption Order 2013, SI 2013/3031 (in force on 1 January 2014), exempts, with conditions, certain rail vehicles from specified requirements of the Rail Vehicle Accessibility (Non-Interoperable Rail System) Regulations 2010, SI 2010/432, when those vehicles are used on the London Underground Victoria Line.

2124　Railway—safety critical work

The Railways and Other Guided Transport Systems (Miscellaneous Amendments) Regulations 2013, SI 2013/950 (in force on 21 May 2013), further amend the Railways and Other Guided Transport Systems (Safety) Regulations 2006, SI 2006/599, so as to (1) introduce new definitions and alter existing definitions; (2) empower the Office of Rail Regulation ('ORR') to determine, for the purposes of those regulations, that a railway does not form part of the mainline railway and that heritage vehicles that operate over the mainline railway are deemed not to do so; (3) remove the requirement for train operators on the mainline railway to carry out a safety verification procedure in relation to new or altered vehicles; (4) shorten the period during which the ORR is required to notify decisions in relation to applications for the issue or amendment of safety certificates or safety authorisations; (5) provide that a freight wagon may not be used or placed in service on a mainline railway unless it has had assigned to it an entity in charge of maintenance which holds a certificate issued in accordance with Commission Regulation (EU) 445/2011; (6) relieve train operators operating on railway that does not form part of the mainline railway of the requirement to send annual safety reports to the ORR; (7) clarify that controllers of safety-critical work must have suitable and sufficient arrangements in place to monitor the competence and fitness of a person to carry out such work; and (8) allow appeals to be made to the Secretary of State against decisions of the ORR or other bodies relating to certificates issued in accordance with Regulation (EU) 445/2011. SI 2006/557 is further amended and SI 2010/724 is amended.

REAL PROPERTY AND REGISTRATION

Halsbury's Laws of England (5th edn) vol 87 (2012) paras 1–1175

Articles

For articles relating to this title please refer to the Table of Articles at the beginning of the Abridgment.

2125　Conveyancing

See CONVEYANCING.

2126　Covenant—positive covenant—enforceability against successors in title

See *Elwood v Goodman*, para 543.

2127　Covenant—restrictive covenant—covenant running with the land—benefit to covenantee's land—requirement for land to be used for specified purposes

The Perpetuities and Accumulations Act 1964 s 9(2) provides that, in the case of a disposition consisting of the conferring of an option to acquire for valuable consideration any interest in land, the perpetuity period under the rule against perpetuities is 21 years.

Twenty four years before the present proceedings commenced, the defendant local authority transferred freehold land to a broadcaster. The transfer included a covenant which provided that the property was to be solely occupied by the broadcaster for the purpose of a broadcasting centre, subject to a proviso that the covenant could be removed by agreement in return for a payment. In the event that the property became surplus to the broadcaster's requirements, the broadcaster was required to notify the defendant, which then had a pre-emptive right to purchase the freehold at its open market value if, within three months, it served notice on the broadcaster. The broadcaster sold the freehold to the claimant and took a 25-year lease back. The claimant sought a declaration that the covenant and the right of pre-emption were not enforceable against it or any successor in title. *Held*, to be enforceable against successors in title, a restrictive covenant had to be intended to benefit, and be capable of benefiting, the covenantee's land. On the evidence, the purpose of the covenant was twofold, to maintain the broadcaster at the site and to serve as a lever for extracting a payment if the broadcaster decided to relocate. It was not intended to protect or preserve the amenity or value of the defendant's adjacent land, but rather was a money payment obligation. It therefore did not bind the claimant or its successors in title. On the facts, the broadcaster's sale of the freehold did not trigger the defendant's pre-emption rights as the property had not become surplus to the broadcaster's requirements. The 21-year perpetuity period mentioned in the 1964 Act s 9(2) began when the option came into existence, not when the right of pre-emption was conferred. As the trigger for the right of pre-emption had not yet arisen, the defendant had not lost the right to enforce the right of pre-emption by the application of s 9(2). However, the right of pre-emption was not binding on the claimant as a purchaser of the land for value as the right had not been protected by an entry on the register. Judgment would be given accordingly.

Cosmichome Ltd v Southampton City Council [2013] EWHC 1378 (Ch), [2013] 1 WLR 2436, [2013] All ER (D) 306 (May) (Chancery Division: Sir William Blackburn).

2128   Land registration—fees

The Land Registration Fee Order 2013, SI 2013/3174 (in force on 17 March 2014), replaces the 2012 Order, SI 2012/1969, and makes changes to land registration fees by, in particular, (1) reducing by 50 per cent the fee for a number of specified applications where those applications are delivered by electronic means; (2) providing that the lowest scale 1 fee band is £0 to £80,000 and attracts a fee of £40; (3) decreasing, from £120 to £80, the fee for the band £80,001 to £100,000; (4) including a reference to applications to register an alteration of priority of registered charges; (5) designating as a fixed fee the fee for an application to cancel a notice in the register in respect of an unregistered lease which has determined; (6) providing that the fee for inspection and requests for official copies of documents referred to in the register, or kept by the registrar in relation to an application, is £3 per document if made by electronic means and £7 per document if made by any other permitted means; (7) reducing the fee for an application for a copy of a historical edition of an individual register or registered title; (8) omitting provisions relating to credit accounts; and (9) removing the right to fee exemption in respect of an application to lodge a caution against first registration, or to make a register entry, where the application relates to rights in respect of the repair of a church chancel and is lodged on or before 12 October 2013.

2129   Register—rectification—mistaken modification—adverse possession

The appellant's property included a small piece of land measuring under two metres across at its widest point and four metres long (the 'disputed land'). The disputed land had been registered as part of the appellant's property for almost a century. However, when the respondent's property, which was across the road from the appellant's, was registered, the Land Registry mistakenly included the disputed land in the title. A chain and metal eye were subsequently fixed into a concrete bollard to demarcate the disputed land as a parking space, which was used thereafter by the owners of the respondent's land. Several years later, the Land Registry mistakenly excluded the disputed land from the appellant's property when computerising the title plan. Eight years after that, the appellant applied for the register to be rectified so that the disputed land was excluded from the title plan to the respondent's property. The respondent challenged the application, submitting that it was statute-barred on the basis that her predecessors in title had been in adverse possession of the disputed land for more than 12 years. The deputy adjudicator to the Land Registry made an order refusing rectification, ruling that the respondent and her predecessors had acquired a possessory title to the disputed land. The appellant's appeal against that decision was dismissed on the same grounds. On the appellant's further appeal, *held*, the land register was a system of state-guaranteed registered title. The legislation provided machinery for the correction of mistakes and for indemnity with safeguards to protect the interests of the proprietor in possession and to prevent injustice. That was the machinery which had to be used to establish the true title to registered land before any question arose of establishing possessory title. The previous owners of the appellant's property were not dispossessed of the disputed land by the owners of the respondent's property, and their possession of the disputed land during the relevant period was not 'adverse possession' within the meaning of the Limitation Act 1980. As long as they remained registered proprietors of the disputed land, that possession would be lawful and could not be adverse to the owners of the appellant's property. Just as time had not begun to run against the owners of the appellant's property, so it had not begun to run in favour of the owners of the respondent's property. The fact that the owners of the appellant's property had a right to apply for rectification of the register was besides the point for the purposes of the 1980 Act. That was a right of a different kind than a right of action for the recovery of possession to which the 1980 Act applied a limitation period. The 1980 Act did not apply to the statutory right to apply to rectify the land register. The right to apply for it did not of itself give the owners of the appellant's property a right of action to recover possession of the disputed land from others who had a concurrent registered title to it. Accordingly, the appeal would be allowed.

Parshall v Hackney [2013] EWCA Civ 240, [2013] 3 All ER 224 (Court of Appeal: Mummery, Patten and Treacy LJJ).

2130   Registration—adjudicator—transfer of functions

See para 612.

2131   Registration—first registration—caution against first registration—right of squatter to lodge caution

The Land Registration Act 2002 s 15(1)(a) provides that, subject to s 15(3), a person may lodge a caution against the registration of title to an unregistered legal estate if he claims to be the owner of a qualifying estate. No caution may be lodged under s 15(1) by virtue of ownership of a freehold estate in land: s 15(3)(a)(i).

The claimant had resided in his caravan as a squatter in adverse possession of unregistered land for six years. The defendant chief land registrar dismissed the claimant's application to register a caution against first registration in respect of the land. The claimant sought a declaration that he was entitled to register a caution against first registration under the 2002 Act s 15. *Held*, the claimant would only be entitled to register a caution under s 15 if he was the owner of a 'qualifying estate', and on the facts the only qualifying estate he could claim to own was an estate in land. Under the Law of Property Act 1925 s 1(1), the only types of estates in land were an estate in fee simple absolute in possession and a term of years absolute. It was clear that the claimant did not have a term of years, so that, if he had any estate in the land, it could only be an 'estate in fee simple absolute in possession' or, in modern parlance, the freehold. As a freehold owner, he was precluded by the 2002 Act s 15(3)(a) from lodging a caution. His contention that his estate was not 'absolute', because it was liable to be defeated by the paper owner, was misconceived. In English law, at least in unregistered land, title was a relative concept, so that two or more titles could subsist in the same land. A squatter would acquire title by virtue of his possession but, unless the paper owner's title had been extinguished by the squatter's adverse possession, the squatter's title was subject to the paper owner asserting his better title based on his prior possession. The rationale for the statutory exclusion of the owner of a freehold from lodging a caution was that a caution against first registration was not intended to provide a substitute for first registration. The 2002 Act had not provided for a squatter whose period of possession was insufficient to have extinguished the paper owner's superior title to lodge a caution. Accordingly, the application would be dismissed.

Turner v Chief Land Registrar [2013] EWHC 1382 (Ch), [2013] 2 P & CR 223, [2013] All ER (D) 340 (May) (Chancery Division: Roth J).

2132   Registration—proper office

The Land Registration (Proper Office) Order 2013, SI 2013/1627 (in force on 1 October 2013), replaces the 2010 Order, SI 2010/1635, and designates 14 land registry offices as proper offices for the receipt of specified descriptions of applications under the Land Registration Act 2002.

2133 Registration—unilateral notice—proprietary estoppel—sale of property to fund defence to claim—court's inherent jurisdiction to set-aside

The claimant was the defendant's grandson. He made a claim in equity based on proprietary estoppel to the defendant's farm, stating that the defendant and her late husband had promised him the farm and that the claimant had acted in reliance on those promises. He registered a unilateral notice under the Land Registration Act 2002 s 32. The defendant made an application for an order of the court to cancel the unilateral notice. Her purpose in doing so was to sell or charge part of the property to meet the legal fees of defending the claim. The defendant submitted that the court had inherent jurisdiction to cancel a unilateral notice registered under the 2002 Act. The issue arose as to whether the 2002 Act had abrogated or otherwise affected the jurisdiction. Consideration was given to the Land Registration Act 1925. *Held*, the court had an inherent jurisdiction to cancel notices registered under the 2002 Act. It was the clear philosophy of the case law that the court should not allow the beneficiary of the notice to have the protection of the notice pending trial without the court considering the position of the registered proprietor and whether, and if so how, the proprietor should be protected pending trial. The inherent jurisdiction, recognised and developed by the courts in relation to vacation of cautions registered under the 1925 Act, applied. There was nothing in the scheme of the 2002 Act to suggest that the court's inherent jurisdiction had been abrogated or otherwise affected by the 2002 Act. Further, there was no evidence to suggest that the earlier jurisdiction in its original form was incompatible with the 2002 Act. In the present circumstances, it would be appropriate to regard the case as an appropriate one in which to restrain the defendant from disposing or charging the property. The court would approach the case as it would a case where a claimant claimed an injunction to prevent a defendant interfering with the claimant's property rights. The matter would come down to the balance of injustice of deciding the application against the claimant were he to establish his claim, and deciding the application against the defendant if the claimant was later to fail to establish his claim. The court had the jurisdiction to make the order sought. Justice required the court to exercise that jurisdiction to permit the defendant to raise funds to defend the claim by way of an appropriate sale or an appropriate charge of the land, or a part of it. Accordingly, the application would be allowed.

Nugent v Nugent [2013] EWHC 4095 (Ch), [2014] All ER (D) 92 (Jan) (Chancery Division: Morgan J). *Stein v Stein* [2004] EWHC 3212 (Ch), [2004] All ER (D) 144 (Dec) applied. *Fitzgerald v Williams, O'Regan v Williams* [1996] QB 657, [1996] 2 All ER 171 (1996 Abr para 2427), CA; *Heywood v BDC Properties Ltd (No 2)* [1964] 2 All ER 702, CA; and *Clearbrook Property Holdings Ltd v Verrier* [1973] 3 All ER 614, [1974] 1 WLR 243 considered.

RECEIVERS

Halsbury's Laws of England (5th edn) vol 88 (2012) paras 1–196

2134 Appointment by court—administration of estate—control of administration

The applicant was the claimant in an action against seven defendants. Following the death of the first defendant five executors were named. Three of the executors declined to apply for a grant of probate. The applicant applied for the appointment of a receiver in relation to the first defendant's estate and proposed two named persons. The remaining two executors were the respondents to the application. *Held*, there was no one in post to represent the estate and things might need to be done without further delay such that it was appropriate to have receivers in position to act on behalf of the estate. Therefore, it was appropriate to appoint a receiver to the estate. The court was concerned with the question of what was in the best interests of the estate and interested parties in the estate, who included the beneficiaries under the will, but who also included creditors and possible potential creditors. In the circumstances, it was right to appoint the proposed two named persons. Accordingly, the application would be allowed.

Joint Stock Co Aeroflot Russian Airlines v Berezovsky [2013] EWHC 1209 (Ch), [2013] All ER (D) 141 (May) (Chancery Division: Morgan J). For related proceedings see para 2135.

2135 Appointment by court—gap in representation—risk of dissipation of assets

The claimant, a Russian company, brought proceedings against the defendant and other parties who were suspected of committing large-scale financial fraud. The defendant died during the course of the proceedings. The defendant had apparently executed a valid will regarding his estate in which a number of executors were named. Three of the named executors renounced the office of executor and two had not identified the course they intended on taking. As a result, for approximately four weeks there was a gap in the representation of the defendant's estate. The claimant applied without notice for an order appointing two insolvency practitioners as receivers of the deceased's estate. The order would confer extensive powers on the receivers, including the power to defend the action, the power to take delivery of a range of assets from third parties, and the power to enter premises to search for documents. In support of the application, the claimant submitted evidence that it had been the defendant's long-term practice to put his assets beyond the reach of his creditors and bodies such as the claimant. Consideration was given to the Senior Courts Act 1981 s 37, which gave the court jurisdiction to appoint a receiver in relation to an estate in any case where it was just and convenient to do so. *Held*, a typical case where it was appropriate for the jurisdiction under s 37 to be exercised was where the estate was entitled to an income, but, in the absence of the receiver, there was no-one to collect it. An alternative case was where the estate had liabilities which needed to be serviced on a continuing basis and, if there was neglect in that respect, then a third party could claim a forfeiture or enforce a security depriving the estate permanently of a valuable asset. The order sought by the claimant had unusual and disturbing features. What was needed was a decision as to who was to represent the estate in what might be a transitional period between the death of the defendant and a formal grant of representation to a fit and proper person. One of the essential weaknesses in the far-reaching application was that it seemed to be implicit that, if the executors took a grant of probate, the claimant's interest in having a receiver would fall away and all the consequential orders which were sought would also fall away. It was entirely back to front to appoint a receiver to fill a gap in representation and then, just because one was filling a gap, suddenly to give the receiver far-reaching powers but without satisfying the court that it was anything like an appropriate case for a freezing injunction in the first place. The need for the order to be made as a justification for an application ex parte in accordance with conventional principles had simply not been demonstrated. Accordingly, the application would be dismissed.

Joint Stock Co 'Aeroflot Russian Airlines' v Berezovsky [2013] EWHC 1210 (Ch), [2013] All ER (D) 158 (May) (Chancery Division: Morgan J). For related proceedings see para 2134.

2136 Legal proceedings—costs—payment to third party—right to be indemnified

An action was brought by a company against a number of persons, one of whom subsequently died. The deceased's will named five executors, three of whom renounced probate. The two remaining executors were his former partner, who was the first defendant in the present proceedings, and his daughter, who was the second defendant. The two executrices did not take out a grant of probate and nobody was appointed to act as an administrator of the estate. In the event, the company successfully applied for the court to appoint receivers of the estate, who were the claimants in the present proceedings. The appointment order also directed that, until further order, the estate should pay such reasonable remuneration and reasonable costs and expenses properly incurred. The claimants later brought proceedings seeking an order requiring the deceased's solicitors to transfer certain business documents to them, and an order that would entitle them to take possession of a number of different settlement agreements which the deceased had entered into, including an agreement with the fourth to seventh defendants. After those proceedings were concluded, the claimants applied to the court for an order directing that the sums which they would have to pay to the solicitors and the fourth to seventh defendants, together with their own costs and expenses in connection with the application, should be paid to them out of the assets of the estate. Issues arose as to whether (1) a receiver, appointed by the court, should be dealt with in a different way to the way the court approached a case involving a liquidator or a trustee or a personal representative who initiated proceedings against a third party; and (2) the receivers should pay the second respondent's costs of the application. *Held*, it was a basic principle of receivership that the

The Finance Act 2009, Sections 101 and 102 (Machine Games Duty) (Appointed Day) Order 2013, SI 2013/67, appoints 1 February 2013 as the day on which ss 101 and 102 come into force for the purposes of machine games duty.

The Finance Act 2009, Sections 101 and 102 (Annual Tax on Enveloped Dwellings) (Appointed Day) Order 2013, SI 2013/2472, appoints 1 October 2013 as the day on which ss 101 and 102 come into force for the purposes of annual tax on enveloped dwellings and penalties assessed in relation to that tax.

For a summary of the Act, see 2009 Abr para 2498. See also the commencement table in the title STATUTES AND LEGISLATIVE PROCESS.

2148   Finance Act 2012—appointed day

The Finance Act 2012, Schedule 14 (Appointed Day) Order 2013, SI 2013/587, appoints 1 April 2012 as the day from which the 2012 Act Sch 14 Pts 2 (paras 2–11) and 3 (paras 12–20) (gifts to the nation) have effect. Savings are also made.

The Finance Act 2012, Schedule 22 (Reduction of Supplementary Charge for Certain Oil Fields) (Appointed Day) Order 2013, SI 2013/744, brings the remaining provisions of Sch 22 into force on 1 April 2013.

The Finance Act 2012, Schedule 38 (Tax Agents: Dishonest Conduct) (Appointed Day and Savings) Order 2013, SI 2013/279, appoints 1 April 2013 for the coming into force of the 2012 Act Sch 38.

For a summary of the Act, see 2012 Abr para 2160. See also the commencement table in the title STATUTES AND LEGISLATIVE PROCESS.

2149   Finance Act 2013

The Finance Act 2013 grants certain duties, alters other duties, and amends the law relating to the national debt and the public revenue, and makes further provision in connection with finance. The Act received the royal assent on 17 July 2013 and certain provisions came into force on that day. For details of commencement, see the commencement table in the title STATUTES AND LEGISLATIVE PROCESS.

Part 1 (ss 1–79) Income Tax, Corporation Tax and Capital Gains Tax

Chapter 1 (ss 1–7) Charges, rates etc
Section 1 provides for the income tax charge for 2013–14, and s 2 sets at £9,440, for 2013–14, the amount of the personal allowance for those born after 5 April 1948. The amount of the basic rate limit for income tax for 2013–14 is set by s 3 at £32,010. Section 4 sets the main rate of corporation tax for the financial year beginning 1 April 2014 at 30 per cent on oil and gas ring fence profits and at 21 per cent on non-ring fence profits. The small profits rate of corporation tax for the financial year beginning 1 April 2013 is set by s 5 at 20 per cent for all profits apart from ring fence profits of North Sea oil companies, where the rate is set at 19 per cent; the fraction used in calculating marginal relief from the main rate is set at 3/400ths for all profits apart from ring fence profits where the fraction is set at 11/400ths. The corporation tax main rate for profits other than ring fence profits is set at 20 per cent for the financial year beginning 1 April 2015: s 6. Section 7, Sch 1 introduce provisions to increase, from £25,000 to £250,000, for a temporary period of two years, the maximum amount of the annual investment allowance.

Chapter 2 (ss 8–28) Income tax: general
Section 8 provides for an exemption from income tax for non-UK resident competitors in the British Athletics London Anniversary Games held at the Olympic Stadium in London in July 2013, and s 9 provides a similar exemption in relation to non-UK resident competitors in the Glasgow 2014 Commonwealth Games. A new income tax exemption for certain travel expenses paid or reimbursed to members of the Scottish Parliament, members of the National Assembly for Wales, and members of the Legislative Assembly in Northern Ireland is introduced by s 10. An employee's exemption from income tax on pension contributions made to a registered pension scheme by his employer is restricted by s 11 so that the exemption only applies to such contributions made by an employer to the employee's arrangements under such a scheme. By virtue of s 12, tax relief for employer-supported childcare continues where a child is in receipt of a personal independence payment rather

than a disability living allowance. Universal credit is added by s 13 to the table of social security benefits that are wholly exempt from income tax. Section 14, Sch 2 amend the legislation relating to share incentive plans, Save As You Earn Option Schemes, company share option plans and enterprise management incentives in order to simplify the employee share scheme rules where they may create undue complexities or unnecessary administrative burdens for scheme users. Section 15 abolishes income tax relief for certain payments of patent royalties. Section 16, Sch 3 limit the income tax reliefs that an individual may deduct in the calculation of his income tax liability. Section 17, Sch 4 enable the profits of a trade, profession or vocation to be calculated on the cash basis; and s 18, Sch 5 enable persons carrying on a trade, profession or vocation to claim deductions for certain expenses at a fixed rate. Section 19, Sch 6 make provision enabling employees who perform employment duties in the United Kingdom and overseas to apportion on a just and reasonable basis their earnings from such employment. Provision is made by s 20, Sch 7 about the application of the remittance basis in relation to exempt property so that property which is lost, stolen or destroyed will not trigger a taxable remittance to the United Kingdom and any compensation payment relating to the loss, theft or destruction of such property will not be treated as a remittance provided such payments are taken offshore or used to make a qualifying investment within 45 days of being received; and the public access rule extends to any property which is brought to the United Kingdom and put on public display at an approved establishment or in transit to or from such display, for no more than two years or such longer period specified by Her Majesty's Revenue and Customs ('HMRC'). By virtue of s 21, certain repayments made in specified circumstances are not treated as a taxable remittance to the United Kingdom provided a sum equal to the amount repaid is taken offshore by 15 March following the end of the tax year in which that amount is repaid. Provisions applying to workers under arrangements made by intermediaries are extended by s 22 to office holders. Section 23 revises the appropriate percentage bands and carbon dioxide emissions thresholds and introduces two new bandings in respect of low emission vehicles. The rules for time apportioned reductions from gains made on life insurance policies for periods when the policyholder is resident outside the United Kingdom are extended to life insurance policies issued by United Kingdom insurers and the time-apportioned reductions will be calculated by reference to the residence history of the person liable to income tax on the gains and not by reference to the residence history of the legal owner of the policy: s 24, Sch 8. Provision is made by s 25, Sch 9 for the implementation of a new annual premium limit of £3,600 on qualifying insurance policies. A new exemption is introduced by s 26, Sch 10 in relation to the anti-avoidance legislation concerning the transfer of assets abroad for genuine transactions where EU treaty freedoms are engaged. Changes are made by s 27, Sch 11 to tax rules on deduction of income tax from interest relating to compensation payments, specialty debt and interest in kind. Provision is made by s 28, Sch 12 for the taxation as income of amounts from arrangements that produce returns that are economically equivalent to interest.

Chapter 3 (ss 29–46) Corporation tax: general
Chargeable profits of a controlled foreign company that are apportioned to a surrendering company are included in the threshold which specified amounts must exceed before group relief is available: s 29. The restrictions on when companies resident in the European Economic Area may surrender losses attributable to their United Kingdom permanent establishments as group relief from corporation tax in the United Kingdom are extended by s 30 so as to apply for EEA resident companies based on whether their losses are relieved in another country in any period, rather than on whether they could potentially be relieved in another country. A change is made by s 31 to the types of arrangements that are exempt from certain anti-avoidance rules affecting group relief. The relief available for carry forward of trading losses of a company whether a transfer of a trade occurs before or after a change in ownership of the company is restricted by s 32. The scope of the loss buying rules is extended by s 33, Sch 13 so as to restrict the availability of non-trading debits, non-trading loan relationship deficits and non-trading losses on intangible fixed assets after a change of ownership of a shell company. Section 34, Sch 14 restrict the circumstances in which deductible amounts may be brought into account where there has been a qualifying change in relation to a company. A new scheme, introduced by s 35, Sch 15, and which is initially optional but will become mandatory on 1 April 2016, enables large companies and certain small or medium-sized enterprises with sub-contracted or subsidised qualifying

research and development expenditure, to claim research and development relief as a taxable above the line credit, to the value of 10 per cent of their qualifying research and development expenditure; the credit will be fully payable, net of tax, to companies with no corporation tax liability. Section 36, Schs 16–18, introduce relief from corporation tax for television production and video games development; the credit is based on a company's qualifying expenditure on the production of a qualifying animation, high-end television programme or video game of which at least 25 per cent of the qualifying expenditure is on goods or services used or consumed in the United Kingdom and must be certified as a culturally British product to qualify for the tax credit. Section 37 ensures that certain new health service bodies will be exempt from corporation tax; and s 38 ensures that chief constables and the Commissioner of Police of the Metropolis are similarly exempt. Under s 39, Sch 19, the income from a United Kingdom real estate investment trust ('UK REIT') investing in another UK REIT may be treated as income of the investing UK REIT's tax exempt property rental business so that the property income distribution that a UK REIT receives from another UK REIT in which it invests will be tax exempt and, for the purpose of the balance of business test, the investment by a REIT in another REIT will be included as an asset of the investing REIT's property rental business; the investing REIT must distribute 100 per cent of the property income distribution received by it from investing in another REIT to its investors. The rules on availability of corporation tax deductions where companies award shares or grant share options to their employees are revised by s 40 to make it clear that, except in specified circumstances, no corporation tax deduction is available in relation to an employee share option unless shares are acquired pursuant to the option and no other corporation tax deductions should be made in cases where statutory corporation tax relief is available. Section 41 amends provisions applying to swap contracts relating to land or to an index over the value of land in order to prevent such provisions from being used to produce losses which are unrelated to real exposure to movements in property prices. Section 42, Sch 20 amend provisions relating to loan relationships and derivative contracts by blocking schemes where a company benefits from a tax advantage by creating a mismatch using a loan relationship or derivative. Section 43 prevents the payments on banks' and parent undertakings of banks' Tier Two regulatory capital debt instruments from being treated as distributions for corporation tax purposes and ensures that the issue of such instruments does not break the banks' corporate group for corporation tax group relief purposes. Changes are made by s 44 to the conditions which a company must satisfy in order to make an election for its financing expenses and financing income to be excluded from the group's debt cap computation and to how the election applies to financing expenses and financing income so that financing expense or income amounts are excluded if the company is a group treasury company during the worldwide group's period of account. One of the conditions for a company to be an investment trust is amended by s 45 so that all, or substantially all, of the company's business must be investing its funds in shares, land or other assets with the aim of spreading investment risk and giving members of the company the benefit of the results of the management of its funds. The conditions which a club must meet in order to be a registered community amateur sports club are amended by s 46, Sch 21.

Chapter 4 (ss 47–54) Pensions
A power to amend the transitional protection regime in relation to the lifetime allowance is introduced by s 47 for the purpose of ensuring that an individual does not lose fixed protection in circumstances outside his control; and a new standard lifetime allowance is introduced, and transitional provision is made, by s 48, Sch 22. Section 49 reduces the level of the annual allowance for United Kingdom tax relieved pensions for the tax year 2014–15 and subsequent tax years. By virtue of s 50, the amount of authorised pension which a drawdown pensioner may choose to receive from his registered pension scheme is increased. Under s 51, a registered pension scheme may continue to pay a bridging pension until a member reaches state pension age. Certain provisions of pensions tax legislation are repealed by s 52 in order to reflect the abolition of contracting out of the state second pension through a defined contribution pension scheme. The provisions concerning qualifying recognised overseas pension schemes are amended by s 53 in order to enable HMRC to require overseas pension schemes to provide information which is necessary to ensure the proper operation of the legislation relating to such schemes and new rules provide for when a pension scheme may be excluded from being a qualifying recognised

overseas pension scheme. Certain information and inspection powers in relation to overseas pension schemes are amended by s 54 so that they are similar to those for United Kingdom pension matters.

Chapter 5 (ss 55–79) Other provisions
By virtue of s 55, Sch 23, subject to certain conditions, gains on disposals of employee shareholder shares worth up to £50,000 on receipt will be exempt from capital gains tax and no income tax will be chargeable on the first £2,000 of share value received when an individual becomes an employee shareholder although, for corporation tax purposes, companies will be entitled to relief against the £2,000 amount where the general conditions for the relief are met. The legislation relating to the calculation of income tax liability where seed enterprise investment scheme ('SEIS') relief has been given is clarified by s 56 which amends the SEIS independence requirement in order to prevent the disqualification of off-the-shelf companies established by a corporate formation agent. The capital gains tax relief for reinvesting chargeable gains into SEIS shares is extended by s 57 to gains realised on disposals of assets in the tax year 2013–14 but only half, rather than the whole, of the qualifying reinvested amount will be able to be set against chargeable gains. Under s 58, a company may claim disincorporation relief so that no corporation tax charge arises to the company on the transfer of goodwill and interests in land to some or all of its shareholders provided that the transfer is a qualifying business transfer, defined in s 59, and takes place within the specified five-year period. A claim for disincorporation relief is to be made jointly by the company and all of the shareholders to whom the business is transferred, it is irrevocable and must be made within the period of two years of the business transfer date: s 60. Section 61 gives effect to disincorporation relief claims. An anti-avoidance provision dealing with assets held through non UK-resident closely controlled companies is modified by s 62 in order to secure compatibility with EU law by excluding from the scope of charge gains arising from assets used in genuine business activities, clarifying the treatment of furnished holiday accommodation for the purposes of the provision and raising the threshold at which the charge applies to unconnected minority participators. Section 63 extends the circumstances in which certain anti-avoidance provisions do not apply where trustees of a heritage maintenance settlement could have made an election that income arising in the year from the heritage maintenance property comprised in the settlement, which would otherwise be treated as income of the settlor, is not to be so treated, but have not made such an election, so that the provisions do not apply regardless of whether such an election has been made. Section 64, Sch 24 extend entrepreneurs' relief to the disposal by an employee or officer of a company of shares in the company or a company in the same trading group when the shares meet the requirements of the enterprise management incentives scheme and to similar disposals that take place within three years of the company ceasing to be a trading company. A charge to capital gains tax is introduced by s 65, Sch 25 on both UK and non-UK resident non-natural persons in respect of gains accruing on the disposal of interests in high value residential property that are the subject of the annual tax on enveloped dwellings. Under s 66, a company must compute its chargeable gains and losses on disposals of shares, ships, aircraft and interests in shares in the currency which is its functional currency or, if it is a UK resident investment company which has made a designated currency election, that designated currency, at the time of the disposal. Section 67 applies to Northern Ireland. Section 68 extends the 100 per cent first-year allowance for expenditure incurred on cars with low carbon dioxide emissions and electric cars, which is due to expire on 31 March 2013, for an additional two years to 31 March 2015, reduces the emission thresholds that determine the rates of capital allowances available on cars and the restriction of lease rentals and aligns the treatment of cars with other assets provided for leasing by excluding expenditure on cars provided for leasing from qualifying for first-year allowances. The scheme for 100 per cent first-year allowance for expenditure incurred on natural gas, biogas and hydrogen refuelling equipment, that was due to expire on 31 March 2013, is extended by s 69 to 31 March 2015. The general exclusions to first-year allowances for expenditure incurred on railway assets and ships are removed by s 70. Section 71, Sch 26, impose further restrictions on allowance buying. The definition of a disabled person for the purposes of a provision concerning hire cars for disabled persons is amended by s 72 to include reference to recipients of the personal independence payment and to recipients of the armed forces independence payment. The capital allowances rules for future pooling of expenditure and claims for allowances are amended by s 73 so as to confirm that

contribution allowances are available in relation to a contribution of a capital sum to capital expenditure on the provision of plant or machinery in the recipient's hands, the contributor's capital contribution being treated as capital expenditure on the provision of plant or machinery for use in the contributor's business and the contributor, not the recipient, being able to claim capital allowances. In order to ensure that the community investment tax relief scheme comes within EU rules authorising unnotified state aid if it meets de minimis criteria, s 74, Sch 27 restrict the amounts of relief that individuals and corporate investors may receive under the scheme. Section 75, Sch 28 limit lease premium relief available to a trader or intermediate landlord where a lease is of more than 50 years' duration. Schemes where part of a manufactured payment is paid in the form of an intra-group loan write-off, or other non-taxable form, to avoid tax charges which would otherwise arise on the manufactured payment, are blocked by s 76. The tax treatment of manufactured dividends for corporation tax purposes, and of all manufactured payments for income tax purposes, are amended by s 77, Sch 29, and certain rules setting out the current tax treatment of manufactured dividends and repos are repealed. Changes are made by s 78 to income tax and corporation tax provisions governing the relationship between the rules prohibiting and those allowing deductions from profits of a trade or property business so that, in cases involving tax avoidance arrangements, the order of priority in determining if a deduction is allowable will be reversed so that a prohibitive rule will have priority over a permissive rule. Section 79, Sch 30 amend provisions in relation to close companies by imposing a tax charge when close companies enter arrangements with a tax avoidance purpose and restricting the relief available to close companies in certain circumstances.

Part 2 (ss 80–93) Oil
Sums due under decommissioning relief agreements are to be paid out of money provided by Parliament (s 80) and 'decommissioning expenditure' is defined for this purpose (s 81). Section 82 requires the Treasury to make an annual report to Parliament containing information which includes an estimate of the maximum amount liable to be paid under any decommissioning relief agreement. By virtue of amendments made by s 83, no tax relief may be obtained by a company in respect of expenditure for which relief has already been obtained under a decommissioning relief agreement. Where a company with rights under such an agreement incurs decommissioning expenditure as a consequence of another company's default on a decommissioning liability, any allowable unrelievable field loss that would otherwise arise is not to be regarded as arising: s 84. There is no consequential reduction of profits by virtue of relief by way of oil allowance: s 85. Section 86 removes the charge to inheritance tax on property held in decommissioning security settlements. Under s 87, loan relationship debits and credits are not brought into account in respect of a company's loan relationships where they arise in relation to a decommissioning security settlement. The accounting period for which a deduction from profits is given is amended by s 88 so that the period is that for which an addition to profits is provided in respect of decommissioning expenditure. Section 89, Sch 31 make provision about expenditure on and under abandonment guarantees and abandonment expenditure and about calculating the profits of a ring fence trade carried on by a person who incurs expenditure on meeting another person's decommissioning liabilities. The meaning of 'general decommissioning expenditure' for plant and machinery allowances is extended by s 90 to include onshore assets used for the purposes of offshore oil and gas production. By virtue of amendments made by s 91, plant or machinery which was redundant when acquired incidentally to the acquisition of an installation is regarded as having been brought into use for the purposes of the ring fence trade so that expenditure on the decommissioning of the plant or machinery qualifies for relief. Relief is provided by s 92 under the mineral extraction allowances code for expenditure on site restoration incurred by a person who is or has been carrying on a ring fence trade. Section 93, Sch 32 make provision in connection with restrictions on allowances for certain oil-related expenditure.

Part 3 (ss 94–174) Annual tax on enveloped dwellings
A tax, called 'annual tax on enveloped dwellings', is chargeable on companies, collective investment schemes and partnerships with company members who hold UK residential dwellings valued at greater than £2m on specified valuation dates: s 94. Section 95 describes entitlement to interests for the purposes of Pt 3. The chargeable person, defined in s 96, is liable to pay the tax. Where there are one or more joint owners with a company, the

company and other person or persons are jointly and severally liable for the tax charged and, where a company is entitled to a single dwelling interest as a member of a partnership, and another person who is not a partner is jointly entitled to the single dwelling interest on the first day the responsible partners are chargeable, the person is jointly and severally liable for the tax: s 97. Under s 98, where tax is charged in relation to a single dwelling interest held for the purposes of a collective investment scheme, the persons who are major participants in the scheme on the first day in a chargeable period on which the chargeable person is within the charge to the tax are jointly and severally liable for the tax charged in relation to such interest. The amount of tax charged for a chargeable period with respect to a single-dwelling interest is stated in s 99. Interim relief may be claimed before the end of the chargeable period in specified circumstances: s 100. Section 101 provides for an indexation of annual chargeable amounts. The taxable value of a single-dwelling interest is equal to the market value on the last previous valuation date: s 102. By virtue of s 103, an acquisition or a part disposal of a chargeable interest is substantial for the purposes of s 102 only if the chargeable consideration is £40,000 or more. Tax in respect of a given single-dwelling interest is charged only once for any chargeable day even if more than one person is the chargeable person with respect to the tax charged: s 104. Under s 105, where the adjusted chargeable amount is greater than the initial charged amount, the amount of tax charged is taken to be increased at the end of the chargeable period. Where tax is charged for a chargeable period with respect to a single-dwelling interest and the adjusted chargeable amount is greater than the initial charged amount, the amount of tax charged is taken to be increased to the adjusted chargeable amount: s 106. Section 107 defines 'chargeable interest' and lists the exempt interests for these purposes; and s 108 defines 'single-dwelling interest'. Provision is made by s 109 for different interests held in the same dwelling in respect of the chargeable period, and by s 110 for interests held by connected persons. Section 111 prevents the application of s 110 to public bodies and bodies established for national purposes or to aggregate interests held by charitable companies, providers of social housing or where property is conditionally exempt from inheritance tax. Section 112 states when a building or part of a building counts as a dwelling and states that, when land such as a garden or grounds (including any buildings or structures on the land) that is or is intended to be occupied or enjoyed with the dwelling, it is to be part of the dwelling; and s 113 provides for where, in the case of a contract for the acquisition of a chargeable interest in or over land that consists of or includes a building, or part of a building, that is to be constructed or adapted for use as a single dwelling, substantial performance is treated as constituting the acquisition of the chargeable interest in the building and construction or adaptation of the building, or the part of the building, has not begun by the time the contract is substantially performed. The Treasury has power to amend the meaning of the expression 'use as a dwelling': s 114. By virtue of s 115, the fact that a part of a building is suitable for use as a dwelling does not prevent that part from forming part of a larger single dwelling. Section 116 sets out the conditions to be met for a main dwelling and an associated dwelling to be treated as a single dwelling. Sections 117, 118 provide for dwellings in the same building to be treated as linked dwellings when they meet the common ownership condition and there is private access between them; and, for these purposes, any structure (such as a terrace of houses or a pair of semi-detached houses) that is composed of or includes dwellings is regarded as a building (s 119). Section 120 provides for references to the acquisition of a chargeable interest. The effective date of acquisition or disposal of an interest in land is defined by s 121. Section 122 applies to contracts, to be completed by conveyance, to acquire a relevant chargeable interest, and s 123 to contracts, to be completed by conveyance, for disposal of such an interest. The valuation date for a new dwelling that is or has been constructed is set out in s 124. Section 125 deals with dwellings produced from other dwellings as a result of structural alteration. Sections 126–129 apply where an old dwelling is demolished without replacement (s 127) or where a new dwelling is built on the site of the old dwelling (ss 128, 129): s 126. Where a building, or any part of it, which has previously been suitable as a dwelling is then altered so as to make it unsuitable to use as a dwelling, it is a question of fact whether the alterations render it or part of it unsuitable for use as a dwelling: s 130. Section 131 applies if damage occurs to a dwelling, resulting in the dwelling becoming temporarily unsuitable for occupation as a dwelling.

Where tax is charged, in respect of a single-dwelling interest, for a chargeable period (or for more than one such period) that includes one or more days that are relievable as a result of any of s 133 (property rental businesses), s 134 (rental property: preparation for sale etc), s 137 (dwellings opened to the public), s 138 (property developers), s 139 (property developers: exchange of dwellings), s 141 (property traders), s 143 (financial institutions acquiring dwellings in the course of lending), s 145 (occupation by certain employees or partners), 148 (farmhouses), s 150 (providers of social housing), for any such period, the adjusted chargeable amount is to be calculated on the basis that the chargeable person is not within the charge with respect to the interest on any relievable day: s 132. Where, on a day in a chargeable period, a single-dwelling interest is being exploited in a property rental business or steps are being taken to exploit it, if a non-qualifying individual (defined in s 136) is permitted to occupy the dwelling, and where the continuity of ownership condition is met, no further day in that chargeable period or the subsequent three chargeable periods will be a relievable day unless and until there is a day of qualifying use: s 135. Supplementary provision is made by ss 140 (in relation to s 139), 142 (in relation to s 141), 144 (in relation to s 143), 146 (meaning of 'qualifying employer' and 'qualifying partner' in s 145), 147 (meaning of '10 per cent or greater share in a company' in s 146), and s 148 applies where on a day in a chargeable period a farmhouse forms part of land occupied for the purposes of a qualifying trade of farming, and a person carrying on the trade is entitled to, or connected with a person who is entitled to, a single-dwelling interest in the farmhouse. Section 149 defines 'farm worker' and 'former long serving farm worker'. A day in a chargeable period is, by virtue of s 151, a relievable day if a charitable company is entitled to the single dwelling interest and the interest is held for charitable purposes but relief is prohibited if a substantial donor or an associate, defined by s 152, is permitted to occupy the dwelling. Neither a public body (s 153) nor certain bodies established for national purposes (s 154) is regarded as a company for the purposes of Pt 3. If a single-dwelling interest (or a part of it) has been designated under specified provisions of the Inheritance Tax Act 1984, its taxable value is deemed to be zero: 2013 Act s 155. The Treasury has power under s 156 to amend Pt 3 to provide further reliefs or exemptions. Provision is made by s 157 for alternative property finance arrangements entered into between a financial institution and another person, where the institution purchases one or more dwellings.

The Commissioners for HMRC are responsible for the collection and management of annual tax on enveloped dwellings: s 158. Under s 159, a person is required to make a return within a specified period with respect to an interest he holds in a dwelling for a chargeable period and, under s 160, a further return is required if liability for the year is altered by an event after the end of the year if the adjusted chargeable amount is greater than the amount initially charged, when no interim relief has been claimed, and a claim or claims to interim relief have been made and the adjusted chargeable amount is greater than the amount payable. A return under s 158 or 159 must include a self-assessment: s 161. Provision is made by s 162, Sch 33 about returns, inquiries and related matters. The tax charged must be paid by the required date: s 163. Section 164, Sch 34 make provision for information and inspection powers and penalties. Section 165 makes provision for the collection of annual tax on enveloped dwellings, s 166 defines 'company' and s 167 defines 'partnership', for the purposes of Pt 3. Section 168, Sch 35 make miscellaneous amendments and transitory provision about the chargeable period beginning on 1 April 2013. Provision is made by s 169 for the making of orders and regulations under Pt 3. Section 170 defines 'chargeable day' and 'within the charge' with respect to a single-dwelling interest for the purposes of Pt 3. For those purposes, a state of affairs obtaining on a particular day is assumed to have existed throughout the day: s 171. References to connected persons and which persons are connected with a collective investment scheme are to be determined in accordance with s 172, and which person is to be treated as connected to a cell company is to be determined in accordance with s 173. Section 174 provides for the interpretation of Pt 3.

Part 4 (ss 175–205) Excise duties and other taxes
Under s 175, trustees may switch United Kingdom assets held in settlement made by non-UK domiciled individuals to investments in open-ended investment companies and authorised unit trusts without incurring inheritance tax. Restrictions and conditions that must be met before a liability is allowed as a deduction from the value of an estate for inheritance tax purposes are introduced by s 176, Sch 36. Under s 177, an individual who is not domiciled in the United Kingdom but who is, or has been, married to, or in a civil partnership with, a person who is domiciled in the United Kingdom may elect to be treated

as domiciled in the United Kingdom for inheritance tax purposes. The lifetime limit on transfers from one United Kingdom domiciled spouse or civil partner to another not so domiciled that are exempt from inheritance tax is increased by s 178.

The rates of duty and rates of rebate on products charged to duty under the Hydrocarbon Oil Duties Act 1979 are revised so that increases in duties provided by the Finance Act 2011 will not become payable: 2013 Act s 179. Increases are made by s 180 in the rates of excise duty charged on spirits, wine and made-wine, and cider and perry, and there is an overall reduction in the rates of excise duty on beer. The rates of excise duty on tobacco products are revised by s 181 and, by s 182, the general exemption granted to herbal smoking products is granted only to products used exclusively for medical purposes. Section 183 increases the gross gaming yield bands for gaming duty, and s 184 defines the payments that may be taken into account for the purpose of calculating the duty liability from combined bingo and makes amendments enabling bingo promoters in the United Kingdom to offer games in conjunction with promoters outside the United Kingdom without affecting their own bingo duty liability. The reduced and standard rates of air passenger duty to certain destinations are increased (s 185) and special accounting arrangements may be made in relation to annual accounting and to specify the detail of such arrangements in regulations (s 186). Certain rates of vehicle excise duty are increased (s 187) and a 14-day period of grace for not exhibiting a newly issued tax disc within a vehicle is introduced (s 188). Section 189 removes the requirement to renew annually a statutory off-road notification in order for a vehicle to remain appropriately covered. By virtue of s 190, Sch 37, a 50 per cent discount to rates of vehicle excise duty is given to persons receiving the standard mobility component of personal independence payment, and a complete exemption is given to those receiving either the enhanced mobility component of personal independence payment or the armed forces independence payment. The National Health Service Commissioning Board, clinical commissioning groups, the Health and Social Care Information Centre and the National Institute for Health and Care Excellence are added by s 191 to the list of bodies within the definition of government departments which may claim refunds of the value added tax they pay on certain goods and services. Section 192, Sch 38 make provision about the valuation of certain supplies of fuel for the purposes of VAT. The scope of the legislation relating to the reduced VAT rate for the installation of energy-saving materials to residential accommodation is reduced by s 193, and buildings intended for use solely for a relevant charitable purpose are removed. Section 194 makes it clear that certain types of stamp duty land tax avoidance schemes involving an onward sale (ie a subsale or other transfer of rights) which is not to be completed for a number of years are ineffective. Relief for intermediate purchasers where rights under a land transaction are transferred by way of an assignment of rights and/or qualifying subsale is retained by s 195, Sch 39, by virtue of which the end purchaser is charged with stamp duty land tax, the types of transactions that qualify for relief are specified and the legislation is clarified to protect against avoidance schemes which seek to circumvent the stamp duty land tax charge. Provision is made by s 196, Sch 40 for a number of reliefs from the higher rate of stamp duty land tax. Section 197, Sch 41 make special provision for stamp duty land tax on certain types of lease transactions so as to abolish the rules on abnormal rent increases and simplify the reporting requirements where a lease continues after the expiry of its fixed term and where an agreement for a lease is substantially performed before the actual lease itself is granted.

The standard rate of landfill tax for disposals of waste made or treated as made on or after 1 April 2014 is increased (s 198) and the rates of climate change levy are increased with effect from 1 April 2014 (s 199). Section 200, Sch 42 provide for the introduction of the carbon price floor in Great Britain, as it applies to coal and other solid fossil fuels, gas and liquefied petroleum gas used in most forms of electricity generation. Under s 201, insurance premium tax reliefs which apply to vehicles used by persons who are in receipt of the mobility component of a disability living allowance also apply to vehicles used by persons who receive the mobility component of a personal independence payment or receive an armed forces independence payment

The rates at which the bank levy is charged are amended from 1 January 2013 (s 202) and from 1 January 2014 (s 203). Recharges of the bank levy are not an allowable deduction for the purposes of income tax and corporation tax whether recharged directly or via a third party and foreign bank levies are not an allowable deduction for the purposes of income tax or corporation tax: s 205.

Part 5 (ss 206–215) General anti-abuse rule
Part 5 has effect for the purpose of counteracting tax advantages arising from tax arrangements that are abusive and it applies to income tax, corporation tax including amounts chargeable/treated as corporation tax, capital gains tax, petroleum revenue tax, inheritance tax, stamp duty land tax and annual tax on enveloped dwellings; the rules of Pt 5 are collectively to be known as the general anti-abuse rule ('GAAR'): s 206. Section 207 defines 'tax arrangements' and 'abusive'; s 208 defines 'tax advantage'. Section 209 explains that the tax advantages arising from abusive tax arrangements are to be counteracted by the making of just and reasonable adjustments, whether in respect of the tax in question or any other tax to which the GARR applies, and tax is to be charged in accordance with any adjustment that imposes or increases a liability to tax; and the procedural requirements set out in Sch 43 must be complied with before any such adjustments are made by an officer of HMRC. The process by which consequential relieving adjustments may be made are set out in s 210; and information relating to proceedings before a court or tribunal are set out in s 211. By virtue of s 212, any priority rule has effect subject to the GARR (despite the terms of the priority rule (ie a rule (however expressed) to the effect that particular provisions have effect to the exclusion of, or otherwise in priority to, anything else)). Consequential amendment is made by s 213 to certain administrative provisions so that procedural requirements relating to certain claims do not apply to consequential adjustment claims under the GAAR. Section 214 provides for the interpretation of Pt 5, and s 215 provides for the commencement of the GARR and makes transitional provision in relation to it.

Part 6 (ss 216–234) Other provisions
Section 216, Sch 44 make provision about trusts which have a vulnerable beneficiary so that, in particular, for the purposes of defining a vulnerable beneficiary trust, a disabled person includes an individual in receipt of personal independence payment by virtue of entitlement to the daily living component, and rules limiting how the capital and income of such trusts may be applied are harmonised. Power is conferred on the Treasury by s 217 to make provision by regulations about the treatment of the trustees or unit holders of unauthorised unit trusts for the purposes of income tax, corporation tax, capital gains tax or stamp duty land tax. Section 218, Sch 45, introduce a statutory residence test for determining an individual's residence for tax purposes; and s 219, Sch 46, make provision removing or replacing rules relating to ordinary residence. Amendments to the controlled foreign companies regime in the Taxation (International and Other Provisions) Act 2010 are made: 2013 Act s 220, Sch 47. The UK-Swiss Confederation Taxation Co-operation Agreement set out in the Finance Act 2012 Sch 36 is amended so that certain transfers made under the Agreement will not give rise to a taxable remittance where they are made by a person who is taxed on the remittance basis: 2013 Act s 221. Power is conferred on the Treasury by s 222 to make regulations for, or in connection with, giving effect to, or enabling effect to be given to, international agreements to improve tax compliance. Section 223 adds new information provisions relating to the disclosure of tax avoidance schemes. Certain powers under the Proceeds of Crime Act 2002 concerning the recovery of cash in summary proceedings and investigations are extended by the 2013 Act s 224, Sch 48, so that they may be exercised by an officer of HMRC in respect of a limited number of functions when such officer is exercising a function which is not an excluded matter. The definition of 'goods' for certain customs purposes (s 225) and provisions as to detention, seizure and condemnation of goods etc (s 226) are amended. The level of financial penalties that may be imposed by HMRC on larger ships where a responsible officer has been complicit or negligent in respect of customs or excise offences committed on board his ship is increased: s 227. Section 228 amends HMRC data-gathering powers, and s 229, Sch 49 make provision for, and in connection with, deferring the payment by a company of certain corporation tax in circumstances where income, profits or gains arise. Section 230, Sch 50, make provision for, and in connection with, penalties for late filing, late payment and errors. The overpayment relief provision for income tax and capital gains tax that restricted the provision if the tax overpaid was charged contrary to EU law is removed: s 231. By virtue of s 232, the time limit for claims to relief for tax which has been over assessed as a result of a mistake in a return runs from the tax year or chargeable period to which the mistake relates. Section 233, Sch 51 confer power on HMRC to withdraw a notice to file a self-assessment tax return (individual, partnership and trustee) on request in certain circumstances and

provide for cancelling liability to a penalty where a notice is withdrawn. Section 234 imposes restrictions on interim payments in proceedings relating to taxation matters.

Part 7 (ss 235, 236) Final provisions
Section 235 provides for interpretation, and s 236 for the short title, of the Act.

2150 Inheritance tax

See INHERITANCE TAXATION.

2151 Stamp duties

See STAMP TAXES.

2152 Supply and Appropriation (Anticipation and Adjustments) Act 2013

The Supply and Appropriation (Anticipation and Adjustments) Act 2013 authorises the use of resources for the service of the year ending with 31 March 2014. The Act received royal assent 26 March 2013 and came into force on that day. The amount up to which there is authorisation for the use of those resources is, for current purposes £216,006,686,000, and for capital purposes £21,552,454,000. The amount up to which the Treasury has authorisation to issue money out of the Consolidated Fund, and apply it to the year ending with 31 March 2014, is £209,612,302,000.

2153 Supply and Appropriation (Main Estimates) Act 2013

The Supply and Appropriation (Main Estimates) Act 2013 authorises the use of resources for the service of the year ending with 31 March 2014. The Act received royal assent on 17 July 2013 and came into force on that day. The amount up to which there is authorisation for use of those resources is increased by £272,996,671,000. The amount up to which the Treasury has authorisation to issue sums out of the Consolidated Fund, and to apply in the year ending 31 March 2014 is increased by £244,640,963,000.

2154 Tax law rewrite Acts—unintended changes—amendment

The Tax Law Rewrite Acts (Amendment) Order 2013, SI 2013/463 (in force on 1 April 2013), makes amendments to the Inheritance Tax Act 1984, the Local Government Finance Act 1988, the Finance Act 1990, the Taxation of Chargeable Gains Act 1992, the Finance Act 1994 and the Income Tax (Trading and Other Income) Act 2005 in consequence of certain provisions rewritten in the Corporation Tax Act 2010 and the Taxation (International and Other Provisions) Act 2010, so as to undo unintended changes to the operation of group relief from corporation tax and the operation of two limitations on the available total profits of a company against which relief may be claimed.

2155 Value added tax

See VALUE ADDED TAX.

RIGHTS AND FREEDOMS

Halsbury's Laws of England (5th edn) vol 88A (2013) paras 1–660

Articles

For articles relating to this title please refer to the Table of Articles at the beginning of the Abridgment.

2156 Data protection

See CONFIDENCE AND INFORMATIONAL PRIVACY.

2157 European Convention on Human Rights—jurisdiction—extraterritorial application—degree of control and authority—funding of legal representation

The European Convention on Human Rights art 1 provides that contracting states must secure to everyone within their jurisdiction the rights and freedoms contained in arts 2–18.

The claimant, a British national, was convicted in Indonesia of drug-trafficking offences and sentenced to death. She brought proceedings seeking judicial review of the defendant Secretary of State's policy not to fund legal representation for British nationals facing the death penalty abroad. The claimant contended that, through the activities of the Foreign and Commonwealth Office and its officials in connection with her case, she fell within the 'jurisdiction' of the United Kingdom for the purpose of the European Convention on Human Rights art 1 and the Secretary of State was in breach of art 6. She further contended that the Secretary of State's policy never to fund legal representation in death penalty cases was irrational. Her application was dismissed and she appealed. *Held*, the acts and omissions of diplomatic and consular agents would only bring an individual within the 'jurisdiction' of the United Kingdom where those acts and omissions came within the scope of control and authority by the state in question. The acts of diplomatic and consular agents might amount to an act of jurisdiction when those agents exerted authority and control over others, but their mere involvement would not be sufficient. Whether the involvement amounted to the exercise of control and authority was a question of fact and degree. However, in circumstances where the individual was completely under the control of and detained by the foreign state, it was difficult to see how the necessary degree of authority and control could be exercised by diplomatic and consular agents. Where a policy was made in the exercise of prerogative or common law powers, as opposed to a statutory discretion, there was no rule of law which required the decision-maker to consider the facts of every case with a view to deciding whether, exceptionally, to depart from the policy in a particular case. In the present case, the practical problems associated with funding legal advice or representation for British nationals facing criminal proceedings abroad demonstrated that the policy was not irrational. Accordingly, the appeal would be dismissed.

R (on the application of Sandiford) v Secretary of State for Foreign and Commonwealth Affairs [2013] EWCA Civ 581, [2013] 3 All ER 757 (Court of Appeal: Lord Dyson MR, Elias and Patten LJJ). Application 55721/07 *Al Skeini v United Kingdom* (2011) 30 BHRC 561 (2011 Abr para 1402), ECtHR, applied. *R (on the application of Elias) v Secretary of State for Defence* [2006] EWCA Civ 1293, [2006] 1 WLR 3213, [2006] IRLR 934 (2006 Abr para 2947) considered. Decision of Queen's Bench Divisional Court [2013] EWHC 168 (Admin), [2013] All ER (D) 122 (Feb) affirmed.

2158   Freedom of assembly—demonstration—Parliament—authorisation

See *R (on the application of Gallastegui) v Westminster City Council*, para 656.

2159   Freedom of expression—injunction to restrain publication—breach of undertaking not to publish

See *McCann v Bennett*, para 518.

2160   Freedom of expression—restrictions—political advertising—television advertisement

The applicant was a non-governmental organisation that campaigned against the use of animals in commerce, science and leisure. It sought to achieve changes in law and public policy and to influence public and parliamentary opinion to that end. The applicant wished to screen a television advertisement as part of a campaign against the keeping and exhibition of primates and their use in television advertising. The Broadcast Advertising Clearance Centre ('BACC') refused to clear the advertisement on the basis that its transmission would breach the prohibition on political advertising in the Communications Act 2003 s 321(2). The BACC's decision was upheld on appeal. On a complaint by the applicant that the statutory prohibition of paid political advertising on television and radio was too wide to be proportionate, *held*, in order to determine the proportionality of a general measure, the legislative choices underlying it had to be assessed. The quality of the parliamentary and judicial review of the necessity of the measure was of particular importance in that respect. It was also relevant to take into account the risk of abuse if a general measure were to be relaxed. The more convincing the general justifications for the measure were, the less importance the court would attach to its impact in a particular case. The core issue was whether, in adopting the measure and striking the balance it did, the legislature acted within the margin of appreciation afforded to it. Access to alternative media was key to the proportionality of a restriction on access to other potentially useful media. The reasons adduced to justify the prohibition in the present case had to be both relevant and sufficient and the interference had to correspond to a pressing social need and be proportionate to the legitimate aim pursued. In the circumstances, the reviews of the ban by both parliamentary and judicial bodies were exacting and pertinent. The prohibition was specifically circumscribed to address the precise risk of distortion the state sought to avoid with the minimum impairment of the right of expression. The ban only applied to advertising and the applicant had access to alternative media. Further, the lack of European consensus on how to regulate paid political advertising in broadcasting broadened the margin of appreciation to be accorded as regards restrictions on public interest expression. Overall, the reasons given for the prohibition of the advertisement were relevant and sufficient. The prohibition was not therefore a disproportionate interference with the applicant's right to freedom of expression and there was no violation of the European Convention on Human Rights art 10.

Application 48876/08 *Animal Defenders International v United Kingdom* [2013] All ER (D) 21 (May) (European Court of Human Rights). For earlier related proceedings see *R (on the application of Animal Defenders International) v Secretary of State for Culture, Media and Sport* [2008] UKHL 15, [2008] 1 AC 1312, [2008] 3 All ER 193 (2008 Abr para 1735).

2161   Freedom of religion—hoteliers—beliefs—refusal to let double-bedded rooms to unmarried couples—sexual orientation discrimination

See *Hall v Bull*, para 878.

2162   Freedom of religion—practice or observance of religious belief—compulsory value added tax filing—exemption

See *Blackburn (t/a Cornish Moorland Honey)*, para 2558.

2163   Freedom of religion—practice or observance of religious belief—employment—requirement to work Sunday

The claimant, a practising Christian, worked as a care assistant in a children's home run by the defendant authority. A dispute arose as to whether she would be required to work on Sundays. Disciplinary proceedings were commenced against her when she refused to do so. Later, she resigned. She commenced proceedings in an employment tribunal, alleging constructive unfair dismissal and indirect religious discrimination. The tribunal identified the relevant provision, criterion or practice as the requirement that staff worked Sunday shifts. It found that it was necessary to weigh the discriminatory impact of the criteria on the claimant. While the criteria had impacted on her genuinely and deeply held religious belief, the defendant had made efforts to accommodate her in that respect for two years and had been prepared to organise shifts so that she was able to attend church every Sunday. It further found that the claimant's belief, that no paid employment should be carried out on Sundays, was not a core component of the Christian faith, and that the imposition of the criteria had been proportionate and the claim of indirect discrimination failed. The claimant appealed unsuccessfully to the Employment Appeal Tribunal. On further appeal, *held*, the fact that the defendant had made efforts to accommodate the claimant had been irrelevant factors to consider in the proportionality exercise. Equally, the fact that the defendant would accommodate church worship was no answer to the claim that it should accommodate her genuinely held belief that she ought not to work on Sunday. While those factors showed that the defendant had been acting in good faith and had gone some way towards meeting her concerns, the issue had been whether it had gone far enough, and those factors did not help in answering that question. The question was whether the tribunal had been entitled to take into account the fact that the refusal to work on Sunday was not a core component of the Christian faith. Were the case to be considered purely as a domestic law indirect discrimination case, independently of considerations about the European Convention on Human Rights art 9, it would at least indirectly be a legitimate factor for the tribunal to consider. Therefore, an evaluation of the impact had to include its extent. The tribunal ought not to have taken into account the fact that the claimant's refusal to work on Sunday had not been a core component of her faith. Furthermore, the protection of freedom of religion conferred by art 9 did not require a claimant to establish any group disadvantage, the question was whether the interference of that individual right by the employer was proportionate given the legitimate aims of the employer. Domestic law had to be read so as to be consistent with Convention rights where possible. It was simply not possible to read down the concept of indirect discrimination to ignore the need to establish group disadvantage. But there was no reason why the concept of justification should not be read compatibly with art 9 where that provision was in play. In that context it did not matter whether the claimant was disadvantaged along with others, and it could not in any way weaken her case with respect to justification that her beliefs were not more widely shared or did not constitute a core belief of any particular religion. It was the art 9 part of the case that made it inappropriate for the tribunal, when assessing justification, to weigh in the employer's favour the fact that the appellant's religious belief was not a core belief of her religion so that any group impact was limited. However, that had been a peripheral part of the proportionality analysis of the tribunal and not materially affected its conclusion. Accordingly, the appeal would be dismissed.

Mba v Merton LBC [2013] EWCA Civ 1562, [2014] 1 All ER 1235 (Court of Appeal: Maurice Kay VP, Elias and Vos LJJ). Applications 48420/10, 59842/10, 51671/10 and 36516/10 *Eweida v United Kingdom* [2013] IRLR 231, ECtHR (para 2165); and *Homer v Chief Constable of West Yorkshire Police* [2012] UKSC 15, [2012] 3 All ER 1287 (2012 Abr para 907) applied.

2164 Freedom of religion—right to manifest religious beliefs—persecution—establishing refugee status

See Cases C-71/11 and C-99/11 *Germany v Y; Germany v Z*, para 1456.

2165 Freedom of religion—right to manifest religious beliefs—workplace— proportionality of restriction—balance between competing Convention rights

The four applicants were Christians who had brought cases claiming that their right to manifest their religion pursuant to the European Convention on Human Rights art 9 had been contravened. The first applicant worked for an airline in a customer-facing role and for several years had worn a cross at work concealed under her uniform. After she started wearing the cross openly, as a sign of her commitment to her faith, her manager asked her to remove or conceal it. She refused. She was offered administrative work without customer contact, which would not have required her to wear a uniform, but she rejected the offer. The first applicant brought a claim before an employment tribunal for indirect discrimination contrary to the Employment Equality (Religion or Belief) Regulations 2003, SI 2003/1660, reg 3. The tribunal dismissed her claim, finding that the airline's uniform policy had not put Christians generally at a disadvantage as the visible wearing of a cross was the first applicant's personal choice rather than a requirement of the Christian faith, and there was no evidence of any complaint by any of the airline's other 30,000 uniformed employees. The second applicant also wished to wear a cross in a visible fashion while performing her duties as a nurse on a hospital ward, but was prevented from doing so on health and safety grounds. Her complaint to an employment tribunal of both direct and indirect discrimination was dismissed on grounds that, on the facts, there had been no discrimination and, in any event, the policy against wearing jewellery was proportionate. In the third case, the applicant was a registrar of births, deaths and marriages. After the Civil Partnership Act 2004 came into force, despite not being required to do so, the local authority responsible for the third applicant designated all of its registrars as civil partnership registrars. Although the authority initially permitted her to make informal arrangements to avoid conducting civil partnership ceremonies, it later told her that her refusal could put her in breach of its code of conduct and its equality and diversity policy. The third applicant's complaint to an employment tribunal was successful but overturned on appeal on the ground that the authority had acted proportionately in achieving the legitimate aim of providing the registrar service on a non-discriminatory basis. The fourth applicant believed that homosexual activity was sinful. He worked for a private organisation which provided a confidential sex therapy and relationship counselling service. A dispute arose over whether he was prepared to work on sexual issues with homosexual couples. He was dismissed for gross misconduct because his employer did not trust him to comply with its policy of not discriminating on the ground of sexual orientation. The fourth applicant complained to an employment tribunal of direct and indirect discrimination. The tribunal dismissed his complaint on the basis that the dismissal was not because of his faith but rather because his employer believed that he would not comply with its policies and that a commitment to equality was fundamental to the organisation's work. *Held*, in cases involving restrictions placed by employers on an employee's ability to observe religious practice, the possibility of the employee resigning from the job and changing employment should be weighed in the overall balance when considering whether the restriction was proportionate. The state had a certain margin of appreciation in deciding whether and to what extent an interference was necessary, particularly when it came to striking a balance between competing Convention rights. In the first applicant's case, the refusal by the airline to allow her to remain in her post while visibly wearing a cross amounted to an interference with her right to manifest her religion. On the facts, a fair balance had not been struck between the first applicant's desire to manifest her religion and the airline's desire to project a certain corporate image. The cross was discreet and could not have detracted from her professional appearance, and there was no evidence that the wearing of other, previously authorised, items of religious clothing, such as turbans and hijabs, by other employees, had had any negative effect on the airline's corporate image. In those circumstances, the state's failure to protect the first applicant's right to manifest her religion breached the positive requirement of art 9. By contrast, the requirement in the second case for the applicant to remove the cross on health grounds was proportionate in view of the protection of health and safety on a hospital ward. With regard to the third applicant, the requirement that all registrars be designated as civil partnership registrars had a particularly detrimental impact on her because of her religious beliefs. Set against this was the consideration that same-sex couples were in a relevantly similar situation to different-sex couples as regards their need for legal recognition and protection of their relationship, though as a developing area contracting states enjoyed a wide margin of appreciation in the way in which that might be achieved. The local authority's policy therefore pursued a legitimate aim. The strength of the third applicant's religious convictions had to be balanced against the rights of others which were also protected under the Convention. In the circumstances, the authority had not exceeded the wide margin available to it in striking a balance between competing Convention rights. The most important factor in the fourth applicant's case was that the employer's action was intended to secure the implementation of its policy of providing a service without discrimination. In all the circumstances, the authorities had not exceeded their wide margin of appreciation in deciding where to strike the balance between the applicant's right and the employer's interest in securing the rights of others.

Applications 48420/10, 59842/10, 51671/10 and 36516/10 *Eweida v United Kingdom* [2013] IRLR 231 (European Court of Human Rights). For previous proceedings see *Eweida v British Airways plc* [2010] EWCA Civ 80, [2010] IRLR 322 (2010 Abr para 996).

2166   Freedom of thought—harassment of suspected terrorist—injunction

The Human Rights Act 1998 s 12(1), (3) provides that any relief which, if granted, might affect the exercise of the right under the European Convention on Human Rights art 9 to freedom of thought must not be granted so as to restrain publication before trial unless the court is satisfied that the applicant is likely to establish that publication should not be allowed.

The claimants were the wife and children of a man ('the suspect') who was believed to be involved in terrorist activities although he had never been convicted of an offence. Two of the five children were aged under 16. The suspect was released from custody under bail conditions to reside with his family in London. Since his release, the claimants had been subjected to a sustained campaign of protests directly outside their home by individuals apparently affiliated with the defendants, which were nationalist organisations. Such protests had involved, among other things, demonstrators knocking on the door of the property and shouting racist abuse through megaphones. There was also evidence that demonstrators had stopped passersby to tell them that terrorists lived in the property. The claimants successfully applied for an injunction preventing the defendants from harassing the claimants within a prescribed distance of the property and an injunction restraining the defendants from disclosing personal matters in relation to the claimants, including their names, residential address, images of them or the address of any school attended by them. The claimants applied to continue the injunctions, submitting that, while the demonstrations took place, they were effectively prisoners in their own home. The defendants submitted that their protests were lawful and that the continuation of the injunctions would infringe their rights to freedom of thought, under the Convention art 9, and to freedom of expression, under art 10. Consideration was also given to the Protection from Harassment Act 1997 and the 1998 Act s 12. *Held*, each of the Convention rights had to be considered in the light of the associated reservations. The defendants were unable to rely on art 9 because freedom of thought, conscience and religion was awarded subject to limitations provided by law, for example in the 1997 Act. In relation to the Convention art 10, the court was satisfied that the threshold set in the 1998 Act s 12(3) would be likely to be reached. Moreover, the claimants' private information was protected by their right to a private life under the Convention art 8, and the court was satisfied that the exception in art 10 in relation to the protection of the rights of others was overwhelming and that the balancing exercise leaned towards non-disclosure. It was therefore appropriate for both injunctions to remain in force. Accordingly, the applications would be allowed.

The wife and children of Omar Othman v English National Resistance [2013] All ER (D) 290 (Feb) (Queen's Bench Division: Silber J).

2167   Human rights claim—proceedings against public authority—child at children's home—victim attacked by child on supervised visit—liability of local authority

The defendant local authority had assumed care responsibilities for a child under the Children Act 1989 s 20 and placed him in a children's home. In its monthly reports to the defendant, the home noted that the child's behaviour was a concern, but did not suggest that the placement was not appropriate. He was taken on an escorted trip from which he absconded. The child and two others encountered the claimant and his girlfriend who were both 13 years old. The claimant was severely beaten and left unconscious, and his girlfriend was repeatedly raped. The child was subsequently convicted of causing grievous bodily harm with intent and of rape. A claim made through the Criminal Injuries Compensation Authority was accepted in principle, though the award was subject to a maximum cap. Over seven years later, in the erroneous belief that the limitation period had not yet expired but was about to expire, the claimant brought a claim against the defendant under the Human Rights Act 1998 for breaching his rights under the European Convention on Human Rights art 8. *Held*, although the claim had been presented as a claim under art 8, on the facts it was in essence a claim under art 3 and, arguably, art 2. Whether framed as a breach of his rights under art 3 or art 8, the threshold of risk had to be the same; a real and immediate risk of serious harm to the claimant had to be identified. The risk manifesting itself was 'real' but it was not 'immediate'. More pertinently, however, it had not been a risk specific to the claimant; it had been a risk to the public in general. Further, the defendant could not be regarded as being vicariously liable for the acts and omissions of the home. While a local authority owed continuing obligations in relation to strategic/policy decisions relating to looked-after children, it could cede day-to-day decisions of an operational nature to an appropriate children's home unless facts had been drawn to the authority's attention that would merit an intervention in those operational decisions. The decision to allow the child out of the home on the day in question had been an operational decision for the home and not a decision for the defendant. Finally, in all the circumstances, it would not be equitable to extend the one-year limitation period specified by the 1998 Act s 7. By specifying a one-year limitation period rather than the ordinary three-year common law limitation period, the legislature had clearly intended that claims under the 1998 Act should be dealt with swiftly and economically. There had been a number of periods of apparent delay that had not been explained. The whole tempo had been dictated by the erroneous belief that the limitation period did not expire until the claimant's twenty-first birthday. It was also relevant to take into account the fact that a claim under the Criminal Injuries Compensation Scheme had been accepted. Accordingly, the claim would be dismissed.

Bedford v Bedfordshire CC [2013] EWHC 1717 (QB), [2014] LGR 44 (Queen's Bench Division: Jay J). Application 23452/94 *Osman v United Kingdom* [1999] 1 FLR 193, ECtHR (1998 Abr para 1801), applied.

2168   Human rights claim—sanctions—restrictive measures against named individuals

See Case T-383/11 *Makhlouf v Council of the European Union*, para 2678.

2169   Prohibition of human trafficking—status of 'victim'—reasonable grounds for belief that claimant was victim of trafficking

The claimant, a Nigerian national, sought asylum in the United Kingdom or, alternatively, the right to remain on humanitarian or human rights grounds. The defendant certified the claimant's asylum claims as clearly unfounded pursuant to the Nationality, Immigration and Asylum Act 2002 s 94, with the result that she would be removed to Nigeria with a right to bring only an out-of-country appeal. The defendant considered whether there were reasonable grounds for believing that the claimant had been the victim of human trafficking in accordance with a policy document which provided guidance to the competent authorities. She decided that the claimant had been the 'victim' of trafficking, but that she was no longer a victim of trafficking in need of protection under the Convention on Action against Trafficking in Human Beings. The decision contained a statement that, as there was no evidence that the claimant had made a complaint to the police or that there was any on-going police investigation, the claimant was not required a period of leave in the United Kingdom to co-operate with police inquiries. Following her removal to Nigeria, the claimant sought an order quashing the decision and a declaration that she was a 'victim' of trafficking. It fell to be determined whether the guidance was unlawful because it misinterpreted arts 4 and 10(2), whether the decision was unlawful and whether there had been a failure by the UK Border Agency to take proper steps to initiate an effective investigation into the offence of trafficking of the claimant. *Held*, the present tense was used in art 4(e) in the sense that the person concerned had attained the status of 'victim' of trafficking because she was someone who was or had been the subject of any form of trafficking as defined in art 4(a). There was no further qualification to the meaning of 'victim'. It followed that the passages of the guidance relied on by the defendant concerning reasonable grounds consideration were based on a misinterpretation of the Trafficking Convention. Properly construed, art 10(2) provided that, once there were reasonable grounds for believing that a claimant had the status of a victim of trafficking, he could not be removed until the identification process as a victim of an offence provided for in art 18 had been completed. As the guidance had wrongly interpreted arts 4 and 10(2), the decision had been based on an erroneous policy as set out in the guidance and had been unlawful. Therefore, the decision would be quashed and a declaration would be made that there had been reasonable grounds for believing that the claimant had been the victim of human trafficking. The Agency had failed in its duty to initiate or trigger an effective investigation by the police into the offence that had been committed against the claimant in respect of her trafficking into the United Kingdom. There was an indirect connection between this failure and the decision, in that one of the reasons for the conclusion that there had been no reasonable grounds for believing that the claimant had been a victim in need of protection under the Trafficking Convention had been that she had made no complaint to the police and so there had been no police investigation. A further declaration would be made that the claimant's right under the European Convention on Human Rights art 4 to an effective investigation had been breached. Judgment would be given accordingly.

R (*on the application of Atamewan*) *v Secretary of State for the Home Department* [2013] EWHC 2727 (Admin), [2013] All ER (D) 61 (Sep) (Queen's Bench Division: Aikens LJ and Silber J).

2170   Prohibition of human trafficking—trafficking people for exploitation—protection of complainants

See para 665.

2171   Right to fair and public hearing—care proceedings—care and placement orders— mental capacity of parent

The applicant, who had learning difficulties, had a child which was born prematurely and suffered significant health problems. A local authority commenced care proceedings following concerns about the applicant's ability to care for the child. The applicant's solicitor became concerned that the applicant was unable to understand the advice she was being given in respect of the proceedings and a psychologist was instructed, who concluded that the applicant would find it very difficult to understand the advice given by her solicitor and would not be able to make informed decisions on the basis of that advice. The Official Solicitor formally consented to act as the applicant's guardian ad litem. The local authority subsequently recommended that the child be adopted outside the family and, following a hearing, care and placement orders were made in respect of the child. The applicant's appeal against the orders was dismissed by the Court of Appeal and she was refused leave to appeal to the House of Lords. The applicant complained to the European Court of Human Rights that the appointment of the Official Solicitor to act as her litigation friend violated her right to a fair trial under the European Convention on Human Rights art 6(1) because the decision on whether she had litigation capacity had not been fully tested by a court and she had not had a full opportunity to challenge that decision. *Held,* the decision to appoint the Official Solicitor had only been taken after the applicant had been thoroughly assessed by a psychologist and, while there was no formal review procedure, in practice further assessment had been made of the applicant's litigation capacity in the course of the proceedings. Adequate safeguards had been in place to ensure that the nature of the proceedings had been fully explained to the applicant and, had she sought to challenge the appointment of the Official Solicitor, procedures had been in place to enable her to do so. While the procedures set out by the Official Solicitor fell short of a formal right of appeal, in view of the finding that the applicant lacked litigation capacity, they would have afforded her an appropriate and effective means by which to challenge the appointment or the continued need for the appointment of the Official Solicitor. Further, in the course of the proceedings in the Court of Appeal the applicant had been afforded ample opportunity to put her views before the court, and her arguments had been fully addressed in the court's judgment. The very essence of the applicant's right of access to a court had not been impaired and there had been no violation of her rights under art 6(1).

Application 38245/08 *RP v United Kingdom* [2013] 2 FCR 77 (European Court of Human Rights).

2172   Right to fair and public hearing—care proceedings—care order—application for judicial review by mother

See *R (on the application of CB) v Sheffield CC,* para 1634.

2173   Right to fair and public hearing—care proceedings—child habitually resident abroad—jurisdiction of court

See *Re B (a child) (care order: jurisdiction),* para 214.

2174   Right to fair and public hearing—care proceedings—judge visiting private residence

See *AMV v RM (children: judge's visit to private home),* para 176.

2175   Right to fair and public hearing—company proceedings—private hearing—necessity

See *Global Torch Ltd v Apex Global Management Ltd; Apex Global Management Ltd v Fi Call Ltd,* para 315.

2176   Right to fair and public hearing—criminal proceedings—murder charge—undue delay in bringing prosecution

Scotland
The appellants were convicted of a number of sexual offences, including offences against a minor, and sentenced to a period of imprisonment. They were later questioned under caution about the disappearance of the victim of a murder. Both appellants gave 'no comment' interviews and were not arrested or charged during or at the end of the interviews. After their release on licence, the appellants were formally charged with the murder of the victim and with concealing and disposing of her body in an attempt to pervert the course of justice. They were also charged with a number of sexual offences against children. Separate trials were conducted in respect of the sexual offences and the murder charges, both trials taking place before the same judge, but with different juries. The appellants were convicted of some of the sexual offences, but sentence was adjourned until the outcome of the murder trial, in relation to which the appellants were convicted and sentenced to life imprisonment. On their appeals, it fell to be determined whether, for the purposes of their right to a fair trial within a reasonable time, guaranteed by the European Convention on Human Rights art 6(1), the appellants were charged in the interview, and whether, in relation to the first appellant, the conduct of the judge could be said to have given rise to a legitimate concern as to the appearance of bias. *Held,* the appellants had certainly not been charged in the formal sense at any stage of their interviews. They had

both been asked directly whether they had killed the victim. The attitude of the police at the interview had been entirely understandable as it had not yet been established that the victim was dead. In the absence of any evidence to show where, when and how she had died, the police had been in no position to initiate criminal proceedings against the appellants for her murder. It followed that the date when reasonable time began was when the appellants were formally charged and not when they had been detained and interviewed. Moreover, it would only have been if the judge expressed outspoken opinions about the first appellant's character that were entirely gratuitous, and only if the occasion for making them had been plainly outside the scope of the proper performance of his duties in conducting the trial, that the professional judge's ability to perform his duties with an objective judicial mind would be doubted. Nothing like that had occurred. The judge had been asked to make a risk assessment order and had been asked to defer his consideration of that until after the trial of the murder charges. The judge's comments on the appellant's character had been directly relevant to that issue. The informed observer would have understood that, if the judge had been passing sentence on the appellants, the remarks he had made would have been entirely appropriate as background to the sentences which he would have been obliged to pass. It followed that there was no basis for the suggestion that the judge was apparently biased. Accordingly, the appeals would be dismissed.

O'Neill v HM Advocate (No 2); Lauchlan v HM Advocate [2013] UKSC 36, [2013] 2 Cr App Rep 409, [2013] All ER (D) 110 (Jun) (Supreme Court: Lord Hope DP, Lord Kerr, Lord Wilson, Lord Hughes and Lord Toulson SCJJ).

2177   Right to fair and public hearing—criminal proceedings—presumption of innocence—conviction quashed—court's refusal to grant compensation

The Criminal Justice Act 1988 s 133(1) provides that when a person has been convicted of a criminal offence and when subsequently his conviction has been reversed on the ground that a new or newly discovered fact shows beyond reasonable doubt that there has been a miscarriage of justice, the Secretary of State must pay compensation for the miscarriage of justice to the person who has suffered punishment as a result of such conviction.

The applicant was convicted of the manslaughter of her four-month-old son and sentenced to three years' imprisonment. New medical evidence came to light which might have affected the jury's decision to convict. The conviction was quashed after the applicant had served time in prison. She claimed compensation pursuant to the 1988 Act s 133. The claim was refused and the applicant brought judicial review proceedings challenging the decision. Her application was dismissed and she appealed. Her appeal was also dismissed and leave to appeal further was refused. She subsequently complained to the European Court of Human Rights, contending that the reasons given in the decision not to award her compensation had breached her right to presumption of innocence in violation of the European Convention on Human Rights art 6(2). *Held*, the 1988 Act s 133 did not require the applicant's criminal guilt to be assessed and did not question her innocence. The courts had considered whether any 'miscarriage of justice' had taken place and had concluded that the existence of a miscarriage of justice had not been established beyond reasonable doubt. They had not questioned the conclusion that her conviction was unsafe and had not commented on whether the applicant should have been, or would likely have been, acquitted or convicted on the basis of the new evidence which had led to the quashing of her conviction. They had consistently repeated that it would have been for a jury to assess the new evidence, had a retrial been ordered. Therefore the language used by the courts in their decisions to decide on compensation had not undermined the applicant's acquittal or treated her in a manner inconsistent with her innocence. Accordingly, the application would be dismissed.

Application 25424/09 *Allen v United Kingdom* [2013] All ER (D) 222 (Jul) (European Court of Human Rights: Grand Chamber). *R (on the application of Mullen) v Secretary of State for the Home Department* [2004] UKHL 18, [2004] 3 All ER 65 (2004 Abr para 693) considered.

2178   Right to fair and public hearing—extradition proceedings—right to be heard by judicial authority issuing arrest warrant

See Case C-396/11 *Criminal proceedings against Radu*, para 1169.

2179   Right to fair and public hearing—extra-territorial jurisdiction—British citizen facing death sentence abroad—funding of legal representation

See *R (on the application of Sandiford) v Secretary of State for Foreign and Commonwealth Affairs*, para 2157.

2180   Right to fair and public hearing—independent and impartial tribunal—extradition—evidence of judicial corruption in foreign state—admissibility

See *Kapri v the Lord Advocate representing the Government of the Republic of Albania*, para 1179.

2181   Right to fair and public hearing—independent and impartial tribunal—overseas territory—combined judicial and legislative powers

See *R (on the application of Barclay) v Secretary of State for Justice*, para 343.

2182   Right to fair and public hearing—medical practitioner—disciplinary proceedings—evidence challenging allegation

See *Perry v Nursing and Midwifery Council*, para 1864.

2183   Right to fair and public hearing—prisoner—revocation of licence—Parole Board—oral hearing

See *Osborn v Parole Board, Booth v Parole Board, Re Reilly's Application for Judicial Review*, para 2103.

2184   Right to free elections—right to vote—British citizen resident overseas

See Application 19840/09 *Shindler v United Kingdom*, para 993.

2185   Right to free elections—right to vote—disenfranchisement—prisoners

See *R (on the application of Chester) v Secretary of State for Justice; McGeoch v The Lord President of the Council*, para 979.

2186   Right to liberty—lawfulness of detention—autistic and epileptic young adult

See *ZH v Metropolitan Police Comr*, para 1872.

2187   Right to liberty—lawfulness of detention—mental patient—review of detention

See *R (on the application of Modaresi) (FC) v Secretary of State for Health*, para 1886.

2188   Right to liberty—lawfulness of detention—prisoner—release on licence—delay in determination by Parole Board

See *R (on the application of Faulkner) v Secretary of State for Justice; R (on the application of Sturnham) v Parole Board of England and Wales*, para 2101.

2189   Right to liberty—lawfulness of detention—terrorism suspect—right to presence of solicitor

See *Elosta v Metropolitan Police Comr*, para 2087.

2190   Right to liberty—release of prisoner on licence—revocation—review—unlawful—bail pending reconsideration

See *Re Corey for Judicial Review (Northern Ireland)*, para 2104.

2191   Right to life—duty to investigate cause of death—independence of investigation—death caused by British servicemen

The claimants were Iraqi citizens who claimed that they had been ill-treated by the British armed forces in Iraq or were relatives of those who were killed by the British armed forces. They established by judicial review that the investigation by the defendant through the Iraq Historic Allegations Team ('IHAT') was not independent. The defendant reconstituted the investigation by removing members of the Royal Military Police and replacing them mostly with retired police officers, but also them with members of the Royal Navy Police. On a further application for judicial review, the claimants contended that the investigation as reconstituted was still not independent and sought a more far-reaching public inquiry. *Held*, there was no objection, in principle, to a service police force investigating service personnel of the service which they policed or another service police force. The only question was whether, on the facts of a given case, the service police were independent of the events or personnel being investigated. On the evidence in the present case, the IHAT was independent and, objectively, could be seen as independent. There should be some form of effective official investigation when individuals had been killed as a result of use of force by agents of the state. The essential purpose of such an investigation was to secure the effective implementation of the domestic laws safeguarding the right to life and, in those cases involving state agents or bodies, to ensure their accountability for deaths occurring under their responsibility. The investigative duty of the state, under the European Convention on Human Rights art 2, in the case of deaths in custody would only be discharged by a full, fair and fearless investigation, accessible to the victims' families and to the public, into each death, which had to look into and consider the immediate and surrounding circumstances in which each of the deaths had occurred. Those circumstances would ordinarily include the instructions, training and supervision given to soldiers involved in the interrogation of those who had died in custody in the aftermath of the invasion. It should also identify the culpable and discreditable conduct of those involved, including their acts and omissions, as well as identifying the steps needed for the rectification of dangerous practices and procedures. The IHAT investigation had not fulfilled the obligations under art 2. In relation to the cases involving deaths, the defendant had to within six weeks state what further progress had been made in investigating the deaths and when a decision would be made as to whether any prosecutions would be brought. Where there would not be a prosecution, consideration would have to be given as to how art 2 should be complied with. Once it was determined that there were cases in which there would be no prosecution, the procedure for cases under art 3 had to be reviewed by the defendant in the light of the experience in the cases under art 2. Judgment would be given accordingly.

R (on the application of Mousa) v Secretary of State for Defence (No 2) [2013] EWHC 1412 (Admin), [2013] All ER (D) 302 (May) (Queen's Bench Division: Sir John Thomas P and Silber J).

2192   Right to life—prisoner with serious medical condition—discharge from hospital wing

The claimant pleaded guilty to being knowingly concerned in the fraudulent evasion of the prohibition on the importation of a Class A drug and was sentenced to three years' imprisonment. He suffered from Friedreich's ataxia, which affected many of the major systems of the body, causing progressive disablement. While in prison, he was detained in a hospital wing, where he required the constant attendance of two assistants. The claimant commenced judicial review proceedings, contending that the prison regime to which he was subject amounted to inhuman and degrading treatment contrary to his rights under the European Convention on Human Rights art 3. He was shortly afterwards transferred to a different hospital which eventually decided that the claimant was fit to be discharged to a non-medical section of the prison. The claimant brought a second judicial review claim, submitting that his discharge would put his life at risk in breach of art 2. *Held*, it was settled law that the duty under art 2 included, in the context of persons detained by the state, an obligation to preserve life and to provide the necessary care to preserve life. However, art 2 was engaged only where there was a real and immediate risk of death. There was no possible evidential basis whatsoever for the assertion that the claimant had been at imminent risk of death while in prison, that his treatment had reduced his life expectancy or that he would be at such risk if he was discharged from the hospital wing. It followed that the art 2 claim failed. In the circumstances, the claimant's claim under art 3 was also untenable. In the light of the claimant's medical condition, detaining him and providing him with the care which he had needed had been clearly challenging for the prison. However, merely because the level of care he had received had fallen below that to which he had been accustomed did not make it contrary to his human rights. Looking at the treatment to which he had been subject at the prison as a whole, it had clearly fallen far short of the minimum level of severity that art 3 required, even given the claimant's state of health and the fact of his detention by the state. Accordingly, the application would be dismissed.

R (on the application of Hall) v University College London Hospitals NHS Foundation Trust [2013] EWHC 198 (Admin), [2013] All ER (D) 119 (Feb) (Queen's Bench Division: Hughes LJ, Wyn Williams and Hickinbottom JJ).

2193   Right to life—protection from physical injury—duty of police—time taken to attend scene of incident

A log was created from an emergency telephone call made by a first caller reporting that a number of men were smashing the windows of a house with baseball bats and were chasing an individual whom they had already assaulted earlier that night. The first caller suggested that the police should go to the premises quickly. He stated that the men were beating up his nephew and that they had also beaten the claimant with baseball bats. During a second emergency telephone call, the second caller stated that her boyfriend had been beaten up by the men and requested the police to send a riot van. During the second call, the claimant was mentioned by name. The second caller also told the police that the claimant had been battered with a bat and that he needed an ambulance. The claimant sustained a serious head injury which caused short and long-term memory loss. He brought proceedings alleging that the defendant chief constable had been in breach of his statutory duty under the Human Rights Act 1998 s 6 in that, in breach of the European Convention on Human Rights art 2 and/or art 3, his police officers had failed, without justification, to take reasonable steps to protect the claimant and his family from physical violence at the hands of the men. The claim was struck out as having no prospect of success. On appeal by the claimant, *held*, there was no reason in principle for limiting the scope of the defendant's duty. Such a limitation would be inconsistent with the idea that the provisions of the Convention should be interpreted and applied in such a way as to make its safeguards practical and effective. The duty to provide protection arose when the first emergency call was made when it was impossible to know whether and, if so, how quickly an assault would take place. There had been no reason at the time for the police to believe that immediate attendance was not required. The time and contents of the first call suggested that there was every reason to think that there was an imminent likelihood that the men would injure or kill one or more persons who were in the vicinity. Although it was accepted that, if it were established that a timeous response by the police in the circumstances would have made no difference, it would be relevant to quantum. A finding that a response would have made no difference might mean that there was no right to damages but it was not relevant to liability. It went without saying that, if the police were told that a person had been killed, it was too late to take measures to prevent the risk of death materialising. However, if the police were told that there was a gang which was threatening and/or committing acts of violence and the incident was on-going, there was no basis for saying that there was no duty to take operational measures to avert the risk of further violence. There was no support for such a proposition. If the police were or should have been aware that there was a real and immediate risk to a person's life, they were under a duty to take reasonable measures to prevent the risk from materialising, and it made no difference that the risk had arisen during an incident which had already commenced. Accordingly, the appeal would be allowed.

Sarjantson v Humberside Police Chief Constable [2013] EWCA Civ 1252, [2013] All ER (D) 205 (Oct) (Court of Appeal: Lord Dyson MR, McFarlane and Sharp LJJ). Application 23452/94 *Osman v United Kingdom* [1999] 1 FLR 193, ECtHR (1998 Abr para 1801), applied.

2194   Right to life—soldier—death while on active duty overseas

See *Smith v Ministry of Defence; Ellis v Ministry of Defence; Allbutt v Ministry of Defence*, para 77.

2195   Right to life—state's obligation to investigate death—delay in investigation

The deceased were shot in Northern Ireland by soldiers from a specialist unit of the British Army. The Director of Public Prosecutions decided not to prosecute the soldiers involved in the shooting. Material concerning the incident was forwarded to a coroner and over two years went by before the coroner made his first contact with the applicants, the relatives of the deceased. An additional four and a half years passed before the coroner requested the relevant soldiers' statements from the police. The applicants wrote to the coroner asking when the inquest would be listed and seeking pre-inquest disclosure. Two sets of judicial proceedings were subsequently brought by the applicants and the inquest was effectively postponed pending the resolution of the judicial review actions. The inquest hearing did not begin until more than 21 years after the deaths. The applicants maintained that the post-operation investigation, which had not led to any prosecution, lacked independence and had been ineffective. The applicants complained to the European Court of Human Rights under the procedural aspect of the European Convention on Human Rights art 2, in relation to the length of the investigation. *Held,* art 2 required investigations to begin promptly and to proceed with reasonable expedition, and that was required quite apart from any question of whether the delay actually impacted on the effectiveness of the investigation. The fact that it was necessary to postpone the applicants' inquest so frequently and for such long periods pending clarifying judicial review actions demonstrated that the inquest process itself was not structurally capable at the relevant time of providing the applicants with access to an effective investigation which would commence promptly and be conducted with due expedition. Further, by the time the inquest hearing began, the delay was such that the High Court considered itself obliged to raise the threshold of leave to apply for judicial review, which made the clarification of the procedural rights of the applicants exceedingly difficult and rendered inescapable another post-inquest judicial review action. The delays could not be regarded as compatible with the state's obligation under art 2 to ensure the effectiveness of investigations into suspicious deaths, in the sense that the investigative process, however it be organised under national law, had to be commenced promptly and carried out with reasonable expedition. To that extent, the finding of excessive investigative delay, of itself, entailed the conclusion that the investigation was ineffective for the purposes of art 2. Accordingly, the application would be allowed.

Application 43098/09 *McCaughey v United Kingdom* [2013] All ER (D) 260 (Jul) (European Court of Human Rights). *Re McKerr* [2004] UKHL 12, [2004] 2 All ER 409 (2004 Abr para 1466); and *Jordan v Lord Chancellor; McCaughey v Chief Constable of the Police Service of Northern Ireland* [2007] UKHL 14, [2007] 2 AC 226 considered.

2196   Right to life—suicide—complicity in another's suicide—liability to prosecution

See *R (on the application of Nicklinson) v Ministry of Justice; R (on the application of AM) v DPP,* para 666.

2197   Right to peaceful enjoyment of possessions—deprivation of possessions—public interest—proportionality—excessive taxation of severance pay

The applicant, a Hungarian national who had been a civil servant for 30 years, was dismissed. On dismissal, she was entitled to receive eight months' severance pay. Approximately one year before her dismissal, the Hungarian parliament adopted an Act introducing a new tax on certain payments to public sector employees whose employment had been terminated. The aim of the Act was to fight against excessive severance payments and to protect the public finances in times of economic hardship. The Act was challenged before the Constitutional Court, which found the relevant provisions unconstitutional for being confiscatory. The court annulled the relevant provisions retroactively. A further amendment was made ten weeks before the dismissal of the applicant which provided that any severance pay over 3.5 million Hungarian forints ('HUF') would be taxed at 98 per cent. The exceeding part was HUF 2.4m, which represented an overall tax burden of approximately 52 per cent on the entirety of the severance, as opposed to the general personal income tax rate of 16 per cent in the relevant period. The tax amount in question was never disbursed to the applicant, but was withheld by the employer and directly transferred to the tax authority. The applicant complained to the European Court of Human Rights that the imposition of a 98 per cent tax on the upper bracket of her severance constituted an unjustified deprivation of property, or else taxation at an excessively disproportionate rate, contrary to the First Protocol to the Convention for the Protection of Human Rights and Fundamental Freedoms 1950 art 1. It was agreed that the impugned taxation represented an interference with the applicant's right to peaceful enjoyment of possessions. It therefore fell to be determined whether that interference was reasonably proportionate to the aim sought to be realised. *Held,* the tax was determined in a statute that was enacted and entered into force some ten weeks before the termination of the applicant's civil service relationship, and the tax was not intended to remedy technical deficiencies of the pre-existing law, nor had the applicant enjoyed the benefit of a windfall in a changeover to a new tax-payment regime. In conclusion, the specific measure in question, as applied to the applicant, even if meant to serve social justice, could not be justified by the legitimate public interest relied on by the government. It affected the applicant, and other dismissed civil servants in a similar situation, being in good-faith standing, and deprived her of the larger part of a statutorily guaranteed, acquired right serving the special social interest of reintegration. Those who acted in good faith on the basis of law should not be frustrated in their statute-based expectations without specific and compelling reasons. The measure could not be held reasonably proportionate to the aim sought to be realized. There had, therefore, been a violation of art 1. Accordingly, the application would be allowed.

Application 66259/11 *NKM v Hungary* [2013] STC 1104 (European Court on Human Rights: Second Section).

2198   Right to peaceful enjoyment of possessions—income taxation—late return—penalty

See *Revenue and Customs Comrs v Bosher*, para 1561.

2199   Right to peaceful enjoyment of possessions—property—erection of barrier preventing vehicular access to property

See *Cusack v Harrow LBC*, para 1382.

2200   Right to peaceful enjoyment of possessions—property—registration of land as town or village green

See *R (on the application of Newhaven Port and Properties Ltd) v East Sussex CC (No 2)*, para 341.

2201   Right to private and family life—assisted suicide—right of health care professionals to defence of necessity

See *R (on the application of Nicklinson) v Ministry of Justice; R (on the application of AM) v DPP*, para 666.

2202   Right to private and family life—asylum-seeker—refusal of asylum—legitimate need to control immigration

See *Zoumbas v Secretary of State for the Home Department*, para 1406.

2203   Right to private and family life—care proceedings—care order—application for judicial review by mother

See *R (on the application of CB) v Sheffield CC*, para 1634.

2204   Right to private and family life—care proceedings—care order—balancing exercise—proportionality

See *Re G (a child) (care proceedings: welfare balancing exercise: proportionality)*, para 170.

2205   Right to private and family life—child—father convicted of sexual offence against sibling

See *CW v SG*, para 222.

2206   Right to private and family life—children—care proceedings—exclusion of media

A family was travelling in their car on holiday in France when they were attacked by a gunman. The three adults in the car were killed and the children were orphans with no person having parental responsibility for them. Initially, it was not possible for them to be placed into the care of members of the extended family because one line of the police investigation concerned the possible involvement of family members in the murders. As a result, the applicant local authority started care proceedings in respect of the children. The principal issue arising in the substantive proceedings was whether the children should be placed with two members of the extended family, who had been joined to the proceedings. The sixth respondent newspaper asked the fifth respondent Chief Constable to confirm whether he would be making any application to exclude accredited press representatives from a substantive hearing. The fifth respondent brought proceedings seeking to exclude the media, relying on the European Convention on Human Rights arts 2, 8, and the need to maintain judicial secrecy in France pursuant to provisions of the French penal code, which involved art 6. It fell to be determined whether there was a real and immediate risk to the children's lives and whether permitting the press to attend the hearing would give rise to a materially increased risk to life. *Held*, it was incumbent on a court to compare the importance of the specific rights being claimed. That involved an intense focus on the circumstances that were said to create a risk to life so as to engage art 2. In the period immediately after the killing, there had manifestly been a real and immediate risk to the lives of the children. Since then, the French authorities, the British police, the local authority and the court had taken a series of measures, separately and together designed to reduce the risk. There was no longer any real and immediate risk to the children's lives. There was no likelihood that the attendance of accredited representatives of the media at the substantive hearing would materially increase the risk to the children's lives. The court and the parties retained the right and the duty to keep the issue of their attendance under review at all points. The police had not demonstrated that there was a general risk of leakage and any specific risk could be addressed as it arose. Thus, the court was not under a positive obligation under art 2 to take steps to reduce the risk by excluding the media from the outset of the hearing. The attendance of the media would not substantially interfere with the rights under art 8 of the children, their carers, or members of their extended family. Nor would it interfere with any rights under art 6 in the substantive proceedings. Accordingly, the application would be dismissed.

Re Al-Hilli (*children: reporting restrictions*) [2013] EWHC 2190 (Fam), [2014] 1 FLR 403, [2013] All ER (D) 31 (Aug) (Family Division: Baker J).

2207　Right to private and family life—confidential information—criminal records—disclosure

See *R* (*on the application of A*) *v Chief Constable of Kent Constabulary*, para 2282.

2208　Right to private and family life—confidential information—criminal records—disclosure

See *R* (*on the application of T*) *v Chief Constable of Greater Manchester; R* (*on the application of JB*) *v Secretary of State for the Home Department; R* (*on the application of AW*) *v Secretary of State for Justice*, para 2285.

2209　Right to private and family life—criminal proceedings—17-year-old person—detention and questioning—treatment as adult

See *R* (*on the application of HC*) *v Secretary of State for the Home Department* (*Coram Children's Legal Centre and The Howard League intervening*), para 205.

2210　Right to private and family life—deportation order—criminal

See *MF* (*Nigeria*) *v Secretary of State for the Home Department*, para 1424.

2211　Right to private and family life—deprivation of citizenship—child born in member state—parents third country nationals—rights of residence for parents

The present proceedings concerned two references for a preliminary ruling from the European Court of Justice. In the first case the applicant, a national of Ghana who lived in Finland on the basis of a permanent residence permit, married a Finnish national, with whom she had a child. The child had Finnish nationality and lived in Finland. The applicant had sole custody of the child and later divorced. During her stay in Finland, the applicant had studied, taken maternity leave, qualified for a trade, and been gainfully employed. Her second marriage was to a national of Côte d'Ivoire. Her second husband had applied to the respondent Immigration Office for a residence permit on the basis of the marriage. Subsequently, a child of the marriage was born in Finland. The child had Ghanaian nationality and the spouses had joint custody of the child. The second husband had entered into a contract of employment. He had not, however, produced documents to show that he worked in accordance with the contract. The Immigration Office refused the second husband's application for a residence permit on the ground that he had not had secure means of subsistence. It further considered that there had been no reason to make an exception to the requirement of means of subsistence, as permitted by Finnish law. The Administrative Court dismissed the action brought by the second husband for the decision of the Immigration Office to be annulled. The applicant and second husband appealed against that judgment to the Supreme Administrative Court. In the second case, the applicant, a national of Algeria, had resided lawfully in Finland. She obtained a permanent residence permit there following her marriage to a Finnish national. The child of that marriage had dual Finnish and Algerian nationality and lived in Finland. The spouses divorced and the applicant was granted sole custody of the child. The applicant had married a second husband, an Algerian national who had arrived lawfully in Finland and sought asylum there. The second husband had been returned to his country of origin. The applicant applied to the Immigration Office for her spouse to be granted a residence permit in Finland on the basis of their marriage. Subsequently, a child of the marriage had been born in Finland. The child had Algerian nationality and was in the joint custody of both parents. The applicant had never been in gainful employment during her stay in Finland. Her means of subsistence came from subsistence support and other benefits. Her husband was not known to have been gainfully employed in Finland. The Immigration Office rejected the application for a residence permit for the second husband on the ground that he had not had secure means of subsistence. The Administrative Court allowed the applicant's application for that decision to be annulled. The Immigration Office appealed against that judgment to the referring court. The referring court decided to stay the proceedings and to refer certain questions to the court for a preliminary ruling. *Held,* (1) TFEU art 20 should be interpreted as not precluding a member state from refusing to grant a third country national a residence permit on the basis of family reunification where that national sought to reside with his spouse, who was also a third country national and resided lawfully in that member state and was the mother of a child from a previous marriage who was an EU citizen, and with the child of their own marriage, who was also a third country national, provided that such a refusal did not entail, for the EU citizen concerned, the denial of the genuine enjoyment of the substance of the rights conferred by the status of citizen of the EU, that being for the referring court to ascertain. Should that court find that such a denial did not follow from the refusals of residence permits at issue in the main proceedings, that would be without prejudice to the question whether, on the basis of other criteria, by virtue of the right to the protection of family life, the second husbands in both cases could not be refused a right of residence. That question should be addressed in the framework of the provisions on the protection of fundamental rights which were applicable in each case. (2) Applications for residence permits on the basis of family reunification such as those at issue in the main proceedings were covered by Council Directive (EC) 2003/86. Article 7(1)(c) should be interpreted as meaning that, while member states had the faculty of requiring proof that the sponsor had stable and regular resources which were sufficient to maintain himself and the members of his family, that faculty should be exercised in the light of the Charter of Fundamental Rights of the European Union arts 7, 24(2), (3), which required the member states to examine applications for family reunification in the interests of the children concerned and also with a view to promoting family life. It was for the referring court to ascertain whether the decisions refusing residence permits at issue in the main proceedings had been taken in compliance with those requirements.

Cases C-356/11 and C-357/11 *O v Maahanmuuttovirasto* [2012] All ER (D) 122 (Dec) (ECJ: Second Chamber).

2212 Right to private and family life—discrimination—damages for fatal accident— couple cohabitating for less than two years

See *Swift v Secretary of State for Justice*, para 790.

2213 Right to private and family life—employee—dismissal—fair hearing

The applicant had been appointed to the post of judge of a district court in Ukraine. Subsequently, he was elected president of the Military Chamber of the Supreme Court. The Assembly of Judges of Ukraine elected the applicant to the post of member of the High Council of Justice. The chairman of the parliamentary committee, who was also a member of the High Council of Justice, refused to allow the applicant to take the oath of office.

Meanwhile, the chairman and two members of the parliamentary committee lodged requests with the High Council of Justice, asking it to carry out preliminary inquiries into possible professional misconduct by the applicant. Another member lodged a request asking the High Council of Justice to determine whether the applicant could be dismissed from the post of judge for 'breach of oath', claiming that the applicant had reviewed decisions delivered by a relative. The High Council of Justice submitted to Parliament that the applicant be dismissed. Parliament voted for the dismissal of the applicant from the post of judge for breach of oath. The applicant challenged his dismissal before the Higher Administrative Court. The Higher Administrative Court found that the decision had been unlawful. However, the Higher Administrative Court refused to quash the High Council of Justice's acts, noting that it was not empowered to take such a measure. The applicant complained to the European Court of Human Rights of violations of his rights under the European Convention on Human Rights arts 6, 8. *Held*, the proceedings before the High Council of Justice had not been compatible with the principles of independence and impartiality. There were a number of serious issues pointing both to structural deficiencies in the proceedings before the High Council of Justice and to the appearance of personal bias on the part of certain members. The European Court of Human Rights had held previously that, where at least half of the membership of a tribunal was composed of judges, including the chairman with a casting vote, that was a strong indicator of impartiality. However, only three of the members who determined the applicant's case were judges. The presence of the prosecutor general on a body concerned with the appointment, disciplining and removal of judges created a risk that judges would not act impartially in such cases. The further determination of the case by Parliament, the legislative body, had served to contribute to the politicisation of the procedure and to aggravate the inconsistency of the procedure with the principle of the separation of powers. The procedure at the plenary meeting had not been an appropriate forum for examining issues of fact and law, assessing evidence and making a legal qualification of facts. The Higher Administrative Court's review of the applicant's case was not sufficient. There were violations of art 6(1) as regards the principle of legal certainty. The lack of time bars on proceedings for dismissal of a judge for 'breach of oath' also posed a serious threat to the principle of legal certainty. There was a violation of art 6(1) as the chamber dealing with the applicant's case was not set up and composed in a legitimate way which satisfied the requirement that it be a 'tribunal established by law'. The dismissal of the applicant constituted an interference with his right to respect for private life within the meaning of art 8. That interference was not justified. The present case disclosed serious systemic problems as regards the functioning of the Ukrainian judiciary. In particular, the violations found suggested that the system of judicial discipline had not been organised in a proper way, as it did not ensure the sufficient separation of the judiciary from other branches of state power. Having regard to the exceptional circumstances of the case and the urgent need to put an end to the violations of art 6, 8, Ukraine had to secure the applicant's reinstatement at the earliest possible date.

Application 21722/11 *Volkov v Ukraine* [2013] IRLR 480 (European Court of Human Rights).

2214   Right to private and family life—extradition—person facing longer sentence in requesting territory

See *Fridenberga v Public Prosecutor, Prosecutor General Office for the Republic of Latvia*, para 1178.

2215   Right to private and family life—famous person—publication of photograph without consent—freedom of expression

At a private birthday party attended by the claimant a series of photographs were taken by another guest ('the guest'), some of which showed the claimant partially naked. The claimant later married a well-known actress. The photographs came to the attention of the defendant news group, which sought to publish them, together with a description of their contents, in a national newspaper. The defendant notified the claimant of its intention to do so and stated that it intended to pixillate the part of any published photographs which showed the lower half of the claimant's body. The guest assigned the copyright in the photographs to the claimant. The claimant applied for an interim injunction to restrain their publication by the defendant, or the publication of a description of their contents, relying both on his status as copyright owner by assignment, and on his right to a private life under the European Convention on Human Rights art 8. He submitted that he had a reasonable expectation of privacy in relation to the photographs and their content, that they would not contribute anything of substance to any debate of general interest in a democratic society, and that their publication would risk causing real harm and distress, both to him, to his new wife and to her children. *Held*, it was very unlikely that the defendant would be able to establish at trial that no useful purpose would be achieved by a restraint on publication of the photographs or their contents, or that there was no longer anything by way of privacy left to be protected. The claimant was not in that narrow category of persons who, although engaged in no public office, might be regarded as having reduced expectations of privacy due to their important role in national affairs. Further, the consequences of publication, in terms of risk of harm and distress to the children of the claimant's wife, were matters tending towards a conclusion that the claimant's privacy should prevail. With regard to the copyright issue, it was in theory possible that the propensity of an injunction restraining a threatened breach of copyright to impinge on a defendant's art 10 right to freedom of expression might occasionally incline the court, on particular facts, to decline the discretionary remedy of an injunction, and leave the claimant to a claim in damages. The claim in copyright would merely prohibit the actual copying of photographs, rather than the publication of a description in words of their content. In those circumstances an injunction merely to restrain copying of photographs would constitute no disproportionate fetter on the defendant's art 10 rights, which could sufficiently, albeit not fully, be vindicated by a description of their contents. Applying that test, on the evidence as it stood, the claimant had a much better than even chance of obtaining an injunction to restrain the breach of copyright inherent in the threatened publication of the photographs as such. Accordingly, the application would be allowed.

Rocknroll v News Group Newspapers Ltd [2013] EWHC 24 (Ch), [2013] All ER (D) 98 (Jan) (Chancery Division: Briggs J).

2216   Right to private and family life—father—child conceived by artificial insemination—mother in same-sex relationship

See *Re G (a child) (sperm donor: contact order); Re Z (a child) (sperm donor: contact order)*, para 201.

2217   Right to private and family life—freedom of movement—restriction of freedom—exclusion of EU national on public security grounds

See Case C-300/11 *ZZ (France) v Secretary of State for the Home Department*, para 1435.

2218   Right to private and family life—immigration—adult children of Gurkha soldiers

See *R (on the application of Sharmilla) v Secretary of State for the Home Department*, para 1441.

2219   Right to private and family life—immigration—leave to enter—English language requirement

See *R (on the application of Bibi) v Secretary of State for the Home Department; R (on the application of Ali) v Secretary of State for the Home Department*, para 1439.

2220   Right to private and family life—immigration—leave to remain—marriage—policy

See *MM v Secretary of State for the Home Department*, para 1446.

2221   Right to private and family life—immigration—refusal of leave to remain—withdrawal of accommodation and support

The claimant, a Nigerian national, entered the United Kingdom illegally and her husband joined her. The claimant and her husband had three children, all born in the United Kingdom. They applied for leave to remain, which was refused. An application was made for reconsideration of the decision. The claimant placed reliance on the European Convention on Human Rights art 8, and sought, in the alternative, that an immigration decision should be made within six weeks. The claimant and her family were told to leave the country by a specified date. She issued a letter before action in respect of the defendant authority's failure to assess and provide for the claimant under the Children Act 1989. The authority carried out a needs assessment of the children and concluded that the family had rights pursuant to art 8, but as the family would be returning to Nigeria, there would be no breach of their rights. Further, the children would no longer be classified as being in need once they had returned to Nigeria and, accordingly, the authority terminated accommodation and support under the 1989 Act. The claimant wrote again to the authority setting out the intention to prepare a further application for leave to remain in the event that an immigration decision was not made beforehand. The authority stated that it had not seen any evidence suggesting that the family had a strong case in any challenge against any future decision as to their removal, and that there was no application pending with the United Kingdom Border Agency. Therefore, the authority denied that it was obliged to provide support under the 1989 Act. The claimant issued an application for judicial review. The claimant submitted that under the Nationality, Immigration and Asylum Act 2002, the statutory framework had included a right of appeal on Convention grounds against an immigration decision for the issue of removal directions. *Held,* it was established law that the Convention art 8 provided expressly for the rights to family and private life, but that implicitly included the right for procedural protection which was fair and effective. The 2002 Act required an authority to consider whether the provision of support under the 1989 Act was necessary to avoid a breach of an individual's rights under the Convention. The procedural safeguard for art 8 rights under the 2002 Act included the opportunity for appeal against removal directions following the refusal of leave to remain. The effect was that, save where the case was obviously hopeless or abusive, an authority could not generally deny support under the 1989 Act if the effect would be to negate the procedural right for protection of the Convention right. Where on the facts of the case it was demonstrated that a person had a substantive Convention claim that would found an appeal against removal directions if made, a decision that effectively deprived the person of that protection would be in breach of his Convention procedural right. The existence of judicial review would not be a complete answer to the denial of that procedural right. In the circumstances, it would be material for an authority to consider whether the provision of support was necessary to avoid a breach of that procedural right for protection of art 8. In the present case, in principle the procedural right to appeal against removal directions if and when they were made would be a right of significance and one to which the claimant and her family would be entitled in protection of their rights under art 8. The authority had been aware at the time of its decision that the claimant and her family would not voluntarily return to Nigeria, that they had been seeking an immigration decision to enable an appeal to the tribunal, and that in any event, they had been preparing a further application for leave to remain, supported by new evidence. Thus, there had been a substantive Convention procedural right comprised in the statutory right to appeal against the immigration decision for removal directions which would be required for the removal of the claimant and her family in the absence of any other supervening event. It was equally plain that the decision to remove support had been made in recognition that the consequence would be the return of the claimant and her family to Nigeria, and, in effect, that that would deprive them of their procedural right of appeal under the 2002 Act against the immigration decision when it was made. The decision had been flawed in that it had not taken into account adequately or at all the effect on the claimant's and her family's Convention right to procedural protection. Accordingly, the appeal would be allowed and the decision would be quashed.

R (on the application of KA (Nigeria)) v Essex CC [2013] EWHC 43 (Admin), [2013] 1 WLR 1163, [2013] LGR 363 (Queen's Bench Division: Robin Purchas QC). *R (on the application of Murdock) v Secretary of State* [2011] EWCA Civ 161, (2011) Times, 02 March, [2011] All ER (D) 254 (Feb) (2011 Abr para 1485) applied. *R (on the application of Nasseri) v Secretary of State for the Home Department* [2009] UKHL 23, [2010] 1 AC 1, [2009] 3 All ER 774, (2009 Abr para 253) considered.

2222   Right to private and family life—incest between siblings—criminal conviction of brother—conflict between private rights and public interest

The applicant was adopted at the age of seven. As a young adult, he re-established contact with his family of origin and discovered that he had a biological sister born after his adoption. Following their mother's death, the relationship between the two siblings intensified and they had consensual sexual intercourse. They lived together for several years

2232   Torture or inhuman or degrading treatment or punishment—extradition—mental and physical condition

See *Edwards v Government of United States of America*, para 1174.

2233   Torture or inhuman or degrading treatment or punishment—extradition—prison conditions

See *Lutsyuk v Govt of Ukraine*, para 1175.

2234   Torture or inhuman or degrading treatment or punishment—extradition—prospect of imprisonment in foreign state—effect on mental health

The applicant was detained in a high security psychiatric hospital. He had been indicted in the United States of America as a co-conspirator in respect of a conspiracy to establish a jihad training camp and had been arrested in the United Kingdom following a request by the United States authorities. He had unsuccessfully contested the order for his extradition. He applied to the European Court of Human Rights, claiming that his extradition, possibly to a high security detention facility, would violate his right to protection from inhuman and degrading treatment under the European Convention on Human Rights art 3. The last forensic psychiatrist reports in his case indicated that while his condition was well-controlled on anti-psychotic medication, his detention in hospital was required for his medical treatment and such treatment was necessary for his health and safety. *Held*, in light of the medical evidence, there was a real risk that the applicant's extradition to the United States of America and to a different, potentially more hostile prison environment, would result in a significant deterioration in his mental and physical health. Such deterioration would be capable of amounting to treatment in breach of the Convention art 3. The court gave full consideration to the submissions of the United States Department of Justice and observed, in particular, that it could not be determined with certainty in which detention facility or facilities the applicant would be placed if extradited to the United States of America, either before or after trial. It was also unclear how long he might expect to remain on remand pending trial. As for his detention following a possible conviction, the court observed that although the applicant would have access to mental health services regardless of which prison he was detained in, his extradition to a country where he had no ties and where he would face an uncertain future in an as yet undetermined institution, and possibly also be subject to a highly restrictive regime would, accordingly, violate art 3.

Application 17299/12 *Aswat v United Kingdom* (2013) Times, 24 April (European Court of Human Rights).

2235   Torture or inhuman or degrading treatment or punishment—prisoner—medical condition—relevance to overall length of sentence

See *R v Hall*, para 2292.

2236   Torture or inhuman or degrading treatment or punishment—prisoner—medical treatment

See *R (on the application of Hall) v University College London Hospitals NHS Foundation Trust*, para 2192.

ROAD TRAFFIC

Halsbury's Laws of England (5th edn) vol 89 (2011) paras 1–693, vol 90 (2011) paras 694–1253

Articles

For articles relating to this title please refer to the Table of Articles at the beginning of the Abridgment.

2237   Accident—personal injury claim—injuries sustained in France—English proceedings—expert evidence

See *Wall v Mutuelle De Poitiers Assurances*, para 431.

2238   Commercial road transport workers—breach of rest breaks—request for secondary legislation to provide civil remedy

The claimant trade union applied for judicial review of the defendant Secretary of State's refusal to accede to the claimant's request that he introduce secondary legislation to provide commercial road transport workers with a civil remedy, in particular in the form of access to an employment tribunal, if they were required to work in contravention of regulations providing for breaks and rest periods. The claimant's complaint was that the refusal to introduce any such secondary legislation in respect of commercial road transport workers, so as to bring their situation into line with the access to a tribunal available for the generality of other workers in a comparable situation, was a breach of the principle of equivalence and/or the principle of effectiveness. The judge dismissed the claim on the basis that commercial road transport workers had a right to redress through the Vehicle and Operator Services Agency ('VOSA'). The claimant appealed. Held, the judge had reached the right conclusion on both issues. In respect of the principle of equivalence, *Oyarce v Cheshire CC* was decisive on the issue and the ground of appeal had to fail. In respect of the principle of effectiveness, any employee had access to VOSA to make any relevant complaint. If he was threatened with dismissal, he might further rely on the protected disclosure provisions of the relevant employment legislation. If instructed to act in breach of the Road Transport (Working Time) Regulations 2005, SI 2005/639, he would also have a potential civil claim against his employer for breach of implied duty in the contract of employment. All of that told strongly against the principle of effectiveness being infringed. On the facts, the enforcement provisions under the 2005 Regulations did not infringe the principle of effectiveness. Accordingly, the appeal would be dismissed.

R (on the application of United Road Transport Union) v Secretary of State for Transport [2013] EWCA Civ 962, [2013] IRLR 890 (Court of Appeal: Jackson, Elias and Davis LJJ). *Oyarce v Cheshire CC* [2008] EWCA Civ 434, [2008] 4 All ER 907 (2008 Abr para 1234) applied. Decision of Hickinbottom J [2012] EWHC 1909 (Admin) [2012] IRLR 941 affirmed.

2239   Drink-driving—rehabilitation courses—Wales

The Rehabilitation Courses (Relevant Drink Offences) (Wales) Regulations 2013, SI 2013/372 (in force in part on 15 March 2013 and in part on 24 June 2013), make provision about drink-driver rehabilitation courses, specifically, by (1) providing for application to the Welsh Ministers for approval of a rehabilitation course; (2) making provision about the Welsh Ministers' decision on such an application; (3) providing for the payment of fees; (4) providing for withdrawal of approval of courses in the event of a course provider failing to observe a condition of approval, disregarding guidance or ceasing to be an appropriate person to provide the course or administer its provision efficiently or effectively; (5) providing that, save where the Welsh Ministers believe the course provider, or a person acting with the provider's authority, has been guilty of serious misconduct meriting immediate withdrawal, a warning notice must first be given allowing the provider an opportunity to reply to the proposal to withdraw approval; (6) providing for appeals against the refusal of an application for approval, the imposition of a condition on the grant of approval or the withdrawal of an approval; (7) requiring appeals to be made within a specified period to the First-tier Tribunal, which has the power to make such orders as it thinks fit; (8) setting out a minimum course fee of £150 and a maximum course fee of £250; (9) specifing when and how course fees are to be paid; (10) empowering the Welsh Ministers to require information from course providers about their administration and conduct of courses and also their compliance with the Road Traffic Offenders Act 1988 ss 34A–34C; (11) setting out the form of a certificate of completion of a course and of a notice of non-compliance and also the circumstances in which such a notice is to be treated as having been given; and (12) empowering the Welsh Ministers to publish, free of charge, information about courses, including their cost.

2240   Driving licence—exchangeable licences

The Driving Licences (Exchangeable Licences) (Amendment) Order 2013, SI 2013/22 (in force in part on 11 January 2013 and in part on 19 January 2013), designates countries and territories for the purpose of allowing driving licences issued in those countries or territories in respect of specified vehicles to be exchanged for a driving licence issued in Great Britain.

2241   Driving without insurance and licence—causing death by driving—fault or otherwise blameworthy act

The appellant was driving his family in his camper van along a single-carriageway trunk road. A third party's car crashed into the appellant's van, tipping it over and trapping some of the occupants inside. The third party died from injuries he suffered in the impact. He was found to have been a drug user and under the influence of heroin. It was accepted on all sides that there was nothing the appellant could have done to avoid the collision. Although his manner of driving could not be criticised, the appellant had been without insurance and without a full driving licence. However, rather than being prosecuted for driving uninsured and driving without a full licence, contrary to the Road Traffic Act 1988 ss 87 and 143, the appellant was prosecuted for two offences under s 3ZB of causing the death of the third party at a time when he had been uninsured and without a full driving licence. The recorder ruled that the appellant had not committed either offence because he had not caused the death of the third party. The Crown appealed and the Court of Appeal considered itself bound to allow the appeal by the decision in *R v Williams*, ruling that the appellant had, in law, caused the death. On appeal by the appellant, *held*, it would plainly have been possible for Parliament to legislate in terms which left it beyond doubt that a driver was made guilty of causing death whenever a car which he was driving was involved in a fatal accident if he were at the time uninsured, disqualified or unlicensed. However, it had not and had used the expression 'causes ... death ... by driving'. That imported the concept of causation. The gravity of a conviction for homicide, for which the sentence might be a term of imprisonment, was such that if Parliament wished to displace the normal approach to causation recognised by the common law and substitute a different rule, it had to do so unambiguously. Where Parliament had plainly chosen not to adopt unequivocal language which had been readily available, it followed that an intention to create the meaning contended for by the Crown could not be attributed to it. There was no logical or satisfactory intermediate position between the holding that the law imposed guilt of homicide whenever the unlicensed motorist was involved in a fatal accident and that he was guilty of causing death only when there was some additional feature of his driving which was causative on a common sense view and the latter entailed there being something in the manner of his driving which was open to proper criticism. The statutory expression could not be given effect unless there was something to be criticised in the driving of the defendant, which contributed in some more than minimal way to the death. Juries ought to be directed that it was not necessary for the Crown to prove careless or inconsiderate driving, but that there had to be something open to proper criticism in the driving of the defendant, beyond the mere presence of the vehicle on the road and which contributed in some more than minimal way to the death. The recorder had been correct to rule that the appellant had not in law caused the death by his driving. There was no suggestion that there had been anything which the appellant had either done or omitted to do in the driving of the car which had contributed to the least extent to the fatality. The driving of the appellant had been, no doubt, a 'but for' cause of the death. By the test of common sense, while the appellant's driving had created the opportunity for his car to be run into by the third party, what had brought about the latter's death had been his own dangerous driving under the influence of drugs. Accordingly, the appeal would be allowed.

R v Hughes [2013] UKSC 56, [2014] 1 Cr App Rep 46, [2013] All ER (D) 388 (Jul) (Supreme Court: Lord Neuberger P, Lord Mance, Lord Kerr, Lord Hughes and Lord Toulson SCJJ). *R v Hennigan* [1971] 3 All ER 133, CA, applied. *R v Williams* [2010] EWCA Crim 2552, [2010] All ER (D) 19 (Nov) (2010 Abr para 2421) considered. Decision of Court of Appeal [2011] EWCA Crim 1508, [2011] All ER (D) 135 (Jun) (2011 Abr para 2122) reversed.

2242   Fixed penalty—offences

The Fixed Penalty Offences Order 2013, SI 2013/1565 (in force on 16 August 2013), provides for the offence of driving a mechanically propelled vehicle on a road or other public place without due care and attention, or without reasonable consideration for other persons using the road or place, to be a fixed penalty offence for the purposes of the Road Traffic Offenders Act 1988.

The Fixed Penalty (Amendment) Order 2013, SI 2013/1569 (in force on 16 August 2013), further amends the 2000 Order, SI 2000/2792, by specifying the amount of fixed penalty payable in relation to an offence of driving a vehicle on a road or other public place without due care and attention, or without reasonable consideration for other persons using the road or place. The order also increases the amount of fixed penalty prescribed for certain offences, including graduated fixed penalties.

The Fixed Penalty (Amendment) (No 2) Order 2013, SI 2013/1840 (in force on 15 August 2013), amends the principal 2013 Order above to correct an error with the effect that fixed penalty levels for parking offences outside Greater London remain unchanged.

2243   HGV Road User Levy Act 2013

The HGV Road User Levy Act 2013 makes provision charging a levy in respect of the use or keeping of heavy goods vehicles on public roads in the United Kingdom. The Act received the royal assent on 28 February 2013 and came into force in part on that day. The remaining provisions come into force in accordance with provision made by order. For details of commencement, see the commencement table in the title STATUTES AND LEGISLATIVE PROCESS.

Section 1 introduces a duty of excise, called HGV road user levy, charged in respect of any heavy goods vehicle which is used or kept on a public road in the United Kingdom. A 'heavy goods vehicle' is defined in s 2 as a mechanically propelled vehicle with a revenue weight of 12,000 kg or more, or a heavy motor car within the meaning of the Road Traffic Act 1988 s 185 in respect of which vehicle excise duty is charged at the applicable rate or would be so charged but for an exception granted on the basis that the vehicle is only temporarily in the United Kingdom. The 2013 Act s 3, which provides that the Act applies to public roads in the United Kingdom, empowers the Secretary of State, by order, to disapply the levy in relation to specified roads or roads of a specified description. The persons liable for the levy, whether the vehicle is a UK heavy goods vehicle or a non-UK heavy goods vehicle, are described in s 4. Sections 5, 6 and Sch 1 set out the payment requirements for UK and non-UK heavy goods vehicles in respect of the levy, including details of when it is to be paid and the amount to be paid for each vehicle. A person who has paid the levy is entitled to a rebate if his vehicle has been stolen, destroyed, sold or no longer kept or used on a road to which the 2013 Act applies, provided the levy has been paid for more than one month and at least one month of the levy period remains: s 7. Exemptions and reductions are specified by s 8, which also empowers the Secretary of State to make regulations exempting certain heavy goods vehicles from paying the levy or allowing them to pay it at a reduced rate. By virtue of s 9, for the purpose of collecting HGV road user levy, the Secretary of State and his officers (including any individual or body authorised by the Secretary of State to act as his agent for these purposes) have the same powers, duties and liabilities as the Commissioners for Her Majesty's Revenue and Customs and their officers have with respect to duties of excise (other than duties on imported goods), and other matters (except matters relating only to duties on imported goods). A stopping officer has power to stop a vehicle appearing to be a heavy goods vehicle in order to check whether the levy is unpaid in respect of the vehicle: s 10. Using or keeping a heavy goods vehicle on a road if the levy has not been paid is an offence: s 11. The arrangements for legal proceedings in relation to an offence under s 11 are provided by s 12, Sch 2. An offence under the 2013 Act is a fixed penalty offence: s 13. The Secretary of State is required by s 14 to set up and keep a register of the heavy goods vehicles in respect of which HGV road user levy has been paid; the register must show the prescribed information on a website indicating that it is kept by or on behalf of the Secretary of State. By virtue of s 15, the Secretary of State may refuse to issue a vehicle licence if the levy has not been paid. A highway authority has power under s 16 to install equipment for the detection of offences under s 11. Sections 17, 18 provide for the making of regulations and orders under the Act, s 19 provides for interpretation and ss 20–22 provide for extent, commencement and short title.

2244   International road traffic—visitors' driving permits—local border traffic permit— multiple visits

The claimant was a Ukrainian national who had a local border traffic permit which authorised him to enter the border area of Hungary. During the relevant five-month period, the claimant entered Hungary on 105 separate occasions, staying on each occasion for several hours. Since the claimant had stayed in the Schengen area for more than three months during a six-month period, the local border police authority decided to refuse him entry into Hungarian territory pursuant to Hungarian law. The claimant challenged that decision before a county court, which ruled that there was no limit on the number of entries to which the holder of a local border traffic permit was entitled, and that the three-month limit laid down in the Schengen Convention applied only to uninterrupted stays. A preliminary ruling was sought as to (1) whether European Parliament and Council Regulation (EC) 1931/2006 (laying down rules on the local border traffic at the external land borders of the member states) was to be interpreted in the light of the Schengen Convention, or whether it should be given an autonomous interpretation; and (2) how frequently it was acceptable for there to be interruptions of stay on the part of the holder of a local border traffic permit for the purposes of Regulation 1931/2006 art 5. *Held*, Regulation 1931/2006 was an integral part of the Schengen acquis. The rule under which the duration of short stays of third-country nationals exempt from visa requirements was limited to a total of three months over a six-month period had to take precedence over any other provision. It followed that holders of a local border traffic permit who were exempt from visa requirements under Regulation 1931/2006 were not excepted from that rule. Regulation 1931/2006 had to be interpreted as meaning that the holder of a local border traffic permit granted under the special local border traffic regime should be able to move freely within the border area for a period of three months if his stay was uninterrupted and to have a new right to a three-month stay each time that his stay was interrupted. Regulation 1931/2006 also had to be interpreted as meaning that there was an interruption of stay on the crossing of the border between the neighbouring member state and the third country in which the holder of the local border traffic permit resided, in accordance with the conditions laid down in that permit, irrespective of the frequency of such crossings, even if they occurred several times daily.

Case   C-254/11   *Szabolcs-Szatmar-Bereg   Megyei   Rendorkapitanysag   Zahony Hatarrendeszeti Kirendeltsege v Oskar Shomodi* [2013] All ER (D) 10 (May) (ECJ: Fourth Chamber).

2245   London Local Authorities and Transport for London Act 2013

See para 1811.

2246   Road vehicles—superseded provisions—revocation

The Road Traffic, Public Passenger Transport and Vehicles (Revocations) Order 2013, SI 2013/2987 (in force on 31 December 2013), revokes, because they are redundant, have been superseded or are no longer required, the Motorcycles (Sound Level Measurement Certificates) Regulations 1980, SI 1980/765, the Public Service Vehicles (London Local Service Licences) Regulations 1986, SI 1986/1691, the Cycle Racing on Highways (Tour de France 1994) Regulations 1994, SI 1994/1226, the Public Service Vehicles (Lost Property) Regulations 1978, SI 1978/1684, the Road Traffic (Carriage of Dangerous Goods and Substances) (Amendment) Regulations 1992, SI 1992/1213, the Road Traffic (Training of Drivers of Vehicles Carrying Dangerous Goods) (Amendment) Regulations 1993, SI 1993/1122, the Parking Attendants (Wearing of Uniforms) (London) Regulations 1993, SI 1993/1450, the Drivers' Hours (Passenger and Goods Vehicles) (Exemption) Regulations 1996, SI 1996/240, and, in relation to England, the Vehicles (Conditions of Use on Footpaths) Regulations 1963, SI 1963/2126.

2247   Motor vehicles—competitions and trials—Wales

The Motor Vehicles (Competitions and Trials) (Amendment) (Wales) Regulations 2013, SI 2013/2496 (in force on 25 October 2013), further amend the 1969 Regulations, SI 1969/414, so as to (1) appoint the Royal Automobile Club Motor Sports Association Ltd, in place of the Royal Automobile Club, as the authorising body for events consisting of a competition or trial taking place wholly or partly in Wales and involving the use of motor vehicles on a public highway; (2) permit that body to determine its own application fees, which must not exceed a reasonable amount; and (3) rename one of the specified events.

2248   Motor vehicles—disabled persons—badges—England

The Disabled Persons (Badges for Motor Vehicles) (England) (Amendment) Regulations 2013, SI 2013/2203 (in force on 8 October 2013), further amend the 2000 Regulations, SI 2000/682, so as to (1) provide that a disabled person's badge must now be in a form specified or approved by the Secretary of State; (2) change references to a local authority, or to residence in the area or a local authority, for the purposes of a new power under the Disabled Persons' Parking Badges Act 2013 for the Secretary of State to issue badges to members of Her Majesty's Armed Forces and certain other persons who are resident in specified places; (3) apply to recognised badges issued outside Great Britain the provisions which enable an authority to refuse to issue a badge where the applicant already holds a badge issued by another authority, and which require the return of a badge where the holder is issued with a badge by more than one authority; (4) introduce a new requirement that a badge retained by a constable or enforcement officer in certain circumstances, pursuant to the 2013 Act, must be returned to the holder as soon as reasonably practicable; and (5) omit certain provisions concerning appeals and provisions which have been made redundant by the amendment described in head (1) above.

2249   Motor vehicles—disabled persons—badges—Wales

The Disabled Persons (Badges for Motor Vehicles) (Wales) (Amendment) Regulations 2013, SI 2013/438 (in force on 8 April 2013), further amend the 2000 Regulations, SI 2000/1786, so as to (1) modify the description of persons to whom a disabled person's badge may be issued by adding a new class of eligibility comprising persons who are in receipt of personal independence payments at prescribed levels; and (2) make changes as regards the photographic requirements for persons with disabilities which prevent them from looking directly at the camera, opening their eyes or closing their mouth by providing that where these requirements cannot be fulfilled, a photograph will still be accepted, provided it is accompanied by a written statement explaining the reasons for non-compliance.

2250   Motor vehicles—driving licences

The Motor Vehicles (Driving Licences) (Amendment) Regulations 2013, SI 2013/258 (in force on 8 March 2013), further amend the 1999 Regulations, SI 1999/2864, so as to change the medical standards applicable for driver licensing of applicants and licence holders in relation to eyesight and epilepsy, as specified in Council Directive (EC) 2009/113. In particular, the regulations (1) make provision so there is no longer a single description of epilepsy as a prescribed disability for both groups of licences; (2) in relation to Group 1 licences, (a) prescribe impairment of vision as a relevant disability, where an applicant for, or holder of, a Group 1 licence fails to meet visual acuity standards or visual field standards, or in the case of a person with diplopia or sight in only one eye fails to meet the adaptation standard for those conditions; (b) provide that a licence must not be refused on the basis that a person fails to meet visual field standards, where conditions prescribed under the Road Traffic Act 1988 s 92(4)(b) are met; (c) make epilepsy a prescribed disability for Group 1, where there has been more than one epileptic seizure in the previous five years, and prescribe the circumstances in which a licence can be granted to a person who has had two or more epileptic seizures in the previous five years where the condition is controlled; and (d) prescribe an isolated seizure or isolated epileptic seizure as a relevant disability, where that seizure has occurred in the previous six months (or one year if there is an underlying causative factor that may increase future risk); a Group 1 licence must not be refused on the grounds of an isolated seizure, which occurred outside those prescribed periods, provided additional conditions are also met; (3) in relation to Group 2 licences, (a) prescribe impairment of vision as a relevant disability, where an applicant for, or holder, of a Group 2 licence fails to meet Group 2 visual acuity, visual field or corrective lenses standards, or has sight in only one eye or uncontrolled diplopia, unless a person is excepted from a standard; (b) amend the Group 2 additional visual acuity standard; (c) prescribe the Group 2 visual field standard and the corrective lenses standard for visual acuity; (d) prescribe conditions to be satisfied by certain categories of person with sight in one eye where there is an existing entitlement to drive; (e) make epilepsy a prescribed disability for Group 2, where there has been more than one seizure, or medication to treat epilepsy has been prescribed, in the previous ten years; a Group 2 licence must not be refused on grounds of epilepsy where the conditions for an isolated seizure are met; or in any other case, where no seizure has occurred and no epilepsy medication has been prescribed in the ten-year period immediately before the date when the licence is granted and additional conditions are met; and (f) also prescribe an isolated seizure as a relevant disability for Group 2, where such a seizure has occurred, or medication has been prescribed to treat epilepsy or a seizure, during the previous five-year period; a Group 2 licence must not be refused on grounds of an isolated seizure, provided no seizure has occurred and no relevant medication has been prescribed, in the five-year period immediately before the date on which the licence is granted and provided additional conditions are also met; (4) amend the prescribed disability relating to impairment of vision, for the purposes of the 1988 Act s 94(5)(b)(i) (examination by officer nominated by the Secretary of State); and (5) require the Secretary of State to review the operation and effect of the regulations and publish a report within five years after they come into force and within every five years after that.

The Motor Vehicles (Driving Licences) (Amendment) (No 2) Regulations 2013, SI 2013/1013 (in force on 1 June 2013), further amend the 1999 Regulations above so as to provide that, in certain circumstances, the Secretary of State may require a person who has been disqualified from driving by a court for failing, without reasonable excuse, to give permission for a laboratory test of a specimen of blood taken pursuant to the Road Traffic Act 1988 s 7A to undergo a medical examination, provide an authorisation for a medical practitioner to release information, or undergo a driving test.

The Motor Vehicles (Driving Licences) (Amendment) (No 3) Regulations 2013, SI 2013/2184 (in force on 7 October 2013), further amend the 1999 Regulations so as to provide that the minimum age for holding or obtaining a licence for a small car driven without a trailer is 16 for persons in receipt of the mobility component at the enhanced rate of the allowance known as personal independence payment ('PIP'). Recipients of the higher rate component of the disability living allowance ('DLA') will also benefit from the entitlement to hold or obtain a driving licence aged 16 provided that they comply with the three requirements, which are (1) that a person has received an award of the higher rate component of DLA; (2) that the award was in force immediately before his sixteenth birthday; and (3) that he has made a claim for PIP, whether or not an award of PIP is subsequently made.

See para 2466.

2251   Motor vehicles—insurance

See INSURANCE.

2252   Motor vehicles—international circulation

The Motor Vehicles (International Circulation) (Amendment) Order 2013, SI 2013/3150 (in force on 12 December 2013), further amends the 1975 Order, SI 1975/1208, so as to exempt a vehicle from excise duty when it is used for certain types of cabotage operations which are not already exempt.

2253   Motor vehicles—off-road events—Wales

The Motor Vehicles (Off Road Events) (Amendment) (Wales) Regulations 2013, SI 2013/2494 (in force on 25 October 2013), further amend the 1995 Regulations, SI 1995/1371, by making changes to the list of bodies appointed to authorise off-road events in Wales, so that the Association of Rover Clubs Limited is replaced by the Association of Land Rover Clubs Limited, the Auto-Cycle Union is replaced by the Auto-Cycle Union Limited and the Royal Automobile Club is replaced by the Royal Automobile Club Motor Sports Association Limited. The regulations also make additional provision in relation to the setting of application fees by authorising bodies.

2254   Motor vehicles—registration—tax—vehicle used in two member states—freedom of establishment

The appellant was a Belgian national who lived and worked in the Netherlands for part of each year. She spent the rest of the year in Belgium. The appellant owned a car which she had purchased in Belgium but which she used in both Belgium and the Netherlands for private and professional purposes. Although the appellant had registered her car in Belgium and paid car registration tax there, the Dutch tax authorities decided that the appellant should also pay vehicle tax in the Netherlands. Accordingly they issued a tax assessment notice to the appellant. The appellant's challenge against the notice was dismissed on the basis that the appellant had been resident in the Netherlands and had been using her car on the Dutch public road network. The case reached the Dutch Supreme Court, which decided to stay the proceedings and refer for a preliminary ruling the question of whether TFEU art 49, which guaranteed the right to freedom of establishment, should be interpreted as precluding legislation of a member state under which a motor vehicle, which had been registered and had already been the subject of taxation as a result of its registration in another member state, had been the subject of a tax when it had first been used on the national road network, where that vehicle had been intended, essentially, to be actually used on a long-term basis in both those member states or had, in fact, been used in that manner. *Held*, in the absence of harmonisation at European Union level, the disadvantages which could arise from the parallel exercise of tax competences by different member states, to the extent that such an exercise was not discriminatory, did not constitute restrictions on the freedom of movement. Further, assuming that the chargeable event for the vehicle tax and the car registration tax was the same, member states were not obliged to adapt their own tax systems to the different systems of tax of other member states in order to eliminate double taxation. The contested legislation did not put the appellant at a disadvantage compared to self-employed persons who were already subject to the vehicle tax, since each Netherlands resident, whether self-employed or not, was subject to that tax either when a motor vehicle was registered in the Dutch vehicle register or when such a vehicle, registered in another member state, was first used on the road network in the Netherlands. It followed that the tax disadvantage suffered by the appellant, which resulted only from the non-discriminatory exercise of the tax systems of both member states concerned, did not contravene art 49. Article 49 therefore had to be interpreted as not precluding legislation of the type in question provided the tax was not discriminatory.

Case C-302/12 *X v Minister van Financien* [2013] All ER (D) 240 (Nov) (ECJ: Second Chamber).

2255   Parking—contraventions—approved devices—Wales

The Civil Enforcement of Road Traffic Contraventions (Approved Devices) (Wales) Order 2013, SI 2013/360 (in force on 25 March 2013), replaces the 2008 Order, SI 2008/1215, and specifies a description of a device which is an approved device for the purposes of the Civil Enforcement of Road Traffic Contraventions (General Provisions) (Wales) Regulations 2013, SI 2013/362 (see para 2261).

2256   Parking—contraventions—enforcement

The Bus Lane Contraventions (Approved Local Authorities) (England) (Amendment) and Civil Enforcement of Parking Contraventions Designation Order 2013, SI 2013/992 (in force on 30 May 2013), designates specified parts of five county council areas as civil enforcement areas for parking contraventions and special enforcement areas for the purposes of the Traffic Management Act 2004 Pt 6 (ss 72–93). SI 2002/2186 and SI 2008/2567 are revoked, SI 2005/2755 is further amended, and SI 2011/2431 is amended.

2257   Parking—contraventions—guidelines—levels of charges—Wales

The Civil Enforcement of Road Traffic Contraventions (Guidelines on Levels of Charges) (Wales) Order 2013, SI 2013/1969 (in force 2 November 2013), replaces the 2008 Order, SI 2008/613, and sets out the guidelines given by the Welsh Ministers for the setting by enforcement authorities of the level of charges for parking contraventions.

2258   Parking—parking places—designation—resident permits—increase in charges— lawfulness

The Road Traffic Regulation Act 1984 s 45(2)(a) entitles a local authority to designate by order a parking place for use only by such persons or vehicles, or such persons or vehicles of a class specified in the order, as may be authorised for the purpose by a permit from the authority operating the parking place. Except in the case of a public service vehicle, the authority may make such charge in connection with the issue or use of the permit, of such amount and payable in such manner, as the authority by whom the designation order was made may by order prescribe: s 45(2)(b).

The defendant local authority decided to increase the charges for resident parking permits and visitor vouchers in controlled parking zones in the borough pursuant to the 1984 Act s 45. The claimant, who was a resident of the borough, brought a judicial review claim against the defendant, contending that the increase in charges was unlawful because its purpose was to generate a surplus, beyond the money needed to operate the parking scheme, to fund other transport expenditure such as road repair and concessionary fares. The defendant submitted that there were no restrictions on the charging power in s 45(2)(b) other than those imposed by the general principles of administrative law. It argued that an increase could not be irrationally high, but that aside an authority was entitled to exercise its charging powers in order to generate a surplus to defray the cost of other transport expenditure, provided it came within the scope of s 122. The defendant sought to rely on s 55, which it claimed expressly provided for any surplus to be used for other road traffic purposes. *Held*, the 1984 Act was not a taxing statute, although the permit charges generated revenue for local authorities. A public body had to exercise a statutory power for the purpose for which the power had been conferred by Parliament, and not for any unauthorised purpose. The defendant's purpose in increasing the charges for resident parking permits and visitor vouchers was to generate additional income to meet projected expenditure for road maintenance and improvement, concessionary fares and other road transport. The 1984 Act was not a fiscal measure and did not authorise an authority to use its powers to charge local residents for parking in order to raise surplus revenue for other transport purposes funded by the authority's general fund. The intention was to transfer the surplus on the special parking account to the general fund, to defray other road transport expenditure and reduce the need to raise income from other sources, such as fines, charges and council tax. That was not authorised under the 1984 Act. It followed that the defendant's decision was unlawful and, accordingly, the application would be allowed.

R (on the application of Attfield) v Barnet LBC [2013] EWHC 2089 (Admin), [2014] 1 All ER 304 (Queen's Bench Division: Lang J).

2259   Road safety—financial penalty deposit—appropriate amount

The Road Safety (Financial Penalty Deposit) (Appropriate Amount) (Amendment) Order 2013, SI 2013/2025 (in force on 16 August 2013), further amends the 2009 Order, SI 2009/492, by (1) increasing the appropriate amounts of financial deposits (a) for fixed penalty offences (except those relating to parking offences); (b) where a person has been given notification that it appears likely that proceedings will be brought against him; and (c) in respect of any single occasion in circumstances where more than one financial penalty deposit requirement is imposed; and (2) specifying £100 for the deposit for the fixed penalty offence of driving a mechanically propelled vehicle on a road or other public place without due care and attention, or without reasonable consideration for other persons using the road or place.

2260   Road Safety Act 2006—commencement

The Road Safety Act 2006 (Commencement No 10) Order 2013, SI 2013/1012, brings s 13 into force on 1 June 2013. For a summary of the Act, see 2006 Abr para 2491. See also the commencement table in the title STATUTES AND LEGISLATIVE PROCESS.

2261   Road traffic contraventions—civil enforcement—general provisions—Wales

The Civil Enforcement of Road Traffic Contraventions (General Provisions) (Wales) Regulations 2013, SI 2013/362 (in force on 25 March 2013), replace the Civil Enforcement of Parking Contraventions (General Provisions) (Wales) (No 2) Regulations 2008, SI 2008/1214, and the Civil Enforcement of Parking Contraventions (Penalty Charge Notices, Enforcement and Adjudication) (Wales) Regulations 2008, SI 2008/609, and provide for the civil enforcement of road traffic contraventions in Wales in accordance with the Traffic Management Act 2004 Pt 6 (ss 72–93). In particular, the regulations (1) make provision for the service of a penalty charge notice by post; (2) enable a penalty charge to be imposed for specified types of road traffic contravention; (3) provide that a penalty charge is payable by the owner of the vehicle concerned, except where the vehicle is hired a vehicle hiring firm under a vehicle hiring agreement; (4) specify that a penalty charge is not to be imposed except on the basis of a record produced by an 'approved device' or information given by a civil enforcement officer as to conduct observed by that officer; (5) provide that a penalty charge is not to be payable for a road traffic contravention where the contravention is the subject of criminal proceedings or a fixed penalty notice has been given under the Road Traffic Offenders Act 1988, but, if a penalty charge is in fact paid in either of those circumstances, it must be refunded by the enforcement authority; (6) define a penalty charge notice and make detailed provision as to the form and content of such notices; (7) enable a civil enforcement officer, where that officer has reason to believe that a penalty charge is payable for a stationary vehicle in a civil enforcement area, to fix a penalty charge notice to the vehicle or hand one to the person appearing to him to be in charge of it; (8) make provision for the service of a penalty charge notice by post, on the basis of the evidence of an approved device or where a civil enforcement officer has been prevented by some person from serving one, or had begun to prepare a penalty charge notice, but the vehicle was driven away before it had been served, and for time limits applicable to notices served by post; (9) make it an offence to interfere with a penalty charge notice served by its being fixed to a vehicle, except by or under the authority of the owner or person in charge of the vehicle or the enforcement authority; (10) in relation to the immobilisation of vehicles for parking contraventions, define when an immobilisation device may be fixed to a vehicle, require a notice to be fixed to the vehicle at the time of immobilisation and create the offences of interfering with the notice or the immobilisation device; (11) specify exceptions to the general power to immobilise and specify the pre-requisites for the release of a vehicle from an immobilisation device; (12) in relation to provision for the appointment of adjudicators by enforcement authorities and for the functions of those authorities relating to adjudicators to be discharged through joint committees, require the Welsh enforcement authorities to act through one or more joint committees and also provide for arrangements under the Road Traffic Act 1991 to be continued as between Welsh and, where required, English enforcement authorities until superseded; (13) require enforcement authorities to appoint a sufficient number of adjudicators and provision is made for parking adjudicators holding office under the 1991 Act immediately before the coming into force of the regulations to continue in office; (14) deal with the expenses of the relevant authorities, provide for the Welsh enforcement authorities to refer decisions concerning the apportionment of expenses to an independent arbitrator and give the Welsh Ministers power to give directions to the joint committee to refer such matters for arbitration; (15) in connection with the enforcement of penalty charges, provide for the service of a notice to owner by an enforcement authority in respect of an unpaid penalty charge and specify the contents of a notice to owner and the time limit for service; (16) provide for the service of charge certificates in respect of unpaid penalty charges, where a notice to owner or penalty charge notice has been served and the avenues of appeal have not been pursued or have been pursued unsuccessfully, for charge certificates to be enforced through a county court and for county court orders to be set aside where the respondent serves a witness statement stating one of the specified matters; (17) apply the Road Traffic Regulation Act 1984 s 55 with modifications, to the income and expenditure of enforcement authorities from parking places under the 2004 Act Pt 6; (18) make provision for separate accounts to be kept in respect of the income and expenditure from bus lane and moving traffic contraventions respectively; (19) provide that a surplus in an account kept under the 1984 Act s 55 must be carried forward and specify the purposes for which those funds, and any surplus resulting from bus lane and moving traffic contraventions, must be applied; and (20) deal with revocation of previous legislation and amendment to the 2004 Act Sch 7 to allow further traffic signs to be included for moving traffic contravention purposes.

2262 Road traffic contraventions—civil enforcement—representations and appeals—Wales

The Civil Enforcement of Road Traffic Contraventions (Representations and Appeals) (Wales) Regulations 2013, SI 2013/359 (in force on 27 February 2013), replace the 2008 Regulations, SI 2008/608, and make provision entitling a person who is or may be liable to pay a penalty charge in respect of a road traffic contravention or who secures the release of a vehicle from an immobilisation device which has been fixed to it on account of such a contravention, to make representations to the enforcement authority regarding liability for those charges and to appeal to an adjudicator if those representations are not accepted. The regulations concern representations and appeals against penalty charge notices and notices to owner and, in particular, (1) specify the information to be given to the recipients of penalty charge notices and notices to owner; (2) confer on the recipient of a notice to owner or penalty charge notice the right to make representations to the enforcement authority which served it; (3) set out the duties of an enforcement authority to which representations are made; and (4) enable a person who has made representations to appeal to an adjudicator against an enforcement authority's rejection of those representations. The regulations also make equivalent provisions for representations and appeals in relation to vehicles which have been immobilised and, in particular, (a) confer, on the owner or person in charge of a vehicle who secures its release from an immobilisation device, a right to make representations to the enforcement authority and to appeal to an adjudicator, where those representations are rejected; the enforcement authority is required to inform the person securing the release of the vehicle of their rights in writing; (b) specify the basis for making representations; (c) set out the duties of an enforcement authority to which representations are made; and (d) provide for an appeal to be made to an adjudicator where representations are rejected. Further, the regulations relate to offences and procedure and, in particular, (i) create an offence of making false or reckless representations; and (ii) make provision as to the procedure to be followed in adjudication proceedings, the service of documents in such proceedings and the requirements to keep a register; otherwise the procedure is in the discretion of the adjudicator.

The Civil Enforcement of Road Traffic Contraventions (Representations and Appeals) Removed Vehicles (Wales) Regulations 2013, SI 2013/361 (in force on 27 February 2013), replace the 2008 Regulations, SI 2008/615, so as to (1) allow a person whose vehicle has been removed from a civil enforcement area under the Road Traffic Regulation Act 1984 s 99 to make representations to the enforcement authority and to appeal to an adjudicator where such representations are rejected; (2) set out the duties of the enforcement authority to which representations are made; (3) provide for an appeal to be made to an adjudicator where the representations are rejected; and (4) apply the Civil Enforcement of Road Traffic Contraventions (Representations and Appeals) (Wales) Regulations 2013, SI 2013/359, Schedule, to procedure and the service of documents in adjudicator proceedings under the regulations.

2263   Road user charging—penalty charges, adjudication and enforcement—England

The Road User Charging Schemes (Penalty Charges, Adjudication and Enforcement) (England) Regulations 2013, SI 2013/1783 (in force on 2 September 2013), make provision for the civil enforcement of a penalty charge imposed in respect of a motor vehicle by a road user charging scheme made under the Transport Act 2000 Pt 3 (ss 163–200). The regulations (1) prescribe the circumstances in which a penalty charge will be payable; (2) require that the rates of penalty charge imposed by a charging authority are to be specified in the charging scheme or communicated to users of the road over which they apply; (3) specify the maximum level of penalty charge that a charging scheme may impose for the use of a designated road; (4) provide that primary liability for a penalty charge resides with the registered keeper of a vehicle, but may be transferred to another person in specified circumstances; (5) prescribe when a penalty charge notice can be served and what information it must contain; (6) empower the recipient of a penalty charge notice to make representations to the charging authority, which may accept the representations and cancel the penalty charge notice or reject the representations; (7) provide for a right of appeal to an adjudicator against a refusal by the charging authority to accept any representations made; (8) make provision for the appointment of road user charging scheme adjudicators, the procedure they must follow and the recovery of sums that are the subject of an adjudicator's award; (9) provide that, where a penalty charge remains unpaid after the period specified, the charging authority may issue a charge certificate, after which, if the penalty charge continues to remain unpaid, the sum due may be enforced as if it were payable under a county court order; (10) provide that any sum to be paid under an adjudication or unpaid penalty charge which in either case is recoverable as if it was payable under a county court order may be enforced in accordance with the Enforcement of Road Traffic Debts Order 1993, SI 1993/2073; (11) detail the range of enforcement powers in respect of motor vehicles that a charging authority may provide for in a charging scheme; (12) create powers to examine and enter motor vehicles, which apply to any motor vehicle where the charging scheme so provides; (13) enable an authorised person to ascertain that any document or equipment required by the charging scheme to be carried, used or displayed in a motor vehicle is being properly carried, used or displayed; (14) allow items to be seized (if the charging scheme so provides) if they are evidence of the commission of an offence under the Transport Act 2000 s 173(5) or (6); (15) provide that, where there are three or more unpaid penalty charges in respect of a vehicle, the registered keeper's address cannot be ascertained, a period of 14 days from the date on which the third unpaid penalty charge was imposed has elapsed, and the charging scheme so provides, the motor vehicle may be immobilised, removed, and, if not released or returned, disposed of to recover the unpaid penalty charges (and, where the charging scheme provides, any unpaid road user charges); (16) authorise a person to take possession of a removed motor vehicle, subject to stated conditions including the payment of all unpaid road user charges and penalty charges; (17) allow the keeper of a motor vehicle that has been disposed of to recover any excess proceeds following payment of all unpaid road user charges and penalty charges provided the claim is made within one year of such disposal; (18) allow for representations to be made to the charging authority, and appeals to be made to an adjudicator, arising from the exercise of the powers to immobilise, remove or dispose of a motor vehicle; (19) provide that the charging authority may accept such representations and make an appropriate refund, or reject them; (20) provide for an appeal to an adjudicator where the charging authority rejects the representations; and (21) detail the procedure for appeals to an adjudicator against the issue of a penalty charge notice or the exercise of powers in respect of a motor vehicle.

2264   Road vehicles—registration and licensing

The Road Vehicles (Registration and Licensing) (Amendment) Regulations 2013, SI 2013/2909 (in force on 16 December 2013), further amend the 2002 Regulations, SI 2002/2742, so as to (1) provide for first nil licences for vehicles to run for a period of 12 months plus a further period commencing on the 10th, 17th or 24th day of the month in which the licence first has effect; and (2) replace the requirement to make an annual statutory off-road notification in respect of a vehicle with a requirement to make a statutory off-road notification that will have effect indefinitely until such time as a vehicle licence or nil licence is taken out for the vehicle. If the vehicle keeper of an unlicensed vehicle is changed, and the new keeper wishes to keep the vehicle unlicensed, the new keeper is required to make a new statutory off-road notification.

2265   Road vehicles—testing

The Road Vehicles (Testing) (Miscellaneous Amendments) Regulations 2013, SI 2013/271 (in force on 20 March 2013), further amend (1) the Road Vehicles (Construction and Use) Regulations 1986, SI 1986/1078, by (a) revising the braking efficiencies for M1 vehicles; and (b) requiring the Secretary of State to review the operation and effect of provisions relating to the efficiency of brakes, and to publish a report; (2) the Goods Vehicles (Plating and Testing) Regulations 1988, SI 1988/1478, by (a) making compliance with the Road Vehicles (Display of Registration Marks) Regulations 2001, SI 2001/561, part of the annual roadworthiness test, and providing for a free retest of any vehicle that fails its annual roadworthiness test as a result of a failure to comply with those requirements; (b) adding requirements for batteries, electrical connections, supplementary restraint systems and electronic stability control to the prescribed construction and use requirements so that the new requirements form part of the annual roadworthiness test; and (c) requiring the Secretary of State to review the operation and effect of the prescribed construction and use requirements, and to publish a report; and (3) the Motor Vehicles (Tests) Regulations 1981, SI 1981/1694, by (a) adding the battery and electrical wiring as matters for which a free retest of a vehicle will be allowed; (b) adding requirements for batteries, electrical connections and wiring, supplementary restraint systems and electronic stability control to the prescribed statutory requirements for Class IV vehicles and ensuring that such requirements apply to Classes IVa, V, VI and VIa vehicles; and (c) requiring the Secretary of State to review the operation and effect of the prescribed statutory requirements, and to publish a report.

2266   Traffic commissioners—consequential amendments

The Local Transport Act 2008 (Traffic Commissioners) (Consequential Amendments) Order 2013, SI 2013/1644 (in force on 3 July 2013), amends various primary and secondary legislation in consequence of the removal of the link between traffic commissioners and traffic areas and the creation of the office of senior traffic commissioner.

SALE OF GOODS AND SUPPLY OF SERVICES

Halsbury's Laws of England (5th edn) vol 91 (2012) paras 1–409

Articles

For articles relating to this title please refer to the Table of Articles at the beginning of the Abridgment.

2267 Commercial debt—late payment

The Late Payment of Commercial Debts Regulations 2013, SI 2013/395 (in force on 16 March 2013), implement European Parliament and Council Directive (EU) 2011/7 (on combating late payment in commercial transactions). In particular, they amend the Late Payment of Commercial Debts (Interest) Act 1998 by (1) introducing a maximum payment period of up to 30 days where the purchaser is a public authority, and in other cases a payment period of up to 60 days or longer as otherwise agreed; where the payment period is longer than 60 days, the period must not be grossly unfair to the supplier; (2) introducing a period of either up to 30 days or longer as otherwise agreed and provided it is not grossly unfair to the supplier, for a purchaser to confirm that the goods or services they have received from the supplier conform with the contract before the payment period commences; and (3) introducing a right to compensation for the reasonable costs to the supplier of recovering a debt incurred if that amount exceeds the fixed sums.

The Late Payment of Commercial Debts (No 2) Regulations 2013, SI 2013/908 (in force on 14 May 2013), further amend the 1998 Act above so as to remove, in relation to contracts made on or after that date, an additional 30-day period in which a purchaser may confirm that goods or services received conform with the contract.

2268 Consumer protection

See CONSUMER PROTECTION.

2269 Sale of goods—action for price—availability of remedy—retention of title

The Sale of Goods Act 1979 s 49(1) provides that, where, under a contract of sale, the property in the goods has passed to the buyer and he wrongfully neglects or refuses to pay for the goods according to the terms of the contract, the seller may maintain an action against him for the price of the goods.

The claimant company manufactured and sold generator sets and spare parts, together with associated services. The defendant company purchased generators and spare parts from the claimant for export to Nigeria by way of resale to its Nigerian subsidiary, which itself then resold the goods to its customers. Following the defendant's failure to pay invoices for deliveries made, the claimant purported to exercise its rights under a retention of title clause and sought summary judgment in respect of the amount allegedly owed. The retention of title clause provided that title would not pass until the claimant had received payment, that, until the title passed, the defendant held the goods as the claimant's fiduciary agent, and that the defendant was entitled to resell the goods in the ordinary course of business but would then be required to account to the claimant for the proceeds of sale. The claimant's standard terms and conditions also contained a no set-off clause. The judge ruled that the claimant could maintain an action for price and that the no set-off clause satisfied the requirement of reasonableness. The defendant appealed against that decision, submitting that property had never passed to it because, pursuant to the retention of title clause, the defendant had been acting as fiduciary agents for the claimant when the defendant resold the goods. *Held*, a natural construction of the retention of title clause as a whole was that title would not pass to the defendant until the claimant had received payment in full. While there was nothing in the clause to state that the defendant was to resell as agent, that had been the inevitable consequence of the application of its terms. The natural reading of the clause was that property had never passed to the defendant; immediately before and at the moment of the sub-sale, the goods remained the property of the claimant. The entitlement to resell had been expressly described as being in the period prior to title passing. During the whole of that period, the goods had been held by the defendant as the claimant's fiduciary agent. That conclusion was entirely consistent with the fact that the entire proceeds of sale were to be held for the claimant. The no set-off clause governed the terms of payment and made it clear that payment when due could not be withheld or reduced on the grounds of some counterclaim or set-off. The ability of the claimant to sue for the price was a different question which depended on the construction of the 1979 Act s 49(1) and the question of whether it had provided an exhaustive code for the recovery of the price. The claimant would have had a claim against the defendant as a fiduciary agent to account for the proceeds of sale. The defendant could not set up a counterclaim and set-off against its liability as a fiduciary to account for the proceeds of sale. Accordingly, the appeal would be allowed.

FG Wilson (Engineering) Ltd v John Holt & Co (Liverpool) Ltd [2013] EWCA Civ 1232, [2013] All ER (D) 179 (Oct) (Court of Appeal: Longmore, Patten and Floyd LJJ). Decision of Popplewell J [2012] EWHC 2477 (Comm), [2013] 1 All ER (Comm) 223 (2012 Abr para 2260) reversed.

2270　　Supply of services—licensing—sex establishment—licence fee—charge for costs of enforcement of licensing regime—lawfulness

The claimants were licensed sex establishments in London. Historically, the defendant local authority had charged an application fee for new and renewed sex establishment licenses which covered the costs of processing the application, monitoring the compliance of those with licenses, and enforcing the licensing regime against unlicensed operators. For a number of years, neither the licensing sub-committee nor the major licensing applications committee considered the fees for licenses for sex establishments and, consequently, the same fee was charged to the claimants for a number of years. Following the coming into force of the Provision of Services Regulations 2009, SI 2009/2999, the claimants made a CPR Pt 36 offer to the defendant. That offer was refused. Soon after, the claimants applied for judicial review of the licence fee charged by the defendant. It was found that the defendant had not determined a licence fee for any year after the year ending 31 January 2006. The judge also found that the effect of reg 18(4) was that the defendant was no longer entitled to include the cost of the enforcement process in the fee as that cost did not fall within the costs of the 'authorisation procedure'. It was also found that the claimants were entitled to restitution of overpayments made in respect of the fee with the amount to be repaid to be calculated on a cumulative year by year basis and as the judgment was more advantageous to the claimants than the Pt 36 offer, the claimants were entitled to their costs on the indemnity basis. On appeal by the defendant, *held*, it was not possible to regard the prosecution of those who were not licensed as an authorisation procedure. The costs of a regulator's authorisation procedures were only a part of its administration costs and, if the general administrative cost to a regulatory body of implementing the licensing regime did not qualify as part of its administrative costs, it was difficult to see how the cost of enforcement could qualify as part of the authorisation procedure. Although the judge had not had the benefit of extensive citation of European jurisprudence, his approach to the provisions of Council Directive (EC) 2006/123 (on services in the internal market) reflected that jurisprudence. Therefore, the conclusion as to the impact of the Directive and 2009 Regulations had been correct. The defendant's appeal on the restitution issue should be allowed in part. It had been entitled to determine the fee in the way it proposed between the year ending 31 January 2007 and the year ending 31 January 2010. At that stage, the cost of the enforcement process could no longer be reflected in the fee, and such part of the sums received would have been repayable forthwith, and should have been so treated. However, the cost of the authorisation and monitoring processes could have continued to be determined in the way the defendant proposed. It could continue to roll deficits and surpluses forward in respect of them until the date the proceedings were issued. In respect of those elements, it was at that point that the calculation of the difference between the amount received in respect of those categories and the reasonable fees and thus the amount repayable should be determined. The appeal in respect of costs would be dismissed. Accordingly, the appeal would be allowed in part.

R (on the application of Hemming (t/a Simply Pleasure Ltd)) v Westminster City Council [2013] EWCA Civ 591, [2013] LGR 593 (Court of Appeal: Dyson MR, Black and Beatson LJJ). *M v Croydon LBC* [2012] EWCA Civ 595, [2012] 3 All ER 1237 (2012 Abr para 1631) applied. Decision of Keith J [2012] EWHC 1260 (Admin), [2012] All ER (D) 158 (May) (2012 Abr para 1707) affirmed in part.

SENTENCING AND DISPOSITION OF OFFENDERS

Halsbury's Laws of England (5th edn) vol 92 (2010) paras 1–820

Articles

For articles relating to this title please refer to the Table of Articles at the beginning of the Abridgment.

2271   Appeal against sentence—grounds—sentence manifestly excessive—fatal attack on school boy

The deceased, a school boy, was chased by 20 teenagers and attacked with bladed weapons before falling down a flight of stairs into a station ticket hall. While he was on the ground, a core group of those who had chased him attacked him by stabbing or cutting him with knives, and kicking and punching him with force. Five trials were conducted involving twenty attackers, the result of eight of the defendants being relevant to the present case. The first to third defendants were convicted of murder and conspiracy to cause grievous bodily harm and sentenced to be detained with a minimum term specified of 18 years for the murder offence and concurrent terms of eight years' detention in a young offender institution for the conspiracy offence. The fourth defendant was convicted of conspiracy to cause grievous bodily harm and violent disorder and sentenced to seven years' detention for conspiracy with a concurrent term of three years for violent disorder, and the fifth to seventh defendants were convicted of manslaughter and conspiracy to cause grievous bodily harm, with the fifth and seventh defendants sentenced to 12 years' detention for manslaughter and concurrent terms of seven years' detention for conspiracy, and the sixth defendant sentenced to 12 years' detention for manslaughter and a concurrent term of eight years' detention for conspiracy. The eighth defendant was convicted of conspiracy to cause grievous bodily harm and violent disorder and was sentenced to seven years' detention with no separate penalty for violent disorder. The second, fourth and eighth defendants appealed against sentence and the first, third, fifth, sixth and seventh defendants sought to renew their applications following refusal of leave. *Held,* in respect of the first and third defendants, the judge had been of the view that they attacked the deceased with knives and, having regard to the acts recorded on CCTV along with the nature and location of the injuries, the intention could only have been to kill. That view was shared by the court. Although it was recognised that for the first and third defendants the sentences imposed might appear to be overwhelming in length, the need to punish and deter others made them inevitable. Moreover, in relation to the second defendant, the judge should have differentiated slightly between those who carried knives to the scene and, with the intention to kill, no doubt formed in the heat of the moment, caused death, and the case of the second defendant who might have played a greater role in the organisation of the confrontation but in respect of whom it could not be said that he intended death, however great the risk of that outcome. It followed that the minimum term in the second defendant's case would be reduced by two years to 16 years. In relation to the fifth defendant, he had been one of the group of killers, had been armed and had struck the deceased. The need for a deterrent sentence was undeniable and, even making every allowance for the antecedents, background and references which the fifth defendant amassed, in light of all the circumstances, it was impossible to say that the sentence imposed was wrong in principle or manifestly excessive. In respect of the sixth defendant, the premise that the sentence imposed for murder had been manifestly excessive so that the sentences for manslaughter ought to be adjusted was rejected. The fact that a plea to manslaughter had been offered was no mitigation unless the plea was openly tendered in court and before the jury, which it had not. The fact that the sixth defendant's role came to an end before the events at the station should not have led to a lesser sentence for manslaughter. The sentence for conspiracy had not reflected the fact that the knives he acquired had been used in the subsequent attack and that fatal injury resulted. With regard to the seventh defendant, he played no part in the planning, joined the conspiracy on the spur of the moment and did not have a weapon. On the other hand, he had been convicted on the basis that he had known that at least one of the group was armed with a knife or other bladed weapon and foresaw it might be used to cause some harm. Further, although not using a knife, he utilised another weapon, namely his shod foot, and it followed that the deterrent sentence received was not arguably wrong in principle or manifestly excessive. There was force in the submission that for the offence of conspiracy by the fourth and eighth defendants, with their more limited involvement, a different approach had been justified from that adopted for those convicted of homicide. The sentences imposed did not adequately reflect that different position which, bearing in mind their youth, good character and positive reports did not need to be as long as seven years. It followed that the sentences of the fourth and eighth defendants would be quashed and sentences of five and half years would be put in their place. Accordingly, the appeals of the first, third, fifth, sixth and seventh defendants would be dismissed and the appeals of the second, fourth and eighth defendants would be allowed.

R v Odegbune [2013] EWCA Crim 711, [2013] All ER (D) 255 (May) (Court of Appeal: Leveson LJ, Foskett and Hickinbottom JJ).

2272 Arson—attempt—recklessness as to whether life endangered—appropriate sentence

The defendant and the victim were former friends who had fallen out. On the day of the victim's wedding, pieces of slightly burnt paper and burnt-out matches were found behind the front door of the victim's house. The defendant denied any involvement in the incident, but her fingerprints were found on the burnt papers and her name and address were also found on some of those pieces of paper. CCTV footage also showed the defendant on the street where the victim's home was located around the time the incident had taken place. The defendant was convicted of attempted arson being reckless as to whether life was endangered. A psychiatrist subsequently diagnosed the defendant as suffering from chronic adjustment disorder and assessed her offending as not being a result of her mental issues but as a result of anger and alcohol abuse. In sentencing the defendant to two years' imprisonment, the sentencing judge focused on the defendant's behaviour on the relevant day and described it as spiteful and destructive. A probation report was later prepared which recommended a custodial sentence on the basis that the defendant had a medium risk of causing serious harm to others unless she received assistance for her alcohol problem, anger management and dealing with grievances. Another probation officer examined the defendant and concluded that an alternative to an immediate custodial sentence could be considered provided certain conditions were met, notwithstanding that the risk of the defendant causing serious harm within the community remained high. During her custody, the defendant successfully completed numerous courses including a cognitive behaviour course and an understanding behaviour course. The defendant appealed against sentence, submitting that it was manifestly excessive. Held, although the defendant's actions had been dangerous, her attempts at starting a fire were crude. Undoubtedly, the defendant had longstanding mental health issues, and she also had family responsibilities and, until the present offence, had been of previous good character. The overall effect of the mitigating features particular to the defendant and the final probation report required a reduction in the sentence imposed to one of 12 months' imprisonment. Accordingly, the appeal would be allowed.

R v Humphries [2013] All ER (D) 163 (Sep) (Court of Appeal: Fulford LJ and Cox J).

2273 Banning orders—football spectators—regulated matches

See para 2341.

2274 Conditional cautions—financial penalties

The Criminal Justice Act 2003 (Conditional Cautions: Financial Penalties) Order 2013, SI 2013/615 (in force on 8 April 2013), replaces the 2009 Order 2009, SI 2009/2773, and prescribes descriptions of offences in relation to which a financial penalty condition may be attached to a conditional caution imposed under the Criminal Justice Act 2003 s 22. The order also sets different maximum amounts of penalty that the offender may be required to pay, depending on the description of offence.

2275 Confiscation order—proceeds of crime—benefit obtained—calculation—value of estate

The testator had left a professionally drawn will by which he left everything to his then wife, or in the event of her predeceasing him, which she did, his estate was to be divided equally between the defendant, who was his daughter by a former wife, and his nephew. Subsequent to the date of that will the testator executed an enduring power of attorney that appointed the defendant his sole attorney with general powers in relation to his property and affairs. Following the testator's death a further will emerged. It was drawn on an over the counter will form and bore a more recent date. It appeared to be properly signed and attested. It appointed the defendant sole executor and left the whole of the residuary estate to her. The defendant instructed solicitors to collect in the estate. However, the most recent will was a forgery by the former wife. Probate was granted to the defendant of the forged will. By the time the true facts came to light and the defendant was charged with the offence of fraud contrary to the Fraud Act 2006 s 1, the solicitors had begun the administration of the estate but it was incomplete. The defendant had given no instructions and no distribution had been made. A restraint order was made following the defendant's arrest. It was alleged that the defendant had been party to the forgery of the will by her mother and had knowingly sworn a false affidavit giving her solicitors instructions to obtain probate of what she knew to be a forged will. The prosecution sought a confiscation order in respect of a sum representing 50 per cent of the value of the estate. The judge considered that the defendant had benefited from criminal conduct under the Proceeds of Crime Act 2002 s 6(4)(c) and made a confiscation order. The defendant appealed. *Held,* a grant of probate while unrevoked was conclusive evidence of the execution and validity of a will. Therefore, in the present case, it established the defendant as sole executrix and beneficiary until such time as it was revoked. The defendant had acquired full legal and beneficial title to the estate property as well as a power of disposition and control. In the circumstances the defendant had obtained property within the 2002 Act. There was no requirement under the 2002 Act that the offender enjoy the benefit of property obtained. The purpose of confiscation proceedings was to recover the financial benefit that the offender had obtained by their criminal conduct. In the present case, the Crown had identified the benefit as the sum represented by the nephew's 50 per cent share. The Crown's argument that the testator might have altered his will, had he known of the defendant's behaviour was merely speculative. The court was only concerned with the actual consequences of the defendant's criminal conduct. Previous authority made it clear that where property obtained by a criminal had been restored or stood ready to be restored where there had been no additional benefit to the offender a confiscation order would be disproportionate. Therefore, the confiscation order would be quashed. Accordingly, the appeal would be allowed.

   R v Hursthouse [2013] EWCA (Crim) 517, [2013] WTLR 887 (Court of Appeal: Treacy LJ, Henderson and Saunders JJ). *R v Waya* [2012] UKSC 51, [2013] 1 AC 294, [2013] 1 All ER 889 (2012 Abr para 2272) applied.

2276   Confiscation order—proceeds of crime—benefit obtained—lifting corporate veil

The defendant was the managing director of a company which traded with a wide range of well-known established companies. The defendant offered and gave gifts to an employee of a national rail company in order to secure commercial favour. Consequently, the employee arranged for the award of a number of high value contracts to the company. There was no suggestion that the company was anything other than a legitimate business except in relation to its dealings with the rail company. Following a police investigation into the matter the defendant pleaded guilty to corruption and fraud by false representation. Confiscation proceedings were brought under the Proceeds of Crime Act 2002. Although all the payments from the rail company under the contracts had been made to the company and not to the defendant, the judge ruled that it was right and just to lift the corporate veil as the defendant had performed the criminal acts in the name of the company. Accordingly, a confiscation order was made in the total sum paid to the company. The defendant appealed against the confiscation order. *Held,* the principle that the court might be justified in piercing the corporate veil if a company's separate legal personality was being abused for the purpose of some relevant wrong doing was well established. In the present case, the defendant was the sole controller and there was a very close inter-relationship between his corrupt actions and steps taken by the company in advancing those corrupt acts and intentions. The reality was that the activities of both the defendant and the company were so interlinked as to be indivisible. It followed that the court had been entitled to see what the realities of the defendant's criminal conduct were. A confiscation order under the 2002 Act would generally be disproportionate if it would require the defendant to pay for a second time money which he had fully restored to the loser. However, the present case was not analogous to one where goods or money had been entirely restored to the loser. The defendant had obtained contracts for his company by corrupt means on a continuing basis so that every contract was tainted by it. Existing contractors with the rail company had been cheated out of the tendering process. However, the total amount paid to the company did not reflect the pecuniary advantage obtained by obtaining a market position and similar advantages at the expense of legitimate competitors. The present case, therefore, was not one where the defendant could claim to have put matters right by fully recompensing the victim and divesting himself of the benefit of his crimes. A proportionate confiscation order would need to reflect those additional pecuniary advantages. The amount of the confiscation order would be reduced. Accordingly, the appeal would be allowed in part.

R v Sale [2013] EWCA Crim 1306, [2014] 1 WLR 663, [2013] All ER (D) 367 (Jul) (Court of Appeal: Treacy LJ, Macduff and Dingemans JJ). *R v Waya* [2012] UKSC 51, [2013] 1 AC 294, [2013] 1 All ER 889 (2012 Abr para 2272); and *Prest v Petrodel Resources Ltd* [2013] All ER (D) 90 (Jun) (para 1819) applied. *Jennings v Crown Prosecution Service* [2008] UKHL 29, [2008] 1 AC 1046, [2008] 4 All ER 113 (2008 Abr para 2637); and *R v Seager; R v Blatch* [2009] EWCA Crim 1303, [2010] 1 WLR 815, [2009] All ER (D) 283 (Jun) (2009 Abr para 940) considered.

2277   Confiscation order—proceeds of crime—benefit obtained—multiple recovery against co-conspirators—proportionality

The defendants were convicted of conspiracy to defraud. The fraud involved a company buying goods and obtaining services on credit, payments never being made and the goods being sold on. Confiscation proceedings were brought against the defendants and confiscation orders were made against each of them by reference to the total benefit arising from the conspiracy. The defendants appealed. *Held*, it was firmly established that, where there had been a finding of jointly obtained benefit, that benefit was to be valued in the whole amount of the property so obtained in respect of each defendant. There could be no question of apportionment of the benefit obtained at that stage of the assessment. If apportionment was appropriate at all, then that could only be at the final stage, on the grounds of proportionality, of determining the recoverable amount in which the confiscation order was to be made. It was settled law that it could not be regarded as disproportionate to make an order depriving a defendant of a benefit which he had in fact and in law obtained, within the limits of his realisable assets. The right conclusion to be drawn in a joint benefit case was that an order requiring a defendant to pay the whole of the sum which he had obtained jointly with others was not disproportionate even if the others were also ordered to pay the same sum. Lack of proportionality was not to be assessed simply by focusing on orders also made against others, or of payments made by others, or by focusing on the potential 'profit' accruing to the Crown by reason of prospective multiple recovery. On the contrary, such an approach detracted from the scheme and objective of the Proceeds of Crime Act 2002, which required the focus of attention to be on depriving each defendant of the proceeds of his crime. If a confiscation order were to be apportioned, there was a real risk that ultimately the order would not be satisfied in full as defendants often would fail to make the payment ordered under a confiscation order. Further, apportionment of benefit between co-conspirators at any stage would potentially involve impracticable inquiries into financial dealings between criminals and could lead to evasion, manoeuvring and chicanery on the part of defendants. On the facts, each of the defendants had obtained the joint benefit of the proceeds of the conspiracy and no apportionment or deduction was required on the ground of proportionality. Accordingly, the appeals would be dismissed.

R v Fields [2013] EWCA Crim 2042, [2014] 2 WLR 233, [2013] All ER (D) 19 (Dec) (Court of Appeal: Davis LJ, Spencer J and Judge Rook QC). *R v May* [2008] UKHL 28, [2008] 1 AC 1028, [2008] 4 All ER 97 (2008 Abr para 2272); and *R v Waya* [2012] UKSC 51, [2013] 1 AC 294, [2013] 1 All ER 889 (2012 Abr para 2272) applied.

2278   Confiscation order—proceeds of crime—benefit obtained—proportionality— disposal of controlled waste

The defendant operated a scrap vehicle recovery business. He had the necessary licences to bring waste on to parts of his land but not a particular farm ('the farm'). The defendant pleaded guilty to depositing controlled waste without a licence contrary to the Environmental Protection Act 1990 s 33(1)(a) and (6). He also pleaded guilty to knowingly permitting the operation of a regulated facility contrary to the Environmental Permitting (England and Wales) Regulations 2007, SI 2007/3538, reg 38(1)(a) and knowingly causing controlled waste to be submitted to a listed operation without an environmental permit contrary to the 1990 Act s 33(1)(b). All offences related to the deposit of waste material at the farm. The defendant had pleaded guilty on a basis of plea which stated that to his knowledge, the waste was inert construction and demolition waste, the deposits were to improve the land for agricultural purposes and he had received no monies for the deposits. Confiscation proceedings were subsequently commenced. Following a previously rejected application to stay the confiscation proceedings and the submission of export reports from both sides on the nature of the operations undertaken at the farm, the defendant made a second application to stay the confiscation proceedings on the ground that they were an abuse of process. That argument was rejected. At the full confiscation hearing, the judge heard from two experts who reported on issues concerning the nature of the waste deposited. It was found that the waste deposited at the farm was 'inert' with no more than minimal amounts of 'active' waste in it and that the operation at the farm had not been a 'recovery' operation as there had not been drainage or agricultural improvement to the land. It was also found that the fact that the defendant had received no payment for the tipping of the material had been a relevant factor and a useful indication in cases as to whether the landowner had obtained a benefit and relevant to the issue of whether that was a 'deposit' or a 'recovery' case. However, the fact that he had received no payments had been 'overborne' by other factors. It was agreed that the relevant range of sums saved by the defendant had been between £156,500 and £207,000. The judge determined the lowest figure had been the benefit obtained by the defendant's criminal conduct, so that the recoverable amount was £156,500. The defendant appealed against the confiscation order. *Held*, the concept of 'abuse of process' was not appropriate to the argument being advanced. Rather, the key question was whether the confiscation order made was 'disproportionate' so as to amount to a breach of the defendant's rights under the European Convention on Human Rights Protocol 1 art 1. On the assumption that the judge had been correct to conclude that the defendant had engaged in a 'disposal' operation, he had also been correct to conclude that he had, by engaging in unlawful unlicensed activity, thereby obtained a pecuniary advantage. On the basis of the definition of 'property' in the 1990 Act s 84(1)(a) and the application of the assumption in s 10(3), that pecuniary advantage constituted 'property' obtained by the defendant as a result of his general criminal conduct and thus the 'benefit' obtained from such conduct for the purposes of s 6(4). Given the proper use of the assumptions and the findings of fact of the judge, there could be no 'very unusual circumstances' to court the danger of the confiscation order being disproportionate. Further, there was no basis on which it could be argued that the judge's conclusion of fact had been unreasonable, or based on a misunderstanding of the evidence or perverse. Accordingly, the appeal would be dismissed.

R v Morgan [2013] EWCA Crim 1307, [2014] 1 All ER 1208 (Court of Appeal: Aikens LJ, Cranston J and Judge Pert QC). *R v Waya* [2012] UKSC 51, [2013] AC 294, [2013] 1 All ER 889 (2012 Abr para 2272) applied.

2279   Confiscation order—proceeds of crime—compensation order

The defendant and two co-accused were convicted of a money laundering offence connected with frauds on a bank. The defendant's benefit was deemed, pursuant to the lifestyle provisions of the Proceeds of Crime Act 2002, to be anything obtained from criminal conduct generally and not limited to the proceeds of the count of which he had been convicted. Before the judge the amount of the benefit was agreed. The agreed benefit figure had been arrived at by adding together the sum directly obtained through the frauds and sums resulting from the statutory assumptions provided for by the 2002 Act s 10. Assets available to the defendant comfortably exceeded the agreed benefit figure. The judge made a confiscation order in the sum of the agreed benefit, and at the request of the prosecution also made a compensation order in favour of the bank. On the defendant's appeal against the confiscation order, *held*, a confiscation order made under the 2002 Act would generally be disproportionate if it required the defendant to pay for a second time money which he had fully restored to the loser. If there was no additional benefit beyond that sum, any confiscation order was likely to be disproportionate. If there was additional benefit, an order which double-counted the sum which had been repaid was likely, to that extent, to be disproportionate, and an order for the lesser sum which excluded the double counting should generally be the right order. However, the mere fact that a compensation order was made for an outstanding sum due to the loser, and thus that money might be restored, was not enough to render disproportionate a confiscation order which included that sum. What would bring disproportion was the certainty of double payment. If it remained uncertain whether the loser would be repaid, a confiscation order which included the sum in question would not ordinarily be disproportionate. A loser who took advantage of his opportunity to invite the prosecution to ask the court to make a compensation order could not in any known sense of the word be said to have started, or to be intending to start, proceedings against the defendant in respect of the loss. Furthermore, it was plainly wrong that benefit from general and from particular criminal conduct were concepts which were mutually exclusive. In a lifestyle case, general criminal conduct plainly included the particular conduct charged in the count of which the defendant had been convicted. There was nothing in s 6 to say otherwise and it would be nonsense if there had been. If within 28 days the defendant repaid to the bank the amount owed, together with the interest properly payable on it, then the appeal would be allowed to the extent of reducing the confiscation order. If he did not, the appeal would be dismissed. Judgment would be given accordingly.

R v Jawad [2013] EWCA Crim 644, [2014] 1 Cr App Rep (S) 85, [2013] All ER (D) 55 (May) (Court of Appeal: Hughes LJ, Foskett J and Judge Radford). *R v Waya* [2012] UKSC 51, [2013] 1 AC 294, [2013] 1 All ER 889 (2012 Abr para 2272) applied.

2280 **Conspiracy to pervert course of justice—police officer—falsifying result of drugs test—appropriate sentence**

The defendant, a serving police officer, arrested a woman after finding what he suspected to be drugs on her person. A test carried out by the co-accused at the police station confirmed that the substance was cocaine. However, feeling sympathetic towards the woman, the co-accused suggested to the defendant that they record the test as a negative result. The defendant agreed, and in due course a decision was made to take no further action against the woman. Shortly afterwards, the co-accused confessed to what they had done. The defendant and the co-accused were charged with conspiracy to pervert the course of justice. The co-accused admitted fault, but the defendant maintained his innocence until the day of the trial, when he pleaded guilty. The co-accused was sentenced to 12 months' imprisonment, suspended for 24 months with an unpaid work requirement of 250 hours. The defendant was sentenced to two years' imprisonment. The defendant appealed against sentence, contending that it was manifestly excessive. *Held*, in cases of conspiracy to pervert the course of justice, three factors had to be taken into consideration: (1) the seriousness of the underlying offence to which the conspiracy was directed; (2) the degree to which the conspiracy offence persisted; and (3) the effect on the course of justice. The present case was unusual. It was not one in which a police officer had given false evidence against an innocent person. Nor was it one in which an officer had made personal gain through his offending. The defendant's actions had been spontaneous; he had not thought of the serious consequences. The defendant's sympathy towards the woman had been misplaced. It had not been for the defendant to decide to put the woman in a position where prosecution would be unlikely. There had been a serious abuse of power. The fact that the defendant was a serving a police officer at the time of the offence was an aggravating feature. Nevertheless, had the defendant maintained his plea of not guilty and been convicted he would have received a sentence of between 12 and 15 months' imprisonment, and that would have been appropriate. The defendant was entitled to a modest deduction for his late guilty plea. In the circumstances, the appropriate term of imprisonment was 12 months. Accordingly, the appeal would be allowed.

R v Evans-Keady [2013] EWCA Crim 1546, [2013] All ER (D) 160 (Aug) (Court of Appeal: Davis LJ, Keith and Lewis JJ).

2281 **Criminal record certificates—applications—disclosure of relevant matters**

The Police Act 1997 (Criminal Record Certificates: Relevant Matters) (Amendment) (England and Wales) Order 2013, SI 2013/1200 (in force on 29 May 2013), amends the Police Act 1997 s 113A so as to introduce new rules for the disclosure of relevant criminal record information by the Disclosure and Barring Service in response to applications for criminal record certificates and enhanced criminal record certificates which take into account factors including the type of offence committed, the disposition imposed and the person's age when the disposition was imposed.

2282   Criminal record certificates—enhanced criminal record certificates—disclosure— unproven allegations

The claimant, who was a registered nurse employed at a care home, had allegations of mistreatment made against her. She was dismissed from her role, but subsequently reinstated on appeal as no supporting evidence to any of the allegations was found. The Independent Safeguarding Authority concluded that it was not appropriate to include the claimant on the children's barred list or the adults' barred list, but the Nursing and Midwifery Council imposed an interim conditions of practice order on her. The allegations were also investigated by the police and the claimant was charged with four separate charges of ill treatment and neglect, but, following an investigation, the Crown Prosecution Service offered no evidence and the claimant was acquitted. The claimant applied for a new job and the Criminal Records Bureau requested the defendant to provide an enhanced check in respect of the claimant's proposed employment as a registered nurse. The defendant supplied an enhanced criminal record certificate which detailed the allegations that had been made against the claimant and that she had been found not guilty of all criminal charges. The claimant applied for judicial review of the defendant's decision to disclose the allegations and issued a claim under the Human Rights Act 1998. The judge allowed the application, deciding that the disclosure amounted to a disproportionate interference with the claimant's right to respect for her private life and was an unlawful interference with her right to private life under the European Convention on Human Rights art 8. The defendant appealed, contending that the judge had gone beyond the higher intensity review which was required in a claim for judicial review of a decision where Convention rights were at issue and that the judge had relied on material which could not have been available to the defendant at the time the decision to disclose had been made or on the date of the disclosure. *Held*, the judge had considered that the defendant applied the wrong legal tests and her conclusion on that matter had not in terms been challenged. Even if the judge erred in considering the defendant's decision-making process, she had herself assessed the proportionality of the disclosure. The established authorities required the court itself to make an objective assessment of proportionality and the judge had done so. Moreover, although parts of the judgment appeared to be, or were very close to being, fact finding of the sort which was inappropriate in the context of a reviewing jurisdiction, the judge had not in fact and had not purported to make any findings of fact in her judgment in the sense of findings that a particular event had happened or had not happened. She had followed the appropriate guidance which gave importance to reliability as a factor in assessing the proportionality of disclosure. Further, if the court was required to scrutinise material which could not have been available to the decision-maker at the time of the decision, it was difficult to see how the process could be characterised as one of a review of a decision made by the public authority which had been given primary responsibility for a subject-matter. Although established authority provided that the court's powers of review could extend to considering for itself facts which had arisen since the issue of proceedings, those authorities did not require the conclusion that, in the circumstances of the present case, the court was required to or should have considered post-decision or post-disclosure material. Once the relevant report had been published, it had been open to the claimant to seek a further enhanced criminal record certificate which had taken account of it. The defendant would then have been able to decide whether a report in fact made a difference to the assessment. It followed that the judge had fallen into error in her assessment of proportionality because of the reliance she had placed on the Council's decision that had been made after the relevant disclosure by the defendant. In the circumstances, the court could itself consider whether the defendant's disclosure had been a proportionate interference with the claimant's rights under art 8. The information had clearly been relevant to the application and the central issue had been its reliability. The fact that the Crown Prosecution Service had decided not to proceed and that the claimant had been acquitted of the criminal charges and that the Independent Safeguarding Authority had decided not to bar her were all relevant factors, but they were in no way conclusive. In the light of all the material that had been available at the time of the disclosure, the decision to disclose had been disproportionate and the judge's order would not be set aside. Judgment would be given accordingly.

R (on the application of A) v Chief Constable of Kent Constabulary [2013] EWCA Civ 1706, [2013] All ER (D) 228 (Dec) (Court of Appeal: Pitchford, Beatson and Gloster LJJ). *Manchester City Council v Pinnock* [2010] UKSC 45, [2011] 1 All ER 285 (2010 Abr para 1857); *Re B (a child) (care order: proportionality: criterion for review)* [2013] UKSC 33, [2013] 3 All ER 929 (para 171); and *Booth v Parole Board* [2013] UKSC 61, [2014] 1 All ER 369 (para 2103) applied. Decision of Lang J [2013] EWHC 424 (Admin), [2013] All ER (D) 94 (Mar) affirmed on other grounds.

2283   Criminal record certificates—enhanced criminal record certificates—fees

The Protection of Freedoms Act 2012 (Consequential Amendments) No 2 Order 2013, SI 2013/1196 (in force on 17 June 2013), amends the Police Act 1997 (Criminal Records) (Fees) Order 2004, SI 2004/1007, by (1) replacing references to the Secretary of State with references to the Disclosure and Barring Service; and (2) requiring the costs of providing up-to-date information to volunteers about criminal record certificates and enhanced criminal record certificates to be taken into account when determining the amount of any fees specified for providing such information.

2284   Criminal record certificates—enhanced criminal record certificates—general provisions

The Police Act 1997 (Criminal Records) (Amendment No 2) Regulations 2013, SI 2013/2669 (in force on 2 December 2013), further amend the 2002 Regulations, SI 2002/233, by providing that an enhanced criminal record certificate may be required for the purposes of considering a person's suitability to work with children or for assessing a person's suitability for any office or employment relating to national security. The regulations also further amend the 2009 Regulations, SI 2009/1882, by substituting a new prescribed purpose for which suitability information in relation to children must be included in an enhanced criminal record certificate.

2285   Criminal record certificates—enhanced criminal record certificates—information—disclosure

The Rehabilitation of Offenders Act 1974 provided a scheme whereby criminal convictions, cautions, warnings and reprimands in respect of certain offences were deemed to be spent after specified periods of time. Thereafter, the person convicted or cautioned was to be treated as if he had never committed the offence in question and did not have to make reference to the conviction or caution in answering any question which might otherwise have required its disclosure. The first claimant, when aged 11, received two warnings from the police in connection with two stolen bicycles. Issues subsequently arose when he sought to enrol on a sports studies course which involved teaching and contact with children. In judicial review proceedings, the first claimant contended that the scheme for issuing criminal record certificates and for requiring a person to disclose spent warnings to certain future employers was incompatible with the European Convention on Human Rights art 8. His application was dismissed. The second claimant had received a caution for stealing. She was told that she would be not be offered employment in the care sector as her criminal record rendered her inappropriate for work with vulnerable people. Permission to apply for judicial review of the decision was refused. In both cases, an enhanced criminal record certificate ('ECRC') had been obtained revealing the relevant caution or warning. The third claimant had carried out a car-jacking and was given concurrent sentences of five years' detention for manslaughter and four years' detention for robbery. She sought permission to apply for judicial review of the 1974 Act s 5(1)(b) on the ground that it was incompatible with the Convention art 8. Permission was refused. The three claimants appealed. *Held*, in respect of the first claimant, the disclosure of the warning on an ECRC had interfered with his rights under art 8(1) in two ways. Firstly, it had involved the disclosure of sensitive information about him which he had wished to keep to himself. The information about the warning was properly to be regarded as an aspect of his private life. Secondly, disclosure had been liable to affect his ability to obtain employment and to form relationships with others. The disclosure regime was introduced in order to protect children and vulnerable adults. Disclosure that was irrelevant, or at best of marginal relevance, was counter to the interests of re-integrating ex-offenders into society so that they could lead positive and law-abiding lives. In respect of the first claimant, the fact that he was only 11 years of age when he received his warnings made his case that the disclosure of the warnings seven years later was a disproportionate interference with his art 8 rights even stronger than it would have been if he had been an adult at the time of the warnings. Save for the fact that the second claimant was an adult at the time of her offending, all the arguments deployed on behalf of the first claimant in relation to the disclosure provisions of the Police Act 1997 would seem to apply with equal force. Her offence was of a trivial nature committed some eight years before she had applied for a post working with vulnerable people. In respect of the third claimant, the decision of Parliament had fallen within its area of discretionary judgment. It had been entitled to take the view that some offences were so serious that they should never be regarded as 'spent'. That was not a blanket policy. It discriminated between offences which were very serious and those which were not. The court was not persuaded that Parliament's response to a question of social policy had been disproportionate. The disclosure provisions of the 1997 Act and the Rehabilitation of Offenders Act 1974 (Exceptions) Order 1975, SI 1975/1023, were incompatible with the Convention art 8. Accordingly, the appeals of the first and second claimants would be allowed and the appeal of the third claimant would be dismissed.

R (on the application of T) v Chief Constable of Greater Manchester; R (on the application of JB) v Secretary of State for the Home Department; R (on the application of AW) v Secretary of State for Justice [2013] EWCA Civ 25, [2013] 2 All ER 813 (Court of Appeal: Lord Dyson MR, Richards and Davis LJJ). R (on the application of L) v Metropolitan Police Comr [2009] UKSC 3, [2010] 1 AC 410, [2010] 1 All ER 113 (2009 Abr para 902) applied. Applications 55480/00, 59330/00 Sidabras v Lithuania (2004) 42 ECHR 104, ECtHR, adopted. R (on the application of JF) v Secretary of State for the Home Department [2010] UKSC 17, [2011] 1 AC 331, [2010] 2 All ER 707 (2010 Abr para 2513); R (on the application of Smith) v Secretary of State for the Home Department [2005] UKHL 51, [2006] 1 AC 159, [2006] 1 All ER 407 (2005 Abr para 2795) considered. R (on the application of X) v Chief Constable of the West Midlands Police [2004] EWCA Civ 1068, [2005] 1 All ER 610 (2004 Abr para 703) distinguished. Decisions of Kenneth Parker J [2012] EWHC 147 (Admin), [2012] All ER (D) 154 (Feb) (2012 Abr para 2283) and Judge Gosnell [2011] EWHC 2197 (Admin), (unreported, 13 June 2011) reversed.

2286 Criminal records—miscellaneous provisions

The Police Act 1997 (Criminal Records) (Amendment) Regulations 2013, SI 2013/1194 (in force on 17 June 2013), further amend the 2002 Regulations, SI 2002/233, by (1) revising the prescribed purposes for which an enhanced criminal record certificate may be required in accordance with a statement made by a registered person under the Police Act 1997 s 113B(2)(b), including adding the consideration of a person's suitability to work with adults; (2) prescribing the fees for requesting up-to-date information about a person's criminal conviction certificate, criminal record certificate or enhanced criminal record certificate under s 116A; and (3) setting out certain conditions which must be satisfied before a copy of a criminal record certificate or an enhanced criminal record certificate can be provided to a registered person in response to a request for such a copy.

2287 Custodial sentence—duration—crediting of periods on remand—curfew and electronic monitoring conditions

The defendant was released on bail, and subjected to a qualifying curfew condition and an electronic monitoring condition. He subsequently committed offences of burglary and breaching a non-molestation order, for which he was sentenced to a two-year community order with a requirement to attend an integrated domestic abuse programme, a six-month drug rehabilitation requirement and a six-month electronically monitored curfew order. Following breaches of the orders, the community order was revoked and the defendant was resentenced to 12 months' imprisonment. The sentencing judge intended that the defendant should receive credit for 38 days he had spent on remand and for half the number of days that he had spent on bail while subject to the relevant conditions. However, the judge did not give a direction on those terms because he believed credit would be given automatically following the coming into force of amendments to the Criminal Justice Act 2003 ss 240 and 240A. An attempt was later made to invite the judge to give a direction in relation to the days spent on bail, but the application was made out of time. The defendant appealed against sentence, and it fell to be determined whether there should have been a direction under s 240A, and, if so, how many days spent on qualifying curfew and electronic monitoring conditions should have counted towards service of the prison sentence. *Held*, the judge had been right to conclude that, in accordance with s 240ZA, the 38 days which the defendant had spent on remand in custody would automatically count towards the service of his sentence. However, the judge had erred in concluding that no direction had been required in relation to the days that the defendant had spent on bail while subject to qualifying curfew and electronic monitoring conditions. A direction complying with s 240A was required. In the circumstances, 47 days would be ordered to count towards the service of the defendant's sentence. Accordingly, the appeal would be allowed.

R v Hoggard [2013] EWCA Crim 1024, [2013] All ER (D) 184 (Jun) (Court of Appeal: Hughes VP, Sweeney J and Judge Radford).

2288   Custodial sentence—duration—crediting of periods on remand—custody—date from which sentence runs

Guernsey

The defendant was convicted of assault by an acting magistrate in Guernsey and sentenced to three months' imprisonment with no credit given for ten days during which he had been remanded in custody awaiting trial. Five days after his sentence, the defendant gave notice of appeal against conviction and remained in custody until he was granted an open remand. At that stage, there had been only 18 days of his sentence left to serve, taking into account the normal grant of one third remission. Soon after, the defendant's appeal was listed but he did not attend. The appeal was dismissed and it was ordered that when apprehended the defendant should serve the sentence of three months imprisonment imposed on him less the period of five days already served. On learning of the judgment the defendant left Guernsey and did not return. Following a number of unsuccessful appeals, the defendant appealed again. He applied for leave to appeal against his sentence imposed by the magistrates' court because it had failed to take into account the ten days served before conviction. It was also claimed that the court had made an obvious error in recording that he had served only five days of his sentence, whereas he had served 43 days as a convicted person or 53 days since his arrest. He also claimed relief under Guernsey human rights law. Those applications were dismissed. As to the first claim it was found that the delay had been inordinate and largely unexplained and that it would be wrong to take the exceptional step of granting leave to appeal out of time. With regard to the second claim, it appeared that there had been no obvious or glaring error by the court. As to the third claim, it had not been shown that the defendant's human rights had been violated by the proceedings and the human rights law did not apply to violations that had taken place before it had come into force. On further appeal by the defendant, *held*, anyone contemplating an appeal against the order of a magistrates' court could have been informed that if he did not succeed, the court could decide the date from which his sentence was to run, whether from the date of its own order or from the date which it had been imposed, or from some other date which would take into account the time already served. Unless that was a case in which the court thought that the sentence should be increased, it appeared to have been the usual practice to give credit for the portion of the sentence already served, but in most cases not for any time spent in custody after the notice of appeal had been given. The risk had clearly been there to be appreciated and taken into account by anyone contemplating an appeal against a magistrates' decision. Traditionally, there had always been a large measure of discretion in sentencing, because of the infinite variety of circumstances in which such decisions had to be made. Further, it had not been incompatible with the European Convention on Human Rights for the authorities in Guernsey to implement the court's order. Accordingly, the appeal would be dismissed.

R v Sherry [2013] UKPC 7, [2013] 5 LRC 118, [2013] All ER (D) 75 (Mar) (Privy Council: Lord Neuberger, Lady Hale, Lord Kerr, Lord Wilson and Lord Sumption). Application 6538/74 *Sunday Times v United Kingdom* (1979) 2 EHRR 245, ECtHR (1979 Abr para 1459), applied.

2289   Custodial sentence—duration—crediting of periods on remand—reduction in days credited—lawfulness of deduction

The appellant pleaded guilty to conspiracy to commit fraud. In the plea in mitigation, counsel for the appellant asked the judge to give the appellant credit for 120 of 184 days spent on remand while he had been serving another sentence. The judge reduced the sentence by two months to take account of the period spent on remand, which was stated in court as 184 days. Neither the parties nor the judge realised that the period of 184 days was an error and that figure ought to have been reduced by the time spent serving the other sentence. In fact, the time spent on remand, leaving out of account the time spent serving the other sentence, was 115 days, something which was subsequently realised by the prison authorities. The court order was duly amended to provide that 115 days should count against sentence, and the appellant's release date was corrected accordingly. The appellant appealed, submitting that the court lacked power to make the amendment order. The prosecution contended that the effect of the Criminal Justice Act 2003 s 240(4)(a) was clear and that the court had no power to count the time spent serving another sentence as time on remand. *Held*, it was clear from the terms of s 240(4) that, if a prisoner was serving a sentence for another offence at the time at which he was remanded for the offence for which he was to be sentenced, the application of the rules was mandatory: the court had neither the power, nor the discretion under s 240(3), to allow that period to count as time on remand. The effect of s 240(6) was that, where a court gave a direction for less than the number of days for which the prisoner had been remanded in custody, or gave no direction under s 240(3), it had to make clear that it had complied with the mandatory provisions of s 240(4)(a) as to the time being served with respect to another sentence of imprisonment and give its reasons for not making a direction under s 240(3). The intention of Parliament was clear: a court could not count the time spent serving another sentence, but had to give reasons as to why otherwise the full period of time on remand did not count. In effect, there was to be no diminution in the punishment for the earlier offence, but time awaiting trial should normally count in full. Thus understood, it was clear that there was no separate order under s 240(4); the only order a court could make was an order under s 240(3). Section 240(4)(a) of the Act merely restricted the discretion of the court, and s 240(4)(b) made it clear that, if an order was not made under s 240(3), reasons had to be given. It was settled law that the court was able to reconsider decisions made when it was clear that the decision made on an earlier occasion had been made without the benefit of all the material matters being drawn to the attention of the court. It followed that the court had had power to correct the error in the order made under s 240(3). Accordingly, the appeal would be dismissed.

R v Leacock [2013] EWCA Crim 1994, [2013] All ER (D) 180 (Nov) (Court of Appeal: Lord Judge CJ, Mackay and Sweeney JJ). *R (on the application of Hicks) v Snaresbrook Crown Court* [2012] EWCA Crim 2515, [2012] All ER (D) 309 (Nov) (2012 Abr para 2292) considered.

2290 Custodial sentence—duration—fraud—guidance

In two cases which raised common issues about sentencing in fraud cases, questions arose as to (1) whether and to what extent the Sentencing Council's guideline on sentencing for statutory offences of fraud were relevant to the task of sentencing for an offence of conspiracy to defraud; (2) what extent the absence of loss might constitute mitigation of the seriousness of the offence; and (3) the appropriate use of the power to impose consecutive sentences for substantive offences of fraud and for conspiracy to defraud. *Held*, there was no ambiguity in the principles to be applied in sentencing for the most serious offences of fraud, nor in the assessment whether consecutive sentences ought to be imposed to reflect the overall seriousness of similar offending. While the guideline on statutory offences of fraud did not apply to offences of conspiracy to defraud, the underlying principles of sentencing for fraud applied both to the substantive offence and to conspiracy to defraud. The fact that the maximum sentence for the statutory offence and for conspiracy to defraud was the same made the comparison of some, if ultimately limited, value. The 'seriousness' element of an offence comprised both culpability and harm. Harm was to be treated as harm which had been intended by the offender, or had been caused or might foreseeably have been caused by the offence. The guideline on the statutory offence recognised that a fraud which resulted in substantial financial loss, particularly if the loss was suffered by vulnerable victims deliberately targeted, was more serious than a fraud which had not.

R v Kallakis; R v Levene [2013] EWCA Crim 709, [2014] 1 Cr App Rep (S) 140, [2013] All ER (D) 201 (May) (Court of Appeal: Pitchford LJ, Evans and Turner JJ).

2291 Custodial sentence—duration—fraud—motor insurance claim

The defendant and his two co-accused lodged motor insurance claims in relation to a road traffic accident. The defendant claimed to be a passenger in the first co-accused's car when he lost control and drove into the second co-accused's car. The defendant and the first co-accused claimed to have sustained whiplash injuries. The insurance claim was found to be fraudulent and the defendant and both co-accused were convicted of fraud. The defendant's employer provided a good reference, describing him as a devoted family man. His wife suffered from bipolar disorder and the judge acknowledged the devastating impact the defendant's case had had on her. The trial had taken many weeks to conclude because the matter involved complex investigations and a large number of people. Both the defendant and the first co-accused were sentenced to 15 months' imprisonment and the second co-accused was sentenced to two years' imprisonment. The judge also ordered the defendant to contribute toward the prosecution costs. The defendant appealed against sentence and the costs order. *Held*, although it was difficult to classify the offence into a particular sentencing category, the defendant's contention that the judge should have treated it as a single fraud offence was questionable. The judge had had regard to the deterrent effect that the sentence would have had pursuant to the Criminal Justice Act 2003 s 142(1) and this approach could not be faulted. The judge had been justified in taking the starting point in excess of 15 months and discounting it by reason of the defendant's personal mitigation and the long time it had taken to hear the case. Accordingly, the appeal against sentence would be dismissed. An order that a defendant should pay towards prosecution costs could only be made if the defendant had the means and capability to pay. In the present case, it had not looked like the judge had been provided with the means of the defendant. Further, it was unclear whether the defendant would be able to return to his employment after serving his sentence. On the facts, while the defendant had the means to pay something, he did not have the means to pay the amount ordered. Accordingly, the costs order would be quashed and substituted for an order to pay a smaller sum.

R v McKenzie [2013] All ER (D) 167 (Aug) (Court of Appeal: Davis LJ, Keith and Lewis JJ).

2292 Custodial sentence—duration—medical condition—consideration in determining overall length of sentence

Since childhood the defendant had suffered from a rare hereditary condition known as Friedreich's ataxia. The condition resulted in progressive, irreversible and incurable degeneration of the spinocerebellar tract, which affected the nervous system and often resulted in multi-system disorders of the body. On returning from a holiday to Peru, the defendant was found with a large amount of cocaine hidden in the cushion of his wheelchair. He eventually admitted to planning the importation, and stated that he had been motivated more by the desire to demonstrate an independence in his life rather than by financial gain. At the sentencing hearing, an issue arose as to whether the imprisonment of the defendant would contravene the prohibition of torture or inhuman or degrading treatment or punishment enshrined in the European Convention on Human Rights art 3. The judge decided that, provided the normal arrangements for special care of prisoners with medical conditions were applied, imprisonment would not infringe the defendant's art 3 rights. The judge arrived at a notional sentence of seven years' imprisonment. That term was reduced by two-and-a-half years because of the defendant's early guilty plea, and by a further one-and-a-half years on the basis of the defendant's medical condition. The defendant appealed against sentence, submitting that his imprisonment breached his rights under arts 2 and 3, and that a three-year term was manifestly excessive in view of his medical condition. The defendant relied in part on an episode that had occurred seven weeks after entering prison in which he had developed a degree of arterial fibrillation. *Held*, the medical needs of prisoners were a well understood factor in the administration of prisons. A court which was passing sentence ought not to concern itself with the adequacy of those arrangements in an individual case, except where the mere fact of imprisonment would inevitably expose the prisoner to inhuman or degrading treatment contrary to art 3. Independently of that exceptional possibility, the sentencing court was fully entitled to take account of a medical condition by way of mitigation as a reason for reducing the length of the sentence. On the facts, there was no basis on which the art 2 and 3 submissions could possibly be arguable. None of the medical reports suggested that the defendant would be unable to cope with imprisonment. The fibrillation and supervening toxicosis had nothing to do with the care provided in prison. However, while that episode did not demonstrate any breach of art 2 or 3, it did serve to underline and illustrate the unstable combination of conditions from which the defendant suffered and the real potential for unexpected deterioration over a short period. Had the judge known of them he would have felt able to make a significantly greater reduction in the sentence. Bearing in mind the additional blow which life had dealt the defendant, his was an appropriate case for an exceptional application of mercy. On that basis it was appropriate to reduce the defendant's sentence by a further 18 months. Accordingly, the appeal would be allowed.

R v Hall [2013] EWCA Crim 82, [2013] All ER (D) 92 (Feb) (Court of Appeal: Hughes LJ, Wyn Williams and Hickinbottom JJ). *R v Qazi* [2010] EWCA Crim 2579, [2011] 2 Crim App Rep (S) 32, [2010] All ER (D) 54 (Nov) (2011 Abr para 2188) applied.

2293   Custodial sentence—duration—mitigating factors—supply of drugs

The defendant and the deceased were very close friends for a long time. Once a month, they spent time with each other, during which they took drugs. The responsibility for buying the drugs alternated between the defendant and the deceased. When it was the defendant's turn to purchase the drugs, he unknowingly purchased a drug that was more toxic than the drug that he intended to purchase. Both the defendant and the deceased suffered adverse effects from taking the drug, and the deceased subsequently died. The defendant pleaded guilty to a charge of supplying a controlled Class A drug contrary to the Misuse of Drugs Act 1971 s 4(3)(a). At sentencing, the judge had a large number of references for the defendant, and a letter from the father of the deceased expressing the hope that the court would be merciful towards him. A pre-sentence report stated that there was very little chance of the defendant re-offending. The defendant was sentenced to nine months' imprisonment. On appeal against sentence, *held*, the case was a tragic one. The judge was correct to categorise the offence as within category four of the relevant sentencing guidelines, which provided a sentencing range of a high level community order to three years' imprisonment with a starting point of one-and-a-half years' imprisonment. The mitigating features of the offence were the defendant's remorse and his previous positively good character. Leaving aside the death of the deceased, the offence would have attracted a sentence at the bottom end of the range. The deceased's death was a significant aggravating feature, but that was moderated by the effect it had on the defendant. It appeared that the judge had taken a starting point of 15 months' imprisonment. Considering the exceptional circumstances of the case, the appropriate starting point was nine months, which would be reduced to six months to reflect the early guilty plea. Accordingly, the appeal would be allowed.

R v Harrod [2013] All ER (D) 224 (Sep) (Court of Appeal: Pitchford LJ, Saunders and Spencer JJ).

2294   Custodial sentence—duration—multiple offending—conspiracy

On an application by the Attorney General for leave to review the sentences of offenders who have been convicted of conspiracy to burgle more than 40 dwelling houses, it has been held that it is an established principle of multiple offending that sentencing has to reflect the seriousness of the overall offending. Sometimes in a case of conspiracy, it is appropriate to lay more than one conspiracy charge or charge several substantive offences in lieu of conspiracy charges. Consecutive sentences should not be imposed merely because the term of the maximum sentence is too low.

R v Connors [2013] All ER (D) 192 (Sep) (Court of Appeal: Pitchford LJ, Blake and Carr JJ).

2295   Custodial sentence—restrictions—persons not represented

The Powers of Criminal Courts (Sentencing) Act 2000 s 83(1)(a) provides that a magistrates' court on summary conviction, or the Crown Court on committal for sentence or on conviction on indictment, may not pass a sentence of imprisonment on a person who is not legally represented in that court.

The claimant was found guilty of two offences of harassment and two offences of criminal damage. He was sentenced to 28 days' imprisonment for the harassment offences and to seven days' imprisonment for the criminal damage offences, suspended for 12 months. He appealed against conviction to the Crown Court. His appeal was dismissed and he was re-sentenced to twelve weeks' imprisonment for the harassment offences and to four weeks' imprisonment for the criminal damage offences. The claimant was not represented in either court. At the Crown Court, the claimant asked the court to appoint a solicitor to mitigate on his behalf, but the judge, commenting that the claimant had always refused legal representation previously and concluding that the material that he wished to put forward was either irrelevant or could be put by witnesses present, failed to respond to the request and, by implication, rejected it without giving reasons. The claimant subsequently asked the court to state a case on whether it was entitled to sentence the claimant to imprisonment when he was unrepresented. The court refused to do so, on the basis that it had been an appeal against conviction and sentence, which did not fall within the 2000 Act s 83. The claimant sought judicial review challenging the court's refusal to state a case. *Held*, if the Crown Court could impose a custodial sentence on an unrepresented defendant on the dismissal of his appeal against conviction in the magistrates' court, in circumstances where the magistrates could not themselves have imposed such a sentence as a result of s 83, that would be a lacuna which Parliament could not rationally have intended. There was no discernible policy reason for imposing restrictions on a magistrates' court, but not on an appeal from it. As it was clear that s 83 prevented the magistrates' court from sentencing the claimant, as an unrepresented defendant, to a sentence of imprisonment, the restrictions contained in s 83 also applied to the Crown Court as its powers were no greater than those of the magistrates' court. Accordingly, the application would be allowed.

R (on the application of Ebert) v Crown Court at Wood Green [2013] All ER (D) 12 (Mar) (Queen's Bench Division: Toulson LJ and Silber J). *R v Birmingham Justices, ex p Wyatt* [1975] 3 All ER 897, DC (1978 Abr para 887), criticised; *Sunworld Ltd v Hammersmith and Fulham LBC; R v Crown Court at Blackfriars, ex p Sunworld Ltd* [2000] 2 All ER 837, DC (2000 Abr para 812), applied.

2296   Injunction to prevent gang-related violence—exclusion from area—alternative injunctions

Following a gang-related incident, the applicant city council obtained an injunction against the respondent under the Policing and Crime Act 2009 s 34 prohibiting him from entering a prescribed area of the city and associating with named persons or gathering with them in any public place in the city. The respondent appealed, arguing that the court should have considered alternative injunctions, such as an anti-social behaviour injunction under the Housing Act 1996 or the Crime and Disorder Act 1998. *Held*, it could not have been the intention of Parliament that, when considering whether it was necessary to grant a gang-related violence injunction, the court had to ask itself whether an anti-social behaviour order would provide an adequate remedy. If the conditions for granting an injunction preventing gang-related violence had been met then it was appropriate to grant one. Further, it was inappropriate to invite the appellate court to trawl through the legislation in a quest for alternative injunctions. The principal issue, and usually the only live issue, in any appeal for which permission had been granted would be whether the statutory conditions were satisfied. Accordingly, the appeal would be dismissed.

Birmingham City Council v James [2013] EWCA Civ 552, [2013] All ER (D) 218 (May), (2013) Times, 8 July (Court of Appeal: Maurice Kay, Moore-Bick and Jackson LJJ).

2297   Life sentence—discretionary life sentence—serious offence—public protection

The defendant pleaded guilty to six counts of robbery. In sentencing him, the judge noted that the defendant demonstrated a real danger to the public, particularly to those owning and working in small shops, and that significant determinate sentences had not deterred him. The defendant was sentenced to life imprisonment for each count, to run concurrently, with a minimum term of eight years. On appeal against sentence, *held*, the judge was wrong to approach the discretionary life term in the way that he did, in effect as a substitute for an order for imprisonment for public protection. A sentence of imprisonment for public protection was available, and that sentence would have achieved the necessary element of public protection. On the other hand, there was no basis for interfering with the minimum term. Accordingly, the appeal would be allowed to the extent of replacing the sentence of life imprisonment with a sentence of imprisonment for public protection.

R v Saunders [2013] EWCA Crim 1027, [2013] All ER (D) 17 (Jul) (Court of Appeal: Lord Judge CJ, Lloyd Jones LJ and Openshaw J).

2298   Plea of guilty—factual basis of plea—sentence—guidance

See *R v Cairns; R v Morris; R v Rafiq; R v Firfire*, para 728.

2299   Proceeds of crime—appeals

The Proceeds of Crime Act 2002 (Appeals Under Part 2) (Amendment) Order 2013, SI 2013/24 (in force on 8 February 2013), further amends the 2003 Order, SI 2003/82, so as to ensure consistency between appeals to the Court of Appeal and then on to the Supreme Court under the Proceeds of Crime Act 2002 Pt 2 (ss 6–91) and those which relate to external requests and orders. The order applies to appeals that are both ongoing at the time the order comes into force and those commenced after. In particular, the order (1) makes provision corresponding to the Criminal Appeal Act 1968 s 18 and gives the time limit for giving notice of application for leave to appeal to the Court of Appeal; (2) makes provision corresponding to s 22 and provides when and how a person is permitted to be at the hearing of an appeal by the Court of Appeal; (3) makes provision corresponding to s 23 and sets out the Court of Appeal's powers to order the production of documents and other evidence and require witnesses to attend; (4) makes provision corresponding to s 31 and sets out which of the Court of Appeal's powers may be exercised by a single judge; (5) makes provision corresponding to s 31A and sets out which of the Court of Appeal's powers may be exercised by the registrar; (6) makes provision about transcripts; (7) makes provision corresponding to s 31B and sets out which of the Court of Appeal's procedural directions powers may be exercised by a single judge and the registrar; (8) makes provision corresponding to s 31C and sets out appeals to a single judge in respect of decisions by the registrar concerning procedural directions; (9) makes provision corresponding to s 44A about appeals in the case of death; and (10) makes provision corresponding to s 38 and deals with when and how a person is permitted to be at the hearing of an appeal by the Supreme Court.

2300   Rehabilitation of offenders—spent convictions—exceptions

The Rehabilitation of Offenders Act 1974 (Exceptions) Order 1975 (Amendment) (England and Wales) Order 2013, SI 2013/1198 (in force on 29 May 2013), further amends the 1975 Order, SI 1975/1023. The effects of the amendments are that (1) the Rehabilitation of Offenders Act 1974 applies to service offences which are not recordable service offences; (2) a caution or conviction is to be treated as a protected caution or a protected conviction depending on a person's age at the date of the caution or conviction, the time which has passed since the date of the caution or conviction, the nature of the offence resulting in the caution or conviction and the type of sentence imposed in respect of a conviction; (3) except in certain specified circumstances, the 1974 Act is no longer disapplied in respect of a protected caution or protected conviction when a question is asked to assess a person's suitability for certain purposes or when a decision is made for certain purposes; and (4) specified provisions of the 1974 Act do not apply in relation to questions asked to assess a person's suitability for purposes concerning offices or employment in Jersey, Guernsey or the Isle of Man.

2301   Restraining order—protection from harassment—person acquitted of offence—finding of not guilty by reason of insanity

The Protection from Harassment Act 1997 s 5A(1) provides that a court before which a person ('the defendant') is acquitted of an offence may, if it considers it necessary to do so to protect a person from harassment by the defendant, make an order prohibiting the defendant from doing anything described in the order.

The defendant had a history of paranoid schizophrenia. His mental health started to deteriorate. In the early hours of one morning, he began to act irrationally, speaking of demons, of the family being angels and going to a better place. A member of the family called the police, who tried to calm him. While in that state, he picked up his seven-month-old daughter and stabbed her four times in the chest before making stabbing motions to his own throat and wrist causing injury. The police subdued him using CS spray. The defendant's injuries were minor. His young daughter received emergency surgery for life threatening injuries. A five-year restraining order was imposed on the defendant, pursuant to the 1997 Act. The defendant applied for leave to appeal against the restraining order on the ground that a person who had been found not guilty by reason of insanity had not been 'acquitted' for the purposes of s 5A. *Held*, a person found not guilty by reason of insanity had, as a matter of ordinary language, been acquitted of the offence charged. The purpose of a restraining order was to protect a person from harassment by an acquitted defendant. However, the court first had to be satisfied that the defendant was likely to pursue a course of conduct which would amount to harassment within the meaning of s 1. On the facts, there was no relevant course of conduct. The incident was a single one and did not satisfy the requirements of the 1997 Act. Further, the defendant was not suffering from disability at the time of sentence that pertained at the time of the incident. It could not, therefore, be said that repetition, even of a single act, as opposed to a course of conduct, was likely. Accordingly, the leave to appeal and the appeal would be allowed and the restraining order would be quashed.

R v R (AJ) [2013] EWCA Crim 591, [2013] 2 Cr App Rep 128 (Court of Appeal: McCombe LJ, Saunders J and Judge Collier QC). *R v Smith (Mark)* [2012] EWCA Crim 2566, [2013] 2 All ER 804 (2012 Abr para 2311) applied.

2302   Restraint order—breach—perverting the course of justice

See *R v Kenny*, para 727.

2303   Sentencing principles—effect of crime on victim—personal and family impact statements

See *R v Perkins*, para 714.

2304   Sentencing principles—seriousness of offence—culpability—gross negligence manslaughter—medical negligence

The deceased's mother called a healthcare service provider and explained the deceased's condition as muddled, mumbling, sunken eyes, erratic breathing and a breath smelling of pear drops. The defendant, an out of hours doctor working for the provider, was sent to see the deceased. The mother described the symptoms and asked the defendant if the deceased was in a coma and had an infection or might be diabetic, as his father was diabetic. The defendant shook his head to all those questions. He had no equipment with him and did not examine the deceased. He said that the deceased was depressed and had a headache and should see his own doctor on the following day. In his attendance log, the defendant recorded a history of depression and stated that, on examination, the deceased's general condition had been fair, that he had not been communicating but had been comfortable. The defendant recorded a normal temperature and pulse rate but did not record blood pressure or undertake a urine analysis. The following morning, the deceased passed away. A post-mortem examination concluded that the death had been due to diabetic ketoacidosis. The defendant pleaded not guilty to a charge of manslaughter. He informed the court that he admitted a breach of duty and causation but not gross negligence as to which he was awaiting an expert report. Subsequent expert evidence from a professor of forensic medicine, a retired professor of clinical diabetes and a consultant physician found that the deceased had displayed classic symptoms of ketoacidosis, that the defendant had failed to take an adequate history, to recognise the symptoms and to undertake adequate examinations. His failure to diagnose the condition had been the main cause of death and his breach of duty had been appalling and gross. The defendant changed his plea to guilty. The judge gave a starting point of three years' imprisonment and, following a discount, for the defendant's guilty plea and mitigating factors, sentenced him to two and a half years' imprisonment. On the defendant's appeal against sentence, consideration was given to the Criminal Justice Act 2003 s 143(1), which provided that, in considering the seriousness of any offence, the court had to consider the offender's culpability in committing the offence and any harm which the offence had caused, had intended to cause or might foreseeably have caused. *Held*, the judge had taken the view that the evidence pointed clearly and unequivocally in the case to manslaughter by way of gross negligence and, therefore, the defendant had not needed expert opinion. The starting point of three years had not been manifestly excessive. It had been within the appropriate range for the offending of the nature and facts of the present case and, accordingly, the appeal would be dismissed.

R v Kovvali [2013] All ER (D) 48 (Jun) (Court of Appeal: Pitchford LJ, Griffith Williams J and Judge Ford QC). *R v Holtom* [2010] EWCA Crim 934, [2011] 1 Cr App

Rep (S) 128, [2010] All ER (D) 124 (Apr) (2010 Abr para 2497); and *R v Garg* [2012] EWCA Crim 2520, [2012] All ER (D) 21 (Dec) (2012 Abr para 2313) considered.

2305   Sexual offence—rape—aggravating features

The defendant befriended his victims, who were 22 and 28 years of age, through a social networking website. On separate occasions, he took each victim to a hotel and gave her drinks. Following the consumption of a small quantity of their drinks, the victims became unconscious and woke up several hours later semi-naked or naked. They both failed to recollect what happened in the interim. The police were contacted and the defendant was arrested. A film of his activities with one of the victims was discovered on his mobile phone together with images of his activities with the other victim. The defendant was charged with two counts of assault by penetration (counts 1, 3) and one count of rape (count 2). During the trial, the judge found that both victims were disabled by drugs applied by the defendant. The defendant was convicted on all counts. A pre-sentence report stated that the offences were planned, and that the defendant maintained that sexual activity was consensual and initiated by the victims, denied lacing the victims' drinks, and regretted making the images only to the extent of the impact it had on him and his family. In sentencing, the judge said that the relevant sentencing guidelines were not easy to apply to the unusual circumstances of the case. The judge also took into account the question of totality and reduced the total sentence to one that was appropriate. The defendant was sentenced to three years' imprisonment for count 1, three and a half years' for count 2 and three years' for count 3. The sentences for counts 2 and 3 were to run concurrently and consecutive to count 1. The Attorney General applied for leave to review the sentence on the ground that it was unduly lenient. *Held*, there were a number of aggravating features in the case, which included (1) the use of substances for the purpose of facilitating the offences, which reflected an element of deliberation and planning; (2) the photographs and filming of the offences; and (3) the fact that on the same occasion, in respect of one of the victims, the defendant committed the further offence of assault by penetration following rape. Considering count 2 in isolation, the sentence ought not to have properly fallen below seven years. Further, having regard to the offending behaviour as a whole, it ought not to have fallen below nine years. Accordingly, the application would be granted and the sentence for count 2 would be substituted by a sentence of six years' imprisonment.

R v Master [2013] All ER (D) 149 (Sep) (Court of Appeal: Pitchford LJ, Blake and Carr JJ).

2306   Sexual offence—sexual offences prevention order—appropriateness—indecent
        assault and attempted buggery involving child

The offender was a teacher who was actively involved in the church. The first victim was a ten-year-old boy whom the offender met through school and church. On numerous occasions the offender invited the first victim to visit him at his home, where he gave him sweets and meals, and, on later visits, cigarettes and alcohol. On some occasions, the first victim was allowed to stay with the offender overnight. Over a period of two years, when the first victim was aged between 12 and 14, the offender assaulted him sexually on several occasions. The second victim, who was the first victim's brother, was subjected to a similar process of grooming by the offender. Over a course of three years beginning when the second victim was aged 11, the offender carried out between eight and ten sexual offences on the second victim. Suspicions were raised about the offender, and, although he lost his position as a teacher, no criminal proceedings were brought against him at the time. Several years later, it was discovered that the offender was giving private music lessons at his home. The offender was arrested and indecent images of young boys of uncertain age were discovered on his computer. The offender was convicted of one count of attempted buggery in relation to the first victim, and six counts of indecent assault in relation to both victims. He was sentenced to a total of six years' imprisonment, but the judge declined to impose a sexual offences prevention order ('SOPO') in addition. The Attorney-General was granted leave to refer the sentences as unduly lenient. *Held*, in the circumstances, the sentences were unduly lenient. The appropriate sentence in respect of the attempted buggery, had the offence stood alone, would have been in the region of five years' imprisonment. The appropriate sentence after trial in respect of the other offences would also be five years' imprisonment. The principle of totality had to be applied to the total of ten years' imprisonment. An adjustment ought to be made in order to produce a final sentence of eight years' imprisonment. With regard to the SOPO, there had been a specific necessity to ensure that the offender was prevented from accessing the internet for the purpose of sexual fantasising about children. A SOPO would therefore be made forbidding the offender from using the internet for sexual purposes and requiring any use made by him of the internet to be retained and made available for inspection by the police. The SOPO would also constrain the offender's access to any male children under the age of 16. Judgment would be given accordingly.

A-G's Reference (No 59 of 2013); R v Lillis [2013] EWCA Crim 2200, [2013] All ER (D) 132 (Nov) (Court of Appeal: Pitchford LJ, Nicola Davies J and the Recorder of Leeds).

2307   Sexual offence—sexual offences prevention order—variation—power of court

The defendant pleaded guilty to four charges of distributing indecent photographs of children and six charges of making indecent photographs. He was sentenced to two years' imprisonment concurrent on each count. A sexual offences prevention order ('SOPO') was also made in relation to the defendant. Pursuant to the Sexual Offences Act 2003 s 108, the defendant applied to the Crown Court for the SOPO to be varied, submitting that it was unreasonable in view of the guidance given in later authority. The application was refused on the basis that s 108 existed to deal with difficulties arising from an order due to unforeseen circumstances, which did not include objections in principle to the terms of the order. The judge held that such objections should be raised by way of appeal. The defendant appealed against that decision. *Held*, guidance given in later authorities could not provide the basis for a successful appeal against a SOPO which had been made with every justification. Sentence was imposed on the basis of the relevant legislation, the principles, practice and guidance which were current at the date when the sentence was imposed. An existing sentence should not be varied on appeal because of changes to them. Although the express terms of the 2003 Act were broad in relation to the court's power to make a variation order, a judge had to have regard not only to the express terms of the legislation, but also to the principles which the Court of Appeal had said should be applied. Objections in principle to the terms of a SOPO imposed by the Crown Court ought to be raised by an appeal to the Court of Appeal and not by subsequent applications to vary to the Crown Court. On the facts, the defendant's attack on the breadth of the order could not properly be made through the vehicle of an application to vary it, but could be launched only by means of an appeal against the original order. Accordingly, the appeal would be dismissed.

R v Spencer [2013] EWCA Crim 2286, [2013] All ER (D) 50 (Dec) (Court of Appeal: Davis LJ, Nicol J and Judge Elgan Edwards). R v Instone [2012] All ER (D) 161 (Jul) applied.

2308   Terrorism—imprisonment—length of sentence

The defendants came to the attention of the security services after becoming fundamentalists who wished to support and commit acts of terrorism. They were monitored using covert surveillance techniques and devices. Although from different parts of the country, they met together. They were recorded meeting in a park. Although limited material was available as to precisely what transpired, the meeting was alleged to have covered ideological discussion and general ambitions concerning terrorist activities. Later, the third defendant and the four co-accused met and discussed targets for attack. Thereafter, two of the co-accused were recorded discussing the construction of explosive devices. Soon after, the first, second, fourth and fifth defendants were recorded discussing jihad overseas. The defendants then met in a park where discussions included how to advance plans for an attack with the first defendant monitored in conversation about how to construct a pipe bomb from a recipe referred to in a terrorist publication. In turn, two of the co-accused were engaged in experimentation using the pipe bomb recipe. It was at that point that the defendants and co-accused were arrested. Subsequently, the defendants all pleaded guilty to various offences. The first defendant was sentenced to detention for public protection with a minimum custodial term of eight years, the second defendant was sentenced to five years' imprisonment and the third defendant was sentenced to an extended sentence of 15 years and four months with a custodial term of 10 years' imprisonment and an extension period of five years. The fourth and fifth defendants were both sentenced to imprisonment for public protection with minimum custodial terms of eight years. All were subject to terrorist notification periods imposed pursuant to the provisions of the Counter Terrorism Act 2008 Pt 4 (ss 40–61) of 30 years, save for the second defendant whose period was 15 years. All appealed against their sentence. *Held*, the decision which the judge had made had been to the effect that the position of the first, second, fourth and fifth defendants was equally serious. The judge had been fully entitled to reach that conclusion and its implementation in the sentencing decisions reached for those defendants could not be impeached. However, the indeterminate sentences would be quashed and determinate terms passed such that in the case of the fourth defendant the substituted sentence was an extended sentence of 22 years and eight months of which the custodial term was 17 years eight months with an extension period of five years. For both the first and fifth defendants, the sentence was an extended sentence of 21 years of which the custodial term was 16 years' imprisonment, in each case with an extension period of five years. In all three cases, the notification provisions would continue. Having reduced the sentence on the first, fourth and fifth defendants by removing the sentence of imprisonment for public protection, it would be right to make a marginal adjustment to the second defendant's sentence. The appeal would be allowed and the sentence would be reduced to four-and-a-half years, recognising that that would reduce the notification period from 15 years to 10 years. There was no reason in the third defendant's case for interfering with the sentencing decision. Judgment would be given accordingly.

R v Khan [2013] EWCA Crim 468, [2013] All ER (D) 90 (Apr) (Court of Appeal: Leveson LJ, Mitting and Sweeney JJ).

2309   Terrorism—prevention—notification requirements—compatibility with right to private and family life

The claimant pleaded guilty to engaging in conduct with the intention of assisting in the commission of acts of terrorism contrary to the Terrorism Act 2006 s 5(1), and was sentenced to four years' imprisonment. On his release, he became subject to the notification requirements in the Counter-Terrorism Act 2008 ss 47–52, under which a person sentenced to less than five years' imprisonment was subject to notification requirements for a ten-year period following release with no right of review. The claimant applied for judicial review of the requirements on the basis of *F*, in which similar notification requirements in relation to convicted sex offenders pursuant to the Sexual Offences Act 2003 which endured for the rest of a person's life without a right of review were held to be incompatible with the European Convention on Human Rights art 8. The court refused the application on the ground that there was no incompatibility with art 8. On the claimant's appeal, *held*, the ratio of *F* was limited to the disproportionality of a lifetime notification requirement with no right of review and the decision was not binding authority to the effect that any notification requirement of significant finite duration with no right of review was, without more, disproportionate. There was nothing disproportionate about the ten-year notification requirement, even in the absence of a right of review. In the circumstances, given the relatively moderate intrusion caused by the interference of the requirements with the private lives of convicted terrorists generally, and having particular regard to the interference with the private life of the claimant, it could not be said that either the notification scheme or its application to the claimant was disproportionate. The 2008 Act was not therefore incompatible with art 8 and, accordingly, the appeal would be dismissed.

R (on the application of Irfan) v Secretary of State for the Home Department [2012] EWCA Civ 1471, [2013] QB 885, [2012] All ER (D) 158 (Nov) (Court of Appeal: Maurice Kay, Munby and Tomlinson LJJ). *R (on the application of F (a child)) v Secretary of State for the Home Department; R (on the application of Thompson) v Secretary of State for the Home Department* [2010] UKSC 17, [2011] 1 AC 331, [2010] 2 All ER 707 (2010 Abr para 2513) distinguished.

2310   Terrorism—prevention and investigation measures—proportionality of restrictions

The appellant, a Somali national, had engaged in terrorist activities abroad, and on his return to the United Kingdom the Secretary of State imposed restrictions on him under the Terrorism Prevention and Investigation Measures Act 2011 s 3. The measure limited who the appellant could associate with and where he could go, as well as imposing reporting duties, overnight residence and restrictions on the kind of electronic communications device he could possess. At the annual review meeting the appellant requested a variation of the measure so that he could begin a university course and could reply to offers of part-time work without seeking prior approval. The request was refused, and the appellant appealed against that decision. *Held*, it was settled law that the question of whether it was necessary to impose any particular obligation on an individual in order to protect the public from the risk of terrorism involved the customary test of proportionality. Applying established principles, the residence requirements satisfied the tests both of necessity and proportionality and would not be varied. In relation to the device requirement, acknowledging the deference to be paid to the Security Service, the measure was necessary. Further, the current restriction passed the test of proportionality and would not be varied. The work or studies measure was also necessary. As for proportionality, it was not disproportionate to require the appellant not to start work for two days in order to give the Secretary of State the opportunity to check whether the security issues which it legitimately had did not arise, or could be sufficiently managed to permit the appellant to undertake that work. The work or studies measure would also therefore not be varied. In relation to the reporting measure, bearing in mind the deference the court ought to pay to the views of the Security Service based on its expertise and experience, the daily reporting requirement at a police station was necessary, as were the restrictions in the association measure. However, the association restrictions did not satisfy the requirements of proportionality. They imposed a chilling effect on the appellant's participation in the life of a student on his course, without any apparent beneficial effect on national security. Some variation in those requirements was therefore necessary to satisfy the test of proportionality. Accordingly, the appeal would be allowed in part.

CF v Secretary of State for the Home Department (proceedings under the Terrorism Prevention and Investigation Measures Act 2011) [2013] EWHC 843 (Admin), [2013] All ER (D) 71 (Apr) (Queen's Bench Division: Wilkie J). *De Freitas v Permanent Secretary of Ministry of Agriculture, Fisheries, Lands and Housing* [1999] 1 AC 69; and *Secretary of State for the Home Department v AF* [2009] UKHL 28, [2010] 2 AC 269, [2009] 3 All ER 643 (2009 Abr para 953) applied.

2311　Unduly lenient sentence—reference by Attorney General—cases which may be referred—trafficking for sexual exploitation

The Protection of Freedoms Act 2012 (Consequential Amendments) Order 2013, SI 2013/862 (in force on 13 May 2013), (1) further amends the Criminal Justice Act (Reviews of Sentencing) Order 2006, SI 2006/1116, so as to empower the Attorney General to refer to the Court of Appeal where he considers that an unduly lenient sentence has been imposed for an offence of trafficking people for sexual exploitation, contrary to the Sexual Offences Act 2003 s 59A; (2) amends the Armed Forces (Review of Court Martial Sentence) Order 2009, SI 2009/1168, so that the Attorney General may refer to the Court Martial Appeal Court where he considers that an unduly lenient sentence has been imposed by a Court Martial in respect of an offence under the 2003 Act s 59A, or an offence of administering a substance with intent, contrary to s 61; and (3) amends the Criminal Legal Aid (Remuneration) Regulations 2013, SI 2013/435, by adding offences under the 2003 Act s 59A to the list of serious sexual offences contained in those regulations.

2312　Unduly lenient sentence—reference by Attorney General—sexual offence against children—indecent assault—deliberately false statement to the media

The defendant was charged with 14 counts of indecent assault, contrary to the Sexual Offences Act 1956 s 14, on 13 different victims who were females aged between nine and 17, over a twenty-year period. When the offender had been arrested he had said that the complaints were completely untrue and he made a statement to the media outside the magistrates' court that the victims' claims were 'pernicious, callous, cruel and, above all, spurious'. However, the defendant pleaded guilty to all the charges and was sentenced to 15 months' imprisonment. The Attorney General sought leave to refer the sentence to the Court of Appeal as unduly lenient. *Held*, a deliberately false statement to the media claiming that the assertions of victims were spurious was a seriously aggravating feature to be taken into account when sentencing. The defendant had been attempting to use the media perhaps to influence potential jurors, but whether his comments might have had that effect they affected the victims who described themselves as absolutely incensed, upset and concerned that people would have been unduly influenced by his statement. The sentencing decision facing the judge had been far from straightforward. For so-called 'historic' offences the maximum sentence for most of the offences was two years' imprisonment, although for those offences committed against victims under 13 the maximum term was five years. Since the offences had been committed sentences had been significantly increased. The court considered the discount to be allowed for the guilty pleas. The offender did plead guilty but not before he had publicly attacked his victims. The appropriate way to proceed was to reflect that behaviour in assessing the overall sentence and then to make the deduction for the guilty pleas. The impact of those offences on the victims had been lifelong, although manifested differently. Account was taken of all the features identified by the Attorney General and counsel for the offender but it was also recognised that there was public concern about the molestation of children and an increasing public understanding of the consequences to such victims. Therefore, leave would be granted to the Attorney General pursuant to the Criminal Justice Act 1988 s 36. The overall sentence would be increased to 30 months. Judgment would be given accordingly.

R v Hall (A-G's Reference (No 38 of 2013)) [2013] EWCA Crim 1450, (2013) Times, 17 October (Court of Appeal: Lord Judge CJ, Rafferty LJ and Macur J).

2313 Unduly lenient sentence—reference by Attorney General—sexual offence against children—indecent assault and attempted buggery—sexual offences prevention order

See para 2307.

2314 Unduly lenient sentence—reference by Attorney General—sexual offence against children—social media

The defendant was arrested and charged on an indictment containing 17 counts which involved inciting, or attempting to incite, children to engage in sexual activities and making indecent photographs of children. The defendant committed the majority of those offences by setting up Facebook accounts in which he described himself as a teenage girl or boy. He befriended a number of younger boys through those accounts and incited and/or caused eight of them to perform sexual activities in front of a web camera so that he could see them. He also incited up to 220 others to perform in a similar way, although they did not do so. He was charged and released on bail. While he was on bail, the defendant committed a further eight offences. At the plea and case management hearing, he pleaded guilty to all 17 counts and asked for the eight offences committed while on bail to be taken into consideration. At sentencing, reference was made to victim impact statements and other similar statements from the numerous victims who described their incidences as having made them 'feel bad, scared, sick and angry'. The judge sentenced the defendant to a total sentence of 16 months' imprisonment. The Attorney General made an application for leave to refer the sentence, contending that the sentence imposed was unduly lenient. *Held*, there were not any sentencing guidelines specifically tailored to such offences, namely 'cyber sex' offences. The closest analogy was the part of the guidelines directed to the Sexual Offences Act 2003 s 8 and was part of the range of sentences for non-consensual sexual offences. The victims did not know the identity of the other person they were in contact with through Facebook. Cyber sex offences, although serious, were less serious than physical contact offences. However, the court, in no way, would dilute the seriousness of the present offences based on their own facts. The offences were difficult to prevent and the court could envisage some contact offences less serious than some cyber offences as the victims might develop serious psychological effects. There was the aggravating factor that the defendant had committed a further eight offences while on bail. The sentence was unduly lenient. Accordingly, the application would be allowed and the sentence would be quashed and substituted with a sentence of four years' imprisonment.

R v Knight [2013] All ER (D) 138 (Aug) (Court of Appeal: Rafferty LJ, Griffith Williams and Thirlwall JJ). *R v Butcher* [2009] EWCA Crim 1458; and *A-G's Reference (No 24 of 2011)* [2011] EWCA Crim 1960 considered.

2315 Young offender—remand to youth detention—recovery of costs

The Recovery of Costs (Remand to Youth Detention Accommodation) Regulations 2013, SI 2013/507 (in force on 1 April 2013), make provision for and in connection with payment by local authorities to the Youth Justice Board for England and Wales of the cost of a child being subject to a remand to a secure children's home, a secure training centre or a young offender institution. SI 2012/2822 is revoked.

The Recovery of Costs (Remand to Youth Detention Accommodation) (Amendment) Regulations 2013, SI 2013/2243 (in force on 1 October 2013), amends the 2013 Regulations, SI 2013/507 (see above), by inserting new amounts which local authorities are liable to pay the Youth Justice Board for England and Wales in respect of each night on which a child is detained on remand in a secure training centre on or after 1 October 2013 and 1 December 2013.

SHIPPING AND MARITIME LAW

Halsbury's Laws of England (5th edn) vol 93 (2008) paras 1–590, vol 94 (2008) paras 591–1254

2316　Carriage by sea

See CARRIAGE AND CARRIERS.

2317　Limitation of liability—time limit—agreement—waiver of limitation period

A collision occurred between two ships and a collision jurisdiction agreement was concluded between the claimant owners of one of the ships, the defendant owners of the other ship and her demise charterers. A formal agreement to settle was signed, providing that the defendant was 75 per cent to blame for the collision and was to pay 75 per cent of the claim of the claimant as proved or agreed, together with interest. Similar provisions provided for the claimant's liability. The parties' claims were to be referred to the Admiralty Registrar failing agreement. The claimant repeatedly provided the defendant with its claim and issued a claim form seeking damages for the loss caused by the collision. The defendant advised the claimant that, since the writ had been issued after the expiry of the second anniversary of the collision, a time bar defence would be raised. The claimant issued an application notice, seeking an order that the claim was not time-barred and seeking permission to add the demise charterers of the defendants' ship as defendants to the claim form under CPR 19.2. It was contended that the true construction of the agreement was that each party was precluded from saying that proceedings to claim damages for the loss caused by the collision had to be commenced within two years. The obligation entered into by each party that it would pay the agreed percentage of the other side's claim was inconsistent with either party being able to claim that it did not have to pay the agreed percentage of the other side's claim in the event that proceedings by that party were not commenced within two years of the date of the collision under the Merchant Shipping Act 1995 s 190. *Held*, the obligation that had been assumed by each party that it would pay the agreed percentage of the other's claim was inconsistent with an obligation not to pay in the event that it proved to be the case that the other had not issued a claim form within two years of the date of the collision. It followed that each party was precluded by agreement from relying on the time bar provided by s 190. Any such reliance would be inconsistent with the express obligation accepted by each party that it would pay the agreed percentage. The 1995 Act provided for a two year time bar, but a ship owner might waive his right to rely on that time bar and the parties had done so. It had been the true construction of the agreement that neither party would take any steps which would make it impossible to have the quantum of the claims determined by the Registrar. Further, it was fair and just to add the demise charterers as a new party. The demise charterers had been party to the agreement. Therefore, the demise charterers had promised that they would pay 75 per cent of the claim. In those circumstances, there was no hardship or prejudice to the demise charterers in granting permission to add them as a party. If they were not added, a fresh action could be issued against the demise charterers who could not, by reason of the agreement, assert that they had not had to pay 75 per cent of the claim in circumstances where a claim form had not been issued within two years of the claim. Accordingly, the claim would be allowed.

Owners of the Ship Theresa Libra v Owners of the Ship MSC Pamela [2013] EWHC 2792 (Admlty), [2013] All ER (D) 175 (Sep) (Queen's Bench Division: Teare J).

2318   Marine insurance

See INSURANCE.

2319   Marine Navigation Act 2013

The Marine Navigation Act 2013 makes provision in relation to marine navigation and harbours. The Act received the royal assent on 25 April 2013 and came into force in part on that day. Further provisions came into force on 26 June 2013 and 1 October 2013: SI 2013/1489, SI 2013/2006. The remaining provisions come into force on a day or days to be appointed. For details of commencement, see the commencement table in the title STATUTES AND LEGISLATIVE PROCESS.

Section 1 gives the appropriate national authority power by order to remove the pilotage functions of a harbour authority. By virtue of s 2, the restriction under which only the master or first mate of a ship may hold a pilotage exemption certificate is removed so that any deck officer of a ship may hold a certificate provided the harbour authority is satisfied that he has the skill, experience and local knowledge, and sufficient knowledge of English for safety purposes, to be capable of piloting specified ships within its harbour. Section 3 extends the circumstances in which a harbour authority may suspend or revoke a pilotage exemption certificate so that an authority may now do so where (1) an event has occurred as a result of which the authority is no longer satisfied that the holder of the certificate meets the requirements of holding the certificate; (2) the authority thinks that the holder has provided false information; (3) the authority thinks that the holder has been guilty of professional misconduct while piloting a ship; and (4) the certificate has been misused in circumstances where an act of pilotage is undertaken by an unauthorised person. Under s 4, the master of a ship commits an offence if he does not give a pilotage notification before a ship is navigated in an area for which a pilotage direction is in force.

Section 5 provides that the appropriate national authority may by order designate harbour authorities so that they can give harbour directions to ships, sets out the procedure applicable to harbour directions, and makes it an offence for the master of a ship to fail without reasonable excuse to ensure compliance with harbour directions. Section 6 empowers the Secretary of State and the Welsh Ministers to make closure orders relieving harbour authorities of maintaining harbours which are no longer commercially viable or necessary, sets out the content and procedure applicable to such orders, and provides that orders may include provision for the transfer of the property, rights and liabilities of harbour authorities.

The jurisdiction of ports police forces may be extended with the consent of the chief officer of the local police force under s 7 to enable ports police to carry out specified policing tasks without the assistance of regular police forces. Pursuant to s 8, the area in which each general lighthouse authority may operate includes the area for which the United Kingdom has jurisdiction for the prevention of pollution from ships. General lighthouse authorities are authorised by s 9 to enter into agreements for others to use their assets and to provide consultancy and other services. Section 10 permits greater flexibility in drafting the provisions of regulations that determine the standards that must be met by seafarers for them to be qualified for the purposes of the manning requirements on ships. Harbour authorities and conservancy authorities have power by virtue of s 11 to mark wrecks that are a danger to navigation either by physical devices such as buoys or lights or by broadcasting relevant information that can be used to show locations on electronic devices and charts.

Section 12 deals with extent, s 13 with commencement and s 14 with short title.

Amendments and repeals

The list below, which is not exhaustive, mentions repeals and amendments which are or will be effective when the Act is fully in force.

Specific provisions of the following Acts are amended, added or repealed: Harbours Act 1964 ss 1A(1), 17A–17F, 40A–40D, 44(9), 54(5), (6), 57(1); Pilotage Act 1987 ss 1(4A), (4B), (5)–(7), (8A), (8B), 8(1), 8A, 8B, 10(3), 15(1), (3)–(5), 20(1), 31(1); Merchant Shipping Act 1995 ss 47(4A), (4B), 193(6), 197(8)–(11), 197A, 252(2), (3A), 255C(4), (5), 255F(4).

2320   Merchant shipping—accident reporting and investigation

The Merchant Shipping (Accident Reporting and Investigation) (Amendment) Regulations 2013, SI 2013/2882 (in force on 31 December 2013), further amend the

2012 Regulations, SI 2012/1743, by (1) correcting the definition of 'EMCIP'; (2) excluding the Maritime and Coastguard Agency from the requirement to provide a report to the Chief Inspector; and (3) enabling the Chief Inspector to provide, at his discretion, information obtained from a voyage data recorder taken from a ship by an inspector in the course of a safety investigation to the ship's owner without the need for the owner to apply to a court.

2321　Merchant shipping—health and safety—asbestos

The Merchant Shipping and Fishing Vessels (Health and Safety at Work) (Asbestos) (Amendment) Regulations 2013, SI 2013/1473 (in force on 12 July 2013), further amend the 2010 Regulations, SI 2010/2984, so as to bring the regulations into line with the Control of Asbestos Regulations 2012, SI 2012/632, regs 2 and 4(8).

2322　Merchant shipping—health and safety—boat used in course of employment

Scotland

The claimant was instructed by the first defendant, her employer, to conduct an audit at a lighthouse. For that purpose she was required to travel to the lighthouse by boat. Transport was provided by the second defendant under a contract with the first defendant. The claimant was injured during the crossing to the lighthouse, and she brought proceedings against the defendants at common law and under the Merchant Shipping and Fishing Vessels (Health and Safety at Work) Regulations 1997, SI 1997/1962, reg 5. The second defendant contended that the claim was governed by the Convention relating to the Carriage of Passengers and their Luggage by Sea (Athens, 13 December 1974). As the Convention imposed a two-year time limit on bringing claims, the second defendant argued that the proceedings were time barred. *Held*, the defendants owed a strict duty under the 1997 Regulations reg 5 to ensure the health and safety of workers. The claimant was a worker on the boat in the course of her employment, and it followed that the liability of both defendants under reg 5 was clear. Although the Convention was in theory applicable to the second defendant, the second defendant had not mentioned it in the pleadings and so it could not rely on it. The claimant's application was therefore not time barred. In view of the applicability of the 1997 Regulations reg 5, the claimant's common law case was not of practical importance, but on the facts her case was made out against the second defendant but not the first defendant. The defendants were therefore jointly and severally liable for the claimant's injury, but as the second defendant was obliged under the contract to indemnify the first defendant against any liability incurred by it as a result of a breach of reg 5, the second defendant was liable for the full amount in damages. Accordingly, the application would be allowed.

　Cairns v Northern Lighthouse Board [2013] CSOH 22, 2013 SLT 645 (Outer House).

2323　Merchant shipping—Maritime Labour Convention—survey and certification

The Merchant Shipping (Maritime Labour Convention) (Survey and Certification) Regulations 2013, SI 2013/1785 (in force on 15 August 2013), (1) further amend the Merchant Shipping (Vessels in Commercial Use for Sport and Pleasure) Regulations 1998, SI 1998/2771, and the Merchant Shipping (Small Workboats and Pilot Boats) Regulations 1998, SI 1998/1609, so as to add a reference to the 2013 Regulations which has the effect of disapplying the requirements of the regulations as regards ships which comply with certain codes of practice; (2) require United Kingdom ships over 500 gross tonnage to be surveyed for the purposes of issuing a Maritime Labour Certificate; (3) make further provision regarding surveys and the issuing of certificates; (4) require (a) certain documents to be carried on board a United Kingdom ship and to be made available; and (b) on-board and on-shore complaint procedures to be available to seafarers on the ship; (5) make provision for arbitration on the outcome of surveys for United Kingdom ships; (6) make provision for enforcement in relation to United Kingdom ships; (7) require ships which are not United Kingdom ships to comply with requirements of the Maritime Labour Convention relating to the documents to be carried on board the ship and on-board and on-shore complaints procedure, and make provision for enforcement; and (8) require the Secretary of State to review the operation and effect of the regulations and publish a report within five years after they come into force and within every five years after that.

2324   Merchant shipping—pollution
See ENVIRONMENTAL QUALITY AND PUBLIC HEALTH.

2325   Merchant shipping—port security
The Port Security (Amendment) Regulations 2013, SI 2013/2815 (in force on 29 November 2013), amend the 2009 Regulations, SI 2009/2048, and further transpose European Parliament and Council Directive (EC) 2005/65 (on enhancing port security). Specifically, the regulations (1) alter the definition of 'port' to include port facility locality and introduce the word 'specified'; (2) move responsibility from the port security authority to the Secretary of State for ensuring that the port security assessment is done; (3) require the Secretary of State to review the operation and effect of the regulations and publish a report before 29 November 2018 and within every five years after that; and (4) make consequential amendments.

2326   Merchant shipping—registries—categorisation
The Merchant Shipping (Categorisation of Registries of Relevant British Possessions) (Amendment) Order 2013, SI 2013/1115 (in force on 12 June 2013), further amends the 2003 Order, SI 2003/1248, so as to enable the registration, in certain British possessions, of ships of no more than 400 tons, provided that certain conditions relating to survey and inspection are satisfied.

2327   Merchant shipping—safety convention—legislation—revocation
See para 1146.

2328   Shipowner's liability—limitation—constitution of limitation fund—acceptability of guarantee
The Convention on Limitation of Liability for Maritime Claims art 11(1) (London, 1 November 1976) provides that any person alleged to be liable may constitute a fund with the court or other competent authority in any state party in which legal proceedings are instituted in respect of claims subject to limitation. The fund must be constituted in the sum of such of the amounts payable as are applicable to claims for which that person may be liable, together with interest thereon from the date of the occurrence giving rise to the liability until the date of the constitution of the fund: art 11(1). A fund may be constituted either by depositing the sum or by producing a guarantee acceptable under the legislation of the state party where the fund is constituted and considered to be adequate by the court or other competent authority: art 11(2). The provisions of the 1976 Convention have the force of law in the United Kingdom: Merchant Shipping Act 1995 s 185(1).
    The owners of a bulk carrier sought to limit their liability in respect of the loss of the carrier under the 1976 Convention and the 1995 Act until a limitation fund was constituted. They applied for an interim declaration that they were entitled to constitute a limitation fund by the provision of a P & I club guarantee for the purposes of the 1976 Convention art 11(2), the 1995 Act s 185(1) and CPR Pt 61. It fell to be determined whether any guarantee was acceptable under the legislation of the United Kingdom. *Held*, in the absence of a specific statutory provision that a guarantee was acceptable, the rule remained that a limitation fund might only be constituted by making a payment into court. There was nothing in the 1995 Act or CPR Pt 61 to justify reversing the previous well-established practice, and nothing that made the provision of a guarantee acceptable under the legislation of the United Kingdom. Accordingly, the application would be dismissed.
    Cosmotrade SA v Kairos Shipping Ltd [2013] EWHC 1904 (Comm), [2013] All ER (D) 151 (Sep) (Queen's Bench Division: Simon J).
    This decision has been reversed on appeal: [2014] EWCA Civ 217, [2014] All ER (D) 59 (Mar).

SOCIAL SERVICES AND COMMUNITY CARE
Halsbury's Laws of England (5th edn) vol 95 (2013) paras 1–240

2329   Care Quality Commission—additional functions
The Care Quality Commission (Additional Functions) Amendment Regulations 2013, SI 2013/1413 (in force on 15 July 2013), amend the 2011 Regulations, SI 2011/1551, so as

to reflect the fact that the High Security Psychiatric Services (Arrangements for Safety and Security at Ashworth, Broadmoor and Rampton Hospitals) Directions 2011, have been replaced by the High Security Psychiatric Services (Arrangements for Safety and Security) Directions 2013.

2330   Care Quality Commission—membership

The Care Quality Commission (Membership) (Amendment) Regulations 2013, SI 2013/2157 (in force on 1 October 2013), further amend the 2008 Regulations, SI 2008/2157, so as to increase the maximum number of members of the Care Quality Commission from 12 to 14.

2331   Care Quality Commission—regulated activities

The Health and Social Care Act 2008 (Regulated Activities) (Amendment) Regulations 2012, SI 2012/1513 (in force in part on 18 June 2012, in part on 1 October 2012 and in part on 1 October 2013), amend the 2010 Regulations, SI 2010/781, which prescribe the kinds of activities that are regulated activities for the purposes of registration in respect of the provision of health or social care. In particular, the regulations (1) allow service providers which are partnerships to meet the fitness requirements collectively rather than individually; (2) define 'medical device'; (3) ensure service providers have suitable arrangements in place where the service user lacks capacity to consent to care and treatment provided for them; (4) amend the defence of due diligence for specified offences; (5) require the Secretary of State to review the operation and effect of the 2010 Regulations and publish a report; and (6) amend the 2010 Regulations Schs 1, 2 which respectively set out the activities that will be regulated activities for the purposes of the Health and Social Care Act 2008 and those which are exempt.

2332   Community care—carers' and children's services—direct payments—residential accommodation—England

The Community Care, Services for Carers and Children's Services (Direct Payments) (England) (Amendment) Regulations 2013, SI 2013/2270 (in force on 1 November 2013), further amend the 2009 Regulations, SI 2009/1887, so as to provide that (1) specified local authorities are not prohibited from making direct payments for the provision of certain residential accommodation for a period of more than four consecutive weeks in any period of 12 months; and (2) a person who receives a direct payment from a specified local authority is deemed to have been provided with accommodation under the National Assistance Act 1948 Pt III (ss 21–36) for the purposes of determining their ordinary residence and making financial adjustments between local authorities. The regulations also further amend the Social Security (Attendance Allowance) Regulations 1991, SI 1991/2740, the Social Security (Disability Living Allowance) Regulations 1991, SI 1991/2890, and the Social Security (Personal Independence Payment) Regulations 2013, SI 2013/377 (see para 2646), to ensure that payments of attendance allowance, disability living allowance and personal independence payment cease in respect of a person who is resident in a care home for a period of more than four weeks in any 12-month period and who receives a direct payment for that purpose from a specified local authority.

2333   Community care—social care charges—means assessment and determination—Wales

See para 2338.

2334   Disabled Persons' Parking Badges Act 2013

The Disabled Persons' Parking Badges Act 2013 amends the Chronically Sick and Disabled Persons Act 1970 s 21. The Act received the royal assent on 31 January 2013 and came into force on 8 October 2013: SI 2013/2202.

Section 1 removes the requirement for the Secretary of State to prescribe in regulations the form of a parking badge and replaces it with a requirement that badges issued under the 1970 Act s 21 must be in a valid form, that is, a form specified or approved by the Secretary of State. The 2013 Act s 2 further amends the 1970 Act s 21 so as to provide that a local authority may cancel a badge issued by them if it appears to the authority that the person to whom it was issued no longer holds the badge, either because the person notifies the authority that it has been lost or stolen, or for any other reason. The 2013 Act s 3 makes it an offence to drive a vehicle displaying a badge that should have been returned to the issuing authority or which has been cancelled. Under s 4, there is a power for a constable or enforcement officer to retain a badge that has been presented to them and which appears not to have been issued under the 2013 Act or which has been cancelled, should have been returned or is being misused. Section 5 removes a person's right of appeal to the Secretary of State in cases where an authority refuses to issue a badge or requires the return of a badge, in each case, for reasons relating to the misuse of badges. Section 6 establishes the Secretary of State as a badge issuing authority for members of the armed forces and persons employed in support of those forces, together with members of the same household of such persons, resident overseas in places to be prescribed. Section 7 deals with extent, commencement and short title.

2335   Domiciliary care agencies—Wales

The Domiciliary Care Agencies (Wales) (Amendment) Regulations 2013, SI 2013/225 (in force on 28 February 2013), (1) further amend the 2004 Regulations, SI 2004/219, so as to require managers of domiciliary care agencies to hold a required qualification and to be registered with the Care Council for Wales; and (2) make consequential amendments to the Registration of Social Care and Independent Health Care (Wales) Regulations 2002, SI 2002/919.

2336   Her Majesty's Chief Inspector of Education, Children's Services and Skills—fees and frequency of inspections

See para 220.

2337   National assistance—assessment of resources—England

The National Assistance (Sums for Personal Requirements and Assessment of Resources) Amendment (England) Regulations 2013, SI 2013/518 (in force on 8 April 2013), further amend (1) the National Assistance (Assessment of Resources) Regulations 1992, SI 1992/2977, so as to provide that earnings derived from employment and self-employment are to be disregarded when calculating the amount a person is liable to pay for accommodation arranged under the National Assistance Act 1948 Pt III (ss 21–36); and (2) the National Assistance (Sums for Personal Requirements) (England) Regulations 2003, SI 2003/628, so as to increase, from £23·50 to £23·90, the weekly sum which local authorities in England are to assume, in the absence of special circumstances, that residents in such accommodation will need for their personal requirements.

2338   National assistance—assessment of resources—Wales

The National Assistance (Sums for Personal Requirements) and National Assistance (Assessment of Resources) (Amendment) (Wales) Regulations 2013, SI 2013/631 (in force on 8 April 2013), amend the National Assistance (Sums for Personal Requirements) (Assessment of Resources and Miscellaneous Amendments) (Wales) Regulations 2012, SI 2012/842, and the National Assistance (Assessment of Resources) Regulations 1992, SI 1992/2977, which concern the assessment of the ability of a person to pay for accommodation arranged by local authorities under the National Assistance Act 1948 Pt III (ss 21–36). In particular, the 2013 Regulations (1) prescribe £24·50 as the sum needed for personal requirements under the 1948 Act s 22(4); (2) disregard the earnings of employed and self employed earners when calculating the amount a person is liable to pay for accommodation arranged under Pt III; and (3) provide that the capital limit, which is the maximum amount of capital a person may have before that person becomes liable to pay for, or contribute towards the cost of any accommodation arranged, becomes £23,750.

The National Assistance and Social Care Charges (Wales) (Miscellaneous Amendments) Regulations 2013, SI 2013/633 (in force on 8 April 2013), further amend in relation to Wales (1) the National Assistance (Assessment of Resources) Regulations 1992, SI 1992/2977, so as to (a) disregard any armed forces independence payment in its entirety and a guaranteed income payment in its entirety, rather than only partially, from the calculation of income other than earnings for the purposes of assessing a person's ability to pay for that accommodation; and (b) disregard the first £10 of a survivor's guaranteed income payment made under the Armed Forces and Reserve Forces (Compensation Scheme) Order 2011, SI 2011/517; and (2) the Social Care Charges (Means Assessment and Determination of Charges) (Wales) Regulations 2011, SI 2011/962, and the Social Care Charges (Direct Payments) (Means Assessment and Determination of Reimbursement or Contribution) (Wales) Regulations 2011, SI 2011/963, so as to disregard any guaranteed income payment and armed forces independence payment, in their entirety, from the calculation of a person's ability to pay for non-residential social care services.

The National Assistance (Assessment of Resources) (Miscellaneous Amendments) (Wales) Regulations 2013, SI 2013/634 (in force on 8 April 2013), further amend in relation to Wales the 1992 Regulations above so as to disregard personal independence payments and payments made under council tax reduction schemes from the calculation of income other than earnings for the purpose of assessing a person's ability to pay for accommodation arranged by local authorities under the National Assistance Act 1948 Pt III (ss 21–35).

2339 Social work services—providers—regulation and registration—England

See para 229.

SPORTS LAW

Halsbury's Laws of England (5th edn) vol 96 (2012) paras 1–300

Articles

For articles relating to this title please refer to the Table of Articles at the beginning of the Abridgment.

2340 Disputes—arbitration—arbitral proceedings—hearing before appeal panel of governing body

See *England and Wales Cricket Board Ltd v Kaneria*, para 49.

2341 Football—spectators—banning orders—regulated matches

The Football Spectators (Prescription) (Amendment) Order 2013, SI 2013/1709 (in force on 2 August 2013), further amends the 2004 Order, SI 2004/2409, so as to (1) revise the definition of association football match for the purposes of football banning orders to reflect the merger of the Scottish Football League and the Scottish Premier League to form the Scottish Professional Football League; (2) clarify that an association football match is a regulated football match where the match involves clubs whose home grounds are outside England or Wales but they are playing in England or Wales; and (3) delete a historic reference to matches played as part of the 2012 Olympic Games.

2342 Football—spectators—seating

The Football Spectators (Seating) Order 2013, SI 2013/1568 (in force on 22 July 2013), directs the Sports Grounds Safety Authority to include an 'all-seater' condition in any licence granted to admit spectators to Goldsands Stadium, which is the home of AFC Bournemouth Limited.

2343 Football club manager—contract—early termination—compensation

See *Berg v Blackburn Rovers Football Club & Athletic plc*, para 239.

2344 Sports grounds—football stadium—policing—special police services—area outside stadium

See *Leeds United Football Club v Chief Constable of West Yorkshire Police*, para 2068.

2345 Sports grounds and sporting events—control of alcohol—designated grounds

The Sports Grounds and Sporting Events (Designation) (Amendment) Order 2013, SI 2013/1710 (in force on 2 August 2013), further amends the 2005 Order, SI 2005/3204, for the purposes of designating sporting events to which the Sporting Events (Control of

Alcohol etc) Act 1985 applies and making it clear that an association football match is designated where the match involves clubs whose home grounds are outside England or Wales but they are playing within England or Wales.

STAMP TAXES

Halsbury's Laws of England (5th edn) vol 96 (2012) paras 301–600

Articles

For articles relating to this title please refer to the Table of Articles at the beginning of the Abridgment.

2346   Finance Act 2013

See para 2149.

2347   Stamp duty—exemption—collective investment schemes

The Stamp Duty and Stamp Duty Reserve Tax (Collective Investment Schemes) (Exemptions) Regulations 2013, SI 2013/1401 (in force on 28 June 2013), amend (1) the Finance Act 1986 s 90 so as to (a) except from stamp duty reserve tax agreements to transfer chargeable securities in certain prescribed circumstances; and (b) disapply the exceptions where an agreement forms part of arrangements to avoid stamp duty or stamp duty reserve tax; and (2) the Finance Act 1999 Sch 13 so as to (a) exempt from a stamp duty charge transfers on sale in certain prescribed circumstances; and (b) disapply the exemptions where a transfer forms part of arrangements to avoid stamp duty or stamp duty reserve tax.

2348   Stamp duty—relief—ICE Clear Europe Ltd

The Stamp Duty and Stamp Duty Reserve Tax (ICE Clear Europe Ltd) Regulations 2013, SI 2013/1382 (in force on 1 July 2013), give relief from stamp duty and stamp duty reserve tax to certain transfers of, or agreements to transfer, traded securities or options made in the course of trading in those traded securities or options either on a facility or over the counter. The transfers and agreements eligible for relief are those involving ICE Clear Europe Ltd ('ICE Clear Europe'), and its nominees, (through whom transactions on the facility are cleared) or clearing participants of ICE Clear Europe and its nominees. In particular, the 2013 Regulations (1) prescribe ICE Clear Europe as a recognised clearing house for the purposes of the relief; and (2) prescribe the circumstances in which the stamp duty and stamp duty reserve tax will not be charged.

2349   Stamp duty land tax—avoidance schemes—information

See para 1567.

2350   Stamp duty land tax—exemption—transfer to partnership of interest in land— sub-sale of lease

A company contracted to purchase the head leasehold interest in a property. In order to avoid paying stamp duty land tax on the transaction, the company sold the lease to the taxpayer, a partnership that had been created for that purpose. The company owned the vast majority of the shares in the taxpayer. By virtue of the Finance Act 2003 ss 44 and 45, tax was not chargeable on the contract between the company and the seller, but on a deemed contract where the taxpayer was the purchaser. Since the sub-sale to the taxpayer fell within Sch 15 para 10, it would be a transaction excluded from tax because it was a transfer by a partner of an interest in land to a partnership. The Revenue decided that Sch 15 para 10 did not apply because ss 44 and 45 eliminated the company as the transferor of a chargeable interest to the taxpayer. The matter came before the First-tier Tribunal, which ruled in the taxpayer's favour. That decision was affirmed by the Upper Tribunal. On further appeal by the Revenue, *held*, when the company had entered into the original contract, s 44(2) had applied. Thus, the company had not been regarded as having entered into a land transaction. It followed that the company had not been regarded as having acquired a chargeable interest. When the company entered into the contract with the taxpayer, s 45(2) applied. Thus, the taxpayer had not been regarded as having entered into a land transaction and, just as in the case of the company, had not been regarded as having acquired a chargeable interest. However, it had been regarded as having entered into a contract for a land transaction, the consideration for which was so much of the consideration under the original contract as was referable to the subject matter of the transfer of rights. The contract between the original seller and the company was the 'original contract' and the contract between the company and the taxpayer was the 'secondary contract'. Section 44 therefore took effect subject to modifications made by s 45. In the circumstances, completion of the original contract had to be disregarded. That disregard had to be made for the purpose of s 44. Consequently, the company had not acquired a chargeable interest by entering into the contract with the original seller. Section 44(3) had not applied to completion of that contract, therefore, it followed that the company had not entered into a land transaction for the purposes of stamp duty land tax. Therefore, for the purposes of stamp duty land tax, the company had never acquired a chargeable interest. When the secondary contract had been completed, s 44(3) had applied to the taxpayer's acquisition of a chargeable interest. The effective date of its land transaction had, therefore, been the date of completion of its contract with the company. Schedule 15 para 10 only applied if a partner transferred a chargeable interest to a partnership. Since, for the purposes of stamp duty land tax, the company had not acquired a chargeable interest, that paragraph did not apply. It followed that the taxpayer was not entitled to rely on the exemption. Therefore, the taxpayer had been liable to pay stamp duty land tax on the consideration which it had given for its own acquisition. Accordingly, the appeal would be allowed.

DV3 RS Ltd Partnership v Revenue and Customs Comrs [2013] EWCA Civ 907, [2013] STC 2150 (Court of Appeal: Maurice Kay VP, Lewison and Gloster LJJ). Decision of Upper Tribunal [2012] UKUT 399 (TCC), [2013] STC 430 (2012 Abr para 2443) reversed.

2351　Stamp duty land tax—relief—charity—entitlement to partial relief

The first taxpayer was a trustee of a trust, shares in which were freely alienable. Its major beneficiaries were the Church Commissioners and the Secretary of State for Defence in his role as trustee for a hospital. Both the Church Commissioners and the hospital were registered charities but the remaining beneficiaries under the trust were not. The first taxpayer bought four commercial properties on behalf of the trust and sought an exemption from stamp duty land tax under the Finance Act 2003 Sch 8 in respect of the proportion of the properties attributable to the charitable beneficiaries and under s 107 in respect of the proportion attributable to the hospital. The second taxpayer was a well-known university institution and charity, which operated a shared equity scheme under which it participated in the acquisition of homes for its employees in return for an equitable interest in the property acquired proportionate to its contribution. An employee of the second taxpayer bought a lease of a flat with the help of a contribution from the second taxpayer towards the purchase price. The employee executed a declaration of trust by which he declared that he held the flat as a specified amount for the second taxpayer and a specified amount for himself. The second taxpayer sought partial relief from stamp duty land tax under Sch 8 in respect of the proportion of the property attributable to it. The Commissioners for Her Majesty's Revenue and Customs denied both taxpayers partial relief on the basis that relief from stamp duty land tax was only available in the case of joint purchasers where all of them were entitled to the relief. The taxpayers' appeals were dismissed, with the effect that, if a charity acquired property in furtherance of its charitable purposes, or as an investment, it was entitled to relief against liability to pay stamp duty land tax on the purchase price. The same applied if a non-charity bought the property as bare trustee for the charity, but if the non-charity also had a beneficial interest in the property, then the charity was not entitled to any relief at all. The taxpayers' further appealed. *Held*, the tribunal had correctly identified the chargeable interest by reference to which stamp duty land tax was levied. The only people who acquired a chargeable interest as a bare trustee had been the first taxpayer or the second taxpayer's employee. The taxpayers' submissions mistakenly read the deeming provision as having deemed the trustees to have acquired what the beneficiaries, individually, acquired. That was to read the deeming provision the wrong way around. In addition there was only one equitable estate in each case. It was held by a number of tenants in common in undivided shares, but the crux was that the shares were undivided. Since the shares were undivided, the equitable estate was not divided. It followed that the correct reading of Sch 8 para 1 was that a land transaction was exempt from charge to the extent that the purchaser was a charity. That reading had the consequence that a land transaction was partially exempt but only to the extent of a charity's interest. Accordingly, the appeal would be allowed.

Pollen Estate Trustee Co Ltd v Revenue and Customs Comrs [2013] EWCA Civ 753, [2013] STC 1479 (Court of Appeal: Laws, McFarlane and Lewison LJJ). *Inco Europe Ltd v First Choice Distribution (a firm)* [2000] 2 All ER 109, HL (2000 Abr para 209), applied. Decision of Upper Tribunal [2012] UKUT 277 (TC), [2012] STC 2443 (2012 Abr para 2444) reversed.

2352   Stamp duty reserve tax—exemption—collective investment schemes
See para 2347.

2353   Stamp duty reserve tax—relief—ICE Clear Europe Limited
See para 2348.

STATUTES AND LEGISLATIVE PROCESS
Halsbury's Laws of England (5th edn) vol 96 (2012) paras 601–1219

Articles

For articles relating to this title please refer to the Table of Articles at the beginning of the Abridgment.

2354   Act of Parliament—repeal—implied repeal—overlapping powers
See *Snelling v Burstow Parish Council*, para 8.

2355   Act of Parliament—repeal—transitional provision—intention of Parliament with regard to subsequent enactment

Scotland
The appellants operated a children's nursery in Scotland. As it was a 'care service' within the meaning of the Regulation of Care (Scotland) Act 2001, it was required to be registered by the respondent Commission. The appellants' application for registration was granted but the respondent became concerned with the way the nursery was being operated and gave notices to the appellants of its decisions to cancel the nursery's registration. The appellants disputed the basis for the respondent's concerns and appealed against the decisions. Under new legislation, the Public Services Reform (Scotland) Act 2010, the respondent was to be dissolved and its functions were to be transferred to a new body. Two transitional orders were made. At the appeal hearing, the appellants submitted that the respondent could no longer be a party to the appeal as it had been replaced by the new body which had no title or interest to enter the proceedings as it was concerned only with things that had been done under the 2001 Act. It was held that, as the respondent had ceased to exist and there was no provision in either of the transitional orders for the decisions to be treated as if they had been made by the new body, the decisions could no longer have any effect. The respondent's appeal was allowed. Further notices of decisions to implement proposals to cancel the nursery's registration were served by the new body, one in the name of the respondent under the 2001 Act and one in the new body's own name under the 2010 Act. The appellants appealed further. *Held,* the effect of the transitional provisions was that the proceedings should be adjudicated on as if the 2001 Act remained in force; the new body should be held to have taken over the conduct of the proceedings and the respondent was no longer the proper party to the proceedings. The effect of the first transitional order was to resurrect the respondent and its purpose was to ensure that only the substantive law was applied in the course of the proceedings. The second transitional order, looked at on its own terms, left the problem unsolved; there was a gap in its provisions that had to be filled. The first order, on the other hand, contained a provision which dealt with the question as to what was to happen where applications made for registration had not been determined by the respondent before the hearing of the appeal. The first order stated that, in that situation, if the application related to a care service, all references to the respondent were to be read as

references to the new body. Applying established principles, the gap that was left by the second order could be filled by reading all references to the respondent as references to new body in that context too. To do otherwise would leave the dissolved respondent in existence for some of the purposes of the 2001 Act and require a reference to the respondent to be read as a reference to new body for others. That would be very untidy. It could safely be assumed that, if the draftsman had considered the point, he would have written into the second order the words he had used in the first order. The most recent notice of the decision that had been given under the 2010 Act had to be regarded as ineffective. The second order provided in the clearest terms that the 2001 Act was to continue to apply for the purposes of the care service until the final determination of the appeals that had been taken against the earlier decisions of which notice had been given. The nursery was still registered under the 2001 Act, so it was with reference to the provisions of the 2001 Act, not those of the 2010 Act, that any steps with a view to the cancellation of the nursery's registration would have had to have been taken until the final determination of the appeals. It was in the public interest, and especially in the interests of those who wished to make use of those services, that national care standards were adhered to and that prompt steps were taken to address a failure to do so and, if necessary, remove the service from the register. The time had come for the court to intervene in order to minimise further delay and expense. In the very unusual circumstances of the case it was open to it to proceed on the basis that, if the new body were to adhere to the earlier decisions, that would be an abuse of process and, in the interests of appropriate case management, to take steps to prevent such an abuse. The court would direct that the earlier decisions would not have effect. That meant that the appeal proceedings against those decisions had been finally determined and the nursery had to be treated as if it had been registered under the 2010 Act. The appeal against the most recent decision had to proceed under the 2010 Act. Judgment would be given accordingly.

Davies t/a All Stars Nursery v Scottish Commission for the Regulation of Care (Scotland) [2013] UKSC 12, 2013 SLT 577, [2013] All ER (D) 325 (Feb) (Supreme Court: Lord Hope DP, Lord Kerr, Lord Wilson, Lord Reed and Lord Carnwath SCJJ). *Inco Europe Ltd v First Choice Distribution (a firm)* [2000] 2 All ER 109, HL (2000 Abr para 209), applied. *Tonner v Reiach* [2007] CSIH 48, 2008 SC 1 considered. Decision of Inner House [2012] CSIH 7, 2013 SC 1 affirmed in part.

2356   Commencement of statutes

The following table contains detailed commencement provisions of all public statutes passed in 2013. Repealed provisions are omitted. Schedules are included but not those sections which simply introduce schedules. The table also contains details of all commencement orders made in 2013, which in certain cases relate to statutes passed before 2013. Revoked orders are omitted.

An asterisk (*) indicates that a section, subsection or schedule is in force only in part or only for certain purposes.

The table refers to statutes only in so far as they relate to England and Wales.

STATUTE	IN FORCE	AUTHORITY
Active Travel (Wales) Act 2013		
• ss 3–11	no date	s 14(1)
• ss 1, 2, 12–15	5 November 2013	s 14(2)
Antarctic Act 2013		
• ss 1–3, 5–13	no date	s 18(3)
• ss 14–16, 18	26 May 2013	s 18(4)
• Schedule	no date	s 18(3)
Apprenticeships, Skills, Children and Learning Act 2009		
• ss 2, 7–10, 11*, 12*, 18–22, 28–31, 39*	10 May 2013	s 269(3); SI 2013/1100
• ss 145, 146	31 May 2013	s 269(4); SI 2013/975

STATUTE	IN FORCE	AUTHORITY
• Sch 16*	31 May 2013	s 269(4); SI 2013/975
Armed Forces Act 2011		
• ss 9, 10*, 11(1)*, (2), 16(1)	1 November 2013	s 32(3); SI 2013/2501
• s 25	6 April 2013	s 32(3); SI 2013/784
Charities Act 2011		
• Sch 9 (paras 7, 10, 11, 13, 15–18, 20–22, 25)*	1 September 2013	Sch 9 (para 29); SI 2013/1775
Child Maintenance and Other Payments Act 2008		
• ss 17*, 18*	29 July 2013	s 62(3); SI 2013/1860
• ss 17*, 18*	25 November 2013	s 62(3); SI 2013/2947
• Schs 4 (paras 1–3*, 4, 5–10*), 7 (paras 1(1)*, (2), (28), (29)*), 8*	25 November 2013	s 62(3); SI 2013/2947
• Schs 4 (paras 1–3, 5–10)*, 7 (para 1(1), (2), (29))*, 8*	29 July 2013	s 62(3); SI 2013/1860
Children and Families (Wales) Measure 2010		
• ss 57*, 58(1)*, (3)–(5)*, (6)(a)*, (7)–(14)*, 59*, 60(2)*, 61*, 62(1)*, 64*, 65*	1 February 2013	s 75(3); SI 2013/18
• ss 58(10)*, 59(2)*	19 July 2013	s 75(3); SI 2013/1830
• ss 57*, 58(1)*, (3)–(5)*, (6)(a)*, (7)–(9)*, (11)–(14)*, 59–62*, 64*, 65*	31 July 2013	s 75(3); SI 2013/1830
Children and Young Persons Act 2008		
• ss 1*, 4*	12 November 2013	s 44(4); SI 2013/2606
Children, Schools and Families Act 2010		
• s 8	15 April 2013	s 29(5); SI 2013/668
• s 10	3 July 2013	s 29(5); SI 2013/1573
Church of England Marriage (Amendment) Measure 2012		
• s 1	1 June 2013	s 3(2); instrument dated 21 May 2013
• ss 2, 3	19 December 2012	s 3(2)
City of London (Various Powers) Act 2013	18 December 2013	
Civil Aviation Act 2012		
• ss 1–12, 14–46, 48, 50–54, 56–75, 76(1)*, 77, 100, 103, 104	6 April 2013	s 110(1), (4); SI 2013/589
• ss 76(1)*, 102	1 April 2014	s 110(1), (4); SI 2013/589
• Schs 1–8, 9 (paras 2, 3*, 5–8, 10–13, 14*, 15, 16, 17*), 10 (paras 2–6, 8–18)	6 April 2013	s 110(1), (4); SI 2013/589

STATUTE	IN FORCE	AUTHORITY
• Sch 9 (paras 1, 3*, 4, 9, 14*, 17*)	1 April 2014	s 110(1), (4); SI 2013/589
Clergy Discipline (Amendment) Measure 2013		
• ss 1–8, 9(2)–(8)	no date	s 10(2)
• s 10	26 March 2013	s 10(2)
• Schedule (paras 1–9, 11–13)	no date	s 10(2)
• Schedule (para 10)	1 July 2013	s 10(2); instrument dated 31 May 2013
Competition Act 1998		
• s 1(a)	10 March 2013	s 76(3); SI 2013/284
Constitutional Reform and Governance Act 2010		
• Sch 6 (paras 35(3), 38–41, 47(2)*)	1 November 2013	s 52(2); SI 2013/2826
Consumer Insurance (Disclosure and Representations) Act 2012		
• ss 2–11	6 April 2013	s 12(2); SI 2013/450
• Schs 1, 2	6 April 2013	s 12(2); SI 2013/450
Co-operative and Community Benefit Societies and Credit Unions Act 2010		
• ss 4–7	1 December 2013	s 8(2); SI 2013/2936
Coroners and Justice Act 2009		
• ss 1–10, 13–17, 24, 36*, 42, 46	25 July 2013	s 182(4); SI 2013/1869
• ss 43, 45	3 July 2013	s 182(4); SI 2013/1628
• s 117(4)–(8)	22 April 2013	s 182(4), (5); SI 2013/705
• s 148	18 November 2013	s 182(4); SI 2013/2908
• Schs 1–3, 5 (paras 1, 2, 6, 7), 6, 7, 10 (paras 1, 3, 5), 21 (paras 1–51*), 23 (Pt 1*)	25 July 2013	s 182(1); SI 2013/1869
• Sch 17 (paras 4, 5)	28 May 2013	s 182(5); SI 2013/1104
• Sch 23*	12 February 2013	s 182(4); SI 2013/250
Crime and Courts Act 2013		
• ss 17(1)–(3), 18, 25(1)–(3), (4)*, (6), (7), (9), 26(1), (3)–(8), 28, 34–42, 46, 47, 48(6)(a), 49, 55(3)*, (4)(a), 56	no date	s 61(2), (3)
• ss 1(1), (2), 3, 4(2)–(9), 6(2)	27 May 2013	s 61(2); SI 2013/1042
• ss 1(3)–(11), 2, 4(1), 5, 6(1), (3), (4), 7–10, 11(1)–(5), (6)*, (7), (8), 12, 13, 15	7 October 2013	s 61(2); SI 2013/1682
• ss 11(6)*, 14, 16, 51	8 May 2013	s 61(2); SI 2013/1042
• s 17(4)	4 September 2013	s 61(3); SI 2013/2200

STATUTE	IN FORCE	AUTHORITY
• s 19	26 April 2013	s 61(5)
• ss 21, 30	1 October 2013	s 61(3); SI 2013/2200
• s 22	1 November 2013	s 61(3); SI 2013/2200
• ss 23, 25(4)*, (5), (8), 29, 32	15 July 2013	s 61(3); SI 2013/1725
• s 24	7 January 2014	s 61(3); SI 2013/3176
• ss 26(2), 31, 33, 52–54, 55(1), (2), (3)*, (5)–(13)	25 June 2013	s 61(6); SI 2013/1042
• s 27	11 December 2013	s 61(2); SI 2013/2981
• ss 43, 48(1)–(5), (6)(b), (7), (8), 58–61	25 April 2013	s 61(11)
• s 57	1 February 2014	s 61(2); SI 2013/2981
• Schs 9 (paras 1–20, 21(3), 22–26, 28, 29, 31–140), 10, 11 (paras 1–30, 32–210), 12, 13 (paras 41*, 49*), 15, 16 (paras 11–21, 37), 17, 18 (paras 1–3), 19, 20 (paras 10–15), 21 (paras 14*, 15–18, 20–29), 22, 23	no date	s 61(2), (3)
• Schs 1 (paras 1–5, 8–15), 2 (paras 2, 3, 6(1), (2), 7, 8(1), (2)), 3 (paras 1–11, 16–23, 26–33, 35, 36), 4 (paras 2, 3, 5), 5 (paras 1–3, 6–13, 15–26), 6 (paras 3, 4, 5(1)–(4), 6–17), 7, 8 (paras 6–10, 12–26, 28–36, 38–51, 55–60, 64–100, 104–114, 121–170, 173–190)	7 October 2013	s 61(2); SI 2013/1682
• Schs 1 (para 7), 2 (paras 1, 4, 5), 5 (para 4), 8 (paras 101–103)	27 May 2013	s 61(2); SI 2013/1042
• Schs 3 (para 34), 4 (para 1), 5 (paras 5, 27–30), 6 (paras 5(5), (6)), 8 (paras 1–5, 13)	8 May 2013	s 61(2); SI 2013/1042
• Schs 9 (paras 21(1), (2), 27, 30), 13 (paras 1–8, 29–40, 41*, 42–48, 49*, 50–81), 14	1 October 2013	s 61(6); SI 2013/1042, 2200
• Sch 13 (paras 9–15, 83–89)	15 July 2013	s 61(6); SI 2013/1042
• Sch 13 (paras 16–28)	4 September 2013	s 61(3); SI 2013/2200
• Schs 13 (para 82), 18 (paras 4–6)	25 April 2013	s 61(11)
• Sch 16 (paras 1–10, 22–36, 38)	11 December 2013	s 61(2); SI 2013/2981
• Sch 20 (paras 1, 2, 3*, 4, 5, 6*, 7–9)	14 October 2013	s 61(2); SI 2013/2349
• Sch 20 (paras 3*, 6*)	18 September 2013	s 61(2); SI 2013/2349
• Sch 20 (paras 10–15)	29 July 2013	s 61(2); SI 2013/1682
• Sch 21 (paras 1–13, 14*, 19, 30–43)	25 June 2013	s 61(6); SI 2013/1042

STATUTE	IN FORCE	AUTHORITY
Criminal Justice Act 2003		
• Schs 3 (paras 2–12*,16–18*, 20(3)–(14)*, 21*, 23–36*, 41–52*, 54–56*, 57(1)*, (3)–(7)*, 58–64*, 66–69*, 71(a)–(c)*, 72–75*), 37 (Pt 4*)	28 May 2013	s 336(3); SI 2013/1103
Criminal Justice and Immigration Act 2008		
• Schs 9 (para 3*), 26 (para 60*), 28 (Pt 4*)	8 April 2013	s 153(7); SI 2013/616
Defamation Act 2013		
• ss 1–14, 16(1)–(3)	1 January 2014	s 17(4); SI 2013/3027
• ss 15, 16(4)–(8), 17	25 April 2013	s 17(6)
Diocese in Europe Measure 2013		
• s 1	1 January 2014	s 3(2); instrument dated 10 June 2013
• s 2	1 July 2013	s 3(2); instrument dated 10 June 2013
• s 3	26 March 2013	
Disabled Persons' Parking Badges Act 2013	8 October 2013	s 7(2); SI 2013/2202
Domestic Fire Safety (Wales) Measure 2011		
• s 1*	30 April 2014	s 9(3); SI 2013/2727
• s 1*	1 January 2016	s 9(3); SI 2013/2727
Education and Skills Act 2008		
• ss 1*, 2–8, 10–14, 16–18, 39(1), (2), 62(1), (2), (5), (6), 64(1), (2), (5), 66	28 June 2013	s 173; SI 2013/1204
• s 1*	26 June 2015	s 173; SI 2013/1204
Education (Wales) Measure 2011		
• ss 22–25	22 August 2013	s 33(2); SI 2013/2090
Electoral Registration and Administration Act 2013		
• ss 1, 2(1)–(5), 3–5, 7–9, 12–14, 16, 18–21	no date	s 27(1)
• s 6	23 April 2013	s 27(1); SI 2013/969
• ss 10, 15, 17, 22, 23	2 April 2013	s 27(1); SI 2013/702
• s 11	25 March 2013	s 27(1); SI 2013/702
• ss 24–28	31 January 2013	s 27(3)
• Schs 1, 3, 4, 5 (paras 1–3, 4(1)–(3), (5), 5–8, 9(2)–(4), 10–27, 29, 30)	no date	s 27(1)
• Schs 2, 5 (paras 4(4), 9(1), (5)–(7))	5 February 2013	s 27(1); SI 2013/219
• Sch 5 (para 28)	31 March 2013	s 27(2)
Energy Act 2011		
• ss 1*, 2*, 4*, 5*, 7–9*, 11(2)*, 12*, 13*, 14(1)–(5)*, (9)*, 23–28, 29*	28 January 2013	s 121(1); SI 2013/125

STATUTE	IN FORCE	AUTHORITY
Energy Act 2013		
• ss 67–82, 84–99, 101–112, 114(2)–(5), 116(3), (4), 117, 119–130, 138(1), (4), (5), 148, 150	no date	s 156(1)
• ss 1–43, 55, 63–66, 113, 114(1), 118, 151–157	18 December 2013	s 156(3)
• ss 45–54, 56–62, 116(2), 131–137, 138(2), (3), 139–143, 145–147, 149	18 February 2014	s 156(2)
• Schs 6–10, 12, 13	no date	s 156(1)
• Schs 1, 2, 11	18 December 2013	s 156(3)
• Schs 3–5, 14	18 February 2014	s 156(2)
Enterprise and Regulatory Reform Act 2013		
• ss 7, 9, 11, 16, 25(3), 24–26, 29–37, 39, 40, 42–51, 54–58, 60, 61, 66, 71, 72, 74, 83–89, 90(1)–(6), (8), 91	no date	s 103(3)
• ss 1–6, 12, 13, 15, 17–22, 62, 64, 72(1), 97	25 June 2013	s 103(2); SI 2013/1455
• ss 10, 24, 28, 52, 53, 59, 75–78, 92–96, 98–104 and any other provision so far as is necessary for enabling the exercise on or after 25 April 2013 of any power to make provision by regulations, rules or order made by statutory instrument	25 April 2013	s 103(1)
• ss 14, 15(10), 23	29 July 2013	s 103(3); SI 2013/1648
• ss 25(1), (2), (4), 27, 65, 67–70, 79–82, 90(7)	31 October 2013	s 103(3), (4); SI 2013/2227
• s 72(2), (3)	16 December 2013	s 103(3), (4); SI 2013/2979
• Schs 1–3, 4 (paras 19, 29* 30, 33, 36–50, 51–53*, 54–58, 61*), 5, 6 (paras 1–8, 15–44, 52–148), 7–13, 14 (paras 1–22), 15 (paras 1–52), 16, 17 (paras 11, 14–19), 18, 19, 20 (para 2*)	no date	s 103(3)
• Sch 4 (paras 1–18, 20–28, 29*, 31, 32, 34, 35, 51–53*, 59, 60, 61*, 62–65), 17 (paras 1–6, 10, 12, 13), 21 (para 5)	31 October 2013	s 103(3), (4); SI 2013/2227
• Schs 17 (paras 7–9, 20), 21 (paras 1–4)	25 June 2013	s 103(2); SI 2013/1455
• Sch 20 (paras 1, 2*)	1 October 2013	s 103(3); SI 2013/1455, 2271
• Sch 20 (para 2*)	16 December 2013	s 103(3); SI 2013/2979
• Sch 20 (para 2*)	31 March 2014	s 103(3); SI 2013/2979

STATUTE	IN FORCE	AUTHORITY
• Sch 22	25 April 2013	s 103(1)
European Union (Approvals) Act 2013	28 February 2013	s 3(2)
European Union (Croatian Accession and Irish Protocol) Act 2013	31 January 2013	s 6(2)
Finance Act 2009		
• appointed date for the purposes of ss 101*, 102*	1 February 2013	s 104(3); SI 2013/67
• appointed date for the purposes of ss 101*, 102*	1 October 2013	s 104(3); SI 2013/2472
• appointed date for the purposes of s 101*	1 April 2013	s 104(3); SI 2013/280
Finance Act 2012		
• appointed date for the purposes of Sch 14 (para 36(1))	1 April 2012	Sch 14 (para 6); SI 2013/587
• Schs 22 (paras 1–13, 16(1), (2), (4), (5), 17–20), 38	1 April 2013	s 223(2), Sch 22 (para 21(2)); SI 2013/279, 744
Finance Act 2013		
• s 52(6)*	no date	s 52(12)
• ss 8, 52(1), (3)–(5), (7)–(9)	6 April 2013	ss 8(6), 52(10)
• s 38	16 January 2012	s 38(2)
• s 43	26 October 2012	s 43(6)
• s 47(2)(b), (c)	6 April 2012	s 47(4)
• s 50(3)(a), (c)	26 March 2013	s 50(5)
• s 52(2)	6 April 2015	s 52(11)
• s 52(6)*	6 April 2016	s 52(12)
• appointed date for the purposes of s 66	1 September 2013	s 66(4); SI 2013/1815
• s 86	20 March 1993	s 86(4)
• s 175(1)	16 October 2002	s 175(2)
• ss 179, 191(1)	1 April 2013	ss 179(8), 191(2)
• s 180	25 March 2013	s 180(7)
• s 181(1)	20 March 2013 (*at 6pm*)	s 181(2)
• s 201	8 April 2013	s 201(5)
• ss 202(2)–(4), 221(1)	1 January 2013	ss 202(5), 221(2)
• s 203(1)–(7)	1 January 2014	s 203(8)
• Schs 17*, 18*, 21*	no date	Schs 17 (para 2(2)), 18 (para 22(1)), 21 (para 9(2))
• Sch 2 (para 31(1))	31 October 2013	Sch 2 (para 31(2)); SI 2013/2796
• Sch 9 (para 6(1))	6 April 2013	Sch 9 (para 6(2))
• appointed date for the purposes of Schs 16*, 18*	19 July 2013	Schs 16 (para 2(2)), 18 (para 22(1)); SI 2013/1817

STATUTE	IN FORCE	AUTHORITY
• appointed date for the purposes of Sch 23	1 September 2013	Sch 23 (para 38); SI 2013/1755
• Sch 29 (paras 3–50)	1 January 2014	Sch 29 (para 52)
• Sch 30 (paras 2, 4, 9–11, 13)	20 March 2013	Sch 30 (paras 2(2), 4(2), 12, 13(5))
• Sch 37	8 April 2013	Sch 37 (para 7)
• Sch 42 (paras 1(2), 2–21)	26 March 2013	Sch 42 (paras 1(3), 21)
• Sch 47	1 January 2013	Sch 47 (para 21)
• Sch 49*	11 Decemebr 2012	Sch 49 (para 8(1))
• remaining provisions (subject to the exception that certain provisions are expressed to take effect on various dates)	17 July 2013	see specific provisions of the Act
Financial Services Act 2012		
• ss 1*, 2, 3, 4*, 6*, 10, 11*, 13, 14*, 16–19*, 20–23, 24*, 25, 26, 27*, 28, 29*, 30*, 31, 32, 33*, 34, 36, 37*, 38*, 40*, 43*, 47, 48(1)(a)–(c), (e)–(i), (k)–(m), (o)–(t), 53–56, 58–63, 65*, 66*, 68–79, 80*, 81, 82, 84–87*, 88–92, 95, 97, 103–105, 107, 110*, 111, 112*	1 April 2013	s 122(3), (4); SI 2013/423
• ss 1*, 4–6*, 108, 113	19 February 2013	s 122(2)–(4); SI 2013/113
• ss 4*, 6*, 7–9, 11*, 14*, 16*, 18*, 19*, 24*, 27*, 29*, 30*, 33*, 37*, 38*, 40*, 43*, 48(1)(d), (j), (n), (2), (3), 49–52, 57, 64, 65*, 66*, 67, 80*, 83, 84–87*, 93, 94, 110*, 112*	24 January 2013	s 122(3), (4); SI 2013/113
• ss 17*, 18*	19 March 2013	s 122(3), (4); SI 2013/651
• Schs 1–3, 4*, 5 (paras 1–3, 4*, 5–9, 10–14*, 15, 16, 17*, 18*), 6, 7*, 8 (paras 1–10, 11*, 12, 13, 14*, 15*, 16–39), 9 (paras 1–9, 10*, 11–16, 17–19*, 20, 21*, 22, 23*, 24–33, 34*, 35*, 36–41), 10 (paras 1, 2, 3*, 4–6, 7*, 8–15), 11, 12 (paras 1–4, 5*, 6*, 7, 8*, 9*, 10–25), 13–17, 18 (paras 1–4, 5*, 6–9, 10*, 11–144), 19	1 April 2013	s 122(3), (4); SI 2013/423
• Sch 4*	27 February 2013	s 122(3), (4); SI 2013/423
• Schs 4 (paras 7, 17, 24, 26(4))*, 5 (paras 4, 10–14, 17, 18)*, 7*, 8 (paras 11, 14, 15)*, 9 (paras 10, 17–19, 21, 23, 34, 35)*, 10 (paras 3, 7)*, 12 (paras 5, 6, 8, 9)*, 18 (paras 5, 10)*, 20, 21	24 January 2013	s 122(3), (4); SI 2013/113

STATUTE	IN FORCE	AUTHORITY
• Sch 11 (para 28*)	19 March 2013	s 122(3), (4); SI 2013/651
Financial Services (Banking Reform) Act 2013		
• ss 1–5, 7–34, 36–120, 121(3), 122–128, 130, 132–140	no date	s 148(3)–(5)
• s 131	18 February 2014	s 148(2)
• ss 142–148	18 December 2013	s 148(1)
• Schs 1–8, 10	no date	s 148(5)
• Sch 9	18 February 2014	s 148(2)
Flood and Water Management Act 2010		
• Sch 4 (paras 2–29, 33–36, 41)*	30 July 2013	s 49(3)(h); SI 2013/1590
Food Hygiene Rating (Wales) Act 2013		
• s 2*	no date	s 27(2)
• ss 3(2)*, (3)(c)*, (d)*, (5)*, 5(4)*, (10)(d)*, 6(2)*, (3)*, 7(3)*, (4)*, 12(2)*, (9)(d)*, 15(1)*	28 October 2013	s 27(2); SI 2013/2617
• ss 1, 2*, 3(1), (2)*, (3)(a), (b), (c)*, (d)*, (4), (5)*, 4, 5(1)–(3), (4)*, (5)–(9), (10)(a)–(c), (d)*, 6(1), (2)*, (3)*, (4), 7(1), (2), (3)*, (4)*, (5), (6), 8–11, 12(1), (2)*, (3)–(8), (9)(a)–(c), (d)*, (10), (11), 13, 14, 15(1)*, (2)–(5), 16–26, 28	28 November 2013	s 27(2); SI 2013/2617
• s 27	4 May 2013	s 27(1)
• Schedule	28 November 2013	s 27(2); SI 2013/2617
Groceries Code Adjudicator Act 2013		
• ss 1–21	25 June 2013	s 25(1); SI 2013/1236
• ss 22–26	25 April 2013	s 25(2)
• Schs 1, 2	25 June 2013	s 25(1); SI 2013/1236
Growth and Infrastructure Act 2013		
• ss 1*, 8*, 27, 34	no date	s 35(1)
• s 1*	9 May 2013	s 35(1); SI 2013/1124
• ss 1*, 4, 7, 9, 16, 19, 26, 32, 33, 35, 36	25 April 2013	s 35(2)
• ss 1*, 2(1)–(6), 28	31 October 2013	s 35(1); SI 2013/2143
• ss 2(7), 3, 6, 8*, 10–12, 13*, 15*, 17, 18, 22–25 (10)*, 27, 29, 30	25 June 2013	s 35(1), (3); SI 2013/1124, 1488
• s 5	9 December 2013	s 35(1); SI 2013/2878
• ss 13*, 14, 15*	1 October 2013	s 35(1); SI 2013/1488, 1766
• s 20*	19 June 2013	s 35(1); SI 2013/1488
• s 20*, 21(1)–(3)	31 July 2013	s 35(1); SI 2013/1488
• s 31	1 September 2013	s 35(1); SI 2013/1766

STATUTE	IN FORCE	AUTHORITY
• Sch 1 (paras 1–11*, 12)	31 October 2013	s 35(1); SI 2013/2143
• Schs 1 (paras 1–11)*, 3	25 June 2013	s 35(1); SI 2013/1124
• Schs 2, 4	25 April 2013	s 35(2)
Health Act 2006		
• s 34*	9 May 2013	s 83(5)(b); SI 2013/1112
Health and Social Care Act 2008		
• s 141(1)	1 April 2013	s 170(3), (4); SI 2013/159
• Sch 15*	1 April 2013	s 170(3), (4); SI 2013/159
Health and Social Care Act 2012		
• ss 1*, 2–7, 9(1)*, 10*, 11, 12, 13(1)–(5)*, (6), (7), 14*, 16, 17(1)–(9), (10)*, (11), (12), (13)*, 18, 19, 22–24*, 25(1)*, 26*, 27*, 28–34, 35(6), 38, 40(1)–(4)*, (5)–(7), (8)*, 41, 43, 45–54, 56–58, 60, 62(1)–(5)*, (6)(a)*, (b), (7)–(11)*, 66*, 67(3), 68(1)–(3)*, (4)–(8), 69, 74(7), 72, 73, 75–77, 80, 81*, 82, 85–87*, 88, 89, 90(1)(b), (2), (3), 91(1)(b), (2)–(4), 92(1)(b), (2), (3), 93, 94, 95(1)(a), (2)–(5), 97*, 98(1)*, (2)*, (3), (5), (6), 99, 102, 103(1)*, (2)*, (3)*, 104(2)(b), (e), (4)(b)*, (c), 105(1)(b), (c), (2)(b), (c), (3), 106(1)(b), (c), (2)–(5), 108(1)–(4)*, (5), 114, 116*, 117(1)–(3), 118*, 119*, 147*, 148(6)(a), 151(2)–(6), (8), 152, 153, 156(5), (6), 157, 159(1)–(3), (5)–(9), 161, 162, 163(1)*, (2)–(9), 164(4), (5), 167–172, 173(2), 181*, 182–189, 190(1)–(8), (10), 191–200, 202–206, 207(1)–(7), (9), (11), (12), 232–276, 280, 282, 284–287, 288(3), 289(1)*, (5), 290(3)(b), (c), 292, 293, 295*, 296*, 300–302*	1 April 2013	s 306; SI 2013/160, 671
• ss 85, 86	1 January 2014	s 306; SI 2013/2896
• ss 95(1)(b), (6), 96(1)(c), 100, 101(1)*, (2)*, (3), (4), (5)*, (6)*, (7), 103(1)*, (2)*, (3), 105(2)(a), (4), (5)	1 July 2013	s 306; SI 2013/671
• ss 104(4)(b)*, 116, 117(1)–(3)*, 127	1 December 2013	s 306; SI 2013/2896
• ss 120–123*	1 September 2013	s 306; SI 2013/671

STATUTE	IN FORCE	AUTHORITY
• Schs 1*, 2*, 3, 4*, 5*, 7, 9, 11 (paras 1, 2(1), (2), (3)(a), (b), (d), (e), 3(1), (2)(a), (b), (d), (e), (3), (4), 4(a), (c), 5, 6, 7(1), (2)(b), 8(b), 9–14), 13 (paras 8*, 14–17), 16–19, 20 (paras 9–13), 21 (paras 1*, 2(1)*, (2), (3)(d), (g), (i), (j), (4), 3, 4(a), (c), 5*, 7, 11, 12*, 13(a), (b), 14–17, 22–32, 34–37, 38(1)(c), (d), 39–42, 43(1)*, (2)(a)(i), (ii), (f)), 22*, 23*	1 April 2013	s 306; SI 2013/160, 671
• Sch 11 (paras 2(3)(c), (4), (5), 3(1), (2)(c), 4(b), 7(2)(a), 8(a))	1 July 2013	s 306; SI 2013/671
• Sch 12*	1 September 2013	s 306; SI 2013/671
Healthy Eating in Schools (Wales) Measure 2009		
• ss 1–3, 5–11	2 September 2013	s 12(3); SI 2013/1985
• s 4	8 August 2013	s 12(3); SI 2013/1985
HGV Road User Levy Act 2013		
• ss 1–16	no date	s 21(1)
• ss 17–22	28 February 2013	s 21(3)
High Speed Rail (Preparation) Act 2013	21 November 2013	s 3(2)
Housing and Regeneration Act 2008		
• s 318*	10 July 2013	s 325(1); SI 2013/1469
• Sch 16*	10 July 2013	s 325(1); SI 2013/1469
Human Transplantation (Wales) Act 2013		
• ss 3–20	no date	s 21(1)
• ss 1, 2, 21, 22	10 September 2013	s 21(4)
Jobseekers (Back to Work Schemes) Act 2013	26 March 2013	s 3(2)
Justice and Security Act 2013		
• ss 1–18	25 June 2013	s 20(1); SI 2013/1482
• ss 19(2), 20	25 April 2013	s 20(2)
• Schs 1, 2, 3 (paras 1–3, 5)	25 June 2013	s 20(1); SI 2013/1482
• Sch 3 (para 4)	25 April 2013	s 20(2)
Legal Aid, Sentencing and Punishment of Offenders Act 2012		
• ss 1–18, 19(1)–(3), (5), (6), 20–30, 32–39, 41–43, 44*, 45(1)–(7)*, (9)–(13)*, 46*, 47, 49–54, 56, 57, 59	1 April 2013	s 151(1); SI 2013/77, 453, 773
• ss 44*, 45(1)–(7)*, (9)–(13)*, 46*, 48	19 January 2013	s 151(1); SI 2013/77
• ss 58, 60	4 March 2013	s 151(1); SI 2013/453
• ss 88, 133–138	8 April 2013	s 151(1); SI 2013/453

STATUTE	IN FORCE	AUTHORITY
• s 148	14 May 2013	s 151(1); SI 2013/1127
• Schs 1–3, 5	1 April 2013	s 151(1); SI 2013/453
• Sch 4	4 March 2013	s 151(1); SI 2013/453
• Schs 23, 24	8 April 2013	s 151(1); SI 2013/453
Local Government (Democracy) (Wales) Act 2013		
• ss 55–58, 63, 68, 69	no date	s 22(2), (3)
• ss 1, 70, 71, 72, 75, 76	30 July 2013	s 75(1)
• ss 2–54, 59–62, 64–67, 74	30 September 2013	s 75(2)
• Schs 1, 2	30 September 2013	s 75(2)
• Sch 3	30 July 2013	s 75(1)
Local Transport Act 2008		
• ss 2, 3(1)*, 4(4)–(9), 5	3 July 2013	s 134; SI 2013/685
• s 4(2), (3)	6 April 2013	s 134; SI 2013/685
Localism Act 2011		
• s 122*	17 December 2013	s 240(2), (7); SI 2013/2931
• ss 180(1)*, (2), (3), 181, 182	1 April 2013	s 240(2), (7); SI 2013/722
• Schs 9–11*, 12 (paras 1–21, 23–31)*	6 April 2013	s 240(2), (7); SI 2013/797
• Sch 15	1 October 2013	s 240(2), (7); SI 2013/797
London Local Authorities and Transport for London Act 2013		
• ss 4(1)–(12), (14), (15), 5, 7–14	no date	s 1(2), (3)
• ss 1–3, 4(13), 6, 15–20	18 February 2013	s 1(2)
Marine and Coastal Access Act 2009		
• Sch 4 (paras 1–5)	31 March 2014	s 342(3), (4); SI 2013/3055
Marine Navigation Act 2013		
• ss 1–6	1 October 2013	s 13(1); SI 2013/1489, 2006
• ss 7–11	26 June 2013	s 13(1); SI 2013/1489
• ss 12–14	25 April 2013	
Marriage (Same Sex Couples) Act 2013		
• ss 1–3, 4*, 5–11, 13	no date	s 21(3)
• ss 4*, 14, 17(1)–(3), 18–20	31 October 2013	s 21(2); SI 2013/2789
• ss 15, 16, 21	17 July 2013	s 21(2)
• Schs 1*, 2 (paras 2(1), 3–5), 3, 4 (paras 1–4, 5*, 6, 7, 8*, 9–13, 14*, 15–26, 27(1)*, (2)), 5–7	no date	s 21(3)

STATUTE	IN FORCE	AUTHORITY
• Schs 1*, 2 (paras 1, 2(2)), 4 (paras 5*, 8*, 14*, 27(1)*, (3), (4))	31 October 2013	s 21(2); SI 2013/2789
Mental Health (Discrimination) Act 2013		
• ss 1, 3	28 April 2013	s 4(1)
• s 2	15 July 2013	s 4(2); SI 2013/1694
• s 4	28 February 2013	
• Schedule	28 April 2013	s 4(1)
Mobile Homes Act 2013		
• ss 8, 13, 14	no date	s 15(2)
• ss 1–7	1 April 2014	s 15(1)
• ss 9–12, 15	26 May 2013	s 15(3)
Mobile Homes (Wales) Act 2013		
• ss 1–57	no date	s 64(2)
• ss 58–65	5 November 2013	s 64(1)
• Schs 1–3	no date	s 64(2)
• Schs 4, 5	5 November 2013	s 64(1)
Offender Management Act 2007		
• ss 28*, 29*	6 January 2014	s 41(1); SI 2013/1963
Pensions Act 2011		
• Sch 4 (paras 1*, 21–36)	13 March 2013	s 38(4); SI 2013/585
Police and Justice Act 2006		
• s 17(1), (2)*, (3), (4)	8 April 2013	ss 49(3), 53(1); SI 2013/592
Political Parties and Elections Act 2009		
• s 27(1), (2), (4)	22 January 2013	s 43(1); SI 2013/99
• s 27(3)	1 January 2014	s 43(1); SI 2013/99
Presumption of Death Act 2013		
• ss 1–8, 9*, 10–14, 15(1)–(3), 16	no date	s 22(2)
• ss 9*, 17–24	26 March 2013	s 22(1)(a), (c)–(e)
• Schs 1*, 2	no date	s 22(2)
• Sch 1*	26 March 2013	s 22(1)(b)
Prevention of Social Housing Fraud Act 2013		
• ss 1–9*, 11*	15 October 2013	s 12(3); SI 2013/2622
• ss 1–9*, 11*	5 November 2013	s 12(3); SI 2013/2861
• s 12	31 January 2013	
• Schedule	15 October 2013	s 12(3); SI 2013/2622
Prisons (Interference with Wireless Telegraphy) Act 2012		
• s 1–4	21 October 2013	s 5(3); SI 2013/2460
Prisons (Property) Act 2013		
• s 1	no date	s 2(2)
• s 2	28 February 2013	s 2(3)

STATUTE	IN FORCE	AUTHORITY
Protection of Freedoms Act 2012		
• ss 1–12, 13*, 14*, 15–19, 20(2)–(9), 21, 23–25	31 October 2013	s 120(1); SI 2013/1814
• s 13*	31 January 2014	s 120(1); SI 2013/1814
• ss 26–28	1 September 2013	s 120(1); SI 2013/1566, 2104
• ss 79(2)(b)*, (3)*, 83	17 June 2013	s 120(1); SI 2013/1180
• s 102*	1 August 2013	s 120(1); SI 2013/1906
• ss 102*, 103, 106–108	1 September 2013	s 120(1); SI 2013/1906
• ss 109, 110	6 April 2013	s 120(1); SI 2013/470
• Sch 1 (paras 1(1)–(3), (4)*, (5)–(8), 2–6)	31 October 2013	s 120(1); SI 2013/1814
• Sch 1 (para 1(4)*)	31 January 2014	s 120(1); SI 2013/1814
• Schs 9 (paras 1–4), 10 (Pt 1)	31 October 2013	s 120(1); SI 2013/2104
• Schs 9 (paras 108, 109(2)(a), 110(2), (4)–(6), 111(4), 113, 118*, 119–128), 10 (Pt 6)	17 June 2013	s 120(1); SI 2013/1180
• Sch 9 (paras 136–142)	6 April 2013	s 120(1); SI 2013/470
Public Audit (Wales) Act 2013		
• ss 1, 8, 10, 12–16, 17(2), (3), 18, 20, 24–28, 29(1), (2), (3)(b), (c), (4), 31, 32	4 July 2013	s 35(2), (3); SI 2013/1466
• ss 2–7, 9, 11, 17(1), 19, 21–23, 29(3)(a)	1 April 2014	s 35(2), (3); SI 2013/1466
• ss 30, 35, 36	29 April 2013	s 35(1)
• Schs 1 (paras 1–13, 26–28, 29(1), 30–32), 2 (paras 1, 2, 5–14), 3 (paras 4, 13), 4 (para 79(2) (in part))	4 July 2013	s 35(2), (3); SI 2013/1466
• Schs 1 (paras 14–25, 29(2), (3), 33–36), 2 (paras 3, 4), 3 (paras 1–3, 5–12), 4 (paras 1–78, 79(1), (2) (in part), (3)–(6), 80–92)	1 April 2014	s 35(2), (3); SI 2013/1466
Public Service Pensions Act 2013		
• ss 1–9, 10*, 11(1), (2)–(4)*, (5), 12(1), (2)–(5)*, (6), (7), (8)*, (9)*, 13, 14(1), (2)*, (3)*, (4), (5), (6)*, 15, 17(1)*, 18, 19, 22, 24–26, 28, 30–32, 34	no date	s 41(2)
• ss 10*, 36	24 June 2013	s 41(2); SI 2013/1518
• ss 11(2)–(4)*, 12(2)–(5)*, (8)*, (9)*	1 December 2013	s 41(2), (3); SI 2013/2818
• ss 14(2)*, (3)*, (6)*, 16, 17(2)–(5), 21, 23, 35	1 November 2013	s 41(2), (3); SI 2013/2818

STATUTE	IN FORCE	AUTHORITY
• ss 37–42	25 April 2013	s 41(1)
• Schs 1–3, 4 (paras 1*, 2–13, 14–16*, 17, 18*, 19–21, 22*), 5–7, 8 (paras 1–20, 22–31), 10	no date	s 41(2)
• Sch 4 (paras 1, 14–16, 18, 22)*	1 November 2013	s 41(2), (3); SI 2013/2818
• Sch 8 (para 21)	1 February 2014	s 41(2), (3); SI 2013/2818
• Schs 9, 11	25 April 2013	s 41(1)
Road Safety Act 2006		
• s 13	1 June 2013	s 61; SI 2013/1012
School Standards and Organisation (Wales) Act 2013		
• ss 2–17, 19–31, 40–83, 96	no date	s 100(4)
• ss 1, 100, 101	5 March 2013	s 100(1)
• ss 32–37, 91, 94, 95, 97*, 98*	4 May 2013	s 100(3)
• ss 38*, 39*, 97*, 98*	26 April 2013	s 100(4); SI 2013/1000
• ss 38*, 39*	19 July 2013	s 100(4); SI 2013/1800
• ss 40–83	1 October 2013	s 100(4); SI 2013/1800
• ss 84–87	3 December 2013	s 100; SI 2013/3024
• ss 88–90, 92, 93	1 April 2013	s 100(2)
• Schs 1, 4 (para 8), 5 (paras 1–13, 32, 34(2))	no date	s 100(4)
• Schs 2, 3, 4 (paras 1–7, 9–39), 5 (paras 14–30)	1 October 2013	s 100(4); SI 2013/1800
• Sch 5 (paras 31, 33, 34(1), (3), 36, 36)	4 May 2013	s 100(3)
Scrap Metal Dealers Act 2013		
• ss 1(1), (2), 2–4, 6, 7, 8(1)–(8), (11), 10(1)–(4), 11(1)–(3), 12–14, 15(1)–(3), 16–19, 21, 22	1 October 2013	s 23(2); SI 2013/1966
• ss 1(3), 8(9), (10), 10(5), 11(4)–(7), 15(4)–(6)	1 December 2013	s 23(2); SI 2013/1966
• ss 20, 23	28 February 2013	
• Sch 1 (paras 1, 2, 3(1)–(4), 4, 7—9)	1 October 2013	s 23(2); SI 2013/1966
• Schs 1 (paras 3(5), (6), 5), 2	1 December 2013	s 23(2); SI 2013/1966
• Sch 1 (para 6)	1 September 2013	s 23(2); SI 2013/1966
Statute Law (Repeals) Act 2013	31 January 2013	s 3(2)
Succession to the Crown Act 2013		
• ss 1–4	no date	s 5(2)
• s 5	25 April 2013	s 5(1)
• Schedule	no date	s 5(2)
Supply and Appropriation (Anticipation and Adjustments) Act 2013	26 March 2013	

STATUTE	IN FORCE	AUTHORITY
Supply and Appropriation (Main Estimates) Act 2013	17 July 2013	
Traffic Management Act 2004		
• s 71*	1 October 2013	s 99(1); SI 2013/2408
Tribunals, Courts and Enforcement Act 2007		
• ss 62(1)*, 64(2)–(4)*, 73(8)*, 77(4)*, (6)*, 78(2)*, 81(5)*, (6)*, 90	15 July 2013	s 148(5); SI 2013/1739
• Sch 12 (paras 3(1), 7(2), (4), 8, 11(2), 12(1), 13(3), 14(3), 15(3), 22(1), 24(1), 25(1), (2), 28(2), (3), 31(2), (4), 32(1), (2), 33(2), 34(4), 35(2), 36, 39(2), 40(2), (3), 41(3), (5), 42, 43(1)–(3), 48, 49(3), (4), 50(3), (4), (7), 53(3), 54(2), 56(3), 60(4), (5), 62)*	15 July 2013	s 148(5); SI 2013/1739
• Schs 8 (paras 24, 27*), 23 (Pt 1*)	19 August 2013	s 148(5); SI 2013/2043
Trusts (Capital and Income) Act 2013		
• ss 1–3	1 October 2013	s 5; SI 2013/676
• s 4*	6 April 2013	s 5; SI 2013/676
• s 4*	1 January 2014	s 5; SI 2013/2461
• ss 5, 6	31 January 2013	s 5(3)
Welfare Benefits Up-rating Act 2013		
• ss 1, 2	1 October 2013	s 3(4); SI 2013/2317
• s 3	26 March 2013	s 3(3)
• Schedule	1 October 2013	s 3(4); SI 2013/2317
Welfare Reform Act 2012		
• ss 2(2), 4(2), (3), (5)–(7), 5*, 6(1)*, (3)*, 7(2), (3), 8(3)*, 9(2), (3), 10(2)–(5), 11(3)–(5), 12(1)*, (3), (4), 14(5)*, 15(2), (3), 17(3)–(5)*, 18(3)*, (5)*, 19(2)*,(3), (4), 20(1)*, 22(2)*, 24(1), (5), (6), 25, 26(2)*, (6)–(8), 27(4), (5), (9), 28, 32, 37(3)–(7), 39(3)(a), 40, 42, 43, 49(3)*, (6), 54(6), 57(2)*, (6), 77(3)*, 78(3), (4), 79(3), (4), (7), 80, 81, 83(3)*, 85, 86, 87*, 92–94, 95*, 98–100, 101(1)*, 102(2)–(5), (6)*, 104, 118(5)*, (8)*	25 February 2013	s 150(3); SI 2013/358
• ss 29, 37(1), (2), (8), (9), 38, 39(1), (2), (3)(b), (c)	29 April 2013	s 150(3); SI 2013/983
• s 101(2)	1 April 2013	s 150(3); SI 2013/358
• s 66*	1 November 2013	s 150(3); SI 2013/2534
• ss 77–79*, 82–84*, 87–89*, 95*	8 April 2013	s 150(3); SI 2013/358
• s 110*	17 June 2013	s 150(3); SI 2013/1250

STATUTE	IN FORCE	AUTHORITY
• s 110*	1 October 2013	s 150(3); SI 2013/1250
• ss 117(1)*, (3), 120(1)*, (2)*, (3), (5)	6 April 2013	s 150(3); SI 2013/178, 358
• s 120(1)*, (2)*, (4)	1 February 2013	s 150(3); SI 2013/178
• ss 136, 140, 141	25 November 2013	s 150(3); SI 2013/2947
• Schs 1 (paras 1, 3, 4, 5, 7), 2 (paras 2*, 4*, 5–7, 23*, 26, 31–34*, 36, 43*, 45*, 46, 47*, 48, 49*, 51, 55*, 56*, 58*, 59(1)*, (3), 61(1)*, (2)–(4), 63*), 5 (paras 2, 3), 6 (paras 1*, 3*, 4*, 5*, 6*), 9 (paras 9, 26, 32*, 39*, 40, 41*, 42), 10, 11 (paras 1–11*, 15–18*), 14*	25 February 2013	s 150(3); SI 2013/358
• Schs 2 (paras 1, 2, 3*, 4, 8–12, 14–22, 23*, 25, 27–30, 31–34, 35*, 37–42, 43*, 44, 45*, 47*, 49*, 50(1)*, (2), 52–54, 55*, 65), 5 (para 1), 11 (paras 1–11, 15–18)*, 14*	29 April 2013	s 150(3); SI 2013/358, 983
• Sch 14*	1 April 2013	s 150(3); SI 2013/358
• Sch 9 (paras 1–3, 5–25, 27–50)*	8 April 2013	s 150(3); SI 2013/358
Welsh Language (Wales) Measure 2011		
• ss 120(2), (3), 123–125, 127, 128, 131, 133	7 January 2014	s 156(2); SI 2013/3140
• Sch 11 (paras 1–8, 10–17)	7 January 2014	s 156(2); SI 2013/3140
Youth Justice and Criminal Evidence Act 1999		
• s 28*	30 December 2013	s 68(3); SI 2013/3236

2357   Statute Law (Repeals) Act 2013

The Statute Law (Repeals) Act 2013 promotes the reform of the statute law by the repeal, in accordance with recommendations of the Law Commission and the Scottish Law Commission, of certain enactments which, except in so far as their effect is preserved, are no longer of practical utility. The Act received royal assent on 31 January 2013 and came into force on that day.

Section 1, Schs 1–12 effect the repeals and revocations and deal with savings. Section 2 deals with extent and s 3 with short title.

TELECOMMUNICATIONS

Halsbury's Laws of England (5th edn) vol 97 (2010) paras 1–300

Articles

For articles relating to this title please refer to the Table of Articles at the beginning of the Abridgment.

2358   Broadcasting

See BROADCASTING.

2359   Electronic communications—electronic communications code—conditions and restrictions

The Electronic Communications Code (Conditions and Restrictions) (Amendment) Regulations 2013, SI 2013/1403 (in force on 27 June 2013), further amend the 2003 Regulations, SI 2003/2553, by introducing a more permissive regime for installation above ground of fixed-line broadband electronic communications apparatus. The new regime will apply for a limited period of five years as required by the Growth and Infrastructure Act 2013 s 9. In particular, the regulations (1) add definitions of 'fixed-line broadband', 'fixed-line broadband cabinet', 'fixed-line broadband pole', 'narrowband' and 'overhead fixed-line broadband line'; (2) extend the existing categories of lines which may be deployed overhead to include all fixed-line broadband lines; (3) provide that sites and areas of special scientific interest and other protected areas remain subject to the more restrictive regime for deployment of overhead lines; (4) require an electronic communications network provider ('code operator') to notify and consult with a planning authority where he intends to install fixed-line broadband cabinets, fixed-line broadband poles and overhead fixed-line broadband lines (other than service lines); (5) provide that the requirement in conservation areas for the code operator to obtain prior approval from the planning authority in order to install, above ground, electronic communications apparatus is now a requirement, as respects specified fixed-line broadband apparatus, merely to notify and consult the planning authority; (6) provide that the requirement to obtain prior approval when installing electronic communications apparatus in proximity to a listed building is now, as respects specified fixed-line broadband apparatus, a requirement merely to notify and consult; and (7) provide that, in specified protected areas, the requirement to obtain prior approval is now, as respects the installation of specified fixed-line broadband apparatus, a requirement merely to notify and consult.

2360   Growth and Infrastructure Act 2013

See para 2022.

2361   Mobile telephones—networks—roaming

The Mobile Roaming (European Communities) (Amendment) Regulations 2013, SI 2013/822 (in force on 1 May 2013), further amend the 2007 Regulations, SI 2007/1933, so as to implement European Parliament and Council Regulation (EU) 531/2012 on roaming on public mobile communications networks within the European Union. The effect of the amendments is to (1) set out a substituted definition of 'EU Mobile Roaming Regulation'; (2) introduce provisions relating to breaches of obligations and remedying of breaches; (3) empower the Office of Communications ('OFCOM') to give directions in relation to the obligation placed on mobile network operators to allow other providers access to their networks for wholesale roaming; (4) give OFCOM powers to obtain information; (5) align enforcement procedures in the 2007 Regulations with those contained in the Communications Act 2003; (6) enable OFCOM to impose daily penalties for continuing breaches; (7) increase, from £50,000 to £2m, the maximum civil penalty for breach of information requirements; (8) allow OFCOM to involve other national regulatory authorities and the Body of European Regulators for Electronic Communications in disputes involving other member states; (9) make new provision relating to the giving of notifications and the sending of other documents; and (10) require the Secretary of State to review the operation of the 2007 Regulations. Transitional provision is also made.

2362   Service provider—price control—change in mechanism—reference to Competition Commission

The proceedings concerned charges applied to wholesale mobile voice call termination services provided by mobile and fixed communications providers. Price control was exercised through conditions pursuant to the Communications Act 2003. The Office of Communications ('OFCOM') was under a statutory obligation to consider the effect on efficiency and competition of any regulatory control of price and to confer the greatest possible benefits on end-users of public electronic communications services. Following a market review and consultations, OFCOM decided to change the price control mechanism from so-called 'LRIC-plus' to 'LRIC', which was predicted to lose operators significant revenue from their wholesale termination charges. The appellant and other national mobile communications companies appealed various of OFCOM's conclusions to the Competition Appeal Tribunal. The Tribunal referred questions to the Competition Commission seeking a determination on the merits and of whether OFCOM was wrong to impose LRIC. The Commission stated that, since the question of consumer responses to price increases was a key issue in the determination, it would normally expect a robust survey to have been important evidence that a regulator would seek to rely on, but that there had not appeared to be any reliable survey evidence that directly addressed the magnitude of customer loss that would flow from the type of price changes expected. The Commission also determined that, while the customer response to price increases had been a key issue, it had not been determinative of the question of allocative efficiency, and concluded that, while there had been errors in OFCOM's reasoning, it had not been shown that there was convincing evidence that the scale of decline in the number of users would be significant. The Commission therefore determined that OFCOM had not been mistaken in respect of the appropriateness or otherwise of its choice for promoting efficiency in choosing a LRIC cost standard. The appellant appealed against that decision, submitting that, in light of the Commission's disagreement with OFCOM, it should have referred the matter back for reconsideration. *Held*, it was for the appellant to establish that OFCOM's decision had been wrong on one or more of the grounds specified in s 192(6). It was for the appellant to marshal and adduce all the evidence and material on which it had relied to show that OFCOM's original decision had been wrong. The appellant's appeal had been against the decision, not the reasons for that decision. It had not been enough to identify some error in reasoning; the appeal could succeed only if the decision could not stand in light of that error. If it was to succeed, the appellant had to first, demonstrate that the facts, reasoning or value judgments on which the ultimate decision had been based were wrong and, second, show that its proposed alternative price control measure should have been adopted by the Commission. If the Commission had concluded that the original decision could be supported on a basis other than that on which OFCOM had relied, then the appellant would not have shown that the original decision had been wrong. The Commission had demonstrated its view that, although the customer response to price increases had been a key issue, it had by no means been determinative of the question of allocative efficiency. In any event, the Commission had not felt inhibited, by any absence of evidence, from making judgments on an array of issues, all of which went to its rejection of the challenge before it. Accordingly, the appeal would be dismissed.

British Telecommunications plc v Competition Commission [2013] EWCA Civ 154, [2013] All ER (D) 46 (Mar) (Court of Appeal: Longmore, Moses and Patten LJJ).

2363   Telecommunications—interception of communications
See POLICE AND INVESTIGATORY POWERS.

TIME
Halsbury's Laws of England (5th edn) vol 97 (2010) paras 301–400

2364   Computation of time—notice of appeal—time limit—specified number of days—calendar or working days
See *R (on the application of Adesina) v Nursing and Midwifery Council*, para 1869.

TORT
Halsbury's Laws of England (5th edn) vol 97 (2010) paras 401–800

Articles
For articles relating to this title please refer to the Table of Articles at the beginning of the Abridgment.

2365   Conspiracy—unlawful means—procuring breach of duty—loss
See *Alpstream AG v PK Airfinance Sarl*, para 1895.

2366   Economic torts—inducing breach of contract—contract of sale—sale of goods to separate purchaser

The claimant company, whose shares were owned by two individuals (the 'owners'), was in the business of purchasing aircraft from China and selling them in Iran. The owners hired a broker to represent the claimant in all technical matters relating to the purchase and sale of the aircraft. The claimant entered into a contract with the defendant to buy six aircraft and five engines, with payment to be made in three instalments. The claimant was unable to pay the full amount of the first instalment, leading the defendant to decline to make delivery of the first three aircraft. The parties eventually entered into a supplemental agreement under which the defendant agreed to deliver the first aircraft. Around that time, the broker started the process of incorporating a South African company, which the broker and the second owner intended should replace the claimant as purchaser of the remaining aircraft. Shortly afterwards, the defendant gave notice to the claimant that it was terminating the agreement for the claimant's failure to perform. The claimant brought proceedings claiming damages for breach of contract and inducement of breach of contract, alleging that there had been a series of secret agreements whereby the defendant and the second owner had conspired to prevent the claimant proceeding with the purchase of the aircraft. *Held*, on the facts, neither the broker nor the second owner had owed the claimant any relevant obligations, nor had they breached them. Further, even if there had been relevant contractual obligations, the defendant had not known enough about them to found the tort of inducement. The defendant had not breached its contracts with the claimant, while the claimant had been in substantial and continuous breach of its contractual obligations to the defendant. There was no real evidence of any secret agreements of the type alleged by the claimant. The defendant had not needed a pretext to terminate the agreement and mitigate its loss by selling to another purchaser. It had been entitled to terminate the agreement, and it had made good commercial sense that, before it did so, it knew it would be able to sell the aircraft to another purchaser for a comparable price. The defendant had been doing little more than trying to mitigate the loss which had been caused by the claimant's continued breach of contract. Accordingly, the claim would be dismissed.

Tigris International NV v China Southern Airlines Co Ltd [2013] EWHC 2211 (Comm), [2013] All ER (D) 342 (Jul) (Queen's Bench Division: Simon J).

2367   Harassment—defence—preventing or detecting crime—test of rationality

The Protection from Harassment Act 1997 s 1(3)(a) provides that a course of conduct is not harassment if the person who pursued it shows that it was pursued for the purpose of preventing or detecting crime.

The defendant made serious but unsubstantiated allegations against the claimant in relation to the alleged disposal of assets of companies which the claimant controlled. The defendant conducted a lengthy and persistent campaign of correspondence and investigation over seven years. In particular, the defendant made complaints to the Department of Trade and Industry, the Official Receiver, the police, and other public bodies. Those authorities declined to take action, taking the view that the allegations were unfounded. The claimant brought an action under the 1997 Act s 1. It was held that the defendant had established the defence under s 1(3)(a) that the purpose of his conduct had been the prevention or detection of crime, even though not all of his acts had been reasonable. The claimant's appeal was allowed and he was granted an injunction. The defendant appealed. *Held*, Lord Reed dissenting, it could not be the case that the mere existence of a belief, however absurd, in the mind of the harasser that he was detecting or preventing a possibly non-existent crime would justify him in persisting in a course of conduct which the law characterised as oppressive. Some control mechanism was required, even if it fell short of requiring the alleged harasser to prove that his alleged purpose was objectively reasonable. In the context of s 1(3)(a), the necessary control mechanism was to be found in the concept of rationality. Rationality was not the same as reasonableness. A test of rationality applied a minimum objective standard to the relevant person's mental processes. It imported a requirement of good faith, a requirement that there should be some logical connection between the evidence and the ostensible reasons for the decision and an absence of arbitrariness, of capriciousness or of reasoning so outrageous in its defiance of logic as to be perverse. Before an alleged harasser could be said to have had the purpose of preventing or detecting crime, he had to have sufficiently applied his mind to the matter. He had to have thought rationally about the material suggesting the possibility of criminality and formed the view that the conduct said to constitute harassment had been appropriate for the purpose of preventing or detecting it. If he had done those things, then he had the relevant purpose. The court would not test his conclusions by reference to the view which a hypothetical reasonable man in his position would have formed. If, on the other hand, he had not engaged in those minimum mental processes necessary to acquire the relevant state of mind, but proceeded anyway on the footing that he was acting to prevent or detect crime, then he acted irrationally. In that case, two consequences followed. Firstly, the law would not regard him as having had the relevant purpose at all. He had simply not taken the necessary steps to form one. Secondly, the causal connection which s 1(3)(a) posited between the purpose of the alleged harasser and the conduct constituting the harassment would not exist. The defendant had not had the protection of the defence offered by s 1(3)(a). His vendetta against the claimant had been more than objectively unreasonable. It had been irrational and his persistence had been obsessive. He had no longer been guided by any objective assessment of the evidence of the claimant's supposed criminality and there had no longer been any logical connection between his supposed purpose and his acts. He had proceeded with his campaign for its own sake, regardless of the prospect of detecting any crimes. Accordingly, the appeal would be dismissed.

Hayes v Willoughby [2013] UKSC 17, [2013] 2 All ER 405 (Supreme Court: Lord Neuberger P, Lord Mance, Lord Wilson, Lord Sumption and Lord Reed SCJJ). *EDO MBM Technology Ltd v Axworthy* [2005] EWHC 2490 (QB), [2005] All ER (D) 77 (Nov) (2005 Abr para 2987); and *Howlett v Holding* [2006] EWHC 3758 (QB), [2006] All ER (D) 162 (Jan) (2006 Abr para 1708) considered. Decision of Court of Appeal [2011] EWCA Civ 1541, [2012] 1 WLR 1510, [2011] All ER (D) 144 (Dec) (2011 Abr para 2352) affirmed on other grounds.

2368   Harassment—injunction—suspected terrorist

See *The wife and children of Omar Othman v English National Resistance*, para 2166.

2369   Harassment—vicarious liability of employer—act within course of employment— murder of colleague

Scotland

An employee ('the victim') of the defendant supermarket wrote a letter of complaint to his team leader that he was being harassed by another member of staff ('the offender') because of his nationality. No action was taken by the defendant's staff. After discovering that the victim had complained about him, the offender started an argument with the victim which culminated in the offender stabbing the victim to death on the defendant's premises. The claimants, who were relatives of the victim, brought proceedings against the defendant alleging that it was vicariously liable for the offender's acts, which they claimed constituted harassment under the Protection from Harassment Act 1997 s 8. They contended that everything about the harassment, including the murderous assault and the taking of a knife from the place of work, had been connected with the employment situation. An application by the defendant for the proceedings to be dismissed as irrelevant was rejected, the judge stating that there was a sufficient connection between the crime and the fact that the persons involved were employed by the defendant. The defendant appealed against that decision, arguing that the judge had erred in proceeding on the basis that it was sufficient to establish a connection between the murder and the offender's employment in the broader sense, when the close connection which had to be established in order to found vicarious liability was between the harmful act and the wrongdoing employee's duties. *Held*, the court had to determine whether there was a connection, and if so whether it was a close one, between what the wrongdoing employee was asked to do and the wrong he committed, having regard to the risks involved in the employee's work. It was equally possible to achieve the same result from a practical point of view simply by reverting to the traditional formula of asking whether the wrongful actions were, on the other hand, a 'frolic' of the employee's own devising and execution and thus unconnected with what he was employed to do. The mere bringing together of persons as employees was not sufficient to impose vicarious liability for all the actions of each employee towards another. In the present case, no matter how broadly the context of the offender's employment was looked at, it was not possible to hold that the defendant's activities carried any special or additional risk that employees be harassed or otherwise come to harm as a result of the deliberate and violent actions of co-employees. The risk was no greater than that involved when engaging any two or more employees to work together. It was not possible to categorise the offender's actions as so closely connected with what he was employed to do that they could have been seen as ways of carrying out the work which he was authorised to do. The fact that the offender had a known propensity to be violent to immigrant workers was not relevant to the issue of vicarious liability, although it may well have been in the context of a direct liability case based on the duty of an employer to take reasonable care to employ competent staff and to supervise their activities while on its premises. It followed that the claimants' action had to be dismissed as irrelevant, and, accordingly, the appeal would be allowed.

Vaickuviene v J Sainsbury plc [2013] CSIH 67, [2013] IRLR 792 (Inner House).

2370 Joint tortfeasors—liability—common design—campaign against illegal fishing—use of violence

The second defendant was a conservation charity that was involved in a campaign against the illegal fishing of Atlantic blue fin tuna. As part of that campaign, using a boat owned by the first defendant, the second defendant caused a collision at sea involving that boat and a vessel owned by the claimant, which operated a fish farm. Members of the second defendant were successful in damaging a tuna fish cage and releasing fish into the sea. The third defendant was the master of the first defendant's boat at the time of the collision. The claimant issued proceedings against the defendants seeking damages for trespass to and/or conversion of its property. It alleged that the actions against its property had been taken pursuant to a common design between the defendants to commit those acts, and that the first defendant was a joint tortfeasor because it had acted in furtherance of the common design by making the vessel available to the campaign, by paying the crew, and by processing and remitting donations received to the second defendant. A preliminary issue was tried as to whether the first defendant could be jointly liable for the damage caused. The judge decided that, although the first defendant had been aware of and had generally approved of the campaign, and that that campaign had envisaged the possibility of violent intervention against property such as cutting fishing nets, the purpose of the campaign had been to investigate, document and take action when necessary to expose and confront illegal fishing activities. That had involved a preparedness to use violent intervention, but had not meant that any action would necessarily have been taken. He concluded that, once the third defendant and the crew had been found to have been acting on behalf of the second defendant rather than the first defendant, the participation that the claimant relied on had been remote in time and place, of minimal importance and had played no effective part in the commission of the tort. On the claimant's appeal against that decision, *held*, once a common design had been established, the question was whether the defendant who was said to be a joint tortfeasor had done something that had furthered that common design. Providing that the act that furthered an undoubted common design was more than de minimis, there was no further hurdle that required it to have been an essential part of or of real significance to the commission of the tort. On the evidence, it was difficult to regard the cutting of fishing nets and freeing fish from them and the cages as not an objective or purpose of the campaign, even if the campaign also had other purposes. In inferring from the documents that had been before him that the purpose of the campaign had been investigation, documentation and exposure of illegal activities but that it had not, notwithstanding the content of the documents that had been before him, encompassed violent intervention, the judge had fallen into error. Accordingly, the appeal would be allowed.

Fish & Fish Ltd v Sea Shepherd UK [2013] EWCA Civ 544, [2013] All ER (D) 191 (May) (Court of Appeal: Mummery, McCombe and Beatson LJJ).

2371 Joint tortfeasors—settlement of claim—reservation of right to sue

A local authority and a fire authority hired the first and second defendant property firms to market a disused fire station and adjoining land. The claimant company contended that it was induced by the third and fourth defendants, who were employees of the first and second defendants, to bid for and then contract to purchase the properties in question. The claimant submitted that it subsequently obtained confirmation that there were planning problems in respect of the intended redevelopment of the properties, on which basis it declined to complete either contract. The authorities served notices to complete, and the fire authority later issued proceedings against the claimant seeking specific performance. Negotiations took place, and in due course a settlement agreement was made under which the claimant was to be paid a specified sum. The agreement stated that the payment was in satisfaction of all claims by the claimant against the fire authority and the local authority in respect of damages, interest, costs and repayment of deposits, and was in full and final settlement of all and any existing or potential claims of any nature, whether or not contemplated, that the claimant had against the other parties. In the event, the claimant received the sum, but the authorities retained the deposits paid by the claimant under the purchase contracts. The difference between those two sums therefore represented payment on account of the claimant's damages claim, its costs of the claim and its out of pocket expenses of the aborted sale. The claimant then issued a second claim against the defendants for fraudulent misrepresentation. The defendants applied to strike out the second claim, submitting that the claim was precluded by the terms of the settlement agreement. The judge decided that there had been no basis for implying a reservation of a right to sue the defendants in the settlement agreement and struck out the second claim. The claimant appealed against that decision, submitting that the settlement agreement had not released the claimant's cause of action against the defendants. *Held*, the fact that the authorities and the defendants had all been joint rather than concurrent tortfeasors had been the cardinal aspect of the contextual background to the case. The established legal consequence of a release of one or more joint tortfeasors was that there was a release of all of them. By contrast, the legal consequence of a release of one or more concurrent tortfeasors was precisely the opposite. The effect of the settlement agreement had been that the claimant had succeeded both in its defence to the claim for specific performance, and in recovering agreed compensation for misrepresentation. There was no reason why a reservation of the right to sue the defendants should be implied in the settlement agreement. The undoubted legal consequence of the express terms of the settlement agreement had been to release the defendants. If the reservation of a right to sue the defendants was to be implied, the authorities had been giving up a specific performance claim worth significantly less than the value of the properties, and by implied agreement exposing themselves to the likelihood of contribution claims from the defendants, if sued thereafter by the claimant. That the authorities should be regarded as having agreed by implication to do so while professionally represented seemed to be an altogether improbable hypothesis. It simply showed that no such common intention could sensibly be presumed. Accordingly, the appeal would be dismissed.

Gladman Commercial Properties v Fisher Hargreaves Proctor [2013] EWCA Civ 1466, [2013] All ER (D) 187 (Nov) (Court of Appeal: Longmore, Ryder and Briggs LJJ). Decision of Arnold J [2013] EWHC 209 (Ch), [2013] All ER (D) 256 (Feb) affirmed.

2372   Malicious prosecution—elements—withdrawn civil claim alleging deceit and conspiracy

Cayman Islands

The appellant was an individual resident in the Cayman Islands. A hurricane caused extensive damage to a development of a number of residential units in Grand Cayman. The properties of the village were insured with the respondent company. It accepted that much of the damage was covered by the insurance policy. The appellant was appointed to act as the respondent's loss adjuster in relation to the claim. Partly due to infrastructure destruction and shortages, paperwork to the project was lacking. The company chosen to do the work gave a preliminary estimate of which the respondent was made aware. A number of advance payments were made to the company. Three final payments had also been approved by another loss adjuster instructed by the respondent although he expressed concern about the lack of detail in the appellant's report. The appellant was close to finalising his adjustment of the respondent's liability under the policy. He put forward figures, which the respondent appeared to accept, for the total cost of the works, of which the respondent would be liable for a percentage. At the same time, an individual joined the respondent as senior vice-president. He began a detailed study of its liability for losses caused by the hurricane and in particular for the cost of the works at the village. After it had completed about half the work, the individual fired the company and stated that he intended to drive the appellant out of business. The individual instructed a chartered surveyor and loss adjuster to assess the value of the company's work at the village. It was alleged that work done by the company was defective so that the value of the work should be reduced. Both the respondent and the proprietors of the village instructed attorneys to issue proceedings on their behalf. It was alleged that the appellant and the company had made fraudulent misrepresentations about the value of the works. The respondent claimed damages against them for deceit and conspiracy. However, the proprietors amended their claim so that it was brought only against the company and only for breach of contract or by way of restitution. Like the company, the appellant filed a defence in which all allegations were denied. The company made disclosure of invoices and other documentation which indicated its extensive payments to subcontractors and suppliers. The respondent discontinued the action and judgment was entered for the appellant and the company. The respondent was ordered to pay the appellant's and the company's costs on the indemnity basis. Leave was granted to the appellant to amend the counterclaim so as to include a claim for damages for abuse of process. The company brought a separate claim for malicious prosecution. Following two unsuccessful hearings, the appellant appealed to the Privy Council. *Held*, the respondent had committed the tort of malicious prosecution. It did not challenge the judge's conclusion that, if the tort applied to civil proceedings, all four of its ingredients had been present. The predominant purpose of the individual amounted to malice. Moreover, the fact that he believed that the appellant had defrauded the respondent counted for nothing because of the absence of reasonable cause of any such belief. Therefore, the appeal would be allowed and judgment entered for the appellant. However, the respondent had not committed the tort of abuse of process. The predominant factor which had led it to allege fraud and conspiracy had been the individual's obsessive determination to destroy the appellant professionally. Judgment would be given accordingly.

Crawford Adjusters (Cayman) Ltd v Sagicor General Insurance (Cayman) Ltd [2013] UKPC 17, [2013] 3 WLR 927, [2013] All ER (D) 38 (Jul) (Privy Council: Lord Neuberger, Lady Hale, Lord Kerr, Lord Wilson and Lord Sumption).

2373   **Malicious prosecution—no case to answer—assessment of damages—loss of liberty and damage to reputation**

Trinidad and Tobago
The appellant was charged with robbery and rape. Bail was fixed but the appellant failed to provide a surety and was remanded in custody until his trial. A summary trial on the robbery charge took place and the appellant was acquitted of that charge following the grant of a direction of no case to answer. Despite the evidence against him on the charge of rape having been the same as that on the charge of robbery, and despite the officer in charge of the prosecution recommending that the rape charge be discontinued, the appellant remained in custody and stood trial on the charge of rape. He was subsequently acquitted of that charge following the grant of a direction of no case to answer. The appellant instituted proceedings for malicious prosecution and the judge held that, after the dismissal of the robbery charge, the appellant should not have been prosecuted on the rape charge and the trial on that charge amounted to malicious prosecution. The judge awarded the appellant compensation, including as his reasons for that award consideration of the appellant's character and reputation. The appellant appealed against the award amount and the court held that the grant of bail was, in law, a sufficient ground to disentitle the appellant to an award under the head of claim of loss of liberty, on the basis that granting bail interposed a judicial act between the prosecution and the continued detention of the appellant and that the prosecution was no longer the cause of the deprivation of liberty. Further, the court decided that the appellant's failure to apply for variation of the bail endangered his own liberty. On further appeal, *held*, the judge failed to advert directly to the fact that the appellant had a good character and that the malicious prosecution had been in respect of a very serious offence, and that led him to underestimate the significance of that aspect of the appellant's claim. Further, it was true that the appellant's reputation already suffered damage as a result of his having been prosecuted for robbery. However, that circumstance ought not to have operated to diminish the compensation to which the appellant was entitled. He was, therefore, entitled to be compensated on the basis that he had been of unblemished reputation when he was prosecuted for rape. Moreover, neither the trial judge nor the appellate court had been correct in the approach that they had taken to the appellant's claim for compensation for loss of liberty. The judge's analysis had to be

presumed to have proceeded on the premise that, if the appellant had been remanded in custody, he would have been entitled to recover damages but that those damages would be reduced because he failed to take steps to secure his release. That was a classic mitigation of loss situation. However, the prosecution had not pleaded nor made the case that the appellant failed to mitigate his loss. If a failure to mitigate loss had been pleaded, it would have been for the prosecution to prove it. Without such an examination of the matter it had not been open to the judge to make a finding adverse to the appellant on the issue. It was, moreover, very far from certain that the appellant would have been able to have persuaded a court to alter the conditions of his bail as to enable him to avail it. Further, a claimant's failure to take up a grant of bail was not a judicial act. Although a judicial act precluded liability in false imprisonment, it did not relieve the prosecutor of liability in malicious prosecution. Furthermore, the conclusion that it had been the appellant's failure to apply for a variation of his bail conditions which endangered his liberty was erroneous. Accordingly, the appeal would be allowed.

Calix v A-G of Trinidad and Tobago [2013] UKPC 15, [2013] 5 LRC 600 (Privy Council: Lord Hope, Lord Kerr, Lord Wilson, Lord Reed and Sir John Sheil). *Flint v Lovell* [1935] 1 KB 354, PC; and *Nance v British Columbia Electric Rly Co Ltd* [1951] AC 601, [1951] 2 All ER 448, PC, applied.

2374   Trespass—trespass to land—licensee not in occupation—right to sue for trespass

See *Vehicle Control Services Ltd v Revenue and Customs Comrs*, para 2544.

TRADE AND INDUSTRY

Halsbury's Laws of England (5th edn) vol 97 (2010) paras 801–1024

Articles

For articles relating to this title please refer to the Table of Articles at the beginning of the Abridgment.

2375   Aircraft and Shipbuilding Industries Arbitration Tribunal—abolition

The Public Bodies (Abolition of the Aircraft and Shipbuilding Industries Arbitration Tribunal) Order 2013, SI 2013/686 (in force in part on 22 March 2013 and in part on 23 March 2013), abolishes the Aircraft and Shipbuilding Industries Arbitration Tribunal and makes consequential repeals, revocations and amendments.

2376   British Shipbuilders—abolition

The Public Bodies (Abolition of British Shipbuilders) Order 2013, SI 2013/687 (in force in part on 22 March 2013 and in part on 23 March 2013), (1) abolishes British Shipbuilders and its subsidiaries; (2) transfers the property, rights and liabilities of British Shipbuilders and its subsidiaries to the Secretary of State for Business, Innovation and Skills; (3) makes provision supplemental to those transfers; and (4) makes consequential repeals, revocations and amendments.

2377   Competition

See COMPETITION.

2378   Export of goods—control—prohibited goods

The Export Control (Amendment) Order 2013, SI 2013/428 (in force on 20 March 2013), further amends the 2008 Order, SI 2008/3231, in implementation of Commission Directive (EU) 2012/47, by substituting the list of military goods, software and technology which are subject to export controls with a list which reflects changes made by the directive to the Common Military List of the Union.

2379   **Export of goods—control—trade with Iran**

The Export Control (Iran Sanctions) (Amendment) Order 2013, SI 2013/340 (in force on 12 March 2013), amends the 2012 Order, SI 2012/1243, so as to create offences for the contravention of additional trade sanctions against Iran introduced by Council Regulation (EU) 1263/2012.

2380   **Export of goods—control—trade with North Korea, Ivory Coast and Syria**

The Export Control (North Korea and Ivory Coast Sanctions and Syria Amendment) Order 2013, SI 2013/3182 (in force on 7 January 2013), makes provision for the enforcement of certain trade restrictions against North Korea specified in Council Regulation (EC) 329/2007, and provides for the enforcement of trade restrictions against the Ivory Coast specified in Council Regulation (EC) 174/2005. The order sets out offences in relation to these prohibitions and provides that those offences can be committed by any person in the United Kingdom and, around the world, by any United Kingdom person, as defined in the Export Control Act 2002 s 11. In particular, the order replaces the Export Control (North Korea) Order 2007, SI 2007/1334, and the Export Control (Iraq and Ivory Coast) Order 2005, SI 2005/232, and (1) creates offences for contravention of the trade restrictions of Regulations 329/2007, and 174/2005; (2) sets out the penalties relating to the specified offences and makes some consequential modifications to the Customs and Excise Management Act 1979 to ensure that the offences covered by that Act are subject to the same penalties as those in the order; and (3) provides for the ancillary provisions which apply to the enforcement of customs and excise legislation to also apply to the enforcement of this order. The order also amends (a) the Export Control Order 2008, SI 2008/3231, so as to include Syria in the list of countries in Sch 4 Pt 4, so that the exemption for transit controls in that order does not apply when the goods in transit are those listed in Sch 1 Pt 2 and they are being exported to Syria; and (b) the Export Control (Syria Sanctions) Order 2013, SI 2013/2012, to expressly provide that a person carrying out any of the activities described in arts 4, 5 without the authority of a United Kingdom licence commits an offence and may be arrested. The Secretary of State must review the operation and effect of the order and publish a report within five years after the order comes into force and within every five years after that.

2381   **Export of goods—control—trade with Syria**

The Export Control (Syria Sanctions) Order 2013, SI 2013/2012 (in force on 6 September 2013), replaces the Export Control (Syria Sanctions) and (Miscellaneous Amendments) Order 2012, SI 2012/810, makes provision for certain trade restrictions against Syria and certain Syrian persons and makes provision for the enforcement of certain new trade sanctions against Syria specified in Council Regulation (EU) 36/2012, concerning restrictive measures in view of the situation in Syria. In particular, the order, which applies to any person in the United Kingdom as well as to any United Kingdom person anywhere in the world (1) imposes export, transfer and brokering controls in relation to equipment, goods or technology which could be used for internal repression in Syria, and in relation to the manufacture or maintenance of such products; (2) creates offences in relation to the trade restrictions set out in Regulation 36/2012 and sets out penalties relating to those offences, as well as to certain offences contained in the Customs and Excise Management Act 1979; (3) provides for the ancillary provisions which apply to the enforcement of customs and excise legislation to apply to the enforcement of the order; and (4) requires the Secretary of State to review the operation and effect of the order and to publish a report within five years of its commencement and within every five years after that. SI 2011/1304 is further amended. SI 2012/2125 is revoked.

2382   **Industrial relations**

See EMPLOYMENT.

2383   **Misleading marketing—business protection**

The Business Protection from Misleading Marketing (Amendment) Regulations 2013, SI 2013/2701 (in force on 14 November 2013), further amend the 2008 Regulations, SI 2008/1276, so as to (1) give the Gas and Electricity Markets Authority ('GEMA') certain powers as an enforcement authority, including the power to bring proceedings for an injunction in certain circumstances; (2) require GEMA to notify the Office of Fair Trading ('OFT') of its intention to apply for an injunction; (3) enable the OFT to direct which enforcement authority is to bring proceedings for an injunction, or decide that only it may do so, in cases where more than one enforcement authority is contemplating bringing such proceedings; and (4) clarify that the power to make test purchases, the power of entry and investigation and the power to enter premises with a warrant are powers which do not apply to GEMA.

2384 Restrictive measures—financial restrictions—Burma/Myanmar

The Burma/Myanmar (Financial Restrictions) (Revocation) Regulations 2013, SI 2013/1096 (in force on 8 May 2013), revoke the 2009 Regulations, SI 2009/1495, and the Burma/Myanmar (Financial Restrictions) (Suspension) Regulations 2012, SI 2012/1302, so that criminal penalties do not continue in place in United Kingdom law following the revocation of certain EU financial restrictions.

2385 Scrap metal dealers—prescribed documents and information

The Scrap Metal Dealers Act 2013 (Prescribed Documents and Information for Verification of Name and Address) Regulations 2013, SI 2013/2276 (in force on 2 October 2013), prescribe the documents and information which are sufficient to verify the name and address of the Small Charitable Donations Act 2012 person supplying scrap metal, for the purpose of the Scrap Metal Dealers Act 2013 s 11(3)(a).

2386 Scrap metal dealers—prescribed relevant offences—relevant enforcement action

The Scrap Metal Dealers Act 2013 (Prescribed Relevant Offences and Relevant Enforcement Action) Regulations 2013, SI 2013/2258 (in force on 1 October 2013), prescribe relevant offences and relevant enforcement action for the purposes of the Scrap Metal Dealers Act 2013 s 3(3)(b), (c).

2387 Scrap Metal Dealers Act 2013

The Scrap Metal Dealers Act 2013 amends the law relating to scrap metal dealers. The Act received the royal assent on 28 February 2013 and came into force in part on that day. Further provisions came into force on and between 1 September 2013 and 1 December 2013: SI 2013/1966. The remaining provisions come into force on a day or days to be appointed. For details of commencement, see the commencement table in the title STATUTES AND LEGISLATIVE PROCESS.

Section 1 requires a person carrying on business as a scrap metal dealer to obtain a scrap metal licence and provides that carrying on business as a scrap metal dealer without a licence is an offence. A licence is to be issued by a local authority and there are two types of licence, a site licence, which authorises the licensee to carry on business as a scrap metal dealer at the sites listed in it, and a collector's licence, which authorises the licensee to carry on business as a scrap metal dealer within the local authority area: s 2. A local authority must not issue or renew a scrap metal licence unless it is satisfied that the applicant is a suitable person to carry on business as a scrap metal dealer: s 3. Further, a local authority may include conditions relating to opening hours and quarantine scrap metal in a licence if the applicant or site manager has been convicted of an offence prescribed by the Secretary of State, or if the licensee or site manager is convicted of such an offence: ss 3, 4. Section 4 empowers a local authority to revoke a licence if it is (1) satisfied that the licensee does not carry on business at any of the sites identified in the licence; (2) satisfied that a site manager named in the licence does not act as site manager at any of the sites identified in the licence; (3) no longer satisfied that the licensee is a suitable person to carry on business as a scrap metal dealer. Section 5 introduces Sch 1, which provides that a licence will be issued for a period of three years, provides for the variation of licences, allows local authorities to charge a licence fee and makes provision as to the application process. Section 6 requires a local authority to supply any such information as requested relating to a scrap metal licence to any other local authority in England and Wales, the Environment Agency, the Natural Resources Body for Wales and to police forces. A register of scrap metal licences issued in England must be maintained by the Environment Agency and a register of those issued in Wales must be maintained by the Natural Resources Body for Wales, and those registers must be open to inspection by the public: s 7. Under s 8, an applicant is required to notify the relevant environmental body of any changes which materially affect the accuracy of any information which the applicant has provided in connection with the application. Section 9 introduces Sch 2, which makes provision for the closure of sites at which a scrap metal business is carried on without a licence. A scrap metal dealer who holds a site licence must display a copy of the licence at each site identified in the licence in a prominent place in an area accessible to the public, and a scrap metal dealer who holds a collector's licence must display a copy of the licence on any vehicle that is being used in the course of the dealer's business: s 10. Section 11 requires scrap metal dealers, site managers and employees who have been delegated the responsibility to do so, to verify the identity of the person they are receiving metal from and the person's address, and provides that failure to do so is an offence. Section 12 re-enacts with modifications provision creating the offence of purchasing scrap metal for cash. Sections 13–15 set out the record-keeping requirements in respect of any scrap metal received by a scrap metal dealer in the course of their business and in respect of records of metal being disposed of by a site licensee or collector. Police constables or officers of a local authority are, by s 16, empowered to enter and inspect the premises of licensed and unlicensed scrap metal dealers. Where an offence under the Act is committed by a body corporate and is proved to have been committed with the consent or connivance of a director, manager, secretary or other similar officer, or to be attributable to any neglect on the part of any such individual, the individual as well as the body corporate is guilty of the offence: s 17. Section 18 requires the Secretary of State to review the Act within five years of the licensing requirement coming into force and publish a report. Section 19 makes consequential amendments, s 20 deals with orders and regulations, ss 21, 22 deal with interpretation and s 23 deals with extent, commencement and short title.

Amendments, repeals and revocations
The lists below, which are not exhaustive, mention repeals and amendments which are or will be effective when the Act is fully in force.

The following Act is repealed in full: Scrap Metal Dealers Act 1964. The following provisions of the following Acts are amended or repealed: Local Government (Wales) Act 1994 Sch 9 para 6; Vehicle Excise and Registration Act 1994 Sch 3 para 1; Vehicles (Crime) Act 2001 ss 1–16, 35, Schedule paras 1, 2; Communications Act 2003 Sch 17 para 168; Legal Aid, Sentencing and Punishment of Offenders Act 2012 ss 145–147; Regulatory Enforcement and Sanctions Act 2008 Sch 3.

2388   Trade restrictions—trade with Burma—European Community common foreign and security policy—offences and penalties

The Export Control (Burma Sanctions) Order 2013, SI 2013/1964 (in force on 28 August 2013), makes provision for the enforcement of the remaining trade sanctions against Myanmar/Burma specified in Council Regulation (EU) 401/2013 (concerning restrictive measures in respect of Myanmar/Burma). In particular, the order (1) sets out the enforcement of the trade restrictions; (2) creates new offences in relation to those prohibitions; (3) specifies the penalties; (4) provides for the ancillary provisions which apply to the enforcement of customs and excise legislation to apply also to the enforcement of the order; and (5) requires the Secretary of State to review the operation and effect of the order and publish and report within five years after 28 August 2013 and within every five years after that. SI 2008/1098 is revoked.

2389   Trade restrictions—trade with Zimbabwe—European Community common foreign and security policy—financial sanctions—suspension

The Zimbabwe (Financial Sanctions) (Suspension) Regulations 2013, SI 2013/795 (in force on 5 April 2013), further amend the 2009 Regulations, SI 2009/847, so as to provide for the suspension, until 20 February 2014, of criminal penalties under those regulations for any breach of the freeze of funds and economic resources of certain persons, entities and bodies connected with the government of Zimbabwe.

2390   Trade unions

See EMPLOYMENT.

2391　Transfer of undertakings

See EMPLOYMENT.

2392　Welsh Development Agency—general

The Welsh Development Agency Act 1975 (Amendment) (Wales) Order 2013, SI 2013/2948 (in force on 21 November 2013) amends the Welsh Development Agency Act 1975 so as to authorise the Welsh Ministers to override easements and other rights restricting the use of land which they have acquired under the 1975 Act s 21A.

TRADE MARKS AND TRADE NAMES

Halsbury's Laws of England (5th edn) vol 97A (2014) paras 1–476

Articles

For articles relating to this title please refer to the Table of Articles at the beginning of the Abridgment.

2393　Hallmarks—assay offices—powers and duties

The Legislative Reform (Hallmarking) Order 2013, SI 2013/251 (in force on 8 February 2013), further amends the Hallmarking Act 1973 so as to (1) enable assay offices to strike hallmarks outside the United Kingdom and for items bearing those marks to be treated in the same way as items bearing marks struck in the United Kingdom; (2) remove the requirement that a registered manufacturer's or sponsor's mark must include the initial letters of the name of the manufacturer or sponsor; and (3) permit articles of silver, gold or platinum bearing a mark to be coated with platinum without the written consent of an assay office.

2394　Passing off—goodwill—geographical name—Greek yoghurt

The claimant companies sold strained yoghurt in the United Kingdom which was made in Greece and had been marketed as Greek yoghurt for over 20 years. It was common ground that all yoghurt sold in the United Kingdom with descriptions including 'Greek yoghurt' was strained yoghurt made in Greece. Other yoghurt which was not made in Greece, but bore similarities to the yoghurt sold as Greek yoghurt was, by an unwritten industry-wide labelling convention, sold as Greek style yoghurt, which was not usually strained yoghurt but was made through the addition of thickening agents. The defendant companies manufactured and distributed strained yoghurt made in America for many years and sold it in America as Greek yoghurt with no difficulties. The defendants started selling and promoting its yoghurt as Greek yoghurt in the United Kingdom and the claimants commenced proceedings for extended passing off, seeking an injunction to prevent the defendants from selling yoghurt not made in Greece as Greek yoghurt. It fell to be determined whether the phrase 'Greek yoghurt' had, when used in the United Kingdom marketplace, come to have attached to it sufficient reputation and goodwill as denoting a distinctive type of yoghurt made in Greece, such that the use of the same phrase to describe yoghurt not made in Greece, however otherwise similar, would involve a damaging misrepresentation sufficient to support a claim in passing off. *Held*, a substantial proportion of those who bought Greek yoghurt in the United Kingdom thought that it was made in Greece and the proportion of those Greek yoghurt buyers to whom that mattered was substantial. It followed that the claimants succeeded in demonstrating that substantial goodwill had become attached to the use of the phrase 'Greek yoghurt' in the sense that it created pulling power, rather than merely denoting a geographical origin to which buyers were indifferent. Further, it was clear that if sufficient goodwill was shown to be attached to the phrase 'Greek yoghurt', then the use of that phrase to describe yoghurt not made in Greece plainly involved a material misrepresentation. Accordingly, the claim would be allowed.

　　FAGE UK Ltd v Chobani UK Ltd [2013] EWHC 630 (Ch), [2013] All ER (D) 267 (Mar) (Chancery Division: Briggs J). *Diageo North America Inc v InterContinental Brands (ICB) Ltd* [2010] EWCA Civ 920, [2011] 1 All ER 242 (2010 Abr para 2703); and *Interflora Inc v Marks and Spencer plc* [2012] EWCA Civ 1501, [2012] All ER (D) 228

(Nov) (2012 Abr para 2509) considered. *Reckitt & Colman Products Ltd v Borden Inc* [1990] 1 All ER 873, HL (1990 Abr para 2478), applied.

2395   Passing off—goodwill—goodwill generated by licensees

The claimant companies provided marketing services to estate agents using the name 'Fine & Country' which was registered both as a United Kingdom trade mark and an EU trade mark. The defendant companies, which operated a number of estate agency brands, adopted a branding strategy for their higher value property wing that used the word 'FINE' in gold letters to distance itself from their other lower value property business. The claimants alleged that valuable goodwill and reputation in their registered trade marks attached to the claimants' own name and logo, which they licensed to a number of estate agents, but was owned by at least one of the claimants. An injunction was granted against the defendants prohibiting them from passing off any services which were not the services of, or services connected with any of, the claimants and from infringing the claimants' mark. The defendants appealed. *Held*, all use of the simple word 'FINE' had not been prohibited as a brand name. What persuaded the judge that passing off had been established was the combination of the name, the font, the capitalisation, the underlining, the use of gold, the strap line and the overall impression. Had the defendants stayed with an italicised flowing 'fine' sign, the judge might well not have reached the conclusion that he had. In other words, the claimants might well not have been able to object to the mere fact that the defendants used the single word 'fine' as their brand name. The misrepresentation had been to represent themselves as successors to, or part of, the network licensed by 'Fine & Country'. In relation to the distinctiveness of the marks, the judge's assessment had been a qualitative rather than a quantitative assessment. He had found, as a fact, that the marks had been highly distinctive. There had been no error of principle demonstrated in his approach such as would entitle interference with his assessment of acquired distinctiveness. Given the judge's findings on confusion and, in particular, his findings that, in some cases, it had been the appearance of the sign that had caused the confusion, it could not be said that his assessment as to whether the marks had been infringed was plainly wrong. The judge had been entitled to conclude that, in all the circumstances, the defendants' use of the sign had not involved 'tolerable confusion'. Accordingly, the appeal would be dismissed.

Fine & Country Ltd v Okotoks Ltd (formerly Spicerhaart Ltd) [2013] EWCA Civ 672, [2013] All ER (D) 137 (Jun) (Court of Appeal: Lloyd, Lewison and Gloster LJJ). *Phones 4u Ltd v Phone4u.co.uk Internet Ltd* [2006] EWCA Civ 244, [2007] IP & T 439 considered. Decisions of Hildyard J [2012] EWHC 2230 (Ch), [2012] All ER (D) 149 (Aug) (2012 Abr para 2480); and [2012] EWHC 2528 (Ch), [2012] All ER (D) 85 (Oct) affirmed.

2396   Passing off—likelihood of confusion—relevant persons—significant number of actual and potential customers

The claimant sold anti-aging skin care products using the word mark 'LUMOS'. The defendants launched nail care products under the same mark. Their products were much cheaper than those of the claimant and were aimed at a mass market. The products of both the claimant and defendants reached both professional and retail customers. The defendants' products were advertised, with the word LUMOS, in magazines aimed at the beauty trade and then at a trade fair. A trade customer of the claimant emailed the claimant asking how the products as advertised fitted in with the claimant's other products, the impression being that the customer thought the defendants' products were the claimant's. The claimant received emails from two further trade customers who, while understanding that the defendants' products were not those of the claimant, expressed concerns about the use of the word LUMOS by the defendants. The claimant issued proceedings alleging passing off and seeking an injunction. The judge held that the claimant had proved that it had established a goodwill for its business to which the mark related, and that, if the defendants had represented their products as being those of the claimant, or as being associated with the claimant, then it would have been likely that the claimant would have suffered damage to its reputation. The judge dismissed the claim for lack of evidence of confusion. The claimant appealed. *Held*, Sir Bernard Rix dissenting, the end-users of the claimant's products were relevant as people who might have been affected by any representation made by the defendants. The judge, when asking the question whether relevant persons would have been deceived by the defendants' use of the same mark, had misdirected himself by treating only the claimant's trade customers as the relevant people. In concluding that no-one would think that the defendants' nail care products were associated with the claimant's skincare products, despite the use of the same mark, he had wrongly ignored the evidence that, in some well-known instances, the same brand name was used for both kinds of product. He had also wrongly concluded that the customer's email did not show that she assumed that the defendants' LUMOS products had come from, or were associated with, the claimant, and that he could not have come to that conclusion without having seen her give oral evidence. Further, the judge had been wrong not to draw the inference, from the fact that a person in the trade could express herself in the way she had in the email, that an end-user familiar with the claimant's product who came across the defendants' LUMOS products might well have thought that they came from, or were associated with, the claimant. The evidence had justified the inference that a significant number of the claimant's actual and potential customers would be likely to be misled by the defendants' use of the LUMOS mark into thinking that the defendants' nail care products were products of, or associated with, the claimant. The claimant had made out the necessary elements of the tort of passing off and, accordingly, the appeal would be allowed.

Lumos Skincare Ltd v Sweet Squared Ltd [2013] EWCA Civ 590, [2013] All ER (D) 42 (Jun) (Court of Appeal: Lloyd and McFarlane LJJ and Sir Bernard Rix). *Neutrogena Corpn v Golden Ltd* [1996] RPC 473, CA (1996 Abr para 3138) considered. Decision of Recorder Douglas Campbell [2012] EWPCC 22, [2012] All ER (D) 265 (May) (2012 Abr para 2482) reversed.

2397   Passing off—likelihood of confusion—trade magazine

A dispute arose out of the launch by the defendant of a trade newspaper. The claimant published a magazine with a similar name. It was alleged by the claimant that the defendant was liable for passing off its magazine title and trading name and trade mark infringement in relation to its United Kingdom registered trade mark. The claimant's evidence submitted at the time of the registration of the trade mark contained an error as to the extent of the use of the trade mark, before its registration. In its counterclaim, the defendant sought revocation of the trade mark and a declaration that the registration of the trade mark was invalid. *Held*, to establish passing off, first, a claimant had to establish a goodwill or reputation attached to the goods or services which he supplied in the mind of the purchasing public by association with the identifying 'get-up'. Secondly, he had to demonstrate a misrepresentation by the defendant to the public leading or likely to lead the public to believe that goods or services offered by him were the goods or services of the claimant. Thirdly, he had to demonstrate that he had suffered or was likely to suffer damage by reason of the erroneous belief engendered by the defendant's misrepresentation that the source of the defendant's goods or services was the same as the source of those offered by the claimant. The action was not in confusion but misrepresentation. In the circumstances, the claimant had goodwill and reputation which was vested in its publication. However, the evidence of confusion was of a low level. It was not necessary to consider whether damage had been suffered or whether it was likely to be suffered. There had been no deception. It followed that there was no damage or risk of it. Therefore, the claim in passing off would be dismissed. In relation to trade mark infringement, taking account of all of the relevant factors in the global assessment of the trade mark, the average consumer of publications of the category to which the claimant's publication belonged, including both readers and advertisers, who was reasonably well informed and reasonably observant and circumspect was not likely to be confused by the alleged similarity between the trade mark as presented to the public and the sign. The claim for infringement of trade mark would be dismissed. Further, although the evidence submitted at the time of the registration of the trade mark contained an error as to the extent of the use of the trade mark before its registration, the actual length of use which was in the region of seven or eight years, was sufficient for the purposes of distinctiveness. The distinctiveness, therefore, was attached to features of the masthead itself. The evidence in relation to the reputation and goodwill of the claimant, which was for the most part based on the use of the trade mark, supported that conclusion. That was the case despite the descriptive nature of the title itself. Therefore, the counterclaim had to fail. Judgment would be given accordingly.

Evegate Publishing Ltd v Newsquest Media (Southern) Ltd [2013] EWHC 1975 (Ch), [2013] All ER (D) 132 (Jul) (Chancery Division: Asplin J). Case C-533/06 *o2*

Holdings Ltd v Hutchison 3G UK Ltd [2008] IP & T 1069, ECJ (2008 Abr para 2894); *Reckitt & Colman Products Ltd v Borden Inc* [1990] 1 All ER 873, HL; *Fine & Country Ltd v Okotoks Ltd (formerly Spicerhaart Ltd)* [2013] EWCA Civ 672, [2013] All ER (D) 137 (Jun) (para 2395) applied.

2398 Passing off—likelihood of confusion—unauthorised use of celebrity's image

The claimant was an internationally famous pop star who was regarded as a style icon by many people, especially teenagers and young women. Through her companies, she ran a very large merchandising and indorsement operation. A separate company paid a significant sum for the right to sell the claimant's branded merchandise, including clothing. The defendant, a fashion retailer, began selling a t-shirt with an image of the claimant on it. The defendant had a licence in respect of the image from the photographer who took it, but had no licence from the claimant. The claimant brought an action for passing off, contending that the sale of the t-shirt without her permission infringed her rights. It fell to be determined whether there was a general right of a person, famous or otherwise, to control the reproduction of his image. The defendant submitted that there was nothing on the t-shirt which represented that it was an item of official merchandise and customers did not think that it was. The claimants accepted that, as a general proposition, it was not the case that the presence of an image of her on a product necessarily made a representation that the product had been authorised by her or her companies. However she submitted that, in the particular circumstances of the case, customers would be misled. *Held*, the mere sale by a trader of a t-shirt bearing an image of a famous person was not, without more, an act of passing off. There was no such thing in England as a freestanding general right by a famous person, or anyone else, to control the reproduction of their image. A celebrity might control the distribution of particular images in which he owned the copyright, but that right was specific to the particular photographs in question. If goods were sold in circumstances in which the purchasers understood there to be a representation that the goods were authorised by the claimant or were in that sense 'official' merchandise, but in fact that representation was a false one, then as long as the false representation was operative, passing off could be established. On the evidence, the actions of the defendant constituted passing off. If the claimant was seen to wear or approve of an item of clothing, that was an indorsement of that item in the mind of those people. The public links between the defendant and famous persons in general, and more importantly the links to the claimant in particular, would enhance the likelihood in the purchaser's mind that the garment had been authorised by her. The fact that there was no indication of artist authorisation on the swing tag or neck label was not strong enough to negate the impression that the garment was authorised. A substantial portion of those considering the product would be induced to think it was a garment authorised by the artist. Accordingly, the claim would be allowed.

Fenty v Arcadia Group [2013] EWHC 2310 (Ch), [2013] All ER (D) 410 (Jul) (Chancery Division: Birss J).

2399 Registered design—time limits

See para 2458.

2400 Trade mark—EU trade mark—appeal—procedure—irregularity

Commission Regulation (EC) 216/96 art 1(d)(2) provides that if a case is referred to another Board of Appeal, that Board must not comprise members who were party to the contested decision.

The applicant had filed an application for registration of a Community trade mark at the Office for Harmonisation in the Internal Market (Trade Marks and Designs) ('OHIM'). An intervener filed a notice of opposition against registration on the basis of its earlier trade marks, which was upheld by the Opposition Division. The applicant appealed and, on concluding that there had been a likelihood of confusion on the part of the average consumer, the Second Board of Appeal of OHIM dismissed the appeal. The applicant brought an action for annulment of that decision before the General Court of the European Union, which annulled the decision in part. The case was subsequently remitted to the First Board of Appeal of OHIM. The First Board rejected the application for a Community trade mark in respect of certain goods and dismissed the appeal against the Opposition Division's decision. The applicant then sought annulment of the First Board's decision on the ground that one of its members was a member of the Second Board responsible for the previous decision, contrary to Commission Regulation (EC) 216/96 art 1(d)(2). *Held*, there had been a contravention of art 1(d)(2) in that one of the members of the Second Board at the time of the adoption of the first decision had been a member of the First Board at the time of the adoption of the contested decision. In the light of this irregularity, the contested decision would be annulled.

Case T-106/12 *Cytochroma Development Inc v Office for Harmonisation in the Internal Market* [2013] All ER (D) 113 (Jul) (EGC: Third Chamber).

2401   Trade mark—EU trade mark—distinctive character—descriptive nature of mark

The applicant company filed an application for registration of an EU trade mark at the Office for Harmonisation in the Internal Market under Council Regulation (EC) 207/2009. The mark for which registration was sought was the word mark 'ecoDoor'. The goods in respect of which registration was sought were machines and devices that fell within of the 1957 Nice Agreement concerning the International Classification of Goods and Services for the Purposes of Registration of Marks Classes 7, 9 and 11 as well as the components for those machines and devices. The examiner refused the application for registration for certain of the goods that fell within those classes on the basis that the trade mark applied for was descriptive for the purposes of Regulation art 7(1)(c) and devoid of any distinctive character for the purposes of art 7(1)(b). The applicant unsuccessfully appealed to the Board of Appeal. The Board found that the mark applied for would be perceived by the public as meaning 'a door the construction and mode of operation of which are ecological'. The applicant brought an action before the European General Court seeking annulment of the Board's decision, arguing that the relevant public would not immediately take 'eco' to mean 'environmentally friendly' or 'cost effective in terms of energy'. Secondly, the applicant claimed that the meaning of the mark applied for, perceived overall, was vague. Thirdly, concerning the descriptive character of the mark applied for, the applicant claimed that, as a result of its limitation of the list of goods in the application, the mark no longer covered components of the machines and devices, such as doors, but only the machines and devices themselves. In those circumstances, it was alleged that the mark applied for was not descriptive of the goods which it covered, including the goods in respect of which registration was refused, but at most, of one of their components. *Held*, for a sign to be caught by the prohibition set out in art 7(1)(c) there should be a sufficiently direct and specific link between the sign and those goods or services to enable the public concerned immediately to perceive, without further thought, a description of the goods and services in question or one of their characteristics. The descriptiveness of a trade mark should be assessed, first, by reference to the goods or services in respect of which registration of the sign was sought and, secondly, by reference to the perception of the relevant public, which was composed of the consumers of those goods or services. The Board had been entitled to find that 'eco' would have been perceived by the relevant public as meaning 'ecological' and that 'ecodoor' would be understood immediately by the relevant public to mean 'a door the construction and mode of operation of which are ecological'. The mark applied for was descriptive of an essential characteristic of the goods in respect of which registration had been refused, namely their ecological character. In relation to the submission of vagueness, irrespective of the relevant public's exact interpretation of the mark applied for, it would be perceived as describing directly an essential quality of the goods concerned. Consequently, the Board had rightly held that the mark applied for had been descriptive of the goods in respect of which registration had been refused for the purposes of art 7(1)(c).

Case T-625/11 *BSH Bosch und Siemens Hausgerate GmbH* [2013] All ER (D) 79 (Jan) (EGC: Fourth Chamber).

2402   Trade mark—EU trade mark—identical sign for identical or similar goods— parties sharing use of trade mark—consent

The applicant manufactured small leather goods and the respondent manufactured handbags. Both parties used the same trade mark for their respective goods. The applicant had also been affixing such a mark to other goods. The applicant had a Benelux figurative mark registered and a work sign registered as a Benelux trade mark. The respondent issued proceedings against the applicant, seeking to have the marks declared invalid or a ruling that those marks were valid only with respect to small leather goods. The application was dismissed. The applicant's application for an order to stop the respondents using the signs was also dismissed and the court ordered the applicant not to manufacture or put on the market, under the signs, handbags which were identical or similar to those distributed by the respondent. The court of appeal held that the respondent could not use signs which were identical or similar to the marks for goods other than handbags and shoes, and that the applicant could not use the marks for handbags and shoes. The referring court questioned whether the Court of Appeal, without erring in law, could have deprived the applicant of the possibility of invoking its marks against the respondent and of the possibility of itself using its marks in respect of handbags and shoes. The question was referred to the European Court of Justice. *Held*, Council Directive (EC) 89/104 art 5 precluded a proprietor of a trade mark which, in a situation where there had been shared use with a third party, had consented to the use by that third party of signs which were identical to its marks in respect of certain goods in classes for which those marks were registered and which no longer consented to that use, from being deprived of any possibility of asserting the exclusive right conferred on it by those marks against that third party and of itself exercising that exclusive right in respect of goods which were identical to those of that third party.

Case C-661/11 *Martin Y Paz Diffusion SA v Depuydt* [2013] All ER (D) 208 (Sep) (ECJ: Fourth Chamber).

2403 Trade mark—EU trade mark—infringement—application of mark on labelling or packaging—necessity to re-package or re-label

It has been held, in proceedings concerning parallel imports and re-branding in relation to a pharmaceutical product, that the test to be applied was quite clear after the decision in *Boehringer*. It was settled law that it was for the national courts to examine whether the circumstances prevailing at the time of marketing made it objectively necessary to replace an original trade mark with that of the importing member state in order that the product in question could be placed on the market in that state by the parallel importer. That condition of necessity was satisfied if, in a specific case, the prohibition imposed on the importer against replacing the trade mark hindered effective access to the markets of the importing member states. Replacement packaging of pharmaceutical products was objectively necessary within the meaning of the case-law if, without such re-packaging, effective access to the market concerned, or to a substantial part of that market, was considered to be hindered as the result of strong resistance from a significant proportion of consumers to re-labelled pharmaceutical products. The question in relation to re-packaging was whether there was effective access to the market concerned or a substantial part of that market. The question remained whether, in all the circumstances prevailing at the time of marketing, it was objectively necessary to replace the original trade mark with that used in the importing member state, in order to gain effective access to the relevant market in the United Kingdom.

Speciality European Pharma Ltd v Doncaster Pharmaceuticals Group Ltd [2013] EWHC 3624 (Ch), [2013] All ER (D) 291 (Nov) (Chancery Division: Asplin J). Case C-379/97 *Pharmacia and Upjohn SA (formerly Upjohn SA) v Paranova A/S* [1999] All ER (EC) 880, ECJ; and *Boehringer Ingelheim KG v Swingward Ltd* [2008] EWCA Civ 83, [2008] IP & T 842 (2008 Abr para 2889) applied.

2404 Trade mark—EU trade mark—infringement—counterclaim for partial revocation—lack of genuine use

It has been held, on a counterclaim in trade mark infringement proceedings for partial revocation of the EU trade mark concerned for lack of genuine use, that (1) genuine use means actual use of the mark by the proprietor or a third party with authority to use the mark; (2) the use must be more than merely token; (3) the use must be consistent with the essential function of a trade mark; (4) the use must be by way of real commercial exploitation of the mark on the market for the relevant goods or services; (5) all the relevant facts and circumstances must be taken into account in determining whether there is real commercial exploitation of the mark; (6) use of the mark does not need always to be quantitatively significant for it to be deemed genuine; (7) the tribunal's first task is to find as a fact in relation to what goods or services there has been genuine use of the trade mark during the relevant period; (8) the tribunal must arrive at a fair specification having regard to the use made; (9) in arriving at a fair specification, the tribunal is not constrained by the existing working of the specification of goods or services and it should strike a balance between the respective interests of the proprietor, other traders and the public, having regard to the protection afforded by a registered trade mark; (10) in order to decide what a fair specification is, the tribunal should inform itself about the relevant trade and then decide how the average consumer would fairly describe the goods or services in relation to which the trade mark has been used; (11) in deciding what a fair description is, the average consumer must be taken to know the purpose of the description; (12) what is a fair description depends on the nature of the goods, the circumstances of the trade and the breadth of use proved; and (13) the exercise of framing a fair specification is a value judgment.

Stichting BDO v BDO Unibank Inc [2013] EWHC 418 (Ch), [2013] All ER (D) 39 (Mar) (Chancery Division: Arnold J).

2405   Trade mark—EU trade mark—infringement—damages for infringement

The claimant, a Gibraltar-registered company, operated an on-line casino under the brand '32Red' and was the registered owner of EU trade marks for the word '32Red' and for a device consisting of a stylisation of '32Red' in a roulette ball. The defendants acquired a domain name '32Vegas' and any associated marks, whether registered or unregistered. The claimant successfully brought proceedings against the defendants for infringement of its trade mark and the court considered questions relating to the 'user principle' for assessing damages: firstly, the importance of the specific characteristics and circumstances of the parties and, second, how far was it appropriate to have regard to alternative courses of action which would have been available to the parties at the date of the hypothetical negotiation. *Held*, the parties should be taken to have been willing to make a deal even if one or both of them would not in reality have been prepared to do so and it should be assumed that the parties would have acted reasonably. A defendant's financial circumstances were not material as such and particular character traits of the parties could be disregarded. The courts did have regard to the circumstances in which the individual parties were placed at the time of the hypothetical negotiation. The availability of a non-infringing alternative was a relevant factor in the calculation of a reasonable royalty for the claimant. If the parties could be expected to have taken such an alternative into account in their hypothetical negotiation, the court had to do so as well. An alternative did not need to have had all the attributes of the '32Vegas' name to be relevant. What mattered was what impact the possibility of rebranding would have had on the hypothetical negotiation, not whether a substitute mark would have shared the attributes of '32Vegas'. Damages for infringement were assessed in three main ways. First, if the claimant exploited the invention by manufacturing and selling goods at a profit, and the effect of the infringement had been to divert sales to the defendant, the measure of damages would normally be the profit which would have been realised by the owner of the patent if the sales had been made by him. Second, if the claimant exploited his patent by granting licences in return for royalty payments, the measure of damages the defendant had to pay would be the sums which he would have paid by way of royalty if, instead of acting illegally, he had acted legally. Third, where it was not possible to prove either that there was a normal rate of profit or a normal royalty, damages fell to be assessed by considering what price could reasonably have been charged for permission to carry out the infringing acts. On the facts, damages would be assessed in accordance with the amount that the licence fee would have been. Judgment would be given accordingly.

32Red plc v WHG (International) Ltd [2013] EWHC 815 (Ch), [2013] All ER (D) 93 (Apr) (Chancery Division: Newey J).

2406   Trade mark—EU trade mark—infringement—internet search engine—keyword advertising—keyword identical with trade mark

The claimant operated the best-known flower delivery network in the United Kingdom and owned registered trade marks associated with its name. The defendant was a well-known retailer. Both parties operated internet websites which took orders for the delivery of flowers. The defendant paid a search engine to display advertisements for its flower delivery service on the search engine results page when a user searched for names associated with the claimant. A question arose as to whether the defendant thereby infringed the claimant's trade mark. *Held*, applying settled law, the defendant had infringed the trade marks under

Council Directive (EEC) 89/104 art 5(1) and Council Regulation (EC) 40/94 (on the Community trade mark) art 9(1)(a). Three particular factors had to be considered. The first factor was whether the reasonably well-informed and reasonably observant internet user was deemed to be aware, on the basis of his general knowledge of the market, that the defendant's flower delivery service was not part of the claimant's network, but was in competition with it. That was not generally known at the relevant time. The second factor was whether the defendant's advertisements enabled the reasonably well-informed and reasonably observant internet user to tell that the defendant's flower delivery service was not part of the claimants' network. They did not do so. There was nothing in any of the defendant's advertisements in issue to inform the reader that the defendant's flower delivery service was not part of the claimant's network. The third factor to be considered was the nature of the claimant's network. The nature of the claimant's network might make it particularly difficult for the reasonably well-informed and reasonably observant internet user to determine, in the absence of any indication in the advertisement, whether the defendant's service was part of the network. It was a feature of the claimant's network that a member traded under its own name. In addition, the claimant had commercial tie-ups with several large retailers. That made it all the more plausible that there should be a connection between the defendant's flower delivery service and the claimant's network. The use of signs adversely affected the origin function of the trade marks if they did not enable reasonably well-informed and reasonably observant internet users, or enable them only with difficultly, to ascertain whether the defendant's flower delivery service originated from the claimant, or an undertaking economically connected with the claimant, or originated from a third party. The defendant's advertisements did not enable reasonably well-informed and reasonably attentive internet users, or enabled them only with difficulty, to ascertain whether the service referred to originated from the proprietor of the trade marks, or an undertaking economically connected with it, or originated from a third party. It followed that the defendant's use of the signs had an adverse effect of the origin function of the trade marks. Judgment would be given accordingly.

Interflora Inc v Marks and Spencer plc [2013] EWHC 1291 (Ch), [2013] IP & T 931 (Chancery Division: Arnold J). For related proceedings see Case C-323/09 *Interflora Inc v Marks and Spencer plc* [2013] All ER (EC) 519, ECJ (2011 Abr para 2381).

2407   Trade mark—EU trade mark—infringement—likelihood of confusion—distinctive character—television service

The claimant registered the word 'NOW' as an EU trade mark and used it in connection with a television service in Hong Kong. The defendant intended to launch a new television service in the United Kingdom under the name 'NOW TV'. Following the launch of that service, the claimant brought proceedings against the defendant alleging that the use of the chosen name infringed its trade mark. The judge dismissed the claim and found that the mark was invalid on the ground that, in relation to a television service, it designated a characteristic of the service. *Held*, the mark 'NOW' was devoid of distinctive character that served to identify the claimant's service and to distinguish it from the service offered by other undertakings. The fact that there were other instances in which the word 'now' was distinctive of a service or a product did not assist the court in deciding its character in the present case. Context was not everything, but it counted in determining whether a word was being used in a distinctive way or in a descriptive way. For reasons inseparable from perceived commercial advantage, the claimant chose as its trade mark a commonplace, easily understood, ordinary English word, which was also used by other undertakings in relation to other products or services. It must have been obvious to the claimant that, in making that choice, it was running the risk of invalidating the mark on the ground that the message conveyed by the everyday word to the average consumer designated a characteristic of its service. The characteristic of the claimant's service that was likely to attract the average consumer was the offer of something new and different. The essential appeal of the service was that programmes of choice were available on demand, without waiting for the arrival of the scheduled time set by someone else for the broadcast of a programme. That 'nowness' was not a characteristic possessed by an ordinary television service broadcasting scheduled programmes at pre-set times. The judge's assessment that, when viewed from the position of the hypothetical average consumer of the claimant's service, the mark 'NOW' would be understood as designating the attractive immediate characteristic of the service for which it was registered was correct. Accordingly, the appeal would be dismissed.

Starbucks (HK) Ltd v British Sky Broadcasting Group plc (No 2) [2013] EWCA Civ 1465, [2014] IP & T 128, [2013] All ER (D) 214 (Nov) (Court of Appeal: Patten and Pitchford LJJ and Sir John Mummery). Decision of Arnold J [2012] EWHC 3074 (Ch), [2013] IP & T 251 (2012 Abr para 2487) affirmed.

2408   Trade mark—EU trade mark—infringement—likelihood of confusion—use of colour

The defendant company, which owned a chain of supermarkets, decided to sell optical products. It launched an advertising campaign using the slogans 'Be a real spec saver at Asda' and 'Spec savings at ASDA', and two logos. The claimant, which operated the largest chain of opticians in the United Kingdom, brought proceedings against the defendant alleging that the slogans and logos infringed its trade marks in the word 'Specsavers' and figurative marks in shaded and wordless logos. The court dismissed the application, but that decision was largely overturned on appeal. In the course of those proceedings, the appellate court decided that, in order to rule on the aspect of the dispute concerning the wordless logo mark, it was necessary for it to refer to the European Court of Justice for a preliminary ruling the questions of whether Council Regulation (EC) 207/2009 art 9(1)(b), (c) should be interpreted as meaning that (1) where an EU trade mark was not registered in colour, but the proprietor had used it extensively in a particular colour or combination of colours so that it had become associated in the mind of a significant portion of the public with that colour or combination of colours, the colour or colours which a third party used in order to represent a sign alleged to infringe that trade mark were relevant in the global assessment of the likelihood of confusion or unfair advantage under those provisions; and (2) the fact that the third party making use of a sign which allegedly infringed the registered trade mark was itself associated, in the mind of a significant portion of the public, with the colour or particular combination of colours which it used for the representation of that sign was relevant to the global assessment of the likelihood of confusion and unfair advantage for the purposes of that provision. *Held*, the fact that the defendant used a colour similar to that used by the claimant with the intention of taking advantage of the distinctive character and reputation of the claimant's trade marks was a factor which should be taken into account in order to ascertain whether it could be held that unfair advantage was being taken of the distinctive character or reputation of the trade mark. It followed that the first question should be answered in the affirmative. With regard to the second question, the global assessment should take account of the precise context in which the sign which was allegedly similar to the registered trade mark had been used. In those circumstances, the fact that the third party making use of a sign which had allegedly infringed the registered trade mark was itself associated, in the mind of a significant portion of the public, with the colour or particular combination of colours which it used for the representation of that sign was a factor which, among others, might have a certain importance while determining the existence of a likelihood of confusion or unfair advantage under art 9(1)(b) or (c). The fact that the defendant was itself associated with the colour green, which it used for the signs alleged to infringe the trade marks of the claimant, could result in a reduction of the likelihood of confusion or association between those signs and the trade marks of the defendant, to the extent that the relevant public could perceive that the colour green of those signs was that of the defendant, a matter which was to be determined by the referring court.

Case C-252/12 *Specsavers International Healthcare Ltd v Asda Stores Ltd* [2013] All ER (D) 355 (Jul) (ECJ: Third Chamber).

2409   Trade mark—EU trade mark—infringement—name—gambling company

The claimant company was registered in Monaco and carried out business there. It was the owner of a casino. Its business also extended to the ownership of hotels and the provision of a range of leisure services, which it had done for many years. It owned a number of trade marks, including a Community trade mark for the words 'MONTE-CARLO' covering computer programs, software, playing cards and other gambling apparatus, and an international trade mark, for the words 'CASINO DE MONTE-CARLO' and covering software, gambling paraphernalia, online registration services for casino gambling and the provision of gambling facilities. The defendant company traded under the name 'Monte Carlo Casino Entertainment'. It provided tables and croupiers for playing 'fun' casino games at weddings and other events. No real gambling took place at its events. It did not have premises where games could be played. The claimant brought proceedings, contending that the defendant's name infringed its registered marks and amounted to passing off. The defendant counterclaimed. *Held*, the average consumer for the defendant's services would be any member of the general public in the United Kingdom who wished to organise entertainment for an event of some description. On the evidence, the services offered by the defendant were identical to services offered by the claimant, and the defendant's signs were quite similar to those of the claimant. The amount of attention that the average user of the defendant's services would give to the defendant was quite high, partly because of the price charged, but also because the defendant's services would be normally booked for a one-off event. The consumer would be likely to exercise a good deal of care in choosing the defendant, and would pay a higher level of attention than usual to the transaction. That would help to distinguish the defendant from the claimant. Further, there was no evidence of confusion before the court. Despite the notional identity or similarity of the services, the full circumstances of use would preclude any likelihood of confusion. There was no likelihood of confusion on the part of the average consumer in the sense that there was a risk that the public might believe that the services came from the same undertaking or one economically linked to the mark's proprietor. The claim under Council Regulation (EC) 207/2009 art 9(1)(b) would be dismissed. In order for infringement to be found, the trade mark had to have a reputation in the relevant territory. On the evidence, there was no reputation in the Monte-Carlo mark. However, there was reputation in the Casino de Monte-Carlo mark, in that it had a reputation regarding gambling services in a significant part of the public having an interest in such services. It was possible that the mark would be called to mind by the defendant's signs. However, there was no likelihood of confusion for art 9(1)(b), and no misrepresentation made by the defendant's use of its signs. Its use did not cause dilution or tarnishment or adversely affect the function of the mark. In the circumstances, even if there was a possibility of detriment, the defendant's use was not without due cause. The claim under art 9(1)(c) would fail. Judgment would be given accordingly.

Société Anonyme des Bains de Mer et du Cercle des Etrangers à Monaco v Anglofile International Ltd t/a Monte Carlo Entertainment [2013] EWPCC 38, [2013] All ER (D) 89 (Sep) (Patents County Court: Recorder Amanda Michaels).

2410   Trade mark—EU trade mark—opposition to registration—genuine use

The applicant company, established in the United Kingdom, was granted registration of a figurative Community trade mark 'Al bustan'. An intervener company filed an application with the Office for Harmonisation in the Internal Market for a declaration of invalidity in respect of the mark 'Al bustan' based on a figurative mark 'ALBUSTAN', which was covered by an earlier Greek registration. The Cancellation Division granted the application for a declaration of invalidity in respect of the part of the goods covered by the contested mark. The applicant appealed, disputing the proof of use of the earlier mark and the similarity of the trade marks at issue. The appeal was dismissed, the Second Board of Appeal concluding that genuine use of the earlier mark had been proven for part of the goods covered by the mark but not for others, and that there was a likelihood of confusion for all the goods in respect of which the Cancellation Division had granted the application for a declaration of invalidity. The applicant commenced proceedings, seeking annulment of the contested decision on the basis that the evidence submitted by the intervener company had not been sufficient to establish genuine use of the earlier trade mark. *Held*, in the assessment of whether use of a trade mark was genuine, regard should be had to all the facts and circumstances relevant to establishing whether the commercial exploitation of the mark was real, particularly whether such use was viewed as warranted in the economic sector concerned in order to maintain or create a share in the market for the goods or services protected by the mark, the nature of those goods or services, the characteristics of the market and the scale and frequency of use of the mark. As to the extent of the use to which the earlier trade mark had been put, account should be taken, in particular, of the commercial volume of the overall use, as well as the length of the period during which the mark had been used and the frequency of use. The intervener company provided a number of third party documents, such as certificates of origin or shipment records, as well as invoices, on the basis of which it had been possible to establish the sale of a significant quantity of cans bearing the 'ALBUSTAN' trade mark. Consequently, the evidence produced had been sufficient to establish the extent of use of the earlier mark. It followed that the applicant failed to establish that the evidence submitted by the intervener company had been insufficient for the purpose of demonstrating genuine use of the earlier mark. Accordingly, the appeal would be dismissed.

Case T-454/11 *Luna International Ltd v Office for Harmonisation in the Internal Market (Trade Marks and Designs)* [2013] All ER (D) 180 (Apr) (EGC: Seventh Chamber). Case C-40/01 *Ansul BV v Ajax Brandbeveiliging BV* [2005] Ch 97, [2003] IP & T 970, ECJ; Case T-325/06 *Boston Scientific Ltd v Office for Harmonisation in the Internal Market (Trade Marks and Designs)* [2008] All ER (D) 52 (Sep), CFI; and Cases T-493/07, T-26/08 and T-27/08 *GlaxoSmithKline SpA v Office for Harmonisation in the Internal Market (Trade Marks and Designs)* [2009] All ER (D) 145 (Sep), CFI, considered.

2411   Trade mark—EU trade mark—registration—distinctive character

The applicant filed an application under Council Regulation (EC) 207/2009 for registration of an EU trade mark in relation to the word mark 'CONTINENTAL'. The goods and services in respect of which registration was sought related to the keeping and breeding of dogs. An examiner of the defendant regulatory body refused registration. The applicant's appeal against that decision was dismissed on the ground that the word mark was, for the goods and services claimed, descriptive within the meaning of art 7(1)(c), as well as devoid of any distinctive character within the meaning of art 7(1)(b). The applicant applied to the General Court of the European Union seeking an annulment of that decision. *Held*, authority established that it was enough for a word sign to designate a characteristic of the goods or services concerned in at least one of its potential meanings in order for it to be refused registration under art 7(1)(c). It followed that the defendant had not erred in finding that the trade mark applied for was directly understood by the relevant public as a description of a breed of bulldogs or, in relation to the services targeted, as a specification in so far as it concerned dogs of that same breed. The applicant's other claims did nothing to invalidate that conclusion. It followed that the defendant had not erred in finding that the word 'continental' had been descriptive of the goods and services at issue within the meaning of art 7(1)(c). Since art 9(1) made it clear that it was sufficient that one of the absolute grounds for refusal listed in that provision applied for the sign at issue not to be registrable as an EU trade mark, it was no longer necessary to consider the second plea raised alleging breach of art 7(1)(b). Accordingly, the application would be dismissed.

Case T-383/10 *Continental Bulldog Club Deutschland eV v Office for Harmonisation in the Internal Market (Trade Marks and Designs)* (OHIM) [2013] All ER (D) 03 (May) (EGC: Second Chamber).

2412   Trade mark—EU trade mark—registration—distinctive character—colour mark

The intervener company filed an application for registration of a Community trade mark with the Office for Harmonisation in the Internal Market under Council Regulation (EC) 207/2009 (on the Community trade mark). The contested mark was identified in the application as a colour mark and a description of the colours applied for had been provided by means of a colour code. The applicant company filed an application for a declaration of invalidity against the contested mark on the basis of art 52(1)(a), (b). The application was granted on the basis of art 7(1)(b), and the intervener company successfully appealed to the appellate board, which held that the contested mark was composed of a figurative sign consisting of a two-dimensional shape made up of colours, not a colour mark, and that it was of sufficiently distinctive character. The applicant brought proceedings seeking an annulment of the contested decision, contending that the board had been wrong to re-categorise the contested mark as a figurative mark and, in consequence, its assessment of the distinctive character of the contested mark had also been incorrect. *Held*, in order to constitute a trade mark, colours or colour combinations had to satisfy three conditions. First, they should be a sign. Secondly, that sign had to be capable of graphic representation. Thirdly, the sign had to be capable of distinguishing the goods or services of one undertaking from those of other undertakings. As regards the question whether colours or combinations of colours were capable of distinguishing the goods or services of one undertaking from those of other undertakings, it had to be determined whether those colours or combinations of colours were capable of conveying specific information, particularly as regards the origin of a product or service. In that regard, while colours were capable of conveying certain associations of ideas, and of arousing feelings, they possessed little inherent capacity for communicating specific information. Save in exceptional cases, colours did not initially have a distinctive character, but might be capable of acquiring such character as the result of the use made of them in relation to the goods or services covered by the Community trade mark application. Further, in assessing the potential distinctiveness of a given colour or combination of colours as a trade mark, regard had to be had to the general interest in not unduly restricting the availability of colours for the other traders who offered for sale goods or services of the same type as those in respect of which registration was sought. The board had made an error of assessment by finding that the contested mark had not been a colour mark but rather a two-dimensional figurative mark made up of colours. It followed that the board's decision had been based on a mistaken perception of the nature and characteristics of the mark at issue, which was sufficient to vitiate the entirety of the assessment. Accordingly, the application would be allowed.

Case T-245/12 *Gamesa Eólica SL v Office for Harmonisation in the Internal Market* (*Trade Marks and Designs*) [2014] IP & T 286 (EGC: Fourth Chamber).

2413   Trade mark—EU trade mark—registration—distinctive character—commercial
        origin of goods

The applicant company filed an application for registration of a Community trade mark for the wordmark 'INNOVATION FOR THE REAL WORLD' with the Office for Harmonisation in the Internal Market ('OHIM') pursuant to Council Regulation (EC) 40/94 (on the Community trade mark). Objections to the registrability of the mark were raised by the OHIM's examiner. In response, the applicant submitted that the mark applied for had been inherently distinctive, on the ground that the word 'WORLD' was a vague term, that the expression 'REAL WORLD' was not distinctive, promotional or laudatory, and that several similar marks had already been registered. Pursuant to Regulation 40/94 arts 7(1)(b), (2), the examiner refused to register the mark on the ground that it was devoid of distinctive character. The applicant's appeal was dismissed on the ground that the mark applied for was not an indication of the commercial origin of the goods concerned. Nothing in the expression 'innovation for the real world', beyond its promotional meaning, would enable the relevant public to memorise the mark applied for easily and instantly as a distinctive mark. In that regard, the appellate board pointed out that the mark applied for was not a play on words and was not imaginative, surprising or unexpected. The applicant sought annulment of the board's decision. *Held*, for a mark to possess distinctive character within the meaning of art 7(1)(b), it had to serve to identify the goods in respect of which registration was applied for as originating from a particular undertaking, and thus to distinguish those goods from those of other undertakings in order to enable the consumer who acquired the goods to repeat the experience, if it proved to be positive, or to avoid it, if it proved to be negative, on the occasion of a subsequent acquisition. The distinctive character of a mark had to be assessed, first, by reference to the goods or services in respect of which registration had been applied for and, second, by reference to the perception which the relevant public had of those goods or services. With respect to the determination of the relevant public, the goods were everyday consumer goods for which the relevant public was the average reasonably well-informed and circumspect consumer. Further, the board had been justified in finding that, in respect of the goods at issue the relevant public would perceive the sign 'innovation for the real world', directly and without further consideration, as an allusion to innovative goods and not as an indication of the commercial origin of those goods. The registration of the mark applied for had been caught by the ground of refusal set out in art 7(1)(b). The board had been correct in finding that the registration of the mark applied for in respect of the goods at issue had been incompatible with Regulation 40/94, and that the applicant could not usefully rely on earlier decisions of OHIM to undermine that finding.

Case T-515/11 *Delphi Technologies Inc v Office for Harmonisation in the Internal Market* (*Trade Marks and Designs*) (*OHIM*) [2013] All ER (D) 89 (Nov) (EGC: Sixth Chamber).

Council Regulation (EC) 40/94 replaced by Council Regulation (EC) 207/2009.

2414   Trade mark—EU trade mark—registration—distinctive character—descriptive nature of mark

The applicant sought registration of an EU trade mark in respect of the word sign 'fluege.de' in relation to travel services. The application was refused on the ground that, pursuant to Council Regulation (EC) 207/2009 art 7(1)(b), (c), (2), the mark was descriptive and devoid of any distinctive character. In an action challenging the refusal, the applicant submitted that (1) the term 'fluege' was a verbal composition alien to the German language, the latter featuring only the word 'flüge', in which the letter 'ü' appeared, with the result that, by reason of the unusual spelling of the term 'fluege', the average consumer would identify an indication of commercial origin in the trade mark; and (2) in view of the unusual nature of the term 'fluege' in German and of the particular attention paid by the relevant public as a result of the unique character of the registration of an internet domain, the trade mark had the minimum distinctive character required to justify its registration. *Held*, (1) for a sign to be caught by the prohibition in Regulation 207/2009 art 7(1)(c) there had to be a sufficiently direct and specific relationship between the sign and the goods or services in question to enable the public concerned immediately to perceive, without further thought, a description of the goods or services in question or one of their characteristics. Further, a sign's descriptive nature could only be assessed by reference to the way in which it was understood by the relevant public and to the goods or services concerned. The present trade mark might have been perceived spontaneously by the relevant public as a domain name referring to the address of an internet page in the aviation and air-travel field, and conveyed to the relevant public clear and direct information as to the nature of the services at issue, and it was by virtue of that fact descriptive of those services. (2) In relation to art 7(1)(b), the overlap between the absolute grounds for refusal implied that a word mark which was descriptive of characteristics of goods or services might, on that account, be devoid of any distinctive character in relation to those goods or services, without prejudice to other reasons why it might be devoid of distinctive character. The trade mark was descriptive with regard to the services at issue. The fact of joining a descriptive term devoid of distinctive character to a dot and a group of letters corresponding to a top-level domain did not confer on the resulting sign, which was then readily identifiable by the relevant public as a domain name referring to an internet address, a distinctive character. Accordingly, the action would be dismissed.

Case T-244/12 *Unister GmbH v Office for Harmonisation in the Internal Market (Trade Marks and Designs) (OHIM)* [2013] All ER (D) 185 (May) (EGC: Second Chamber).

2415   Trade mark—EU trade mark—registration—distinctive character—invalidity

The applicant filed an application for registration of a EU trade mark pursuant to Council Regulation (EC) 40/94 on the European Union trade mark. The sign was registered as a European Union trade mark. The intervener company filed a request for a declaration of invalidity of the sign on the grounds that it had been registered in breach of art 7(1)(b), (c). The Office for Harmonisation in the Internal Market Cancellation Division rejected the application for a declaration of invalidity. It found that the sign, taken as a whole, was neither descriptive nor devoid of any distinctive character. The First Board of Appeal upheld the intervener's appeal, annulled the Cancellation Division's decision and declared the EU trade mark invalid on the bases that it was descriptive for the purposes of art 7(1)(c) as well as devoid of distinctive character for the purposes of art 7(1)(b). The applicant applied for the annulment of the board's decision. *Held*, for a sign to be caught by the prohibition set out in s 7(1)(c), there should be a sufficiently direct and specific relationship between the sign and the goods or services in question to enable the public concerned immediately to perceive, without further thought, a description of the goods and services in question or one of their characteristics. Since the smooth movement of an iron across clothes, which resulted from the steam, corresponded to what the consumer might expect from a product of that type, the description of that movement by the word in question did not conjure up an image of hovering but was clearly descriptive of a very real characteristic of the goods in issue. Therefore, each of the words of which the expression 'steam glide' was composed, taken in isolation, was descriptive of a characteristic of the goods. Further, from the point of view of syntax, there was nothing unusual in English about the combination of the words 'steam' and 'glide' in the expression 'steam glide'. It followed that the two complaints forming the first part of the first plea were without substance. Further, for the purposes of art 7(1)(c) it was necessary only to consider, on the basis of the relevant meaning of the sign, whether, from the viewpoint of the target public, there was a sufficiently direct and specific relationship between the sign and the goods for which registration was sought. Therefore, the second part of the first plea would be rejected as unfounded. Furthermore, in rejecting the first plea in law put forward, the court had confirmed the board's finding that the absolute ground for refusal set out in art 7(1)(c) had applied. That being so, it did not appear necessary to rule on the plea for annulment, in order to give a decision on the substance of the action. In those circumstances, the second plea appeared to be manifestly unfounded. Accordingly, the application would be dismissed.

Case T-544/11 *Spectrum Brands (UK) Ltd v Office for Harmonisation in the Internal Market (Trade Marks and Designs)* [2013] All ER (D) 156 (Jan) (EGC: Second Chamber).

2416   Trade mark—EU trade mark—registration—distinctive character—lack of distinctive character

The applicant company sought registration of the word sign 'ECO PRO' pursuant to Council Regulation (EC) 207/2009 in relation to goods which fell within the Nice Agreement concerning the International Classification of Goods and Services for the Purposes of the Registration of Marks Class 9 (electric and electronic apparatus for controlling, indicating, accumulating and regulating, data processing apparatus and computers) and Class 12 (motor vehicles and parts thereof). The Office for Harmonisation in the Internal Market (Trade Marks and Designs) refused the application on the ground that the sign was devoid of distinctive character in relation to the goods concerned. On appeal, the Board of Appeal considered that the sign ECO PRO might describe a variety of goods, environmentally friendly and designed for professional use, the relevant consumer not perceiving it as an indicator of commercial origin. The Board therefore concluded that the sign was devoid of any distinctive character within the meaning of the Regulation art 7(1)(b) and dismissed the appeal. The applicant brought proceedings seeking the annulment of that decision. *Held*, art 7(1)(b) prevented the registration of marks which were regarded as incapable of performing the essential function of a trade mark, which was of identifying the commercial origin of the goods or services at issue. The distinctive character of a sign should be assessed, first, by reference to the goods or services in respect of which the application for registration had been made and, second, by reference to the relevant public's perception of the sign. A mark would not meet the conditions laid down by art 7(1)(b) if the relevant public perceived a sign as providing details of the type of goods but not as indicating the origin of those goods. What had to be determined was whether the association established by the Board between the semantic content of the sign for which registration had been sought, on the one hand, and the goods in question, on the other, was sufficiently concrete and direct to prove that that sign enabled the relevant public to identify certain characteristics of those goods immediately. The relevant public would perceive the semantic content of that sign as providing information on certain characteristics of the goods concerned and not as indicating their origin. Accordingly, the sign ECO PRO was necessarily devoid of any distinctive character with regard to those goods. Further, neither the sign ECO PRO nor the elements of which it consisted would be perceived by the relevant public as an indication of the commercial origin of the goods at issue. The fact that the sign ECO PRO might have meanings other than that of 'ecological professional' or 'ecological supporting', as the applicant claimed, did not preclude the application of the absolute ground for refusal provided for in art 7(1)(b). A word sign should be refused registration under that provision if at least one of its possible meanings designated a characteristic of the goods or services concerned. Accordingly, the action would be dismissed.

Case T-145/12 *Bayerische Motoren Werke AG v Office for Harmonisation in the Internal Market (Trade Marks and Designs)* [2013] All ER (D) 73 (May) (EGC: Sixth Chamber).

2417   Trade mark—EU trade mark—registration—distinctive character—relationship between mark and associated goods

The applicant company applied to the defendant to have the word sign 'CARBON GREEN' registered as an EU trade mark. An examiner found that the impact of the mark on the relevant public was primarily descriptive, with the result that its trade origin might not be perceived by the public. The examiner therefore concluded that the mark applied for was devoid of any distinctive character within the meaning of Council Regulation

(EC) 207/2009 art 7(1)(b). The applicant appealed to the defendant's Board of Appeal against the examiner's refusal to register the mark. The Board dismissed the appeal, ruling that, in the light of the technical nature of the goods concerned, the relevant public consisted of specialised English-speaking consumers, and that the individual words 'carbon' and 'green', as well as the sign CARBON GREEN as a whole, were descriptive of the goods in question, which were goods manufactured from carbon obtained in an environmentally friendly manner. According to the Board, the sign at issue was made up of standard words which were not capable of indicating the trade origin of the mark to the relevant public, with the result that the mark applied for was devoid of distinctive character in respect of the goods concerned. The applicant brought proceedings seeking annulment of that decision, submitting that (1) the Board had failed to assess the relationship between the word 'carbon' and the goods covered by the application; (2) the Board had not based its assessment of the descriptive character of the mark applied for on any evidence; and (3) while the Board had been obliged to take account of the public interest in descriptive signs being freely used by all, it should have analysed the sector in question so as to establish the likelihood of other traders wanting to use the sign in the future. *Held*, the Board had assessed the relationship between the word 'carbon' and the goods at issue by maintaining that that word on its own had a sufficiently immediate and direct link with those goods. The Board had therefore been correct to consider that the word 'carbon' should be considered, from the point of view of the relevant public, as descriptive of a characteristic of the goods concerned. Moreover, it was settled law that the registrability of a sign as an EU trade mark should be assessed only on the basis of the relevant EU legislation. The Board had applied the descriptiveness test and the case law relating thereto to reach the conclusion that the sign CARBON GREEN had a direct and specific relationship with the goods concerned without any evidence being necessary for that purpose. In terms of the third of the applicant's contentions, in the context of the application of art 7(1)(c), it should be determined whether a descriptive sign was currently associated in the mind of the relevant class of persons with the category of goods concerned, or whether it was reasonable to assume that such an association might be established in the future. It was quite reasonable to envisage that the sign CARBON GREEN might, in future, be associated in the mind of the relevant class of persons with similar goods. Indeed, the direct and specific relationship with the goods concerned had been established, so that the relevant public might immediately perceive, without further thought, a description of the characteristics of those goods. The Board had therefore not erred in its assessment. Accordingly, the application would be dismissed.

Case T-294/10 *CBp Carbon Industries Inc v Office for Harmonisation in the Internal Market (Trade Marks and Designs) (OHIM)* [2013] All ER (D) 100 (Apr) (EGC: Fifth Chamber).

2418   Trade mark—EU trade mark—registration—distinctive character—relevant
        consumers—comprehension of word signs in various member states

The applicant company filed applications for registration of the word signs 'méditation transcendantale' and 'transcendantal meditation' as EU trade marks. The examiner rejected the applications on the basis that under Council Regulation (EC) 207/2009 art 7(1)(b) the marks were devoid of any distinctive character and under art 7(1)(c) they were descriptive of the goods and services in question, and that art 7(1)(b) and (c) could not be disapplied pursuant to art 7(3) because the applicant had failed to establish that the marks had acquired distinctive character through use in the part of the European Union where they lacked such character. The relevant member states considered were Belgium and France in respect of the first mark and Ireland, Malta and the United Kingdom in respect of the second mark. The applicant appealed to the Second Board of Appeal of the Office for Harmonisation in the Internal Market (Trade Marks and Designs) ('the Board'). The Board affirmed the decision that the marks lacked distinctive character and were descriptive. The Board considered the examiner's conclusion that the marks had not acquired distinctive character through use pursuant to art 7(3). It found that in considering the relevant consumers, the examiner had erroneously restricted the relevant territory to France and Belgium, in respect of the first mark, and Ireland, Malta and the United Kingdom, in respect of the second mark. This was because the words 'méditation' and 'transcendantale' were words with a Latin origin present in almost all languages of the EU, in identical or very close terms which would allow the public to recognise them, and because basic English could be understood in a number of countries where English was not the native language. On the facts, the relevant consumers were the general public in all countries except Bulgaria and Greece. The Board therefore remitted the case for further prosecution. The applicant sought annulment of the Board's decision. *Held*, although in certain languages adjectives generally preceded the noun and in others it was the other way around, the public in the relevant member states, and particularly the public in romance language countries, was accustomed to inversion of the normal syntax of words, for rhetorical, poetic or other purposes. The inversion observed in certain languages, compared with the normal position of the words 'méditation' and 'transcendantale' in French, and the words 'transcendental' and 'meditation' in English, was therefore not such as to hinder comprehension of the expression in question by the relevant public of the member states concerned. Further, while there were certain differences, both visually and with regard to pronunciation, between the words translated into the various languages referred to, those differences did not outweigh the fact that they had a common Latin stem. Consequently, the information contained in the signs applied for would be understood not only by a consumer who spoke French or English, but consumers in almost all members states, because of the closeness of those signs to the equivalent words in their national language. Also, there were a number of countries where English was not the native language but where there was a basic understanding of the language by the general public. The sign applied for conveyed a message which was immediately understandable and which could serve to indicate the subject-matter or purpose, and therefore the characteristics of the goods and services for which registration had been sought. It followed that the Board had correctly concluded that the word sign applied for was descriptive within the meaning of art 7(1)(c) with regard to the goods and services at issue. In the light of the rejection of the plea in respect of art 7(1)(c), it was unnecessary to examine the plea alleging infringement of art 7(1)(b). Accordingly, the action would be dismissed.

Cases T-412/11, 426/11 *Maharishi Foundation Ltd v Office for Harmonisation in the Internal Market (Trade Marks and Designs)* [2013] All ER (D) 180 (Feb), [2013] All ER (D) 181 (Feb) (EGC: Second Chamber).

2419   Trade mark—EU trade mark—registration—distinctive character—visual perception of mis-spelled word

The applicant company obtained an international registration designating the European Community for the word sign 'RELY-ABLE'. The services in respect of which international registration was obtained related to pharmaceutical information. An examiner of the defendant trade mark registration body refused protection of the mark on the basis of Council Regulation (EC) 207/2009 art 7(1)(b), (2) (on the EU trade mark), under which protection was not to be awarded to marks which lacked distinctive character. That decision was affirmed by the defendant's appeal board, which concluded that the mark could not be perceived and memorised by the relevant consumer as a trade mark and that the sign as a whole would be perceived as nothing more than a promotional message whose aim was to highlight an important positive aspect of the services, namely that they were reliable. The appeal board took the view that the relevant public would directly and unambiguously perceive the sign as a deliberate mis-spelling of the English word 'reliable' to make it more catchy, but would not perceive that spelling as particularly fanciful or arbitrary. The board also found that the relevant public would directly perceive the message communicated by the sign as a banal, laudatory one relating to an important characteristic of clinical trial services for pharmaceutical products, namely their reliability. The obvious promotional meaning of the sign eclipsed any impression that the sign could indicate commercial origin. The applicant brought proceedings seeking an annulment of the board's decision, submitting that it had erred in deciding that the mark lacked distinctive character. *Held*, for a finding that a mark lacked distinctive character, it was sufficient that the semantic content of the mark indicated to the consumer a characteristic of the goods or service which, while not specific, represented promotional or advertising information which the relevant public would perceive first and foremost as such, rather than as an indication of the commercial origin of the services. Further, the mere fact that the semantic content of the word mark applied for did not convey any information about the nature of the goods concerned was not sufficient to make that sign distinctive. The board had in no way failed to have regard to the importance of the relevant public's visual perception of the sign at issue. It had devoted particular attention to the deliberate mis-spelling of the English word 'reliable', and that 'spelling' related to visual perception rather than phonetic perception. Consequently, the applicant's claim that visual perception prevailed over phonetic perception in the field of clinical trials, even on the assumption that it was well founded, was not capable of calling into question the board's assessment, which had taken due account of the relevant public's visual perception of the sign at issue in respect of the services concerned. Nor had the board erred in respect of its other findings. Accordingly, the application would be dismissed.

Case T-640/11 *Boehringer Ingelheim International GmbH v Office for Harmonisation in the Internal Market (Trade Marks and Designs)* [2013] All ER (D) 72 (May) (EGC: First Chamber).

2420   Trade mark—EU trade mark—registration—distinctive character—word mark

The applicant filed an application for registration of the word mark 'NEO' as an EU trade mark. The goods and services for which registration was sought were in the Nice Agreement Classes 7, 12, 39. The defendant notified the applicant that its application was not eligible for registration under Classes 7, 12, but was allowed to proceed for the services in Class 39. The First Board of Appeal of the defendant dismissed the applicant's appeal. As a preliminary point, the Board found that, pursuant to Council Regulation (EC) 207/2009 art 64(1), it could re-open ex officio the examination of the application in the light of all the absolute grounds for refusal set out in art 7, without being limited in any manner whatsoever by the examiner's reasoning. It inferred from that that it had the power to re-open the examination also as regards the services which had been accepted for registration by the examiner. The Board concluded that the mark applied for was devoid of any distinctive character to distinguish the goods and services for which registration had been sought within the meaning of art 7(1)(b), (c), 7(2) and that, therefore, the examiner had acted correctly when he had refused the registration. The applicant brought an action seeking annulment of the Board's decision. *Held*, the Board had exceeded the limits of its powers as defined in art 64(1), read in conjunction with the first sentence of art 59, inasmuch as it ex officio had re-opened the examination of the application for registration of the EU trade mark in respect of the services referred to in that application in the light of the absolute grounds for refusal set out in art 7 and found that the mark applied for had been devoid of any distinctive character to distinguish those services within the meaning of art 7(1)(b), (c), 7(2). As regards the goods covered by the application for registration, the Board had been right to find that the sign NEO was descriptive from the point of view of the relevant public with a command of modern Greek. The sign NEO had been devoid of any distinctive character for the purposes of art 7(1)(b), 7(2) in respect of the goods covered by the application for registration. Contrary to the applicant's claims, the assessment of its application had been made in a manner consistent with the case law, on the basis of a correct interpretation and application of art 7(1)(b), (c), 7(2). Consequently, since the legality of the contested decision regarding the registrability of the sign NEO as an EU trade mark for the goods in question was established directly on the basis of art 7(1)(b), (c), 7(2), it was apparent from the relevant case law that the contested decision could not be called into question by virtue of the mere fact that the Board had not followed the Office for Harmonisation in the Internal Market's ('OHIM') decision-making practice in the present case. The Board had based its conclusion as to the descriptive and non-distinctive character of the mark, in particular, the finding that in modern Greek the word 'neo' existed on its own and meant 'new', with the result that the relevant consumer would deduce from the sign NEO in modern Greek, as regards the goods covered by the application, that that sign referred to something new, modern or in line with the latest technological developments. That finding constituted a sufficient ground for refusing registration pursuant to art 7(1)(b), (c), 7(2). Further, the fact remained that the applicant had not provided specific and substantiated information to show that the sign NEO could have distinctive and non-descriptive character in the mind of the relevant public in modern Greek as regards the goods covered by the application. Consequently, the arguments alleging infringement of the principle of examination of the facts by OHIM of its own motion pursuant to art 76 could not succeed. As the plea alleging infringement of arts 59, 64(1) was well founded, the contested decision would be annulled in so far as the mark in respect of which registration had been applied for had been declared descriptive and devoid of any distinctive character within the meaning of art 7(1)(b), (c), 7(2) as regards the services in Class 39, in respect of which the examiner had allowed registration. Accordingly, as the other pleas were unfounded, the action would be dismissed as to the remainder.

Case T-236/12 *Airbus SAS v Office for Harmonisation in the Internal Market (Trade Marks and Designs)* [2013] All ER (D) 156 (Jul) (EGC: Third Chamber).

2421   Trade mark—EU trade mark—registration—earlier EU trade mark—distinctive character

An application was made to the defendant body for registration of an EU trade mark in the figurative sign 'dialdi'. The applicant company opposed registration, contending that there was a likelihood of confusion with its own mark 'ALDI', which was used in the same market. The applicant submitted that its own mark had a reputation throughout the EU and was highly distinctive. The defendant rejected the opposition claim, deciding that there were manifest differences between the marks notwithstanding the fact that the goods covered were identical. The applicant's appeal was dismissed by the defendant's Second Board of Appeal, which took the view that, from an overall assessment of the marks at issue from a visual, phonetic and conceptual point of view, they were not similar. The applicant brought proceedings before the General Court of the European Union, seeking annulment of the Board's decision. It claimed that the Board had been wrong to conclude that there had been no likelihood of confusion between the marks within the meaning of Council Regulation (EC) 207/2009 art 8(1)(b). *Held*, for the purposes of applying art 8(1)(b), a likelihood of confusion presupposed both that the marks at issue were identical or similar and that the goods or services which they covered were identical or similar. Those conditions were cumulative. Further, the more distinctive the earlier mark, the greater would be the likelihood of confusion. Consequently, marks with a highly distinctive character, either inherently or because of the reputation they possessed on the market, enjoyed more extensive protection than marks with a less distinctive character. Where the protection of the earlier trade mark extended to the entirety of the EU, it was necessary to take into account the perception of the marks in dispute by the consumer of the goods or services in question in that territory. The marks in question certainly had a degree of visual and phonetic similarity. In the circumstances, when ruling on the existence of a likelihood of confusion, the Board had failed to assess all the relevant factors and, in particular, to determine whether the applicant had demonstrated the enhanced distinctive character acquired through use of the earlier mark, or even its renown. Accordingly, the application would be allowed.

Case T-505/11 *Aldi GmbH & Co KG v Office for Harmonisation in the Internal Market (Trade Marks and Designs)* (OHIM) [2013] All ER (D) 266 (Jun) (EGC: Second Chamber).

2422   Trade mark—EU trade mark—registration—earlier EU trade mark—likelihood of confusion—alcoholic beverages

The applicant filed an application for registration of an EU trade mark at the Office for Harmonisation in the Internal Market ('OHIM'), pursuant to Council Regulation (EC) 40/94 (on the EU trade mark). The mark in respect of which registration was sought was the word sign 'CA' MARINA'. The goods in respect of which registration was sought were in the Nice Agreement (concerning the International Classification of Goods and Services for the Purposes of the Registration of Marks) class 33 and corresponded to the following description: 'alcoholic beverages, in particular wine, sparkling wine, spirits, liqueurs'. The defendant filed a notice of opposition to the registration of the trade mark applied for in respect of all of the goods in Class 33. That opposition was based, in particular, on the earlier EU word mark 'MARINA ALTA', the disputed mark. That mark was registered for goods in Class 33 corresponding to the following description: 'alcoholic beverages (except beers)'. The grounds relied on in support of the opposition were those referred to in Regulation 40/94 art 8(1)(b). The Opposition Division upheld the opposition. The First Board of Appeal of OHIM dismissed the applicant's appeal. The applicant sought the annulment of the contested decision as well as the decision of the Opposition Division. *Held*, it was well established that the global assessment of the likelihood of confusion entailed some interdependence between the factors taken into account and, in particular, between the similarity of the trade marks and the similarity of the goods or services concerned. Accordingly, a lesser degree of similarity between those goods or services might be offset by a greater degree of similarity between the marks, and vice versa. Given the identical nature of the goods at issue and the significant visual, phonetic and conceptual similarity of the signs at issue, for at least part of the relevant public, the Board had been correct in considering that there was a likelihood of confusion between the marks at issue. Indeed, consumers exposed to wines sold under the earlier mark could believe that the wines sold under the mark applied for came from the same undertaking or connected undertakings. It followed that the applicant was wrong to claim that art 8(1)(b) had been infringed on the grounds that the earlier mark had not been sufficiently analysed, that there was no likelihood of confusion between the conflicting signs, that there was no identity between the goods and that the distribution channels and the targeted public had not been taken into account. Accordingly, the action would be dismissed.

Case T-393/11 *Masottina SpA v Office for Harmonisation in the Internal Market (OHIM)* [2013] All ER (D) 200 (May) (EGC: First Chamber).

Council Regulation (EC) 40/94 art 8(1)(b) now Council Regulation (EC) 207/2009 art 8(1)(b).

2423   Trade mark—EU trade mark—registration—earlier EU trade mark—likelihood of confusion—relevant public

The applicant filed an application for registration of a Community trade mark with the defendant Office for Harmonisation in the Internal Market ('OHIM'). Later, the intervener filed a notice of opposition based on an earlier Community word. The grounds relied on in support of the opposition were those referred to in Council Regulation (EC) 207/2009 (on the Community Trademark) arts 8(1)(b) and 8(5). In rejecting that opposition, the Opposition Division found that the goods and services covered by the signs at issue were said to be partially identical and partially different. The signs were visually and phonetically different and were slightly similar conceptually for a section of the relevant public. As the signs were globally dissimilar, it was said that there was no likelihood of confusion between the signs under art 8(1)(b), and as the signs were different, art 8(5) was not applicable. On appeal by the intervener, the first board of the OHIM considered that the relevant public was made up of the general public in the European Union and concluded that the marks at issue were identical, or, 'at the least', were conceptually extremely similar. Finally, there was a likelihood of confusion or association between the signs at issue in respect of the identical goods, and there was no likelihood of confusion for the different goods and it had not been necessary to consider art 8(5). Following that determination, the parties sought varying orders from the General Court of the European Union. *Held*, the assessment of the likelihood of confusion on the part of the relevant public depended on various factors and should be appreciated globally, taking into account all factors relevant to the circumstances of the case. That global assessment had to, as regards the visual, aural or conceptual similarity of the marks in question, be based on the overall impression which they created, bearing in mind, in particular, their distinctive and dominant components. In the context of the global assessment of the likelihood of confusion, account should be taken of the average consumer of the category of goods or services concerned, who was reasonably well informed and reasonably observant and circumspect. It should also be borne in mind that the average consumer's level of attention was likely to vary according to the category of goods or services in question. In the circumstances, the board had found that the public was composed of average consumers, in the European Union, reasonably well informed and reasonably observant and circumspect. Therefore, contrary to what the applicant claimed, it relied on a public having a normal level of attention. Further, the board's assessment of the visual and phonetic comparison of the signs at issue was correct. However, the board had been wrong to consider that the signs were conceptually extremely similar or identical. Those signs had, at most, a weak degree of conceptually similarity for the reasonably informed and observant relevant public. Furthermore, the board had been wrong to find the existence of a likelihood of confusion on the part of the relevant public. Due to the fact that the signs were in different languages, a manifest distinction was created between them so that the average consumer would not immediately associate them without undergoing an intellectual process of translation.

Case T-437/11 *Golden Balls Ltd v Office for Harmonisation in the Internal Market (Trade Marks and Designs)* [2013] All ER (D) 182 (Oct) (EGC: First Chamber).

The applicant company applied to the defendant to register a European trade mark in respect of the word sign 'BOOMERANG'. The sign was used in connection with telecommunications and entertainment services. A notice was filed opposing the registration on the ground that there was a likelihood of confusion with an earlier trade mark which was used in connection with film production. The defendant's Opposition Division found that there had been a likelihood of confusion and upheld the opposition. The applicant's appeal against that decision was dismissed by the Second Board of Appeal, which concluded that there was a likelihood of confusion even though certain consumers might have a higher than average level of attention. The applicant brought proceedings seeking an annulment of that decision. It submitted that the services referred to by its own mark were directed to the general public, which would be reasonably well-informed, observant and circumspect, whereas the services covered by the earlier mark were directed at a more specialised public, namely, to individuals and business entities involved in the production and commercialisation of films, with a high level of attention, and not to the general public. *Held*, the only services covered by the earlier mark that had been taken into consideration by the Board when it had compared the services covered by the conflicting marks were film production services. Film production services were aimed solely at professionals in the audiovisual sector. Although the general public watched the films produced, it did not itself use film production services. The Board had therefore been wrong to take the view that the film production services covered by the earlier mark had also been addressed to the general public. However, when it was taken into account that the services in question might be supplied by the same undertakings and that they were complementary from the point of view of those who received the services, the Board had been correct to take the view that the services covered by the two marks had a degree of similarity. Taking into account the fact that the services in question were similar and that the conflicting marks were similar, the Board had found that, even though certain consumers might have a higher than average level of attention, a likelihood of confusion could not be excluded. It followed that the Board had found that there had been a likelihood of confusion both for the general public and for the part of the relevant public composed of professionals with a high level of attention. Consequently, the error which the Board had made in including the general public in the definition of the relevant public had no consequence for that finding. Accordingly, the application would be dismissed.

Case T-285/12 *Cartoon Network v Office for Harmonisation in the Internal Market* (*Trade Marks and Designs*) [2013] All ER (D) 227 (Oct) (EGC: Seventh Chamber).

2424 Trade mark—EU trade mark—registration—earlier EU trade mark—likelihood of confusion—weak distinctive character

In proceedings opposing the registration of an EU trade mark on the basis of the likelihood of confusion with an earlier trade mark, it has been held that the finding of a weak distinctive character for the earlier trade mark does not preclude a finding that there is a likelihood of confusion. Although the distinctive character of the earlier mark should be taken into account when assessing the likelihood of confusion, it is only one factor among others involved in the assessment. It follows that, even in a case involving an earlier mark of weak distinctive character, there may be a likelihood of confusion on account of a similarity between the signs and between the goods or services covered.

Case T-624/11 *Yueqing Onesto Electric Co Ltd v Office for Harmonisation in the Internal Market* [2013] IP & T 801 (EGC: Third Chamber). Case T-443/05 *El Corte Ingles SA v Office for Harmonisation in the Internal Market* [2007] All ER (D) 152 (Jul), CFI; and Case C-256/04 *Mundipharma AG v Office for Harmonisation in the Internal Market* [2007] All ER (D) 159 (Feb), CFI, considered.

Regulation 40/94 replaced by Council Regulation (EC) 207/2009.

2425 Trade mark—EU trade mark—registration—earlier EU trade mark—likelihood of confusion—well-known character of mark

A company sought registration for an EU trade mark, 'Caffe KIMBO', for goods corresponding to the description 'coffee, tea, cocoa, sugar, rice, tapioca, sago, coffee substitutes; flour and preparations made from cereals, bread, pastry and confectionery, ices; honey, treacles; yeast, baking-powder; salt, mustard; vinegar sauces (condiments); relish; ice'. The applicant filed a notice of opposition against registration, based on the Spanish word mark 'BIMBO', which was a registered trade mark in respect of 'cereals, milling industry, baking, pastry and starch', reputation being claimed in Spain in respect of all of those goods, and on an earlier mark BIMBO, well known in Spain in respect of the same goods. The opposition was upheld in respect of part of the goods at issue. On appeal by the company that decision was annulled in so far as it had rejected the application in respect of 'flour, confectionery, ices, yeast and baking-powder'. However, the rejection of the application as regards preparations made from 'cereals, bread, pastry' was confirmed. The applicant sought the alteration or annulment of the appeal decision. *Held*, the appeal had set out the grounds on which the well-known character of the earlier mark was considered to have been demonstrated only for 'packaged sliced bread' and on which it was considered, on account of their intrinsic characteristics, that the various goods examined had been identical or different. Sufficient reasons had been given for the contested decision. In respect of the obligation provided for by Council Regulation (EC) 207/2009 art 75, pursuant to which opposition decisions were to be based only on reasons or evidence on which the parties concerned had had an opportunity to present their comments, it had to be observed that, although the right to be heard covered all the matters of fact or of law and the evidence which formed the basis for the decision, it did not apply to the final position which the administration intended to adopt. That was true in the present case because the applicant had been aware of the evidence taken into consideration on appeal, since it had been produced during the opposition proceedings. The appellate tribunal had not infringed art 8(1)(b) in holding, on the basis of an overall assessment of the likelihood of confusion, that the opposition decision should be annulled in part in so far as the opposition had initially been upheld for 'flour, confectionery, ices, yeast and baking-powder'. Accordingly, the action in its entirety would be dismissed.

Case T-277/12 *Bimbo, SA v Office for Harmonisation in the Internal Market (Trade Marks and Designs)* [2013] ALL ER (D) 09 (May) (EGC: First Chamber).

2426 Trade mark—EU trade mark—registration—geographical location—likelihood of confusion—eligibility for registration

The word mark 'CASTEL' was registered as a Community trade mark in respect of goods described as 'alcoholic beverages (except beers)'. The applicant filed an application for a declaration that the disputed mark was invalid pursuant to Council Regulation (EC) 207/2009 arts 7(1), 52 based on the geographical indication 'Castell', protected for wines in Germany, France, Greece, Italy and Spain. The Office for Harmonisation in the Internal Market (Trade Marks and Designs) ('OHIM'), in dismissing the application, determined that the term 'castell' was a German indicator of geographical provenance for wines, protected in the relevant countries and perceived as such by the relevant public, and the disputed mark had differed from the earlier geographical indication by the use of a single 'l', rather than two, in its spelling. It also stated that the disputed mark, in light of its being commonly used in the wine sector and meaning 'castle', was perceived by the relevant public as having that meaning, whereas the earlier geographical indication was perceived by the relevant public as designating a place in Germany which was renowned for wine production and that it was therefore not descriptive of the geographical origin of the goods concerned for the purposes of art 7(1). The applicant appealed. *Held*, in order for a sign to be caught by the prohibition set out in art 7(1)(c), there had to be a sufficiently direct and specific link between the sign and the goods or services in question to enable the public concerned immediately to perceive, without further thought, a description of those goods or services or one of their characteristics. Contrary to the OHIM's claims, the term 'castell' had designated a place which was sufficiently known to the relevant public for the production of wines and was therefore associated, for that public, with the category of goods concerned. Further, the difference in spelling that the OHIM had identified between 'castel' and 'castell' had not been sufficient to outweigh the resemblance which had existed between the two words. The relevant public, which was aware of the earlier geographical indication and therefore of the existence of the wine-producing municipality of Castell in Germany, when confronted with goods bearing the mark 'CASTEL', would think immediately, without further thought, that what they had in front of them was a wine which came from that wine-producing municipality. Consequently, the disputed mark had to be held to be descriptive of the goods at issue and it followed that it had been ineligible for registration as a Community trade mark. Accordingly, the appeal would be allowed and the contested decision would be annulled.

Case T-320/10 *Furstlich Castell'sches Domaenenamt Albrecht Furst zu Castell-Castell v Office for Harmonisation in the Internal Market (Trade Marks and Designs)* [2013] All ER

(D) 171 (Sep) (EGC: Sixth Chamber). Case C-191/01P *Office for Harmonisation in the Internal Market (Trade Marks and Designs) v WM Wrigley Jnr Co (Doublemint)* [2004] All ER (EC) 1040, ECJ (2003 Abr para 2686); and Case C-383/99 P *Procter & Gamble Co v Office for Harmonisation in the Internal Market (Trade Marks and Designs)* [2002] All ER (EC) 29, ECJ (2001 Abr para 3101), applied.

2427   Trade mark—EU trade mark—registration—opposition—absence of likelihood of confusion with earlier mark

A company filed an application for registration of an EU trade mark with the Office for Harmonisation in the Internal Market ('OHIM') pursuant to Council Regulation (EC) 40/94 on the EU trade mark. The trade mark for which registration was sought was the word sign 'Fitcoin'. The applicant filed a notice of opposition to registration of the mark applied for in respect of all the goods and services covered by the application for registration. That opposition was based on the earlier rights granted for the registration of several previous marks being variations of the mark 'COIN'. The ground relied on in support of the opposition was that specified in art 8(1)(b). It was found by the Opposition Division of OHIM that there was no likelihood of confusion within the meaning of art 8(1)(b). The applicant's appeal against the decision was dismissed by the First Board of Appeal of OHIM. The applicant brought proceedings before the European General Court seeking annulment of that decision. *Held*, the Board had erred in finding that none of the meanings of the English word 'fit' other than 'in good health' had been in direct relation to any of the goods and services covered by the mark applied for. Therefore, the Board had erred in finding that there was no likelihood of confusion, for English consumers as regards the 'clothing, including footwear and slippers' in the Nice Agreement Class 25. However, the Board had been correct in finding that as regards the goods and services in Classes 16, 28, 35, 36 and 41, the differences between the marks at issue introduced by the presence of the letters 'f', 'i', 't' at the beginning of the mark applied for outweighed the similarity limited to their coinciding in four letters. It followed that firstly, the Board had erred in rejecting the opposition as regarded, the 'clothing, including footwear and slippers' in Class 25 and that secondly, it had been correct to reject the opposition as to the remainder. The action would be upheld in part and the contested decision annulled in part.

Case T-272/11 *Coin SpA v Office for Harmonisation in the Internal Market (Trade Marks and Designs) (OHIM)* [2013] All ER (D) 134 (Feb) (EGC: Seventh Chamber).

Regulation 40/94 replaced by Council Regulation (EC) 207/2009.

2428   Trade mark—EU trade mark—registration—opposition—genuine use—relevant territory

The applicant company filed a notice of opposition to the registration of a trade mark relating to beverages. The opposition was based on the earlier international figurative mark which produced effects in various European countries. On being asked to provide proof of use of the earlier trade mark, the applicant stated that it was maintaining the opposition only in respect of the German part of the international registration, and submitted a number of documents as proof of use in Switzerland. It relied, in that regard, on the Convention between Switzerland and Germany on the reciprocal protection of patents, designs and trade marks (Berlin, 13 April 1892) pursuant to which use in Switzerland was equivalent to use in Germany. The defendant's Fourth Board of Appeal rejected the application of the 1892 Convention, and therefore dismissed the opposition application. The Board found that the only relevant legal framework was that of Council Regulation (EC) 207/2009, and, more specifically, art 42(2), (3), under which an earlier trade mark should have been put to genuine use in the member state in which it was protected. The General Court of the European Union dismissed the applicant's application for annulment of that decision, and the applicant appealed to the European Court of Justice. Consideration was given to the Agreement concerning the International Registration of Marks (Madrid, 14 April 1891), and to European Parliament and Council Directive (EC) 2008/95. *Held*, the Madrid Agreement art 4 provided that the protection of the mark in each of the contracting parties concerned was to be the same as if the mark had been deposited direct with the office of that contracting party. By virtue of those provisions, 'trade marks registered under international arrangements which have effect in a member state' in Regulation 207/2009 art 8(2)(a)(iii) were subject to the same system as the 'trade marks registered in a member state' referred to in art 8(2)(a)(ii). It followed that the General Court had not erred in law by applying art 42(3) to the trade mark. That being so, the applicant could not claim that the General Court's reasoning in the judgment under appeal was contradictory. Also, the EU trade mark system was an autonomous system with its own set of objectives and rules peculiar to it; it applied independently of any national system. However, Directive 2008/95 art 10(1), which was intended to harmonise the national laws on trade marks, provided that, after a certain period, a trade mark which had not been put to genuine use by its proprietor in a member state was to be subject to the sanctions provided for in that directive, including invalidity. The General Court had not erred in law in ruling that the concept of use of a trade mark in the EU was exhaustively and exclusively governed by EU law. Provision was also made in Regulation 207/2009 for exceptions to the principle of the unitary character of a trade mark. In particular, art 111(1) allowed the proprietor of an earlier right which applied only to a particular locality to oppose the use of a European trade mark in the territory where his right was protected, in so far as the legislation of the member state concerned so permitted. The General Court had therefore been right to find that the principle of the unitary character of a trade mark was not absolute. Accordingly, the appeal would be dismissed.

Case C-445/12P *Rivella International AG v Office for Harmonisation in the Internal market (Trade Marks and Designs)* [2013] All ER (D) 141 (Dec) (ECJ: First Chamber).

2429   Trade mark—EU trade mark—registration—opposition—likelihood of confusion—conceptual similarity

An application was made to the defendant body for registration of a European trade mark in respect of the figurative sign 'Cultra', which was used in relation to a variety of products in the beauty, cosmetic and medical industries. The applicant company opposed registration, relying on the existing word mark 'SCULPTRA', which was used in the same markets. The applicant contended that there was a likelihood that customers would confuse the two marks. The defendant's Opposition Division rejected the opposition application, deciding that there was only a certain degree of similarity between the two marks which was not sufficient to find that there was a likelihood of confusion. The applicant's appeal against that decision was dismissed by a Board of Appeal, which ruled that the earlier trade mark had an inherently distinctive character and that the relevant public's degree of attention was relatively high. The applicant brought proceedings seeking an annulment of the Board's decision, submitting that it had erroneously ruled out the possibility of a likelihood of confusion on the basis of the purportedly low degree of similarity between the signs at issue. *Held*, the Board had been correct in its findings concerning the member states in which the relevant public was situated, the high degree of attention of the relevant public, the similarity between the goods covered by the trade marks, and the low degree of visual similarity between the marks. However, any conceptual similarity between the signs at issue could not be excluded in relation to that part of the relevant public which associated the words 'cultra' and 'sculptra' respectively with the concepts of culture and sculpture, since those two concepts might be linked to each other. The Board had done no more than find that those words were conceptually different, without providing any explanation in support of its statement, even though it conceded that they might refer to those concepts. It followed that the Board's finding to the effect that the signs at issue were conceptually different could not be upheld. Similarly, the Board's finding that the signs at issue were globally similar to a low degree could not be upheld, since it had been founded on the incorrect premises that the signs at issue had been phonetically similar only to a low degree and that they had been conceptually different. Furthermore, the Board had excluded the existence of a likelihood of confusion, despite the identity or similarity of the goods or services at issue. Since the goods and services covered by the trade marks at issue were similar or identical, the exclusion of the existence of a likelihood of confusion between those marks necessarily flowed from the inadequate assessment which had led the Board to its incorrect findings as regards the assessment of the phonetic and conceptual similarity of those trade marks. Accordingly, the application would be allowed.

Case T-142/12 *Aventis Pharmaceuticals Inc v Office for Harmonisation in the Internal Market (Trade Marks and Designs)* [2013] All ER (D) 244 (Jul) (EGC: Sixth Chamber).

2430   Trade mark—EU trade mark—registration—opposition—likelihood of confusion—earlier EU trade mark

A company filed an application for registration of an EU trade mark in the word 'KMIX'. The applicant company filed a notice of opposition against registration of the mark on the basis of likelihood of confusion with the earlier EU word mark 'BAMIX'. The Office for Harmonisation in the Internal Market (Trade Marks and Designs) ('the Office') rejected the opposition. It took the view that the goods at issue had been identical or similar and that the signs at issue had a medium degree of visual similarity, a high degree of phonetic similarity and a certain degree of conceptual similarity inasmuch as they both contained the element 'mix'. However, the Office considered that the element 'mix' had a very limited distinctive character and as the other elements of those signs – 'ba' and 'k' – had been different, there had been no likelihood of confusion. The decision was affirmed by the Second Board of Appeal of the Office for Harmonisation in the Internal Market (Trade Marks and Designs) ('the Board'), which considered that the signs at issue had not been similar overall. The applicant sought annulment of that decision. *Held*, the global assessment of the likelihood of confusion, as far as concerned the visual, phonetic or conceptual similarity of the marks in question, should be based on the overall impression given by the marks, bearing in mind, in particular, their distinctive and dominant components. Further, it was well established that the consumer generally paid greater attention to the beginning of a mark than to the end and that the brevity of the marks at issue enabled consumers to better grasp the variations in their spelling. The visual, phonetic and conceptual aspects of the signs did not always have the same weight. It was appropriate to examine the objective conditions under which the marks might be present on the market. The extent of the similarity or difference between the signs might depend, in particular, on the inherent qualities of the signs or the conditions under which the goods or services covered by the opposing signs were marketed. In the present case, the goods covered by the signs at issue were intended for the general public and could be bought in department stores and speciality shops. Those shops often operated on a self-service basis, even though they employed personnel to assist customers in their choices. The marks at issue therefore would generally be perceived visually prior to purchase. Further, oral communication would take place, where necessary, with qualified sales personnel who were capable of informing customers about the various brands. It followed that the visual similarity between the signs at issue had more weight than the phonetic similarity in the assessment of the overall similarity. Consequently, the fact that the Board had not taken into account the pronunciation 'kamix' of the mark applied for in the assessment of the phonetic similarity of the signs at issue was not liable to affect the assessment of the overall similarity of those signs. Finally, since the signs at issue were meaningless, a conceptual comparison of the signs was not possible. It was clear that the Board had not erred in finding that the signs at issue had not been similar overall and so was also entitled to conclude that there had been no likelihood of confusion. Accordingly, the action would be dismissed.

Case T-444/10 *Esge AG v Office for Harmonisation in the Internal Market (Trade Marks and Designs)* [2013] All ER (D) 297 (Feb) (EGC: Seventh Chamber).

An application for registration of an EU trade mark was filed with the Office of Harmonisation in the Internal Market under Council Regulation (EC) 2007/2009 (on the EU trade mark). The goods in respect of which registration had been sought were in the Nice Agreement Classes 18 and 25. The applicant filed a notice of opposition against registration of the trade mark in respect of some of the goods referred to in those classes. The Board of the Office of Harmonisation dismissed the appeal, deciding when assessing overall the likelihood of confusion that, despite the identical nature of the goods concerned, there had been no likelihood of confusion given the visual dissimilarity of the marks at issue, the below average degree of their phonetic similarity, the average distinctiveness of the earlier marks and the normal level of attentiveness of the relevant public. On appeal by the applicant, *held*, the risk that the public might believe that the goods or services in question came from the same undertaking or from economically-linked undertakings constituted a likelihood of confusion. The likelihood of confusion should be assessed globally, according to the relevant public's perception of the signs and the goods or services concerned and account being taken of all factors relevant to the circumstances of the case, including the interdependence between the similarity of the signs and that of the goods or services covered. For the purposes of applying art 8(1)(b), a likelihood of confusion presupposed both that the marks at issue were identical or similar and that the goods or services which they covered were identical or similar. Those conditions were cumulative. In the circumstances, the Board had correctly assessed the importance of the alphanumeric combination of the marks at issue when it had made the visual, phonetic and conceptual comparisons of them. It followed that in light of the examination of the similarity between the marks at issue, the Board had been correct to find that it could not be considered that there had been a likelihood of confusion. Further, the earlier marks in question had the level of inherent distinctiveness of any mark which did not describe the goods it referred to and their level of distinctiveness was not above average. Therefore, the second complaint, alleging the failure to take into account the supposedly inherently distinctive character of the earlier marks, would be dismissed. Accordingly, the action would be dismissed.

Case T-231/12 *Rocket Dog Brands LLC v Office for Harmonisation in the Internal Market (Trade Marks and Designs)* [2013] All ER (D) 189 (Jun) (EGC: Seventh Chamber).

An application was made to the defendant body for the registration of an EU trade mark in relation to the figurative sign 'eventer EVENT MANAGEMENT SYSTEMS'. The applicant company filed a notice of opposition against registration of the mark, contending that there was a likelihood that the sign would be confused with the earlier German word mark 'Event'. The defendant's Opposition Division found that the relevant public consisted, in respect of some of the services at issue, of German professionals whose level of attention was high, and, in respect of the other services at issue, of the German general public. The defendant decided that there was no likelihood of confusion, even in respect of the services which were similar, given the high degree of attention of the relevant public in relation to those services, the low degree of distinctive character of the earlier mark, the insufficient degree of similarity between the signs at issue and the unusual nature of the element 'eventer' in the mark applied for. The applicant's claim was refused and its appeal against that decision was dismissed. The applicant appealed further to the European General Court, seeking an annulment of the defendant's decision. It disputed the defendant's assessments relating to the definition of the relevant public, the similarity of the services, the similarity of the signs and the global assessment of the likelihood of confusion. *Held*, the risk that the public might believe that the goods or services in question came from the same undertaking or from economically linked undertakings constituted a likelihood of confusion. The likelihood of confusion should be assessed globally, according to the relevant public's perception of the signs and goods or services concerned, and taking into account all factors relevant to the circumstances of the case, and in particular the interdependence between the similarity of the signs and that of the goods or services covered. The word element 'eventer' of the mark applied for had not exactly reproduced the earlier mark. While the latter was included in the phrase 'event management systems', in respect of the second verbal component of the mark applied for, the relevant public would not isolate the word 'event' from the two others which followed it in that phrase, but would retain the overall meaning thereof. Since the relevant public for similar services was made up of professionals, who had a high degree of attentiveness, it was necessary to uphold the finding that the similarities between the signs were insufficient for there to be a likelihood of confusion with respect to the services which should be held to be similar. Accordingly, the appeal would be dismissed.

Case T-353/11 *Event Holding GmbH & Co. KG v OHIM* [2013] All ER (D) 123 (Jun) (EGC: Sixth Chamber).

2431 Trade mark—EU trade mark—registration—opposition—likelihood of confusion—global assessment

The applicant company filed an application with the Office for Harmonisation in the Internal Market for registration of the figurative sign 'SNICKERS' as a Community trade mark for goods in the Nice Agreement concerning the International Classification of Goods and Services for the Purposes of the Registration of Marks Classes 8, 9 and 25. An intervener company filed a notice of opposition to the registration in Class 25, which related to 'clothing, footwear, headgear; workwear, coveralls, vests, braces for clothing (suspenders), belts (clothing)', based on its earlier Italian word mark 'KICKERS', which covered 'clothing items, shoes, headgear', on the ground of likelihood of confusion within the meaning of Council Regulation (EC) 207/2009 art 8(1)(b). The Opposition Division upheld the opposition and its decision was upheld by the Board of Appeal. The Board found, in particular, that since the earlier mark was an Italian mark, the relevant territory for the purposes of analysing the likelihood of confusion was Italy. It took the view that the signs had an average degree of visual and phonetic similarity, that they were conceptually neutral and that the inherent distinctive character of the earlier mark should be regarded as normal, since the word 'kickers' did not have meaning for the goods concerned. The applicant brought proceedings before the European General Court seeking annulment the Board's decision. *Held*, it was clearly established that the likelihood of confusion had to be assessed globally. A global assessment of the likelihood of confusion implied some interdependence between the factors taken into account, and in particular between the similarity of the trade marks and the similarity of the goods or services concerned. In the present case, the goods covered by the signs at issue were identical and the signs showed an average degree of similarity from a visual and phonetic perspective. In those circumstances, the Board had been correct to conclude that there had been a likelihood of confusion between the marks. That conclusion could not be invalidated by the argument concerning the high distinctive character of the mark applied for, since it was not a relevant factor to be taken into account in the assessment of the likelihood of confusion. It was only the distinctive character of the earlier mark that should be taken into account in the global assessment of the likelihood of confusion because its distinctiveness would determine the scope of the protection of the earlier mark. It followed that the single plea of infringement of art 8(1)(b) would be rejected.

Case T-537/11 *Hultafors Group AB v Office for Harmonisation in the Internal Market* (*Trade Marks and Designs*) [2013] All ER (D) 267 (May) (EGC: Seventh Chamber). Case C-39/97 *Canon Kabushiki Kaisha v Metro-Goldwyn-Mayer Inc (formerly Pathe Communications Corpn)* [1998] All ER (EC) 934, ECJ, considered.

The applicant company filed an application with the defendant pursuant to Council Regulation (EC) 40/94 for registration of a European trade mark. A notice of opposition was subsequently filed which opposed registration on the basis that there was a likelihood of confusion with an earlier trade mark under art 8(1)(b). The defendant's Opposition Division rejected the opposition. An appeal to the First Board of Appeal was also dismissed, the Board finding that, as the conceptual comparison did not influence the assessment of the similarity of the signs, the visual and phonetic differences were sufficiently relevant to exclude a likelihood of confusion, even for identical goods. A successful application was then made to the European General Court seeking an annulment of that decision. On the applicant's appeal, it submitted that the European General Court had failed to apply correctly the case law relating to the global assessment of the likelihood of confusion. *Held*, the global assessment of the likelihood of confusion, in relation to the visual, aural or conceptual similarity of the marks in question, should be based on the overall impression given by those marks, bearing in mind, in particular, their distinctive and dominant components. The perception of the marks by the average consumer of the goods or services in question played a decisive role in the global assessment of that likelihood of confusion. In that regard, the average consumer normally perceived a mark as a whole and did not proceed to analyse its various details. In the present case, the European General Court itself had drawn a distinction between goods within the same class on the basis of the conditions under which they were marketed. Consequently, it was incumbent on the European General Court to set out reasons for its decision with regard to each group of goods which it had established within that class. Since such reasoning was lacking with regard to the goods in one particular class, the judgment did not enable the persons concerned to know the grounds on which the European General Court had based, in that regard, its annulment of the contested decision or provide the present court with sufficient material for it to exercise its powers of review within the context of the appeal. Accordingly, the appeal would be allowed.

Case C-597/12P *Isdin SA v Office for Harmonisation in the Internal Market* (*Trade Marks and Designs*) [2013] All ER (D) 225 (Oct) (ECJ: Seventh Chamber).

The applicant filed a notice of opposition to the registration of a European trade mark in the class of non-alcoholic beverages, fruit drinks and fruit juices. The mark in question was the figurative sign 'PANINI'. The applicant contended that, pursuant to Council Regulation (EC) 207/2009 art 8(1)(b), there was a likelihood that the sign would be confused with the earlier Community and German word mark 'GRANINI'. The defendant's Opposition Division rejected the opposition in its entirety, and the applicant appealed to the defendant's Second Board of Appeal. The Board of Appeal ruled that, although the signs at issue were slightly similar from a visual and phonetic point of view, and in some member states there was a clear conceptual difference between those signs, the dissimilarities between the signs outweighed the similarities and the signs were dissimilar overall. The applicant brought an action before the General Court of the European Union seeking annulment of that decision. It submitted that the degree of similarity of the signs at issue was average, or even high, and taking into account the identical nature or high degree of similarity of the goods in question, the Board had been wrong in concluding that there had been no likelihood of confusion. *Held*, having regard to the low degree of phonetic similarity between the signs at issue, to their lack of visual similarity, to their lack of conceptual similarity or to the absence of a possible comparison between the signs from a conceptual point of view, the signs were dissimilar overall. Overall, they did not have a high, or even average, degree of similarity. The Board had therefore correctly concluded that the signs had been different or different overall, its error in the assessment of the visual similarity between the signs not being capable of vitiating the finding relating to the overall comparison of the signs. It followed that, within the context of the global assessment of the trade marks at issue, assuming that use of the earlier marks had been demonstrated with regard to the goods for which they had been registered, the signs in question were dissimilar and, in accordance with the relevant case law, the existence of a likelihood of confusion on the part of the consumer concerned was excluded. Accordingly, the application would be dismissed.

Case T-487/12 *Eckes-Granini Group GmbH v Office for Harmonisation in the Internal Market (Trade Marks and Designs)* [2013] All ER (D) 140 (Dec) (EGC: Eighth Chamber).

2432   Trade mark—EU trade mark—registration—opposition—likelihood of
        confusion—global assessment—average consumer

The respondent had applied to register an EU trade mark at the Office for Harmonisation in the Internal Market, under Council Regulation (EC) 40/94 (on the EU trade mark), in respect of the figurative sign 'KSPORT' for goods in the Nice Agreement concerning the International Classification of Goods and Services for the Purposes of the Registration of Marks Classes 18, 25 and 28. The applicant filed a notice of opposition against registration of the mark applied for based on existing marks 'K2 SPORTS' for goods in Classes 18, 25 and 28 on the basis of likely confusion contrary to Regulation 40/94 art 8(1)(b). The opposition was rejected and the applicant's appeal was dismissed on the ground that, even though the goods covered by the marks were similar or identical, there was no likelihood of confusion between them since they were identical only with regard to the word 'sport'. The applicant sought the annulment of the decision on the basis of a breach of art 8(1)(b). *Held*, the risk that the public might believe that the goods or services in question came from the same undertaking or from economically linked undertakings constituted a likelihood of confusion. The likelihood of confusion should be assessed globally, according to the perception which the relevant public had of the signs and the goods or services in question, account being taken of factors including the interdependence between the similarity of the signs and that of the goods or services covered. For the purposes of art 8(1)(b), a likelihood of confusion presupposed both that the two marks were identical or similar and that the goods or services which they covered were identical or similar. Those conditions were cumulative. The global assessment of the likelihood of confusion, in relation to the visual, phonetic or conceptual similarity of the signs at issue, should be based on the overall impression given by the signs, in particular, their distinctive and dominant components being borne in mind. The perception of the marks by the average consumer of the goods or services at issue played a decisive role in the global assessment of that likelihood of confusion. The average consumer normally perceived a mark as a whole and did not proceed to analyse its various details. Two marks were similar when, from the point of view of the relevant public, they were at least partially identical with regard to one or more of the visual, phonetic and conceptual aspects. When considered as a whole, the two marks at issue were not visually similar because the term 'sport' at the end of the mark applied for was not decisive and would not attract the attention of consumers who only rarely had the chance to make a direct comparison between the different marks and could rely on an imperfect recollection of them. The signs were phonetically identical only in respect of their final component 'sport', which would be pronounced identically in the relevant languages, differing slightly as a result of the sound made by the final letter 's' in some languages such as English and German. However, it should be borne in mind that the consumer generally paid greater attention to the beginning of a mark than to the end. Thus, it was correct to find that the overall impression created by the marks at issue was different. The cumulative conditions for the application of art 8(1)(b) was not fulfilled and, accordingly, the action would be dismissed.

Case T-54/12 *K2 Sports Europe GmbH v Office for Harmonisation in the Internal Market (Trade Marks and Designs)* [2013] All ER (D) 262 (Feb) (EGC: Fifth Chamber).

Regulation 40/94 art 8(1)(b) replaced by Council Regulation (EC) 207/2009 art 8(1)(b).

2433   Trade mark—EU trade mark—registration—opposition—likelihood of confusion—global assessment—cumulative conditions

The respondent had filed an application for registration of an EU trade mark at the Office for Harmonisation in the Internal Market (Trade Marks and Designs) under Council Regulation (EC) 207/2009 (on the EU trade mark). The mark in respect of which registration was sought was the word mark 'DIGNITUDE'. The goods in respect of which registration was sought were in the Nice Agreement concerning the International Classification of Goods and Services for the Purposes of the Registration of Marks Classes 5, 24 and 25. The applicant filed a notice of opposition to registration of the mark, alleging infringement of Regulation 207/2009 art 8(1)(b) because of likely confusion of the public with respect to the goods. The opposition was based on a registered right for the EU word mark 'Dignity' for goods in Classes 5 and 10. The Opposition Division upheld the opposition in part, with regard to the goods in Classes 5, 24 covered by the application for registration but it dismissed the opposition in respect of the goods in Class 25, finding that those goods were not similar to the goods covered by the earlier marks. The applicant sought the annulment of the decision dismissing its appeal, arguing that the conclusion that the goods covered by the application for registration and the goods covered by the earlier trade marks were not similar within the meaning of art 8(1)(b) was wrong as the goods had the same purpose, the same nature and the same distribution channels. Further, according to the applicant, the goods covered by the application for registration and those covered by earlier trade marks had a competitive relationship or, at least, a complementary relationship. *Held*, the risk that the public might believe that the goods or services in question came from the same undertaking or from economically linked undertakings constituted a likelihood of confusion. The likelihood of confusion should be assessed globally, according to the relevant public's perception of the signs and goods or services concerned and taking into account all factors relevant to the circumstances of the case, in particular the interdependence between the similarity of the signs and that of the goods or services designated. For the purposes of applying art 8(1)(b), a likelihood of confusion presupposed both that the two marks were identical or similar and that the goods or services which they covered were identical or similar. Those conditions were cumulative. Relevant factors should be considered, including the intended purpose of the goods, their nature, their method of use and whether they were in competition with each other or were complementary and also how they would be distributed. Having considered the relevant factors, the Board had not erred in finding that the goods covered by the marks at issue had not been similar. Further, the Board had been correct in finding that there had been no likelihood of confusion between the marks for the purpose of art 8(1)(b). Accordingly, the action would be dismissed.

Case T-504/11 *Paul Hartmann AG v Office for Harmonisation in the Internal Market (Trade Marks and Designs)* [2013] All ER (D) 261 (Feb) (EGC: First Chamber).

2434   Trade mark—EU trade mark—registration—opposition—likelihood of confusion with earlier mark—aural and visual differences

The applicant company filed an application for registration of a Community trade mark with the Office for Harmonisation in the Internal Market, pursuant to Council Regulation (EC) 40/94 on the Community trade mark. The trade mark in respect of which registration was sought was the figurative sign, 'Metro Kids Company', and the goods and services in respect of which registration was sought were in the Nice Agreement Concerning the International Classification of Goods and Services for the Purposes of the Registration of Marks Classes 24, 25 and 39. The intervener company filed a notice of opposition to the registration, based on the international registration of the figurative mark, 'Metro', which had effect in Bulgaria, the Czech Republic, Hungary, Poland, Romania, Slovenia and Slovakia and had been filed and registered in respect of Classes 1 to 45. The Opposition

Division of the Office for Harmonisation in the Internal Market upheld the opposition on the ground that there had been a likelihood of confusion on the part of the target public between the goods and services covered by the Community trade mark application and those covered by the earlier international figurative mark. The applicant filed an appeal against that decision and the First Board of Appeal decided that the relevant territory had been that of Bulgaria, the Czech Republic, Hungary, Poland, Romania, Slovenia and Slovakia, that the relevant public consisted of the public at large in those states displaying an average level of attentiveness, that the goods in Classes 24, 25 and 39 covered by the trade mark application and by the earlier trade mark had been identical and that, in view of the visual and aural similarities between the signs at issue and despite the inappositeness of any conceptual comparison, there had been a likelihood of confusion and, mainly, a likelihood of association between the signs. The applicant brought proceedings before the General Court of the European Union seeking annulment of the contested decision, contending that the First Board of Appeal had merely considered the element, 'Metro', which was the common element of the signs at issue, without examining the signs as a whole and that, due to the presence of visual and aural differences between the signs that outweighed the identity between them arising from the presence of the common element 'Metro', there was no likelihood of confusion. *Held,* regarding the similarity of the goods and services concerned, as the First Board of Appeal rightly observed, the goods covered by the trade mark application and by the earlier mark were identical. Moreover, regarding the similarity of the signs, as the First Board of Appeal correctly observed, those signs were visually similar because they both contained the element 'Metro'. It followed that the contested decision should be upheld as regards the analysis of the visual similarity of the signs. Further, there was an even stronger aural similarity between the signs because their figurative elements would not be pronounced. It followed that the contested decision should be upheld as regards the analysis of the aural similarity of the signs. With respect to the conceptual comparison, it should be found, as the First Board of Appeal rightly observed, that it was not possible to carry out any relevant conceptual comparison between the signs. Consequently, notwithstanding the absence of any relevant conceptual comparison, the signs were, by reason of their visual and aural similarities, similar overall.

Case T-50/12 *AMC-Representacoes Texteis Lda v Office for Harmonisation in the Internal Market (Trade Marks and Designs)* [2013] All ER (D) 146 (Feb) (EGC: Eighth Chamber).

Regulation 40/94 replaced by Council Regulation (EC) 207/2009.

The applicant company applied for registration of the word sign 'ENDURACE' as a Community trade mark for goods and services in the Nice Agreement concerning the International Classification of Goods and Services for the Purposes of the Registration of Marks Classes 12, 35 and 37. An intervener company filed a notice of opposition to the registration based on its earlier figurative mark 'ENDURANCE' for goods in Class 12, on the ground of likelihood of confusion within the meaning of Council Regulation (EC) 40/94 art 8(1)(b). The opposition was upheld on the basis that such a likelihood of confusion existed, in particular, as regards the non-English-speaking section of the relevant consumers, who would not understand the meaning of the word 'endurance'. This decision was upheld by the Board of Appeal. The applicant sought annulment the Board's decision. *Held,* it was well established that the global assessment of the likelihood of confusion with respect to the visual, aural or conceptual similarity of the marks in question should be based on the overall impression given by the marks, bearing in mind, in particular, their distinctive and dominant components. However, the comparison should be made by examining each of the marks as a whole. Only where all the other components of the mark were negligible in the overall impression created by that mark could an assessment of similarity be carried out solely on the basis of the dominant element. There was nothing to prevent a determination as to whether there was any visual similarity between a word mark and a figurative mark, since the two types of mark had graphic form capable of creating a visual impression. In the absence of any possibility of comparing the marks at issue conceptually, since the non-English or non-French speaking public would not derive any meaning from either of the marks at issue, the visual similarity and virtual phonetic identity led to the conclusion that there was a likelihood of confusion between those marks as regards the goods and services found to be identical or similar. Due to the strong similarities in question, such a likelihood of confusion could not be excluded even for a consumer who was highly attentive when purchasing the goods or choosing the services at issue. Accordingly, the action would be dismissed.

Case T-109/11 *Apollo Tyres AG v Office for Harmonisation in the Internal Market (Trade Marks and Designs) (OHIM)* [2013] All ER (D) 75 (May) (EGC: Second Chamber). Regulation 40/94 art 8(1)(b) now Council Regulation (EC) 207/2009 art 8(1)(b).

2435   Trade mark—EU trade mark—registration—opposition—likelihood of confusion with earlier mark—obligation to state reasons

The applicant company filed an application with the Office for Harmonisation in the Internal Market for registration of the word sign 'METROINVEST' as an EU trade mark for services in the Nice Agreement concerning the International Classification of Goods and Services for the Purposes of the Registration of Marks Class 36. Those services included financial services relating to real estate services. An intervener company filed a notice of opposition to the registration based on its earlier figurative mark 'METRO' in so far as that mark was registered in respect of certain services in Class 36, on the ground of likelihood of confusion within the meaning of Council Regulation (EC) 207/2009 art 8(1)(b). The Opposition Division upheld the opposition on the ground that there was a likelihood of confusion on the part of the relevant public between the signs at issue. Its decision was upheld by the Board of Appeal. The applicant sought annulment of the Board's decision. *Held*, the signs at issue displayed some degree of visual similarity because they both contained the element 'metro'. Further, there was a certain conceptual similarity between the two signs, albeit very weak, since the sign METROINVEST might be broken down into two elements, each of which had a particular meaning, one of them having the same meaning as the single element comprising the earlier mark. In the context of an overall assessment of the mark, 'metro' was the distinctive and dominant element of the overall impression conveyed to the relevant public. This was because it was at the beginning of the mark and was devoid of any meaning in relation to the services at issue, while 'invest' was descriptive of those services. There was a likelihood of confusion between the two marks because the distinctive and dominant element of those signs was identical and the services concerned were also identical. On the basis that, as stated by established case law, the distinctive character of a sign should be determined by reference to the service to which it related, the challenge to the Board's finding that the word 'metro' was distinctive and the word 'invest' was descriptive did not concern infringement of the obligation to state reasons, but a potential error of law under art 8(1)(b). It followed that the complaint alleging infringement of the obligation to state reasons would be rejected. Accordingly, the application would be dismissed.

Case T-284/11 *Metropolis Inmobiliarias y Restauraciones, SL v Office for Harmonisation in the Internal Market (Trade Marks and Designs)* [2013] All ER (D) 91 (May) (EGC: Eighth Chamber).

2436   Trade mark—EU trade mark—registration—opposition—time-limit for supply of documents

The intervener company filed an application for registration of a Community trade mark with the Office for Harmonisation in the Internal Market ('OHIM') pursuant to Council Regulation (EC) 40/94 (on the Community trade mark). The rules implementing Regulation 40/94 were laid down by Commission Regulation (EC) 2868/95. Later, the applicant filed a notice of opposition against registration of the mark applied for in respect of the goods in question. The opposition was based on earlier rights in the form of two German word marks. That opposition was rejected by the Opposition Division, on the ground that the applicant had failed to prove, within the time-limit set, the existence and validity of the earlier marks relied on in support of the opposition. As regards documents submitted, the Opposition Division refused to take them into account, on the basis of Regulation 2868/95 r 20(1), because they had been submitted late. The applicant's appeal against that decision was dismissed by the Board of Appeal without assessing the merits of the opposition. It was found that the Opposition Division had been correct to conclude that the applicant had not duly substantiated, within the time-limits laid down, the existence and validity of the earlier marks relied on in support of the opposition. The Board further stated that neither the Opposition Division nor the Board itself had discretion under Regulation 40/94 art 74(2) to take into account documents that had not been filed before expiry of the time-limit set by OHIM, having regard to Regulation 2868/95 r 20(1). It further stated that even if it was to be found that it enjoyed discretion to accept documents filed late with the Opposition Division, it would have exercised such discretion against the applicant. The applicant sought annulment of the contested decision before the General Court of the European Union ('EGC'). It was decided that, if the evidence to establish the existence, validity and scope of the earlier mark, which could not be taken into account by the Opposition Division when it was filed late, could nevertheless be taken into consideration by the Board by virtue of its discretionary power under Regulation 40/94 art 74(2), the legal consequence laid down expressly in Regulation 1041/2005 for that type of deficiency, namely the rejection of the opposition, might, in certain cases, have no practical effect. It was concluded that the Board had not erred by finding that, in the circumstances, there had been a provision which had prevented evidence submitted late to OHIM by the applicant from being taken into account and that the Board had not had any discretion under art 74(2). *Held*, the EGC had found that the Board had been bound to apply Regulation 2868/95 r 20(1) and, therefore, to find that the submission of evidence after the expiry of the period specified for that purpose by OHIM, in order to establish the existence, validity and scope of protection of the earlier mark, entailed the rejection of the opposition, and the Board had no discretion in that regard. In so doing, the EGC had adopted an incorrect interpretation of r 50(1), which misconstrued the scope of the third sub-paragraph of that provision. In finding that the Board did not have discretion under Regulation 40/94 art 74(2) for the purposes of taking into account that evidence, the EGC had committed an error of law which vitiated its judgment. However, that error in law had no effect on the examination of the appeal, since the EGC's rejection of the applicant's plea in law alleging infringement of art 74(2) was well founded on legal grounds other than those given by the EGC, and could not therefore lead to the setting aside of that judgment.

Case C-120/12P *Rintisch v Office for Harmonisation in the Internal Market (Trade Marks and Designs)* [2013] All ER (D) 95 (Oct) (ECJ: Fourth Chamber).

The intervener company filed an application for registration of a Community trade mark with the Office for Harmonisation in the Internal Market pursuant to Council Regulation (EC) 40/94 (on the Community trade mark). Later, the applicant filed a notice of opposition against registration of the mark applied for in respect of the goods in question. The opposition was based on earlier rights in the form of two German word marks and a German figurative mark. That opposition was rejected on the ground that the applicant had failed to prove, within the time-limit set, the existence and the validity of the earlier marks relied on in support of the opposition. Documents submitted at a later date were rejected on the basis that they had been submitted late. The applicant's appeal against that decision was dismissed by the Board of Appeal without assessing the merits of the opposition. It was found that the Opposition Division had been correct to conclude that the applicant had not duly substantiated, within the time-limits laid down, the existence and the validity of the earlier marks relied on in support of the opposition. The Board further stated that neither the Opposition Division nor the Board itself had discretion under Regulation 40/94 art 74(2) to take into account documents that had not been filed before expiry of the time-limit set. It was further stated that, in any event, even if it was to be found that it enjoyed discretion to accept documents filed late, the Board would have exercised such discretion against the applicant. The applicant sought annulment of the contested decision before the General Court of the European Union ('EGC'). It was found that, if the evidence to establish the existence, validity and scope of an earlier mark could nevertheless be taken into consideration by the Board by virtue of its discretionary power under art 74(2), the legal consequence laid down expressly in Commission Regulation (EC) 2868/95 for that type of deficiency, namely the rejection of the opposition, might, in certain cases, have no practical effect. The EGC therefore concluded that the Board had not erred in finding that, in the circumstances, there had been a provision which had prevented evidence submitted late to the Office of Harmonisation in the Internal Market ('OHIM') by the applicant from being taken into account and that, therefore, the Board had not had any discretion under Regulation 40/94 art 74(2). The applicant appealed. *Held*, the EGC had found that the Board had been bound to apply Regulation 2868/95 r 20(1) and, therefore, to find that the submission of evidence after the expiry of the period specified for that purpose by OHIM, in order to establish the existence, validity and scope of protection of the earlier mark, entailed the rejection of the opposition, and the Board had no discretion in that regard. In so doing, the EGC had adopted an incorrect interpretation of r 50(1), which misconstrued the scope of the third sub-paragraph of that provision. Consequently, in finding that r 20(1) had constituted a provision to the contrary which had prevented evidence submitted late to OHIM by the applicant from being taken into account by the Board, with the result that the Board had not had any discretion under Regulation 40/94 art 74(2) for the purposes of taking into account that evidence, the EGC had committed an error of law which vitiated its judgment. However, that error in law had no effect on the examination of the appeal, since the EGC's rejection of the applicant's plea in law alleging infringement of art 74(2) was well founded on legal grounds other than those given by the EGC, and could not therefore lead to the setting aside of that judgment.

Case C-121/12P *Rintisch v Office for Harmonisation in the Internal Market (Trade Marks and Designs)* [2013] All ER (D) 96 (Oct) (ECJ: Fourth Chamber).

The intervener company filed an application for registration of a Community trade mark with the Office for Harmonisation in the Internal Market pursuant to Council Regulation (EC) 40/94 (on the Community trade mark). The rules implementing Regulation 40/94 were laid down by Commission Regulation (EC) 2868/95. The applicant filed a notice of opposition against registration of the mark based on earlier rights in the form of two German word marks and a German figurative mark. The Opposition Division rejected the opposition on the ground that the applicant failed to prove, within the time-limit set, the existence and the validity of the earlier marks. As regards certain documents submitted by the applicant, the Opposition Division refused, on the basis of Regulation 2868/95 r 20(1), to take them into account as they had been submitted late. The applicant's appeal against that decision was dismissed by the Board of Appeal, which found that the Opposition Division had been correct to conclude that the applicant had not duly substantiated, within the time-limits laid down, the existence and the validity of the earlier marks relied on in support of the opposition. The Board further stated that neither the Opposition Division nor the Board had discretion under Regulation 40/94 art 74(2) to take into account documents that had not been filed before the expiry of the time-limit set by the Office for Harmonisation, having regard to Regulation 2868/95 r 20(1), and that, even if it was found that it enjoyed such discretion, it would have exercised it against the applicant. The applicant sought annulment of the contested decision before the European General Court, contending that the Board of Appeal infringed Regulation 40/94 and had misused its powers. The European General Court decided that the Board had not erred by finding that there had been a provision which prevented evidence submitted late to the Office for Harmonisation by the applicant being taken into account and that the Board, therefore, had not had any discretion under art 74(2). Moreover, it decided that the applicant's complaint relating to the Board's misuse of powers was inadmissible. The applicant appealed. *Held*, the European General Court had found that it followed from Regulation 2868/95 r 50(1) that the Board had been bound to apply r 20(1) and, therefore, to find that the submission of evidence after the expiry of the period specified for that purpose by the Office for Harmonisation, in order to establish the existence, validity and scope of protection of the earlier mark, entailed the rejection of the opposition, and the Board had no discretion in that regard. In so doing, the European General Court adopted an incorrect interpretation of r 50(1), which misconstrued the scope of the third sub-paragraph of that provision. Consequently, in finding that r 20(1) constituted a provision to the contrary which had prevented evidence submitted late to the Office for Harmonisation by the applicant from being taken into account by the Board, with the result that the Board had not had any discretion under art 74(2) for the purposes of taking into account that evidence, the European General Court had committed an error of law which vitiated its judgment. However, that error in law had no effect on the examination of the appeal, since the European General Court's rejection of the applicant's plea in law alleging infringement of art 74(2) was well founded on legal grounds other than those given by the European General Court, and could not therefore lead to the setting aside of that judgment. Moreover, in respect of the applicant's submission that the Board misused its powers, the applicant had confined itself to general assertions and had in no way identified the paragraphs of the judgment under appeal which it criticised. Further, it had not stated the legal requirements relied on in support of that ground of appeal. Since that ground of appeal had not met the relevant requirements, it would be rejected as being inadmissible. Accordingly, the appeal would be dismissed.

Case C-122/12 P *Rintisch v Office of Harmonisation in the Internal Market (Trade Marks and Designs)* [2013] All ER (D) 97 (Oct) (ECJ: Fourth Chamber).

Council Regulation (EC) 40/94 replaced: Council Regulation (EC) 207/2009.

2437   Trade mark—EU trade mark—registration—opposition proceedings—invalidity on basis of earlier mark

Council Regulation (EC) 207/2009 art 53(1)(c) provides that a European Union trade mark must be declared invalid where there is an earlier right as referred to in art 8(4) and the conditions set out in art 8(4) are fulfilled.

The applicant filed an application with the defendant for registration of an EU trade mark in respect of the word sign 'macros'. Before a decision was made, the defendant granted registration of the figurative sign 'makro' (the 'conflicting mark') for goods and services in the same classes as the applicant's mark. The owner of the conflicting mark filed a notice of opposition to registration of the applicant's mark. The applicant applied for a declaration of invalidity in relation to the conflicting mark, based in particular on the German company name 'macros consult GmbH'. It claimed that that company name constituted an earlier mark which invalidated the conflicting mark by virtue of Regulation 207/2009 art 53(1)(c). The application was rejected on the grounds that the applicant had not indicated with sufficient precision what earlier right it relied on, and that the existence of an earlier right could not be established from the evidence presented by the applicant. The applicant brought proceedings seeking annulment of that decision, submitting that, at the date on which the application for registration of the conflicting mark had been lodged, it had already been using the designation 'macros consult' as a name, company name and trade sign. *Held*, from the very wording of art 53(1), (2), applications for a declaration of invalidity based on those provisions depended on the existence of an earlier right. Further, 'earlier' was defined in art 8(4) as meaning that the right on which the application for a declaration of invalidity was based should have been acquired prior to the date of application for registration of the EU trade mark in respect of which the declaration of invalidity was sought or the date of the priority of the latter. The applicant had failed to show that the defendant had wrongly found that it had not established the existence of an earlier right on which an application for a declaration of invalidity brought under art 53(1)(c) could be based. Accordingly, the application would be dismissed.

Case T-579/10 *macros consult GmbH – Unternehmensberatung für Wirtschafts- und Finanztechnologie v Office for Harmonisation in the Internal Market (Trade Marks and Designs)* [2013] All ER (D) 164 (May) (EGC: First Chamber).

2438   Trade mark—EU trade mark—registration—opposition proceedings—likelihood of confusion—identical services

The applicant filed an application for registration of an EU trade mark with the Office for Harmonisation in the Internal Market, pursuant to Council Regulation (EC) 40/94 on the EU trade mark in respect of the word sign 'babilu' for goods and services in the Nice Agreement concerning the International Classification of Goods and Services for the Purposes of the Registration of Marks Class 35. An intervener company filed a notice of opposition to the registration of the mark based on an earlier EU word mark 'BABIDU' for services in Class 35 claiming likely confusion in breach of Regulation 40/94 art 8(1)(b). The Opposition Division upheld the opposition. The applicant unsuccessfully appealed to the Second Board of Appeal, which found that the relevant public consisted of professionals who had a higher than average level of attentiveness. It further held that the services covered by the marks at issue were identical, and observed that those marks displayed a high degree of similarity visually and aurally, and that they had no meaning conceptually. It therefore considered that there was a high degree of similarity overall between those marks. It added that the earlier trade mark displayed a normal degree of distinctiveness and concluded that, in a global assessment of the evidence in the case, the Opposition Division had not erred in finding that there had been a likelihood of confusion between the marks at issue. The applicant applied to the European General Court to annul the decision, alleging infringement of art 8(1)(b). *Held*, in order to assess the similarity of the goods or services concerned, all the relevant features of the relationship between those goods or services should be taken into account, including their nature, their intended purpose, their method of use and whether they were in competition with each other or were complementary. For the purposes of art 8(1)(b), the group of goods or services protected by the marks at issue should be taken into account, and not the goods or services actually marketed under those marks. The services in question were identical. It followed that the Board had been correct in its conclusion. In making a global assessment of the likelihood of confusion, account should be taken of the average consumer of the category of products concerned, who was reasonably well informed and reasonably observant and circumspect. The average consumer's level of attention was likely to vary according to the category of goods or services in question. It should be based on the overall impression given by the marks, bearing in mind their distinctive and dominant components. The average consumer normally perceived a mark as a whole and did not proceed to analyse its various details. Since the services were identical, there was a high degree of similarity overall between the marks at issue and the earlier trade mark had a normal inherent distinctiveness. The Board had been right to conclude that there had been a likelihood of confusion even though the relevant public had a higher than average level of attentiveness. Accordingly, the action would be dismissed.

Case T-66/11 *Present–Service Ullrich GmbH & Co KG v Office for Harmonisation in the Internal Market (Trade Marks and Designs)* [2013] All ER (D) 263 (Feb) (EGC: Fifth Chamber).

Regulation 40/94 art 8(1)(b) replaced by Council Regulation (EC) 207/2009 art 8(1)(b).

2439   Trade mark—EU trade mark—registration—refusal—likelihood of confusion with earlier mark

The applicant company filed an application for registration of an EU trade mark under Council Regulation (EC) 207/2009 (on the EU trade mark). The mark in respect of which registration was sought was the word sign 'Gigabyte'. The goods in respect of which registration was sought were in the Nice Agreement Classes 37, 42 (concerning the International Classification of Goods and Services for the Purposes of the Registration of Marks), and corresponded to IT services. The intervener company filed a notice of opposition against registration of the mark applied for in respect of the goods in Classes 37, 42 based on the earlier EU word mark 'GIGABITER'. That mark had been registered for goods in Class 42. The ground relied on in support of the opposition was that referred to in Regulation 207/2009 art 8(1)(b) (likelihood of confusion). The intervener's opposition was upheld on the basis that the services were similar to those in Class 42 covered by the earlier mark, and that the mark applied for was visually and aurally similar to the earlier mark. The applicant's appeal against the decision was dismissed on the ground that there had been a likelihood of confusion between the mark applied for and the earlier mark. The applicant sought annulment of the contested decision on the basis of errors in the assessment of the likelihood of confusion between the signs at issue. *Held*, global assessment of the likelihood of confusion implied some interdependence between the relevant factors and, in particular, a similarity between the trade marks and between the services designated. Accordingly, a lesser degree of similarity between the services designated might be offset by a greater degree of similarity between the marks, and vice versa. In the present case, the assessment on appeal was well founded. The signs in question were visually, aurally and conceptually similar. Further, the services covered by the marks in question were similar. In the context of a global assessment, there was a likelihood of confusion between the signs at issue. Accordingly, the action for annulment would be dismissed.

Case T-451/11 *Gigabyte Technology Co Ltd v Office for Harmonisation in the Internal Market (Trade Marks and Designs)* [2013] All ER (D) 161 (Jan) (EGC: Third Chamber).

2440   Trade mark—EU trade mark—registration—requirements—relevance of distinctive character

European Parliament and Council Directive (EC) 2008/95 (to approximate the laws of the member states relating to trade marks) art 2 provides that a trade mark may consist of any signs capable of being represented graphically, particularly words, including personal names, designs, letters, numerals, the shape of goods or of their packaging, provided that such signs are capable of distinguishing the goods or services of one undertaking from those of other undertakings.

The claimants owned a registered trade mark associated with the popular board game 'Scrabble'. The description of the mark was that it consisted of a three-dimensional ivory-coloured tile on the top surface of which was shown a letter of the Roman alphabet and a numeral in the range one to ten. The mark was registered in respect of computer game adaptations of board games. The claimants alleged infringement of the mark by the defendant in connection with the exploitation of a digital game 'Scramble with Friends'. The defendant counterclaimed for revocation of the mark on the ground that it was not a sign capable of graphic representation because of the large variety of representations encompassed by it. On the defendant's application for summary judgment, the judge declared that the registration of the mark was invalid as it did not comply with Directive 2008/95 art 2. On appeal, the claimants submitted that the judge was wrong to decide summarily that the distinctiveness of the mark was irrelevant in determining the requirements in art 2 for a sign and for the sign to be capable of graphic representation. *Held*, the judge did not misapply the law to the facts. The mark was not a sign as required by art 2. It potentially covered many signs achievable by numerous permutations, presentations and combinations of the subject matter of the registration. Further, there was no graphic representation of a sign as required by art 2 that met the requirements of clarity, precision and objectivity. Accordingly, the appeal would be dismissed.

JW Spear & Sons Ltd v Zynga Inc [2013] EWCA Civ 1175, [2014] IP & T 228 (Court of Appeal: Lewison LJ, Sir John Mummery and Sir Timothy Lloyd). Decision of Arnold J [2012] EWHC 3345 (Ch), [2012] All ER (D) 326 (Nov) affirmed.

2441   Trade mark—EU trade mark—registration—sign capable of being graphically represented—specified colour applied as predominant colour on packaging

The defendant company applied to register a trade mark for chocolate which featured a specified shade of the colour purple. The application comprised a swatch of the relevant colour along with a verbal description of the mark sought which described the purple shade as being 'applied to the whole visible surface' or being 'the predominant colour applied to the whole visible surface' of the packaging of the goods. The application was accepted and the mark registered. The claimant company appealed on the ground that the colour mark described in the application was not registrable because it was not a sign and was not capable of being represented graphically. The judge concluded that single colours were capable of being signs, of being represented graphically and of distinguishing and that the mark in question was capable of being a mark within Parliament and Council Directive (EC) 2008/95 art 2. He further found that the words of the description were not too vague as the description of 'predominant' in respect of the colour required the decision-taker to make a judgment as to whether a colour was the 'predominant' colour used on the visible packaging for a product. The appeal was dismissed and the claimant appealed further. *Held*, the description of the trade mark did not constitute 'a sign' that was 'graphically represented' within art 2. The crucial point stemmed from the misinterpretation of the verbal description of the graphic representation of the mark for which application had been made. The description referred not only to the colour as applied to the whole visible surface of the packaging of the goods, but also to the colour purple 'being the predominant colour' applied to the whole visible surface. The use of the word 'predominant' opened the door to a multitude of different visual forms as a result of its implied reference to other colours and other visual material not displayed or described in the application and over which the colour purple might predominate. If the colour purple was less than total, the application would cover other matter in combination with the colour, but not graphically represented or verbally described in the specific, certain, self-contained and precise manner required. The result would not be an application to register 'a sign', but to register multiple signs with different permutations, presentations and appearances, which were neither graphically represented nor described with any certainty or precision, or at all. To allow a registration so lacking in specificity, clarity and precision of visual appearance would offend against both the principle of certainty and the principle of fairness by giving a competitive advantage to the defendant. Accordingly, the appeal would be allowed.

Cadbury UK Ltd v Société des Produits Nestlé SA [2013] EWCA Civ 1174, [2014] IP & T 214 (Court of Appeal: Lewison LJ, Sir John Mummery and Sir Timothy Lloyd). Decision of Judge Birss QC [2012] EWHC 2637 (Ch), [2012] All ER (D) 06 (Oct) reversed.

2442   Trade mark—EU trade mark—revocation—genuine use

A medical services company held a European trade mark in relation to its former company name. The goods and services in question fell within Classes 10, 37 and 42 of the Nice Agreement 1957 as amended. In respect of Class 10, the goods and services for which registration was sought included various medical instruments and equipment such as infusion pumps, controllers, and blood pressure measurement instruments. In relation to Classes 37 and 42, the goods and services corresponded respectively to the service and repair of instruments and equipment, and also the leasing and rental of such items. The applicant filed a request for revocation of the mark on the basis of Council Regulation (EC) 207/2009 art 51(1)(a), pursuant to which a mark was to be revoked if it had not been put to genuine use. The respondent's Cancellation Division rejected most of the applicant's request and the applicant appealed to the respondent's Board of Appeal. The appeal was not successful, and the applicant brought proceedings before the European General Court seeking annulment of the Board's decision. It alleged that (1) genuine use of 'controllers' in Class 10 had not been expressly proved; and (2) the Board had arbitrarily bundled all of the goods falling within Class 10 into a single category and so extended the protection conferred by registration of the trade mark. In the second plea, the applicant alleged that the evidence taken into account by the Board did not make it possible to establish sufficient use of the mark with regard to the services falling within Class 37. *Held*, in the circumstances, the Board had been correct not to declare the rights of the proprietor of the trade mark at issue revoked in respect of 'controllers'. Further, with regard to the other products covered by that mark, the applicant did not contest that genuine use of disposable thermometers and thermometers had been proved, and genuine use should be considered as established for those goods. However, this had not been proved for the other goods covered by the mark in question falling within Class 10 and the Board had been wrong not to revoke the rights of the proprietor in respect of those goods. As to the second ground of appeal, the examination of whether an earlier trade mark had been put to genuine use entailed a degree of interdependence between the factors taken into account and that test could not rely solely on usage or a de minimis approach. When it served a real commercial purpose, even minimal use of the trade mark could be sufficient if demonstrated by solid and objective evidence of effective and sufficient use of the trade mark to maintain or create a share in the market concerned. However, the applicant had failed to adduce any evidence which would substantiate its claims of infringement of art 51(1)(a) in respect of services in Class 37. Further, it did not contest the probative nature of the evidence submitted to the Board. Therefore, the contested decision would be annulled in so far as it rejected the application for revocation in relation to the products covered by the trade mark falling within Class 10 other than those specified. Accordingly, the application would be allowed in part.

Case T-353/12 *Aleris Holding AB v Office for Harmonisation in the Internal Market (Trade Marks and Designs)* [2013] All ER (D) 263 (May) (EGC: Fifth Chamber). Case T-203/02 *Sunrider v OHIM – Espadafor Caba (VITAFRUIT)* [2004] All ER (D) 129 (Jul), CFI, applied. Case T-126/03 *Reckitt Benckiser (España) v OHIM – Aladin (ALADIN)* [2005] All ER (D) 198 (Jul), CFI, explained.

2443   Trade mark—genuine use—non-use of registered trade mark—trade mark use as part of composite mark

Council Regulation (EC) 40/94 art 15(1) provides that if, within a period of five years following registration, the proprietor has not put the Community trade mark to genuine use in the Community in connection with the goods or services in respect of which it is registered, or if such use has been suspended during an uninterrupted period of five years, the Community trade mark is subject to sanctions unless there are proper reasons for non-use. Use of the Community trade mark in a form differing in elements which do not alter the distinctive character of the mark in the form in which it was registered constitutes use within the meaning of art 15(1): art 15(2)(a).

The applicant was the proprietor of a German word and figurative mark for trousers, shirts, blouses and jackets which contained the word element 'LEVI'S' in a red rectangular element at the left upper edge of a pocket. It was also the proprietor of a Community figurative mark, in red and blue, which consisted of a rectangular red label, made of textile, sewn into and protruding from the upper part of the left-hand seam of the rear pocket of trousers, shorts or skirts. The respondent placed trousers on the market with small rectangular red fabric tags on which appeared certain brands or the word 'SM JEANS', sewn into the upper part of the outer right seam of the right rear pocket. The applicant sought an order from the competent German court to restrain the respondent from offering or marketing such trousers or stocking them for those purposes. In the course of proceedings it was found that there was a likelihood of confusion between the respondent's mark and the applicant's Community mark, but the question arose whether the applicant had put that mark to genuine use within the meaning of Regulation 40/94 art 15. A preliminary ruling was sought as to whether a trade mark could be put to genuine use, within the meaning of art 15(1), where it was used only in conjunction with another mark, the public considered the two marks to be independent distinctive signs, and the combination of the two marks was itself registered as a trade mark. *Held*, it was settled that the distinctiveness of a mark meant that the mark served to identify the goods in respect of which registration was applied for as originating from a particular undertaking, and thus to distinguish those goods from those of other undertakings. The essential function of the mark was to identify, in the eyes of consumers, the undertaking of origin of the goods. Therefore, regardless of whether the sign was used as part of a registered trade mark or in conjunction with the registered trade mark, the fundamental condition was that, as a consequence of that use, the sign for which registration as a trade mark was sought might serve to identify the goods to which it related as originating from a particular undertaking. The 'use' of a mark, in its literal sense, generally encompassed both its independent use and its use as part of another mark taken as a whole or in conjunction with that other mark. It followed that the condition of genuine use of a trade mark, within the meaning of art 15(1), might be satisfied where a registered trade mark, which had become distinctive as a result of the use of another composite mark of which it constituted one of the elements, was used only through that other composite mark, or where it was used only in conjunction with another mark, and the combination of those two marks was itself registered as a trade mark.

Case C-12/12 *Colloseum Holding AG v Levi Strauss & Co* [2013] IP & T 705 (ECJ: Fifth Chamber). Case C-245/02 *Anheuser-Busch Inc v Budejovicky Budvar, narodni podnik* [2007] IP & T 348, ECJ; Case C-488/06 *L & D SA v Office for Harmonisation in the Internal Market (Trade Marks and Designs) (OHIM)* [2008] All ER (D) 260 (Jul), ECJ; Case C-311/11P *Smart Technologies ULC v Office for Harmonisation in the Internal Market (Trade Marks and Designs)* [2012] All ER (D) 192 (Jul), ECJ (2012 Abr para 2493); and Case C-553/11 *Rintisch v Eder* [2013] Bus LR 318, [2012] All ER (D) 343 (Oct), ECJ, considered.

Regulation 40/94 art 15 now Council Regulation (EC) 207/2009 art 15(1).

2444　　Trade mark—infringement—injunction—general injunction

In earlier proceedings, it had been found that the defendant had infringed the claimant's trade marks. Consequential issues, including the form of an injunction sought by the claimant, fell to be determined. The conventional form of injunction to restrain trade mark infringement granted by the court was a general injunction. However, the rival drafts of the injunction specified the particular acts which were to be restrained. The claimant stated that it would be content with an injunction in conventional form and did not pursue the request for a more specific injunction. By contrast, the defendant resisted the grant of an injunction in conventional form. *Held*, European Parliament and Council Directive (EC) 2004/48 art 3(2) required that any remedy granted by way of relief for trade mark infringement had to be proportionate. However, it did not follow that the court's normal practice of granting a general injunction was contrary to art 3(2), since it was not necessarily the case that a general injunction was disproportionate, although there might be specific circumstances in which a general injunction would be disproportionate. The conventional form of injunction to restrain trade mark infringement granted by the court was a general injunction. A general injunction would not be disproportionate, or create a barrier, to legitimate trade in the circumstances. The defendant had not proved that use of the signs did not affect, and was not liable to affect, the functions of the EU trade mark in member states other than the United Kingdom. Therefore, the general rule stated by the European Court of Justice, that a prohibition against further infringement or threatened infringement of an EU trade mark must, as a rule, extend to the entire area of the EU, should be applied. A general injunction would be granted to restrain infringement of the trade marks. In the case of the EU trade mark, an EU-wide injunction would be granted. Judgment would be given accordingly.

Interflora Inc v Marks and Spencer plc (No 3) [2013] EWHC 1484 (Ch), [2013] IP & T 1023 (Chancery Division: Arnold J). Case C-235/09 *DHL Express France SAS v Chronopost SA* [2011] IP & T 403, ECJ (2011 Abr para 2382), considered. For related proceedings see [2013] EWHC 1291 (Ch), [2013] IP & T 931 (para 2406).

2445   Trade mark—infringement—likelihood of confusion—similarity of signs

The claimant, which was a lay corporation that constituted a world-famous University, had a law faculty which operated under the name 'Oxford Law'. The defendant company, which offered short-term tuition for courses administered by separate professional regulatory bodies, traded under the name 'Oxford Law School'. The claimant sought to establish a Community trade mark infringement under Council Regulation (EC) 207/2009 (on the Community trade mark) art 9(1)(b) or (c) and an infringement of its United Kingdom registered trade marks under the Trade Marks Act 1994 s 10(2) or (3). It brought proceedings seeking injunctive relief and orders that the defendant transfer ownership of its domain name and change its registered company name to no longer include 'Oxford' or any confusingly similar name. The claimant submitted that there was a high degree of visual, aural and conceptual similarity and a likelihood of initial interest confusion and actual confusion between the parties' signs. Moreover, the claimant contended that the defendant had been taking advantage and causing detriment to the distinctive character of the claimant's registered trade marks and that the necessary elements of passing off were satisfied. *Held,* in the circumstances, there was an infringement of the claimant's registered United Kingdom and Community trade marks. Given the very high degree of visual, aural and conceptual similarity between the parties' signs, there was a strong likelihood of initial interest and actual confusion by the average consumer. Although the parties generally operated in slightly different markets and did not compete with each other, the average consumer would not have considered the differences sufficient to distinguish the services. The defendant's sign took unfair advantage of, and was detrimental to, the distinctive character and repute of the claimant's trade marks. In respect of the passing off claim, the claimant had established that the use of the defendant's sign took unfair advantage of, and was detrimental to, the distinctive character and repute of the claimant's trade marks. The claimant had an established and historic worldwide reputation. The defendant was making a misrepresentation to the public so as to lead them to believe that the services were either those of the claimant or associated with, approved, authorised or endorsed by the claimant. The claimant was likely to suffer genuine and substantial damage to its reputation and goodwill by reason of the material misrepresentation. It followed that there had been an infringement of the claimant's registered United Kingdom and Community trade marks and the claimant would be granted an injunction. Accordingly, the appeal would be allowed.

University of Oxford v Oxford Law School Ltd [2014] All ER (D) 104 (Jan) (Intellectual Property Enterprise Court: Judge Lambert). *Och-Ziff Management Europe Ltd v Och Capital LLP* [2010] EWHC 2599 (Ch), [2011] Bus LR 632, [2010] All ER (D) 07 (Nov) (2010 Abr para 2709); Case C-323/09 *Interflora Inc v Marks and Spencer plc* [2013] All ER (EC) 519, ECJ (2011 Abr para 2377); and Case C-252/12 *Specsavers International Healthcare Ltd v Asda Stores Ltd* [2013] All ER (D) 355 (Jul), ECJ (para 2408), applied.

2446   Trade mark—infringement—likelihood of confusion—use of sign in respect of identical or similar products

The claimant registered the sign 'Ideal Home' in respect of a variety of house wares, domestic electrical goods and appliances, garden equipment, plants and furniture and home furnishings. The claimant also published a magazine entitled 'Ideal Home'. The defendant launched an online shop which sold home interest goods and used the words 'Ideal Home' in exhibitions or shows. The claimant brought proceedings alleging that the defendant's activities infringed its trade mark contrary to the Trade Marks Act 1994 s 10(1), (3). The defendant counterclaimed, contending that the claimant's trade mark was invalid. It submitted that the mark lacked distinctive character and that it consisted exclusively of signs or indications which served to designate the kind, quality and intended purpose of the goods or services. The defendant further submitted that, in so far as the mark encompassed services provided in connection with or in the context of the defendant's ideal home show, its use was liable to be prevented by the law of passing off and the registration was and remained contrary to s 5(4)(a). *Held,* in the circumstances, the attack on the validity of the trade mark failed. The sale of home interest goods by either party under the Ideal Home name was sufficiently in the middle of the spectrum between the respective core businesses for neither party to be able to succeed against the other in a passing off claim. With regard to infringement, it was settled law that a proprietor of a trade mark could succeed in a claim for infringement only if (1) there was a use of a sign by a third party within the relevant territory; (2) the use was in the course of trade; (3) the use had been without the consent of the proprietor of the trade mark; (4) the sign was identical to the trade mark; (5) the sign was in relation to goods or services which were identical to those for which the trade mark was registered; and (6) the sign affected or was liable to affect the functions of the trade mark. A sign was to be regarded as identical with the trade mark where it reproduced, without any modification or addition, all the elements constituting the trade mark or where, viewed as a whole, it contained differences so insignificant that they might go unnoticed by an average consumer. On the facts, the claimant failed to establish double identity. The average consumer would perceive that the sign being used in connection with the online offering was the Ideal Home Show. Although there might be some confusion caused by use of Ideal Home Show as a trade mark for online retail shopping, that confusion was no more than might be expected by reason of the concurrent trading by the parties in their core businesses using Ideal Home, and was not such as to affect the function of the claimant's trade mark more adversely that it was already affected by virtue of the longstanding uses by the separate businesses. Further, Ideal Home, as a mark, did not denote the retail services of the proprietor alone. Accordingly, the claim and the counterclaim would be dismissed.

IPC Media Ltd v Media 10 Ltd [2013] EWHC 3796 (IPEC), [2013] All ER (D) 56 (Dec) (Chancery Division: Mr John Baldwin QC).

2447   Trade mark—infringement—likelihood of confusion—use of similar trade mark—stay of proceedings

The claimant was an American university based in Virginia. The defendant was a private university in London. The defendant had previously been known as 'Regent's College'. The defendant formally applied to change its name to 'Regent's University London'. After the consultation deadline had passed, the claimant wrote to the defendant enclosing details of its Community trade mark in respect of the name 'Regents University'. The defendant denied any possibility of confusion and made it clear that it intended to continue with its name change, which was approved. The defendant filed an application for the revocation of the claimant's mark. The claimant commenced proceedings in England, alleging infringement of its mark. The defendant applied for a stay of the proceedings pursuant to Council Regulation (EC) 207/2009 art 104 pending the outcome of its revocation proceedings. The claimant opposed that application, but also applied for provisional and protective measures under art 104(3) in the form of an injunction should the stay be granted. Held, when considering an application to stay under art 104, the first task was to identify what, if any, special grounds there were, and if there were any, to ask whether they were sufficiently compelling to outweigh the strong presumption in favour of granting a stay. In doing so, it was necessary to bear in mind both the underlying rationale of art 104 to minimise the risk of irreconcilable judgments, and also the potential availability in an appropriate case of protective and provisional measures under art 104(3). There were potential consequences of infringement that had the potential to transform the possibilities of confusion into special features for the purposes of art 104(1). However, the likely frequency or seriousness were not such as to weigh heavily in the balance. Further, there was some possibility of confusion taking place, but the nature of the business conducted by the respective parties was such that the vast majority of people involved or potentially involved with either of the parties would take great care over their selection of the university they approached. The word 'London' in the defendant's name was an important factor in distinguishing it from a university based in the United States. Although the claimant had a respectable argument that there were special grounds, they were not sufficiently weighty to outweigh the strong presumption in favour of granting a stay to avoid the risk of irreconcilable decisions. In respect of provisional and protective measures, if no injunction were granted, some of the damage that the claimant would sustain would have been unquantifiable, but it was not likely to be very extensive or very serious. On the other hand, some of the consequences of the grant of an injunction restraining the defendant from calling itself 'Regent's University London' would have been both unquantifiable and serious. If, in order to comply, it dropped the use of the word 'Regent's' it would lose much of the advantage of its existing reputation as Regent's College. Similarly, dropping 'University' would have lost the prestige associated with that word which the defendant had worked so hard to obtain. The risk of unquantifiable damage to the defendant if an injunction were wrongly granted greatly outweighed the risk of such damage to the claimant if an injunction were wrongly refused. Accordingly, the stay would be granted and the application for an injunction dismissed.

Regents University v Regent's University London [2013] EWPCC 39, [2013] All ER (D) 50 (Sep) (Patents County Court: Recorder Alastair Wilson QC). *Starbucks (HK) Ltd v British Sky Broadcasting Group plc; EMI (IP) Ltd v British Sky Broadcasting Group plc* [2012] EWCA Civ 1201, [2013] IP & T 222 (2012 Abr para 2490) applied. Case C-159/02 *Turner v Grovit* [2005] 1 AC 101, [2004] 2 All ER (Comm) 381 (2004 Abr para 558) considered.

2448 Trade mark—infringement—proceedings—evidence—surveys

In trade mark infringement proceedings, a judge granted the claimants permission to adduce evidence from 13 witnesses who, the claimants said, would give evidence of confusion in the real world in relation to advertisements of the defendant. The evidence comprised witness statements based on answers given by the witnesses to a questionnaire produced by the claimants. The defendant appealed, submitting that the judge had erred in concluding that the evidence was admissible. *Held*, a judge should not let in such evidence unless the party seeking to call the evidence satisfied the judge that it was likely to be of real value and that the likely value of the evidence justified the cost. The judge had been misled by the impression created by the witness statements when compared to the raw data on which they were based. He had left it to the defendant to amplify the range of responses from the questionnaire, imposing on it the burden of disproving the validity of the selection of witnesses. The judge should have asked himself whether the evidence was likely to be of real value. He had conducted a flawed analysis of the nature of the claimants' application, the quality of the raw data that supported the witness statements, and had ultimately applied too lax a test. Accordingly, the appeal would be allowed.

Interflora Inc v Marks and Spencer plc [2013] EWCA Civ 319, [2013] All ER (D) 14 (Apr) (Court of Appeal: Longmore and Lewison LJJ and Sir Robin Jacob). *Interflora Inc v Marks and Spencer plc* [2012] EWCA Civ 1501, [2012] All ER (D) 228 (Nov) (2012 Abr para 2509) applied. Decision of Arnold J [2013] EWHC 273 (Ch), [2013] All ER (D) 273 (Feb) reversed.

2449 Trade mark—infringement—proceedings—expert evidence

See *Interflora Inc v Marks and Spencer plc*, para 298.

2450 Trade mark—infringement—trade mark use—concurrent goodwill

The claimant company made boots and shoes which it branded with a fox and boot logo using a device previously used for the same purpose by a second company, another boot maker. The second company had supplied shoes to the defendant company which was based in the United States. The second company ceased trading and sold the goodwill of its business and the use of its name, as well as its rights and interest in the device to the defendant. The defendant made no use of the device in the United Kingdom. A respected shoe maker who had formerly worked for the second company went to work for the claimant which thereafter used the device on shoes, leather goods and stationery and made mention of the shoe maker's connection to the second company. The defendant opened a shop in the United Kingdom and began to sell shoes branded with the device. The claimant complained to the defendant before issuing proceedings for infringement of its Community trade mark and for passing off. *Held*, with regard to the issue of goodwill, the device did not lack distinctive character. The fact that the device was used along with the name of the claimant did not preclude a claim in passing off. The device and the name were not indivisible parts of a single logo. They were separate entities. There could be no serious doubt that the claimant's customers would recognise the device as the claimant's logo and the name as the claimant's name. The use of the device by the defendant on products sold from its shops or through its website in the United Kingdom amounted to passing off of those products. Regarding deception, it was most unlikely that many customers would think it coincidental that two companies had adopted the same logo for high quality shoes. It was highly likely that a substantial number of customers with whom the claimant had goodwill would be deceived, by the presence of the logo on the defendant's shoes and other products, into believing either that they were manufactured by the claimant or that they were connected or associated with the claimant in some other way. It was not necessary to be precise about the nature of the connection that the customers would believe existed. The distinctiveness of the logo and the degree of similarity were very high. The only obvious explanation was therefore that the logo was being used to indicate some kind of commercial connection. In the circumstances, damage was inevitable, at least in the sense of the blurring, diminishing or erosion of the mark. Regarding honest concurrent use, although the defendant had technically purchased the equipment necessary to keep the established business going in the United Kingdom, it was clear that it had allowed those assets to be dissipated or destroyed. By promoting, through agreement with the second company, the destruction of the second company's business, by failing to take any steps to preserve a business in the United Kingdom, and by allowing the market to assume that the second company no longer existed, the defendant had abandoned any and all the goodwill associated with the second company. The defendant had no defence based on concurrent goodwill. Accordingly, the claim would be allowed.

WS *Foster & Son Ltd v Brooks Bros UK Ltd* [2013] EWPCC 18, [2013] All ER (D) 232 (Mar) (Patents County Court: Iain Purvis QC).

2451   Trade mark—international registration—fees

The Trade Marks (International Registration) (Amendment No 2) Order 2013, SI 2013/2237 (in force on 1 October 2013), further amends the 2008 Order, SI 2008/2206, so as to (1) impose a £100 fee for a notice of opposition to the conferring of protection on an international registration where the grounds of opposition are based solely on either or both of the Trade Marks Act 1994 s 5(1) or (2); (2) provide that a fee of £100 is payable on giving notice of fast track opposition to the conferring of protection on an international registration; (3) require a fee of £100 to be paid on an application to add grounds other than those contained in s 5(1), (2) to an opposition to the conferring of protection on an international registration; and (4) provide that a fee of £250 is payable on an appeal to the person appointed under s 76 in proceedings between two or more parties.

2452   Trade mark—international registration—time limits

The Trade Marks (International Registration) (Amendment) Order 2013, SI 2013/445 (in force on 31 March 2013), further amends the 2008 Order, SI 2008/2206, so as to exclude the date on which a relevant event occurred for the purpose of computing a period of time by reference to the relevant event.

2453   Trade mark—legislation—application to Isle of Man

The Trade Marks (Isle of Man) Order 2013, SI 2013/2601 (in force on 11 November 2013), replaces the Trade Marks Act 1994 (Isle of Man) Order 1996, SI 1996/729, and modifies the Trade Marks Act 1994 in its application to the Isle of Man. SI 2002/3148 and SI 2004/1497 are revoked.

2454   Trade mark—registration—fast track opposition—procedure

The Trade Marks (Fast Track Opposition) (Amendment) Rules 2013, SI 2013/2235 (in force on 1 October 2013), further amend the Trade Marks Rules 2008, SI 2008/1797, so as to provide for an additional fast track procedure under the Trade Marks Act 1994. In particular, the rules (1) specify that a fast track opposition (a) may only be brought on grounds set out in s 5(1) or (2); (b) must be based on no more than three earlier trade marks which are registered or protected in the United Kingdom or European Union; (c) applies only where proof of use of the earlier marks can be provided with the notice of opposition; and (d) can be used only where the opponent considers that the opposition may be determined without the need for further evidence and without an oral hearing; (2) set out the procedure for filing a notice of fast track opposition and require such notice to be filed electronically using the prescribed form; (3) disapply certain provisions of the 2008 Rules in relation to fast track oppositions, but clarify that the rule providing that the registrar may at any time give leave to either party to file on such terms as the registrar thinks fit continues to apply; (4) set out rules concerning the amendment of the statement of case and the consolidation of proceedings for fast track oppositions; (5) provide that a dispute relating to a fast track opposition may be heard before the registrar only if the Intellectual Property Office so requests or if either party to the proceedings so requests and the registrar considers that oral proceedings are necessary; (6) require the registrar, where no oral hearing is held, to give the parties an opportunity to set out their arguments in writing before a decision is reached; and (7) prescribe the notice to be used when an appeal arises in proceedings between two or more parties.

2455   Trade mark—registration—fees

The Trade Marks (Fees) (Amendment) Rules 2013, SI 2013/2236 (in force on 1 October 2013), further amend the 2008 Rules, SI 2008/1958, so as to (1) impose a £100 fee for a notice of opposition to the registration of a mark where the grounds of opposition are based solely on either or both of the Trade Marks Act 1994 s 5(1) or (2); (2) provide that a fee of £100 is payable on giving notice of fast track opposition to registration; (3) require a fee of £100 to be paid on an application to add grounds other than those contained in s 5(1), (2) to an opposition to registration; and (4) provide that a fee of £250 is payable on an appeal to the person appointed under s 76 in proceedings between two or more parties.

2456   Trade mark—registration—opposition to registration

The defendant company traded in the United Kingdom selling drainage products and washroom products. Many of its products had been used in noted buildings, some of which were in London. The claimant company was a Canadian corporation, which also sold washroom products but had always been based in Canada. The claimant filed a European Union trade mark relating to the word 'Frost' in relation to a number of bathroom fittings. The defendant registered eight United Kingdom trade marks relating to the use of the word 'Frost' in connection with its own products. The defendant contended that the claimant's mark was invalid for two main reasons. The defendant could have successfully sued the claimant for an injunction to restrain its use of the word 'Frost' in relation to the sale of washroom products, especially because the claimant had acted in bad faith when it filed its application for its mark. The main argument revolved around the questions of whether the defendant would have had any or any sufficient goodwill or reputation in washroom products to have brought a passing off action, whether the sign 'Frost' had been of more than mere local significance, and whether it could be properly regarded as the defendant's own name. The defendant submitted that it had used the name 'Frost' for over forty years. *Held*, on the evidence, the defendant had been trading in washroom products for over forty years. It had built up a good reputation and had run a highly successful washroom products business supplying major buildings in the United Kingdom and beyond. It was unrealistic to suggest that the defendant's business or reputation had only local significance. The relevant territory had to be seen as England and Wales. The defendant could have prohibited the use of the sign 'Frost' in the course of trade in washroom products in the jurisdiction by an action for passing off against the claimant. Bad faith was generally implied or involved but was not limited to actual or constructive fraud. It could be a design to mislead or deceive another, or involve any other sinister motive. It also included unfair practices involving a lack of any honest intention. On the evidence, the claimant had known about the defendant's washroom product business. It had sought to try to prevent the defendant from using its 'Frost' trading name from the start, and could not have been unaware of the defendant's business. There could be no doubt that the claimant had acted in bad faith in applying for its mark. Therefore, the claimant's mark would be declared invalid. Judgment would be given accordingly.

Frost Products Ltd v FC Frost Ltd [2013] EWPCC 34, [2013] All ER (D) 323 (Jul) (Patents County Court: Vos J).

2457   Trade mark—revocation—non-use—assessment of use

The claimant company sold cycling clothing, creams for treatment to relieve discomfort during cycling and some bicycles and accessories. It sold the goods worldwide but had not encouraged sales on the internet and preferred its distributors to sell through retail stores. The defendant company operated a global online fashion and beauty retail company and was purely an online internet retailer. The claimant applied for registration of a Community trade mark for the mark 'Assos'. Registration was sought under three classes, namely class 3 to cover the creams and treatments, class 12 to cover the bicycles and accessories, and class 25 to cover clothing, footwear and headgear. The defendant claimed that there were many kinds of clothing to which the claimant had never fixed its mark and that the broad category of clothing, footwear and headgear which it had sought to include by way of class 25 was too wide. The claimant accepted that there had been partial non-use in class 3 and class 12 and that those classes therefore fell to be cut back, but, in regard to class 25, it asserted that it had always sold clothing beyond the narrow class of specialist cycling gear and there was no appropriate sub-classification which properly described its range. The claimant also alleged that the defendant's use of the sign 'ASOS' constituted infringement. The defendant alleged that the claimant's mark 'Assos' was partially invalid because it would have been able to oppose the registration of the mark at the relevant priority date. *Held*, the claimant had maintained a much focused approach, limiting the kinds of clothing to which its brand name was attached. It had kept the sales almost entirely to specialist stores, advertised them largely in specialist cycling magazines and had not marketed its clothes online. An ordinary customer would not have regarded the claimant as a company selling 'clothing' but as selling a distinct sub-set of clothing. The registration of the mark under class 25 should be revoked for non-use outside that range. With regard to classes 3 and 12, the trade mark would be revoked for non-use apart from items that fell within a defined description. The only goodwill which the defendant had built up was in relation to an online clothing store selling other brands of clothing and celebrity look-alike styles. It had not by the priority date had sufficient goodwill as a supplier of goods bearing the brand name 'ASOS' for it to have succeeded in showing that the average 'ASOS' customer would, if confronted with clothing bearing the 'Assos' mark, have mistakenly thought that the clothing was made by the defendant or that it was made by someone associated with the defendant. The defendant's goodwill as at the priority date would not have enabled it to succeed in a passing off claim against the claimant if it had begun to make fair use of the mark which it was seeking to register. As both the parties sold different products for different uses, the relevant average consumer was not likely to be confused into thinking that the defendant's products were linked to the claimant's mark. It was also clear that the 'Assos' and 'ASOS' names and logos were similar. However, there was no evidence that the presence of 'ASOS' in the market had actually diluted the ability of 'Assos' to be associated with its mark. Accordingly, the counterclaim by the defendant under Council Regulation (EC) 207/2009 art 51 for the partial revocation for non-use of the claimants' trade mark would succeed to a limited extent; the counterclaim by the defendant for the partial invalidity of the claimant's trade mark under art 8(4) would be dismissed; and the claim for infringement of the claimant's mark under art 9(1)(b), (c) would be dismissed.

Maier v ASOS Plc [2013] EWHC 2831 (Ch), [2013] All ER (D) 185 (Sep) (Chancery Division: Rose J). *West (t/a Eastenders) v Fuller Smith & Turner plc* [2003] EWCA Civ 48, [2003] IP & T 768 (2003 Abr para 2708) applied.

2458　　Trade mark—time limits

The Trade Marks and Registered Designs (Amendment) Rules 2013, SI 2013/444 (in force on 31 March 2013), further amend the Trade Mark Rules 2008, SI 2008/1797, and the Registered Designs Rules 2006, SI 2006/1975, so as to exclude the date on which a relevant event occurred for the purpose of computing a period of time by reference to the relevant event. The rules also correct a drafting error in the 2006 Rules.

TRANSPORT

2459　　Bus services—operators grants—England

The Bus Service Operators Grant (England) (Amendment) Regulations 2013, SI 2013/2100 (in force on 1 October 2013), further amend the 2002 Regulations, SI 2002/1015, so as to (1) add new service definitions; (2) provide that certain services are always, rather than normally, available to the public; and (3) end eligibility for the grant under the Transport Act 2000 s 154 for (a) temporary services; (b) London franchised services; (c) services for which a special amenity element fare is charged; (d) services operated primarily for the purposes of tourism or because of the historical interest of the vehicle used to deliver the service; (e) local authority services; and (f) rail replacement services.

2460   Channel Tunnel—safety

The Channel Tunnel (Safety) (Amendment) Order 2013, SI 2013/407 (in force on 26 March 2013), further amends the 2007 Order, SI 2007/3531, so as to give effect to a bi-national regulation made by the Intergovernmental Commission. In particular, the order (1) places restrictions on the scope of the verifications required by the safety authority before it issues additional authorisations, where these are required; (2) requires the safety authority to deal with applications for safety authorisations for railway undertakings within certain time limits; (3) provides that railway vehicles already certified as complying fully with the technical specifications for interoperability will no longer need further authorisation in order to be used within the Tunnel if and when the Tunnel itself becomes fully compliant with the specifications, or when the trains run under the conditions specified in any corresponding specifications; (4) provides for the authorisation of railway vehicles to cover all types, as well as individual vehicles; (5) prescribes that no person may place a railway vehicle in service in the Tunnel unless an entity in charge of maintenance has been assigned to it, with the entity in charge of maintenance, in the case of a freight wagon, having to hold an 'ECM certificate'; (6) provides the entity in charge of maintenance must also set up a maintenance system to ensure the railway vehicle is in a safe state of running; and (7) revises the common safety indicators.

2461   Goods vehicles—licensing—operators—exemption

See para 2463.

2462   Goods vehicles—licensing—operators—general provisions

The Goods Vehicles (Licensing of Operators) (Amendment) Regulations 2013, SI 2013/1750 (in force on 15 August 2013), further amend the 1995 Regulations, SI 1995/2869, by adding, to the specified classes of vehicles the use of which is exempted from the requirement to hold an operator's licence under the Goods Vehicles (Licensing of Operators) Act 1995, vehicles used in Great Britain for the specific type of cabotage operation when engaged in the carriage of motor vehicles of types M1 (motor vehicles designed and constructed for the carriage of passengers and comprising no more than eight seats in addition to the driver's seat) and N1 (motor vehicles designed and constructed for the carriage of goods and having a maximum mass not exceeding 3·5 tonnes) as they are categorised under the applicable European framework type approval directive for motor vehicles. The exemption is limited to carriage only between 22 February and 31 March and between 25 August and 30 September. During such prescribed periods, and where the vehicle is being employed for the specified use, the haulier is not subject to a time limit on the number of cabotage operations or unloadings that may be conducted.

2463   Goods vehicles—test vehicles—training loads

The Motor Vehicles (Driver Testing and Vehicle Load) Regulations 2013, SI 2013/1753 (in force on 15 August 2013), further amend (1) the Motor Vehicles (Driving Licences) (Amendment) Regulations 1999, SI 1999/2864, by (a) adding new definitions of 'IBC' (intermediate bulk container), 'training load' and 'training load package', setting out the nature of loads to be carried on vehicles used during driving tests, and 'fire engine'; (b) providing for test vehicles to carry the training loads, the minimum weight of the training loads to be carried, and whether the load is to be carried on the motor vehicle or the trailer, or both; and (c) permitting such training loads to be carried during driving tests during a transitional period from 15 August 2013 and requiring the loads to be carried from 15 November 2013; (2) the Vehicle Drivers (Certificates of Professional Competence) Regulations 2007, SI 2007/605, by permitting test vehicles to carry the training loads during CPC tests during a transitional period from 15 August 2013 and requiring the loads to be carried from 15 November 2013; and (3) the Goods Vehicles (Licensing of Operators) Regulations 1995, SI 1995/2869, by exempting vehicle users from the requirement to hold an operator's licence in relation to any goods vehicle carrying the training loads during tests, where the vehicle is being used for a practical driving test, for driving instruction or for testing or training for the CPC test. The Secretary of State is required to review, within five years of 19 January 2013 and within every five years thereafter, the operation and effect of these amendments and to publish a report of his conclusions.

2464   Guided transport systems—safety

See para 2124.

2465   Local Transport Act 2008—commencement

The Local Transport Act 2008 (Commencement No 3) Order 2013, SI 2013/685, brings s 4(1) (in part), (2), (3) into force on 6 April 2013. The appointed day for the coming into force of ss 2, 3 (so far as not already in force), 4(1) (in part), (4)–(9) and 5 is the day after the day on which the Secretary of State first makes an order under s 6. For a summary of the Act, see 2008 Abr para 2914. See also the commencement table in the title STATUTES AND LEGISLATIVE PROCESS.

2466   Passenger and goods vehicles—tests—certificates of professional competence

The Vehicle Drivers (Certificates of Professional Competence) (Amendment) Regulations 2013, SI 2013/2667 (in force on 13 November 2013), further amend the 2007 Regulations, SI 2007/605, so as to (1) disapply the 2007 Regulations where (a) a person is driving a relevant vehicle to or from a relevant test for the purposes of technical development, repair or maintenance; (b) a relevant vehicle is being driven by a person whose principal work activity is not driving such vehicles; (c) apart from any fixed items, no goods or passengers are being carried; and (d) the vehicle is only being driven within a limited area; and (2) apply a new exemption to vehicles being driven in accordance with specified conditions.

2467   Public passenger transport—revocation of provisions

The Control of Fuel and Electricity, Local Government and Transport (Revocations and Savings) Order 2013, SI 2013/2986 (in force on 31 December 2013), revokes, because they are redundant, have been superseded or are no longer required, (1) the Public Passenger Transport Policies (Anticipatory Exercise of Powers) Order 1986, SI 1986/81, the Traffic Control System (Transfer) Order 1988, SI 1988/166, as amended, the Regulation of Bus Services in Greater London (Transitional Provisions) Order 2000, SI 2000/1462, the Transport Holding Company (Transfer of Assets) Order 1971, SI 1971/1254, the Passenger Car Fuel Consumption Order 1983, SI 1983/1486, as amended, the Transport Act 1985 (Modifications in Schedule 4 to the Transport Act 1968) Order 1985, SI 1985/1903, as amended, and the National Bus Company (Dissolution) Order 1991, SI 1991/510; (2) in relation to England only, the Public Transport Companies (Permitted Maximum and Required Minimum Numbers of Directors) Order 1985, SI 1985/1901, and the London Regional Transport Levy (General Rate Act 1967) (Modification) Order 1988, SI 1988/2153; and (3) in part, the Transport Act 1985 (Exclusion of Bus Operating Powers and Exemption for Councils Running Small Bus Undertakings) Order 1985, SI 1985/1902.

2468   Public service vehicles—buses and coaches—rights of passengers—exemptions

The Rights of Passengers in Bus and Coach Transport (Exemptions and Enforcement) Regulations 2013, SI 2013/1865 (in force on 19 August 2013), replace the Rights of Passengers in Bus and Coach Transport (Exemptions) Regulations 2013, SI 2013/228. Specifically, the 2013 Regulations implement European Parliament and Council (EU) Regulation 181/2011 (concerning the rights of passengers in bus and coach transport) (1) art 2(4), which permits member states, on a transparent and non-discriminatory basis, to exempt domestic regular services from the application of specified aspects of Regulation 181/2011 for a maximum of four years; (2) art 2(5), which permits member states, on a transparent and non-discriminatory basis, to exempt from the application of Regulation 181/2011 particular regular services because a significant part, including at least one scheduled stop, is operated outside the European Union for a maximum of four years; (3) art 12, by designating certain bus and coach terminals at which assistance for a disabled person and persons with reduced mobility must be provided; (4) art 16(2), which permits member states to exempt drivers from certain disability-related training requirements for a maximum of five years; (5) art 28(1), by designating certain bodies which are responsible for enforcement of Regulation 181/2011 and giving those bodies the right to ask for information to assist them in carrying out their functions; (6) art 28(3), by designating certain bodies to which complaints can be made by passengers about alleged infringements of Regulation 181/2011; and (7) art 31, by establishing enforcement measures, including penalties applicable to infringements of Regulation 181/2011. In addition, the regulations (a) enable persons who have suffered an infringement of their rights under Regulation 181/2011 to seek compensation separately from any penalty that can be imposed; (b) modify the Public Passenger Vehicles Act 1981 to disapply criminal offences that would otherwise attach to contraventions of licences held by public service vehicle operators and to empower traffic commissioners to hold and summon witnesses to attend public inquiries for the purpose of the regulations; (c) ensure, by amending the Unfair Contract Terms Act 1977, the Equality Act 2010, and the Unfair Terms in Consumer Contract Regulations 1999, SI 1999/2083, consistency with Regulation 181/2011; and (d) require the Secretary of State to review the operation and effect of the regulations and make public a report within five years after 1 March 2013 and within every five years after.

2469   Public service vehicles—London local service licences—superseded provisions—revocation

See para 2246.

2470   Public service vehicles—lost property—revocation of provisions

See para 2246.

2471   Public service vehicles—operator's licence—carrying passengers for hire or reward—vehicle not in motion

The appellant owned a passenger transport business, in which capacity he had a public service vehicle ('PSV') operator's licence authorising the use of a maximum of four PSVs. Four operator's discs were issued with the licence. The business had eight PSVs but, on the evidence of the appellant, it operated no more than four of them at any one time, transferring the operator's discs between vehicles as necessary. It was the appellant's case that the business had a strict policy whereby a driver taking a vehicle which needed a disc would sign out the disc before leaving the depot and would sign in the disc upon his return. The proceedings arose out of an occasion where the system did not work. A bus was due to be taken out to pick up children at a school. That school bus service was provided pursuant to a contract between the appellant and the respondent authority, which provided that the respondent might be entitled to terminate the contract by written notice having immediate effect in circumstances where a PSV was used without an operator's licence disc. The disc intended for use on that bus was not available, having been used on a different vehicle in the course of the morning. A technician was sent to collect the disc and take it to the bus at its school pick-up point. The bus driver's evidence was that he had travelled to the school to await the arrival of the technician. Once parked, an inspector from the respondent approached the bus and began carrying out checks on the vehicle, escort and driver. Before the children boarded the bus, the driver informed the inspector that he was awaiting the arrival of the operator's disc. Before the arrival of the technician, the children were ushered on to the bus. Within a short space of time, the technician arrived with the disc. The driver showed the disc to the inspector, placed the disc on the windscreen and proceeded out of the school. By a letter, the respondent relied on the Public Passenger Vehicles Act 1981 s 12(1) as a ground for terminating the contract with the appellant, stating that the appellant's actions in supplying a bus without an operator's licence disc left it with no alternative but to give notice of termination of the contract. The appellant brought proceedings seeking a declaration that the respondent had not been entitled to terminate the contract and claiming damages for breach of contract. That claim was dismissed, the judge finding that the bus was being used, at the time when it was parked and the children were boarding, for carrying passengers for hire or reward. On appeal by the appellant, *held*, the use of a vehicle for carrying passengers was not limited to the time or times when the vehicle was in motion. A vehicle was being used for carrying passengers throughout the period when it had passengers on board for the purpose of being transported from one place to another. That encompassed the time when the passengers had boarded the vehicle but it had not moved off and the time when it had arrived at its destination but the passengers had not yet got off. The position was not altered by the fact that the driver had not intended to move until the arrival of the disc. While it was acknowledged that the breach of the statutory requirements had been of a very technical nature, that had not assisted the appellant in relation to the question of whether the respondent had been entitled to proceed on the basis that there had been a breach of the statutory duty to display a disc. Accordingly, the appeal would be dismissed.

　　Grey (t/a Citytax) v City and County of Swansea [2013] EWCA Civ 1057, [2013] All ER (D) 123 (Aug) (Court of Appeal: Richards, Davis and Lloyd-Jones LJJ).

2472　Railways
See RAILWAYS AND TRAMWAYS.

2473　Road traffic
See ROAD TRAFFIC.

2474　Transport Holding Company—capital debts
The Transport Holding Company (Capital Debts) (Revocations) (England and Wales) Order 2013, SI 2013/2844 (in force on 20 December 2013), revokes the Transport Holding Company (Capital Debts) Order 1972, SI 1972/1024, the Transport Holding Company (Capital Debts) Order 1973, SI 1973/290, and the Transport Holding Company (Commencing Capital Debt) (Extinguishment) Order 1973, SI 1973/366, which are spent as a result of the dissolution of the Transport Holding Company.

TRUSTS AND POWERS
Halsbury's Laws of England (5th edn) vol 98 (2013) paras 1–723

Articles
For articles relating to this title please refer to the Table of Articles at the beginning of the Abridgment.

2475　Breach of trust—dishonest assistance—proof
The claimant investors paid money to a brokerage for investment with the defendant company. The brokerage collapsed when one of its clients ran up a deficit. The brokerage used funds paid by and due to its other clients, including the claimants, to finance its liabilities. The claimants sought to recover losses on the basis that three employees of the defendant had dishonestly assisted in breaches of fiduciary duty by the brokerage arising from its failure to hold the claimants' funds on a segregated basis and to use those funds only for the purpose of supporting the claimants' individual trading and for no other purpose; and that the defendant had acted in dishonest assistance. *Held*, the employees had been truthful, reliable and accurate witnesses and had taken the relationship between the brokerage and the defendant at face value, as they had been entitled to do, and had proceeded on the basis that the brokerage was trading with the defendant as a principal and on terms that title in all money transferred to the brokerage under the agreement would pass to the defendant. The employees did not think or suspect that the brokerage was putting the claimants' money at risk. The claimants had failed to establish that the employees had dishonestly participated in the wrongdoing practices of the brokerage and, accordingly, the claim would be dismissed.

　　Stokors SA v IG Markets Ltd [2013] EWHC 631 (Comm), [2013] All ER (D) 300 (Mar) (Queen's Bench Division: Field J). *Royal Brunei Airlines Sdn Bhd v Tan* [1995] 2 AC 378, [1995] 3 All ER 97, PC (1995 Abr para 2982); *Twinsectra Ltd v Yardley* [2002] UKHL 12, [2002] 2 AC 164, [2002] 2 All ER 377, HL (2002 Abr para 3025); *Barlow Clowes International Ltd (in liq) v Eurotrust International Ltd* [2005] UKPC 37, [2006] 1 All ER (Comm) 478 (2006 Abr para 2880); and *Brown v Innovatorone plc* [2012] EWHC 1321 (Comm), [2012] All ER (D) 273 (May) (2012 Abr para 1240), considered.

2476　Constructive trust—fiduciary duty—duty not to profit
The first company owned a hotel in France. Its share capital was owned by a second company, incorporated in the British Virgin Islands, which wanted to sell either the hotel or the first company. The first defendant had established the second defendant company with the intention of providing consultancy services to the hotel industry. A number of the

claimants were among the first defendant's clients and contacts. The first defendant had learnt of the second company's plans in respect of the hotel and encouraged the claimants to investigate the possibility of purchasing the hotel. A memorandum prepared by the first defendant for the claimants told them that the second company was offering the hotel for sale through the second defendant on an off-market basis. Under an exclusive brokerage agreement between the second company and the second defendant, the latter had an exclusive right, for a defined period, to sell the hotel and, if a sale was made to the claimants, the second defendant would be paid a fee. The second defendant was to introduce the second company to the claimants and advise them but it was not to be involved in negotiations on behalf of the second company of any of the terms of sale. The second defendant was to disclose its appointment under the agreement to the claimants. A sale to the claimants took place in the form of a share purchase of the issued share capital of the first company. The claimants issued proceedings for the recovery of a sum which it had paid to the defendants at a time when they were acting as the claimants' agents with the result that the defendants were in breach of their duty as fiduciary agents not to profit from their position or to put themselves in a position where their interest and duty were in conflict. It fell to be determined whether the second defendant had made sufficient disclosure of its relationship with the second company, so that it could be said that it had acted with the informed consent of the claimants. The judge found that there had been insufficient disclosure. It was determined that the claimants were not entitled to a proprietary remedy against the second defendant, but were only entitled to the personal remedy of an account in equity. The judge did not accept that secret commissions were to be characterised as assets of the beneficiary and determined that it would be artificial to describe the agreement as the second defendant having taken advantage of an opportunity which had properly been that of the claimants as principals, and that the relevant opportunity had been the opportunity to purchase for a lesser price. On appeal by the claimants, *held*, the facts brought the case within the second category of exceptions to the rule that a beneficiary of a fiduciary's duties could not claim a proprietary interest, but was entitled to an equitable account, in respect of any money or asset acquired by a fiduciary in breach of his duties to the beneficiary, unless the benefit had been obtained by the fiduciary having taken advantage of an opportunity which had been properly that of the principal. That conclusion reflected principle, because the agreement, and the fact that it had not been disclosed by the second defendant to the claimants, had diverted from the claimants the opportunity to purchase the hotel at the lowest possible price, namely, a price lower than the price they had ultimately agreed to pay. It was also a conclusion that was consistent with precedent. Accordingly, the appeal would be allowed.

FHR European Ventures v Mankarious [2013] EWCA Civ 17, [2014] Ch 1, [2013] All ER (D) 219 (Jan) (Court of Appeal: Sir Terence Etherton C, Pill and Lewison LJJ). *Sinclair Investments (UK) Ltd v Versailles Trade Finance Ltd (in administration)* [2011] EWCA Civ 347, [2012] Ch 453, [2011] 4 All ER 335 (2011 Abr para 2401) applied.

2477   Constructive trust—money lent pursuant to business enterprise—personal liability of director

The claimant was compulsorily wound up when petitioners demanded payment of an alleged debt. The debt was in respect of payments that they had made to a Swiss subsidiary of the claimant in reliance on advice that an imminent initial public offering ('IPO') of shares in the Swiss company would be traded in Germany and was a good investment opportunity. The petitioners paid the claimant tranches after it was represented to them that the German financial supervisory authority would likely decline permission for the listing of the Swiss company. The claimant was to be substituted as the vehicle for the IPO. The claimant brought proceedings against the defendant, who was the claimant's sole director and controlling shareholder and also the controller of the Swiss company. The claimant contended that the defendant was accountable as constructive trustee of the claimant. *Held*, certain questions raised fell into the *Quistclose* line of cases, on the footing that the sum did not fall into and form part of the assets of the recipient pending exercise of a power to apply the fund as directed in default of which it resulted to the petitioners. In *Quistclose* cases, the resulting, or secondary, trust did not operate on the conscience of the recipient so as to impress the recipient with an obligation in the nature of a trust to repay or return a fund, until and unless the primary trust had failed. A further question was whether the Swiss company's obligation to repay had become the claimant's obligation. The inviolability of the principle of separate legal personality save in the most exceptional cases was unquestioned. Under the law, the defendant's duties in relation to the claimant could not be treated as identical to or corresponding with his like duties in relation to the Swiss company or vice versa. Neither could the defendant's knowledge as a director of the Swiss company be attributed to him as a director of the claimant or vice versa. It had neither been pleaded, nor was there evidence that the Swiss company, with the petitioner's agreement, novated its liability to the claimant. There was no reliable evidence that the Swiss company had ever been a subsidiary of the claimant. The defendant's control of both companies enabled the court to assume relevant knowledge, but only if the Swiss company tranches had actually been transferred to or received by the claimant, of which there was no evidence. It followed that, at the time the tranches had been paid, the defendant had de facto control over the Swiss company and the Swiss company held the sum on constructive trust for the petitioners. The defendant procured a breach of trust when he procured or permitted the Swiss company to pay funds away. However, the defendant was not liable to repay or compensate the claimant in respect of such breach. Accordingly, the claim would be dismissed.

Tag Capital Ventures Ltd (in liq) v Potter [2013] EWHC 2338 (Ch), [2013] All ER (D) 18 (Aug) (Chancery Division: Martin Mann QC). *Barclays Bank Ltd v Quistclose Investments Ltd* [1970] AC 567, [1968] 3 All ER 651, HL, applied.

2478   Fiduciary powers—exercise—control by court—trustees failing to understand tax implications

See *Pitt v Holt; Futter v Futter*, para 2480.

2479   Resulting trust—investment money—release of money to pay loan—breach of trust

The second defendant was a chartered surveyor and director of a company. Together with his colleague, he ran a series of investment opportunities. It was a fundamental feature of the schemes that the investors would have or be entitled to control the special purpose vehicle ('SPV') used as part of the schemes. It was a feature of the schemes that the investors would rely on the solicitors advising the SPV both to safeguard their interests as future equity participants and also to ensure that their subscription money would not be released unless and until the investors' participation and control of the SPV was safely arranged. One of the schemes concerned land which had been acquired by an SPV. The land was acquired with the assistance of substantial lending from a bank. That lending included a short term bridging loan, half of which was to be repaid after three months. The first defendant solicitors were the solicitors to the SPV. The principal of the first defendant was responsible for dealing with the scheme. In turn the second defendant proceeded to obtain investments in the scheme from the claimants, who all paid their investment funds into the client account of the first defendant. The investments were classified as loans to the SPV. It was expected that the first defendant would act for the investors as well as the SPV and look after the claimants' interests. On receiving those funds, prior to either final agreement as to the terms of the loan or the claimant's participation and control of the SPV being secured, the first defendant released the funds to pay off the bridging loan. The claimants commenced proceedings against the defendants. It was asserted that the money paid into the client account was at all material times held subject to escrow conditions, and further or alternatively, on a form of resulting trust for them or otherwise to their order and that the payment of that money out of the client account was a breach of contract and/or trust for which the first defendant was liable. *Held*, it was clear that the objective intention was that the money paid into the client account was not immediately to have belonged to the SPV, and that it was to have been parked pending finalisation of formal authorisation on its behalf. Objectively, the provision by the first defendant of the client account, and the instructed use of it by the claimants for the purposes of the transaction, had been plainly and unequivocally referable to a shared intention that the money paid in should have been retained separately from the money of the SPV, and that payment out to or at the direction of the SPV should have awaited some further event or instruction, pending which the money would have been held safe for the claimants. However, the evidence was insufficient, and lacking the requisite certainty and detail as to the terms on which the money would have been available to the SPV, to establish a contract of escrow. Further, the crucial question was as to the terms on which the first defendant had received the claimants' money into its client account and whether such terms negated any intention that such money should have belonged immediately to the SPV. It was to be inferred from the evidence that if the scheme failed, or no definitive agreement could be reached as to the terms of the loan, then the money should have been remitted to the claimants. Once in that trust with the principal or the first defendant as trustee, she had been bound to establish with certainty who the beneficiary was, and to act only in accordance with directions from that beneficiary. The principal had been certain of neither and in proceeding as she had, she had breached her duties. Therefore, on the basis of a form of resulting trust of which the principal had been in breach, the claimants succeeded on their primary case. Judgment would be given accordingly.

Challinor v Juliet Bellis & Co [2013] EWHC 347 (Ch), [2013] All ER (D) 06 (Mar) (Chancery Division: Hildyard J). *Barclays Bank Ltd v Quistclose Investments Ltd* [1970] AC 567, [1968] 3 All ER 651, HL; and *Twinsectra Ltd v Yardley* [2002] UKHL 12, [2002] 2 AC 164, [2002] 2 All ER 377 (2002 Abr para 3025) applied.

2480   Trustee—power and duties—exercise of powers—relevant considerations—tax implications

The first appeal arose from the exercise of powers of enlargement and advancement by the trustees under discretionary trusts. Each trust fund contained assets with 'stockpiled gains'. Each trust was located offshore for United Kingdom tax purposes, so as not to be subject to capital gains tax while funds remained offshore. The enlargement and advancements were made on the basis that losses incurred for capital gains tax purposes by the beneficiary could be set off against the stockpiled gains. However, the trustees' solicitors had overlooked a statutory provision that provided that losses could not be set off against gains attributed to beneficiaries in such circumstances. In the second appeal, the claimant's husband was badly injured in an accident. His personal injury claim resulted in a structured settlement and, on professional advice, the proceeds of the settlement were placed in a special needs trust for the husband's benefit. Acting as the husband's receiver, the claimant entered into a deed of settlement which created discretionary trusts. The husband subsequently died. In the meantime, it was realised that the terms of the special needs trust were such that inheritance tax applied to it. In both cases, the judge set aside the relevant acts under the rule in *Hastings-Bass*. On appeal, the Court of Appeal found that the rule in *Hastings-Bass* was not applicable because the respective trustees had acted reasonably in reliance on what they supposed to be competent professional advice. It dismissed the second appeal based on mistake. On appeal by the trustee in the first appeal and the claimant in the second appeal, *held*, for the *Hastings-Bass* rule to apply, the inadequate deliberation on the part of the trustees had to be sufficiently serious as to amount to a breach of fiduciary duty. In the first appeal, the essential issue was whether the trustees of the settlements, in deciding to take the steps which they had, had failed in their duty to take relevant considerations into account. Capital gains tax had been not only a relevant consideration, but the paramount consideration and the trustees had given it a great deal of thought. However, the tax advice which they received and acted on had been wrong because an amendment to the Taxation of Chargeable Gains Act 1992 had been overlooked. The only complication had been that one of the trustees had been both one of the solicitors who had given the erroneous advice and a trustee who had acted on it. It would be artificial to distinguish between the two trustees, who had acted together in making and effectuating their decisions. In the second appeal, the claimant, as her husband's receiver, had been in a fiduciary position but there was no suggestion that she had had any professional qualifications. She had taken supposedly expert advice and followed it. There was no reason to find that she had personally failed in the exercise of her fiduciary duties. Consequently, the appeal in the first case would be dismissed while the second appeal would also be dismissed so far as it turned on the rule in *Hastings-Bass*. Further, the Court of Appeal had accepted that the claimant had had an incorrect conscious belief, or had made an incorrect tacit assumption, that the proposed trust had had no adverse tax consequences. The trust could have complied with the Inheritance Tax Act 1984 s 89 without any artificiality or abuse of the statutory relief. Therefore, the test for setting aside a voluntary disposition on the ground of mistake had been satisfied in the second appeal. The second appeal would be allowed on the ground of mistake and the trust would be set aside. Judgment would be given accordingly.

Pitt v Holt; Futter v Futter [2013] UKSC 26, [2013] 2 AC 108, [2013] 3 All ER 429 (Supreme Court: Lord Neuberger P, Lord Walker, Lady Hale, Lord Mance, Lord Clarke, Lord Sumption and Lord Carnwath SCJJ). *Re Hastings-Bass; Hastings-Bass v IRC* [1975] Ch 25, [1974] 2 All ER 193, CA (1974 Abr para 2599), considered. *Re Barr's Settlement Trusts; Abacus Trust Co (Isle of Man) v Barr* [2003] EWHC 114 (Ch), [2003] Ch 409, [2003] 1 All ER 763 approved. *Sieff v Fox* [2005] EWHC 1312 (Ch), [2005] 3 All ER 693 (2005 Abr para 2467), criticised. *Gibbon v Mitchell* [1990] 3 All ER 338 (1990 Abr para 1630) doubted. Decision of Court of Appeal [2011] EWCA Civ 197, [2012] Ch 132, [2011] 2 All ER 450 (2011 Abr para 2406) reversed in part.

2481   Trustee—removal of trustee—jurisdiction—application to strike out on principle of non-justiciability

The claimants and the defendants were members of the Sikh community. Most either were or had been trustees of one or other of two meeting places for religious worship. The meeting places were subject to trust deeds. The trust deeds conferred on the First Holy Saint or his successor a power to remove trustees and to appoint new trustees to take their place. In the present proceedings, the claimants sought declarations that the defendants had been removed from their positions of trustees and officers of the meeting places and replaced by the claimants as lawfully appointed trustees and officers. The key question in the proceedings was whether the ninth claimant was 'the Third Holy Saint' and whether he was the successor to the First Holy Saint. The defendants applied to strike out the proceedings on the ground that a determination of whether the ninth claimant was the successor turned on matters of religious faith, doctrine and practice on which the parties held differing beliefs, that a secular court would not adjudicate on the truth of disputed tenets of religious belief and faith, or the correctness of religious practices, and, therefore, the issues were non-justiciable. The judge dismissed the defendants' application and the defendants appealed. *Held,* it was established law that the courts would abstain from adjudicating on the truth, merits or sincerity of differences in religious doctrine. Generally, the courts would also exercise caution in adjudicating on the fitness of a particular individual to carry out the spiritual duties of a religious office. There were matters on which a court was not competent to speak with authority, because of the limitations inherent in the nature of the judicial process, and therefore, should not speak. That was so where questions were not matters of law at all, such as subjective inward matters incapable of proof by direct evidence or by inference. In the present case, the court had been asked to pronounce on matters of religious doctrine and practice. The trusteeship turned on who had been the successor of the original founder of the temple trusts. The resolution of that issue had depended on the religious beliefs and practices of Sikhs. The issue had not depended solely on the construction of the trust deeds governed by English law, but it had been necessary to ascertain and apply objective criteria before a court had been in a position to decide whether a person who had claimed to be the successor within the meaning of the trusts deeds had been what he had claimed to be. The English courts had not been equipped to adjudicate on the issue of succession by reference to religious beliefs and practices. The trust deeds were silent on the criteria to be applied by another person who had been asked to decide the question. The matter of succession had essentially been a matter of professed subjective belief and faith on which secular municipal courts could not possibly have reached a decision, either as a matter of law or fact. Therefore, the judge had erred in treating the particular core issue in the proceedings as one that had been properly justiciable by the English courts. It followed that the court would allow the appeal and put a halt to the proceedings. Accordingly, the appeal would be allowed.

Shergill v Khaira [2012] EWCA Civ 983, [2012] All ER (D) 167 (Jul) (Court of Appeal: Mummery, Hooper and Pitchford LJJ).

2482   Trusts (Capital and Income) Act 2013

The Trusts (Capital and Income) Act 2013 amends the law relating to capital and income in trusts. The Act received the royal assent on 31 January 2013 and came into force in part on that day. The remaining provisions came into force on and between 6 April 2013 and 1 January 2014: SI 2013/676, SI 2013/2461. For details of commencement, see the commencement table in the title STATUTES AND LEGISLATIVE PROCESS.

2483

The 2013 Act s 1 disapplies specified statutory and equitable rules of apportionment for all trusts created or arising on or after 1 October 2013. Where a trust receives a tax-exempt corporate distribution, it is to be treated as a receipt of capital rather than income: s 2. Trustees are empowered by s 3 to compensate income beneficiaries where there has been a tax-exempt distribution classified as capital under s 2. Section 4 enables the trustees of a charity with permanent endowment to invest on a total return basis by making a resolution to adopt a Charity Commission total return investment scheme, where they consider that it is in the interests of the charity to do so. Section 5 deals with commencement and extent, and s 6 specifies the short title.

VALUE ADDED TAX
Halsbury's Laws of England (5th edn) vol 99 (2012) paras 1–500

Articles
For articles relating to this title please refer to the Table of Articles at the beginning of the Abridgment.

2483 Exempt supply—association—representations to government—primary purpose

The taxpayer, which was in the business of representing and promoting its members who were engaged in the business of amusement parks, arranged for its members to attend exhibitions and produced magazines highlighting particular rides or providing a summary as to the location of various amusement parks. The taxpayer claimed that it had been entitled to be repaid allegedly overpaid output tax in respect of membership subscriptions received by it and on which output tax had been charged and accounted for. The taxpayer claimed that at all material times it had been exempt from value added tax pursuant to the Value Added Tax Act 1994 Sch 9 Pt II Group 9 item 1(d). The issue to be determined before the First-tier tribunal was whether as regards all or any part of the period covered by the claim the taxpayer had been a body falling within Sch 9 Pt II Group 9 item 1(d). The First-tier tribunal decided that, during the relevant period, the taxpayer had not shown that its primary purpose had been to make representations to the government in the way required by Sch 9 Pt II Group 9 item 1(d) and, therefore, the taxpayer's claim to be repaid output tax failed for the entirety of the claim. The taxpayer appealed. *Held,* the reference to 'primary purpose' in Sch 9 Pt II Group 9 item 1(d) did not require the taxpayer to show that the purpose referred to in Sch 9 Pt II Group 9 item 1(d) was the sole purpose of the association but the purpose referred to in Sch 9 Pt II Group 9 item 1(d) should be its main or principal purpose. It was possible for a body to have multiple objects so that no single object could be said to be the predominant or the primary purpose. The primary purpose test involved an objective inquiry, not a subjective one, and the matter was to be determined primarily by an examination of the stated objects and the actual activities of the body in question. The inquiry as to the primary purpose of the body normally involved the tribunal looking at the constitutional documents of that body and other materials from which the purposes of the body could be derived tested against the reality of what the body did. It was accepted that it was appropriate for the First-tier tribunal, when seeking to ascertain the primary purpose of the taxpayer, to look at the constitutional documents of the taxpayer. The First-tier tribunal paid close attention to what the taxpayer did throughout the period covered by the claim, had made detailed findings on that subject and then came to its overall conclusion in light of those findings. It had considered all of the evidence and was entitled to reach the conclusion that it had expressed. Accordingly, the appeal would be dismissed.

British Association of Leisure Parks, Piers and Attractions Ltd v Revenue and Customs Comrs [2013] UKUT 0130 (TCC), [2013] STC 1410 (Upper Tribunal: Morgan J). *Edwards (Inspector of Taxes) v Bairstow* [1956] AC 14, [1955] 3 All ER 48, HL, considered. *British Association for Shooting and Conservation Ltd v Revenue and Customs Comrs* [2009] EWHC 399 (Ch), [2009] STC 1421 (2009 Abr para 2917) applied.

The taxpayer was a non-profit making organisation made up of tour operator members and associate members. Its objectives included establishing relations with European institutions, acting as a forum for the international inbound tour operators based in Europe, and maintaining good relations with the suppliers to the industry. Members paid an annual subscription. The taxpayer accounted for value added tax on its membership subscription

1013

income. It submitted a voluntary disclosure of VAT overpaid, claiming that membership subscriptions were exempt under the Value Added Tax Act 1994 Sch 9 Pt II Group 9 item 1(d) on the basis that the taxpayer was an organisation whose primary purpose was to make representations to the United Kingdom and other European governments on legislation and other public matters which affected the business or professional interests of its members. The taxpayer was a representational body whose membership was made up of corporate bodies whose business or professional interests were directly connected with the purposes of the taxpayer, and therefore the exemption was not disapplied by Sch 9 Pt II Group 9 note (5)b. The Commissioners for Her Majesty's Revenue and Customs rejected the claim on the basis that the primary purpose of the taxpayer was to provide an avenue for networking; while the taxpayer made representations to the government, that was not its main purpose. Accordingly, the membership income was not exempt. The taxpayer appealed to the First-tier Tribunal which considered that it had to determine the primary purpose of the taxpayer. It held that the test was subjective; the primary purpose of the taxpayer was what its directors and members considered to be the most important matter it was seeking to achieve or doing in return for membership subscriptions; the associations professed purposes had to be tested against what happened in reality. The taxpayer's appeal was allowed. The Revenue appealed. *Held*, it was wrong to regard the primary purpose test as a subjective one. The relevant inquiry was an objective one, to be answered primarily by an examination of the stated objects and the actual activities of the body in question. The tribunal had thus erred in law by directing itself that the primary purpose of the taxpayer was what its directors and members considered to be the most important matter that it was seeking to achieve or doing in return for membership subscriptions. It was not clear if the tribunal would have reached the same conclusion had it not misdirected itself in law about the nature of the test to be applied, and had it clearly taken into account the possibility that the taxpayer might have multiple objects, no single one of which could be said to be predominant. The present case was not one where it could be said that only one conclusion was reasonably open to the tribunal, on the basis of the primary findings of fact, if it had correctly directed itself in law. It followed that the matter would be remitted to the tribunal for it to reconsider and amplify its reasoning and conclusions about the primary purpose of the taxpayer.

Revenue and Customs Comrs v European Tour Operators' Association [2012] UKUT 377 (TCC), [2013] STC 1060 (Upper Tribunal: Henderson J).

2484　Exempt supply—betting, gaming and lotteries—gaming machine—multi-terminal machine

The Value Added Tax Act 1994 Act Sch 9 Pt II Group 4 item 1 note 3 defines the term 'gaming machine' as meaning a machine in respect of which the following conditions are satisfied: (1) it is constructed or adapted for playing a game of chance by means of it; (2) a player pays to play the machine, either by inserting a coin, token or other thing into the machine or in some other way; and (3) the element of chance in the game is provided by means of the machine.

The taxpayer operated slot machines in which the element of chance was provided by a component that was separate and remote from, but linked to, the terminal used by the player. The machines were multi-terminal machines, an arrangement where a single remote random number generator was linked by a cable to a number of gaming machines. The Revenue described the disputed machines as reconfigured machines. The taxpayer contended that the disputed machines were regulated by the Gaming Act 1968 s 21. If the machines were covered by s 16, then they were entitled to a value added tax exemption under the 1994 Act Sch 9 Pt II Group 4 item 1, which referred to 'the provision of any facilities for the placing of bets or the playing of any games of chance'. The effect of that provision was to exempt from VAT the takings of all machines used for gaming. The effect of Sch 9 Pt II Group 4 item 1 note 3 was to bring the takings from gaming machines within the scope of VAT. The Revenue contended that the machines were regulated by the 1968 Act Pt III (ss 26–39). If the machines were Pt III machines, they were not entitled to the tax exemption. A tribunal allowed the taxpayer's appeal against the Revenue's decision to reject its claim for the repayment of tax which the taxpayer alleged had been overpaid, having decided that the provision of gaming facilities by multi-terminal products was exempt from VAT as a matter of law. The Revenue's appeal was dismissed. On further appeal, it was common ground that the taxpayer was entitled to invoke the EU principle of fiscal neutrality to assert that the takings on different machines which had fallen to be taxed under the domestic VAT provisions ought not to have been taxed and it was, therefore, entitled to reclaim the VAT it had paid in respect of such takings. *Held,* the correct legal characterisation of the multi-terminal systems was that they were gaming machines within the meaning of the 1994 Act Sch 9 Pt II Group 4 item 1 note 3. There was no doubt that the definition of 'gaming machine' in note 3 was drawn from the definition of a 'machine' in the 1968 Act s 26. If the word 'machine' referred to in s 26 was to be given a sensible effect that would enable it to achieve its obvious purpose, it had to be interpreted as including equipment ancillary, and connected, to the playing terminal that automatically provided the element of chance that determined the outcome of the game played on the terminal. Anyone who sought to evade the 1968 Act Pt III by segregating the random number generator from the playing terminal was doing so with his eyes wide open and, unless he had obtained a prior clearance, he took the risk that he had misread the legislation. It followed that a purpose built system that comprised a terminal with a separate, but connected, random number generator was also properly characterised as a 'machine'. The terminal could not be used for gaming purposes except by being linked to the random number generator and the random number generator was designed to be linked to the terminal in order to enable the game to be played. Although two separate items of equipment, they were being used together for the purpose of playing a game on the terminal and the random number generator formed an essential element of that system. There was no reason to treat the multi-terminal systems any differently. The fact that there was only one random number generator that served several terminals did not make a material difference. Accordingly, the appeal would be allowed.

Revenue and Customs Comrs v Rank Group plc [2013] EWCA Civ 1289, [2014] STC 470 (Court of Appeal: Rimer, Beatson and Floyd LJJ). Decision of Norris J [2009] EWHC 1244 (Ch), [2009] STC 2304 (2009 Abr para 2907) reversed.

1968 Act repealed by Gambling Act 2005 Sch 17.

2485   Exempt supply—building land—payment of transfer duties

An agreement for the sale of a plot of land was entered into. At that time there was a building on the land. Next to the building there was a public, surfaced car park. The contract of sale stipulated that the property sold would be supplied in an improved condition in view of the intention to have homes built on the land, possibly combined with offices with parking facilities. It was agreed that the vendor would be responsible for the demolition of the building as well as for the removal of the surface of the car park. Later, the vendor had the building demolished and the resulting building rubble removed. The land was supplied to the purchaser at the time of the transfer of ownership. On that date, the car park was still in use, as the surface had yet to be removed and the purchaser had not obtained the necessary planning permission for its construction plans for the land. Under national law, in order to avoid double taxation, if a purchase of real estate was subject to value added tax, it was exempted from the transfer duty calculated on the sale price. The supply of building land was subject to VAT. By contrast, the supply of land which had not been built on was exempt from VAT and remained subject to transfer duty. The purchaser paid VAT to the vendor for the supply of the land at issue, as it considered that it was building land and was, therefore, subject to VAT, meaning that transfer duties were not due. However, the tax inspector considered that the supply at issue concerned land which had been built on, exempting it as such from VAT and thus subjecting it to the payment of transfer duty. The purchaser received an assessment of the outstanding transfer duty. When the objection lodged against that assessment was rejected by decision of the tax inspector, the purchaser brought an action against that decision before the national court. That court dismissed the action and the purchaser's appeal was also dismissed. On further appeal the national appeal court decided to stay the proceedings and seek a preliminary ruling from the European Court of Justice. It fell to be determined whether Council Directive (EC) 2006/112 (on the common system of VAT) art 135(1)(k), read in conjunction with art 12(1), (3), should be interpreted as meaning that the exemption from VAT covered a supply of land which had not been built on, following the demolition of the building situated on it, even where, at the time of that supply, improvement works on the land, apart from that demolition, had not been carried out, but the land at issue had been intended to be built on. *Held*, it was for the referring court to carry out an overall assessment of the factual circumstances surrounding the transaction and prevailing at the time of supply, including the intention of the parties, provided that it was supported by objective evidence, in order to determine whether the transaction concerned building land. It followed that art 135(1)(k), read in conjunction with art 12(1), (3), should be interpreted as meaning that the exemption from VAT did not cover the supply of land which had not been built on following the demolition of the building situated on it, even where, at the time of that supply, improvement works on the land, apart from that demolition, had not been carried out, where it was apparent from an overall assessment of the factual circumstances surrounding that transaction, including the intention of the parties when it was supported by objective evidence, that, at that time, the land at issue had in fact been intended to be built on, which was for the referring court to determine.

Case C-543/11 *Woningstichting Maasdriel v Staatssecretaris van Finaanciën* [2013] All ER (D) 155 (Jan) (ECJ: Eighth Chamber).

2486　Exempt supply—cultural services—students' union—entertainment events

The taxpayer was the students' union of a university. It was a charity and was registered for value added tax. Under its constitution, the taxpayer's policy was formulated and decided by the council, with the day-to-day running delegated to an executive committee. The members of the council were the members of the executive committee, the student officers, and the representatives of the halls of residence and the colleges. The executive committee included nine sabbatical officers, who were salaried employees. The taxpayer claimed repayment of VAT relating to certain supplies which it claimed should have been treated as exempt. The taxpayer's primary claim was that supplies of the right of admission to entertainment events, specifically the two balls that were held every year, were exempt under the Value Added Tax Act 1994 Sch 9 Pt II Group 13 item 2. The taxpayer made an alternative claim that supplies of goods and services in connection with certain fund-raising events were exempt under Council Directive (EC) 2006/112 art 132(1)(o). The Revenue refused to make any repayment to the taxpayer. The taxpayer's appeal to the First-tier Tribunal was dismissed on the ground that the cultural services exemption had not applied because the taxpayer had not met the condition that it should be managed and administered on an essentially voluntary basis. The tribunal further held that the fund-raising exemption did not apply because the evidence did not show that the balls met the conditions laid down in the 1994 Act Sch 9 Pt II Group 12 item 1 that their primary purpose had been the raising of money and that they had been promoted as being primarily for the raising of money. On the taxpayer's appeal against that decision, *held*, the tribunal had been entitled to find, on the evidence before it, that the salaried sabbatical officers had played a significant part in the higher decision-making processes of the taxpayer both before and after the change in the constitution. On the basis of that finding, the tribunal had been right to conclude that the taxpayer had not been managed and administered on an essentially voluntary basis. It followed that the taxpayer's supplies of the right of admission to entertainment events had not fallen within the cultural services exemption. The tribunal's decision had proceeded on the basis that the restrictions in Sch 9 Pt II Group 12 item 1 had not been ultra vires the requirements of EU law. In some circumstances, an implicit decision on such a point might be enough but, in the present case, the absence of any discussion of the point in the decision meant that there was real doubt that the issue had been given proper consideration by the tribunal. The only course open in the circumstances was to remit the appeal for a further hearing at which the parties might adduce further evidence and make submissions on the issue. Judgment would be given accordingly.

Loughborough Students Union v Revenue and Customs Comrs [2013] UKUT 517 (TCC), [2013] All ER (D) 42 (Nov) (Upper Tribunal: Judge Sinfield and Judge Sadler).

2487　Exempt supply—education—educational services supplied by private company

The taxpayer company sought to benefit from an exemption from value added tax on the ground that it provided educational services. The taxpayer was a private company and was not entered in the register of schools and non-public institutions in accordance with Polish Law. Questions arose as to whether (1) Council Directive (EC) 2006/112 art 132(1), read in conjunction with arts 133 and 134, should be interpreted as meaning that educational services provided for commercial purposes by bodies not governed by public law were precluded from exemption from VAT; and (2) whether a taxable person might rely on the fact that the exemption from VAT provided for by national law was incompatible with art 132(1) in order to claim a right to deduct input VAT, provided for by art 168, and benefit at the same time from that exemption for the supplies of professional educational and training services which it supplied. *Held*, under art 132(1) the supply of educational services referred to was exempt only if those services were provided by educational bodies governed by public law or by other organisations recognised by the member state concerned as having similar objects. Article 132(1) did not permit member states to grant the supply of the educational services exemption to all private organisations providing such services, by including also those whose objects were not similar to those of bodies governed by public law. Therefore, an exemption as sought by the taxpayer was incompatible with art 132(1). Article 132(1) did not specify the conditions or procedures for defining similar objects and it was for the national law of each member state to lay down the rules. It also was for the national courts to examine whether the member states had observed the limits of their discretion in applying the principles of EU law, in particular the principle of equal treatment, which, in the field of VAT, took the form of the principle of fiscal neutrality. Articles 132(1), 133 and 134 should be interpreted as not precluding educational services supplied for commercial purposes by bodies not governed by public law from being exempt from VAT. However, art 132(1) precluded a general exemption of all supplies of educational services, without consideration of the objects pursued by non-public organisations supplying those services. A taxpayer might not claim, in accordance with art 168 or the national provision transposing it, a right to deduct input VAT where, as a result of an exemption provided for by national law in breach of art 132(1), the input supply of its educational services was not subject to VAT. That taxpayer might rely, however, on the incompatibility with art 132(1) of the exemption provided by national law, so that the exemption was not applied to it where, notwithstanding the discretion granted to member states, the taxpayer could not objectively be regarded as an organisation having objects similar to those of an educational body governed by public law. In such a case, the educational services supplied by that taxpayer would be subject to VAT and that person could then benefit from the right to deduct input VAT.

Case C-319/12 *Minister Finansow v MDDP sp zoo Akademia Biznesu, sp komandytowa* [2013] All ER (D) 37 (Dec) (ECJ: Third Chamber).

2488   Exempt supply—education—eligible body—provider of services to university

The taxpayer was an institution which provided certain educational services, including services provided pursuant to an arrangement with a university. The taxpayer claimed that the services provided by it in relation to the university courses were exempt from value added tax by virtue of the exemption conferred by the Value Added Tax Act 1994 Sch 9 Pt II Group 6. In order to be able to rely on that exemption, the taxpayer had to establish that it was an 'eligible body' within the meaning of that provision, which referred to 'a United Kingdom university, and any college, institution, school or hall of such a university'. The taxpayer took the view that, pursuant to the arrangements it had made with the university, it was a college or institution of the university in relation to those courses. It accepted that it was not a college or institution of the university in relation to the remainder of its activities. The First-tier Tribunal decided that that the taxpayer was not a college or institution of the university, even in relation to the university courses, and, in any case, it was not possible to be an eligible body in relation to only some of the activities of a body. The taxpayer appealed against that decision. *Held*, the relevant established authorities supported an approach which involved asking of a particular body whether it was a college or an institution of a university. On that approach, it would not be possible to conclude that a body was a college or an institution of a university and at the same time that it was not such a college or institution. The approach did not permit one to distinguish between the possible different capacities of a body when deciding whether the body was an eligible body. Further, the approach did not permit one to hold that a body was an eligible body in one capacity and at the same time not an eligible body in another capacity. The approach contended for by the taxpayer was not permissible as a matter of law. Further, no support for the taxpayer's approach was to be derived from considering the purpose of the provisions. If, as the taxpayer accepted, it was not a college or institution of the university when one took account of all of the circumstances, including all of its activities, then it was not within the definition of 'an eligible body'. It could not in law be an eligible body and, at the same time, not an eligible body. If it was not an eligible body, it could not claim exemption even on those occasions when it provided services which would be exempt services if they had been provided by an eligible body. Accordingly, the appeal would be dismissed.

Finance and Business Training Ltd v Revenue and Customs Comrs [2013] UKUT 594 (TCC), [2014] All ER (D) 84 (Jan) (Upper Tribunal: Morgan J presiding).

2489   Exempt supply—education—eligible body—research

The Value Added Tax (Education) Order 2013, SI 2013/1897 (in force on 1 August 2013), amends the Value Added Tax Act 1994 Sch 9 Pt II Group 6 item 1 to remove the supply of research by an eligible body to another eligible body from exemption from value added tax.

2490   Exempt supply—finance—management of authorised contractual schemes

The Value Added Tax (Finance) Order 2013, SI 2013/1402 (in force on 28 June 2013), amends the Value Added Tax Act 1994 Sch 9 Pt II Group 5 so as to (1) include as an exempt supply the management of authorised contractual schemes; and (2) provide that, for the purposes of applying the exemption, authorised contractual schemes are to be defined in accordance with the Financial Services and Markets Act 2000 s 237.

2491   Exempt supply—finance—special investment funds—fund pooling assets of occupational pension schemes

The manager of an investment fund pooling the assets of occupational pension schemes established by an employer charged the trustee of the fund value added tax on its services and accounted for the VAT to the Revenue. The fund manager claimed repayment of the VAT on the ground that it came within the exemption laid down in Council Directive (EC) 2006/112 (on the common system of value added tax) art 135(1)(g). On the trustee's appeal against the Revenue's rejection of the claim, a question arose as to whether and under what conditions assets of a retirement pension scheme, and the investment fund in which they were pooled, were a 'special investment fund' within the meaning of art 135(1)(g). *Held*, it was settled law that funds constituting undertakings for collective investment in transferable securities within the meaning of Council Directive (EEC) 85/611 (on the co-ordination of laws, regulations and administrative provisions relating to undertakings for collective investment in transferable securities) were special investment funds. Undertakings for collective investment in transferable securities were undertakings that had as their sole object, in accordance with the objective of Directive 2006/112 art 135(1)(g), the collective investment in transferable securities of capital raised from the public. Further, funds which, without being collective investment undertakings, displayed identical characteristics and carried out the same transactions or, at least, displayed features that were sufficiently comparable for them to be in competition with such undertakings, also had to be regarded as special investment funds. However, a fund in which the assets of a retirement pension scheme were pooled could not be regarded as a collective investment undertaking. Such a fund was not open to the public, but constituted an employment-related benefit which employers granted only to their employees. It was not identical to funds that constituted special investment funds, nor was it sufficiently comparable with collective investment undertakings to be in competition with them. Therefore such a fund was not a special investment fund within the meaning of Directive 2006/112 art 135(1)(g) where the members of the scheme did not bear the risk arising from the management of the fund and the contributions that the employer paid into the scheme were a means by which it complied with its legal obligations towards its employees.

Case C-424/11 *Wheels Common Investment Fund Trustees Ltd v Revenue and Customs Comrs* [2014] STC 495 (ECJ: First Chamber).

2492   Exempt supply—financial services—management of special investment funds

The taxpayer was an undertaking whose objects were the dissemination of information and recommendations relating to the stock market. The taxpayer concluded a contract with an investment management company which managed a retail investment fund in the form of a special investment fund under the German law on investment management companies. The taxpayer undertook to advise the company in the management of the fund and constantly to monitor the fund and to make recommendations for the purchase or sale of assets. The parties had agreed that the taxpayer would be paid for its advice on the basis of a percentage calculated by reference to the average monthly value of the investment fund. Pursuant to the contract, the taxpayer provided the company at issue in the main proceedings, by telephone, fax or email, with recommendations concerning the purchase and sale of securities. The company entered the recommendations into its purchase and sale order system and, after checking that they had not infringed any statutory investment restriction applicable to special investment funds, implemented them, often within a few minutes of receiving them. Although the company had made no selection of its own in the management of the investment fund, the final responsibility had continued to lie with it. In the context of the fiscal procedure relating to turnover tax, the taxpayer had requested that its advisory services to the company be exempted from value added tax as outsourced services for the management of a special investment fund. The request was refused on the ground that the services supplied by the taxpayer had not been covered by the 'management of special investment funds' within the meaning of Council Directive (EEC) 77/388 art 13(B)(d)(6) and, therefore, could not warrant such exemption. In legal proceedings challenging the decisions taken against the taxpayer, questions arose as to whether and under what conditions advisory services provided by a third party to an investment management company concerning investment in transferable securities fell within the concept of 'management of special investment funds' for the purposes of the exemption laid down in art 13(B)(d)(6). *Held,* it was settled law that, in order to determine whether advisory services provided by a third party to an investment management company concerning investment in transferable securities fell within the concept of 'management of special investment funds' for the purposes of the exemption laid down in art 13(B)(d)(6), it was necessary to examine whether the advisory service provided by a third party concerning investment in transferable securities was intrinsically connected to the activity characteristic of an investment management company, so that it had the effect of performing the specific and essential functions of management of a special investment fund. Services consisting in giving recommendations to an investment management company to purchase and sell assets were intrinsically connected to the activity characteristic of the investment management company, which consisted in the collective investment in transferable securities of capital raised from the public. Article 13(B)(d)(6) should be interpreted as meaning that advisory services concerning investment in transferable securities, provided by a third party to an investment management company which was the manager of a special investment fund, fell within the concept of 'management of special investment funds' for the purposes of the exemption laid down in art 13(B)(d)(6).

Case C-275/11 *GfBk Gesellschaft fur Borsenkommunikation mbH v Finanzamt Bayreuth* [2013] All ER (D) 118 (Mar) (ECJ: First Chamber). Case C-44/11 *Finanzamt Frankfurt am Main V-Hochst v Deutsche Bank AG* [2012] STC 1951, ECJ considered.

Directive 77/388 art 13(B)(d)(6) now Council Directive (EC) 2006/112 art 135(1)(g).

2493   Exempt supply—health and welfare—provision of pharmaceutical products

The European Commission informed Spain that it considered the application of the regime of reduced rates of value added tax provided by the Spanish law on VAT to be in breach of its obligations under Council Directive (EC) 2006/112 (on the common system of value added tax). Spain submitted that the application of the rates to the goods referred to in the relevant provisions was permissible under Directive 2006/112 Annex III points 3, 4. Spain first of all relied on the need to interpret the concept of 'pharmaceutical products', within the meaning of Annex III point 3, in accordance with the definition of pharmaceutical products applicable under Spanish law, which included not only medicinal products, but also medical appliances and devices. Next it submitted that finished medicinal products, magistral formulas, officinal formulas, active substances and pharmaceutical forms, as defined in national legislation, should be regarded as pharmaceutical products within the meaning of Annex III point 3. Finally, Spain submitted that the concept of 'disabled' within the meaning of Annex III point 4 should be understood, in accordance with the relevant guidelines of the World Health Organisation, as referring to any person suffering from an illness resulting from disability. The Commission was not convinced and called on Spain to take appropriate measures to comply with the reasoned opinion within two months. The Spanish authorities repeated that the national provisions were in conformity with Directive

2006/112. The Commission sought a declaration that by applying a reduced rate of VAT to (1) medicinal substances which could be used habitually and suitably in the manufacturing of medicinal products; (2) medical devices, material, equipment and appliances which, viewed objectively, could be used only to prevent, diagnose, treat, alleviate or cure human or animal illnesses or ailments, but which were not normally intended to alleviate or treat disability, for the exclusive personal use of the disabled; (3) aids and equipment which might be used essentially or primarily to treat physical disabilities in animals; and (4) aids and equipment essentially or primarily used to treat human disabilities, but which had not been intended for the exclusive personal use of the disabled, Spain had failed to fulfil its obligations under art 98. *Held*, (1) Annex III point 3 permitted a reduced rate of VAT to be applied to medicinal substances only if they were likely to be used directly by final consumers for health care, prevention of illnesses and as treatment for medical and veterinary purposes. (2) It was apparent that neither Annex III point 3 nor Annex III point 4 authorised a reduced rate of VAT to be applied to 'medical devices, material, equipment and appliances used only to prevent, diagnose, treat, alleviate or cure human or animal illnesses or ailments'. (3) Neither Annex III point 3 nor Annex III point 4 authorised a reduced rate of VAT to be applied to apparatus and accessories which might be used to treat physical disabilities in animals. (4) A reduced rate of VAT, under Annex III point 4, might not be applied to apparatus and accessories used essentially or primarily to alleviate physical disability in humans, but which were not intended for the exclusive personal use of the disabled. Accordingly, the declaration sought by the Commission would be made.

Case C-360/11 *European Commission v Spain* [2013] All ER (D) 268 (Jan), [2013] STC 2236 (ECJ: Third Chamber).

2494   Exempt supply—plastic surgery and cosmetic treatments—provision of medical care

Under Council Directive (EC) 2006/112 art 132(1)(b) and (c), member states must exempt from value added tax hospital and medical care and closely related activities undertaken by bodies governed by public law or, under social conditions comparable with those applicable to bodies governed by public law, by hospitals, centres for medical treatment or diagnosis and other duly recognised establishments of a similar nature; and the provision of medical care in the exercise of the medical and paramedical professions as defined by the member state concerned.

The taxpayer offered medical services in the field of plastic surgery and cosmetic treatments. It had provided services involving both cosmetic reconstructive plastic surgery and also some skincare services. It claimed the refund of input tax. The tax authority refused both the refund and the deduction of the tax on the ground that VAT could not be refunded in respect of exempt transactions nor could a deduction of VAT be granted since cosmetic and reconstructive surgery constituted medical care exempt from taxation. The taxpayer's appeal was allowed on the basis that the services offered by the taxpayer in respect of plastic surgery and cosmetic treatments did not constitute medical care. The authority's appeal was allowed in part on the ground that surgery and treatments which were reconstructive or carried out for psychological reasons were exempt from taxation if they were carried out by persons specially licensed to practice as medical professionals. On further appeal by the authority, questions arose as to the manner in which the expressions 'medical care' and 'the provision of medical care' in Directive 2006/112 art 132(1)(b) and (c) were to be applied in the context of medical services consisting of surgery and various treatments. *Held*, art 132(1)(b) and (c) should be interpreted as meaning that supplies of service, consisting of plastic surgery and other cosmetic treatments, fell within the concepts of 'medical care' and 'the provision of medical care' within the meaning of art 132(1)(b) and (c) where those services were intended to diagnose, treat or cure diseases or health disorders or to protect, maintain or restore human health. The subjective understanding that the person who underwent plastic surgery or a cosmetic treatment had of it was not in itself decisive in order to determine whether that intervention had a therapeutic purpose. The fact that services such as those at issue were supplied or undertaken by a licensed member of the medical profession or that the purpose of such services was determined by such a professional might influence the assessment of whether interventions such as those at issue fell within the concept of 'medical care' or 'the provision of medical care' within the meaning of art 132(1)(b) and (c). In order to determine whether supplies of services such as those at issue were exempt from VAT, all the requirements laid down in art 132(1)(b) or (c) should be taken into account as well as the other relevant provisions as far as concerned arts 132(1)(b), 131, 133 and 134.

Case C-91/12 *Skatteverket v PFC Clinic AB* [2013] STC 1253 (ECJ: Third Chamber).

2495   Exempt supply—rental of grass sports pitches—conversion of pitches to artificial surfaces—effect on charge to tax

Council Directive (EC) 77/388 art 5(7)(a) provides that member states may treat as supplies made for consideration the application by a taxable person for the purposes of his business of goods produced, constructed, extracted, processed, purchased or imported in the course of such business, where the value added tax on such goods, had they been acquired from another taxable person, would not be wholly deductible.

The taxpayer, a Dutch entity, owned open-air sports pitches that it rented to sports associations. The transactions were exempt from VAT. The taxpayer replaced the grass on the pitches with an artificial surface and continued to rent them. The taxpayer paid VAT on the invoices from the contractors who carried out the resurfacing work, but it did not deduct VAT from its rental activities. The tax authority assessed the taxpayer's rental activities following the resurfacing of the pitches for VAT. On the taxpayer's appeal, a question arose as to the interpretation of Directive 77/388 art 5(7)(a). *Held*, art 5(7)(a), read in conjunction with art 11(A)(1)(b), meant that the application by a taxable person, for the purposes of an economic activity exempt from VAT, of sports pitches that he owned and that he had transformed by a third person, could be subject to VAT calculated on the basis of the aggregate arrived at by adding to the transformation costs the value of the ground on which the pitches lay, to the extent that the taxable person had not yet paid the VAT relating to that value or to those costs, and provided that the pitches were not covered by the exemption in relation to land that was not built on provided for in art 13(B)(h).

Case C-299/11 *Staatssecretaris van Financiën v Gemeente Vlaardingen* [2013] STC 478 (ECJ: First Chamber).

Directive 77/388 arts 5(7)(a), 11(A)(1)(b), 13(B)(h) now Council Directive (EC) 2006/112 arts 18(a), 74, 135(1)(k).

2496   Exempt supply—right to deduct—refusal of refund—fiscal neutrality

The taxpayer submitted an invoice to a company relating to the sale and renovation of a building. The invoice set out the prices of the building and its renovation, the amounts of purchase tax and stamp duty, together with the amount of value added tax. Since the sale of the building had been considered to be exempt from VAT, the tax had been calculated on the basis of the other items on the invoice. The taxpayer included the invoice in its tax return. The company exercised its right to deduct the VAT entered on the invoice. Following an audit by the Bulgarian tax authority, the company was refused the right to deduct the VAT entered on the invoice on the basis that, as all of the transactions entered on the invoice were exempt, there was no justification for the VAT entry on the invoice. The taxpayer's application for a refund of the amount improperly invoiced was refused on the ground that payments of VAT had not been wrongly made so that the VAT entered on the invoice was payable by the taxpayer as the person who had entered the tax on the invoice. The taxpayer claimed that, in view of the fact that the tax authority had earlier refused the company the right to deduct the VAT paid but not due in respect of the exempt supply, the tax authority had wrongly refused to refund the tax. It fell to be determined whether the principle of the neutrality of VAT precluded a tax authority from refusing a refund in such circumstances. *Held*, Council Directive (EC) 2006/112 art 203 provided that any person who entered VAT on an invoice was liable to pay the tax entered on the invoice. Any such person was liable to pay the VAT entered on an invoice independently of any obligations to pay it on account of there being a transaction subject to VAT. The VAT neutrality principle would be interpreted as precluding a tax authority from refusing, on the basis of a provision of national law intended to transpose art 203, the supplier of an exempt supply the refund of VAT invoiced in error to a customer, on the ground that the supplier had not corrected the incorrect invoice, in circumstances where that authority had definitively refused the customer the right to deduct that VAT and such definitive refusal resulted in the system for correction provided for under national law no longer being applicable. The VAT neutrality principle, if necessary, might be relied on by a taxable person against a provision of national law, or the application of that provision, that failed to have regard to the principle. It might also be relied on by a taxable person in order to contest a provision of national law that made the refund of VAT invoiced in error conditional on the correction of the incorrect invoice, in circumstances where the right to deduct that VAT had definitively been refused and such definitive refusal resulted in the system for correction provided for under national law no longer being applicable.

Case C-138/12 *Rusedespred OOD v Direktor na Direktsia 'Obzhalvane i upravlenie na izpalnenieto' – Varna pri Tsentralno upravlenie na Natsionalnata agentsia za prihodite* [2013] All ER (D) 190 (Apr) (ECJ: Fifth Chamber).

2497   Finance Act 2013
See para 2149.

2498   General regulations
The Value Added Tax (Amendment) Regulations 2013, SI 2013/701 (in force on 15 April 2013), further amend the 1995 Regulations, SI 1995/2518, (1) by adding to the list of specified communications that may be made using an electronic communication system a reference to a notification of the arrival in the United Kingdom of motorised land vehicles and payment of value added tax; (2) by providing for a new notification system for arrivals in the United Kingdom of means of transport that are motorised land vehicles and making provision as to how and when any acquisition VAT due on such an arrival is to be paid to the Commissioners for Her Majesty's Revenue and Customs; (3) so that the notification scheme for acquisitions of new means of transport is limited to new ships and new aircraft with a revised time limit for notification to match the time limit for the new notification scheme; and (4) extending, from seven to fourteen days, the time for notification after the later of the date of the acquisition or the arrival of the goods in the United Kingdom.

The Value Added Tax (Amendment) (No 2) Regulations 2013, SI 2013/2241 (in force on 1 October 2013), further amend the 1995 Regulations above so as to correct an error in reg 129 in relation to the implementation of Council Directive (EC) 2006/112 (on the common system of value added tax) art 146(1)(b). In addition, the regulations substitute reference to the Excise Goods (Holding, Movement, Warehousing and REDS) Regulations 1992, SI 1992/3135, in reg 135 for reference to the Excise Goods (Holding, Movement and Duty Point Regulations 2010, SI 2010/593.

The Value Added Tax (Amendment) (No 3) Regulations 2013, SI 2013/3211 (in force on 1 January 2014), further amend the 1995 Regulations by adding the territories of Mayotte and Saint-Martin to, and removing the territory of St Pierre and Miquelon from, the list of territories which are treated as being excluded from the territory of the member states and the European Union for the purposes of the Value Added Tax Act 1994.

2499   Input tax—attribution—partial exemption—income from charitable investment fund—input tax on investment management fees
The taxpayer was a charity and, as such, was required to expend all of its income in the deliverance of its charitable aims. Its main activity, the provision of education, was an exempt supply, but it also undertook taxable activities, including commercial research, publishing and consultancy. The taxpayer received donations which were invested through an endowment fund in a range of securities including equities, property and bonds. The income produced was distributed across all of the taxpayer's activities. Where a taxpayer made both taxable and exempt supplies, input tax which did not have a direct and immediate link to the supplies was treated as residual input tax, and was attributable in appropriate portions between the taxpayer's taxable and exempt supplies. The taxpayer had come to an arrangement with the Commissioners for Her Majesty's Revenue and Customs for calculating and apportioning its residual input tax, under which input tax incurred on investment management fees relating to the fund was not treated as residual input tax. The taxpayer sought to have that input tax included on the basis that it was an overhead cost which related to raising funds to support all of its activities, and so tax was recoverable to the extent that its activities were carried out for taxable purposes. The Commissioners refused the claim and the taxpayer appealed. *Held*, there was clearly a link between the taxpayer's investment activity and its overall economic activity. Costs associated with the

investment activity had been in reality components of the price of the taxpayer's taxable research and publications on the one hand and educational and other exempt activities on the other. The fact that the investment activity might have raised, primarily, income rather than capital was of no relevance. The value added tax system achieved the greatest degree of simplicity and neutrality when the tax was levied in as general a manner as possible and when its scope covered all stages of supply. It could not be accepted that overheads relating to a non-economic activity undertaken for the purchase of an economic activity should not be regarded as recoverable because the non-economic activity might technically be capable of falling within the definition of 'a supply'. Accordingly, the appeal would be allowed.

Chancellor, Masters & Scholars of the University of Cambridge v Revenue and Customs Comrs [2013] UKFTT 444 (TC), [2013] All ER (D) 52 (Sep) (First-tier Tribunal: Judge Michael Connell presiding). Case C-465/03 *Kretztechnik AG v Finanzamt Linz* [2005] 1 WLR 3755, [2005] STC 1118, ECJ (2005 Abr para 3145), applied; *Fleming (t/a Bodycraft) v Revenue and Customs Comrs; Condé Nast Publications Ltd v Revenue and Customs Comrs* [2008] UKHL 2, [2008] 1 All ER 1061 (2008 Abr para 2965); and Case C-437/06 *Securenta Gottinger Immobilienanlagen und Vermogensmanagement AG v Finanzamt Gottingen* [2008] STC 3473, ECJ, considered.

2500   Input tax—deduction—right to deduct—abusive practice—discretionary trust

The taxpayer was a university which decided to redevelop a derelict mill in which it had previously acquired a leasehold estate. It opted to tax the lease of the mill and grant a taxable 20-year lease of it to a discretionary trust. The taxpayer elected to waive the exemption from value added tax over the mill pursuant to the Value Added Tax Act 1994 Sch 10 para 2(1) and charged VAT on the supplies made under the lease. The trustees of the trust also elected to waive exemption over the property and charged VAT on the supplies made under the terms of the leaseback. The arrangements took the form of a 'cash flow' VAT scheme, which enabled the taxpayer to deduct input tax incurred in respect of the redevelopment of the mill when the input tax was incurred, but exposed the taxpayer to the obligation to account for output tax on the rent payable under the lease. The Revenue issued an assessment which represented the input tax which the taxpayer had deducted in respect of the supply to it of standard rated construction services. The transactions had been entered into with the sole intention of obtaining a fiscal advantage. The lease involved the supply of goods or services and amounted to an economic activity. It fell to be determined whether the taxpayer's tax arrangements constituted an abusive practice. *Held*, to allow taxable persons to deduct all input VAT even though, in the context of their normal commercial operations, no transactions conforming with the deduction rules of national and European law would have enabled them to deduct only a part, would be contrary to the principle of fiscal neutrality and, therefore, contrary to the purpose of those rules. In the circumstances, the taxpayer's arrangements had not been contrary to the purposes of the legislation. Although it was accepted that the exercise of the option to tax had amounted to the obtaining of a tax advantage, it had been an advantage entirely consistent with the domestic legislation. By paying the irrecoverable input tax and the rent on the sublease by the trust, the taxpayer had been paying the tax for which it would have been liable on the refurbishment costs of the mill had it carried out the works itself. The tax advantage obtained had not been abusive for it had not been absolute and, further, it had been balanced by the liability to account for output tax. Accordingly, the appeal would be allowed.

University of Huddersfield Higher Education Corpn v Revenue and Customs Comrs [2013] UKFTT 429 (TC), [2013] All ER (D) 150 (Aug) (First-tier Tribunal: Judge David Demack). For earlier related proceedings see Case C-223/03 *University of Huddersfield Higher Education Corpn v Customs and Excise Comrs* [2006] Ch 387, [2006] STC 919, ECJ (2006 Abr para 2909).

2501   Input tax—deduction—right to deduct—abusive practice—insurance services

A scheme designed to minimise the overall liability to value added tax of a group of companies involved in motor breakdown insurance was intended to enable the VAT element of the cost of repairs to be recovered by any member of the group, thereby reducing costs and enabling the insurer to offer lower premiums and redressing a perceived competitive disadvantage. Motor breakdown insurance policies were issued to members of the public by an English company. Under the contract of insurance, the English company undertook to the insured that it would meet the cost of the repair. It did not undertake to repair the vehicle. The English company reinsured its liabilities under those policies with a company based in Gibraltar that retroceded 85 per cent of the reinsurance to the second appellant, another company based in Gibraltar. The second appellant contracted with the first appellant, an English company, to supply claims-handling services, namely to instruct garages to carry out any works required to be effected under the policies, and to pay for such works. The garages were to make supplies of labour and parts to the first appellant and then invoice the first appellant for the supplies. The first appellant then invoiced the second appellant for claims-handling services and the latter invoice covered the amounts invoiced by the garages. The first appellant would be able to recover the VAT charged by the garage, input VAT, and would not have to charge VAT on its onward supply of claims-handling services to the second appellant. The first appellant contended that it was entitled to claim repayment of the input tax. A question arose as to whether the scheme was abusive. Consideration was given to the agreements between the appellants and the garages, to Council Directive (EEC) 67/227 (on the harmonisation of legislation of member states concerning turnover taxes) and Council Directive (EC) 77/388 (on the harmonisation of the laws of the member states relating to turnover taxes). *Held*, decisions about the application of the VAT system were highly dependent on the factual situations involved. When determining the relevant supply in which a taxable person engaged, regard had to be had to all the circumstances in which the transaction in question took place. In cases where a scheme operated through a construct of contractual relationships, it was necessary to look at the matter as a whole in order to determine its economic reality. The question should be answered in the negative in the present case: there was no supply of repair services by the garages to the first appellant. Having regard to all the circumstances, although the transaction of particular importance was that between the garage and the first appellant, it had to be understood in the wider context of arrangements between the insured, the Gibraltar company, the English company, the appellants and the garage. There was no indication in the relevant agreements that the first appellant's role included undertaking responsibility for the carrying out of repairs. Further, turning to the relationship between the first appellant and the garages, there was no finding that the garage had undertaken to the first appellant to carry out repairs. Under the contract of insurance, the English company undertook to the insured that it would meet the cost of the repair. The garage supplied a service to the uninsured by repairing his vehicle, and the English company met the cost of that supply because it had undertaken to the insured that it would do so, and had received premiums from the insured as the consideration for its giving that undertaking. The cost of the repair was the cover. In economic reality, when the first appellant paid for the repairs it was merely discharging on behalf of the insurer the latter's obligation to the insured to pay for the repair. The interposition of the first appellant did not transmute the discharge of the insurer's obligation to the insured into the consideration for a service provided to the reinsurer's agent. The final consumer of the services supplied by the garage was the insured and VAT was borne on that supply. Accordingly, the appeal would be dismissed.

WHA Ltd v Revenue and Customs Comrs [2013] UKSC 24, [2013] 2 All ER 907, [2013] STC 943 (Supreme Court: Lord Hope DP, Lord Walker, Lord Mance, Lord Reed and Lord Carnwath SCJJ). Decision of Court of Appeal [2007] EWCA Civ 728, [2007] STC 1695 (2007 Abr para 3007) affirmed.

Directive 67/227 repealed. Directive 77/388 replaced by Council Directive (EC) 2006/112.

2502   Input tax—deduction—right to deduct—adjustment of deduction—recovery of amounts due after adjustment

Council Directive (EEC) 77/388 art 20(1)(a) (on the harmonisation of the laws of the member states relating to turnover taxes–common system of value added tax: uniform basis of assessment) provides that an initial deduction of value added tax must be adjusted according to the procedures laid down by the member states, in particular where the deduction is higher or lower than that to which the taxable person is entitled.

It has been held, on a reference for a preliminary ruling on the interpretation of Directive 77/388, that art 20(1)(a) means that, in the event of the adjustment of a VAT deduction applied by a taxable person, the amounts due in that regard must be paid by the taxable person. A contrary interpretation, according to which the adjustment of a VAT deduction can be imposed on a taxable person other than the person who has benefited from the supply, is incompatible with the objectives pursued by Directive 77/388. Directive 77/388 therefore precludes the recovery of amounts due following the adjustment of a VAT deduction from a taxable person other than the person who applies the deduction.

Case C-622/11 *Staatssecretaris van Financen v Pactor Vastgoed BV* [2013] All ER (D) 246 (Oct) (ECJ: Second Chamber).

Directive 77/388 art 20(1)(a) now Council Directive (EC) 2006/112 art 184.

2503   Input tax—deduction—right to deduct—appeal—legitimate expectation— jurisdiction

The Value Added Tax Act 1994 s 83(1)(c) provides that an appeal lies to the tribunal with respect to the amount of any input tax which may be credited to a person.

The taxpayer took legal action against a builder whom he had engaged to construct a building. A reference was made to adjudication before the building was completed. As a result, the taxpayer received three invoices from the solicitors whom he had instructed in the action and an invoice from the adjudicator. The taxpayer registered for value added tax so as to be able to claim input tax in respect of the costs incurred on the construction of the property. The Revenue decided that the taxpayer was not entitled to deduct the VAT shown on the invoices as input tax because of the effect of the Value Added Tax Regulations 1995, SI 1995/2518, reg 111(2)(d) on the basis that the VAT was in respect of services which had been supplied to the taxpayer more than six months before his effective date of registration. He was allowed a deduction in respect of the building works themselves as a different time limit applied under reg 111(2)(b). The taxpayer's appeal was allowed on the basis that the conclusion of the judge in *Oxfam v Revenue and Customs Comrs* to the effect that he considered that the 1994 Act s 83(1)(c) covered all issues regarding the amount of input tax, had been a necessary part of the judge's reasoning and therefore of binding effect on the First-tier Tribunal which concluded that it had jurisdiction to consider 'the issue of legitimate expectation' in the taxpayer's statutory appeal, and that the taxpayer had an enforceable legitimate expectation that he could recover the input tax shown on certain identified invoices. The Revenue appealed, contending that the First-tier Tribunal had no jurisdiction, when dealing with a VAT appeal, to consider a taxpayer's claims based on the public law concept of 'legitimate expectation'. It also contended that, if that was wrong, the First-tier Tribunal had been wrong, as a matter of law, to conclude that the taxpayer had a right to payment of the VAT based on the alleged legitimate expectation. *Held*, the First-tier Tribunal was not bound by the judge's decision in *Oxfam* nor did it believe that, although not bound, it should follow that decision. The relevant factors pointed strongly to the conclusion that Parliament had not intended to confer a judicial review function on a VAT and duties tribunal or on the First-tier Tribunal in relation to appeals under s 83. Further, the First-tier Tribunal had no jurisdiction over the taxpayer's claim to a credit in respect of VAT on the invoices. That was a claim based on legitimate expectation. In so concluding, the decision of the judge in *Oxfam* was disagreed with and departed from. His principal reason for arriving at his decision had been his perception of the 'ordinary meaning of the language' of s 83(1)(c) and the importance which he had attached to the words 'with respect to'. The 'ordinary meaning of the language' was not that which the judge attributed to s 83(1) and the words 'with respect to' did not bear the weight with which he burdened them. Accordingly, the appeal would be allowed.

Revenue and Customs Comrs v Noor [2013] UKUT 071 (TCC), [2013] STC 998 (Upper Tribunal: Warren J and Judge Colin Bishopp). *Revenue and Customs Comrs v Hok Ltd* [2012] UKUT 363 (TCC), [2013] STC 225 (2012 Abr para 1535) applied. *Oxfam v Revenue and Customs Comrs* [2009] EWHC 3078 (Ch), [2010] STC 686 (2010 Abr para 1830) disapproved. Decision of First-tier Tribunal (Tax Chamber) [2011] UKFTT 349 (TC), [2011] SWTI 195 reversed.

2504   Input tax—deduction—right to deduct—deductible portion—construction of building comprising commercial and residential parts—turnover method

The taxpayer company built and let a building which included both living accommodation and commercial premises. The letting was partly exempt, and partly subject to, value added tax. In its VAT declaration, the taxpayer carried out a partial deduction of the input tax in relation to the building. It calculated the amount of deductible VAT by applying a proportion determined by reference to the ratio between the turnover in relation to the commercial letting and that arising from other letting transactions. Following a tax inspection, the applicant tax authority took the view that, in accordance with domestic law, the amount of deductible input VAT had to be determined by reference to the ratio between the area of the commercial premises and that of the premises used for living accommodation. It sent an amendment notice to the taxpayer. In proceedings by the taxpayer against the amendment notice, a question arose as to whether one of the possibilities set out in Council Directive (EC) 77/388 art 17(5)(c) (on the harmonisation of the laws of the member states relating to turnover taxes—common system of value added tax: uniform basis of assessment) authorised member states to restrict allocation arising from the application of the turnover-based method by providing that this method might only be used where no other economic allocation was possible. It fell to be determined whether art 17(5)(c) was to be interpreted as authorising the member states to prescribe primarily an apportionment criterion other than the turnover-based method for apportioning the input tax on the construction of a mixed-use building other than that based on turnover appearing in art 19(1). *Held,* art 17(5) had to be interpreted as allowing member states, for the purposes of calculating the proportion of input VAT deductible for a given operation, such as the construction of a mixed-use building, to give precedence, as the key to allocation, to an allocation key other than that based on turnover appearing in art 19(1), on condition that the method used guaranteed a more precise determination of the said deductible proportion.

Case C-511/10 *Finanzamt Hildesheim v BLC Baumarkt GmbH & Co KG* [2013] STC 521 (ECJ: First Chamber).

Directive 77/388 arts 17(5), 19(1) now Council Directive (EC) 2006/112 arts 173–175.

2505　Input tax—deduction—right to deduct—economic activity—sale of shares—transfer of totality of assets

The taxpayer sold the entirety of its shareholding in a company. A number of services were supplied to the taxpayer in conjunction with the sale, and the invoices provided for value added tax to be charged. The taxpayer deducted that VAT in its tax returns, on the basis that the disposal of its shareholding constituted the transfer of a totality of assets and of services and that the costs incurred by the taxpayer in connection with that transaction had to be considered part of the general costs associated with its entire economic activity and were, therefore, fully deductible. The Dutch tax authority rejected that deduction and issued a notice of additional assessment. The taxpayer's appeal against that decision was allowed, and the tax authority appealed, submitting that the disposal of the shares, which had occurred in conjunction with the cessation of management activities in respect of the company, was an economic activity and should be exempt pursuant to Council Directive (EC) 77/388 art 13(B)(d)(5). The appeal court decided to stay the proceedings and refer to the European Court of Justice for a preliminary ruling the questions (1) whether arts 5(8) and/or 6(5) should be interpreted as meaning that the disposal of the shares in a company to which the transferor supplied services that were subject to VAT constituted the transfer of a totality of assets or services or part thereof within the meaning of those provisions; and (2) if not, whether the conditions for the application of those provisions were nonetheless satisfied if, on the one hand, the other shareholders transferred all the other shares in that company to the same person at practically the same time, and, on the other, disposal was closely linked to management activities carried out for that company. *Held,* the mere acquisition, holding and sale of shares in a company did not, in themselves, amount to an economic activity within the meaning of Directive 77/388, since the mere acquisition of financial holdings in other undertakings did not amount to the exploitation of property for the purpose of obtaining income from it on a continuing basis. Any dividend yielded by that holding was merely the result of ownership of the property. It was otherwise where the holding was accompanied by direct or indirect involvement in the management of the companies in which the holding had been acquired, if that entailed carrying out transactions which were subject to VAT, such as the supply of administrative, financial, commercial and technical services. It followed that the transfer of shares in a company could not, irrespective of the size of the shareholding, be regarded as equivalent to the transfer of a totality of assets or part of it within the meaning of art 5(8) unless the holding was part of an independent unit which allowed an independent economic activity to be carried out, and that activity was carried on by the transferee.

Case C-651/11 *Staatssecretaris van Financien v X BV* [2013] All ER (D) 50 (Jun) (ECJ: Ninth Chamber).
Directive 77/388 arts 5(8), 6(5), 13(B)(d)(5) now Council Directive (EC) 2006/112 arts 19, 29, 135(1)(f).

2506 Input tax—deduction—right to deduct—economic activity—statutory body—supplies to government

The taxpayer was a statutory body established in South Africa by South African domestic legislation to promote tourism in South Africa. The taxpayer's day-to-day management was in the hands of its board and it was fully commercial and professional in its approach to its operations. Although the South African government could control who sat on the taxpayer's board, in practice, it had chosen not to do so. The majority of the taxpayer's income was provided by the South African government. The taxpayer established a branch in the United Kingdom. The Revenue decided that the value added tax incurred by the taxpayer's United Kingdom branch in respect of the portion of the income it derived from the South African government was irrecoverable because the activities from which it derived that income were not business activities. On the taxpayer's appeal, it fell to be determined whether its activities in providing supplies to the South African government were business activities. *Held*, the receipt by a statutory body of funds from the government in order to carry out the purpose for which it had been established could not be an economic activity. Where a government established a statutory body to carry out a specific task, it would be impossible for that statutory body to make a profit at the expense of the government. It was not in the same position as an independent entity to which the government had outsourced a task, as such an entity was free to make a profit, or carry on other activities. In the present case, the taxpayer had not been a taxable person acting as such when receiving government funding to carry out its statutory duties. Accordingly, the appeal would be dismissed.

Re South African Tourist Board [2013] UKFTT 780 (TC), [2013] All ER (D) 52 (Jan) (First-tier Tribunal: Judge Barbara Mosedale presiding). *Institute of Chartered Accountants of England and Wales v Customs and Excise Comrs* [1999] STC 398 applied; Case 89/81 *Staatssecretaris van Financiën v Hong Kong Trade Development Council* [1982] ECR 1277, ECJ (1983 Abr para 1442); Case 102/86 *Apple and Pear Development Council v Customs and Excise Comrs* [1988] STC 221, ECJ (1988 Abr para 2758); Case C-284/04 *T-Mobile v Austria* [2008] STC 184, ECJ (2008 Abr para 2960); and Case C-369/04 *Hutchison 3G UK Ltd v Revenue and Customs Comrs* [2008] STC 218, ECJ (2007 Abr para 3009), considered.

2507 Input tax—deduction—right to deduct—invoices concerning supplies—bona fide purchaser

The taxpayer was a company incorporated under Bulgarian law, the main economic activity of which was trade in animals. The taxpayer declared nine invoices concerning the supply of calves for slaughter from a particular supplier, in order to obtain, in the form of a tax credit, the deduction of the value added tax relating to those invoices. In order to provide proof of the acquisition of the animals at issue, in addition to the nine invoices, the taxpayer produced weight certificates, bank statements relating to payment of those invoices and the contract concluded with the supplier for the supply of calves. Following a tax investigation into the supplier, which revealed certain gaps in its accounting and in its compliance with the veterinary formalities relating, in particular, to titles of ownership of the animals and to their ear tags, the authorities took the view that it had not been proved that those supplies had in fact been carried out and that, consequently, the taxpayer was not entitled to claim a right to deduction of the VAT relating to those supplies. The taxpayer's appeal was dismissed and it appealed further. The taxpayer argued that it acted as a bona fide purchaser, and that the question of the right to deduct VAT was independent of the question as to the ownership of and the origin of the goods acquired. The referring court decided to stay the proceedings and to refer certain questions to the European Court of Justice for a preliminary ruling. *Held*, (1) Council Directive (EC) 2006/112 on the common system of value added tax should be interpreted as meaning that, in the context of the exercise of the right to deduct VAT, the concept of 'supply of goods' for the purposes of Directive 2006/112 and evidence that such a supply had in fact been carried out were not linked to the form of the acquisition of a right of ownership of the goods concerned. It was for the referring court to carry out, in accordance with the national rules relating to evidence, an overall assessment of all the facts and circumstances of the dispute before it in order to determine whether the supplies of goods at issue in the main proceedings had actually been carried out and whether, as the case might be, a right to deduct might be exercised on the basis of those supplies. (2) Article 242 should be interpreted as meaning that it did not require taxable persons who were not agricultural producers to show in their accounts the subject matter of the supplies of goods which they made, when animals were concerned, and to prove that those animals had been subject to control in accordance with the standards set out in the annex to Commission Regulation (EC) 1725/2003 (adopting certain international accounting standards in accordance with European Parliament and Council Regulation (EC) 1606/2002). (3) Directive 2006/112 art 226(6) should be interpreted as meaning that it did not require a taxable person who carried out supplies of goods concerning animals which were subject to the identification and registration system established by Regulation 1760/2000 to mention the ear tags of those animals on the invoices relating to those supplies. (4) Directive 2006/112 art 185(1) should be interpreted as allowing a deduction of VAT to be adjusted only if the taxable person concerned had previously benefited from a right to deduct that tax under the conditions laid down in art 168(a).

C-78/12 'Evita-K' Food v Direktor na Direktsia 'Obzhalvane i upravlenie na izpalnenieto' – Sofia pri Tsentralno upravlenie na Natsionalnata agentsia za prihodite [2013] All ER (D) 378 (Jul) (ECJ: Second Chamber).

2508   Input tax—deduction—right to deduct—knowledge of fraud—circumstances surrounding transaction

In July 2006, the taxpayer company had purchased mobile phones in two transactions. The Revenue and Customs Commissioners (the Revenue) denied the taxpayer credit for input tax in respect of those purchases. The basis for the Revenue's refusal was that those purchases had been connected to the fraudulent evasion of VAT by a company called Softlink Ltd, and that the taxpayer knew or should have known of the connection to VAT fraud. That was a further example of cases which had been described as missing trader intra-Community fraud (or MTIC) cases which had fallen to be considered on a number of occasions by the courts and tribunals. The taxpayer's appeal to the First-tier Tribunal (Tax Chamber) (the FTT) was dismissed. The FTT found that such a connection to VAT fraud had been made out, and that the taxpayer should have known that its purchases had been connected with the fraudulent evasion of VAT. Following submissions of the parties following the release of the FTT's decision on the appeal, the FTT subsequently released a further decision refusing the taxpayer's application that a reference be made to the Court of Justice of the European Union (the Court). The taxpayer appealed to the Upper Tribunal (Tax and Chancery Chamber) (the tribunal). The primary ground of appeal was that the FTT had erred in its analysis of the operation of the legal regime in European Union law and case law of the Court covering the right of a person who purchased goods (and paid VAT on the purchase) and then sold them on in the course of his trade, to claim back the VAT paid as input tax. In the taxpayer's submission, the FTT should have found that the taxpayer had been entitled to claim the VAT it had paid in relation to those transactions as input tax, and that its entitlement in that regard had been acte clair in the taxpayer's favour. In the alternative, if not acte clair in the taxpayer's favour, the taxpayer submitted that the position was unclear so that a reference should be made to the Court under art 267 of the Treaty on the Functioning of the European Union. As a further, distinct ground of appeal, the applicant submitted that the FTT had erred in law in its assessment regarding the taxpayer's state of mind in relation to its purchase transactions and its conclusion that the taxpayer should have appreciated that those transactions had been connected with VAT fraud, and that certain of its conclusions on those matters had been irrational. Consideration was given to Council Directive (EEC) 77/388 (on the harmonisation of the laws of the member states relating to turnover taxes – Common system of value-added tax) (the Sixth Directive). Held, (1) it was settled EU law that a taxable person who knew or should have known that, by his purchase, he had been taking part in a transaction connected with fraudulent evasion of VAT should be regarded as a participant in that fraud, irrespective of whether or not he had profited by the resale of the goods. Where it was ascertained, having regard to objective factors, that the supply was to a taxable person who knew or should have known that, by his purchase, he had been participating in a transaction connected with fraudulent evasion of VAT, it was for the national court to refuse that person entitlement to the right to deduct. In the instant case, the FTT had identified the legal principles correctly and had directed itself appropriately as to the law when deciding the case before it. Further, there was no sound basis on which it would be appropriate to make a reference to the Court for the purposes of deciding the outcome of the instant appeal. (2) Taking all the objective factors known to the taxpayer into account, the FTT had been entitled to conclude that the transactions at issue could not be explained by reference to ordinary commercial trading, but that the only reasonable explanation was that purchases had been connected with VAT fraud. Accordingly, the FTT had been entitled to find, as it had that the taxpayer should have known that its purchases had been connected with fraudulent evasion of VAT at the time it had made them. Accordingly, the appeal would be dismissed.

Fonecomp Ltd v Revenue and Customs Comrs [2013] UKUT 599 (TCC), [2014] All ER (D) 126 (Jan) (Upper Tribunal: Sales J presiding). *Mobilx Ltd (in administration) v Revenue and Customs Comrs; Blue Sphere Global Ltd v Revenue and Customs Comrs; Calltel Telecom Ltd v Revenue and Customs Comrs (No 2)* [2010] EWCA Civ 517, [2010] STC 1436 (2010 Abr para 2765) applied.

Directive 77/388 now Council Directive (EC) 2006/112.

2509 Input tax—deduction—right to deduct—pension fund set up by employer—operation costs

The taxpayer was a Dutch company that had set up a pension scheme for its employees with a certain pension fund. A subsidiary of the taxpayer entered into contracts with suppliers of services established in the Netherlands relating to the administration of the pensions and the management of the assets of the pension fund. The costs associated with those contracts were paid by that subsidiary and not passed on to the pension fund. The taxpayer deducted the amounts of VAT relating to those costs as input tax. However, the Dutch tax authority issued the taxpayer with an additional assessment to VAT for the relevant period in relation to those amounts. The taxpayer appealed against the assessment, submitting that the costs relating to the pensions of its members' employees were general costs of the undertaking, and that the VAT invoiced to it was therefore eligible for deduction according to Dutch law. The tax authority argued that the taxpayer could not itself be regarded as being the recipient of the services which it had transferred to the pension fund without invoicing any consideration, and was not therefore entitled to deduct the VAT invoiced to it in that connection. The court decided to stay the proceedings and refer to the European Court of Justice for a preliminary ruling the question of whether Council Directive (EC) 77/388 art 17 should be interpreted as meaning that a taxable person who had set up a pension fund in the form of a legally and fiscally separate entity, in order to safeguard the pension rights of his employees and former employees, was entitled to deduct the VAT he had paid on services relating to the management and operation of the fund. *Held*, where there was no direct and immediate link between a particular input transaction and an output transaction or transactions giving rise to the right to deduct, a taxable person had a right to deduct input tax where the costs of the services in question were part of his general costs and were, as such, components of the price of the goods or services he supplied. Such costs had a direct and immediate link with the taxable person's economic activity as a whole. By setting up the fund, the taxpayer had complied with a legal obligation imposed on it as an employer, and, in so far as the costs of the services acquired in that connection formed part of its general costs, which was for the referring court to verify, they were, as such, component parts of the price of the taxpayer's products. If there was no right to deduct the input tax paid, not only would the taxable person be deprived, by reason of the legislative choice to protect pensions by a legal separation of the employer from the pension fund, of the tax advantage resulting from the application of the deduction system, but the neutrality of VAT would also no longer be guaranteed. The contrary view would amount to restricting the freedom of taxable persons to choose the organisational structures and the form of transactions which they consider to be most appropriate for their economic activities and for the purposes of limiting their tax burden. It followed that the question would be answered in the affirmative and that a right to deduct input tax arose in the circumstances of the present case.

Case C-26/12 *Fiscale eenheid PPG Holdings BV cs te Hoogezand v Inspecteur van de Belastingdienst/Noord/kantoor Groningen* [2013] All ER (D) 258 (Jul) (ECJ: Fourth Chamber).

Directive 77/388 now Council Directive (EC) 2006/112.

2510   Input tax—deduction—right to deduct—recipient of services—incomplete invoice

The taxpayer, which was the main company in a group of companies in terms of staff, provided numerous services to other companies within that group. Contracts were concluded to regulate the use of staff in the context of the intra-group services, which provided for remuneration for those services on the basis of hours worked by staff. During inspections, the Belgian tax authority questioned, both as regards direct taxes and VAT, the intercompany invoices and resulting deductions, the main reason being that the invoices were incomplete and could not be shown to correspond to actual services. Consequently, the tax authority disallowed the deductions made by the companies receiving services on the ground of non-compliance with the requirements laid down in the relevant Belgian law. Although additional information was subsequently provided by those companies, it was not accepted by the tax authority as a sufficient basis to allow the deduction of the various VAT amounts. The Court of First Instance ruled in favour of the taxpayer in the case of certain invoices, but also upheld the refusal to allow the deduction of VAT in respect of companies receiving services. The court subsequently decided to reopen the procedure following new applications seeking a refund of charges paid by the service providers, and delivered judgment in the joined cases, dismissing the refund applications as unfounded. On appeal, the court stayed proceedings and referred for preliminary ruling questions whether the provisions of Council Directive (EC) 77/388 on the harmonisation of legislation of member states concerning turnover taxes should be interpreted as precluding national legislation under which the right to deduct VAT might be refused to taxable persons who were recipients of services and in possession of invoices which were incomplete, in the case where those invoices were then supplemented by the provision of information seeking to prove the occurrence, nature and amount of the transactions invoiced, and whether the principle of fiscal neutrality should be interpreted as precluding a tax authority from refusing to refund the VAT paid by a company providing services, in the case where the exercise of the right to deduct the VAT on those services had been denied to the companies receiving those services by reason of the irregularities confirmed in the invoices issued by that service providing company. *Held,* Directive 77/388 must be interpreted as not precluding national legislation under which the right to deduct VAT might be refused to taxable persons who were recipients of services and were in possession of invoices which were incomplete, even if those invoices were supplemented by the provision of information seeking to prove the occurrence, nature and amount of the transactions invoiced after such a refusal decision was adopted. Moreover, the principle of fiscal neutrality did not preclude the tax authority from refusing to refund the VAT paid by a company providing services, in the case where the exercise of the right to deduct the VAT levied on those services had been denied to the companies receiving those services by reason of the irregularities confirmed in the invoices issued by that service providing company.

Case C-271/12 *Petroma Transport SA v Belgium* [2013] STC 1466 (ECJ: Second Chamber).

Directive 77/388 replaced by Council Directive (EC) 2006/112.

2511   Input tax—deduction—right to deduct—special tax on turnover

The taxpayer company operated gaming machines in gaming halls in Hamburg, Germany. Pursuant to the local legislation of the municipalities concerned, the operation of such machines was subject to an entertainment tax which was calculated using rates and bases of assessment which differed from municipality to municipality. The balance of cash box contents for each gaming machine namely, the money inserted by players less the money paid out as winnings, plus withdrawals less replenishment of machines, was noted by the taxpayer each month using an electronic monitoring device. The taxpayer took the yearly total of monthly cash receipts from all its gaming machines and applied the standard value added tax rate to calculate a taxable amount for VAT, and turnover on the operation of gaming machines, representing almost the entirety of the VAT owed. The taxpayer paid the VAT due. The defendant tax office sent a notice to the taxpayer of further VAT owed. A question arose as to the validity of the notice, the taxpayer arguing that the methods used to tax gaming machine turnover were contrary to European Union law and, in particular, contrary to the principles of proportionality, pass-through and VAT neutrality. *Held,*

Council Directive (EC) 2006/112 art 401, read in conjunction with art 135(1)(i), should be interpreted as meaning that VAT and a special national tax on games of chance might be levied cumulatively, provided that the special national tax could not be characterised as a tax on turnover. Articles 1(2), 73 should be interpreted as not precluding a national provision or practice whereby, in the operation of gaming machines, the amount of the cash receipts from those machines was used after a set interval as the basis of assessment. Article 1(2) should be interpreted as not precluding a national system regulating an unharmonised tax, under which the VAT owed was to be set in full against that tax.

Case C-440/12 *Metropol Spielstätten Unternehmergesellschaft (haftungsbeschränkt) v Finanzamt Hambury-Bergedorf* [2014] STC 505 (ECJ: First Chamber).

2512   Input tax—disallowance—economic activity—direct and immediate link to taxable supplies

In the course of a successful bid to acquire the entire issued share capital of the taxpayer, bankers and legal advisers made taxable supplies of services to a company. The company joined the taxpayer's value added tax group, which made taxable supplies, thereby becoming a taxable person with a VAT registration. The taxpayer, as representative member of the group, then claimed recovery, as input tax, of the VAT incurred and paid by the company on the supplies to it prior to the acquisition of the taxpayer and prior to joining the group. It was claimed that the supplies were made to the company in the course of an 'economic activity' carried on by it at the relevant time and that its economic activity had been preparatory to the acquisition of the taxpayer. It was further claimed that the taxpayer group's subsequent tax outputs should be attributed to the company's prior tax inputs, that the VAT incurred by the company was part of the general overheads of the group and that there was a direct and immediate link between the taxable supplies made to the company in connection with the acquisition and the taxable supplies made by the group. The Commissioners for Her Majesty's Revenue and Customs disallowed, as part of the group's general overheads, the claim for recovery of the input tax incurred by the company on the acquisition. On the taxpayer's appeal, it was found that the company had been carrying on an economic activity at the relevant time and that the taxpayer had been entitled to claim the input VAT incurred by the company as part of the taxpayer's general overheads. There had been a direct and immediate link between the supplies on which the company had incurred input tax and the supplies on which the taxpayer had charged output tax. It was determined by the First-tier Tribunal that there was no evidence before it of the making of taxable supplies or of an intention, at the relevant date, to make taxable supplies. On appeal by the Revenue, it was found that the company had been carrying on an economic activity at the relevant time, but the appeal was allowed on the ground that there had been no direct and immediate link between the supplies of professional services on which the company had incurred liability to VAT and the taxable output supplies on which the taxpayer had charged VAT. The taxpayer appealed. *Held*, it had not been correct in law for either the First-tier Tribunal or the Upper Tribunal to have found that the company had been carrying on an economic activity at the relevant date. The relevant date had been the date on which the company had incurred the liability to VAT on the services supplied to it. The company's only evidence and proven intention at that time had been to acquire the taxpayer. Acquiring the taxpayer's shares had been an act which would have economic consequences, but that was not the same as carrying on an economic activity for VAT purposes. The company's activities at that time had neither involved the making of, nor even had the intention of making, taxable supplies of goods or services. Further, the First-tier Tribunal had erred in finding that there had been a direct and immediate link between the input tax on the supplies of services to the company and the output tax on the supplies of taxable services made by the taxpayer. The taxpayer's outward supplies and the VAT charged on them could not have been attributed to the company to produce the requisite direct and immediate link between them. It was a general rule that inputs of one taxable person acquired for its own purposes might not be treated as the cost components of the supplies of another taxable person made for its own purposes. Where there was a transfer of a going concern, the transferee stood for VAT purposes in the shoes of the transferor and the inputs of the taxable transferor might be treated as having been acquired for the purposes of the taxable supplies of the transferee. In the circumstances, the taxpayer had not been the successor of the company and the inputs acquired by the company had not been acquired for the purposes of the taxpayer's taxable supplies. Accordingly, the appeal would be dismissed.

BAA Ltd v Revenue and Customs Comrs [2013] EWCA Civ 112, [2013] STC 752 (Court of Appeal: Mummery and Patten LJJ and Kenneth Parker J). Case C-137/02 *Finanzamt Offenbach am Main-Land v Faxworld Vorgründungsgesellschaft Peter Hünninghausen und Wolfgang Klein GbR* [2005] STC 1192, ECJ, considered.

2513   Input tax—disallowance—economic activity—supply of electricity from photovoltaic installation

The taxpayer had a photovoltaic installation fitted on the roof of his house, which he used as a dwelling. It had no storage capacity and the whole of the electricity produced was supplied to the network on the basis of a contract, granting access to that network. The consideration for that supply was the market price and subjected to value added tax. Such electricity as was necessary to meet the taxpayer's household needs was bought back from the company at the same price as the price of the supply. The taxpayer applied for reimbursement of input VAT in connection with his purchase of the photovoltaic installation. The German tax office took the view that the taxpayer was not entitled to deduct the input VAT on the ground that he had not carried out any economic activity by operating his photovoltaic installation. On appeal by the taxpayer, it was found that the taxpayer had been carrying out an economic activity as defined by the Council Directive (EC) 77/388 (on the harmonisation of the laws of the member states relating to turnover taxes) art 4(1), (2). On appeal by the German tax office the court decided to stay the proceedings and refer a question to the European Court of Justice for a preliminary ruling. It fell to be determined whether the operation of a network-connected photovoltaic installation with no independent power storage capability on or adjacent to a privately-owned house used for private residential purposes, which was technically designed such that the power generated by the installation was below the total quantity of power privately consumed by the installation was below the total quantity of power privately consumed by the installation operator in the privately-owned house, an economic activity of the installation operator within the meaning of art 4. *Held*, an analysis of the definitions of 'taxable person' and 'economic activities' showed that the scope of the term 'economic activities' was very wide, and that the term was objective in character, in the sense that the activity was considered per se and without regard to its purpose or results. The issue of whether that activity was designed to obtain income on a continuing basis was an issue of fact which should be assessed having regard to all the circumstances of the case, which included the nature of the property concerned. That property was suitable only for economic exploitation would normally be sufficient for a finding that its owner was exploiting it for the purposes of economic activities and, consequently, for the purpose of obtaining income on a continuing basis. Article 4(1), (2) should be interpreted as meaning that the operation of a photovoltaic installation on or adjacent to a house which was used as a dwelling, which was designed such that the electricity produced was always less than the electricity privately consumed by its operator and supplied to the network in exchange for income on a continuing basis, fell within the concept of economic activities as defined by art 4.

Case C-219/12 *Finanzamt Freistadt Rohrbach Urfahr v Unabhangiger Finanzsenat Außenstelle Linz* [2014] STC 114 (ECJ: Second Chamber).

Directive 77/388 replaced by Council Directive (EC) 2006/112.

2514   Input tax—disallowance—full costs shifting regime

The taxpayer was a business trading in electronic goods. By three decisions, the Commissioners for Her Majesty's Revenue and Customs denied input tax repayment claims made by the taxpayer on the ground that the taxpayer's transactions in respect of which input tax had been incurred were connected with fraud, and the taxpayer had known, or should have known, of that connection. The Commissioners were of the opinion that transactions undertaken by the taxpayer involved the taxpayer acting as the exporter or broker, and that some of the transactions were connected with a fraudulent trader. In acting as a dishonest contra-trader, the trader had acted as a knowing party to the fraudulent series of transactions. Following the conviction and sentencing of the trader's director, the taxpayer challenged the decisions to refuse input tax repayment. The Commissioners sought to adduce material with regard to the conviction of the director. Their application was dismissed by the First-tier Tribunal. On the Commissioners' appeal, it was found that the

First-tier Tribunal had erred in law as the application by the Commissioners had been made as soon as was practicable after the sentencing of the director. The Upper Tribunal exercised its discretion and allowed the material to be admitted. On appeal by the taxpayer, *held*, the conviction of the director related to the same period which included the time-scale for the taxpayer's transactions which were the object of the proceedings. That was not stale evidence. Until the conviction had been entered, the material relating to the facts in issue would have been no more than material in a separate criminal action. While it might have been true that the evidence on which the convictions were based was old, that could not be said of the fact of the convictions themselves. The Upper Tribunal had concluded that the First-tier Tribunal had identified the prejudice to the taxpayer that the admission of the material could have caused but had failed to refer to, let alone consider, the prejudice to the Revenue by its exclusion. Although it had been correct that the First-tier Tribunal had referred to the principles by directing its mind to a previous detailed exposition of those principles, that had not cured the lack of application of the principles to the facts in the First-tier Tribunal's decision. The reasons identified by the Upper Tribunal had been sufficient to amount to an error of law justifying the interference by the Upper Tribunal in the First-tier Tribunal's case management decision. The Upper Tribunal had adopted the correct approach to the admission of the material. It had assessed whether the evidence had been relevant and had applied the presumption that all relevant evidence should be admitted unless there was a compelling reason to the contrary. The Upper Tribunal had clearly understood the limited purpose to which the prosecution opening note in the criminal proceedings could have been put and the issues to which it might have gone. That had been within the purpose and terms of the Tribunal Procedure (First-tier Tribunal) (Tax Chamber) Rules 2009, SI 2009/273, r 15(2)(a) and, therefore, was admissible. The Upper Tribunal had been right to conclude that the opening note and statement of evidence to which it had been attached had been relevant to an issue before the First-tier Tribunal, had been admissible, and, having regard to the balance of prejudice should have been admitted. That had been fair, just and proportionate. Accordingly, the appeal would be dismissed.

Revenue and Customs Comrs v Atlantic Electronics Ltd [2013] EWCA Civ 651, [2013] STC 1632 (Court of Appeal: Arden, Beatson and Ryder LJJ). *T&N Ltd* (*in administration*) *v Royal & Sun Alliance Insurance plc* [2002] EWCA Civ 1964, [2003] All ER (D) 105 (Jan); and *R* (*on the application of Mobile Export 365 Ltd*) *v Customs and Revenue Comrs* [2006] STC 1069 (2006 Abr para 2911) applied. Decision of Upper Tribunal [2012] UKUT 45 (TCC), [2013] STC 856 (2012 Abr para 2570) affirmed.

2515   Input tax—disallowance—missing trader intra-Community fraud—knowledge

The taxpayer was involved in a number of commercial transactions in which it acted as the broker in the purchase and sale of a large number of mobile phones. In those transactions, the taxpayer bought goods from value added tax registered traders in the United Kingdom and sold them to VAT registered traders in other European Union member states. In regard to those transactions, the Commissioners for Her Majesty's Revenue and Customs refused to pay input tax that the taxpayer had incurred on the basis that the taxpayer's trades in the course of the transactions were connected to missing trader intra-Community fraud. The taxpayer appealed. In the course of the hearing before the tribunal, the tribunal stated that the evidence that the taxpayer's transactions were connected with fraud had been overwhelming, and that the taxpayer had not challenged that evidence and had been right not to have done so. The tribunal dismissed the appeal on the grounds that the transactions were connected with the fraudulent evasion of VAT, and the taxpayer should have known that its transactions were connected with those VAT frauds. The tribunal did not find that the taxpayer knew of the connection, but that it should have known. The taxpayer appealed further. *Held*, while the tribunal had made errors in admitting evidence on a flawed understanding of the position and in concluding that the issues of tax loss, fraudulent evasion of VAT and connection to fraud had not been challenged or had effectively been conceded, on an assessment of the evidence properly before the tribunal, there had been sufficient evidence to establish that, as found by the tribunal, the taxpayer should have known of the connection of its relevant transactions to the fraudulent evasion of VAT. That finding had been one that the tribunal had been fully entitled to make on the evidence that had properly been before it and no error of law could be discerned in the conclusion reached by the tribunal. Accordingly, the appeal would be dismissed.

Eyedial Ltd v Revenue and Customs Comrs [2013] UKUT 432 (TCC), [2014] STC 520 (Upper Tribunal: Judge Roger Burner and Judge Charles Hellier). Decision of Judge Colin Bishopp [2011] UKFTT 47 (TC) affirmed.

2516   Input tax—recovery—customer loyalty points

The taxpayer was the promoter company behind a popular customer loyalty rewards programme. Members of the public who joined the programme were issued with a card which allowed them to collect points to use in future purchases. In order to operate the programme the taxpayer entered into separate contracts with (1) retailers of goods and services ('sponsors'), who paid a specified sum together with an annual fee for marketing the scheme for their customers, on production of the card, to have points credited to their accounts with the taxpayer when they had purchased goods or services; (2) individuals who had joined the scheme; and (3) other retailers of goods and services ('redeemers') from whom collectors received goods and services at no cost or at a reduced cost, when points were debited from their accounts. It was common ground that the provision of points to collectors in return for payment by the sponsors was a taxable supply by the taxpayer. Accordingly, the taxpayer charged VAT on the payments which it received from the sponsors and in turn the redeemers charged VAT on the service charges which they received from the taxpayer. However, the Revenue decided that the service charges were third party consideration for the redeemers' supply of goods and services to collectors, and that any VAT charged on such a supply was therefore not deductible by the taxpayer as input tax. There followed a series of appeals culminating in a reference to the European Court of Justice, after which the matter returned to the Supreme Court for final determination. The principal issue was whether the taxpayer was entitled to deduct as input tax the VAT element of the service charges. The taxpayer contended that the payments were the consideration for the redeemers' supply to it of the services for which it had contracted. Since that supply was made to the taxpayer for the purpose of its business, the taxpayer maintained that it was entitled to deduct the VAT as input tax in accordance with the Value Added Tax Act 1994. Consideration was given as to how the court should apply the ruling of the European Court. *Held*, Lords Carnwath and Wilson dissenting, in the exceptional circumstances of the present case, the court could not treat the ruling of the European Court as dispositive of its decision; rather, the court had to reach its decision with such guidance as could be derived from the judgment of the European Court. The European Court had focused on the relationship between redeemers and collectors. However, the taxpayer's business was of an unusual character: through the programme, it provided collectors with a contractual right to obtain goods and services from redeemers in exchange for points. The counterpart of that right supplied to collectors was an obligation on the part of the taxpayer to procure that redeemers provided goods and services in exchange for points. Accordingly, the payments made to redeemers constituted the cost of fulfilling that obligation, and were therefore a cost of the taxpayer's business. Applying established principles, VAT should have been chargeable on the taxpayer's taxable supplies only after the deduction of the VAT borne by its necessary costs. The taxpayer should therefore have been authorised to deduct from the VAT for which it was accountable the VAT charged by the redeemers, so that it accounted for VAT only on the added value for which it was responsible. Only in that way would VAT be completely neutral as regards the taxpayer. Accordingly, the appeal would be dismissed.

Revenue and Customs Comrs v Aimia Coalition Loyalty UK Ltd [2013] UKSC 15, [2013] 2 All ER 719 (Supreme Court: Lord Hope DP, Lord Walker, Lord Wilson, Lord Reed and Lord Carnwath). *Customs and Excise Comrs v Redrow Group plc* [1999] 2 All ER 1, HL (1999 Abr para 3431); and *Customs and Excise Comrs v Plantiflor Ltd* [2002] UKHL 33, [2002] All ER (D) 365 (Jul) (2002 Abr para 3067) applied. Case C-185/01 *Auto Lease Holland BV v Bundesamt für Finanzen* [2003] All ER (D) 75 (Feb), ECJ, considered. For earlier related proceedings see Cases C-53/09 and C-55/09 *Revenue and Customs Comrs v Loyalty Management UK Ltd* [2010] STC 2651, ECJ (2010 Abr para 2789). Decision of Court of Appeal sub nom *Loyalty Management UK Ltd v Revenue and Customs Comrs* [2007] EWCA Civ 965, [2008] STC 59 (2007 Abr para 3011) affirmed.

2517   Input tax—recovery—share issue—group company

A subsidiary company in a group of companies issued shares in order to raise finance. At the time the money was raised, such a share issue was considered to be an exempt supply with consequent restrictions on input tax deduction. Seventeen years later, the taxpayer company purchased the subsidiary. The following year, the subsidiary ceased to be a member of the group and was put into members' voluntary liquidation. The liquidators of the subsidiary recorded that they had declared and paid first and final distribution to the taxpayer. However, although there had been an assignment of book debts, there had been no assignment of the value added tax claim by the liquidators. The subsidiary was dissolved. The taxpayer made a claim for credit for input tax in respect of the costs of the share issue made by the subsidiary, more than 20 years previously. The Revenue accepted that certain share issues were outside the scope of VAT and that the VAT incurred on associated costs was recoverable to the extent that they were used for the purpose of the company's taxable transactions. The subsidiary had not, however, make a claim for under-claimed input tax when it had gone into liquidation. The Revenue rejected the taxpayer's claim, deciding that (1) any right to deduct VAT, and any right to a VAT credit, properly belonged to the subsidiary, not the taxpayer; (2) there had been no valid assignment of any such right to the taxpayer; and (3) the taxpayer had failed to provide sufficient evidence to support the claim. The taxpayer appealed, submitting that, as the representative member of the VAT group of which the subsidiary had been a member, it should recover the input tax VAT which the subsidiary had incurred following clarification that it had been deductible, otherwise the Revenue would be holding money to which it had not been not entitled. *Held*, there had been no evidence as to the overpayment of VAT either generally or as to its amount. The taxpayer had not established that there had been an overpayment of VAT, and, if there had been (which had not been shown), the taxpayer had not established the amount of such alleged overpayment. The onus was on the taxpayer to establish that and, on the balance of probabilities, it had failed to do so. That on its own was sufficient to dispose of the appeal. Accordingly, the appeal would be dismissed.

Chubb Ltd v Revenue and Customs Comrs [2013] UKFTT 579 (TC), [2013] All ER (D) 40 (Nov) (First-tier Tribunal: Judge Adrian Shipwright presiding).

2518   Input tax—reduced rate charge—installation of energy-saving materials

The taxpayer business installed, improved and repaired domestic central heating installations. The installations included components which the taxpayer claimed fell within the definition of 'energy saving materials' in the Value Added Tax Act 1994 Sch 7A Pt II Group 2 note 1. Value added tax was accounted for by the taxpayer on the components, and on an apportioned element of the labour charges applicable to their installation, at the reduced rate of five per cent provided for by s 29. The respondent Revenue conducted an audit of the taxpayer's VAT returns. In turn, the respondent wrote to the taxpayer expressing the view that while the components would qualify for VAT at the reduced rate if they had been installed 'in their right', where they have been installed as part of a larger installation, such as a boiler or a central heating system, the whole supply was a supply taxable at the standard rate. Subsequently, the respondent raised an assessment in respect of the taxpayer's accounting periods. The taxpayer unsuccessfully sought a review of the decision. On appeal by the taxpayer, *held*, the question whether there was one supply or two was a question of law on which the court was entitled and bound to form its own view. In deciding whether there was one supply or two where two separate elements were present, the test was whether one element was 'incidental to, or an integral part' of the other. Further, a supply comprising different elements was a single supply for VAT purposes where some of the elements were ancillary to the principal element, or where the elements were so closely linked that in objective economic terms they formed a single supply which it would be artificial to split. The taxpayer's supplies of energy-saving materials along with boilers or central heating systems were complex single supplies and could not be described as supplies 'of' installing energy-saving materials listed in Group 2, though the supplies included that. Section 29A referred to a reduced rate for a supply and reinforced that the supply had to be of a description contained within Sch 7A. To read the provisions as applying the reduced rate applied to elements within a supply would be to depart from the meaning of the words used. In the circumstances, when the taxpayer installed energy-saving materials along with a replacement boiler or as part of the installation of a central heating system, it was making a standard-rated supply of which the energy-saving materials were elements. That conclusion had to follow whether the taxpayer was itself installing an individual item, such as a thermostat, which fell within the definition of energy-saving materials or installing a larger item, such as a boiler, into which energy-saving materials such as insulation had been incorporated by its manufacturer. Accordingly, the appeal would be dismissed.

AN Checker Heating & Service Engineers v Revenue and Customs Comrs [2013] UKFTT 506 (TC), [2013] All ER (D) 72 (Dec) (First-tier Tribunal: Judge Nicholas Paines).

2519   Input tax—repayment—exemption—financial services—booking fees

The taxpayer owned and operated an exhibition centre which was used for a variety of public events. It had always treated all of facility fees, booking fees and transaction fees as consideration for standard-rated supplies for the purposes of its value added tax returns but later considered that the booking fees levied in respect of credit card and debit card payments on tickets sold for events were consideration for a supply of payment processing services which was exempt from VAT under Council Directive (EEC) 77/388 art 13(B)(d)(3). The taxpayer's claims for repayment of overpaid output tax in respect of the booking fees were refused and the taxpayer appealed, contending that the output tax was repayable because the charges it made to its customers in relation to ticket booking fees, being the provision of financial services, were correctly exempt supplies under Directive 77/388. *Held,* the criteria for a service to fall within the VAT exemption for financial services under art 13(B)(d)(3) were well established. The critical test was whether the transaction carried out by the taxpayer truly effected a transfer. A number of principles were relevant to determining the issue. Firstly, a transfer was the execution of an order for the transfer of a sum of money from one bank account to another. Secondly, it involved a change in the legal and financial situation existing between the person giving the order and the recipient and between those parties and their respective banks. Thirdly, there was no requirement for the supplier to be a bank. Fourthly, there was no requirement for a direct contractual link between the person executing the transfer and the ultimate customer of the bank. Fifthly, the test whether a transaction constituted a transfer was a functional one that asked whether the transaction in question was one which had effected the movement of money and changed the legal and financial situation of the parties. The cause of the transaction was not in itself a relevant consideration. The booking fees were exempt supplies pursuant to art 13(B)(d)(3). That conclusion flowed from a number of findings. The booking fees were received by the taxpayer on its own behalf for services it provided, and not as agent for the promoter. The evidence did not show that the booking fees were charged for a taxable supply made by the promoter to the customer, with the taxpayer acting merely as an agent of the promoter in the collection of the sums charged. Rather, it showed that a customer would have been aware that he had been charged not only the face value of the chosen ticket but also that other charges were made. The money paid by a customer comprised both a ticket price collected by the taxpayer as agent for the promoter, and other charges collected by the taxpayer on its own behalf as principal. The booking fees were consideration for a card handling service provided by the taxpayer. Although there were exceptions where a booking fee was not charged when a card was used, such as when a customer paid for a ticket in person at the box office or when he purchased car parking in addition to a ticket, the general practice from the point of view of the typical customer would have been that a booking fee was charged if he chose to pay by card and not if he chose to pay by cash. On that basis, the evidence showed that a service provided by the taxpayer and remunerated by the booking fee related to provision of card processing services. The booking fees satisfied the requirements of art 13(B)(d)(3), as detailed in Case C-2/95, which made it clear that, for the VAT exemption for financial services to apply, it was not necessary that the supplier be a bank. The booking fees did not fall outside the VAT exemption under art 13(B)(d)(3) on the basis that they were consideration for debt collection. Given that the booking fees were received by the taxpayer as principal, it received sums properly due to itself from the customer for services immediately performed by the taxpayer. That action, of a supplier receiving money due from its own customer, could not be construed as debt collection. Accordingly, the appeal would be allowed.

National Exhibition Centre Ltd v Revenue and Customs Comrs [2013] UKFTT 289 (TC), [2013] All ER (D) 47 (Nov) (First-Tier Tribunal: Judge Peter Kempster presiding). Case C-2/95 *Sparekassernes Datacenter (SDC) v Skatterministeriet* [1997] All ER (EC) 610, ECJ, followed. Case C-349/96 *Card Protection Plan Ltd v Customs and Excise Comrs* [1999] 2 AC 601, [1999] All ER (EC) 339, ECJ (1999 Abr para 3419); Case C-276/09 *Everything Everywhere Ltd, formerly T-Mobile (UK) Ltd v Revenue and Customs Comrs* [2011] STC

316, [2010] All ER (D) 80 (Dec), ECJ (2010 Abr para 2790); Case C-350/10 *Proceedings brought by Nordea Pankki Suomi Oyj* [2011] STC 1956, ECJ (2011 Abr para 2413); *College of Estate Management v Customs and Excise Comrs* [2005] UKHL 62, [2005] 4 All ER 933 (2005 Abr para 3154); *Bookit Ltd v Revenue and Customs Comrs* [2006] EWCA Civ 550, [2006] All ER (D) 151 (May) (2006 Abr para 2895); and *Revenue and Customs Comrs v AXA UK plc* [2011] EWCA Civ 1607, [2012] STC 754 (2011 Abr para 2414) considered.

Directive 77/388 art 13(B)(d)(3) now Council Directive (EC) 2006/112 art 135(1)(d).

2520   Input tax—repayment—subsidised project

The applicant company concluded a subsidy contract with the Hungarian government. Under government guidelines, the eligible expenditure of a subsidised project included, for the purposes of calculating the aid, part of the VAT corresponding to a percentage of the project financed by that aid. The eligible expenditure of the project at issue in the present proceedings therefore included an amount in respect of non-deductible VAT. The assessment of VAT relating to development expenditure had been included in the applicant's monthly VAT returns. Hungarian law did not permit a taxpayer to deduct, proportionally to the amount of the aid, the part of input VAT paid on costs relating to the subsidised project. The applicant was therefore unable to exercise its right to deduct the amount of VAT relating to development expenditure paid in advance and calculated in the return. The applicant subsequently applied for repayment of the VAT which the limitation on the right to deduct had prevented it from deducting. The application was refused and the applicant challenged the decision. It fell to be determined whether the principle of repayment of taxes levied by a member state in breach of the rules of EU law should be interpreted as meaning that it enabled that state to refuse to repay part of the VAT, the deduction of which had been precluded by a national measure contrary to EU law, on the ground that that part of the tax had been subsidised by aid granted to the taxable person and financed by the EU and by that state. *Held*, the right to a refund of charges levied in a member state in breach of EU law was the consequence and complement of the rights conferred on individuals by provisions of EU law as interpreted by the European Court of Justice. The member state was therefore in principle required to repay charges levied in breach of EU law. The right to the recovery of sums unduly paid helped to offset the consequences of the duty's incompatibility with EU law by neutralising the economic burden which that duty had unduly imposed on the operator who, in the final analysis, had actually borne it. However, by way of exception, such repayment could be refused where it entailed unjust enrichment of the persons concerned. In the absence of EU rules governing claims for the repayment of taxes, it was for the domestic legal system of each member state to lay down the conditions under which those claims might be made, subject, nevertheless, to observance of the principles of equivalence and effectiveness. Observance of the principle of effectiveness required that the conditions under which an action might be brought for recovery of sums unduly paid be fixed by the member states, pursuant to the principle of procedural autonomy, in such a way that the economic burden of the duty unduly paid could be neutralised. It was therefore on condition that the economic burden that the tax unduly paid imposed on the taxable person had been completely neutralised, that a member state might refuse to repay part of that tax on the ground that such repayment would give rise to unjust enrichment for the benefit of the taxable person. The principle of repayment of taxes levied in a member state in breach of EU law should be interpreted as meaning that it did not preclude that state from refusing to repay part of the VAT, the deduction of which had been precluded by a national measure contrary to EU law, on the ground that that part of the tax had been subsided by aid granted to the taxable person and financed by the EU and by that state, provided that the economic burden relating to the refusal to deduct VAT had been completely neutralised, which was for the national court to determine.

Case C-191/12 *Alakor Gabonatermelo es Forgalmazo Kft v Nemzeti Ado- es Vamhivatal Eszak-alfodi Regionalis Ado Foigazgatosaga* [2013] All ER (D) 265 (May) (ECJ: Seventh Chamber).

2521   Output tax—conspiracy to commit fraud—damages—resident in another member state

See Case C-49/12 *Revenue and Customs Comrs v Sunico ApS*, para 440.

2522 Output tax—deductible proportion—turnover of branches in other member states

The claimant bank had its principal establishment in France and had branches in European Union member states and other states. Following an examination of the accounts of the claimant, and two adjustment notices, the French tax administration assessed it for arrears of value added tax. The arrears resulted from that administration's refusal to take account, unlike the claimant, in its declaration, of the interest on loans granted by the claimant's principal establishment to its branches established outside France, in the numerator and the denominator of the deductible proportion laid down in French tax law. The claimant lodged its first objection to the declaration of the arrears, claiming that the amount of the interest in question could be taken into account in calculating the deductible proportion of VAT. In a second objection, it asked for a refund of the sums which it had considered it had overpaid for the periods in question and of those which it had paid. The claimant maintained that, while the amount of interest invoiced by the principal establishment to the branches could not be taken into account on the ground that its principal establishment, together with its foreign branches, all formed part of one and the same entity, the income from the transaction which the branches carried out with third parties should be regarded as their own income and be taken into account in calculating the deductible proportion applied to it. Since those complaints had been rejected by the administration, the claimant appealed to the national court in France. The appeal was dismissed. Its appeal against the judgment also having been dismissed, the claimant appealed on a point of law. It fell to be determined how the deductible proportion of VAT of the principal establishment of a company established in France fell to be ascertained and also how the deductible proportion of the branches of that company established outside that member state should be determined. *Held*, Council Directive (EC) 77/338 arts 17(2), (5) and 19(1) would be interpreted as meaning that, in determining the deductible proportion of VAT applicable to it, a company, the principal establishment of which was situated in a member state, might not take into account the turnover of its branches established in other member states. Articles 17(3)(a), (c) and 19(1) would be interpreted as meaning that, in determining the deductible proportion of VAT applicable to it, a company, the principal establishment of which was situated in a member state, might not take into account the turnover of its branches established in third states. Article 17(5) would be interpreted as not permitting a member state to adopt a rule for the calculation of the deductible proportion per sector of business of a company subject to tax, which had authorised that company to take into account the turnover of a branch established in another member state or in a third state.

Case C-388/11 *Le Crédit Lyonnais v Ministre du Budget* [2014] STC 245 (ECJ: First Chamber).

Directive 77/388 replaced by Council Directive (EC) 2006/112.

2523 Output tax—overpayment—repayment—set-off

For a number of value added tax periods the taxpayer theatre had accounted for output tax on supplies which should have been treated as exempt but for a two-year period had received a repayment of input tax, which, because its outputs should have been treated as exempt, should not have been made. The taxpayer made a claim for the repayment of its overpaid output tax for those periods in which its claim was not barred by time limits. However, the Revenue was, by that stage, out of time to claim repayment of the input tax wrongly repaid. The repayments exceeded the overpaid output tax. The Revenue sought to deny the taxpayer's claim on two grounds. Firstly, that such a repayment would give rise to a result contrary to the provisions of Council Directive (EEC) 77/388 (on the harmonisation of the laws of the member states relating to turnover taxes). It argued that the claim was incongruent with Directive 77/388. Secondly, on the basis that that was the effect of the set-off provisions of the Value Added Tax Act 1994 s 81(3A). On the taxpayer's appeal, it was found that there was not a generally applicable principle that taxpayer claims that happened to produce an advantageous result for the taxpayer constituted abusive practices which would permit the claim to be denied. However, it was also found that s 81(3A) entitled the Revenue to offset the input tax erroneously repaid against the output tax claim so as to reduce the amount payable to the taxpayer to nil. The taxpayer appealed. *Held*, the words of s 81(3A) did not require any restriction of the periods in which the liabilities or amounts payable arose. There was nothing in the relevant explanatory notes or the statutory context relevant to matters within s 81(3A) which suggested a different interpretation.

Section 81(3A) hinged around a particular mistake. Extending the ambit of the provisions to matters other than a particular mistake would not go with the grain of the legislation. Therefore, s 81(3A) could not be interpreted in that way. It was true that the limitation of the effect of s 81(3A) to adjustments by reason of a particular mistake might mean that a taxpayer paid more or less tax than it otherwise should have under Directive 77/388. However, that was the result of the operation of time limits from which the 1994 Act s 81(3A) was an exception. Given that the time limits were not precluded either by Directive 77/388 or by European Union principles, the loss of rights entailed by that limitation in the 1994 Act s 81(3A) could not be precluded either. It was settled law that time limits were permissible even though their effect was to deny a right or to curtail the obligation under Directive 77/388. That raised the issue as to whether construing the 1994 Act s 81(3A) as requiring the Revenue to consider all previous periods in determining the set-off conflicted with legal certainty. Further, it was clear that domestic procedural rules such as s 81(3A), in the context of matters subject to Community law such as VAT, might also be affected by the primacy of Community law. Therefore, while it could be expected that within the period for which domestic law required records to be kept a taxpayer had the onus of showing the amount of net effect of the relevant mistakes, in periods before that, the onus of proof had to be on the authority alleging otherwise. In the circumstances, there had been a mistake, namely that of treating the taxpayer's ticket sales as standard rated, which had been the reason for both the output claim and the repayment. Consequently, s 81(3A) applied. Accordingly, the appeal would be dismissed.

Birmingham Hippodrome Theatre Trust Ltd v Revenue and Customs Comrs [2013] UKUT 57 (TCC), [2013] STC 1079 (Upper Tribunal: Proudman J presiding).

Directive 77/388 replaced by Council Directive (EC) 2006/112.

2524   **Overpayment—recovery—claim by end consumer—charge on services subsequently held to be exempt**

The claimants were investment trust companies which paid investment management companies for management services. Under value added tax legislation then in force, it was thought that the services were not exempt from VAT. Subsequently, the European Court of Justice decided that supplies of the management services should have been exempt from VAT as from a date specified. Under the Value Added Tax Act 1994 s 80, the managers claimed refunds from the Commissioners for Her Majesty's Revenue and Customs for the input tax paid by them in relation to the services, taking account of output tax charged on the provision of those services. An issue arose as to whether the claimants should be confined to a modified version of the *Woolwich* cause of action, established in *Woolwich Equitable Building Society v IRC,* in order to satisfy their directly effective EU rights to recover from the Commissioners that part of the consideration paid by them to the managers that represented VAT mistakenly thought to be due and which the managers themselves had been unable to recover from the Commissioners and pass on to the claimants. The court adjourned determination of the issue until after the Supreme Court had given its judgment in *Test Claimants in the FII Group Litigation v Revenue and Customs Comrs.* In the light of that judgment, the claimants made further submissions to the court, contending that it was clear, as a matter of principle and logic, that a *Woolwich* claim was available only to a taxpayer properly so called, and that it was irrelevant that the claimants were persons who had borne the economic burden of the tax. The claimants further submitted that the *Woolwich* principle was in large part a constitutional one and that it could only be invoked by a person against whom the state could bring its coercive power to bear. *Held,* the *Woolwich* cause of action was not in principle available to the claimants. Properly understood, the principle was confined to claimants who were themselves liable for the overpaid tax, and to claimants who were in principle subject to the coercive power of the state in relation to the exaction and recovery of such tax. The critical distinction was that the only obligation of the claimants to pay the VAT was a purely contractual one as between them and the managers. For some purposes, the fact that the claimants bore the economic burden of the tax made it appropriate to align their position with that of taxpayers properly so called. However, there was no logical reason why the same approach had to be followed in relation to the question of remedies. The direct claim that was available to the claimants against the Commissioners was, on any view, a last resort which ought to have been invoked only if and to the extent that recovery from the managers themselves proved impossible. If such a claim were to be characterised as a *Woolwich* claim, it would seem to follow that any end user of goods or services who had borne the burden of unlawfully levied VAT would be able, as a first rather than a last resort, to maintain a direct action against the Commissioners to recover it. That would be inappropriate, and would tend to undermine the constitutional significance of the *Woolwich* principle. The scope of the *Woolwich* remedy was to be confined to those persons who had paid to a public authority the sums which it sought to recover in response to an apparent statutory requirement to do so. Judgment would be given accordingly.

   Investment Trust Companies (in liquidation) v Revenue and Customs Comrs (No 2) [2013] EWHC 665 (Ch), [2013] STC 1129 (Chancery Division: Henderson J). *Woolwich Equitable Building Society v IRC* [1993] AC 70, [1992] 3 All ER 737, HL (1992 Abr para 1398), applied. *Test Claimants in the FII Group Litigation v Revenue and Customs Comrs* [2012] UKSC 19, [2012] 2 AC 337, [2012] 3 All ER 909 (2012 Abr para 2659); and Case C-591/10 *Littlewoods Retail Ltd v Revenue and Customs Comrs* [2012] STC 1714, [2012] All ER (D) 267 (Jul), ECJ (2012 Abr para 2574), considered.

2525   Overpayment—recovery—claim by member of group

The taxpayer was the representative member of a value added tax group and accounted for tax in full on its subsidiary's turnover. The taxpayer transferred its business and assets to the subsidiary which became the generating taxpayer. The subsidiary left the group and made a claim for repayment of overpaid output tax under the Value Added Tax Act 1994 s 80. The taxpayer applied for retrospective disbandment of the group. Before the group was disbanded, the Commissioners for Her Majesty's Revenue and Customs repaid to the taxpayer a sum of overpaid VAT plus statutory interest. Soon after, the Commissioners issued an assessment against the taxpayer for recovery of those sums, relying on ss 78A and 80(4A), asserting that the claim had been incorrectly paid to it. The Commissioners intimated that claims made by the subsidiary would not be paid to the taxpayer. The taxpayer appealed, contending that it could recover the sums claimed in its subsidiary's timely claim as it was the representative member of the group of which its subsidiary had been a member. The taxpayer further contended that the disbandment of the group had been purely an administrative exercise and that it had still been the group representative when the payments had been made. *Held*, it was settled law that, for there to be liability on the part of the Revenue under s 80 to a particular taxpayer, it had to be faced with a claim by or on behalf of that taxpayer, his successor or assignee, asserting the right to repayment, such claim having been made within the prescribed time scale. The taxpayer had never made a claim under s 80 and, therefore, could not rely on the claims made by its subsidiary. The subsidiary had not made the claims by or on behalf of the taxpayer. The Revenue had no liability to make repayment to the taxpayer of the sums claimed. The claims made by the taxpayer in the appeal had been time-barred. Further, the subsidiary had left the group so that the taxpayer could no longer have represented it and had no right to claim repayment of overdeclared output tax generated by the subsidiary. Accordingly, the appeal would be dismissed.

   Re Taylor Clark Leisure plc [2013] UKFTT 792 (TC), [2013] All ER (D) 59 (Jan) (First-tier Tribunal (Tax Chamber): J Gordon Reid QC presiding). *Midlands Co-operative Society Ltd v Revenue and Customs Comrs* [2008] EWCA Civ 305, [2008] STC 1803 (2008 Abr para 2964); and *Reed Employment Ltd v Revenue and Customs Comrs* [2011] UKFTT 200 (TC), [2011] SFTD 720 applied.

2526   Overpayment—recovery—interest—official error—time limit

The claimant, a Romanian company, had a negative balance on its value added tax returns for two consecutive months. The defendant, which was the national tax authority of Romania, therefore approved a refund of VAT to be paid to the claimant. However, the defendant proceeded unlawfully to impose two supplementary tax charges on the claimant in respect of VAT and by way of penalty for default. It subsequently issued two notices by which it refunded the excess VAT by setting it off against those two tax liabilities, thereby purportedly settling them. The claimant challenged the lawfulness of the defendant's notices, and the defendant was ordered to refund to the claimant the sum claimed as its principal claim. On the basis of the unlawfulness of the notice of set-off and the delayed refund of the amount of VAT unlawfully set off, the claimant then made a further claim against the defendant for the payment of interest on that amount, calculated with effect from the date of expiry of the statutory period of 45 days for reaching a determination on VAT returns until the date of the actual refund of that amount. The defendant rejected the claim, and the claimant successfully brought proceedings to require the defendant to pay it an amount by way of statutory interest up to the specified date. On the defendant's appeal against that decision, the national court decided to stay the proceedings and refer to the European Court of Justice for a preliminary ruling the question of whether Council Directive (EC) 2006/112 art 183 should be interpreted as precluding a situation in which a taxable person, having made a claim for refund of excess input VAT over the VAT which it had been liable to pay, could not obtain from the tax authorities of a member state default interest on a refund made late by those authorities in respect of a period during which administrative measures precluding the refund, which had been subsequently annulled by a court ruling, had been in force. *Held*, where the calculation of the interest payable did not take as its starting point the date on which the excess VAT would have had to be repaid in the normal course of events in accordance with Directive 2006/112, that would in principle be contrary to the requirements of art 183. Further, from the taxable person's perspective, the reason why the refund of excess VAT had been delayed was irrelevant. There was no material difference in that situation between a refund delayed because a claim had been dealt with administratively after the expiry of the time limits and one delayed by administrative measures which unlawfully precluded the refund and were subsequently annulled by a court ruling. Article 183 should therefore be interpreted as precluding the situation outlined in the referring court's question.

Case C-431/12 *Agentia Nationala de Administrare Fisacala v SC Rafinaria Steaua Romana SA* [2013] All ER (D) 304 (Oct) (ECJ: Tenth Chamber).

2527   Overpayment—recovery—time limit—compatibility with principles of EU law

The taxpayer made various claims for repayment of overpaid value added tax. The Commissioners for Her Majesty's Customs and Revenue refused some of the claims on the basis that they were made outside the applicable three-year time limit specified by the Value Added Tax Act 1994 s 80(4). The taxpayer appealed, contending that the Revenue's reliance on the expiry of the three-year cap offended various principles of EU law. The taxpayer argued that it had been denied an effective remedy, in that the combined effect of the absence of implementation of Council Directive (EC) 77/388 art 4(5) coupled with the Revenue's public position made it impossible for the taxpayer to discover that it had any right of recovery until after the claims had been barred. Further, the taxpayer argued that the decision contravened the requirement of legal certainty and breached the principle of equivalence. *Held*, although art 4(5) had not been implemented, it was a provision which, so long as it was sufficiently precise, had direct effect. The taxpayer could, therefore, have relied on it irrespective of the absence of implementation. Further, it was not arguable that the Revenue's public position had rendered it impossible or excessively difficult for the taxpayer to assert its rights within a period of three years from payment of the disputed amounts. Had the taxpayer considered that the Revenue had been wrong about any one or more of the relevant supplies, it could have sought a ruling and then appealed against it. The argument that the taxpayer had been deprived of an effective remedy would be rejected. The argument that there was or had been lack of certainty would also be rejected. The reality had been that the taxpayer's failure to make an earlier claim or to pursue the claims it had made to a conclusion had nothing to do with uncertainty about the limitation period but had been attributable to uncertainty about the correct tax treatment of the supplies. The authorities relating to a breach of the principle of equivalence showed that what was required was discrimination between rights derived from EU law and similar rights derived from domestic law. It was not enough that the period laid down for the recovery of overpayments of VAT was shorter than the period prescribed for the recovery of overpayments of some other taxes. In the circumstances, where the applicable time limit for the recovery of overpayments of VAT had previously been more generous than that applicable to other taxes, there was no breach of the principle of equivalence. Accordingly, the appeal would be dismissed.

Leeds City Council v Revenue and Customs Comrs [2013] UKUT 596 (TCC), [2014] All ER (D) 127 (Jan) (Judges Colin Bishopp and Nicholas Aleksander).

Directive 77/388 art 4(5) now Council Directive (EC) 2006/112 art 13.

2528   Reduced rate—cable-suspended passenger transport systems

The Value Added Tax (Reduced Rate) (Cable-Suspended Passenger Transport Systems) Order 2013, SI 2013/430 (in force on 1 April 2013), amends the Value Added Tax Act 1994 Sch 7A so as to apply a reduced rate of value added tax for the transport of passengers by means of certain cable-suspended vehicles designed or adapted to carry no more than nine passengers.

2529   Reduced rate—independence payment

The Value Added Tax (Independence Payment) Order 2013, SI 2013/601 (in force on 8 April 2013), amends the Value Added Tax Act 1994 Sch 7A (charge at reduced rate) so that the value added tax reliefs that apply to persons who are in receipt of a disability living allowance by virtue of entitlement to the mobility component will additionally apply to persons who no longer receive that benefit but instead receive either the personal independence payment or the armed forces independence payment.

2530   Refund—bad debt relief—assessment of claims

Scotland
The taxpayer was a firm of solicitors that provided legal services in respect of insurance claims. In such matters, they were instructed by insurers, but also had a professional responsibility towards the insured person. The taxpayer initially sent its fee notes to the insurers that instructed them with the expectation that the insurers would pay value added tax on the fees as well as the fees themselves. Following an agreement between the Commissioners for Her Majesty's Revenue and Customs and the insurers' trade association in respect of such fees, the taxpayer issued its fee notes in duplicate in cases where the insured was registered for VAT. The principal fee note claiming payment only of fees was sent to the insurer and a duplicate was sent to the insured, who was asked to pay only the VAT on the fees. In the covering letter, it was made clear that the insured would not be out of pocket because they should be able to recover as input tax what they were being asked to pay. If payment of unpaid VAT could not be obtained, the taxpayer claimed bad debt relief. The Commissioners suggested that the taxpayer had been incorrectly calculating relief in that it had claimed the full relief on the invoices that showed a VAT-only amount instead of partial relief, and issued an assessment to the taxpayer for the difference. The taxpayer's challenge to the assessment was dismissed on the basis that the Value Added Tax Act 1994 s 36, read in the context of s 19, meant that because there was a single supply of services, the consideration was the aggregate of fees and the VAT on them. As s 36 only provided for bad debt relief on the outstanding amount of the consideration written off, the taxpayer was limited to claiming the VAT portion of the amount written off. The Upper Tribunal allowed the taxpayer's appeal. On further appeal by the Commissioners, *held*, the refund to which the taxpayer was entitled was stipulated in s 36(2) as the 'amount of VAT chargeable by reference to the outstanding amount'. The words 'outstanding amount' were defined in s 36(3) by reference to the amount of the consideration, or the extent to which the consideration has been written off. But as s 19 made plain, the consideration was an amount inclusive of VAT. There was nothing in the text which gave any warrant for an exercise of seeking to identify the extent to which the amount was demonstrably all VAT. Moreover, there was nothing that required any consideration of 'elementary fairness' to which the Upper Tribunal had referred and which it had regarded as dictating a purposive approach. The taxpayer had provided a taxable service for which they had received partial payment of the consideration and there was no real basis on which it was inequitable, or contrary to elementary fairness, that they should not be responsible, in the normal way, for the proportionate amount of VAT on the part-consideration which they had received. Accordingly, the appeal would be allowed.

Simpson & Marwick (a firm) v Revenue and Customs Comrs [2013] CSIH 29, [2013] STC 2275 (Inner House). Decision of Upper Tribunal [2011] UKUT 498 (TCC), [2012] STC 611 (2011 Abr para 2431) reversed.

2531   Refund—Natural Resources Body for Wales

The Value Added Tax (Refund of Tax to the Natural Resources Body for Wales) Order 2013, SI 2013/412 (in force on 19 March 2013), specifies the Natural Resources

Body for Wales as a body which is entitled to claim refunds of value added tax charged on supplies, acquisitions or importations which are not for the purpose of any business carried on by it.

2532 Registration—application—refusal—suspicion that registration number would be used fraudulently

The taxpayer, a Latvian company, applied to the Latvian tax authority to be entered on the register of taxable persons subject to value added tax. The application was refused on the basis that the taxpayer did not have the material, technical and financial capacity to carry out its declared economic activity. A number of questions arose as to the interpretation of Council Directive (EC) 2006/112 arts 213 and 214, on the identification of taxable persons, and art 273, concerning other obligations to ensure the correct collection of VAT and to prevent evasion. *Held*, it was well established that the registration of a taxable person in the register of taxable persons subject to VAT was a formal requirement, such that a taxable person could not be prevented from exercising his right of deduction on the ground that he had not been identified as a taxable person for VAT purposes before using the goods purchased in the context of his taxed activity. Therefore, the refusal to assign a VAT identification number could not, in principle, have any effect on the taxable person's right to deduct input VAT if the material conditions which gave rise to that right had been fulfilled. In order to be considered proportionate to the objective of preventing evasion, a refusal to identify a taxable person by an individual number should be based on sound evidence giving objective grounds for considering that it was probable that the VAT identification number assigned would be used fraudulently. Such a decision should be based on an overall assessment of all the circumstances of the case and of the evidence gathered when checking the information provided by the undertaking concerned. Therefore, where a tax authority had not established sound evidence leading to the suspicion that the VAT identification number assigned would be used fraudulently, it could not refuse to assign a VAT identification number to a company solely on the ground that the company did not have at its disposal the material, technical and financial resources to carry out the economic activity declared, and that the owner of the shares in that company had already obtained, on various occasions, such an identification number for companies which never carried out any real economic activity.

Case C-527/11 *Valsts ienemumu dienests v Ablessio SIA* [2013] All ER (D) 275 (Mar) (ECJ: Second Chamber).

2533 Registration—limits—increase

The Value Added Tax (Increase of Registration Limits) Order 2013, SI 2013/660 (in force on 1 April 2013), amends the Value Added Tax Act 1994 Schs 1 and 3 so as to increase (1) the registration values, from £77,000 to £79,000; (2) the deregistration value for taxable supplies, from £75,000 to £77,000; and (3) the deregistration value for acquisitions, from £77,000 to £79,000.

2534 Supply of goods and services—agreement to construct building—chargeable event—relevant date

Four property owners granted a building right to the taxpayer company to construct a building on its land and to become the sole owner of certain parts of that property. By way of consideration, the taxpayer undertook to design the plans for the building, to build it at its own cost and to deliver on a turn-key basis certain real property situated in that building to the owners, without any additional payment being required of the owner, the owners having retained and mutually established a building right on the property. The taxpayer sent an invoice to each of the owners relating to the transaction. A tax audit found that the taxable amount of the transaction had been determined by reference to the tax value of the building right in accordance with a certified document and not by reference to the open market value. Further, the taxpayer had not included those invoices in its sales log for the relevant tax period or in value added tax declarations. The tax authorities issued a tax adjustment notice. They took the view that the taxpayer had been supplying construction services and that, under national law, the chargeable event for VAT on that transaction had occurred on the date the building right had been established. The taxpayer unsuccessfully brought an administrative action and subsequently successfully brought proceedings to set aside the notice. On appeal by the tax authorities, the court referred for a preliminary ruling questions as to whether (1) Council Directive (EC) 2006/112 (on the common system of value added tax) arts 63, 65 meant that where a building right was established in favour of a company in order to erect a building, and by way of consideration for construction services of certain real property in that building that company had undertaken to deliver that real property, on a turn-key basis to the persons who had established that building right, that precluded the VAT on those construction services from becoming chargeable as from the moment when the building right was established; (2) arts 73, 80 had to be interpreted as precluding a national provision under which, when the consideration for a transaction was made up entirely of goods or services, the taxable amount of the transaction was the open market value of the goods or services supplied; and (3) arts 63, 65 and 73 had direct effect. *Held*, (1) the principle of equal treatment, of which the principle of fiscal neutrality was a particular expression at the level of secondary EU law and in the specific area of taxation, required similar situations not to be treated differently unless differentiation was objectively justified. Thus, the principle of fiscal neutrality, which was a fundamental principle of the common system of VAT, precluded treating similar supplies of services, which were thus in competition with each other, differently for VAT purposes. Directive 2006/12 arts 63, 65 did not preclude the VAT on the construction services from becoming chargeable as from the moment when the building right was established, namely, before those services were performed, provided that, at the time that right had been established, all the relevant information concerning the future supply of services had already been known, and therefore the services in question had been precisely identified. (2) The taxable amount for the supply of goods or services effected for consideration was represented by the consideration actually received for them by the taxable person. Further, that consideration had to be capable of being expressed in monetary terms. Where the transaction was not completed between parties having ties within the meaning of art 80, which it was for the national court to verify, arts 73, 80 had to be interpreted as precluding a national provision under which, when the consideration for a transaction was made up entirely of goods or services, the taxable amount of the transaction was the open market value of the goods or services supplied. (3) Article 65 set out in a clear and unconditional manner the circumstances in which VAT became chargeable before the goods or services were supplied and the amount on which it became chargeable. Accordingly, arts 63, 65 and 73 had direct effect.

Case C-549/11 *Direktor na Direktsia 'Obzhalvane i upravlenie na izpalnenieto' – grad Burgas pri Tsentralno upravlenie na Natsionalnata agentsia za prihodite v Orfey Balgaria EOOD* [2013] STC 1239 (ECJ: Eighth Chamber).

2535   Supply of goods and services—complex storage services—immovable property—liability for tax

As part of its business, the respondent company provided to traders, who were subject to value added tax and established in member states other than Poland, a complex service relating to the storage of goods. That service covered admission of the goods to a warehouse, placing them on the appropriate storage shelves, storing those goods, packaging the goods for customers and issuing, unloading and loading the goods. The respondent subsequently submitted an application for individual interpretation concerning the determination of the place of the supply of a complex storage service for the purposes of calculating VAT. It was stated that the place where a supply of services of the kind which it provided was carried out should be the place where the service recipient was established. Consequently, the respondent argued, the services which it offered should not be subject to VAT in Poland. In its individual interpretation, the appellant Polish tax authority stated, however, that the services relating to the storage of goods had been in the nature of services connected with immovable property and therefore came within Polish tax law. In those circumstances, the place where those services had been supplied had been the place where the immovable property used for warehousing purposes had been. The respondent brought an action against that individual interpretation, contending that the interpretation supported by the appellant had departed from the wording and interpretation of Council Directive (EC) 2006/112 (on the common system of value added tax) art 47, and that it had been contrary to the principle of consistency of EU law, and that it had called into question the uniform application of that law in the member states. It fell to be determined whether art 47 should be interpreted as meaning that a supply of complex storage services constituted a supply of services connected with immovable property within the terms of art 47. *Held*, art 47 should be interpreted as meaning that the supply of a complex storage service, comprising admission of goods to a warehouse, placing them on the appropriate storage shelves, storing them, packaging them, issuing them, unloading and loading them, came within the scope of art 47 only if the storage constituted the principal service of a single transaction and only if the recipients of that service were given a right to use all or part of expressly specific immovable property.

Case C-155/12 *Minister Finansów v RR Donnelley Global Turnkey Solutions Poland sp zoo* [2014] STC 131 (ECJ: First Chamber).

2536 Supply of goods and services—deemed supplies—cessation of taxable economic activity

Under Bulgarian law, a person was deemed at the time of his removal from the VAT register to have carried out taxable transactions through the medium of all the existing goods and/or services in respect of which he had deducted input tax in full or in part. The taxable amount of those transactions was the open market value, meaning the amount, exclusive of VAT and excise duty, that would be payable under the same conditions on the same or similar goods or services in an arm's-length transaction. The applicant was removed from the VAT register for non-payment of VAT. The Bulgarian tax authorities believed that, at the time of the removal, the applicant had carried out taxable transactions for the purposes of the relevant national law. The applicant contested the evaluation in so far as it did not take into account the condition of the assets. It claimed that the depreciation in value of the assets since their acquisition should have been taken into account, and the value of the assets should have been determined in accordance with the accounting standards applicable on the day of its removal from the register. The tax authorities rejected the applicant's claim, deciding that the open market value mentioned in the relevant provision was the purchase price to which Council Directive (EC) 2006/112 art 74 referred. The applicant brought an action before the local administrative court, which referred for a preliminary ruling the questions of (1) whether the national law in question was compatible with arts 74 and 80; (2) if so, to what extent depreciations in value which had occurred since the assets were acquired were to be taken into account in determining the taxable amount; and (3) whether removal from the VAT register came within the scope of art 18(c). *Held*, art 18(c) covered all cessation of taxable economic activity without differentiating between the causes or circumstances of that cessation. That was consistent with the main objective of the provision, which was to avoid the situation where the final consumption of goods on which the VAT became deductible was untaxed following the cessation of the taxable economic activity. It followed that transactions carried out on goods retained after the removal of the taxpayer from the VAT register for non-payment of the VAT due and in respect of which VAT had been deducted could be treated as supply of goods for consideration. Transactions carried out on goods retained after the removal of the taxpayer from the VAT register for non-payment of the VAT due and in respect of which VAT have been deducted could be treated as supply of goods for consideration. Moreover, art 80 did not apply to transactions contemplated in art 18(c). Also, the taxable amount of transactions contemplated in art 18(c) was governed by art 74, which referred to the residual value of the goods at the time of allocation. Therefore, the taxable amount of transactions carried out on goods retained after the removal of the taxpayer from the VAT register for non-payment of the VAT due and in respect of which VAT had been deducted had to be determined taking into account the change in value of the assets retained by the taxpayer after the cessation of his taxable activity between their acquisition and the cessation.

Case C-142/12 *Marinov v Direktor na Direktsia 'Obzhalvane i upravlenie na izpalnenieto' – grad Varna pri Tsentralno upravlenie na Natsionalna agentsia za prihodite* [2013] All ER (D) 163 (May) (ECJ: Eighth Chamber).

2537 Supply of goods or services—deemed supplies—small business gift—medal awarded to professional footballer

Scotland
The taxpayer was the body responsible for organising and promoting professional football in Scotland. Members of the three divisions of the national league paid the taxpayer a small

annual subscription. Under the taxpayer's rules, the winning teams in each division received 20 gold medals to be distributed to the players. The recovery of input value added tax on the medals had been blocked because output tax had not been declared. The taxpayer eventually sought to argue that the award of medals had not constituted a gift, and that the input tax on their purchase had been deductible but no output tax on their disposal was payable. It further argued that such output tax had already been accounted for on its other income streams. The Revenue disagreed, disallowing the recovery of input tax on the cost of the medals on the basis that no output tax had been expressly accounted for on the supply by way of the disposal of the medals when the awards had been made. On the taxpayer's appeal against that decision, the tribunal concluded that the award of the medals was a supply by way of a business gift for the purposes of the Value Added Tax Act 1994, notwithstanding the taxpayer's obligation to supply the medals. Relying on the 1994 Act Sch 4, the tribunal also concluded that output tax was due on the disposal of the medals by the taxpayer to the appropriate member clubs. On that basis the tribunal dismissed the appeal. The taxpayer appealed against that decision. *Held*, the medals were, as the taxpayer accepted, goods forming part of the assets of its business, and once awarded were no longer part of its business assets. In awarding the medals, the taxpayer was making a supply of goods other than for a consideration, and that was so whether the supply in law was made as a gift or, as the taxpayer contended, pursuant to some kind of obligation. Once that point was clear, the tribunal's other conclusions followed. Also, a taxable person could not avoid liability to account for output tax on a discrete transaction falling within Sch 4 para 5(1) by asserting that the output tax had been accounted for in some other unspecified transaction or series of transactions. The concept of consideration required a reciprocal or direct link between the goods or services provided and the consideration received. There was no reasonable correlation between the value of the medals awarded and the value of the other supplies such as sponsorship, copyright and broadcasting fees and membership subscriptions. The membership fees were insignificant in comparison with the taxpayer's other individual income streams. Further, no link existed between the sponsorship, copyright or television rights income, each of which related to the whole season and all the member clubs, and the award of the medals, which related to three events involving the three championship clubs at or about the end of the season. On that basis, the input VAT which the taxpayer had paid on the purchase of the medals could be recovered from the VAT accounted for in relation to the supply comprised by the award of the medals. If the taxpayer failed to account for such VAT, the Revenue was entitled to set off its liability to give credit for the input VAT paid by the taxpayer on its purchase of the medals. Accordingly, the appeal would be dismissed.

Scottish Football League v Revenue and Customs Comrs [2013] UKUT 160 (TCC), [2013] All ER (D) 224 (Apr) (Upper Tribunal: Gordon Reid QC presiding).

2538   Supply of goods and services—evidence of supply—finding that supply had occurred—rationality of finding

The Commissioners for Her Majesty's Revenue and Customs refused to allow the taxpayer's claim for zero-rating in respect of certain alleged export transactions on the ground that they were not satisfied that the goods in question had been exported. On the taxpayer's appeal, the First-tier Tribunal held that the conditions for zero-rating had been met for three of the six invoices. The Commissioners appealed. *Held*, a pure finding of fact could be set aside as an error of law if it was found without any evidence or if the facts found were such that no person acting judicially and properly instructed as to the relevant law could have come to the determination under appeal. On the evidence, there was nothing to suggest that the First-tier Tribunal had erred in its approach to the three invoices and it had been entitled to reach the conclusions that it had. Accordingly, the appeal would be dismissed.

Revenue and Customs Comrs v Arkeley Ltd (in liq) [2013] UKUT 0393 (TCC), [2014] STC 309 (Upper Tribunal: Judge Roger Berner and Judge John Clark). *Edwards (Inspector of Taxes) v Bairstow* [1956] AC 14, [1955] 3 All ER 48, HL; and Case C-409/04 *R (on the application of Teleos plc) v Customs and Excise Comrs* [2008] QB 600, [2008] STC 706, ECJ (2007 Abr para 3036), applied.

2539   **Supply of goods and services—exchange of services—supply of services for consideration—fitting out and furnishing of property**

The taxpayer was a one person limited liability company belonging to its director. The company's business activities included the letting of property. The director, together with his wife ('the owners') purchased two apartments. They concluded two identical contracts with the taxpayer, under which he granted the taxpayer a 'right in rem to use' the 'shells' of his immovable property, including the two apartments in question, for a period of five years with the possibility of extension. It was envisaged that the taxpayer would let the apartments to third parties. Under the contracts, the taxpayer was not bound to pay rent to the owners during the term of the contracts. However, it undertook to carry out in its own name, at its expense, and according to its own assessment, fitting-out and assembly work in order to complete the apartments and put them into service for occupation. It was envisaged that at the end of the contracts, the owners would recover the apartments along with the fixtures and fittings. The tax authorities carried out an inspection and issued a tax adjustment notice, on the basis that the taxpayer had supplied services to the owners free of charge and that the taxable amount of that supply corresponded to the value of the expenditure incurred by the taxpayer for the purposes of that supply. The taxpayer appealed and the authorities annulled the tax adjustment notice, having decided that what had actually taken place was an exchange of services, namely fitting-out and furnishing services on the part of the taxpayer and a letting service on the part of the owners, and that the taxable amount of the services of fitting out and furnishing the apartments was the open market value of those services, which had to be determined and reassessed. The taxpayer submitted that there had been no exchange of services, but that it had provided a supply of services free of charge. On a reference for a preliminary ruling on the interpretation of Council Directive (EC) 2006/112 art 2(1)(c) (on the common system of value added tax), *held*, the possibility of classifying a transaction as a transaction for consideration required only that there be a direct link between the supply of goods or the provision of services and the consideration actually received by the taxable person. Directive 2006/112 art 2(1)(c) had to be interpreted as meaning that a supply of services to fit out and furnish an apartment was to be regarded as having been carried out for consideration if, under a contract concluded with the owner of that apartment, the supplier of those services, first, undertook to carry out that supply of services at its own expense and, secondly, obtained the right to have that apartment at its disposal in order to use it for its business activities during the term of that contract, without being required to pay rent, whereas the owner recovered the improved apartment at the end of that contract.

Case C-283/12 *Serebryannay vek EOOD v Direktor na Direktsia 'Obzhalvane i upravlenie na izpalnenieto' – Varna pri Tsentralno upravlenie na Natsionalna agentsia za prihodite* [2014] STC 427 (ECJ: Eighth Chamber).

2540   **Supply of goods and services—fuel for private use—consideration**

The Value Added Tax (Consideration for Fuel Provided for Private Use) Order 2013, SI 2013/659 (in force on 1 May 2013), amends the Value Added Tax Act 1994, in relation to prescribed accounting periods starting after 30 April 2013, so as to substitute a new table of flat rate values, based on vehicle CO_2 emissions, which are payable where road fuel constituting a business asset is used for private motoring.

2541   **Supply of goods and services—fuel for private use—flat-rate valuation**

The Value Added Tax (Flat-rate Valuation of Supplies of Fuel for Private Use) Order 2013, SI 2013/2911 (in force on 1 February 2014), makes provision for the flat-rate valuation of supplies of road fuel acquired by a business which is provided for, or appropriated to, private use. In particular, the order (1) sets out a valuation table, accompanied by notes, in accordance with which the flat-rate basis for the valuation of supplies of road fuel for private use must be determined; (2) requires the Commissioners for Her Majesty's Revenue and Customs to revalorise the amounts of the flat-rate charge, in accordance with a prescribed method, within a specified timeframe and at least once in every 12-month period thereafter; (3) provides for an updated valuation table to take effect following each revalorisation; and (4) requires the Commissioners to publish any updated valuation table and a statement specifying the date from which the table is to take effect.

2542   Supply of goods and services—goods—relief—secondhand motor cars

Under a scheme for the sale of demonstration cars, the taxpayer purchased new cars from the manufacturer and sold them as used cars to customers resulting in a low or non-existent profit margin. The scheme used several captive companies under the taxpayer's control and a bank resident in Jersey and independent of the taxpayer. Cars were purchased by the taxpayer from the manufacturer and sold as new cars which were destined as demonstrator cars to captive leasing companies. The captive companies leased the cars pursuant to a hybrid hire purchase or lease agreement to dealership companies within the taxpayer's group under a vehicle demonstrator hire agreement. The captive companies then assigned the lease agreements and title in the cars to the bank which paid the companies a sum of money. The bank entered into a facility agreement with its United Kingdom parent in relation to the facility to finance the assignments and granted its United Kingdom parent an assignment of the assets to be assigned to it as a form of security. The bank transferred as a going concern the lease agreements and titles in the cars to one of the captive companies, which resolved to purchase the relevant hire business carried on by the bank. The bank contracted with the captive company to sell it the business of the hire cars said to have been carried on by the bank. The sale was the transfer of a business as a going concern. On various dates thereafter, the cars were sold to customers by the dealerships acting as undisclosed agents of the captive company in which title to the cars was vested. When the captive company sold the vehicles to the retail customer, the captive company accounted for value added tax only on the difference between the cost of the car on the purchase from the bank and the price at which it sold the car to the customer. The Revenue notified the taxpayer that the dealership companies were obliged to account for VAT on the full sale price when sold to retail customers. It maintained that the proper VAT treatment of the sequence of events was that VAT was chargeable on the sale to the retail customer on the full sale price of the car. Such analysis was disputed by the taxpayer. The First-tier Tribunal concluded that the essential aim of the scheme was to obtain finance and not to obtain a tax advantage. The Revenue's appeal succeeded on the ground that the First-tier Tribunal was in error and the aim of the scheme had been to achieve an illegitimate tax advantage. On appeal by the taxpayer, *held*, there was no basis on which the Upper Tribunal could have found that the First-tier Tribunal had erred in law in its treatment of the taxpayer's evidence and, therefore, no reason to interfere with the First-tier Tribunal's conclusion with regard to such evidence. The tax advantage of the scheme was to be taken as read, and the focus of attention had to be on whether there was another explanation for the transactions, or at any rate for the elements in them that were said to have been artificial. The Upper Tribunal had not been able to identify any error in the First-tier Tribunal's assessment of the taxpayer's position as regards borrowing needs. The tribunal had been entitled to reach the conclusion which it had and, accordingly, the appeal would be allowed.

Revenue and Customs Comrs v Pendragon plc [2013] EWCA Civ 868, [2013] All ER (D) 278 (Jul) (Court of Appeal: Lloyd, Lewison and Gloster LJJ). Case C-255/02 *Halifax plc v Customs and Excise Comrs*; Case C-223/03 *University of Huddersfield Higher Education Corpn v Customs and Excise Comrs* [2006] Ch 387, [2006] STC 919, ECJ (2006 Abr para 2909), applied. Decision of Upper Tribunal [2012] UKUT 90 (TCC), [2012] STC 1638 reversed.

2543   Supply of goods and services—loan broking services—abusive practice

The taxpayer, which traded as a partnership carrying on a loan-broking business, wished to avoid input tax on supplies of advertising services. For that purpose it created a new company which was wholly owned by the taxpayer and was incorporated in Jersey. The taxpayer and the Jersey company entered into a services agreement under which the taxpayer agreed to provide loan processing services to the Jersey company and allow it to use the partnership name in its advertisements for the sole purpose of soliciting applications from the public. The taxpayer was paid a fee by the Jersey company for the processing services. The Jersey company then entered into various agreements with third-party lenders in the United Kingdom to provide loan-broking services. All payments of commission for those services were made by the lenders to the Jersey company. The Commissioners for Her Majesty's Revenue and Customs determined that it was the taxpayer who supplied the loan-broking services, that the advertising supplies were made to it, and that the scheme was an abuse. This resulted in a significant reverse charge arising to the taxpayer which was not recoverable as it related to the exempt loan broking services. The taxpayer appealed to the First-Tier Tribunal, which ruled that the supplies of the loan broking and advertising services to the lenders were made by the Jersey company, and that there was no purpose in the establishment of the Jersey company other than to obtain a tax advantage. However, the structure was not contrary to the purposes of Council Directive (EC) 2006/112 so that the scheme was not abusive and did not need to be redefined. On the Commissioners appeal, a preliminary ruling was sought as to the legality of the scheme. *Held*, contractual terms, even though they constituted a factor to be taken into consideration, were not decisive for the purposes of identifying the supplier and the recipient of a 'supply of services' within the meaning of Directive 2006/112. They might be disregarded, in particular, if it became apparent that they did not reflect economic and commercial reality, but constituted a wholly artificial arrangement which did not reflect economic reality and was set up with the sole aim of obtaining a tax advantage, which was for the national court to determine. Even if the contractual terms mentioned the Jersey company as the supplier of the loan services and the recipient of the advertising services, the economic reality of the business relationships seemed to be different. It was conceivable that the effective use and enjoyment of the services at issue were in the United Kingdom and that the taxpayer profited from them.

Case C-653/11 *Newey v Revenue and Customs Comrs* [2013] All ER (D) 254 (Jun) (ECJ: Third Chamber). Case C-255/02 *Halifax plc v Customs and Excise Comrs* [2006] STC 919, ECJ (2006 Abr para 2909), considered.

2544 Supply of goods and services—parking control services—penalty charges—supply of services or damages

The taxpayer was contracted by owners and lawful occupiers of land or car parks to provide parking control services. Under the contracts, the car park owner was obliged to pay a registration fee and an annual fee for warning signs, and the taxpayer was obliged to inspect the car park and to take parking enforcement procedures against vehicles not clearly displaying parking permits, including the issue of parking charge notices, vehicle immobilisation and towing away. The taxpayer collected and retained all parking enforcement charges. The Revenue decided that the taxpayer was liable to pay value added tax on the parking penalty charges. On appeal, the First-tier Tribunal found that the penalty parking charges were consideration for a supply of services, that service being the provision of parking to motorists, and hence were subject to VAT. The Upper Tribunal affirmed that decision, but on the basis that the services were services of parking control that the taxpayer supplied to car park owners and the parking penalty charges formed part of the taxpayer's remuneration. The taxpayer further appealed. *Held*, the issue was whether the parking penalty charges were consideration for a supply of services, in which case they would be liable to VAT, or damages, in which case they would not. The Upper Tribunal had confused the making of a contract with the power to perform it. While a contracting party could be sued in damages for failure to honour its contractual obligations, the validity of a contract was not dependent on the contracting parties being able to perform those obligations. The terms and conditions on which the permit was issued amounted in law to an offer. Acceptance of the offer took place when the motorist first parked the vehicle after the issue of the permit. The consideration moving from the taxpayer to the motorist was the provision of the permit itself. Therefore, all the necessary elements of a contract were in place when the motorist parked his car. While the taxpayer received small fees in its contract with the cark park owner, its principal benefit was the right to exploit the opportunity to make money from the motorists. The fruits of that exploitation could not sensibly be described as payment by the cark park owner. The monies that the taxpayer collected from motorists by enforcement of parking charges were not consideration moving from the landowner in return for the supply of parking services. A principle which emerged from authority was that a licensee not in occupation could claim possession against a trespasser if that was necessary to vindicate his legal rights granted by the licence. In the present case, the contracts between the taxpayer and the car park owners gave the taxpayer the right to eject trespassers. Further, the contracts between the taxpayer and the motorists gave the taxpayer the same right. In order to vindicate those rights, it was necessary for the taxpayer to have the right to sue in trespass. It followed that if, instead of towing away a vehicle, the taxpayer imposed a parking charge, that charge could be regarded as damages for trespass. Accordingly, the appeal would be allowed.

Vehicle Control Services Ltd v Revenue and Customs Comrs [2013] EWCA Civ 186, [2013] STC 892 (Court of Appeal: Hallett, Lewison and Treacy LJJ). *Hill v Tupper* (1863) 2 H & C 121 considered. *Carlill v Carbolic Smoke Ball Co* [1893] 1 QB 256, HL; and *Manchester Airport plc v Dutton* [2000] QB 133, [1999] 2 All ER 675, CA (1999 Abr para 2762), applied. Decision of Upper Tribunal [2012] STC 2065 (2012 Abr para 2587) reversed.

2545   Supply of goods and services—place of supply—intellectual property—private vehicle registration mark

The taxpayer purchased a personalised vehicle registration mark at an auction through an agency and value added tax was added to the hammer price and buyer's premium at a standard rate by the auctioneer, who was acting on behalf of an executive agency of the Secretary of State for Transport. The Value Added Tax Act 1994 s 1(1)(a) provided that VAT would be charged on supplies of services in the United Kingdom. The taxpayer was resident in Saudi Arabia when he purchased the registration mark. The taxpayer entered into correspondence with the Commissioners for Her Majesty's Revenue and Customs concerning the charge to VAT and the Commissioners confirmed that VAT had been properly charged. The taxpayer appealed to the First-tier Tribunal, which decided that the supply of the registration mark would be treated as made in the United Kingdom as it had been the place where the supplier had been based and the underlying supply had not been outside the European Union member states, and that it would be standard rated, not zero-rated, for VAT purposes. On appeal, the taxpayer contended that the First-tier Tribunal had been wrong to conclude that the supply did not fall within Sch 5 para 1, that it had been wrong to conclude that the underlying supply had not been one made outside the European Union, and that it failed to take into account that the agency, acting through the auctioneer, was not acting as a taxable person within the meaning of Council Directive (EC) 2006/112 art 9, as the issuing of licences pursuant to the Sale of Registration Marks Regulations 1995, SI 1995/2880, was essentially regulatory and not an economic activity, with the consequence that the supply had not been made by a taxable person acting as such and was not chargeable to VAT. *Held,* the primary focus of the 1994 Act Sch 5 para 1 was on recognised forms of intellectual property whereby legal protection was afforded to certain defined products of human skill, endeavour or invention. The United Kingdom system of vehicle registration did not involve the creation of intellectual property rights in any recognisable shape or form. The grant of a registration mark did not confer any private right on its owner to prevent anybody else from using it. That being the essential nature of a vehicle registration mark, its characterisation for VAT purposes could not be transmuted into something akin to a form of intellectual property merely because there were certain marks which people were prepared to pay good money to acquire, and because such marks could become articles of commerce. Moreover, the sale of particular registration marks, although by definition regulated by statute, was in substance an ancillary activity of a profit-making nature, and the Secretary of State was in effect a participator in the same market for personalised registration marks as were independent dealers in the same field. The sale of registration marks was a separate economic activity which fell outside the core regulatory functions of the Secretary of State. It followed that the sale of registration marks, through the agency, was an economic activity within the meaning of Directive 2006/112 art 9. Accordingly, the appeal would be dismissed.

Tanjoukian v Revenue and Customs Comrs [2012] UKUT 361 (TCC), [2013] STC 825 (Upper Tribunal: Henderson J). *R v International Stock Exchange of the United Kingdom and the Republic of Ireland Ltd, ex p Else* (1982) Ltd; *R v International Stock Exchange of the United Kingdom and the Republic of Ireland Ltd, ex p Roberts* [1993] QB 534, [1993] 1 All ER 420, CA (1992 Abr para 2501); and Case C-369/04 *Hutchison 3G UK Ltd v Revenue and Customs Comrs* [2008] STC 218, ECJ (2007 Abr para 3009), considered.

1994 Act Sch 5 para 1 now Sch 4A para 16(2)(a).

2546   Supply of goods and services—sale of goods through agents—consideration—deduction of agents' commission

Council Directive (EC) 67/228 art 8(a) provides that the basis of assessment for value added tax is, in the case of supply of goods, everything which makes up the consideration for the supply of the goods, including all expenses and taxes except the VAT itself.

The taxpayers were members of a value added tax group comprised of mail order companies. The taxpayers used the services of agents, who arranged purchases of the taxpayers' goods by third parties. The taxpayers paid the agents' commission on the purchases, and on the agents' own purchases from them. The commission was given to the agents in different ways, which included cheque payments and credits applied against the balance of their accounts with the taxpayers so as to reduce the debts they owed to the taxpayers in relation to goods purchased from them. The taxpayers accounted for VAT on the price of the goods, including in that price the commissions paid to the agents. The taxpayers claimed repayments of VAT in relation to the commissions. The Revenue refused to repay the VAT on commissions earned by the agents in relation to third party transactions. The taxpayers appealed. On a reference for a preliminary ruling, a question arose as to the interpretation of Directive 67/228 art 8(a). *Held*, art 8(a) did not confer on a taxable person the right to treat the basis of assessment of a supply of goods as retrospectively reduced where, after the time of that supply of goods, an agent received a credit from the supplier that the agent elected to take either as a payment of money or as a credit against amounts owed to the supplier in respect of supplies of goods that had already taken place. Directive 67/228 did not provide for the occurrence of the chargeable event to be set at a subsequent time or its deferral in another manner, nor for the alteration of a tax debt that had arisen. A taxable person's VAT debt therefore arose in an amount derived from a basis of assessment that had to be determined at the time of delivery.

Case C-310/11 *Grattan plc v Revenue and Customs Comrs* [2013] STC 502 (ECJ: Second Chamber).

Directive 67/228 art 8(a) now Council Directive (EC) 2006/112 art 73.

2547   Supply of goods and services—single supply or separate supplies—grant of lease of land and supply of water—indispensable and inseparable elements

The taxpayer was the Middle Temple, one of the four Inns of Court. It held land and buildings in the western part of the Temple and most of its buildings were let. The taxpayer had opted to tax its land under the Value Added Tax Act 1994 Sch 10 para 2 so that the grants of leases in relation to its buildings were supplies chargeable to value added tax at the standard rate. For historical reasons, the taxpayer owned a network of underground pipes through which cold water was supplied to its buildings. Cold water was supplied to the network by Thames Water. The supply was metered and Thames Water charged the taxpayer for it. The taxpayer thereafter supplied cold water to its tenants. The cold water supplied by the taxpayer to the premises let by it was not metered. Each tenant was provided with a quarterly invoice, which separately itemised rent for the premises and the charge for cold water. The amount of the charge for cold water was calculated by reference to the area occupied. The supply of cold water was zero-rated under Sch 8 Pt II Group 2 item 2. The taxpayer did not account for VAT on the amount charged for cold water. The cold water was supplied by the taxpayer because there was no practical choice of a supply from anyone other than it as landlord. However, it was possible for the taxpayer's tenants to have agreed, at the time of taking their leases, to have separate meters for their water supplies and the water would have been provided by a third party and invoiced by that third party once the meters had been read. The Commissioners for Her Majesty's Revenue and Customs decided that the grant by the taxpayer of leases of land, subject to an option to tax, together with the provision of cold water, for which separate charges had been made, had been a single supply chargeable to VAT at the standard rate. The taxpayer contended that it had made two separate supplies to its tenants, namely, a standard-rated supply of the letting of land and a zero-rated supply of cold water. The taxpayer's appeal to the First-tier Tribunal (Tax Chamber) succeeded on the basis that the grant of a lease of land and the provision of a supply of cold water were separate supplies. The Commissioners appealed. *Held*, it was well established that the key principles for determining whether a particular transaction should be regarded as a single composite supply or as several independent supplies were that (1) every supply should normally be regarded as distinct and independent, although a supply which comprised a single transaction from an economic point of view should not be artificially split; (2) the essential features or characteristic elements of the transaction should be examined in order to determine whether, from the point of view of a typical consumer, the supplies constituted several distinct principal supplies or a single economic supply; (3) there was no absolute rule and all the circumstances should be considered in every transaction; (4) formally distinct services, which could be supplied separately, should be considered to be a single transaction if they were not independent; (5) there was a single supply where two or more elements were so closely linked that they formed a single, indivisible economic supply which it would be artificial to split; (6) in order for different elements to form a single economic supply which it would be artificial to split, from the point of view of a typical consumer, they should be equally inseparable and indispensable; (7) there was also a single supply where one or more elements were to be regarded as constituting the principal services, while one or more elements were to be regarded as ancillary services which shared the tax treatment of the principal element; (8) a service should be regarded as ancillary if it did not constitute for the customer an aim in itself, but was a means of better enjoying the principal service supplied; and (9) the ability of the customer to choose whether to be supplied with an element was an important factor in determining whether there was a single supply or several independent supplies, although it was not decisive, and there should be a genuine freedom to choose which reflected the economic reality of the arrangements between the parties. The tenants had no choice but to obtain water from the taxpayer. As both accommodation and water were essential if the tenants were to occupy and use the premises, they would be assumed to require a combination of those two elements if the premises were to fulfil their economic purpose. From the point of view of the typical tenant, both the premises and the water were equally indispensable and inseparable. It followed that they formed a single indivisible economic supply which it would be artificial to split. That supply was a single supply of the leasing of immovable property which was chargeable to VAT by virtue of the taxpayer's option to tax and, accordingly, the appeal would be allowed.

Honourable Society of the Middle Temple v Revenue and Customs Comrs [2013] UKUT 250 (TCC), [2013] STC 1998 (Upper Tribunal: Judge Greg Sinfield and Judge Jill C Gort). Case C-349/96 *Card Protection Plan Ltd v Customs and Excise Comrs* [1999] STC 270, ECJ (1999 Abr para 3419); Case C-41/04 *Levob Verzekeringen BV v Staatssecretaris van Financien* [2005] All ER (D) 328 (Oct), ECJ; Case C-572/07 RLRE *Tellmer Property sro v Financni reditelstvi v Usti nad Labem* [2009] All ER (D) 120 (Sep), ECJ (2009 Abr para 2915); Case C-44/11 *Finanzamt Frankfurt am Main V-Hochst v Deutsche Bank AG* [2012] All ER (D) 32 (Sep), ECJ (2012 Abr para 2548); Case C-117/11 *Purple Parking Ltd v Revenue and Customs Comrs* [2012] STC 1680, ECJ (2012 Abr para 2548); and Case C-392/11 *Field Fisher Waterhouse LLP v Revenue and Customs Comrs* [2012] All ER (D) 163 (Sep), ECJ (2012 Abr para 2592), considered.

2548   Supply of goods and services—single supply or separate supplies—leasing transaction including insurance

The applicant was a Polish leasing company that allowed its customers to pay an additional sum in order to insure the items that were leased. Where a customer decided to take up that offer, the applicant subscribed to the corresponding insurance with an insurer and re-invoiced the cost of the insurance. The applicant took the view that the re-invoicing of the cost of the insurance for the leased item was exempt from value added tax. However, the regional tax office decided that the transaction consisting in the supply of insurance cover was a supply of services ancillary to the leasing service so that the transaction was subject to VAT in the same way as the principal service. The national court dismissed the applicant's appeal against that decision, ruling that the taxable amount of a supply of services also included incidental costs, such as insurance costs charged by the supplier to the customer. The court stated that a supply which comprised a single service from an economic point of view should not be artificially split, so as not to distort the functioning of the VAT system. On the applicant's further appeal, the court decided to stay the proceedings and refer for a preliminary ruling the questions of whether (1) the supply of leasing services and of insurance for a leased item were, for VAT purposes, a single supply to which a single rate of VAT should be applied, or whether they were independent transactions which should be assessed separately; and (2) Council Directive (EC) 2006/112 art 135(1)(a), which obliged member states to exempt insurance and reinsurance transactions from VAT, should be interpreted as meaning that a transaction under which the lessor ensured the leased item with a third party and re-invoiced the cost of that insurance to the lessee constituted an exempt insurance transaction. *Held*, the supply of insurance services for a leased item and the supply of the leasing services themselves should, in principle, be regarded as distinct and independent supplies of services for VAT purposes. It was for the referring court to determine whether, having regard to the specific circumstances of the case, the transactions concerned were so closely linked that they should be regarded as constituting a single supply or whether they constituted independent services. Where the lessor insured the leased item itself and re-invoiced the exact cost of the insurance to the lessee, such a transaction constituted, in circumstances such as those at issue, an insurance transaction within the meaning of art 135(1)(a).

Case C-224/11 *BGZ Leasing sp z.o.o v Dyrektor Skarbowej Warszawie* [2013] All ER (D) 273 (Jan) (ECJ: Sixth Chamber).

2549   Supply of goods and services—supply for a consideration—fraudulent transactions—repayment of tax

See Case C-494/12 *Dixons Retail plc v Revenue and Customs Comrs*, para 2556.

2550   Supply of goods and services—supply for a consideration—health clubs—recovery of late membership fees

The taxpayer operated health and fitness clubs. Membership of the clubs was initially for a 12-month 'commitment period', with fees paid monthly in advance. If any monthly fee was not paid then the member would not be permitted to use the facilities while the payment was outstanding. However, the member would remain liable to make the monthly payments for the commitment period. The taxpayer recovered arrears of membership fees from club members who had failed to make the required monthly payments. The taxpayer did not account for value added tax on those late fees, believing that no relevant supply had been made within the meaning of the Value Added Tax Act 1994 s 5(2) as there had been no consideration. The Revenue determined a supply for consideration had been made. The First-tier Tribunal allowed the taxpayer's appeal against that decision, ruling that the late fees were not consideration for any supply made by the taxpayer, but were instead compensation due to it. On the Revenue's appeal, it submitted that the denial of access to the facilities did not amount to a cessation of the supply for VAT purposes. *Held*, it was clear from the membership agreements that the monthly payments were part payments or instalments of the membership fee for the commitment period. Each monthly payment was not consideration for membership for that month, but was part of the consideration for supplies of services by the taxpayer during the commitment period. It followed that the payment of an outstanding monthly payment was not consideration for retrospective access to the facilities for a particular month, but part of the consideration for services supplied during the commitment period. The extent to which a member availed himself of the facilities to which the taxpayer provided access could vary during the commitment period; the fact that the right of access to the facilities was denied for some months did not break the link between the late paid fees and the services provided by the taxpayer when access was allowed. The correct analysis was that the monthly payments were consideration for supplies of services by the taxpayer, namely the grant of the right to enter the premises of the clubs and to use the facilities and services provided there, subject to availability. The monthly payments were consideration for the supply of the services whether they were paid in advance, on time or late. The same analysis applied where the unpaid fees were recovered after the commitment period had ended, as then the payment was also late payment for services that had been supplied during the commitment period. Accordingly, the appeal would be allowed.

Revenue and Customs Commissioners v Esporta Ltd [2013] UKUT 173 (TCC), [2013] STC 2139 (Upper Tribunal: Judge Sinfield and Judge Sadler).

2551   Supply of goods and services—supply for a consideration—pass to buy goods at reduced rate—monthly fee

The taxpayer was an internet-based retail supplier of goods. A prospective customer viewing its website for the first time was offered a choice between paying what was described as the normal retail price, or a lower website price. A customer who chose to buy goods and elected to pay the lower price was offered a pass, at no cost for the first 30 days, and thereafter at a specified price per month. Even though the customer had benefited, free of charge, from the lower price as many times as a purchase had been made in the 30-day period the pass might be cancelled, during that period, without penalty. Once the 30 days had expired, the monthly fee was charged automatically to the customer's credit card or bank account until the customer cancelled the arrangement, again without penalty. The pass could be used, so as to access the lower price, as many times as the customer chose during the first month and during every month thereafter in respect of which the fee had been paid. It was agreed by the parties that the monthly fee charged to a customer who made a purchase during the month in respect of which that fee had been paid represented the consideration for a taxable supply, the right to buy goods at a lower than normal retail price. The Revenue took the view that those fees were taxable at the standard rate and assessed the taxpayer for additional tax for which, considering the supply to be exempt, the taxpayer had not accounted. The taxpayer appealed to the First-tier Tribunal. *Held*, the monthly payment had not been part payment for goods, it had been of the same amount irrespective of the value of goods bought, and had been payable even if the customer had bought no goods. No part of the payment had been appropriated to the cost of the discounted goods. Moreover, if the customer had already bought goods of such value that the difference between the ordinary retail price and the website price had exceeded the value of the monthly fee, he had nevertheless been able to continue buying at the website price without having to pay an additional fee. The fee had not been a payment made in order to reserve something and could not be regarded as a deposit nor as full payment, since it had not been and could never constitute payment or part payment for the goods. The fee paid represented the consideration for the taxable supply of the right to purchase goods at a preferential price. Whether the customer chose to exercise the right was immaterial, he had paid for it. No part of what he paid was the consideration for the inchoate supply of the goods which he might choose to buy. Accordingly, the appeal would be dismissed.

Re Nettexmedia.com Ltd [2013] UKFTT 050 (TC), [2013] All ER (D) 217 (Jan) (First-tier Tribunal: Judge Colin Bishopp presiding). *Leisure Pass Group Ltd v Revenue and Customs Comrs* [2008] EWHC 2158 (Ch), [2008] STC 3340 (2008 Abr para 2977) applied.

2552   **Supply of goods and services—taxable amount—price established without reference to VAT**

The taxpayers concluded numerous contracts for the sale of land, but neither made provision for value added tax at the time the contracts were concluded. The tax authorities found that the taxpayers were taxable persons subject to VAT which they calculated by adding that amount to the price agreed by the contracting parties, plus overdue interest. The first taxpayer argued that the tax authorities' practice of calculating VAT infringed a number of legal principles, including the principle of contractual freedom. The second taxpayer contended that the addition of VAT to the amount paid as consideration for the sale disregarded the subject-matter of the contract concluded by the parties and produced effects contrary to the objective pursued by VAT. Moreover, he submitted that VAT could not be borne by the supplier since it was, by its very nature, a tax on consumption which had to be borne by the end consumer and, when a contract of sale made no reference to VAT, the tax owing should be applied to an amount equal to the price agreed by the parties, minus the total tax, with the result that the amount paid by the purchaser covered both the price owing to the supplier and VAT. Both actions were dismissed and the taxpayers appealed. On a reference for a preliminary ruling, a question arose as to whether, in light of Council Directive (EC) 2006/112 arts 73, 78, when the price of a good had been established by the parties without any reference to VAT and the supplier of that good was the taxable person for the VAT owing on the taxed transaction, the price agreed should be regarded as already including VAT or as not including VAT, which should be added thereto. *Held*, Directive 2006/112, in particular arts 73, 78, had to be interpreted as meaning that, when the price of a good had been established by the parties without any reference to VAT and the supplier of that good was the taxable person for the VAT owing on the taxed transaction, in a case where the supplier was not able to recover from the purchaser the VAT claimed by the tax authorities, the price had to be regarded as already including VAT.

Cases C-249/12 and C-250/12 *Tulica v Agentia Nationala de Administrare Fiscala–Directia Generalia de Solutionare a Contestatilor* [2013] All ER (D) 121 (Nov) (ECJ: Third Chamber).

2553   **Supply of goods and services—taxable amount—price reduction after supply—principle of fiscal neutrality**

The taxpayer was a mail order company whose agents earned commission in respect of purchases by third party customers. The question arose whether commission earned by the agents gave rise to a retrospective reduction in the value of the supplies made by the taxpayer prior to 1 January 1978 when European Council Directive (EEC) 77/388 superseded European Council Directive (EEC) 67/228. Directive 77/388 art 11(C)(1) introduced conditions under which the taxable amount would be reduced retrospectively. There was no equivalent provision in Directive 67/228. The European Court of Justice ruled that Directive 67/228 could not be interpreted as permitting the regularisation of the basis of assessment, or of the output tax, after the supplies in question had been delivered. On the question whether the principles of fiscal neutrality and/or equal treatment would, either in conjunction with Directive 67/228 or on their own, require such an adjustment to be made, the court stated that the principle of fiscal neutrality was not a rule of primary law which enabled on its own the basis of assessment. Further, it ruled that the amount of value added tax to be collected by the tax authority had to correspond exactly to the amount of VAT declared on the invoice and paid by the final consumer to the taxable person. It fell to be determined whether the effect of the ruling was that the principle of fiscal neutrality required a retrospective reduction in the value of taxable supplies made by the taxpayer to its agents prior to 1 January 1978. *Held*, the statement that the principle of fiscal neutrality was not a rule of primary law that enabled the basis of assessment to be determined was not limited to the principle in its equal treatment sense. If the court had intended to draw the distinction between the effects of the two different senses of the principle of fiscal neutrality, it would not have chosen to do so otherwise than by plain words. The Directives gave rise to the principles on which the VAT system was based; the principles themselves did not have independent effect but were developed at the evolving stages of harmonisation. The principle of fiscal neutrality in its neutral tax burden sense had been left to be determined by the member states. It followed that the European Court's ruling did not allow the basis of assessment to be retrospectively reduced in respect of purchases by third party customers. Accordingly, the appeal would be dismissed.

Grattan plc v Revenue and Customs Comrs [2013] UKFTT 488 (TC), [2013] All ER (D) 227 (Nov) (First-tier Tribunal: Judge Roger Berner presiding). For previous proceedings see Case C-310/11 *Grattan plc v Revenue and Customs Comrs* [2013] STC 502, ECJ (para 2546).

Directive 77/388 now Council Directive (EC) 2006/112.

2554   **Supply of goods and services—taxable amount—screening of commercial advertising—inclusion of screening tax**

The applicant screened commercial advertising and invoiced its clients for the supply of its services, adding a percentage by way of screening tax to the price charged. To calculate the value added tax payable, the applicant applied the specified rate to the full amount invoiced. The revenue accruing by way of screening tax was paid pursuant to Portuguese legislation for the benefit an organisation for the cinematographic arts. The applicant unsuccessfully sought a review of the VAT assessment on the basis that the taxable amount for VAT should not have included the amount payable by way of screening tax. The court dismissed the applicant's challenge to that decision. On appeal, the appellate court made a reference for a preliminary ruling in relation to the interpretation of Council Directive (EC) 2006/112 arts 73, 78(1)(a), 79(1)(c). *Held*, the court previously stated that, in order for taxes, duties, levies and charges to be included in the taxable amount for VAT, even though they did not represent any added value and did not constitute the financial consideration for the supply of services, they had to have a direct link with that supply. The screening tax did not constitute the financial consideration for the supply of commercial advertising screening services and did not represent any added value. As for whether the screening tax had a direct link with the supply of commercial advertising screening services, the court consistently held that the question whether the chargeable event for the tax at issue coincided with that for VAT was a decisive factor for the purposes of establishing the existence of such a direct link. It followed from the Portuguese legislation that the chargeable event for the screening tax coincided with that for the VAT payable on commercial advertising screening services. The screening tax became chargeable as soon as the services were provided and only became chargeable if such services were provided. Consequently, a tax such as the screening tax had a direct link with the supply of commercial advertising screening services, since the chargeable events for the screening tax and for the VAT coincided. It therefore fell within the concept of 'taxes, duties, levies and charges' referred to in Directive 2006/112 art 78(1)(a). On a proper construction of arts 73, 78(1)(a), 79(1)(c), a tax such as the screening tax had to be included in the taxable amount for the purposes of the VAT payable on services consisting of the screening of commercial advertising.

Joined Cases C-618/11, C-637/11, C-659/11 *TVI–Televisao Independente SA v Fazenda Publica* [2013] All ER (D) 76 (Dec) (ECJ: Third Chamber).

2555　Supply of goods and services—time of supply—transport and shipping services

Council Directive (EC) 2006/112 art 66 provides that, by way of derogation from arts 63–65, member states may provide that VAT is to become chargeable, in respect of certain transactions or certain categories of taxable person (1) no later than the time the invoice is issued; (2) no later than the time the payment is received; or (3) where an invoice is not issued, or is issued late, within a specified period from the date of the chargeable event.

Under Polish law, liability to pay VAT arose when the services were supplied or, where an invoice was required, when the invoice was issued, provided that it was issued within seven days of the chargeable event. However, liability to pay VAT on transport and shipping services arose on receipt in full or in part payment, but no later than 30 days from the date on which the services were supplied. The taxpayer, a provider of courier, postal, transport and shipping services, issued VAT invoices to its customers which covered all services supplied for a particular period. Invoices were payable in either 7, 14 or 21 days from the date on which the invoice was issued. The taxpayer asked the Polish Finance Minister to issue an individual interpretation confirming that it had the right to take account of turnover in the taxable period in which the invoice was issued, even though it did not receive any payment in that period and 30 days had not elapsed since the service was supplied. The Minister considered that the liability to pay tax on courier and postal services arose under the general rules, but liability to pay on transport and shipping services was fixed so that the tax due had to be included in the VAT return for the month in which the liability to pay the tax arose. The taxpayer appealed against that decision, submitting that the relevant law infringed Directive 2006/112 art 66. The appeal was dismissed and, on the taxpayer's further appeal, the court decided to stay the proceedings and refer to the European Court of Justice for a preliminary ruling the question of whether art 66 precluded national legislation which provided that, in respect of transport and shipping services, VAT was to become chargeable on the date on which payment was received in full or in part, but no later than 30 days from the date on which those services were supplied, even where the invoice had been issued earlier and specified a later deadline for payment. *Held*, although the legislature had substantially extended the scope of the permitted derogations, that did not allow the inference that a member state had a discretion to establish a time at which the VAT became chargeable other than one of those specified in art 66. The legislature had not made it possible for a member state which chose the option under art 66(b) to establish a time period in which the tax was to become chargeable. Further, the application of art 66(c), and the time period that it envisaged, could be coupled only with the application of art 66(a), since the time period was conditional on an invoice not having been issued or having been issued late, and not on the non-receipt or late receipt of payment. Article 66 was therefore to be interpreted as precluding national legislation of the type in dispute.

Case C-169/12 *TNT Express World wide (Poland) sp zoo v Minister Finansow* [2013] All ER (D) 264 (May) (ECJ: Sixth Chamber).

2556　Supply of goods and services—transactions made fraudulently—repayment of tax paid

The claimant was the representative member of a value added tax group. It had an agreement with a number of card issuers under which, if one of the claimant's customers used a card issued by the card issuer as a means of payment, the claimant was obliged to accept the card and the card issuer undertook, subject to compliance with the procedures laid down, to pay it the price of the goods purchased by that customer with the card. After declaring and paying the VAT relating to transactions carried out, the claimant claimed repayment of VAT from the respondent Commissioners for Her Majesty's Revenue and Customs, who rejected its claim. The claimant appealed to the First-tier Tribunal. The appeal concerned card transactions in respect of which, although they subsequently turned out to have been paid for by means of cards used in a fraudulent manner, the claimant had received payment of the price. Despite the fraudulent use of cards, the card issuers had not exercised recourse against the claimant or made a chargeback. The claimant had therefore retained the payments made, which had included a VAT element. It fell to be determined whether the physical transfer of goods to a purchaser who fraudulently used a bank card as a means of payment constituted a 'supply of goods' within the meaning of Council Directive (EC) 77/388 (on the harmonisation of the laws of the member states relating to turnover taxes) art 5(1) and Council Directive (EC) 2006/112 (on the common system of value added tax) art 14(1) and whether, in the context of such a transfer, the payment made by a third party, under an agreement concluded between it and the supplier of those goods by which the third party had undertaken to pay the supplier for the goods sold by the latter to purchasers using a card as a means of payment, constituted 'consideration' within the meaning of Directive 77/388 art 11(A)(1)(a) and Directive 2006/112 art 73. *Held*, the concept of 'supply of goods' covered any transfer of tangible property by one party which empowered the other party actually to dispose of it as if he was its owner. The concept was objective in nature and applied without regard to the purpose or results of the transactions concerned and without it being necessary for the tax authorities to carry out inquiries to determine the intention of the taxable person in question or for them to take account of the intention of a trader other than that taxable person involved in the same chain of supply. Transactions constituted supplies of goods provided that they satisfied the objective on which that concept was based and were not vitiated by VAT fraud. In the circumstances, the fraudulent use of a bank card when those transactions had been carried out did not affect the ability to classify them as supplies of goods. Therefore, a 'transfer', existed between the claimant and its customers even though the latter, when the transactions had been carried out, had fraudulently used a bank card. Further, the fact that payment of the price of the goods supplied had been made by third parties, the card issuers, could not lead to the conclusion that that payment did not constitute the consideration obtained by the claimant for the supply of those goods. Likewise, inasmuch as the claimant had complied with the procedures laid down by the agreements concluded with the card issuers and, in addition, the sales at issue satisfied the objective criteria of which the concept of 'supply of goods' was based, the fact that those sales had subsequently turned out to have been paid for by means of cards used in a fraudulent manner could not have the consequence that the payment of the price of those sales did not constitute the consideration obtained by the claimant in respect of the sales.

Case C-494/12 *Dixons Retail plc v Revenue and Customs Comrs* [2014] STC 375 (ECJ: Second Chamber).

Directive 77/388 arts 5(1), 11(A)(1)(a) now Directive 2006/112 arts 14(1), 73.

2557   Tax return—inclusion of incorrect invoice—imposition of tax penalty—legality of penalty

The taxpayer was a Bulgarian company liable to value added tax. It entered an invoice issued in error in its accounts and monthly tax return and obtained a deduction of its VAT liability in respect of the invoice. The invoice was subsequently cancelled. The taxpayer did not take account of the cancellation in its tax return for the month of cancellation. It did, however, account for it in its tax return two months later, and repaid the deduction in full with interest. The tax authorities issued the taxpayer with a fine equivalent to the amount of VAT in the invoice. On a reference for a preliminary ruling in proceedings arising out of the taxpayer's challenge to the fine, a question arose as to whether the principles of fiscal neutrality and proportionality in Council Directive (EC) 2006/112 arts 242, 273 precluded the tax authorities from imposing the fine. *Held*, the principle of fiscal neutrality did not preclude the tax authorities of a member state from imposing on a taxable person who did not fulfill within the period prescribed by national legislation his obligation to record in the accounts and to declare matters affecting the calculation of the VAT for which he was liable a fine equal to the amount of the VAT not paid within that period where the taxable person subsequently remedied the omission and paid all the tax due, together with interest. It was for the national court to determine, in view of Directive 2006/112 arts 242, 273, if in the

light of the circumstances, in particular the period within which the irregularity was
rectified, the seriousness of the irregularity, and the presence of any evasion or any
circumvention of the applicable legislation that was attributable to the taxable person, the
amount of the penalty imposed went beyond what was necessary to attain the objectives of
ensuring the correct collection of tax and preventing evasion.

Case C-259/12 *Teritorialna direktsia na Natsionalnata agentsia za prihodite–Plovdiv v
Rodopi-M 91 OOD* [2013] All ER (D) 253 (Jun) (ECJ: Eighth Chamber).

2558   Tax return—online filing—exemption—religious beliefs

By virtue of the Value Added Tax Regulations 1995, SI 1995/2518, reg 25A(6)(a), a person
who the Commissioners for Her Majesty's Revenue and Customs are satisfied is a practising
member of a religious society or order whose beliefs are incompatible with the use of
electronic communications is not required to make a return using an electronic return
system.

The taxpayers traded in partnership as beekeepers and were registered for value added
tax. Their VAT registration was voluntary as their supplies were zero-rated. They chose to
be registered as it enabled them to recover the input tax charged on supplies made to them
in the course of their business. Because of their religious beliefs, the taxpayers shunned
computers, the internet, television and mobile telephones. The Commissioners refused the
taxpayers' request for exemption from compulsory VAT online filing. It was stated that the
wording of the 1995 Regulations reg 25A(6) had to be construed according to the words
which had been used and that there had been no intention to broaden the basis of
exemption to include constructions of scripture which fell outside the tenets of a definable
faith. On appeal by the taxpayers, *held*, applying reg 25A(6)(a) to the taxpayers, if seen
purely as a question of the normal rules of construction and without reference to the effect
of the Human Rights Act 1998, the taxpayers were not entitled to the religious exemption
from liability to file online contained within the 1995 Regulations reg 25A(6)(a). It was
accepted that using a computer, or having an agent use it on their behalf, was contrary to
the taxpayers' religious beliefs. By entirely shunning computers, the taxpayers had
considered they had been acting in accordance with their religious conscience. They had
been manifesting their religious beliefs by refusing to use computers. There was a close and
direct nexus between the manifestation of the taxpayer's religious belief and the underlying
belief. The taxpayers were acting in what they saw as fulfilment of a duty mandated by their
religion. That was clearly within the meaning of 'manifestation' in the European Convention
on Human Rights art 9 which guaranteed freedom of religion. The right to recover input tax
was a fundamental right under European Union law. It could not be proportional to require
the appellants to give up this right and suffer the financial consequence of doing so as the
cost of abiding by their religious beliefs and refusing to use a computer. That had to be all
the more so when the United Kingdom law actually provided an exemption for persons with
certain religious beliefs, albeit not for the taxpayers. Therefore, the requirement to file
online was a restriction under the Convention art 9(1) so far as the taxpayers were
concerned in their right to manifest their religion. In particular, it restricted the
manifestation of their belief that they should shun the use of computers, and that
manifestation had been in fulfilment of a duty imposed on them by their religion and/or had
been intimately linked with their religion. The taxpayers had no proportionate means to
circumvent the requirement. The next step was to consider whether the restriction was
justified. Article 9(2) set out the grounds on which a restriction on the right to manifest
religion might be justified. The Revenue accepted that none of the grounds in art 9(2) could
apply and it did not seek to justify the restriction. It followed that the 1995 Regulations
reg 25 was in breach of the taxpayer's rights under the Convention art 9. Accordingly, the
appeal would be allowed.

Blackburn (t/a Cornish Moorland Honey) [2013] UKFTT 525 (TC), [2013] All ER (D) 16
(Nov) (First-tier Tribunal: Judge Barbara Mosedale). Applications 48420/10, 59842/10,
51671/10 and 36516/10 *Eweida v United Kingdom* [2013] IRLR 231, ECtHR (para 2165),
considered.

2559   Tax return—supply of false information—imposition of tax penalty—legality of additional criminal penalty

The Charter of Fundamental Rights of the European Union art 50 provides that no one is liable to be tried or punished again in criminal proceedings for an offence for which he has already been finally acquitted or convicted within the European Union in accordance with the law.

The taxpayer was found to have submitted false information in a value added tax return and was subject to a surcharge of 40 per cent of the tax under-reported. He was subsequently charged with criminal offences of intentionally filing false returns. The taxpayer claimed that he already had a tax surcharge levied against him and that the surcharge amounted to a criminal charge. On a reference for a preliminary ruling as to whether the tax surcharge constituted a criminal penalty, an issue arose as to whether the court had jurisdiction to answer the question referred. *Held*, the fundamental rights guaranteed in the legal order of the European Union were applicable in all situations governed by EU law, but not outside such situations. Tax penalties and criminal proceedings for tax evasion constituted implementation of Council Directive (EC) 2006/112 arts 2, 250(1), 273 and TFEU art 325 and, therefore, of EU law for the purposes of the Charter art 51(1). The fact that the national legislation on which the tax penalties and criminal proceedings were founded was not adopted to transpose Directive 2006/112 could not call that conclusion into question. However, where a court of a member state had to review whether fundamental rights were complied with by a national provision which, in a situation where action of the member states was not entirely determined by EU law, implemented the latter for the purposes of art 51(1), national authorities and courts remained free to apply national standards of protection of fundamental rights, provided that the level of protection provided for by the Charter and the primacy, unity and effectiveness of EU law were not compromised. The court therefore had jurisdiction to answer the question referred. The double jeopardy principle in the Charter art 50 did not preclude a member state from imposing successively, for the same acts of non-compliance with declaration obligations in the field of VAT, a tax penalty and a criminal penalty in so far as the tax penalty was not criminal in nature, a matter which was for the national court to determine. The relevant criteria for the purpose of assessing whether tax penalties were criminal in nature were the legal classification of the offence under national law, the nature of the offence, and the nature and degree of severity of the penalty that a person was liable to incur.

Case C-617/10 *Aklagaren v Fransson* [2013] STC 1905 (ECJ: Grand Chamber).

2560   Taxable person—company in group—suppliers of financial and insurance services—European law requirements

Council Directive (EC) 2006/112 art 11 provides that each member state may regard as a single taxable person any persons established in the territory of that member state who, while legally independent, are closely bound to one another by financial, economic and organisational links. A member state exercising such an option may adopt any measures needed to prevent tax evasion or avoidance through the use of this provision: art 11.

The European Commission sent a formal notice to the Swedish tax authorities stating that it believed that Swedish value added tax law was in contravention of the requirements of Directive 2006/112 art 11. Specifically, it submitted that Swedish law restricted, in practice, the possibility of forming a group of persons which could be regarded as a single taxable person for VAT purposes to suppliers of financial and insurance services. The Swedish authorities denied that there was any infringement of art 11. The Commission therefore brought proceedings seeking a declaration that Sweden had failed to fulfil its obligations under art 11. It contended that a national VAT grouping scheme should apply to all the undertakings established in the member state concerned, whatever their type of activity. It also believed that, since the common VAT system was a uniform system, the introduction of a special scheme within that system should, as a rule, be of general application. *Held*, it was not apparent that art 11 was a derogating or special provision which should be interpreted narrowly. The European Union legislature had intended, either in the interests of simplifying administration or with a view to combating abuses such as, for example, the splitting up of one undertaking among several taxable persons so that each might benefit from a special scheme, to ensure that member states would not be obliged to treat as taxable persons those whose 'independence' was purely a legal technicality. The measures authorised by art 11 might, however, be taken only in compliance with EU law. It followed that, with that reservation, it was permissible for member states to restrict the application of the scheme provided for under art 11 to combat tax evasion or avoidance. In the present case, the member state submitted that, in order to prevent tax evasion and avoidance, it had decided to restrict the possibility of forming a VAT group to those undertakings which were placed, directly or indirectly, under the supervision of the Finance Inspectorate and which were therefore covered by a public monitoring system. The Commission had failed to show convincingly that, in the light of the need to combat tax evasion and avoidance, that measure was not well founded. It followed that the Commission had failed to show that the restriction of the application of the scheme provided for in art 11 to undertakings in the financial and insurance sector had been contrary to EU law. Accordingly, the application would be dismissed.

Case C-480/10 *European Commission v Sweden* [2013] All ER (D) 62 (Nov) (ECJ: Fourth Chamber).

2561   Taxable person—group of persons—economic activity

The European Commission sought a declaration that United Kingdom legislation permitting non-taxable persons to be members of a group of persons regarded as a single taxable person for the purposes of value added tax was incompatible with Council Directive (EC) 2006/112 (on the common system of value added tax) arts 9, 11. The Commission submitted that art 11 meant that non-taxable persons for VAT purposes could not be included in a VAT group and that the word 'persons' in art 11 referred only to persons who satisfied the necessary conditions to be regarded as taxable persons. It argued that art 11 did not contain a derogation from art 9, which defined a 'taxable person' as 'any person who, independently, carries out … any economic activity'. *Held*, it was apparent from the wording of art 11 that Directive 2006/112 permitted each member state to regard a number of persons as a single taxable person if those persons were established in the territory of that member state and if, although they were legally independent, they were closely bound to one another by financial, economic and organisational links. The application of art 11 was not made subject to other conditions, in particular to the condition that those persons could themselves, individually, have had the status of a taxable person within the meaning of art 9(1). As it used the word 'persons' and not the words 'taxable persons', the first paragraph of art 11 did not make a distinction between taxable persons and non-taxable persons. Consequently, it was not apparent that non-taxable persons could not be included in a VAT group. The Commission had not established that the objectives of art 11 meant that non-taxable persons could not be included in a tax group. It was not evident that the possibility for member states to regard as a single taxable person a group of persons including one or more persons who might not individually have the status of a taxable person ran counter to those objectives. It was, on the contrary, conceivable that the presence, within a VAT group, of such persons contributed to administrative simplification both for the group and for the tax authorities and made it possible to avoid certain abuses, and that that presence might even be indispensable to those ends if it alone established the close financial, economic and organisational links which should exist between the persons constituting that group in order for it to be regarded as a single taxable person.

C-86/11 *European Commission v United Kingdom* [2013] STC 2076 (ECJ: Fourth Chamber).

2562   Taxable person—registration as self-employed bailiff—other economic activity

The taxpayer, a self-employed private bailiff in Bulgaria, was registered for the purposes of value added tax pursuant to Bulgarian law. Under a contract of agency concluded with a company, the taxpayer undertook to make bids in the context of three auctions of three plots of partially built-on land. The contract provided that the taxpayer would retain the remuneration if the bids were unsuccessful. The taxpayer acquired ownership of the plots. According to a tax adjustment notice drawn up by the tax inspectorate, the taxpayer had received his remuneration in consideration for a taxable supply of services, had made the supply as a taxable person for VAT purposes and was therefore required to pay VAT on such remuneration. The taxpayer claimed that he had provided the service on an occasional basis and not in connection with his economic activity as a self-employed private bailiff, the only activity for which he had been registered for VAT. It fell to be determined whether Council Directive (EC) 2006/112 (on the common system of value added tax) art 9(1) was to be interpreted as meaning that a person who was taxable for VAT purposes in respect of his activities as a self-employed bailiff should be regarded as a taxable person in respect of any other economic activity carried out occasionally. *Held*, art 12(1) should be interpreted as referring only to a person who was not already a taxable person for VAT purposes in respect of his main economic activities. In the case of such a taxable person, like the taxpayer, it would not be consistent, in particular, with the objective that VAT should be levied with simplicity and in as general a manner as possible, to interpret art 9(1) as meaning that the term 'economic activity' appearing in art 9(1) did not encompass an activity which, while carried out only occasionally, fell within the general definition of that term in art 9(1) and was carried out by a taxable person who also carried out, permanently, another economic activity for the purposes of Directive 2006/112. Therefore, art 9(1) was to be interpreted as meaning that a natural person who was already a taxable person for VAT purposes in respect of his activities as a self-employed bailiff should be regarded as a 'taxable person' in respect of any other economic activity carried out occasionally, provided that the activity constituted an activity within the meaning of art 9(1).

Case C-62/12 *Kostov v Direktor na Direktsia 'Obzhalvane i upravlenie na izpalnenieto' – Varna pri Tsentralno upravlenie na Natsionalnata agentsia za prihodite* [2013] All ER (D) 53 (Jul) (ECJ: First Chamber).

2563   **Taxable person—reverse charge—compulsory sale—immovable property—**
        insolvency proceedings

The applicant company had been declared insolvent. In the course of voluntary insolvency proceedings, the insolvency administrator provided a report on the assets and liabilities of the applicant to its creditors and to the court. The opportunity to sell two of the applicant's properties arose and the applicant, on the basis of a favourable report from the administrator and with the consent of the purchaser, requested authorisation to carry out the sale under Spanish law. The sale was authorised by court order on the basis that it was timely and conducive to the interests of the general body of creditors. The sale, which was an integral part of the applicant's commercial activity, gave rise to a chargeable event for the purposes of value added tax. A question arose as to whether the applicant or the purchaser was liable for payment of the VAT. The question was relevant for the purposes of determining precisely the terms on which the sale was to be carried out. It fell to be determined whether Council Directive (EC) 2006/112 (on the common system of value added tax) art 199(1)(g) was to be interpreted as meaning that every sale of immovable property carried out by the debtor in the course of insolvency proceedings came within the concept of 'compulsory sale procedure', including where the sale was carried out in the course of the first phase which did not form part of the liquidation proceedings and was carried out pursuant to a voluntary agreement between the parties. *Held*, it was settled law that the wording used in one language version of a provision of European Union law could not serve as the sole basis for the interpretation of that provision, or be made to override the other language versions in that respect. Where there was a divergence between the various language versions, the provision in question should then be interpreted by reference to the purpose and general scheme of the rules of which it formed part. Although the Spanish-language version of Directive 2006/1112 used the term 'liquidation', examination of the different language versions revealed that the most commonly used expression was 'compulsory sale procedure'. Such a concept encompassed a broader scope of the term 'liquidation' by itself. The general scheme of art 199(1)(g) constituted an exception to the principle, set out in art 193, according to which VAT was payable by any taxable person carrying out a taxable supply of goods or services. Article 199(1)(a)–(g) allowed member states to introduce a reverse charge mechanism whereby the person liable for the payment of VAT was the taxable person who had been the recipient of the transaction subject to VAT. The derogations which served as the basis for the drafting of art 199(1)(g) had been justified by the fact that taxable persons, in the situations referred to by those derogations, had generally been unable to pay the VAT imposed because of the financial difficulties which they faced. Article 199(1)(g) should be interpreted as meaning that every sale of immovable property by a judgment debtor carried out not only in the course of the liquidation of the debtor's assets but also in the course of insolvency proceedings occurring before such liquidation, came within the concept of a compulsory sale procedure, provided that such a sale had been necessary in order either to settle creditors' claims or to enable the debtor to re-establish its economic or professional activities.

Case C-125/12 *Promociones y Construcciones BJ 200 SL* [2013] All ER (D) 177 (Sep) (ECJ: Sixth Chamber).

2564 Zero-rating—equipment and appliances for use by handicapped person—design solely for use by handicapped person

The taxpayer charity bought two light aircraft for use by disabled persons. No aircraft manufacturer produced aircraft specifically manufactured for disabled persons nor could any such modification be requested from the manufacturer. Any such modification had to be carried out after manufacture. The taxpayer purchased the two aircraft for sums which included value added tax. The first aircraft was modified for use by disabled persons by a third party on the day after the aircraft was purchased. The second aircraft had been leased by the taxpayer prior to purchase; it had been modified for use by disabled persons during the lease period. The Commissioners for Her Majesty's Revenue and Customs decided that the supplies to the taxpayer of the two aircraft were chargeable to VAT. On appeal by the taxpayer, it was held that the supplies of both aircraft were zero-rated as they fell within (1) the Value Added Tax Act 1994 Sch 8 Pt II Group 12 item 2(g) as a supply to a charity of equipment designed solely for use by a handicapped person; and (2) Sch 8 Pt II Group 15 item 5 as a supply of relevant goods to a charitable institution providing care for handicapped persons in a relevant establishment. On appeal by the Commissioners, *held*, for the purpose of Sch 8 Pt II Group 12 item 2(g), the word 'designed' could not mean merely intended or destined for some purpose. Such an interpretation would mean that the liability for the supply could only be interpreted by looking at the intentions of the parties. That would create obvious difficulties where the parties had different intentions or where their intentions had been difficult to ascertain. Looking at the other paragraphs of Sch 8 Pt II Group 12 item 2, 'designed' was used in conjunction with 'adapted' and referred to the physical characteristics of an item rather than its intended use. The required intended use was described in the opening words of Sch 8 Pt II Group 12 item 2 and it would, therefore, be unnecessary to refer to it again. For those reasons, 'designed' in Sch 8 Pt II Group 12 item 2(g) referred to the physical characteristics of the equipment that made it suitable for use by a handicapped person. The question of whether an item had the physical characteristics to qualify as designed solely for use by a handicapped person should be decided by reference to the item's physical characteristics at the time of supply. Since the second aircraft had been adapted for use by disabled persons prior to its sale to the taxpayer, it followed that it was designed solely for use by a handicapped person and its supply to the taxpayer was zero-rated. However, the first aircraft had not been designed solely for use by a handicapped person at the time of its supply to the taxpayer and its supply was, therefore, chargeable to VAT at the standard rate. Accordingly, the appeal would be allowed in so far as it related to the supply of the first aircraft; the appeal in relation to the second aircraft would be dismissed.

British Disabled Flying Association v Revenue and Customs Comrs [2013] UKUT 162 (TCC), [2013] STC 1677 (Upper Tribunal: Judge Sinfield and Judge Barlow). *The Expert Witness Institute v Customs and Excise Comrs* [2001] EWCA Civ 1882, [2002] 1 WLR 1674, [2002] STC 42 (2001 Abr para 3158) applied. *InsuranceWide.com Services Ltd v Revenue and Customs Comrs* [2010] EWCA Civ 422, [2010] All ER (D) 145 (Apr) considered.

WATER AND WATERWAYS

Halsbury's Laws of England (5th edn) vol 100 (2009) paras 1–452, vol 101 (2009) paras 453–851

Articles

For articles relating to this title please refer to the Table of Articles at the beginning of the Abridgment.

2565 Bathing water—quality—management

The Bathing Water Regulations 2013, SI 2013/1675 (in force in part on 31 July 2013 and in part on 24 March 2015), replace the 2008 Regulations, SI 2008/1097, and implement European Parliament and Council Directive (EC) 2006/7, concerning the management of bathing water quality, and Commission Implementing Decision (EU) 2011/321, establishing a symbol for information to the public on bathing water classification and any bathing prohibition or advice against bathing. In particular, the regulations (1) provide that the appropriate agency is the Environment Agency in relation to England and the Natural Resources Body for Wales in relation to Wales; (2) set out a list of surface waters at which no permanent advice against bathing is currently in force; (3) specify criteria which must be applied to the identification of such surface waters and other matters which must be given consideration; (4) require the Secretary of State and the Welsh Ministers to publish, annually and before the start of the bathing season, a list of all bathing waters within their respective areas and a list of all surface waters at which permanent advice against bathing has been issued and which are therefore no longer bathing waters; (5) provide that the bathing season lasts from 15 May to 30 September each year; (6) require all bathing waters to reach a minimum classification of 'sufficient' by the end of the 2015 bathing season; (7) set out duties in relation to public participation which are imposed on the Secretary of State, the Welsh Ministers and the appropriate agency; (8) require the appropriate agency to establish a suitable monitoring programme for every bathing water, to assess bathing water quality data gathered under the programme and to classify each bathing water as 'poor', 'sufficient', 'good' or 'excellent'; (9) make provision in relation to the dissemination of specified information by local authorities and the appropriate agency in order to give effect to signage requirements in the Decision; (10) provide for the management measures which the appropriate agency, sewerage undertakers and local authorities must take in the event of certain pollution events occurring at a bathing water and impose obligations on the appropriate agency and on local authorities to inform the public when such events occur; (11) require the appropriate agency, in certain circumstances, to issue permanent advice against bathing at a bathing water and require the appropriate agency and local authorities to publicise such advice, together with reasons for the declassification of the bathing water; (12) set out obligations on the appropriate agency and local authorities to make specified information available to the public in relation to short-term pollution at relevant bathing waters; (13) contain enforcement provisions and set out the measures which may be taken against a local authority or private operator; (14) state that the appropriate Minister may give guidance to the appropriate agency or any local authority as regards the implementation of the Directive; (15) make transitional provision; and (16) require the Secretary of State to review the regulations and to publish a report containing the conclusions of the review. SI 1991/1597 and SI 2003/1238 are revoked. SI 2003/3242 is further amended. SI 2004/99 is amended.

2566 Flood and Water Management Act 2010—commencement

The Flood and Water Management Act 2010 (Commencement No 2, Transitional and Savings Provisions) (England) Order 2013, SI 2013/1590, brings s 33 (in part), Sch 4 paras 2–29, 33–36 and 41 into force on 30 July 2013. For a summary of the Act, see 2010 Abr para 2798. See also the commencement table in the title STATUTES AND LEGISLATIVE PROCESS.

2567 Inland waterways—British Waterways Board—power to move vessel

The claimant owned four vessels which he moored on a stretch of a canal. Each of the vessels was moored alongside riparian land which was in the possession or occupation of the claimant. The vessels were occupied as the sole residential home of the occupants, and therefore, were moored otherwise than for a temporary purpose ancillary to navigation of the canal. The defendant was the statutory navigational authority for the canal. Purporting to act as such authority for the management of the canal, the defendant served notices on the claimant, pursuant to the British Waterways Act 1983 s 8, demanding the removal of the vessels on the ground that they had been moored 'without lawful authority'. The claimant issued proceedings seeking a declaration that the notices had been unlawful and that he had a right to moor the vessels without the defendant's permission by reason of his riparian ownership. It was submitted that riparian ownership had created a common law right to moor permanently. The judge found that a riparian owner had no entitlement, simply by reason of that riparian ownership, to moor a vessel alongside their riparian land otherwise than temporarily to facilitate access and for loading and unloading the vessel. Therefore, the judge upheld the defendant's notices and ordered the claimant to move the vessels. On appeal by the claimant, *held*, there was no common law riparian right to moor vessels permanently to the canal bank. Therefore, the judge had correctly found that the claimant had no riparian right to moor the vessels permanently. However, s 8 did not confer a general statutory power to require the removal of vessels moored without permission. The power under s 8 was exercisable only in a case where the vessel was there without lawful authority. If the recipient of a notice served under s 8 was doing nothing wrong in mooring his vessel alongside his part of the bank, then he had acted within the law, not contrary to it. If what he did was lawful, there was no power under s 8 to compel him to remove his vessels from their moorings. Therefore, if what the claimant had been doing was not a legal wrong, he had been entitled to do it. If he had been entitled to it, he had not been doing it without lawful authority within s 8, because the law had allowed him to do what it did not prohibit at common law or by statute. In the circumstances, it had not been possible to identify what unlawful act the claimant had committed that had entitled the defendant to serve a notice under s 8. The defendant had no power under s 8 to require the claimant to remove vessels, the mooring of which had been lawful, with the effect that the notices were invalid. Accordingly, the appeal would be allowed.

Moore v British Waterways Board [2013] EWCA Civ 73, [2013] Ch 488, [2013] 3 All ER 142 (Court of Appeal: Mummery, Jackson and Lewison LJJ).

2568   Inland waterways—regulation—England

The Environment Agency (Inland Waterways) (Amendment) Order 2013, SI 2013/1888 (in force on 23 August 2013), amends the 2010 Order, SI 2010/699, so as to allow the Environment Agency to regulate the safety of boats moored in marinas on the River Medway.

2569   Marine and Coastal Access Act 2009—commencement

The Marine and Coastal Access Act 2009 (Commencement No 6) Order 2013, SI 2013/3055, brings into force on 31 March 2014 s 41 and Sch 4 Pt 1 (paras 1–5). For a summary of the Act, see 2009 Abr para 2963. See also the commencement table in the title STATUTES AND LEGISLATIVE PROCESS.

2570   Marine licences—delegation of functions—Wales

The Marine Licensing (Delegation of Functions) (Wales) Order 2013, SI 2013/414 (in force on 1 April 2013), delegates to the Natural Resources Body for Wales the exercise of functions of the Welsh Ministers as a licensing authority under the Marine and Coastal Access Act 2009 Pt 4 (ss 65–115) and Schs 7–9, including functions under subordinate legislation made under Pt 4, and, in consequence, (1) amends the Marine Licensing (Exempted Activities) (Wales) Order 2011, SI 2011/559, so as to refer to the Natural Resources Body for Wales instead of to the licensing authority; (2) amends the Marine Licensing (Appeals Against Licensing Decisions) (Wales) Regulations 2011, SI 2011/925, so as to require a person who sends notice of an appeal to the Welsh Ministers to send at the same time a copy of the notice to the licensing authority; and (3) makes transitional provisions and savings.

2571   Marine licences—exempted activities—England

The Marine Licensing (Exempted Activities) (Amendment) Order 2013, SI 2013/526 (in force on 6 April 2013), amends the 2011 Order, SI 2011/409, and applies in relation to any area, and any licensable marine activity carried on in that area, in relation to which the Secretary of State is the appropriate licensing authority by virtue of the Marine and Coastal Access Act 2009 s 113. In particular, the order (1) modifies the conditions subject to which certain activities relating to (a) shellfish propagation and cultivation, (b) marine chemical substances, marine oil treatment substances and substances for removing surface fouling matter, and (c) scientific instruments, reagents and tracers, are not to need a marine licence; (2) includes the deposit of a marker as an activity which is not to need a marine licence; (3) specifies a removal activity carried on for the purpose of taking a sample for testing or analysis, and a removal activity carried on for the purpose of removing objects accidentally deposited on the seabed, as not needing a marine licence; (4) provides that a dredging activity carried on for the purpose of conserving or maintaining the navigation of an area of the sea is an activity which is not to need a marine licence; (5) specifies an additional activity relating to the use of vehicles by local authorities to remove seaweed or litter from beaches as an activity which is not to need a marine licence; (6) makes modifications relating to activities carried on by or with the consent of a lighthouse authority or harbour authority for the purpose of providing or removing a mooring of a certain description or an aid to navigation to insert an additional condition subject to which such activities are not to need a marine licence; (7) specifies the deposit or removal of a pontoon by or with the consent of a harbour authority as an activity which is not to need a marine licence; and (8) specifies the deposit or removal of a temporary marker as an activity which is not to need a marine licence.

2572   Marine limits—exclusive economic zone—declaration
See para 1103.

2573   Marine limits—territorial sea
The Territorial Sea (Limits) (Amendment) Order 2013, SI 2013/3164 (in force on 31 March 2014), amends the 1989 Order, SI 1989/482, so as to reflect an agreement between the United Kingdom and France that the co-ordinates of the points defining the territorial sea boundary between those countries in the Straits of Dover should be reformulated in World Geodetic System 1984 Datum.

2574   Natural Resources Body for Wales—functions
See para 1918.

2575   Pollution—control—silage, slurry and agricultural fuel oil—England
See para 1147.

2576   Reservoirs—exemptions, appeals and inspections—England
The Reservoirs Act 1975 (Exemptions, Appeals and Inspections) (England) Regulations 2013, SI 2013/1896 (in force on 28 July 2013), provide, for the purposes of the Reservoirs Act 1975, for (1) specified things not to be treated as large raised reservoirs; (2) rights of appeal against designations of large raised reservoirs as high risk; (3) rights of appeal against notices given by the Environment Agency either to appoint an engineer or to carry out a recommendation of an engineer; (4) the timings of inspections; (5) savings and transitional arrangements for inspections; and (6) a review of the requirements.

2577   Reservoirs—miscellaneous provisions—England
The Reservoirs Act 1975 (Capacity, Registration, Prescribed Forms, etc) (England) Regulations 2013, SI 2013/1677 (in force on 30 July 2013), provide, for the purposes of the Reservoirs Act 1975, for (1) the calculation of the capacity of a large raised reservoir; (2) registration of a large raised reservoir; (3) notification of changes to, and the keeping and inspection of, the English register; (4) transitional arrangements in relation to the English register; (5) the making and content of reports by the Environment Agency to the Secretary of State; (6) the form of record to be kept for a high-risk reservoir and the information to be given in that record; (7) the form of certificates of engineers, the forms of reports of engineers and the forms of directions of engineers; (8) the information to be provided by undertakers when intending to construct or bring back into use a large raised reservoir; and (9) the making of reports by undertakers to the Agency in relation to incidents relating to the uncontrolled release of water from a large raised reservoir and emergency measures.

2578   Reservoirs—referees—appointment, procedure and costs—England
The Reservoirs Act 1975 (Referees) (Appointment, Procedure and Costs) (England) Rules 2013, SI 2013/1676 (in force on 30 July 2013), replace the Reservoirs Act 1975 (Referees) (Appointment and Procedure) Rules 1986, SI 1986/467, and make provision for

the time within which any appointment of a referee by agreement between the undertakers and the engineer must be made and the manner in which any request to the Secretary of State to appoint a referee in default of agreement must be made. The 2013 Rules also provide for procedure and for the payment of costs of the investigation.

2579   Water and sewerage undertakers—discharge of sewage into canal—right of discharge—effect of privatisation

The defendant company was a sewerage undertaker and, as such, held an implied power to discharge the contents of sewers on to third party property without the owner's consent pursuant to the Public Health Act 1875. The defendant discharged water into two canals owned by the claimant via numerous outfalls. A significant number of the outfalls pre-dated the commencement of the Water Act 1989 and the Water Utilities Act 1991. Under the 1989 Act, provision was made for sewage services to be privatised and for a transfer scheme to take place between the incumbent and new undertakers. Section 4 provided for the transfer of the water authorities' functions to water undertakers and sewerage undertakers, and for there to be schemes for the division of the property, rights and liabilities of those authorities between their successor companies and the National River Authority. The transfer scheme took effect on the transfer date, which was also the date on which the relevant provisions of the 1989 Act came into effect. It followed that, if the implied right of discharge had been repealed by the 1989 Act, the repeal and the transfer scheme had been simultaneous. The claimants issued proceedings seeking declarations that, as regards a large number of outfalls, the defendant had no right of discharge. The issue between the parties was whether the implied right of discharge had been permanently saved from repeal in the 1989 Act or the 1991 Act as respects outfalls from sewers in place in 1989, because it had been transferred under statutory transfer schemes by the transfer of property, rights and liabilities from the then sewerage undertakers to successor companies in 1989. The judge held that, where outfalls had been transferred to a sewerage undertaker under the transfer scheme entered into as part of the privatisation process implemented under the 1989 Act, the sewerage undertaker had acquired the implied right of discharge from that outfall that had existed prior to the 1989 Act. The claimants appealed. *Held*, it was clear from s 4 that the transfer scheme was intended to apply to the whole of the transferor's sewerage undertaking. It was clearly the purpose of the transfer scheme to ensure that all assets and rights were vested in the successor company by a single document. Therefore, the transfer scheme was not limited to matters for which a written agreement was required, or to transfers of non-assignable contracts or to property-related rights and liabilities. Parliament had not intended a transfer scheme to have been used to vest a right which had itself been creating and vesting in the transferee by other provisions in the 1989 Act. It followed that the transfer scheme had not encompassed the implied right of discharge. The purpose of the 1991 Act had been to ensure the survival of acts done under the earlier legislation, and not to remove rights that had been in force while that legislation was in force. The rights transferred had not had an existence under the transfer scheme which was independent of the enactment from which they had derived. In addition, if the repeal of the implied right of discharge was effected by the 1989 Act, the repeal occurred at exactly the same time as the transfer scheme took effect. On that basis, the implied right of discharge could never have been transferred under the scheme as a pure matter of timing. It followed that the transfer scheme had been ineffective to freeze the position as it had stood immediately at the date of the transfer scheme. Accordingly, the appeal would be allowed.

Manchester Ship Canal Co Ltd v United Utilities Water plc [2013] EWCA Civ 40, [2013] 1 WLR 2570, [2013] All ER (D) 72 (Feb) (Court of Appeal: Arden, Sullivan and Patten LJJ). *British Waterways Board v Severn Trent Water Ltd* [2001] EWCA Civ 276, [2002] Ch 25, [2001] 3 All ER 673 applied.

2580   Water fluoridation—proposals and consultation—England

The Water Fluoridation (Proposals and Consultation) (England) Regulations 2013, SI 2013/301 (in force on 1 April 2013), impose procedural requirements on local authorities in the exercise of their functions in relation to the consideration of proposals for new fluoridation schemes and the variation, termination or maintenance of existing schemes. In particular, the regulations (1) require a local authority which makes a proposal to increase the fluoride content of water or a proposal to vary or terminate an existing fluoridation scheme to notify any other local authorities which may be affected by the proposal and give them relevant information to enable them to decide whether to vote in favour of further steps being taken in relation to the proposal; (2) provide that further steps may be taken in relation to a proposal where there is a majority of 67 per cent or more among the authorities affected by the proposal in favour of the decision; (3) set out the procedure to be followed by a proposing authority or a joint committee of affected local authorities to determine a proposal; (4) require a decision made in relation to a proposal to be notified to the Secretary of State; (5) provide for the circumstances in which consultation is required on whether to maintain existing arrangements for fluoridation and set out the procedure for the maintenance of such arrangements; (6) require the Secretary of State to give notice to a water undertaker to terminate fluoridation arrangements where a decision is made not to propose that such arrangements be maintained; (7) provide that where a variation proposal does not concern the boundary of an area to which fluoridation arrangements relate or where it does concern the boundary of the area but the number of houses affected by the variation would be 20 per cent or less of the number of houses within the area, there is no requirement to consult or ascertain opinion or to establish a joint committee of affected local authorities; (8) empower the Secretary of State to give notice to a water undertaker to terminate fluoridation arrangements without a termination proposal having being made where he is satisfied that a significant risk to health has been identified in connection with the fluoridation of water; and (9) provide for a minimum term of 20 years between the making of termination proposals. The Water Fluoridation (Consultation) (England) Regulations 2005, SI 2005/921, are revoked.

2581 Water industry—specified infrastructure projects—English undertakers

The Water Industry (Specified Infrastructure Projects) (English Undertakers) Regulations 2013, SI 2013/1582 (in force on 28 June 2013), implement the Water Industry Act 1991 Pt 2A (ss 36A–36G) in relation to water and sewerage undertakers whose appointment areas are wholly or mainly in England. The regulations (1) apply, with modification, the general duty on the Secretary of State and the Water Services Regulation Authority ('Ofwat') with respect to the water industry for the purposes of their functions exercised under the regulations or, in certain cases, the 1991 Act; (2) give the Secretary of State and Ofwat powers to specify by notice in writing an infrastructure project in certain circumstances; (3) require Ofwat to publish guidance to be followed by it in determining whether to specify an infrastructure project; (3) prohibit the incumbent water or sewerage undertaker from undertaking that infrastructure project, but authorise the Secretary of State or Ofwat to permit or require it to undertake preparatory work; (4) empower the Secretary of State and Ofwat to vary or revoke notices issued by them under the powers; (5) require the incumbent undertaker to put a specified infrastructure project out to tender; (6) limit companies associated with the water or sewerage undertaker from bidding in the tender process except where agreed by the Secretary of State or Ofwat by notice in writing; (7) give the Secretary of State and Ofwat power to designate by notice in writing a person wholly or partly responsible for a specified infrastructure project which has been put out to tender; (8) make provision for the licensing and regulation of infrastructure providers; (9) require water and sewerage undertakers and infrastructure providers to provide the Secretary of State with such information as may be reasonably required for the purposes of carrying out their functions under the regulations; (10) provide for civil enforcement of the requirements; and (11) require the Secretary of State to review the operation and effect of the provisions and to publish a report within five years after they come into force.

2582 Water supply and quality—fees

The Public Bodies (Water Supply and Water Quality Fees) Order 2013, SI 2013/277 (in force on 12 February 2013), (1) provides for fees to be payable for the carrying out of certain functions under the Water Industry Act 1991 by an inspector, including functions that are related to the investigation and reporting requirements of (a) checking water sampling and analysis arrangements; (b) checking water supply management arrangements; (c) investigating an event, incident, emergency or other matter arising from the quality or sufficiency of water; (d) checking the handling and reporting of consumer complaints about water quality; and (e) checking compliance with requirements to furnish information to, or to notify, the Secretary of State concerning these arrangements and matters; and (2) sets out the circumstances and manner in which such fees are payable, approved, published and reviewed.

WELFARE BENEFITS AND STATE PENSIONS

Halsbury's Laws of England (5th edn) vol 104 (2014) paras 1–663

Articles

For articles relating to this title please refer to the Table of Articles at the beginning of the Abridgment.

2583   Armed forces independence payment—general

The Armed Forces and Reserve Forces Compensation Scheme (Consequential Provisions: Subordinate Legislation) Order 2013, SI 2013/591 (in force in part on 8 April 2013 and in part on 6 May 2013), give full effect to the Armed Forces (Pensions and Compensation Scheme) Act 2004 s 1(2) consequential on the Armed Forces and Reserve Forces (Compensation Scheme) (Amendment Order) 2013, SI 2013/436. In particular, the regulations further amends (1) the Social Security Benefit (Persons Abroad) Regulations 1975, SI 1975/563, so as to provide that persons in receipt of armed forces independence payment will not be disqualified from receiving a benefit in respect of incapacity by reason of temporary absence from Great Britain in certain circumstances; (2) the Social Security (Invalid Care Allowance) Regulations 1976, SI 1976/409, so as to provide that entitlement to Carer's Allowance can continue where the claimant is not present in Great Britain provided the absence is temporary and for the purpose of caring for a severely disabled person in receipt of armed forces personal independence payment; (3) the Social Security (Overlapping Benefits) Regulations 1979, SI 1979/597, so as to (a) allow for adjustment where both armed forces independence payment and any benefit to be adjusted by reference to armed forces independence payment are payable in respect of the same person; and (b) permit the adjustment of armed forces independence payment where certain other benefits are payable in respect of the same person; (4) the Income Support (General) Regulations 1987, SI 1987/1967, to make a number of consequential amendments; (5) the Council Tax (Discount Disregards) Order 1992, SI 1992/548, so as to include armed forces independence payment in the definition of a 'qualifying benefit'; (6) the Council Tax (Additional Provisions for Discount Disregards) Regulations 1992, SI 1992/552, so as to add armed forces independence payment to the list of qualifying benefits in respect of the person being cared for; (7) the Child Support (Maintenance Assessments and Special Cases) Regulations 1992, SI 1992/1815, so as to provide that armed forces independence payment, or any other payment to compensate for the non-payment of armed forces independence payment, is disregarded when calculating the net income of a non-resident parent and parent with care; (8) the National Assistance (Assessment of Resources) Regulations 1992, SI 1992/2977, so as to make provision for how armed forces independence payments are to be treated in the calculation of income and earnings, and requires local authorities to disregard armed forces independence payment in the financial assessment of what a person pays for their residential care; (9) the Social Security (Incapacity Benefit) Regulations 1994, SI 1994/2946, to provide that persons in receipt of armed forces independence payments will not have their benefits reduced under the Social Security Contributions and Benefits Act 1992 s 30DD(1); (10) the Jobseeker's Allowance Regulations 1996, SI 1996/207, so as to make consequential amendments; (11) the Housing Renewal Grants Regulations 1996, SI 1996/2890, to deal with the impact of armed forces independence payments on means testing for receipt of disabled facilities grants; (12) the Social Security Benefit (Computation of Earnings) Regulations 1996, SI 1996/2745, so as to make provision for payments of armed forces independence payments to be taken into account in the determination of applications for departures from the standard child maintenance formula; (13) the Education (Student Loans) Regulations 1998, SI 1998/211, so as to include armed forces independence payment to the definition of 'disability related benefits'; (14) the Social Security and Child Support (Decisions and Appeals) Regulations 1999, SI 1999/991, so as to make provision for the date on which certain decisions regarding entitlement to armed forces independence payments take effect; (15) the Maternity and Parental Leave etc

Regulations 1999, SI 1999/3312, so as to provide that where an employee is a parent of a person in receipt of armed forces independence payment, they are entitled to certain additional rights in respect of parental leave; (16) the Child Support (Variations) Regulations 2000, SI 2000/156, so as to provide that a person receiving armed forces independence payment comes within the definition of a 'disabled' person, and allow armed forces independence payment to be taken into account when calculating special expenses for the purposes of the Child Support Act 1991; (17) the Community Legal Service (Financial) Regulations 2000, SI 2000/516, to include armed forces independence payment in the list of payments to be disregarded when calculating disposable income; (18) the Representation of the People (England and Wales) Regulations 2001, SI 2001/341, to provide that, where a person is in receipt of armed forces independence payment, they are exempted from the requirement to obtain medical attestation when applying to vote by proxy; (19) the Social Security (Loss of Benefit) Regulations 2001, SI 2001/4022, to provide that the definition of a 'person in hardship' and a 'couple in hardship' includes persons in receipt of armed forces independence payment; (20) the State Pension Credit Regulations 2002, SI 2002/1792, so as to make a number of consequential amendments; (21) the Working Tax Credit (Entitlement and Maximum Rate) Regulations 2002, SI 2002/2005, so as to provide that persons in receipt of armed forces independence payment may be entitled to a disability element or a severe disability element for the purposes of working tax credit; (22) the Tax Credits (Definition and Calculation of Income) Regulations 2002, SI 2002/2006, so as to provide that armed forces independence payment is disregarded when calculating income; (23) the Child Tax Credit Regulations 2002, SI 2002/2007, so as to provide that, for the purposes of child tax credit, where a child or qualifying young person is in receipt of armed forces independence payment a severe disability element may be payable; (24) the Tax Credits (Claims and Notifications) Regulations 2002, SI 2002/2014, so as to make provision for the date on which decisions regarding entitlement to armed forces independence payment take effect for the purposes of entitlement to the severe disability element of child tax credit; (25) the Flexible Working (Eligibility, Complaints and Remedies) Regulations 2002, SI 2002/3236, so that the definition of 'disabled' includes someone entitled to armed forces independence payment; (26) the Government Resources and Accounts Act 2000 (Rights of Access of Comptroller and Auditor General) Order 2003, SI 2003/1325, so as to provide that the Comptroller and Auditor General cannot access documents in the custody or control of an individual relating to grants of armed forces independence payment to individuals; (27) the European Parliamentary Elections Regulations 2004, SI 2004/293, to provide that, where a person is in receipt of armed forces independence payment, they are exempted from the requirement to obtain medical attestation when applying to vote by proxy in European parliamentary elections; (28) the Non-Contentious Probate Fees Order 2004, SI 2004/3120, so as to include armed forces independence payment in the definition of 'excluded benefits'; (29) the Social Fund Maternity and Funeral Expenses (General) Regulations 2005, SI 2005/3061, so as to include armed forces independence payment in the definition of 'arrears of benefits excluded' from a deceased's assets; (30) the Criminal Defence Service (Financial Eligibility) Regulations 2006, SI 2006/2492, so as to include armed forces independence payment in the list of payments to be disregarded when calculating gross annual income; (31) the Housing Benefit Regulations 2006, SI 2006/213, so as to make a number of consequential amendments; (32) the Housing Benefit (Persons who have attained the qualifying age for state pension credit) Regulations 2006, SI 2006/214, so as to make a number of consequential amendments; (33) the National Assembly for Wales (Representation of the People) Order 2007, SI 2007/236, so as to provide that, where a person is in receipt of armed forces personal independence payment, they are exempted from the requirement to obtain medical attestation when applying to vote by proxy in National Assembly for Wales elections; (34) the Employment and Support Allowance Regulations 2008, SI 2008/794, so as to make a number of consequential amendments; (35) the Magistrates' Court Fees Order 2008, SI 2008/1052, to include armed forces independence payment in the definition of 'excluded benefits'; (36) the Civil Proceedings Fees Order 2008, SI 2008/1053, to include armed forces independence payment in the definition of 'excluded benefits'; (37) the Criminal Defence Service (Contribution Orders) Regulations 2009, SI 2009/3328, so as to include armed forces independence payment in the list of payments to be disregarded when calculating gross annual income; (38) the Education (Student Loans) (Repayment) Regulations 2009, SI 2009/470, so as to include armed forces independence payment in the definition of 'disability-related benefits';

(39) the Supreme Court Fees Order 2009, SI 2009/2131, so as to include armed forces independence payment in the definition of 'excluded benefits'; (40) the Social Security (Contributions Credits for Parents and Carers) Regulations 2010, SI 2010/19, so as to include armed forces independence payment in the definition of 'relevant benefit'; (41) the Upper Tribunal (Immigration and Asylum Chamber) (Judicial Review) (England and Wales) Fees Order 2011, SI 2011/2344, so as to include armed forces independence payment in the definition of 'excluded benefits'; (42) the Police and Crime Commissioner Elections Order 2012, SI 2012/1917, so as to provide that, where a person is in receipt of armed forces independence payment, they are exempted from the requirement to obtain medical attestation when applying to vote by proxy in the Police and Crime Commissioner Elections; (43) the Child Support Maintenance Calculation Regulations 2012, SI 2012/2677, so as to provide that the definition of a 'disabled' person includes persons in receipt of armed forces independence payment; (44) the Benefit Cap (Housing Benefit) Regulations 2012, SI 2012/2944, so as to provide that a person will not be subject to the housing benefit cap where that person, their partner or a young person for whom they or their partner is responsible is in receipt of armed forces independence payment; (45) the Civil Legal Aid (Financial Resources and Payment for Services) Regulations 2013, SI 2013/480, so as to provide that armed forces independence payments are to be disregarded in the calculation of disposable income or gross income; (46) the Criminal Legal Aid (Financial Resources) Regulations 2013, SI 2013/417, so as to provide that armed forces independence payments are to be deducted in the calculations of disposable income and gross income; (47) the Employment and Support Allowance Regulations 2013, SI 2013/379, so as to provide that the definition of a 'person in hardship' includes persons in receipt of armed forces independence payment; (48) the Jobseeker's Allowance Regulations 2013, SI 2013/378, so as to provide that armed forces independence payment is included in the definition of 'remunerative work'; (49) the Universal Credit (Transitional Provisions) Regulations 2013, SI 2013/386, so as to provide that armed forces independence payment is included in the definitions of 'existing benefits' and 'other incapacity benefits'; and (50) the Universal Credit Regulations 2013, SI 2013/376, so as to provide that armed forces independence payment is included in the list of universal benefits.

2584   Assistance fund for disabled persons—decision to close—lawfulness

See *Bracking v Secretary of State for Work and Pensions*, para 862.

2585   Attendance allowance—residence and presence conditions

See para 2614.

2586   Benefits—age-related payments

The Transfer of Functions (Age-Related Payments) Order 2013, SI 2013/1442 (in force on 11 July 2013), provides that the regulation-making function under the Age-Related Payments Act 2004 is to be exercisable concurrently by the Secretary of State and the Treasury in specified circumstances.

The Age-Related Payments Regulations 2013, SI 2013/2980 (in force on 28 November 2013), make provision for the Treasury to make payments to qualifying Equitable Life annuitants. Specifically, the regulations (1) define 'qualifying Equitable Life annuitant'; (2) set out the conditions under which a qualifying Equitable Life annuitant is entitled to a payment of £5,000, or an equivalent amount in the currency of the country in which the qualifying Equitable Life annuitant is resident, and the circumstances in which the payment can be made to a qualifying Equitable Life annuitant's personal representative; (3) provide for a qualifying Equitable Life annuitant to be entitled to a further payment of £5,000, or an equivalent amount in the currency of the country in which the qualifying Equitable Life annuitant is resident, if that person was in receipt of state pension credit on 1 November 2013; (4) provide for procedural matters; and (5) ensure that payments made under the regulations are to be tax-free in the hands of recipients and do not affect eligibility for state funded means-tested support.

2587   Benefits—amount—cap—human rights

The Welfare Reform Act 2012 s 96 introduced a cap on the total amount of state benefits that individuals and couples could receive. The claimants were single mothers who had at least three children living with them. Following the introduction of the cap, they were all subjected to a reduction in their state benefits to bring them within the cap. The claimants applied for judicial review of the decision to enact the cap, submitting that it was (1) discriminatory contrary to the European Convention on Human Rights art 14 taken with art 8 and/or the First Protocol art 1; and (2) a direct breach of the claimants' rights under art 8. In respect of the discrimination issue, it was common ground that the cap had a disproportionate adverse impact on women and that the critical issue was whether the cap could be justified. *Held*, with regard to discrimination, it was an established principle that the question to be answered was whether, having regard to the fact that some children would plainly be disadvantaged by the cap, the decision to impose it was manifestly without reasonable foundation. The cap could not possibly have been said to be manifestly without reasonable foundation. The diversion of the resources of the state and more particularly the question of the extent to which state funds should be made available to those in need for one reason or another was a political question. In respect of the art 8 issue, it was settled law that all that was necessary was to give appropriate weight to the interests of children as a primary consideration in the overall balancing exercise. It could not conceivably have been said that there had been any failure to appreciate the impact of the cap on children nor could it have been inferred from the mere fact that in certain circumstances children were adversely affected that their interests were not treated as a primary consideration. The cap was entirely consistent with those interests being given that status; it was simply outweighed by countervailing considerations. Accordingly, the claim would be dismissed.

R (on the application of JS) v Secretary of State of Work and Pensions (Child Poverty Action Group intervening) [2013] EWHC 3350 (QB), [2013] All ER (D) 37 (Nov) (Queen's Bench Division: Elias LJ and Bean J).

2588   Benefits—claims and payments—mortgage interest—deductions from benefits

The Social Security (Claims and Payments) Amendment Regulations 2013, SI 2013/456 (in force on 1 April 2013), further amend the 1987 Regulations, SI 1987/1968, so as to reduce from £0·38 to £0·35 the fee which qualifying lenders pay for the purpose of defraying administrative expenses incurred by the Secretary of State in making payments in respect of mortgage interest direct to qualifying lenders.

2589   Benefits—entitlement—habitual residence

The Jobseeker's Allowance (Habitual Residence) Amendment Regulations 2013, SI 2013/3196 (in force on 1 January 2014), further amend the 1996 Regulations, SI 1996/207, in relation to the definition of a 'person from abroad', with the effect that the habitual residence test cannot be satisfied unless the claimant has been living in the common travel area for the past three months, in addition to the existing requirement that he has a right to reside in the common travel area.

2590   Benefits—entitlement—migrant worker—application for unemployment benefits in country of last employment

See Case E-3/12 *The Norwegian State v Jonsson*, para 2687.

2591   Benefits—entitlement—migrant worker—Croatia

The Social Security (Croatia) Amendment Regulations 2013, SI 2013/1474 (in force on 1 July 2013), further amend the Jobseeker's Allowance Regulations 1996, SI 1996/207, the Income Support (General) 1987 Regulations, SI 1987/1967, the State Pension Credit Regulations 2002, SI 2002/1792, the Housing Benefit Regulations 2006, SI 2006/213, the Housing Benefit (Persons who have attained the qualifying age for state pension credit) Regulations 2006, SI 2006/214, and the Employment and Support Allowance Regulations 2008, SI 2008/794, in consequence of the accession of Croatia to the European Union on 1 July 2013. Specifically, the regulations insert a new category of persons who are exempt from the habitual residence test, nationals of Croatia who are subject to the worker authorisation scheme established by the Accession of Croatia (Immigration and Worker

Authorisation) Regulations 2013, SI 2013/1460, and who are treated as workers. In addition, the regulations further amend the Social Security (Immigration and Asylum) Consequential Amendment Regulations 2000, SI 2000/636, in order to update the reference to the Agreement on the European Economic Area.

2592 Benefits—entitlement—parent of child born in EU member state—refusal of interim payments

See R (on the application of Sanneh) v Secretary of State for Work and Pensions, para 1460.

2593 Benefits—income-related—subsidy to authorities

The Income-related Benefits (Subsidy to Authorities) Amendment Order 2013, SI 2013/266 (in force on 18 March 2013), further amends the 1998 Order, SI 1998/562, by (1) revising the figures to be used in the calculation of administration subsidy for the year beginning on 1 April 2011; (2) changing, from 31 May in the relevant year to 30 April in the relevant year, the date on which a subsidy claim must be sent to the Secretary of State; (3) making new provision for whether an authority is liable to a deduction from rent rebate subsidy payable for 201213; (4) with respect to authorities in England, revising the calculation so that the rent for a dwelling in an authority's Housing Revenue Account which is part of the Affordable Rent programme is not included (and so is not subject to the subsidy limitation on weekly rents); and (5) with respect to authorities in Wales, revising the specified amount and the guideline rent increase used when calculating deductions from subsidy.

The Income-related Benefits (Subsidy to Authorities) Amendment (No 2) Order 2013, SI 2013/2989 (in force on 28 January 2014), amends the 1998 Order above so as to (1) provide that certain overpayments that were made between 9 April 2012 and 19 April 2012 can be treated as departmental error overpayments rather than administrative delay overpayments; (2) set out new figures to be used in the calculation of subsidy for the year beginning on 1 April 2012; (3) provide that the subsidy in respect of council tax benefit will be nil on and after 1 April 2013 even if the claim relates to a period before that date; and (4) set out the specified amount 'O' and the guideline rent increase used when calculating deductions from subsidy.

2594 Benefits—industrial injuries—employment training schemes and courses

The Industrial Injuries Benefit (Employment Training Schemes and Courses) Regulations 2013, SI 2013/2540 (in force on 31 October 2013), (1) prescribe employment training schemes and courses for the purposes of the Social Security Contributions and Benefits Act 1992 s 95A; (2) clarify that an employer, within the meaning of s 95A(2), is any person providing a prescribed employment training scheme or course; (3) make provision for the payment of industrial injuries benefit to persons previously in receipt of payments under the Employment and Training Act 1973 s 11(3); and (4) provide for claims for payments under that provision which have been made but not yet determined to be treated as claims for industrial injuries benefit.

2595 Benefits—information-sharing

The Social Security (Information-sharing in relation to Welfare Services etc) (Amendment) Regulations 2013, SI 2013/41 (in force on 11 February 2013), amend the 2012 Regulations, SI 2012/1483, so as to prescribe additional purposes to allow for the sharing of relevant information for prescribed purposes relating to council tax.

The Social Security (Information-sharing in relation to Welfare Services etc) Amendment and Prescribed Bodies Regulations 2013, SI 2013/454 (in force on 1 April 2013), prescribe information-sharing permitted in relation to welfare services, council tax and social security benefits. In particular, the regulations prescribe Welsh bodies under the Welfare Reform Act 2012 s 131 and ensure that the Welsh Ministers are Welsh bodies for those purposes. The regulations also further amend the Social Security (Information-sharing in relation to Welfare Services etc) Regulations 2012, SI 2012/1483, so as to (1) permit the use and supply of information for purposes connected to a troubled families programme; (2) allow local authorities and social landlords to provide assistance to any person in receipt of a relevant social security benefit affected by the benefit cap or rules relating to under-occupation; (3) make provision relating to the use and supply of relevant information by the Department of Health and its service providers for purposes relating to the healthy start scheme and also to the use and supply of relevant information by qualifying persons for purposes relating to local welfare provision; (4) prescribe qualifying persons for the purposes of troubled families programmes, the healthy start scheme and local welfare provision; (5) make provision in relation to information supplied or held for purpose connected to offences relating to a council tax reduction; and (6) prescribe purposes for which relevant information must be held by a qualifying person in order for them to supply the Secretary of State or persons providing services to the Secretary of State for purposes relating to a relevant social security benefit.

2596 Benefits—loss of benefit—consequential amendments

The Social Security (Loss of Benefit) (Amendment) Regulations 2013, SI 2013/385 (in force in part on 1 April 2013, in part on 8 April 2013 and in part on 29 April 2013), further amend the 2001 Regulations, SI 2001/4022, so as to make provision as to how the loss of benefit regime will apply to universal credit. In particular, the regulations (1) deal with the appropriate start date for disqualification period for persons entitled to universal credit; (2) specify the amount of the reduction in universal credit; (3) set out entitlement to, and recoverability of, hardship payments where universal credit is reduced either by virtue of provision made by the regulations or sanctions under the Welfare Reform Act 2012 s 26 or 27; (4) specify what is to be the start date for the disqualification period where the offender is in receipt of a benefit which is payable neither wholly in advance nor in arrears; (5) prescribe the offences, conviction for which will result in a three year loss of benefit penalty; (6) make provision relating to the amount of reduction where an offender is in receipt of an income-related employment and support allowance; (7) update a reference to persons over the age of 16 in respect of whom child benefit is payable; (8) allow an income-related employment and support allowance to be payable to an offender or an offender's family member at a reduced rate where it would otherwise not be payable by operation of the Social Security Fraud Act 2001 if they would be entitled to hardship payment under the Employment and Support Allowance Regulations 2008, SI 2008/794; and (9) update the list of benefits which are not sanctionable to reflect the current references in armed forces pensions legislation.

2597 Benefits—offences—enforcement—persons required to provide information

The Social Security (Persons Required to Provide Information) Regulations 2013, SI 2013/1510 (in force on 1 October 2013), prescribe the following descriptions of persons, in addition to those listed in the Social Security Administration Act 1992 s 109B(2), (2A), from whom authorised officers may require certain information about the possible or actual commission of offences relating to social security benefits: (1) those who provide relevant childcare; (2) those to whom a person in receipt of universal credit is liable to make rent payments in respect of accommodation which he occupies, or purports to occupy, as his home where his award includes an amount in respect of such payments; (3) rent officers to the extent that the information required relates to their functions under the Housing Act 1996 s 122 (functions in relation to universal credit and housing benefit); and (4) local authorities which administer council tax reduction schemes to the extent that the information required relates to such a scheme. Relevant definitions are also provided.

2598 Benefits—overpayment—recovery

The Social Security (Overpayments and Recovery) Regulations 2013, SI 2013/384 (in force in part on 8 April 2013 and in part on 29 April 2013), make provision relating to recovery of amounts which are recoverable under social security legislation. Specifically, the regulations (1) prescribe that overpayment of universal credit, jobseeker's allowance and employment and support allowance under the Social Security Administration Act 1992 s 71ZB, subject to provision as to their calculation, and overpayments of tax credits under the Tax Credits Act 2002 are recoverable amounts for the purpose of the regulations; (2) make provision as to whom certain overpayments are recoverable from where it is necessary to recover from a person instead of, or in addition to, the person to whom it was paid; (3) make provision as to when overpayments made under an award will still be recoverable if there has been no revision or supersession of that award; (4) prevent duplication of payment of universal credit where income which would be taken into account in a universal credit claim is paid after the prescribed date for payment of that income; (5) make provision, where an overpayment of universal credit relates to the amount of a person's capital, for the amount of that overpayment to be reduced to take account of diminution in that capital; (6) allow for the recoverable amount of the benefits to be reduced to take account of any universal credit which should have been paid to the person concerned or their partner; (7) make provision relating to calculating the amount of an overpayment of housing costs in universal credit where a claimant changes dwelling; (8) allow recovery of recoverable amounts to take place by deduction from certain benefits; (9) prescribe limitations on such recovery; (10) make provision confirming when an obligation of a tenant is taken to have been discharged when recovery of an overpayment of housing costs has been obtained by deduction from a landlord's benefit; (11) allow, where a decision awarding benefit is reversed, varied, revised or superseded, for the offsetting of arrears of entitlement against subsequent payments of universal credit, jobseeker's allowance or employment and support allowance; (12) make provision for recovery of recoverable amounts by deduction from earnings; (13) prescribe what details a notice requiring the employee to make deductions from earnings must contain and when it takes effect; (14) specify the amounts to be deducted by the employer from the amount paid to the liable person each pay-day; (15) allow the employer to deduct a charge not exceeding £1 in respect of any administration costs; (16) require the employer to notify the liable person of the amount of the deduction including any deduction in respect of the employer's administrative costs; (17) provide that the employer must pay the amount of the deduction to the appropriate authority which sent the employer the notice by any of the specified methods; (18) require the employer to keep records of amounts deducted and of persons in respect of whom such deductions have been made; (19) specify that the liable person must inform the appropriate authority within seven days if they leave the employment of an employer who has received a notice in respect of them or when they become employed or re-employed; (20) require a person to notify the appropriate authority if a notice is received on the assumption that they are the employer of a liable person but it transpires that they are not or if they think the exemption applies to them; (21) require the employer to notify the appropriate authority if the liable person ceases to be in their employment; (22) allow the appropriate authority to vary notices to decrease or, if agreed, to increase amounts included in them or to substitute a new employer for a previous one and requires the employer to comply with the notice as varied; (23) provide for a notice to be discharged in certain circumstances if no further payments are due under it, it is ineffective as a means of recovery or it is defective; (24) allow for notices to lapse if the employer no longer has the liable person in their employment; (25) make provision relating to those in employment of the Crown; (26) make provision as to priority where employers are obliged to make deductions under more than one notice under the regulations; and (27) provide that it is a criminal offence to fail to comply with certain provisions. The regulations also further the Social Security (Payments on account, Overpayments and Recovery) Regulations 1988, SI 1988/664, to ensure that overpayments of benefits coming within the 1992 Act s 71 can be recovered by deduction from universal credit and personal independence payment and by deduction from earnings. The regulations also clarify the rules on what sums are deducted in calculating the amount of a recoverable overpayment, and further amend the Social Fund (Recovery by Deductions from Benefits) Regulations 1988, SI 1988/35, by adding universal credit to the list of benefits from which social fund awards may be recovered by deduction.

2599　Benefits—payments on account

The Social Security (Payments on Account of Benefit) Regulations 2013, SI 2013/383 (in force in part on 1 April 2013 and in part on 29 April 2013), make provision for the circumstances when payments on account of benefit may be made. Specifically, the regulations (1) specify that in certain circumstances payments on account of benefits can be made; (2) provide for payments to persons for the purpose of defraying intermittent expenses where those persons are in receipt of universal credit and have been receiving it or its predecessor benefits for a continuous period of at least six months; (3) prescribe that a person must satisfy certain conditions as to their earnings; (4) provide that a budgeting advance is payable only if there is no amount of budgeting advance outstanding and the Secretary of State is also satisfied that the budgeting advance can reasonably be expected to be recovered; (5) set out the maximum and minimum amount payable by way of a budgeting advance; (6) prescribe that capital over £1,000 is offset against the amount of a budgeting advance which would otherwise be awarded; and (7) make provision for budgeting advances. In addition, the regulations further amend the Social Security (Payments on account, Overpayments and Recovery) Regulations 1988, SI 1988/664, by revoking Pt 2 under which payments on account are currently made, subject to a saving provision consequent to which those provisions continue to apply for applications made before 29 April 2013 and to payments on account made pursuant to such applications. Consequential amendments are made to the Social Security and Child Support (Decisions and Appeals) Regulations 1999, SI 1999/991.

2600 Benefits—recovery—decisions and appeals

The Social Security, Child Support, Vaccine Damage and Other Payments (Decisions and Appeals) (Amendment) Regulations 2013, SI 2013/2380 (in force on 28 October 2013), further amend the Vaccine Damage Payments Regulations 1979, SI 1979/432, the Child Support (Maintenance Assessment Procedure) Regulations 1992, SI 1992/1813, the Social Security and Child Support (Decisions and Appeals) Regulations 1999, SI 1999/991, the Mesothelioma Lump Sum Payments (Claims and Reconsiderations) Regulations 2008, SI 2008/1595, and the Child Support Maintenance Calculation Regulations 2012, SI 2012/2677, so as to (1) provide that a right of appeal to the First-tier Tribunal against certain decisions relating to vaccine damage payments, child support, certificates of recoverable benefits, certificates of recoverable lump sum payments and mesothelioma claims only exist where an application for reversal, revision, review or reconsideration, as the case may be, of the decision has been considered by the Secretary of State; (2) enable the Secretary of State to treat a purported appeal as an application for reversal, revision, review or reconsideration; (3) require the Secretary of State to provide written statements of reasons for a decision to be provided on the request of any person seeking its reversal, review or reconsideration; (4) in relation to vaccine damage payments, allow an application for the reversal of a decision to be made at any time, rather than within six years of the date of notification of the decision; and (5) in relation to mesothelioma claims, enable the Secretary of State to extend the time limit for reconsideration of applications. The regulations also make various consequential amendments.

2601 Benefits—up-rating

The Social Security Benefits Up-rating Order 2013, SI 2013/574 (in force on various dates on and between 1 April 2013 and 11 April 2013), replaces the 2012 Order, SI 2012/780, and (1) alters the benefits and increases of benefits under the Social Security Contributions and Benefits Act 1992; (2) increases the rates and amounts of certain pensions and allowances under the 1992 Act; (3) increases, on account of increases in guaranteed minimum pensions, the sums payable as part of a Category A or Category B retirement pension under the Pension Schemes Act 1993; (4) specifies the dates from which the sums specified for rates or amounts of benefits under the 1992 Act or the 1993 Act are altered; (5) specifies earnings limits for child dependency increases; (6) increases the weekly rate of statutory sick pay, statutory maternity pay, ordinary and additional statutory paternity pay and statutory adoption pay; (7) increases the rate of graduated retirement benefit and disability living allowance; (8) increases, subject to an exception, the weekly rates of age addition to long-term incapacity benefit; (9) increases, subject to an exception, the weekly rates of transitional invalidity allowance; (10) increases the rates of widowed mother's allowance, widow's pension, widowed parent's allowance and bereavement allowance; (11) states the amount of sums relevant to the applicable amount for the purposes of income support, and sets out the personal allowances, premiums and other miscellaneous amounts; (12) provides for the percentage increase of sums payable by way of special transitional additions to income support; (13) states the sum by which any income support of a person involved in a trade dispute is reduced; (14) states the amount of the sums relevant to the applicable amount for the purposes of housing benefit, and sets out the personal allowances and premiums; (15) states the amount of the sums relevant to the applicable amount for the purposes of housing benefit for certain persons over the qualifying age for state pension credit, and sets out the personal allowances and premiums; (16) increases the age-related amounts for contribution-based jobseeker's allowance; (17) states the amount of sums relevant to the applicable amount for the purposes of income-based jobseeker's allowance, and sets out the personal allowances, premiums and other miscellaneous amounts; (18) states the sum by which any jobseeker's allowance of a person involved in a trade dispute is reduced; (19) specifies the amounts relevant to state pension credit; and (20) states the amount of sums relevant to the applicable amount for the purposes of employment and support allowance, and sets out the premiums and other miscellaneous amounts.

The Social Security Benefits Up-rating Regulations 2013, SI 2013/599 (in force on 8 April 2013), contain provisions in consequence of an order under the Social Security Administration Act 1992 ss 150 and 150A. Specifically, the regulations (1) provide that where a question has arisen about the effect of the Order 2013 above on a benefit already in payment, the altered rates will not apply until that question is determined by the Secretary of State, the First-tier Tribunal or the Upper Tribunal; (2) restrict the application of the increases specified in the 2013 Order in cases where the beneficiary is not ordinarily resident in Great Britain; (3) raise from £215 to £220, and from £28 to £29, the earnings limits for child dependency increases payable with a carer's allowance; and (4) increase from £23·25 to £23·50 the amount allowed for personal expenses for a person in accommodation for which benefit is paid to their accommodation provider. SI 2012/819 is revoked.

2602　Child support

See CHILDREN AND YOUNG PERSONS.

2603　Contributions—credits

The Social Security (Crediting and Treatment of Contributions, and National Insurance Numbers) (Amendment) Regulations 2013, SI 2013/3165 (in force on 6 April 2014), further amend the 2001 Regulations, SI 2001/769, so as to provide that Class 2 contributions collected through the Pay As You Earn tax code are to be treated as paid on 5 April of the tax year in which they are paid. The regulations also describe the circumstances in which contributions paid in this way satisfy the contribution conditions for the purpose of entitlement to contributory benefits.

2604　Contributions—general provisions

The Social Security (Contributions) (Amendment) Regulations 2013, SI 2013/718 (in force on 18 April 2013), further amend the 2001 Regulations, SI 2001/1004, so as to make provision to enable voluntary contributors who will reach pension age on or after 6 April 2016 to be able to take advantage of the extended time limits for paying voluntary contributions and the limit on the rates that apply to the payment of voluntary Class 2 and Class 3 National Insurance contributions.

The Social Security (Contributions) (Amendment No 2) Regulations 2013, SI 2013/1142 (in force on 10 June 2013), further amend the 2001 Regulations above so as to provide a disregard for (1) the fee and the renewal fee for the up-date service of the Disclosure and Barring Service where those fees are paid or reimbursed by an employer; and (2) the fee for criminal record certificates and enhanced criminal record certificates where an application is made at the same time as an application to the up-date service and the fee is paid or reimbursed by an employer.

The Social Security (Contributions) (Amendment No 3) Regulations 2013, SI 2013/1907 (in force on 1 September 2013), further amend the 2001 Regulations above in order to ensure that National Insurance contributions are payable on the amount treated as earnings for the purposes of income tax in relation to the receipt of shares as part of the new employee shareholder employment relationship. The regulations, in particular, (1) provide for certain payments to be disregarded in the calculation of earnings for the purposes of earnings-related contributions; (2) provide that there is no liability to National Insurance contributions in respect of the expenses of elected officials for travel within the United Kingdom; and (3) provide that there is no liability to National Insurance contributions in respect of the reimbursement of reasonable legal costs associated with obtaining the advice required to be able to enter into a proposed shareholder agreement.

The Social Security (Contributions) (Amendment No 4) Regulations 2013, SI 2013/2301 (in force on 6 October 2013), further amend the 2001 Regulations above so as to (1) require employers who employ no more than 49 employees and who are required to deliver specified real time information to the Revenue before making a payment of general earnings to deliver, during the period beginning on 6 October 2013 and ending on 5 April 2014, such information by the end of the tax month in which the payment is made; and (2) make it clear that such an employer which does not deliver the real time information to the Revenue until after 19 May following the tax year in question will be liable to a penalty from that date.

The Social Security (Contributions) (Amendment and Application of Schedule 38 to the Finance Act 2012) Regulations 2013, SI 2013/622 (in force in part on 6 April 2013 and in part on 6 April 2014), further amend the 2001 Regulations above in consequence of the simplified deduction scheme for personal employers being closed to new employers by virtue of amendments to the Income Tax (Pay As You Earn) Regulations 2003, SI 2003/2682. In particular, the regulations (1) make further provision in relation to the provision of real time information ('RTI') to the Commissioners for Her Majesty's Revenue and Customs on or before the making of a payment to an employee; (2) exclude certain employers from becoming RTI employers; (3) set out the information required where the employee is one whose earnings are below the lower earnings level; (4) make provision for exceptions from the requirement to report information on or before the making of a payment; (5) require the employer, in certain circumstances, to report the payment by the end of a period of seven days beginning with the day after the day on which the payment is made; (6) make provision for employers who make a specified payment of general earnings to deliver the information required as soon as practicable and no later than 14 days after the end of the tax month in which the payment is made; (7) require an employer who makes a notional payment to report the payment no later than 14 days after the end of the tax month in which the payment is made; (8) detail the information which an employer must provide when making a payment of general earnings by an approved method of electronic communication; (9) require a service provider who receives notification from the employer that the payment is one of general earnings to report the information that it holds to HRMC; (10) include in those who are not required to make a return those employers who the Commissioners are satisfied are unable to file using an approved method of electronic communications; (11) make provision for specified employers to file as non-RTI employers for the tax year 2013–14; (12) expand the information which an employer must provide when making a return to include details of information omitted from an earlier return; (13) make provision for the situation where an employer has failed to make a return of information; (14) require the employer to provide the information in the next return for the tax year in question; (15) provide that if the information has not been included in such a return before 20 April following the tax year to which the information relates, the employer is required to report the information before 20 May; (16) make provision for the Taxes Management Act 1970 s 98A to apply if the return is not made before 20 May following the end of the tax year to which the information relates; (17) provide that an employer who has not reported all the payments may be liable to a penalty for late filing; (18) make provision for an employer to notify the Commissioners that for a particular tax period the employer was not required to make any returns under RTI or that the employer has made the final return for the tax year and to notify the date of cessation of the scheme; (19) enable the Commissioners to seek security in respect of any amount due as a consequence of the rectification of an error or omission; (20) make provision for employees, in certain circumstances, to continue to submit paper returns for the tax year 2013–14; (21) set out the information which must be provided to the Commissioners by an employer when making a payment to an employee; (22) require any employer who has more than 250 employees on the day on which it becomes an RTI employer to provide certain information to the Commissioners at that time; (23) provide that the employer must provide the information specified in head (22) to the Commissioners with the information specified within one month of making the first return; (24) require a large employer to provide specified information before any return is made; (25) provide that an employer who is not a large employer may, but is not required, to provide the specified information; (26) remove the disregard from Class 1 National Insurance contributions on the first 15 pence per working day of a meal voucher provided by an employer to an employee; (27) ensure that redundant legislation is removed from the statute book; (28) extend the period of time in which to make voluntary contributions for contributors who, as a consequence of the unavailability of pension statements between the tax years 2013–14 and 2016–17, will not be in a position to make an informed decision regarding payment of voluntary contributions for the tax years 2006–07 to 2016–17 and who will reach pension age on or after 6 April 2017; (29) give effect to the extended time period for Class 3 contributions by allowing, subject to conditions, contributions to be paid between 6 April 2013 and 5 April 2023, and disapply the relevant higher rate provision; (30) give effect to the extended time period for voluntary Class 2 contributions by allowing, subject to conditions, contributions to be paid between 6 April 2013 and 5 April 2015, and disapply, until 5 April 2019, the relevant higher rate provision; (31) reflect a change to the reduced rates of primary Class 1 National Insurance contributions in respect of members of certain contracted-out pension schemes in relation to contributions paid with effect from the tax year 2012–13 and subsequent tax years; (32) provide for the return of National Insurance contributions paid in excess of the annual maximum prescribed; (33) reflect a change to the reduced rates of primary Class 1 National Insurance contributions in respect of members of certain contracted-out pension schemes from 10·4 per cent to 10·6 per cent; (34) provide for the computation of the amount of a person's Class 2 National Insurance contributions where it is paid in the tax year to which an Income Tax Pay As You Earn code ('PAYE') relates if the PAYE code was determined in order to effect recovery of the contributions that should have been paid in an earlier tax year; (35) allow certain payments to be disregarded in the calculation of earnings for the purpose of establishing liability for earnings-related National Insurance contributions; (36) provide that payments made under the Armed Forces Early Departure Scheme 2005, SI 2005/437, are disregarded when calculating a person's earnings for those purposes; and (37) provide for tax agents who engage in dishonest conduct to be subject to penalties and for officers of Revenue and Customs to obtain relevant documents from such agents.

2605   Contributions—migrant workers—applicable national law—self-employed persons

Council Regulation (EEC) 1408/71 art 13(2)(b) (on the application of social security schemes to employed persons, to self-employed persons and to members of their families moving within the Community) provides that, subject to specified provisions, a person who is self-employed in the territory of one member state is subject to the legislation of that state even if he resides in the territory of another member state. A person who is simultaneously employed in the territory of one member state and self-employed in the territory of another member state is subject in specified cases to the legislation of the member state in the territory of which he is engaged in paid employment and to the legislation of the member state in the territory of which he is self-employed: art 14c(b).

A company had its registered office in Belgium and was subject to Belgian corporation tax. Two directors each owned half of the company's capital. One of the directors lived in Portugal and was employed or in receipt of benefit there before becoming self-employed. The Belgian authorities served an order requiring payment of sums corresponding to contributions owed by the director for the period of his residence in Portugal. The company brought proceedings opposing the order. On a reference for a preliminary ruling, a question arose as to whether Regulation 1408/71 arts 13(2)(b), 14c(b), precluded national law that allowed a member state to presume irrebuttably that management from another member state of a company subject to tax in the first member state took place in the first member state. *Held*, arts 13(2)(b), 14c(b) precluded national law that allowed a member state to presume irrebuttably that management from another member state of a company subject to tax in the first member state took place in the first member state. The concept of the location of an activity had to be understood, in accordance with the primary meaning of the words used, as referring to the place where, in practical terms, the person concerned carried out the actions connected with that activity. By irrebuttably presuming that persons designated as agents of a company or association which was liable to pay Belgian corporation tax or the Belgian tax on non-residents pursued in Belgium a professional activity as self-employed persons, national law was liable to lead to a definition of the location of an activity that did not correspond to that understanding and was thus liable to be contrary to EU law.

Case C-137/11 *Partena ASBL v Les Tartes de Chaumont-Gistoux SA* [2013] 1 CMLR 395, [2012] All ER (D) 177 (Sep) (ECJ: Fourth Chamber).

2606   Contributions—national insurance—avoidance

The Revenue agreed that two group companies of an international investment bank would pay outstanding national insurance contributions of some of their employees on the basis that the Revenue would forego interest on the payment. The claimant, a campaigner against tax avoidance, applied for a declaration that the agreement infringed the Revenue's litigation and settlement policy as it was a package deal and did the opposite of encouraging taxpayers to behave positively and that, in approving the agreement, the Revenue's officers had taken account of immaterial considerations relating to potential embarrassment of the Chancellor of the Exchequer. The Revenue accepted that embarrassment to the Chancellor was an irrelevant consideration to have taken into account, but submitted that it was not a factor that had influenced its decision to enter into the agreement. *Held*, the agreement did not infringe the policy. The Revenue looked at each issue separately and a single payment undifferentiated as between different issues was not made. Interest and principal were treated as separate issues. In principle, if one of two decision-makers took account of an irrelevant matter, that would be sufficient to render the decision unlawful. Further, even where the irrelevant factor played a significant part in the decision-maker's thinking, the decision might exceptionally still be upheld if the court was satisfied that it was clear that, even without the irrelevant factor, the decision-maker would have reached the same conclusion. Applying established authority, both officers had to take into account only relevant considerations. However, the decision would have been the same even if one of them did not take account of potential embarrassment to the Chancellor. The officer concerned gave other independent and substantial reasons why the approval decision was taken. That those would, separately from the irrelevant consideration, have led to the same decision was supported by the fact that the other officer had reached her decision without regard to it. Further, it was not irrational for them to have taken into account damage to the Revenue's relationship with the companies, damage if the companies withdrew from the government's code of practice on taxation for banks and damage to the wider reputation of the Revenue. Accordingly, the application would be dismissed.

R (on the application of UK Uncut Legal Action Ltd) v Revenue and Customs Comrs [2013] EWHC 1283 (Admin), [2013] STC 2357 (Queen's Bench Division: Nicol J).

The National Insurance Contributions (Application of Part 7 of the Finance Act 2004) (Amendment) Regulations 2013, SI 2013/2600 (in force on 4 November 2013), amend the 2012 Regulations, SI 2012/1868, so as to introduce new disclosure obligations for promoters and users of national insurance contribution avoidance schemes by (1) requiring users to provide prescribed information to promoters within a prescribed period; and (2) empowering the Commissioners for Her Majesty's Revenue and Customs to require a promoter to provide further information where that promoter has provided a client list which is suspected of being incomplete. The regulations also provide that a promoter is not liable to pay a penalty for failure to disclose proposals or arrangements which relate to the period before the regulations come into force, but which become notifiable as a consequence of the regulations.

2607 Contributions—national insurance—employer's contributions—earnings-related contribution—payments to be disregarded—gratuities

The taxpayer company operated an employee benefit trust for the benefit of its employees. Consequent on the planned takeover of the taxpayer's corporate group, the trustees of the employee benefit trust decided to make cash payments to employees ('the payments'). Income tax was deducted from all those payments but no deduction was made in respect of primary and secondary Class 1 National Insurance contributions ('NICs'). The Commissioners for Her Majesty's Revenue and Customs decided that the taxpayer was liable to pay primary and secondary NICs in respect of those payments. That decision was reversed on appeal and the Commissioners appealed further. The issue was whether the payments had constituted gratuities under the Social Security (Contributions) Regulations 2001, SI 2001/1004, Sch 3 Pt X para 5, which provided for payments in respect of gratuities to be disregarded in the calculation of earnings for the purposes of earnings-related contributions. *Held*, it was well established that a gratuity meant a voluntary payment given in return for services rendered where the amount of the gratuity depended on the donor and where there was no obligation on the part of the donor to make the payment. A voluntary payment by a third party who had received an indirect benefit from the provision of the employee's services could not amount to a gratuity. The essence of a gratuity was that it was a token of thanks for the services provided directly and personally to the donor, and this was reinforced by the wording of Sch 3 Pt X para 5(2) and (3), which sought to implement the policy that the exemption should only apply in respect of payments designed to reward the recipient personally for that aspect of his services which constituted a personal service to the person making the payment. Any other payment that the employee received in the course of his employment should reasonably be characterised as earnings from his employment, akin to a bonus if it was voluntary rather than a contractual payment. Therefore, the payments had not been gratuities within Sch 3 Pt X para 5. Accordingly, the appeal would be allowed.

Knowledgepoint 360 Group Ltd v Revenue and Customs Comrs [2013] UKUT 007 (TCC), [2013] STC 1690 (Upper Tribunal: Judge Timothy Herrington and Judge John Walters). Channel 5 TV Group Ltd v Morehead (Inspector of Taxes) [2003] STC (SCD) 327 disapproved. Calvert (Inspector of Taxes) v Wainwright [1947] KB 526, [1947] 1 All ER 282; and Annabel's (Berkeley Square) Ltd v Revenue and Customs Comrs [2009] EWCA Civ 361, [2009] 4 All ER 55 (2009 Abr para 1358) considered. Decision of First-tier Tribunal [2011] UKFTT 438 (TC), [2011] SFTD 977 reversed.

2608   Contributions—national insurance—employer's contributions—employed earners—payments by way of salary

The Revenue determined that actors engaged by the appellant television company under certain types of contract were to be treated as 'employed earners' for National Insurance purposes and that, in consequence, the appellant was liable to secondary Class 1 National Insurance contributions in respect of the payments it made to the actors. Various contracts were of concern. The Equity Contracts contained a term which entitled the actor to receive attendance day payments as set out in an agreement between the appellant and Equity, the trade union for professional performers and creative practitioners, in the event that they were required to attend post-synchronisation sessions following the completion of filming. Other contracts known as 'PACT Contracts' expressly incorporated an agreement with the Producers Alliance for Cinema and Television, which included a right to production day payments at a fixed rate for each day worked beyond the first ('the daily rate clause'). One of the PACT contracts, the 'Bespoke Agreement', also included an entitlement to payment at either a daily or weekly rate in the event that principal photography was required beyond the agreed dates ('the extension clause'). The appellant appealed and the appeal was dismissed twice. The appellant appealed further. Held, in respect of the Social Security (Categorisation of Earners) Regulations 1978, SI 1978/1689 Sch 1 para 5A(d) when the draftsman used the words 'work has been performed' he was to be taken as having chosen them deliberately, and to have intended to convey a sense different from what Sch 1 para 5A(d) would or might have meant if he had instead used the words 'services. rendered'. He was identifying what he regarded as the key criterion for determining whether 'any payment' forming part of the total remuneration for the services rendered was salary. The focus was on 'work has been performed' in the ordinary sense of those words and the inquiry was as to whether any payment forming part of the total remuneration paid to the actor qualified under it. The condition in Sch 1 para 5A(d) would be satisfied if at least part of the payments to be made to the actor could be identified as computed by reference to the time for which work was to be done. In respect of the PACT Contracts, the daily rate clause clearly provided for the payment to the actor of a fee that included a reward at the fixed rate in respect of any production days worked. Viewed at the outset, that meant that the PACT contracts included an obligation by the appellant to make payments to the actor by way of salary. Further, the extension clause in the Bespoke Agreement provided for a payment by way of salary. It could be seen that the Bespoke Agreement contemplated that part of the remuneration in respect of the engagement for the production in question was an overage payment, which was clearly a payment by way of salary. In respect of the Equity Contracts, the actor's entitlement to a payment under the post-synchronisation clause amounted to a right to payment by way of salary. Accordingly, the appeal would be dismissed.

ITV Services Ltd v Revenue and Customs Comrs [2013] EWCA Civ 867, [2014] STC 325 (Court of Appeal: Sir James Munby P, Rimer LJ and Sir Stanley Burnton). Decision of Sales J [2012] UKUT 47 (TCC), [2012] STC 1213 affirmed.

2609   Contributions—national insurance—personal liability notice—meaning of 'neglect'

The respondent was the finance director of a company. After one year of trading the company had entered into administration. At the time of going into administration, the company had a liability in respect of National Insurance Contributions ('NIC'). Soon after, the company went into Creditors' Voluntary Liquidation. Subsequently, a personal liability notice was issued by the Revenue to the respondent in respect of the NIC. On appeal against the notice, the respondent submitted that his actions, at the time of the company's failure to pay NIC, had been affected by mental illness and that ought to be considered when assessing whether he was culpable. He sought to adduce medical evidence to substantiate that claim and its effects. The judge excluded the medical evidence as being irrelevant. Subsequently, the respondent caused the issue to be referred to a differently constituted First-tier Tribunal. After submissions on a preliminary issue as to the true meaning of the term 'neglect', the tribunal resolved the issue in favour of the respondent. It found that set in context and construing the Social Security Administration Act 1992 s 121C purposively and in a way which was compatible with the European Convention on Human Rights, 'neglect' imported a subjective standard and should be read as requiring proof that the relevant officer had acted knowingly and deliberately. It was also found that s 121C was penal in nature, and that the mens rea of the individual formed an essential ingredient of assessing liability under it. The proposed medical evidence from the respondent was ruled relevant and admissible. The Revenue appealed against that decision. *Held*, the anchor of the tribunal's approach was their characterisation of s 121C as being criminal for the purposes of the Human Rights Act 1998 and in any event essentially punitive, and was thereby attracting the common law presumption that mens rea was an essential ingredient of the offence. However, the characterisation of s 121C as 'criminal' for those purposes could not provide a reliable guide to the intention of the domestic legislature in choosing 'neglect' as an alternative basis on liability. The presumption could not be based on a characterisation of the provision as criminal for the purposes of the Convention art 6 if it would not be so characterised under domestic law. Further, given that under domestic law the provision would not be characterised as criminal, its depiction for the purposes of domestic law as 'punitive' or 'penal in nature' did not trigger the presumption. The question to be posed was whether there was any proper basis why 'neglect' should bear anything other than its ordinary meaning of an objectively tested departure from a standard of care. The most obvious possible indication that some subjective ingredient was required was the use of the word 'culpable' and the provision for apportionment of liability depending on the degree of 'culpability' of each other. However, the clear view was that that did not signify any different test than that ordinarily applied in establishing neglect, and that the provision for apportionment simply reflected the possibility that some officers might have had particularly relevant responsibilities, or been in a position to do more than others. Therefore, the word 'neglect' was to be given its usual objective meaning: it was a standard of conduct, not a subjective state of mind. Judgment would be given accordingly.

Revenue and Customs Comrs v O'Rorke [2013] UKUT 0499 (TCC), [2014] STC 279 (Upper Tribunal: Hildyard J).

2610 Contributions—primary and secondary Class 1 contributions—limits and thresholds

The Social Security (Contributions) (Limits and Thresholds) (Amendment) Regulations 2013, SI 2013/558 (in force on 6 April 2013), further amend the Social Security (Contributions) Regulations 2001, SI 2001/1004, so as to (1) specify the levels of the lower and upper earnings limits for primary Class 1 contributions and the primary and secondary thresholds for primary and secondary Class 1 contributions for the 2013–14 tax year; and (2) provide for equivalents of the upper earnings limit, primary threshold and secondary threshold where the earnings period is a month or a year.

2611 Contributions—re-rating

The Social Security (Contributions) (Re-rating) Consequential Amendment Regulations 2013, SI 2013/619 (in force on 6 April 2013), further amend the Social Security (Contributions) Regulations 2001, SI 2001/1004, by increasing, from £3·30 to £3·35, the special rate of any Class 2 contributions payable by share fishermen.

The Social Security (Contributions) (Re-rating) Order 2013, SI 2013/559 (in force on 6 April 2013), (1) increases (a) from £2·65 to £2·70, the rate of Class 2 contribution specified in the Social Security Contributions and Benefits Act 1992 s 11(1); (b) from £13·25 to £13·55, the rate of Class 3 contribution specified in s 13(1); (c) from £5,595 to £5,725, the amount of earnings, specified in s 11(4), below which an earner may be excepted from liability for Class 2 contributions; and (d) from £7,605 to £7,755, the lower limit of profits, specified in s 15, between which Class 4 contributions are payable at the main Class 4 percentage rate; and (2) decreases, from £42,475 to £41,450, the upper limit of profits, specified in s 18, between which Class 4 contributions are payable at the main Class 4 percentage rate.

2612   Council tax benefit—abolition—consequential provision

The Council Tax Benefit Abolition (Consequential Provision) Regulations 2013, SI 2013/458 (in force on 1 April 2013), amend various enactments as a consequence of the abolition of council tax benefit.

2613   Council tax benefit—abolition—transitional provisions—Wales

See para 1766.

2614   Disability living allowance—residence and presence conditions

The Social Security (Disability Living Allowance, Attendance Allowance and Carer's Allowance) (Amendment) Regulations 2013, SI 2013/389 (in force in part on 7 April 2013 and in part on 8 April 2013), further amend the Social Security (Invalid Care Allowance) Regulations 1976, SI 1976/409, the Social Security (Attendance Allowance) Regulations 1991, SI 1991/2740, and the Social Security (Disability Living Allowance) Regulations 1991, SI 1991/2890, so as to alter the residence and presence conditions for the disability benefits so that they align with the conditions that are being introduced for Personal Independence Payment and, in particular, (1) the test of ordinary residence is changed to habitual residence; (2) the past presence test is altered so that a period of presence in Great Britain of 104 out of the past 156 weeks is required before entitlement can be established to any of the disability benefits; (3) for Disability Living Allowance and Attendance Allowance, the temporary absence rule is reduced to 13 weeks and the rule for temporary absence for medical reasons is reduced to a maximum of 26 weeks; (4) for Disability Living Allowance and Attendance Allowance, serving members of the armed forces are treated as being habitually resident in Great Britain when they are serving and stationed abroad; and (5) include reference to the 'genuine and sufficient link' for those arriving in Great Britain from another EEA state or Switzerland or moving abroad to one of those states.

2615   Employment and support allowance—claims and payments

See para 2662.

2616   Employment and support allowance—decisions and appeals

See para 2664.

2617   Employment and support allowance—general provisions

The Employment and Support Allowance Regulations 2013, SI 2013/379 (in force on 29 April 2013), provide for a social security benefit to be known as an employment and support allowance, which replaces the existing benefit of the same name. Most claimants will be required to serve an assessment phase which will normally last for 13 weeks from the start of the claim. Once the assessment phase is complete and subject to satisfying the assessment of 'limited capability for work' claimants will move onto the main phase of the benefit. Specifically, the regulations (1) set out detailed provisions on when the assessment phase will end; (2) deal with conditions of entitlement; (3) deal with the determination of whether a claimant has limited capability for work; (4) provide for the circumstances in which a claimant is to be treated as having limited capability for work; (5) deal with the determination of whether a claimant has limited capability for work-related activity; (6) provide for the circumstances in which a claimant is to be treated as having limited capability for work-related activity; (7) provide for the circumstances in which the work a claimant does affects the claimant's entitlement; (8) make provision in relation to the claimant's responsibilities; (9) set out details on which requirements apply to which claimants, how those requirements are met and circumstances in which they do not apply;

(10) deal with the claimant's responsibilities where they are entitled to Universal Credit as well as an employment and support allowance; (11) make provision for accepting the claimant commitment which is usually a condition of entitlement; (12) make provision relating to the reduction of benefit where a claimant fails to meet their responsibilities without good reason; (13) specify the amounts of employment and support allowance which are payable; (14) deal with the calculation of a claimant's income and earnings; (15) provide that a claimant must wait a number of days at the start of a period of limited capability for work before becoming entitled to employment support allowance; (16) enable two periods of limited capability for work separated by not more than 12 weeks to be linked together; (17) provide for the circumstances in which a claimant may be disqualified from receiving an employment and support allowance; (18) make provision to deal with the situation where this would leave a person in hardship; and (19) enable the amount of employment and support allowance to be calculated where the claimant is entitled for a period of less than a week.

2618 Employment and support allowance—work capability assessment—mental health patients at a disadvantage

See R (on the application of MM) v Secretary of State for Work and Pensions, para 853.

2619 Guardian's allowance—up-rating

The Guardian's Allowance Up-rating Order 2013, SI 2013/716 (in force on 8 April 2013), (1) increases, from £15·55 to £15·90, the weekly rate of guardian's allowance prescribed by the Social Security Contributions and Benefits Act 1992 Sch 4 Pt 3 para 5; and (2) states that no change is made in relation to the rates of child benefit which were substituted in the Child Benefit (Rates) Regulations 2006, SI 2006/965, reg 2(1) by the Child Benefit Up-rating Order 2010, SI 2010/982.

The Guardian's Allowance Up-rating Regulations 2013, SI 2013/746 (in force on 8 April 2013), which supersede the Guardian's Allowance Up-rating Regulations 2012, SI 2012/845, (1) provide that where a question has arisen about the effect of the 2013 Order above on a guardian's allowance already in payment, the altered rates will not apply until that question is determined by the Commissioners for Her Majesty's Revenue and Customs, an appeal tribunal or a Commissioner; and (2) apply certain provisions of the Social Security Benefits (Persons Abroad) Order 1975, SI 1975/563, so as to restrict the application of the specified increases in cases where the beneficiary lives abroad.

2620 Housing benefit—benefit cap

The Benefit Cap (Housing Benefit) (Amendment) Regulations 2013, SI 2013/546 (in force on 15 April 2013), amend the 2012 Regulations, SI 2012/2994, so as to (1) provide that where the welfare benefit is housing benefit, the local authority will use the amount of nil in any case where the dwelling is exempt accommodation within the meaning of the Housing Benefit and Council Tax Benefit (Consequential Provisions) Regulations 2006, SI 2006/217, Sch 3 para 4(10); and (2) exempt a claimant who is receiving universal credit from the benefit cap in housing benefit.

2621 Housing benefit—calculation—appropriate maximum benefit—statutory changes—lawfulness

The Social Security Contributions and Benefits Act 1992 s 130A(3) provides that regulations may provide for the appropriate maximum housing benefit ('AMHB') to be ascertained in the prescribed manner by reference to rent officer determinations. A rent officer determination is a determination made by a rent officer in the exercise of functions under the Housing Act 1996 s 122: 1992 Act s 130A(7).

Pursuant to the Rent Officers (Housing Benefit Functions) Order 1997, SI 1997/1984, the levels of rent charged in each broad rental market area were ascertained by rent officers. The median result so ascertained was used to set the local housing allowance. The local housing allowance so determined constituted the AMHB, on the basis of which housing benefit for private sector tenants was calculated. The Housing Rent Officers (Housing Benefit Functions) (Amendment) Order 2012, SI 2012/646, amended the 1997 Order by capping the AMHB by reference to the consumer price index. The claimant organisation was concerned that rental inflation would rise faster than the general inflation indicated in the consumer price index and that some tenants would therefore be forced to move to more deprived areas. It brought judicial review proceedings challenging the lawfulness of the 2012 Regulations, submitting that they were ultra vires the enabling power in the Housing Act 1996 s 122(1). In particular, it submitted that (1) the reference in the 1992 Act s 130A(3) to a rent officer determination meant an expert decision of a rent officer about rents based on actual evidence of market rents, rather than a mechanical exercise based on a price index; and (2) a person was not entitled to receive housing benefit unless there was an AMHB in his case. The application was dismissed, and, on the claimant's appeal, *held*, the Secretary of State had to be entitled to specify the functions which he required rent officers to carry out in connection with housing benefit under the 1997 Order in such a way as to enable him to achieve what he regarded as the right balance. When rent officers were making expert determinations, fixing fair rents for private sector tenants, there was no such balance to be struck. There were, therefore, sound reasons why the functions which might be specified in an order made under the 1996 Act s 122 were not limited to functions within the established expertise of rent officers in respect of fair rent determinations. While rent officers did have an expertise, their office was a creature of statute and their functions were defined by statute. With regard to the claimant's second submission, while the regulations had to prescribe the manner in which the AMHB was to be determined, they did not have to reinvent the wheel. They could provide for the AMHB to be ascertained in the prescribed manner, by reference to rent officer determinations. If that was done, there would be no need to repeat in detail in the regulations the manner in which rent officers were required to make their determinations, because, subject to the claimant's first submission, the 1992 Act s 130A(7) defined a rent officer determination as a determination made by a rent officer in the exercise of functions under the 1996 Act s 122. By specifying the functions that rent officers were required to carry out in connection with housing benefit, the 1997 Order set out the manner in which rent officer determinations had to be made. Parliament had expressly authorised the regulations to prescribe the manner in which AMHB was to be determined by reference to rent officer determinations, and the manner in which rent officers had to make their determinations was set out in an order which was subject to Parliamentary scrutiny. Accordingly, the appeal would be dismissed.

R (on the application of Zacchaeus 2000 Trust) v Secretary of State for Work and Pensions [2013] EWCA Civ 1202, [2013] All ER (D) 284 (Oct) (Court of Appeal: Maurice Kay VP, Sullivan and Ryder LJJ). Decision of Underhill J [2013] EWHC 233 (Admin), [2013] All ER (D) 186 (Feb) affirmed.

**2622		Housing benefit—disability discrimination—additional requirements of disabled person**

See *R (on the application of MA) v Secretary of State for Work and Pensions*, para 858.

**2623		Housing benefit—discretionary financial assistance**

The Welfare Reform Act 2012 (Consequential Amendments) Regulations 2013, SI 2013/1139 (in force on 10 June 2013), further amend the Discretionary Financial Assistance Regulations 2001, SI 2001/1167, so as to (1) enable local authorities to make discretionary housing payments to persons entitled to universal credit that include an amount in respect of housing costs relating to rent, and limit the monthly amount of such payments to the amount of housing costs included in the calculation of universal credit; and (2) enable discretionary housing payments to be made where persons are entitled to universal credit that has not been calculated that include amounts in respect of housing costs because the person is in exempt accommodation, and limit the monthly amount of such payments to the aggregate of the payments the person is liable to make that would otherwise be eligible to be met by way of universal credit.

**2624		Housing benefit—general provisions**

The Housing Benefit (Amendment) Regulations 2013, SI 2013/665 (in force on 1 April 2013), further amend the 2006 Regulations, SI 2006/213, so as to (1) insert definitions of 'member of the armed forces away on operations' and 'qualifying parent or carer'; (2) ensure that an additional bedroom will be included in the determination where the claimant or their partner is a qualifying parent or carer; (3) ensure that a member of the armed forces away on operations will continue to be included as an occupier when assessing the number of rooms for which housing benefit may be paid; (4) make provision for the determination of the amount of rent eligible to be met by way of housing benefit for claimants renting in the private sector to whom the local housing allowance applies; (5) ensure that a referral to a rent officer will be made if a claimant or their partner becomes, or ceases to be, a qualifying parent or carer; (6) provide that a non-dependent deduction will not be made in respect of a member of the armed forces away on operation; and (7) ensure that a case if not referral to a rent officer for a new determination where the only change has been that the claimant's non-dependent has become, or ceased to be, a member of the armed forces away on operations. Similar amendments are made to the Housing Benefit (Persons who have attained the qualifying age for state pension credit) Regulations 2006, SI 2006/214.

See para 2665.

2625   Housing benefit—rent officers—functions

The Rent Officers (Universal Credit Functions) Order 2013, SI 2013/382 (in force on 29 April 2013), confers functions on rent officers in connection with universal credit. In particular, the order (1) confers functions relating to the determination of local housing allowances, which will be used in calculating the amount of a person's housing costs for universal credit where the landlord is not a registered provider of social housing, registered social landlord or local authority; (2) requires that the rent officer determines broad rental market areas; (3) specifies that the rent officer determines local housing allowances each year for each broad rental market area; (4) makes transitional provisions to establish broad rental market areas and local housing allowances from 29 April 2013 until 1 April 2014; (5) provides that the rent officer must determine the level of reasonable payments in accordance with specified provisions; (6) makes provision for redetermination of broad rental market area determinations and local housing allowance determinations where the rent officer has made an error; (7) provides for the redetermination of housing payment determinations where the rent officer made an error, used inaccurate information, or where the Secretary of State has requested a redetermination; (8) makes provision for circumstances where the rent officer under the order has received incomplete or inaccurate information; and (9) makes provision for any notice given by a rent officer to be given by electronic means, unless the Secretary of State requests that it is given in writing.

The Rent Officers (Housing Benefit Functions) Amendment Order 2013, SI 2013/666 (in force on 1 April 2013), further amends the 1997 Order, SI 1997/1984, so as to require a rent officer to include an additional bedroom where the local authority making an application for a determination states that the tenant or the tenant's partner is a qualifying parent or carer within the meaning of the Housing Benefit Regulations 2006, SI 2006/213.

The Rent Officers (Housing Benefit Functions) Amendment (No 2) Order 2013, SI 2013/2827 (in force on 4 December 2013), further amends the 1997 Order above so as to require a rent officer, provided certain conditions are satisfied, to allow an additional bedroom for a child who would normally be expected to share a room under the size criteria but is unable to do so because of their disability.

The Rent Officers (Housing Benefit and Universal Credit Functions) (Local Housing Allowance Amendments) Order 2013, SI 2013/2978 (in force on 13 January 2014), (1) further amends the 1997 Order above, and amends the principal 2013 Order above so as to provide (a) for the calculation of local housing allowance rate; (b) that the rate will be determined differently depending on the category of dwelling for which the rate is being determined and the broad rental market area in which the dwelling is situated; and (c) that the determinations made by the rent officers will be based on the list of market rents payable in the 12-month period ending on the preceding 30 September; and (2) amends the principal 2013 Order above by changing the date that the local housing allowance determinations and broad rental market area determinations take effect.

2626   Housing benefit—size criteria

The Housing Benefit and Universal Credit (Size Criteria) (Miscellaneous Amendments) Regulations 2013, SI 2013/2828 (in force on 4 December 2013), further amend the Housing Benefit Regulations 2006, SI 2006/213, and the Housing Benefit (Persons who have attained the qualifying age for state pension credit) Regulations 2006, SI 2006/214, so as to (1) define a 'child who cannot share a bedroom' as being a child who is entitled to the care component of disability living allowance at the highest or middle rate and is, by reason of their disability, not reasonably able to share a bedroom with another child; (2) in relation to SI 2006/213 only, provide that a person who is a qualifying parent or carer is not a young individual and is not subject to the shared accommodation rate when calculating the amount of rent eligible to be met by housing benefit for claimants in the private sector; (3) in relation to SI 2006/213 only, ensure that (a) where one of the occupiers of a dwelling rented in the social sector is a child who cannot share a bedroom, a bedroom is allowed under the size criteria applicable; and (b) when determining whether such a dwelling is under-occupied for the purposes of applying a reduction, a room is included where a joint tenant, or a joint tenant's partner, requires overnight care or is a qualifying parent or carer; (4) ensure that, where one of the occupiers of a dwelling rented in the private sector by a claimant to whom the local housing allowance applies is a child who cannot share a bedroom, a bedroom is allowed under the size criteria applicable; and (5) require a referral to a rent officer to be made if a child becomes, or ceases to be, a child who cannot share a bedroom. The regulations also further amend the Universal Credit Regulations 2013, SI 2013/376 (see para 2665), in order to (a) ensure that only children for whom a renter is responsible are treated as part of the extended benefit unit and allocated a room under the size criteria; (b) clarify that only non-dependants who normally live with a renter can be allocated a room under the size criteria; and (c) allow for an additional room to be allocated for a child who is a member of the renter's extended benefit unit and would usually have to share a room, where that child is entitled to the care component of disability living allowance at the highest or middle rate and is, by reason of their disability, not reasonably able to share a room with another child.

2627　Income support—deductions—fines

The Fines, Council Tax and Community Charges (Deductions from Universal Credit and Other Benefits) Regulations 2013, SI 2013/612 (in force on 29 April 2013), further amend (1) the Fines (Deductions from Income Support) Regulations 1992, SI 1992/2182, so as to (a) add universal credit to the list of benefits from which deductions can be made to recover both fines and amounts payable under compensation orders; (b) ensure that such deductions are to be made when after the deduction, there will remain at least one penny of universal credit in payment; (c) specify that the amount of deduction is to be a minimum of five per cent of the appropriate universal credit standard allowance for the relevant assessment period up to a maximum deduction of £108·35; (d) make provision as to the circumstances when such deductions can made by the Secretary of State, the timing of such deductions, when they are to cease and for rounding of the five per cent figure; (e) alter the rate of deduction where the offender is entitled to contribution-based jobseeker's allowance or contributory employment and support allowance from one-third of the relevant age-related amount to 40 per cent; (f) make provision excluding from the scope of head (e) above persons in respect of whom applications to recover fines by deductions are received by the Secretary of State before 29 April 2013; and (g) remove the relevant rounding rule which is no longer necessary; (2) the Council Tax (Deductions from Income Support) Regulations 1993, SI 1993/494, by making amendments corresponding to those set out under head (1) above; and (3) the Community Charges (Deductions from Income Support) (No 2) Regulations 1990, SI 1990/545, by adding universal credit to the list of benefits from which community charges may be recovered by deduction.

2628　Income support—general provisions

The Social Security (Miscellaneous Amendments) Regulations 2013, SI 2013/443 (in force in part on 2 April 2013, in part on 8 April 2013 and in part on 29 April 2013), further amend the Income Support (General) Regulations 1987, SI 1987/1967, so as to (1) ensure that certain types of payment will not be taken into account when calculating housing costs for all income-related benefits; (2) provide that certain payments made by local government, for welfare purposes and/or to assist with council tax liability, should be disregarded when assessing the claimants income and/or capital when assessing eligibility; (3) disregard liable relative payment for rent in respect of a claimant's dwelling made directly to a third party and for which housing benefit is payable; and (4) disregard the new local welfare payments,

non-dependent of the claimant include the situation where the non-dependent is aged less than 25 and is entitled to universal credit on the basis that the non-dependent does not have any earned income as defined in the principal 2013 Regulations above. The regulations also further amend the principal 2013 Regulations and the Jobseeker's Allowance Regulations 2013, SI 2013/378, so as to provide for an extra category of claimant who can claim universal credit as a single person when his partner is not eligible to claim and make provision for the period of a hardship payment where an award has been reduced for a sanctionable failure. In relation to child support, the regulations further amends (i) the Child Support (Maintenance Assessment and Special Cases) Regulations 1992, SI 1992/1815, so as to provide that, where a parent with care or absent parent is awarded universal credit on the basis that he has no earned income he will be treated as having 'no assessable income' for the purposes of a maintenance assessment; (ii) the Child Support (Maintenance Calculations and Special Cases) Regulations 2000, SI 2000/155, and the Child Support Maintenance Calculation Regulations 2012, SI 2012/2677, so as to provide that where a non-resident parent or his partner is awarded universal credit on the basis that the non-resident parent has no 'earned income', then he will be liable to pay the flat rate of maintenance unless the conditions for payment of the nil rate of maintenance apply, and the latter conditions include a reference to the situation where a non-resident parent or his partner is awarded universal credit; (iii) the Employment Protection (Recoupment of Jobseeker's Allowance and Income Support) Regulations 1996, SI 1996/2349, so as to provide for the recoupment of an award of universal credit where the award was paid for a period in respect of which an employment tribunal has made an order, where the award would not have been paid if the person's earnings had not been reduced or stopped; (iv) the Housing Renewal Grants Regulations 1996, SI 1996/2890, so as to provide that, in relation to a 'relevant person' with respect to whom an application for a housing renewal grant is made, where the person or his partner, with certain exceptions, is entitled to universal credit, then he is to be regarded as having no income, and as having an 'applicable amount' of £1, with the result that there will be no reduction in grant with respect to that person; (v) the Rent Repayment Orders (Supplementary Provision) Regulations 2007, SI 2007/572, so as to provide for the tribunal to be able to alter the amount of a rent repayment order where an award of universal credit which included the housing element with respect to occupation of part of the house in question has been altered in a material way; and (vi) the Social Security (Credits) Regulations 1975, SI 1975/556, so as to provide that a person entitled to universal credit will be credited with a Class 3 National Insurance contribution.

The Universal Credit (Miscellaneous Amendments) Regulations 2013, SI 2013/803 (in force on 29 April 2013), amend the principal 2013 Regulations above and the Universal Credit (Transitional Provisions) Regulations 2013, SI 2013/386, above so as to set out changes to the size criteria that are applied in the calculation of the housing costs element. In particular, the regulations provide that certain foster parents, as well as adopters who have a child placed with them prior to adoption, will be entitled to one extra bedroom for the purposes of the size criteria assessment and that any person who is the child or step-child of a renter or joint renters and usually lives with them, but is in the armed forces and away on operations will continue to be treated as part of the household during any such period of absence, and no housing costs contribution will be deducted in relation to that person during any such absence. In addition, the regulations specify additional requirements which must be met in order for a person to claim universal credit during the first phase of the introduction of universal credit. A person may not make such a claim if a person who lives in his household is a member of the armed forces who is away from home in connection with that role, and a person is also excluded from making a claim if he is a foster parent.

The Universal Credit (Transitional Provisions) and Housing Benefit (Amendment) Regulations 2013, SI 2013/2070 (in force on 28 October 2013), further amend (1) the principal 2013 Regulations above so as to (a) allow for claimants to be entitled to both universal credit and housing benefit, where the housing benefit is paid in respect of exempt accommodation; (b) enable universal credit to be claimed by persons who have a current account with a credit union; (c) provide that a person who has claimed universal credit, but is not entitled to it for the first assessment period because of the level of their earned income, may become entitled without a further claim if their income falls during the following six months; and (d) remove the temporary exemption for universal credit claimants from the application of the benefit cap, in relation to any assessment period starting on or after the commencement date; (2) the Housing Benefit Regulations 2006, SI 2006/213, so as to allow for circumstances in which a claimant or their partner is in receipt of universal credit and housing benefit at the same time; and (3) the Housing Benefit (Persons who have attained the qualifying age for state pension credit) Regulations 2006, SI 2006/214, so as to ensure that SI 2006/213 applies, rather than SI 2006/214, where a universal credit claimant also receives housing benefit to cover some or all of their housing costs.

2666   Universal credit—size criteria
See para 2626.

2667   Welfare Benefits Up-rating Act 2013
The Welfare Benefits Up-rating Act 2013 makes provision relating to the up-rating of certain social security benefits and tax credits. The Act received the royal assent on 26 March 2013 and s 3 came into force on that day. The remaining provisions came into force on 1 October 2013: SI 2013/2317.

Section 1 requires the Secretary of State, in the 2013–14 and 2014–15 tax years, to make an order by statutory instrument increasing each of the relevant sums by one per cent. In those tax years, the Treasury must make an order by statutory instrument increasing each of the relevant amounts by one per cent: s 2. Section 3 deals with short title, interpretation, commencement and extent.

2668   Welfare Reform Act 2012—commencement
The Welfare Reform Act 2012 (Commencement No 7) Order 2013, SI 2013/178, brings s 120 into force, for certain purposes, on 1 February 2013 and, for remaining purposes, on 6 April 2013.

The Welfare Reform Act 2012 (Commencement No 8 and Savings and Transitional Provisions) Order 2013, SI 2013/358, brings into force (1) on 25 February 2013, ss 2(2), 4(2), (3), (5)–(7), 7(2), (3), 9(2), (3), 10(2)–(5), 11(3)–(5), 12(3), (4), 15(2), (3), 17(3)(f), 19(2)(d), (3), (4), 24(1), (5), (6), 25, 26(6)–(8), 27(4), (5), (9), 28, 32, 37(3)–(7), 39(3)(a), 40, 42, 43, 49(6), 54(6), 57(6), 78(3), (4), 79(3), (4), (7), 80, 81, 85, 86, 92–94, 98–100, 102(2)–(5), 104, Sch 1 paras 1, 3–5, 7, Sch 2 paras 5–7, 26, 36, 46, 48, 56, 58 (in part), 59 (in part), 61 (in part), 63 (in part), Sch 6 paras 1(1), (2)(b), 3(1)(a)–(c), 4(1)(a), 5(1), (2)(c), (d), (3)(a), 6, Sch 9 paras 9, 26, 40, 42, Sch 10; (2) for certain purposes, on 25 February 2013, ss 5, 6(1)(a), (3), 8(3), 12(1), 14(5), 17(4), (5), 18(3), (5), 20(1), 22(2), 26(2)(a), 49(3), 57(2), 77(3), 83(3), 87, 95, 101(1), 102(6), 118(5), (8)(b), Sch 2 paras 2–4, 23, 31–34, 43, 45, 47, 49, 55, Sch 9 paras 32, 39, 41, Sch 11 paras 1–11, 15–18; (3) on 1 April 2013, ss 33(1)(e), 101(2), 117(2), 118 (so far as not already in force), 119, Sch 2 paras 51, 57, 58(2), 59(2), 62, Sch 3 paras 5 (in part), 15–18 (in part), Sch 14 Pts 1 (in part), 11 (in part); (4) on 6 April 2013, s 117 (so far as not already in force); (5) for certain purposes, on 8 April 2013, ss 77, 78(1), (2), (5), (6), 79(1), (2), (5), (6), 82, 83, 84, 87–89, 95, Sch 9 paras 1–3, 5–25, 27–50; and (6) on 29 April 2013, s 105(1) (so far as not already in force), (3), (5), (6), (7) (in part), Sch 2 para 9, Sch 14 Pt 11 (in part). Transitional provisions and savings are also made.

The Welfare Reform Act 2012 (Commencement No 9 and Transitional and Transitory Provisions and Commencement No 8 and Savings and Transitional Provisions (Amendment)) Order 2013, SI 2013/983, brings into force, on 29 April 2013, ss 29, 31 (in part), 35 (in part), 37(1), (2), (8), (9), 38, 39(1), (2), (3)(b), (c), 102(6) (in part) and, so far as they are not already in force, Sch 2 paras 1, 2, 3 (in part), 4, 8, 10–23, 25, 27–35, 37–45, 47, 49, 50(1) (in part), (2), 52–55, 65, Sch 5 para 1 and Sch 11 paras 1–11, 15–18. Transitional and transitory provisions are also made. The Welfare Reform Act 2012 (Commencement No 8 and Savings and Transitional Provisions) Order 2013, SI 2013/358, is amended.

The Welfare Reform Act 2012 (Commencement No 10) Order 2013, SI 2013/1250, brings s 110 into force on 17 June 2013, for regulation-making purposes, and on 1 October 2013, for all other purposes.

The Welfare Reform Act 2012 (Commencement No 11 and Transitional and Transitory Provisions and Commencement No 9 and Transitional and Transitory Provisions (Amendment)) Order 2013, SI 2013/1511, commences, by reference to certain cases, provisions of the Welfare Reform Act 2012 that relate to universal credit and the abolition of income-related employment and support allowance and income-based jobseeker's allowance. Certain transitional provisions in the Welfare Reform Act 2012 (Commencement No 9 and Transitional and Transitory Provisions and Commencement No 8 and Savings and Transitional Provisions (Amendment)) Order 2013, SI 2013/983, are amended.

The Welfare Reform Act 2012 (Commencement No 12) Order 2013, SI 2013/2534, brings s 66 into force, so far as it is not already in force, on 31 October 2013.

The Welfare Reform Act 2012 (Commencement No 13 and Transitional and Transitory Provisions) Order 2013, SI 2013/2657, brings into force, by reference to certain cases, provisions of the Welfare Reform Act 2012 that relate to universal credit and the abolition of income-related employment and support allowance and income-based jobseeker's allowance. A transitional provision in the Welfare Reform Act 2012 (Commencement No 9 and Transitional and Transitory Provisions and Commencement No 8 and Savings and Transitional Provisions (Amendment)) Order 2013, SI 2013/983, is also amended.

The Welfare Reform Act 2012 (Commencement No 14 and Transitional and Transitory Provisions) Order 2013, SI 2013/2846, brings into force, by reference to certain cases, provisions of the Welfare Reform Act 2012 that relate to universal credit and the abolition of income-related employment and support allowance and income-based jobseeker's allowance.

For a summary of the Act, see 2012 Abr para 2406. See also the commencement of statutes table in the title STATUTES AND LEGISLATIVE PROCESS.

2669 Working tax credit—entitlement and maximum rate

The Working Tax Credit (Entitlement and Maximum Rate) (Amendment) Regulations 2013, SI 2013/1736 (in force on 5 August 2013), further amend the 2002 Regulations, SI 2002/2005, so as to (1) provide that where council tax benefit was payable to a person or their partner on 31 March 2013 and the applicable amount of the person entitled to the benefit included a disability premium solely on account of the non-working partner's incapacity, that partner is defined as incapacitated for the purposes of the child care element; (2) ensure that claimants whose entitlement to working tax credit and/or the child care element of working tax credit depended solely on an award of council tax benefit containing a disability premium as part of the applicable amount will continue to be entitled to working tax credit and/or the child care element of working tax credit despite council tax benefit having been abolished; and (3) provide that should claimants cease to be entitled to working tax credit on or after 1 April 2013, they will not be able to rely on the fact that one of them was receiving council tax benefit which included a disability premium on 31 March 2013 if they make a new claim.

WILLS AND INTESTACY

Halsbury's Laws of England (5th edn) vol 102 (2010) paras 1–564, vol 103 (2010) paras 565–1304

Articles

For articles relating to this title please refer to the Table of Articles at the beginning of the Abridgment.

2670 Administration of estates—control of administration—receiver—appointment by court

See *Joint Stock Co 'Aeroflot Russian Airlines' v Berezovsky*, para 2134.

2671 Administration of estates—disclosure and inspection of documents—application by receivers

Following the death of a wealthy Russian businessman, his daughter applied to be appointed as administratrix of the estate. The claimant company served a claim under CPR Pt 8 opposing the application on the grounds that the daughter was unsuitable for the position and the estate was insolvent. In the event, the daughter was appointed as administratrix in relation to some matters. The receivers then applied for an order that they be granted letters of administration ad colligenda bona in respect of the estate, but only for the purposes of allowing them to take possession of all files relating to the affairs of the deceased provided earlier or retained by a number of different persons. The daughter applied for directions from the court that she be permitted to inspect, copy and use, for the purposes of fulfilling her obligations pursuant to the limit of the grant, all the information and/or documents held by the receivers, both at the date of the order, which might be held or received by them, and future times, relating to the estate. The daughter submitted that she expected to make *Beddoes* applications in relation to the defence of the litigation where the estate and others were defendants, and required the disclosure sought to do so. She contended that it was well established that an applicant for *Beddoes* relief had to be candid, and give full and frank disclosure of the strengths and weaknesses of the claim, and that full and frank disclosure of the asset position of the estate was required. *Held*, there would be difficulties in the court making an order as sought by the receivers. There would be expenses involved. The receivers would be obliged, on behalf of the estate, to pay the costs of third parties, that were difficult to ascertain. It was far from clear that the further information which might come into the possession of the receivers would add any significant information to that being put forward at the present time. The court was not satisfied that it was appropriate any longer to pursue the matter raised by the receivers for the purposes for which the information would be used. The way ahead might not be worth pursuing and the costs would appear to be undesirable, unless the benefit justified it, as to which the court was not convinced. It followed that the receivers' application would be adjourned with liberty to restore it. Regarding the daughter's application, if she was not the administratrix because the estate was insolvent, then she would not make a *Beddoes* application and would have no concern about her duties in such an event. If she remained or was appointed administratrix in all respects, she would be able to explain to the court that the question of solvency had been gone into and the court, on a CPR Pt 8 claim, would have taken a certain view and her obligation to give full and frank disclosure would be dealt with in that way. In other words, some of the difficulties which she suggested she would be under in connection with a *Beddoes* claim would disappear or be radically changed by the outcome of the CPR Pt 8 claim becoming relevant. In those circumstances, common sense suggested that the CPR Pt 8 claim ought to go forward to determination before the litigation against the estate was pursued. No order would therefore be made on the daughter's application. Judgment would be given accordingly.

Aeroflot v Berezovsky [2013] EWHC 4348 (Ch), [2014] All ER (D) 166 (Jan) (Chancery Division: Morgan J).

2672   Preparation of will—negligence—liability of solicitor

The claimant was the step-granddaughter of the testatrix. The defendant firm of solicitors had acted for the testatrix in relation to her wills. The claimant was not a beneficiary under earlier wills. The claimant had telephoned a solicitor with the defendant firm, in order to discuss the testatrix's affairs. The testatrix was almost 90 years old and possibly suffering from dementia. There followed a series of telephone calls. The claimant subsequently wrote to the solicitor enclosing a typed copy of what she understood to be the testatrix's instructions, which had been signed by the testatrix. The draft provided that the claimant would receive the remainder of the estate following the payment of two legacies to the testatrix's cousin and a friend. Under the terms of the previous will, the cousin and friend would have each received half of the residuary estate. The solicitor wrote to the testatrix's doctor requesting that he see the testatrix and provide a written report as to whether she had testamentary capacity. The doctor stated that he could find no medical or mental health reason why the testatrix could not make decisions about her will and any changes she wished to make. After a delay, the testatrix asked the claimant herself to prepare a new will for her. The claimant attempted to persuade the testatrix to use a solicitor but she refused and signed a will which had been prepared by the claimant. The will was witnessed by two individuals. Under the new will, the testatrix left her residuary estate to the claimant. After the testatrix's death the cousin and the friend sought to challenge the will. The proceedings were settled, the claimant having made additional payments to the cousin and friend. The claimant brought a solicitors' negligence action against the firm. *Held*, (1) in the circumstances, it had been reasonably foreseeable that if the solicitor failed to carry out his instructions for the testatrix, the claimant would suffer loss. The claimant was entitled to maintain an action in negligence against the firm in establishing breach of duty of care. (2) On the evidence, the testatrix had been, in general, a lady of sound mind in the period from when she had instructed the solicitor until the time when she had signed the new will. The doctor had been instructed to report as a medical practitioner in circumstances where he had expressly been put on notice as to the concern the testatrix was suffering from dementia. His report had been unequivocal. The two individuals who had witnessed the signing of the will both recalled the testatrix as being alert and in control of her mental facilities. The claimant's evidence demonstrated not merely an affection for the testatrix but also a recognition that the testatrix had had, to the end, clear and firm views. The directions given to the claimant on by the testatrix had been precise and detailed and had been repeated in the lead up to the signing of the new will. Further, it was striking that not one of the individuals who had seen the testatrix in that period had doubted her mental capacity. (3) On the evidence, the solicitor had taken on the responsibility for sorting out, and satisfying himself, of the capacity issue. It followed that, having undertaken the issue as part of his brief, it had been the solicitor's obligation to resolve the capacity issue with reasonable expedition. However, it was entirely inadequate for a solicitor instructed by a 90 year old client to alter her will to take the view that, because he was concerned that she might be being taking advantage of by the potential beneficiary under the new will, and because she had not mentioned the will to him when they had spoken on the phone, he would take the matter no further unless she raised it again. Five weeks had passed between the solicitor instructing the doctor and receiving his report. That had been far too long. Case law recognised that where a solicitor was instructed by an elderly client to change a will, and accepted those instructions, he had to act promptly. Further, if the solicitor had drafted the amended will as instructed, there would have been no real prospect of a challenge. The testatrix's decision to ask the claimant to prepare the will rather than the solicitor had reflected the fact that the solicitor had done nothing. Accordingly, the claim would be granted.

Feltham v Bouskell [2013] EWHC 1952 (Ch), [2013] WTLR 1363, [2013] All ER (D) 172 (Jul) (Chancery Division: Charles Hollander QC). *Carr-Glynn v Frearsons (a firm)* [1998] 4 All ER 225, CA (1998 Abr para 3333), considered.

2673   Presumption of Death Act 2013

See para 2138.

2674   Probate—non-contentious probate—fees

The Non-Contentious Probate Fees (Amendment) Order 2013, SI 2013/1408 (in force on 1 July 2013), further amends the 2004 Order, SI 2004/3120, so as to increase the fee for copies of any document which are made available on a computer disk or in other electronic form from £4 to £6 for each copy.

2675   Will—attestation—validity—presumption of due execution of will

The claimant was the only daughter of the testator. The testator had four siblings, who were the third to fourth defendants. The first and second defendants were the testator's first cousins. The third and fourth defendants, at first, refused to acknowledge that the claimant was the testator's daughter. The testator learned that he had terminal cancer and the siblings drafted a will for him, although certain requirements remained uncompleted. The testator was admitted to hospital, during which time he was visited by the siblings and the cousins and a will was executed. The will was written on a stationer's will form and contained a standard form attestation clause. The circumstances surrounding the execution of the will formed the dispute between the claimant and the defendants. Under the will, its beneficiaries were the claimant and the third and fourth defendants. The first and second defendants were nominated as executors of the will. The claimant's case was that the testator's intentions had always been that he would die intestate so that the claimant would inherit his entire estate. The claimant's case was fourfold, namely that there was a lack of execution, lack of capacity, lack of knowledge and approval, and undue influence. *Held*, (1) the disputed will was written on a stationer's will form and contained a standard form attestation clause. It had a signature which purported to be that of the testator, and it professed to be witnessed by the first and second defendants, neither of whom were a beneficiary. From the evidence, the first and second defendants were present on the day that the will was executed. On the balance of probabilities, the testator had executed the will in accordance with the Wills Act 1837 s 9. (2) On the balance of probabilities, the testator had been capable of understanding that he had been making a will. (3) It was settled law that an assertion that the testator did not know and approve of the will required the court, before admitting it to proof, to be satisfied that the testator understood what he was doing and its effect so that the document represented his testamentary intentions. The burden lay on the propounder to show that the testator knew and approved of the will in that sense, and, as a matter of common sense and authority, the fact that a will had been properly executed, after being prepared by a solicitor and read over to the testator, raised a very strong presumption that it represented the testator's intentions at the relevant time. Accordingly, the party challenging the will had to produce evidence of circumstances which aroused the suspicion of the court as to whether the usual strong inference arising from the manner of the signature might be properly drawn. In the present case, the will had not been drawn up by a solicitor, and had instead been encouraged and drawn up by members of the family who stood to benefit under it. However, the law did not require a testator to be shown to have had knowledge and approval of every effect and consequence of the will. (4) The execution of a will as a result of undue influence had to be proved by those who asserted that influence. They had to establish that there was coercion, pressure that had overpowered the freedom of action of the testator without having convinced his mind. If the evidence established only persuasion, then a case of undue influence would not be made out. In the present case, there was plenty of evidence that the third and fourth defendants had had the opportunity to influence the testator in the making of the will, and indeed that they had done so. However, there was no evidence of coercion or pressure so as to have overpowered the testator's freedom of action. Therefore, an order would be made to pronounce in favour of the will in solemn form. Accordingly, the claim would be dismissed.

Re Devillebichot; Brennan v Prior [2013] EWHC 2867 (Ch), [2013] WTLR 1701, [2013] All ER (D) 243 (Sep) (Chancery Division: Mark Herbert QC).

2676   Will—testamentary intentions—rectification—clerical error

Shortly before the deceased's death, she had made a new will. The claimant was one of two executors named in the will and was also a beneficiary of it. The first to fifteenth defendants were individual beneficiaries, the family members, and the sixteenth to nineteenth defendants were charities also named as beneficiaries. The will provided for specific money legacies for all of the beneficiaries with the residue to be divided equally amongst 'such of the beneficiaries ... as shall survive [the deceased] in equal shares'. The deceased's solicitor considered that the deceased's intention had been for the residue to be distributed only among the family members, and further considered that the will as drafted effected that intention. The charities considered, and the family members agreed, that the wording of the will meant that the residue was to be distributed amongst all of the beneficiaries, including the charities. The claimant applied for rectification of the will to provide for the residue to be distributed only among the family members. The issues that fell to be determined, pursuant to the Administration of Justice Act 1982 s 20(1), were (1) the deceased's intentions with regard to the dispositions in respect of which rectification was sought; and (2) whether the will was expressed as it was in consequence of either (a) clerical error; or (b) a failure on the part of someone to whom the testator had given instructions in connection with his will to understand those instructions. *Held,* the distinction between clerical errors and mistakes which were not inadvertent was firmly established and s 20(1)(a) did not extend to errors that were made which were not per incuriam in the sense that they had not resulted from the draftsman having failed to advert to the significance of or effect of the words used in his draft. Taking the evidence as a whole, it was, in combination, sufficiently convincing that the intention of the deceased in preparing her will had been that the residuary estate would be divided among the family members and not among all of the beneficiaries including the charities. However, the evidence of the solicitor had been that he had believed that the will, as drafted, gave effect to the deceased's intentions and he still held that belief. Therefore, the claim for rectification had to fail. Accordingly, the application would be dismissed.

Kell v Jones [2013] WTLR 507, [2013] All ER (D) 153 (Jan) (Chancery Division: Judge Cooke). *Wordingham v Royal Exchange Trust Co Ltd* [1992] Ch 412, [1992] 3 All ER 204

(1991 Abr para 2601); and *Re Segelman* [1995] 3 All ER 676 (1995 Abr para 3084) applied. *Re Morris, Lloyds Bank Ltd v Peake* [1970] 1 All ER 1057 considered.

EUROPEAN UNION

Halsbury's Laws of England (4th edn) vols 51 and 52

Articles

For articles relating to this title please refer to the Table of Articles at the beginning of the Abridgment.

THE UNION

2677 Actions—annulment—Commission decision—construction of underground gas storage facility—obligation to provide access—applicable procedural and substantive law

The applicant company filed an application with the Czech Ministry of Industry and Trade for authorisation to build an underground gas storage facility. It further applied for a temporary exemption from the obligation to provide negotiated third party access for the entire new capacity of the facility. The Ministry authorised the construction of the facility and temporarily exempted the applicant from the obligation to provide negotiated third party access for 90 per cent of the capacity of the facility for 15 years. The decision was notified to the European Commission and the Commission asked the Ministry for additional information and indicated that, if the Commission were to ask the Ministry to amend or withdraw the decision, it would do so by a specified date. After the specified date, the Commission applied European Parliament and Council Directive (EC) 2009/73 art 36 and ordered the Czech Republic to withdraw the decision. The applicant brought proceedings, contending that the General Court of the European Union should annul the Commission's decision on the basis that there were errors in the determination of the applicable procedural and substantive law. It submitted that the Commission should have applied the procedure and substantive criteria laid down in European Parliament and Council Directive (EC) 2003/55 art 22 and not that laid down in Directive 2009/73 art 36, which had subsequently replaced Directive 2003/55 art 22. *Held*, procedural rules were generally held to apply to all proceedings pending at the time when they entered into force, whereas substantive rules were usually interpreted as not applying to situations existing before their entry into force. However, an exception to that principle had been allowed where the legislation contained both procedural and substantive rules which formed an indivisible whole, and the individual provisions of which might not be considered in isolation with regard to the time at which they took effect. In such circumstances, the entirety of the provisions at issue might not be accorded retroactive effect unless sufficiently clear indications led to such a conclusion. The procedural and substantive changes introduced by Directive 2009/73 art 36 formed an indivisible whole, with the result that the entirety of those provisions might not be accorded retroactive effect unless sufficiently clear indications led to such a conclusion. Such indications were not present. In particular, although Directive 2009/73 specified the date from which the rules it laid down applied, it contained no rules for the treatment of procedures pending at the time of its entry into force capable of justifying a derogation from the applicable principle. Consequently, it was the rules of Directive 2003/55 which applied in regard to both the substance and procedure and the Commission's decision would be annulled.

Case T-465/11 *Globula SA v European Commission* [2013] All ER (D) 90 (Sep) (EGC: Fourth Chamber). Case C-251/00 *Ilumitronica – Iluminacao e Electronica Ld v Chefe da Divisao de Procedimentos Aduaneiros e Fiscais/Direccao das Alfandegas de Lisboa* [2002] All ER (D) 210 (Nov), ECJ; and Case T-25/04 *Gonzalez y Diez SA v European Commission* [2007] All ER (D) 66 (Sep), CFI, adopted.

Directive 2003/55 replaced: European Parliament and Council Directive (EC) 2009/73.

2678   Actions—annulment—Council decision—restrictive measures against named individuals—manifest error of assessment

The Council of the European Union, in condemnation of the violent repression of peaceful protests in various locations across Syria, adopted Decision 2011/273, concerning restrictive measures against Syria. The names of the persons responsible for the violent repression against the civilian population in Syria and of the persons associated with them were listed in the annex to Decision 2011/273. The applicant, an officer of the Syrian General Intelligence Directorate, was included in the list. He applied for the annulment of Council Implementing Decision 2011/302, implementing Decision 2011/273. The applicant alleged (1) breach of the rights of defence, the right to a fair hearing and to effective judicial protection; (2) breach of the obligation to state reasons; (3) a manifest error of assessment; and (4) breach of the principle of proportionality, the right to property and the right to respect for private life. In respect of the first issue, the applicant contended that he had had sanctions imposed on him without his having previously been heard, having the opportunity to defend himself or having any knowledge of the basis on which the measures at issue had been taken. He further contended that the Council had failed to comply with its obligation to notify him of its decision. *Held*, due to the precautionary nature and the purpose of the asset freezing measures, their adoption could not be the subject of a preliminary hearing of the persons concerned without thereby running the risk of jeopardizing the effectiveness of those measures and, consequently, of the objective pursued by the European Union. In accordance with the case-law concerning the rights of defence, the European Union authorities could not be required to communicate those grounds before the name of a person or entity was entered on the list imposing restrictive measures. It was apparent that the applicant had been enabled to defend himself effectively against the contested measures following their publication in the official journal since he had brought an action before the court within the prescribed period. With regard to the second issue, it was settled law that the purpose of the obligation to state the reasons on which an act adversely affecting an individual was based, which was a corollary of the principle of respect for the rights of defence, was, first, to provide the person concerned with sufficient information to make it possible to ascertain whether the act was well founded or whether it was vitiated by a defect which might permit its legality to be contested before the European Union Courts and, second, to enable those Courts to review the legality of that act. The plea alleging breach of the obligation to state reasons was rejected. The applicant, as an officer of the General Intelligence Directorate, had full knowledge of the general and specific context in which the measures relating to him had been adopted. The implementation of Decision 2011/302 complied with the rules of the case law and the applicant had not provided any material evidence to justify a finding that the Council had committed a manifest error of assessment in including him in the list. Finally, it was settled law that the fundamental rights to property and private and family life did not enjoy, under European Union law, absolute protection, but had to be viewed in relation to their function in society. Consequently, the exercise of those rights might be restricted, provided that those restrictions corresponded to objectives of public interest pursued by the European Union and did not constitute, in relation to the aim pursued, a disproportionate and intolerable interference, impairing the very substance of the rights thus guaranteed. Accordingly, the application would be dismissed.

Case T-383/11 *Makhlouf v Council of the European Union* [2013] All ER (D) 128 (Sep) (EGC: Sixth Chamber). Case C-417/11 *Council for the European Union v Bamba* (*French Republic and European Commission, intervening*) [2013] 1 CMLR 1434, ECJ; Case C-402/05P; Case C-415/05P *Kadi* (*Spain, interveners*) *Al Barakaat International Foundation v EU Council* [2009] AC 1225, [2010] All ER (EC) 1105, ECJ (2009 Abr para 2982); Case C-199/99P *Corus UK Ltd v European Commission* [2003] All ER (D) 36 (Oct), ECJ; Case C-84/95 *Bosphorus Hava Yollari Turzim Ticaret AS v Minister for Transport, Energy and Communications, Ireland* [1996] 3 CMLR 257, ECJ; and Case T-299/08 *Elf Aquitaine SA v European Commission*, EGC, considered.

2679   Elections—European Parliamentary elections—general

See para 987.

2680   European Union (Approvals) Act 2013

The European Union (Approvals) Act 2013 makes provision approving for the purposes of the European Union Act 2011 s 8 certain draft decisions under the Treaty on the

Functioning of the European Union art 352, and to make provision approving for the purposes of the European Union Act 2011 s 7(3) a draft decision under the Treaty on European Union art 17(5) about the number of members of the European Commission. The Act received the royal assent on 28 February 2013 and came into force on that day.

The 2013 Act s 1 approves Council Regulation (EU) 10222/5/11 and the Multiannual Framework for the European Union Agency for Fundamental Rights for 2013–2017 10449/12. The 2013 Act s 2 approves that the number of members of the European Commission should continue to be equal to the number of member states. Section 3 deals with extent, commencement and short title.

THE COURT OF JUSTICE

2681   General Court—Rules of Procedure—time limits

The first applicant was a European economic interest grouping which represented the interests of companies that were producers and/or importers of polyelectrolytes, polyacrylamide and/or other polymers containing acrylamide. The second applicant was one of its member companies. The Kingdom of the Netherlands (an intervener at first instance in the present proceedings) had submitted to the respondent agency a dossier which it had drawn up concerning the identification of acrylamide as a substance that fulfilled the criteria set out in European Parliament and Council Regulation (EC) 1907/2006 (concerning the registration, evaluation, authorisation and restriction of chemicals), art 57(a), (b). The respondent, following the procedure set out in art 59, identified acrylamide as fulfilling the criteria set out in art 57 and included it on the candidate list of substances ('the contested decision'). Subsequently, the respondent published the candidate list of substances, including acrylamide, on its website. The applicants sought annulment of the contested decision. The respondent and European Commission contended that the applicants had failed to observe the time limit for bringing the action pursuant to TFEU art 263. An extra period of ten days was to be provided for on account of distance in accordance with the Rules of Procedure of the General Court art 102(2). The applicants contended that, under art 102(1), the period for lodging an appeal was to be calculated from the end of the fourteenth day following the date of publication of the contested decision, with the result that the time limit had been complied with. The General Court held that art 102(1) applied only to measures published in the Official Journal of the European Union whereas, under Regulation 1907/2006 art 59(10), the candidate list of substances was to be published on the agency's website and no other form of publication was provided for. The General Court found that the applicants had failed to observe the time-limit for bringing an action in accordance with TFEU art 263 and their application was dismissed as inadmissible. The applicants appealed. *Held*, it was not apparent from the wording of the Rules of Procedure art 102(1) that TFEU art 263 applied only to measures published in the Official Journal. It could not be ruled out that art 102(1) applied to a measure which was published only on the internet. In so far as the wording of the article could give rise to doubts, it was necessary, in the absence of any imperative reasons to the contrary, to favour an interpretation which did not result in the interested parties' being time-barred and therefore depriving them of the right to resort to legal proceedings. It was established that, where the wording of a provision was unclear, account had to be taken of the context of that provision and of the objectives which it pursued. The objective of the 14-day time limit laid down in art 102(1) was to ensure that interested parties had sufficient time within which to bring an action against published measures and, consequently, to observe the right to effective judicial protection. The reference in the article to the Official Journal might be explained by the fact that a publication in the Official Journal was the only form of publication envisaged at the time the Rules of Procedure were adopted. The General Court had erred in law in having found that art 102(1) applied only to measures published in the Official Journal and, consequently, having declared the action brought by the applicants as inadmissible. Accordingly, the order of the General Court would be set aside and the matter would be referred back to the General Court for final judgment.

Case C-625/11 P *Polyelectrolyte Producers Group GEIE v European Chemicals Agency* [2014] 1 WLR 158, [2013] All ER (D) 11 (Oct) (ECJ: Fourth Chamber). Case C-149/11 *Leno Merken BV v Hagelkruis Beheer BV* [2013] IP & T 295, ECJ, considered.

EXTERNAL RELATIONS

2682　Agreements with third countries—applicability of jurisprudence concerning relations between member states—Turkey—freedom to provide services

In the course of a dispute relating to an application by a Turkish national for a visa to visit Germany, a German court referred a question to the European Court of Justice as to whether passive services fell within the scope of the concept of freedom to provide services within the meaning of that phrase in the additional protocol to the Association Agreement between the EEC and Turkey 1963 art 41(1). The court considered the meaning of 'freedom to provide services' within the Treaty Establishing the EEC art 59, which corresponded to the TFEU art 56, and *Luisi v Ministero del Tesoro*. Held, *Luisi* established that the freedom to provide services conferred by the EEC Treaty art 59 on member state nationals and, thus, on the EU citizens, included passive freedom to provide services, which was the freedom for recipients of services to go to another member state in order to receive a service there without being hindered by restrictions. However, in deciding whether a provision of EU law lent itself to application by analogy under an association agreement, a comparison had to be made between the objective pursued by that association agreement and the context of which it formed a part, on the one hand, and those of the EU law instrument in question on the other. There were differences between the association agreement and the additional protocol on the one hand, and the TFEU on the other, on account of the link that existed between freedom to provide services and freedom of movement for persons within the EU. First, the association agreement and the additional protocol were intended to promote the economic development of Turkey. By contrast, under EU law, protection of passive freedom to provide services was based on the objective of establishing an internal market, conceived as an area without internal borders, by removing all obstacles to the establishment of such a market. It was precisely that objective which distinguished the TFEU from the association agreement, which pursued an essentially economic purpose. Secondly, there was nothing to indicate that the contracting parties to the association agreement and the additional protocol had envisaged, when signing those documents, freedom of provision of services as including passive freedom of provision of services. It followed that the court's interpretation of the EEC Treaty art 59, and correspondingly TFEU art 56, could not be extended to the standstill clause in the additional protocol art 41(1). Accordingly, 'freedom to provide services' in art 41(1) could not be interpreted as encompassing freedom for Turkish nationals who were the recipients of services to visit a member state in order to obtain services.

Case C-221/11 *Demirkan v Bundesrepublik Deutschland* [2013] All ER (D) 237 (Sep) (ECJ: Grand Chamber). Cases 286/82, 26, 83 *Luisi v Ministero del Tesoro* [1984] CMLR 52, ECJ (1985 Abr para 3081), considered.

STATE AIDS AND REGIONAL POLICY

2683　State aids—selective measures—subsidies and tax incentives—social housing

See Cases C-197/11 and C-203/11 *Libert v Gouvernement Flamand; All Projects & Developments NV v Vlaamse Regering*, para 2690.

ENVIRONMENT AND CONSUMERS
See ENVIRONMENTAL QUALITY AND PUBLIC HEALTH; CONSUMER PROTECTION.

CUSTOMS UNION AND FREE MOVEMENT OF GOODS
See CUSTOMS AND EXCISE.

AGRICULTURE
See AGRICULTURAL PRODUCTION AND MARKETING.

FREEDOM OF MOVEMENT FOR WORKERS

2684　European Union (Croatian Accession and Irish Protocol) Act 2013
See para 469.

2685   Free movement of persons—border control—local border traffic permit—multiple visits

See Case C-254/11 *Szabolcs-Szatmar-Bereg Megyei Rendorkapitanysag Zahony Hatarrendeszeti Kirendeltsege v Oskar Shomodi*, para 2244.

2686   Free movement of persons—head of member state—entry to another member state—restrictions on entry

The president of Hungary was invited to Slovakia to take part in a ceremony commemorating the first king of Hungary. The Slovak government prohibited the president from entering its territory, citing restrictions in European Parliament and Council Directive 2004/38 on the right of EU citizens to enter a member state for reasons of public policy, public security and public health. The European Commission found that TFEU art 21 and Directive 2004/38, under which EU citizens had the right to move and reside freely within the territory of the member states, did not apply to visits made by the head of one member state to the territory of another member state. Hungary challenged the prohibition. *Held*, it was well established that citizenship of the EU was intended to be the fundamental status of nationals of the member states. However, EU law had to be interpreted in the light of the relevant rules of international law. The status of head of state had a specific character, resulting from the fact that it was governed by international law, with the consequence that the conduct of such a person internationally, such as that person's presence in another state, came under that law, in particular the law governing diplomatic relations. Such a specific character was capable of distinguishing the person who enjoyed that status from all other EU citizens, with the result that the person's access to the territory of another member state was not governed by the same conditions as those applicable to other citizens. Therefore, the fact that an EU citizen performed the duties of a head of state justified a limitation, based on international law, on the exercise of free movement conferred on that person by art 21. Since the president was of Hungarian nationality, he unquestionably enjoyed the status of a citizen of the EU. However, as he was performing the duties of a head of state, neither art 21 nor Directive 2004/38 obliged Slovakia to guarantee him access to its territory. Accordingly, the action would be dismissed.

Case C-364/10 *Hungary v Slovak Republic* [2013] 1 CMLR 651, [2012] All ER (D) 174 (Oct) (ECJ: Grand Chamber).

2687   Free movement of persons—migrant workers—social security—application for unemployment benefits in country of last employment

The respondent was a Swedish national who was employed in Norway. During his last employment, he lived in Norway during work periods and travelled back to Sweden during off-duty periods. He returned to live in Sweden after becoming unemployed. His claim for unemployment benefits in Norway was rejected on the grounds that he no longer lived in Norway and that he had failed to meet the conditions for such benefits under national law. The respondent appealed against the rejection. In the meantime, he was granted unemployment benefits in Sweden, which was lower than that of which he would have received from Norway. The rejection was subsequently annulled on the ground that the requirement that he actually live in Norway was incompatible with Council Regulation (EC) 1408/71 art 71. The Norwegian state appealed. The appellate court sought an opinion from the EFTA Court. *Held*, art 71 precluded a national law pursuant to which entitlement to unemployment benefits was conditional on actual presence in the EEA state concerned. Although EEA states retained the power to organise the conditions of affiliation to their social security schemes, when exercising that power they were required to comply with EEA law, in particular the freedom to provide services and the freedom of movement for workers.

Case E-3/12 *The Norwegian State v Jonsson* [2013] 3 CMLR 236 (EFTA Court). Cases E-11/07 and E-1/08 *Rindal v Norway* [2009] 3 CMLR 32; and Case E-3/04 *Athanasios v Norway* [2005] 1 CMLR 29, EFTA Ct, followed.

2688   Free movement of persons—migrant workers—third-country national—parent of child residing in different member state to child

The applicant was a Japanese national who had married a German national in the United States. They had a daughter who was born in the United States. The family moved to Germany, and the applicant obtained a residence permit for family reunion in accordance with German law. The applicant subsequently secured a full-time job in Germany, and the following year his wife took up employment in Austria. The year after that, the parties separated but did not divorce. The couple exercised joint parental responsibility for their daughter, even though the mother and daughter had taken up habitual residence in Austria. Following the departure of his family, the applicant lost his autonomous right of residence. When his residence permit expired, the applicant applied for an extension on the ground that he was a family member of a European Union citizen. The application was rejected, and the applicant's appeal to a regional court was dismissed. On his further appeal, the court decided to stay the proceedings and refer to the European Court of Justice for a preliminary ruling the question of whether EU law gave a parent who had parental responsibility and was a third-country national, for the purpose of maintaining regular personal relations and direct parental contact, a right to remain in the member state of origin of his child who was an EU citizen if the child moved from there to another member state in exercise of the right of freedom of movement. Consideration was given to Council Directive (EC) 2003/109 (concerning the status of third-country nationals who were long-term residents), European Parliament and Council Directive (EC) 2004/38 (on the right of citizens of the EU and their family members to move and reside freely within the territory of the member states), and TFEU arts 20 and 21, which established the right to move and reside freely within the territory of the member states. *Held*, Directive 2003/109 applied to third-country nationals residing legally in the territory of a member state. In accordance with art 4(1), member states were required to grant long-term resident status to those nationals who, under national law, had resided legally and continuously within their territory for five years immediately prior to the submission of the relevant application. Although in principle the applicant might be granted the status of long-term resident within the meaning of Directive 2003/109, the fact that he had withdrawn his application for a long-term residence permit precluded him from obtaining such a permit. With regard to Directive 2004/38, the applicant could not be regarded as a family member of his daughter within the meaning of art 2(2) and so qualify for protection. Although he could be regarded as a family member of his spouse within the meaning of art 2(2), he could not be classed as a beneficiary, since art 3(1) required that the family member of the EU citizen moving to or residing in a member state other than that of which he was a national should accompany or join him. It followed that the right of a third-country national who was a family member of an EU citizen who had exercised his right of freedom of movement to install himself with that EU citizen pursuant to Directive 2004/38 could be relied on only in the host member state in which that citizen resided. Moreover, TFEU arts 20 and 21 did not confer any autonomous right on third-country nationals. Like the rights conferred by Directive 2004/38 on third-country nationals who were family members of an EU citizen who was a beneficiary, any rights conferred on third-country nationals by the Treaty provisions on EU citizenship were not autonomous rights of those nationals but rights derived from the exercise of freedom of movement by an EU citizen. It followed that, outside the situations governed by Directive 2004/38 and where there was no other connection with the provisions on citizenship of EU law, a third-country national could not claim a right of residence derived from an EU citizen.

Case C-40/11 *Iida v Stadt Ulm* [2013] Fam 121, [2012] All ER (D) 204 (Nov) (ECJ: Third Chamber).

2689   Free movement of persons—restriction—exclusion on public security grounds

See Case C-300/11 *ZZ (France) v Secretary of State for the Home Department*, para 1435.

2690   Free movement of persons—restrictions on right to purchase or rent residential property—social housing policy—requirement for persons to have 'sufficient connection' with local area

Flemish legislation restricted the right of sale, purchase and letting of residential property in specified communes by persons who did not have a 'sufficient connection' with the commune in question. The purpose of the legislation was to protect less affluent population groups from becoming excluded from the local property market. Flemish legislation also imposed a 'social obligation' on developers, requiring them to take steps to ensure the delivery of a supply of social housing. The legislation also gave various tax incentives and subsidies for private undertakings which discharged the social obligation. The legislation was challenged in two sets of proceedings. Issues arose as to the compatibility of the legislation with the rights of free movement and residence of persons and workers under European Parliament and Council Directive (EC) 2004/38 arts 22, 24 and TFEU arts 21, 45, the right of establishment under art 49, the freedom to provide services under art 56 and the free movement of capital under art 63. Those proceedings were stayed and a number of questions were referred for a preliminary ruling, including (1) whether Directive 2004/38 arts 22, 24 and TFEU arts 21, 45, 49, 56 and 63 precluded legislation which restricted the sale or letting of residential property to persons with a sufficient connection with the area; (2) whether art 63 precluded legislation under which a social obligation was imposed on developers; and (3) whether the tax incentives and subsidies afforded to certain undertakings which fulfilled a social obligation amounted to a state aid within the meaning of art 107, requiring notification to the European Commission. *Held*, (1) social housing policy could constitute an overriding reason in the public interest for justifying restrictions, such as those provided for by the Flemish legislation, where those restrictions were a necessary and appropriate measure to attain the objectives pursued by the social housing policy. However, the 'sufficient connection' requirement in the Flemish legislation applied equally to both those who were less affluent and those with no need of social protection on the property market. It followed that the conditions went beyond what was necessary to attain the objective pursued. Therefore, arts 21, 45, 49, 56 and 63 and Directive 2004/38 arts 22, 24 precluded legislation which made the transfer of immovable property in the target communes subject to the existence of a 'sufficient connection' between the prospective buyer or tenant and those communes. (2) TFEU art 63 did not, however, preclude legislation which imposed a social obligation on housing developers in so far as that legislation was necessary and appropriate to attain the objective of guaranteeing sufficient housing for the low-income or otherwise disadvantaged sections of the local population. (3) The tax incentives and subsidy mechanisms were liable to be classified as state aid within the meaning of art 107(1). In determining whether such measures would be so classified the national court would have to determine whether the conditions relating to the existence of state aid were met and, if so, to ascertain whether it was exempt from notification pursuant to Commission Decision (EC) 2005/842.

Cases C-197/11 and C-203/11 *Libert v Gouvernement Flamand; All Projects & Developments NV v Vlaamse Regering* [2013] 3 CMLR 947, [2013] All ER (D) 287 (May) (ECJ: First Chamber).

2691   Free movement of persons—third-country nationals—family members of EU citizen

The applicants were all from Kosovo. The first applicant arrived in Luxembourg at the age of 15 to live with his uncle, a Luxembourg national. Several years later he was joined by his parents and his two brothers, the second to fifth applicants. The first applicant later acquired Luxembourg nationality and the second to fifth applicants sought residence on grounds of family reunification with the first applicant. Those applications were rejected. On appeal, the appellate court referred to the European Court of Justice the question whether TFEU art 20 precluded a member state from refusing to allow third-country nationals to reside in its territory with a family member who was a citizen of that member state and who had never exercised his right of freedom of movement as an EU citizen. *Held*, any rights conferred on third-country nationals under the TFEU were not autonomous rights of those nationals but rights derived from the exercise of freedom of movement by an EU citizen. The purpose and justification of those derived rights were based on the fact that a refusal to allow them would be such as to interfere with the EU citizen's freedom of movement by discouraging him from exercising his rights of entry into and residence in the host member state. It was recognised that there were very specific situations in which a right of residence could not be refused to a third-country national who was a family member of an EU citizen who had not exercised his freedom of movement, if such refusal would effectively oblige that citizen to leave the territory of the EU altogether, thereby denying him the genuine enjoyment of the substance of the rights conferred by virtue of his status. However, the mere desirability for a national of a member state, for economic reasons or in order to keep his family together in the territory of the EU, for the members of his family who were not nationals of the member state to be given residence rights there could not in itself support the view that the EU citizen would be forced to leave EU territory if such rights were not granted.

Case C-87/12 *Ymeraga v Ministre du Travail, de l'Emploi et de l'Immigration* [2013] 3 CMLR 895, [2013] All ER (D) 184 (May) (ECJ: Second Chamber). Case C-256/11 *Dereci v Bundesministerium für Inneres* [2012] All ER (EC) 373, ECJ (2012 Abr para 2642), considered.

2692   Free movement of workers—income tax—exemption—base of employer

The applicants were husband and wife. The husband was a Danish national and owned a holiday home in Denmark. For a number of years, the applicants and their daughter had been officially resident in Germany where they owned an apartment. The husband was employed by an undertaking established in Denmark. He had been seconded to Benin for a period of three years. His employer successfully requested an exemption from the Danish tax authority in respect of the income paid to the husband during his secondment. The applicants asked the respondent tax authority to apply the joint assessment scheme to their income tax and stated that their place of residence was Germany. They claimed that the income received by the husband from his employer ought not to be subjected to income tax in Germany and that the double taxation agreement between Germany and Denmark entitled Denmark alone to tax that income. In the alternative, the applicants requested a tax exemption in respect of the income as it was income derived from employment carried out in another state in the context of development aid activity for an employer established in Denmark that was exempt from income tax under a notice from the Ministry of Finance. The respondent, however, made the entirety of the husband's income subject to income tax. It fell to be determined whether TFEU art 56 ought to be interpreted as precluding national legislation of a member state pursuant to which income received in respect of employment activity by a taxpayer who was resident in that member state and had unlimited tax liability was exempt from income tax if the employer was established in that member state, but was not so exempt if that employer was established in another member state. *Held*, the opportunity provided by the legislation at issue for a resident taxpayer to be exempt from income tax constituted a tax advantage. That advantage was granted only when a taxpayer residing in Germany was employed by an employer established in that member state. It was not granted when the taxpayer was employed by an employer established in another member state. By establishing a difference in treatment for employees' income in that way, depending on the member state in which their employer was established, the national legislation was liable to dissuade those employees from accepting work from an employer established in a member state which was not Germany and thus constituted a restriction on the free movement of workers, which was in principle forbidden by art 45. Therefore, art 45 should be interpreted as precluding national legislation of a member state pursuant to which income received for employment activities by a taxpayer who was resident in that member state and had unlimited tax liability was exempt from income tax if the employer was established in that member state, but was not so exempt if that employer was established in another member state.

Case C-544/11 *Petersen v Finanzamt Ludwigshafen* [2013] STC 1195 (ECJ: First Chamber).

2693   Material scope—equality of treatment—student—paid employment during course—entitlement to student grants

The claimant, an EU citizen, applied for a course of study in Denmark. He subsequently entered Denmark and was offered employment. While in employment, he applied for a student grant. The claimant began his studies and resigned from his job, but carried on other part-time employment. The Danish authorities rejected his application for a grant. The claimant challenged the rejection on the ground that he had the status of a worker within the meaning of TFEU art 45 and was therefore entitled to education assistance. The Danish authorities argued that the claimant was a student and not a worker as his principal objective in coming to Denmark was to pursue a course of study. A question arose as to the interpretation of European Parliament and Council Directive (EC) 2004/38 arts 7(1)(c), 24(2) (on the right of citizens of the EU and their family members to move and reside freely within the territory of the members states). *Held*, arts 7(1)(c), 24(2) had to be interpreted as meaning that an EU citizen who pursued a course of studies in a host member state while at the same time pursuing effective and genuine employment activities such as to confer on him the status of a worker within the meaning of TFEU art 45 could not be refused maintenance aid for studies that was granted to the nationals of that member state. It was for the national court to make the necessary findings of fact in order to ascertain whether the employment activities of a claimant were sufficient to confer that status on him. The fact that the person entered the territory of the host member state with the principal intention of pursuing a course of study was not relevant for determining whether he was a worker within the meaning of art 45 and, accordingly, whether he was entitled to the aid under the same terms as a national of the host member state under Council Regulation (EEC) 1612/68 art 7(2) (on freedom of movement for workers within the EU).

Case C-46/12 *LN v Styrelsen for Videregaende Uddannelser og Uddannelsesstotte* [2013] ICR 715, [2013] All ER (D) 330 (Feb) (ECJ: Third Chamber).

2694   Material scope—migrant worker—accession states—Croatia—right to social security payments

See para 2591.

2695   Material scope—migrant worker—tideover allowance—requirement jobseeker educated in member state

The applicant, a French national, completed her secondary studies in France. She married a Belgian national and settled in Belgium, registering as a jobseeker. Her application for a tideover allowance was rejected on the ground that she had not completed a minimum of six years' study in an educational establishment located in Belgium before obtaining her certificate in secondary education as required by the relevant Belgian law. The applicant commenced proceedings and on appeal, the court found that the applicant was not entitled to tideover allowance and in particular made clear that she was not able to derive such a right either from EC Treaty art 39 or from art 18. The applicant contended that the judgment infringed the rights which arts 12, 17 and 18 and, so far as necessary, art 39, conferred on citizens of the European Union. The referring court decided to stay proceedings and referred to the European Court of Justice for preliminary ruling questions whether art 39, precluded a provision of national law under which entitlement to tideover allowance for a young EU national, who did not have the status as a worker within the meaning of art 39, who completed secondary studies in the EU but not at an educational establishment run, subsidised or approved by one of the communities in Belgium, and who obtained either a document issued by one of those communities establishing the equivalence of those studies to the study certificate issued by the competent authority of one of those communities for studies completed in those Belgian educational establishments, was conditional on the young person in question having previously completed six years study at an educational establishment run, approved or subsidised by one of the communities in Belgium. *Held,* art 39 precluded a national provision which made the right to a tideover allowance for the benefit of young people looking for their first job subject to the condition that the person concerned completed at least six years study in an educational establishment of the host member state, in so far as that condition prevented other representative factors liable to establish the existence of a real link between the person claiming the allowance and the geographic labour market concerned being taken into account and accordingly went beyond what was necessary to attain the aim pursued by that provision, which was to ensure that such a link existed.

Case C-367/11 *Prete v Office National de l'Emploi* [2013] 1 CMLR 1142, [2012] All ER (D) 15 (Dec) (ECJ: Fourth Chamber). Case C-224/98 *D'Hoop v Office National de l'Emploi* [2003] All ER (EC) 527, ECJ (2002 Abr para 2693); and Case C-258/04 *Office National de l'Emploi v Ioannidis* [2006] All ER (EC) 926, ECJ (2005 Abr para 3222), considered.

EC Treaty arts 12, 17, 18, 39 now TFEU arts 18, 20, 21, 45.

2696   Non-discrimination—income tax—transfer of residence—splitting method

The taxpayers worked on a self-employed basis and received all their income in Germany. They transferred their residence to Switzerland. They continued, however, to carry on their business activities in Germany and to receive almost all their income in Germany. They requested, as in previous tax years, to be taxed jointly by the 'splitting' method, stating that they had not obtained any taxable income in Switzerland. According to the German law, the splitting procedure was a tax advantage for spouses subject to income tax in Germany where the income received by one of them was markedly higher than that received by the other. However, the system only applied if the spouses had their permanent or usual residence either in German territory or in the territory of another member state of the European Union or a state to which the European Economic Area Agreement applied. The EEA Agreement did not apply to the Swiss Confederation. In an initial tax notice, the respondent tax office allowed their request. Subsequently, however, it cancelled the notice on the ground that the 'splitting' arrangement should not be applied to the taxpayers because their residence was neither in the territory of a member state of the European Union nor in that of a state party to the Agreement between the European Community and its member states and the Swiss Confederation, of the other, on the free movement of persons (Luxembourg, 21 June 1999) ('the Agreement'). Having failed in her administrative complaint, the wife brought proceedings for annulment of the notice. The court considered that the taxpayers were self-employed frontier workers within the meaning of the Agreement Annex I art 13(1), since they were German nationals resident in Switzerland, working on a self-employed basis in Germany, and returned from their place of business to their place of residence every day. In accordance with the Agreement Annex I art 9(2) in conjunction with art 15(2), self-employed frontier workers enjoyed the same tax and social security advantages in the territory of the state in which they pursued their activity as self-employed nationals. It followed that the principle of non-discrimination, which also applied in tax matters, prohibited not only overt discrimination on grounds of nationality but also all forms of covert discrimination. The court decided to stay the proceedings and refer for a preliminary ruling the question whether the provisions of the Agreement, in particular arts 1, 2, 11, 16 and 21 and Annex I arts 9, 13 and 15, were to be interpreted as precluding the benefit of joint taxation with the use of the 'splitting' procedure from being refused to spouses residing in Switzerland who were subject to taxation in Germany on their entire taxable income. *Held,* (1) the Agreement Annex I art 13(1) was applicable to the situation of the taxpayers. They were nationals 'of a contracting party', namely Germany, were resident in the territory 'of a contracting party', namely the Swiss Confederation, and pursued a self-employed activity in the territory 'of the other contracting party', namely Germany. The taxpayers' situation fell within the scope of the Agreement. (2) Article 21(2), under which no provision of the Agreement might be interpreted in such a way as to prevent the contracting parties from distinguishing, when applying the relevant provisions of their fiscal legislation, between taxpayers whose situations were not comparable, especially as regards their place of residence. Accordingly, that provision allowed different treatment, in tax matters, of resident and non-resident taxpayers, but only where they were not in a comparable situation. A non-resident taxpayer who received all or almost all of his income in the state in which he pursued his business activity was objectively in the same situation, as regards income tax, as a resident of that state who pursued comparable activities there. Article 21(2) could not be relied on by a contracting party in order to refuse spouses who pursued their business activities in that state, received all their income there and were subject to unlimited liability to income tax there the tax advantage, linked to their personal and family situation, consisting in the application of the 'splitting' method. In the present case, by refusing that tax advantage because of the place of residence of the taxpayers, the legislation at issue was contrary to Annex I art 13(1) in conjunction with arts 9(2), 15(2). Consequently, art 1(a) and Annex I arts 9(2), 13(1) and 15(2) had to be interpreted as precluding legislation of a member state which refused the benefit of joint taxation with the use of the 'splitting' method, provided for by that legislation, to spouses who were nationals of that state and subject to income tax in that state on their entire taxable income, on the sole ground that their residence was situated in the territory of the Swiss Confederation.

Case C-425/11 *Ettwein v Finanzamt Konstanz* [2013] All ER (D) 51 (Mar) (ECJ: Third Chamber).

2697   Principle of equal treatment—free movement of persons—students—entitlement to benefits—reduced transport fares

European Parliament and Council Directive (EC) 2004/38 art 24(1) provides that EU citizens residing on the basis of Directive 2004/38 in the territory of the host member state enjoy equal treatment with the nationals of that member state. By way of derogation, the host member state is not obliged to grant maintenance aid for studies consisting in student grants or student loans: art 24(2).

Various federal authorities in Austria had agreed with local transport undertakings fare reductions for students whose parents received family assistance in respect of their studies.

This assistance was only available to parents who lived in Austria. The European Commission sought a declaration that, by granting reduced fares on public transport only to students whose parents were in receipt of Austrian family allowances, Austria had failed to fulfil its obligations under the combined provisions of TFEU arts 18, 20 and 21, and European Parliament and Council Directive (EC) 2004/38 art 24. *Held*, it was settled law that the status of citizen of the EU, as provided by TFEU art 20, was destined to be the fundamental status of nationals of the member states, which enabled such nationals who found themselves in the same situation to receive the same treatment in law as nationals of the member state irrespective of their nationality, subject to such exceptions as were provided for in that regard. The prohibition of discrimination on grounds of nationality under art 18 covered all situations which fell within the material scope of the TFEU, which included the exercise of the freedom conferred by art 21 to reside within the territory of member states. Having regard to the fact that national aid granted to students to cover their maintenance costs and certain social benefits provided for by national legislation had been held to come within the scope of art 18, a scheme providing for reduced transport fares for students also came within the scope of art 18 in so far as it enabled them to cover their maintenance costs. The contention that the reduced transport fares should be categorised as a 'family benefit' did not rule out the existence of discrimination on grounds of nationality, contrary to art 18 and the Directive art 24. The condition relating to students' parents receiving Austrian family allowances gave rise to unequal treatment because it was more easily fulfilled by Austrian students. Taking into account the requirement for art 24(2), as a derogation from the principle of equal treatment, to be interpreted narrowly, reduced transport fares could not be considered to be a maintenance aid for studies 'consisting in student grants or student loans'. Although a national system requiring a student to provide a genuine link with the host member state could, in principle, reflect a legitimate objective capable of justifying restrictions on the right to move and reside freely within the territory of the member states provided for in TFEU art 21, the genuine link should not be fixed in a uniform manner for all benefits, but should be established according to the constitutive elements of the benefit in question, including its nature and purpose. By granting reduced fares on public transport in principle only to students whose parents were in receipt of Austrian family allowances, Austria had failed to fulfil its obligations under the combined provisions of arts 18, 20 and 21 TFEU and Directive 2004/38 art 24.

Case C-75/11 *European Commission v Austria (re student benefit)* [2013] 1 CMLR 567, [2012] All ER (D) 133 (Oct) (ECJ: Second Chamber). Case C-73/08 *Bressol v Gouvernement de la Communauté Française; Chaverot v Gouvernement de la Communauté Française* [2010] 3 CMLR 559, [2010] All ER (D) 48 (Apr), ECJ (2010 Abr para 2839); and Case C-224/98 *D'Hoop v Office National d'Emploi* [2002] 3 CMLR 309, ECJ (2002 Abr para 2693), considered.

2698   Professional qualifications—recognition

The European Communities (Recognition of Professional Qualifications) (Amendment) Regulations 2013, SI 2013/732 (in force on 18 April 2013), further amend the 2007 Regulations, SI 2007/2781, which implement in part Council Directive (EC) 2005/36 on the recognition of professional qualifications, as amended by Council Directive (EC) 2006/100, so as to alter the implementation of Directive 2006/100 art 14(3) in relation to the derogation from the choice of the compensation measures, for midwives and nurses responsible for general care who do not meet the professional requirements which would grant them acquired rights.

RIGHT OF ESTABLISHMENT AND FREEDOM TO PROVIDE SERVICES

2699   Freedom to provide services—Association Agreement with Turkey—applicability of jurisprudence relating to freedom to provide services between member states

See Case C-221/11 *Demirkan v Bundesrepublik Deutschland*, para 2682.

2700   Freedom to provide services—financial services—measures to ensure effectiveness of fiscal supervision—necessity

Under Belgian law, interest payments, up to a specified level, from savings deposits paid by banks established in Belgium were exempt from tax. Belgium conceded that this constituted an obstacle to the free movement of services but contended that it was justified by the need to guarantee the effectiveness of fiscal supervision and the need to protect small savings. The European Commission was not satisfied with this justification and issued proceedings against Belgium for failure to fulfil its obligations regarding the freedom to provide services and the free movement of capital under the EC Treaty arts 49 and 56. *Held*, it was established that the need to guarantee the effectiveness of fiscal supervision was capable of justifying a restriction on fundamental freedoms. However, the existing machinery for mutual assistance between the authorities of the member states was sufficient to check the truthfulness of taxpayers' returns relating to their income earned in another member state. Member states could not rely on possible difficulties in obtaining the information required or on shortcomings on co-operation between their tax authorities in order to justify a restriction on fundamental freedoms. The law in question went beyond what was necessary to secure the objective of ensuring the effectiveness of fiscal supervision and, in particular, the prevention of tax avoidance and evasion. It also restricted the legitimate exercise of the freedom to provide services where taxpayers proved that their objective was not tax avoidance and evasion. In view of those conclusions, there was no need for a separate examination of the effect of the legislation on the free movement of capital.

Case C-383/10 *European Commission v Belgium (re tax exemption on interest of resident banks accounts)* [2013] 3 CMLR 1305 (ECJ: Fifth Chamber).

EC Treaty arts 49, 56 now TFEU arts 56, 63.

2701   Freedom to provide services—financial services—reporting requirements—national legislation duplicating EU reporting requirements for financial institutions operating but not established in member state

See Case C-212/11 *Jyske Bank Gibraltar Ltd v Administración del Estado*, para 1204.

2702   Right of establishment—discriminatory taxation—advance corporation tax

See Case C-362/12 *Test Claimants in the Franked Investment Income Group Litigation v Revenue and Customs Comrs*, para 1487.

2703   Right of establishment—discriminatory taxation—corporation tax—dividend payment to non-resident companies

The proceedings concerned a test case brought by the claimants concerning the legality of the United Kingdom's rules on the taxation of dividends received by United Kingdom-resident companies on shareholdings which were held by them as investments and allocated to their pension business and life assurance business. The fundamental issue concerning the lawfulness of a charge to corporation tax on dividends paid by a subsidiary resident in a European Union member state to its United Kingdom-resident parent had remained open, pending a decision of the Supreme Court. The Supreme Court overruled the Court of Appeal on two procedural issues, which had led to the adjournment of the present trial. First, the court held that the Finance Act 2007 s 107 infringed the EU principle of protection of legitimate expectations in so far as it retrospectively excluded mistake-based claims which had been commenced before a certain date. Second, the Supreme Court held that the Taxes Management Act 1970 s 33 was inapplicable to claims for recovery of tax which had been paid contrary to EU law. Therefore, it became clear that the procedural obstacles to the prosecution of the present claims in the High Court had largely disappeared. The test trial was ordered to resume. The Finance Act 1989 s 89 set out the rules for calculating the policy holders' share of the profits of life assurance business, which were chargeable to tax at the basic rate of income tax, while the shareholders' share, representing the profit derived from carrying on the business, was charged to tax at the full corporation tax rate. The effect of those deductions from the Case I profits was to increase by a corresponding amount the policy holders' share which was taxed at the lower rate. Issues arose as to (1) whether s 89 infringed the claimants' treaty rights; (2) whether the claimants were entitled to rely on the TFEU art 63 in relation to dividends from third countries in respect of which the United Kingdom had no entitlement to obtain information relevant for ascertaining the amount of tax paid on the foreign profits; (3) the approach to remedying the invalidity under EU law of the charge to corporation tax on portfolio dividends; (4) whether the advance corporation tax ('ACT') charge on the onward distribution in the United Kingdom of portfolio dividends received from abroad infringed the TFEU art 63;

and (5) remedies in relation to each of the above. *Held*, the 1989 Act s 89 did infringe the claimant's treaty rights. The deduction afforded by s 89(2) for unrelieved franked investment income and foreign income dividends brought a corresponding tax advantage by increasing the size of the policy holders' share, whereas no such advantage could be obtained in respect of foreign portfolio dividends. That difference in treatment was plainly discriminatory, and no justification for it had been advanced by the Revenue. The question, therefore, was how the discrimination should be remedied. The right solution was not to allow a further deduction for foreign portfolio dividends under s 89(2), but rather to leave them in the computation and grant a tax credit for the dividends. With regard to the second issue, EU law required the United Kingdom to grant a tax credit for foreign portfolio dividends which was based on the foreign nominal rate of tax. There was no reason to exclude any third countries from the relief. The claimants were entitled to a credit based on the nominal rate for the underlying tax actually paid. In relation to the third issue, it was settled law that, firstly, whatever mechanism a member state chose to adopt in order to prevent or mitigate economic double taxation, the treaty freedoms of movement prohibited treating foreign-sourced dividends less favourably than nationally-sourced dividends, unless the less favourable treatment either (a) concerned situations which were not objectively comparable, or (b) was justified by overriding reasons in the general interest. Secondly, there was no reason in principle why a member state should not operate a dual system of exemption for national dividends and imputation for foreign dividends provided that the member state did not impose a higher rate of tax on foreign dividends than it did on national dividends and it gave a credit for the amount of tax paid by the foreign company. Thirdly, the mere fact that an imputation system imposed additional administrative burdens on taxpayers, when compared with an exemption system, did not infringe the TFEU art 63, because such burdens were an intrinsic part of the operation of a tax credit system. With regard to the fourth issue, the United Kingdom legislation would have been compliant with EU law if it had provided for the grant of dual credit for portfolio dividends. The grant of the further credit for withholding tax was not, in itself, a requirement of EU law. However, there could be no doubt that a credit for withholding tax had also to be granted, as a matter of domestic law. In relation to remedies to the above issues, the obligation on the English courts to construe domestic legislation consistently with EU law obligations was far-reaching. In particular, the obligation was not to be constrained by conventional rules of construction and did not require ambiguity in the legislative language. It fell well within the scope of conforming interpretation to construe the Income and Corporation Taxes Act 1988 s 790 as providing for the grant of a tax credit for foreign dividends to the extent necessary to secure compliance with EU law. Since s 790 already provided for the grant of tax credits, in the case of both portfolio and non-portfolio dividends, the grant of a further tax credit for portfolio dividends would not go against the grain of the United Kingdom tax legislation. EU law required the United Kingdom to grant a tax credit for foreign portfolio dividends which was based on the foreign nominal rate of tax. On the facts, the test claimants had failed to prove their entitlement to a tax credit for the underlying tax actually paid. That failure involved no breach by the United Kingdom of the principle of effectiveness and there was, therefore, no reason either to disapply the requirement of proof, or to grant a tax credit at the nominal rate as a proxy. The claim had to fail because it was based on the flawed assumption that the relevant portfolio dividends would have been exempt from corporation tax and could therefore be left out of account in the tax computation. The right analysis was that the dividends should not be treated as exempt, but rather as carrying a tax credit to set against the tax otherwise chargeable. The court rejected the Revenue's submission that the claimants' only entitlement was to simple interest pursuant to the Senior Courts Act 1981 s 35A. In each case the Revenue was enriched by the overpaid tax, and in each case full restitution required an award of compound interest as part of the principal sum which the claimant was entitled to recover. It was not disputed that the award of compound interest computed on the conventional government basis would satisfy the requirement of effectiveness under EU law, and provide the claimants with an adequate indemnity. The ACT claims were deemed to have been commenced on the same date as the original claims, and they were not time barred. Judgment would be given accordingly.

Prudential Assurance Co Ltd v Revenue and Customs Comrs [2013] EWHC 3249 (Ch), [2013] All ER (D) 335 (Oct) (Chancery Division: Henderson J). *Test Claimants in the FII Group Litigation v Revenue and Customs Comrs* [2012] UKSC 19, [2012] 2 AC 337 (2012 Abr para 2659) applied.

1988 Act s 790 replaced by provisions of Taxation (International and Other Provisions) Act 2010.

2704 Right of establishment—discriminatory taxation—vehicle registration tax—car used in two member states

See Case C-302/12 *X v Minister van Financien*, para 2254.

2705 Right of establishment—married couple—joint assessment—tax advantage

See Case C-303/12 *Imfeld v Belgium*, para 1542.

FREEDOM OF MOVEMENT OF CAPITAL

2706 Capital movement—income tax credits—dividends from company established in other member state

For a number of years, the taxpayer, who was resident in Germany, received dividends on shares in companies established in the Netherlands and Denmark. He applied to the German tax authority for a credit against his income tax. The application was made pursuant to German national law provisions relating to the avoidance of double taxation, whereby a credit, equal in amount to the corporation tax already paid on dividend distributions to a person, could be made in calculating that person's income tax liability on those dividends. That application was refused. The matter was referred to the European Court of Justice. It was found that national legislation by virtue of which the corporation tax already paid on dividend distributions was credited to taxpayers by means of income tax credits equal to the prior corporation tax charge, had to be applied equally to domestic dividends from dividends from other member states. The original referring German court sought to clarify that judgment, and made a further reference to the European Court of Justice on the interpretation of the EC Treaty arts 56 and 58 in relation to the set-off of corporation tax imposed on dividends from a company established in one member state against corporation tax payable in the taxpayer's member state of residence, and the degree of detail of evidence which the taxpayer could be required to provide in order to benefit from the tax credit. *Held*, in terms of the calculation of the amount of tax credit, arts 56 and 58 precluded the application, if evidence required under the legislation of the first member state was not adduced, of a provision of national law under which the corporation tax on foreign dividends was set off against a taxpayer's income tax to the level of the fraction of corporation tax on gross dividends in that member state. The calculation of the tax credit had to be made in relation to the rate of corporation tax applicable to the dividend-paying company in its member state of establishment. However, the amount of the calculated corporation tax could not exceed the amount of the income tax that had to be paid on the dividends in the member state in which the tax credit was sought. As regards the degree of detail which the evidence required had to meet in order to benefit from the tax credit, art 56 and 58 precluded the application of national law provisions under which the degree of detail and the form of evidence to be adduced by such a taxpayer had to be the same as those required where the dividend-paying company was established in the member state of taxation. Further, where the rules for restitution of national taxes were amended by national law with retroactive effect, the principle of effectiveness required new legislation to include transitional arrangements allowing an adequate period of time for lodging claims for repayment which persons were entitled to submit under the original legislation. The principle of effectiveness thus precluded legislative amendments such as those in the current circumstances, as they did not grant taxpayers a reasonable period of time to make their claim during a transitional period.

Case C-262/09 *Meilicke v Finanzamt Bonn-Innenstadt* [2013] STC 1494 (ECJ: First Chamber).

EC Treaty arts 56 and 58 now TFEU arts 63 and 65.

2707   Capital movement—prohibition of restriction on movement—corporation tax—deductibility of loan interest

See Case C-282/12 *Itelcar – Automoveis de Aluguer Lda v Fazenda Publica*, para 1496.

2708   Capital movement—prohibition of restriction on movement—differential treatment—inheritance tax—tax-free allowance

The applicant was a Swiss national who had lived with his wife ('the deceased') in Switzerland. The deceased had been born in Germany but had become a Swiss national after their marriage. The deceased had owned a piece of land in Germany, and had funds in both German and Swiss bank accounts. In relation to inheritance tax, German law provided for a significantly smaller tax-free allowance to be applied to the estates of resident persons than the estates of non-residents. The effect of that provision was that the applicant was required to pay a substantial amount of inheritance tax in Germany. If the deceased or the applicant had been resident in Germany on the date of the deceased's death, the applicant would not have had to pay any inheritance tax. The applicant brought proceedings contesting the inheritance tax assessment, submitting that the unequal treatment of resident and non-resident taxpayers was incompatible with the principle of free movement of capital guaranteed by TFEU arts 63, 65. The national court decided to stay proceedings and to refer the question to the European Court of Justice for a preliminary ruling. *Held*, where the legislation of a member state made the grant of a tax advantage dependent on satisfying requirements, compliance with which could be verified only by obtaining information from the competent authorities of a third country, it was in principle legitimate for the member state to refuse to grant that advantage if it proved impossible to obtain such information from that country. However, death certificates and other documents issued by civil registrars in the state where the succession took place could be forwarded by the heirs or, if necessary, by the tax authorities of that state as part of the application of a bilateral agreement for the avoidance of double taxation and did not, as a general rule, require a complex assessment. In any event, in accordance with the national legislation, an heir residing in Germany received the full tax-free allowance when he acquired by succession an immovable property located in that member state from a person who had been residing, at the moment of his death, in a third country. However, such a succession further required the inspection by the competent German authorities of the information concerning a deceased person residing in a third country. Having regard to the relevant legal principles, the German government could not claim that national legislation, in so far as it deprived the heir of an estate passing between residents of a third country, such as the Swiss Confederation, of the benefit of the full tax-free allowance was necessary to preserve the effectiveness of fiscal supervision. It followed that arts 63, 65 should be interpreted as precluding legislation of a member state relating to the calculation of inheritance tax which provided that, in the event of inheritance of immovable property in that state, in a case where the deceased and the heir had a permanent residence in a third country at the time of the death, the tax-free allowance was less than the allowance which would have been applied if at least one of them had been resident in that member state at that time.

Case C-181/12 *Welte v Finanzamt Velbert* [2013] All ER (D) 268 (Oct) (ECJ: Third Chamber). Case C-510/08 *Mattner v Finanzamt Velbert* [2010] 3 CMLR 815, [2010] All ER (D) 167 (Apr), ECJ (2010 Abr para 2858), considered.

2709   Capital movement—prohibition of restriction on movement—dividend—payment by company established in another state—tax credit

See *BT Pension Scheme v Revenue and Customs Comrs*, para 1551.

2710   Capital movement—prohibition of restriction on movement—income tax—foreign withholding tax

The taxpayers were spouses and were jointly assessed for income tax in Germany. In addition to their German income, they received income from capital holdings in various corporate enterprises in other European Union member states as well as other states. In respect of those holdings, the taxpayers received dividends which gave rise to payment, in the various states of origin of those dividends, of foreign tax. The respondent tax office calculated the maximum amount of foreign withholding tax deductible and offset that amount against the income tax due from the taxpayers. The taxpayers sought an amendment to the tax assessment and a reduction of income tax for the relevant tax year. It was submitted that the respondent had based the calculation of the maximum amount deductible on total revenue before general deductions corresponding to special expenditure and extraordinary costs had been taken into account. The request was rejected. It fell to be determined whether TFEU art 63 ought to be interpreted as precluding rules of a member state under which, in the context of a system aimed at limiting double taxation, where persons subject to unlimited tax liability paid on foreign income, in the state where that income originated, a tax equivalent to the income tax levied by the said member state, the foreign tax was offset against income tax in the member state by multiplying the amount of tax due in respect of taxable income in the same member state by the proportion that the foreign income bore to total income, the latter not taking into account special expenditure or extraordinary costs. *Held*, taxpayers resident in one member state who had received one part of their revenue abroad were at a disadvantage compared with taxpayers resident in the same member state who received all of their revenue in that member state and who therefore benefited from all allowances corresponding to special costs and extraordinary charges such as costs relating to lifestyle or to personal and family circumstances. Such a difference in treatment was likely to discourage persons subject to unlimited taxation in a member state from investing their capital in companies having their principal place of business in another member state or in a third state. It followed that rules of a member state such as those contested constituted a restriction on the free movement of capital within the meaning of art 63. Further, the fact that Germany fully granted the benefit of the personal and family allowances to the taxpayers did not undermine the right of a member state to exercise its powers of taxation in relation to activities carried out in its territory. Therefore, art 63 had to be interpreted as precluding rules of a member state under which, where persons subject to unlimited tax liability paid on foreign income, in the state where that income originated, a tax equivalent to the income tax levied by the said member state, the offsetting of that foreign tax against the amount of income tax levied in the said member state was carried out by multiplying the amount of the tax due in respect of taxable income in the same member state, including foreign income, by the proportion that the foreign income bore to total income, that latter sum not taking into account special expenditure or extraordinary costs such as relating to lifestyle or to personal and family circumstances.

Case C-168/11 *Beker v Finanzamt Heilbronn* [2013] STC 1334 (ECJ: Second Chamber). Case C-385/00 *de Groot v Staatssecretaris van Financiën* [2004] STC 1346, ECJ, applied.

TAXATION

2711   Direct internal taxation—merger between parent company and non-resident subsidiary—deduction of subsidiary's losses

See Case C-123/11 *Proceedings brought by A Oy*, para 1497.

2712   Taxes paid but not due—repayment—interest on repayment—pollution tax on purchase of motor vehicle

The applicant purchased a motor vehicle registered in Germany. In order to register it in Romania, she paid pollution tax in compliance with Romanian law. The applicant subsequently sought repayment of the sum paid and interest from the date of payment. According to settled Romanian case law, interest on sums to be repaid from public funds was granted only from the day following the date of the claim for repayment. It fell to be determined whether EU law precluded a national system which limited the interest granted on repayment of a tax levied in breach of EU law to that accruing from the day following the date of the claim for repayment of the tax. *Held*, a system such as that at issue did not meet the requirement in the principle of effectiveness that, in a situation of repayment of a tax levied by a member state in breach of EU law, the national rules referring in particular to the calculation of interest which might be due should not lead to depriving the taxpayer of adequate compensation for the loss sustained through the undue payment of the tax. Such loss depended, among other things, on the duration of the unavailability of the sum unduly levied and therefore occurred, in principle, during the period between the date of the undue payment of the tax and the date of repayment. It followed that EU law precluded a national system which limited the interest granted on repayment of a tax levied in breach of EU law to that accruing from the day following the date of the claim for repayment of the tax.

Case C-565/11 *Irimie v Administratia Finantelor Publice Sibiu* [2013] STC 1321 (ECJ: Third Chamber).

2713   Value added tax
See VALUE ADDED TAX.

SOCIAL POLICY

2714   Employment
See EMPLOYMENT.

2715   Equal pay and treatment
See DISCRIMINATION.

2716   Welfare benefits
See WELFARE BENEFITS AND STATE PENSIONS.

INDEX

The titles under which the Abridgment is arranged are listed on pp 9–10. The references in the list are to paragraphs, not pages.